T0398870

JEWISH MUSIC STUDIES

THE OXFORD HANDBOOK OF

JEWISH MUSIC STUDIES

Edited by

TINA FRÜHAUF

OXFORD
UNIVERSITY PRESS

Oxford University Press is a department of the University of Oxford. It furthers the University's objective of excellence in research, scholarship, and education by publishing worldwide. Oxford is a registered trade mark of Oxford University Press in the UK and certain other countries.

Published in the United States of America by Oxford University Press
198 Madison Avenue, New York, NY 10016, United States of America.

Library of Congress Cataloging-in-Publication Data
Names: Frühauf, Tina, editor.
Title: The Oxford handbook of Jewish music studies / [edited by] Tina Frühauf.
Description: [1.] | New York : Oxford University Press, 2023. |
Series: Oxford handbooks series | Includes bibliographical references and index.
Identifiers: LCCN 2023017633 (print) | LCCN 2023017634 (ebook) |
ISBN 9780197528624 (hardback) | ISBN 9780197528655 | ISBN 9780197528648 (epub)
Subjects: LCSH: Jews—Music—History and criticism. | Music—Political aspects—History. |
Music—Social aspects—History. | Music—Religious aspects—Judaism.
Classification: LCC ML3776 .O94 2023 (print) | LCC ML3776 (ebook) |
DDC 780.89/924—dc23/eng/20230503
LC record available at https://lccn.loc.gov/2023017633
LC ebook record available at https://lccn.loc.gov/2023017634

DOI: 10.1093/oxfordhb/9780197528624.001.0001

Printed by Integrated Books International, United States of America

CONTENTS

Acknowledgments ix
List of Contributors xi
On Transliteration and Translation, Spelling, and Names xiii
About the Cover xv

1. Introduction: Mapping Jewish Music Studies 1
   TINA FRÜHAUF

PART I: LAND—אדמה

2. Adamot—Art Music—Israel 39
   ASSAF SHELLEG

3. Land, Voice, Nation: Jewish Music in the Adamot of Al-Andalus 70
   VANESSA PALOMA ELBAZ

4. "We Shall Sing Songs and Praise to the Lord Who Created Us Last in
   the World": Ḥakham Joseph Ḥayyim of Baghdad, Leadership with
   Poetry and Music 91
   MERAV ROSENFELD-HADAD

PART II: CITY—עיר

5. Jewish Refugees from the Nazi State in Shanghai, 1938–1949 119
   SOPHIE FETTHAUER

6. Jewish Émigré Musicians in Buenos Aires: Integration and Cultural
   Impact, 1933–1945 144
   SILVIA GLOCER

7. From a City of Greeks to Greeks in a City: Migration and Musical
   Taste Cultures between Salonika and Tel Aviv-Jaffa 165
   ODED EREZ

8. Berlin Klezmer and Urban Scenes 185
PHIL ALEXANDER

PART III: GHETTO—גטו

9. Hearing the Ancient Temple in Early Modernity: Abraham
Portaleone and the Cultivation of Music in Seventeenth-Century
Mantua 215
REBECCA CYPESS AND YOEL GREENBERG

10. Sonic Transformations: Urban Musical Culture in the Warsaw
Ghetto, 1940–1942 240
J. MACKENZIE PIERCE

11. Sounding Out the Ghetto: Spatial Aspects of Jewish Musical Life
during the Nazi Era 261
TOBIAS REICHARD

PART IV: STAGE—בימה

12. Hasidic Cantors "Out of Context": Venues of Contemporary
Cantorial Performance 289
JEREMIAH LOCKWOOD

13. Jewish Music and Totalitarianism in the Post-Stalinist Soviet Union 309
JASCHA NEMTSOV

14. Art Music in the Yishuv and in Early-Statehood Israel 335
JEHOASH HIRSHBERG

15. The Yiddish Theater Republic of Sounds and the Performance of
Listening 357
RUTHIE ABELIOVICH

PART V: COLLECTION—זאמלונג

16. The YIVO Sound Archive as a Living Space: Archiving and
Revitalizing Klezmer Music 383
ELÉONORE BIEZUNSKI

17. Jewish Music Sound-Recording Collections in the United States 408
JUDITH S. PINNOLIS

18. Postcustodialism in the Jewish Music Archive   429
    JOSEPH TOLTZ

PART VI: SACRED AND RITUAL SPACES—
עירוב/ חופה/ כותל

19. Reimagining Spiritual Experience and Music: Perspectives from
    Jewish Worship in the United States   449
    JEFFREY A. SUMMIT

20. Sonic Collectivity at the Kotel ha-Ma'aravi (Western Wall)   476
    ABIGAIL WOOD

21. Singing at the Sabbath Table: Zemiroth as a Family History   493
    NAOMI COHN ZENTNER

22. Early Modern Yiddish Wedding Songs: Synchronic and Diachronic
    Functions   512
    DIANA MATUT

23. Bukharian Jewish Weddings and Creative Uses of the Central Asian
    Past   531
    EVAN RAPPORT

PART VII: DESTRUCTION / REMEMBRANCE—
זכר/ חורבן

24. Remembering the Destruction, Re-animating the Collective:
    Romaniote Liturgical Music after the Holocaust   553
    MIRANDA L. CROWDUS

25. "We Live Forever": Music of the Surviving Remnant in Sweden   569
    SIMO MUIR

26. "Ferramonti We Do Not Forget": Jews, Music, and Internment
    in Italy   594
    SILVIA DEL ZOPPO

27. "I Say She Is a *Muṭriba*": Faded Memories of Aleppo's Jewish Women
    Musicians   614
    CLARA WENZ

PART VIII: SPIRIT—שכינה

28. Ultra-Orthodox Women and the Musical Shekhinah: Performance, Technology, and the Artist in North America   637
JESSICA RODA

29. "On a Harp of Ten Strings I Will Sing Praises to You": Envisioning Women and Music in the Oppenheimer Siddur   664
SUZANNE WIJSMAN

30. The Concept of Harmony in Pre- and Early Modern Jewish Literature   698
ALEXANDRE CERVEUX

Index   715

ACKNOWLEDGMENTS

THIS handbook began as an idea to apprehend the universe of topics contained under the umbrella "Jewish music"; it grew during a pivotal time when this domain of research evolved toward becoming an international field of study. I wish to thank Oxford University's former executive editor for Music, Suzanne Ryan-Melamed, for her support and encouragement to find new inroads into this growing domain and the current executive editor, Norman Hirschy, for endorsing the direction I have taken to capture it as a field.

I am indebted to countless people who knowingly or unknowingly helped this project come to fruition: archivists, librarians, and informants all over the world who aided the authors of the volume with their research for the chapters presented here. The contributors worked with me through the worst surges of the COVID-19 pandemic and under truly less-than-ideal conditions finalized their chapters without great delay. None of my work as editor, translator, and contributor would have been accomplished if it were not for my husband, Pryor Dodge, who continually and strongly supported this endeavor. I am grateful that Mark Podwal generously allowed me to use his painting as a window to the highly diverse content that awaits the reader beneath the cover.

CONTRIBUTORS

Ruthie Abeliovich, Tel Aviv University

Phil Alexander, University of Edinburgh

Eléonore Biezunski, YIVO Institute for Jewish Research

Alexandre Cerveux, Wolfson College, University of Oxford

Miranda L. Crowdus, Concordia University

Rebecca Cypess, Rutgers University

Silvia Del Zoppo, Università degli Studi di Milano

Vanessa Paloma Elbaz, University of Cambridge

Oded Erez, Hebrew University of Jerusalem

Sophie Fetthauer, Hochschule für Musik und Theater Hamburg

Tina Frühauf, The CUNY Graduate Center / Columbia University

Silvia Glocer, Universidad de Buenos Aires

Yoel Greenberg, Bar-Ilan University

Jehoash Hirshberg, Hebrew University of Jerusalem

Jeremiah Lockwood, Herbert D. Katz Center for Advanced Judaic Studies, University of Pennsylvania

Diana Matut, Martin-Luther-Universität Halle-Wittenberg

Simo Muir, University College London

Jascha Nemtsov, Hochschule für Musik Franz Liszt Weimar

J. Mackenzie Pierce, University of Michigan

Judith S. Pinnolis, Berklee College of Music—Boston Conservatory at Berklee

Evan Rapport, Eugene Lang College of Liberal Arts at The New School

Tobias Reichard, Hochschule für Musik und Theater München

Jessica Roda, Georgetown University

Merav Rosenfeld-Hadad, University of Cambridge

Assaf Shelleg, Hebrew University of Jerusalem

Jeffrey A. Summit, Tufts University

Joseph Toltz, The University of Sydney

Clara Wenz, Julius-Maximilians-Universität Würzburg

Suzanne Wijsman, University of Western Australia

Abigail Wood, University of Haifa

Naomi Cohn Zentner, Bar-Ilan University

ON TRANSLITERATION AND TRANSLATION, SPELLING, AND NAMES

MANY of the foreign terms used in this volume do not exist in the English language and are left in the original. To make this book accessible to a broad readership, these are glossed en route. The different Hebrew and Yiddish pronunciations—often rendered in various spellings such as "Shalom aleikhem," and "Shuloym aleykhem"—and other divergent spellings were kept intact in quoted and transliterated sources. Otherwise, as with all Hebrew transliteration in this volume, they are reconciled following the standards of the American Library Association–Library of Congress. Yiddish is transliterated according to the Standard Yiddish Orthography established by the YIVO Institute for Jewish Research in New York. Following the YIVO guidelines, the romanization of titles uses initial capitals only for the first word. Personal names and the names of organizations and places are capitalized. Judeo-Spanish is transliterated using the system of the journal *Aki Yerushalayim*, in consultation with Rivka Havassy.

This volume contains numerous other languages. The romanization of Chinese used in the chapter of Sophie Fetthauer follows pinyin and relies on the stylesheet of the *Harvard Journal of Asiatic Studies*. The transliteration of Cyrillic for Tajik Persian in Evan Rapport's chapter is based on Edward Allworth's romanization; the system is applied to both Persian and Russian words. Transliteration from Persian written in the Perso-Arabic script follows a slightly adjusted version of the Library of Congress system; the same applies to Arabic. The transliteration of Cyrillic for Russian is based on a compromise between phonetic transliteration and legibility in English. The handbook follows the system developed by Gerald Abraham for the *New Grove Dictionary of Music and Musicians*, while respecting the accepted spelling of a number of names that, through common usage, have become so established that a different spelling might merely confuse the English-speaking reader. The transliteration of Greek follows the ELOT 743 (type 2) of the conversion system of the Greek Standardization Organization. Exceptions to all these rules pertain to words and concepts that have become an integral part of the English language and are now in common usage (such as Hanukkah), quotations from other works, and sources that already exist in transliteration (such as the journal of the Tel Aviv–based World Center for Aleppo Jews Traditional Culture *Darkhey "Eretz"*).

The *Merriam-Webster's Collegiate Dictionary*, eleventh edition, serves as the authority for assimilated terms. Different spellings of the same personal name, such as Avram Goldfadn, Avrom Goldenfode, and Abraham Goldfaden, were reconciled in the chapters, but are preserved in the index. The *Encyclopaedia Judaica*, second edition (2007), is the last word on all other Hebrew names and common terms, such as tractates and others. Psalm numbers refer to those of the Hebrew Bible, which differ from those of the Vulgate. Geographic terms appear in the form current during the period discussed. Where those differ from the terms used today, current usage is provided as well. Translations and transcriptions, unless marked otherwise, are by the respective authors.

About the Cover

The cover presents an acrylic, gouache, and colored pencil painting by New York–based artist Mark Podwal, entitled *Hebrew Zodiac* and created in 2001. The artwork has been widely exhibited and is featured on a Rosh Hashanah card offered by the Jewish Museum in New York. The artwork is inspired by the mystical ideas of the Kabbalah and Jewish magic regarding the composition of the universe, as well as by the colorful legends from the Talmud and the daily world of prayer and celebrations of the Sabbath and Jewish holidays. Following Jewish mystical thinking that Jerusalem is the center of the universe, the artist draws an imaginary rendition of the city with recognizable houses, trees, and the Temple Mount as shared symbolism, an iconography in line with similar depictions by Jewish artists from the late fifteenth century until today (though in light of recent events in the region, an iconography perceived as problematic by some). Many of the zodiac's themes resurface in various chapters of this volume. Indeed, the choice of the zodiac for a book on music is not arbitrary. Attempts to link the organized knowledge of astronomy and music hark as far back as Plato and Pythagoras, to Johannes Kepler's *Harmonices mundi* of 1619, in which he imagined the musical scale extending along the zodiac which he uses as a comparison to the Greater Perfect System. In this way, the zodiac serves also as a bookend to the last chapter of the volume, which discusses the music of the spheres.

Podwal's drawing is a two-dimensional representation of a three-dimensional reality, created through the artist's use of shadowing. This approach relates to the content of this handbook, which presents the multiple dimensions of music, though only shadows the actual sounds. The zodiac visually encapsulates spatiality and temporality—two of the volume's key concepts. With its metaphors and symbols, it resembles the handbook's structure, which is also rooted in such approach. No other artwork could better capture this volume's subject: a Jewish music that is neither solely sacred nor secular, nor bound to a particular place and time—but a universal and inclusive ontology (and by extension epistemology). There is also an inherent musicality in Podwal's painting, reminiscent of notated music of the ars subtilior and later graphic notations. Given the symbolic meanings of the zodiac, Podwal's painting visually represents ideas *The Oxford Handbook of Jewish Music Studies* seeks to convey as well as an encompassing inclusiveness of Jewishness that, indeed, reaches beyond the perimeters of this world, drawing on the largest spatiality possible: the universe beyond the belt of the zodiac.

1

INTRODUCTION
Mapping Jewish Music Studies

TINA FRÜHAUF

וְהָיָה זַרְעֲךָ כַּעֲפַר הָאָרֶץ
וּפָרַצְתָּ יָמָּה וָקֵדְמָה וְצָפֹנָה וָנֶגְבָּה וְנִבְרְכוּ בְךָ
כָּל-מִשְׁפְּחֹת הָאֲדָמָה, וּבְזַרְעֶךָ

Your seed shall be like the dust of the earth
and you shall burst forth to the west and the east and the north and
the south;
and all the clans of the earth shall be blessed through you and through
your seeds.

Genesis 28:14

THE inner meaning of this verse from Bereshit (Genesis 28:14), which is known as
Ufaratsta (And you shall burst forth) and rendered in a "vivid" language, pertains to
the dissemination of the Jewish people.[1] The term *ufaratsta* appears in this form only
once in the Hebrew Bible. It has been translated and interpreted with slightly different
meanings, as an indication of strength (Rashi, 1040–1105), as an authorization to break
down a wall or fence in order to make a road (Mishnah Sanhedrin 2:4), and, adopting
this reading, as suggestion that God promised Jacob that his descendants would break
through the borders of the Land of Israel (Rabbi Obadiah Sforno, 1468/1473–ca. 1550).
Abraham Ibn Ezra's interpretation of the whole verse as the expansion of Judaism
through growth of numbers represenced itself in the later twentieth century with the
Lubavitcher Hasidim's extensive outreach efforts initiated by its last rebbe, Menachem
Mendel Schneerson (1902–1994), who in 1958 adopted Ufaratsta as the central mission
for the movement.

The Lubavitcher musically eternalized Ufaratsta in the nigun "Daled bavos" (Melody of four stanzas or gates), also known as "Rav's nigun," and "Alter rebbe's nigun," uniquely attributed to the first Lubavitcher rebbe, Schneur Zalman (1745–1812). Solemn and serious in nature, "Daled bavos" sets the fourness of Ufaratsta to music: it consists of four stanzas, each of which intends to elevate the singer and listener to the next spiritual level to ultimately achieve deveḳut, closeness to God. Set in common time, "Daled bavos" reiterates the same four notes before moving stepwise; only occasionally is there a leap.[2] Like most nigunim, "Daled bavos" is not sung on text (only some use psalm texts in Hebrew) but employs various vocables phonemically consistent with Hebrew, Russian, and Yiddish. These are not nonsense syllables but aim to transcend words and soar above semantics (usually for theurgical purposes) to create a deeper connection with the divine. Wordless signifies limitless. In "Daled bavos," the syllables symbolize YHWH, the tetragrammaton of God's name. The pervasive fourness of this nigun has many meanings, and its presence is not arbitrary. Four is an important number in Judaism, signifying completion and fullness. It corresponds and lifts those at the Hasidic tish to each of the four spiritual worlds in the descending chain of existence, as outlined in the Kabbalah. It also corresponds to the four-stage process of deveḳut: closeness to God through awakening, self-evaluation, work, and union.[3] Thus, Ufratsta can be understood in geographic and demographic terms, as well as in a spiritual and cultural sense, as a practice and aesthetic experience; and musically it has burst forth with countless arrangements of the nigun and new settings, many of them in the domain of popular music.

The *Oxford Handbook of Jewish Music Studies* bursts forth with these and further understandings, discovering and uncovering the reach of "Jewish music" in all hemispheres, past and present: to the west, where in North America ultra-Orthodox women have created feminine musical scenes, balancing new technologies and norms of modesty (*tsniut*) to create dynamic artistic spaces; to the east, where Ḥakham Yosef Ḥayyim Ben 'Eliah al-Ḥakham provided spiritual leadership through paraliturgical songs for the Babylonian Jews in Baghdad before they departed Iraq in the early 1950s; to the north, where Jewish Displaced Persons found a temporary or permanent home in Sweden, transplanting Yiddish song and theater from Poland to new environments, rebuilding and revitalizing their culture. To the south, where émigrés sought integration in the city of Buenos Aires, contributing to the local music scenes and the growing cultural industries, with their cultural heritage leaving a permanent mark on the city's musical life. As these snapshots of topics convey, Jewish music can be found around the world, constituting a global phenomenon. It even reaches beyond, to the spheres, as revealed in Alexandre Cerveux's chapter on the concept of harmony in pre- and early modern Jewish literature, or as translocal and transnational phenomena as Ruthie Abeliovich's chapter on the "Yiddish theater republic of sound," and as Evan Rapport's chapter on Bukharian Jewish wedding music affirm. All this is nothing new. Since the early twentieth century, Jewish music studies have had a wide geographic scope, prefiguring the recent trends in the academy to "go global." This reach also extends to their growth and internationalization, with insights from cultural contexts that have both expanded and challenged accepted approaches, priorities, and ideas regarding what has been labeled "Jewish music."

"Jewish Music"

In 1978 at one of the most inclusive congresses on Jewish music held after the Second World War, Israel Adler (1925–2009) proclaimed in his keynote address: "In trying to define the subject of our discussion we shall avoid ambivalent topics such as 'what is Jewish music' or the so-called 'genuine character of Jewish music'. We shall attempt, rather, to provide a workable definition of the scope of subjects related to our field of study, which for reasons of convenience we shall designate under the overall label of 'Jewish music.'"[4] Ever since its scientific use in early modern Europe, that is, since early modernity, "Jewish music" and its many variants—*jüdische Musik, musica hebraica, música judía, Musik der Hebräer, muziḳah yehudit (מוזיקה יהודית), musique juive,* among others— has been a conceptual vessel, exclusive and inclusive, narrow and broad, and as such filled with differing content over time.[5] It is commonly used as the overarching working term in the academy, the synagogue, the Jewish world, and beyond, and as shorthand for an expansive and disparate series of conversations. It has been debated, contested, avoided, defined, and redefined.[6] As such it embodies a dialectical process and the mobility of the same. Indeed, the term has grown to take on different meanings in a wide variety of contexts across the world, for a diverse conglomerate of people at different places and at various times. Accordingly, definitions are reflections, responding to the state of Jewish music in its respective milieu and habitus. In the academic context, they often mirror the anxieties Jewish music studies have faced.

In his aforementioned speech Israel Adler, continues his elaborations, surprisingly stating, by way of agreeing with Batya Bayer, that the "functional definition" by Curt Sachs (1881–1959)—"Jewish Music is that Music made by Jews, for Jews and as Jews"[7]—is most workable (this definition, set forth in 1957, has been repeatedly adopted, although many scholars wrestle with it).[8] (Assaf Shelleg has proposed its expansion to include music about Jews, a category that emerged in the fifteenth century.[9]) Sachs' definition, as it were, echoes a similar phrase Abraham Lincoln used in the Gettysburg Address, which in turn was adopted to the French Constitution of 1958; it assumes an underlying principle of nationalism, which after the foundation of the modern State of Israel has territorially grounded itself. And yet, Jews have represented throughout their history a unique fusion of peoplehood and religion, which cannot be grasped on either side of such dichotomies or by a delimiting to national, racial, cultural, ethnic, religious, linguistic, and other categories. Jewishness was never a simple or unitary identity and in light of the evolving heterogeneity of the Jewish people cannot serve as a marker for what is Jewish music and what is not; especially in light of a long prevalent and increasing participation of non-Jews as well as what Isaac Deutscher termed "non-Jewish Jews" (those who abandoned particular Jewish practices and instead searched for universal solutions to the world's problems), a concept taken further by Yuri Slezkine.[10] Indeed, creators, performers, and audiences and those who study them are as diverse as the sounds themselves.

Another factor in this discourse is music's variable ontology—as performing art, artifact, culture, representation, and so on. As an organized collection of sounds, it can submit to but also resist fixed notation; it can attain, convey, and traverse meaning beyond resounding. As the most abstract of the arts, an art without referentiality, music as a practice and discourse is a cultural reality that functions as a mirror of diverse collectives across the geographical-historical-cultural maze. As other musics, Jewish music is and has always been heterogenous, inherently hybrid, and a work in progress, continuing existing and established expressions and creating new ones. More specifically, it encompasses complex and multifaceted relationships between Jewishness, inwardly and outwardly, and sounds from ancient times to the present day, and not necessarily in linear patterns but rather in discontinuous and fragmentary lines as a result of migrations, persecutions, and exterminations (a discussion of temporality will ensue below). As such, it is the focal point of shared ideas and beliefs. It offers a positive and open term of categorizing a spectrum of musics, whatever they mean to the reader and listener; or as Stefan Wolpe poignantly affirmed in 1940: "The question of Jewish music conceals the questioner. Who asks and who needs the answer."[11] Indeed, there are levels of authenticity that can never be agreed upon due to their subjectivity. Seeking a common denominator, Philip Bohlman asserts that, "at the core of the paradox of defining Jewish music is the frequent belief in authenticity, chosenness, and uniqueness."[12]

What seems like another paradox—there is a field with active scholars, but disputes about the definition and even existence of Jewish music continue to linger—refers to a productive openness and fluidity of a term that relates to musics and musical activities that have been surfacing, persisting or evolving, and expanding in the course of time.[13] Thus the use of the term does not imply any *one* definition as it can be understood in a variety of ways, reflecting a myriad of possible contexts and experiences.

With every chapter being a mediator that thickens the network of Jewish music(s), the *Oxford Handbook of Jewish Music Studies* consciously maintains the term, thus accepting its historical precedence and function, while acknowledging its complexity. It relies on it also as a shorthand for Jewish musical activities and expressions, and with the understanding that it is non-hierarchical with regard to the repertoires and practices generally associated with it. Such equity also expresses itself in the range of musics the handbook chapters include—from Asia to the Americas, from antiquity and early modernity to the very present day, from vernacular and popular to classical repertoires and prevalent in various contexts, as well as to the spectrums filling these bookends. Jewish music requires no rigid definition as its holistic understanding will emerge with sufficient clarity in the chapters that follow this introduction and that together form a meaningful whole. Instead of a singular definition or apologetics of the same, a productive way then to approach "Jewish music" is through a problematization of the issues it faces in our time and through a proposal of how it can be adequately studied.

JEWISH MUSIC *STUDIES*—
THEORIES, METHODOLOGIES

In the early twentieth century Abraham Zvi Idelsohn (1882–1938) advanced an over-arching theory for the study of Jewish music. Born in Latvia, he began as a peripatetic cantor, active in different European cities and in Johannesburg, before emigrating to Ottoman Palestine in 1906. Having settled in Jerusalem in 1907, he observed a great diversity of musics among the resident Jews who had settled there from various places. Supported by the Phonogrammarchiv in Vienna, he engaged in the recording, transcription, and analysis of these oral traditions. Idelsohn discerned unique recurring motifs and progressions, which to him suggested a common origin in the first century CE. The results of his comparative studies present the first encompassing, though still fragmentary, description of the variety of surviving Jewish musical practices. A Zionist in the early stages of his career, Idelsohn proposed the underlying cultural unity of the Jewish people, despite their millenary dispersion among nations, and promoted the view that the music of the various Jewish communities in the present reflects aspects of that unity.[14] Working under a complex and fluid ideological agenda, in his landmark book *Jewish Music in Its Historical Development* (1929) Idelsohn presented a unilineal and linear historical narrative of Jewish music from biblical times to the early twentieth century rooted in essentialism. Written after Idelsohn had moved to the United States, it displays a departure from the primordial theory, toward a more multilayered approach, reflecting a sober balance between diaspora and territorial Zionism.[15] It still lacks the understanding that history is too complex to be fully depicted through a singular representation of events. Despite its problematic assumptions, it is widely consulted; in fact, Idelsohn's basic ideas have shaped Jewish music research for decades, granting him the title of "father of Jewish musicology"—deservedly so in light of his monumental ten-volume *Hebräisch-orientalischer Melodienschatz—Thesaurus of Oriental Hebrew Melodies* (Leipzig: Breitkopf & Härtel et al., 1914–1932), which in its final form covers a universe of over eight thousand Jewish melodies including the musical traditions of Yemenite, Babylonian, Persian, Bukharan, Oriental Sephardi, Moroccan, German, eastern European, and Hasidic Jewish communities in Palestine and elsewhere, laying the groundwork for subsequent generations of scholars.

Apart from Idelsohn's questionable attempt at a metatheory, there have been similarly problematic theories on the relations between Jewish and Christian religious musical practices, solidifying with the work of Eric Werner and lingering on into the 1990s,[16] and turning into a critical approach and broadening toward secular musics with the work of Ruth HaCohen.[17] More specifically, Werner pursued the theory of an active and passive assimilation, categorizing musical examples based on the presence or absence of a "Judaizing" process as Jewish collectives absorb "foreign" musical elements. His student William Sharlin expanded this thinking by way of a third category, that of experiential assimilation, wherein sounds that are not overtly "Judaized" can still be actively absorbed and transformed by a prevailing "Jewish spirit." Apart from this, there have also been attempts at modal theories, though their application is narrow and they do not apply to a broad and inclusive Jewish music.[18] Still, the perpetuation of modality as a widely applicable cross-cultural category pioneered by Idelsohn and furthered by European and American scholars has been an important train of thought that in the twenty-first century culminated in broader methodological ideas.[19] While Jewish music studies, by responding to various disciplines and fields in the course of the later twentieth century, have largely moved away from essentialist approaches—whether or not a piece or practice is studied as Jewish music lies less in the music itself than in the context of its creation and in its meaning as a marker of Jewishness—a new overarching theory has not crystallized and should not be expected to emerge in light of the collapse of disciplinary partitions and with academic crossovers becoming almost unpredictable (and representational methodologies invalid).[20] What often passes for theorizing amounts for the most part to what has been done and suggestions for what might be done rather than statements of relationships to be explored. Edwin Seroussi, in his seminal article "Music: The 'Jew' of Jewish Studies," evaluates what he calls "four key theoretical concepts for a musicology of the Jewish," which are tradition, binaries, genres, and canonization. These he rightfully critiques for implying unifying and homogenous aspects of Jewish music from the Bible to modern times, and yet he does not advance alternatives that take into consideration the transcending of geographical, cultural, and linguistic boundaries.[21] Likewise, in several of his writings, Philip Bohlman has advanced ontologies of Jewish music (such as those relating to religion, text and language, embodiment, geography, and politics and culture) without synthesizing them.[22] In parallel, an ever-increasing number of focused Jewish music studies that populate the musicological landscape outshines the relative paucity of attempts to theorize, asserting a praxis of multiplication, nonsystematic and non-differential proliferation, and most importantly contiguities.

That Jewish music studies have been rather untheoretical mirrors the uncertainty among scholars whether it is a field (provided that fields ought to have theories) or whether it merely represents a domain of interest shared by a conglomerate of scholars. Such theory-lacking Jewish music studies would have no use for a methodology; indeed, a specific system of methods is impossible to outline in the absence of theory. The lingering and artificial division between (historical) musicology and ethnomusicology has added to this uncertainty, even though boundaries have become increasingly permeable. (Musicology is henceforth used as an umbrella term for ethnomusicology, historical musicology, music theory, and systematic musicology.[23]) Indeed, many chapters in this handbook dissolve these presumed boundaries for the sake of broader, integrative, and holistic perspectives. Quite a few have transcended these presumed boundaries previously.[24]

As a field, Jewish music studies has been decentered, and along with it its supporting and adjacent theories. In the twenty-first century, it mirrors the situation of Jewish studies (as well as other fields), which is an even broader umbrella for the academic exploration of Jewish and Judaic subjects in the context of history, literature, philosophy, and ritual and religion across disciplinary boundaries. It has likewise seen expansion and a permeability, creating new conditions as well as debates of its ontology.[25] While Jewish studies does not conform to the norms of classic historical or literary or other disciplines based upon either a specific time, place, or a specific language, Jewish music studies largely focuses on one specific language, that of music (if music is, indeed, viewed as a language). And yet, with musicology not always using music as language or text but veering toward procedures prevalent in philology and cultural studies as well as criticism based on feminist or gender studies, queer theory or postcolonial theory, among others, one easily faces a cul-de-sac. Additionally, the ontology of music itself has recently come under scrutiny.[26]

Although not quite equivalent, Jewish music studies could be regarded as analogous to a field of area studies to which various disciplines are applied, such as history and anthropology, literature and philosophy, and many others. Various chapters in the handbook provide clear examples of the disciplinary contributions to the field. Accordingly, it would be pointless to expect an overarching methodology or consistent methods across the field as a whole, but rather one should be open to a breadth of (cultural) theories and a range of methodological options. Indeed, a different perspective on the current state of Jewish music studies might suggest that no single theory predominates and scholars work with many. If a field requires a unifying paradigm, then Jewish music studies might not qualify, but each of its employed theories would account for or require a "disciplined" methodology.

Jewish music studies have unfolded as a methodological palimpsest by picking and choosing from one or another, instead of creating an integrative methodology demanded by the research subject at large. Few research projects have sought explicitly to synthesize disciplinary approaches. Such an interdisciplinary approach would exceed simply bringing together disciplinary competences, as it implies an intellectual construction that goes beyond the intrinsic value of the methods, in order to take into account the very essence of the complex phenomenon that the different disciplines are intended to illuminate. Many chapters in this handbook have overcome this by way of transdisciplinary approaches, combining, for example, archival research, interviews, musical analysis, participant observation for audio-visual and textual documentation, and transcription in one single study such as the chapter by Miranda Crowdus on liturgical music and the Romaniote Jews; or relying on procedures prevalent in manuscript studies, music iconography, and source criticism, as can be observed in Suzanne Wijsman's chapter on music and the Oppenheimer Siddur that crosses into art history.[27] There is no doubt that Jewish music studies is en route to being ever more dialogic and embracing difference, with researchers consciously or subconsciously relying on interdisciplinarity by synthesizing links between disciplines into a coordinated and coherent whole, or multidisciplinarity by drawing on knowledge from different disciplines but staying within their boundaries. Indeed, a hybrid musical culture warrants a pluralistic approach that overcomes the compartmentalization of disciplines. Georgina Born has advanced similar thinking for musicology, proposing a relational musicology in which music's ontology is related to the social or is a social object, beyond text and practice, in an interdisciplinary framework for the sake of mediations.[28] Adam Newton takes this even further for Jewish studies, envisioning the field to go beyond the disciplines and interdisciplines to an entirely new place "at once an interruption and a sharing-at-the-boundary among its constituent parties and with its university others."[29]

If Jewish music studies is understood as a contraction of and the intersection between Jewish studies and music studies—two bookends between which all disciplined research unfolds—then the choice of methodology must be approached by questions on the nature of music and sound within Jewish contexts or how the sound itself reflects concepts of Jewishness and vice versa. Such objectives can equip the researchers with a richly evocative common ground for substantive and interdisciplinary study.

Jewish music studies should be captured and accepted as a loosely defined and open-ended field at the crossroads of several of the aforementioned disciplines and other fields, first and foremost musicology and Jewish studies, and embedded in the wider humanities and social sciences as well as the performing arts. Relatively unbounded while reflecting the enduring difficulty of bridging disciplinary divides, it is as complex and changing as rapidly as the musical world it purports to study. Jewish music studies, like other academic fields, is constantly being created and re-created through the research, writing, and teaching of scholars. Accordingly, at any given time and working on any given subject, it would be important to ask which paradigms guide the field, what the theoretical and methodological developments in the humanities and social sciences are, and how scholars working in a broad range of disciplines contribute to the field. The trajectories of our aforementioned protagonists—Sachs, Idelsohn, and Adler—point to related issues, namely, the stance of Jewish music studies in the academy and further matters concerning discipline.

INSTITUTIONALIZATION AND CONSOLIDATION

As contributor to musicology and founding father of organology, Curt Sachs, whose degree was in art history, never held a tenured academic appointment in his native Germany for racial reasons, nor in the countries of emigration for reasons too complex to unravel here.[30] In the United States he taught as visiting professor at various universities (New York University, Harvard, Northwestern, and Michigan); beginning in 1952, he lectured regularly at Columbia University on topics of the newly emerging ethnomusicology and systematic musicology. Three years before his death, in 1956, he received an honorary doctorate from the Freie Universität Berlin and was appointed an emeritus professor by the German government. Jewish music was not the basis of any of his appointments, nor was it the core of his research. Indeed, one might wonder whether he would have even received these positions had he devoted himself to it exclusively.

As a contemporary rooted in cantorial practice rather than scholarship, Idelsohn exemplifies a different path. After he left Palestine in 1921, he visited Berlin, Leipzig, London, and Oxford on lecture tours and settled in the United States in 1922. In 1924 he began to teach Jewish liturgy and music at Hebrew Union College in Cincinnati, Ohio, focusing on training the clergy (the school would award him an honorary doctorate in 1933). From this point on, the cantorial school would be the most solid framework for scholars involved in Jewish music studies, at least in the United States.[31]

Israel Adler's institutional inroad took place on the grounds of library science. From 1950 to 1963, he headed the Hebraica-Judaica department of the Bibliothèque nationale de France in Paris. In 1963 Adler returned to the country he had called home since 1936. He was appointed by the Hebrew University of Jerusalem as director of the Music Department of the Jewish National and University Library, and in 1964 founded there the Israeli National Sound Archive and the Jewish Music Research Centre, which he directed from 1964 to 1969 and, after two years of directorship of the library, again from 1971 onward. In 1971 he became associate professor of musicology at Tel Aviv University, followed by an appointment in 1973 at Hebrew University, where he became full professor in 1975, teaching Jewish music from the Middle Ages to the Emancipation of the Jews in Europe, with a focus on written sources, the rabbinic attitude to music, and the dialectic between the oral and written sources of sacred Jewish music.

These three cases, and many more over the course of the twentieth and early twenty-first centuries, suggest that there has been no uniform practice to anchoring Jewish music studies, as its institutional presence is different across and even within the nations in which scholars are active. Jewish music studies is neither firmly nor exclusively practiced by musicologists and embedded in musicology departments nor in any other, although musicologists as trained interpreters of music make for the majority of scholars active in the field. This is underlined by the fact that all three chairs of Jewish music—in Weimar, Hannover, and Los Angeles, established in the years 2013 to 2015—are under the auspices of musicology departments. Outside of musicology, scholars are in quite disparate faculties, in which their interest in Jewish music constitutes only one segment in their intellectual work. In recent years Jewish studies has taken a heightened though still fluctuating interest in music, with the American Jewish Studies Association featuring, for example in 2018, an impressively high number of papers and panels of interest in the areas of music, sound, and performance studies; or with the Oxford Seminar in Advanced Jewish Studies of 2019/2020 being devoted to the theme "Jewish musical cultures in early modern Europe." The quadrennial World Congress of Jewish Studies, which has served as an axis mundus for Jewish music scholars since its second meeting in 1957, foreshadowed this interest, initially scattering music scholarship in topical sections on history, language, literature, and the Bible—and from 1985 on offering a designated art, folklore, and music division. The 2022 World Congress of Jewish Studies offered an ever-more substantial section on music with concerts and workshops as well as papers on music integrated into other sections.

These developments correlate with special-interest or study groups, which have formed mostly within major musicological societies. The Association for Jewish

Studies hosts an interest group as well. The European Association for Jewish Studies accepts an increasingly healthy number of music papers into its quadrennial congress. Subject-specific conferences and the Jewish Music Forum, a project of the American Society for Jewish Music, as well as the recently formed International Forum for Jewish Music Studies, have spun a wide circle, including linguists, historians, pedagogues, practitioners and theologians, and others. All these developments support the presumption that the institutionalization of Jewish music studies has begun to solidify in its being recognized as a field.

While these tendencies can be observed in England, Germany, Israel, and the United States, academic interest has unfolded in other countries of Europe and the Americas, as well as Australia (to a far lesser extent Asia and Africa). Accordingly, and given the nature of its subject, the *Oxford Handbook of Jewish Music Studies* has international participation, with chapters conceived by authors who reside in or stem from Australia, Argentina, Canada, England, France, Germany, Israel, Italy, the Netherlands, Scandinavia, South Africa, the former Soviet Union, and the United States. Such breadth and inclusivity are especially critical in light of the recent discoveries in the field, which have brought to discussion the Jewish music of areas previously treated peripherally—countries behind the former Iron Curtain and Latin America—and of the "double" or post-diasporas. With this, studies emerged that investigate issues of place and space, addressing questions about the effect and meaning of uprooting and dislocation, the significance of belonging to a place (or to several), the emergence of new diasporas, and similar. (Earlier studies have mainly focused on music in places and spaces that people created, occupied, passed through, or endured—the material sites that were essential to the implementation of Jewish music and inseparable from people's experience of it.) Accordingly, reframing the field in a more transnational mode has significant implications for the nature of Jewish music studies, for understanding the past and present, and for shaping it for the future.

In parallel to these developments, a heightened stream of publications emerged at the turn of the twenty-first century, reflecting not only a rise in the field's popularity, but also emerging subjects as well as topical shifts.[32] Holocaust and post-Holocaust subjects are at an all-time peak, and the same is true for modern Israel; the Americas are being approached as a whole as well as by supranational regions, with more attention given to Latin America than ever before; the Islamic world has become of interest anew; and parts of Asia have come into focus. Publications have been increasingly engaging with the role of women, Hasidism, and popular musics. Comparative studies are devoted to Arab-Jewish relations, replacing the earlier focus on Christian-Jewish relations. Specific publications could be mentioned, but a simple keyword search in *RILM Abstracts of Music Literature* will corroborate these observations and unearth specific results (including articles in nearly eighty Jewish studies journals as well as non-music journals published worldwide). This cursory survey underlines that, especially in light of migration and hybridity, any thinking about Jewish music as continuous and unified is not viable, if it ever has been. In order to accept this overarching diversity and multiplicity, it is important to retreat from such ideas, as well as the aforementioned categories scrutinized by Edwin Seroussi.

In his theoretical propositions on twentieth-century Jewish literature, Dan Miron likewise breaks with the idea of a lineage, proposing a "modern Jewish literary complex."[33] Following his proposition, one might think as well of a "Jewish musical complex" that is vast and diffuse. Adapting Miron's theory for Jewish music studies (and following Assaf Shelleg's application of the same that takes into consideration multiple dimensions), nonlinear and noncontinuous contiguities that operate within and across designated spaces—with an abrogation of binary classifications and concurrent retention of differences in mind—can serve as a principle that informs various approaches. Contiguities can be observed in the chapters of this volume that are relational in terms of spatiality and approximate other semblances of significant order, and through links that are more ambivalent and less tangible, or predictable, and yet revealing. Miron captures these links with notions such as "dualities, parallelisms, occasional intersections, marginal overlapping, hybrids, similarities within dissimilarities, mobility, changeability, occasional emergence of patterns and their eventual disappearance, randomness."[34] Other ambivalent and hard-to-define relations between text/music, creator, and the awareness or experience of Jewishness or the sense of being Jewish in the world could be added. Further, contiguity as concept also opens the path to investigating not merely what connects Jewish musics, but what separates and discontinues them.

By embracing contiguities, Jewish music studies circumscribes a new Jewish musical complex based on proximities, unregulated contacts, and moments of adjacency in designated spaces, fathoming the interconnectivity of various collective cultural traditions through various forms of loose or close relations. Such an approach opens the possibility of moving away from various ontological propositions to empirical definitions. As such, a Jewish musical complex implies a new way of thinking about Jewish music as a construct: it suggests that there is no previous, coherent canon to which Jewish music should conform, and there should be no specific, fixed Jewish music canon. By embracing the concept of a musical radicant, the field could move beyond a strict taxonomy of musics and musical activities belonging to a canon, and even a Jewish music without Jewish agency, but conceived in reaction to, for example, the Holocaust—or with regard to text-based musical settings of languages that are in neither Hebrew, Aramaic, Yiddish, nor Ladino. This would not only lead to a great expansion of the Jewish musical complex, but also create the basis for an institutionalized cultural capital (in Bourdieusian and Latourian terms) that would, in return, certify the status and the importance of Jewish music studies as an autonomous field. The question remains how to model Jewish music studies rooted in contiguities.

Modeling Jewish Music Studies

In light of the above examined decenteredness of Jewish music studies and its pursuit of multiplication, nonsystematic and nondifferential proliferation, as well as contiguities, the author wishes to propose a three-dimensional model for the approach to Jewish music studies, as a heuristic device for planning and carrying out research and for thinking and writing about a given subject. Putting disciplinary concerns aside entirely, this model brings forward three conceptual lenses—statements of relationships, as it were—in which contiguities can be explored and ought to be employed to bring into focus Jewish music (each lens has the potential to construct a particular notion of Jewish music, but it does not have to). These lenses exist within or have some relationship with place and space, the quality or state of people being collective, and the state of existing within or having some relationship with time. The model is rooted in the understanding that Jewish music studies, despite its arrival still being en route, paralleling "a Jewish Studies-à-venir."[35]

Spatiality

At its most fundamental, a spatial approach begins with the question *where*, inquiring about place and space. In recent years, in the aftermath of the spatial turn, debates on the distinction between place and space have become increasingly differentiated, de-pendent on the disciplinary context and the subject of interest. Social theorists such as Henri Lefebvre, Michel de Certeau, and others have given much attention to the epistemological and ontological complexities of space and place, and cultural geographers have particularly probed the politics of controlling space and defining place.[36] As Barbara Mann asserts, "space and place depend on one another for defini-tion";[37] and in turn, the engagement with them hinges upon the understanding of these concepts, which have varied over time and in different academic disciplines and fields. Acknowledging them to be interrelated (and in some instances also interchangeable), cultural studies generally sees "place" to designate a particular location, to be actual, a physical, static environment through which we move—while "space" is understood as multi-dimensional and fluid, and as an experience of place, it can also be imagined, metaphorical or symbolic, and abstract, a representation, as it were.[38] For Jewish music studies, the Hebrew designation *ha-maḳom* might be useful. Offering multiple dimensions ha-maḳom allows for middle grounds and in-betweenness to explore contiguities in the (hybridized) ontologies of Jewish music, as the term carries multiple meanings: the relationship to a place, the implied treatment of a place, the act of taking possession thereof, the settlement and development of a place, and even the absence of such relationships to a place. It is also one of God's names.[39] These meanings resonate in the chapters in this volume.

Following the directions other disciplines and fields have taken, spatiality can serve as an important analytical and theoretical lens for Jewish music studies indeed.[40] It proves fruitful not least because some of the most pronounced spatial concepts such as *galut* (exile), shtetl, or ghetto are, if not exclusively, distinctively linked to Jewish music. Focusing on Jewish music in various places and within designated spaces also allows for shifting away from tracing—which implies more of a linear process—toward mapping, which recognizes the palimpsest of layers and allows to point to relationships and to contiguities. Utilized both in a literal sense and as a metaphor, the map is thus also an allegory of space and time.[41] Embracing it as such can uncover the meanings behind seemingly self-evident and unchallenged cultural topographies, as well as representations, versions of place and space that we thought we knew.[42]

In a world of shifting maps, established lenses tied to specific Jewish geographies and their cultures—such as Ashkenaz/Sepharad, East/West, *Erets* or *Medinat Yisrael*/diaspora, and similar—have long served their purpose; they no longer capture the spectrum of places and spaces of Jewish music. This is especially pertinent for developments from the nineteenth century onward when mobility, migration, and displacement began to accelerate, blurring the meanings between these and other spatially derived concepts, although they can be contested in the longue durée given the population shifts from the pre-Christian era onward. Jews were always diasporic, living outside the Land of Israel as well as in it, largely being what we would term today "cosmopolitan."[43] Jewish culture always had multiple centers that have shifted over time and can be expected to shift again. In this, the interactions of Jews and non-Jews, in the various environments in which they have taken place, is a given. With ever-changing (diasporic) maps reordered so many times, musical and other activities began to meld and mutually shape each other.

Although location is a crucial substrate of the many places of Jewish music, it is just one of its many spatial facets. With musical activities and manifestations in material or non-material settings, certain places and spaces are more strongly tied to Jewish music or a container for the same. This handbook proposes specific places and spaces distinct to Jewish music, which will be elucidated in the last part of this introduction, "Organization"—a first comprehensive foray into capturing Jewish music spatially that ought to be expanded over time. More concretely, it focuses on both general or mainstream spaces that are material, such as the concert hall and similar spaces that offer stages, material *Jewish* spaces such as the chuppah, non-material Jewish spaces such as the phenomenological space of *shekhinah*, and spaces that can be captured as either material or non-material such as ghetto. The concept of "Jewish space" is taken literally as opposed to its prevalent post-1945 application, when it began to designate the space occupied by Jewish culture and Jewish memory within mainstream society, entailing the ways in which European countries have begun to integrate Jewish history and memory, and also the Holocaust, into an understanding of their national history, regardless of the current size or activity of the local Jewish population.[44] Jewish studies scholars have scrutinized and proposed many other places and spaces for further study, such as *beit ha-midrash*, cemetery, shtetl, mellah, and other loci of a given Jewish community— as well as imagined and conceptual ones that point to the constructedness of the two notions.[45]

Ultimately, differentiated and undifferentiated spaces can be produced and enacted as Jewish through musical activity by Jews and non-Jews alike. This is significant, given that some spaces may be thought of as neutral before receiving meaning through Jewish music. Related to this is the question of how music and music making are part of performing certain kinds of spaces into being, and the wider significance of people's direct engagements with the material (including sonic) qualities of musical environments. As such, spaces as sites of Jewish musical enactment are dependent on sound, narrative, or similar production while often being bound up in matters of religion, ethnicity, politics, power, and similar. They also have the ability to affirm specific musics as a Jewish space in itself. As such, Jewish music in a given space or place can be composed or improvised, performed, transmitted, staged, maintained, shared, and so on. These are central spatial strategies of Jewish music in their respective places situated in the world at large. And yet, a typology would depend on and correlate with the peoples that inhabit them in and through time.

Temporality

The destruction of the temples, the Inquisition, the birth of the Reform movement and the subsequent reimaginations of Jewish worship, the Holocaust, and the creation of the modern State of Israel—each of these and other moments put their own stamp on the meaning of Jewishness and time, and of the (Jewish) past as well as a given present. In the most recent encyclopedic entry on Jewish music, for *MGG Online*, Edwin Seroussi has addressed the meaning of linear time, cyclical time, and communitarian versus domestic time. For the first, he asserts that it is largely devoid of tangible substance until it enters the stage of European music history during the Enlightenment, followed by a linear development that also swept synagogue music (which begins, I would assert, already in the nineteenth century, not in the early twentieth century). For the second, Seroussi seeks to put aside linear development in favor of a cyclic conception of time that stresses repetition as an ideal rather than development, leaning on the fact that cyclical repetition is the hallmark of liturgy. For the third, Seroussi asserts that communitarian time regulates Jewish musical performances that depend on the concerted effort of the congregation and are carried at fixed times, while domestic time generates musical performances that depend on the rhythms of the life cycle of individuals and their immediate social surroundings. Where is time outside the European concert canon, the congregation, and domestic space in this? What about layers of time that a music scholar can be easily confronted with in the twenty-first century, when contemplating the performance of music created in the late Renaissance, which draws on prayers going back to the Middle Ages or earlier (perhaps to the Bible)? Tradition—in the sense of *tradere* as a process—abolishes time, making all agents contemporaries. And yet the music of Salamone Rossi does not quite belong in the same dimension of reality occupied by us. With research subjects stretching from the Bible to the very present, Jewish music studies requires distinct and multiple understandings of temporality.

Spatiality is adding another layer of complexity, in light of certain cultures in distinct places having had different understandings of time throughout history. As I have argued elsewhere, music studies need to depart from established notions that describe temporal phenomena and related concepts such as "revival" or the prefix "neo," which suggest cycles, but are ultimately bound to linear conceptions of an absolute time.[46] Jewish music studies, with its long temporal (and spatial) reach, needs to think of musical activities within a given place and space in terms of temporal conceptualizations that are in essence conjunctive (in which two or more times follow one another or coincide), disjunctive (a mixture of times beyond any notion of linearity), and heterogenous. Temporal connections can manifest themselves beyond this and in various ways, in concentric circles that imply a fluidity between past, present, and future without closure and in which the previous is also a new beginning; they can render themselves in more distinct circular formations (conceived by or related to space), that is, spiral or curvilinear formations in which Jewish music goes forth and returns, creating moments of simultaneity and coeval-ness of diverse experiences of time, signifying repetition but with a difference.

New and distinct approaches to temporality can cut across established boundaries of historical eras and propose an approach to comprehending Jewish music that counteracts the preponderance of single-period or other narrow thinking. It cultivates an understanding of how Jewish music may be grasped not only in a single moment, during a specific period, but also in the longue durée. Several chapters in this handbook have done so such as Vanessa Paloma Elbaz in connecting historical Al-Andalus and the timeless Sepharad with present-day Morocco and Spain, Phil Alexander in his assessment of klezmer's changing social role, or Yoel Greenberg and Rebecca Cypess as well as Diana Matut, who address synchronic and diachronic temporal manifestations of their subjects. They underline the importance of microhistories (of micromusics) in lieu of grand narratives, with focused narratives beyond linearity.[47]

Collectivity (Rather than Identity)

In 1994 Richard Handler posed the question whether identity is a useful concept and suggested that we should "be as suspicious of 'identity' as we learned to be of 'culture,' 'tradition,' 'nation,' and 'ethnic group.'"[48] His theory of identity as a "communicative process" challenges notions of stability and immutability in much the same way as the rethinking of "community" in recent years.[49] Both concepts are neither monolithic, in geographical or cultural terms, nor fixed. Both are constructed. Both are undoubtedly embedded in collectivity, which as a conceptual container is broad and useful as it veers away from distinguishing between cultures, religious practices, or denominations as lenses of Jewish music studies and aids the overcoming of identity politics. Collectivity also extends to scenes, groups, and other formations of peoples coming together as a body, as well as groupings of individuals and other incongruencies that stem from what might be perceived as a collective.

Theories of collectivity go back to Herbert Spencer and Émile Durkheim—the former's theoretization being broad and extending to concepts of the homogenous and heterogenous, the latter's aiming at more specific features and capacities. Adjacent theories emerged focusing on collective memory, collective agency, and so on.[50] As such collectivity hangs loosely at the intersection of affiliation, demographics, time, and space. It is a social process rooted to some extent in ideology. It is fluid, but its inclusivity implies borders. In this, community, while well theorized, is especially problematic. Just as Jewish music comprises a multitude of meanings, so too does community.

Originally the theoretical property of sociologists, the concept of community remained relatively stable, encompassing the elements of locale, social network, and a shared sense of belonging. The basic tenets were based on the ideas of the founding fathers—Émile Durkheim, Karl Marx, Ferdinand Tönnies, and Max Weber. In the 1980s scholars such as Jean-Luc Nancy, Maurice Blanchot, and Giorgio Agamben began to rethink its basic presumptions with a view on its limits and the tangibility of social interactions, questioning the concept's applicability in modern, globalized contexts, where mobility and technological innovations had rendered relatively fixed social boundaries porous; further theories continued to emerge.[51] These lines of thought transformed community into a *metaphysical* idea (rather than one resting on solid, tangible social foundations) and posed a new conceptual difficulty: the tension between the "real" versus the "imagined."[52] As Fran Tonkiss has poignantly sums it up: "Difficult to define, harder to observe and unvirtuous to reject."[53]

To complicate matters within the Jewish context, the once polar distinctions between Reform and Orthodoxy, Ashkenazim and Sephardim, Zionist and anti-Zionist, and secular Jews and Haredim and Hasidim have diffused into spectrums with many shades, ever more challenging the idea of a "Jewish community." Various chapters in this handbook nonetheless embrace the concept of community, but by focusing on specific and more graspable formations: a specific Jewish community, the musical community, the urban community, and so on. Other contributors to this handbook have focused on smaller sets of collectivities involved with Jewish musical activity, such as congregations, scenes, or groupings such as a movement, wedding party, and family. Most have theoretically bolstered their collectivity-in-focus as well as inscribed performers, composers, and other seminal personalities into their discussions, thus reflecting the reality of collectivities being products of interacting individuals. Scholars might wish to embrace the above-mentioned poles, not as expressions of identity but as (politicized) literary metaphors or cultural constructions, following the example of Sephardism.

Due to its breadth and in light of the broad and diffuse participation in Jewish musical activity, the concept of collectivity is deliberately chosen as a lens. A model focused on *Jewish* collectivities (genetic Judaism, statist Zionism, or potential victimhood) that stress unity around bloodline would exclude the participation of non-Jews so pertinent to Jewish music. And yet it allows for a focus on specific *Jewish* populations (Syrian and Bukharian Jews, and so on) and denominations (reaching from Reconstructionism and Reform to various forms of Orthodoxy), amalgamations of the same, or temporal formations. Mapping collectivities in places and spaces that embody relationships, while acknowledging their existence within or relationship with time, can be a useful procedure for all Jewish music studies.

ORGANIZATION

The volume presents twenty-nine chapters in eight categories, that is, spaces that are actual and concrete as well as conceptual and are roughly organized according to their scale. The inner structure of each section follows distinct criteria, such as the size or composition of the collectives that musically or sonically inhabit them (while reinscribing individuals). For all their variety, the chapters share a common structure and general approach. In each of their chapters, the authors situate their key spatial questions in the context of relevant scholarship and base their observations upon both musical, visual, and/or textual evidence essential for interrogating and representing select spaces of Jewish music. They interrogate to what extent spaces and spatial experiences influenced the course and perception of musical events—and conversely, which actors and which practices were involved in the emergence, change, or disappearance of places or spaces with significance for Jewish musical life. The focus on the places and spaces of Jewish music not only brings to light previously neglected perspectives, but also challenges the question of perspective itself. As with all collections, the sections and chapters could have been organized in other ways, and some of the chapters, reframed, could have been suitably appropriate in different sections.

As such, this conceptual organization, rooted in spatiality, aims at bringing to the fore how Jewish music unfolds within distinct spaces and how they can be understood anew for Jewish music studies. The very purpose of articulating and exploring them is to inspire cultural topographies of Jewish music and to uncover contiguities. Indeed, what does music within the *eruv* share with other Jewish spaces such as the ghetto, the Jewish quarter, and specifically the mellah? With such thinking, the organization of the handbook seeks to defy and transcend binaries and expected designations as well as conceptualizations rooted therein.

Part I: Land—אדמה

The concept of adamah originated in the Hebrew Bible, where it surfaces over 220 times, appearing sixteen times in the first five chapters of Genesis alone. It has been translated predominantly as land, but also as material substance and earth, while also referring to *the* earth.[54] It has also been captured as ground, soil, and territory, as well as country. It recalls the meaning of *arets*, and yet as W. Joseph Stallings asserts, there is a clear differentiation between the two, with the former referring to the "inhabitable land upon the Earth," while adamah designates "the Earth as a plant."[55] Arets evokes immediate association with the Land of Israel, which is first mentioned in 1 Samuel 13:19, following the Exodus, and ever since has occupied various geographies in the Middle East, to describe a somewhat flexible territory with fluid borders on which the tribes of Israel had their settlements. Veering away from Erets Yisrael or *ha-arets* as *the* central land of Jewish music, the chapters in this section look at various lands and territories in the Middle East and North Africa. In his chapter "Adamot—Art Music—Israel," Assaf Shelleg focuses on the lands related to Israeli art music that are neither necessarily national nor refer exclusively to the territories of the UN Security Council Resolution 242. In this he resituates key variables of Hebrew culture at the overlap of modern Jewish culture and contemporary art music, acknowledging that several lands have been conditioning Hebrewism since its outset. Vanessa Paloma Elbaz's chapter, "Land, Voice, Nation: Jewish Music in the Adamot of Al-Andalus," demonstrates how the Jewish relationship to adamah counterpoints the tripartite relationship of Jews to local specificities, to the diverse nation in Spain and Morocco, and to their simultaneous belonging to a larger Jewish polity. She draws on the Jewish voice performed by Jews and non-Jews, but also fertility and burial, to examine these spaces. In " 'We Shall Sing Songs and Praise to the Lord Who Created Us Last in the World': Ḥakham Joseph Ḥayyim of Baghdad, Leadership with Poetry and Music," Merav Rosenfeld-Hadad also captures adamah in its plural, *adamot*—the diasporic lands and the Land of Israel without defined borders in time and space. These are discussed and explored in the works and paraliturgical songs of Ḥakham Joseph Ḥayyim of Baghdad and vis-à-vis the collectives at the heart of this chapter: his followers, the Baghdadi Jewish community, and the Nation (the people of Israel). Overall, the chapters map Jewish music on territories without fixed borders as well as in the context and problematization of territorialization, deterritorialization, and reterritorialization.

Part II: City—עיר

As with the land, the city can be thought of as a neutral space entirely, and yet with Jerusalem, mentioned in Psalm 46:4 as the city of God, the holiest city in Judaism, and the spiritual center of Jews since 10 BCE when the grounds became the place for the Temple, it can be conceived as Jewish place.[56] And yet, just like the lands and territories, cities are by no means static. From antiquity onward, a city was often a space that was protected by a fortified wall, in contrast to open places that could be easily attacked. Indeed, the Hebrew word for city—*iyr*—relates to the verb *yaiyr*, which in the Hebrew Bible means "to protect" (Job 8:6). While in the Hebrew Bible iyr most commonly refers to a permanent dwelling, it also represents those who live in a given place. The city is thus not just a pragmatic infrastructure but, as Jacques Ellul asserts, has its own dynamics.[57] Iyr's semantic polyvalence correlates with the Jewish musical dynamics in the different cities presented in this section. The first two chapters closely lean on the city as a protective shelter: In "Jewish Refugees from the Nazi State in Shanghai, 1938–1949," Sophie Fetthauer focuses on China's "modern Babel," which offered exiles from Germany and Nazi-annexed territories a safe if temporary haven. In prior decades, foreigners living in the city had built a European-style infrastructure that created opportunities for musicians. With its cosmopolitan openness, Shanghai thus offered a relatively heterogenous group of refugees the possibility of connection as well as demarcation, preservation, and remembrance through the music they transferred and performed, while still making it relevant to contemporaneous issues. Silvia Glocer's chapter on "Jewish Émigré Musicians in Buenos Aires: Integration and Cultural Impact, 1933–1945" focuses on a similar environment, but one that offered possibilities for permanence in a then prosperous and stable city. Buenos Aires' different social networks provided the new arrivals with opportunities to truly integrate into the local musical scenes and the growing cultural industries. The powerful local Jewish community helped with contacts and links to social and professional networks. These networks not only facilitated integration, but also led to reciprocity in that the émigré musicians and their cultural heritage would leave their permanent mark on the musical life of Buenos Aires. Oded Erez's chapter, "From a City of Greeks to Greeks in a City: Musical Taste Cultures in Salonika and Tel Aviv-Jaffa," focuses on two urban settings in the early twentieth century tied together by waves of migration that transplanted, transformed, and repositioned the evolving popular music of Salonika Jews. It unravels the complexities of cosmopolitan environments as evident in the identity of perceived collectives as they pertain to ethnicity and class. Phil Alexander's chapter on "Berlin Klezmer and Urban Scenes" brings out another meaning of the term *iyr*, that of excitement (Deuteronomy 32:11 and Psalm 73:20). Klezmer as discovery and development has served as a source of exhilaration in a scene that rapidly grew in the course of a few decades and that navigated the local and the transnational. Focusing mainly on developments in the twentieth and twenty-first centuries, the four chapters in this section map Jewish music in cities as sites of displacement, dislocation, translocation, and creativity. They are followed by chapters that more narrowly focus on spaces within the urban environment: the ghetto, ritual spaces, and the stage, as well as the archive and library and collections therein.

Part III: Ghetto—נטו

The ghetto as a designated "Jewish space" was first called into existence in Renaissance Italy, when in March 1516 Venice confined its Jewish population to the northern part of the city known as the Ghetto Nuovo.[58] In July 1555, with Pope Paul IV's issuing of the *Cum nimis absurdum*, the institution of the legally compulsory and physically enclosed exclusively Jewish enclave spread to Rome, Florence, Mantua, and a host of other Italian towns and cities. Ghetto became a place of restrictions and danger, but also a space of productivity and self-assertion. It formed the basis for internal religious and social coherence and a certain degree of autonomy as well as for cultural interaction with the Christian world of Europe.[59] In line with other scholars who have devoted their research to the ghettos of early modern Europe, Rebecca Cypess and Yoel Greenberg's chapter focuses on the Jewish ghetto in Mantua, showing that the political and social division of urban space did not engender cultural isolation.[60] David Portaleone's *Shilṭei ha-giborim* and the midrashic approach found therein serve as a case study to uncover the paradoxes that unfolded within and beyond the permeable ghetto walls, giving way to a synchronic collectivity through music and sound, while also cultivating a diachronic collectivity among the music-making Jews.

With the emancipation of the Jews of Italy starting in the late eighteenth century, the dissolution of ghettos began, with Rome's being the last one to be dissolved in 1870. In subsequent decades, the word *ghetto* was resurrected and transferred to refer to new big-city Jewish immigrant neighborhoods, such as Manhattan's Lower East Side (once labeled the "New York Ghetto"). Unwalled, these were ever more permeable, marked by density and diversity of populations. During the Second World War, the Nazis reinvented *ghetto* as a space of enforced Jewish segregation, mass starvation, and disease, and eventually of deportation to the camps. In his chapter "Sonic Transformations: Urban Musical Culture in the Warsaw Ghetto, 1940–1942," J. Mackenzie Pierce looks closely at one such ghetto, the one situated in the city of Warsaw, established in November 1940 by the German authorities within the new General Government territory of occupied Poland. He considers this ghetto with its diverse performance venues as a fluid space within its urban setting to which it responds and with which it corresponds. As Tobias Reichard's chapter, "Sounding Out the Ghetto: Spatial Aspects of Jewish Musical Life during the Nazi Era," elucidates, ghettos became spaces in which the persecution of musicians and composers born Jewish took on a new severity. As Reichard asserts, *ghetto* can also refer to a conceptual space as embodied by the Jewish Culture League, which was exclusive and temporary and, as another Jewish space, constructed only to be deconstructed again by the Nazi regime; it was also a symbolic space, standing for creation, creativity, and survival. Problematizing and indeed mapping the term, Reichard ultimately cautions that its application to Jewish musical life in Nazi Germany needs to be approached with great nuance. The chapters map the ghetto as a fluid space with various meanings for Jewish and non-Jewish relations. The subsequent group of chapters fills quite different topographies with content, by way of taking uniquely Jewish spaces as a point of departure.

Part IV: Sacred and Ritual Spaces—כותל / עירוב / חופה

Sacred and ritual spaces as areas of spirituality, ceremony, but also contestation are manifold in Judaism, sounding out and resounding liturgical and paraliturgical as well as secular musics. This section focuses on a modest selection of such spaces, beginning with the Western Wall Plaza, which is most commonly associated with the ancient limestone wall known as *Kotel* in the Old City of Jerusalem. Due to its proximity to the Temple Mount, it is considered closest to the former Holy of Holies and thus to the presence of God (shekhinah). With the adjacent plaza created in 1967, it has become a space of worship and public gathering, celebration and ceremony; it is also a contested space, a source of friction between Jews and Muslims. Much has been written about the Wailing Wall with discussions of its historical, religious, cultural, and political significance. However, approaching it as a space of music and sound has hardly entered this body of literature. Abigail Wood's chapter, "Sonic Collectivity at the Kotel ha-Ma'aravi (Western Wall)," focuses on the changing soundscape of the adjacent plaza at large, thereby highlighting the embodied interaction between a flexible physical and auditory space of religious activity with the politics of individual and collective presence. It thus points to the dynamic processes of contesting discourses and identities that continue to shape it as a contemporary Jewish space of ritual.

If the Kotel has prompted the creation of space, similar can be said of the wire that encloses the eruv. Dating back to the biblical era, *eruv hatserot* (literally, "mixture" or "unification of the courtyards") has come to designate an urban area that symbolically extends the private domain of Jewish households into public spaces, permitting activities within it that are normally forbidden on the Sabbath. It might cover a few blocks or indeed a whole neighborhood. In the Talmud it refers to the symbolic amalgamation of all the residents in houses that surround a common courtyard and thus suggest the extension of a given collective. As a conceptual, imaginary, provisional, and contingent Jewish space, the eruv expands the religious space to include or absorb secular space. Its existence symbolically entangles place with religion and ritual. In Jewish studies, the eruv has become a compelling concept for marking distinct collectives as well as belonging and difference, and interaction and accommodation between Jews and non-Jews.[61] Further, as Charlotte Fonrobert asserts, an eruv maps a space of Jewish collectivity that is dependent on neither sovereignty nor any form of actual political or territorial control.[62] Relying on the image of concentric circles, Fonrobert also articulates how an eruv functions to symbolically demarcate collectivity and space.[63] The eruv's symbolism and concentricity unfolds in Jeffrey A. Summit's chapter, "Reimagining Spiritual Experience and Music: Perspectives from Jewish Worship in the United States." He leans on the concept of Rav Kook's "four-fold song" to suggest a typology of categories that can be employed to consider how Jews in the twenty-first century experience music in worship—the song of self, the song of nation, the song of humanity, and the song of all existence. Summit understands these four areas as expanding concentric circles—analogous to concentric eruvin—domains that move from the individual, to the Jewish people, out to all humanity, and ultimately encompassing all creation. Summit points to the flexibility and even permeability of eruv (the root of the term also connotes "mixture"), which music facilitates; he also points to the eruv facilitating collectivity as it does not separate per se, but rather connects. Fonrobert's assertion, that "the eruv does construct a collective identity with respect to space, but does so in the absence of having control or any form of sovereignty over that space," is challenged in Naomi Zentner Cohn's chapter, "Singing at the Sabbath Table: Zemiroth as a Family History." While zemiroth are historically one of the quintessential collective musical experiences in the private space of the home during the Sabbath, the repertoires used in the families also signify their belonging to ethnic and regional collectives, their affiliation to innovative religious, social, or national movements (specific branches of Hasidism, religious Zionism). In the early twentieth century, zemiroth began to extend beyond the boundaries of the eruv into public spaces, and with it, a specifically religious Zionist repertoire was formalized and popularized.

The third space addressed in this section points to the chuppah, a biblical term that originally referred to a cover in a variety of meanings and contexts.[64] It has come to designate the canopy under which a Jewish couple stands during the two parts of the wedding ceremony, a ritual space that envelops the bridal couple (and the family) in the private space of commitment. In broader terms, it relates to the second stage of the wedding, where it can be also captured as a symbolic space for the home the couple will be building. There are pronounced differences in the physical appearance of the chuppah and practices associated with it, depending on Jewish groups and their customs. The last two chapters in this section engage with the space surrounding the chuppah in distinct contexts. Diana Matut focuses on a period when the contemporary meaning of chuppah as a wedding canopy had just begun to crystalize. Her chapter, "Early-Modern Yiddish Wedding Songs: Synchronic and Diachronic Functions," relies on songs as vehicles for transmitting and instilling social, religious, and ethical norms among the premodern Ashkenazic communities of central and eastern Europe. These songs, rendered by and for members of the wedding party and especially the bride, had an important function within the larger collective as tools of normativization. Evan Rapport's chapter, "Bukharian Jewish Weddings and Creative Uses of the Central Asian Past," focuses on the post-chuppah part of the wedding, the celebratory festivities. Using contemporary Bukharian Jews in the United States as a lens of observation, he shows how the wedding party offers an occasion to relate to the past by performing representations of old Central Asia. His chapter uncovers the wedding as a transgenerational space that provides meaning and distinctiveness to the community's history and experiences, as well as pride. The chuppah is a spatial constant that bridges past and present.

Part V: Stage—בימה

The Hebrew word *bimah* initially referred to a high place and came to designate the platform in the center of the synagogue from which the service is conducted and the Torah is read. Its function as well as its position and design have greatly changed over the centuries, coming in many cases to resemble a theater stage, with the congregation becoming spectators, watching the dramatic action occurring in front of them, reminiscent of the times of the Temples. In modern Hebrew bimah also refers to the secular stage on which music and theater are performed. This dual meaning comes to the fore in Jeremiah Lockwood's chapter, "Hasidic Cantors 'Out of Context': Venues of Contemporary Cantorial Performance," in which he interrogates the performance of cantorial music outside the synagogue, a phenomenon known to have existed since at least the mid-nineteenth century. In the late twentieth century, a group of cantors rooted in Hasidism began to steer their music toward scenes and stages (virtual and actual), where they realized their conception of sacred music. Presenting videos on social media, concertizing in theaters, and performing at private parties offers Hasidic cantors new spaces, in which to resound an ontology of Jewish prayer that features the mediated sounds of early cantorial records upon which they model themselves, prioritizing a musical aesthetic over the social norms of prayer in contemporary synagogues.

In 1917 Habimah became the name of a Hebrew repertory theater company founded in Moscow and permanently reestablished in Tel Aviv in the 1930s. The trajectory of this first professional Hebrew theater in the world points to the stance of staged performances in two places: the Soviet Union and the Middle East. Focusing on the former, in his chapter "Jewish Music and Totalitarianism in the Post-Stalinist Soviet Union," Jascha Nemtsov provides insight into the presence and absence of Jewish music in the public sphere of the post-Stalinist Soviet Union. Jews and non-Jews thematicized, performed, represented, and received Jewish culture through Yiddish theater and songs, art music, and popular music. Concerts and works conceived for the Soviet stages demonstrate that Jewishness mattered, with music taking on new symbolism and becoming imbued with new meaning. Jehoash Hirschberg, in "Art Music in the Yishuv and in Early-Statehood Israel," shows that concert halls, and the compositions that filled them with sound, were spaces of transition for an emerging imagined community that had not yet found itself as a nation. This correlated with a proliferation of diverse compositional styles, especially in the 1950s and 1960s, and a plethora of attempts and approaches that filtered into conception of art music.

These chapters map the various meanings of the stage for Jewish music in the twentieth and twenty-first centuries. But Jewish music as music on the performance stage is manifest much earlier. From the Middle Ages onward it continued to appear first intermittently and later continually, always adapting to changing conditions. Central to the early history is the *badkhn*, the Jewish entertainer who appeared on the wedding stage (bimah) and published versions of his performance.[65] Concert activities of Jewish performers, which have been transmitted in late Renaissance Italy and later in England at the Tudor court, blur the boundaries between meanings of Jewish and non-Jewish stages.[66] The nineteenth century then saw the firm and continuous growth of Jews as audiences, composers, and performers on the stages of Europe in the aftermath of the *Haskalah*, the Jewish Enlightenment.[67] This is the time when Yiddish theater emerged, which is at the core of Ruthie Abeliovich's chapter, "The Yiddish Theater Republic of Sounds and the Performance of Listening." Recognizing that alongside the synagogue, theater and opera houses, the bourgeois salon, and street performances developed as parallel theatrical arenas for Jewish music, she focuses on modes of listening generated by the Yiddish theater beyond the theater stage. As such, the Yiddish theater has encompassed multiple simultaneous spaces: the live theater event, recorded theater songs, and their performances in the public sphere. Together the four chapters in this section provide a glimpse into a wide range of staged performances of Jewish music, which in the course of the twentieth century have diversified resembling rhizome patterns, spanning disparate genres and hybridizations of the same in a wide array of venues.

Part VI: Collection—זאמלונג

In her seminal book on Jewish studies and space, Barbara Mann challenges the normative identification of Jewishness with exile, history, and textuality by demonstrating that while "often viewed as the 'people of the book,' and as somehow lacking geography, spatial thinking has in fact permeated Jewish cultural expression."[68] And yet spaces closely representing the "people of the book," that is, archives and libraries, have become most vital for Jewish music and in more than one way. Since the *zamler* movement, which came out of the nineteenth-century interest in historiography and ethnography and culminated in the founding of the Society for the Promotion of Culture Among the Jews of Russia in 1892 (succeeded by in Jewish Historical Ethnographic Society in 1908) and the Yidisher Visnshaftlekher Institut (YIVO) in 1923, Jewish music became an integral part of archives and libraries, and their collections shaped its various trajectories. Eléonore Biezunski, in her chapter "The YIVO Sound Archive as a Living Space: Archiving and Revitalizing Klezmer Music," surveys some of the early zamler history of YIVO, bringing the reader to watershed moments in the 1970s and 1980s during which the archive saw itself interacting with musicians in the klezmer revitalization movement. Indeed, the archive as a living space serves as a fulcrum that brings in motion and serves as a bridge between a wide variety of peoples regardless of their background—archivists, scholars, musicians, and all recipients of their work. In turn it is performed and archived in itself—all in a temporality of anachronism. In her chapter on "Jewish Music Sound-Recording Collections in the United States," Judith S. Pinnolis widens the archival landscape, focusing on the origins of selected collections and thus providing insight into individual agency of the zamlers and their different understandings of Jewish music. The collection as a constructed space that produces, inhabits, and preserves Jewish music reveals numerous complexities from conservation and preservation to bibliographic control and other issues, and balances the fine line of individuality and collectivity. Turning to Australia, Joseph Toltz, in "Postcustodialism in the Jewish Music Archive," surveys selected repositories of Jewish music and comparatively discusses the Australian Archive of Jewish Music, held at Monash University in Melbourne, and the United States Holocaust Memorial Museum in Washington, DC, through the lens of postcustodialism. This theory considers the changing role of the archive as not inevitably being *the* central repository for collections, with creators retaining custody of their materials, a complex topic in light of musical material that represent the Holocaust experience. The three chapters focus on the presence of material, and yet they allude to the often-faced problem that sources relevant for Jewish music research are often insufficient in quantity or quality to paint a full picture that would do justice to the subject matter—even if the heterogeneity of the sources is fully embraced by way of loosening disciplinary self-restrictions. And thus, the history of Jewish music remains fragmentary and temporally and spatially scattered. As such, the interest in collections and collecting that these chapters convey is strongly related to the Jewish imperative to remember (*zakhor*), which is at the heart of the subsequent section. In what follows, the spatial configurations discussed are less fixed than the previous, with more fluid boundaries and meanings.

Part VII: Destruction/Remembrance—זכר / חורבן

The *ḥurban ha-bayit* (literally, "the destruction of the House") originally referred to the physical destructions of the Jerusalem Temple, first by the Babylonians in 587 BCE and again by the Romans in 70 CE, as well as to the spiritual disconnection. In the twentieth century, ḥurban or in Yiddish, *khurbn*, also became one of the terms—along with Shoah and Holocaust—to refer to the Nazi genocide of the Jews between 1933 and 1945. The biblical term *zekher* takes on various meanings—from remembrance to commemoration, memorial, or invocation—and is part of a long-standing Jewish practice. Important sources of zekher include the invocation to "remember the Sabbath" in the Kiddush text for the Sabbath afternoon and in the Hebrew Bible in the passages describing the punishment of Amalek (Deuteronomy 25:17–19, Amalek will *not* be remembered). The chapters in this section focus specifically on spaces defined by catastrophe or destruction but also remembrance. While spatial analysis of this kind has characterized recent work by historians and geographers, who use techniques of mapping and geo-visualization, there has been less research on cultural examples of space and Holocaust memory.[69] Space is integral to the representation of Holocaust memory, even—or especially—in cases where such spatial imagery might seem only to be implicit or act as a backdrop.

The following four chapters map musical manifestations of ḥurban and zekher, which in some cases are intertwined. Miranda L. Crowdus, in "Remembering the Destruction, Re-animating the Collective: Romaniote Liturgical Music after the Holocaust," focuses on the process of remembering destruction as an intrinsically Jewish practice, taking as a case in point the descendants of the Jews of Ioannina in an "ingathering of the exiles." Her chapter understands zekher as a process, in the sense of remembering and commemorating, but also as the "making present" of no-longer-present Jewish objects, events, and people through religious ritual and the musical transmission of the liturgy. As such ḥurban and zekher are evoked simultaneously, with zekher filling the emptiness that constitutes ḥurban. Similarly, Simo Muir focuses on the aftermath of the Holocaust, engaging with a space of represence. His chapter, " 'We Live Forever': Music of the Surviving Remnant in Sweden," focuses on the Yiddish performances of Polish Jewish singers after 1945, exemplifying the manifold process of zekher: in parallel (and response) to dealing with the trauma of their own persecution and commemorating their perished loved ones, singing and performing was an act of remembering and reconnecting with the prewar Yiddish culture in a new and different environment. The different functions and representations of Yiddish song ultimately suggest both a spatial and a temporal understanding of zekher, as remembrance for the future. Silvia Del Zoppo's chapter, " 'Ferramonti We Do Not Forget': Jews, Music, and Internment in Italy," uncovers further layers of zekher on the grounds of a site that first served as a concentration camp, then as a Displaced Persons camp, and later on as a memorial when an "imaginary," transgenerational community emerged that shared the collective ritual of zekher. In parallel, zekher as memorialization expresses itself in the memories of those who had left Ferramonti behind. In his discussion of the concept of zekher, Lawrence A. Hoffman illuminates its deeper meaning by drawing on the Talmud, where in a legal context it has nothing to do with remembering but with pointing. He concludes: "As a 'pointer,' *zekher* can apply across many lines of thought: temporally, it is indeed 'memory'; in arguments, it is an act of logic; spatially, it is like a road sign drawing attention from one place to another."[70] The road sign to the former concentration camp Ferramonti di Tarsia embodies such a pointer. But a pointer is also figurative, alerting the reader to ambivalences and layers of meaning. With regard to zekher and the role music takes therein, the notion of the road sign is indeed fitting, but as a sign pointing in two opposite directions. These oppositions manifest themselves, for example, in the ambivalence that Ferramonti as a concentration camp represented. The pointer of opposites addresses the different stages of Ferramonti as a concentration camp, Displaced Persons camp, and site of remembrance. The meaning of zekher as a pointer also comes to the fore in Clara Wenz's chapter, "'I Say She Is a Muṭriba': Faded Memories of Aleppo's Jewish Women Musicians." The ethno-historical memory of the Khūjahs, musicians who performed songs in Arabic and whose primary performance context was Muslim women wedding celebrations, point to the omission from official records that many of these women were Jewish. In this regard, the concept of zekher, then, implies a fragmentary, dislocated, and at times "suppressed" memory and a form of remembrance that is largely absent from public and persistently male-dominated modes of commemoration. Zekher, here, refers to a history that lacks official memorials and archivization efforts, but lingers instead in the personal stories of the musicians' dispersed descendants and constituencies. At times, their stories memorialize Aleppo's Khūjahs as members of a great musical community. Diversely, they reenact the loss of their memory. All chapters underline Maurice Halbwachs' assertion that collective memory is not a metaphor but a social reality transmitted and sustained through the conscious efforts and institutions of the group.[71] In this way, Judaism itself may be seen as a space of memory, with a set of transmitted and evolving practices.[72] These equally express themselves in soft memory and hard memory.

Part VIII: Spirit—שכינה

The post-biblical term *shekhinah* literally means "dwelling" or "settling." As a concept that relates to inhabiting, it unequivocally refers to the process of (filling a) space. In classic Jewish thought, since the emergence of rabbinic literature, shekhinah refers to such dwelling or settling in a special sense, namely that of divine presence to the effect that, while in proximity to the shekhinah, the connection to God is more readily perceivable. As such shekhinah is related to the Holy Spirit or *ruah ha-kodesh*. These facets of meaning entered Jewish prayer. In addition, shekhinah also represents the feminine attributes of the presence of God as especially promulgated through the Kabbalah.[73] The chapters in this section respond to the multivalent meanings and understandings of shekhinah. In her chapter, "Ultra-Orthodox Women and the Musical Shekhinah: Performance, Technology, and the Artist in North America," Jessica Roda builds on the kabbalistic concept of feminine principles of the divine, postulating a feminine musical scene as a quasi-musical shekhinah. Indeed, if ultra-Orthodox women claim their productions to be sacred and their manifestation of God's message exclusively available to women, then the shekhinah embraces this feminine attribute of the presence of God in musical production. Roda promulgates an understanding of the shekhinah as active and receptive to matriarchal values, symbolizing the power and status of the ultra-Orthodox woman while also acknowledging its ambivalence, capable not only of challenging the divide between the masculine and the feminine, but also of reinforcing it. Similarly, in her chapter " 'On a Harp of Ten Strings I Will Sing Praises to You': Envisioning Women and Music in the Oppenheimer Siddur," Suzanne Wijsman examines shekhinah as the feminine divine as it is prevalent in early modern iconographical sources, particularly in three illuminations created by Asher ben Yitzḥaq in the siddur he made for his family. Due to rabbinic prohibitions against instrumental music in the synagogue, the inclusion in a Jewish prayer book of figures playing musical instruments, especially women, is enigmatic and loaded with symbolism; two of the illuminations affirm the harmony of love between *kneset Yisrael* and her God, on the one hand, while the other suggests a moral warning inherent in the fifteenth-century allegory of the folly of love, which the artist-scribe was apparently familiar with. Turning to a different facet of shekhinah and using the narrative space of writing as a point of inquiry, Alexandre Cerveux, in his chapter, "The Concept of Harmony in Pre- and Early Modern Jewish Literature," discusses the importance of harmony in a Jewish context, which corresponds to its connection with and a manifestation of shekhinah, here understood as the divine presence of God in the world. In his philological approach he considers what music, or harmony specifically, has to do with matters that are diametrical opposites, such as the microcosm and the macrocosm, terrestrial and celestial beings, or Israel and the shekhinah. He asserts that since biblical times, harmony in its universal (and analogous musical) understanding has served as a link between Jews and the shekhinah, which ultimately transcends space.

Overall, the chapters take into consideration how Jewish music performs or is part of performing and listening Jewish and mainstream spaces into being, or address the wider significances of people's direct engagements with the material (including sonic) qualities of musical environments. They map the stages as spaces of presence and absence, transition, and expansion of Jewish music. With these chapters, which exemplify a broad range of approaches and disciplinary perspectives in the context of select spaces relevant for Jewish music studies (and further spaces within, such as utopias, dystopias, and heterotopias), the handbook seeks to propagate inclusiveness. And yet a number of areas, subjects, and perspectives could not be included by twists of circumstance. There is thus, for instance, neither a separate chapter on Jewish music in India or African countries, nor comprehensive coverage of the flourishing subject of art music in Europe and in the United States, or on twentieth-century modernism beyond the Holocaust, although brief discussions in other chapters, suggested readings (select bibliographies), and judicious use of the index might provide help to those who wish to investigate some topics further.

It is the editor's hope that the categories proposed here will encourage researchers to think about further spaces of and for Jewish music studies as the field evolves. As such, these categories are intended as an initial step to inspire scholars in considering how and in which directions they might expand their research. Indeed, mapping Jewish music in these given spaces is only a first step in a much larger project, that is, the collective work of charting Jewish music-related areas of scholarship and practice for the purpose of facilitating new entry points for researchers and illuminating connections across disciplines and fields. Indeed, cohesion does not come from inward focus, but from looking outward in many directions. Ultimately, it is the editor's wish that this volume will trigger the immense possibilities Jewish music studies offers as a field of inquiry and help establish the foundation for the systematic scholarly exploration of Jewish music.

ACKNOWLEDGMENTS

I would like to extend warmest thanks to my colleagues across the globe for the many discussions and debates over the years that have helped inform this introductory chapter. In particular, I would like to thank Assaf Shelleg, Mark Slobin, and the anonymous reviewers for providing valuable feedback on earlier drafts.

NOTES

1. Robert Alter, *The Five Books of Moses: A Translation with Commentary* (New York: W.W. Norton, 2008), 150.
2. For a detailed analysis of "Daled bavos," including a transcription, see Ellen Koskoff, *Music in Lubavitcher Life* (Champaign: University of Illinois Press, 2000), 88–91.
3. See also Raffi Ben-Mosheh, *Experiencing Devekut: The Contemplative Niggun of Habad in Israel /* חוויית הדבקות: בניגוני חסידות חב"ד בישראל, trans. Jonathan Chipman, Yuval Music Series 11 (Jerusalem: Jewish Music Research Centre, Hebrew University of Jerusalem 2015).
4. Israel Adler, "Problems in the Study of Jewish Music," in *Proceedings of World Congress on Jewish Music, Jerusalem 1978*, ed. Judith Cohen (Tel Aviv: Institute for the Translation of Hebrew Literature, 1982), 15.
5. The earliest documented scientific engagement can be traced back to sixteenth-century Germany and Italy. Noteworthy is a manuscript of 1599, by the Italian scholar, mathematician, poet, music theorist, architect, and composer Ercole Bottrigari (1531–1612), "Il Trimerone de' fondamenti armonici, overo, Lo Essercitio mvsicale: Dialoghi . . . ne' qvai si ragiona de' Tuoni antichi e moderni, e de' Caratteri diuersi vsati da Musici in tutti i tempi," in which he addresses "il Canto degli Hebrej" (chant of the Hebrews) and the musical rendition of the Masoretic accents that govern the singing of the Hebrew Bible in synagogue liturgy; MS B44, 1–23, Civico Museo Bibliografico Musicale G. B. Martini, Bologna. A discussion of other early sixteenth-century tractates can be found in Edwin Seroussi, "Jewish Music and Diaspora," in *The Cambridge Companion to Jewish Music*, ed. Joshua S. Walden, Cambridge Companions to Music (Cambridge: Cambridge University Press, 2015), 33–34.
6. For a discourse on various definitions and complications, albeit limited to the German-speaking world and the nineteenth century, see Heidy Zimmermann, "Was heißt 'jüdische Musik'? Grundzüge eines Diskurses im 20. Jahrhundert," in *Jüdische Musik? Fremdbilder—Eigenbilder*, ed. Eckhard John and Heidy Zimmermann, Reihe Jüdische Moderne 1 (Cologne: Böhlau, 2004), 11–32. For a broader, categorizing perspective, see Frank Alvarez-Péreyre, "Sur le concept de musique juive," in "Studies in Honour of Israel Adler," ed. Eliyahu Schleifer and Edwin Seroussi, special issue, *Yuval* 7 (2002): 75–91. These and other

discourses hardly problematize the increasing participation of non-Jews. Similarly, many scholars trace set the onset of "Jewish music" discourses to the nineteenth century, when it in fact began in the sixteenth century; for one such example, see *MGG Online*, s.v. "Jüdische Musik: Schreiben über Jüdische Musik," by Edwin Seroussi, trans. Matthias Müller; https://www.mgg-online.com/mgg/stable/372426 (accessed January 30, 2022).

7. Sachs rendered this definition in a speech at the First International Congress of Jewish Music in Paris, in 1957. It is documented in writing by Batya Bayer, "Music," in *Encyclopaedia Judaica* (Jerusalem: Keter Publications, 1971), 12:555.

8. See Adler, "Problems in the Study of Jewish Music," 16. In 1995 Kay Kaufman Shelemay still arrives at the same conclusions; see "Mythologies and Realities in the Study of Jewish Music," *The World of Music* 37, no. 1 (1995): 35. Other scholars, such as Don Harrán, have embraced this definition without reflection.

9. See Assaf Shelleg, *Jewish Contiguities and the Soundtrack of Israeli History* (New York: Oxford University Press, 2014), 18.

10. See Isaac Deutscher, *The Non-Jewish Jew and Other Essays* (New York, London: Hill and Wang, 1968); and Yuri Slezkine, *The Jewish Century* (Princeton University Press, 2004), 1 and 17.

11. Stefan Wolpe, "What Is Jewish Music," unpublished lecture, February 29, 1940, Stefan Wolpe collection, Paul Sacher Stiftung, Basel. This lecture has been published along with a preface by Austin Clarkson, "What Is Jewish Music?," *Contemporary Music Review* 27, nos. 2–3 (2008): 179–192.

12. Philip V. Bohlman, "Ontologies of Jewish Music," in Walden, *The Cambridge Companion to Jewish Music*, 12. On current views on problems and definitions, see ibid. Bohlman also provides a detailed reading of Sachs. For further paradoxes, see Mark Slobin, "Ten Paradoxes and Four Dilemmas of Studying Jewish Music," *The World of Music* 37, no. 1 (1995): 18–23.

13. For a critique of a broad definition, deemed another paradox, see Alvarez-Péreyre, "Sur le concept de musique juive," 84. "Ce paradoxe tient au fait que les specialistes de la musique juive postulant une definition large, non exclusivement musicale—sachant par experience dans quel paysage culturel plus global s'inserent les donnees sonores—tout en presentant une analyse des donnees qui, majoritairement, semble vite laisser en chemin une analyse detaillee et articulee du complexe d'elements dont ils laissent pourtant entendre qu'il est constitutif de leur objet et de sa definition." (This paradox lies in the fact that specialists in Jewish music postulate a broad, not exclusively musical definition—knowing from experience in which global cultural landscape the sound data are inserted—while presenting an analysis of the data that, for the most part, seems to quickly leave behind a detailed and articulated analysis of the complex of elements which they nevertheless imply is constitutive of their object and its definition.)

14. See also James Loeffler, "Do Zionists Read Music from Right to Left? Abraham Tsvi Idelsohn and the Invention of Israeli Music," *Jewish Quarterly Review* 100, no. 3 (2010): 385–416.

15. See also Judah M. Cohen, "Rewriting the Grand Narrative of Jewish Music: Abraham Z. Idelsohn in the United States," *Jewish Quarterly Review* 100, no. 3 (2010): 417–453.

16. See Regina Randhofer, *Psalmen in einstimmigen vokalen Überlieferungen: Eine vergleichende Untersuchung jüdischer und christlicher Traditionen* (Frankfurt am Main: Peter Lang, 1995); for an overview and discussion on writings by German scholars in the postwar period, see Tina Frühauf, "After the Holocaust: Jewish Music and the Canon in

German Intellectual History," in *Partituren der Erinnerung: Der Holocaust in der Musik*, ed. Wiener Wiesenthal Institut für Holocaust Studien (Vienna: new academic press), 12–40.

17. See Ruth HaCohen, *The Music Libel Against the Jews: Vocal Fictions of Noise and Harmony* (New Haven, CT: Yale University Press, 2011).

18. See Boaz Tarsi, "The Early Attempts at Creating a Theory of Ashkenazi Liturgical Music," in *Jüdische Musik als Dialog der Kulturen / Jewish Music as a Dialogue of Cultures*, Jüdische Musik 12 (Wiesbaden: Harrassowitz, 2013), 59–70; and Boaz Tarsi, "At the Intersection of Music Theory and Ideology: A.Z. Idelsohn and the Ashkenazi Prayer Mode Magen Avot," *Journal of Musicological Research* 36, no. 3 (2017): 208–233.

19. See Yonatan Malin, "Ethnography and Analysis in the Study of Jewish Music," in "Ethnography and Analysis," ed. Yonatan Malin, special issue, *Analytical Approaches to World Music* 7, no. 2 (2019): 108–125.

20. The veering away from an essentialist approach paralleled historical musicology's paradigm shift from a *Kunstwissenschaft* to a *Kulturwissenschaft*, i.e., from a focus on music as art to a focus on music as culture. See also Tobias Janz, "Musikwissenschaft als Kunstwissenschaft?," in *Historische Musikwissenschaft: Grundlagen und Perspektiven*, ed. Michele Calella and Nikolaus Urbanek (Stuttgart: J.B. Metzler, 2013), 15–48.

21. Edwin Seroussi, "Music: The 'Jew' of Jewish Studies," *Jewish Studies /* מדעי היהדות, no. 46 (2009): 43.

22. Subsequently, Bohlman reinforced established ontologies rooted in religion, language, embodiment, space (specified as synagogue and ritual practice), and culture; and, in a second round, translation, diaspora, collection and community (the latter hardly discussed), mass media, and nationalism—instead of creating new ones for more productive discourses of the field. See Bohlman, "Ontologies of Jewish Music," 141–126.

23. Criticism of a separation of ethnomusicology from musicology can be traced back to at least 1977, with Frederic Lieberman; for a recent plea, which received numerous responses, see Stephen Amico, "'We Are All Musicologists Now,' or, The End of Ethnomusicology," *Journal of Musicology* 37, no. 1 (2020): 1–32. See also selected chapters in *The New (Ethno) Musicologies*, ed. Henry Stobart, Europea: Ethnomusicologies and Modernities 8 (Lanham, MD: Scarecrow Press, 2008). The call for a unified discipline has been repeatedly reiterated; see the reprint of Tim Rice's article of 1987, "Toward the Remodeling of Ethnomusicology," in *Modeling Ethnomusicology* (New York: Oxford University Press, 2017), 43–60.

24. A poignant example is the essay by Rebecca Cypess, who is often identified as an early music scholar: "The Community as Ethnographer: Views of Classical Music in the English-Speaking Orthodox Jewish Community," *International Review of the Aesthetics and Sociology of Music* 41, no. 1 (2010): 117–139.

25. For a summary, see Martin Goodman, "The Nature of Jewish Studies," in *The Oxford Handbook of Jewish Studies*, ed. Martin Goodman (Oxford: Oxford University Press, 2002), 1–13.

26. For an overview of various positions, see Stephen Davies, "Works of Music: Approaches to the Ontology of Music from Analytic Philosophy," *Music Research Annual* 1 (2020): 1–19.

27. For recent literature on methods prevalent in historical musicology and music theory, see Stephen A. Crist and Roberta Montemorra Marvin, eds., *Historical Musicology: Sources, Methods, Interpretations*, Eastman Studies in Music (Rochester, NY: University of Rochester Press, 2004); and Eric Clarke and Nicholas Cook, eds., *Empirical Musicology: Methods, Aims, Prospects* (New York: Oxford University Press, 2004). For recent literature

on methods prevalent in ethnomusicology, see Gregory F. Barz and Timothy J. Cooley, eds., *Shadows in the Field: New Perspectives for Fieldwork in Ethnomusicology* (New York: Oxford University Press, 2008); Jonathan McCollum and David G. Hebert, eds., *Theory and Method in Historical Ethnomusicology* (Lanham: Lexington Books, 2014); and Beverley Diamond and Salwa El-Shawan Castelo-Branco, eds., *Transforming Ethnomusicology*, vol. 1, *Methodologies, Institutional Structures, and Policies* (New York: Oxford University Press, 2021).

28. See Georgina Born, "For a Relational Musicology: Music and Interdisciplinarity, Beyond the Practice Turn," *Journal of the Royal Musical Association* 135, no. 2 (2010): 205–243.

29. See Adam Zachary Newton, *Jewish Studies as Counterlife: A Report to the Academy* (New York: Fordham University Press, 2019), 80.

30. For further insights on Sachs, see Martin Else, "Alte Musik in der Neuen Welt: Curt Sachs und die Konzeption eines Musik-Museums," in *Vom Sammeln, Klassifizieren und Interpretieren: Die zerstörte Vielfalt des Curt Sachs*, ed. Wolfgang Behrens, Martin Elste, and Frauke Fitzner (Mainz: Schott, 2017), 277–288; see also Annette Otterstedt, "Curt Sachs und die Entthronung der Linie," ibid., 5–16.

31. See Judah M. Cohen, "Whither Jewish Music? Jewish Studies, Music Scholarship, and the Tilt Between Seminary and University," *AJS Review* 32, no. 1 (2008): 29–48.

32. A quantitative survey reveals that the number of publications that have appeared since the year 2000 exceeds the number of publications issued between 1945 and 2000 (more than six thousand) by a few thousand. For a recent historiography of writings from early modernity to the mid-twentieth century, see Seroussi, "Jüdische Musik." See also Seroussi, "Music," which likewise stops short in the mid-twentieth century. Earlier historiographies similarly present a well-defined body of literature on Jewish music, while revealing political and cultural divergence. A future historiography ought to traverse musicology as well as Jewish studies and musicology, while at the same time considering other disciplines and fields.

33. Dan Miron, *From Continuity to Contiguity: Toward a New Jewish Literary Thinking* (Stanford, CA: Stanford University Press, 2010), 303.

34. Ibid., 276.

35. See Newton, *Jewish Studies as Counterlife*, 15.

36. For broader overviews and discussions, see, for example, Tim Cresswell, *Place: A Short Introduction* (Malden, MA: Blackwell, 2000); Edward S. Casey, *Getting Back into Place: Toward a Renewed Understanding of the Place-World*, 2nd ed. (Bloomington: Indiana University Press, 2009). Philip Ethington, "Placing the Past: 'Groundwork' for a Spatial Theory of History," *Rethinking History* 11, no. 4 (2007): 465–493; and Alan Baker, *Geography and History: Bridging the Divide* (Cambridge: Cambridge University Press, 2003).

37. Barbara E. Mann, *Space and Place in Jewish Studies*, Key Words in Jewish Studies (New Brunswick, NJ: Rutgers University Press, 2012), 153. See also Barbara E. Mann, "Space and Place," in *Routledge Handbook of Contemporary Jewish Cultures*, ed. Laurence Roth and Nadia Valman (New York: Routledge 2015), 18.

38. See Brian Longhurst, Greg Smith, Gaynor Bagnall, Garry Crawford, and Miles Ogborn, *Introducing Cultural Studies*, 3rd ed. (London: Routledge, 2016), 192–193. For further references and definitions, see Tobias Reichard, "'Eine abgeschlossene Sache'? Zu einer Topografie jüdischen Musiklebens im NS-Staat am Beispiel Münchens," in *Jüdische Musik im süddeutschen Raum / Mapping Jewish Music of Southern Germany*, ed. Claus Bockmaier and Tina Frühauf, Musikwissenschaftliche Schriften der Hochschule für Musik und Theater München 16 (Munich: Allitera Verlag, 2021), 35–38.

39. See also Richard I. Cohen, ed., preface to *Place in Modern Jewish Culture and Society*, Studies in Contemporary Jewry 13 (New York: Oxford University Press, 2018), viii.

40. For concise historiographies on recent treatment of place and space in Jewish studies and musicology, see Tina Frühauf, "Resonating Places, Mapping Jewish Spaces: Jews, Music, and Southern Germany," in Bockmaier and Frühauf, *Jüdische Musik*, 15–17; and Reichard, "'Eine abgeschlossene Sache'?," 35–38.

41. This approach should not be confused with the so-called cultural mapping, which refers to a wide range of research techniques and tools used to "map" distinct peoples' tangible and intangible cultural assets within local landscapes around the world. For a recent collection of essays on the subject in the realm of music, see Britta Sweers and Sarah M. Ross, eds., *Cultural Mapping and Musical Diversity* (Sheffield: Equinox Publishing Limited, 2020).

42. See also David Crouch, Simon Naylor, James Ryan, and Ian Cook, *Cultural Turns / Geographical Turns: Perspectives on Cultural Geography* (London: Taylor & Francis, 2018), 333. The term *topography* has been layered with different meaning over time. Originally denoted as a description of places in words, it later came to mean "the art of mapping a place by graphic signs." The now dominant meaning relates simply to "that which is mapped." J. Hillis Miller, *Topographies* (Stanford: Stanford University Press, 1995), 3–19.

43. For a historicizing discourse, see Edwin Seroussi, "Jewish Music and Diaspora," in Walden, *The Cambridge Companion to Jewish Music*, 27–40.

44. See Diana Pinto, "A New Jewish Identity for Post-1989 Europe," *JPR Policy Paper* 1 (1996): 1–15; and "The Jewish Challenge in the New Europe," in *Challenging Ethnic Citizenship: German and Israeli Perspectives on Immigration*, ed. Daniel Levy and Yfaat Weiss (New York: Berghahn Books, 2002), 239–252.

45. For further examples, see Simone Lässig and Miriam Rürup, eds., *Space and Spatiality in Modern German-Jewish History*, New German Historical Perspectives 8 (New York: Berghahn Books, 2019).

46. See Tina Frühauf, introduction to *Postmodernity's Musical Pasts* (Woodbridge, UK: Boydell Press, 2020), 1–14.

47. See also Mark Slobin, *Subcultural Sounds: Micromusics of the West* (Middletown, CT: Wesleyan University Press, 1993).

48. Richard Handler, "Is 'Identity' a Useful Cross-Cultural Concept?," in *Commemorations: The Politics of National Identity*, ed. John R. Gillis (Princeton, NJ: Princeton University Press, 1994), 27.

49. Ibid., 30.

50. A comprehensive overview and reader has yet to be conceived.

51. See, for example, Benedict R. Anderson, *Imagined Communities: Reflections on the Origins and Spread of Nationalism*, 2nd ed. (London: Verso, 2006). See also Anthony P. Cohen, *The Symbolic Construction of Community*, rev. ed. (London: Routledge, 2013).

52. As a consequence of this continued ambiguity, many scholars are ambivalent about community's efficacy as a sociological concept. But the ubiquity of the term in public discourse alone speaks to the continued meaning this concept has for individuals—just as does Jewish music—however vague and undefined its meaning may be in certain contexts. While modern communities may indeed be, as sociologist Tony Blackshaw argues, "weak ontologies"—existing without solid foundations, their bases always in flux and thus contestable—he nonetheless similarly argues for the concept's importance: "[W]e are often deeply committed to [communities] because they have fundamental importance to how we see and reflect on our observations about the world as individuals, our sense

of who we are, and how we want to live their lives with other people." *Key Concepts in Community Studies*, SAGE Key Concepts (London: SAGE, 2009), 11.

53. Fran Tonkiss, *Space, the City and Social Theory: Social Relations and Urban Forms* (Cambridge: Polity, 2005), 24.

54. On the complexities of the term, see Maximillien De Lafayette, *Etymology, Philology and Comparative Dictionary of Synonyms in 22 Dead and Ancient Languages* (Morrisville, NC: Lulu Press, 2017), 1:65.

55. W. Joseph Stallings, *The Genesis Cataclysm: Proposing a Noahic Global Flood Within an Old-Earth Scriptural Paradigm* (Eugene, OR: Wipf & Stock, 2020), 21.

56. For a comprehensive study of twentieth-century Jerusalem as a city of music, see Michael A. Figueroa, *City of Song: Music and the Making of Modern Jerusalem* (New York: Oxford University Press, 2022).

57. See Jacques Ellul, *The Meaning of the City* (1970; Eugene, OR: Wipf & Stock Publishers, 2011).

58. For an in-depth discussion of ghetto's fuzzy etymology, see Daniel B. Schwartz, *Ghetto: The History of a Word* (Cambridge, MA: Harvard University Press, 2019).

59. Salo W. Baron, "Ghetto and Emancipation: Shall We Revise the Traditional View?," *The Menorah Journal* 14 (1928): 515–526.

60. For studies arriving at similar conclusions, see Robert Bonfil, *Jewish Life in Renaissance Italy* (Berkeley: University of California Press, 1994); Benjamin Ravid, *Studies on the Jews of Venice, 1382–1797* (Aldershot, UK: Ashgate, 2003); David B. Ruderman, "The Cultural Significance of the Ghetto in Jewish History," in *From Ghetto to Emancipation: Historical and Contemporary Reconsiderations of the Jewish Community*, ed. David N. Myers and William V. Rowe (Scranton, PA: University of Scranton Press, 1997), 1–16; and Kenneth Stow, *Theater of Acculturation: The Roman Ghetto in the 16th Century* (Seattle: University of Washington Press, 2001). See also Francesco Spagnolo, "The Bimah and the Stage: Synagogue Music and Cultural Production in the Italian Ghettos," in *Venice, the Jews, and Europe*, ed. Donatella Calabi (Venice: Marsilio, 2016), 264–269.

61. See, for example, Yosef Gavriel Bechhofer, *The Contemporary Eruv: Eruvin in Modern Metropolitan Areas* (Jerusalem: Feldheim, 2002); Peter Vincent and Barney Warf, "Eruvim: Talmudic Places in a Postmodern World," *Transactions of the Institute of British Geographers* 27, no. 1 (2002): 30–51; Charlotte Elisheva Fonrobert, "From Separatism to Urbanism: The Dead Sea Scrolls and the Origins of the Rabbinic 'Eruv," *Dead Sea Discoveries* 11, no. 1 (2004): 43–71; Sophie Watson, *City Publics: The (Dis)enchantments of Urban Encounters* (New York: Routledge, 2013); and Manuel Herz, "Eruv Urbanism: Towards an Alternative Jewish Architecture in Germany," in Brauch et al., *Jewish Topographies*, 43–62.

62. See Charlotte Elisheva Fonrobert, "Political Symbolism of the Eruv," *Jewish Social Studies* 11, no. 3 (Spring/Summer 2005): 29.

63. See ibid., 67.

64. Abraham P. Bloch, *The Biblical and Historical Background of Jewish Customs and Ceremonies* (New York: Ktav Publishing House, 1980), 31–33.

65. See Ariela Krasney, "The *Badkhn*: From Wedding Stage to Writing Desk," in *Focusing on Jewish Popular Culture and Its Afterlife*, ed. Michael C. Steinlauf and Antony Polonsky, Polin: Studies in Polish Jewry 16 (Oxford: Littman Library of Jewish Civilization, 2003), 7–28.

66. See selected essays in *Music and Jewish Culture in Early Modern Italy: New Perspectives*, ed. Lynette Bowring, Rebecca Cypess, and Liza Malamut, Music and the Early Modern

Imagination (Bloomington: Indiana University Press, 2022), and Alessio Ruffatti, "Italian Musicians at Tudor Court: Were They Really Jews?" *Jewish Historical Studies: Transactions of the Jewish Historical Society of England* 35 (1996–1998): 1–14.

67. For a comprehensive account, see David Conway, *Jewry in Music: Entry to the Profession from the Enlightenment to Richard Wagner* (Cambridge: Cambridge University Press, 2012).

68. Mann, *Space and Place in Jewish Studies*, 153.

69. See, for instance, in Anne Kelly Knowles, Tim Cole, and Alberto Giordano, eds., *Geographies of the Holocaust* (Bloomington: Indiana University Press, 2014).

70. Lawrence A. Hoffman and David Arnow, *My People's Passover Haggadah: Traditional Texts, Modern Commentaries* (Woodstock, VT: Jewish Lights Pub., 2008), 127.

71. See Maurice Halbwachs, *Les cadres sociaux de la mémoire* (Paris: F. Alcan, 1925), and his posthumously published *La mémoire collective* (Paris: Presses Universitaires de France, 1950).

72. See Yosef Hayim Yerushalmi, *Zakhor: Jewish History and Jewish Memory* (Seattle: University of Washington Press, 1996).

73. See Chani Smith, "The Symbol of the Shekhinah," *The Absent Mother: Restoring the Goddess to Judaism and Christianity*, ed. Alix Pirani and Foosiya Miller (London: Mandala, 1991), 5–13.

SELECT BIBLIOGRAPHY

Bodenhamer, David J., John Corrigan, and Trevor M. Harris, eds. *The Spatial Humanities: GIS and the Future of Humanities Scholarship*. Bloomington: Indiana University Press, 2010.

Bohlman, Philip V. "Inventing Jewish Music." In *Studies in Honour of Israel Adler*, edited by Eliyahu Schleifer and Edwin Seroussi, 33–68. Yuval 7. Jerusalem: Magnes, 2002.

Bohlman, Philip V. "Music." In *The Oxford Handbook of Jewish Studies*, edited by Martin Goodman, Jeremy Cohen, and David Sorkin, 852–869. Oxford and New York: Oxford University Press, 2002.

Born, Georgina. "Introduction: Music, Sound and Space: Transformations of Public and Private Experience." In *Music, Sound and Space: Transformations of Public and Private Experience*, edited by Georgina Born, 1–70. Cambridge: Cambridge University Press, 2013.

Brauch, Julia, Anna Lipphardt, and Alexandra Nocke, eds. *Jewish Topographies: Visions of Space, Traditions of Place*. Aldershot: Routledge, 2008.

Cohen, Judah M. "Whither Jewish Music? Jewish Studies, Music Scholarship, and the Tilt between Seminary and University." *Association of Jewish Studies Review* 32, no. 1 (2008): 29–48.

Cohen, Richard I., ed. *Place in Modern Jewish Culture and Society*. Studies in Contemporary Jewry 13. New York: Oxford University Press, 2018.

Cole, Tim. *Holocaust City: The Making of a Jewish Ghetto*. New York: Routledge, 2003.

Goldman, Wendy Z., and Joe William Trotter, eds. *The Ghetto in Global History: 1500 to the Present*. New York: Routledge, 2018.

Knowles, Anne Kelly, Tim Cole, and Alberto Giordano, eds. *Geographies of the Holocaust*. Bloomington: Indiana University Press, 2014.

Landau, Annette, and Claudia Emmenegger, eds. *Musik und Raum: Dimensionen im Gespräch*. Zurich: Chronos, 2005.

Lodahl, Michael E. *Shekhinah/Spirit: Divine Presence in Jewish and Christian Traditions*. Eugene, OR: Wipf & Stock Publishers, 2012.

Mann, Barbara E. *Space and Place in Jewish Studies*. Key Words in Jewish Studies. New Brunswick, NJ: Rutgers University Press, 2012.

Miron, Dan. *From Continuity to Contiguity: Toward a New Jewish Literary Thinking*. Stanford, CA: Stanford University Press, 2010.

Newton, Adam Zachary. *Jewish Studies as Counterlife: A Report to the Academy*. New York: Fordham University Press, 2019.

Paolo, Giaccaria, and Claudio Minca, eds., *Hitler's Geographies: The Spatialities of the Third Reich*. Chicago: University of Chicago Press, 2016.

Seroussi, Edwin. "Music: The 'Jew' of Jewish Studies." *Jewish Studies /* מדעי היהדות, no. 46 (2009): 3–84.

Zimmermann, Heidy. "Was heißt 'jüdische Musik'? Grundzüge eines Diskurses im Jahrhundert." In *Jüdische Musik? Fremdbilder, Eigenbilder*, edited by John Eckhard and Heidy Zimmermann, 11–32. Jüdische Moderne 1. Cologne: Böhlau, 2004.

PART I

LAND—אדמה

2

ADAMOT — ART MUSIC — ISRAEL

ASSAF SHELLEG

THE song "Moladeti" had been popularized in the Jewish community of Palestine in the 1920s, at a time when adjectives like "folk" and "popular" were used synonymously. It was but a part of a wider emergence that saw the importation, borrowing, appropriation, confiscation, and adaptation of musics from Palestine's Semitic spaces (be they Arab or Jewish), but also from the respective diasporas of the arrangers, composers, and compilers involved in the making and perpetuating of this repertoire. Distinctions between newly composed songs and those concocted from Palestine's variegated oral musical traditions were therefore blurred; as such, they could sustain the rhetoric of separatism that had constituted Hebrew culture (heretofore Hebrewism), namely, separation from both exilic Jewries and the Arab community of Palestine. As long as this rhetoric was sustained, it concealed procedures of hybridization,[1] thereby allowing the Jewish community of Palestine (the Yishuv) to validate "Hebrew" adjectives and subsequently anchor territorial nationalism and expansionism in biblical, post-biblical, and modern Hebrew. An actualization of this kind, etched in a linguistic register that shaped a national Hebrew culture, subsequently deemed eighteen centuries of Jewish exile (from the destruction of the Second Temple to the emergence of political Zionism) a mere nocturnal episode, *rhetorically* repressing the worlds that defined Jewishness through innumerable symbioses with non-Jewish host societies. Indeed, at least part of this teleology is rehearsed in "Moladeti," whose lyrics read "My homeland, the land of Canaan / my goal, the fields of Ḥoran" (Example 2.1).

Like many other early pre-statehood songs, the land in "Moladeti" is referred to as the biblical land of Canaan,[2] thereby symbolically bridging Joshua's conquests and the Zionist project, and in effect suggesting the actualization of biblical sovereignty in the Zionist present. Cementing this connection are the "fields of Ḥoran," a location that could refer to Ḥauran, a northeastern region located in the East Bank (according to Ezekiel 47:16–18), which during pre-statehood years had been part of Transjordan, a

EXAMPLE 2.1 "Moladeti" (My homeland), in *Mi-zimrat ha-arets: Kovets zemirot Artsi-Yisraeliyot im tave-neginah* (From the song of the land: A collection of Erets-Yisrael songs with sheet music), ed. Solomon Rosowsky (Warsaw: Jewish National Fund, 1929), 31.

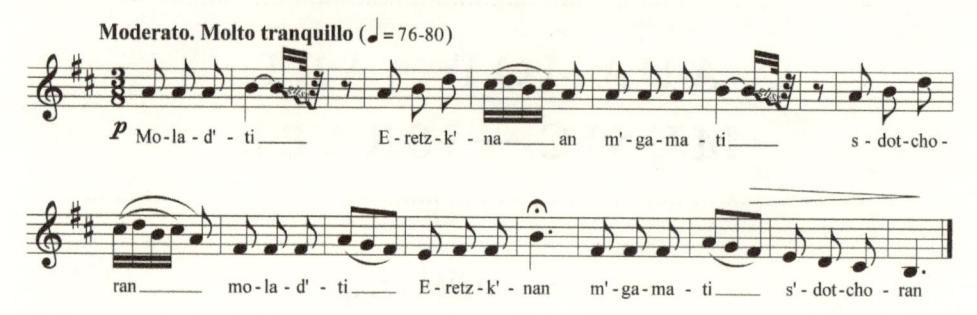

British protectorate from 1921 to 1946; alternatively, the "fields of Ḥoran" might refer to Beth-Ḥoron, a pass located in the West Bank and known as the Valley of Ajalon, where hailstones wreaked havoc on the coalition army of the five kings fighting Joshua's army (Joshua 10:10–11).[3] In post-biblical times, the same Beth-Ḥoron witnessed the defeat of Cestius Gallus' Twelfth Legion in the autumn of 66 CE during the early phases of the First Roman-Jewish War,[4] which became another source of selective narrativization in Zionist historiography.[5] Regardless of the exact location of Ḥoran, these events (which the Zionist historiographical hand had disproportionally augmented as the long forgotten and now coveted qualities of the "new Jew"—active, heroic, rebellious, and nationally zealous) were all potentially encoded in "Moladeti." Notwithstanding hindsight readings that saw the conquests of the Six-Day War of June 1967 as part of a historical continuity operating on particular and only partly conscious cultural, military, and theological premises rooted in the early 1940s,[6] territorial expansionism had been steering Hebrew culture much earlier, temporarily taming the religious to the national and facilitating the nationalization of the theological,[7] four decades at least before the conquests of biblical regions in the West Bank would unleash dormant theological ambitions that had been instilled in and transmitted through the Hebrew language. As for "Moladeti," its appearance in print for the first time in a 1929 songbook titled *Mi-zimrat ha-arets* indeed attested to its oral circulation and popularity, but not without flickering discrepancies that once again marked the gap between rhetoric and processes of hybridizations, beginning with the fact that the melody of this song bore the traces of what had originally been an Arab peasant song. And yet such discrepancies did not prevent the editor, Solomon Rosowsky, from placing "Moladeti" in a section titled "Longing for Zion." Like many other equivalent cases, "Moladeti" seeped into the Jewish community of Palestine, becoming part of its quest for Hebrew indigenousness in a Semitic space where Jews had been living among a non-Jewish majority.[8]

While this chapter aims at recalibrating the perception and understanding of art music in British Palestine and the State of Israel, "Moladeti" is packed with constituent key variables that had been catalyzing the making of Hebrewism even before the

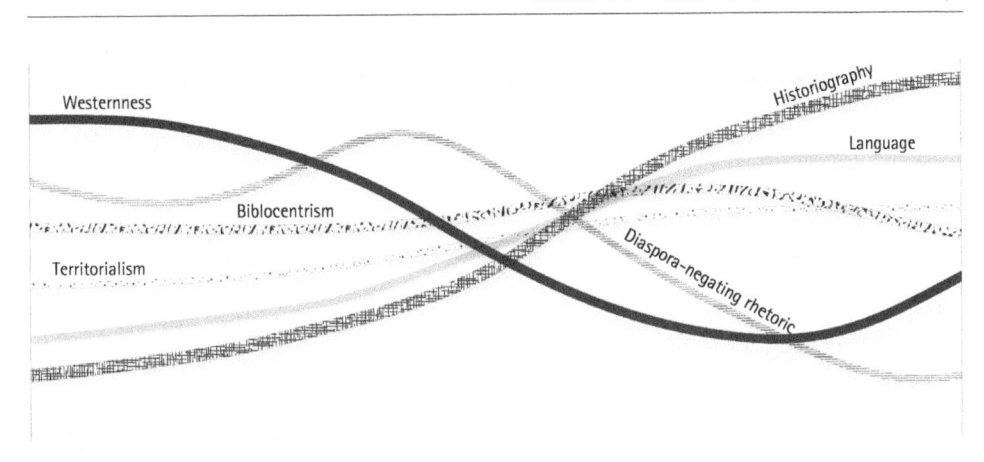

FIGURE 2.1 Key variables of Hebrewism.

institutionalization of art music would take place during the second half of the 1930s, when emigrant composers and musicians from central and western Europe would arrive in unusual numbers to Palestine following the Nazis' rise to power.[9] These key variables include territorialism, biblocentrism, language, historiography (which later would be characterized here as the Zionist management of Jewish history), and diaspora-negating rhetoric. Figure 2.1 visualizes these vectors (with no specifiable Xs and Ys), revealing their simultaneities, interdependencies, fluxes, and subsequently the inability to discuss one constituent exclusively of the other. As such, Figure 2.1 also functions as a monitor for the entire chapter.

The non-linear proliferation of meanings stemming from these variables (in addition to Westernness, which is discussed below) will be addressed with regard to this chapter's main topic, *adamot*—namely, lands (but also territories, yet neither of which is necessarily national or refers exclusively to *the* territories of the UN Security Council Resolution 242)—and the way they have conditioned the entire ecosystem under discussion. Indeed, even when certain variables become mute (and specifically by postmodern patrimonies and remodernist aesthetic, as the last subhead of this chapter suggests), they continue to narrate the dilution of the heteronomy of territorial nationalism as it transitions into autonomous aesthetics, shifting to modernist practices (*sans* its utopianism) while resituating Hebrewism at the overlap of modern Jewish culture and contemporary art music. Before that could happen, however, Hebrewism would gradually separate from the heteronomy of the territory (but not from the space in which hybrids came to be), and Jewish ethnography would progressively outgrow the national and historiographical receptacles that tamed it. And yet despite the transitions unfolded here, despite their simultaneities and meaningful disharmonies (including the turn to exilic histories and cultures that undermined the territorial foundation around which Hebrew nativism has been constituted), Hebrewism writ large still pertains to an ethnocratic setting in which a dominant Jewish group promotes its expansionism in a contested territory while its domination of power structures maintains a democratic façade.[10]

ADAMOT—BIBLICAL, EXILIC, SOVEREIGN

Zionist biblocentrism, the selective appropriation of biblical texts that reenacted Hebrew sovereignty through the Hebrew language (the single surviving linguistic component of ancient Jewish independence), conferred directionality to the Zionist project. Literal reading of selected biblical texts facilitated a Zionist national allegory that actualized tropes of return and returning, of redemption, and of territorial expansionism.[11] The Bible validated the Zionist story by attesting to Israel's primordial ownership of the land: it anticipated the return of the country's inhabitants ("And there is hope for your future—said the LORD—and the sons shall come back to their place [country]"; Jeremiah 31:16), the building of the land ("Yet will I rebuild you and you will be built, O Virgin Israel"; Jeremiah 31:3), and the gathering of exiles ("And I will take you from the nations and gather you from all the lands and bring you to your soil"; Ezekiel 36:24).[12] At the same time, Zionism exalted the Bible by actively fulfilling its prophecies and confirming its eternal truth—be it the decree given to Abraham (Genesis 12:1–2), the exodus from Egypt, the feebleness of the generation sentenced to perish in the desert (Numbers 14:31–32), the stoutness of the conquerors of Canaan, the wars of the judges, or the institution of Israelite monarchy.[13] The realization of biblical sovereignty in Zion of the twentieth century therefore shaped an imposing Zionist allegory; so much so that in a 1936 memorandum submitted to the Palestine Royal (Peel) Commission, which convened following the first stage of the Arab Rebellion, the Jewish Agency traced the origin of the association of the Jewish people with the land of Palestine in the "early pages of the biblical record," specifically Genesis 15:13–14, 46:4, 40:15, Leviticus 26:44–45, and Deuteronomy 30:3–5.[14] Transcribing the sacred into the secular allowed Zionists to conquer and monopolize the diachronic spaces of Jewish presence and absence in the land of Israel while stripping biblical texts of exilic post-biblical rabbinic literature (Mishnah, Talmud, Midrash, Responsa, Zohar, Hasidic literature, etc.),[15] texts that did not promote territorial expansionism.

Several lands (adamot) have been conditioning Hebrewism since its outset. The national territory (whose contested borders are still etched in our daily news) activated biblical and eschatological promises of return, and (political) redemption, while musical settings of such texts rehearsed these national territorial topoi—irrespective of composers' stylistic and aesthetic penchants. It is therefore unsurprising to find both Erich Walter Sternberg and Paul Ben-Haim setting to music Ezekiel's Vision of the Dry Bones (Ezekiel 37:1–14) in the late 1950s; notwithstanding their distinctive compositional approaches, both animated Ezekiel's vision, which the Zionist interpretative community had read and heard as an unequivocal metaphor for the restoration of Israel (much like the way post-biblical commentary, too, had interpreted it literally).[16] Verses like "The breath came into them and they lived, and they stood up on their feet, a very very great legion" (Ezekiel 37:10), or "Thus said the Master, the LORD: I am about to open your graves, and I will bring you up, My people, from your graves and bring you to

Israel's soil" (Ezekiel 37:12) lent themselves quite naturally to Zionist literalist readings.[17] Correspondingly, musicalized prophecies envisioning gaping graves and the slain breathed with life, growing flesh, and forming skins were belated extensions of the predominant paradigm of the living dead in modern Hebrew poetry, which a decade earlier had equated burial with espousal, and internment with sprouting and blossoming.[18] Politically obedient and with limited command of Hebrew (a lack that among other things determined his choice of this text), Ben-Haim's *Vision of a Prophet* (1958–1959), a cantata for tenor solo, choir, and orchestra, would amount to a triumphal monument cemented by bare fifths growing tonal skins and making audible the oncoming resuscitated marching multitude (Example 2.2, mm. 236–253). These emerge most conspicuously with the setting of Ezekiel 37:11 ("Man, these bones are all the house of Israel") as the choir pierces this processional march with a secco non-pitched parlando ("Our bones are dry and our hope is lost; we have been cut off"). Ben-Haim modulates this setting into choric shouts against the background of chromatic passages (Example 2.2, mm. 258–268) that consolidate with Ezekiel's reply into an aria, whose pentatonic scaffolds the speaker announces with glaring fanfares (Ezekiel 37:12).[19]

Only that this pentatonic macroharmony (beginning with the last measure shown in Example 2.2) is soon revealed as yet another shroud in the tonal becoming of the prophecy's redemptive ascension. It begins with Ezekiel's instructive *hineh* ("see," "here," "lo," or "look") as in "Here is the day, here it comes, the gyre has turned around" in Ezekiel 7:10, or as in Isaiah 7:14, where it acquires the meaning of a divine sign: "Therefore the Master Himself shall give you a sign: [*hineh*] the young woman is about to conceive and bear a son."[20] It is with this prevalent visual prophetic idiom, which appears twice in the Vision of the Dry Bones (Ezekiel 37:5, 37:12), that one has to read modern Hebrew poetry. Nathan Alterman's poem "Hineh tamoo yom ḳrav ve'aravo" (Here end the day of battle and its evening) is one example (and to which we will return), but also Haim Gouri's proclamation of the 1948 War dead, "Here [*hineh*] lie our bodies in a long row—and we do not breath," and even Aharon Amir's "Shirat erets ha-ivrim" (Poetry of the Land of the Hebrews, 1947–1949), whose most noticeable caesurae read "My country's great tomorrow, lo [*hineh*] it comes," and "lo [*hineh*] it comes, the great day" (drawing most likely on Jeremiah 7:32, "Therefore, look, a time is coming, said the LORD," or Jeremiah 9:24, "Look, a time is coming—said the LORD").[21] And so while Ben-Haim's choral *parlando* is a useful illustration for the slain whose breath has just been restored (see Example 2.2), this effect ultimately functions as a negative harmonic marker, following which celebratory fanfares become an apotheotic precursor for the delivery of the promise that stands at the core of Zionist biblical literalism, buttressed in Ben-Haim's formulation by tonal distilment.

And it is here where one touches upon the key variable of language (see Figure 2.1)— the language and its messianic stings. Indeed, for Gershom Scholem, the so-called secularization of Hebrew was "*façon de parler*, a phrase!" In a letter to Franz Rosenzweig, dated December 12, 1926, written a year after he settled in Jerusalem, Scholem, who would soon advocate binationalism (which he perceived as anticolonialism) in order to prevent Zionism's turn to Sabbateanism and avert its usage of religious politics for

EXAMPLE 2.2 Paul Ben-Haim, *The Vision of a Prophet* (1958–1959), cantata for mixed choir and symphony orchestra, mm. 236–276. "... and they lived, and they stood up on their feet, a very very great legion; And He said to me, 'Man, these bones are all the House of Israel. They say 'Our bones are dry and our hope is lost; we have been cut off.' Therefore, prophesy and say to them ...'" (Ezekiel 37:10–11). Copyright © 2001 Israel Music Institute. All rights reserved. International copyrights secured.

EXAMPLE 2.2 Continued

EXAMPLE 2.2 Continued

political purposes,[22] argued that "language is name. In the name rests the power of language, its abyss is sealed with its name. We have no right to conjure up the old names day by day without calling forward their hidden power."[23] As a Kabbalah scholar who studied the meanings and combinations of words and letters, he viewed the "the 'actualization' of Hebrew" as a more sinister threat to the Zionist project than the conflict with the Arabs. It is "impossible to empty out words which are filled to the breaking point with specific meaning," he wrote:

> *Fraught with danger is the Hebrew language!.* It cannot remain and will not remain in its present state! . . . We have no right to conjure up the old names day by day without calling forward their hidden power. They will appear, since we have called upon them, and undoubtedly they will appear with vehemence! . . . God will not remain silent in the language in which He has affirmed our life a thousand times and more.[24]

Before language would appear with vehemence, the nationalization of the theological channeled all cultural constructs to the national territory and subsequently to Hebrewist nativism, thereby rendering *the* Diaspora (always in the singular in the Zionist grammar) a diacritical sign of abnormality, anomaly, and degeneration. (Having rejected both the traditional and modern "spiritualization" of exile as a delusory obfuscation of its intrinsically tragic nature, Zionists deemed exilic Jewish life untenable and therefore "negated" it spiritually, and ultimately politically, through the systematic dissembling of Jewish life outside the national territory).[25] If the richness of biblical pastoral and agrarian imagery was a testimony and "a model of Jewish contact with nature from which ghetto life had been severed," it was at the same time "a combat weapon against 'retrograde' Talmud-centered forces in traditional Jewish society"; having transformed the Jew into a Hebrew, the Bible was no longer the narrative of God's history, but rather of the history of the Jewish people, the product of Jewish genius whose "luster had paled in exile, but that shone again on its Land."[26] For David Ben-Gurion, the Bible "constituted the ideal common heritage for young Israelis of Ashkenazi origin cut off from Eastern European Jewish culture, and for young immigrants from Islamic countries, for whom Zionist ideology was largely alien."[27]

Westernness as Duty (Rather Than Identity)

The Hebrewist project of acculturation imposed on the self (on itself) obligatory diagnostic tools like "acculturation" and "normalization" with which it located defects and deficiencies, so that cultural prescriptions could administer a developmental regime. This self-imposed technology of correction and development in turn became the supervising apparatus that classified and controlled societal anomalies: It allowed the agents of the field (usually a minority of Ashkenazi origin, and usually of a particular social class and political affiliation) to experience themselves as the historic spokesmen of a critical and subversive order, even though their critique was interweaved in—and monitored by—the core of the nationalist canonic discourse. Acculturation of this kind, according to Sara Chinski, became a unidirectional track that incessantly vilified the mechanisms capable of manufacturing difference while nonetheless attempting their colonization.[28] Hebrew nativism, at the same time, embodied a new beginning, which *ipso facto* entailed the repression of Jewish exiles; "The fact that the beginning occurred here, in the Eretz-Israeli space, constituted an erasure of everything that did not exist 'here' but elsewhere, in exile—which is itself summarily denied, because it is not the space of beginning."[29] And yet there is a wrinkle in this attentive critique, as the singularization of *the* Diaspora (as noted above) had by itself been constituent; not only because it "admitted *de facto* the strong theological conception of the Jews as an exiled people upon which modern Jewish territorial nationalism built its foundations,"[30] or since this very discourse underscored the phenomenological dimension of exile spoke in political terms of rupture and dislocation,[31] but also since the mere addition of the definite article, *the* Diaspora underwent dehistoricization and functioned as a universal threshold that rendered the times, cultures, and identities of diasporic Jews a single temporality—ahistorical, contextless, and outside the teleological time of Zionism. The act of universalizing the Diaspora, in other words, denied the retrospective existence of Jewish collectives (alongside their histories and cultures) while imposing on them the specific meaning stemming from the Ashkenazi diasporic experience in Europe.[32]

But the paradox grows more marked since a return to the East involved identification with, and commitment, to the West, to Westernness (see Figure 2.1), which saw the denial of both the Arab East and diasporic Judaism (and this apparatus in turn would deny the diasporic past of non-European Jews and facilitate their subjugation).[33] Westernness in art music written in the Yishuv and the ensuing state had been usually manifested through quotations of popular or folk songs, or otherwise, through transcriptions of non-Western Jewish musical traditions, disciplined by (auto)exoticist formulations that (much like other national peripheries) were marketed as autochthonous.[34] Having undergone such "corrections" so that premodern oral musical traditions would complement the Zionist project of Westernness, such musical earmarks relied on the immediacy of recognizable exotic (and, equally, extroversive) semiotics that more often than not were contingent upon a tonal infrastructure (as in Ben-Haim's *Vision of a Prophet*; Example 2.2).

Tonal constellations featuring (auto)exoticist signifiers communicated Otherness to several interpretive communities, inside the state and outside of it. Yet by the time Mordecai Seter had completed his *Motets* (1939–1951), which he based on transcriptions from Idelsohn's *Hebräisch-orientalischer Melodienschatz* (*HOM*), he could align the latter's ethnographic materials with a rhetoric couched in biblical idioms and literalism at the service of an eschatological national narrative. Only that Seter's semiotics eschewed the immediate symbolism evident in works like *Vision of a Prophet* and dozens of similar compositions from that period that practiced similar mimesis. The first motet, for example, set Psalm 137 after a corresponding dirge, drawn, symbolically, on its Babylonian Jewish musical rendition (Example 2.3a). But having rhythmically augmented Idelsohn's transcription with no strict duration ratio, Seter deemed this import unrecognizable and its psalmodic parallelism defective (Examples 2.3a–b): only the intervals were left intact, thus giving birth to a cantus firmus whose imitations in the surrounding vocal parts not only distanced themselves from the transcribed source, but also circumvented what Seter had called "immediate folklore."[35] At once, then, psalmodic receptacles were made inoperative and the ethnographic import was stripped of, and dissociated from, manifestations of auto-exoticism. Concomitantly, a chiaroscuro harmonic scheme was the result of a linear voice leading, featuring faded allusions to decontextualized triads or partly formed ones, flickering amid continuously moving melodic planes and modal networks.

Seter's precursory departure from a peripheralism communicated by tropes of difference signaled new aesthetic horizons for emigrant composers (and soon enough for native composers as well). But even this breakaway from the political plights of auto-exoticism could not withstand the lure of national redemptive trajectories—even if Seter's case was far less obvious than Ben-Haim's setting of Ezekiel's Vision of the Dry Bones, which under the purview of Zionist biblocentrism could be set to music *as is*. Seter devised (indeed, compiled) a different track: Psalms 137 and 144, the outer

EXAMPLE 2.3A "'Al naḥărôt baḇel" (By Babylon's streams), in Abraham Zvi Idelsohn, *Hebräisch-orientalischer Melodienschatz: Gesänge der babylonischen Juden* (Berlin: Benjamin Harz, 1922), 111. (Psalm 137:1–2)

movements of *Motets*, realized a redemptive trajectory that moved from the low point of exilic lamentation ("By Babylon's streams, there we sat, oh we wept, when we recalled Zion"), which Seter projected poetically when verse 3 was communicated amid a murky *fugato* ("For there our captors had asked of us words of song, and our plunderers—rejoicing: 'Sing us from Zion's song'"), to the royal victory hymn of Psalm 144 ("Blessed is the LORD, my rock, Who trains my hands for battle, my fingers for the fray").[36] And bridging these two psalms were the last three verses from Exodus 2 set according to a Samaritan reading of this same text, which was also transcribed by Idelsohn.[37] But then the biblical text from Exodus 2:23–25 was the meaningful choice here, as it cemented Seter's redemptive design:

> And it happened when a long time had passed that the king of Egypt died, and the Israelites groaned from the bondage and cried out, and their plea from the bondage went up to God. And God heard their moaning, and God remembered His covenant with Abraham, with Isaac, and with Jacob. And God saw the Israelites, and God knew.[38]

Up to this point in the biblical story of Exodus, God has not been evident, writes Robert Alter; but "Now He is the subject of significant verbs—hear, remember (which in the Hebrew has the strong force of 'take to heart'), see, and know." Presumably, God knew "the suffering of the Israelites, the cruel oppression of history in which they are now implicated, the obligations of the covenant with the patriarchs, and the plan He must take undertake to liberate the enslaved people. And so, the objectless verb prepares us for the divine address from the burning bush and the beginning of Moses' mission."[39] Seter, who surely had come across this text in the Passover Haggadah, harnessed its mystifying transition from the exilic lamentation of Psalm 137 to the victory hymn of Psalm 144, all while redeeming the transcriptions from their materiality and symbolic immediacy. Nowhere in his early works did he confirm the hidden protocol between aesthetics and politics and the Zionist nationalization of the theological more so than in the *Motets*. While this kind of national heteronomy would continue to subjugate his

EXAMPLE 2.3B Mordecai Seter, *Motets* (1939–1951). I: "'Al naharot bavel" (By Babylon's streams), mm. 1–15. Copyright © 1962 by Israel Music Institute. All rights reserved. International copyrights secured.

compositional narratives, Seter's setting of biblical and post-biblical texts through the 1960s began to undermine the negated historical time of Zionism (particularly in his oratorio *Tikun ḥatsot* [Midnight vigil] and *Jerusalem*, a symphony for mixed choir, brass, and strings), even if its teleological directionality was yet to be renounced. In parallel, semiotic procedures were persistently furthered and experimented with in instrumental works, where, among other things, psalmodic edifices would be free from the texts that conditioned their eschatology.

DEFLATIONS

Equivalent formulations whose linearity was not as subjugated as Seter's to redemptive trajectories were written by other composers during the 1950s and 1960s. Unlike Seter's *Motets*, these designs would weaken the nationalization of the theological and subsequently decenter territorial nationalism and its complementing diaspora-negating rhetoric (Figure 2.1). Josef Tal's 1955 opera, *Saul at Ein-Dor*, was seemingly the ideal Hebrewist actualization of a biblical text as its libretto was word-for-word the text from 1 Samuel 28:3–25. The text narrates King Saul's visit to the ghostwife of Ein Dor, following the Philistines' camping at Shunem and after God had not answered him "neither by dreams nor by the Urim nor by prophets" (1 Samuel 28:6); but his visit takes a turn as Saul learns through the necromancer of his impending death in the battle of the following day.

There were enough precedents in the Yishuv and the young Jewish state that rewrote Saul's demise under the purview of biblocentrism. "Hineh tamoo yom ḳrav ve'aravo," the previously mentioned poem by Alterman, restaged Saul's final moments following the 1948 War, while sanctifying the meaning of death on (and over) the land of Israel. In a setting "echoing the galloping of horses," as Dan Miron writes, Alterman "declared that a people vanquished on its native soil is never fully vanquished," and that the kingdom's fate will not be identical to its king, since he ran himself through a sword supported by the land to which he belonged.[40] Alterman offered the comfort of the symbol and its potential to immortalize the fallen and the wounded through an immediate symbolism that lacked the internalization by which the cessation of the dead and the deficiency of the wounded (physical and mental) are acknowledged (this maybe the literary equivalent to what Seter called "immediate folklore"). Devoid of the sublimation of shock and mourning, and emptied of their emotional and contemplative content, the blood of Saul's armor bearer who informs his mother of the defeat turns in the poem into a decorative, repulsive-in-its-beauty, crimson (the symbolic blood of the people), which covers the mother's legs at whose feet the armor bearer subsequently collapses. But Alterman's inversion becomes automatic, swift, and declarative, as the mother (yet another immediate symbol standing-in for the nation) orates in a near emotionless manner that a people beaten on its soil "would rise sevenfold."[41]

A decade later, however, Yehudah Amichai's poem "Hamelekh Shaul ve'ani" (King Saul and I, 1958) sounded very different. Using King Saul as "a contrasting backdrop against which the speaker defines his otherness" (as Miron remarks),[42] the latter appears as a tired man entrenched in his bed, which he likens to his kingdom: "I am tired, / My bed is my kingdom. / My sleep is my justice / My dream, a verdict."[43] Neither romantic agony, nor stoic courage, nor identifying with or recoiling from Saul's horrible heroic death is on display. Amichai contrasts Saul's wild energy, uncontained strength, and ego-istic and relentless insistence on royal prerogatives with the almost exact opposite quali-ties of his speaker:[44] if the king's heartbeats "pound like hammers in a new construction," the speaker's heartbeats are likened to a leaking faucet; if Saul's arms arc like armor chains in the harbor, the speaker's arms are too thin and too short. But of the two it is the speaker who inadvertently finds the asses Saul had been sent to retrieve, while they kick the speaker who does not know how to handle them.[45] If the asses are metonyms for the unmanageable disheveled reality of the early statehood years and the legacy left by the golden dream of kingship, then aggrandizement of the king's qualities is undermined by the shadowy texts that relate to his reign. Amichai's juxtapositions carry the effect of both overt literalism and the deflating of the sacred in an associative logic that Ziva Shamir dubs "delayed understanding."[46] Yet these procedures do not push toward a synthesis of any sort, but rather form an unstable mixture in which a dissimilarity of imagery is underscored as much as it concurrently undergoes deconstruction. Poetic components therefore enrich familiar portrayals through figurative, analytical, and Midrashic com-mentary, disclosing the inorganic and the chaotic while unrecognizably expanding the particles' semantic fields, which Amichai knowingly leaves undisciplined.[47] Amichai's intertextual agency thus amounts to a resignifying that confers a disobedient response to statist interpellations but is nevertheless inextricably linked to their discursive function-ality. And yet, what Amichai brings back to his vocabulary, following disarticulations and startling collocations that require leafing through concordances,[48] does not end with a discrete series of speech acts in relation to statist language, but rather expands the discourse to a "ritual chain of resignifications whose origin and end remain unfixed and unfixable," signaling, as Judith Butler writes, that "agency begins where sovereignty wanes."[49] And it is this waning that constitutes Amichai and Tal's deflations.

Despite Tal's embeddedness in the biblocentric discourse and the national rewritings of Saul's demise, his use of a primary biblical source stripped of oversized national fonts was a constituent violation of Hebrewist paradigms that colored *Saul at Ein-Dor* in its entirety. Knowingly aiming at the human tragedy behind Saul's demise, Tal em-ployed periodic signals governed by post-tonal arrays that substituted representational paradigms with a self-referential cellular context consisting mostly of 016/056 sets (the intervallic content of a perfect fourth and a tritone). These cells acquire motivic qualities through myriad projections of their intervallic properties while undergoing modifications that do not abrogate traditional compositional tools and formations.[50] At the same time, periodic signals emerge and remain identifiable despite unsystem-atic incremental expansions, decremental contractions, near transpositions, and near inversions that are saturated enough throughout the musical score to generate direc-tionality. Amid these continuously transitioning schemes, Tal managed to decenter biblocentrism and render his setting impenetrable to mimesis and extrovert semiotics that could relegate cellular elasticity to representational paradigms and other stand-ins for the nation. Add to that the fact that this was an opera concertante, and the setting as a whole becomes almost an ideologically indifferent psychological drama that continu-ously deflates national references and shuns transcendence.

Still, deflation of this kind was not an empty soundboard; employing a biblical linguistic register colonized by the state was also an act of biblical literalism—one that Tal pushes to the point of reductionism, as his deflation negates nationalist adulations and renders inoperative assertions of meaningfulness in Saul's death. Tal's low panoramic view generates inner referential projections pertaining to the psyches of his protagonists, with occasional intervening musical commentaries: these include incremental and decremental transformations around 016/056 sets that gradually color the horror shared by Saul and the ghostwife, or the inner references pertaining to the difference between what is being said and what is known in the dialogue unfolding between these two protagonists. But as far as King Saul is concerned, his appearance on Tal's compositional planes arises from an interpellation, the repetition of which (according to Butler) announces the Hebrewist circumscribed field of linguistic possibilities at the gap between redundancy and repetition.[51] Put differently, Tal's agency becomes a reformulated disobedient reiteration that is nevertheless caught in the ideological apparatus. Which means that the negation embedded in regard to the biblocentric discourse marks Tal's simultaneity of adjacency and oppositionality, beginning with his importation of Schoenbergian serialism to British Palestine and employment of cellular harmony in works written in the 1930s and 1940s—works that epitomized his conscious attempt to avoid mechanisms of signification.

Tal's pairing of nonrepresentational aesthetic and post-tonal devices alongside nationalized theological topoi does not necessarily attest to his familiarity with contemporaneous anti-Romantic poetic formulations of this period (Amichai's deflations of biblocentrism, for example), but it is the connectivity of these elements "circulating inside tiny conduits," as Latour writes, that amount to a "trail of associations" of heterogeneous components that follow the actors themselves so as to learn from them "what the collective existence has become in their hands."[52] And so rather than staging formations in which actors are made to fit in a privileged group (which in the annals of Israeli art music also concerns the somewhat positivistic attempts to partition composers according to generational affiliations),[53] they should be assembled as pulsating networks of actors' own ways, starting with the "traces left behind by the their activity of forming and dismantling groups,"[54] and continuing, in this case, with Tal's oeuvre from the mid-1930s and through the mid-1950s, where a steady consolidation of syntactic linearity destabilizes national constructs while still remaining within their aesthetic orbit.

Such simultaneities anticipated anti-Romanticist readings of North African and Near Eastern Jewish musical traditions in the 1950s. Readings of this kind were announced by Seter's previously discussed *Motets*, yet in Abel Ehrlich's 1953 *Bashrav* for solo violin they appeared devoid of redemptive commitments and immediate national signifiers. Turning to the properties of Eastern music, *Bashrav* records Ehrlich's adaptation of the Ottoman *peşrev*, whose rondo-like form shaped both the simulation of maqāmic principles (quartertones included) and periodic signals that functioned as the *peşrev*'s ritornello and which Ehrlich configured as an incrementally growing cell evolving into a synthetic maqam. The core of this ritornello is palpably displayed at the very opening of the work—a two-note cell descending from G to F-sharp (Example 2.4). This modest

EXAMPLE 2.4 Abel Ehrlich, *Bashrav* (1953) for violin solo, mm. 1–40. Copyright © 2006 by Israel Music Institute. All rights reserved. International copyrights secured.

intervallic content would shape periodic appearances and reappearances of the ritornello in diverse layouts, projections, and permutations, without renouncing the function of this unit within the larger form.

Having considered serial practices from Schoenberg to Messiaen to be the equivalent of artistic quests in Israel, Ehrlich argued that local artistic undertakings were neither "provincial chauvinist isolationism" nor "reactionary entrenchments," but rather manifestations of prioritizing local Eastern melodic and rhythmic properties. And he was very specific: With "Eastern melodic properties" Ehrlich referred to transcriptions of Jewish musical traditions found in the first four volumes of *HOM* (namely, Yemenite, Babylonian, Persian, Bukharan, Dagestani, and Oriental Sephardi Jewish musical traditions). Interested in the mechanism of these traditions' recitatives rather than the fixity of biblical tropes, he discerned motifs that revolve around an axis tone, expanding incrementally to include two to three tones for the entire array, and spawning new motifs while maintaining ties with the primary nucleus.[55]

Ehrlich applied this mechanism to rhythmic irregularities and subsequent asymmetrical accentuations. Rhythm, he maintained, could be employed autonomously, independent of pitch, and develop in the manner of theme and variations, or become a separate part in a two-part texture wherein its timbres and rhythmic configurations would not be constrained by the rhythm of the melody (harmony, subsequently, becomes the product of joining these planes). By applying such musical attributes in both musical pedagogy and compositional practice, he wrote, "we abandon the field of folklore and begin experimenting." And like Seter, this decision, too, relegated harmony to be the mere outcome of joined melodic planes and rhythmic modes: "In music that draws only on melodic and rhythmic features," Ehrlich added, "the 'what' of every part is far more important than the total amassed sound. . . . such music would be first and foremost a polyphony in which the intervals between the voices cease to be a problem." And so regardless of whether these edifices featured perfect intervals, permutating aggregates, or heterophonic textures, the melodic material was to remain equal to the harmonic one: "It is high time we extracted ourselves from the fossilized situation that endangers contemporary Israeli music and turn our back to cheap and shallow optimism," he wrote.[56]

All this was on display in the intervallic information of *Bashrav*'s ritornello. Orbiting around a G axis, its half-step descent is inverted within four measures (Example 2.4) prior to commuting to A, A-flat, B, and C, and before gravitating back to G through yet another inversion of the ritornello (Example 2.4, mm. 5–9). The new melodic element in measure 10 breaks away from the intervallic content of the ritornello with is ascent from G to D, and F, and finally to a G three-quarter flat. At once this phrase manifests a melodic hyperbole whose gravitation to C inverts the ritornello (Example 2.4, mm. 16–17) and shifts the G axis microtonally, thereby refashioning its descent to F (Example 2.4, mm. 12–13); quartertones, in other words, expand here the scope of cellular permutations. After concatenating the intervallic information of the ritornello through measure 30, a two-part texture ensues. Centered on D, this texture reorchestrates elements that earlier were displayed linearly while gravitating to diverse vertical and horizontal variants of the ritornello. And if the ritornello is differentiated from the couplets by its intervallic content (0, -1 and + 7, +3, respectively), Ehrlich progressively infiltrates the latter with permutations of the ritornello, thereby steadily collapsing the differences between both sections (mm. 74–92).

Experiments of this kind with the linear properties of Eastern musics (be they Jewish or not) were inevitable in a culture that perpetuated tropes of return—no matter the discernable gap between Ehrlich's growing aloofness from national musical signifiers and the territorial infrastructure they sustained, and between Seter's theological-cum-national project. Both composers underscored the introversive, nonsignifying semiotics of their ethnographic imports and thus distanced their formulations from immediate symbolism and the territorial functions they had served. But as Seter's case shows, all that did not prevent him from duplicating redemptive national allegories through the 1960s, even when in 1966 he abandoned altogether the use of ethnographic materials, which at that stage he perceived as too extrovert and overtly marked, regardless of the permutations and abstractions he had applied on them. The outcome of this aesthetic choice further de-signified Seter's music; opting for a-thematic melodic proclamations while using the same mechanism that animated *Motets* and his 1961 *Tiḳun ḥatsot*, he breathed life in a musical dramaturgy that used the most rudimentary components—intervals concatenated into monodies and recitatives, or aligned as chords—in two works from 1966, *Dithyramb* for twelve voices a cappella and the aforementioned *Jerusalem*. The latter work compiled biblical texts (mostly from Isaiah 40, 51, and 52), carving an unequivocally bold and redemptive account etched in biblocentrism and in accordance with Seter's perception of the bible as the nation's myth and collectivist ethos.[57] It would be the last time he would install such an allegory. Indeed, take out the compiled biblical texts from *Dithyramb* and *Jerusalem* and the precursory ring of Seter's works from the 1970s becomes apparent, a ring wherein muted Hebrewist visions are substituted with intervallic soliloquies and synthetic modes are bereft of words.

RETURNS TO OTHER LANDS

By the early 1970s, the Hebrewist mechanism spawned returns to the ethnographic spaces in, around, and outside the State of Israel and to the histories that precede national identitarian earmarks. Concomitantly, other returns were becoming politically palpable: ultra-right-wing religious nationalists maximalized the literalist manner in which the Bible was read in earlier decades and shifted it toward messianic territorialism in the newly occupied territories in the West Bank and the Gaza Strip.[58] The abundance of incongruencies stemming at this point from biblocentrism, from the agency of non-Western Jewish musical traditions, and from the subsequent emergence of aesthetic hybrids stained by the theological infrastructure of Zionism, saw dialectical returns to Jewish diasporic pasts alongside imagery overproduction that could no longer serve national functions or abide by territorial nationalism. Returns to diasporic Jewish cultures attenuated immediate national symbolism as much as they anticipated the faltering of symbolization by their sheer pluralities. With the usurpation of diasporic Jewish cultures, national referents were progressively decentered and Hebrewist signifiers ceased to activate the national soundboard (and all the more so when toward the turn-of-the-twenty-first-century composers drew on adjacent non-Jewish soundscapes; seemingly this comes full circle with our discussion on "Moladeti," but the variables that sustained Hebrewism during the statehood era were only partly operative in the early twenty-first century). All this was not commensurate with the thrust of latent messianism in the rank and file of religious Zionism and the subsequent creeping annexation of the occupied territories.

Several prophetic texts from the early 1950s had warned about the radical consequences of too close an overlap between theology and politics,[59] but it took the demise of the (Ashkenazi) political elite in whose image Hebrewism had been conceived, and the ideological vacuum this founding cohort found itself in during the 1970s, before religious Zionists could repurpose Hebrewist theological receptacles and infuse budding messianic ambitions.[60] Indeed, the hegemony's failure to "modernize" Arab Jews (to redeem them from themselves, as it were) undermined the Zionist project of

Westernness through the growing visibility of diasporic alternatives that ultimately resituated Ashkenazy ethnicity. The latter's self-proclaimed universality now underwent *re-ethnicization* alongside additional Jewish collectives: Ashkenazim were placed *in relation* to other Jewish ethnicities (especially those located on the lower rungs of this hierarchy), thereby invalidating the assimilatory apparatus set up by this hegemony for correcting performances (or lack thereof) of Westernness.[61]

Compositions written during the 1970s evinced turns to the narrative leftovers of the materials from which Zionist myths were culled. These included post-biblical literatures that were excluded from the national allegory, and ultimately returns to premodern Ashkenazi diasporic cultures. The person to spell out these tensions most violently was Andre Hajdu, a Holocaust survivor who fled Hungary in 1956 to live and work in Paris (where he studied with Darius Milhaud and Olivier Messiaen) prior to immigrating to Israel in 1966 and becoming a *baal teshuvah*. Hajdu's early European works betray a non-sublimated deconstructive approach that jeers at socialist realism (against whose dictates he received his early musical training), but also at Western art music forms in addition to serial and post-serial compositional approaches. At the same time, the same modest compositional output resounded the disbelief of an ethnomusicologist, who, having trained with Zoltán Kodály, could meticulously transcribe his wildest (spasmatic) improvisatory impulses, but also critically assess the road traveled by ethnographic imports as they become artsy constructs. Hajdu's 1970 *Ludus Paschalis*—where Talmudic excerpts and psalmodic verses were gradually eclipsed and eventually stained by the singing of Christian children performing a mock Easter play—and his setting of *Mishnayot* (third-century redactions of Jewish oral traditions) began staging what Hebrewism had repressed. Having visualized the cultural and religious adjacencies of Jews and Christians while setting texts that undermined the Zionist management of Jewish history (including its denial of Jewish diasporas), Hajdu's returns to Europe (as a composer and an ethnographer) and to Judaism (as an observant Jew) were preoccupied neither with auto-exoticism nor with defamiliarization of post–World War II serialism. Rather, after conducting ethnographic fieldwork in Hasidic Jewish communities and institutions for advanced Talmudic studies (*kolelim*) in Israel, he ethnicized, or rather *re-ethnicized*, Ashkenazi Jewry by returning to the early stages of Western musical literacy, from which he could portray repressed ethnographic and liturgical adjacencies.

In *Ludus Paschalis*, Hajdu's penchant for non-sublimated formulations saw the staging of raw and unvarnished psychic energies in a seemingly unskillful heterophony of Jews and Christians in late medieval times. With no aesthetic debts to Hebrewism and its rhetorical constraints, Hajdu felt distanced from the ideological arguments held at the Israel Composers' League, especially since he saw no contradiction between the experience and loyalty to the land, and everything Jews had created in the Diaspora.[62] The historicist mechanism at the basis of his writing, in other words, was not different from the Hebrewist return to origins (as was the Canaanites' idealization of a pre-monotheistic past, to give another example),[63] but the difference was crucial. Hajdu perceived both Judaism and Western existentialism as part of his "pioneer" vision;[64] having realized that the Israeli elite had been decentered and disoriented, while exilic experiences were still too close and the "instinct to run away from them was strong" (and notice Hajdu's striking offhand relabeling of what Figure 2.1 lists as "diaspora-negating rhetoric"),[65] he could now unload the imports that had been simmering within him since the late 1950s.

Set for a (Jewish) men's choir (with occasional flickering solo parts), and a (Christian) boys' choir whose members also play percussion instruments (bells, cymbals, whistle, rattle, bullroarer, small casserole, and side drums), *Ludus Paschalis* sought the ethnographic reproduction of the sonic spaces shared by Jews and Christians. A production inseparable from the autobiography of the composer-ethnomusicologist, the work set tractates from the Babylonian Talmud alongside passages from medieval Passions and Easter plays that called for the participation of impersonated Jews while sampling the Holy Week violence. Hajdu's main source for such texts was Ernst August Schuler's 1951 *Die Musik der Osterfeiern, Osterspiele und Passionen des Mittelalters*, in whose spirit of mock or corrupt Hebrew Hajdu took the liberty to further decontextualize several words and refashion others, amid a *gemore-nign* (Talmud melody), which he studied during an ethnographic fieldwork in Israel.[66] By fleshing out frictions of this kind, Hajdu's main attention was given to the unsublimated and ultimately violent energies stemming from such religious and sonic adjacencies. Having interpreted Zionist diaspora-negating rhetoric as disingenuous, given the gap he discerned between national rhetoric and the ethnographic findings he had been exposed to in his ethnographic fieldwork, Hajdu staged what had been repressed in Hebrewism, namely the texts, musics, and temporalities of the Mishnah and the Talmud. Both were granted the status of a motif amid the staging of unwanted Christian contiguities. In addition to the blatantly non-biblocentric narrative and the performance of an Eastern European (exilic) soundscape that set Mishnaic Hebrew, *Ludus Paschalis* allowed neither Zionist diaspora-negating rhetoric nor "symptoms of a linear march toward intolerance" (in David Nirenberg's words) to be easily converted into a territorial Zionist paradigm.[67] Hajdu was most likely the only person capable of transcribing such musics *about* Jews, while being indifferent to—and disinterested in—national compulsions. With this alone he accomplished the separation of Jewish ethnography from the iron grip of territorial nationalism.

Between 1972 and 1973 Hajdu set fifty-six Mishnaic tractates to music, returning not only to miniature forms (where he had always been at his best), but also to a temporality alien to Hebrewist paradigms. Being a collection of rabbinic traditions redacted at the beginning of the third century and mostly indifferent to Hebrew scriptures, the Mishnah did not lend itself to ideological commandeering. Indeed, it would cause puzzlement to someone who had never seen it before, as it provides contextless information and presents "disputes about facts hardly urgent outside a circle of faceless disputants," while permitting only slight variation in its authorities' patterns of language and speech, as authors do what they must to efface all traces of not only individuality, but also their participation in the formation of the document.[68] With no attempt to imitate biblical Hebrew or attribute its saying to biblical heroes, prophets, and holy men, the Mishnah "does not claim to emerge from a fresh encounter with God through revelation, as is not uncommon in Israelite writing of the preceding four hundred years."[69] Being the foundation of the Babylonian and Palestinian Talmuds, the Mishnah's descriptive rules (dealing with agriculture rules, laws governing Sabbaths and festivals, laws on the transfer of women and property, a civic and criminal legal system, laws for conduct of the cult and the Temple, and laws on the preservation of cultic purity in the temple and under certain domestic circumstances)[70] were thus deemed inferior, not to say irrelevant, in a Zionist biblocentric discourse. The oral nature of the Mishnah's encyclopedic law code, Hajdu argued, took forms that were suggestive of folksongs, with characteristic symmetric phrases and rhyme schemes[71] whose formulary units lent themselves to the staging of irregular phrasing corresponding to the variants of recurring cognitive units. In Hajdu's settings such structures are complemented by harmonic tessituras whose tonalities draw on various musics that remain contextually uncommitted—much like the Mishnah itself. Semiotically distancing his settings from constraining Jewish musical earmarks while relying on the Mishnah's lack of emotional context, Hajdu deemed his abundance of stylistic allusions, pastiches, and citations ethnographic raw materials; and through these rebranded raw materials he conveyed a remarkable openness to what was otherwise an assortment of cognitive units resorting to a "limited repertoire of formulary patterns" (according to Neusner).[72] Hajdu's adamot subsequently not only manifested the temporalities and oralities denied by Hebrew culture, but also featured a radial musical view traversing through art, popular, folk, vernacular, and post-vernacular musics whose animation of Mishnaic tractates defied the identitarian signifiers that sustained Zionist territorialism by mere multiplication.

"Eppur Si Muove"

The last two works to be discussed here in this network of Hebrewism (including its adamot) and the meanings its key variables have accrued and lost were written by Betty Olivero and Chaya Czernowin. Both received their undergraduate training at the Tel Aviv University Music Academy in the late 1970s (Olivero) and early 1980s (Czernowin) during a post-ideological age that author Yaakov Shabtai had meticulously recorded in his 1977 novel *Past Continuous*.[73] Both had close acquaintance with Ehrlich's undisciplined linearity (and aloofness from Zionism), with Seter's disillusionment with the nationalization of the theological, and with Hajdu's unsublimated ethnographic deconstructions. The aesthetic penchants Olivero and Czernowin have been developing since the 1980s and cannot be considered apart from the aftermath of the key variables of Hebrewism shown in Figure 2.1, particularly due to their demonstrably dissimilar compositional approaches. Because rather than resistance to these variables, whose spiritual dominance has already become dim and their ideological grip frail, a sense of disbelief in such constructs has led these two composers to render Hebrewism and its territorial corollaries irrelevant and hence ideologically invalid. Indeed, the overt political content of more than three decades of statehood discloses a gap between the Zionist commitment to Westernness and the reality of its social structure, which had been dominated by the state itself and the Labor movement. But if the statist subject superseded or subsumed any competing political project that threatened its universality or pecking order, while weightily perpetuating imaginary worlds fettered in politics, then by the 1980s such self-referential heteronomous acts were losing their ability to confer homogeneity and project the monologic of Hebrewism and its *telos*.[74] Art music, too, ceased to function as a receptacle for national ideology or a site for its reproduction, beginning with the turn to exilic histories and cultures whose very multiplicities and disorderliness threatened both territorial Zionism and the Zionist management of Jewish history (in the 1980s, this coincided with the appearance of contesting narratives by the so-called New Historians Benny Morris, Ilan Pappé, Gershon Shafir, Avi Shlaim, and others). Toward the turn of the twentieth century, practices drawing on modernist aesthetics in addition to asynchronous temporalities bequeathed from postmodernism were knowingly distanced from the dictates of heteronomous national narrations, and mostly without the need for its abstract negation. Musical formulations were no longer subjugated stencils—no longer stand-ins. Both the self and the cultural spaces one resounded and radically juxtaposed now formed the autonomous canvas—free from *opposing* (and hence, from rendering present) national and territorial tropes.

Thus Olivero's 2004 *Bashrav* for nine players sets up a half-century-long corridor wherein both the distance traveled by this form and its mutable aesthetic functions are measurable. If Ehrlich's 1953 *Bashrav* was a pretext for syntactic common denominator that could challenge the metaphors conditioned by the heteronomy of Hebrewism, his employment of linear devices manifested at the same time his objection to the folkish morphology that epitomized a desirable Western self-image in art music of the 1950s (and which he resisted more vehemently in his diaries when he deemed Marc Lavry's practice of citing folkish themes a "photographic undertaking").[75] It is against this negative soundboard that Ehrlich consolidates mosaic-like formulations and abstracted maqāmāt devoid of specific collections of notes or motifs. But resistance of this kind does not steer Olivero's aesthetics: her *Bashrav* is launched from a ritornello in the form of a de-arpeggiated major second on the viola (G–A), while each node competes for centricity as the opening unfolds. Indeed, it takes Ehrlich's *Bashrav* 57 measures to de-arpeggiate his ritornello as a major seventh (E-flat–D), yet by the time he does so, this formation is but a mediator in an almost seamless succession of variants. Olivero's harmonic ritornello, comparatively, is but a suggestion for the possibilities arising from the oscillating saturations of each of these nodes while linearly expanding the adjacent half-step between and around both centers, thereby outlining the modal and tonal potentials that she never fully realizes. In fact, it is the simultaneity of these scalar and harmonic possibilities that annuls the very notion of discrepancies in those seemingly bi- or polymodal constellations.[76] Olivero suffices with provisional nodes (and usually by means of rhetoric rather than harmonic syntax) amid aggregates that deform and disfigure modal identities. Among such formations are tonally ambiguous clusters whose saturation impairs traditional directionality while anchoring them in partially static centricities that are tainted for the purpose of (re)brightening. Such tainting is achieved by means of additives whose surveying of chromatic adjacencies produces simultaneous (and hence, murky) modal allusions that Olivero almost always shapes into wounded apparitions of tonal objects. With this she also relativizes the Western disciplining mechanism itself (the same mechanism whose criteria informed both auto-exoticist practices in art music and the very socio-ethnic hierarchy of Zionism); with this she also crisscrosses ethnic spaces in relationships of familiarity or quasi-familiarity while loosely huddling together an interconnected skein of threads that lead unpredictably from one culture to another (Jewish or non-Jewish).[77]

To a certain extent Czernowin's muting of Hebrewist key variables goes even further, especially since she opts for remodernist aesthetics.[78] Much like Olivero, resistance to national topoi is replaced with disinterestedness, while Otherness is consciously circumvented by the very separation of culture from national territory; unlike Olivero, however, there are significantly fewer postmodern patrimonies in a semiotic context wherein pitch competes for centricity with the timbres and sonorities that inundate it. Twelve years after the publication of David Grossman *Ayen erekh: Ahavah* (See Under: Love),[79] Czernowin based her first opera, *Pnima . . . ins Innere* (*Inwards*; 1998/1999) on the first section in Grossman's novel ("Momik"), culling, paraphrasing, and acoustically translating its sonic prelinguistic resources. In a calculated thick of drones ringing incessantly in numerous frequencies and amplitudes, Czernowin complements the obfuscation and garbling that governs this section in the novel by distilling the sounds recorded in its first section into granular textures, and by muddying them altogether so as to prolong the incessant mumbling and humming of Anshel (the demented and incommunicative Holocaust survivor) in numerous textural widths. Such sonic minutiae are realized in *Pnima* through de-signification and a poetics of non-redemption by which Czernowin knowingly distances her music (and this opera in particular) from the Zionist management of Jewish history (much like how Grossman's novel itself disables the very syntax that facilitated the Israeli nationalization of the Holocaust).

Yet with a dense flux of recounted dialogues that are usually reported in the third person by Momik (the young protagonist of this novel) while traversing through thick intertextual, intercultural, and national interpolations that cannot transition into a dialogical libretto,[80] Czernowin's had almost no option other than muting Grossman's text in its entirety and reduce the number of characters on stage to only two. Seemingly these are Momik and Anshel, only that their names and voices are denied of them. Both characters are impersonalized as "boy" and "grandfather" (great-uncle, in fact, but this is a common mistake, given that Momik himself refers to Anshel as "grandfather Anshel"),[81] and their voices are dislocated and duplicated by two male vocalists and two female vocalists, (dis)embodying Anshel and Momik (respectively). The extent by which these two characters are ventriloquized remains arguable, as Czernowin's keeps her four vocalists invisible (in the orchestra pit) and nonsynchronous with the mimes on stage; but then the proximities of voices and non-singing bodies is further disequilibrated by the fact the that none of the vocalists, male or female, utters words or even phonemes, but rather sonorants that decenter vowels and undo phonology. At this level of semiotic atomization, the limit of consonants a single body can produce without vowels is prolonged by the interlacing of two singing bodies whose sonorants involve changing air pressures, different postures of the mouth, and transitions to and from whispers, breaths, singing, and falsettos.

With the absence of a libretto or a plot, and the subsequent disavowal of a linear narrative,[82] Czernowin continuously engages with disnarration, namely, that which relates to the narrating rather than the narrated, that which foregrounds ways of creating a situation or ordering an experience, and most importantly that which emphasized the realities of representation as opposed to the representation of realities (according to Gerald Prince).[83] Czernowin in fact maximalizes Prince's characterization of the disnarrated by muddling those "terms, phrases, and passages that consider what did not or does not take place . . . whether they pertain to the narrator and his or her narration . . . or to one or the characters and his or her actions." As a result, alethic expressions of impossibility or unrealized possibility, purely imagined worlds, desired worlds, intended words, or failed attempts[84] are transcribed while the textural substitutes the textual. And yet the musical textures of *Pnima* are adamantly unstable and discontinuous (which is another way of saying that Czernowin never succumbs to self-indulgent patterning from which she breaks away the moment such arrays could become predictable). But then even Grossman's novel, which by itself is a form of historical, fictive, and intertextual lineaments, endows meaning to a semiotics otherwise nationally orphaned. Would the compositional praxis of Olivero and Czernowin necessitate the redrawing Figure 2.1?

Before it does, we should reconsider the adamot that have traversed through this text. The national land—be it the biblical Greater Israel (*Erets Yisrael*) or the (still) unfinalized borders of the State of Israel—conditioned Hebrew culture and facilitated its expansionism. Complemented by the Zionist management of Jewish history whose telos actualized biblical promises of return while nationalizing theological tropes, this apparatus deemed other non-sovereign Jewish histories and cultures (and lands) a threat to the territorial core of the Zionist project and thus negated the political option of life among host societies, outside the national soil. Concomitantly, anthropomorphic metaphors conflated "the-man-and-his-work with the-man-as-a-work (of art)," thereby camouflaging the strategy of territorializing authenticity and annulling the difference between selfhood and land.[85] But then exilic non-territorial histories usurped to the point of undermining the rhetorical veneer that sustained the negation of *the* Diaspora; and the more visibility these histories gained, the more it became apparent that the network of modern Jewish culture exceeds the territorial paragons that governed it in the Zionist discourse. Indeed, modern Hebrew culture as well as modern Jewish art music preceded and ran parallel to Hebrewism: suffice to think of poet David Vogel's dissociation from Zionism and his refusal to mobilize his version of Hebrew modernism to a national thematics,[86] or the works of Ernest Bloch, Darius Milhaud, Mario Castelnuovo-Tedesco, and even Arnold Schoenberg, who remained safely distanced from the Zionist project (and its territory; the same is true for Leonard Bernstein, even if his command of Hebrew and familiarity with Jewish liturgy was incomparable with the former names listed here in addition to many of the emigrant composers dislocated to British Palestine and Israel). Dialectical returns to Jewish diasporas in art music since the 1970s therefore sought to contain competitive non-territorial histories against the backdrop of diluted Hebrewism (whose territorial foundation was by then thrusted by messianic political theologies in religious Zionist circles) and an aged Eastern European political hegemony facing an ideological vacuum. But amid the inundation of Jewish diasporic cultures that bred contemporary art music, and the realization that a Westernized hegemonic national identity is *not* contingent upon its dissociation from its preceding diasporic pasts, composers were led to other adamot. In this still unfolding phase, Olivero opts for the adjacent Jewish and non-Jewish spaces of the Mediterranean in an attempt to defeat the "symbolic house arrest" of one's culture, ethnicity, or geographic roots,[87] and Czernowin (re)turns to Europe and its current modernist brands while knowingly disabling tropes of Otherness.

NOTES

1. See Bruno Latour, *We Have Never Been Modern*, trans. Catherine Porter (Cambridge, MA: Harvard University Press, 1993).

2. See Natan Shahar, "The Eretz Israeli Song and the Jewish National Fund," in *Modern Jews and their Musical Agendas*, ed. Ezra Mendelsohn, Studies in Contemporary Jewry 9 (New York: Oxford University Press, 1994), 78–91.

3. The absence of the word *beth* in the song could be explained by both its poetic meter and the description of the region in Joshua 21:22 (Beth-Horon and its pastures), which refers to the open area that surrounded a fortified city.

4. See Josephus Flavius, *The Jewish War*, trans. Martin Hammond (New York: Oxford University Press, 2017), 144.

5. See Anita Shapira, "The Religious Motifs of the Labor Movement," in *Zionism and Religion*, ed. Shmuel Almog, Jehuda Reinharz, and Anita Shapira (Hanover, NH: University Press of New England, 1998), 251–272; see also Julius H. Schoeps, "Modern Heirs of the Maccabees: The Beginning of the Vienna Kadimah, 1882–1897," *The Leo Baeck Institute Year Book* 27, no. 1 (1982): 155–170.

6. See Yehouda Shenhav, *Beyond the Two State Solution: A Jewish Political Essay* (Cambridge: Polity Press, 2012), 55–56.

7. See Amnon Raz-Krakotzkin, "A National Colonial Theology: Religion, Orientalism, and the Construction of the Secular in Zionist Discourse," *Tel Aviver Jahrbuch für deutsche Geschichte* 30 (2002): 312–326.

8. Yael Zerubavel, "Memory, the Rebirth of the Native, and the Hebrew Bedouin Identity," *Social Research* 75, no. 1 (2008): 315–352.

9. See Jehoash Hirshberg, "The Germans are Coming! Cultural Pre-Migration Conditions in Palestine," in *Verfemte Musik: Komponisten in den Diktaturen unseres Jahrhunderts*, ed. Joachim Braun, Vladimír Karbusický, and Heidi Tamar Hoffmann (Frankfurt am Main: Peter Lang, 1995), 287–291; Philip V. Bohlman, "The Immigrant Composer in Palestine, 1933–1948: Stranger in a Strange Land," *Asian Music* 17 (1986): 147–167; Yoav Gelber, *Moledet ḥadashah: 'Aliyat Yehude merkaz Eropah ve-ḳeliṭatam, 1933–1948* [New homeland: Immigration and absorption of Central European Jews, 1933–1948] (Jerusalem: Ben-Zvi Institute, 1990), 61.

10. See Oren Yiftachel, *Ethnocracy: Land and Identity Politics in Israel/Palestine* (Philadelphia: University of Pennsylvania Press, 2006), 3.

11. See Anita Shapira, "The Bible and Israeli Identity," *AJS Review* 28, no. 1 (2004): 11–42.

12. Robert Alter, *The Hebrew Bible: A Translation with* Commentary (New York: W.W. Norton, 2019), 2:964, 962, 1162.

13. See Uriel Simon, "Ma'amad ha-mikrah ba-hevra ha-yisraelit: Mi-midrash le'umi lipheshat kiyumi" [The status of the Bible in Israeli society: From national commentary to existential literalism], in *Yeriot: Essays and Papers in the Jewish Studies Bearing on the Humanities and the Social Sciences /* יריעות: ב' ליצחק הס - מסה, עיון ומחקר במדעי היהדות, ed. Elhanan Reiner, Israel Ta-Shema, and Gideon Ofrat (Jerusalem: Orna Hess, 1999), 1:8.

14. Jewish Agency for Palestine, *The Historical Connection for the Jewish People with Palestine*, rev. ed. (Jerusalem: Jewish Agency for Palestine, 1946), 7.

15. See Gershon Shaked, "Modern Midrash: The Biblical Canon and Modern Literature," *AJS Review* 28, no. 1 (2004): 43–62.

16. See Arthur B. Hyman and Shiloni Yitshak, eds., *Yalkut Shim'oni 'al Nevi'im—Nevi'im aharonim: Yesha'yahu, Yirmeyahu, Yehezkel, Tere 'asar* (Jerusalem: Rabbi Kook Institute, 2009), 7:597–601.

17. Alter, *The Hebrew Bible*, 2:1165.

18. See Dan Miron, *The Prophetic Mode in Modern Hebrew Poetry* (New Milford, CT: Toby Press, 2010), 433–443; Hannan Hever, *Nativism, Zionism, and Beyond* (Syracuse, NY: Syracuse University Press, 2014), 21–39.

19. Alter, *The Hebrew Bible*, 2:1165.

20. Ibid., 2:1068, 645.

21. Haim Gouri, *Hashirim* (Tel Aviv: Hakibbutz Hameuchad, 1998), 1:93; Aharon Amir, *The Clouds Return after the Rain: Collected Poems, 1943–1991 /* ושבו העבים אחר הגשם: כל השירים (Jerusalem: Carmel Publishing, 2000), 283–284; Alter, *The Hebrew Bible*, 2: 885, 893.

22. See Amnon Raz-Krakotzkin, "Between Brit Shalom and the Temple: The Dialectics of Redemption and Messianism following Gershom Scholem" / בין "ברית שלום" ובין בית המקדש: הדיאלקטיקה של גאולה ומשיחיות בעקבות גרשם שלום, *Theory and Criticism* 20 / תיאוריה וביקורת (Spring 2002): 105–06.

23. William Cutter, "Ghostly Hebrew, Ghastly Speech: Scholem to Rosenzweig, 1926," *Prooftexts* 10, no. 3 (1990): 417–418.

24. Ibid., 417–418 (emphasis in original).

25. See Paul Mendes-Flor, "Zion und die Diaspora: Vom babylonischen Exil bis zur Gründung des Staates Israel," in *Jüdische Lebenswelten: Essays*, ed. Andreas Nachama, Gereon Sievernich, Julius H. Schoeps, and Edward van Voolen (Frankfurt am Main: Jüdischer Verlag / Suhrkamp, 1991), 257–283; on the differentials involved in Zionist perceptions of the Diaspora see Gideon Shimoni, "Reexamination of the Negation of the Diaspora as an Idea and an Act" / בחינה מחדש של שלילת הגלות כרעיון וכמעשה, in *The Age of Zionism /* עידן הציונות, ed. Anita Shapira, Jehuda Reinharz, and Jacob Harris (Jerusalem: Zalman Shazar Center, 2000), 45–51; and Eliezer Schweid, "The Rejection of the Diaspora in Zionist Thought: Two Approaches," *Studies in Zionism* 5, no. 1 (1984): 43–70.

26. Jean-Christophe Attias, *The Jews and the Bible*, trans. Patrick Camiller (Stanford: Stanford University Press, 2014), 142–144.

27. Ibid., 145.

28. See Sara Chinski, *Kingdom of the Meek: The Social Grammar of the Israeli Art Field /* מלכות הענווים: הדקדוק החברתי של שדה האמנות הישראלי ענווי ארץ (Tel Aviv: Hakibbutz Hameuchad, 2015), 280–287.

29. Hever, *Nativism, Zionism, and Beyond*, 23.

30. Edwin Seroussi, "Jewish Music and Diaspora," in *The Cambridge Companion to Jewish Music*, ed. Joshua S. Walden (Cambridge: Cambridge University Press, 2015), 30.

31. See Paul Mendes-Flohr, "About the Term Exile," *Critical Inquiry* 46, no. 2 (2020): 444.

32. See Chinski, *Kingdom of the Meek*, 215–216.

33. See Amnon Raz-Krakotzkin, "Secularism, the Christian Ambivalence toward the Jews, and the Notion of Exile," in *Secularism in Question: Jews and Judaism in Modern Times*, ed. Ari Joskowicz and Ethan B. Katz (Philadelphia: University of Pennsylvania Press, 2015), 276–298; Raz-Krakotzkin, "The Zionist Return to the West and the Mizrahi Jewish Perspective," in *Orientalism and the Jews*, ed. Ivan Davidson Kalmar and Derek J. Penslar (Waltham, MA: Brandeis University Press, 2005), 162–181.

34. See Susan McClary, "Playing the Identity Card: Of Grieg, Indians, and Women," *Nineteenth-century Music* 31, no. 3 (2008): 217–227; James Parakilas, "How Spain Got a Soul," in *The Exotic in Western Music*, ed. Jonathan Bellman (Boston: Northeastern University Press, 1998), 137–193; Eva Mantzourani, *The Life and Twelve-Note Music of Nikos Skalkottas* (Farnham: Ashgate, 2011); and Ben Earle, "Twelve-Note Music as Music: An Essay in Two Parts," *Music Analysis* 34, no. 1 (2015): 112–126.

35. Mordecai Seter, handwritten notebook, 1961, MUS110 D4, Mordecai Seter Collection, The National Library of Israel, Jerusalem.

36. Alter, *The Hebrew Bible*, 3:326. The transcription used for Psalm 144 was a Bukharan psalmody, no. 135 in the third volume of *HOM*.

37. See Abraham Zvi Idelsohn, *Toldot haneginah ha-ivrit: Mahutah yesodoteha ve-hitpathutah* [History of Hebrew music: Its essence, foundations, and development] (Tel Aviv: Dvir, 1924), 1:57; Idelsohn, "Die Vortragszeichen der Samaritaner," *Monatsschrift für Geschichte und Wissenschaft des Judentums* 61 (1917): 126.

38. Alter, *The Hebrew Bible*, 1:219–220.

39. Ibid., 1:219–220.

40. Miron, *The Prophetic Mode*, 450; Nathan Alterman, *Sefer ha- tevah ha- mezameret* (Tel Aviv: Hakibbutz Hameuchad, 1966), 1:185. Hannan Hever, *Suddenly, the Sight of War: Nationality and Violence in Hebrew Poetry of the 1940s* / לאומיות ואלימות בשירת שנות הארבעים :פתאם מראה המלחמה (Tel Aviv: Hakibbutz Hameuchad, 2001), 92; Shaked, "Modern Midrash," 57–58.

41. Dan Miron, *Facing the Silent Brother: Essays on the Poetry of the War of Independence* / מול האח השותק: עיונים בשירת מלחמת העצמאות (Jerusalem: Keter, 1992), 54.

42. Miron, *The Prophetic Mode*, 474.

43. Yehuda Amichai, "King Saul and I", in *Shire Yehudah ʿAmiḥai*, 5 vols. (Tel Aviv: Schocken, 2002), 1:150.

44. See Miron, *The Prophetic Mode*, 475.

45. Amichai, "King Saul and I," 1:148–150.

46. Ziva Shamir, "The Conceit as a Cardinal Style-Marker in Yehuda Amichai's Poetry," in *The Experienced Soul: Studies in Amichai*, ed. Glensda Abramson (Boulder, CO: Westview Press, 1997), 24–25.

47. See Dan Miron, *More! Cognitive Formations in Early Israeli Poetry* / עוד! תשתיות קוגניטיביות בשירה הישראלית המוקדמת (Ramat Gan: Afik, 2014), 291–295.

48. See Robert Alter, "Yehuda Amichai: At Play in the Fields of Verse," *Jewish Review of Books* (Summer 2011): 39–40.

49. Judith Butler, *Excitable Speech: A Politics of the Performative* (London: Routledge, 1997), 14, 16.

50. See Jack F. Boss, "'Away with Motivic Working?' Not So Fast: Motivic Processes in Schoenberg's op. 11, no. 3," *Music Theory Online* 21, no. 3 (2015); http://www.mtosmt.org/issues/mto.15.21.3/mto.15.21.3.boss.html (accessed December 9, 2020); and Ethan Haimo, *Schoenberg's Transformation of Musical Language* (Cambridge: Cambridge University Press, 2006).

51. See Butler, *Excitable* Speech, 129.

52. Bruno Latour, *Reassembling the Social: An Introduction to Actor-Network-Theory* (Oxford: Oxford University Press, 2005), 5, 12.

53. See Peter Gradenwitz, *The Music of Israel: from the Biblical Era to Modern Times*, 2nd ed. (Portland, OR: Amadeus Press, 1996); Robert Fleisher, *Twenty Israeli Composers: Voices of a Culture* (Detroit, MI: Wayne State University Press, 1997); Ronit Seter, "Israelism: Nationalism, Orientalism, and the Israeli Five," *Musical Quarterly* 97, no. 2 (2014): 238–308; Jehoash Hirshberg, "Art Music in the Yishuv and in Israel," in Walden, *The Cambridge Companion to Jewish Music*, 228–243.

54. Latour, *Reassembling the Social*, 28–29.

55. See Abel Ehrlich, "Ha-musiḳah ha-yisraelit ve-tasbikhiah" [Israeli music and its complexes], *Masa* (April 14, 1954): 12.

56. Ibid.

57. See Mordecai Seter, handwritten notebooks, 1965 and September 1978–February 1980, respectively, MUS 110 D10–11, D19, Mordecai Seter Collection, The National Library of Israel, Jerusalem.

58. See Gershon Shafir, *A Half Century of Occupation: Israel, Palestine, and the World's Most Intractable Conflict* (Berkeley: University of California Press, 2017), 58–60; see also Arie Perliger and Ami Pedahzur, "The Territories in Israeli Politics," in *The Oxford Handbook of Israeli Politics and Society*, ed. Reuven Y. Hazan, Alan Dowty, Menachem Hofnung, and Gideon Rahat (New York: Oxford University Press, 2021), 533–547.

59. See Akibah Ernst Simon, *Are We Still Jews? Essays* / האם עוד יהודים אנחנו: מסות (Tel Aviv: Poalim, 1982), 9–46; Baruch Kurzweil, *Sifrutenu ha-ḥadashah: Hemshekh o mahpekhah?* [Our new literature: Continuity or revolution?] (Jerusalem: Schocken, 1971), 270–300; Yeshayahu Leibowitz, *Judaism, Human Values, and The Jewish State*, trans. Eliezer Goldman (Cambridge, MA: Harvard University Press, 1992), 185–191.

60. See Gadi Taub, *The Settlers and the Struggle over the Meaning of Zionism* (New Haven, CT: Yale University Press, 2010).

61. See Aziza Khazzoom, *Shifting Ethnic Boundaries and Inequality in Israel, or, How the Polish Peddler Became a German Intellectual* (Stanford, CA: Stanford University Press, 2008).

62. See Mira Zakai and Andre Hajdu, *Doors Opening, an Ongoing Conversation* / דלתות נפתחות: מירה ואנדרה ממשיכים לשוחח (Tel Aviv: Hakibbutz Hameuchad, 2015), 79.

63. See David Ohana, *The Origins of Israeli Mythology: Neither Canaanites nor Crusaders*, trans. David Maisel (Cambridge: Cambridge University Press, 2012), 73–100.

64. See Zakai and Hajdu, *Doors Opening*, 80.

65. See ibid., 81.

66. See Ernst August Schuler, *Die Musik der Osterfeiern, Osterspiele und Passionen des Mittelalters* (Kassel: Bärenreiter Verlag, 1951), 290–291, 367–368, 370–371; and Andre Hajdu Collection, MUS 173 A63, The National Library of Israel, Jerusalem. Hajdu's early ethno-musicological publications include: Avigdor Herzog and Andre Hajdu, "A la recherche du

Tonus Peregrinus dans la tradition musicale juive," *Yuval* 1 (1968): 194–203; Andre Hajdu, "Le niggûn merôn: Description d'un patrimoine instrumental juif," *Yuval* 2 (1971): 73–113; Andre Hajdu and Yaacov Mazor, "Hasidim," in *Encyclopedia Judaica* (Jerusalem: Keter, 1971) 7:1422–1432; Yaacov Mazor, Andre Hajdu, and Bathja Bayer, "The Hasidic Dance-Niggûn: A Study Collection and Its Classificatory Analysis," *Yuval* 3 (1974): 136–166.

67. David Nirenberg, *Communities of Violence: Persecution of Minorities in the Middle Ages* (Princeton: Princeton University Press, 1996), 229; see also Chinski, *Kingdom of the Meek*, 128.

68. Jacob Neusner, trans., *The Mishnah: A New Translation* (New Haven, CT: Yale University Press, 1988), xiii.

69. Ibid., xiv.

70. See ibid., xv.

71. See Zakai and Hajdu, *Doors Opening*, 57.

72. Neusner, *The Mishnah*, xx.

73. See Yaakov Shabtai, *Past Continuous*, trans. Dalya Bilyu (Philadelphia, PA: Jewish Publication Society of America, 1985).

74. See Kfir Cohen Lustig, *Makers of Worlds, Readers of Signs; Israeli and Palestinian Literature of the Global Contemporary* (New York: Verso, 2019), 119–122.

75. Abel Ehrlich, notebook "Erinnerungen um die 120 Nummern herum," December 7, 1961, Abel Ehrlich Archiv, file 4010, Akademie der Künste, Berlin.

76. See Paolo Susanni and Elliott Antokoletz, *Music and Twentieth-Century Tonality: Harmonic Progression Based on Modality and the Interval Cycles* (New York: Routledge, 2012).

77. See Benny Ziffer, *Entre nous, les Levantins: Carnets de voyage* (Arles: Actes Sud, 2014).

78. See Claus-Steffen Mahnkopf, "Second Modernity—An attempted Assessment," in *Facets of the Second Modernity*, ed. Claus-Steffen Mahnkopf, Frank Cox, and Wolfram Schurig (Hofheim: Wolke, 2008), 9–16; Chaya Czernowin, "Few Examples from MAIM (Water, 2001/2, 2005, 2006/7): How this Music Thinks," in *Facets of the Second Modernity*, 99–133; Chaya Czernowin, "The Art of Risk Taking: Experimentation, Invention, and Discovery," in *Experimental Encounters in Music and Beyond*, ed. Kathleen Coessens (Leuven: Leuven University Press, 2017), 31–37; see also Robin Van den Akker and Timotheus Vermeulen, "Periodising the 2000s, or, The Emergence of Metamodernism," in *Metamodernism, Historicity, Affect, and Depth after Postmodernism*, ed. Robin van den Akker, Alison Gibbons, and Timotheus Vermeulen. (New York: Rowman & Littlefield, 2017), 1–19.

79. See David Grossman, *See Under: Love*, trans. Betsy Rosenberg (London: Jonathan Cape, 1989).

80. See Naomi Sokoloff, "Reinventing Bruno Schulz: Cynthia Ozick's *The Messiah of Stockholm* and David Grossman's *See Under: Love*," *AJS Review* 13 (1988): 171–199; Yael Feldman, "Whose Story Is It, Anyway? Ideology and Psychology in the Representation of the Shoah in Israeli Literature," in *Probing the Limits of Representation: Nazism and the "Final Solution"*, ed. Saul Friedlander (Cambridge, MA: Harvard University Press, 1992), 223–239; Bruno Arich-Gerz, "Bruno Schulz's Literary Adoptees: Jewishness and Literary Father-Child Relationships in Cynthia Ozick's and David Grossman's Fiction," *European Judaism* 42, no. 1 (2009): 76–89; Naomi Sokoloff, "Rereading David Grossman's *See Under: Love*," *Prooftexts* 35, no. 1 (2015): 1–12; Iris Milner, "The End of Love: Kaniuk's *Adam Resurrected* and Grossman's *See Under: Love* Revisited," *Prooftexts* 35, no. 1 (2015): 37–47; Michael Gluzman, "Shoah ve-zikaron—Bein subyekṭiviut ve-inṭerṭexṭualiut be-ʿAyen

erekh: Ahavah'" [Holocaust and memory— Intersubjectivity and intertextuality in *See Under: Love*], in *A Moment of Birth: Studies in Hebrew and Yiddish Literatures in Honor of Dan Miron /* רגע של הולדת: מחקרים בספרות עברית ובספרות ייריש לכבוד דן מירון, ed. Hannan Hever (Jerusalem: Bialik Institute, 2007), 563–589.

81. Grossman, *See Under: Love*, 11.

82. Chaya Czernowin, *Pnima . . . ins Innere* (1998/1999) (Mainz: Schott, 2002).

83. See Gerald Prince, "The Disnarrated," *Style* 22, no. 1 (1988): 5.

84. Ibid., 3.

85. Donald Preziosi, *Rethinking Art History: Meditations on a Coy Science* (New Haven, CT: Yale University Press, 1989), 109; Chinski, *Kingdom of the Meek*, 75–76.

86. See Chana Kronfeld, *On the Margins of Modernism: Decentering Literary Dynamics* (Berkeley: University of California Press, 1996), 67–70.

87. Nicolas Bourriaud, *The Radicant* (New York: Sternberg Press, 2009), 34.

SELECT BIBLIOGRAPHY

Bohlman, Philip, V. *Jewish Music and Modernity*. New York: Oxford University Press, 2008.

Bohlman, Philip, V. *"The Land Where Two Streams Flow": Music in the German-Jewish Community of Israel*. Urbana: University of Illinois Press, 1989.

Brod, Max. *Israel's Music*. Translated by Toni Volcani. Tel Aviv: Sefer, 1951.

Cohen, Brigid. *Stefan Wolpe and the Avant-Garde Diaspora*. Cambridge: Cambridge University Press, 2012.

Gradenwitz, Peter. *Music and Musicians in Israel*. Jerusalem: Youth and Hechalutz Department of the Zionist Organization, 1952.

Hazan, Reuven Y., Alan Dowty, Menachem Hofnung, and Gideon Rahat, eds. *The Oxford Handbook of Israeli Politics and Society*. New York: Oxford University Press, 2021.

Hirshberg, Jehoash. *Music in the Jewish Community of Palestine 1880–1948: A Social History*. Oxford: Clarendon Press, 1995.

Hochberg, Gil. *In Spite of Partition: Jews, Arabs, and the Limits of Separatist Imagination*. Princeton: Princeton University Press, 2008.

Kimmerling, Baruch. *The Invention and Decline of Israeliness: State, Society, and the Military*. Berkeley: University of California Press, 2001.

Levi, Salli, and Hermann Swet, eds. *Musica Hebraica* 1–2 (1938).

Lucas, Noah. "Israeli Nationalism and Socialism before and after 1948." In *Israel: The First Decade of Independence*, edited by S. Ilan Troen and Noah Lucas, 297–310. New York: State University of New York Press, 1995.

Ohana, David. *The Origins of Israeli Mythology: Neither Canaanites Nor Crusaders*. Translated by David Maisel. Cambridge: Cambridge University Press, 2012.

Raz-Krakotzkin, Amnon. "History Textbooks and the Limits of Israeli Consciousness." *Journal of Israeli History* 20, nos. 2–3 (2001): 155–172.

Seroussi, Edwin. "Yam Tikhoniyut: Transformations of Mediterraneanism in Israeli Music." In *Mediterranean Mosaic: Popular Music and Global Sounds*, edited by Goffredo Plastino, 179–198. New York: Routledge, 2003.

Shelleg, Assaf. "Composition in the Aftermath of Hebrew Culture: The Musics of Betty Olivero and Chaya Czernowin." *Israel Studies* 28, no. 1 (2023): 200–214.

Shelleg, Assaf. "Imploding Signifiers: Exilic Jewish Cultures in Art Music in Israel, 1966–1970." *Hebrew Studies* 60 (2019): 260–266.

Shelleg, Assaf. *Jewish Contiguities and the Soundtrack of Israeli History*. New York: Oxford University Press, 2014.

Shelleg, Assaf. "Josef Tal on the Cusp of Israeli Statehood, or, The Simultaneity of Adjacency and Oppositionality." *Acta Musicologica* 91, no. 2 (2019): 146–167.

Shelleg, Assaf. *Theological Stains: Art Music and the Zionist Project*. New York: Oxford University Press, 2020.

Youngerman, Irit. "'A Melody That Doesn't Exist Anymore': Negation, Erasure, and Void in Israeli Art Music, as Reflected in Hanoch Jacoby's *Mutatio*." *Musical Quarterly* 103, no. 1–2 (2020): 139–183.

3

LAND, VOICE, NATION

Jewish Music in the Adamot of Al-Andalus

VANESSA PALOMA ELBAZ

SEPHARAD and Al-Andalus and the idea of its peaceful idyllic past inhabit present-day Spain and Morocco through culture and music. These geographies' Jewish music has become a symbol for coexistence and peaceful relations between Jews, Muslims, and Christians in the post-9/11 period, as numerous musicians throughout the world have created a syncretism between the cultural legacy from Al-Andalus with Judeo-Andalusian and Sephardic musics. Particularly in North Africa and Spain, the most direct geographic heirs of Al-Andalus, Jewish and non-Jewish musicians, the collective at the heart of this chapter, deploy these repertoires in official, public, and private performances as part of their definition of local and national identities. Not only are these Jewish musics presented as important for the construction of the diverse nation, but Jewish languages, accents, and ritual sounds occasionally appear as sonic grounding for the centrality of the Jew in a national space some construct as hostile. Both governments and multiple civil-society nonprofit organizations that operate outside of governmental structures (such as the Mimouna Foundation, Marocains Plurielles, and Association des Amies de la Fondation du Judaïsme du Maroc in Morocco; and Casa de Sefarad and Radio Sefarad in Spain) are building on the long-standing local history of Jewish connection to *adamah* (earth) and thus to the contemporary nation. This belonging to the adamah is further complicated with the Jewish relationship to transnational Judaism, as embodied by *Erets Yisrael*, the land (*arets*) of Israel, which is of central importance for observant Jews because of the teaching of its intrinsic holiness and divine connection to Jewish pasts and futures.

Tradition within Orthodox Judaism brings together the local and the transnational, saying that an unbroken connection in religious and musical practice has been kept alive through oral transmission within Mediterranean Jewry for thousands of years after the destruction of the Second Temple in the year 70 CE. The actual unruptured transmission and its veracity are not what will be credited or discredited in this chapter, but the relationship of generations of Sephardim to the *idea* of an unruptured transmission of religious and musical practices, and the proxy of their connection through musical liturgical orality to Erets Yisrael. Jewish communities in Spain and North Africa have integrated local popular music into their vernacular repertoires for centuries, adding it to what they perceive is an ancient sonic core, and invariably soon after, into their liturgical ritual as contrafactum.[1]

Today, Sephardic communities in double and triple diasporas have added multiple musical layers tracing various *adamot* to which they are connected—in the case here presented, Judeo-Spanish and Judeo-Andalusian denoting Iberia and North Africa.[2] Both Spain and Morocco have launched diversity initiatives, similarly to the United States and various countries in Western Europe, following the terrorist attacks of 9/11 and later 2003 in Casablanca, and 2004 in Madrid. A public integration of Jewish music and even ritual sounds entered the political "toolbox" to establish local and international political capital as well as to control a growing swell of radicalized youth. As an effective antidote to Islamism and fascist right-wingers, soft-power initiatives of cultural capital used a syncretism between Sephardic music, music from Iberia, and Arabic music from Al-Andalus, which "together formed a classical stage preceded by the music of the Mediterranean."[3]

The region of the Strait of Gibraltar has diversity firmly entangled into its geography, in so much that the very name Gibraltar is known to Arabic speakers as *Jabal Ṭāriq*, the mountain of Ṭāriq ibn Ziyād, the general who led the Muslim army across the Strait in 711. The histories of invasion, Reconquista, conversion, and expulsion are still active in political and social negotiations throughout the region with supporters and detractors to policies of diversity and ethnic "purity." This may have been why post-Franco Spain and post-Years-of-Lead Morocco entered transnational expressions of Mediterraneanism and *convivencia* so easily into their national narratives through performances either of Jewish music or of the music of Jews, Muslims, and Christians in conversation.[4]

Music serves as a manner to re-create an idyllic moment in the national history, a moment remembered as diverse and exemplary in the coexistence of various religious and political groups. These musical encounters have been discussed in the scholarship by authors from anthropological angles exploring musical intimacies, performativities, colonial encounters, and contemporary unmutings.[5] Ethnomusicologists have addressed the contemporary afterlives of these musical and intercultural encounters through analysis of festivals, cultural policy, and use of music for integration of migrant populations in recent years.[6] As the literature insinuates, the historical reality of these collaborations was more uneven than the current political mythology would imply. Notwithstanding, the core issue is the manner that an idealized memory of the past is used as a sonic trope, desiring to create an emotional reality in large numbers of the population who are meant to translate it into their daily attitudes and lives.

This chapter proposes that Al-Andalus is evoked as a "component" of temporal disconnection to the contemporary fractured state of othering non-homogenous cultural elements within current nation-states. This evocative "component of the Europe that we know to be the matrix for the West and that jumped from the Middle Ages in Al-Andalus to live a first renaissance" appears most easily through musical collaborations.[7] Music awakens the sensibilities of connection, the elusive transported "component" from the Middle Ages that can be easily embodied centuries later to soften the fractures of identity politics.

The silence surrounding Jewish religious philosophy in current scholarship of the music of this region reveals that current musicology has hidden local distinctiveness under a European-aesthetic lens. Most previous scholarship from the early and mid-twentieth century on this material focused on knowledge preservation, such as the work of Spaniards Ramón Menéndez Pidal,[8] Manuel Alvar,[9] and Arcadio Larrea Palacín;[10] the French scholars Alexis Chottin,[11] Jules Rouanet,[12] and Paul Bénichou;[13] and the collaborative publications of Samuel Armistead and Joseph Silverman, who preponderantly brushed over or completely ignored texts on religious and mystical significance, which are of core importance for local communities.[14] More recent work on Sephardic repertoire by hispanists and ethnomusicologists, such as Paloma Díaz-Mas,[15] Oro Anahory Librowicz,[16] Judith R. Cohen,[17] and Susana Weich-Shahak,[18] have addressed the societal and gendered dynamics of this music.

Integrating emic philosophy as the theoretical frame, this chapter uncovers manners in which the communities themselves interact with the region's epistemological relationship to music. Crucially, the interaction and impact of religious texts stem from integral expression of self in the first instance, which only later appears in diplomacy, politics, and national identity. Incorporating religious philosophy into the central epistemology of ethnomusicological understanding of current musical production, answers to the decolonizing direction that academic study of this region is moving toward,[19] recalibrating its relationship to history, and ensuring that the long-standing epistemologies of local thought enter current analysis. Because issues of power and the definition of relevant "knowledge lie at the epistemic core of colonialism. The challenge for researchers of decolonizing methodologies is to simultaneously work with colonial and Indigenous concepts of knowledge, decentering one while centering the other."[20]

AL-ANDALUS AND SEPHARAD:
REPERTOIRE AND PLACE

Al-Andalus was the name given to Muslim territories in the Iberian Peninsula under the Umayyad Caliphate of Córdoba (711–1031); after this initial period, the peninsula fluctuated between the split rule of different Islamic kingdoms (the taifas) and temporary unification under the rule of the Almoravids (1085–1145) and Almohads (1232–1287).[21] *Al-Andalus* as a term, however, often covers the entire period between 711 and 1492, which saw a flourishing of poetry, music, and learning. One of its enduring cultural legacies has been the perception of peaceful coexistence and cultural collaboration of Muslims, Christians, and Jews: convivencia, often evoked to invite multicultural or intercultural initiatives. At the helm of this imagined past is the cultural giant of 'Alī ibn Nāfi' Ziryāb, who is posited as the "inventor" of Andalusian music and the larger-than-life symbol of musical and aesthetic creativity until today.[22] Ziryāb traveled to Umayyad Córdoba in 822 at the invitation of the Caliph, accompanied by a Jewish court musician, Mansūr al-Yahūdī. He was fleeing Baghdad after an altercation with his mentor, when he was proclaimed as a better performer than his teacher in the court and fled for his life.

The fact that Ziryāb and al-Yahūdī were collaborators at the seminal moment of the founding of Andalusian music and culture reiterates the validity and "pedigree" of Jewish Andalusian claims within Arabo-Andalusian culture in the Maghreb after the expulsion of 1492 and until today. This fact is often muted in the discourse around Andalusian music, and only brought up by experts and practitioners when speaking directly to Jews. Architecture, music, poetry, and dress from Al-Andalus are said to continue living through closely guarded Andalusian family lineages, who often maintain a close relationship to contemporary Spain.

Moroccan culture maintains a mythical narrative about the grandeur of Al-Andalus being transported directly to Morocco, especially to the cities of Rabat, Salé, and Tetuan,[23] after the expulsion of the Moriscos (Muslim converts to Catholicism) in 1609 from the Iberian Peninsula. For centuries these cities have housed a large Muslim and Jewish Andalusian population. These populations maintained a shared nostalgia for the lost days of Al-Andalus, keeping traditions, foods, and music. In Rabat and Salé their local Andalusian music, Gharnati music, the Andalusian music from Granada, was jealously kept alive by Jews and Muslims.[24]

Sepharad, which is the modern Hebrew name for the Iberian Peninsula, taken from the Book of Obadiah 1:20, became a mythical, timeless land without physical contours that existed in Jewish collective memory after the expulsion of 1492. It has continued to exist as part of the imaginary, supra-national geography that the Jewish people called their own during millennia of diaspora from Erets Yisrael. Sepharad was transported beyond geography through lineages, cuisine, dress, language, religious ritual, and music. Sephardic Jews, then, have emotional attachments both to Erets Yisrael and to the ancestral land of their cultural specificity: Sepharad. This gives Sephardim an added layer of operation within a transnational geography of defined identity in the larger Jewish world. The space of relationship between these two lands, that of national belonging and that of memory, is where the vector of connection between adamah and music becomes crucial, together with the elements of nationalist and inner-group dynamics, the collective and the individual. The question of diaspora then becomes pertinent, as "diaspora, partaking always of the local, but by definition never confined to it, thus suggests itself as a place where that interaction can be grasped."[25]

Jewish communities in Morocco represent both Sepharad and Al-Andalus. Some of the exiles from the 1492 expulsion, called *megorashim*, chose to maintain Judeo-Spanish, its music and culture, as a distinctive differentiation from the Arabic-speaking Jews in the Maghreb. Others, coming from the Arabic-speaking areas of Al-Andalus, integrated easily into the autochthonous Moroccan Jewish community called the *toshavim*, while bringing Andalusian culture and music in Arabic and Hebrew, into their Moroccan practice.[26]

The Jewish communities in Spain today are predominantly Moroccan and have a complex relationship with citizenship after centuries of state-sponsored anti-Semitism.[27] Their integration into the national fabric is often presented through their historical connection to national popular literatures in the vernacular, especially the *romances*. Other Jewish customs, such as the pre-wedding henna celebration, known in Spanish as *la noche de Berberisca*, are accompanied by specific songs in Hebrew and Judeo-Spanish. At the center of this ceremony is a ritual dress embroidered in gold thread in the same manner as a Torah scroll cover. This celebration appears in Spanish movies, novels, and television documentaries as an example of Jewish practice of ancient medieval traditions or their exotic connection to Morocco, maintained in contemporary Spain.[28]

The way Sephardi Jews name their own Judeo-Spanish repertoire plays on the nuanced fluctuation between an inner transmissibility and the historical and traumatic relationship to the ongoing memory of the rupture in their Spanish past. The denomination given to this repertoire by the members of the community is significant because it demonstrates the internal discourse of a connection to a long arm of history within the oral traditions of the Jews from northern Morocco currently living in both Morocco and Spain.

The internal manners of categorization and nomenclature of repertoires, then, define the relationship that the emic group has to its own musical contribution within the historical narratives that occupy their communities. The Judeo-Spanish community itself refers to its repertoire by way of three designations: "los cantares antiguos de Castilla" (the ancient songs from Castile), "los cantares del tiempo de la Reina Isabel la Católica" (the songs from the time of Queen Isabel the Catholic), and "los cantares de las judias antiguas (the songs of the ancient Jewish women). These three classifications show the ongoing preoccupations within the Jewish community about space and temporality. Place is represented by the mythical evocation of Castilla. Time is represented in the reification of the traumatic period of the Catholic monarchs and the rupture the Catholic monarchs created. Unbroken transmission addresses what is perceived as the legacy of older Jewish women to the younger generations. The old Jewesses serve as the repositories of the community's oral traditions and Judeo-Spanish local cultural specificity in Spain or northern Morocco.

Today, Jewish music in Spain is most often performed in the public sphere by non-Jewish Spaniards, such as Mara Aranda, Ana Alcaide, and Begoña Olavide. Their performances, drawing heavily from medieval music-performance practice are often in historical spaces, equating the Sephardi voice with a medieval space and a historic polity, excising living Judaism from the current nation, demonstrating that "[t]hese regenerating acts depend not on the recuperation of ancient identities but on the production of new affiliations and the creation of new remnants."[29]

To add to the complexity at hand, Spain's relationship to the historical Jewish presence and its intrinsic belonging to the land is confronted by the five centuries of systematic official excision of Jewish bodies from the territory. Sephardim often reiterate a nostalgic longing for Sepharad despite the painful history mourned yearly on the anniversary of the expulsion, which coincided with the national Jewish mourning day, the ninth of Av, also commemorating the destruction of the First and Second Temples of Jerusalem. Sepharad is celebrated daily through liturgical poetry in the synagogal ritual—Judah Halevi, Solomon ben Judah ibn Gabirol, and Samuel ibn Nagrela are part of the daily and yearly liturgical cycles—and with popular Sephardic music in the vernacular. The repackaging of this moment in Spanish and Jewish history shows how "the Spanish state's efforts to downplay expulsion and the Inquisition and to promote pride in Spanish Jewish history intermingles, to a limited extent, with some Sephardi's interest in origins lost after the catastrophe of 1492, which is mourned by observant Jews every year on the fasting day of Tisha B'Av."[30]

Earth and Land and the Performance of Jewish Indigeneity

The reasons for musical syncretism between Al-Andalus, Sepharad, Judeo-Andalusian *nubat* (modes),[31] and Sephardi music in recent years, are informed by the Jewish relationship to adamah, arets, fertility, and burial. In Judaism, adamah is intrinsically bound with the human, because the very word for man, *adam*, bears the root of the Hebrew word for earth. In the story of creation from Genesis, after eating from the forbidden tree of knowledge of good and evil, Adam, the first man, is cursed to work and to remember that "By the sweat of your brow, shall you get bread to eat, until you return to the ground. For from it you were taken. For dust you are, and to dust you shall return."[32] The boundedness between the human, labor, earth, birth, and death is made clear in the biblical text. Notwithstanding, adamah is not exclusively masculine in Judaism, as the term *adam* may imply. Adamah as earth is also referred to as feminine when alluding to the cycles in agricultural seasons and the land's fertility, as well as its connection to lunar cycles, which determine the Jewish ritual calendar.

Fertility represents both the fertility and bounty of the earth as well as that of the Jewish couple in bringing forth new generations. In Judaism, this fertility is considered crucial, as it is the communal fortress against annihilation. The existence of Judaism depends on its continuity through generations. The fertility of the land is also rhetorically bound with the voicing of prayers,[33] dramatically demonstrated by the organization of the foundational text of the Mishnah, the first major work of rabbinic literature that annotated Jewish oral tradition (ca. 200 CE) to avert the potential loss of Jewish legal tradition; it starts the initial section on the fertility of the land, Zeraim (Seeds), with chapters on blessings and prayer, most often chanted or sung. Thus, the earth's fertility is bound to agricultural, lunar, female, and life cycles—entangling the Jewish community, its women, human life and death cycles, and the adamot on which they live.

Burial reconnects the body to the earth and thus, to the land. Michel Serre has stated in *Le mal propre* that one of the fundamental living issues in the right to ownership are to pollute or mark one's space.[34] In other words, only by leaving an individual marking is full ownership established. This marking or pollution of ownership is shown in its most extreme animalistic manners through bodily fluids—however, the "polluting" of a land for ownership can be done through bones, the buried bones of ancestors, which "pollute" the land but also mark it as a sacred space of belonging for generations to come. Here the sacredness of belonging through burial intersects with the belonging through the voicing of sacred sounds and songs.

Singing and shofar blowing in Morocco during the burial of community members or the celebration of ancestral rabbis through pilgrimages enacts an "owning" of the land through the buried bones of the deceased, which I call "sonic pollution." In Morocco communal pilgrimages to the sites of burial of holy men (and in rare cases women) are called *hilulot*, and are celebrated throughout the country in cities and far-flung mountainous areas. These celebrations include a grand festive meal and live musical entertainment as well as speeches from rabbinic leaders and descendants of the rabbinic line being celebrated. The hilulot celebrations that happen around the country year-round bring a Jewish presence to areas that often have no extant Jewish community. The three-day celebrations include, food, music, prayer, and the fire of devotional candles, expected to awaken the *tsadik*'s intervention for the pilgrim's plight directly with God.[35] The pilgrimage is an occasion to reiterate historical Jewish presence, and to invite members from the government to celebrate and receive the Jewish blessing. During most hilulot, blessings from the Jewish community to the king and the whole royal family are intoned in a highly ritualized manner by rabbis from the country's rabbinical tribunal. Some of the hilulot are in centers of political or religious power, such as those of Salé and Ouezzane, the spiritual capital and the home to many Sufi brotherhoods; others are in the desert or in the High Atlas Mountains, as distant outposts of Jewish belonging throughout the Moroccan land.

Taking Serre's idea of belonging to the land through the burial of ancestral bones, Spain's dearth of historical cemeteries seems to demonstrate that ancient Jewish ownership of the land through burial was eradicated following the expulsion and centuries of the Inquisition. Even though Jewish spaces such as ritual baths and synagogues have reappeared, inviting Jewish tourism through the government's Red de Juderías project, the oldest active cemetery is that of Madrid, established in 1922. The medieval cemetery of Montjuïc in Barcelona was excavated in the nineteenth century during an archaeological dig. Today, some of these medieval tombstones are in the Museu d'Historia of Barcelona, and others can be found as stones for construction in some city walls. A medieval Jewish cemetery was excavated in 2006 in Lucena, Andalucía, and today is marketed for Jewish tourism.

In Morocco, especially after the founding of the State of Israel, Jews were seen by many as Zionists first and Moroccans second.[36] Even though Jewish presence in Morocco predates Islam, Moroccan Jews living in Casablanca today are occasionally told by young Muslim Moroccans, "Marhababik" (Welcome!), as if to imply that they are visitors and not equal citizens. Jewish Moroccans find this insulting, and some retort back, in perfect Moroccan Arabic, known as Darija: "My ancestors were here before the Arabs came."

Immediately an apology ensues, and a murmured memory about how their parents or grandparents had a Jewish neighbor, merchant, doctor, business partner, and so on. This perception of non-belonging is often publicly countered by Jews themselves through performances of sonic belonging, thus establishing their undeniable indigeneity to the land. This is one of the fundamental reasons that continuous performances of Jewish singers—Haim Botbol singing "Ana el maghribī" (I am Moroccan), Salim Halali singing "'Arjaa lebladek" (Come back to your land), Sami El Maghribi singing "Allāh, watanī ou soulṭanī" (God, my nation and my sultan), and recently Maxime Karoutchi singing "Massira el khadra" (The green march [referring to the Sahara])—carry such symbolic weight. The presentation of an undeniable allegiance of Jews to the Arabic language through musical performance in what is often called Judeo-Arabic roots Jews to the Moroccan earth in the eyes of the larger Moroccan citizen.[37] Jewish singers today continue to sing various musics in Arabic despite the erosion of Arabic speakers in younger generations thanks to the French-dominant education system that has existed in the Jewish community since the mid-nineteenth century.[38] These repertoires are primarily Judeo-Andalusian repertoire (classical), *chgoury* repertoire (popular music), and paraliturgical repertoires.

Contrary to the often-cited diasporic nature of Jews, the manners in which Jews in Morocco and Spain establish their sonic territoriality to both land and nation overturn the idea of Jew as a deterritorialized, nomadic, or cosmopolitan element of these societies. In establishing their very indigeneity, Jewish sounds thus become *of* the nation. Especially when physical Jewish presence is diminishing, as in Morocco, or feeble after centuries of enforced ethnic cleansing, as in Spain, the music of the Jews of both nations has established an undeniable sonic presence in the twenty-first century. Music serves as a manner to reinsert the phantoms of a Jewish presence into empty physical spaces, where the Jews are "a phantom memory, the felt presence of an absent limb."[39] In fact, this confirms that "the cosmopolitan has come to be threatened by its old foe, the local, the national, the autochthonous, the Indigenous."[40] Now the cultural capital of cosmopolitanism is replaced with a hierarchy to deeply rooted Indigenous belonging to land, nation, territory, and state. However, this belonging is often grounded in an idea of capitalist contribution to the nation: "The concepts of cosmopolitanism and nomadism take on quite different meanings when the index is Jews—in particular, when they are symbolically defined by capital."[41] The Indigenous Jew, their beliefs and cultural traditions, are thus an anchor to a past of cultural diversity lost to the homogenous nation, be it pre-expulsion Iberia or the heady years of the nationalist struggle in Morocco in the 1950s before pan-Arabism. By celebrating the entrenched indigeneity of the Jew, both Morocco and Spain are trying to address the religiously conservative elements in their societies as they build narratives of historical national diversity. Religious conservatives claim a need for purity, going as far back as the racial laws of *pureza de sangre* in fifteenth-century Spain or exemplified by the recent controversy in Morocco around the Minister of Culture of the PJD Islamist party advocating for *l'art propre*, clean or pure art, which leads toward a "pure language" and, finally, a "pure citizen."[42]

This is when the indigeneity of the Jew is brought out to counter the homogenizing forces of religious conservatism. The Jew, as Indigenous religious minority, with a deep historical connection to the land, becomes indispensable to the larger nation. One of the manners to establish this has become through vocal music, which has come to stand as, following Kay Kaufman Shelemay's conception, a "sentinel."[43] The performance of the "Jewish voice"—be it sung, spoken, or written—then represents the complexity of belonging to the nation, the wisdom of a longstanding history of diversity, complexity, and multilingualism in the face of the reductive pull that homogenous belonging elicits among the masses. In a televised interview from 2021 with local Moroccan Jewish star singer Maxime Karoutchi, he responds to the question "what is Judeo-Moroccan music?" as follows: "It's our accent, a bit like Yiddish . . . Except that we add a little of everything [implying Arabic, Hebrew, French, Spanish] we sing it with love . . . we took the music which is originally Andalusian music, and we added our *voice* which is sung from the depth of our gut, with a *mawwal* [initial improvisatory section] and that is a bit our voice, our style."[44]

Karoutchi's evoking of *voice* as the very Moroccanness of the Jew echoes the division of voice in political philosophy into *phone* and *logos*,[45] separating sounded voice from language, one animalistic, the other political. However, as Giorgio Agamben explains, this binary is a contradiction because the exception falls into an interiority and the excluded thus forms part of the *core* of belonging. Meaning that through phone, the Other belongs to the core of the larger nation, and the sovereignty of the Other is defined in its relationship to the sacred. Thus, both phone and logos that are perceived as having a connection to the sacred bestow a political sovereignty even to the excluded Other who nevertheless belongs to the core of the nation through "extimacy." In trans-Gibraltar the Jewish "voice" is recognized by the majority in Jewish accents in Judeo-Arabic or the endangered Jewish Romance language Haketia, through Hebrew-inflected Andalusian melodies, or more generally through vocal music in the manner of inflecting timbre, florid ornamentation, and in popular repertoires, a sultry playfulness with sexuality, an intimate "extimacy"—recognizable, owned, but separate as demonstrated in the televised interview of the current Judeo-Moroccan musical star Maxime Karoutchi.

One of the major cultural players in the regional initiative to establish a contemporary musical convivencia is the Fundación Tres Culturas. The Fundación was established to create cultural content embodying the diverse links between Morocco and Spain, through its Andalusian, Jewish, and Muslim cultures. Very often these connections are done through concerts that are meant to promote peace throughout the Mediterranean, evoking the syncretic Mediterraneanism in musical choices by musicians and cultural programmers. A statement on the website of the Fundación Tres Culturas reads:

> This foundation is called to grow even more, to continue to consolidate itself in the Euro-Mediterranean panorama, to assert more strongly its strategic role in Spanish-Moroccan relations be stronger, and to walk side by side with sister institutions to quickly advance its original guiding objectives: to promote dialogue, peace, and

tolerance amongst the people of the Mediterranean; to maintain this space of coexistence in which cultural and religious diversity not only does not separate us, but unites and helps us grow.[46]

In this endeavor, music and concerts play a fundamental role.

Jewish, Muslim, and Catholic music is often performed for public representations of coexistence or convivencia narratives,[47] or in statements of longing for the shared cultural spaces that appear to have existed during the late Middle Ages in Abbasid and Castilian courts. Often, the connecting points between the Spanish and the Sephardic communities are found in the Sephardi economic or political elites. During the push for Spanish colonialism, Spain's philo-Sephardism engaged mostly with Sephardim from the Muslim Mediterranean, and not with Sephardim from major European cities such as London, Amsterdam, or Florence. This is in line with the "Orientalization" of Jews, who were considered foreign in peninsular Spain and Indigenous in the Spanish enclaves of northern Morocco.[48]

The ongoing development since the nineteenth century to integrate Jewish voices into national narratives of diversity in Spain is complicated by the occasional suppression of local Jewish life, such as was felt during the Franco regime.[49] In November of 1940, Franco established the Consejo de la Hispanidad and with it a cultural policy where "Spain's cultural contributions extolled; public education advocated; anti-Semitism denounced, and a conscious pro-Semitism practiced."[50] The following two cases studies—the first, of Ana Alcaide, a Spanish performer of Sephardi repertoires, and the other, of the ensemble Kinor David Maroc from Morocco, which focuses on Jewish liturgical poetry—demonstrate how in Spain and Morocco, different approaches to land, nation, memory, continuity and burial interact with the performance of Jewish repertoires by Jews and non-Jews.

THE CONTRASTS OF SINGING SEPHARDI MEDIEVAL NEW AGE AND MAROCANITÉ

Ana Alcaide (1976–) has been one of the most popular Spanish musicians performing Sephardic music in recent decades. Her style, drawing heavily from New Age sound, incorporates a mixture of medieval and contemporary instruments such as the psaltery and nyckelharpa, together with guitars, flute, and synthesizer. Often performing in Spanish medieval spaces, be they Jewish (Toledo's historical Sinagoga del Tránsito), Muslim (Toledo's Mudéjar palace, which now houses the Taller del Moro), or Catholic (Córdoba's Antiguo Convento de Santa Clara), Alcaide has created an aesthetic style that blends New Age mysticism, convivencia narratives, and medieval instrumentation. Her second album, *Como la luna y el sol* (2007), featuring Sephardic music, was completed as her final project for a degree in Sweden at the Malmö Academy of Music, where she specialized in a Swedish medieval instrument, the nyckelharpa, which has become part of her signature sound.

Alcaide's engagement with Sephardic repertoire stems from her own connection to the adamah of her hometown of Toledo. She says that having lived for many years in the *judería* or Jewish quarter propelled her to learn something about the community that had once been there but was expelled centuries ago. Her deep attachment to the city, its history, and its people brought her to the musical exploration and sonic collage for the introduction to the album, a piece called "Intro: Sefardíes."[51] Beginning with a recorded teaching of the *alef-bet* with an older man's voice teaching a child, two short sections from oral histories sounding out older women's *judezmo* accent from the Eastern Mediterranean with overlaps of synthesizer and disembodied vocals follow. Alcaide's introduction demonstrates the perception of a dreamy, magical relationship of contemporary Spaniards to Sephardim in Spain. In this introduction to her album there is a dramatic contrast between the ancient Sephardic and the contemporary musician. A woman's voice opens, reminiscing in spoken voice about a tradition that she remembered where people would follow to guess the gender of a pregnant woman's child. Immediately after, another voice says, you do not look well; she says, yes, it is the longing for my childhood. The older Jews, teaching, remembering, and longing, appear sonically in the background as the earthy, ancient voices with the timeless ethereal musical sounds provided by Alcaide and her group. After this initial introductory section, the full album ensues, with titles about the longing for the impossible reunion between the moon and the sun, metaphors for Sephardim and contemporary Spaniards.

One example of Ana Alcaide's use of repertoire and space to cross religious boundaries is the 2018 concert *Otoño Sefardí en Córdoba* (Sephardi Autumn in Córdoba). It was held in the ancient convent of Santa Clara, breaking down boundaries between a Catholic church and Jewish sounds. One hour and thirteen minutes into the concert, Alcaide mentions the final set of three songs she will sing, starting with "Como la luna y el sol," which gave the name to her best-selling Sephardic album. During the concert Alcaide describes what she perceives as the Sephardi experience of yearning for Sepharad and the relationship to the loss. In her words, it is a "deep longing for the land, that Sepharad that is lost, and that has been idealized. It is a very universal feeling, to search for what we do not have, and the search becomes the motor that keeps us alive." The song and the album's title thus symbolize her perception of a tragic reality of an impossible Sephardi yearning for lost Sepharad "like the moon and the sun which look for each other and can never meet."[52]

In 2015, three years before the concert in the Toledan convent, the Spanish government had granted Sephardic descendants of those who had suffered the expulsion a right of return, and thousands applied and received citizenship. When the law was announced in November 2015, the Spanish monarch, King Felipe VI, declared, "How we have missed you!," explicitly inviting the descendants of those who were expulsed back to Spain.[53] It appears that the premise of an impossible reunion between Sephardim (the moon) and Sepharad (the sun) that Alcaide's Sephardi musical exploration proposed had overcome the odds of history. Why did she continue to repeat the narrative of an impossible reunion after the watershed moment for Sephardi reintegration into Spain?

Alcaide and her Spanish audiences seem to yearn for the mythical Sepharad, the medieval and unreachable place, and not the integrated contemporary nation state.

And yet, it is important to note that in the preamble of the actual text of the Spanish law, the expulsion is not presented as such, but as a "drastic" decision taken by those Jews who chose to not convert to Catholicism. As Alfons Aragoneses has aptly summarized it:

> According to the preamble, then, Spain bore no responsibility for the expulsion of Jews; the liberal Monarchies were Jewish-friendly and Spain was on the side of the good guys during the Holocaust. No reference was made to the royal decree expelling the Jews in 1492 or to the fact that Spanish Constitutions in the nineteenth century both defined Spain as a Catholic country and banned other religions. Poignantly, neither are there references to the period between 1868 and 1874 when liberal and republican politicians like Emilio Castelar publicly defended the Sephardic Jews. The preamble does not mention the efforts of the Second Republic in Spain that helped thousands of Jewish refugees from Central Europe. Most important, however, is the lack of any reference to the complicity of Francisco Franco with Adolf Hitler and Spanish cooperation in the deportation of Jews from Spain to concentration camps until at least 1944.[54]

The performance of Sephardi repertoires, then, remains ossified into ancient medieval spaces and sounds, and is used as a sentinel of Spain's medieval history and not its recent past nor its present. In contrast, Morocco's relationship to its Jewish music balances between popular music and Judeo-Andalusian repertoires. The Judeo-Andalusian examples bridge the long gap from postcolonial Morocco to the shared moments of musical communion in Al-Andalus, grounding Jews into the traumatic loss of the Muslim Empire.

The last Judeo-Andalusian group in Morocco today, Kinor David Maroc, consists of *paytanim*, that is, liturgical soloists. These, in turn, form the core of the local *hevrah kadisha*, the Jewish burial society, which customarily consists of a select group of observant Jews (both men and women) who prepare the bodies of the deceased for proper ritual burial, linking voice, adamah, and burial. Being that Jewish voices in Morocco are often highly choreographed, appearing nationally and internationally as representatives of Morocco's commitment to diversity and religious tolerance, Judeo-Andalusian music plays a perfect role in this quest, with its textual intermingling of Hebrew and Arabic, called *matrouz*. Considered by Jewish and Muslim descendants of those who were expelled after the fall of Granada to be Morocco's classical repertoire from Al-Andalus, and an index of high culture and refinement, Jewish interpretations of 'ala, as Arabo-Andalusian music is called by practitioners, are considered to embody the continuous living link to an unbroken chain of convivencia from Al-Andalus through to contemporary Morocco[55]. The intermingling of Kinor David Maroc's Jewish representative voices with their commitment to proper burial rites exemplifies the deep symbolism in their representation of Morocco in national and international stages, reminiscent of Serre's idea of ownership, linking burial and voice as binaries of "polluting," owning, and belonging, a sonic pollution. The popular history magazine *Zamane* reiterated the integrality of Jews to Morocco in an issue from 2013 called *Maroc, terre juive* (Morocco,

Jewish land).[56] In Morocco, "territory is deeply intertwined with social identity, bled [territory/earth] is not just physical territory, however regionalized, but a terrain of interaction, a domain of complex and crosscutting social relationships."[57] Despite the firm claim of Zaman's cover article, during the establishment of a Moroccan postcolonial national identity, the acceptance of Jewish Moroccans as equal citizens throughout society was not immediate. The years 1959 to 1961 saw a controversy about the status of Jews as citizens or *dhimmi*. Indeed, the relationship of Morocco's Jews to post-Independence national identity demonstrates that their inclusion into the postcolonial national narrative was not straightforward.[58] During this period, between the early 1950s until the mid-1980s, Jewish musicians played a key role in crossing the socio-political boundaries put in place by Zionism and pan-Arabism. However, it took fifty-five years, with the post–Arab Spring 2011 constitution, for a watershed moment of legalized integration. The diverse elements forming Moroccan identity-composition were specifically named and ratified, including the "Hebraic" element as one of its affluents, plunging Morocco into a new self-definition of what and how to construct *marocanité*. Jewish voices have since performed a crucial role for the public campaign of official national diversity. The Jewish voice, performed by Jews and non-Jews, is often included in festivals, movies, television, and radio throughout Morocco with increasing visibility since the establishment of the constitution. Today, Judeo-Andalusian repertoire is performed by the last members of the generation that still experienced a thriving Jewish community before the vertiginous emigrations that occurred between the 1950s and the 1980s.

In November 2014, Kinor David Maroc performed at the Institut du Monde Arabe in Paris with the Arabo-Andalusian orchestra from Fez, directed by Mohammed Briouel, as part of a series accompanying a large-scale exhibit on Morocco's history and cultural traditions.[59] It was the second concert that the ensemble had traveled for internationally since their founding in 2009 by a group of Arabo-Andalusian music-loving Jewish men, who served as the Board of Directors, and who delighted in the honors and political capital they were garnering. I was invited, as a professional singer, to join the ensemble in 2013 and remained an active member until 2018, when I moved away from Casablanca. I participated in hundreds of hours of rehearsals with the group, in discussions, concerts, and travels, which afforded multiple opportunities for conversations and insights.[60]

The music director of the group, Michel Abitan, often struggled to balance the ideas of Kinor David Maroc's board and singers, as well as the orchestra regarding issues of Jewish musical style and the discrepancies between the Jewish liturgical versions of Andalusian repertoire and the classical tradition sung by Muslims. The board insisted that all Jewish accents be "cleaned" out of the pronunciation of the Arabic, and that the "Jewish" way to sing the pieces would not be acceptable with a "proper" Andalusian orchestra, who followed the non-"corrupted" tradition. There was great concern that the Muslim audiences, knowing the poetry and melodies intimately, would find mistakes in the manner that they sang this repertoire as Jews. Many discussions centered on establishing and learning the Muslim-accepted manner of performance.

During the concert at the Institut du monde arabe, issues of hierarchy and the power asymmetry between the Muslims and the Jews were felt sharply by both Jewish performers and audience members. Briouel had asked Kinor David to perform a *nawba* or *nūba*, as a suite of songs and instrumental pieces in Arabic art music are known, that was not ready in their repertoire until only a few weeks before the concert, leading the group to have to rehearse intensely under great pressure, to perform to their satisfaction. Added to this, the guest soloist was Abderrahim Souiri, one of the most famous Moroccan icons of Andalusian music, slated to perform the same evening for the Kinor David-Briouel concert. Souiri, is from Essaouira, a city on the Atlantic coast known for its close symbiosis between Muslims and Jews in music, and Souiri has publicly declared that he learned much of his style for a Jewish master, and that as a child he was nursed by a Jewish nursemaid, otherwise known in Morocco as a "milk-mother." The general assumption is that he has absorbed some of the "Jewish" sound through both his learning and the ingestion of Jewish milk.

For the concert, the board and singers of Kinor David were thrilled, excited, and honored to be a part of this display of Moroccan Jewish culture on an international cultural stage in Paris, but by the time the evening was over, issues with low vocal microphone levels and other power dynamics between Briouel and Kinor David left many of the singers disappointed at the missed opportunity and the lackluster showing the group appeared to have given. One audience member said afterward, "It looked pretty, the images were great, but we could not hear Kinor singing at all."[61] As a critical point of blindness to Jewish needs by the organizers, the soundcheck had been scheduled on the Sabbath, and as religious Jews, all the singers were respectful of the Sabbath laws. Nobody from Kinor David was able to attend the sound check. The engineers only prepared the orchestral microphones. What was meant as a showcasing of Jewish musicianship of classical Andalusian music transformed during the actual performance into a sonic erasure of the particularities of Jewish musical engagement with Arabo-Andalusian repertoire. The Jews were seen, but their unique contribution was hardly heard as it was subsumed by the instruments and soloists from Briouel's orchestra. The organizers were probably not aiming to erase Jewish sounds that evening. But as often happens to minorities, their specifically different needs did not even enter the equation for decision-making, automatically forcing the Jewish singers choose between their own tradition (Sabbath observance) and the successful appearance of Jewish-Muslim collaboration on a European Muslim stage. The consequence was an obfuscation of the Jewish contribution, leaving some of the Muslim musicians with a feeling of superiority as they walked out that evening.[62]

ADAMOT AND JEWISH MUSIC: INHERITING AL-ANDALUS

The geographic, cultural, and spiritual descendants of the adamot of Al-Andalus continue to grapple with the preponderant memory of the mythical period of cultural flourishing that formed the foundation of the poetico-musical canon in Spain and North Africa. The romancero and Arabo-Andalusian nawba occupy larger-than-life positions within foundational texts of cultural pride, linking contemporary culture to a long literary and musical history. For both, this history is considered to stem from significant and long-standing cultural refinement that is still alive within the national literary and musical traditions transmitted through their oral heritage.

Intimate Jewish musical engagement with the corpus from both canons of Spanish and North African literary culture has entangled the Jewish self with the discourse of national identity construction in contemporary Spain and Morocco, and more recently, with concerns of diversity and discussions of tolerance for the Other. The Jew, carrying the position of intimate Other in both nations, then symbolizes the portability of the strengths within their local national culture, and the centrality of the region's cultural gifts to humanity. These active and unbroken relationships of adamot to Jews to musics are used to firmly establish this region as the matrix for the Mediterraneanism that bestows significant cultural leadership to both nations.

Jewish voices or even only the repertoires known to be sung by Jews, then, represent an ancestral relationship to the land, its fertility, and the unbroken chains of continuity between tradition, bodies, renewal, and regeneration. The recent revitalization of the sonic traces of Jews, either through Ana Alcaide's New Age arrangements of Sephardic melodies or through the deeply rooted Judeo-Andalusian singing of Kinor David Maroc's liturgical singers on Parisian stages representing Morocco's official diversity initiatives, demonstrate these efforts.

If the nation remains "an imagined political community—and imagined as both inherently limited and sovereign . . . because the members of even the smallest nation will never know most of their fellow-members, meet them, or even hear of them, yet in the minds of each lives the image of their communion,"[63] this musical communion between Catholic and Muslim Spaniards to Sephardim, and Muslim Moroccans to Moroccan Jews, establishes deeper links to the political community that stretches from an imagined temporal Al-Andalus into a projected future. The unknowing of Jews by contemporary Catholics and Muslims can be partially remedied by the perceived communion with their culture through the music performed by Jewish performers or known as "of" the Jews. Their music, then, stands by proxy, for them, establishing a sonic belonging of a disembodied presence.[64]

In the words of André Azoulay, the counsellor to the king of Morocco, and president of the Fundación Tres Culturas, "music is the only remaining answer to the current challenges of coexistence."[65] Music has become a living "component" of the legacy of Al-Andalus, its most stable inheritance.[66] The reach that music can afford, through the collapsing of time, place, and religious boundaries, presents the most accessible doorway to the future of stable and prosperous nations in the region of the Strait of Gibraltar. While the two case studies discussed in this chapter seem to highlight some of the ideological and logistical problems surrounding the contemporary performance of Jewish music of Al-Andalus, the deployment of Jewish music in this region remains both problematic and hopeful. The Jewish musics of the adamot of Al-Andalus afford a valuable cultural capital both to nations and to their Jews because of the exemplary power afforded them in the current political environment. A portion of the cultural and political positioning of both nations rests on their lived history as examples for the Western and Arab worlds. The heirs of Al-Andalus present themselves as holding a key for Western societies through the unique relationship they have with musical answers to the political challenges presented by the clash between diversity and intolerance.

ACKNOWLEDGMENTS

This chapter draws on fieldwork that was conducted in person and online between 2013 and 2022 in Casablanca, Paris, Toledo, and Torremolinos. The research was supported by the European Research Commission funded project "Past and Present Musical Encounters Across the Strait of Gibraltar" (MESG_785622) based at the Universities of Aberdeen, Manchester, and Cambridge. I am deeply indebted to the musicians of Kinor David Maroc for their openness and trust in me, allowing me to record hundreds of rehearsals between 2013 and 2018.

NOTES

1. For further discussion on contrafacta in the context of popular melodies within Hebrew liturgy, see Israel J. Katz, "Contrafacta and the Judeo-Spanish *Romancero*: A Musicological View," in *Hispanic Studies in Honor of Joseph H. Silverman*, ed. Joseph Ricapito (Newark: De la Cuesta, 188), 169–187; Edwin Seroussi and Shoshana Weich Shahak, "Judeo-Spanish Contrafacts and Musical Adaptations: The Oral Tradition," *Orbis Musicae*, no. 10 (1990–1991): 164–194; Kay Kaufman Shelemay, "Mythologies and Realities in the Study of Jewish Music," *The World of Music* 37, no. 1 (1995): 24–38.; Judith R. Cohen, "Musical Bridges: The Contrafact Tradition in Judeo-Spanish Songs," *Cultural Marginality in the Western Mediterranean: Selected Proceedings of the International Conference Held at the University of Toronto, June 1–5, 1989*, ed. Frederick Gerson and Anthony Percival (Toronto, ON: New Aurora Editions, 1990), 120–127.

2. In this case a double diaspora would be from Erets Yisrael to Iberia to Morocco/Algeria/Tunisia; a triple diaspora would add another emigration to this line of migratory movement, from the Maghreb to Paris, London, Switzerland, Venezuela, Argentina, Canada, Australia, or the United States. These are the most common patterns for Maghrebi Sephardic Jews; the Sephardim from the Eastern Mediterranean have a different combination of migratory destinations. These points of arrival most often add to the musical palette that is integrated into the group's canon.

3. See Philip V. Bohlman, *Jewish Music and Modernity* (New York: Oxford University Press, 2008), 50.

4. The Years of Lead (*années du plomb* in French) was a period during the reign of King Hassan II, starting in the 1960s through the 1980s, and marked by state violence and repression against political dissidents and activists. It ended with King Hassan II's death in 1999.

5. See Jonathan Glasser, *The Lost Paradise: Andalusi Music in Urban North Africa* (Chicago: University of Chicago Press, 2016); Jonathan Holt Shannon, *Performing Al-Andalus: Music and Nostalgia across the Mediterranean* (Bloomington: Indiana University Press, 2015);

and selected chapters in Samuel Sami Everett and Rebekah Vince, eds., *Jewish-Muslim Interactions: Performing Cultures between North Africa and France* (Liverpool: Liverpool University Press, 2020).

6. See Judith R. Cohen, "Constructing a Spanish Jewish Festival: Music and the Appropriation of Tradition," *The World of Music* 41, no. 3 (1999): 85–113; Ruth F. Davis, ed., *Musical Exodus: Al-Andalus and Its Jewish Diasporas* (Lanham, MD: Rowman and Littlefield, 2015); Matthew Machin-Autenrieth, "'Everyday' Multiculturalism and Moroccan Integration," *Ethnomusicology* 64, no. 3 (2020): 422–446; and Machin-Autenrieth, "*Ziryab and Us*: Tradition and Collaboration in the Interpretation of an Arab-Andalusian Musical Myth," *The Journal of Intercultural Studies* 42, no. 4 (2021): 494–514.

7. "Al Andalus no es un tiempo pasado, sin más; es un componente . . . de la Europa que conocemos como matriz de Occidente y que en Al Andalus saltó del Medioevo para vivir un primer Renacimiento." Emilio González Ferrín, *Historia general de al Andalus: Europa entre Oriente y Occidente* (Córdoba: Almuzara, 2006), 11.

8. See Ramón Menéndez Pidal, *Los godos y la epopeya española: "Chansons de geste" y baladas Nórdicas* (Madrid: Espasa Calpe, 1956); "La primitiva poesía lírica española," *Estudios literarios* (1957): 255–344; and *Estudios sobre el romancero* (Madrid: Espasa-Calpe, 1973).

9. See Manuel Alvar, *Endechas judeo-españolas*, 2nd ed. (Madrid: Instituto Arias Montano, 1969; and *Cantos de boda judeo-españoles* (Madrid: Centro Superior de Investigación Científica, 1971).

10. Arcadio de Larrea Palacín, *Cuentos populares de los judíos del Norte de Marruecos*, 2 vols. (Tetuán: Editora Marroquí, 1952–1953); *Canciones rituales hispano-judías* (Madrid: Consejo Superior de Investigaciones Científicas, 1954).

11. See Alexis Chottin, *Airs populaires recueillis à Fès (airs profanes)*, Hesperis: Archives Berbères et bulletin de l'Institut des Hautes-Etudes Marocaines (Paris: Émile Larose, 1924); *"Les visages" de la musique marocaine* (Rabat: Imprimerie nouvelle, 1928), *Corpus de musique marocaine*, vol. 2, *Musique et danses berbères du pays Chleuh* (Casablanca: Librairie livre service, 1931); and *Tableu de la musique marocaine* (Paris: Paul Geuthner, 1939).

12. Jules Rouanet, "La musique arabe au Maghreb," in *Encyclopédie de la musique et dictionnaire du Conservatoire*, ed. Albert Lavignac and Lionel de La Laurencie (Paris: C. Delagrave, 1922), 5:2813–2944.

13. Paul Bénichou, *Romancero judeo-español de Marruecos* (Madrid: Castalia, 1968).

14. Samuel G. Armistead and Joseph H. Silverman, *Romances judeo-españoles de Tánger recogidos por Zarita Nahón* (Madrid: Cátedra-Seminario Menéndez Pidal, 1977); *El romancero judeo-español en el Archivo Menéndez Pidal (Catálogo-índice de romances y canciones)*, 3 vols. (Madrid: Cátedra-Seminario Menéndez Pidal, 1978); and *Judeo-Spanish Ballads from Oral Tradition. I: Epic Ballads* (Berkeley: University of California Press, 1986).

15. See Paloma Díaz-Mas and Elisa Martín Ortega, "Romances y canciones sefardíes en la colección de partituras de la Biblioteca Tomás Navarro Tomás del CSIC," in *Actas del XVIII Congreso de Estudios Sefardíes* (Madrid: Editorial CSIC, 2017), 55–74; and Paloma Díaz-Mas, "Los romances tetuaníes del manuscrito de Luna Bennaim," in *De balada y lírica*, 2. *3er. Coloquio Internacional del Romancero*, ed. Diego Catalán, Jesús A. Cid, and Beatriz Mariscal (Madrid: Universidad Complutense de Madrid, 1994), 255–262.

16. See Oro Anahory Librowicz, *Florilegio de romances sefardíes de la diáspora (una colección malagueña)* (Madrid: Cátedra-Seminario Menéndez Pidal, 1980; and *Cancionero séphardi du Québec*, vol. 1 (Montreal: Cégep du Vieux Montréal, 1988).

17. See Judith R. Cohen, "'Ya salió de la mar': Judeo-Spanish Wedding Songs among Moroccan Jews in Canada," in *Women and Music in Cross-Cultural Perspective*, ed. Ellen Koskoff (Westport, CT: Greenwood Press, 1987), 55–67; and "Women and Judeo-Spanish Music," *Bridges* 3, no. 2 (1993): 113–119; "'No so komo las de agora' (I'm Not Like Those Modern Girls): Judeo-Spanish Songs Meet the Twenty-first Century," *European Judaism* 44, no. 1 (2011): 150–164.

18. See Susana Weich-Shahak, *Cantares judeo españoles de Marruecos para el ciclo de la vida* (Jerusalem: The Jewish Music Research Center, 1989); and "Canciones acumulativas sefardíes y congéneres hispánicas," *Revista de dialectología y tradiciones populares* 50, no. 1 (1995): 73–91.

19. See Abdelaziz El Amrani, "The Postsecular Turn: Interrogating Postcolonialism after 9/11," *Interventions: International Journal of Postcolonial Studies* (2021): 533–566.

20. Linda Tuhiwai Smith, *Decolonizing Methodologies: Research and Indigenous Peoples*, 3rd ed. (London: Zed Books, 2021), xii.

21. See Daniele Conversi and Matthew Machin-Autenrieth, "The Musical Bridge—Intercultural Regionalism and the Immigration Challenge in Contemporary Andalusia," *Genealogy* 4, no. 1 (2020): [19].

22. For further details on Ziryāb, see Carl Davila, *The Andalusian Music of Morocco: Al-Āla—History, Society and Text* (Wiesbaden: Reichart, 2013); Dwight Fletcher Reynolds, *Medieval Arab Music and Musicians: Three Translated Texts* (Leiden: Brill, 2021); Jonathan Holt Shannon, "Performing Al-Andalus, Remembering Al-Andalus: Mediterranean Soundings from Mashriq to Maghrib," *The Journal of American Folklore* 120, no. 477 (Summer 2007): 308–334.

23. Salé is situated across the Bouregereg River from Rabat, the political capital of Morocco since the installment of the French Protectorate in 1912. Before the arrival of the French, the center for the Sultan's power was Fez. However, Rabat was kept as the political capital after independence in 1956. Politically Salé was known, together with Fez, as a center for opposition to the French-imposed Berber Dahir, to hard-core Arab nationalists, to various intellectuals from the left during the twentieth century.

24. Mohammed Guedira, in discussion with the author, June 3, 2013. Guedira is the founder and president of the Andalusian Music Association Ribat el Fath in Rabat. He is the nephew of Ahmed Reda Guedira, the former Moroccan minister of state and counsellor to the palace and part of an important political family in Morocco.

25. Jonathan Boyarin and Daniel Boyarin, *Powers of Diaspora: Two Essays on the Relevance of Jewish Culture* (Minneapolis: University of Minnesota Press, 2002), 5.

26. See Simon Lévy, S. 2011, *Parlers arabes des juifs du Maroc: Histoire, sociolinguistique et géographie dialectale* (Zaragoza: Instituto de Estudios Islámicos y del Oriente Próximo, 2011).

27. See Maite Ojeda Mata, *Identidades ambivalentes: Sefardíes en la España contemporánea* (Madrid: Sefarad Editores, 2018).

28. For a representation of a Berberisca in a novel, see Ignacio Martínez de Pisón, *La buena reputación* (Madrid: Seix Barral, 2014). For television and film, see *Shalom: Noche de Berberisca tradición sefardí* (2018), RTVE, https://www.rtve.es/play/videos/shalom/shalom-noche-berberisca-ceremonia-sefardi/4790598/; and Miguel Angel Nieto's documentary *Tu boca en los cielos* (2019). For the popular press, see the blog post by Mar Flore, "Vivir una auténtica Noche Berberisca," *Hola*, June 18, 2018, https://blog.hola.com/mar-flores/06/18/vivir-una-autentica-noche-berberisca/ (accessed September 24, 2022).

29. Dalia Kandiyoti, *The Converso's Return: Conversion and Sephardi History in Contemporary Literature and Culture* (Stanford, CA: Stanford University Press, 2020), 125.

30. See ibid., 126.

31. There are twenty-four nubat, one per hour of the day; however, many have been forgotten or "lost," and only eleven remain actively performed in Morocco. In the eighteenth century the entirety of the texts of the Moroccan nuba were published by Al-Haik in Tetuan.

32. Genesis 3:19, *Sefaria*, https://www.sefaria.org/Genesis.3.19?lang=bi&with=all&lang2=en (accessed September 23, 2022).

33. See Richard Hidary, "Classical Rhetorical Arrangement and Reasoning in the Talmud: The Case of Yerushalmi Berakhot 1:1," *AJS Review* 34, no. 1 (2010): 33–64.

34. See Michel Serre, *Le mal propre: Polluer pour s'approprier?* (Paris: Pomier, 2008).

35. See Issachar Ben-Ami, *Culte des saints et pèlerinages judéo-musulmans au Maroc* (Paris: Maisonneuve & Larose, 1990).

36. See Samir Ben-Layashi and Bruce Maddy-Weitzman, "Myth, History and Realpolitik: Morocco and Its Jewish Community," *Journal of Modern Jewish Studies* 9, no. 1 (2010): 98.

37. For an in-depth discussion of Judeo-Arabic and the recent scholarly controversies around the use of this term, see Ella Shohat, "The Question of Judeo-Arabic," *The Arab Studies Journal* 23, no. 1 (2015): 14–76.

38. See Michael M. Laskier, "Aspects of the Activities of the Alliance Israélite Universelle in the Jewish Communities of the Middle East and North Africa: 1860–1918," *Modern Judaism* 3, no. 2 (1983): 147–171. And specifically for Morocco, see Laskier, *The Alliance Israelite Universelle and the Jewish Communities of Morocco: 1862–1962* (Albany: State University of New York Press, 1983).

39. Lawrence Rosen, *The Culture of Islam: Changing Aspects of Contemporary Muslim Life* (Chicago: University of Chicago Press), 103.

40. Cathy Gelbin and Sander Gilman, "How Did We Get Here from There?," in *Cosmopolitanisms and the Jews*, ed. Cathy Gelbin and Sander Gilman (Ann Arbor: University of Michigan Press, 2017), 2.

41. Ibid., 30.

42. See Loubna Bernichi, "Marocain(e)s libres . . . les interdits vous guettent," *Telquel*, May 2, 2012, https://telquel.ma/2012/05/02/Marocaines-libres-les-interdits-vous-guettent_518_2 275 (accessed May 28, 2021).

43. See Kay Kaufman Shelemay, *Sing and Sing On: Sentinel Musicians and the Making of the Ethiopian American Diaspora* (Chicago: University of Chicago Press, 2022).

44. See "Maxime Karoutchi: La musique judéo marocaine 'se chante du fond des tripes,'" January 1, 2021, YouTube video, https://youtu.be/zu2gZr9xhA0.

45. See Giorgio Agamben, *Homo sacer: L'intégrale* (Paris: Seuil, 1997), 15–16.

46. "Pero esta fundación está llamada a crecer aún más, a seguir consolidándose en el panorama euromediterráneo, a hacer valer con más fuerza su papel estratégico en las relaciones hispano-marroquíes y a caminar del lado de instituciones hermanas para avanzar más rápido en los objetivos que la guían desde sus orígenes: promover el diálogo, la paz y la tolerancia entre los pueblos del Mediterráneo; mantener este espacio de convivencia en el que la diversidad cultural y religiosa no solo no nos separa, sino que nos une y nos engrandece." Fundación Tres Culturas, http://tresculturas.org/fundacion/bienvenida/ (accessed May 19, 2021).

47. One recent noteworthy example is the pope's visit to Morocco in late March 2019, when a gala concert with the Moroccan Philharmonic orchestra accompanied a Muslim, Christian, and Jewish singer in a performance for the king and the pope. For a video that

captures this moment, see "Visite du pape François à l'Institut Mohammed VI," March 19, 2019, YouTube video, https://youtu.be/FYIdvqo2dWQ, starting at minute 28' (accessed May 24, 2021).

48. See Ojeda Mata, *Identidades ambivalentes*, 159.

49. See ibid., 341.

50. See Bailey W. Diffie, "The Ideology of Hispanidad," *The Hispanic American Historical Review* 23, no. 3 (1943): 458.

51. This and other titles can be accessed in Alcaide's YouTube channel, https://www.youtube.com/user/anaalcaidemusica/channels.

52. See "Otoño Sefardí en Córdoba 2018: Concierto de Ana Alcaide," November 6, 2018, YouTube video, https://youtu.be/8QscKE2Qwgs at 1′13″.

53. Quoted after Miquel Alberola, "El rey, a los sefardíes: '¡Cuánto os hemos echado de menos!,'" *El país*, November 30, 2015, https://elpais.com/politica/2015/11/30/actualidad/1448887588_869275.html.

54. Alfons Aragoneses, "Convivencia and Filosefardismo in Spanish Nation-building," *Max Planck Institute for European Legal History Research Paper Series*, no. 2016-0 (2016): 3.

55. See two recent articles by Mohamed Chtatou regarding convivencia and the connections of contemporary Jewish music in Morocco to these legacies from al-Andalus: "Al-Andalus: Multiculturalism, Tolerance and Convivencia," *Funci*, May 1, 2021, https://funci.org/al-andalus-multiculturalism-tolerance-and-convivencia/?lang=en (accessed September 24, 2022); and "Jewish Music And Singing in Morocco: Analysis," *EurasiaReview: New and Analysis*, September 1, 2022, https://www.eurasiareview.com/01092022-jewish-music-and-singing-in-morocco-analysis/ (accessed September 24, 2022)

56. *Zamane* 30 (May 2013), https://zamane.ma/fr/maroc-terre-juive (accessed September 24, 2022).

57. Lawrence Rosen, *Bargaining for Reality: The Construction of Social Relations in a Muslim Community* (Chicago: University of Chicago Press, 1984), 7.

58. See Jonathan Wrytzen, "Colonial Legacies, National Identity and Challenges for Multiculturalism in the Contemporary Maghreb," in *Multiculturalism and Democracy in North Africa: Aftermath of the Arab Spring*, ed. Moha Ennaji (Abingdon, UK: Routledge, 2014), 17–34; Eric Calderwood, "Moroccan Jews and the Spanish Colonial Imaginary, 1903–1951," *Journal of North African Studies* 24, no. 1 (2019): 86–110; and Christopher Silver, "Nationalist Record: Jews, Muslims, and Music in Interwar North Africa," in Everett and Vince, *Jewish-Muslim Interactions*, 61–80.

59. See "Musiques: L'art judéo-marocain," February 24, 2016, YouTube video, https://youtu.be/s84ieUpTlxk.

60. Most of the rehearsals are recorded and stored in KHOYA: Jewish Morocco Sound Archive, which is not yet available online, but the group's website can be accessed at http://www.kinordavidmaroc.com/

61. [name withheld], in discussion with the author, November 8, 2014.

62. [name withheld] We couldn't hear any of the Jews, we only heard ourselves. In conversation with the author. November 8, 2014.

63. See Benedict Anderson, *Imagined Communities: Reflections on the Origin and Spread of Nationalism* (London: Verso, 1983), 6.

64. This is often played out in film, as described in Vanessa Paloma Elbaz, "Connecting the Disconnect: Music and its Agency in Moroccan Cinema's Judeo-Muslim Interactions," in *Jewish-Muslim Interactions Performing Cultures between North Africa and France*, ed. Sami Everett and Rebekah Vince (Liverpool: Liverpool University Press, 2020), 201–221.

65. André Azoulay, in discussion with the author, January 23, 2020. This very statement, which Mr. Azoulay made during the conversation in preparation for a trip to the United Kingdom for both the Yallah Conference on Judeo-Arabic music at SOAS and a conference at St. John's College Old Divinity School lecture hall, then became the title for the conference he gave on February 11, 2020, at Cambridge University: "Music Instead of Politics: The Remaining Answer to the Current Challenges of Coexistence?," which can be viewed at YouTube, https://youtu.be/5D7oZDHCmIE.

66. See Ferrín, *Historia general de Al Andalus*, 11.

SELECT BIBLIOGRAPHY

Aydoun, Ahmed. *La musique juive du Maroc*. Casablanca: Marsam, 2021.

Cohen, Judith R. "Constructing a Spanish Jewish Festival: Music and the Appropriation of Tradition." *The World of Music* 41, no. 3 (1999): 85–113.

Conversi, Daniele, and Matthew Machin-Autenrieth, "The Musical Bridge—Intercultural Regionalism and the Immigration Challenge in Contemporary Andalusia." *Genealogy* 4, no. 1 (2020): [19].

Davis, Ruth F., ed. *Musical Exodus: Al-Andalus and its Jewish Diasporas*. Lanham, MD: Rowman and Littlefield, 2015.

Díaz-Mas, Paloma. "El romancero, vínculo entre sefardíes y españoles." In *Rostros judíos del occidente medieval*, 29–52. Pamplona: Gobierno de Navarra, 2019.

Elbaz, Vanessa Paloma. "A Common Language: Popular Music in Morocco." In *Jews and Muslims in Morocco: Their Intersecting Worlds*, edited by Joseph Chetrit, Jane Gerber, and Drora Arussy, 189–216. Lanham, MD: Lexington Books, 2021.

Elbaz, Vanessa Paloma. "Imagining a Sonic Al-Andalus through Sound, Bones, and Blood: The Case of Jewish Music in Morocco and Spain." *Jewish Culture and History* 22, no. 4 (2021): 336–357.

El Haddaoui, Mohammed. *La musique judéo-marocaine: Un patrimoine en partage*. Casablanca: La Croisée des chemins, 2014.

Glasser, Jonathan. *The Lost Paradise: Andalusi Music in Urban North Africa*. Chicago: University of Chicago Press, 2016.

Glasser, Jonathan. "Musical Jews: Listening for Hierarchy in Colonial Algeria and Beyond." *Anthropological Quarterly* 90, no. 1 (2017): 139–166.

Guettat, Mohammed. *La musique classique du Maghreb*. Paris: Sindbad, 1980.

Reynolds, Dwight. "The Music of Al-Andalus: Meeting Place of Three Cultures." In *A History of Jewish-Muslim Relations: From the Origins to the Present Day*, edited by Abdelwahab Meddeb and Benjamin Stora, 970–984. Princeton, NJ: Princeton University Press, 2013.

Reynolds, Dwight. *The Musical Heritage of Al-Andalus*, SOAS Studies in Music. Abington, UK: Routledge, 2021.

Roda, Jessica, and Stephanie Tara Schwartz. "Home beyond Borders and the Sound of Al-Andalus: Jewishness in Arabic—The Odyssey of Samy Elmaghribi." *Religions* 11, no. 11 (2020): [17].

Shannon, Jonathan Holt. *Performing Al-Andalus: Music and Nostalgia across the Mediterranean*. Bloomington: Indiana University Press, 2015.

Weich-Shahak, Susana. *Romancero sefardí de Marruecos*. Madrid: Alpuerto, 1997.

4

"WE SHALL SING SONGS AND PRAISE TO THE LORD WHO CREATED US LAST IN THE WORLD"

Ḥakham Joseph Ḥayyim of Baghdad, Leadership with Poetry and Music

MERAV ROSENFELD-HADAD

ḤAKHAM Joseph Ḥayyim ben Eliyah al-Ḥakham (1835–1909) was the last spiritual leader of the Babylonian Jews before they departed Iraq in the early 1950s.[1] He is considered one of the most prominent and prolific *hakhamim* (rabbis) in their history. Although he lacked an official public position, his leadership was unquestioned in Iraq and beyond. Ḥakham Joseph Ḥayyim's followers venerated him for his exceptional rabbinic scholarship and unique piety, as well as for his personal qualities, all of which also earned him respect among Muslims. During his lifetime, Ḥakham Joseph Ḥayyim published a few dozen of books. More than forty additional books have been published posthumously, each in several editions, and many more still await publication. Ḥakham Joseph Ḥayyim passed away on August 30, 1909. His funeral was the largest ever seen in Baghdad and was attended by many Muslims and Christians. The Jews of Baghdad decreed seven days of public mourning, and leading rabbis both in and outside of the city lamented his death, describing his departure as a giant void that could never be filled. Jewish communities across the Middle East and North Africa, Europe, and the United States follow his teachings and commemorate his life and work by singing his exceptionally large repertoire of songs, which the Babylonian Jews call *shbaḥoth*.

Out of his estimated two hundred songs, only seventy-three are known. They are published in various anthologies of paraliturgical songs and in his own works.[2] The paraliturgical song genre is one of the most ancient and valuable religious-cultural assets of the Judeo-Arabic heritage, in general, and of the Babylon Jews, in particular, and its practice is not regulated by any halakhic rulings. This genre typically takes the form of a Hebrew religious poem expressing Jewish values and ethics, mixed with idiosyncratic Arabo-Islamic poetic features of form, style, and, often, even content. It is frequently set to a melody of an already existing Arabic song and is sung on private and public Jewish occasions outside liturgical settings, such as Sabbath meals and weddings. The texts of this genre, which emerged as early as the ninth century in Abbasid Baghdad and which continue to be written until the present day, are documented in numerous collections published over the course of many centuries by Arab-Jewish communities throughout the Arabo-Islamic Empire, including the Babylonian Jewish community. The melodies, on the other hand, were orally transmitted, varied at different times and in different places, and were never documented in any kind of notation. Hakham Joseph Hayyim continues the millennium-old legacy of his predecessors—who, like him, were important rabbis of historical significance, mostly adapting the style of Israel ben Moses Najara (1555–1625), who was also a musician. Hakham Joseph Hayyim's songs mark an important chapter in the history of this genre, as he was the last prominent figure to create paraliturgical songs in the Babylonian diaspora.

The period between the mid-nineteenth and mid-twentieth centuries marks the last phase of two and a half millennia of Jewish presence in the area known today as Iraq. During this period, Babylonian Jews went through critical changes and challenges that were far more dramatic than they had ever experienced. Iraq's exposure to Western culture, around the mid-nineteenth century, resulted in some fundamental changes to Iraqi society, in general, and to the Jewish community, in particular. The fast growth of the Jewish population in Baghdad, expanding from 2,500 in 1794 to 50,000 in 1893 (from 3.3 percent to 35 percent of the Baghdadi population, respectively), together with its robust governing bodies and successful social, commercial, and education systems, had significantly improved the lives of the Jews and consequently increased their prominence in the wider Iraqi society. However, a series of successive political and social instabilities culminated with around 120,000 Jews departing en masse, mostly to Israel in the early 1950s.

The new acquaintance with Western culture in Iraq during the second half of the nineteenth century raised questions about the central issues of secularism, modernism, and nationalism, which soon became subjects of intense debate within the Jewish communities. Among many Jews, this encounter with the West instigated significant changes in both lifestyle and conceptions of Jewishness and identity. As a result, the relationship between the community and its rabbinic leadership went through some difficulties that neither side had experienced before.

Hakham Joseph Hayyim operated within this new reality. Fascinated by the innovative technology and knowledge that the new culture offered, and keen to preserve the Jewish culture of his community, he presents a new alternative through his versatile rabbinic work, which also includes songs, sermons, and teaching. He forged a path that would enable his followers both to adhere to their ancient heritage and to keep up with the changes taking place in wider society, many aspects of which he supported.

This chapter is the first to explore Ḥakham Joseph Ḥayyim's leadership and his relationship with his followers through his paraliturgical songs, while taking into account the ethos reflected in his other rabbinic work. This exploration is supported by studies on both Jewish Middle Eastern and Babylonian history, religion, *halakhah*, and music. It examines Ḥakham Joseph Ḥayyim's view on the bond between the Jewish people (henceforth the Nation) and its land (namely, the Land of Israel) and the role of the paraliturgical songs in building this bond and in bringing about God's salvation of His Nation, an event that is inherently connected to the return of the Nation to its promised land.

It is almost impossible to explore the scope and scale of this topic in a single chapter. Nonetheless, this chapter provides a succinct yet panoramic outlook of this ḥakham and his songs, with the hope that it will encourage further exploration of his leadership, songs, and the world that he still represents. It considers rabbinic writing in general as a critical source of both historical and cultural, as well as social and political, importance. As such, it serves as a source that provides new and authentic information, offering wider perspectives and deeper understanding of Ḥakham Joseph Ḥayyim's leadership and songs in the context of Middle Eastern Judaism. The chapter thus offers a unique look at religious leadership through both the leader's poetry and his musical taste, as well as through his views on songs and singing as they are expressed in three of his seminal works, which cover two fields of his rabbinic scholarship. In the field of halakhah the chapter draws on *Rav pe'alim* (Mighty deeds); a four-volume work containing responsa (*Shut*, a Hebrew acronym for questions and answers), which comprises answers to his followers' questions; and *Ben ish ḥay halakhot* (Halakhic rulings of the living man), in which he focuses on halakhic issues that he finds important. In the field of commentary, the chapter draws on *Even shelemah* (A complete stone), which is the first part of a seminal trilogy and contains a kabbalistic commentary on the Song of Songs.[3] The analysis of these three sources in this chapter presents Ḥakham Joseph Ḥayyim's core view on the religious status, values, and merits of songs and of singing songs of praise to God.

STUDIES ON THE MUSIC OF THE JEWS ORIGINATING IN ARAB-MUSLIM COUNTRIES

Studies on the history, religion, and culture of Jewish communities originating in Arab-Muslim countries is still in its infancy. This fact is in stark contrast to the extensive research that has been undertaken on Jewish communities in Europe. There has yet to appear a coherent synthesis of Babylonian Jewish history, in both the ancient and modern periods, that includes a balanced and comprehensive narrative of both the Middle Eastern and the European Jewish communities, and thus reflects the contribution of Babylonian Jewry to Jewish history as a whole. Additionally, only during the last few decades has music gained some recognition as a significant field within Jewish studies, as an art form composed and performed by Jews of all origins. Similarly, Arabic music, as the music of Arab-Jewish communities, has hardly been explored. The music of the Babylonian Jews was examined by scholars such as Amnon Shiloah, who looked into their religious songs; Yeheskel Kojaman, who focused on Iraqi music in general and its Jewish musicians; and Esther Warkov and Dafna Dori, who focused on a few of their musicians.[4]

In the field of rabbinic scholarship, the gap between studies on European rabbis and studies on Middle Eastern and North African rabbis is equally striking. Zvi Zohar argues that it is important for both Jews and non-Jews to understand that Judaism is a Middle Eastern phenomenon and that many of its ideas and values were cultivated and developed in the Middle East and as an integral part of Judaism's history.[5] He further asserts that the flexible and creative rabbinic ethos characteristic of Middle Eastern Judaism was totally forgotten and, instead, the rigid and insular Ashkenazi halakhic approach has become the dominant halakhic line among both Ashkenazic and Middle Eastern Orthodox rabbis and communities. Furthermore, Zohar stresses that, without the unique halakhic ethos of the Middle Eastern rabbinic leadership, Judaism is impoverished and stagnated. Haviva Pedaya points out the absence of a textbook on the history of *maḥshevet yisrael* (Jewish thought) that includes a balanced representation of both Middle Eastern and European rabbinic thinking.[6] She adds that only the occurrence of a balanced and genuine discourse in the mainstream Israeli academic, cultural, and political arenas can rectify this historical misrepresentation. Indeed, only recently, studies on Middle Eastern rabbinic work and leadership have emerged in seminal writings. One central view depicted by leading scholars such as Daniel Elazar, Zvi Zohar, and Yaron Harel emphasizes the attentive and flexible qualities of Middle Eastern rabbinic leadership.[7] Based on their strong belief in the greatness of the Torah and its unlimited potential to implement its values in any circumstances, Middle Eastern ḥakhamim decreed flexible, practical, and balanced halakhic rulings down the centuries. They thereby preserved close relationships with their respective communities and strengthened the unity within those communities, regardless of their members' levels of observance. This halakhic approach is strongly reflected in Rabbi Ovadiah Yosef's (1920–2013) leadership and rulings, in general, and in his view on using Arabic music in Jewish worship, in particular.

Despite the prominence of Babylonian rabbinic leaders in Jewish history, they have until fairly recently been little studied.[8] In the past two decades, studies on the Babylonian rabbinic scholarship in general and that of Ḥakham Joseph Ḥayyim in particular have emerged across a range of disciplines addressing various aspects of their work.[9] This plethora of studies on Ḥakham Joseph Ḥayyim's versatile work, which do not include any studies of his songs, strongly reflects the still-negligible status of music in Jewish studies. One exceptional study is the monumental work of Abraham Ben-Jacob, who lists all the known sources of Ḥakham Joseph Ḥayyim's work, including his songs, and presents the texts of the known songs, adding a short description of their formal poetic characteristics, although with no reference to any of the songs' melodies.[10]

ḤAKHAM JOSEPH ḤAYYIM'S LIFE, WORK, AND LEADERSHIP

Born into a distinguished rabbinic dynasty and gifted with a refined persona and piety, Ḥakham Joseph Ḥayyim followed his ancestors' footsteps in both rabbinic scholarship and community support and leadership. During the few years following his bar mitzvah, he studied in the prestigious rabbinic academy Midrash Zelkhah at the feet of its founder and head, the renowned leader Ḥakham Abdallah ben Abraham Somekh (1813–1889). He then continued his studies on his own, with no students and direct disciples, in his private, home library, which, according to some records, contained a few thousand books. However, Ḥakham Joseph Ḥayyim was not isolated and detached from his community and followers. He gave Torah lessons every morning, delivered sermons every Sabbath before hundreds of followers, replied to halakhic questions sent to him by hundreds of people from all over the Jewish world, and maintained an ongoing correspondence with many rabbinic scholars across the Middle East, North Africa, and Europe.

Ḥakham Joseph Ḥayyim's work covers all types and genres of rabbinic writing, mostly in Hebrew but also in the Baghdadi Judeo-Arabic dialect, demonstrating his remarkable knowledge of the entire rabbinic literature penned by both Middle Eastern and Ashkenazi rabbis, his predecessors and also contemporaries. Furthermore, Ḥakham Joseph Ḥayyim's work also shows his acquaintance with many genres of the indigenous Iraqi literature and music that were prevalent in his immediate Arabo-Islamic environment, which he uses particularly in his inspirational sermons as well as his songs. Ḥakham Joseph Ḥayyim's life and work, including his songs, also reflect a wide knowledge of kabbalistic sources and particularly works of the leading kabbalist the Ari, Rabbi Isaac ben Solomon Luria (1534–1572), who also wrote songs for the Sabbath.

Ḥakham Joseph Ḥayyim's unofficial leadership is characterized by both his pedigree and his personal qualities. Max Weber describes this type of leader as one who combines traditional and charismatic features.[11] The charismatic side emanates from the belief in the leader's special powers, a belief that leads followers to fear that any disobedience to him is likely to bring about immediate divine punishment. However, as will be demonstrated below, Ḥakham Joseph Ḥayyim conveys ideas and messages, in both his written and spoken language, that are connected to neither threat of punishment nor warning. On the contrary, it was not fear of punishment that made Ḥakham Joseph Ḥayyim a loved and admired leader. In his simple, clear, and inviting spoken and written language, intended for both erudite and lay audiences, he endorses Jewish values and ethics, and encourages Jewish lifestyle and identity, by reassuring his followers that this path will lead to a speedy salvation, which is inherently connected to the return of the Nation to its Land of Israel. Ḥakham Joseph Ḥayyim's message reflects his deep involvement in and care for his followers, men, women, and children alike, and it expresses a strong conviction in both their noble qualities and bright future. His guidance is always attached to positive and encouraging rewards and, therefore, gained him the love and trust of his followers, who acknowledged his unequivocal authority to guide them in every aspect of their lives.

Ḥakham Joseph Ḥayyim's work mirrors the following main characteristics of his leadership, a part of which he also describes in the prologues of many of his books. Understanding that his position makes him a role model for his followers, he adds a note to many of his rulings, explaining that he acts according to his own decree, and advising gently that his ruling is highly recommended rather than binding.[12] Confident in his halakhic leadership, Ḥakham Joseph Ḥayyim describes an ideal halakhic leader as an innovative, open-minded, and original thinker, a leader who produces rulings that meet the needs of his community, even if his opinion is not shared by any other halakhic authority. He asserts that this is the rabbinic ethos of *ḥakhmey ha-sefaradim* (the Sephardic/Middle Eastern rabbis/sages).[13] With his clear commitment and mission, Ḥakham Joseph Ḥayyim constantly expresses his strong pledge to God and His Nation, and conveys his gratitude to God for granting him the ability to produce his work. He vows to publish his work, which he describes as food for every person that has "zekhut ha-rabim ṭepi" (the power to increase the merits of everyone), and he considers himself privileged to pass on God's message.[14] Being aware of his status and position, Ḥakham Joseph Ḥayyim asserts in the introductory part of many of his books that he never sought to gain power through his halakhic learning, nor did he exploit it for financial or any other gain; instead, he engages in Torah learning for its own sake and "le-shem shamayim" (for the sake of heaven).[15]

As a leader who is deeply attentive to the natures and needs of his followers, Ḥakham Joseph Ḥayyim develops, with his remarkable communication skills, methods of both spoken and written rhetoric and aesthetics that enables him to pass on his message to his followers in a manner that would appeal to them and hold their attention. Through his sermons and books, he communicates messages that are specifically tailored to his followers, while employing the unique advantages of each form of media.[16] His sermons are intended for the Baghdadi lay audience, whose members find halakhic talks unappealing.[17] Hence, he delivers them in a clear and entertaining manner and in their spoken Baghdadi Judeo-Arabic dialect. Ḥakham Joseph Ḥayyim combines halakhic, kabbalistic, and Torah sources with lighter ones, such as stories, parables, and riddles taken from Baghdadi Jewish social and cultural life. This distinctive presentation sets the stage for the most important aspect of his sermons, that is, his halakhic message, which occupies only a small part of his presentation and appears with perfect timing, when the audience is ready both emotionally and intellectually to absorb its content.[18] His books, on the other hand, are targeted at *talmidey ḥakhamim* (religious sages); hence, they are divided into their specific rabbinic branches of scholarship. Ḥakham Joseph Ḥayyim's care for the wellbeing of all members of the community is also reflected in the importance he attributes to a good education system for the children, which includes both religious and secular knowledge, and an accommodating learning environment. Furthermore, he writes a special book of Torah studies for children, *Imrey binah* (Words of wisdom), which includes sources and accommodating methods of teaching, and is intended, as he explains, for sharpening the children's minds.[19] For women, Hakham Joseph Hayyim writes a book in the Baghdadi Judeo-Arabic dialect that they speak, titled *Kanun al-nisa* (The law for women), which appeared in Livorno in 1906. He offers them guidance and advice, encouraging them to lead both their families and their communities with wisdom and knowledge. In the vast majority of his work, Hakham Joseph Hayyim offers men a complete religious path that covers all aspects of life—guiding them both as individuals and as members of the community, as well as a part of what he considers the Jewish people, and even includes advice regarding their interaction and relationship with the wider Muslim society. Hakham Joseph Hayyim's work displays deep trust and conviction in God and His Nation. He believes in the strong relationship between the two, and in the good nature of the Nation and its prosperous fortune. As will be demonstrated in the following parts of this chapter, Hakham Joseph Hayyim's typical traits of leadership, which are strongly reflected in his rabbinic writing, are equally reflected in his songs.

HAKHAM JOSEPH HAYYIM'S VIEW ON THE PARALITURGICAL SONGS

In his *Rav pe'alim, Ben ish hay halakhot*, and *Even shelemah*, which are the focus of this chapter, Hakham Joseph Hayyim does not mention songs, singing, or music as such, and he rarely mentions the centuries-old debate among leading rabbinic authorities on the various aspects of the use of music in Jewish life and worship. Instead, through his ruling and commentary, he presents the virtue of singing praises to God. Hakham Joseph Hayyim uses the term *shirot ve-tishbahot* (songs and praises [to God])[20] to denote both liturgical hymns and paraliturgical songs, and the halakhic difference between the two types can be recognized either by their title or by his description of the occasion on which they are performed. The words "ne'imah"[21] or "nigun"[22] are mentioned to denote melody, verbs such as "likro" (to read) "lomar" (to say) or "lenagen" (to play)[23] are used to denote singing, and the sound of singing appears as "kol zemer."[24] Hakham Joseph Hayyim never promotes his own songs but rather encourages this practice both in and outside of the liturgy, while covering myriads of daily activities that should be accompanied by songs and praises to God. He explains much of his view using kabbalistic reasoning influenced by the Ari, who attributes to songs a power to evoke *yir'at hashem* (reverence of God) among believers.[25]

Hakham Joseph Hayyim outlines the merits of shirot ve-tishbahot in the most optimistic and positive way. He creates a strong link between the Nation's salvation and return to the Promised Land, and the importance of shirot ve-tishbahot in helping to produce the right conditions for this deliverance. Hakham Joseph Hayyim emphasizes the power of shirot ve-tishbahot to draw both the Nation and the worshipper closer to God, who, he says, will then bring salvation to His beloved Nation and restore its life in the Land of Israel. He bestows a significant religious status on these songs, equating them with Torah study, which is one of the most important obligations in Judaism, asserting that learning the Torah at night sounds like a pleasant song to God's ears.[26] Hence, both activities are equally rewarded with God's protection and salvation.[27]

Ḥakham Joseph Ḥayyim thinks that shirot ve-tishbaḥot can cultivate and refine the Nation's and the worshipper's good traits and piety, and redeem their sins.[28] These songs are a "singing" proof, so to speak, that despite the destruction of the Temple and the Nation's expulsion from its Land of Israel, God never *geresh* (divorced) and abandoned His people. He still resides among them and listens to their songs of praise, which are more powerful in bringing about the salvation than many other commandments, including Torah study. Hence, for the merits of their singing, God will bring speedy deliverance to His beloved Nation.[29]

According to Ḥakham Joseph Ḥayyim, shirot ve-tishbaḥot can defeat the Nation's enemies and thus bring salvation. The quality of these songs reflects the Nation's condition and circumstances; therefore, at the time of salvation the Nation would be able to produce songs that are more powerful.[30] Furthermore, the ability to compose and sing these songs appears to be a required trait for *ha-melekh ha-mashiaḥ* (the Messiah), who will, equipped with these musical skills, bring salvation to the Nation. This talented musician will be none other than King David, who is "ne'im zemirot yisrael" (the most beloved of Israel's singers) and who has the power to defeat the Nation's enemies with his songs and praises to God.[31] The voice of the Nation singing praises to God is, in Ḥakham Joseph Ḥayyim's view, the most genuine way to draw closer to Him. He argues that no other nation can forge the unique imprint of this voice and that the Nation's special characteristics enable its voice to reach the highest levels in heaven and to separate between the sacred and the profane on earth. Because of this, Ḥakham Joseph Ḥayyim claims that God recognizes His Nation's voice, and therefore, touched by its earnestness, He will bring speedy salvation and renew the Nation's life in the Land of Israel.[32]

In order to benefit from the reward that shirot ve-tishbaḥot offer, Ḥakham Joseph Ḥayyim explains how to perform these songs and presents the following instructions. They must be performed with humility, which can be achieved only if we remember how insignificant we are, because God created us last in this world. Only then can the *shekhinah* (God's presence) be drawn down to reside among us; otherwise, the Shekhinah would leave, as God is reported to say that "he (the proud man) and I cannot dwell together in the same place."[33] The songs should be sung with great joy, and deep "kavanah" (conviction) that unites the worshipper's body, mind, soul, and deeds in purity, and enables him or her to focus on the deep meaning of the text.[34] The language of the songs has to be Hebrew. Any translation into Arabic will impair the meaning of their texts, potentially causing them to be misunderstood as "shirey 'agavim" (promiscuous songs), which are prohibited by the halakhah.[35] A beautiful melody has the power to redeem the worshipper's sins, uplift and enhance the song's meaning, and ultimately to draw him or her closer to God.[36] Special attention must be given both to the right pronunciation of the words,[37] and to the correct order of the songs' renditions, as well as to the number of repetitions for each song, to the pitch of each rendition,[38] and even to the use of certain gestures[39] that accompany the singing.[40] Drinking wine does not impair the quality of the singing but, rather, can enhance its holiness and religious importance; however, this is only true of the paraliturgical realm.[41] With great trust in and love for the Nation and its people, Ḥakham Joseph Ḥayyim promises that adhering to this guidance and singing songs of praise to God will bring salvation to both the individual worshipper and the Nation.[42]

ḤAKHAM JOSEPH ḤAYYIM'S PARALITURGICAL SONGS

The present study focuses on those of Ḥakham Joseph Ḥayyim's songs that were published in the 1954 *Miṣḥaf al-shbaḥot* (The holy book of praises), or the *Miṣḥaf* in short. It was the first collection to be edited and published in Jerusalem by the Baghdadi-born Tsaleḥ ben Rabbi Ya'aḳov Mantsur (1895, Baghdad–1987, Jerusalem), only three years after the mass immigration of Babylonian Jews to Israel.[43] The book includes fifty-two of Ḥakham Joseph Ḥayyim's songs, the highest number to appear in any known collection of paraliturgical songs published by the Babylonian Jews, and covers songs for both private and communal celebrations (Table 4.1).[44]

The songs that are presented for these different occasions can also be sung at other events, as the worshippers see fit. The greatest number of songs appear in the sections for the Sabbath and for Simchat Torah, reflecting Ḥakham Joseph Ḥayyim's view on the significance of these occasions and the values they represent in Judaism.

Most of the songs are in Hebrew, one is in Aramaic, and four are in the Baghdadi Judeo-Arabic dialect.[45] Ḥakham Joseph Ḥayyim is the first known poet to write paraliturgical songs in Judeo-Arabic. He uses simple and clear language, employing vocabulary that is known to his followers from biblical, liturgical, and midrashic sources, from other known and loved paraliturgical songs including his own, and from their spoken Judeo-Arabic dialect. Most songs are written in the poetic genre known as *shir me'eyn 'ezori*, which is a derivative of the Arabic *muwashshaḥ* form. It has a flexible structure and equally flexible rhythmic pattern that is based on the *mishḳal havarati foneti* (phonetic-syllabic meter), which allows the same number of syllables for each line of the song, regardless of their length, and was adapted to Hebrew verse for the first time, by Najara. Therefore, these songs can be easily adjusted to many melodies. Drawing on Iraqi indigenous folk and popular songs that also inspired his sermons, such as the *zuhayrī* and the *'atāba*, Ḥakham Joseph Ḥayyim makes his own songs even more familiar and approachable. In addition, he often creates an acrostic that runs through the entire Hebrew alphabet, which can help the worshipper to remember the song's text by heart, rather than a more prevalent acrostic, in which the successive first letter of each of the song's lines comprises a sequence of letters that spells out a phrase or a name of

Table 4.1 Ḥakham Joseph Ḥayyim's Paraliturgical Songs in the 1954 *Miṣḥaf*

Occasion No.	Occasion	Number of songs
1	*Baḳashot* (supplications)	1
2	Sabbath	8
3	*Motsa'ey Shabbat* (The end of Sabbath)	6
4	Rosh Ḥodesh (The head of each month)	2
5	Tu Bi-Shevat (The fifteenth day of Shevat, the new year for trees)	1
6	Purim	1
7	Passover	1
8	Lag ba'Omer (The thirty-third day of the counting of the Omer)	3
9	Ezekiel the Prophet	1
10	Joshua the High Priest	1
11	Ezra the Scribe	2
12	Jerusalem and The Land of Israel	2
13	Pentecost and The Ten Commandments	3
14	*Yamim Nora'im ve-'Aseret Yemey Teshuvah* (The High Holy Days and Ten Days of Repentance)	1
15	Tabernacles	2
16	Simchat Torah (The celebration of the Torah)	14
17	Bar mitsvah	1
18	Various occasions	2
Total		52

a person. This complex technique, which is adopted by Ḥakham Joseph Ḥayyim and demonstrates another aspect of his talent, is inspired by the Ari, who asserts that the Hebrew alphabet comprises the letters of the Torah with which God created the world, therefore, covering the entire Hebrew alphabet in a song symbolizes the creation's perfection.

THE RELIGIOUS ETHOS EXPRESSED IN THE PARALITURGICAL SONGS

Ḥakham Joseph Ḥayyim's strong support of the practice of singing paraliturgical songs is reflected in both his relatively large number of songs and in their content. Being aware of the centrality of this genre among his followers, and the vast repertoire of songs already intensely practiced, he creates an additional channel through which he passes on his ethos. Similar to his other rabbinic work, his songs mirror his deep commitment to, love for, and trust in both God and the Nation, his strong conviction in the special bond between them, and his unreserved trust in the virtuous nature of the Nation together with its glorious future prospects as a free Nation living in its own Land of Israel. Equally, Ḥakham Joseph Ḥayyim expresses his ideas in the same accommodating and encouraging manner that appears in his other work. Four main protagonists appear in the songs: God, the Nation, the Torah, and the salvation, the last of which involves Ḥakham Joseph Ḥayyim's belief in a return to the Land of Israel. He argues that the relationship between God and the Nation relies on the ancient covenant between Him and the Nation's forefathers. Only with the Nation's adherence to the Torah that God gave as a present to His Nation will salvation arrive, uniting its people with its land. Typically in the paraliturgical song genre, the Nation turns to God (the dominant protagonist of this genre), both as a collective and as individuals, and with words of exaltation and supplication plead for His forgiveness and rescue.

Ḥakham Joseph Ḥayyim's rich, affirmative, reassuring, and warm language that appears even in the songs' acrostics[46] helps worshippers to create an empowering and inspirational atmosphere. He emphasizes and praises the Nation's virtuous nature and well-deserved glorious future, encouraging its people to follow the Torah, love and trust God, and believe in the speedy salvation that will lead to them living freely in the Land of Israel, worshipping Him with joy in His reinstated Temple in Jerusalem.

Ḥakham Joseph Ḥayyim portrays both God and the Nation, as well as their relationship, with heartfelt words, such as "joy," "rejoice," "love," "friendship," "peace," "celebrations," "light," "songs," "praises," "singing," "blessings," and "kindness."[47] Phrases such as "rejoicing with song," and particularly "I shall sing a new song,"[48] are often linked to the days of salvation M(105;146). The Nation's painful present is often described only briefly, and with a great sense of sympathy and compassion.[49] God is described as the Nation's shepherd M(118;161), and as its redeemer and lover,[50] who encourages, supports, and protects his wife, namely, the people of Israel M(167;233). He is depicted as a merciful father, forgiving, healing, gracious, patient, and close and attentive to His Nation: He will never forget His covenant with its forefathers and will never forsake their offspring. Hence, He will forgive the Nation's sins, and with mercy and support He will bring salvation to its people and gather them in the Land of Israel M(64;90). At the time of salvation, the Nation is portrayed as a powerful woman with a glorious crown on her head M(85;118). All its people are "distinguished," "majestic," "modest," "righteous," and "pure" M(156;216). In one single song the Nation's qualities are described in twenty-four adjectives, such as "honest," "decent," "clever," "erudite in the Torah," "great," "good," "kind," "pure," "beautiful," and "pleasant" M(157;217). In these songs, the Nation views God as its father and king, asks for His forgiveness and love, and pleads for His rescue M(64;91). Its people thank God with great joy and songs for His care, love, and mercy M(148;205), and they celebrate His glory and kindness with utter delight M(213;318).

Every aspect connected to the Torah is described with heartening and joyous words. The Torah is seen as the source of happiness, wisdom, and light M(128;174), encompassing the entire world, as a crown on the head of those who seek its knowledge and adhere to its words M(129;175). The Torah's message is "clear," "pleasant," "uplifting," "precious," and "wise," and it gives life to the entirety of God's creation M(168;235). It is "sweet," "deep," "pure," and "forgiving" M(171;239), a special gift given by God, and delivered by Moses, to His most beloved Nation who received the Torah wholeheartedly M(168;235), with commitment and gratitude M(171;239). At the time of salvation, King David will lead the Nation, in its own Land of Israel, for long and happy years filled with love, justice, and wisdom, according to the Torah M(63;89). Ḥakham Joseph Ḥayyim describes the strong bond between God, the Torah, and the Nation with great festivity. He declares that there is no one like God, who is mighty, pure, and the savior; there is nothing like the sacred and perfect Torah, and there is no Nation like the people of Israel, who love, zealously study, and rely upon and trust the Torah M(157;218).

To further support the Nation and fortify its spirit and its hope for God's speedy salvation, Ḥakham Joseph Ḥayyim often enrolls the forefathers of the Nation and a large group of the most holy and righteous figures in Judaism, to advocate on behalf of the Nation before God. His wish to enroll them is based on the Jewish belief that "These are the righteous who in their death are called alive" (Babylonian Talmud, Berakhot, 18a), and they still have the power to plead before God for the welfare of the Nation. These figures have four roles in Ḥakham Joseph Ḥayyim's songs. The first is to remind God of His covenant to protect their offspring;[51] the second is to advocate for the Nation's future.[52] The third role is to argue that their good virtues and deeds merit God's forgiveness and salvation of the Nation.[53] The fourth and final role is to ask God that His unreserved protection be provided equally to all members of the Nation.[54] In many of the songs, Ḥakham Joseph Ḥayyim asks the Nation to rejoice and trust in God's salvation M(85;118). He also adds his own benedictions, wishing its people long and happy years blessed by the forgiving God, who will grant His Nation a good life filled with peace, renewal, joy, and celebration in both festive and ordinary days M(172;240).

THE MELODIES

Since the melodies of the paraliturgical songs were transmitted from one generation to the next only orally, and they were often replaced by other melodies, we do not know with certainty whether those used today are the original melodies to which Ḥakham Joseph Ḥayyim wrote his songs. The endeavor to discover all the known melodies for Ḥakham Joseph Ḥayyim's fifty-two songs in the 1954 *Miṣḥaf*, which was conducted in the framework of this study, reveals that all of them are taken from the Baghdadi Jews' religious-cultural environment. Twenty-five percent of Ḥakham Joseph Ḥayyim's songs share the same melodies as songs of Najara, who is their most beloved poet. For example, Ḥakham Joseph Ḥayyim's song for bar mitzvah celebrations "Barukh el ḥay eloheynu" (Blessed be our living God) M(213;318) is sung to the melody of Najara's *baḳashah*

"Yihyu ke-mots" (They shall become as chaff before the wind) M(14;6). Ten percent of his songs share melodies with various hymns in the liturgy, which the Baghdadi Jews regularly recite, like all Jewish communities. The rest of his songs share melodies with other paraliturgical songs that they love and frequently sing. These melodies are known from Ḥakham Joseph Ḥayyim's other popular paraliturgical songs, or songs by other prominent poets, such as the poets of Muslim Spain, Solomon ben Judah Ibn Gabirol (1020–1057), Abraham ben Meir Ibn Ezra (1089–1164), and Judah Halevi (1075–1141), as well as prominent eighteenth- and nineteenth-century Baghdadi poets.

The melodies used for Ḥakham Joseph Ḥayyim's songs strongly reflect his approachable and accommodating manner of communication with his followers, which was revealed earlier in his work in general, and in the texts of his paraliturgical songs, in particular. The religious-cultural surroundings of the Baghdadi Jews that is reflected in his songs' vocabulary and content is equally embodied in their melodies.

In addition, the high percentage of melodies that are shared with Najara's songs also attests to Najara's influence on Ḥakham Joseph Ḥayyim, which can be seen in the striking structural and linguistic similarities between their songs.[55] Hence, it is highly likely that the melodies known today were originally chosen by Ḥakham Joseph Ḥayyim. Furthermore, bearing in mind that he is still considered an important rabbinic leader by Babylonian Jews and that, after their immigration to Israel, they were eager to preserve their culture as it was, it would be reasonable to assume that most of the melodies that were chosen by Ḥakham Joseph Ḥayyim for his songs are those used today. Nevertheless, the melodies' origins are yet to be determined.

The following example demonstrates the difficulty in identifying the original melodies that were chosen by Ḥakham Joseph Ḥayyim. The song "Az tit'anag 'al adonay" (Then you can seek the favor of the Lord) M(65;73), following Isaiah 55:14, included in the songs for the Sabbath is sung today to the same two melodies that are used for Najara's baḳashah "Ana elekh me-ruḥakha" (Where shall I hide from Your [the Lord's] presence) M(20;16). These are melodies of two Arabic love songs that are still popular in the Arab world today. The poets of both songs, which are written in the muwashshaḥ genre, are unknown; however, both of the melodies' composers were contemporaries of Ḥakham Joseph Ḥayyim. The first song is "Ya ṭira ṭirī ya ḥamāmah" (Fly, fly away [my] dove) in maqām rāst, which was composed by the Turkish-born Syrian musician and playwright Aḥmad Abu Khalīl al-Qabbānī (1835–1902). The second song is "Qadduka al-mayyās ya 'umrī" (Your graceful waist o my life [love]) in maqām ḥijāz, composed by the Mosul-born Sufi poet and musician Mulla 'Uthmān al-Mauṣilī (1854–1923). Al-Mauṣilī spent much of his time in Baghdad and was a prominent Koran reciter, and a composer and singer of many religious and non-religious songs, which are still prevalent in the repertoire of the Iraqis. It is more likely that al-Mauṣilī's music was more popular among the Jewish Baghdadi community at Ḥakham Joseph Ḥayyim's time. However, we do not know why we have two melodies for this song, and which of them was chosen by Ḥakham Joseph Ḥayyim, or whether he chose both of them.

ḤAKHAM JOSEPH ḤAYYIM'S SONG
"AZ YERANEN 'ETS HA-YE'ARIM"

"Az yeranen 'ets ha-ye'arim" (On that day the tree of the forest shall shout for joy), for Tu Bi-Shevat,[56] is a prime example of Ḥakham Joseph Ḥayyim's leading through poetry and music. With his familiar and warm language, he aims to create a positive and uplifting atmosphere, which emerges through the optimistic and hopeful idea that celebrates the bond between God, the Nation, and its fertile and prosperous Land of Israel. This idea is saturated with words about songs and singing and hence demonstrates their centrality in this bond.

אָז יְרַנֵּן עֵץ הַיְעָרִים   לִפְנֵי אֵל אַדִּיר אַדִּירִים
יָעִיר זְמִירוֹת וְשִׁירִים   אָשִׁיר שִׁיר חָדָשׁ
יִתְפָּאַר אֵל חַי צוּרֵנוּ   וּשְׁמוֹ יִתְקַדֵּשׁ

בָּרוּךְ אֵל שׁוֹכֵן עֲרָבוֹת   הַבּוֹרֵא נְפָשׁוֹת רַבּוֹת
וּבָרָא אִילָנוֹת טוֹבוֹת   אָשִׁיר שִׁיר חָדָשׁ
יִתְפָּאַר אֵל חַי ...

רָם אֵל בִּשְׁמֵי מְעוֹנִים   בָּרוּךְ מְבָרֵךְ הַשָּׁנִים
מַצְמִיחַ עִנְבֵי גְפָנִים   אָשִׁיר שִׁיר חָדָשׁ
יִתְפָּאַר אֵל חַי ...

כַּבְּדוּ אֵל בָּאוּרִים   הִגְדִּיל עֲנָפִים וּזְמִירִים
וּבָרָא זֵיתִים וּתְמָרִים   אָשִׁיר שִׁיר חָדָשׁ
יִתְפָּאַר אֵל חַי ...

יִתְבָּרַךְ חַי דָּר מְעוֹנָה   מַצְמִיחַ פְּרִי תְּאֵנָה
נוֹדֶה לוֹ בְּשִׁיר וּרְנָנָה   אָשִׁיר שִׁיר חָדָשׁ
יִתְפָּאַר אֵל חַי ...

הַלְלוּ אֵל חַי בְּזְמִירוֹת   הַמַּגְדִּיל עַל מֵי נְהָרוֹת
רִמּוֹנִים וּמִינֵי פֵרוֹת   אָשִׁיר שִׁיר חָדָשׁ
יִתְפָּאַר אֵל חַי ...

חִזְקוּ לְבָבוֹת שׁוֹבֵבוֹת   שִׂמְחוּ בָּנִים עִם הָאָבוֹת
כֹּה נִזְכֶּה לְשָׁנִים רַבּוֹת   אָשִׁיר שִׁיר חָדָשׁ
יִתְפָּאַר אֵל חַי ...

On that day, the trees of the forest shall shout for joy[57] A[58]	Before the LORD the mighty of the mightiest[59] A
(The trees of the forest) shall rouse hymns and songs A	(O LORD) I shall sing a new song[60] B
The name of our living God[61] our rock shall be glorified C	And His name shall be sanctified B

Blessed be the LORD who dwells in clouds[62] D
And creates bountiful trees[64] D

Mighty is the LORD who dwells in heaven

Who makes the grapes of the vine grow[66]

Honor the LORD with light[67]

And created olives and dates

Blessed be the LORD Who dwells in heaven
We shall glorify You with songs and joyful singing

Praise the living God with songs
Pomegranate and abundant fruits

Be strong Oh ye rebellious hearts[69]
Thus, we shall all be blessed (by the LORD)
          with many long years

Who creates many souls[63] D
(O LORD) I shall sing a new song B
          The name of our living God . . .

Blessed be the LORD who blesses
the years[65]
(O LORD) I shall sing a new song
          The name of our living God . . .

Who raised branches (of trees)
and twigs[68]
(O LORD) I shall sing a new song
          The name of our living God . . .

Who makes the fig tree grow
(O LORD) I shall sing a new song
          The name of our living God . . .

God who makes grow on riverbanks
(O LORD) I shall sing a new song
          The name of our living God . . .

Rejoice sons with fathers[70]

(O LORD) I shall sing a new song
          The name of our living God . . .

The song comprises seven stanzas, each of which aside from the first has two lines. The first stanza alone has three lines, the last of which functions as a refrain. Each line is divided over two hemistiches. The rhythmic pattern of the song is identical in all the stanzas and different in the refrain. The first line in each of the stanzas comprises sixteen syllables, with eight syllables in each hemistich, and the second line comprises thirteen syllables, with eight and five syllables in each hemistich, respectively. The last line (in the first stanza), the refrain, has the same rhythmic pattern as the second line of the stanza. The rhyming scheme, as indicated in the body of the text, shows that each hemistich in the stanza ends with the same syllable except for the last hemistich of the second line, which rhymes with the second hemstitch of the refrain: AAABCB, DDDBCB, and so on.

Ḥakham Joseph Ḥayyim produces a joyous and celebratory song, aimed at creating an elevating atmosphere, saturated with words of praise to God for the rich and fruitful land he created for His Nation, all expressed through songs and singing, and welcoming the followers with a warm acrostic, "I shall bless the Lord wholeheartedly." His close communication with his followers, which was revealed earlier in his work and leadership as well as in his songs' texts and melodies, is mirrored here in the text of this song.

Ḥakham Joseph Ḥayyim uses a vocabulary that is taken from, or inspired by, a number of familiar sources: biblical verses that describe lofty ideas and refer to happy events in the history and future of the Nation in its land; the familiar liturgy; and popular paraliturgical songs, written mainly by Najara but also by himself.

The following analysis will focus on a few of the main aspects conveyed in Ḥakham Joseph Ḥayyim's complex and rich text. Inspired by Psalm 96:12–13, "Az yeranen" describes God's blessing of the world, in general, and His blessings of Land of Israel, in particular, all accompanied by the Nation's praise for His actions. It expresses the idea that the renewal and blossoming of nature evoke in the Nation feelings of gratitude to God and a need to praise Him with hymns and songs. The song opens with the word "az" (on that day), namely, the day of salvation when God "will rule the world justly, and its peoples in faithfulness." The word "az" is also connected to a formative event in the Nation's history, when God liberated its people from the Egyptian oppressor, as described in *Shirat ha-yam* (The song of the sea),[71] which also begins with this word and expresses gratitude by means of song to God for His salvation (Exodus 15:1).

Psalm 68:5 inspired Ḥakham Joseph Ḥayyim's description of God's almightiness both in heaven and on earth. It is reflected in the references to God's dwelling in clouds (stanza 2, line 1) and in heaven (stanzas 3 and 5, line 1, respectively), and His power on earth, as the creator of the world and nature, is described throughout the song. In the first stanza, nature with its trees and forest(s) praises and sings to God, the mighty of the mightiest, and incites all to praise Him with songs and hymns. God creates many souls (lives), both humans and animals as well as bountiful trees (stanza 2, lines 1 and 2). He blesses the years and makes the grapes of the vine to grow (stanza 3, lines 1 and 2), an image that also symbolizes a successful match between a virtuous woman and man (Babylonian Talmud, Pesaḥim, 49a). God creates and nurtures branches and twigs of trees (stanza 4, line 1), suggesting that they grow and bring light and blessing to the world just like the light of the righteous. Ḥakham Joseph Ḥayyim describes God's glorious creation by mentioning five of *shivʿat ha-minim* (the seven agricultural products) with which God blessed the Land of Israel, and which are the only agricultural products considered acceptable for offerings in the times of the Temple.[72] These are grapes (stanza 3, line 2), olives, dates (stanza 4, line 2), figs (stanza 5, line 1), and pomegranates (stanza 6, line 2). God also creates plentiful fruits to grow on riverbanks (stanza 6, lines 1 and 2). Ḥakham Joseph Ḥayyim's typical and central descriptions of God also appear here, according to which God is mighty of the mightiest (stanza 1, line 1) and a living God (refrain). His solid and truthful relationship with the Nation is emphasized and contrasts with the false relationship between other gods and their Nations.

Songs of praise to God appear throughout. Each stanza ends with the phrase "ashir shir ḥadash" (I shall sing a new song) emphasizing, through the act of singing, God's miraculous actions in nature, which are also linked to the salvation, and the refrain that glorifies and sanctifies God's name then follows. To further emphasize the strong bond between the Nation and God, Ḥakham Joseph Ḥayyim encourages his followers to sing to and praise God and glorify Him with songs and joyful singing (stanza 5, line 2) and, again, to praise the living God with songs (stanza 6, line 1).

Ḥakham Joseph Ḥayyim's method of presentation in his *derashot* (sermons)—as described earlier, where he conveys his main halakhic message in brief, wrapped with many familiar and cherished sources that set the stage for its presentation—is also apparent in this song. After almost an entire song saturated with joyous ideas and descriptions, Ḥakham Joseph Ḥayyim presents a sensitive and subtle request in the last stanza, which is concentrated in a three-word phrase, "ḥizeḵu levavot shovavot" (Be strong Oh ye rebellious hearts). It is inspired by Jeremiah (3:22), "shuvu banim shovavim" (repent rebellious sons); however, Ḥakham Joseph Ḥayyim softens this phrase. He changes the term "rebellious sons" to "rebellious hearts," which sounds more intimate, and replaces the verb "repent" with "be strong," which is more encouraging, gently suggesting that this time of celebration of God's glory in heaven and on earth is also the time for repentance. According to a Jewish belief that Ḥakham Joseph Ḥayyim endorses here, such repentance would result in the Nation's salvation and return to its rich and blessed Land of Israel. This request is also connected to the period in which Tu Bi-Shevat is taking place. It is called *yemey shovavim* (the period of the mischievous),[73] commencing two weeks after Hanukkah and ending at the beginning of the month of Adar. This period is designated for the repentance of sins that were committed in one's youth, hence the word *shovavim*.

Ḥakham Joseph Ḥayyim's succinct and sensitive request is followed by a heart-felt blessing, "Rejoice sons with fathers," reassuring his followers that their repentance will lead to the days of salvation, when sons will rejoice with their fathers, a quote from Malachi, who was the last prophet to prophesy about the day of salvation. Ḥakham Joseph Ḥayyim ends his song with a further extended blessing, which is based on the most prevalent blessing among the Babylonian Jews for every celebratory occasion: "tizku le-shanim rabbot ṭovot u-ne'imot" (May you be blessed [by the Lord] with long, good, and pleasant years). It is borrowed from the hymn El nora alilah (God of awesome deeds) by the poet Moses Ibn Ezra (Muslim Spain, 1055–1138), which is recited on Yom Kippur. Ḥakham Joseph Ḥayyim wishes his followers "koh nizekeh le-shanim rabot" (Thus, we shall all be blessed [by the Lord] with many long years) (stanza 7, line 2), namely, the days of salvation and the return to the Land of Israel.

"Az yeranen" appears in the repertoire of both the Babylonian and the Yemenite Jews, and, in the past few decades, many other communities inside and outside of Israel have been singing this song, which was also set relatively recently to a new Western melody.[74] The melody used by the Babylonian Jews is in maqām *ḥusaynī* and comprises five melodic phrases. Based on the rendition of Mordekhay and Mal'akhi Yitshar, the tune is in maqām ḥusaynī on e. The first musical phrase (set to the first hemistich of line 1 of the song) is based on the upper *jins* (tetrachord) of ḥusaynī, jins rāst (here, A–D). This phrase includes the ḥusaynī's typical feature of lowering the sixth scale degree in descending (here, from C half-sharp to C-sharp), which adds to the song's sense of festivity at its very beginning. The second musical phrase (set to the second hemistich of line 1) remains on jins rāst and emphasizes its lower tone (here, A), and the third musical phrase (set to the first hemistich of line 2) presents a full and moderate descent of maqām ḥusaynī (here, from D to e). The fourth musical phrase (set to the second hemistich of line 2) focuses on the lower jins of ḥusaynī, *bayāt* (here, e–A), descending from its upper tone (here, A) to the tonic of the ḥusaynī (here, e), with the festive C-sharp.

The fifth and last musical phrase of the song (set to the first hemistich of line 3 of the song) emphasizes the dominant of ḥusaynī (here, B), and the fourth melodic phrase is repeated again (for the second hemistich of line 3) descending smoothly to the tonic of ḥusaynī (here, e). Both phrases five and then four constitute the song's refrain. The melodic line of "Az yeranen" includes relatively few subtle ornamentations. It features a relatively simple contour, which is easy to sing. Its bouncy and lively rhythmic pattern, 7/8, adds to the celebratory and optimistic meaning of the song's text. This rhythmic pattern appears only rarely in Iraqi music; it is more popular in Turkish or Ottoman music, which was strongly prevalent in Baghdad at Ḥakham Joseph Ḥayyim's time.

In the paraliturgical realm this melody is also used for two other songs, both sung on Purim, the most cheerful religious event in Judaism. The first is Ḥakham Joseph Ḥayyim's "'Ovedey ha-el be-emunah" (They who worship God with devotion) M(105;146), in which the phrase "I shall sing a new song" is also prominent. The second song is "'Ezer mi-tsaray" ([My] rescuer from my foe) M(96;135), written by Ezra ben Sasson ben Ezra (first half of the nineteenth century), who also uses the phrase "I shall sing a new song." Ḥakham Joseph Ḥayyim might have borrowed this melody from him; however, the original song to which this melody was written is unknown.

CONCLUSION

Ḥakham Joseph Ḥayyim was a rabbinic leader "of the old type."[75] He was revered by virtue both of his family pedigree and his greatness in the Torah, as well as his charisma. His leadership was based on the long tradition of rabbinic halakhic authority that, to his followers, symbolized stability and continuity. Indeed, despite the dramatic changes that the Babylonian Jews went through as a result of their exposure to Western culture, it seems that their wish to uphold the community's stability was vital. For them, enthusiastically embracing values of modernity and progress was aimed at improving their life conditions. It never meant embracing Western culture exclusively and abandoning their sense of Jewish belonging and identity. For the most part, Babylonian Jews did not develop any anti-religious feelings or the notion that Judaism is inherently crude and therefore no longer relevant to their lives. Instead, they wished to make modern changes in line with the spirit of Judaism by creating a balanced combination of these two cultures.[76] One interesting fact that can demonstrate the richness of Jewish religious life in Ḥakham Joseph Ḥayyim's time is that the number of synagogues in Baghdad increased over the course of the nineteenth century, from three to over thirty; and even then, the synagogues were often overcrowded. Likewise, the number of *batey midrash* (houses of Torah learning) reached an unprecedented number of a few dozen.

It seems that Ḥakham Joseph Ḥayyim, who was close and attentive to his followers' needs, understood their wish to bring Western culture into their lives while simultaneously adhering to their Jewish values and keeping the community's atmosphere of stability and continuity. With both his rabbinic writings and sermons, as well as his songs, he emphasized in the most approachable and familiar manner his positive and optimistic outlook on Jewish values and identity, on the Nation's special relationship with God, and on its unique traits and its imminent salvation. Hakham Joseph Hayyim neither rejected nor opposed modern changes in Jewish life, as long as they did not impair Jewish values. Rather, his ethos suggests that these changes do not alter or remove their core essence. With his keen stress on these particularly optimistic ideas, Hakham Joseph Hayyim established a balanced view of the new reality, in which the strong influence of a foreign culture that is posing a seeming threat to the old and known world can be stabilized and balanced by an equally strong and optimistic Jewish outlook. Thus, Hakham Joseph Hayyim offered his followers an inclusive path that combines the old with the new and provides for much-needed continuity and stability. He encouraged them to adhere to their ancient Jewish values and to strengthen their trust in God, promising them that this path will lead to a better future of salvation as a free Nation in its own Land of Israel suggesting that while the new culture improves present life, the old culture guarantees a better life in both the present and the future. Therefore, both cultures can coexist together as they complement rather than contradict each other.

Both the accommodating approach and the optimistic and encouraging ethos mirrored in Hakham Joseph Hayyim's songs further affirm findings described in previous studies, mentioned above, regarding the uniquely close and attentive relationship that Middle Eastern and North African hakhamim had, and still have, with their respective communities. His view on songs and singing and the content and melodies of his unprecedented number of paraliturgical songs attest to his conviction that this genre of songs, which were central in his followers' lives for generations, can also support his ethos. These songs have the power to strengthen and preserve their Jewish life and identity, and thus to help in creating a balanced and stable environment—one that accommodates both their past and their present as well as their future.[77] To make this genre even more appealing, Hakham Joseph Hayyim created a particularly approachable and familiar language and cheerful content, and adapted cherished melodies for these songs. Altogether, his view and approach produced an encouraging and inspiring atmosphere that enhanced his followers' sense of their Jewishness with ideas and values that are hopeful and inviting and by no means overbearing.

Hakham Joseph Hayyim's paraliturgical songs mirrored both the past and the present as well as the future of the Nation, in general, and of the Babylonian Jews, in particular. His songs are saturated with cultural features of form, style, and music that were prevalent in the wider Arabo-Islamic cultural environment of the Babylonian Jews. However, the content of these songs is entirely Jewish, emphasizing and celebrating the values that Hakham Joseph Hayyim wished to promote among his followers. These are the strong bond between God, His Nation, and its salvation and return to its Land of Israel, and they thus represent their future. In this future, the time of salvation, the Babylonian Jews will no longer be a small diasporic community, but rather a fortunate group of people uniting with its larger collective, namely, the Jewish people, and their land will no longer be Iraq, but rather their own Land of Israel. Therefore, it seems that Hakham Joseph Hayyim believed that singing these prized songs assists in creating a coherent coexistence between the diasporic community, facing different cultural and social changes, and its future life as a free Nation in its homeland. It is a coherent combination of present and future only if the ancient core essence of Jewish life and identity is preserved. As Ḥakham Joseph Ḥayyim suggested gently but clearly in his songs, only following the Torah's path and preserving a strong sense of Jewish belonging will improve life in the present and eventually bring about salvation. In other words, the Nation's commitment to Judaism as a collective must remain stable and strong, as it will ultimately enable the transition from the present diasporic land to the future homeland, and will serve as a strong foundation for the Nation's life in its ancient and simultaneously renewed land.

It seems that this is the kind of stability and continuity that Ḥakham Joseph Ḥayyim wished to create for his followers. Their possessing a strong notion of Jewishness that can cope with all the drastic changes that they had to face, including the following decades of endless turmoil in their lives, proved that he was right in many respects. His legacy seems to have crossed the boundaries of both time and place, as his teachings and songs penned in the diasporic land still provide the stability and continuity for his followers in the State of Israel, long after they have left Iraq. Ḥakham Joseph Ḥayyim is still a central figure in the Babylonian Jews' religious-cultural life and identity, regardless of the level of their religious observance, and his legacy now attracts many other communities originating both in and outside of the Middle East who eagerly adhere to his path and songs. His unique ethos and songs rendered his leadership almost immortal, as he continues to be significant in a completely different reality and cultural environment. In the new environment, a strong sense of Jewishness, whether Middle Eastern or another form of Jewishness that was cultivated in diaspora, can coexist in the modern settings of the State of Israel, which is mostly Western and secular. In this sense, Ḥakham Joseph Ḥayyim's life and leadership mark another important chapter not only in the history of rabbinic leadership in the Middle East and North Africa but also in the history of rabbinic leadership in Judaism.

Acknowledgments

I would like to thank Professor Shaul Regev (Bar Ilan University) for his invaluable help and advice regarding several aspects of this chapter. I would also like to thank Cantor Mosheh Ḥabushah for his kind and generous help in discovering the known melodies to which Ḥakham Joseph Ḥayyim's paraliturgical songs have been sung.

Notes

1. The phrase in the chapter's title is quoted from Ḥakham Joseph Ḥayyim's *Even shelemah* [A complete stone] (Livorno: n.p., 1870), 5a. Here he explains that the notion of being created last in the world produces humbleness, which is considered a necessary trait for drawing closer to God by praising Him with songs.

2. Abraham Ben-Jacob mentions the lost *Sefer ha-pizmonim* (The book of songs) and asserts that it probably included over 150 songs; see *ha-Rav Yosef Ḥayyim mi-Bagdad: Toledot ḥayyav u-reshimat ketavav* [Rabbi Joseph Hayyim of Baghdad: His life and writings] (Or Yehuda: Iraqi Jews Traditional Culture Center Institute for Research on Iraqi Jewry, 1984), 40. For different assessments of the number of songs, see ibid., 87, and Abraham Ben-Jacob, *Otsar ha-shirim, ha-ḥiburim veha-derashot ve-sipurey ha-maʿasiyot shel ha-Rav Yosef Ḥayyim zʿl* [The collected songs, essays, books, sermons, and tales of Rabbi Joseph Hayyim of blessed memory] (Jerusalem: Haktav Institute, 1994), 16. For their location, see Ben-Jacob, *ha-Rav Yosef Ḥayyim*, 30–40 and 103–130.

3. The second part is *Em ha-melekh* (The king's mother/The king's path), a commentary on the Scroll of Ruth, and the third part is *Ķeren yeshuʿah* (Power of salvation), on the Scroll of Esther.

4. See Amnon Shiloah, *The Musical Tradition of Iraqi Jews* (Or Yehuda: The Babylonian Jewry Heritage Center, The Institute for Research on Iraqi Jewry, 1983); Yeheskel Kojaman, *The Maqam Music Tradition of Iraq* (London: Y. Kojaman, 2001); Esther Warkov, "Revitalization of Iraqi-Jewish Instrumental Tradition in the Persistent Centrality of an Outsider Tradition," *Asian Music* 17, no. 2 (1986): 9–31; and Dafna Dori, *The Brothers Al-Kuwaity and the Iraqi Song 1930–1950* (Uppsala: Uppsala University Publication, 2022).

5. See Zvi Zohar, *Rabbinic Creativity in the Modern Middle East* (London: Bloomsbury, 2013), 369.

6. See Haviva Pedaya, "Mizraḥ hu mizraḥ" (East is East) (*Maʿariv*, 2005), https://www.mako rrishon.co.il/nrg/online/1/ART/989/500.html.

7. See Daniel J. Elazar, *The Other Jews: The Sephardim Today* (New York: Basic Books, 1989); and Daniel J. Elazar, "Can Sephardic Judaism Be Reconstructed?," *Judaism* 41, no. 3 (1992): 217–228; Zohar, *Rabbinic Creativity*; and Yaron Harel, *Intrigue and Revolution: Chief Rabbis in Aleppo, Baghdad, and Damascus, 1774–1914* (Oxford: Littman Library of Jewish Civilization, 2015).

8. The most notable work on Ḥakham Abdallah ben Abraham Somekh was that of Abraham Ben-Jacob, *Toledot ha-Rav ʿAbdallah Somekh* [The history of Rabbi Abdallah Somekh] (Jerusalem: Matmon Press, 1949); and Zvi Zohar, "Yaḥaso shel ha-Rav ʿAbdallah Somekh le-temurot ha-meʾah ha-teshʿa ʿesreh ka-mishtaķef bi-yetsirato ha-hilkhatit" [Rabbi Abdallah Somekh's approach towards changes in the nineteenth century as reflected in his halakhic writings], *Peʿamim: Studies in Oriental Jewry* 36 (1988): 89–107. On Ḥakham Joseph Ḥayyim, Ben-Jacob, *ha-Rav Yosef Ḥayyim*, and Ben-Jacob, *Otsar ha-shirim*; Norman A. Stillman, *Sephardi Religious Responses to Modernity* (Luxembourg: Harwood Academic Publishers, 1995); and Shaul Regev, "Ha-derashot shel Rabbi Yosef Ḥayyim— Ben Ish Ḥay" [The sermons of Rabbi Joseph Ḥayyim—*Ben ish ḥay*], in *Rabbi Joseph Ḥayyim: Chapters of Research and Exploration on the Ninetieth Anniversary of His Death*, ed. Zvi Yehudah (Or Yehudah: The Babylonian Jewry Heritage Center, Research Institute of Babylonian Jewry, 1999), 11–16.

9. On his halakhah and leadership, see Zvi Zohar, *He'iru peney ha-mizraḥ* [The luminous face of the East] (Tel Aviv: Hakibbutz Hameuchad, 2001); and Harel, *Intrigue and Revolution*. On his Kabbalah, see Jonathan Meir, "Toward the Popularization of Kabbalah: R. Joseph Ḥayyim of Baghdad and the Kabbalists of Jerusalem," *Modern Judaism* 33, no. 2 (2013): 148–172. On the literary aspects of his work, see Itamar Drori, "Encoding and Decoding Secret Signs in the Stories of Rabbi Joseph Hayyim of Baghdad," *Journal of Jewish Studies* 71 (2020): 345–364; and Rivka Kadosh, *Sipurey ha-Rav Yosef Ḥayyim mi-Bagdad: Hebeṭim*

po'etiyyim ide'im ve-ḥevratiyyim [The literary writings of Rabbi Joseph Ḥayyim of Baghdad: Poetic and socio-ideological aspects] (Ramat Gan: Bar-Ilan University, 2021). On his approach to women, see Nahem Ilan, "Ḳanun al-nisa' (Ḥoḳ ha-nashim): ḥiburo ha-yaḥid shel ha-Rav Yosef Ḥayyim le-nashim be-'Arvit-yehudit" [Ḳanun al nisa (The law for women): Rabbi Joseph Ḥayyim's only work for women in Judeo-Arabic], *Pe'amim: Studies in Oriental Jewry* 109 (2006): 33–57.

10. See Ben-Jacob, *Ha-Rav Yosef Ḥayyim*, and Ben-Jacob, *Otsar ha-shirim*.

11. See Max Weber, *On Charisma and Institutions Building* (Chicago: University of Chicago Press, 1968), 28.

12. See, for example, Ḥakham Joseph Ḥayyim, *Ben ish ḥay halakhot* (Baghdad: n.p., 1904) Year 1, *va-Yeshev, Hilkhot Ḥanukkah, siman* 13, and *siman* 18.

13. See the introduction to *Rav pe'alim* (Baghdad: n.p., 1901–1912), vol. 1.

14. See, for example, the introduction to *Ben ish ḥay halakhot*.

15. Ibid.

16. On the sermons, see Ḥakham Joseph Ḥayyim, *Ben ish ḥayil* [The brave man], 2 vols. (Jerusalem: n.p., 1901–1909), vol. 2, *Petiḥah* 2. On his books and his halakhic answers, see the introduction to *Rav pe'alim*, vol. 1.

17. See, for example, the introduction to *Ben ish ḥay halakhot*.

18. In the introduction to *Ben ish ḥay halakhot*, Ḥakham Joseph Ḥayyim states clearly that the most important message in a sermon, i.e., the halakhic one, must be succinct because the audience does not wish to hear too much about it.

19. See the introduction to *Imrey binah* (Jerusalem: n.p., 1904), part 1.

20. See, for example, *Ben ish ḥay halakhot*, Year 1, *va-Yishlaḥ, siman* 3.

21. Ibid., Year 2, *va-Yira, siman* 2.

22. See, for example, *Rav pe'alim*, vol. 2, *Oraḥ ḥayyim, she'elah* 25.

23. See, for example, *Ben ish ḥay halakhot*, Year 2, *va-Yira, siman* 2; ibid., *Toledot, siman* 3; ibid., Year 1, *Devarim, siman* 5, respectively.

24. Ibid., Year 1, *Bo, siman* 13.

25. Meir Benayahu, "Rabbi Yisrael Najara" [Rabbi Israel Najara], *Asufot* 4 (1990): 203–284, 229.

26. *Rav pe'alim*, vol. 2, *Sod yesharim, she'elah* 9.

27. *Even shelemah*, 27a.

28. *Ben ish ḥay halakhot*, Year 1, *va-Yigash, siman* 14.

29. *Even shelemah*, 6a.

30. Ibid., 26b.

31. Ibid.

32. Ibid., 27a–28b.

33. Ibid., 5a. See the quotation in this chapter's title.

34. Ibid., 5a and 5b.

35. See, for example, *Rav pe'alim*, vol. 1, *Yoreh de'ah, she'elah* 56.

36. *Ben ish ḥay halakhot*, Year 1, *va-Yigash, siman* 14, and *siman* 15.

37. Ibid., *siman* 14.

38. See, for example, ibid., Year 2, *va-Yira, siman* 1, and *siman* 2.

39. See, for example, *Even shelemah*, 5b, and *Ben ish ḥay halakhot*, Year 1, *va-Yigash, siman* 15.

40. For the symbolic meaning of this manner of rendition, see *Ben ish ḥay halakhot*, Year 2, *va-Yira, siman* 1, and *siman* 2.

41. *Even shelemah*, 15a and 15b.

42. Ibid., 6a.

43. Tsaleḥ ben Rabbi Yaʿaḳov Mantsur, ed., *Sefer shirim tehilat-yesharim ha-shalem, pizmonim, baḳashot ve-tishbaḥot* [The complete book of songs, in praise of the righteous songs, supplications, and praises] (Jerusalem: Tsaleḥ ben Rabbi Yaʿaḳov Mantsur, 1954).

44. Each poem in the 1954 *Miṣḥaf* is coded here in the following form: M(x;y), whereby the letter "M" is an abbreviation for the word "miṣḥaf," "x" denotes the page number on which the poem appears, and "y" the poem number. Both "x" and "y" are changed from Hebrew letters to numbers.

45. In Aramaic M(108;150); in Judeo-Arabic: M(18;14), which is also written in Hebrew, and M(79;112), M(80;113), and M(81;114).

46. Examples of such warm messages spelled out in acrostics are "I shall bless God," M(91;126); "Love (and) companionship," M(168;235); and "Joy," M(214;320).

47. E.g., M(91;126), M(105;146), M(129;175), M(148;205), M(177;250), M(177;251), and M(178;252).

48. A variation of Isaiah 42:10; and Psalms 33:3, 40:4, 96:1, 98:1, 144: 9, and 149:1.

49. See, for example, M(63;89), M(118;161), and M(125;169).

50. See, for example, M(18;14), which is the only baḳashah written by Ḥakham Joseph Ḥayyim that appears in this collection, and M(132;181).

51. See, for example, the forefathers Abraham and Jacob M(64;90) and King David M(78;111).

52. See, for example, the prophet Elijah M(77;109) and Rabbi Shimon bar Yoḥai M(113;156).

53. See, for example, the forefathers/matriarchs of the Nation, Abraham, Isaac, and Jacob M(136; 186), and Rachel M(170;238). The prophets Moses M(136;186), Elijah M(77;110), Ezekiel M(116;159), and Ezra M(117;160). Holy figures such as Aaron, Joseph, and King David M(136;186).

54. See, for example, Joseph M(66;95) and M(132;181).

55. Ḥakham Joseph Ḥayyim's interest in Kabbalah and Jewish mysticism might explain his interest in Najara's songs, despite the fact that not much is known about Najara's involvement in these fields. According to *Sefer toledot ha-Ari* (The chronicles of the Ari), a source of uncertain provenance, Najara was in close contact with the Ari, who appreciated Najara's musical traits and attributed a highly kabbalistic power to his talent. The Ari guided Najara, through one of his disciples, with particular advice on how to apply this power and musical talent in a righteous way. See also Meir Benayahu, *Toledot ha-Ari* [The chronicles of the Ari] (Jerusalem: The Ben-Zvi Institute of Yad Izhak Ben-Zvi and the Hebrew University of Jerusalem, 1967), 230.

56. This occasion originally had no religious significance, and the Talmud does not describe any celebration or liturgical observance associated with the fifteenth of Shevat (the eleventh month in the Jewish calendar). It is only since the seventeenth century, and partly under the influence of the kabbalists of Safed, who saw a strong affinity between mankind and trees, that this special celebration emerged. In this month, marking the approaching end of winter in the Land of Israel, it is celebrated among Jewish communities of the Middle East and North Africa with the eating of fifteen different fruits, accompanied by reading various passages from the Bible, the Talmud, and the Zohar.

57. Psalm 96:12.

58. The capital letter in each hemistich indicates its position in the rhyming scheme.

59. A variation of a phrase in the Kedushah (Holiness), which is one of the most important parts of the liturgy. It appears in the *Musaf* prayer for Jewish festivals and the Sabbath that follows the morning prayer, *Shaḥarit*.

60. A version of Psalm 96:1.
61. Joshua 3:10; Hosea 2:1; and Psalm 84:3.
62. Psalm 68:5.
63. From *Birekat bore nefashot rabot* (Benediction of the creator of many souls), which is the *Berakhah aḥaronah* (Final benediction [over food]) recited after eating a meal that does not include food made with dough (bread and cakes), wine, or the seven agricultural products that the Land of Israel was blessed with.
64. From *Birekat ha-ilanot* (Benediction of the trees), recited during the month of Nisan when the first bloom of the trees appears.
65. From *Birekat ha-shanim* (Benediction of the years), which is the ninth blessing in the ʿAmidah prayer, asking God for a successful livelihood and bountiful crops and also, in winter, for rain. This prayer is recited a few times every day.
66. Babylonian Talmud, Pesaḥim, 49a.
67. Isaiah 24:15.
68. The Hebrew word *uzemirim* can be interpret either as twigs, the plural form of *zemorah* (Numbers 13:23), or as zemiroth (Isaiah 24:17) referring to the singing of the righteous.
69. A variation of Jeremiah 3:22.
70. Malachi 3:24.
71. It appears in the Torah portion *be-Shalaḥ* that is read on *Shabbat shirah* (The Sabbath of song), which is the Sabbath close to Tu Bi-Shevat.
72. Deuteronomy 8:8. Not including wheat and barley.
73. The word *shovavim* also constitutes an acronym of the first six portions of Exodus that are read every Sabbath, during this period.
74. The most prominent renditions of the song, known today are the Babylonian melody, performed by Cantor Mosheh Ḥabushah (2016), https://youtu.be/-kMfqFCCc4Y and by Mordekhay and Malʾakhi Yitshar, May 25, 2020, YouTube video, https://youtu.be/hallgOP_BN4; the Yemenite melody, performed by Cantor Yitshak Nahari (n.d.), https://web.nli.org.il/sites/nlis/he/Song/Pages/song.aspx?songid=133#6,58,7233,459; and a new Western melody, composed and sung by Yehudah Kadari, November 21, 2011, YouTube video, https://youtu.be/tPiMrrHSkAU.
75. See Harel, *Intrigue and Revolution*, 341.
76. For this process in the Middle Eastern Muslim society, and the completely different process in Jewish communities in Europe, see Zohar, *Rabbinic Creativity*, 357.
77. Eighty years after his departure, in the new State of Israel, Rabbi Ovadiah Yosef also encourages his followers who originated in Muslim countries to sing paraliturgical songs as a means of restoring their Jewish identity and heritage, which had been marginalized and undermined in Israel for many years.

Select Bibliography

Ben-Jacob, Abraham. *A History of the Jews in Iraq from the End of the Gaonic Period (1038 CE) to the Present Time /* יהודי בבל מסוף תקופת הגאונים עד ימינו. Jerusalem: The Ben-Zvi Institute of Yad Izhak Ben-Zvi and the Hebrew University of Jerusalem, 1965.

Deshen, Shlomo. "Baghdad Jewry in Late Ottoman Times: The Emergence of Social Classes and of Secularism." *AJS Review* 19, no. 1 (1994): 19–44.

Deshen, Shlomo, and Walter P. Zenner, eds. *Jewish Societies in the Middle East: Community, Culture and Authority.* Washington, DC: University Press of America, 1982.

Kligman, Mark L. *Maqām and Liturgy: Ritual, Music, and Aesthetics of Syrian Jews in Brooklyn.* Detroit: Wayne State University Press, 2009.

Leon, Nisim. "Mi-Masoret ʿadatit ketanah le-masoret datit gedolah: Ha-sipur ha-dati shel yehudey ʿIraḳ be-Yisrael." [From communal tradition to a large religious tradition: The religious story of Iraqi Jews in Israel]. *Israel* 17 (2010): 211–237.

Regev, Shaul. "Hanhagot u-minhagim she-hidesh ha-Rav Yosef Ḥayyim be-Bavel: Beyin halakhah le-Kabbalah" [Practices and customs ruled by Rabbi Joseph Ḥayyim in Babylon: Between halakhah and Kabbalah]. In *Ḥalamish Le-maʿayno Mayim: Studies in Kabbalah, Halakhah, Customs and Thought, Presented to Professor Ḥalamish,* edited by Avi Elkayam and Haviva Pedaya, 516–541. Jerusalem: Karmel Press, 2016.

Rosenfeld-Hadad, Merav. *Judaism and Islam One God One Music: The History of Jewish Paraliturgical Song in the Context of Arabo-Islamic Culture as Revealed in Its Jewish Babylonian Sources.* Leiden: Brill, 2019.

Rosenfeld-Hadad, Merav. "*Misḥaf al-Shbaḥot*: The Holy Book of Praises of the Babylonian Jews One Thousand Years of Cultural Harmony between Judaism and Islam." In *The Convergence of Judaism and Islam: Religious, Scientific, and Cultural Dimensions,* edited by Michael M. Laskier and Yaacov Lev, 241–271. Gainesville: University Press of Florida, 2011.

Rosenfeld-Hadad, Merav. "'There on the Poplars [Arabs] We Hung Up [Rely On] Our Lyres [Jewish Music]': Rabbi ʿOvadyah Joseph's Halakhic Rulings on Arabic Music." In *Muslim-Jewish Relations in Past and Present: A Kaleidoscopic View,* edited by Yousef Meri, 172–205. Leiden: Brill Academic Publishers, 2017.

Rotman, David. "'Kakh nivra'ti': nashim u-migdar be-sipurey ha-Rav Yoseph Ḥayyim mi-Bagdad." ["This is how I was created": Women and gender in Rabbi Joseph Ḥayyim of Baghdad's sorties]. *Mikan* 15 (2015): 669–700.

Seroussi, Edwin. "Rabbi Yisra'el Najara: Meʿatsev zimrat ha-ḳodesh aḥarey gerush sefarad." [Rabbi Israel Najara: Molder of Hebrew sacred singing after the expulsion from Spain]. *Asufot* 4 (1990): 285–310.

Shabat, M. Mosheh, and Yaʿaḳov Zamir. *Yeshivot Bagdad hithavutan ve-hashpaʿatan le-dorot* [Rabbinic academies in Baghdad, their formation and long-lasting impact]. 2 vols. Jerusalem: self-published, 2016 and 2019.

PART II

CITY—עיר

5

JEWISH REFUGEES FROM THE NAZI STATE IN SHANGHAI, 1938–1949

SOPHIE FETTHAUER
TRANSLATED BY TINA FRÜHAUF

SHANGHAI was politically, socially, and culturally one of the most challenging cities for Jews seeking refuge from Nazi persecution. Since the mid-nineteenth century a treaty port, the metropolis with its predominantly Chinese population had long been dominated by Great Britain, the United States, and France in the International Settlement and the French Concession. From 1937, Japan, the occupying power, was in charge, first in the suburbs and from the end of 1941 in the entire city. In addition, complicated power relations marked by inner-Chinese conflicts between nationalists and communists as well as mafia-like gangs, overpopulation, wartime destruction, precarious working conditions, and a strenuous climate made Shanghai a difficult place for exiles from Central Europe, also in terms of housing, care, and health. The only advantage was that the refugees were allowed to work.

In early 1940 the pianist Hans Baer published his article "10 Monate juedische Musik in Shanghai" in the German-language exile newspaper *Shanghai Jewish Chronicle* in which he reported on the musical activities of the refugees during the first months of their stay in Shanghai. He wrote that experiences in the city weighed heavier and characterized Shanghai as a modern Babel—referring both to the origin myth in Genesis meant to explain why the world's peoples speak different languages, and to the idea that it was the Babylonian exile that gave rise to a Jewish identity in the first place.[1] Baer went on to explain that, upon arrival, the impoverished refugees were only aware that they had to create a new existence for themselves on this foreign soil. Some occupational groups had succeeded in this, others had not. Detailing the situation of the musicians, he asserted that in Shanghai, less than a year was enough to write history, the history of Jewish art activities. Baer then provided information on the organization of the cultural life as well as on ensembles founded by the refugees and professional integration in the established music institutions. He concluded: "We Jewish artists have come to Shanghai, bringing here our skills and energy. We will continue to give our best to this city, its people and its institutions, to which we owe much, and thus consolidate the recognition of Jewish musicians as a group in Shanghai!"[2]

Baer equated the "Jewish music" mentioned in the title of his article quite naturally with all the refugees' musical activity of the previous months. Given his artistic aspiration, this excluded, however, popular music performed in the city's entertainment venues. That he did not cite his own ambitions as a composer and interpreter of specifically "Jewish music," which he had presented to the public at performances at the American Women's Club in 1939, seems ambiguous, however.[3] Perhaps he did not want to be self-referential. It even seems that he was not quite as certain of "Jewish music"; other musical identifications, especially the Classical-Romantic music tradition of Europe, were ultimately more important to him.

Hans Baer was not the only refugee in Shanghai who touched on the question of Jewish music as an author, composer, and performer. This was a subject that would continuously play a role in the musical life of the refugees. The subject of Jewish music thus arises in concert programs and concert reviews, in newspaper articles written by music critics who discussed facets of the same in the German-speaking exile press from a historical or cultural-political perspective. These publications hardly provide a coherent discourse on the subject; rather, they are isolated statements made at different times and on different occasions. Nevertheless, they allow for a full picture to emerge.

Only fragments of the original materials documenting the musical life of the Nazi refugees in Shanghai are still available today. They can be found scattered all over the world in libraries, archives, and private collections, some of which have been brought together in special Shanghai collections.[4] For some topics there is a considerable quantity and depth of sources, for others not. At least in phases, the newspapers and journals published in higher circulation are well preserved, but only selected concert programs have survived. Correspondence of organizers, artists, and organizations is rarely available. In addition, information on classical, popular, and religious music events can be found in all kinds of often unpublished autobiographical reports, interviews with contemporary witnesses, and private collections. Scattered through the sources are also indications of works of Jewish music composed in Shanghai; autographs, however, can only be found in some instances.

Historical research on Shanghai has considerable scope and includes the cultural life of the refugees from Nazi Germany. Initial research on the musical activities of the refugees mainly relied on contemporary reports from Shanghai.[5] Articles by some of Baer's colleagues, like Erwin Felber, Martin Hausdorff, and Henry Margolinski, who primarily tried to prove that the refugees had asserted themselves in Shanghai and that they had been able to maintain their cultural level, served as a reference.[6] Over time, works with more far-reaching scientific questions have emerged. Beginning in the 1980s, Chinese scholars have shown an interest in the relations between the refugees and the Chinese musical world. Buzeng Xu, for example, has focused on the influence of music educators, a theme that resurfaced in Christian Utz's and Hartmut Krones' writings on Wolfgang Fraenkel and Julius Schloß as representatives of musical modernism in Shanghai. Other studies are more inward-looking, that is, they concentrate on the refugee community itself and its cultural life. With regard to drama and operetta, Michael Philipp found that these genres served the refugees primarily for the entertainment and self-assurance of German-Austrian culture, while political concerns hardly played any role. In this context, he also refers to the demarcation of the Western-assimilated refugees from the Yiddish theater of the Eastern European Jewish refugees. Yvonne Liao has studied the popular music culture in the bars of the Hongkou Ghetto, interpreting it as an expression of an imagined Vienna;[7] she overlooked the fact that the entertainment culture of the Shanghai refugees also corresponded with other regional, namely Berlin, as well as Yiddish and Chinese practices, and that this process was already underway since the arrival of the refugees in Shanghai 1938/39. In several surveys, Tang Yating has examined the different facets of musical life from concerts and stage productions to popular music events and activities of cantors, arguing that music was an important factor in maintaining the cultural identity of the refugees in the confines of Shanghai exile, but that the commonality of being Jewish was eclipsed by the heterogeneous origins of the refugees from Germany, Austria, Poland, and so on. The musical life of the Jewish refugees in Shanghai has thus been explored from various perspectives, yet the question of a specifically *Jewish* music has not played a central role thus far.

A COMMUNITY OF REFUGEES

When Hans Baer spoke in his aforementioned article of "we," he was referring to the circa 18,000 mostly Jewish refugees who had fled the Nazi regime's territory for Shanghai in the preceding months in the face of intensified anti-Jewish measures. After immigration controls had been suspended as a result of the war between Japan and China in 1937, most of them had used the opportunity to enter Shanghai without passport checks and visas until free access ended in mid-1939 with the introduction of a restrictive permit system and the beginning of the Second World War in Europe, which allowed only few refugees to enter the city until the travel route via Siberia closed with Germany's invasion of the Soviet Union in summer 1941.[8] Baer could not yet have known anything about the circa 900 Polish Jewish refugees who would escape the German occupation of Poland and only arrive in Shanghai via Japan in autumn 1941.[9]

Unlike other places of exile, researchers, especially from China, often approach the subject of the migration from the Nazi state to Shanghai as a refugee rather than an exile issue.[10] The reason is that hardly any of the refugees assumed that Shanghai could be a permanent place of residence. The opportunity to flee to Shanghai resulted from the coincidental timing of the intensification of persecution measures and the suspension of immigration controls in Shanghai in 1938. Shanghai offered a sudden opportunity for rescue, but it was not a desired destination. Germany, after all, continued to exert control over the refugees through the Consulate General and a loyal long-extant German community.[11] Further, during the Japanese occupation, Jews assumed the status of "stateless refugees,"[12] and in the postwar period they were considered "Displaced Persons," which meant that they were still in the "wrong place." Thus, Shanghai always remained a temporary solution, a kind of *Wartesaal* (waiting room).

There are probably few communities of refugees that have been documented as precisely as the one in Shanghai. One reason for this is that the refugees lived continually in the city for several years as there were few opportunities to escape to other countries, Chinese cities, or even the outskirts of Shanghai due to the war and strict immigration regulations in other places. It was not until the postwar period that refugees were able to leave the city. With few exceptions, the endpoint of Shanghai's exile was the communists' seizure of power in 1949. Another reason lies in the veritable refugee quarter created in the Hongkou district. In 1943 the Japanese occupiers proclaimed a part of this district as "designated area." In this so-called Hongkou Ghetto, they separated the stateless refugees, thus further increasing their concentration in a few streets of Hongkou. Even refugees who had lived in other areas had to live in the district until the end of the Pacific War. The ghetto, which was also inhabited by many Chinese, was not bounded by a wall. But there were exit controls and the refugees could only leave it with special passes that had to be applied for in advance.[13]

Based on the shared experience of Nazi persecution and the resulting flight, the Shanghai refugee community is thus clearly defined in terms of space and time. Apart from that, their unity had limits. From data collected over time by the German Consulate General, municipal authorities, aid organizations, or for the purpose of compiling address books, it is clear that the refugees were quite heterogeneous in composition.[14] As previously mentioned, they had different nationalities. Most had German passports, but many had been Austrians until the *Anschluss* in 1938. There were also other European citizens and stateless persons. Indeed, citizenship, which was forcibly withdrawn from the refugees by the German Reich in 1941, said little about their heritage. Some of the refugees, like the Jewish populations of Germany and Austria in general,[15] had a family history in eastern Europe. This resulted in cultural differences between those who had been acculturated into Western Europe and those who had grown up more or less influenced by the Yiddish culture of eastern Europe.

Differences also existed in religious practice. Apart from the ones who were not religious or converted to Christianity, or who had gone into exile as non-Jewish spouses, the refugees were divided between those who followed liberal Judaism and those who adhered to more traditional practices. Despite some of the refugees' connections to eastern Europe, few of them were Orthodox, discounting, of course, those who arrived directly from occupied Poland in 1941. Politically, the refugees were largely indifferent; the group of refugees active in left-wing politics was rather small. Professionally, however, they represented all areas from trade and crafts to academic and artistic occupations. As a result of the aid organizations' information policy, however, doctors and musicians were overrepresented.[16] There was also an imbalance in gender distribution, with a greater number of men refugees and an even stronger disparity among musicians.[17]

In 1938 officials, relief organizations, and the press quickly noticed that the number of refugees from the Nazi state in Shanghai was steadily increasing and that a new community was emerging. Mainly settling in Hongkou, the newcomers soon became visible in the city not only through business activities of all kinds, but also quite obviously through musical performances. Music, in the refugees' self-image and reinforced by the large number of musicians, played an important role in the formation of the refugee community. It marked who the refugees were and where they came from, created opportunities for contact, and enabled exchange with the long-established population groups and their musicians. At the same time, it served as a means of demarcation, preservation, and remembrance. In the following, this chapter will highlight the role Jewishness played in this process, at least to some extent.

THE MUSICAL LIFE OF THE REFUGEES IN SHANGHAI

When the refugees arrived in Shanghai in 1938/39, they found an already wide variety of musical activities. The traditional music of the Chinese population remained largely inaccessible to them, but in the decades before, the foreigners living in the city had built a Western-style musical life that offered job opportunities. In classical music, these included the Shanghai Municipal Orchestra; private (mainly Russian) opera, operetta, and ballet ensembles; British, French, German, and Yiddish amateur theater groups; several choirs; and other instrumental ensembles, including a number of military bands. Shanghai also had a large entertainment sector ranging from large ballrooms, cabarets, and nightclubs to smaller restaurants, cafes, and bars where live music accompanied dinner, dance, and floor shows. The musical life was driven by a few hundred musicians, among them many Russians, Filipinos, Americans, all kinds of touring musicians, and increasingly also Chinese. Since there was no musicians' union to prevent newcomers from taking up employment, the opportunities for swift integration into the cultural landscape of Shanghai were comparatively good. In both the classical and popular sectors, musicians from the refugee community found permanent work and public recognition.

With more than 450 people, musicians were overrepresented within the refugee community, and their number was therefore too large to be fully absorbed by the already established Shanghai music life. In the refugee district of Hongkou, the establishment of bars, cafés, stores, workshops, and public facilities for education, religion, and sports subsequently gave rise to an independent music and theater life. Live music was regularly played in cafés and bars founded by the refugees. In addition, evenings of diverse entertainment (with music, theater sketches, recitations, and dance), concerts of classical music, theater and operetta performances as well as performances by the cantors in synagogue and in concert were established. Some of these were organized in the refugee shelters, but as early as spring 1939 efforts were made by some musicians, actors, and journalists to create a central cultural association. The Artist Club and, from 1940 on, the European Jewish Artist Society tried to centralize cultural activities, following the model of the Jewish Culture League, first mainly in the field of theater, later with greater focus on music through the creation of ensembles and a visitors' organization. Until 1941, events were held more or less regularly. Nevertheless, they never fulfilled the claim of comprehensiveness formulated in 1939/40. Alfred Dreifuß (1902–1993), for example, had called for the Artist Club to have its own theater building, stage ensemble, orchestra, and choir. Besides the theater and operetta some people even had ambitions to organize opera productions. Later on, there was too little audience for regular events, and there were no permanent subsidies or support from patrons to maintain them.[18] In addition, there was competition from privately run ensembles and artistic initiatives. During the Japanese occupation the events of the European Jewish Artist Society were further reduced and then ended in 1946, when the refugee community began to disintegrate through further migration and remigration.

Shanghai was an "exile of the little people,"[19] as those who had money, rank, and name could choose other places of refuge.[20] For all their individual qualities, the musicians who fled to Shanghai were essentially those without pronounced careers and special celebrity status. They played for an equally average audience. Their repertoire was therefore predominantly mainstream. This applied to classical concerts as well as to the popular music sector and religious music practices. In concert, whether in Hongkou, the International Settlement, or the French Concession, the core repertoire of classical music programs ranged from Bach and Händel to Mozart, Beethoven, Schubert, Mendelssohn Bartholdy, and Schumann to Brahms, Wagner, Tchaikovsky, Dvořák, Verdi, and Puccini. Only seldom did works by contemporaries such as Richard Strauss, Sergei Rachmaninov, Ernst Toch, or Erich Wolfgang Korngold appear on the program, or Yiddish and cantorial song. Likewise, operetta was marked by the standard repertoire of German and Austrian stages, for example by works of Johann Strauß, Emmerich Kálmán, and Franz Lehár. In the venues of Hongkou, entertainment music was in demand, which included a broad repertoire ranging from contemporaneous hits, operetta melodies, older dances and marches to popular classical works. Yiddish song repertoire was also partly included. In the entertainment establishments in the city center, the musicians also performed salon-like and classical repertoire. There, American swing music, some of which influenced by Chinese and Japanese musical elements, was mainly in demand and had to be adapted by the newcomers.[21] In classical music, however, influences of Chinese music were limited. Wolfgang Fraenkel and Julius Schloß wrote works for the concert hall in which they drew on Chinese poems and melodies, respectively, but these were never performed in Shanghai.[22]

In his aforementioned article about the musical activities of the refugees in Shanghai during their first ten months in the city, Hans Baer designated *all* repertoires played by the refugees in Shanghai as "Jewish." This, of course, bears the issue that it also and above all includes music composed by non-Jews. What he might have meant is the Jewish artistic activity, which he also referred to in the article, that is, the musical life of the Jewish refugees. Literally read, however, Baer's understanding of "Jewish music" could also be seen as an indication of the character of the refugee community as a *Jewish* refugee community. The Western European understanding of music, which the majority embraced, was an expression of the community's previous acculturation and thus an integral part of Jewish identity. This point of view was widespread, but it did not remain unchallenged.

In early 1940 the journalist Günther Lenhardt reported on the Artist Club in *Die Tribüne*, a journal launched by Heinz Petzall and Kurt Lewin in 1940, predicting that it would develop in roughly the same way as the Jewish Culture League in Germany. A varied theater schedule was expressly wished for, without limiting it to being Jewish. The refugees arrived in Shanghai with the understanding that they "had come from countries that had a high level of art and culture, and in many cases had had an epoch-making effect on the world in these areas." One need not be "ashamed of this tradition because we are bringing to Shanghai something that it has never had before."[23] The statement was, of course, an exaggeration. It not only shows that the ambiguous character of the Jewish Culture League and the fact that Jews in Germany were increasingly *not* allowed to perform "German" culture were ignored, but also suggests that the refugees felt culturally superior even to the foreign societies in Shanghai. Lenhardt made his statement in the course of a controversy that flared up after Alfred Dreifuß, secretary of the Artist Club and former employee of the Berlin Jewish Culture League, had argued in a lecture on the establishment of a cultural life in Hongkou, that the Artist Club's theater program must be based primarily on German cultural achievements. Other representatives of the Artist Club, however, preferred to emphasize Jewish, specifically Yiddish, culture.[24] The Jewish Culture League had carried out similar debates about Yiddish culture.[25] Dreifuß resigned from his post as a result of the dispute, only to be reinstated shortly thereafter at the European Jewish Artist Society, which was founded as the successor organization to the Artist Club.

The European Jewish Artist Society hardly differed from its predecessor organization in its programming. Yiddish songs played an occasional role during diverse entertainment evenings organized by the society; and also a Hanukkah singspiel entitled *Jeder trägt sein Pinkerl* was successfully brought to the stage. Significantly, it was based on a selection of music by Leo Fall (composer of the title song "Jeder trägt sein Pinkerl" from the operetta *Der Fidele Bauer*), Georges Bizet, Jacques Offenbach, and Ruggero Leoncavallo, that is, Jewish and non-Jewish composers. The piece thus again underlined the refugees' will to preserve the musical culture they had lived with in Germany and Austria.[26] Overall, the European Jewish Artist Society focused on repertoires that had made an impact on the stages of German-speaking Europe, as well as on classical music concerts. When the society had to limit its activities in 1941 for lack of funding, the focus shifted to the organization of chamber music concerts as well as opera and operetta evenings.[27]

The largest event organized by the European Jewish Artist Society during the existence of the ghetto was a guest performance by the Shanghai Philharmonic Orchestra (former Shanghai Municipal Orchestra), which had come under the administration of the Japanese and was conducted by Henry Margolinski (1902–1980) as a charity concert in Hongkou in 1944. The repertoire selection for the concert had a programmatic character, featuring Symphony No. 5 by Ludwig van Beethoven, the Overture to *Oberon* by Carl Maria von Weber, the Violin Concerto op. 64 by Felix Mendelssohn Bartholdy with the soloist Ferdinand Adler, the symphonic poem *Má vlast* by Bedřich Smetana, and the Prelude to the *Meistersinger von Nürnberg* by Richard Wagner. The selection certainly had something to do with feasibility in light of short rehearsal times (the orchestra had previously played all of these compositions), but it also hints at the musical understanding of the refugees.[28] The composers Beethoven, Weber, and Wagner stood for "German" culture. Wagner's anti-Semitism was deliberately ignored, and his performance made it clear that the refugees would not allow anybody to take this music away from them. Mendelssohn Bartholdy represented acculturation. As a Czech composer, Smetana stood for nationalism in music. The resemblance of *Má vlast* to the Zionist anthem "Hatikvah" was the only, admittedly quite covert, "Jewish" musical moment of the evening. Against the background of persecution and exile, such a concert program may seem paradoxical from today's perspective, but from the refugees' point of view it certainly was not—it reflected their European and Jewish background, which for them was not a contradiction.

The classical concert repertoire as well as operetta and well-known light music were dominant facets of the musical life of Shanghai's refugees, not only in terms of reassuring their own audience of where they came from, but also in terms of how the refugees presented themselves to the society in the city at large. The musical repertoires performed and heard by the refugees, however, reveal further facets that also have to do with their Jewish heritage.

"Jewish" Concert Music

Shanghai's musical life was strongly influenced by the cosmopolitan origin of its population. For instance, the international character of the Shanghai Municipal Council revealed itself in the Shanghai Municipal Orchestra, which was financed by the government of the International Settlement. The orchestra members came from various countries; the chief conductor Mario Paci and the concertmaster Arrigo Foa, for example, were from Italy, while at the same time Russian emigrants made up the majority.[29] Likewise, much of the orchestra's contemporary repertoire stemmed from composers of different countries. Further, it was shaped by grants and sheet music contributed by Italy, France, and Great Britain.[30] Performances often featured programs that emphasized national heritage.[31] Some people were critical of the orchestra's emphasis on the national aspect and even identified it as a kind of "obsession."[32]

The refugee musicians tried to integrate in such an environment with their own conceptions. This was mainly done through Classical and Romantic repertoires, which were perceived as universal and belonging to the whole world, and which hardly identified them as Germans or Austrians, and certainly not as Jews. Remarkably, Hans

Baer briefly tried a different approach in concerts at the American Women's Club. He was only one of a number of instrumentalists and singers from the circle of refugees who during the early days of exile were given the opportunity to introduce themselves to Shanghai audiences through the help of foreign circles. In April 1939 he gave his first performance, playing works by Chopin, Liszt, and Musorgsky, as well as pieces from the early Baroque period and his own composition. His *Variations on a Palestinian Theme* did not go over well with the critic of the *North China Daily News*.[33] However, this did not stop Baer from giving an entire concert entitled *Jewish Music* in October 1939 under the auspices of the Ashkenazi Zionist Organization Kadimah and the sports club IRC Maccabi.[34] In addition to Yiddish and Hebrew songs, the program included piano pieces by Hans Baer, variations for piano and violin by Israel Brandmann, piano pieces on Yemenite themes by Eduard Moritz, and several short pieces by Joachim Stutschewsky and Shulamith Shafir.

Ossi Lewin was born in Boryslav (Galicia) and had been a resident of Vienna. He was the editor of the *Shanghai Jewish Chronicle*. As a member of the Kadimah, he was not impartial.[35] Thus he wrote that the concert had, in part, introduced the listeners "to a somewhat unfamiliar musical world of feelings." The Yiddish and Hebrew songs were not the pivotal moments of the program, but rather the pieces by those composers, "who consciously work on creating a music that is emotionally Jewish." Especially in the first part of the concert, "a path to a future country" emerged. These are not yet "immortal masterpieces," but this music clears "the path for the arrival of a purely Jewish art, and thus the composers could rightly be called pioneering." All this was unfamiliar to the audience, but Lewin hoped that something could come of it; only then would "the Jewish artist in Shanghai fulfill his special task."[36] The critic of the Jewish Community's newsletter, Albert Trum (1902–1988), was more skeptical. He, too, believed in the possibility of a modern "Jewish music," but he thought that the composers' Jewish heritage was insufficient, that their roots in the "homeland's soil" were missing. He stated that "a *national* Jewish music [emphasis in the original] does not yet exist and cannot yet exist, since the main prerequisite for this, the Jewish soil, is missing."[37] The comments of the critics indicate that the compositions had transferred cultural-political discourses to Shanghai, in this case the question of a Jewish national music or the development of a Jewish musical tradition in modern times. However, as in Europe, perhaps intensified by the experience of foreignness in Shanghai, the coupling of Jewish music to the "homeland" or "soil" created an involuntary connection to *völkisch* views.[38]

Ossi Lewin's hoped-for "path to a future country" never came to fruition in Shanghai. Hans Baer still often played at the American Women's Club, but subsequently the subject of "Jewish music" only surfaced occasionally, for example when he played an arrangement of Max Bruch's *Kol Nidrei* op. 47 and Niccolò Paganini's *Mosé-Fantasia* together with the cellist Mór Porgé (1888–ca. 1948).[39] Both works associate Jewishness by relying on related melodies and subjects, respectively. In the following years Baer only occasionally presented his own "Jewish" works. In a text written in 1949, he wrote about them as "the artistic expression of a Jew in the *galut*." But he also explained that he was not sure whether they were "really Jewish, truly characteristic";[40] above all, he considered them to be the result and expression of experiencing persecution. In his unpublished memoirs from 1950, these compositions, as well as their performance in Shanghai, received no mention. Apart from the simple exercise *March of the Chaluzim*, the compositions themselves have not survived in Baer's estate.[41]

During their time in Shanghai, refugees created all kinds of compositions that could be labeled "Jewish music." Most of them were vocal works written for special occasions and not as part of a large compositional work, for publishing or earning a profit. Some of them were based on texts in Hebrew and were intended for religious celebrations; others addressed Palestine, expressing hope for the establishment of a new Jewish state in the Middle East. These works did not give way to the development of a modern Jewish concert music. Even when in March 1946 the Shanghai refugees joined the "Jewish Music Week" organized in the United States with an event under the title *Purim Oneg Shabbat*, this issue was not in the foreground.[42] Besides different works by Ernest Bloch, Salomon Jadassohn, Emanuel Kirschner, Benno Peissachowitsch, Janot S. Roskin, Anton Rubinstein, and the non-Jewish composer Joseph Kromolicki, only one composition by a Shanghai refugee was included, the song *Shoshanas Jaacob* by the singer and cantor Max Warschauer (1911–1961).[43] Neither this piece nor Erwin Felber's introductory words to the event have been transmitted.

Music in line with Jewish nationalism or cultural Zionism did not shape the cultural life of the refugees. As such, it was obviously not suitable to represent the refugee community as a whole. Objectives that were wholeheartedly presented at the beginning of exile, for example by Ossi Lewin and Albert Trum, did not result in a tangible music style of their own or even in a school of composition. Indeed, those composers who developed a modernist musical style tended more to explore China's path into musical modernism. Wolfgang Fraenkel (1897–1983) and Julius Schloß (1902–1972), both trained in the music of Arnold Schoenberg and Alban Berg, respectively, pursued this direction as private teachers and professors at the Shanghai Conservatory.[44] Neither of them appears in the context of Jewish music. One written statement from Fraenkel has been preserved, which shows respect for China and the music of the country, but abstaining from any nationalistic insinuations.[45]

While "Jewish music" on the concert stage depended largely on individual interests, the situation of synagogue music was different. Here, the institutional framework played an important role with a view to the preservation of a familiar repertoire.

SYNAGOGUE MUSIC

Soon after their arrival, the refugees began to organize Jewish communal life and worship. They founded the Jüdische Kultusgemeinde, later renamed Jüdische Gemeinde, also known as Jewish Community of Central European Jews. From 1939 on they organized so-called Einheitsgottesdienste (unified services), which combined new and traditional styles of worship. When a section split off in 1940 and formed the Jüdisch-liberale

Gemeinde (Jewish-Liberal community) services were held separately.[46] Lutz Wachsner, a representative of the Jewish Community of Central European Jews, explained that the split sought to help avoid hurting "the feelings of those who think differently and not to open up a gulf where all forces must be united and not fragmented."[47] Nearly forty cantors were among the refugees, more than half of them involved in religious services held in the synagogues of the long-established Baghdadi-Sephardic and Russian-Ashkenazi communities, as well as in cinemas, schools, pubs, and the prayer rooms of the refugee shelters and at cemeteries (Figure 5.1).

Hardly any documentation exists that details the prayer-songs and other musical repertoire used in worship. Advertisements in the press only indicate that mixed choirs and a harmonium accompanied liberal services, and male choirs for traditional services.[48] Some indication of the repertoire can be found in concerts—titled *Jewish Concert* or *Jewish Evening*—organized by the Gemeinschaft Jüdischer Kantoren, also known as the Association of Jewish Precentors, which was founded in 1940.[49] On these occasions, the choir and soloists of the association presented works by key composers

FIGURE 5.1 The Shanghai refugee cantors at one of the Shanghai cemeteries, undated photograph. Werner von Boltenstern Shanghai Photograph and Negative Collection, no. 50, box 6d, LML_MS-050-005650001, Department of Archives and Special Collections, William H. Hannon Library, Loyola Marymount University, Los Angeles. Reproduced by permission.

of nineteenth-century synagogue music—Salomon Sulzer, Louis Lewandowski, and Samuel Naumbourg—and their contemporaries, such as Israel Meyer Japhet and Max Goldstein. In addition, there were works by younger generations of composers, including Samuel Alman, Jankel Dymont, Aron Friedmann, Mordechai Hershman, Leon Kornitzer, and Arno Nadel. The Shanghai cantors themselves also contributed to the repertoire, for example Jakob Kaufmann (1892–1977) with a setting of Psalm 121 and *Weschomru*[50] and Mendel Lewkowitz (1915–1976) with *J'he raawoh Kodomoch*.[51] Kaufmann's *Psalm 121: Esso enaj*, which is transmitted in a copy from a foreign hand, closely adheres to the features of liberal synagogue music.[52]

This repertoire, which followed the styles of Classical and Romantic music and chorale music of the church, emphasized the acculturation of many refugees or their ancestors. It was precisely for this reason that it soon aroused opposition (as it had previously in Central Europe) among Shanghai's long-established Orthodox Jewish congregations, culminating in a ruling of the Shanghai Beth Din in the summer of 1940. The ruling stated that the involvement of women and instrumentalists violated *halakhah*, and that anyone who attended such services acted against the sacred tradition and should never count on the help of the established Jewish congregations. The rabbinical court considered the playing of instruments in Jewish worship a violation of the Sabbath and also criticized the introduction of non-Jewish and ecclesiastic customs. It did not specifically justify the rejection of women singing in the synagogue. Finally, the judgment included the demand to refrain from such taboo-breaking in order to halt the inner decay of the Jewish community as a whole in view of the persecution of millions of Jews.[53] In reality, the Nazi refugees did not respond to this warning. They continued their religious services as usual, and there is no record of them being subjected to sanctions.

In addition to these threats, there was skepticism in the refugee's own ranks. The music critics Martin Hausdorff from Breslau and Erwin Felber from Vienna were less concerned with breaking taboos than with the question of the originality of synagogue music. In his article on the transformation of synagogue music, published in the *Gemeindeblatt der Jüdischen Kultusgemeinde* in September 1939 on the occasion of the High Holidays, Martin Hausdorff (1901–1956) described the process of acculturation of synagogue music in the Diaspora, starting with the destruction of the Jerusalem Temple. In his view, the acculturation amounted to a distortion of the original musical traditions. He soberly viewed the music of the European reformers of synagogue song as "compositions from the Romantic era" and thus not as old as Jewish worshippers presumed. He did not want to judge the value of this music, "because we all grew up with this music and we live with it."[54] This was true for Hausdorff himself, who had been previously the director of a synagogue choir in Breslau and was the leader of a men's choir in Shanghai during worship.

Music critic Erwin Felber (1885–1964), a trained lawyer and aspiring musicologist who had already studied non-European music and the question of Jewish music in Vienna,[55] gave a more detailed assessment in his article on Jewish music in ancient times, published in the *Shanghai Jewish Chronicle* in 1942. He described processes of acculturation in secular and religious spheres, and concluded the article by questioning whether the reformers of synagogue music had captured "the real spirit, the right style of the texts . . . Or did they make a well-intended attempt with stylistically completely unsuitable means, on an object completely unsuited for this purpose?"[56] Felber did not have an answer at this point in time. Only in 1943 did he continue his reflections in an article on the nature of synagogue song. He detailed the constants of synagogue song and its influence on the song of other religions as well as changes that had caused the desire for reforms and a return to the origins of synagogue music. He deemed Salomon Sulzer's attempts at reform to be "not the least impeccable from the standpoint of tradition and style," because "in his harmonic arrangement, which is rich in spite of all caution and almost concertante, [he approximated] the Protestant chorale." Referring to the widespread distribution of Sulzer's music and to the congregation who appreciated it, he then continued: "Apparently, the people, who often enough rely on healthy instinct, are not so much concerned with stylistic purity and piety of religious music, but rather with pomp and splendor, with the necessary musical solemn ceremony when confronting the very highest being."[57] Hausdorff and Felber agreed that reformed synagogue music, in the sense of a restored century-old tradition, had no claim to originality. In contrast to Hausdorff, who cited the socialization of worshippers as the reason for adhering to reformed synagogue music, Felber saw the cause in their (justified) desire for representation.

The refugee community, insofar as it was interested in religion, was clear in its standpoint and in its demarcation from Shanghai's Orthodox Jewish communities, that is, the Baghdadi-Sephardic, Russian-Ashkenazi, and, from 1941, the Polish. There were few points of contact; accordingly, the Association of Jewish Precentors had no Orthodox cantors among its members. During their years in Shanghai, the cantors held on to the synagogue music they knew and insisted on their assimilationist stance in the face of external attacks. That this music had little in common with the original music of the Jerusalem Temple was a contradiction that was integrated into the refugee community's claim to acculturation.

YIDDISH SONGS—ZIONIST SONG

Yiddish theater was the subject of fierce controversy in Shanghai exile. After the 1940 debate over the extent to which the Artist Club's program should be based on "German cultural assets," an attack followed by Alfred Dreifuß on Yiddish theater in general and on the Yiddish theater director and actor Boris Sapiro (1910–1960), who was active in Shanghai with the Sapiro-Bühne, in particular. In an article published in *Die Tribüne*, Dreifuß emphasized the antagonism between Western and Eastern Jewry and promulgated an allegedly higher cultural level of Western Jewry. He found Yiddish theater too popular and too deeply rooted in the private sphere or milieu of the shtetl.[58] A personal attack on Boris Sapiro, who had staged a play by the American writer Upton Sinclair in Yiddish translation, ensued. Because most of the actors and especially the audience did not speak Yiddish, Dreifuß considered such performances unnecessary. In return, he demanded a commitment to European culture, "to continue in the tradition of the great European cultural assets that we have inherited as our spiritual heritage, to be promoters of the youth who have something to say and to strive with all our senses to make us emigrants aware of our cultural obligations."[59] Sapiro did not allow himself to be intimidated and reacted with an open letter, written in a moderate tone.[60] He continued to appear in theater for some time and probably only had to give it up when financial aid from abroad ceased in the course of the Japanese occupation.

Such disputes have not been transmitted in connection with the performance of Yiddish songs. Perhaps this was due to the fact that in concert, Yiddish song was paired with other genres, a flexibility that full-length theater performance could not offer. Additionally, language played a greater role in the theater than in songs, which could captivate with their melodies alone. And while Yiddish song repertoire did not hold a dominant position in the musical life of the refugees, it nevertheless regularly surfaced in very different contexts, serving quite different functions. The Association of Jewish Precentors, for example, presented not only the aforementioned synagogue music in its *Jewish Concerts*. In addition to occasional instrumental performances, such as Henryk Wieniawski's Violin Concerto No. 2, Max Bruch's *Kol Nidrei*, and Hans Baer's *Lied "Schir"* for piano, the programs of all concerts of the Association of Jewish Precentors included Yiddish songs, for example by Israel Bacon, Julius Jaffe, Janot S. Roskin, and Sholom Secunda.[61] Presumably these songs attracted a much-needed wider audience and provided variety and entertainment—after all, the concerts served to improve the financial situation of the Association of Jewish Precentors. They also functioned as a kind of reinsurance of tradition. The press never critiqued the mix of different repertoires.

Yiddish songs also surfaced in other kinds of concerts. Nikolai Schwarz (1888–1946), who had had a career as an opera singer, combined opera repertoire with Yiddish and Hebrew songs as well as his own compositions in his solo recitals.[62] Hersch Friedmann (1898–1969), who had previously worked as an actor in Breslau, gave entire Yiddish song recitals together with Grete Kleiner and Lia Morgenstern.[63] Schwarz and Friedmann, who also served as cantors in Shanghai, both stemmed from eastern Europe; Schwarz was born in Riga and Friedmann in Zduńska Wola. Some of their concerts took place at the Shanghai Jewish Club, where they were probably geared primarily toward a Russian Jewish audience. The Yiddish song served there as a unifying moment between the Nazi refugees and the Jewish immigrants from Russia.

In Hongkou it was above all Raya Zomina (1914–2010) who provided a stage for Yiddish song. She had previously worked in Vilnius and Warsaw and was one of the Polish Jewish refugees who came to Shanghai in 1941. She appeared regularly with the Berlin cabaret artist and singer Herbert Zernik (1903–1972) and at the piano accompanied by Siegfried Sonnenschein (1909–1980) from Dresden in Hongkou's bars, advertised as "Die zwei 'Z.'" The duo soon experienced a sort of musical convergence: While Zomina began to perform non-Yiddish repertoire, Zernik tried his hand at Yiddish songs—first as a duet, later individually. The critics, who were normally full of praise for Zomina and Zernik and, like Alfred Kahn (1902–1959), saw in Zomina the "herald of Jewish suffering and Jewish joy,"[64] found this switching back and forth between eastern and western European repertoires somewhat incongruous: "Both artists," so Ludwig Schaefer, "should not forget the field in which they have achieved their immense popularity."[65]

In the postwar period, further signs of convergences emerged (and were critically perceived). Thus it became fashionable to teach children Yiddish songs, which the Polish actor Moshe Elbaum found questionable in view of the teachers' lack of Yiddish.[66] Alfred Dreifuß meanwhile accepted Yiddish on the theater stage, but thought it should not be mixed with the German language,[67] and the Yiddish actress Rose Shoshano, who fled from Poland to Shanghai, now performed in Hongkou for audiences from Germany and Austria, which she had rejected before.[68]

In 1946 Martin Hausdorff summarized these developments in an article on eastern Jewish song. He found it shameful that Jews from different regions looked down on one another: those in Western Europe, especially France and England, on Germans and Austrians, the latter on eastern Europeans, and the Polish on the Lithuanian Jews. He stated that disdain had an effect on many areas of life, including culture, and that this was particularly evident in the Yiddish song. According to Hausdorff it was "the child of pain of the Jews originating from Central Europe and at the same time their secret love." Jews would often kill "the soul of our people, which speaks, calls, cries, and implores from the songs of the ghetto in fervent prayers to God through their haughty irony." Nevertheless, they would fall back on the Yiddish song "if they themselves felt a shadow of all the suffering that their brothers and sisters in the East had to endure in the times of the pogroms," that is, if they themselves were "brutally reminded that they are Jews, nothing but Jews." But Hausdorff also said that people had been purified in the meantime through shared suffering, so that understanding for the eastern Jewish world was growing: "Perhaps it will not be too long before this understanding becomes a genuine understanding. It would no longer be considered right and proper; for the old truth still applies: 'Ex oriente lux.' "[69]

The reference to the motto "Ex oriente lux" stemmed from a discourse on the question of Orientalism that had begun in the nineteenth century and had also been discussed in connection with the question of "Jewish music," including, as Heidy Zimmermann has pointed out, in a debate triggered by Heinrich Berl's 1926 Zionist publication *Das Judentum in der Musik*. This debate had been about the question of the extent to which music of the West could be enlivened in its development by elements of music from the East.[70] Hausdorff's colleague in Shanghai Erwin Felber had also taken part in this debate. In his essay on the existence of a Jewish music, which appeared in 1928 in the *Musikblätter des Anbruch*, he had argued that "a decidedly Jewish music will only be cultivated on the basis of a *pan-Asian* [emphasis in the original] musical feeling in conscious contrast to the *pan-European* [emphasis in the original] musical language."[71] Once again the Shanghai debate on "Jewish music" reflected parallels with earlier debates in Europe.

Martin Hausdorff, in his article on eastern Jewish Song, saw the unifying moment above all in the suffering expressed in the Yiddish songs. By this he probably meant songs like "Eyli, Eyli, lomo azavtoni" (My god, my god, why hast thou forsaken me?) by Boris Thomashevsky and Jacob Koppel Sandler, which tells of Jews being burned by fire and flame and punished with contempt, or "Kadish" by Levi Yitshak of Barditshev, which represents the plea to God to end the suffering of the Jews.[72] Hersh Friedmann, for example, sang these songs in his recitals.[73] Raya Zomina, on the other hand, performed a song that specifically referred to the flight to Shanghai. The title of the otherwise unidentified song was "Von Warscze nach Shanghai."[74] In 1946, when Hausdorff was writing his article, contacts to Europe were still rare and he could therefore not have known that Yiddish song had also become an expression of the most recent catastrophe, the Holocaust. In time, however, news from the ghettos and concentration camps reached Shanghai, and at least two songs that had played a role there reached the Chinese port city. At a commemoration of the Jewish Workers' Party Bund on the third anniversary of the Warsaw Ghetto Uprising in April 1946, Hersch Friedmann sang the "Lied der Wilnaer Partisanen," which presumably referred to Hirsh Glick's song "Zog nisht keynmol" (Never say), written in the Vilnius Ghetto in 1943 to a melody by Dmitrij and Daniil Pokrass.[75] The following year, Josef Fruchter (1900–1976) sang Mordechai Gebirtig's song "S'brent" (written in 1938 in response to a pogrom in Poland) and a "Partisanen-Hymne" (probably the aforementioned "Zog nisht keynmol") at an event of the Yiddish Scientific Institute in Shanghai in honor of the "Heroes of the Warsaw Ghetto."[76] In 1948 the latter song was also printed in a German translation by Ossi Lewin in the *Shanghai Echo*.[77]

The performance of the songs from the ghettos and concentration camps connected the Shanghai exiles with their relatives who had stayed behind in Europe and was an expression of their shared mourning. But there was another aspect of topicality in the song repertoire. In one of Hersch Friedmann's concerts, for example, the song "Ikh for aheym" was on the program, which responds to the Zionist quest.[78] Moreover, new compositions were created that took up this subject as well. Max Retzler (1901–1971) presented his song "Erez Israel" in the summer of 1946 at a composers' competition held by and for refugees.[79] At a New Palestine Melody Contest held at the Shanghai Jewish Club in January 1947 to mark the forty-fifth anniversary of the Jewish National Fund (Keren Kayemeth LeIsrael), the jury divided the first prize between the singer Fritz Philippsborn (1915–2006), who had submitted the composition "Eli . . . Eli . . .," and the violinist Henry Sattler (n.d.), who had entered the competition with the melody "Triumph March."[80] Pianist Siegfried Sonnenschein might have submitted a composition as well. In any case, the *Shanghai Echo* in February 1947 stated that Sonnenschein had learned from the Jewish National Fund that his song "Jüdische Heimkehr" had been sent to Jerusalem for further use as one of the best compositions submitted.[81]

In contrast to music for the synagogue, which was more or less dependent on liturgy and its texts, or that for the concert hall, which was of more selective interest and not marked by any specific development, the song repertoire shows that something was in motion in the Jewish refugee community. This development, however, had less to do with the music itself than with the acceptance that was generated by getting used to the language on the one hand and common themes on the other. That these compositions also had a rather occasional character finally becomes clear in that none of the performers and composers mentioned moved to Palestine/Israel after the end of the Pacific War. Baer, Friedmann, Philippsborn (later again in Shanghai, then in Australia), Retzler, Sonnenschein (temporarily remigrated), and Zernik (remigrated) moved to the United States; Sapiro to South America (remigrated); and Zomina to Australia. The United States was the main destination of the Shanghai refugees after the war, accounting for around 65 percent of the musicians in Shanghai, while only about 4 percent of the musicians went to Israel, a good proportion of whom also left the country again.[82]

"Jewish Music" as Marker of Continuity and Topicality

In 1948, when it had long been clear that the refugees would not stay in Shanghai permanently in view of the political situation and increasing emigration, some younger refugees who had arrived in Shanghai as children or adolescents formed a theater group at the Jewish Recreation Club. One of the plays that the Amateur Dramatic Section brought to the stage was the radio show *On the Air*. Pianist Gino Smart (1912–1959), who in previous years had been successful in the entertainment venues in the center of the city and who had embraced swing music, took part in it as an actor and pianist. In this context, during a short scene, he brought up what he jokingly introduced as "classical music with a 'slightly Jewish touch.'"[83] For the accomplished musician, it was apparently no problem to create a "Jewish" idiom on the piano with a few strokes, perhaps by inserting augmented seconds, though the *Shanghai Echo* critic did not corroborate this. The audience laughed about this demonstration of "Jewish music." It was obviously self-ironic enough to accept it as a construct.

What was jokingly presented in this context, however, had a serious core: in Shanghai, "Jewish music" was what the refugees were accustomed to think of as being conveyed through certain musical signs, texts, and subject matters, or the Yiddish and Hebrew languages. This in turn reflected who the refugees in Shanghai were. The reformed synagogue music was an expression of their acculturation in Germany and Austria and of their ancestors', and it signaled in Shanghai, in demarcation from the long-established Jewish communities, the desire to cling to their heritage. "Jewish" concert music, on the other hand, expressed the wish to establish a new, modern musical repertoire and to distinguish oneself "nationally" from other musical communities in Shanghai—the conditions in the Chinese port city and also the composers who were present, however, did not prove suitable for such aim. In various contexts, Yiddish song served as a reassurance in the tradition of eastern European Jewish culture and, beyond that, as a means of establishing contact with the Russian Jewish emigrants in Shanghai. At the same time, it served to address current issues, such as the suffering of refugees, the result of persecution and exile, and, in particular, the mourning for the relatives and friends murdered in the ghettos and concentration camps. In contrast, Zionist songs, in whatever language, pointed to the future of a Jewish state. They underpinned the provisional nature of the Shanghai refugee community. In journalism, it is evident how earlier discourses from Europe continued in Shanghai without reflection despite having experienced persecution and having been dislocated to a new environment. These statements on the various types of "Jewish music" and much of the repertoire that defined the community of refugees show how little the refugees as a whole were influenced by the new surrounding culture. One reason might be that they were confined to Shanghai without possibility to disperse throughout the country in addition to being concentrated in the Hongkou district. But due to the heterogeneous composition of the refugee community, the refugees' concept of "Jewish music" was rather loose and also not free of internal and external conflicts.

Acknowledgment

This chapter is based on research conducted by the author in the context of the project "Musicians in Shanghai Exile, 1938–1949" at the Institute for Historical Musicology at the University of Hamburg, funded by the Deutsche Forschungsgemeinschaft (German Research Foundation), 2014–2019.

Notes

1. See Genesis 11:1–9; Christina von Braun, "Die Zugehörigkeit zur jüdischen Gemeinschaft," in *Handbuch Jüdische Studien*, ed. Christina von Braun and Micha Brumlik (Cologne: Böhlau, 2018), 23–29.
2. "Wir juedischen Kuenstler sind nach Shanghai gekommen, dem wir unser Koennen und unsere Tatkraft mitgebracht haben. Dieser Stadt, ihrer Bevoelkerung und ihren Institutionen, denen wir vieles zu verdanken haben, werden wir auch in Zukunft unser Bestes geben und somit die Anerkennung juedischer Musiker als Gruppe in Shanghai festigen!" Hans Baer, "10 Monate juedische Musik in Shanghai," *Shanghai Jewish Chronicle* 2, no. 19 (January 20, 1940): 4, private collection Axel Schüttauf, Sindorf. Clippings from rare newspapers or journals are followed by a reference to the collections in which they are located.
3. See O. L. [Ossi Lewin], "Juedische Musik im American Women's Club," in *Shanghai Jewish Chronicle* [1939]: 8, private collection Axel Schüttauf, Sindorf.
4. See, e.g., Shanghai Collection, RG 243, YIVO Archives, New York; Jews in Shanghai Collection, AR 2509, Leo Baeck Institute Archives, New York.
5. See David Kranzler, *Japanese, Nazis & Jews: The Jewish Refugee Community of Shanghai, 1938–1945* (New York: Yeshiva University Press, Sifria, 1976), 363–388; Alfred Dreifuß, "Schanghai—Eine Emigration am Rande," in *Kunst und Literatur im antifaschistischen Exil 1933–1945*, ed. Eike Middell (Frankfurt am Main: Röderberg, 1980), 3:497–501; Stephan Stompor, *Künstler im Exil in Oper, Konzert, Operette, Tanztheater, Schauspiel, Kabarett, Rundfunk, Film, Musik- und Theaterwissenschaft sowie Ausbildung in 62 Ländern* (Frankfurt am Main: Peter Lang, 1994), 2:713–726.

6. See, e.g., Martin Hausdorff, "Das Musikleben der Immigranten," *The Shanghai Herald: German Language Supplement*, special issue (April 1946): 16–17; [Erwin Felber], "Cultural Life and Emigration," in *Almanac—Shanghai 1946/47*, ed. Ossi Lewin (Shanghai: Shanghai Echo, [1947]), 64–67; and Henry Margolinski, "Musical Characters in Shanghai Commissions," in *Almanac—Shanghai 1946/47*, ed. Ossi Lewin (Shanghai: Shanghai Echo, [1947]), 68.

7. See Yvonne Liao, "'Die gute Unterhaltungsmusik': Landscape, Refugee Cafés, and Sounds of 'Little Vienna' in Wartime Shanghai," *The Musical Quarterly* 98, no. 4 (2015): 350–394.

8. See Irene Eber, *Wartime Shanghai and the Jewish Refugees from Central Europe: Survival, Co-Existence, and Identity in a Multi-Ethnic City* (Berlin: De Gruyter, 2012), 84–86.

9. See David Kranzler, *Japanese, Nazis & Jews*, 347–362.

10. See Françoise Kreissler: "Europäische Emigranten (1933–1945) in der chinesischen Geschichtsschreibung. Zwischen Politik und Geschichte," in: *Exilforschungen im historischen Prozess*, ed. Claus-Dieter Krohn and Lutz Winkler (Munich: text & kritik, 2012), 228.

11. See Astrid Freyeisen, *Shanghai und die Politik des Dritten Reiches* (Würzburg: Königshausen & Neumann, 2000).

12. See Kranzler, *Japanese, Nazis & Jews*, 490.

13. See ibid., 477–519.

14. See Jewish emigrants in Shanghai, passports, R 98.713–98.725, and passes for Jews in China, R 99.621, Department of Germany, Politisches Archiv des Auswärtigen Amtes, Berlin; diverse lists of names, RI–41, DAL/195–DAL/200, Central Archives for the History of the Jewish People, Jerusalem; *Exil Shanghai 1938–1947: Jüdisches Leben in der Emigration*, ed. Georg Armbrüster, Michael Kohlstruck, and Sonja Mühlberger (Teetz: Hentrich & Hentrich, 2000); *Emigranten Adressbuch fuer Shanghai: Mit einem Anhang: Branchen-Register* (1939; repr., Hong Kong: Old China Hand Press, 1995).

15. See Angelika Kipp, *Jüdische Arbeits- und Berufsfürsorge in Deutschland 1900–1933* (Berlin: Metropol, 1999), 54.

16. See Sophie Fetthauer, "The Far Eastern Jewish Central Information Bureau in Harbin and Shanghai: Nachrichtensteuerung und individuelle Beratung für NS-verfolgte Musiker und Musikerinnen mit dem Fluchtziel Shanghai bzw. Ostasien," in *Musik und Migration*, ed. Wolfgang Gratzer and Nils Grosch (Münster: Waxmann, 2018), 5–65.

17. See Georg Armbrüster, Michael Kohlstruck, and Sonja Mühlberger, "Exil Shanghai: Facetten eines Themas," in Armbruster, Kohlstruck, and Mühlberger, *Exil Shanghai 1938–1947: Jüdisches Leben in der Emigration*, 12–19; and Christiane Hoss, "Abenteurer: Wer waren die Shanghai-Flüchtlinge aus Mitteleuropa?," ibid., 103–132.

18. See Alfred Dreifuss, "Juedische Kunstbestaetigung [Kunstbetätigung] in Shanghai," *Shanghai Jewish Chronicle* (July 16, 1939): 5, Alfred Dreifuß Archiv, 481, fol. 2–3, Akademie der Künste, Berlin; anon., "Das Privattheater hat das Wort! Die 'Ejas' stellt ihre Theateraufuehrungen ein," *Shanghai Jewish Chronicle* (May 9, 1941): 6, Shanghai Collection, RG 243, folder 67, I, fol. 857, YIVO Archives, New York.

19. See *Das Exil der kleinen Leute: Alltagserfahrungen deutscher Juden in der Emigration*, ed. Wolfgang Benz (München: Beck, 1991).

20. See Armbrüster, Kohlstruck, Mühlberger, "Exil Shanghai," 15.

21. See Steve Hochstadt, interview with Henry Rossetty, June 8, 1990, Shanghai Jewish Community Oral History Project, Edmund S. Muskie Archives & Special Collections Library, Lewiston; Sharon Weisberg, interview with Eric Rosenow, August 5, 1982,

The Voice/Vision Holocaust Survivor Oral History Archive, University of Michigan-Dearborn, Mardigian Library, Dearborn, MI.

22. See Wolfgang Fraenkel, *Drei Orchesterlieder*, 1941, Mus.ms.19654, Department of Music, Bayerische Staatsbibliothek, Munich; Julius Schloß, *First Chinese Rhapsody*, 1947–1948, *Second Chinese Rhapsody*, 1948–1949, Julius Schloss Collection, S2.5_F18_SC231.1–10; and S2.5_F19_SC232.1–7, Marvin Duchow Music Library, McGill University, Montreal.

23. "Wir sind nach Shanghai gekommen in dem Bewusstsein, aus Ländern zu stammen, die einen Hochstand an Kunst und Kultur zu verzeichnen hatten, und vielfach für die Welt auf diesen Gebieten epochemachend gewirkt haben. Wir brauchen uns dieser Tradition nicht zu schämen. Denn wir bringen Shanghai damit etwas, was es bisher nicht hatte." gl. [Günther Lenhardt], "Um die jüdische Kunst," *Die Tribüne*, no. 4 (5th week of February 1940): 89–90.

24. Anon., "Kulturvereinigung Hongkew," [journal unknown] [1940], Alfred Dreifuß Archiv, 481, fol. 84, Akademie der Künste, Berlin; gl. [Günther Lenhardt], "Diskussionsabend in der Kulturgemeinschaft," [journal unknown] [1940], Alfred Dreifuß Archiv, 481, fol. 86–87, Akademie der Künste, Berlin; G. L. [Günther Lenhardt], "Zur Erklaerung des Artist Club," in [journal unknown] [1940], Alfred Dreifuß Archiv, 481, fol. 85, Akademie der Künste, Berlin.

25. See Lily E. Hirsch, *A Jewish Orchestra in Nazi Germany: Musical Politics and the Berlin Jewish Culture League* (Ann Arbor: University of Michigan Press, 2010), 37–59.

26. See Alfred Kahn, "Jeder traegt sein Pinkerl. Auffuehrung im Alcock-Theatersaal," *Shanghai Jewish Chronicle* 5, no. 349 (December 29, 1943): 3.

27. See anon., " Das Privattheater hat das Wort! Die 'Ejas' stellt ihre Theaterauffuehrungen ein," *Shanghai Jewish Chronicle* (May 9, 1941): 6, Shanghai Collection, RG 243, folder 67, I, fol. 857, YIVO Archives, New York; anon., "'EJAS' und ihre Plaene," *Shanghai Jewish Chronicle* (August 3, 1941), Shanghai Collection, RG 243, folder 67, I, fol. 1007, YIVO Archives, New York.

28. See Jewish Community, Department of Culture with the EJAS, Symphony Concert of the Shanghai Philharmonic Orchestra, Eastern Theatre, May 30, 1944 [program], Ferdinand Adler album, private collection Christina Adler, Kufstein; Erwin Felber, "Margolinski dirigiert die Philharmoniker," *Shanghai Jewish Chronicle* (June 4, 1944), Ferdinand Adler album, private collection Christina Adler, Kufstein.

29. See Tang Yating 汤亚汀, *Diguo feisan bianzouqu: Shanghai Gongbuju Yuedui shi / Variations of Imperial Diasporas: A History of Shanghai Municipal Orchestra (1879–1949)* 帝国飞散变奏曲：上海工部局乐队史 (1879–1949) (Shanghai: Shanghai Conservatory of Music Press, 2014), 102–106.

30. See anon., "Italian Concert by Orchestra Today: Gesture in Gratitude to Rome for Gift," *The North-China Daily News*, December 11, 1938, 5; Shanghai Municipal Council, *Report for the Year 1938 and Budget for the Year 1939* (Shanghai: North-China Daily News, 1939), 270; Shanghai Municipal Council, *Report for the Year 1939 and Budget for the Year 1940* (Shanghai: North-China Daily News & Herald, 1940), 228.

31. See, e.g., "Municipal Orchestra: 19th Symphony Concert [advertisement]," *The North-China Daily News*, February 24, 1938, 8; "Municipal Orchestra: Twelfth Symphony Concert [advertisement]," *The North-China Daily News*, January 6, 1938, 7.

32. Anon., "S'hai Municipal Orchestra Concerts: Subject of Nationality Becoming Obsession; Fine Sunday Programme," *The North-China Daily News*, March 12, 1940, 9.

33. See H., "Piano Recital by Mr. Hans Baer: Programme Built with Unusual Components," *The North-China Daily News*, April 14, 1939, 2.

34. See anon., "Aus dem Kunstleben," *Gemeindeblatt der Jüdischen Kultusgemeinde* 1, no. 3 (September 29, 1939): 4.

35. See Wilfried Seywald, "Der vergessengemachte Zeitungsmacher Ossi Lewin und seine Zeit im Exil in Shanghai," *IWK: Mitteilungen des Instituts für Wissenschaft und Kunst* 44, no. 3 (1989): 22–27.

36. "Das Konzert . . . fuehrte den Hoerer zum Teil in eine etwas ungewohnte musikalische Gefuehlswelt ein. Es handelte sich in dieser Veranstaltung in der Hauptsache nicht *darum*, bekannte jiddische oder hebraeische Lieder zum Vortrag zu bringen, vielmehr sollten einige Ergebnisse einer Anzahl juedischer Komponisten gezeigt werden, welche mit Bewusstsein daran arbeiten, eine gefuehlsmaessig juedisch betonte Musik zu schaffen. So war der erste Teil des Programms ausschliesslich—von den jiddischen Liedern abgesehen—modernen Komponisten gewidmet. Der Weg, welcher hier beschritten wird, ist ein Weg in ein Zukunftsland. Es soll nicht behauptet werden, dass die aufgefuehrten Kompositionen bereits unsterbliche Meisterwerke waeren, aber diese Werke oeffnen den Weg fuer eine kommende rein juedische Kunst, und so haben die Komponisten Anspruch darauf, als bahnbrechend bezeichnet zu werden. . . . Dann wird der juedische Kuenstler in Shanghai seine besondere Aufgabe erfuellen." O. L. [Ossi Lewin], "Juedische Musik im American Women's Club," *Shanghai Jewish Chronicle* [1939]: 8, private collection Axel Schüttdorf, Sindorf.

37. "so ist hierzu zu sagen, dass es eine nationale juedische Musik noch nicht gibt und noch nicht geben kann, da die Hauptvoraussetzung hierfuer, der juedische Boden, fehlt. Jede national bedingte und national betonte Musik wurzelt mehr oder weniger in der Heimaterde, sie ist es, die auch einer juedischen Kunst einmal den Stempel des Juedischen' aufdruecken wird." Atr. [Albert Trum], "Aus dem kulturellen Leben: Zu dem Konzert 'Juedische Musik' im American Women's Club am 12. Oktober 1939," *Gemeindeblatt der Jüdischen Kultusgemeinde* 1, no. 6 (October 20, 1939): 2.

38. See Heidy Zimmermann, "Was heißt 'jüdische Musik'? Grundzüge eines Diskurses im 20. Jahrhundert," in *Jüdische Musik? Fremdbilder—Eigenbilder*, ed. Eckhard John and Heidy Zimmermann (Cologne: Böhlau, 2004), 27.

39. See "American Women's Club [advertisement]," *The North-China Daily News*, November 22, 1939, 5.

40. "die künstlerische Aeusserung eines Juden in der Galuth . . . wirklich jüdisch, wahrhaft characteristisch." Hans Baer, "Ein Vorwort", February 17, 1949, private collection Axel Schüttauf, Sindorf.

41. See Hans Baer, *March of the Chaluzim*, 1946, private collection Axel Schüttauf, Sindorf.

42. See Irene Heskes, *Passport to Jewish Music: Its History, Traditions, and Culture* (Westport, CT: Greenwood Press, 1994), 215, 225.

43. See Jewish Music Week, Purim Oneg Shabbat, Shanghai Jewish School, March, 15, 1946 [program], Shanghai Collection, RG 243, folder 63, fol. 6, YIVO Archives, New York.

44. See Sang Tong (Zhu, Jingqing) 朱镜清 (桑桐), "Jinian Fulanke'er yu Xu Luoshi: Remembering My Teachers Wolfgang Fraenkel and Julius Schloss," *Yinyue yishu: Shanghai Yinyue Xueyuan xuebao / Art of Music: Journal of the Shanghai Conservatory of Music* 音乐艺术：上海音乐学院学报, no. 1 (1990): 10–12.

45. See Wolfgang Fraenkel, Music-Development, October 1945, Wolfgang Fraenkel collection, Ana 496, box 3, folder: Music-Development, Department of Manuscripts and Rare Books, Bayerische Staatsbibliothek, Munich.

46. See Heinz Ganther, "Das religioese Leben," *The Shanghai Herald: German Language Supplement*, special issue (April 1946): 3–4.

47. "die Gefühle anders Denkender nicht zu verletzen und keine Kluft aufzureissen, wo es gilt, alle Kräfte zu vereinen und nicht zu zersplittern." Lutz Wachsner, "Die Aufgaben des Kultusdezernates," *Jüdisches Nachrichtenblatt* 1, no. 1 (August 2, 1940): 8.

48. See, e.g., "Der liberale Gottesdienst der Juedischen Gemeinde [advertisement]," *Jüdisches Nachrichtenblatt* 1, no. 2 (August 16, 1940): 4.

49. See Gemeinschaft Jüdischer Kantoren, Erster Jüdischer Abend, Alcock-Heim, December 14, 1940 [program], Shanghai Collection, RG 243, folder 32 I, fol. 15, YIVO Archives, New York; Gemeinschaft Jüdischer Kantoren: 2nd Jewish Evening, Shanghai Jewish School, February 2, 1941 [program], Shanghai Collection, RG 243, folder 32 I, fol. 28, YIVO Archives, New York; Choir of Cantors, Jewish Concert, Alcock-Heim, January 24, 1943 [program], Shanghai Collection, RG 243, folder 32 V, fol. 143, YIVO Archives, New York; Choir of Cantors: Jewish Concert, Broadway Theatre, March, 5, 1944 [program], Shanghai Collection, RG 243, folder 32 V, fol. 158, YIVO Archives, New York; Community of Jewish Cantors: Concert, SJYA School, January 27, 1946 [program], Shanghai Collection, RG 243, folder 32 I, fol. 24, YIVO Archives, New York.

50. See Choir of Cantors, Jewish Concert, Broadway Theatre, March 5, 1944 [program], Shanghai Collection, RG 243, folder 32 V, fol. 158, YIVO Archives, New York.

51. See Association of Jewish Precentors: Concert, SJYA School, January 27, 1946 [program], Shanghai Collection, RG 243, folder 32 I, fol. 24, YIVO Archives, New York.

52. See the collection of cantorial and Yiddish choral music for Jakob Kaufmann, Shanghai 1947, 2021/23, Wiener Holocaust Library, London.

53. See Beth-Din, Rabbinate Shanghai, "'Harmonium-Gottesdienst und Frauenchor religionsgesetzlich unzulaessig,'" *Gelbe Post*, July 5, 1940, 4, Shanghai Collection, RG 243, folder 67 II, fol. 2, YIVO Archives, New York.

54. "Kompositionen aus der romantischen Epoche . . . denn wir alle sind mit dieser Musik aufgewachsen und wir leben in ihr." Martin Hausdorff, "Wandlungen der synagogalen Musik," *Gemeindeblatt der Jüdischen Kultusgemeinde* 1, no. 3 (September 29, 1939): 3–4.

55. See Erwin Felber, "Gibt es eine jüdische Musik?" *Musikblätter des Anbruch* 10, no. 8 (October 1928): 282–287.

56. "den echten Geist, den richtigen Stil der Texte . . . Oder haben sie einen gutgemeinten Versuch mit stilistisch voellig untauglichem Mittel, an einem hierfuer voellig untauglichen Objekt unternommen?" Erwin Felber, "Juedische Musik in alter Zeit," *Shanghai Jewish Chronicle* 4, no. 250 (September 11, 1942): xi–xii.

57. "vom Standpunkt der Tradition und des Stiles auch nicht im mindesten einwandfrei . . . in seiner trotz aller Vorsicht reichen, schon fast konzertanten harmonischen Bearbeitung den alten Weisen stark dem protestantischen Gemeinde-Choral . . . Anscheinend geht es dem Volk, das oft genug aus gesundem Instinkt schoepft, in der religioesen Musik nicht so sehr um Stilreinheit und Pietaet, als vielmehr um Prunk und Glanz, um das notwendige musikalische feierliche Zeremoniell, wenn es dem allerhoechsten Wesen gegenuebertritt." Erwin Felber, "Vom Wesen der Synagogalgesaenge," *Shanghai Jewish Chronicle* 5, no. 263 (September 29, 1943): 9.

58. See Alfred Dreifuss, "Der Spielplan: Eine Betrachtung," *Die Tribüne*, no. 2 (3rd week of February 1940): 1–4.

59. "Fortzufahren in der Ueberlieferung der grossen europaeischen Kulturgüter, die wir als geistiges Erbe mit übernommen haben, Förderer zu sein der Jungen, die etwas zu sagen haben[,] und mit all unseren Sinnen darauf hinzustreben, dass wir Emigranten unserer

kulturellen Verp[f]lichtungen bewusst sind." Alfred Dreifuss, "Sapiro," *Die Tribüne*, no. 12 (4th week of April 1940): 405.

60. See Boris Sapiro, "Open letter to Dr. Alfr. Dreifuss," *Die Tribüne*, no. 13 (1st week of May 1940): 441–442.

61. See Gemeinschaft Jüdischer Kantoren, Erster Jüdischer Abend, Alcock-Heim, December 14, 1940 [program], Shanghai Collection, RG 243, folder 32 I, fol. 15, YIVO Archives, New York; Gemeinschaft Jüdischer Kantoren: 2nd Jewish Evening, Shanghai Jewish School, February 2, 1941 [program], Shanghai Collection, RG 243, folder 32 I, fol. 28, YIVO Archives, New York; Choir of Cantors, Jewish Concert, Alcock-Heim, January 24, 1943 [program], Shanghai Collection, RG 243, folder 32 V, fol. 143, YIVO Archives, New York; Choir of Cantors: Jewish Concert, Broadway Theatre, March, 5, 1944 [program], Shanghai Collection, RG 243, folder 32 V, fol. 158, YIVO Archives, New York; Community of Jewish Cantors: Concert, SJYA School, January 27, 1946 [program], Shanghai Collection, RG 243, folder 32 I, fol. 24, YIVO Archives, New York.

62. See t. [Albert Trum], "Concert Nicolai Schwarz," *Jüdisches Nachrichtenblatt* 3, no. 3 (January 30, 1942): 5.

63. See Hersch Friedmann, Yiddish Folk Songs, Shanghai Jewish Club, April 17, 1940 [program], Shanghai Collection, RG 243, folder 56, fol. 2, YIVO Archives, New York.

64. "Kuenderin juedischen Leides und juedischer Freude." Alfred Kahn, "Raja Zomina und Herbert Zernik im Alcock Saal," *Shanghai Jewish Chronicle* 5, no. 300 (November 9, 1943): 3.

65. "Beide Kuenstler sollten nicht vergessen, auf welchem Gebiet sie ihre ungeheure Beliebtheit errungen haben." L. Sch. [Ludwig Schaefer], "Zomina-Zernik-Veranstaltung im Alcock-Theatersaal," *Shanghai Jewish Chronicle* 5, no. 335 (December 14, 1943): 2.

66. See M. [Moshe] Elbaum, "Shanghaier Bemerkungen," *Shanghai Journal: Die neue Zeit* 1945, no. 5 (December 2, 1945): 2.

67. See A. [Alfred] Dreifuss, "'Mit dem Strom' (Scholem Asch)," *Shanghai Journal: Die neue Zeit* 1946, no. 2 (January 7, 1946): 4.

68. See Klewing [Kurt Lewin], "Rund um die Shoshano. 'Heimbewohner fuer Heimbewohner' im Chaoufo[o]ng-Heim," *Shanghai Journal: Die neue Zeit* 1946, no. 48 (February 25, 1946): 4.

69. "das Schmerzenskind der aus Mitteleuropa stammenden Juden und zugleich ihre heimliche Liebe . . . die Seele unseres Volkes, die aus den Liedern des Ghetto spricht, ruft, schreit und in inbruenstigem Beten zu Gott fleht . . . ihre hochmuetige Ironie . . . wenn sie selber einen Schatten all des Leides ueber sich zu spueren glaubten, das ihre Brueder und Schwestern im Osten in den Zeiten der Pogrome erdulden mussten . . . auf brutalste Art daran erinnert wurden, dass sie Juden, nichts als Juden sind . . . Vielleicht wird es nicht mehr allzu lange dauern, bis aus diesem Verstaendnis ein echtes Verstehen wird. Es waere nicht mehr als recht und billig; denn immer noch gilt die alte Wahrheit: 'Ex oriente lux.'" Martin Hausdorff, "Das ostjuedische Lied," *Shanghai Journal: Die neue Zeit* 1946, no. 27 (February 2, 1946): 4.

70. See Zimmermann, "Was heißt 'jüdische Musik'?," 23–24.

71. "Aber eine ausgesprochen jüdische Musik wird erst auf dem Boden eines panasiatischen Musikempfindens in bewußtem Gegensatz zur paneuropäischen Tonsprache hoch-gezüchtet werden können," Erwin Felber, "Gibt es eine jüdische Musik?," *Musikblätter des Anbruch* 10, no. 8 (October 1928): 287.

72. See *Anthology of Yiddish Folksongs*, ed. Aharon Vinkovetzky, Abba Kovner, and Sinai Leichter, 3rd ed. (Jerusalem: Mount Scopus Publications by the Magnes Press, 1989), 4:164–170.
73. See Hersch Friedmann, Yiddish Folk Songs, Shanghai Jewish Club, April 17, 1940 [program], Shanghai Collection, RG 243, folder 56, fol. 2, YIVO Archives, New York.
74. See L. Sch. [Ludwig Schaefer], "Zomina-Zernik-Veranstaltung im Alcock-Theatersaal," *Shanghai Jewish Chronicle*, December 14, 1943.
75. See *Anthology of Yiddish Folksongs*, 65–66.
76. See Ludwig Schaefer, "YIWO-Gedenkfeier fuer die Warschauer Helden," *Shanghai Echo* 2, no. 113 (April 26, 1947): 3.
77. See Hersch Glick, "Niemals Sprich," *Shanghai Echo* 4, no. 81 (April 25, 1948): 2.
78. See Hersch Friedmann, Yiddish Folk Songs, Shanghai Jewish Club, April 17, 1940 [program], Shanghai Collection, RG 243, folder 56, fol. 2, YIVO Archives, New York.
79. See Wolfgang Fischer, "Komponisten-Wettstreit," *Shanghai Echo* 1, no. 233 (August 23, 1946): 4.
80. See anon., "New Palestine Melody Contest," *The North-China Daily News*, January 10, 1947, 3.
81. See W. [Wolfgang] Fischer, "Von Gestern bis Heute," *Shanghai Echo* 2, no. 54 (February 25, 1947): 4.
82. See Sophie Fetthauer, *Musiker und Musikerinnen im Shanghaier Exil 1938–1949* (Neumünster: von Bockel Verlag, 2021), 685–686.
83. See dl., "Festvorstellung 'On the Air,'" *Shanghai Echo* 4, no. 76 (April 20, 1948): 3.

SELECT BIBLIOGRAPHY

Armbrüster, Georg, Michael Kohlstruck, and Sonja Mühlberger, eds. *Exil Shanghai 1938–1947: Jüdisches Leben in der Emigration*. Teetz: Hentrich & Hentrich, 2000.
Eber, Irene, ed. *Jewish Refugees in Shanghai 1933–1947: A Selection of Documents*. Göttingen: Vandenhoeck & Ruprecht, 2018.
Eber, Irene. *Wartime Shanghai and the Jewish Refugees from Central Europe: Survival, Co-Existence, and Identity in a Multi-Ethnic City*. Berlin: de Gruyter, 2012.
Fetthauer, Sophie. "The Far Eastern Jewish Central Information Bureau in Harbin and Shanghai: Nachrichtensteuerung und individuelle Beratung für NS-verfolgte Musiker und Musikerinnen mit dem Fluchtziel Shanghai bzw. Ostasien." In *Musik und Migration*, edited by Wolfgang Gratzer and Nils Grosch, 5–65. Münster: Waxmann, 2018.
Fetthauer, Sophie. "'GEZA und GINO': Musik und Unterhaltung im Shanghaier Exil" / "'GEZA and GINO': Music and Entertainment While in Shanghai Exile." In *Die Wiener in China: Fluchtpunkt Shanghai: Little Vienna in Shanghai*. Katalog zur Ausstellung des Jüdischen Museums Wien 2020 bis 2021, edited by Daniela Pscheiden and Danielle Spera, 52–57, Vienna: Almathea, 2020.
Fetthauer, Sophie. *Musiker und Musikerinnen im Shanghaier Exil 1938–1949*. Neumünster: von Bockel Verlag, 2021.
Freyeisen, Astrid. *Shanghai und die Politik des Dritten Reiches*. Würzburg: Königshausen & Neumann, 2000.
Kranzler, David. *Japanese, Nazis & Jews: The Jewish Refugee Community of Shanghai, 1938–1945*. New York: Yeshiva University Press, Sifria, 1976.

Krones, Hartmut, ed. *An: Karl Steiner, Shanghai: Briefe ins Exil an einen Pianisten der Wiener Schule*. Wien: Böhlau, 2013.

Krones, Hartmut. "'Es waere die Erfuellung eines meiner ernstesten Wuensche und Pflichten, die *Lulu* zu vollenden': Der Alban-Berg-Schüler Julius Schloß—Von Saarlouis über Wien und Shanghai nach Belleville." In *Musik—Transfer—Kultur: Festschrift für Horst Weber*, edited by Stefan Drees, Andreas Jacob, and Stefan Orgass, 269–292. Hildesheim: Olms, 2009.

Philipp, Michael. "Exiltheater in Shanghai 1939–1947." In *Handbuch des deutschsprachigen Exiltheaters 1933–1945*, Volume 1, *Verfolgung und Exil deutschsprachiger Theaterkünstler*, edited by Frithjof Trapp, Werner Mittenzwei, Henning Rischbieter, and Hansjörg Schneider, 457–476. Munich: Saur, 1999.

Philipp, Michael, *Nicht einmal einen Thespiskarren: Exiltheater in Shanghai 1939–1947*. Hamburg: Hamburger Arbeitsstelle für deutsche Exilliteratur, 1996.

Philipp, Michael, ed. *Zwischenwelt: Literatur—Widerstand—Exil. Little Vienna I und II* 18, nos. 1 and 2 (February and August 2001).

Ristaino, Marcia R. *Port of Last Resort: The Diaspora Communities of Shanghai*. Stanford, CA: Stanford University Press, 2001.

Tang, Yating. "Musical Life in the Jewish Refugee Community in Shanghai: Popular and Art Music." *Journal of Music in China* 4, nos. 1–2 (2002): 167–186.

Tang, Yating. "Reconstructing the Vanished Musical Life of the Shanghai Jewish Diaspora: A Report." *Ethnomusicology Forum* 13, no. 1: *Silk, Spice and Shirah. Musical Outcomes of Jewish Migration into Asia c. 1780–c. 1950* (2004): 101–118.

Tang, Yating 汤亚汀. *Shanghai youtai shequ de yinyue shenghuo, 1850–1950, 1998–2005 / Musical Life of Shanghai Jewish Communities* 上海犹太社区的音乐生活. Shanghai: Shanghai yinyue xueyuan chubanshe, 2007.

Utz, Christian. "Cultural Accommodation and Exchange in the Refugee Experience: A German Jewish Musician in Shanghai." *Ethnomusicology Forum* 13, no. 1: *Silk, Spice and Shirah: Musical Outcomes of Jewish Migration into Asia c. 1780–c. 1950* (June 2004): 119–151.

Xu, Buzeng. "The Influence of Jewish Refugees on the Musical and Intellectual Life of Shanghai." *Points East* 5, no. 2 (August 1990): 1, 10–12.

Xu, Buzeng 许步曾. *Xunfang youtairen; Youtai wenhua jingying zai Shanghai / The Jewish cultural elite of Shanghai* 寻访犹太人: 犹太文化精英在上海. Shanghai: Shanghai shehui kexueyuan chubanshe, 2007.

6

JEWISH ÉMIGRÉ MUSICIANS IN BUENOS AIRES

Integration and Cultural Impact, 1933–1945

SILVIA GLOCER

IN the early twentieth century, Nazism and other totalitarian regimes triggered an exodus of artists and intellectuals to an extent unprecedented degree in the history of Europe. A great number of musicians, mostly from Germany and Austria, were forced into exile and sought refuge in various countries, particularly those of the Americas. Among the destinations was Argentina, which some initially considered to be a waystation, but later adopted as a permanent residence. After the United States, Argentina was the country in the Americas that received the largest number of Jewish refugees. (From 1933 to 1945, between 28,000 and 38,000 Jews escaped European fascism and the Shoah by fleeing to Argentina, where they arrived through legal as well as clandestine pathways.[1]) Like the United States, it was historically a nation of immigrants, due to the state policy of 1880 (various later restrictions notwithstanding). However, the waves of immigration during the 1930s and 1940s also generated xenophobia, conservative nationalism, and anti-Semitism, reactions that especially permeated the discourse of the Catholic nationalists. Indeed, Argentina—then in the hands of a conservative and authoritarian government—leaned more toward fascism than democracy.

Despite overt local expressions of anti-Semitism, many factors contributed to Argentina being an attractive destination for Jewish refugees. For instance, there already existed a considerable Jewish population in Argentina prior to the Second World War, due to previous waves of immigration dating back to the late nineteenth century. Consequently, the Jewish community of Argentina was endowed with immigrant-friendly organizations and infrastructures supporting institutions and community endeavors. Members of the Sociedad de Protección a los Immigrantes Israelitas (Society for the Protection of Israelite Immigrants, or Soprotimis), which was founded in Buenos Aires in 1922, would meet arrivals at the harbor to help them through customs, offering moral, material, and legal support. In 1933 the Hilfsverein deutschsprechender Juden

(Society for Aid to German-Speaking Jews) was established as an immigrant-aid society dedicated to helping with employment and providing loans to Jewish refugees.

Deliberately avoiding restrictive or prescriptive definitions of Jews and Judaism, this chapter offers a broad approach to Jewish collectivity. It considers all émigrés of Jewish ancestry who came to Argentina between 1933 and 1945, regardless of patrilineal or matrilineal descent, given that their persecution was not dependent on halakhic definitions of Jewishness. Also included are Jewish Argentines who had been in Europe for study and work and then returned to Argentina with the rise of Nazism. Part of this collectivity are also non-Jewish musicians married to Jews. As the Nazis considered certain so-called mixed marriages to be unlawful, they pursued families through coercive measures.

In spite of its importance to the cultural and social history of the nation, Argentina has hardly been researched as a harbor for Jewish émigré musicians. Since the 1980s, scholars in Europe and the United States have produced a good number of studies on Jewish musicians who fled Europe with the rise of Nazism, however their work has mostly focused on musicians who left for the United States or England.[2] Between 1985 and 2012, the study group *Exilmusik*, formed by faculty and students from the Institute of Musicology of the University of Hamburg, dedicated itself to the study of musicians persecuted during Nazism, researching the phenomenon of exile and its consequences both for German cultural life and the countries of immigration, including Argentina.[3] Still, many of these musicians—one might think of Joseph Kumok (later known as George Andreani, 1901–1979) of Warsaw, and Sophie (Sofía) Knoll (1908–1970) and Victor Schlichter (1903–1986) of Vienna—are found neither in music dictionaries nor in bibliographies dedicated to the twentieth-century music history of Argentina.[4] The extent to which Jewish émigré musicians have been overlooked is evident in their omission in canonical reference books such as the *New Grove Dictionary of Music and Musicians* and *MGG Online* (to a lesser extent the *Diccionario de la música española e hispanoamericana*). In the few biographical articles that do exist, no reference is made to their Jewish heritage nor to their arrival to Argentina as émigrés, a double condition of identity that not only caused them to self-identify as itinerants, but also marked their lives in Argentina in distinctive ways.[5] Even volumes with an explicit focus on Jewish musicians in Argentina, such as the *Trayectorias musicales judeo argentinas*, omit reasons for their migration.[6] In writings on the history of Judaism in Argentina, musicians do receive mention, though without any in-depth analysis of their life and work.[7] Undoubtedly, however, the musicians themselves left traces.

The largest number of musicians entered Argentina through Buenos Aires between 1935 and 1939, and the last émigrés arrived in 1943. Fleeing the Racial Laws of Nuremberg, the Anschluss, the Sudeten Crisis, and the invasion of Poland that led to the Second World War, from 1938 onward they faced greater restrictions upon entering Argentina.[8] Beginning in 1941 the number of Jewish immigrants arriving in Buenos Aires decreased significantly. Some had left their countries of origin years earlier to arrive in Argentina from Spain or Portugal. Others came illegally with transit visas for Paraguay or on tourist visas traveling in first class, if they could afford the ticket.

Among the conditions that facilitated entry into the country were an employment contract and personal connections with residents of Argentina. Aside from being a legal document, the contract had the advantage of professional continuity and being part of a network from early on. In some cases, family members were already in the country, awaiting the arrival of their relatives. In other cases, an association for immigrants or the Jewish community was ready to lend support.[9] In yet again other instances, a combination of these conditions facilitated immigration.

Of the Jewish émigré musicians who arrived at the port of Buenos Aires between 1933 and 1943, three went to live in the city of Córdoba: the Viennese brothers Otto and Ernst Meisels, and conductor Teodoro Fuchs, who stayed there for ten years before moving to Buenos Aires. The Munich-born conductor and composer Richard Engelbrecht settled in the city of Rosario. About 140 musicians settled in Buenos Aires.[10]

The majority of the Jewish musicians who arrived in Buenos Aires came with a strong background in European art music and had studied in conservatories and schools of music with renowned teachers. Pianist, composer, and conductor George Andreani had studied with Xaver Scharwenka and Sergey Aleksandrovich Trailin; pianist, composer, conductor Wilhelm (Guillermo) Graetzer (1914–1993) of Vienna took lessons with Paul Hindemith and Paul Pisk; conductor and pianist Robert (Roberto) Kinsky (1910–1977) of Budapest studied with Zoltán Kodály; Viennese pianist Dora (Dolly) Schlichter's teachers included Arnold Schoenberg and Eduard Steuermann; and her brother, the violinist, composer, and conductor Victor Schlichter, had also worked with Schoenberg. Finally, the violinist Ljerko Spiller (1908–2008) of Crikvenica was a student of Jacques Thibaud, George Enesco, and Diran Alexanian. Their education evidences the rich and varied backgrounds that these musicians brought with them. Some had won international prizes such as Spiller, who had received the fifth prize in the Henryk Wieniawski International Violin Competition in 1935.[11] Aside from musicians trained in European art music, among the émigrés were also performers of popular music and of Yiddish theater, composers, conductors, and music researchers and critics, as well as music teachers.

In his book *Art Worlds*, Howard Becker argues persuasively that art is a product of collective action that involves the labor, coordination, and creativity of many individuals. Applying his theoretical concept of network—a spatial metaphor for understanding cultural production—this chapter unravels the set of links that bound together Jewish émigré musicians in Buenos Aires as members of a social system, while reinserting the individual within the framework of scenes and social relations in which they moved. Both art world and scene focus on relationships and are therefore instances of networks, but they are neither equivalent nor diametrically opposed.[12] According to Benjamin Brinner "scene implies a relatively loose form of affiliation, diffuse in organizations, whereas art world rests on an extensive support system for the production and distribution of art."[13] Given the different and ambiguous understandings and treatments of "scene," it is important to note that this chapter understands it as a concept that accounts for musical practices within a set geographical space, the city of Buenos Aires, and its art world at large. The various music scenes discussed here are understood as unbounded and fluid collectivities in which people bond and belong through music. As such, the concept of scene does not serve as a substitute for community as the collectivity at the center of this chapter is already delineated as Jewish émigré musicians, but as alternative group formation in a network. Conceiving of artistic practices as a network of collaborations among individuals interprets the activities of the Jewish émigré musicians in Buenos Aires as an art world, that is, a model of collective activity organized and later reified in the creation of or participation in diverse musical institutions, such as chamber ensembles, orchestras, educational institutions, and professional associations.[14] As a collectivity, with music being the center of its network, Jewish émigré musicians were found in Buenos Aires, the capital of Argentina and the port entry for immigrants, the ideal city to continue developing their profession.[15]

Buenos Aires and Its (Jewish) Cultural Infrastructure

At the beginning of the twentieth century, the city of Buenos Aires counted around 800,000 inhabitants. With enormous and incessant migratory flows, it grew to 1,500,000 by the time the First World War broke out in Europe. Buenos Aires gradually transformed and became a modern city as well as the center of Argentina's political, institutional, and cultural power.[16] As lyrist Manuel Romero captured it in the famous tango of 1923 sung by Carlos Gardel with music by Manuel Jovés: "Buenos Aires la reina del Plata" (Buenos Aires, the queen of El Plata). Buenos Aires, like Paris, Berlin, or New York, began to enjoy the status of a cultural metropolis. As a space of cultural activity, it attracted individuals from a variety of places, and Argentine artists and intellectuals frequently traveled to Europe and North America on tour from the 1920s onward. As a place of cultural exchange, Buenos Aires was situated within a broader, transatlantic cultural map due to the proliferation of artistic activities and the circulation of cultural goods.[17]

The Teatro Colón, inaugurated in 1908, and the even older Teatro de la Ópera, reopened in 1936 after renovation, were important spaces of musical activity. There was also the Teatro Odeón, where operettas were staged by local theater companies such as Enrique Telémaco Susini's troupe, as well as European theater companies on tour to visit Buenos Aires. As such, the city maintained prosperous cultural industries with immigrant populations eager to see shows that connected them to their countries of origin. Similarly, radio stations like Splendid, Stentor, or El Mundo, which opened in 1935, its deco design inspired by the BBC building in London, were key organizations in the city's cultural life.

With the continual arrival of Jewish musicians, performances increased not only quantitatively but also qualitatively. Singers and instrumentalists, conductors and stage managers brought with them a solid training in their professions, and many had previous work experience in Europe. Their presence in the various music scenes also diversified performances of musical genres; melodramas, café concerts, musical comedies, or shows became part of the cultural life of the city.

Buenos Aires offered Jewish émigrés the opportunity both to join familiar musical circles as well as to establish roots in a new professional environment. Some musicians immediately began work upon arriving at Río de la Plata, having contracts signed before their departure, with the Teatro Colón or radio stations. Musicians would also find work in several cultural and religious establishments in Buenos Aires.

Newcomers often collaborated with Jewish musicians already in Buenos Aires, such as Jacha Galperin, Herman Kumok, Sam Liberman, or Jacobo Ficher (1896–1978), a composer born in Odessa and trained in Russia. He had come to the Argentine capital in 1923 and later trained several generations of musicians in Argentina.[18] Other newly arrived émigrés worked with Jewish musicians born in Argentina, including Miguel Ficher, Samuel Slivskin, Raúl Spivak, Bernardo Stalman, and Valentín Zubrisky. The émigrés also collaborated with non-Jews who had come to Argentina to escape the Nazi regime, including Fritz Busch, Carl Ebert, and Erich Kleiber, as well as those who fled the Franco dictatorship in Spain, such as Julián Bautista. Émigrés also worked with non-Jewish Argentine musicians including composers Juan Carlos Paz and Juan José Castro.

The musicians who arrived in Buenos Aires in the 1930s found a Jewish community that had been evolving since the late nineteenth century. In the 1930s about 131,000 Jews lived in the city of Buenos Aires, making it the city with the highest concentration of Jews in Argentina.[19] This population stood out for its ethnic, political, and linguistic diversity, the result of previous waves of migration. Jews had come from different parts of Europe, the Middle East, and North Africa at different times. The different groups had settled in distinct neighborhoods. The Jews of eastern Europe (Russia, Poland, Lithuania, Hungary), whose native language was Yiddish, had first settled near the Congregación Israelita de la República Argentina, in San Nicolás, and later in neighborhoods like Balvanera and Villa Crespo. For its part, the Moroccan Jews (Spanish-speakers born in Tetouan, Tangier, or Gibraltar) lived in the neighborhood of Constitución. The Jews from Damascus lived in La Boca, Barracas, and Flores, and those of Aleppo in Balvanera. Ladino speakers settled in Villa Crespo and later in Colegiales, Flores, and Villa Urquiza. Generally, the Argentines called all those who had come from eastern Europe, that is the Ashkenazi Jews, "Russians," and the Sephardic Jews "Turks." Ideologically, this heterogenous conglomerate of people was naturally divided as reflected in some of its institutions, such as schools. In the 1920s some schools had responded to progressive Zionism and were named after Dov Ber Borochov, a Marxist Zionist and one of the founders of the Labor Zionist movement; while other schools pursued a cosmopolitan agenda and were named after great Yiddish writers. At the end of that decade, the Bialik schools emerged, where Hebrew was privileged, and in the 1930s secular Jewish schools were promoted.

Buenos Aires also boasted several synagogues, sprinkled around the city. Among them was the Sinagoga de la Congregación Israelita de la República Argentina, also known as Templo Libertad and located just two blocks from the Teatro Colón. As the home of liberal Judaism, the Byzantine-style synagogue had a two-manual organ with twenty-six stops, built in 1931/1932 by the German company E.F. Walcker & Cie as op. 2339. In line with liberal practices, the Templo Libertad also hired women to sing. Upon her immigration the renowned operatic soprano Hilde Mattauch landed her first job there as lead principal at weddings. The Gran Templo Paso in Balvanera, the Sephardic synagogue Templo Israelita Or Torah in Barracas, and the prayer rooms of the Asociación Hebrea Dr. Max Nordau (later becoming the Templo Dr. Max Nordau) in Villa Crespo were central institutions for other congregations of the greater Jewish community of Buenos Aires.

By the time of the 1930s wave of immigration, the Jewish community of Buenos Aires counted about 120 affiliated institutions, among them schools, hospitals and health centers, aid and social assistance associations, societies, clubs, and cultural associations. With an increase of the Jewish population in Villa Crespo, by 1936 many settled in Balvanera, which at the time accounted for 22 percent of Buenos Aires' Jewish population. Given that many Jews worked in the textile industry, the factories and workshops in Balvanera were conveniently close to home. (In contrast, those who worked in carpentry and furniture making or in artificial silk industries settled in Paternal). As the commercial center of Buenos Aires' Jewish population, Balvanera counted a large number of Jewish institutions, from synagogue and schools to cultural institutions, theaters, and clubs, cultural institutions; though each of the aforementioned Jewish groups maintained their separate institutions in their respective neighborhoods.

By the 1930s, the Jewish community was firmly organized and thus had the capacity to centralize Jewish institutional life, attend to its internal needs, and also represent itself before the official Argentine authorities and world Jewry.[20] When the German Jews arrived, they began to establish cultural organizations that reflected their unique heritage. The year of 1937 saw the foundation of the first German-Jewish establishment, the Jüdische Kulturgemeinschaft, later renamed to Asociación Cultural Israelita de Buenos Aires. It organized concerts, theater performances, and cabarets, all in the German language. It also took care of the education of German Jews, offering courses in Spanish for all levels, organizing religious education for the children, and promoting courses in Argentine and Jewish history. (This indicates the gradual change from the cultural separation of the first generation of German Jews born in Argentina to the mélange of cultural practices of the post-immigration generation). In 1937 the Zionist Theodor Herzl Gesellschaft formed as well, and soon other establishments emerged, among them Zionist groups and the Jewish sports organization Bar Kochba. There were also plenty of establishments linked to other Jewish groups: the Sociedad Hebraica Argentina, Asociación Hebrea Macabi, Ateneo Juvenil Sionista "Kadima," Asociación Benefactora Argentina "Bene Berith Tradición," Keren Kayemeth Leisrael, and the Organización Sionista Femenina Argentina.

A large number of the émigré musicians participated in events, concerts, and benefits organized by and for these establishments. Paul Walter Jacob and Guillermo Graetzer were especially active in the Zionist circles of Buenos Aires and as such contributed to cultural events sponsored by Zionist groups and antifascist organizations, especially the

Theodor Herzl Gesellschaft. Graetzer played piano at political events organized by the Forum Zionista Buenos Aires or in recitals of Yiddish songs sung by Dvora Rosemblum and Nuchim Melnik. Works of Graetzer's first compositional period, which comprises the years 1935 to 1957, are specifically linked to Zionist cultural associations; they include musical settings of biblical, mystical, and poetic texts in Yiddish and Hebrew. Graetzer also composed works specifically for festivities and events, such as *Y Jacobo llegó a la casa de Laban* for the Asociación Hebrea Macabi, or the lied "Wir bauen den Turm der Gemeinschaft," on a text by fellow émigré Hans Silber, for a Hanukkah celebration organized by the Nueva Comunidad Israelita and the Theodor Herzl Gesellschaft.

Other musicians who participated in some of these institutions' recitals, concerts, dances, and parties were Artur (Arturo) Wolken from the Vienna State Opera, León Golzmann (Dajos Béla) and his orchestra, Ljerko Spiller, Julián Olevsky, Hermann Ludwig, Walter Rosenberg, Victor Schlichter, Freya Wolfsbruck, Boris Levy (Germán Weil), Leo Schwarz, and Herman Geiger-Torel. They presented a broad repertoire, comprising a wide spectrum of genres and composers from early to Classical and Romantic music. Some concerts were dedicated to Jewish composers; entertainment events were accompanied by jazz and foxtrot. One such event, a so-called *Kulturabend: Heitere Musik aus zwei Jahrhunderten: Vom Rokoko zum Tonfilm* organized by the Jüdische Kulturgemeinschaft in August 1939, featured soprano Lili Heinemann (1909–2006), baritone Arturo Wolken, pianist Walter Selbiger, cellist Kurt Hindermann, and others in a program that included works by Bach, Haydn, Mozart, Beethoven, Rossini, Schubert, Gounod, Offenbach, Nicolai, Johann Strauss, Linke, Benatski, Wiedoeft, Abraham, and Kálmán—a repertoire that could be found on the concert programs of other music scenes and certain in other cities of the world.

As such cultural events were not merely focused on Buenos Aires. In June 1941, for instance, the Gurs Relief Committee organized a concert at the Teatro Astral for the benefit of those interned in French concentration camps. Lili Heinemann and other singers from the Teatro Colón performed alongside pianist Sofía Knoll and violinist Anita Sujovolsky. In July 1941 the Sección Juvenil de la Unión Sionista organized a violin recital featuring Julián Olevsky, accompanied on piano by Jascha Rein, to support the financial campaign and fundraising activities of Keren Hayesod, the preeminent organization for Israel, which was established in London in 1920.

All the events were publicized by local papers, from the *Argentinisches Tageblatt* to *Jüdische Rundschau* and *La Semana Israelita*, from *Mundo Israelita* to *Porvenir*, which distributed announcements of concerts, conferences, festivals and dances taking place in clubs or cultural associations run by the Jewish community at large.

Aside from these specifically *Jewish* spaces, the activities of the émigrés extended to mainstream musical and cultural venues—from the Teatro Colón to cultural centers— that are henceforth discussed in no particular order as they all were equally important as workplaces. In fact, many musicians worked in different spaces during the same time period, singing on the radio and also in a theater or in a Jewish cultural association. Within the network of Buenos Aires' music world, several scenes stand out, from the opera stage to the Yiddish theater, from the avant-garde to the cultural industry.

MUSIC SCENES AS NETWORK

The Teatro Colón was the hegemonic center of classical music in Argentina, an important and elite place for opera, one that gradually expanded its programs to include symphonic music as well. Recognized globally, its international prestige made it one of the preferred destinations for émigré musicians. In the 1930s the theater engaged internationally acclaimed guest conductors, among them Erich Kleiber and Fritz Busch, both non-Jews in conflict with the Nazi regime. Busch conducted the orchestra of the Teatro Colón from 1933 to 1936 and again from 1941 to 1945, and Kleiber in 1926 and from 1937 to 1949. Kleiber, Erich Engel, and Floro Ugarte, director of the Teatro Colón at the time, helped many émigré musicians to find work at the theater. Artists such as alto Lydia Kindermann and sopranos Lili Heinemann and Edytha Fleischer, conductors Roberto Kinsky and Thomas Mayer, among others, joined the theater staff either permanently or in interim positions. Some of them had held important positions in their home countries. Engel, for instance, had served as assistant to Leo Blech and Bruno Walter at Berlin's prestigious Deutsche Oper, and Roberto Kinsky had worked at the equally respected Dresden Opera.

Among the émigrés were also music directors—Otto Erhardt, Herman Geiger-Torel, Georg Pauly, Josef Gielen, and Hans Philipp Wenning—whose work led to important transformations at the Teatro Colón. They introduced ideas that influenced new approaches to staging, turning the stage into a much more dynamic space for movement and singing, while emphasizing the scenic performance of singers and different lighting techniques. Previously, the opera chorus was static, singing without movement; however, this approach was transformed by new ideas introduced by the Jewish émigrés. Subsequently, choruses would move around on stage, or, even if standing, singers would articulate their hands, arms, and heads like actors to express the dramatic moment.

With the participation of émigré musicians, German-language productions dramatically increased in Buenos Aires at large. During 1930s and 1940s, the Colón produced all of Wagner's operas and selected operas by Mozart and Richard Strauss. Some of these works received their Argentine premiere during this time. Aside from Kleiber and Busch, émigrés such as Roberto Kinsky, Alexander (Alejandro) Szenkar (1896/1897–1971), Thomas Mayer, and Wolfgang (Enrique) Vacano (1906–1985) also conducted concerts. Outdoor concerts, which the Colón began to organize monthly in various places around the city beginning in the summer of 1934, took place in the gardens of the Palermo neighborhood, in front of the Spanish Monument, the football stadiums of the River Plate and Boca Juniors teams, or the site of the Sociedad Rural Argentina. Kinsky and Szenkar conducted some of these concerts. In 1937 the Escuela de Ópera del Teatro Colón (today known as the Instituto Superior de Arte del Teatro Colón) was founded and directed by Erich Engel and began operations the following year.

Another important haven for the émigrés was the antifascist Freie Deutsche Bühne (Free German Stage), founded in the spring of 1940 by fellow émigré Paul Walter Jacob

(1905–1977), a theater director, actor, musician, and critic. Jacob was a pivotal figure who created spaces for meeting and exchange in which ideas were shared among participants with common languages, origins, or nationalities.[21] Populated almost entirely by European refugees, the theater staged German-language dramas and avant-garde plays, most of which had been banned in Nazi Germany. As such, it was the only regularly performing German resistance theater in the world. During its eight-month season, the ensemble premiered more than twenty-five plays, many staged for the first time in Latin America. For the first four seasons the Casa del Teatro at 1243 Santa Fe Avenue housed the Freie Deutsche Bühne, with seating for 350 spectators. It became a dedicated space for music, especially for the avant-garde and operetta circles.

In June 1943, the Freie Deutsche Bühne staged Jean Gilbert's musical comedy *Dorine und der Zufall*, under the musical directorship of Enrique Vacano and accompanied on the piano by Hermann Ludwig (1896–1978). In April 1946 it began producing operettas along with the Teatro Húngaro under Andor László, which consisted of musicians and actors, most of whom were Hungarian Jewish émigrés. This included the singer Marguerite Gellert and the pianist Paul Lukas, among others. A few years later, the Freie Deutsche Bühne formed the Conjunto de Operetas under the musical direction of Hermann Ludwig; émigrés with experience in the genre joined, among them Lili Heinemann. Performances took place at the Casal de Cataluña in the San Telmo neighborhood, at the Teatro Municipal, and the Teatro El Nacional in the center of town. Under the direction of Paul Walter Jacob, the group also toured Porto Alegre in Brazil in July 1949 and in May 1951.

In their efforts to rebuild their professional lives on the stage, many émigré musicians were able to establish ties to and deepen their participation in certain social networks alongside other displaced Jewish artists arriving from Europe, including dancers, actors, choreographers, set designers, and theater directors. Some of them found employment in the very same places as the émigré musicians, and as a result, they often worked on various artistic projects. Among them were the actor and director Jacques Arndt, the architect and director Martín Eisler, the actress and director Hedy Crilla, the actress and dancer Erni Vacano, and the choreographer and dancer Otto Werberg. Eisler worked as a set designer at the Teatro Colón as well. These expansive networks in which music connects with the other arts affirm the Beckerian concept of "art world" as collective activity.

A different space for such collective activity is the Yiddish theater, whose history in Argentina begins in 1901 with a performance of Abraham Goldfaden's operetta *Der fanatik oder beyde Kuni-Lemls* (The fanatic or the two Kuni-Lemls) by the Compañía de Artistas Israelitas Aficionados, a company of Jewish amateur artists, at the Doria Theater at 2330 Rivadavia Avenue. By the 1930s Buenos Aires counted several Jewish and Yiddish theaters, among them the Mitre at 5424 Corrientes Avenue, the Excelsior at 3234 Corrientes Avenue, the Soleil at 3150 Corrientes Avenue, the Lasalle at 2283 Cangallo Street, and the Ombú at 641 Pasteur Street. The theaters were spread over different neighborhoods throughout Buenos Aires, but were more concentrated in Balvanera and Almagro. For some of the émigrés these theaters were an entry point to the professional musician network of Buenos Aires. From 1939 onward performances of Yiddish operettas and other musical shows gradually increased, with five shows per week, and, on some days, two performances a day as reported by the newspapers *La Prensa*, *Argentinisches Tageblatt*, *Mundo Israelita*, *Jüdische Wochenschau*, and others.

In 1932 Buenos Aires saw the formation of the first independent Yiddish theater troupe, then known as the Ídishe Dramatishe Stude. From 1938 onward it operated under the name Ídisher Folks Teater and was also known as Teatro IFT.[22] In June 1938 the troupe staged *Boytre*, written in 1936 by the acclaimed Yiddish poet, novelist, and dramatist Moyshe Kulbak. Hermann Ludwig, who had arrived a few months earlier, conducted the orchestra during the premiere. Ludwig's addition to the IFT troupe coincided with another recent arrival, that of theater director David Licht. Both would work together at the IFT for many years, with Ludwig also working actively as a composer of theater pieces such as *Pasada la tormenta* (After the storm, 1938), *Bar Kojba* (1941), *La sonata de Beethoven* (Beethoven's sonata, 1941), *Judith* (1941), and *El mercader de Venecia* (The merchant of Venice, 1944). As such, Ludwig and Licht launched the golden era of Yiddish theater. In addition, Ludwig also founded a chamber orchestra consisting of Austrian and German émigrés, and they performed concerts at the Teatro Lasalle, which featured mainstream classics and works with a Jewish association, such as the *Kol Nidrei* by Max Bruch or *Hebrew Melody* by Joseph Achron, as well as some of Ludwig's own compositions. Noteworthy musicians of this "immigrant orchestra" were the violinists Ernst (Ernesto) Blum and Josef Zimbler, and cellist Kurt Hindermann. From the 1940s onward Ludwig also conducted a symphony orchestra that regularly performed at the Teatro El Nacional.

The IFT was not the only troupe devoted to Yiddish theater. There was the Ídishe Operetn-Geselschaft, a Yiddish operetta company that not only staged productions in Buenos Aires, but also toured in Uruguay and Chile. Many of the émigrés (such as the singers Max Perlman and Gitta Galina) joined the troupe, with pianist Leo Schwarz serving for years as conductor.[23] And there were also operetta companies, often named after the theater at which their performances were staged or after the director who ran the troupe. All of them were important anchors for musicians continuing to arrive to Buenos Aires, and in turn the troupes appreciated the influx of musicians who in their home countries had been active in operetta and other theatrical genres. The (Yiddish) theater scene served as a network and provided them with employment. In turn, the Yiddish theater in Buenos Aires recovered the moments of splendor that it had achieved during the first two decades of the twentieth century, until it was interrupted by the economic crisis of the 1930s.[24]

Among the spaces in Buenos Aires that facilitated a network to absorb newly arrived musicians were also the circles that focused on avant-garde music, which had been labeled "degenerate" by the Nazi regime. Many Jewish émigrés attached themselves to the Argentine composer and critic Juan Carlos Paz, who was an important and powerful figure in Argentine art music and avant-garde circles with an enduring impact on the wider scene of Latin American art music. Musicians performed in the concerts sponsored by the Grupo Renovación, an Argentine composers' association founded in

1929 to promote modern music.[25] The Grupo Renovación was established by composers Juan Carlos Paz, Jacobo Ficher, Juan José Castro, José María Castro, and Gilardo Gilardi. According to the foundational manifesto, they formed the group to foster avant-garde aesthetics in compositional practices, disseminate works by avant-garde composers through public concerts, publish these works, and debate aesthetic matters. Since the beginning of the twentieth century, tensions had arisen among composers who emphasized Argentine folkloric musical heritage in the vein of musical nationalism and others who favored a more "universal" approach to composition by incorporating elements of the musical styles of the European avant-garde. The violinists Ernesto Blum, Alejandro Scholz, León Spierer, Ljerko Spiller, and Anita Sujovolsky; pianists Ruwin Erlich, Michael Gielen, Guillermo Graetzer, Sofía Knoll, and Lily Saslavsky; conductor and pianist Teodoro Fuchs; singers Hilde Mattauch and Freya Wolfsbruck; violists Hilde Heinitz and Jacobo Tuffman; cellist Germán Weil; and the oboist León Mames were among those who participated.

The inclusion of these musicians immediately upon their arrival and as newcomers to the city's avant-garde scene is due to the preexisting, international network of composers and musicians. Juan Carlos Paz had maintained close relationships with musicians from Europe, especially in those countries where the International Society for Contemporary Music (ISCM) was active. Through this network, the works of composers active in the Grupo Renovación became known abroad. (The Grupo Renovación became ISCM's Argentine section in 1932, just after Alfredo Casella conducted Juan José Castro's orchestral work *Allegro, lento y vivace* at the ISCM International Festival held in London in the summer of 1931.) Some of the émigrés had established contact with Paz before coming to Argentina through Paul Pisk, who had headed the Austrian Section of the ISCM before emigrating to the United States. Viennese pianist Sofía Knoll, for instance, arrived in Buenos Aires in early 1936 with a letter of recommendation from Pisk in hand and went straight to Paz, seeking help. Until 1945 she remained linked to the Agrupación Nueva Música, which had formed in 1937 and acted under the direction of Juan Carlos Paz, offering professional opportunities, organizing concerts in different theaters of Buenos Aires, like the Teatro del Pueblo and others concert halls.[26] Under the auspices of the Agrupación Nueva Música, Knoll premiered a large number of works in Buenos Aires by Béla Bartók, Henry Cowell, Paul Hindemith, Philipp Jarnach, Paul Pisk, Francis Poulenc, Sergei Prokofiev, Gerald Strang, Igor Stravinsky, and Jean Wiéner. Others, such as Guillermo Graetzer, who was a student of Pisk and had been referred to Paz by his teacher, participated in these concerts not only as performers, but also as composers. In 1940 Knoll premiered Graetzer's *Tres toccatas* (1937/38), and in subsequent years further works would receive their world premiere, attesting to Graetzer having established himself on the avant-garde scene of Buenos Aires thanks to the existence of this network of composers and musicians.

A similar mode of integration can be observed with Paul Walter Jacob. Beginning with his arrival in 1939, he fostered an interest in avant-garde music through his lectures on music prohibited by the Nazi regime, as well as through his writings on Schoenberg and twelve-tone technique, which appeared in the *Argentinisches Tageblatt*. He thereby strengthened the ties between the European-derived avant-garde and the evolving scene in Buenos Aires.

Aside from these three scenes—the classical, the Yiddish, and the avant-garde—Buenos Aires had a rich and evolving cultural industry, especially in the areas of radio and film. Émigrés who had previously produced recordings for various European record labels were able to continue their work. Those who had conducted jazz orchestras in Europe would find work at the radio stations of Buenos Aires such as Belgrano, El Mundo, Municipal, Splendid, Stentor, and similar. Others found work in the film industry. Among those musicians who reestablished their careers in these industries was the violinist Ljerko Spiller. Already a few months after arriving in Buenos Aires in 1935, he participated in the inaugural concert of the Radio El Mundo Symphony Orchestra for its radio station, under the baton of Argentine composer Juan José Castro. Spiller was eventually hired as concertmaster of this orchestra. Other radio stations hired émigrés as well. George Andreani became conductor of the Radio Splendid's orchestra in 1937, succeeding another immigrant, Dajos Béla (1897–1978), who had moved on to Radio El Mundo, where he worked on a daily radio show for many years.

In March 1935 Béla had arrived in Buenos Aires with a whole crew of musicians he had been working with—Howard Osmond MacFarlane (trumpet), Iura Naum Kramer (piano), Alexandre (Jacha) Beregowsky (violin), Leon Collier (percussion), and Wolf Gradis (saxophone)—all possessing a contract with Radio Splendid. Already in 1934, the station had hired Friederike "Fritzi" Schlichter Lindberg. She and her group, known under various names such as The Singing Babies, moved on to Radio Municipal in 1938. Aside from the circulation of musicians within the broadcasting network, it is noteworthy that radio stations were able to hire entire musical ensembles. For example, Radio El Mundo recruited a quartet consisting of Fritzi's brother Victor Schlichter (violin), Paul Lukas (pianist), Ferry Hilscher (violinist and singer), and László Hirschl (cellist, accordionist, pianist), shortly after the musicians' arrival to Argentina in December 1936. The group eventually became known as Los Bohemios Vieneses (Figure 6.1). Other noteworthy hires were Sándor Horváth, who arrived from Hungary with a contract in hand to direct Radio Belgrano's orchestra beginning in 1938, and Victor Schlichter, who later became the director of the El Mundo's orchestra, a position he held until 1966. Schlichter also composed music for the radio and collaborated with comedians. Beginning in 1938, he led and accompanied the Melodian Harmonists (a nod to the acclaimed German vocal ensemble Comedian Harmonists), which consisted of Bernardo Salno (bass), Mario Sologne (baritone), Tino Dani (tenor), and Walter Fall (tenor), who performed together on Radio Splendid. Other musicians who worked for various radio stations were the violinists Ilia Lifschakoff, Siegmund Olewsky, Efim Schachmeister, Alejandro Scholz, Jorge Urbansky, Iván Weishaus, the violist Hilde Heinitz, the cellist Germán Weil, the pianist Ivan Bank, the percussionist Teddy Fisher, and the saxophonist Gerardo Cahn.

Radio stations also facilitated continuity of repertoires, broadcasting Schlager and operetta and some other musical genres that had been banned in Nazi Germany after being classified as *Entartete Musik* (degenerate music). Radio Belgrano offered an all-operetta

FIGURE 6.1 Los Bohemios Vieneses, Argentina, 1937. From left to right: Paul Lukas, László Hirschl, Victor Schlichter, and Ferry Hilscher. Private collection of Andrés Schlichter. Reproduced by permission of Andrés Schlichter.

program called *Federal*, and Radio El Mundo had a series known as *Atkinsons* dedicated to the genre. On May 4, 1939, renowned Hamburg-born operetta composer Jean Gilbert (1879–1942) arrived in Buenos Aires from Madrid and soon thereafter assumed a position as orchestra conductor at Radio El Mundo. In his new position, he continued to foster operetta programs, featuring excerpts during concerts that took place three times a week.

In addition to the radio, émigrés also established themselves in the film industry, with George Andreani serving as one of the most successful examples. Before his emigration, he had worked as a director and film-music composer at Prague's Barrandov Studios and Berlin's UFA, collaborating with such notable directors as Vladimír Slavínský and Jaroslav Švára (also known as Julián Duvivier). This precondition enabled him to resume his work right after his arrival in 1937, creating the score for the Argentine thriller *Fuera de la ley* (Outside the law, 1937), directed and written by Manuel Romero. Andreani arrived with the onset of the golden age of Argentine cinema, which comprised the years 1937 to 1959. In the course of his long career, he created scores for some seventy-five

Argentine films and contributed music to a dozen Chilean films. At Buenos Aires' Estudios Lumiton, Andreani worked with notable Argentine directors such as Enrique Susini, Arturo García Buhr, and Carlos Hugo Christensen. Andreani was not the only émigré to meld into the Argentine film scene. Dajos Béla composed for the Río de la Plata studios and collaborated with such notable directors as Lucas Demare, Gerardo Húttula, and Antonio Momplet, the latter two stemming from Germany and Spain. Jean Gilbert and Victor Schlichter wrote film music for the San Miguel studios and for Argentina Sono Film, collaborating with Argentine directors such as Luis Saslavsky, Luis César Amadori, or Carlos Schlieper. Indeed, the film industry represented a network in itself, in which émigrés from various European countries, especially Spain, would intersect, meet, and collaborate with Argentines more than in any other.

Aside from these open scenes, émigré musicians permeated the popular mainstream venues of Buenos Aires, performing in luxury hotels such as the Alvear Palace Hotel and dance halls and cafés such as the Restaurante Werthein, the Confitería El Galeón, Confitería Cristal, Bar Richmond, Embassy, or the Gath & Chaves and Harrods department stores. These venues usually employed salon orchestras to entertain visitors with foxtrots, waltzes, and tangos. Pianists also found work in dance schools. Ernesto Epstein and Stella Knoll de Pfeiffer worked as pianists in the Academia de Danza de Ekaterina Galanta.

None of these professional opportunities required linguistic skills as music was the language for employment. Indeed, except for those who immigrated from Spain, many arrived to Buenos Aires with little or no knowledge of Spanish, and its particular variant spoken in Argentina and Uruguay. For those wishing to pursue their activities as music critics in their native tongue, Buenos Aires offered German-language newspapers such as the *Argentinisches Tageblatt* or the *Jüdische Wochenschau*. Between 1939 and 1949 Paul Walter Jacob contributed about forty articles and reviews to the *Argentinisches Tageblatt*. But with the acquisition of language skills, émigrés eventually also contributed to Spanish-language papers, headed by Kurt Pahlen, who became a regular contributor to *La Nación*. The linguistic transition and its effect on music criticism is perhaps most obvious in the contributions of the Viennese critic Curt B. M. Weißstein, who wrote for the *Argentinisches Tageblatt* and *Jüdische Wochenschau*, and later also for *Correo Musical Argentino, La Nación, Polifonía, Semanario Israelita*, and *Tribuna Musical* under the adapted name of Weissstein. Ernesto Epstein and Erwin Leuchter, both of whom held doctorates in musicology, also engaged in music journalism.[27] They also engaged in musicological research, surpassed only by fellow émigré Kurt Pahlen, who authored dozens of books in the fields of history, pedagogy, and others.[28]

Buenos Aires' different social networks provided the newly arrived émigré musicians with opportunities to integrate quickly into the local musical scenes and the growing Argentine culture industries. These networks were familial (as in case of Guillermo Graetzer or Victor Schlichter, whose relatives were already in the country), institutional (such with Marcelo Koc, who received help from Jewish institutions to enter the country), and professional (as in the cases of Dajos Béla and Sofía Knoll, who arrived with work contracts or letters of recommendation). Solidarity networks enabled the exiles to obtain personal contacts, help with cover letters, work contracts, and similar assistance within their professional realm.

The émigrés commonalities—persecution based on Jewish descent, profession, and immigration status—led them to establish contacts with one another and to organize themselves within several networks. These networks would extend to mentor-student relationships and professional connections related to their participation in orchestras, choruses, and ensembles, as well as associations. Across the scenes, commonalities with others—nationality, ethnicity, religion, or professional affinities—led to solidarity and alliances as well as cross-fertilization. Such dynamic exchanges also facilitated social mobility.

THE CITY AS A MUSICAL NETWORK FOR JEWISH ÉMIGRÉS

Buenos Aires offered multiple spaces for Jewish émigré musicians and for audiences as well. Music lovers wandering the streets of the city in 1939 in search of events may have stumbled over a chamber music concert organized by the IFT and conducted by Hermann Ludwig at the Teatro Lasalle, or an evening with symphonic music under the baton of Kurt Pahlen at the Teatro El Nacional. They may have come across an evening of social dance organized by Bar Kochba at Prince George Hall to the jazzy sounds of Dajos Béla's band, or to Viennese music by Istvan Weishaus' orchestra, or to the profound bass of Arturo Wolken. Those who preferred cinema might have watched an Argentine film with music by George Andreani. Theater lovers had the choice between Yiddish and German stages. Those who opted for dance halls or tea rooms would have heard music at the Embassy on the pedestrian shopping street Florida where Efim Schachmeister conducted the salon orchestra. Others seeking intellectual stimulation over entertainment might have attended a lecture by Paul Walter Jacob on "degenerate music" at Pestalozzi-Schule, which Germans opposed to the Nazi regime had founded in 1934;[29] or they might have heard one of Erwin Leuchter's presentations on the history of music. If the weather allowed, they might have ventured to the Palermo neighborhood, where the Colón orchestra appeared for outdoor concerts, either under the direction of Alejandro Szenkar or Roberto Kinsky. Due to its rich cultural infrastructure, Buenos Aires offered music events for all tastes on a given day, all announced by the city's newspapers. Indeed, the music scenes of the Argentine capital offered a broad variety of choices and this is also due to Jewish émigrés, who transformed the musical map of Buenos Aires within a few years upon their arrival.

The absorption of émigré musicians into various music scenes throughout Buenos Aires, largely accomplished by about 1939, led to noticeable changes indeed. For one there was a surge of operetta and other musical genres on the Yiddish stages of the city, especially the Teatro IFT and at the Freie Deutsche Bühne. The number of classical music concerts increased as well due to the newly founded chamber music ensembles and symphony orchestras, such as the Orquesta de Cámara del Teatro IFT under Hermann Ludwig, which formed in 1938. The year of 1939 alone saw the emergence of several new performing organizations: the Asociación General de Músicos de la Argentina under Jacobo Ficher, the Orchestra Filarmónica Metropolitana under Kurt Pahlen, the Orquesta de la Asociación Filarmónica de Buenos Aires under Juan José Castro. With the formation of new performing bodies, a notable variety of avant-garde repertoires came to be played by highly qualified musicians, some of whom maintained direct links with composers and instrumentalists who promoted these repertoires in Europe.[30] Performances of Renaissance and Baroque music saw an increase as well. In turn, tango, the ultimate local genre, swept the émigré musicians, with Szymsia (Simón) Bajour (1928–2005) being a prominent example. Having arrived in Buenos in 1937, he became part of a tango orchestra at the age of thirteen, only to advance in the 1950s as violinist in Astor Piazzolla's Quinteto Nuevo Tango.

In parallel, Buenos Aires began to witness innovations in music education instigated by Guillermo Graetzer, who, inspired by his teacher Paul Hindemith, introduced the concept of *Volkshochschule*, an education center where amateurs could acquire, among other subjects, knowledge in music. In this vein, Graetzer created in 1946, together with Erwin Leuchter and Ernesto Epstein, the Collegium Musicum de Buenos Aires, still in existence today. The Collegium Musicum introduced audiences to early music, holding outdoor concerts in the garden of the acclaimed émigré architect Martin Eisler, with introductory lectures on composers and works. Other areas of music education received an overhaul as well with the adoption of previously unknown methods such as the Orff Schulwerk and similar approaches that promoted the involvement of gesture and movement as bodily expressions of music and use of the recorder. Ljerko Spiller, who prior to his emigration had carried out morphological, harmonic, stylistic, and interpretive analyses of the works that were to be studied, offered violin and chamber music classes. These courses were inspired by similar classes Alfred Cortot, Curt Schnabel, and George Enescu had given in the old world.[31] At the Teatro Colón, music directors like Herman Geiger-Torel and Georg Pauly instigated approaches in directing new to this institution. And again, other musicians would form important musical associations such as the Asociación Amigos de la Música in 1946, and later on the Asociación de Conciertos de Cámara in 1952, thereby disseminating European-style music schools for piano, violin, and vocal performance. As such, Jewish émigré musicians left their indelible mark on musical life in Buenos Aires in the 1930s and 1940s, and beyond.

As musicians circulated through scenes and networks (Figure 6.2), working in different capacities that allowed their integration into different professional fields, establishing and maintaining connections was by no means an easy task. Indeed, the émigrés encountered a number of hurdles, first and foremost the acquisition of a new language. And yet, the musicians' life stories reveal their ability to integrate into the cultural and social environment of Buenos Aires, and with it to change their status from emigrant (a person leaving their home country) to immigrant, that is, one who moves into a new society, seeking and finding stable work, adapting to a new milieu,

FIGURE 6.2 Ruwin Erlich seated at the piano with Juan José Castro (standing to the left) and Washington Castro (standing to the right), Luis Gianneo (seated on the left), and Jacobo Ficher (seated on the right), Buenos Aires, December 29, 1943. Private collection of Alex Erlich Oliva. Reproduced by permission of Alex Erlich Oliva.

and eventually integrating into a population with unique customs, rules, and values—in short, adapting to a new cultural context.[32] For the vast majority, the possibilities Buenos Aires held, with prospects of social, political, cultural, and economic stability, led them to remain permanently, transforming a collectivity of émigrés to a collectivity of musicians by way of integration.

Notes

1. See Haim Avni, *Argentina y la historia de la inmigración judía (1810–1950)* (Buenos Aires, Jerusalem: Editorial Magnes AMIA, 1983), 490.
2. See, for instance, Reinhold Brinkmann and Christoph Wolff, eds., *Driven into Paradise: The Musical Migration from Nazi Germany to the United States* (Berkley: University of California Press, 1999); Dorothy Lamb Crawford, *A Windfall of Musicians: Hitler's Émigrés and Exiles in Southern California* (Yale: Yale University Press, 2011); and Jutta Raab Hansen, *NS-verfolgte Musiker in England: Spuren deutscher und österreichischer Flüchtlinge in der britischen Musikkultur*, Musik im "Dritten Reich" und im Exil 1 (Hamburg: von Bockel, 1996).

3. Thus far, twenty volumes have appeared in the institute's series Musik im "Dritten Reich" und im Exil; for further information see http://www.bockelverlag.de/Schriftenreihen/Exilmusik.html.

4. Between 2007 and 2018, over a dozen biographical articles were added to the *Lexikon verfolgter Musiker und Musikerinnen der NS-Zeit*, ed. Claudia Maurer Zenck, Peter Petersen, Sophie Fetthauer (Hamburg: Universität Hamburg, 2016), at https://www.lexm.uni-hamburg.de, beginning with Guillermo Graetzer and ending with Ernesto Epstein.

5. For such omission, see Carmen García Muñoz's entry on "Graetzer, Guillermo," in *Diccionario de la música española e hispanoamericana*, ed. Emilio Rodicio Casares (Madrid: SGAE, 2000), 5:809–811.

6. See, for instance, "Guillermo Graetzer," in *Trayectorias musicales judeo-argentinas*, ed. Ana E. Weinstein, Miryam Esther Gover de Nasatsky, and Roberto B. Nasatsky (Buenos Aires: Editorial Milá, AMIA, 1998), 85–90.

7. See, for example, Bronislao Lewin, *Cómo fue la inmigración judía en la Argentina* (Buenos Aires: Editorial Plus Ultra, 1983); and Ricardo Feierstein, *Historia de los judíos argentinos* (Buenos Aires: Planeta, 1993).

8. See Uki Goñi. *La auténtica Odessa: La fuga nazi a la Argentina de Perón* (Buenos Aires: Editorial Paidós, 2003).

9. On the notion of "chain migration" to address issues related to the immigration of these musicians, such as departure from Europe, arrival in Argentina, establishing contacts; see John and Leatrice MacDonald, "Chain Migration, Ethnic Neighborhood: Formation and Social Networks," *The Milbank Memorial Fund Quarterly* 42, no. 1 (1964); 82–97.

10. Henceforth only those émigré musicians who are mentioned several times in this chapter, and thus belong to its core, are provided with their life dates. The biographies of all musicians mentioned in this chapter are detailed in Silvia Glocer, *Diccionario biográfico y bibliográfico de músicos judíos exiliados en la Argentina durante el nazismo (1933–1945)* (Buenos Aires: Facultad de Filosofía y Letras, Universidad de Buenos Aires, 2021).

11. For further biographical details on the individuals mentioned in this chapter, see ibid.

12. See Will Straw, "Scenes and Sensibilities," *Public*, no. 22/23 (2002): 252.

13. Benjamin Brinner, *Playing Across a Divide: Israeli-Palestinian Musical Encounters* (New York: Oxford University Press, 2009), 199.

14. See Howard Becker, *Art Worlds* (Berkeley and Los Angeles: University of California Press, 1982).

15. Only few musicians would remigrate or migrate further, among them Paul Walter Jacob, who returned to West Germany in 1949, or Wolfgang Vacano, who in 1951 moved to the United States, and Herman Geiger-Torel, who in 1948 moved on to Toronto.

16. See Matías Landau, "La ciudad y sus partes: una historia de la institucionalidad local en la Ciudad de Buenos Aires," *EURE* (Santiago) 40, no. 119 Santiago (January 2014): 151–171.

17. See Francis Korn and Luis Alberto Romero, *Buenos Aires / Entreguerras: La callada transformación, 1914–1945* (Buenos Aires: Alianza Editorial, 2006).

18. Ficher's extensive works lists contains a good number of compositions with Jewish themes. See Silvia Glocer, "Jacobo Ficher: Fragmentos musicales olvidados," in *Teatro ídish argentino (1930- 1950) / ‎אַרגענטינער ייִדיש-טעאַטער‎, ed. Susana Skura and Silvia Glocer, Colección Saberes (Buenos Aires: Editorial de la Facultad de Filosofía y Letras, Universidad de Buenos Aires, 2016), 79–98.

19. See Feierstein, *Historia de los judíos argentinos*, 123.

20. See ibid., 248–249.

21. For a similar such figure, see Johanna Hopfengärtner, "Immigrante, pionera, Individualistin: Grete Stern y su obra fotográfica en Argentina," in *La emigración alemana en Argentina (1933–1945): Su impacto cultural*, ed. Regula Rohland and Miguel Vedda, Anuario Argentina de Germanística 2 (Buenos Aires: Asociación Argentina de Germanistas, 2010), 176.

22. On the Ídisher Folks Teater, see Paula Ansaldo, "El teatro como escuela para adultos," in Skura and Glocer *Teatro ídish argentino*, 143–160; Paula Ansaldo, "Teatro popular, teatro judío, teatro independiente: Una aproximación al Idisher Folks Teater (IFT)," *Culturales* 6 (2018): 1–27; Paula Ansaldo, "El teatro judío en la polémica shund/kunst: El IFT y el teatro de arte," *Panambí: Revista de Investigaciones Artísticas* 8 (2019): 35–42; Paula Ansaldo, "Directores europeos en el teatro judío de Buenos Aires: Repertorios y experiencias de dirección en el IFT," *Anagnórisis: Revista de investigación teatral* 19 (2019): 20–41; Paula Ansaldo, "Del jerem a la clausura: El Teatro IFT, la colectividad judía argentina y los conflictos políticos durante los años 50," *Nuevo mundo, mundos nuevos* 25, no. 6 (2020): 1–17.

23. Silva Glocer, "Músicos exiliados por causa del nazismo, en el teatro ídish de Buenos Aires," in Skura and Glocer, *Teatro ídish argentino*, 99–112.

24. On the crisis and its effects on Yiddish theater during the 1930s, see Susana Skura and Silvia Hansman, "Debates en torno a la legitimación del repertorio de teatro ídish argentino," in Skura and Glocer, *Teatro ídish argentino*, 63–78.

25. On the Grupo Renovación, see Guillermo Scarabino, *El Grupo Renovación (1922–1944) y la nueva música en la Argentina del siglo XX*, Cuadernos de Estudio 3 (Buenos Aires: Instituto de Investigación Musicológica Carlos Vega, 2000).

26. On the Agrupación Nueva Música, see Daniela Fugellie and Christina Richter-Ibáñez, "Veinte años de Nueva Música (1937–1957)," in *Diez estudios sobre música culta argentina de los siglos XX y XXI*, ed. Omar Corrado (Buenos Aires: Facultad de Filosofía y Letras, Universidad de Buenos Aires, 2019), 159–234.

27. In 1995 Epstein published his memories, *Memorias musicales* (Buenos Aires: EMECE Editores, 1995).

28. See Omar Corrado, "Historias de la música en la Argentina de mediados del siglo XX: La producción de musicólogos austro-alemanes," *Música e investigación* 25–26 (2017–2018): 127–158.

29. See Hermann Schnorbach, *Por "la otra Alemania": El Colegio Pestalozzi en Buenos Aires (1934–2004)* (Buenos Aires: Asociación Cultural Pestalozzi, 2005).

30. See Daniela Fugellie, *"Musiker unserer Zeit": Internationale Avantgarde, Migration und Wiener Schule in Südamerika*, Kontinuitäten und Brüche im Musikleben der Nachkriegszeit (Munich: edition text + kritik, 2018).

31. See Dina Poch de Grätzer, *Por amor a la música: Collegium Musicum de Buenos Aires— 70 años de una institución pionera e innovadora* (Buenos Aires: Collegium Musicum de Buenos Aires, 2016), 42, 43.

32. Egon Schwarz, "La emigración de la Alemania nazi," in *Paul Zech y las condiciones del exilio en la Argentina*, ed. Regula Langbehn (Buenos Aires: Universidad de Buenos Aires, 1999), 18.

SELECT BIBLIOGRAPHY

Avni, Haim. *Argentina and the Jews: A History of Jewish Immigration*. Tuscaloosa: University of Alabama Press, 2002.

Blanco Bazán, Agustín. "Los artistas musicales emigrados del Tercer Reich a la Argentina." *Revista ciclos* 16, nos. 31–32 (2007): 219–238.

Felbinger, Ildikó, and Sophie Fetthauer. *"Ich glaube an Europa, ich glaube sogar an ein anderes Deutschland": P. Walter Jacobs Remigration und seine Intendanz an den Städtischen Bühnen Dortmund 1950–1962*. Musik und Migration 2. Münster: Waxmann, 2018.

Fugellie, Daniela. *"Musiker unserer Zeit": Internationale Avantgarde, Migration und Wiener Schule in Südamerika*. Kontinuitäten und Brüche im Musikleben der Nachkriegszeit. Munich: edition text + kritik, 2018.

Glocer, Silvia. "Encuentro con el maestro Ljerko Spiller." *Nuestra memoria* 20, no. 38 (August 2014): 181–198.

Glocer, Silvia. "George Andreani: Varsovia, Berlín, Praga, Buenos Aires." *Cuadernos Judaicos* 35 (December 2018): 46–83.

Glocer, Silvia. "Guillermo Graetzer: Judaísmo y exilio: las palabras ausentes." *Latin American Music Review* 33, no. 1 (Spring/Summer 2012): 65–101.

Glocer, Silvia. "Hermann Ludwig: Um músico no teatro." *Contrapunto: Revista do Departamento de Historia e do Programa de Pós Graduação em Historia do Brasil da UFPI* 8, no. 1 (2019): 239–253.

Glocer, Silvia. *Melodías del destierro: Músicos judíos exiliados en Argentina durante el nazismo (1933–1945)*. Buenos Aires: Ediciones Gourmet Musical, 2016.

Glocer, Silvia. "Sofía Knoll: Tras los pasos de la 'Liebling' hebrea—Con un Anexo documental: Cartas de Sofía Knoll a Juan Carlos Paz." In *Inmigrantes alemanas en la Argentina: Siete historias de mujeres*, edited by Regula Rohland de Langbehn, 46–76. Cuadernos del Archivo 3, no. 4. Universidad Nacional de San Martín: Publicaciones del Centro de Documentación de la Inmigración de Habla Alemana, 2019.

Glocer, Silvia, and Kelz, Robert. *Paul Walter Jacob y las músicas prohibidas durante el nazismo*. Buenos Aires: Ediciones Gourmet Musical, 2015.

Henck, Herbert. *Rita Kurzmann-Leuchter, Eine österreichische Emigrantin aus dem Kreis der Zweiten Wiener Schule*. Deinstedt: self-published, 2004. http://www.herbert-henck.de/Internettexte/Kurzmann_I/kurzmann_i.html. http://www.herbert-henck.de/Internette xte/Kurzmann_II/kurzmann_ii.html. http://www.herbert-henck.de/Internettexte/Kurzm ann_III/kurzmann_iii.html.

Kelz, Robert. *Competing Germanies: Nazi, Antifascist, and Jewish Theater in German Argentina, 1933–1965*. Ithaca, NY: Cornell University Press, 2020.

Levin, Elena. *Historias de una emigración (1933–1939): Alemanes judíos en Argentina*. Buenos Aires: Lumiere, 2006.

Mirelman, Victor A. *Jewish Buenos Aires, 1890–1939: In Search of an Identity*. Detroit, MI: Wayne State University Press, 2018.

Nouwen, Mollie Lewis. *Oy, My Buenos Aires: Jewish Immigrants and the Creation of Argentine National Identity*. Albuquerque: University of New Mexico Press, 2013.

Palomino, Pablo. "The Musical Worlds of Jewish Buenos Aires, 1910–1940." In *Mazal Tov, Amigos! Jews and Popular Music in the Americas*, edited by Amalia Ran and Moshe Morad, 5–43. Jewish Latin America 7. Leiden: Brill, 2018.

Pohle, Fritz. "Musiker-Emigration in Lateinamerika: Ein vorläufiger Überblick." In *Musik im Exil: Folgen des Nazismus für die internationale Musikkultur*, edited by Hanns-Werner Heister, Claudia Maurer Zenck, and Peter Petersen, 338–335. Frankfurt am Main: Fischer, 1993.

Ran, Amalia. *"Tristes alegrías"*: The Jewish Presence in Argentina's Popular Music Arena." In *Mazal Tov, Amigos! Jews and Popular Music in the Americas*, edited by Amalia Ran and Moshe Morad, 44–59. Jewish Latin America 7. Leiden: Brill, 2018.

Skura, Susana, and Glocer, Silvia, eds. *Teatro ídish argentino (1930–1950)* / ‏אַרגענטינער ייִדיש־‏ ‏טעאַטער‏. Buenos Aires: Editorial de la Facultad de Filosofía y Letras, Universidad de Buenos Aires, 2016.

Weinstein, Ana E., Miryam Esther Gover de Nasatsky, and Roberto B. Nasatsky. *Trayectorias musicales judeo-argentinas*. Buenos Aires, Argentina: Editorial Milá, AMIA, 1998.

7

FROM A CITY OF GREEKS TO GREEKS IN A CITY

Migration and Musical Taste Cultures between Salonika and Tel Aviv-Jaffa

ODED EREZ

SALONIKA often features in accounts of Mediterranean cities as an emblem of cosmopolitanism, shining in the twilight of the Ottoman Empire only to be extinguished by the dramatic forces of homogenization exerted by the nation-states that inherit it. Cultural realities are, of course, more complex.[1] Between 1912 and 1941 Salonika went from being a four-hundred-year-old bastion of Jewish dominance and one of the largest Jewish urban communities in the world, to becoming a Greek city in which Jews were left as the only significant minority. Recent studies shed new light on how, during these turbulent times of transition, the city's Jews formed hardly a uniform collective. Disparities in economic status as well differences in cultural and political outlook placed old oligarchies, socialists, Zionists, and "moderates" in conflict, rendering the interwar period a time rife with tension in terms of Jewish identification, affiliation, and operation.[2] Such tensions persisted up until the German occupation of the city in 1941 and the subsequent destruction of the community in 1943, when the city's Jews were deported and over 96 percent of them murdered in Auschwitz.

This chapter looks at Salonikan Jews in two temporal and geographical contexts—interwar Salonika and pre- and post-statehood Tel Aviv-Jaffa—tracing the popular music taste cultures as they develop in one urban setting and transpose onto a second urban setting after migration.[3] It offers a musical perspective on these times of transition: How does music facilitate the negotiation of such tumultuous terrains of collective identity or reflect its inherent conflicts? What role does it play in shifting notions of belonging for those wrestling with the imperative of "becoming Greek"? Pertaining to how such questions manifest themselves through the production and consumption of popular music, I focus on cultural affiliations that cut across ethno-religious communities, allowing for an understanding of the Jews of Salonika both through their internal diversity and through their relationship with other groups in the cities. This approach resonates with Rogers Brubaker's critique of what he called "commonsense groupism," that is, "the tendency to take discrete, bounded groups as basic constituents of social life, chief protagonists of social conflicts, and fundamental units of social analysis."[4] As an alternative, Brubaker suggests that collectivity ("groupness") should be understood as an event or process, focusing on "practical categories, cultural idioms, cognitive schemas, commonsense knowledge, organizational routines and resources, discursive frames, institutionalized forms, political projects, contingent events and variable groupness."[5] In this vein, the chapter stresses shared elements of the cultural or aesthetic experience of Jews and non-Jews in Salonika as akin to the mode of musical collectivity that Kay Kaufman Shelemay has called *communities of affinity*, which does not tether musical tastes to the making or breaking of "hard" bounded groups.[6]

Literature on music in the lives of Salonikan Jews often highlighted translocal Judeo-Spanish song repertoires, as well as Hebrew liturgical and paraliturgical music.[7] In turn, general literature on popular music in Salonika during the early twentieth century tends to focus on the rise of the urban Greek-language song style retroactively named *rebetiko*, created through the amalgamation of Ottoman café music that became associated in the 1920s with Asia Minor refugees, and a bouzouki-based style of underground urban folk developed in mainland Greece and the Greek diaspora (the "Piraeus style"). The place of Jews in this history was often limited to the role of prominent Jewish individuals such as singers Roza Eskenazi (ca. 1895–1980) and Stella Haskil (1918–1954) and recording-company representatives Abravanel and Benveniste.[8] The contribution of individuals, however, provides little insight into the place of this music in the lives of the greater Jewish populace.

Rivka Havassy provides a more indicative and nuanced account that highlights internal divisions and tensions as well as the transitional nature of cultural affiliations embodied in musical taste. She does so by investigating the Judeo-Spanish songs produced by musician Sadik Nemaha Gershón (ca. 1888–1943) and writer Moshé Cazés (ca. 1890–1943) also known as Sadik y Gazóz.[9] Between 1924 and 1936, more than one hundred of their contrafacta, or "sung-poems," were published in Ladino newspapers, and in ten or more independent booklets. Havassy's analysis of the source melodies used by Sadik y Gazóz indicates a rise, toward the end of this period, in the inclusion of rebetiko songs—local compositions in an Eastern style, with Greek lyrics—that gradually suppressed the popularity of songs in French.[10] As elucidated further below, the reception of this music among Jews has to do not merely with a general process of acculturation into Greek society, but also with the cultivation of a musical sensibility, often class-based, that was at once Eastern and modern, fighting for its place within the homogenizing national culture of the Greek state. It had a strong appeal in some Jewish milieus, but not in others, where modernity was represented more forcefully by Western popular music styles.

K. E. Fleming has argued that Salonika Jews "became Greek" in a full ("unhyphenated") sense only outside of Greece: at Auschwitz and in Palestine/Israel.[11] This assertion finds a complicated and ambivalent counterpart when it comes to the realm of popular music practices. Now part of a Jewish majority, in Israel Salonika Jews once more needed to find their place within a national culture-in-the-making, grappling with its internal "Eastern" others. Israel was a destination in which the complex cultural endowments they brought with them—Judeo-Spanish, Ottoman, European, Greek—would face a rapidly consolidating ethno-class binary dividing the dominant settler elite (comprised largely of Ashkenazi Jews), with their Eurocentric vision of national culture, from the generic and stigmatized category of 'edot ha-mizrah (diasporas of the East), applied indiscriminately to Middle Eastern and North African Jews who arrived in large numbers in the first two decades after 1948. As we will see, in this environment "becoming Greek" was again an uneven process that echoed many of the classed distinctions carried over from interwar Salonica, while also being subject to the shifting perceptions of Greece and its music in both the local and international cultural imagination.[12]

Longing and Belonging: Jews, Refugees, and Musical Nostalgia in the "Jerusalem of the Balkans"

Jews lived in Salonika since antiquity and into the Ottoman period, but the city only became a prominent center for Jewish life with the arrival Jews expelled from Spain in 1492. Later waves of expelled Jews from Spain, Portugal, and southern Italy kept arriving over the next decades. By the early sixteenth century, Jews numbered over 15,000 and were the majority group in the city, making Salonika the largest Jewish city in the world. Jews enjoyed the benefits of Salonika as a central trading hub of the Ottoman Empire and excelled in the manufacturing and trade of textile, wool, and tobacco. The migration of notable families of rich tradesmen and bankers from Livorno in the early eighteenth century enhanced further the prosperity of the city, while also contributing to the introduction of modernizing and secularizing trends into its Jewish life. Over the second half of the nineteenth century, the Jewish population more than doubled in size, exceeding 50,000 by 1906, and nearing an apex of close to 70,000 by the end of Ottoman rule in 1913. Their numbers remained at these peak levels until the end of the 1910s, when they began to decline, dropping to 55,000 by 1928, and to 40,000 by 1941.[13]

The combined effects of Ottoman reforms, modernization, and the growing presence of European culture in Salonika made the city home to a rich and diverse musical culture. In the early twentieth century, Salonika was a city in which multiple musical traditions could coexist, interact, and compete. As Dafni Tragaki captures it, the city was home to "a manifold urban musical reality featuring western European light orchestras, tango and waltz dancing, French cabaret music hosted in *café-chantants*, local *dhimotiko traghoudhi* [Greek rural folk song], and light popular song, and the Eastern Mediterranean repertory of *café-amans*."[14] With the Greek occupation of Macedonia in 1912, Salonika became part of the Greek state. Another dramatic turning point came in 1917, when the Great Fire of Salonika decimated the old city center, where most of the Jewish neighborhoods and businesses were located. Over 50,000 Jews were left homeless and many left to seek their fortune abroad. Subsequently, the Greek authorities slowly rebuilt the city center, following a modern European layout. A large portion of the Jewish population, especially the poor, were resettled to new neighborhoods on the outskirts of the lower city. The effects of the fire, coupled with a global economic slowdown, led to a massive proletarization of lower-income Jews.[15]

A third landmark occurred in 1923, when the Treaty of Lausanne endorsed comprehensive policies of ethnic cleansing and exchange of populations between Greece and Turkey, which were already in motion over the preceding decade of wars. Subsequently, the well-to-do Muslim minority of Salonika, comprising about one-third of the city's inhabitants, were expelled, and over 100,000 Christian refugees from Asia Minor took their place, settling in the city (many more flowed through its port and were resettled elsewhere). As a result of this dramatic demographic shift, the Jewish population remained the only significant minority in the city. As Eyal Ginio asserts, Greek newspapers depicted them "as the ultimate 'others:' oriental foreigners and an unwelcome vestige of the Ottoman era, who were loath to assimilate by absorbing Greek culture."[16] The Jewish population was initially sympathetic to the newly arrived refugees, collecting donations and extending financial and material aid.[17] While Jews and refugees diverged in their religious customs, they shared many cultural proclivities that organized their work and leisure life (especially for men in the public sphere), and the functions of music and musicians therein. The makam-based interethnic urban musical idioms that were popular in the cafés of Ottoman cities (later subsumed under the name *rebetiko*) thus became both a real and a symbolic "contact zone" between Jews and refugees.

Both populations, Jews and Anatolian refugees, were also affected by the new state's Hellenization program, which focused on education. As Mina Rozen writes, "Greece was a nation-state, not a supranational empire, and like other nation-states, it conceived of education as a peerless tool for forging the 'new Greek.'"[18] From 1921 instruction in Greek and instruction of Greek language, history, and geography became a condition for the operation of Jewish community schools. Despite the fact that it took several more years for this policy to be implemented in practice, by the end of the decade, it had intensified generational and class-based gaps among Salonikan Jews. While the elders remained entrenched in the Ottoman past and continued to speak Judeo-Spanish and Turkish, the youth opened up to Greek culture and its Westernizing trends, as did those who received quality education in Greek.

If both Jews and Anatolian refugees were subject to the cultural policies of Hellenization, the latter benefitted from preferential treatment in access to housing and economic opportunities, while the Jewish population was increasingly marginalized.[19] Even though the two populations were politically and economically at odds, culturally they often had more in common with each other than either had with Salonika's "old" Greek elite. The Westernizing trends among the city's elites that emerged already in the nineteenth century went hand in hand with the rejection of Ottoman ways of life, which were labeled by Greek nationalists as "Turkish" influences that should be weeded out. The imperative of Hellenization and the increasing presence of globally circulating Western popular music converged in shaping a youthful often-middle-class sensibility that favored foxtrots and tangos, in both their original and Greek renditions. At the same time, the proletarization of large portions of the Jewish population and the arrival en masse of refugees from Asia Minor gave rise to a working class whose tastes leaned toward late Ottoman styles of popular music and their Greek successors. Indeed, the sheer size of the refugee community ensured the commercial viability of *alaturka* music while also providing an alternative "Eastern track" for recalculating identities in the now Greek city.

Far from being insular or mutually exclusive, these musically articulated cultural sensibilities—the new, the European, the ethno-national, as opposed to the old, "Oriental," and imperial (i.e., multi-ethnic)—still carried disparate connotations, with the disparity bolstered, among other factors, by the desire of musicians and recording companies to maximize profits by selling different musics to different peoples. And so, in addition to their shared Ottoman ways, these populations had a sense of nostalgia in common: not an "unproductive," romantic form of contemplation of "the good old days," but, rather, as Svetlana Boym suggested, an expression of rupture and displacement that couples "the apprehension of loss with a rediscovery of identity."[20] Jews mobilized song to navigate the turbulent changes and disasters of the first half of the twentieth century. Now refugees inside their own city, Jews wrote new songs (and adapted old ones), about the 1917 fire and its aftermath. Some of these songs followed the poetic tradition of *coplas del fuego*, epic poems that narrated historical events that befell Sephardic communities through the generations.[21] Other songs, such as "Saloniko" by the aforementioned Sadik y Gazóz, first published in 1925, lamented the aftermaths of the fire, and the traditional Eastern customs that died with it.[22] In turn, Anatolian refugees lamented in song the loss of their beloved Smyrna and the hardships that befell them after being driven out of their home in Asia. In addition to composing and adapting songs, Jews and refugees harnessed their sense of loss and nostalgia by cultivating a continued interest in music based on the Ottoman makam. As a result, Salonika remained a key market for Turkish records well into the 1930s, despite a ban on Turkish-style music (including its Greek-language variants) imposed by the Metaxas dictatorship, which crippled their circulation. Rebetiko musicians from Piraeus moved in 1936 to Salonika, where they enjoyed the protection of the local chief of police, and this contributed further to the popularization of their style in the city.[23]

During the interwar period, Jewish instrumentalists of the Ottoman small ensemble (*çalgı*), known as *chalgidjís*, were competing with European-style music bands that used saxophones and other Western instruments, as demand for the foxtrot, tango, and other popular dance rhythms steadily increased.[24] Alongside their efforts to adapt and accommodate these new styles, the chalgidjís also struggled to maintain their makam-based Ottoman musical traditions. In this they were in league with refugee musicians, with whom they also cultivated professional relationships marked by mutual admiration.[25]

Moreover, the status and reputation of these musicians and their craft, both in their own eyes and in that of their Jewish audiences, rested on their cosmopolitan prowess and the respect they garnered among non-Jewish practitioners of their craft. In 1938 Moshé Cazés described his creative partner Sadik as follows:

> With his gifts and talent, it can be said that Sadik is truly an "international" musician, who plays many instruments and sings in Turkish, Greek, Judezmo, and Arabic. The excellent traditional musicians who reached Salonika from Istanbul during the period of the population exchanges categorize Master Sadik as a "gramophone"; it suffices for him to hear any piece of music just once in order for him to learn it; and if it contains mistakes, he will correct them.[26]

Written two and a half decades after the incorporation of Salonika into the Greek nation-state, Cazés offers here—through his reference to refugee musicians—a cosmopolitan cultural horizon harkening back to the geo-cultural imagination of the "Ottoman Ecumene," refusing, in a way, the Greek monoculture promoted by the state.

The topos of nostalgia in the music of Jews and refugees is entangled with both their class position and their complex cultural affinities. As Shai Srougo shows, Jews and Anatolian refugees lived side by side in new neighborhoods on the outskirts of the city. "The two populations had much in common," he adds, noting that "[on] these grounds, the first half of the 1930s saw the first reports of joint organization across ethnic lines."[27] In a similar vein, Mark Mazower describes how "Greek and Jewish children played games like *aiuto* together in the streets, shouting Judezmo terms that refugee kids were quick to pick up."[28] By his own testament, it was principally for these working-class Jews—"the seamstress, the tobacco worker, and the cup girl"—that Cazés, an avowed socialist, devised the Judeo-Spanish sung-poems he created with musician Sadik Gershón.[29]

Sadik y Gazóz also conceived songs that tell of the plight and dreams of poor workers. In their last booklet from 1935, for instance, they included the sung-poem "Mansevo dobro" (Honorable young men) using the tune of the Greek song "O ergátis" (The worker), originally composed by Panayiotis Toundas (1886–1992), a prominent Christian refugee musician from Smyrna. The original lyrics give a first-person account of a young worker, speaking of economic hardship and working-class pride, and fantasizing about a future in which he will marry his sweetheart and enjoy fried fish, retsina, and kisses. Responding to a recent wave of Jewish dockworkers who had immigrated to Palestine to work at the Haifa port, in the Judeo-Spanish lyrics by Cazés, the destination became Palestine and the fish "bananas and oranges"[30] (Example 7.1). Indeed, during the early 1930s, immigration to Palestine was often the only path for destitute Jews, disillusioned by growing animosity from elements of Christian Greek society that culminated in the anti-Jewish Campbell Riots of 1931. A few thousands, including a large group of stevedores and dockworkers, were able to immigrate to Palestine before the 1936 Arab Revolt and changes to the British immigration policy curtailed this possibility.

EXAMPLE 7.1 "Mansevo dobro" (Honest young man), verses 1, 5, and, 9, set to the melody of the Greek model-song "O ergátis" (The worker), as recorded by Kostas Roukounas in 1932 (Parlophone B.21640).

TOWARD TEL AVIV-JAFFA: TO BE (GREEK) OR NOT TO BE (GREEK)?

The musical reverberations of sociocultural structures in Salonika continued to echo among those who left before and after the war. Immigrants from Salonika (together with Jews from other parts of Greece) were the first agents of Greek music in the Jewish community of Palestine and a leading force in the rise of a local Greek music scene in the State of Israel. Consequently, the ways in which they mediated sociomusical structures and taste cultures—or provided a screen onto which other parties "projected" developing sociomusical stereotypes of Greekness—played a significant role in the reception of this music in Israel.[31] The divergent musical sensibilities, which developed in the interwar period, were absorbed and "translated" into the Jewish-Israeli ethno-class system, organized around the discursive binary of Ashkenazim (often appearing simply as the unmarked norm of "Israeliness") versus Mizrahim.

Salonikan Jews, Sephardi sons and daughters of the Ottoman Empire, proud dwellers of what was once "their" city, who had acculturated to different degrees and through several different paths to Greek culture, were again under the pressure of a homogenizing national culture that drew circles of inclusion and exclusion partly based on an ideological East/West dichotomy. In this transition, there is a pronounced difference between those who arrived before and after the war.

As in Salonika, music was central to familial and social gatherings that took place in the small community of Salonikan Jews in Mandatory Palestine. Pnina Nahmias (née Cohen), born 1939 in Palestine, recalled her maternal grandparents' house in the southern Tel Aviv Shapira-neighborhood being a sort of *beit vaad* (in her words)—a location for communal gathering. Several family members played mandolin or oud, and the adults often sang in French (the language of their schooling), Ladino, or Greek (of the latter they had only a weak command and spoke it with a heavy accent). Pnina's future father-in-law, a butcher by trade and an avid dancer, used to frequent Salonika's Western-style dance halls, called *dansinges*.[32] In Palestine, he sometimes tuned his radio to Greek-language stations, but mostly to JCPA—a British Army radio station broadcasting from Cyprus (a British colony at the time)—in order to listen to jazz.[33] His son, Yaakov Nahmias (1933–2018), Pnina's husband, who was also a fan of American popular music and fashion in his youth, remembers that Greek-language songs had an important place at the Sabbath table, alongside Judeo-Spanish songs. Records of Greek music were rare and prized possessions, acquired from sailors in the ports of Tel Aviv and Haifa.[34]

Pnina and Yaakov's families exemplify a Jewish middle-class taste characterized by an inclination toward European and American music, as well as Greek Western-style *elafra* (light songs). These styles were all enjoyed alongside the Judeo-Spanish songs, which, as already discussed, also absorbed their melodies as a source of rejuvenation. Importantly, middle-class immigrants, who came in the 1930s—small business owners, shopkeepers, and professionals—often had little appetite for the "heavier" Ottoman-style café music fused into rebetiko music, or for its successors in postwar *laiko* (Greek popular music), an "idiom of grief and trauma . . . inspired and fertilized by the musical tradition of the East."[35] In contrast, men of working-class background, such as those involved in the port and sea trades (stevedores, boat makers, etc.), were often more strongly invested in these styles. As education had been a key factor in Hellenization, many of the working-class Jews who arrived in Palestine in the 1930s with little or no education "lagged behind" their middle-class counterparts in terms of their formal knowledge of Greek language and culture.[36] The state of affairs was different for those born in the 1920s, who were schooled in the Greek public system in greater numbers.

The arrival of Holocaust survivors from Salonika and other parts of Greece in the late 1940s had significant effects on the community of Salonikan Jews living in Palestine/Israel, as well as on the practice of Greek music there. The survivors were mostly young men and women born and raised in a Greek city. As K. E. Fleming shows, their experience in the camps likewise taught them to consider themselves as Greeks.[37] Consequently, their Greek identity was significantly stronger than that of immigrants who had arrived before the war. They constituted a close-knit group through ties that had been cultivated back in Salonika, in Auschwitz-Birkenau, in refugee and Displaced Persons camps in Italy and Cyprus, and later in Israel. Their heightened Greek identity and the strong solidarity between them made them influential beyond their numbers on the local community of Salonikan immigrants. Importantly, they brought with them a thoroughly Hellenized musical repertoire, ranging from military and partisan folk songs and marches to rebetiko music, which had made significant inroads into main-stream popularity in the late 1930s and early 1940s.

Growing up in the poor Baron Hirsch neighborhood of Salonika, Yaakov "Jako" Maestro (1927–2016) heard music coming from two neighborhood cafes, owned by Moshon Karduan and Mister Arditi.[38] At Arditi's, according to a 1936 newspaper ad-vertisement, one would "find next to the megaphone the latest records in Greek and Turkish."[39] Maestro recalled how as children, he and his friends would cling to the café windows, watching the men play billiards and listen to records by rebetiko pioneer Markos Vamvakaris.[40] Jako's first encounter with live instrumental music was when the owner of the store where he worked as a teenager—an Anatolian refugee—sent him on an errand and he passed by a café where the *rebetes* (followers and performers of rebetiko music) sat and played, to his astonishment, during the day.

Like the vast majority of Salonikan Jews, under German occupation Maestro was deported to Auschwitz-Birkenau and was among the small group of survivors who eventually immigrated to Israel. For the rest of his life, so he told me, he listened to nothing but Greek rebetiko and laiko music. From the moment he achieved economic stability for his family (as the owner of a car repair shop), he regularly visited Piraeus and Cyprus with his wife, where they would enjoy live music and food, and buy new recordings for his collection. Maestro's personal collection of Greek music cassettes was made up largely of the "heavier," Eastern variety of laiko. When I asked him about the "lighter" songs mentioned as old favorites by those who grew up in middle-class families of 1930s Salonikan immigrants, he dismissed these songs as "out of commission" (*lo le-shimush*), or not being "heavy" (in other words, not in the lamentful, makam-based style), implying that the latter was what he liked.[41] As late as the 1970s, Salonikans like Maestro would still ask Greek and Cypriot musicians working in Israel, such as Trifonas Nikolaidis (1944–), to play old Eastern-style rebetiko songs like "Khórepsé mou tsiftetéli" (Dance for me the tsifteteli), "Ta matákia sou ta dyo" (Your two little eyes),

EXAMPLE 7.2 Verse 1 of "Kharikláki" (a diminutive of the female name "Kharikeia") by Toundas, as recorded by Roza Eskenazi in 1933 (Parlophon B.21674).

and "Kharikláki" (Example 7.2), which the Greek musicians themselves deemed inappropriate for the larger, multiethnic audiences following Greek music in Israel by that time.[42]

An important avenue for gleaning the Hellenic sentiment among survivors is the domestic experience of their children born in Israel. The perspective of the second generation famously erupted in Israeli public discourse with the release, in 1988, of Yehuda Poliker's album אפר ואבק (Ashes and dust), and the documentary *Because of That War*—בגלל המלחמה ההיא, directed by Orna Ben Dor. In Ben Dor's film, the making of Poliker's album provides the context for conversations with the artist and his parents (as well as with his artistic partner Yaakov Gilad and with Gilad's mother). In one of the first scenes, Poliker sings "Ánoixe, mána" (Open, mother), a song he had learned at home. Poliker explains how his elders sang this song, listened to it over and over, and translated the lyrics for him. Later in the film he puts this practice in context:

> At home they listened to Greek music. Greek music that isn't happy, that only brings heaviness and depression, these are the songs they heard at home, songs about wars, exile, pain; and I absorbed it. I remember sometimes I would tell my father, "Enough, stop it, I can't listen to this anymore, it makes me cry, it makes me feel bad." And my father would reply: "It makes me feel bad too. It reminds me of the family I had back there. If you only knew what happened, what I've been through, you *need* to listen to this, you *need* to know that your father had brothers, and a sister, and uncles, and that there was happiness, and all that happiness was brought to an end." And he added: "I can't live without this music; I *have* to listen to it."[43]

Part of what makes this testimony by the young Poliker so striking is that the song in question, "Ánoixe, mána," was composed and recorded for the first time in 1958, fifteen years after the destruction of Jewish Salonika by the Nazis and long after his parents had left the city. The song is identified with its first performer, Stelios Kazantzidis (1931–2001), the son of Anatolian refugees who spoke Turkish at home. While Kazantzidis recorded older rebetiko songs, he was the main exponent of a new popular style that reintroduced Eastern influences and the cry of the downtrodden into postwar Greek popular music. Despite its being a distinct postwar phenomenon in Greek popular culture, the lamentful music of Kazantzidis—the hero of the Greek working class—and other musicians of his variety came to represent for Salonikan Jews of a working-class background the sounds of their lost Salonika, now remembered as a Greek city.[44]

Such retroactive effects were not, however, limited to the survivors and their children. A curious aftermath to the survivors' arrival in Israel was that larger circles among the Salonikan immigrants became in some respects retroactively Hellenized, with Greek identity being reinforced even among those born in Israel to parents who had left the city in the 1930s after growing up in what was in many ways still an Ottoman Salonika. This retroactive Hellenization did not occur at once but was spread across at least two decades. During this period, several factors contributed to Hellenization

being desirable, including the emergence of Greece as a model for Mediterranean nationhood in the Israeli (and global) popular imagination, and the consolidation of the
ethnic binary of Mizrahim versus the unmarked norm of a Western-oriented Israeliness
(or, alternatively, the stereotype of Ashkenaziness) in Israeli ethnic discourse. In Israel,
particularly in middle-class contexts, it quickly became clear that being identified with
diasporas of the East was a disadvantage. This may have been another catalyst that drove
some Salonikan Jews and their descendants to cultivate even further their distinct
"Greek" identity rather than become enmeshed in the ethnic "soup" of 'edot ha-mizrah.

By the mid-1960s, "Greek" was an appealing commodity in the Israeli stock market
of cultural identifications. This was in part the product of the "Greek wave": a trend in
which Greek music, film, and Greek-style venues became a pronounced cultural presence in Israel. The venue most strongly associated with this wave was Arianna—a Jaffa
restaurant featuring live Greek music, operated by Salonikan immigrants. Live music at
Arianna started in the 1950s with a house band led by another survivor from Salonika—
David "Daviko" Pitchon (1920–2018)—who received his early musical training from
the çalgıcılar in the Salonika's cafés.[45] Pitchon's band provided music for dancing and
accompanied headlining artists brought over from Greece. Bolstered by the phenom-
enal popularity of Greek films, in the early 1960s, Arianna's success spawned a host
of venues implementing its model in Jaffa and other cities. The circles of Greek music
fandom increased even further with the rise of a local superstar: Greek singer, guitar-
virtuoso, and club-owner Aris San (born Aristides Seisanas, 1940–1992), who became
Israel's top-selling recording artist by the end of the 1960s.

The wide appeal of Greekness at the height of the "Greek wave" turned out to be a
tenuous trend. If in its heyday Greek music and leisure culture was seen as a model
for cosmopolitan Mediterraneanism—the days of globally successful music-driven
Greek films such as *Never on Sunday* (1960) and *Zorba the Greek* (1964)—claiming
one's Greekness seemed like a potential escape route from the "Oriental" stereotype,
soon enough the winds shifted. The mainstream fad gradually turned into a subculture, and the structural entanglement of working-classness and "Orientalness" increasingly haunted the meaning of Greekness, taking its toll on the "bourgeois dignity" of the
Greek signifier.

The enthusiasm with which Middle Eastern Jews adopted the "Oriental" variants
of Greek popular music, as embodied in records by Kazantzidis and performances by
local Greek music superstars like Aris San and Trifonas, was not lost on makers of mainstream Hebrew culture. For example, in his debut performance on the Israeli screen—
Menachem Golan's 1966 film *Fortuna*, פורטונה— Aris San portrayed himself, playing
Greek-style music (composed by Dov Seltzer) at the engagement party of Algerian
immigrants in the city of Dimona. This was a highly improbable scenario in real life, but
it reaffirmed the association of Greek music with the Mizrahi underclasses. For a time,
the "respectable," Judeo-Spanish-speaking, middle-class Sephardic Jew was sheltered
from this devaluation of Greekness through persistent identification with Hispanic
and Francophile tropes. For example, in Haim Hefer's lyrics for the 1963 song "Adon
Leon," Mr. Leon is "always fashionably dressed"; he is the "highest-ranking clerk at the

Discount Bank" and "was appointed honorary consul of Costa Rica." This potential of "Hispanicness" as an escape route from the rapidly consolidating Mizrahi stereotype was later taken up in Ladino-centric popular-culture projects of heritagization such as the musical shows *Romancero Sepharadi* (1969) and *Bustan Sephardi* (1970), both written by Labor-Zionist politician (and later Israel's first Sephardi president) Yitzhak Navon.

The representation of working-class Salonikan Jews was another matter entirely. Long associated with the moving business, their places of assembly on Ha-Kishon Street in Tel Aviv, and their prominence in Jaffa's nightlife, by the latter half of the 1960s the cinematic stereotypes of Greekness were being mobilized in the imagining of these immigrants as local "Zorbas," with music being a key element. A prominent example is found in the Navy Band's 1968 song "Ha-shemesh be-Pireus" (The sun in Piraeus), a humorous "sailor song" with music by Yair Rosenblum and lyrics by Yoram Taharlev. The lyrics comprise a plethora of Greek stereotypes, comically applied as puns, while the music is in the style of *syrtaki*: the globally circulating, pseudo-traditional, Greek dance craze of the day.[46] In 1969 this song was included in an Israeli TV show featuring some of the band's hits, preceded by a short skit in which members of the band played drunken, lazy "mariners" who speak Hebrew with a vaguely Salonikan accent. These characters embody a cluster of overlapping stereotypes ambivalently associated with Mizrahim, with Greekness, and with working-class men: "מושיקו! תפסיק "לעבוד על הסטייק, תבוא אצלנו, תשתה רצינה... מושיקו: העבודה היא לא ארנבת—היא לא תברח—אפשר לשבת" (Moshiko! Stop working on that steak, come here, drink retsina . . . Moshiko—work is not a rabbit—it won't run away, you can sit down.) Another drunk mariner declares—this time *not* with a Salonikan accent but with a 'Mizrahi' guttural *ḥet*: "עובד! חבר יסתדרות" (Worker! member of the Histadrut!).[47]

Coinciding with the peak of Aris San's career, and with his final departure for the United States, the televised version of this skit and song encapsulates both the zenith of the popularity of Greekness and Greek music as a trend in mainstream Israeli culture, and the "spilling over" of their image into the domain of a Mizrahi subculture.[48] The extent to which the working-class "Greek" Jew could be associated in the Israeli cultural imagination with the developing stereotype of Mizrahim was significantly bolstered when this image was installed into what we now recognize as a key representational scheme for ethno-class antagonisms in Israel: the *Bourekas* film.[49] The term denotes a collection of films produced in the 1960s and 1970s that focus on Mizrahi characters and social spaces (generally characterized as poor, uneducated, traditional/ religious, and warm or "folksy"), pitting its marginalized Mizrahi protagonists against a dominant Israeliness represented by Ashkenazim (generally represented as cold, educated, secular, and stuck-up). *Salomonico* (1972, directed by Alfred Steinhardt) and its 1975 sequel *The Father* (in Israel released as יהיה טוב סלומוניקו, i.e., *You can work it out, Salomonico*) were the first films employing this formula to feature Salonikan Jews and their musical cultures, with a specific role reserved for Greek music. *Salomonico* combined two preexisting elements proven to draw audiences to the movie theater during the previous decade: a comedic narrative staging conflict between Sephardim/

Mizrahim Ashkenazim; and the inclusion of Greek music, which enjoyed cross-sector popularity in the local market and catapulted Greek cinema to success in Israel and around the world. Constructing a film around the character of a "Greek" (i.e., Salonikan immigrant) dockworker was a perfect narrative pretext for employing both elements.

While in previous Israeli screen and stage productions such as *Fortuna* (1964) and *Kazablan* (1966) Greek music was established as a generic trait of *Mizrahiyut* (Mizrahiness), "Greekness" as such was never a theme in these films. As previously noted by Fleming, the theme of Jewish Greek identity becomes explicit in *Salomonico*, where working-class Salonikan Jews are afforded an unproblematized Greekness.[50] At the same time, however, the film also solidifies their social position in the Israeli ethno-class system as Mizrahim. In *Salomonico*, making Salomonico Greek (as opposed to "just" Sephardi) and making him Mizrahi turn out to be mutually constructive efforts. When adapting the script, Eli Tavor had at his disposal two ready-made stereotypes: the Israeli Greek music fan, already associated with Mizrahim in Israel, and the Zorba-esque working-class, seafaring, ouzo-drinking macho (as seen in the Navy Band example). Greek music allowed Tavor to tap into both stereotypes.

Following the precedent of the 1966 film *Fortuna*, which featured Greek pop star Aris San, the local Greek star of the early 1970s, Trifonas Nikolaidis was recruited in order to usher "Mizrahified" characters through the gates of musical Greekness. However, the Greek musician performs (again, according to the same precedent) pseudo-Greek melodies newly composed by the Israeli Dov Seltzer.[51]

Trifonas first appears in the movie when Salomonico wallows in desperation in the neighborhood café in Florentin—a space long associated by this point with Salonikans and their leisure culture, thanks to several institutions in the south of Tel Aviv, Jaffa, and other places. Trifonas (who just happens to be there, bouzouki in hand) introduces music into the scene with a bouzoki *taximi* (instrumental improvisation), and then starts to sing the song called "Yesh regaim" (There are moments), composed by Selzer for the film. Salomonico and his comrades are "moved," almost compelled by this song to dance, eventually taking over the frame as Trifonas' voice become background music. The song's syrtaki-like rhythm (a slow duple-meter dance rhythm called *hasapiko*, which then accelerates dramatically), the dance moves performed by the actors, and the trope of dancing when you are sad all point to "Zorba's dance" as a clear refence for this musical scene. The next scene to include Trifonas occurs when Salomonico's family moves to a fancy bourgeois neighborhood uptown and throw a house-warming party. It unfolds along the same lines as the café dance scene, with Trifonas leading the guests in the performance of the song "Saloniki mi amor" (in Hebrew, also composed by Selzer). It is a lively tune, full of nostalgia for the paradise lost of Jewish Salonika. With the bouzouki accompaniment of the Cypriot-Greek Trifonas and more Zorba-style dancing, the remembrance of Salonika is performed here via contemporary musical-cinematic tropes of Greekness. When the stereotypically Ashkenazi neighbors come to complain about the noise, it becomes clear that "Greek" no longer spells something European but its opposite.

From Ottoman to Greek Nostalgia

The formation, negotiation, and representation of popular-music taste cultures among Salonikan Jews in two national and urban contexts reveal apparent continuities. These reflect, however, not only the stability or integrity of traditions or social reproduction, but also similarities between the social conditions produced by the national projects of the Greek and Jewish states, and the precarious position of Sephardi Jews within them. In both cases, the ideal of modern nationhood was premised on the privileging of Western European culture and the rejection of the immediate external other, that is, Turks and Arabs. This ideal created, however, several variants of internal "Eastern" others, often overrepresented in the lower socioeconomic strata (refugees and Jews in Salonika, Mizrahi Jews and Palestinian citizens of Israel in Tel Aviv-Jaffa). These structural similarities, in turn, frame the enculturation of local and incoming marginalized populations, as reflected in both their dynamic music taste cultures and their musical representation. The case of urban Ottoman music's persistence as an inter-ethnic site of affinity during the interwar period, in the face of the empire's demise as a political framework, highlights the nuance of Shelemay's processes of affinity in the musical making and remaking of collectivity, as new ethnonational frameworks resignify the sense of belonging evoked by Eastern sounds.

During the twentieth century, Salonikan Jews found themselves negotiating their identities in the troubled waters of such national cultures-in-the-making, not once but twice. Observed in these contexts, the case of Salonika immigrants highlights the need to understand Jewish collectivities through their intersection with other vectors of identity, which cut across religious/ethnic groupings. As Paris Chronakis notes:

> Most of the current historiography . . . disregards the fact that Jews and Greeks engaged with each other in many different fields and in many capacities: as men and women, employers and employees, sellers and buyers; as refugees, fire victims, and members of common professions . . . Attention to specific social groups further allows us to situate the categories of the "Greek" and the "Jew" at the interstices of other identities, such as those of class and gender, to observe their relations, and eventually to understand how ethnic difference was produced in specific contexts.[52]

Indeed, as the case of the Salonikan Jews advocates, listening to Jewish collectives needs to take into account their internal diversity, and the overlap of Jewish and other identities.

In Israel, between the ideological fable of a Hebrew "melting pot," and the all-too-real ethnic division of labor encapsulated in the category of ʿedot ha-mizrah, everyday realities of ethnic identification, often entailed the assimilation of smaller diasporas into larger ones, for example, Tunisian-Israelis like Kobi Oz were raised on a Moroccan musical diet, and migrants from many former Soviet republics all became "Russians." Still, the case of Salonikan Jews is unique in several respects. As a post-Ottoman, European, urban Sephardi community, Salonikan Jews at times came to embody an identity that was taken as unproblematically "Greek." Historically, however, Greekness had been for most Salonikan Jews who arrived in Palestine or later Israel a far more ambivalent terrain for identification—a route to modernization and a space of negotiation. This, in turn, went on to become a defining trait of the reception of Greek music in Israel at large. The music practiced in Israel during the 1950s and through the 1970s under the label "Greek" likewise became a heterogeneous field straddling styles as disparate as Turkish belly-dance music and contemporary Latin pop. As such, the cosmopolitan soundscape of interwar Salonika—a city at the crossroads between Europe and the Middle East—resonated into the field of popular music in Israel. However, that the Israeli-made category of Mizrahim has been from the outset not a purely ethnic one but, rather, overdetermined by ethnicity, class, and geography meant that some working-class Salonikan Jews and their descendants were subject to both symbolic and real ethnicization as Mizrahim, from which the well-to-do were often exempt. Paradoxically, this ethnic stigma made them the primary heirs of "Greekness" in Israeli cultural imagination—a symbolic endowment whose currency has continued to fluctuate with each passing decade.

NOTES

1. See Henk Driessen, "Mediterranean Port Cities: Cosmopolitanism Reconsidered," *History and Anthropology* 16, no. 1 (2005): 129–141. Salonika (sometimes spelled Salonica) is the most common name out of several used in Judeo-Spanish for the city known today by its Greek name—Thessaloniki. I will refer to the city by its Jewish name throughout this chapter.
2. See Mina Rozen, "On Nationalizing Minorities: The Education of Salonikan Jewry, 1912–1941," in Αρχείων Ανάλεκτα: Περιοδική έκδοση μελέτης και έρευνας αρχείων (δεύτερη περίοδος) 3 (2018): 127–232; Minna Rozen, "Money, Power, Politics, and the Great Salonika Fire of 1917," *Jewish Social Studies* 22, no. 2 (2017): 74–115; Shai Srougo, "The Jewish Workers in the Port of Thessaloniki (1939–1943): Their War Experience as Workers, Greeks and Jews," *Journal of Modern European History* 18, no. 3 (2020): 352–373; and Devin E. Naar, *Jewish Salonika: Between the Ottoman Empire and Modern Greece* (Stanford, CA: Stanford University Press, 2016).
3. This chapter is an adapted and updated version of the article "Music, Ethnicity, and Class between Salonica and Tel Aviv-Jaffa, or How We Got *Salomonico*," *Journal of Levantine Studies* 8 (2018): 85–108.
4. Rogers Brubaker, *Ethnicity without Groups* (Cambridge, MA: Harvard University Press, 2004), 8.
5. Ibid., 11.
6. Kay Kaufman Shelemay, "Musical Communities: Rethinking the Collective in Music," *Journal of the American Musicological Society* 64, no. 2 (2011): 373.
7. In addition to the titles listed in the Select Bibliography, see the following recent publications: Edwin Seroussi, *Ruinas sonoras de la modernidad: La canción popular sefardí en la era post-tradicional* (Madrid: Consejo Superior de Investigaciones Científicas,

2019) / Edwin Seroussi, *Sonic Ruins of Modernity: Judeo-Spanish Folksongs Today* (London: Routledge, 2023), and "Ha-musiḳah shel ha-shir ha-amami be-ladino" [The music of Ladino popular song], *Pe'amim: Studies in Oriental Jewry*, 77 (1998): 5–19. See also Susana Weich-Shahak, *El ciclo de la vida en el repertorio musical de las comunidades Sefardies de Oriente* (Madrid: Editorial Alpuerto, 2012), "Musico-Poetic Genres in the Sephardic Oral Tradition: An Interdisciplinary Approach to the Romancero, Coplas and Cancionero," *European Journal of Jewish Studies* 9, no. 1 (2015): 13–37, and "The Songs and their Music," in *Ventanas altas de Saloniki: Sephardic Songs, Coplas and Ballads from Thessaloniki*, ed. Susana Weich-Shahak (Haifa: University of Haifa, 2013), 24–45. Edwin Seroussi, "Sacred Song in an Era of Turmoil: Sephardic Liturgical Music in Southeastern Europe at the Turn of the 20th Century," *Musica Judaica* 21 (2015): 1–64; Edwin Seroussi, "Musiḳah osmanit klasit be-kerev yehudei Saloniḳi" [Ottoman classical music among the Jews of Salonika], *Ladinar: Mehḳarim ba-sifrut, ba-musiḳah uva-historiya shel dovrei ha-ladino*, ed. Judith Dishon and Shmuel Refael (Tel Aviv: ha-Makhon le-ḥeḳer Yahadut Saloniḳi, 1998), 79–92; David A. Recanati, ed., *Zikhron Saloniki: Grandeza i destruyicion de Yeruchalayim del Balkan / זכרון שלוניקי: גדולתה וחורבנה של ירושלים דבלקן* (Tel Aviv: ha-Vaʿad le-hotsa'at sefer Ḳehilat Saloniḳi, 1985/86); Yitzhak S. Recanati, "'Azkir Tehilot Hashem': The Holy Songs of Thessaloniki's Emigrants in Tel Aviv" / ה תוליהת ריכזא – ביבא לתב יקינולש ילוע לש שדוקה תריש הילא םתיילע סע, *Min-Ad: Israel Studies in Musicology Online* 17 (2020); https://www2.biu.ac.il/hu/mu/min-ad/2020/Y_Recan ati_The-Holy-Songs-Thessaloniki-Emigrants.pdf.

8. See, for example, Nicholas G. Pappas, "Concepts of Greekness: The Recorded Music of Anatolian Greeks after 1922," *Journal of Modern Greek Studies* 17, no. 2 (October 1999): 355–358; Katherine Elizabeth Fleming, *Greece: A Jewish History* (Princeton, NJ: Princeton University Press, 2008), 93.

9. Rivka Havassy, "Musiḳah popularit ba-ḳehilah ha-Yehudit be-Saloniḳi bein shtei milhamot ha-olam: Iyun be-yetsiratam shel Mosheh Ḳazis ve-Tsadiḳ Gershon (Tsadik ve-Gazoz)" [Popular music in the Jewish community of Thessaloniki in the interwar period: A study of the work of Sadik Gershón and Moshé Cazés (Sadik y Gazoz)], in *Garment and Core: Jews and their Musical Experiences / לבוש ותוך: המוסיקה בחוויית היהדות*, ed. Eitan Avitzur, Marina Ritzarev, and Edwin Seroussi (Ramat Gan: Bar Ilan University Press, 2012), 141–164.

10. Ibid., 149–150. Albertos Nar has also documented some remarkable instances of cross-fertilization between rebetiko music and Judeo-Spanish song, including Judeo-Spanish renditions of songs recorded in Greek by Markos Vamvakaris, Antonios Dalkas, and Roza Eskenazi, rebetiko songs about Jewish women, and a song composed by Vasilis Tsitsanis with lyrics describing the deportation of the Jews from Salonika by the Germans. See Albertos Nar, "Evraíoi kai rempétika" [Jews and rebetika], in *Judeo-Espaniol: The Evolution of a Culture*, ed. Raphael Gatenio (Thessaloniki: Ets Haim Foundation, 1999), 139–166 (Greek).

11. See Fleming, *Greece*, chapter 10.

12. While in I focus in this chapter on those who settled in Palestine/Israel (before and after the Holocaust) and their investment in Greek rebetiko and *laiko* (popular) music, it is important to note that music was equally central to the experience of Salonikan Jews deported to the camps, and to commemoration efforts in Israel organized by those who were more invested in Western music, and in the revitalization of the Judeo-Spanish song lore, as previously documented by a set of invaluable studies, autobiographies, and testimonies. See for example Haim Rafael, *Shirat ḥayim* [The song of life] (self-published, 1997); Moshe

Ha-Elion, The Straits of Hell: *The Chronicle of a Salonikan Jew in the Nazi Extermination Camps Auschwitz, Mauthausen, Melk, Ebensee*, Peleus 30 (Mannheim: Bibliopolis, 2005); and Jacques Stroumza, *Violinist in Auschwitz: From Salonika to Jerusalem 1913–1967* (Konstanz: Hartung-Gorre Verlag, 1996). See also Shmuel Rafael, ed., *Routes of hell: Greek Jewry in the Holocaust—Testimonies* (Tel Aviv: ha-Makhon le-ḥeker Yahadut Saloniḳi, 1988); Yitzhak Kerem, "The Music of the Greek Jews in the Holocaust," in *Proceedings of the First International Conference on Jewish Music*, ed. Steve Stanton and Alexander Knapp (London: City University Department of Music, 1997), 46–52; Paris Pachomios Chronakis, " 'We Lived as Greeks and We Died as Greek': Salonikan Jews in Auschwitz and the Meanings of Nationhood," in *The Holocaust in Greece*, ed. Dirk A. Moses and Giorgos Antoniou (Cambridge: Cambridge University Press, 2018), 157–180; and Fleming, *Greece*, 151–156.

13. See Orly C. Meron, "Demografia," in Greece: Jewish Communities in the East in the Nineteenth and Twentieth Centuries/:קהילות ישראל במזרח במאות התשע עשרה והעשרים יוון, ed. Eyal Ginio (Jerusalem: Ben Zvi Institute, 2014), 75–92.

14. Dafni Tragaki, *Rebetiko Worlds* (Newcastle: Cambridge Scholars, 2007), 53.

15. See Minna Rozen, "Money, Power, Politics, and the Great Salonika Fire of 1917," *Jewish Social Studies* 22, no. 2 (2017): 74–115; and Rena Molho, "Jewish Working-Class Neighborhoods in Salonika following the 1890 and 1917 Fires," in *The Last Ottoman Century and Beyond: The Jews in Turkey and the Balkans 1808–1945*, ed. Minna Rozen, 2 vols. (Tel Aviv: Tel Aviv University, 2002), 2:173–94. See also, Mark Mazower, *Salonika, City of Ghosts: Christians, Muslims and Jews, 1430–1950* (New York, Alfred Knopf, 2007), 209–237. On the musical aspects of Westernization, see Tragaki, *Rebetiko Worlds*, 6; and David M. Bunis, *Voices from Jewish Salonika* (Jerusalem: Misgav Yerushalayim, 1999), 283.

16. Eyal Ginio, " 'Learning the Beautiful Language of Homer': Judeo-Spanish-Speaking Jews and the Greek Language and Culture between the Wars," in "Ladino Print Culture," special issue, *Jewish History* 16, no. 3 (2002): 239.

17. See Shai Srougo, *The Jewish Laborers in the Port of Thessaloniki: Between Ottoman world World and the Greek Nation State (1869–1936)/* הפועלים היהודים בנמל סלוניקי: בין העולם היוונית הלאום מדינת של לעולמה מאני העות') 1936–1869 (Jerusalem: Ben Zvi Institute and the Hebrew University of Jerusalem, 2014), 182.

18. Rozen, "On Nationalizing Minorities," 152.

19. See, for example, Paris Papamichos Chronakis, "De-Judaizing a Class, Hellenizing a City: Jewish Merchants and the Future of Salonika in Greek Public Discourse, 1913–1914," in "Salonika's Jews," special issue, *Jewish History* 28, nos. 3–4 (2014): 373–403; Orly C. Meron, "Huṭim meḳashrim? Yevanim, pliṭim ve-yehudaim be-taasiyat ha-ṭeḳsṭil be-Saloniḳi beshnim, 1923–1943" [Connecting threads? Greeks, refugees, and Jews in Thessaloniki's textile industry, 1923–1943], *Zmanim: A Historical Quarterly* 129 (Winter 2015): 78–93; and Srougo, *The Jewish Laborers*.

20. Svetlana Boym, *The Future of Nostalgia* (New York: Basic Books, 2001), xiii–xvi.

21. For a detailed account of the literary tradition of *coplas del fuego*, see Elena Romero, *Entre dos (o mas) fuegos: Fuentes poeticas para la historia de los Sefardies de los Balcanes* (Madrid: Consejo Superior de Investigaciones Científicas, 2008). For a discussion of songs/poems in response to the great fire of 1917—*coplas* and other genres—preserved in both oral and written sources, see Shmuel Refael, "Los Cantis del Insidio: The Great Fire of 1917 and Its Reflection in Judeo-Spanish Folk Song," in *Ladinar*, ed. Judith Dishon and Shmuel Refael (Tel Aviv: Institute for Research of the Jews of Salonika, 1998), 93–117.

22. The song was originally published in the booklet *10 kantes populares de Sadik i Gazoz (sinkena shia), El rizon,* n.d. [ca. 1925], 7–8. For a reprint see Bunis, *Voices,* 286–288.
23. Tragaki, *Rebetiko Worlds,* 59–60.
24. Bunis, *Voices,* 295.
25. Ibid., 299. On Refugee musicians, see Stathis Gauntlett, "Between Orientalism and Occidentalism: The Contribution of Asia Minor Refugees to Greek Popular Song and its Reception," in *Crossing the Aegean: An Appraisal of the 1923 Compulsory Population Exchange between Greece and Turkey,* ed. Rene Hirschon (New York: Berghahn Books, 2003), 247–260.
26. "kon su dono i su talento se pwede dezir ke el es un muzikante enternasyonal ke sona muchos estrumentos i kanta en turko, grego, espanyol i arabo. Los bwenos *chalgidjís* ke vinyeron de Estambol al tyempo del trókido de las populasyones, kwalifikan a si[nyor] Sadik de 'gramofón,' talmente le basta una sola vez de sentir no emporta ke pedaso de múzika para ke lo retenga, i muchas vezes lo koreja si está yerado." In Bunis, *Voices,* 295.
27. Srougo, *The Jewish Laborers,* 318.
28. Mazower, *Salonica,* 389.
29. See Bunis, *Voices,* 283.
30. On the Judeo-Spanish version, see ibid., 292–293.
31. The term "sociomusical structures" refers to patterns that govern the dynamic association of certain musical sounds, styles, or genres with social groups identified by gender, race, ethnicity, class, etc. (or some intersection thereof), either by members of those groups themselves or by others. For a useful overview, see William G. Roy and Timothy J. Dowd, "What Is Sociological about Music?," *Annual Review of Sociology* 36, no. 1 (2010): 183–203.
32. *Dansinges* is the Judeo-Spanish plural form for the (Turkish) colloquial name given to Salonikan dance halls playing Western music. It is derived from the English word "dancing."
33. JCPA was a medium-wave British Forces Broadcasting Station established in Palestine in 1944. With the collapse of the British Mandate in 1948, the British Forces relocated the station to Cyprus.
34. Pnina and Yaakov Nahmias, in discussion with the author, October 31, 2013.
35. Leonidas Economou, "Sentiment, Memory, and Identity in Greek Laiko Music (1945–1967)," in *Made in Greece: Studies in Popular Music,* ed. Dafni Tragaki (London: Routledge, 2018), 23.
36. As Eyal Ginio notes, while the middle class and elites stuck with French or learned Greek, Jewish communists advocated the cultivation of Judeo-Spanish as the authentic vernacular of the Jewish worker. See Ginio, "Learning the Beautiful Language of Homer," 248–249.
37. Fleming, *Greece,* 165.
38. Yaakov "Jako" Maestro, in discussion with the author, September 22, 2014.
39. Quoted in Havassy, "Musiḳah popularit," 142–143.
40. Yaakov "Jako" Maestro, in discussion with the author, September 22, 2014.
41. The use of "heavy" (*varýs*) and "light" (*elafrós*) to distinguish music that is lamentful and "Oriental" from music that is more upbeat and more Western in style is common in Greek. It is used in exactly the same sense in Hebrew with regard to Mizrahi- or Mediterranean-style Israeli pop (*mizrahi kaved,* for the more Turkish or Arabic style of Ofer Levi or Avi

Biter, vs. *mizrahi layt* [using the English world "light"] for the more upbeat, Western-pop-influenced style of Moshe Perez or Dudu Aharon).

42. Trifonas Nikolaidis, in discussion with the author, September 3, 2014.

43. בבית שמעו מוזיקה יוונית, מוזיקה יוונית ש... שלא... לא עושה שמח, לא עושה טוב על הלב, רק מביאה כובד ודיכאון. זה שירים שהם שמעו בבית, שירים שמספרים גם על מלחמות, על ניכר, על פרידות, על כאב, דברים כאלה. וזה היה נורא, נורא... זה נספג בי. אני יודע ואני זוכר שירים שהייתי אומר לאבא שלי "די, תעצור את זה, כי זה מביא לי לבכות, אני לא יכול לשמוע זה עושה לי רע". והוא היה אומר לי "זה גם לי עושה רע, זה מזכיר לי את המשפחה שלי. אם אתה היית יודע מה היה ואיזה דברים אני עברתי... אתה צריך לשמוע, אתה צריך לדעת שלאבא שלך היו אחים ואחות ודודים ודודות ומשפחה, והייתה שמחה והיה אושר והאושר הזה נקטע, האושר הזה נגדע", ו...הוא אמר "אני לא יכול בלי המוזיקה הזאת, אני חייב לשמוע אותה"
Because of That War / בגלל המלחמה ההיא, documentary film by Orna Ben-David (1988).

44. Fleming, *Greece*, 51–52.

45. Daviko Pitchon, in discussion with the author, December 18, 2013.

46. *Syrtaki* is the name given retroactively to the dance performed by Anthony Quinn in the role of Zorba the Greek in the eponymous 1964 film. The music for this dance was composed by Mikis Theodorakis, hybridizing several Greek and Cretan dance rhythms. The syrtaki is therefore, as Lisbet Torp has suggested, a synthetic dance that is "invented" and "Western-orientated." The immense success of the film, and the unprecedented global success of this tune in particular, led to hundreds of recorded versions of it and to a cottage industry of Greek dance manuals, all featuring the nonexistent tradition of syrtaki. See Lisbet Torp, "Zorba's Dance: The Story of a Dance Illusion and Its Touristic Value," *Ethnografika* 8 (1992): 207–210.

47. Founded in 1920, the *Histadrut* was the main labor union for Zionists in Palestine, and later the largest union in the State of Israel. Under the hegemony of Labor Zionism, it functioned both as part of the state apparatus, and as an extension of the ruling party, Mapai.

48. Following the success of the Navy Band, at least two more "Greek" musical parodies were recorded: "Ahavah yam-tikhonit" (Mediterranean love) by Lehakat Pikud Merkaz (Central Command Band) in 1969, and "Haristos haristopoulos," by Tsevet Bidur Heil Avir (The Air Force Entertainment Crew) in 1973.

49. The definitive text on Bourekas films is the third chapter of Ella Shohat, *Israeli Cinema: East/West and the Politics of Representation* (Austin: University of Texas Press, 1989), 115–178. See also Rami Kimchi, *Israeli Shtetls: Bourekas Films and Yiddish Classical Literature* / שטעטל בארץ ישראל: סרטי הבורקס ומקורותיהם בספרות יידיש קלסית (Tel Aviv: Resling, 2012), 59–70.

50. Fleming, *Greece*, 195–196.

51. Of Romanian descent, Seltzer (1931–) made himself a name in the 1950s as the founding musical director of the military band Lehakat Ha-Nahal, for which he composed Hebrew songs that employed the hora, and as an ambassador of Israeli "folk" music in the United States. After his 1966 double triumph, scoring two works involving the representation of Mizrahim and the ethnic tensions in Israeli Jewish society—the stage musical *Kazablan* and Menachem Golan's cinematic melodrama *Fortuna*—Seltzer became something of a go-to for this task. His musical reconstruction of Greek and Mizrahi sounds, filtered through his own compositional ear, is thus the sonic counterpart to the social construction of these identities by the authors of Bourekas films and other avenues of representation.

52. Chronakis, "De-Judaizing a Class," 375–376.

SELECT BIBLIOGRAPHY

Brubaker, Rogers. *Ethnicity without Groups*. Cambridge, MA: Harvard University Press, 2004.

Bunis, David M. *Voices from Jewish Salonika*. Jerusalem: Misgav Yerushalayim, 1999.

Chronakis, Paris Papamichos. "'We Lived as Greeks and We Died as Greeks': Thessalonican Jews in Auschwitz and the Meanings of Nationhood." In *The Holocaust in Greece*, edited by Dirk A. Moses and Giorgos Antoniou, 157–180. Cambridge: Cambridge University Press, 2018.

Economou, Leonidas. "Sentiment, Memory, and Identity in Greek Laiko Music (1945–1967)." In *Made in Greece: Studies in Popular Music*, edited by Dafni Tragaki, 17–27. London: Routledge, 2018.

Fleming, Katherine Elizabeth. *Greece: A Jewish History*. Princeton, NJ: Princeton University Press, 2008.

Gauntlett, Stathis. "Between Orientalism and Occidentalism: The Contribution of Asia Minor Refugees to Greek Popular Song and its Reception." In *Crossing the Aegean: An Appraisal of the 1923 Compulsory Population Exchange between Greece and Turkey*, edited by Rene Hirschon, 247–260. New York: Berghahn Books, 2003.

Havassy, Rivka. "Musiḳah popularit ba-ḳehilah ha-Yehudit be-Saloniḳi bein shtei milhamot ha-olam: Iyun be-yetsiratam shel Mosheh Ḳazis ve-Tsadiḳ Gershon (Tsadik ve-Gazoz)" [Popular music in the Jewish community of Thessaloniki in the interwar period: A study of the work of Sadik Gershón and Moshé Cazés (Sadik y Gazoz)]. In *Garment and Core: Jews and their Musical Experiences* / לבוש ותוך: המוסיקה בחוויית היהדות, edited by Eitan Avitzur, Marina Ritzarev, and Edwin Seroussi, 141–164. Ramat Gan: Bar Ilan University Press, 2012.

Havassy, Rivka, and Edwin Seroussi. "Ha-musiḳah ve ha-shirah" [Music and poetry]. In *Greece: Jewish Communities in the East in the Nineteenth and Twentieth Centuries* / קהילות ישראל במזרח במאות התשע עשרה והעשרים: יוון, edited by Eyal Ginio, 219–240. Jerusalem: Ben Zvi Institute, 2014.

Mazower, Mark. *Salonica, City of Ghosts*. New York: Alfred A. Knopf 2005.

Naar, Devin E. *Jewish Salonika: Between the Ottoman Empire and Modern Greece*. Stanford, CA: Stanford University Press, 2016.

Nar, Albertos. "Evraioi kai rempetika / The Sephardi vs. the 'Rembetico' Folk Song." In *Judeo-Espaniol: The Evolution of a Culture* / η ιστορική πορεία μιας παράδοσης: διεθνές συνέδριο, edited by Raphael Gatenio, 139–166. Thessaloniki: Ets Ahaim Foundation, 1999.

Pennanen, Risto Pekka. "The Nationalization of Ottoman Popular Music in Greece." *Ethnomusicology* 48, no. 1 (2004): 1–25.

Regev, Motti, and Edwin Seroussi. *Popular Music and National Culture in Israel*. Berkeley: University of California Press, 2004.

Shohat, Ella. *Israeli Cinema: East/West and the Politics of Representation*. Austin: University of Texas Press, 1989.

Srougo, Shai. *Jewish Laborers in the Port of Thessaloniki: Between Ottoman World and the Greek Nation State (1869–1936)* / הפועלים היהודים בנמל סלוניקי: בין העולם העות׳מאני לעולמה של מדינת הלאום היוונית (1869–1936). Jerusalem: Ben Zvi Institute and the Hebrew University of Jerusalem, 2014.

Tragaki, Dafni. *Rebetiko Worlds*. Newcastle: Cambridge Scholars, 2007.

8

BERLIN KLEZMER AND URBAN SCENES

PHIL ALEXANDER

ROOTED in eastern European Ashkenazi Jewish social ritual—most notably the wedding—klezmer has historically marked both communal cohesiveness and ethnic difference. Whether accompanying the seating of the bride (*kale bazetsn*), playing a *broyges tants* of anger and reconciliation, or a *skotshne* showpiece from the bandleader—the most famous of whom often only played at the top table (*baym tish*) and left the dance music to their band—the music of the klezmorim delineated space and structured proceedings, beating ritual time and underlaying a gamut of appropriate emotions. Klezmorim not only underpinned Jewish communal events, but were in themselves a community, with their own argot (*klezmerloshn*), their own way of life (*leybns shteyger*), and often their own repertoire passed down within musician families. Klezmorim formed a dynastic caste, producing all male *kapelyes* that ensured a cohesive performing unit and provided a living, of varying degrees.

At the same time, successful European klezmer musicians of the nineteenth and early twentieth centuries often traveled widely, moving between towns and cities, performing regularly for non-Jewish patrons, and in some places interacting regularly with professional Roma *lautari*. As with many musicians, spatial mobility was an important, perhaps inevitable, feature of their working environment, placing many klezmorim in an ambiguous insider-outsider position straddling the inner workings of ethnic cohesion and the farther edges of musical and social outreach. Klezmer music thus denotes in-group exclusivity, while the klezmer *musician*, on the other hand, has historically pointed to a potentially subversive level of transgression.

These paradoxes have their popular cultural parallels. Here, for example, is Sholem Aleichem's description of the deep ritual role played—literally—by violinist Stempenyu, based on the real-life musician Yosele Drucker:

> No pen can describe how beautifully Stempenyu played the accompaniment to the
> bride's enthronement . . . It was as if Stempenyu, having taken his stand in front of the

bride, was desirous of playing on his fiddle a special sermon for her edification—a long, beautiful sermon touching on the life she had led hitherto, and the different life to which she was going, on the threshold of which she now found herself.[1]

And yet, a few pages later, this edifying sermonist is simultaneously revealed as a dangerously flesh-and-blood human:

> Rochalle blushed scarlet. She feared to look into Stempenyu's eyes, and kept her face averted from him. She hardly knew what he was saying, and only with difficulty managed to say one word to his ten. She felt that it was not at all right for a modest young woman to stand talking with a musician before a whole room fell asleep.[2]

Much has changed, however, since the time of Yosele Drucker and friends, even though a connection to the music's eastern European roots remains a constituent part of many contemporary musicians' philosophy and practice. Music that once defined and choreographed lifestage and ritual now operates mostly on the concert stage, in jam sessions, in workshops or dances, or at the more exotic end of street-band repertoire. Klezmer musicians still play weddings, but usually as part of a portfolio evening (as opposed to a week-long community event) that includes a DJ, or perhaps a slick cover band—who may also take care of the "Jewish" requests without the need for klezmer specialists.[3] Klezmorim in New York or London are regularly booked for Haredi *simkhes*, but while the musicians' versatility is acknowledged, the main musical attraction is likely to be the singer, who may well be backing themselves on electric keyboard. And where immigrant Jewish wedding musicians of the early twentieth century may have been more comfortable with a freylekhs or sher than with non-Jewish American repertoire, for twenty-first-century wedding bands it is more likely to be the other way around.

Similarly, the term "klezmer" itself has undergone etymological shifts. Originating as a rabbinical Hebrew term for a musical instrument (a contraction of *kley* and *zemer*, i.e., "vessel of song"), from around the sixteenth century onward the word began in Yiddish eastern Europe to refer instead to a musician, and specifically an instrumental musician for weddings and other celebrations. Set against the modernizing changes of the first half of the twentieth century, the appellation increasingly came to signify a certain type of old-world, implicitly limited, musical perspective—in contrast to the more versatile and upwardly mobile *muzikant*. With one or two important exceptions, it is only from the 1970s onward that klezmer has been widely used to mean a type of music; and while this is by far the most common contemporary usage, specifically musical definitions remain hard to pin down.[4]

Alongside these changing spaces, oscillating repertoires, and linguistic transformations, musical meanings have also morphed. Although still frequently used as a (residual) soundtrack for "things Jewish," klezmer no longer has much semiotic energy as a tight in-group marker, or as a musical signifier of transgressive attitudes (many other subcultural musics fill this role far more dramatically). Moving from specific ritual moments and enacted forms of behavior, klezmer music takes its place in the twenty-first century as part of a broad world-music discourse that promotes eclectic consumption underpinned by a manageably loose sense of cultural specificity. And today's klezmer musicians, while they may travel widely, are by and large unlikely to make any lists of the mad, bad, or dangerous to know. For some, multiple forms of Jewishness remain fundamental to their musical creativity. For others, direct links to klezmer as Jewish music are at best tangential: "a symbol, a tease, a keepsake that pays a small deference to a lost world and then takes its place in a contemporary musical culture that has no use for its historical context."[5]

These changing relationships point to a transformation in the nature of klezmer agency: from the musical expression of a distinct ethnic group to a music that itself generates new communities or scenes both temporary and longer-lasting; from a preexisting social order defined by multiple shared practices to a contingent, fluid, and fleeting connectivity; from a well-defined group enacting recognized elements of cohesive social life to something that creates collectivity through its own processes, where "likeness is not the grounds of this community, *but its effect*."[6]

And with klezmer music, there is one further, disappeared layer. Many of the places from which this music sprang are no longer home to Jewish life, meaning that connections to an "Old Country" inevitably take on a more imaginary, affective dimension. As an appealing sonic marker of Jewish eastern Europe, but cut loose from the knotty details of its daily life, klezmer in this case develops an augmented sediment of the symbolic, and of the romantic. It relies ever more heavily upon desire, as seen in the beguilingly wistful confluence of pragmatism and nostalgia that frames the "Invocation," which opens Walter Zev Feldman's comprehensive volume of klezmer history:

> Klezmer music stands across from us and apart from us. It is a little island just off the shore. On a clear day we can make out trees and pathways, half-ruined houses from the days when it had been inhabited. Sometimes ghostly music wafts our way from the island, almost too faint to hear, but at other times strident and piercing. Some free summer afternoon I think I would like to go out to the island, but there is no bridge and no ferry service. The water is unaccountably deep and turbulent—I don't dare to try to swim. I stare out at the blue, almost cloudless sky, wondering why I cannot traverse that short distance.[7]

Unlike Feldman's island, the overwhelming majority of klezmer music now takes place in cities and is marked by musical cosmopolitanism and participant heterogeneity. This is not just music for and by Jews—it is no longer passed down through dynastic lineage, and in most cases it forms only one aspect of any individual's musical life. Klezmer music has moved from being the ritual instrumental music of ethnically marked communities to an internationalized, widely accessed, and flexible form that unfolds through multiple smaller scenes. It has become a more open signifier, one that can be made to "mean" in different, locally relevant ways—as seen, for example, in the broad array of band names into which the word itself is inserted: from the geographically specific (London Klezmer Quartet, Maxwell St Klezmer Band), to the political (Isle of Klezbos), to the extra-terrestrial (Klingon Klezmer), and beyond.

Since the turn of the twenty-first century, klezmer has attracted increasing amounts of academic attention.[8] The majority of this work has been directed toward the various and often ambiguous identity politics that have in different ways (and at different times) been thrown up by the so-called klezmer revival. Klezmer in some of these cases has at times become a vehicle for a wider, occasionally anxious, conversation that is less relevant here. This chapter, instead, explores the detachment of a music from its clear and bounded social function, and the replacement of its original geographies with a universal availability. It seeks to understand what klezmer can reveal about musical collectivity and spatial rootedness based not in preexisting structures but on affiliation across multiple and varied levels of participation. Specifically, in what ways does musical collectivity remain active and important within environments (be they physical, cultural, or psychological) that are far removed from where the music began and developed?

To understand some of these processes, the second half of the chapter will focus on klezmer and Yiddish music in Berlin from the early 1980s onward, which is when the city's vibrant scenes—the liveliest outside of North America—took root. Like many in the twenty-first century, this is a fluid and rhizomatic musical network, accessed on many levels simultaneously, for many different reasons and with widely differing degrees of affinity, expertise, and interest. Berlin's klezmer scenes, comprised of multiple criss-crossing networks and ties, continue to enfold a number of chronologies and geographies—palimpsests that overlay the revitalization of Yiddish music onto the city's own history of borders and their transgression. This ongoing vibrancy shows that in order to survive—even flourish—in the contemporary city, klezmer music needs to make itself part of that city; it must be heard as meaningful to the bars, jam sessions, and festivals where it now operates. And while recent developments are often tied into international Yiddish musical networks, there is a strong parallel sense of the local that has a direct effect on city-based activities and decisions. Berlin, in other words, is one of the axes where the transnational klezmer community meets the local urban scene.

SHIFTING PARADIGMS

A sense of place is fundamental to the meanings and practice of traditional music, but the relationship is not a static one. And in the case of klezmer music, a connection to the changing city has often been a driving force. Moving outward from a musical expression of eastern European Ashkenazi ritual practice, klezmer has reflected the migrations of the populations from which it sprang—in particular, the move of more than two million Jews across the Atlantic at the turn of the twentieth century.[9] For klezmorim who made this journey, the cramped, heterogeneous surroundings of the *goldene medina* meant inevitable changes in their working lives. Weeklong weddings moved to a single afternoon and evening, immigrant *landsmanshaftn* societies became important sources of work, alongside the Yiddish theater, radio broadcasts, and the strengthening of musicians' unions. The shortening of Jewish weddings—the klezmer's mainstay—also meant the disappearance of many accompanying ritual practices, along with an inevitable contraction of repertoire.

Notwithstanding these changes, klezmer in early twentieth-century America remained functionally rooted in the immigrant Jewish communities of which it was a part.[10] Increasing acculturation over the middle decades of the century, however, paralleled a growing distance from eastern European Ashkenazi roots, and the 1950s onward saw klezmer's cultural stock diminish—overpowered by the move of American Jewry to the mainstream (where a music that sounded eastern European difference was less desirable) and the very different sound of the new state of Israel. Following several decades of mid-century cultural submergence, a younger generation of American-born Jewish musicians would retake klezmer and Yiddish music for themselves, reinvesting the work of older immigrant musicians with a new significance and value, and also imbuing the music with a newly muscular and radicalized political sensibility. The American klezmer revitalization of the 1970s onward enacted an alternative model of collectivity, looking "back" to the Old Country in order to forge a new, and in this context radical, relationship to eastern European Ashkenazi culture. Klezmer was reclaimed from its slump into heritage and nostalgia: although its roots were old, this American Jewish music was fresh and vibrant, provoking what Feldman has called a "major cultural catharsis for New York Jews."[11] It proclaimed a sound of difference and of elsewhere that consolidated new musical groupings while also connecting directly back to the music's original—now largely destroyed—homelands.[12]

With its origins in a number of locales, revitalized klezmer swiftly spread across international channels, connecting parallel movements in Germany, Russia, the United Kingdom, and elsewhere from the mid-1980s onward. In a chapter devoted to "Klezmer as Community," Mark Slobin identifies a number of different manifestations, each articulating a relation to place, but also to Jewishness within that place.[13] Nomadic groups are those bands whose place-ness travels with them—such as the self-aware New York downtown eclecticism that the Klezmatics have brought to their performances since their inception in the late 1980s. More recently, American Yiddish musician Daniel Kahn has taken this process one step further, bringing his own version of Yiddish-inflected Berlin into contact with other similarly powerful musical geographies, such as Psoy Korolenko's Moscow. Kaleidoscopic communities, workshops, and festivals like KlezKamp[14] or Yiddish Summer Weimar unite myriad versions of klezmer behavior and identity under one enthusiastic banner—often at a certain remove from everyday life. Phantom collectives—"chimeric communities of artistic imagination"[15]—are those that have been imagined into being and are largely populated by non-Jews. Krakow's virtual Jewish space is the clearest example, although Berlin has at times been cast in the same light.[16] Paralleling these are phoenix communities like Odessa—reborn centers of Ashkenazi Jewish musical life.

Alongside these place-based relationships, wider cultural channels of dissemination have shifted. The music's engagingly direct emotional aesthetic, its easy danceability, and its virtuosic appeal to classically and jazz-trained musicians have enabled klezmer to take its place as a recognized "world music" genre, accessible not just as performance music but simultaneously across numerous less formal levels of participation—from workshops to jam sessions to festivals.[17] Helped along by commercialized routes of dissemination and consumption, klezmer's global reach from the 1990s onward has broadened its networks and diffused its ethnic specificity. As Hankus Netsky suggests, resurgent klezmer music has now splintered into "mainstream, fusion, downtown, feminist, classical, historical performance, religious, and even 'tourist-oriented.' "[18]

An essential component in this contemporary transnational diversity is, of course, the online community, where, as Sophie Arkette notes, "technology mediates between the physical space of encounters, throwing up in its wake modified representations."[19] But "modified representations" have in fact been a part of transnational Yiddish cultural production across much of the twentieth century, reaching across the Yiddish-speaking Jewish diaspora, supported by ongoing patterns of migration, and—until the Holocaust—a lively East–West exchange of texts and music. Thanks to touring theater, sheet music, and subsequently the phonograph and the internal-combustion engine, a Yiddish operetta song such as Avrom Goldfaden's *Rozhinkes mit mandlen*, written in 1881, was able to attain the status of a beloved folksong within a generation or two. In 1916 Russian-born klezmer violinist Wolff N. Kostakowsky published a book of *International Hebrew Wedding Music*, foregrounding the travel of eastern European klezmer music to the New World, and at the same time pointing to the increased presence of musicians from outside family kapelyes on the bandstand.[20] In the early years of the twentieth century, Yiddish language newspapers such as St. Petersburg's *Der fraynd* carried regular pieces from correspondents in Berlin, Vienna, New York, Buenos Aires, and even Glasgow—highlighting the ongoing transnational communication between global population centers that were home to increasing numbers of immigrant Yiddish-speaking Ashkenazi Jews. And the presence of near-identical klezmer tunes in the Ukrainian ethnographic collections of Zusman Kiselhof, the New York songbooks published by J. & J. Kammen, and the phonographic recordings of Naftule Brandwein show that musicians were sustaining strong international networks of dissemination, in much the same way as the links still maintained between traditional Irish or Scottish musicians either side of the Atlantic.

In the twenty-first century, the international Yiddish music community has increasingly connected through online networks and digital technology. Projects such as "Inside the Yiddish Folksong" (www.yiddishfolksong.com), YIVO's online Ruth Rubin archive (see Biezunski in this volume), and the Kiselgof-Makonovestky digitization project (www.klezmerinstitute.org/kmdmp) make available online the riches of physical archives, but are also based around the ongoing collaboration and use of these archives by an international network of practitioners, scholars, and enthusiasts, physically dispersed but digitally connected. This is a symbiotic digital transnationalism: physical resources dispersed through virtual networks, whose globalism begins to constitute an online (non-physical) community. These digital resources are reflected and textured by local iterations in the form of performances, recordings, and online sessions.

Thus while klezmer music's role within Ashkenazi Jewish community ritual has diminished greatly since the middle of the twentieth century, the music continues to act as a cohering force—straddling the local and the virtual, the amateur and the professional, the specialist and the lay participant. Klezmer in the twenty-first century reveals not so much a fixed social grouping as a shifting and overlapping set of local scenes, articulating collective musical space in a looser but equally meaningful way. Will Straw suggests that where a musical community depends on a link between contemporary practice and musical heritage, scenes instead gain momentum through "the building of musical alliances and the drawing of musical boundaries."[21] In other words, scenes contain an active sense of allegiance, of deliberate agency, a collective affiliation that is, Straw suggests, different from the processes underpinning a musical community, who may often have been brought together through forces other than musical ones. Where, in very broad terms, communities use music to reinforce wider shared experience, scenes come together *because* of the music. Or as Simon Frith argues, "making music isn't a way of expressing ideas; it is a way of living them."[22]

These changing relationships of collectivity and spatiality can be better understood and contextualized by looking at some of the lived experiences of klezmer musical practice within the city of Berlin. Berlin offers a particular perspective here, as its klezmer history is a recent one, stemming from the 1980s. The nineteenth-century eastern European Ashkenazi communities of the Pale of Settlement and neighboring Bessarabia—klezmer's heartlands, so to speak—were many miles farther east and south of the German capital, and Berlin's Jewish population through the nineteenth and early twentieth centuries was largely assimilated and westward-facing. Early twentieth-century eastern European immigrant enclaves in the city were perceived in terms of their exoticized difference to the city's assimilated Jews—as in the Russified nickname "Charlottengrad" given to the western district of Charlottenburg, for example. And although there were numerous prewar performances and recordings of Yiddish music in the city, the context for these was overwhelmingly the theater stage or the concert hall. Klezmer in Berlin has rarely been utilized to express Jewish community coherence, or to structure Jewish ritual events. As a result, the performance of klezmer, and the spaces within which it operates, are constitutive of a more recent set of musical and social meanings, connected to participation and performance at a more subcultural level, and in many ways directly representative of the changing relationship of klezmer to different notions of collectivity. And although these newer manifestations are no longer the expression of a distinct ethnic or religious group, they occasionally overlap with one.

BERLIN'S CHANGING KLEZMER SCENES

Connections between Yiddish culture and German lands stretch back a millennium, just like the linguistic *Mittelhochdeutsch* roots shared by both languages. In the late nineteenth and early twentieth centuries, Berlin's Scheunenviertel district became a hub of eastern European Yiddish cultural activity, and the interwar Weimar Republic was a transnational center of Yiddish literary production. In postwar East Berlin the singer and Holocaust survivor Lin Jaldati and her husband Eberhard Rebling were Eastern Bloc ambassadors for Yiddish song—simultaneously helping to mitigate accusations of cultural suppression by the socialist state—while in the West singers such as Peter Rohland used this same tradition to mount a musical challenge to post-Holocaust silence.

Despite these figures, however, it was the absence of historiographies relating to eastern European Jewish culture—a lack of alternative narratives of the city—that would push the next stage of development, and inspire younger musicians to explore. In the early 1980s, a small number of East German musicians came to klezmer and Yiddish song through varying routes, establishing a somewhat disparate, semi-accidental Berlin Yiddish musical scene. Singer Karsten Troyke (1960–) began to perform at small musical events organized by his cultural activist father, Josh Sellhorn. Although his interest was initially sparked by the chance to write and sing his own songs, Troyke found himself gravitating increasingly to the Yiddish song recordings played at the "Jewish evenings" that his father curated. Troyke went on to study Yiddish with Sara Bialas-Tenenberg, a Holocaust survivor from Częstochowa, also learning and recording songs from her own Yiddish repertoire. Troyke's performances often bring together this lesser-known material with well-known Yiddish favorites, and also his own translations of works by, among others, Leonard Cohen.

In the intervening decades, Troyke has become an international ambassador for Yiddish music, performing and teaching around the world. A multilingual performer possessed of a strikingly gravelly voice, his singing style is intimate and accessible, and his stage persona is witty, warm, and never over-serious or preening. Nevertheless, despite this successful artistic reach, the development of Troyke's career illustrates well the slight "outsider" position held by Berlin's Yiddish musical pioneers of the 1980s: held in high esteem and commanding a great deal of respect, and at the same time no longer a central part of the contemporary scene.

Around the same time that Karsten Troyke was honing his craft as a performer and interpreter, the group Aufwind was also coming together in East Berlin, initially to learn and perform Yiddish songs. The place of klezmer in their repertoire was boosted significantly by the arrival of the clarinettist Jan Hermerschmidt (1966–)—a musician who has always placed exploration at the heart of his aesthetic—in 1988. For both Aufwind and Troyke, the relative absence of musical networks and structures was itself an influence upon their development. Working with limited resources, the band found themselves piecing together repertoire, performance style, and history with whatever they could find, driven by an actively revisionist agenda:

> Firstly what interested us was Yiddish. Later, klezmer music came alongside. Yiddish was important because it was a part of the East and yet one learned nothing about it in school. . . . There were no concerts yet, so we had to seek out recordings anywhere that anyone had them.[23]

In 1993, Aufwind was the first German band to travel to KlezKamp, the long-running festival of Yiddish music in New York's Catskill Mountains. As non-Jewish Germans, they faced inevitable curiosity, and some skepticism, about their motives for performing Jewish music—obstacles that they overcame with a mixture of persistence and good grace. They were not, however, the first group to be playing klezmer music in the city of Berlin. Two decades before Troyke and Aufwind, a trio of West German musical explorers had picked up balalaikas and a fiddle and begun to make a name for themselves within both the city's folk pubs, and also the Russian immigrant enclaves of Charlottenburg and Halensee. Kasbek's choice of music and instruments set themselves directly against the Westernized tide of pop music flowing rapidly into their city, but also against the division of their city itself. In the 1980s the arrival of guitarist and singer Uwe Sauerwein added a more explicit Yiddish musical focus that persists in the band today. Through their fifty-years-and-counting career, Kasbek have been a quietly persistent musical force, whose regular and wide-ranging collaborations have included Turkish, Iranian, and Roma musicians. The band's long history articulates several constitutive and continuing threads of the Berlin klezmer scene: a strongly collaborative ethos, firm rooting in specific local and loyal venues, an interested public that acknowledges a need for context, and a notable lack of emphasis on commercial pressures—helped in this case, like many others, by the fact that music is not their primary income.

While Troyke, Aufwind, and Kasbek share a sense of overlapping histories, they also acknowledge that their own musical approach differs from more recent, workshop-trained klezmer musicians in the city. The fact that all three of these artists were forced by limited resources to piece together their style from whatever materials came to hand, rather than learning their klezmer at workshops and summer courses, means that each has in some senses created their own distinct soundworld—one that is less directly linked to the American influence discussed below. Jan Hermerschmidt relates this directly to the changing urban scenes within which they have been in dialogue over many years, and particularly in relation to the city before reunification:

> Aufwind don't belong at all to that [new klezmer] world. [But] it doesn't bother anyone. There are others who do their own thing, too. Karsten Troyke, for example. These musicians also play a lot together—it's still in some ways an East German scene ... There's also a certain nostalgia.[24]

Where klezmer in East Berlin was largely perpetuated through local musician networks—including the Tage der jiddischen Kultur festival, which ran from 1987 to 1996 and included Lin Jaldati's daughter Jalda Rebling among its organizers—in West Berlin performances and dissemination were often the result of American and Israeli impact. The popular Argentinian-Israeli clarinetist Giora Feidman, and American ensembles such as Kapelye and the Klezmer Conservatory Band, toured West Germany throughout the 1980s—often under the auspices of Jewish community organizations—providing most West Germans with their first exposure to klezmer music and setting the paradigm of international (largely American) influence that continues to this day.

In 1989 the third West Berlin–based Jüdische Kulturtage took the theme *Yiddishkeit* and incorporated performances by Feidman and Kasbek, among many others. And some musicians became more than visitors. For the Bloomington-born Alan Bern (1955–), a chance 1987 meeting with Kasbek's Andreas Karpen led to a prolonged stay in the city and subsequent settlement, and in 1988 Bern, clarinetist Joel Rubin, and Yiddish singer Michael Alpert held a residency at Café Einstein on the Kurfürstenstrasse in West Berlin. Bern is characteristically frank about the cultural and historical ripples surrounding these performances:

> In those days klezmer music didn't have any bad reputation at all, so the highest level artists and writers and theater people were coming to our concert. And I like to think that we were delivering to them a musical evening that had a lot of intellectual integrity as well as emotional integrity. . . . It felt to me that we were being listened to and we were being approached, and asked to be in dialogue with, people who realized that their parents' generation was responsible for the annihilation of this culture and of millions of people along with it, and who had a deeply-rooted interest in working that through, with a lot of integrity and a lot of generosity and a lot of modesty. In those days they were not telling us, they were asking, listening.[25]

As a cultural form that appeared to signify a complex mix of Jewishness, raw emotion, and Eastern Otherness, klezmer and Yiddish music were able to become what Tina Frühauf calls "a common cultural denominator of divided (Jewish) Berlin."[26] This early scene, however, would undergo a change in the 1990s and early 2000s, closely tied to the reunified city and its growing internationalism. This development is also connected to the American klezmer revitalization of the late 1970s and early 1980s, alongside the impressive, if egocentric, efforts of clarinetist Giora Feidman. In the early 1990s, both Feidman and American groups such as Brave Old World held workshops in Germany that were instrumental in disseminating klezmer repertoire and performance practice across the country, and particularly among Berlin-based musicians. Many older players still active on the scene point to these workshops as seminal in their own musical and stylistic development, and to the coherent aesthetic and historical frame that they provided.[27] This is an important shift. Although Karsten Troyke, Aufwind, and Kasbek had built their music and artistic practice upon conscientious and careful work, the materials at their disposal were significantly limited: Germany had no YIVO-like institutional archives to mine, no elderly Bessarabian immigrant klezmorim at whose feet young musicians might sit and learn—rites of passage that had proved highly productive for American musicians such as Zev Feldman, Andy Statman, Michael Alpert, and Joel Rubin. In some senses, the international musicians who visited or settled in Berlin performed this role for German musicians coming of age in the 1990s, variously combining elements of instructor, guru, and musical/stylistic ambassador. One of these musicians, Brave Old World's Alan Bern, continues to exert a strong and generously benign influence through musical projects such as the Other Europeans, but particularly in his work as founder and director of the long-running annual arts festival Yiddish

Summer Weimar, Europe's largest festival of Yiddish culture—an annual four week-long celebration of music, dance, language, cooking, and knowledge exchange.

In the 1990s and early 2000s, a number of musicians, heavily inspired by the work of these international artists, but also seeking to sidestep mere imitation, would take on the exploratory mantle of musicians like Troyke and Aufwind. Importantly, however, their work was now framed by the research and knowledge community that was developing at KlezKamp, Yiddish Summer Weimar, and elsewhere, as well as the stylistic hegemony increasingly driven by American musicians' workshops throughout Germany. For these younger musicians, their researches had a grounding and sense of connectedness that was far more pronounced. In discussing the process of putting together a program of *ganovim lider* (thieves' songs) with her longtime collaborator Fabian Schnedler, accordionist Franka Lampe (1969–2016) enthusiastically conveys the thrill of this sense of discovery and development, but also the confidence with which she approached it:

> This was very very exciting for me working with Fabian on the *ganovim lider*, because there is no recordings, and no other sources than this one *heft* [notebook].[28] No chords, no tempo marking.... So then you have to find out, is it a *terkishe*, what is the kind of rhythm? Incredibly exciting! And one tune we worked a year and then we changed it all, we changed the complete song because it didn't work. That's why we feel like explorers.[29]

Alongside this exploratory aesthetic, the scene itself was rapidly expanding throughout the 1990s and early 2000s. An increase in bands and spaces, pushed along by giddy headlines like "In Today's Berlin, It's Hip to Be Klezmer!," met forcefully with the city's rising stock of twenty-first-century cultural cool.[30] The happy klezmer party began to raise more and more eyebrows, the overwhelming number of non-Jews at its center seeming to parallel a simultaneously cheerful yet paradoxical celebration of absence. To some, the lively sounds of klezmer became an unpleasant mix of historical trauma and unsustainable contemporary optimism.[31] At the same time, this was a period that also saw the fast exponential growth of Germany's Jewish population, boosted massively by an influx from the former Soviet Union. To put some numbers to this change: in 1989, there were 20,000–30,000 Jews in the two German republics combined, with around 6,000 in Berlin; in 2006, at the height of the klezmer "boom," the German Jewish Community announced a membership of more than 100,000, 85 percent of which were from the former Soviet Union.[32] The discrepancy between the quiet, small, and relatively stable postwar Jewish community, large numbers of newer arrivals—many of whom had grown up with very little religious or cultural attachment to Judaism or Jewishness—and a Jewish music scene that appeared to be characterized principally by a lack of Jews gave grist to the mill of criticisms of "virtual Judaism" and (worse) "Jew zoo."[33]

In the early 2000s, then, Berlin's klezmer scene was undergoing a paradoxical acknowledgment of the limits of communal space, changing local klezmer demographics and the city's growing internationalism. Karsten Troyke frames this change within a specifically local–global dialogue:

> I always said, this is not a world city, Berlin. But this changed, I would say, within the last five to eight years. And now [2014], Berlin has changed, for my feeling, and I see that there is a big connection all over the world now, and Berlin is now included. And so the special story of Berlin klezmer scene found an end. It's no longer that Berlin is different from other big towns.[34]

Troyke's observation that Berlin is now part of an internationally connected conversation is undoubtedly true. The "special story of Berlin klezmer," however, has not found an end. Rather, the city's more recent relocation as a central node in transnational Yiddish networks has given impetus to a parallel local scene that is fluid and inclusive. Internationally it embraces musical movements that push Yiddish music in striking new directions, such as the radical Yiddish singer-songwriter politics of Daniel Kahn, the self-consciously retro style of Yiddish and klezmer rock band Forshpil, or the art-music arrangements of twentieth-century Yiddish poetry created by singer Svetlana Kundish and accordionist Patrick Farrell. The provenance of these resident musicians—United States, Latvia, Ukraine/Israel—makes clear the more recent internationalism of Berlin's klezmer scene.

An example of the musical effects of some of these transnational connections can be heard in the recording "Volekhl," which opens the band Forshpil's 2012 album, also titled *Volekhl*. Forshpil began in Riga in 2003 as part of an ongoing collaboration between Yiddish singer Sasha Lurje and keyboardist/arranger Ilya Shneyveys, and has subsequently grown to incorporate musicians from St. Petersburg. Both Lurje and Shneyveys, however, have been closely linked to Berlin's klezmer scene (more on this below) for more than a decade—both, in fact, personify the particular mix of local and global that is central to the city's contemporary klezmer networks. As with much klezmer, nomenclature and definitions vary, but a *volekh* or *volekhl* usually denotes a gentle instrumental tune in 3/4 time, often elegiac or pastoral in character. The name likely refers to the Romanian region Wallachia, although far from every volekhl exhibits Romanian elements or influence. This particular one was originally published in Moisey Beregovsky and Itzik Fefer's 1938 *Yidishe folks-lider* collection,[35] but popularized more recently among klezmer musicians through clarinetist Joel Rubin's 1997 recording *Beregovski's Khasene* (it was from Rubin's recording that former Forshpil guitarist Sasha Aleksandrov learned the tune).[36] Rubin's 1997 rendition is a lyrical one, supported stylishly but unobtrusively by cimbalom and accordion. Taking advantage of the slow tempo, Rubin makes full expressive use of characteristic klezmer ornamentation—stretching, contracting, embellishing, and developing the piece's simple phrases to deliver an interpretation that never loses its melodic character while also remaining wholly personal. In Forshpil's interpretation, however, chamber-ensemble lyricism has been replaced by driving bassline ostinatos, The Doors' Ray Manzarek–inspired keyboard flourishes, and a tight, virtually ornament-free, electric guitar statement of the

FIGURE 8.1 "Volekh" (first part) from Beregovsky and Fefer's 1938 *Yidishe folks-lider*.

tune. The stately 3/4 *moderato* of Beregovsky and Fefer's printed version (and Rubin's recording) has become a more insistent and ambiguously brooding 6/8 pulse, overlaid with atmospheric cymbal splashes and distorted electronics, along with a lengthy improvised middle section. The first example shows the first part of Beregovsky and Fefer's original notation (Figure 8.1), and the second gives a sense of where Forshpil takes it (Figure 8.2).

This kind of self-conscious eclecticism and broad musical literacy places klezmer music within an international creative conversation, one that links tradition and learning with a keen ear for cross-cultural and cross-genre fertilization. At the same time, a number of these relentlessly inventive musicians are also closely involved with their city at a far more local level. This newer iteration of Berlin klezmer connects the local to the transnational—in the process overlapping into a stronger sense of community.

The Contemporary Local

> There is a community here, and we are all in touch. We work on our projects here, but often we perform them somewhere else. But we are all connected, especially at the jam sessions. We all meet in Berlin. (Svetlana Kundish)[37]

Klezmer and Yiddish musicians in Berlin, like many around the world, often need to travel elsewhere to actually make a living. The creative energy and enthusiasm of the reunified city, the increasingly commercialized yet persistent attraction of brand Berlin, combined with what is still a relatively cheap cost of living, has for some time attracted musicians to base themselves there, even while they are compelled to go farther afield

FIGURE 8.2 "Volekhl" (first part) from Forshpil's 2011 album *Volekhl*.

to earn their keep. Over the past twenty-five years, this has produced a klezmer scene grounded in a strong sense of local collectivity and inclusivity, contextualized by an informal ease and sociability as much as formalized performance spaces. These shifting trajectories and affiliations can be tracked through the city's three klezmer jam sessions, which together span nearly three decades of musical activity. A closer look at the particular production of musical space within these sessions reveals how each both reinforces and challenges certain expectations and social relationships. What emerges is an arc that moves klezmer spatial practice in the city from bordered to fluid, while at the same time increasingly connecting the local scene to the transnational klezmer community. The analysis that follows will consider each jam session's function in articulating and structuring certain key elements of the city's changing klezmer scenes, from the 1990s until the time of writing.

Berlin's Klezmerstammtisch began life in 1995. It was set up by three German klezmer musicians: fiddle players Matthias Groh and Petra Kirstein, and accordionist Jenny Wieneke, with the close involvement of fellow band members and musical friends such as accordionist Franka Lampe, clarinetist Stefan Litsche, and bassist Carsten Wegener. Although the Stammtisch finally folded in 2018—and had in fact been on the wane for several years—its particular blend of inclusivity and implicit rules is an important waymarker in the ongoing development of Berlin klezmer.[38]

For almost all its existence, the Klezmerstammtisch took place on the fifteenth of the month in Café Oberwasser, a warm and atmospheric neighborhood bar in Mitte. Oberwasser—with its eclectic and hearty menu, and its regular musical events—was enthusiastically curated by the owner Ursula Weigert, who herself was something of a hub around which the Stammtisch klezmer network operated. The influence of the Klezmerstammtisch as a cohering force for the city's klezmer and Yiddish musicians during the late twentieth and early twenty-first centuries is significant. It allowed neophytes learn and enjoy the music in a semi-structured way, and it connected local German and Germany-based musicians with visiting international artists. At the same time, what some musicians felt was an overly heavy reliance upon structure and predictability also marked this space as increasingly limited in relation to the city's incorporation into transnational klezmer networks. For musicians new to klezmer, the repetitive repertoire and "straight" interpretations often acted as a comfortably manageable entry to the style. For more experienced players, however, these same forces came more and more to symbolize a somewhat mediated version of klezmer, contrasting with the expanding creativity and adventurousness of the newer arrivals to the city's scene.

From 2013, one of the Stammtisch's original founders, Matthias Groh, began to curate an ongoing series of Sunday-afternoon jam sessions in Prenzlauer Berg, not far from the Stammtisch itself. Saytham's Lounge is not an open session but an invited one, constructed around players who have signed up via an online list. It thus exists in a liminal zone between session and concert: the "band" is not an actual band with a rehearsed set (although they will likely know one another), but at the same time audience participation is in the form of listening rather than playing.

Saytham's is a friendly, easy-going klezmer space in the city. It keeps musical and so-cial channels active and also allows musicians to meet and make new connections. The changing and unpredictable personnel allows the accidental and the spontaneous to develop, while the invitation/sign-up participation structure also ensures that there is some level of gatekeeping and quality control in operation. Groh's ethic of inclusivity and collaboration makes it an excellent point of entry for musicians recently arrived in the city. At the same time, Saytham's Lounge is very much centered around experi-enced musicians (particularly those experienced in klezmer). It is effectively not open to those who have not yet learned how to play klezmer, or who do not really know any klezmer tunes.

Over the past decade, however, a new inclusive learning and participative space for klezmer in the city has developed. It is a contact zone that sits more comfortably within Berlin's mix-and-match bar culture, and in recent years it has had a formative influence on both the processes and perceptions of klezmer music in the city. The development of this newer, younger, more international scene reveals the profound effects that in-formal urban encounters can have upon musical process, and in turn how those musical processes can play back into and shape the urban soundworld out of which they are formed.

Throughout 2012 and 2013, three musicians began to meet to play klezmer in an in-formal, jamming way. Unlike the founders of the Klezmerstammtisch and Saytham's Lounge, these three musicians were not from Berlin, and two of them had only very recently made the city their home, pointing to the increased internationalism of the reunified city and its klezmer scenes.[39] One of these, Danish clarinettist Emil Goldschmidt (1983–), explains how these ad hoc meetings developed into a more co-herent collective sensibility:

> And we were like, you know what, Berlin is missing an open jam session for klezmer music. Because at that time you had Courage [Saytham's], but the concert there was a fixed band, it wasn't a jam session. And then you had the Klezmerstammtisch, which was a regular thing also but, for instance, drums weren't allowed. So our thought was to have this open jam session. We talked a lot about how the framing should be, and we really wanted to have more like a living room kind of feel to it.[40]

Neukölln Klezmer Sessions began in late 2013 at Bar Oblomov, on the corner of Holbrechtstraße and Lenaustraße in Neukölln. The area hums pleasantly with bars populated by locals and tourists alike, and the stylish informality of Bar Oblomov itself taps directly into the bricolage aesthetic that remains a recognizable stamp of Berlin se-miotic culture. From the start of the Oblomov sessions, Goldschmidt's "living room feel" was central to the creation of an active sense of local inclusivity, and it also informed sev-eral differences between this newer session and its older counterparts.

While Saytham's and the Klezmerstammtisch have always operated within a larger and well-ordered bar space, the Neukölln sessions happen in the busy, half-lit, atmospheric and deliberately un-ordered side room of Bar Oblomov. Where the Klezmerstammtisch took place—for almost the entirety of its two decade lifespan—without fail on the fifteenth of the month (even moving to a different venue when the fifteenth fell on a Sunday and Oberwasser was closed), the Neukölln Klezmer Sessions are roughly three-weekly, although this is a deliberately loose timetable. Rather than the "three-times-through" convention that roughly underpins many European folk jam sessions, in Oblomov tunes are stretched and twisted into surprising new combinations and forms, with the active participation of as many musicians as possible strongly encouraged.[41] And where the Klezmerstammtisch took place around a particular table (sometimes tables) of Café Oberwasser, and Saytham's Lounge performers play in an albeit informal yet clearly bordered space, in Bar Oblomov there is no clear "stage" at all. Musicians and listeners come and go from the playing end of the room, while still others join in from their positions at tables and chairs (or standing). One of the session's founders, Swedish drummer Hampus Melin (1979–), outlines the spatial thinking behind this as follows:

> Klezmer is more communal than something like jazz. We talked about the effect of having a stage, or not having a stage. . . . And of course, as soon as you step up onto a stage, you're "on" in a different way. And maybe that's something that we weren't really going for. But that it would be something where you could kind of melt in, and it would be "Is that person playing? Does it matter? Maybe a little bit?"[42]

The difference is also one of urban geography. In the recently reunified 1990s city, the—at that time—neglected East Berlin neighborhood of Prenzlauer Berg provided cheap and plentiful accommodation for vibrant and free-thinking artistic collectives. Since then, however, wholesale gentrification and corresponding rocketing rents have sent newer arrivals elsewhere, most notably to Neukölln in the south of the city. Although this district is also increasingly at prey to the sweeping forces of commercialization and gentrification (an ironic outcome, of course, of the same Bohemian cool that continues to attract creative people to the city), it nevertheless continues to provide affordable living and a lively bar/club culture.

These changes manifest at other levels—of agency, self-definition, and self-presentation. While the city's early klezmer and Yiddish music scene formed a series of somewhat accidental groupings, supported more recently by networks of education such as visiting artist workshops and subsequently Yiddish Summer Weimar, this younger, more international grouping sees itself clearly and consciously as a community and actively seeks to present itself as such. In the semi-regular email broadcasts that the "Shtetl Team" send out, visiting musicians and bands are usually referred to as "our friends," the community at large as "the Shtetl" or "our Shtetl" (occasionally the more coy "our little Shtetl"), with nicely knowing references to "good times with klezmer," "the finest klezmer in the hood," or "the historic reunion of Oblomov Trio and other fun stuff." And almost all communication takes place in English—the recognizably international language of the transnational Yiddish musical community—despite the fact that it is not the first language of many of the Shtetl Team, and that the majority are fluent German (and often Yiddish) speakers.

Since the end of 2013, Neukölln Klezmer Sessions has become a central hub of Berlin's klezmer scene.[43] And alongside its committed local urban focus, the strong and sustained international links of many of the current protagonists tie the Berlin scene itself into wider transnational Yiddish musical networks. Partly as a result, these deliberately informal local jam sessions have spawned several more ambitious initiatives, further embedding klezmer within the city. Most notable is the winter festival, concert, and workshop series that now operates under the banner of Shtetl Berlin.[44] Combining local and visiting international artists, attended by participants from across Europe, and operating on a shoestring budget, the festival is built precisely upon the blend of local and global that characterizes Berlin's particular relationship to the transnational klezmer community:

> I would say I am mostly talking about the community in Berlin. But this community also extends to people living in other countries. I mean, we had people who traveled there, just to be part of it. Michael Winograd came, Susi Evans came [Winograd (US) and Evans (UK) are internationally-renowned klezmer clarinetists and teachers], Michael Alpert came. And so we wanted to make sure that they got to share some of their things. And in that sense I do think that the community in klezmer music, or in Yiddish music, or in Yiddish culture, is very strong.[45]

The sense of interaction and support has a bearing on the orientation and framing of events. For the festival organizers, this means capping fees at the bare minimum to ensure the widest possible access, keeping the time commitment short, and also committing to the nurturing of a local network of klezmer musicians. For American violinist Craig Judelman (1985–), a Berlin resident since 2017 and now one of the festival's driving forces, this sense of ongoing education and development is essential to the continuation of a dynamic local scene:

> And so definitely a big part of the festival, apart from just all getting together and playing, it's like doing things to create a larger community of people who actually understand the music. It's one level of getting people to come in and play at the sessions, but then to get them to actually really learn tunes, and learn how to play them, it's like the next step. And, you know, as a community if we don't constantly both reach out to people outside the community and bring them in, and sort of help nurture the growth of the people inside, then we're not going to be a strong community and we're not going to survive.[46]

Berlin's recent brand of relaxed cool is, of course, in strong contrast to much of its border-defined twentieth-century history—a history that remains physically inscribed in the many monuments that help structure the city's unique urban topography. For the Shtetl Team's Sasha Lurje (1985–)—Riga-born but a Berlin resident since the early 2010s—this more recent self-conscious egalitarianism chimes well with local musical intentions, and also contrasts with the perceived cliquey-ness of some other klezmer centers:

I think part of it is conscious. Like, we do constantly talk about it as a community where everybody is more or less equal. We want to share what we have with the community, and in this sentence community means whoever wants to be part of it. These are conscious decisions, but also I think Berlin is a good ground for that. Even though, yes, rents are going up, yes everything is getting more stressful here just like anywhere. But compared to other places it's still quite a relaxed place, and you can still find a place. And I think that makes a big difference, because like if you're in New York, you're running around *all* the time, playing every possible gig, just like trying to make the world happen—because if you stop, you're gone, right?[47]

Ash Amin and Nigel Thrift characterize the city space as a "meshwork" that relies on fluidity and flow as much as on planning and order, owing less to grand structural principles and more to the everyday and the improvisatory: "fine grain is still the chief grain of the city."[48] Set against the weight of the city's top-down historical narrative, the conscious "everydayness" of the Oblomov sessions and associated activities links directly to twenty-first-century Berlin's bottom-up, street-level cultural creativity, locating klezmer within a more contemporary urban paradigm. In 2020, however, this relaxed mix of local and global, familiarity and discovery, was inevitably forced into a radical rethink. Restrictions on live gatherings due to the coronavirus pandemic called a temporary halt to the happy intimacy of the Shtetl Team's face-to-face activities, and the team responded by moving 2020's Shtetl Berlin festival online. Aside from the obvious challenges and changes, this boosted workshop numbers with participants from outside the city who would have been less likely to attend in person. And although the majority of these changes should probably be viewed as successful contingencies, the move online did allow the festival one important shift of emphasis: an opportunity to incorporate Jewish calendrical events that in turn allowed those without any sort of personal Jewish experience to participate in an inclusive and non-voyeuristic way.

THE KLEZMER SCENE AND THE JEWISH COMMUNITY

The relationship between klezmer on German soil and the Jewishness of the culture in which it is rooted has frequently been more nuanced than first impressions have often suggested. In her extensive ethnography of the klezmer revitalization in Poland and Germany, Magdalena Waligórska directly questions popular perceptions of the klezmer scene and the Jewish community as "two parallel universes," suggesting instead that:

> there are more points of contact between the two than critics assume at first glance. Klezmer is popular with non-Jewish heritage tourists and local Jews alike. And since the Jewish communities in Germany are numerous enough to create a demand for

music for Jewish occasions, local klezmer bands are among ensembles that service this segment of the market too.[49]

The "points of contact" to which Waligórska refers are not, by and large, particularly representative of the majority of klezmer activity in Berlin, however. To be sure, some Berlin klezmer musicians are occasionally booked for weddings. The busiest Jewish wedding band in Berlin is probably the Ginzburg dynasty. Of Russian origin, the band also appear at official venues such as the Philharmonie, but largely operate well outside the city's active klezmer networks discussed here. Jossif Gofenberg's Klezmer Chidesch play regularly for functions, but the vast majority of these are for non-Jewish patrons.[50] Weddings and similar engagements, however, form a negligible part of most musicians' diaries—especially the most influential and internationally connected, such as Alan Bern, Dan Kahn, or Sasha Lurje.

In fact, many of Berlin's most experienced and inventive klezmer musicians, while they sit at the center of the transnational Yiddish musical scene, have in fact witnessed a certain lack of interest and involvement from the city's local Jewish community. In less guarded moments, some will speculate that this is partly because Berlin's official Jewish bodies are less than willing to support events and initiatives that will, in practice, be attended by a majority of non-Jews. These are, however, criticisms that the official representatives strongly deny, pointing especially to the large number of concerts that they organize in farther-flung Jewish communities throughout Germany.

The klezmer musician most closely associated with the Jüdische Gemeinde zu Berlin is accordionist and bandleader Jossif Gofenberg (1949–). Gofenberg runs klezmer classes at the community center at Fasanenstraße and his band appears regularly at Charlottenburg's Café Bleibergs, a long-established kosher café and West Berlin Jewish community hub. In discussion, Gofenberg is clear in his views that klezmer is available to all, and indeed the majority of his students and choir are non-Jews. Despite this, he also perceives differences between certain backgrounds and approaches:

> You can't say that klezmer is a music just for Jews. It's a music for everyone, first and foremost. . . . With klezmer, in my opinion, you can learn it, in music school, but that doesn't mean that the melodies will be the same when played by different musicians. I don't believe that the melodies sound the same when a musician is Jewish than when they're not Jewish. You must have a feeling inside, you understand? I can hear this feeling. But you can't describe it. You can't draw it. That's why I don't like the way some people do it. Because they think, "ok we're off!" Everyone is playing Jewish music, but not everything is klezmer.[51]

The newer members of Berlin's klezmer scene, while their connections to international Jewish cultural networks may be strong, have often found any explicitly Jewish aspect of klezmer noticeably absent from their local musical lives. Some individuals, however, are actively working to change this. Shtetl Berlin's 2020 online festival, for example, saw a far more explicit engagement klezmer as Jewish music and as a historical part of Jewish culture. Fiddle player Craig Judelman, in his own words one of the few people on the Berlin scene with a religious attachment to Judaism, contextualizes this change with reference to previous disconnects:

> I think there's generally been an effort to not treat this as "music for Jews," necessarily, in our community, and to make sure that everybody feels welcome. And I think recently some of us have been pushing a little bit to be, like, well let's also make sure that *Jews* feel welcome! [laughs] You know, and try to connect to the culture that's living around us.[52]

Throughout its five-year lifespan, Shtetl Berlin has always taken place around Hanukkah. And while previous years have always marked the occasion in some way—often at the Jewish Museum Berlin[53]—the 2020 festival took this several steps further by making Jewish celebration a central part of its programming. The opening event was a socially distanced Hanukkah tish live from Fraenkelufer Synagogue, replete with Breslover nigunim, latkes, Hanukkah gelt, and a gently non-threatening degree of religious contextualization. For Judelman, this last is more than simply a hook on which to hang an event, and in fact opens up avenues of musical engagement that might otherwise be overlooked:

> I think people seem generally quite happy, in the middle of a music festival, to take a moment and not think about music too much, or talk about some spiritual elements of Hanukkah and everything, so I don't feel like there's too much resistance there. But of course we try to be careful along the way that we're framing it, and not to go too much into something that's just about your relationship with God, but to keep it in a little bit more general spiritual terms. But often the stuff overlaps so much, and you know, music is such an important part of Judaism that it's a good space, it works when we talk.[54]

This more thoughtful and self-conscious inclusion of Jewish religious and ritual culture points to a shift in the relationship, and in particular an implicit confrontation of occasionally sticky historical absences within some of Europe's klezmer revitalization centers. Once again, it suggests a renewed balance between the local and the global that marks out the continued development of Berlin's klezmer scene:

> Yeah, and I think we've been trying to make sure that everybody who's not Jewish—or doesn't care—feels comfortable, but at the same time not let that get to the point where we can't also do Jewish stuff. Like, it *is* Jewish, even though you don't have to be Jewish to play it.[55]

CITY OF KLEZMER

Poised at the intersection of traumatic twentieth-century European histories and twenty-first-century cosmopolitan cool, Berlin is both a paradigmatic European capital and a unique city. The same can be said of the city's changing klezmer scenes of the past thirty years: directly influenced by the international effects of the American revitalization and yet inflected with a distinctly Berlinesque mix-and-match creativity, contextualized by the historical complexities of German-Jewish relations. What, then, does this particular intersection of local musical networks and transnational klezmer connectivity represent in terms of collectivity and spatiality?

Barry Shank describes a musical scene as "an overproductive signifying community."[56] Scenes, in other words, offer up something more than simply musical activities and associated networks: their collectivity is also expressed through style, language, and other shared semiotic systems. Paralleling this, Will Straw writes that scenes pull together "cultural phenomena in ways which heighten their visibility and facilitate their circulation to other places."[57] The optimistic German embrace of klezmer in 1990s Berlin is linked to the enthusiastic excesses of the reunified city's outward-facing perspective, but is only a part of the story. An understanding of the Berlin scene also needs to take account of the arrival *into* the city of a number of highly active and creative musicians— from the United States and also Eastern Europe—who have brought a dynamic internationalism to local networks. These musicians have turned the more formal structures of early jam sessions into a fluid transnational network hub, a self-consciously liminal "lived space"[58] between performance and participation that is appealingly fluid in its practice and simultaneously committed to the sharing and dissemination of musical and cultural knowledge.

Like all scenes, Berlin klezmer is a particular conjuncture of history, demographics, and a combination of internal drive and external influence. But at the same time, Berlin is a very particular city of klezmer. It is rooted in the changing musical networks of the city itself—in the semi-accidental collision of pioneer musicians (from both East and West), in the strong and continued influence of international klezmer "stars," in the distinct post-reunification moment, and in the music's more recent incorporation into ground-level bar culture. These processes also show that some of the most interesting developments frequently happen at a local and informal level, while leading on to measurably larger effects—as in Shtetl Berlin's widening musical, social, and religious networks that emanate from the lived locality of the Neukölln Klezmer Sessions.

The radically changing social, cultural, and musical environments that have surrounded Jewish life of the past three centuries have their multiple reflections in the practice of klezmer music. But more than this, klezmer itself has stepped well beyond the bounds of its Ashkenazi instrumental music origins, into a looser twenty-first-century cosmopolitanism. Klezmer thus continues to articulate a changing relationship to musical space, and the shifting requirements of collectivity. Music that was once used to delineate the boundaries of community now functions within a contemporary urban heterogeneity as a tool of collective musical exchange. And the ethnic specificity of ritual celebration has largely been replaced by numerous local city scenes, simultaneously tied in to transnational dissemination and communication networks. But more than this, the conjuncture of traditional music within a contemporary urban framework can bring an energy and vitality (or revitalization) to both—making the music truly a part of its city. Berlin's klezmer offers a lived example of collectivity that connects local musical life to global musical process. Like Yiddish culture more generally, the ability to exist across several different geographical and historical planes simultaneously may well be one of the necessary elements in klezmer's continued relevance, to Jews and non-Jews, in Berlin and elsewhere.

NOTES

1. Sholem Aleichem, *Stempenyu: A Jewish Romance*, trans. Hannah Berman (Brooklyn, NY: Melville House Publishing, 2008), 21.
2. Ibid., 25.
3. This increasing preference for the cosmopolitan mainstream is far from a modern phenomenon. Hankus Netsky, for example, notes a common postwar tension in the United States between the desires of immigrant parents or grandparents and increasingly assimilated brides, who often did not want any "Jewish." See Hankus Netsky, *Klezmer: Music and Community in Twentieth-Century Jewish Philadelphia* (Philadelphia: Temple University Press, 2015), 85.
4. For a succinct summary of the problems of definition, see Joel E. Rubin, *New York Klezmer in the Early Twentieth Century: The Music of Naftule Brandwein and Dave Tarras* (Rochester, NY: University of Rochester Press, 2020), 5–10. For more on the etymology of the word *klezmer*, see Walter Zev Feldman, *Klezmer: Music, History, and Memory* (New York: Oxford University Press, 2016), xiv and chapter 2.
5. Netsky, *Klezmer*, 16.
6. Sara Ahmed and Anne-Marie Fortier, "Re-Imagining Communities," *International Journal of Cultural Studies* 6, no. 3 (2003): 254.
7. Feldman, *Klezmer*, xi. One of the key figures in New York's klezmer revitalization of the 1970s, Feldman's monograph is the first full-length study of prewar eastern European klezmer music—unpacking the changing linguistic, economic, social, and musical contexts that have framed the working lives of klezmorim since the seventeenth century, as well as an analysis of multiple klezmer genres. The breadth and scope of Feldman's study make it a core text not only on klezmer, but on eastern European Jewish musical life more generally.
8. The study of prewar eastern European Yiddish music and klezmer, however, properly begins with the pioneering work of Ukrainian-born Jewish ethnomusicologist Moisey Beregovsky, whose work is discussed in greater detail in Eléonore Biezunski's chapter in this volume; ever aware of changing traditions, as late as 1937 Beregovsky was advocating filling the marked gap in ethnomusicological knowledge with amateur collecting, and his body of notated klezmer melodies now forms a fundamental part of today's canon.
9. Hankus Netsky shows the different ways that klezmer performed a uniting function for Philadelphia's Jews in the early twentieth century. As the music that they expected to hear and dance to at Jewish events, it also signified Old Country regional specificity: different klezmer families would get different gigs, depending on where they came from. Finally, within a North American context, the relative insularity and conservative nature of Philadelphia's Jewish population—compared to other US cities—meant that this particular klezmer community was also notable for its *difference* to larger centers of Jewish life such as New York. See Netsky, *Klezmer*.

10. Joel Rubin's *New York Klezmer* specifically addresses 1920s America through the work of the two best-known klezmer musicians of the time, clarinetists Dave Tarras (1897–1989) and Naftule Brandwein (1889–1963). Rubin explores the possibilities of defining a distinct musical-structural aesthetic, with detailed reference to motivic development, compositional procedure and playing style, and drawing parallels with ideas of native-speaker competence. He also provides a synthesis of the changing social context and cultural attitudes that surrounded klezmer in its transition from the old world to the new.

11. Feldman, *Klezmer*, xvii.

12. Mark Slobin's edited volume *American Klezmer: Its Roots and Offshoots* (Oxford: Oxford University Press, 2002) looks at this distinct geography firstly from a historical ("roots") perspective, followed by a selection of the music's revitalization ("offshoots"). Noteworthy is Barbara Kirshenblatt-Gimblett's essay "Sounds of Sensibility," in which she argues that it is the experience of rupture and disjuncture as much as continuity and connection that frames the American klezmer resurgence.

13. See Mark Slobin, *Fiddler on the Move: Exploring the Klezmer World* (New York: Oxford University Press, 2000), 75–86.

14. See Henry Sapoznik, "KlezKamp and the Rise of Yiddish Cultural Literacy," in Slobin, *American Klezmer*, 174–186.

15. Slobin, *Fiddler*, 85.

16. See, for example, Magdalena Waligórska, *Klezmer's Afterlife: An Ethnography of the Jewish Music Revival in Poland and Germany* (New York: Oxford University Press, 2013), and Ruth Ellen Gruber, *Virtually Jewish: Reinventing Jewish Culture in Europe* (Berkeley: University of California Press, 2002).

17. For a full discussion of performance and participative music, see Thomas Turino, *Music as Social Life: The Politics of Participation* (Chicago: University of Chicago, 2008).

18. Netsky, *Klezmer*, 9.

19. Sophie Arkette, "Sounds Like City," *Theory, Culture & Society* 21, no. 1 (2004): 164.

20. See Wolff N. Kostakowsky, *International Hebrew Wedding Music* (Brooklyn, NY: Nat Kostakowsky, 1916).

21. Will Straw, "Systems of Articulation, Logics of Change: Communities and Scenes in Popular Music," *Cultural Studies* 6 (1991): 373.

22. Simon Frith, "Music and Identity," in *Questions of Cultural Identity*, ed. Stuart Hall and Paul du Gay (London: Sage, 1996), 111.

23. Jan Hermerschmidt, in discussion with the author, May 19, 2014.

24. Jan Hermerschmidt, in discussion with the author, May 19, 2014.

25. Alan Bern, in discussion with the author, September 13, 2019.

26. Tina Frühauf, *Transcending Dystopia: Music, Mobility, and the Jewish Community in Germany, 1945–1989* (New York: Oxford University Press, 2021), 397.

27. This was true of the work of Brave Old World and Alan Bern's Yiddish Summer Weimar, for example, but much less the case for the self-consciously spiritual (and decidedly ahistoric) perspective put forward by Giora Feidman. Brave Old World are an influential klezmer revival band who have developed concert music rooted in traditional Yiddish musical materials. The band consists of accordionist and pianist Alan Bern, clarinetist Kurt Björling, singer and violinist Michael Alpert, and bassist Stuart Brotman. Clarinetist Joel Rubin was a founding member (playing with the band until 1992). The workshops referred to here all took place once Björling had joined. Both Bern and Rubin settled in Germany (Rubin from 1989 to 2003, Bern from 1987 to the present day).

28. See also Pieśni Zlodsiejów / גנבים־לידער: מיט מעלאדיעס (Warsaw: Graubard, 1928); the anthology consists of 130 songs collected by folklorist Shmuel (Szmil) Lehman from prisoners, thieves, prostitutes, and other underworld characters.

29. Franka Lampe, in discussion with the author, March 4, 2014.

30. Steve Kettmann, "In Today's Berlin, It's Hip to Be Klezmer," *San Francisco Chronicle*, December 20, 1998.

31. See, for example, Rita Ottens and Joel Rubin, "The Sounds of the Vanishing World: The German Klezmer Movement as a Racial Discourse" (lecture, University of Wisconsin–Madison, 2002).

32. These figures stem from Jeffrey Peck, *Being Jewish in the New Germany* (New Brunswick: Rutgers University Press, 2006), 40.

33. This disturbing juxtaposition comes from singer Elisabeth Schwartz. See Yale Strom, *The Book of Klezmer: The History, the Music, the Folklore* (Chicago: A Capella, 2002), 242. Ruth Ellen Gruber's *Virtually Jewish* devotes three chapters to klezmer music in Europe, in particular Giora Feidman and his popular humanist spirituality as expressed through a comfortably dominant code of "laughter-through-tears" Jewish emotion and depth. Against this she cites the efforts of American musicians such as Alan Bern and Yiddishist Michael Wex to ensure that klezmer and Yiddish culture be understood as existential and temporally rooted. In a follow-up 2009 article, Gruber concedes of klezmer in Germany: "The attraction is deep and springs from many sources, partly, of course, but only partly (and less so as time moves on), from an underlying guilty legacy." Ruth Ellen Gruber, "Beyond Virtually Jewish: New Authenticities and Real Imaginary Spaces in Europe," *Jewish Quarterly Review* 99, no. 4 (2009): 503.

34. Karsten Troyke, in discussion with the author, July 20, 2014.

35. See Moisey Beregovsky and Itzik Fefer, *Yidishe folks-lider* (Kiev: Ukrmelukhenatsmindfarlag, 1938). The published book can be viewed online at: https://www.yiddishbookcenter.org/collections/yiddish-books/spb-nybc210708/beregovski-m-fefer-itzik-yidishe-folks-lider.

36. Joel Rubin Jewish Music Ensemble, *Beregovski's Khasene (Beregovski's Wedding): Forgotten Instrumental Treasures from the Ukraine* (Weltmusik, SM 1614-2, 1997). Forshpil's 2012 recording can be accessed on SoundCloud; https://soundcloud.com/forshpil/volekhl?in=forshpil/sets/forshpil (accessed September 9, 2022).

37. Svetlana Kundish, in discussion with the author, September 3, 2019.

38. For a discussion of the "structured informality" of the English folk scene, see Niall Mackinnon, *The British Folk Scene: Musical Performance and Social Identity* (Buckingham: Open University Press, 1993).

39. The three session founders were Riga-born accordionist Ilya Shneyveys (1983–), who lived in Berlin from 2013 to 2016; Danish clarinetist Emil Goldschmidt, who migrates between Berlin and Copenhagen; and drummer Hampus Melin, born in Malmö but a Neukölln resident since the mid 2000s.

40. Emil Goldschmidt, in discussion with the author, September 16, 2019. Goldschmidt also used the Yiddish word "heymish" (homely) several times.

41. This includes beginners and inexperienced players, who—as Hampus Melin notes—simply "sit at the back and play quieter until they feel more confident." Melin, in discussion with the author, July 21, 2014.

42. Hampus Melin, in discussion with the author, Berlin, July 21, 2014.

43. Since 2019, the Neukölln Klezmer Sessions have been led by violinist Craig Judelman and accordionist Patrick Farrell, both of whom are internationally recognized klezmer musicians. Both Judelman and Farrell moved (independently) to Berlin in 2017.

44. For the first three years of its existence, the festival was called Shtetl Neukölln. The name change was partly prompted by pragmatism (Berlin is a more familiar word and concept, and is easier to pronounce), but is also indicative of a desire on the part of the festival organisers to locate their efforts within a city-wide frame.

45. Emil Goldschmidt, in discussion with the author, September 16, 2019.

46. Craig Judelman, in discussion with the author, February 17, 2021.

47. Sasha Lurje, in discussion with the author, February 17, 2021.

48. Ash Amin and Nigel Thrift, *Cities: Reimagining the Urban* (Cambridge: Polity Press, 2002), 87.

49. Waligórska, *Klezmer's Afterlife*, 102.

50. Jossif Gofenberg, in discussion with the author, August 27, 2014.

51. Jossif Gofenberg, in discussion with the author, August 27, 2014.

52. Craig Judelman, in discussion with the author, February 17, 2021.

53. Sasha Lurje, in particular, has worked hard to develop and maintain a strong and symbiotic relationship with the Jewish Museum Berlin, a relationship that connects audiences and spaces that may not otherwise overlap.

54. Craig Judelman, in discussion with the author, February 17, 2021.

55. Sasha Lurje, in discussion with the author, February 17, 2021.

56. Barry Shank, *Dissonant Identities: The Rock 'n' Roll Scene in Austin, Texas* (Hanover, OH: Wesleyan University Press, 1994), 122.

57. Will Straw, "Some Things a Scene Might Be," *Cultural Studies* 29, no. 3 (2015): 478.

58. Michel de Certeau, *The Practice of Everyday Life*, trans. Stephen Rendall (Berkeley: University of California Press, 1984), 96.

SELECT BIBLIOGRAPHY

Alexander, Phil. *Sounding Jewish in Berlin: Klezmer and the Contemporary City*. New York: Oxford University Press, 2021.

Beregovsky, Moisey. *Jewish Instrumental Folk Music: The Collections and Writings of Moshe Beregovski*. Translated and edited by Mark Slobin, Robert Rothstein, and Michael Alpert. Syracuse: Syracuse University Press, 2001.

Feldman, Walter Zev. *Klezmer: Music, History, and Memory*. New York: Oxford University Press, 2016.

Gruber, Ruth Ellen. "Beyond Virtually Jewish: New Authenticities and Real Imaginary Spaces in Europe." *Jewish Quarterly Review* 99, no. 4 (2009): 487–504.

Gruber, Ruth Ellen. *Virtually Jewish: Reinventing Jewish Culture in Europe*. Berkeley: University of California Press, 2002.

Netsky, Hankus. *Klezmer: Music and Community in Twentieth-Century Jewish Philadelphia*. Philadelphia: Temple University Press, 2015.

Peck, Jeffrey. *Being Jewish in the New Germany*. New Brunswick, NJ: Rutgers University Press, 2006.

Rubin, Joel E. *New York Klezmer in the Early Twentieth Century: The Music of Naftule Brandwein and Dave Tarras*. Eastman / Rochester Studies in Ethnomusicology. Rochester, NY: University of Rochester Press, 2020.

Rubin, Joel E. "'With an Open Mind and with Respect': Klezmer as a Site of the Jewish Fringe in Germany in the Early Twenty-first Century." In *Dislocated Memories: Jews, Music, and Postwar German Culture*, edited by Tina Frühauf and Lily E. Hirsch, 31–56. New York: Oxford University Press, 2014.

Sapoznik, Henry. "KlezKamp and the Rise of Yiddish Cultural Literacy." In *American Klezmer: Its Roots and Offshoots*, edited by Mark Slobin, 174–186. Berkeley: University of California Press, 2002.

Slobin, Mark. *Fiddler on the Move: Exploring the Klezmer World*. New York: Oxford University Press, 2000.

Straw, Will. "Systems of Articulation, Logics of Change: Communities and Scenes in Popular Music." *Cultural Studies* 6 (1991): 368–388.

Strom, Yale. *The Book of Klezmer: The History, the Music, the Folklore*. Chicago: A Capella, 2002.

Tonkiss, Fran. *Space, the City and Social Theory*. Cambridge: Polity Press, 2005.

Waligórska, Magdalena. *Klezmer's Afterlife: An Ethnography of the Jewish Music Revival in Poland and Germany*. New York: Oxford University Press, 2013.

PART III

GHETTO—גטו

9

HEARING THE ANCIENT TEMPLE IN EARLY MODERNITY

Abraham Portaleone and the Cultivation of Music in Seventeenth-Century Mantua

REBECCA CYPESS AND YOEL GREENBERG

THE year 1612 saw the completion of construction on the Jewish ghetto in the Italian city of Mantua. Built at the behest of Duke Vincenzo Gonzaga starting in 1610, the ghetto was among the last of its kind to be completed in major Italian cities.[1] The Mantuan ghetto, like most other ghettos on the Italian Peninsula, occupied what Robert Bonfil describes as a "paradoxical" position in the heart of the city.[2] Like all early modern Italian ghettos, the ghetto of Mantua was intended to circumscribe the movements and contain the influence of the city's Jewish population, as the pressures of the Catholic Reformation prompted Italian rulers to crack down on non-normative influences within their domains. However, it stood near the famed Basilica of Sant'Andrea in one of the most bustling cultural and commercial centers of Mantua. Figure 9.1, a detail from the 1628 map of Mantua by Gabriele Bertazzolo, shows the close proximity of the ghetto walls and the basilica. For Bonfil, the central position of this and most other Jewish ghettos within their urban landscapes "led to the crystallization of the Jewish presence within the city's topography."[3] Even as the physical space of the ghetto framed the Jews as negative models for the Christian faithful—a distasteful but necessary component of society—it simultaneously ensured the continued interaction of Jews and Christians within the city. Moreover, as David B. Ruderman has suggested, construction of ghettos had far-reaching cultural implications, in that they "paradoxically opened up new opportunities for cultural dialogue and interaction with the Christian majority as Jews saw themselves a more organic and natural part of their environment than ever before."[4]

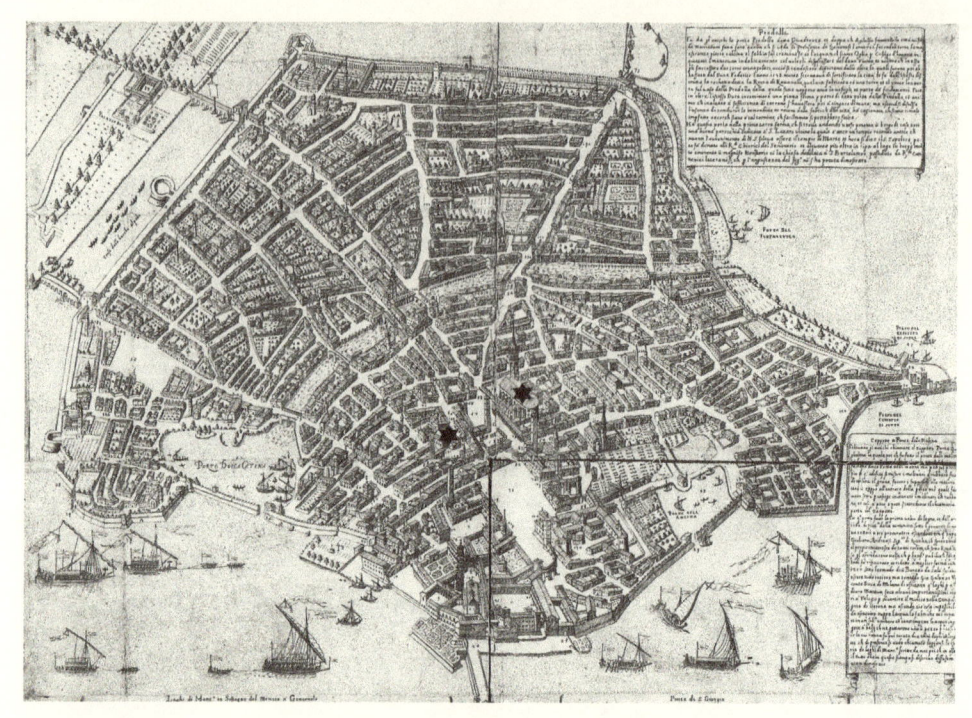

FIGURE 9.1 Detail of Gabriele Bertazzolo, *Urbis Mantua descriptio* (1628). The star on the left shows the position of the Jewish ghetto; the star on the right indicates the location of the Basilica di Sant'Andrea. Prints and Drawings Department, scroll 1, Biblioteca Teresiana. Reproduced by permission of the Biblioteca Teresiana, Mantua.

Incidentally, in the same year that construction of the Mantuan ghetto was completed, the Mantuan Jewish writer Abraham Portaleone (also known by his Hebrew name, Avraham Mi-Sha'ar Aryeh, 1542–1612) published his treatise *Shilṭei ha-giborim* (שלטי הגיבורים, Shields of the heroes, Figure 9.2)— a work concerned with another edifice, from a distant place and time: the ancient Temple in Jerusalem, believed to have been built by King Solomon. Portaleone's Hebrew-language volume anthologized a series of sacred texts from the Hebrew Bible to the Kabbalah and presented them in a manner that would allow their daily study. The purpose of this anthology, he wrote, was to "bring the servants of God . . . to the good, eternal happiness that is promised to all righteous people by the mercy of God."[5] In facilitating the study of sacred texts, the book constituted a new "front" in the "war of Torah" (מלחמתה של תורה)—thus the volume's title.

Yet Portaleone's textual anthology actually occupied only a minor portion of the book. He preceded this anthology with an original account of the construction of the ancient Temple that had stood in Jerusalem centuries earlier, as well as the arts and sciences practiced there.[6] Among these, Portaleone devoted ten chapters to music in the Temple, discussing both speculative music theory and practical music-making, especially among the Levites, who were responsible for singing and playing instruments as

FIGURE 9.2 Internal title page of Abraham Portaleone, *Shilṭei ha-giborim* (Mantua: printed by the author, 1612). Courtesy of the Manuscripts and Rare Books Collection, Bar-Ilan University Library.

part of the Temple service. As Don Harrán has shown, Portaleone's music theory bears striking resemblances to that of Italian humanists from Tinctoris to Zarlino,[7] and, indeed, the inventory of his library indicates that he was familiar with debates on ancient Greek musical theory and its application in modern Italy.[8] He was also well versed in music and owned at least two lutes.[9] In his description of musical practice in the ancient Temple, he made overt reference to modern usage, for example, by likening ancient instruments mentioned in the Hebrew Bible, such as the kinnor (כינור) and 'ugav (עוגב), to modern ones like the lute, cornetto, and viola da gamba. In this general sense, his methodology mirrored that of the Italian humanists of his age, who found precedent for modern musical practice in the imagined music of ancient times. Yet Portaleone's text diverged from those of his non-Jewish contemporaries in significant ways, most importantly by asserting the complexity of ancient Hebrew music, which stood in opposition to the ideal of pastoral simplicity embraced by the humanists, who idolized the music of ancient Greece and Rome. Moreover, in likening ancient Hebrew music to the music of seventeenth-century Mantua, Portaleone elided not only temporal spheres but religious ones: he identified the music of the ancient Israelites as the true ancestor of all music—Christian, Jewish, or secular—in his own day.

While Portaleone's juxtaposition of music of the ancient Temple with the music that he heard in the streets and homes of early modern Mantua might seem jarring from the standpoint of modern readers, we suggest that his approach is best understood not as an attempt at a strictly historical reading, but one rooted in the traditional exegetic methods of midrash. Portaleone reads accounts of Temple music in the Hebrew Bible and reinterprets them through hermeneutic techniques of midrash to make them relevant to the music of his own time and place. Seen against the backdrop of ongoing debates about whether music was permissible in Jewish practice at all—debates that stemmed from Talmudic strictures imposed as a sign of mourning following the destruction of the Temple—Portaleone's midrashic reinterpretations of these ancient texts serve a polemical purpose. By reviving an understanding of music as part of Jewish tradition and practice, Portaleone's readings have the effect of *midrash halakhah* (מדרש הלכה), an application of the midrash's textual-hermeneutic approach that directly affects understandings of Jewish practice. Portaleone's approach sought to collapse past and present, bringing practices of the ancient Temple to bear on modern life.

Moreover, as we will show, the effect of this midrashic approach can be elucidated through the concept of collectivity. The widespread participation of Jews in the musical cultures of northern Italy—well attested in the documentary evidence—rendered music a discursive space that allowed Jews to define themselves both internally and in relation to their non-Jewish neighbors.[10] Even as Jews were sought after as musical performers and as music and dancing masters by both the courts of rulers and members of the wider Christian population, they were increasingly targeted by Catholic authorities for their excursions into Christian society, as Daniel Jütte affirms: "While Jewish musicians frequently crossed the boundaries between two different (sometimes segregated) societies, they were also—and from the late sixteenth century on, increasingly—caught between the front lines of the conflicts that divided those societies."[11] Portaleone's treatise, directed at an "insider" Jewish readership in Mantua and beyond, sought to link contemporary musical practice among the Jews with ancient Jewish practice—not ancient Greek or Roman practice, as it was frequently understood by his non-Jewish humanist contemporaries. Thus, the Jews in his home city may have read the *Shilṭei ha-giborim* as an attempt to bolster their collective experience: seen in the light that Portaleone proposes, music could be reclaimed as a component of Jewish history and a Torah-observant life. In this understanding, rather than weakening the collective Jewish experience by facilitating interaction with non-Jews, music served to link Jews to their ancient forebears, thus fostering a sense of diachronic collectivity, collectivity through time. In addition, it asserted the legitimacy of Mantuan Jews' place in the musical lives of their own day, affirming music as a component of modern Jewish experience and allowing for—even encouraging—Jewish participation in music outside distinctly Jewish contexts. In this sense, Portaleone also fostered a sense of synchronic collectivity, collectivity with others in their own time and place. Music could help Jews to cross the walls of the ghetto even as it was still under construction.

The musical sections of Portaleone's treatise thus address three fundamental and interrelated concepts: collectivity, music, and ghetto. Music already served to connect Jews to their Christian neighbors through professional interactions and traditions of performance; yet these connections were fraught, since the Catholic religious authorities viewed them so skeptically, and since some Jewish authorities likewise discouraged the kind of close interactions that such connections engendered. Portaleone reframed music as an ancient art that strengthened the bonds of Jews to their own ancestors, and in this sense, he heightened the experience of collectivity and community with Jews across the ages. The paradoxical position that music occupied in Portaleone's view—simultaneously bringing Jews into contact with Christians and linking them to their ancestral past—was also embodied in the ghetto itself. The walls of the ghetto were not simply restrictive: they also allowed Jews to foster their own sense of cultural collectivity and communal experience, and they enshrined the place of the Jewish community within the city. In Portaleone's formulation, music could help Jewish readers to view themselves as legitimate, collective heirs to tradition across time and place.

THE *SHILṬEI HA-GIBORIM* AND PORTALEONE'S ENGAGEMENT WITH "GREEK WISDOM"

The *Shilṭei ha-giborim* was not Portaleone's first publication. A physician by training and profession, he had, in 1584, published a volume titled *De Auro dialogi tres*, which pondered the efficacy of gold in curing illness.[12] As Alessandro Guetta has explained, Portaleone used that volume to articulate his ideas on two interrelated themes that were central to the nascent modern scientific epistemology articulated most famously in the following generation by Galileo Galilei, among others: Portaleone considered, first, the relationship between ancient and modern learning and, second, the relative places of experience and reason in epistemology.[13] These interrelated questions were central to all humanist inquiry, and, while Portaleone cites numerous ancient scholars in *De Auro*, his allegiance to experience over the received wisdom gleaned from ancient sources is apparent. Indeed, in the years between Portaleone's two treatises, the balance between the wisdom of the ancient Greeks and the observations and reasoning of the modern natural philosophers tipped, with empirical observation and experience coming to form a central pillar of the nascent scientific method. In this sense, Guetta has interpreted Portaleone's medical treatise as a manifestation of his "radical empiricism."[14]

Despite his break with the authorities of classical learning, *De Auro* is replete with references to those authorities; it is clear that the specter of ancient knowledge loomed large over Portaleone's work as a physician in a humanist environment. Indeed, Portaleone would later claim that his engagement with secular subjects—what the Talmud and other Jewish sources dub "Greek wisdom," using that phrase both literally, in the sense that much of it emanated from Greek scholars, and synecdochally, to stand for all subjects other than Torah learning—was the cause of the terrible illness that he experienced in 1605, which left him paralyzed. Seeking the cause of this illness, Portaleone explained,

> I searched my behavior and saw (after Him who sees all) that in addition to my sins, which were more numerous than the hairs on my head, the clamor of my neglecting the Torah rose before the face of God. For I had dealings with the children of Greek wisdom, I sought to reach the heights through philosophy and medicine, which lured me with their honeyed words to seek salvation in the ways of darkness, and thus prevented me from devoting myself to the heritage of the community of Jacob, as I should have done.[15]

Portaleone explains that his sense of remorse for his neglect of Torah study in favor of "Greek wisdom" is what led him to compile the *Shiltei ha-giborim*, thus enabling other Jews to fulfill their obligation of Torah study easily. While he addresses the volume to his four sons, the fact that it was published indicates that Portaleone intended it as a tool for the entire community. In this sense, his "sons" form a rhetorical device through which he proclaims his familial relationship with his entire Jewish readership.[16]

Nevertheless, in his *Shiltei ha-giborim*, Portaleone does not limit himself to Jewish sources. To be sure, his anthologized texts draw on the Bible—especially the passages from Exodus and Leviticus that deal with the construction of the Tabernacle and its associated rituals, as well as the Book of Psalms, with its accounts of Temple practice and music—in addition to the Mishnah, the Talmud, and later texts, including extensive citation of the Kabbalah. However, in framing these texts from the Jewish tradition, he drew on a wide range of other sources. In this approach he joined a long line of Mantuan Jewish scholars who viewed all forms of learning as not only permissible within a Jewish worldview but, in fact, inherent to Jewish thought. For example, as early as the late fifteenth century, Judah Messer Leon's *Nofet tsufim* had articulated a view of Jewish learning that would "retrieve all of world literature as a means of restoring and recuperating what was once Israel's alone."[17]

Portaleone's adoption of this principle is readily seen in the method that he adopts in his book, which contains references to previous writings in ten languages,[18] as well as in its approach to music. When Portaleone cites neo-Platonic ideas of music theory, when he describes musical notation, or when he identifies modern Italian instruments with ancient Israelite ones, he aims to show that they were, in fact, preceded by practices endemic to Judaism. This rhetorical move was common to Jewish thinkers of the Renaissance, as Abraham Melamed has shown. Throughout the Renaissance, in a wide range of fields, Jewish scholars sought to position their intellectual heritage not only as integral to secular learning but also as preceding Christian scholarship in the major intellectual trends of the age.[19] In the musical theories and practices of his own day, Portaleone claimed that Jews could discern vestiges of their own musical heritage.

The major difference between *De Auro* and the *Shilṭei ha-giborim*, then, is not *whether* the author engaged with subjects that lay outside the immediate domain of Torah, but *how*. Portaleone casts his later work as that of a pious and repentant Jew and frames his presentations of secular subjects in religious terms—not as components of "Greek wisdom," but as aspects of Jewish tradition and practice. While *De Auro* was dedicated to Duke Guglielmo Gonzaga and bore no overt markers of traditional Jewish learning, the *Shilṭei ha-giborim* was clearly intended for an "insider" readership—that is, for other Jews. This is clear not only from Portaleone's use of the Hebrew language, in which Christian scholars were increasingly gaining expertise, but also from his description of the book as an instrument in the "war of Torah," the story of his repentance and renewed commitment to Torah study, and turns of phrase that would have resonated with other Jews, such as his characterization of the Jewish people as "servants of God" (עבדי ה').[20]

From one perspective, it seems only natural that Jewish writers would address music. After all, ancient sources attest that music had formed a central component of Temple practice. This point is clear throughout the book of Psalms, in which introductions to various chapters refer to liturgical usage as well as recitation in certain spaces of the Temple; for example, the title "Song of Ascents," which appears at the heading of Psalms 120–134, may refer to the Levites singing these Psalms as they ascended to the altar. Musical details likewise appear throughout the book of Psalms. Psalm 150, for example, enumerates the many instruments used in worship, and instrumental or modal indicators appear at the beginning of numerous Psalms. These musical aspects of Temple worship are discussed in passages throughout the Mishnah, Talmud, and later texts.

From another perspective, however, Portaleone's extensive engagement with music in the *Shilṭei ha-giborim* is striking—especially in light of the author's claim that he had separated himself from the study of "Greek wisdom." Following the destruction of the Second Temple in Jerusalem in 70 CE, the Mishnah forbade the practice of music as a sign of mourning and in recognition of the Jews' status as a nation in exile. In subsequent generations, Jewish legal authorities had debated the permissibility of music-making: some argued that a total ban on music was required; others took a more lenient position, arguing that the prohibition on music applied only to instruments, or only to instruments in synagogues, or only to the singing of secular songs while the singer is experiencing the intoxicating effects of wine.[21] It is noteworthy that, in these legal discussions, music is described as a component of "Greek" (i.e., vernacular) culture. For example, the Talmud relates that the heretic known as *Aḥer* (literally, "Other," a pseudonym for Rabbi Elisha ben Avuya) was tempted to turn away from Judaism because "Greek song never left his lips."[22] The "othering" of Elisha ben Avuya for having deigned to leave the self-imposed Jewish intellectual ghetto serves as a parable on the double-faceted role that the externally imposed ghetto served a millennium and a half later: it was at once a means for the Christian majority to contain and control the Jewish minority and a means for that self-same Jewish minority to preserve its sense of internal collectivity. Thus, accounts such as that of Elisha ben Avuya served as cautionary tales to warn Jews against integration with non-Jews in their musical practices, since music could serve as a seemingly dangerous vehicle of acculturation.

Purportedly, it was the ancient musical practice of the Temple that formed the topic of these chapters of Portaleone's treatise. Yet the manner in which he treated this topic— juxtaposing this ancient music with practices and theories of his own day—brought to the fore essential questions about Jews' interactions with non-Jews and adoption of their cultural practices. In Portaleone's day, there were some within the Jewish communities of northern Italy who objected to the cultivation of music in the style of Christian or secular Italian music within synagogue practice, and they cited the halakhic prohibition on music in their objections. In 1604 the rabbi and cantor Leon Modena had attempted to introduce polyphonic music into the synagogue practice at Ferrara. Although most listeners were pleased with the result, one communal leader in attendance, Rabbi Moses Coimbram, objected, citing the Talmudic passage prohibiting music from synagogue practice entirely.[23] Modena authored a lengthy halakhic responsum to justify the use of polyphony in synagogue. He later printed this same responsum in the prefatory material to Salamone Rossi's *Ha-shirim 'asher li-Shlomo*, apparently anticipating similar objections to Rossi's polyphonic Hebrew vocal works.[24]

While Portaleone claimed that the objective of his chapters on music in the Temple was to recount what had taken place in the past, he connects these past practices—including the use of instruments, notation, and principles of harmony and counterpoint—to those of his own time and place. Thus, although he does not attempt to defend this mode of writing against those who might object on the basis of the Talmudic prohibitions on music, he was clearly assuming—and tacitly accepting—a level of musical education among his Jewish readership that exceeded the bounds laid out by some Jewish legal texts and authorities. Indeed, in numerous Italian cities, Mantua chief among them, Jews found that performance and teaching of music and dance offered professional opportunities when many other fields were off-limits to them. In addition to Rossi, the Jewish community of Mantua boasted many accomplished musicians and music teachers, including Rossi's sister, the singer known as Madama Europa, as well as members of the Dall'Arpa family, known for their expertise as harpists.[25] The Jewish practices of music and musical theater were so much part of the soundscape of Mantuan society that the Gonzaga family required the Jews to mount a theatrical presentation for them once a year at their court as a form of tribute. The sounds of musical theater as enacted by the Jewish community came to inform the composition of other courtly spectacles, as well.[26]

These circumstances point to an active musical culture among the city's Jewish community, and it is within this context that Portaleone's discussion of ancient music should be understood. When Portaleone included references to contemporary musical instruments, systems of notation, theories, and practices in his *Shiltei ha-giborim*, he was apparently writing from a position of close familiarity and assuming the same from his readers. And although he framed his book as a description of the past, it should, in fact, be considered as a thinly veiled justification of Jewish participation in the musical culture of his time. While this active musical culture had been in development in Mantua for decades or perhaps even centuries, it reached an inflection point in the early seventeenth century. As the duke's plan to build a ghetto became clear, and construction began in 1610, the Jewish population experienced increased pressure over its distinct religious and cultural profile. Portaleone's treatise served to reinforce Jewish participation in modern Italian musical life by locating precedent for such participation in ancient Jewish history.

PORTALEONE ON THE COMPLEXITY OF MUSIC IN THE ANCIENT TEMPLE

On a surface level, it is easy to discern general similarities between Portaleone's approach to music and those of the Italian humanists of his day. Like theorists and historians such as Vincenzo Galilei, Girolamo Mei, and numerous others, Portaleone connected the music of his own lifetime to ancient practices. While the composers and theorists who took inspiration from descriptions of ancient Greece used it to justify developments such as monody and opera, Portaleone claimed that modern Italian music found its true origins in Jewish history—specifically, in the musical practices of the Levites who served in the ancient Temple. Like the Christian humanists, Portaleone cites Plato as an authority on the relationship among *ritmo*, *metro*, and *armonia*, all of which are subservient to *orazione*. And, like Christian writers as well as so many Jewish kabbalists, he adopts aspects of the neo-Platonist understanding of the "sympathies" between sounding music, the music of the human body, and the inaudible music of the spheres.

And yet, the relationship between Portaleone's musical project and that of the Christian humanists is more complex than it might appear at first, since he adopts some aspects of Italian humanist theory while rejecting others. The precise ways in which his argument overlaps with and diverges from the central tenets of his humanist contemporaries highlight significant aspects of his agenda. These points of overlap and divergence attest to his desire to cast ancient Hebrew music, above all, as a complex art—one that, as he understood it, reflected a high level of intellectual and artistic achievement. In locating a precedent for advanced musical learning in Jewish history, Portaleone implied that continued engagement with this art in his own lifetime was not only acceptable, but warranted as a component of Jewish practice.

Portaleone's first discussion of music in the ancient Temple appears in chapter 4 of the *Shiltei ha-giborim*, where he begins by insisting that the ancient Hebrew music was not equivalent to the "songs of field laborers and shepherds"—that is, to folk song.[27] Whereas such rustic, pastoral music is monophonic, Portaleone asserted that the music sung by the Levites in the ancient Temple was polyphonic, and indeed, that it followed the rules of consonance and dissonance as codified by Italian theorists of the late sixteenth century. The Levites, he claimed, employed a rigorous system of training to master these rules of polyphony, and, significantly, he asserted that they used notated part books to transmit the countless musical compositions that they performed. He reasoned that "since there was a great number of all the players and musical instruments and singers, we may assume that the Levites had many books which taught them all sorts of instrumental melodies and all kinds of tunes for the Psalms of David, son of Jesse."[28] In Portaleone's view, music notation was a marker of a complex musical system, as the Levites' notated books transmitted a tradition of "interweaving voices" (קולות מורכבים)—that is, counterpoint. Oral traditions of music-making seemed closer to the practices of the "field laborers and shepherds" whom he dismisses.[29]

Portaleone expounds upon the complexity of the notational systems used by the Levites in the ancient Temple in his discussion of musical instruments. In chapter 11, following a lengthy discussion of the instruments themselves, he asserts that music for chordal instruments was written out in *ḥalukah*, or *partitura*—a word that, like many other Italian musical terms, he spells out in Hebrew. By contrast, the nevel, which he equates to the lute, uses intavolatura notation. He cites the Mishnah, which relates in tractate Arakhin that the musical instruments were kept in the courtyard that led to the women's section of the ancient Temple, and he insists in more than one passage of his treatise that the vocal part books and instrumental *partiture* and *intavolature* were kept in the same location.[30]

Portaleone's motivation for insisting on the musical literacy of the ancient Hebrews becomes clearer in considering his description of the system of cantillation markings (*te'amim*) used for the chanting of scripture—the one type of musical notation that had actually been transmitted to Portaleone's own day. He adheres to the view, commonly accepted by rabbinic authorities, that the te'amim had been used in the Temple (and, indeed, that they derived from the time when the ancient Hebrews had received the Torah on Mount Sinai). However, he needs to contend with the fact that the te'amim are not pitch-specific: like early Christian chant notation, they convey aspects of the directionality of the melody but not its precise pitches. Portaleone takes a two-pronged approach to solving this problem. First, he asserts that the cantillation markings actually form a superior system of notation, since they convey multiple pitches with a single pen stroke: "one *nota* of the six usual *note* (which are *ut, re, mi, fa, sol, la*, like the others), shows the singers only one tone which is distinct from the other singable tones," while "the marking of a single [cantillation] accent . . . always indicates to us many tones together."[31] Second, he explains, the precise pitch content of the cantillation markings was well known to the Levites, but it was forgotten because of the Jews' exile: "When our Messiah comes, He will restore the pristine splendor; our priests, Levites and prophets will teach us, by God's command, the proper intervals of music, which are based on [the cantillation markings] *zarqa*, *sharey*, and the like, which we have forgotten in our exile. God will have pity and be merciful to us."[32]

Portaleone's claim that the music of the ancient Temple had nothing in common with the music of "field laborers and shepherds" leads him to deny the use of certain instruments in the Temple. Among these was the sampogna, which he understood as the bagpipe.[33] The pastoral associations of the sampogna are clear from its description in Italian translations of Ovid's *Metamorphoses*, although its precise identity was debated. The most basic form of the sampogna was widely understood as equivalent to the panpipes; this interpretation would, paradoxically, lead some writers to claim that it was the precursor to the organ, since they imagined the organ pipes as a set of panpipes operated by bellows. In fact, the pastoral associations established in the *Metamorphoses* led to an understanding of the sampogna among Christian writers as encompassing a spiritual dimension. As Ovid relates, in fleeing Pan, the nymph Syrinx prayed to Diana, who turned her into a set of reeds—rendered in Italian as a sampogna. Giuseppe Horologgi, whose commentary on the *Metamorphoses* circulated widely in the late sixteenth and early seventeenth centuries, endowed this story of the sampogna with a mystical overlay. He argued that Pan, whose name (Horologgi contended) derives from the Greek word for "everything," came to be dominated by his love for Syrinx; she, in turn, symbolized "that suave harmony produced by the movement of the spheres, so much beloved by nature."[34] Other interpreters, among them Giambattista Marino, read this interpretation of the sampogna through a distinctly Christian lens. In an interpretation published two years after the *Shiltei ha-giborim*, Marino argued that Pan stood for God, and the seven reeds of the panpipes (the sampogna) symbolized the seven last words of Jesus on the cross.[35] Portaleone owned two copies of sixteenth-century Italian translations of Ovid, and it is quite likely that these included Horologgi's popular commentary, which was nearly ubiquitous.[36] Portaleone's rejection of the sampogna as a component of ancient Temple practice is significant in that it underscores his overarching objective—namely, to show that the music of the Temple was complex and sophisticated, and that it required real training.

The sampogna was not the only instrument with folk associations that Portaleone claimed was excluded from the music-making of the Levites in the ancient Temple. In chapter 5 of the *Shiltei ha-giborim* he enumerates several other "inferior" musical instruments that were known to the ancient Hebrews, some of which were used in ritual, but that were not considered suitable for the more refined music that was performed by the Levites. Among these are the shofar, which was "not blown to make music, but as [a fulfillment of the] obligation on the first day of the seventh month; it is intended to put fear in the heart, and is not for the enjoyment of melody."[37] Similarly, Portaleone argues, the tof (drum) was not used in the temple; for proof, he turns to I Chronicles, where "King David did not mention the tof at all among the instruments he chose for music-making."[38]

In his rejection of these seemingly primitive instruments, Portaleone's approach diverged from that of his Italian humanist contemporaries. As is well known, theorists involved in monody and opera justified their practice through reference to the music of pastoral soundscapes and the musical-dramatic performance practices of ancient Greece. In his valorization of monody over counterpoint, Vincenzo Galilei cited the simple, monodic singing of "peasant farmers cultivating their fields or shepherds tending their flocks."[39] In justifying his invention of recitative, Jacopo Peri admitted that he could not be sure that "this was the type of song used in Greek and Roman plays."[40] Nevertheless, he cited their use of "an intermediate form" between speech and song as a precedent for modern recitative and opera as a whole. Other examples abound. With their central place in the musical and theatrical life of Mantua, many of the Jews of the city must have known of the importance of classical myth and the pastoral mode to contemporary developments. Inventories of their libraries indicate that many Jews owned copies of Ovid, Tasso, Ariosto, Guarini, and others central to the humanist-pastoral tradition.[41]

After establishing that simple instruments such as the sampogna, shofar, and tof were excluded from the Levites' music-making, Portaleone devotes ample space to consideration of the more refined instruments that were used in that context. He identifies the *tsiltsal* (צלצל) or *tsiltsal shema* (צלצל שמע) with the trombone, and he classifies the biblical *ķeren* (קרן) in the same family as the piffero and the flauto.[42] He devotes separate chapters to the minim (מנים), the nevel (נבל), the kinnor, and the 'ugav, all four of which he views as integral to Temple practice. Portaleone claims that the minim (literally, "various types") is the complex and multi-part clavicordo—which, strangely, he claims was identical to the Greek monochord.[43] In light of Portaleone's detailed description of the clavichord, we may assume that its identification with the monochord is no error on his part, but rather the result of his different understanding of the identity of the Greek instrument. Portaleone relies on what appears to be a far-fetched interpretation of the Greek word, which, rather than simply meaning "of one string," becomes "the one instrument suitable for playing, for even with its many parts combined, it forms only one instrument with strings on it; *monos* means 'singular' or 'one,' and *corda* means 'a string suitable for playing.'"[44] If viewed as an etymology, the connection between "min" and "mono" is tenuous, to say the least. Yet making such connections on the basis of similar phonology was common practice in the midrash; the technique is known as *'al tiķri* (אל תקרי; don't read [the word] thus, [but rather thus]). This approach enables the elision of phonetically similar words from different roots to yield spiritually meaningful interpretations. The technique of *'al tiķri* creates bridges between words such as *ben* (בנים, sons) with boneh (בונים, builders) to argue that our offspring are our edifices; or between *morashah* (מורשה, heritage) and *me'orasah* (מאורסה, betrothed) to express the connection between the Jewish people and the Torah in terms of matrimony.[45] Portaleone was therefore quite traditional in exploiting the phonological similarity between minim and mono to the idea of one unifying all. He thus rooted contemporary practice in historical Jewish precedent by using word play in a manner entirely typical of the hermeneutic techniques of midrash.

"The *nevel*," Portaleone writes, "is one of the musical instruments well known to us, called *liuto* in Italian. In our holy language it is called *nevel*; either because it *menabel* [מנבל, puts to shame] all kinds of musical instruments by its great pleasantness, as described in the midrash on Psalms, or because its shape is like that of a *nevel yayin* [נבל יין, wine bottle], which is hollow inside and has a long neck and belly."[46] Here, too, it is clear that the author's awareness of the relative value and complexity of musical instruments was driving his interpretations: the lute was an instrument highly prized by the Italian aristocracy, since the instrument was known for its subtlety, rich tone, and usefulness in accompanying song. Moreover, when Portaleone addresses the *nevel 'asor* (נבל עשור, ten-stringed nevel), he associated it with the ten-course chitarrone, or theorbo: "In my opinion, King David was referring to a[n instrument] such as this when he said: 'I will sing unto Thee upon a *nevel 'asor*' [Psalm 144:9], meaning a *nevel* of ten sets of strings."[47]

Portaleone departs from the traditional Jewish classification of the 'ugav as a wind instrument, preferring instead to identify it as the viola da gamba. His detailed description of the instrument, itemizing the body of the instrument, fingerboard, pegs, bridge, six strings, and "two holes on its front side lengthwise on the belly of the instrument, shaped like the Christian letter called in Italian *esse*" belies his misinterpretation of the role of those holes to allow "the sweet tone of the touched strings to enter the hollow body of the instrument."[48] Portaleone explains his identification of the instrument by reading the word 'ugav as a compound of *ugah* (עוגה, loaf) with *gav* (גב, back, or hump); this derivation results from his use of a midrashic technique known as *notarikon* (נוטריקון), in which a single word is interpreted as a compound of two other words. The tenuous, if imaginative, etymology—similar in approach to the midrash about the etymology of the word *nevel*—once again underscores Portaleone's agenda of identifying the musical instruments of the Temple with complex modern instruments rather than with more rudimentary, folk-based ones. Moreover, his use of a midrashic technique points to his engagement with Jewish methodologies for framing musical history; this is a point to which we will return below.

In light of what Guetta refers to as the "radical empiricism" of Portaleone's scientific practice, his approach to the kinnor—the harp—is of special significance. In his description of this biblical instrument, we may discern his application of empiricism to a musical instrument. Portaleone's teacher, the kabbalist and rabbi Judah Moscato, had already offered an interpretation of the kinnor in a sermon, titled *Higayon be-khinor* (הגיון בכינור, Sounds for contemplation with a lyre, Venice, 1589) that takes as its point of departure the Talmudic story of King David awakening to the sound of this instrument:

> Rav Aha bar Bizna said that Rabbi Shimon Hasida said: A lyre hung over David's bed, and once midnight arrived, the northern midnight wind would come and cause the lyre to play on its own. David would immediately rise from his bed and study Torah until the first rays of dawn. . . . Rav Yitzhak bar 'Adda, and some say Rav Yitzhak, son

of Rav 'Idi, said: From what verse [is this derived?] "Awake, my glory; awake, harp and lyre; I will wake the dawn" [Psalms 57:9].[49]

For Moscato, this passage presented an opportunity for a long metaphorical interpretation with kabbalistic underpinnings. Moscato draws on the possible derivation of the word *kinor* from the word *ken* (straight, upright) to liken the kinnor to human beings seeking to fulfill their potential as "instruments" of God; all individuals must seek to harmonize with the "music" of heaven. Taking his cue from neo-Platonic theories of sympathy and the harmony of the spheres, Moscato is focused not on actual music-making, but on all individuals' quest to fulfill their potential to harmonize with the divine will. As Moscato writes, "David's *kinnor* is already in the hands of all men, for each will gather unto himself his body, spirit, and soul in his being a *kinnor* as ordered as the *kinnor* of David."[50] As Gianfranco Miletto explains, "Moscato describes the Torah as the highest science, the eighth discipline in the learning system of *trivium* and *quadrivium*, the perfect teaching that cannot at all be modified."[51]

In interpreting Moscato's sermon, Harrán explains, "Because humans are fallible, David is offered as a more reasonable example for them to follow: he repaired his sins by endeavoring to walk on 'an upright path,' whereby, in time, his *kinnor*, as stated in the *midrash*, played of itself."[52] This, indeed, is as close as Moscato comes to describing musical practice: he addresses the instrumentalist who acquires the skill of managing an instrument, likening that process to that of a person who learns to behave according to the will of God. In such cases, "as in the practice of playing on a music[al] instrument when from one's training in it one acquired a perfect ability, for one will proceed from the training of one's hands, which will make the playing easier for one, as if one's hands knew how to play on their own."[53]

Although Portaleone also derives the word *kinor* from the Hebrew word for "straight," his discussion of the instrument is entirely different from that of Moscato. Rather than dwelling at length on this mystical interpretation of the kinnor, Portaleone again provides a detailed description of the Italian harp of his day, addressing its construction, the "straightness" of its strings, and the manner in which it is played, what it is made of, and how many strings it has.[54] He cites the same Talmudic story about King David being awakened by the sound of his lyre at midnight, but, significantly, he attempts to provide an empirical proof for it, explaining that if one places the kinnor and other instruments facing the wind, they will not play by themselves. However, he notes,

> if one takes the *arpa* and places it facing the north wind . . . when the wind touches the strings from both sides, it will sound a kind of musical whisper; not a particular melody, arranged and distinct, as created by the harpists with knowledge and intention: for that would be an absolute miracle, which is unnecessary. Our God, blessed [be] His name, will neither rob nature, nor seek miracles, except at special times, for a very special cause, in order to honor His name, His glory, and His magnificence.[55]

In this passage, Portaleone appears to directly address and contradict the interpretation of Moscato. This is true not only in that Moscato's interpretation is mystical while Portaleone's is practical, but also in their understandings of how David's kinnor worked. While Moscato reads the story as miraculous—the kinnor "played itself" in response to King David's "well-tuned" soul—Portaleone sees the story as descriptive of a physical phenomenon.[56]

Portaleone's insistence on the instrument facing the north wind was doubtless prompted by the Talmudic passage that he seeks to explain, but the demonstration itself was one that had already been described in a book that Portaleone owned: *De i miracoli et maravigliosi effeti dalla natura* (Of the miraculous and marvelous effects of nature), by the neo-Platonist writer Giovanni Battista Della Porta.[57] This volume offered a compendium of demonstrations that would show the workings of sympathetic "magic": "To make a *chitara* or *lira* be played by the wind, do thus: When there is a great wind, place the instrument against it, so that the wind will strike it inside; and when there is enough, it will play lightly, and run through all the pipes of the instrument (if it is made of pipes), such that you will hear a most pleasant harmony."[58] This passage from Della Porta's treatise, together with several other excerpts in the same chapter, represents one of the first instances of practical demonstrations with musical instruments.[59] While his neo-Platonist tendencies led him to report a number of questionable effects of music— for example, to ward off the plague, Della Porta suggests playing music on instruments made of vine or poplar wood, "since Wine and Vinegar are very effective against the pestilence"—his drive toward practical experience led him to suggest demonstrations that could be replicated with certainty by his readers.

The same may be said of Portaleone. While he followed his teacher, Moscato, in certain mystical tendencies, their divergent uses of the Talmudic passage about King David's harp reveal their different approaches. For Moscato, music resided almost entirely in the mystical realm; it served a metaphorical purpose that could inspire his readers to a life in "harmony" with God's will. For Portaleone, like Della Porta, David's *arpa* was a real instrument that could be held and tested and played in Mantua in 1612. Portaleone's insistence on reading the Temple's instruments into those sounding around him attests to his wish to hear the ancient Temple in the musical soundscape of early modern Italy.

Portaleone's Midrashic Approach to Music History

In assessing the *Shiltei ha-giborim*, Harrán remarks on its novelty and comprehensive treatment. Still, he claimed, Portaleone interpreted "biblical and rabbinical sources . . . more often whimsically than historically"; moreover, Harrán writes, "[Portaleone's] report is marred by his uncertainty about the topic and his anachronistic approach to it."[60] Thus Harrán assumes that Portaleone's elision of historical eras—his collapsing of the musical practices of the Levites in the ancient Temple with those of musicians in seventeenth-century Mantua—was accidental, a result of a lack of understanding of how times change and how history progresses.

It is certainly true that an objective *ars historica*, which sifts demonstrable, chronological fact from the mythologized fiction received from ancient sources, was only just emerging in the late sixteenth and early seventeenth centuries.[61] This, no doubt, contributed to Portaleone's mode of writing, which, indeed, was more the norm than otherwise. And yet, aspects of the *Shilṭei ha-giborim* indicate that its author was not simply ignorant of or insensitive to the obvious anachronisms it contained. His "radical empiricism" in medicinal practice and writing shows that he was not simply content to accept ancient texts at face value. Even if his renewed religious zeal compelled him to accept the chronologies of the Hebrew Bible as historical fact, the historical writing of his older contemporary and fellow physician Azariah ben Moses dei Rossi had already addressed questions of Jewish history and its reconciliation with demonstrable chronology. Dei Rossi's book of Jewish history, the *Meʾor ʿeinayim* (Mantua, 1578), was controversial, to be sure, but it continued to circulate in Mantua. The rabbinic authorities there declined to ban its reading, choosing instead to limit it to those over twenty-five years old. The *Meʾor ʿeinayim* addressed the history of the ancient Temple, as the *Shilṭei ha-giborim* would later do. Yet the approaches of the two volumes were quite different.[62]

Portaleone owned a copy of the *Meʾor ʿeinayim*; the precedent of this book, together with Portaleone's own empiricism in his scientific writing, suggests that his approach to history in the *Shilṭei ha-giborim* was not simply a matter of historical obliviousness.[63] In fact, as Guetta argues, Portaleone's "collapsing of present and past . . . must be seen alongside the spiritual displacement into the past recommended for the pious Jew. These anachronisms—there are many in the work—indicate an acute perception of historical time rather than great naivety."[64] Indeed, the precedent of the *Meʾor ʿeinayim* suggests that a more objective historical methodology was available to Portaleone, and, given his empirical approach to science, he would likely have known how to apply it if he had wanted to.

But did he want to apply it? As Yosef Hayim Yerushalmi has argued, the controversy around the *Meʾor ʿeinayim* was due to "the use of profane history, which few, if any, would accept as a truth by which the words of the sages might be judged."[65] Dei Rossi's engagement with serious historiography, argues Yerushalmi, was the only instance of its kind in sixteenth-century Jewish literature, leaving "no heirs to his method" and having "no real parallel for the next two hundred years."[66] Dei Rossi was well aware of his "splendid isolation" among his fellow Jews, characterizing their attitude toward historiography as "what was—was" (מאי דהוה הוה), and writing, "for what have we to do with all this considering that what was—was, several thousand years ago or more?" As Dei Rossi was fully aware, the traditional Jewish study of the past was first and foremost a practical endeavor, less interested in an accurate reconstruction of the past than in making the world of the ancients relevant to the present day: "what was—was and there is in it no relevance to law and observance."[67]

Instead, Yerushalmi has argued that Jewish study of ancient sources up to the nineteenth century was characterized by "a merging of historical and liturgical time, of verticality and circularity . . . a fusion of past and present," in which ancient texts are read not in order to reconstruct the past, but rather to read them into the present.[68] The most common manifestation of this practice in ancient rabbinic literature such as the Mishnah and the Talmud appears in the techniques of midrash, which often verify traditionally received practice as well as the derivation of new practices on the basis of the ancient scriptures, or their interpretation through the application of certain hermeneutic rules. In later generations, writers such as Portaleone knew how to deploy these midrashic techniques in order to achieve the same aims.[69]

Rather than viewing Portaleone's discussion of music as historical (or, as some scholars have done, denigrating it as ahistorical), we suggest that he approached his subject using the methodologies of midrash, in which historical accuracy was largely irrelevant. Portaleone did not seek historical verisimilitude in interpreting the minim as a clavichord, or the 'ugav as a viola da gamba, but rather the appropriate hermeneutic "hooks" that would enable his brethren to imagine their contemporary practice as a reenactment of the rites of the ancients. His vivid descriptions of notated part books and his efforts to identify exactly where those books were located did not represent a detached reconstruction of the liturgy of the Temple, but rather the subjective imagination of sixteenth- and seventeenth-century music-making by Jews in Italy as a spiritual time machine, transporting the profane present into the sacred past.

Understanding Portaleone's project as midrashic allows for a clearer distinction between inspiration from the ancients and that of contemporary Christian humanists. For the humanists, the Greeks represented a precedent and an inspiration, one that enabled them to combine renewal with a sense of tradition and provided a venerable pedigree that allowed them to deviate from ecclesiastic traditions of the earlier centuries. For Jews, by contrast, harking back to the Temple as a source of inspiration for their day-to-day practice was a continuous and age-old strategy. The Talmud (Berakhot 26b) claims that the daily prayers were substitutes for the *temidim*, the daily sacrifices offered at the Temple; the prohibition of work on the Sabbath was interpreted in the Talmud (Shabbat 96b) as the cessation of all the actions necessary for the erection of the temporary temple, the tabernacle, a precursor to the Temple in Jerusalem; the Jewish seder night on Passover replaced the sacrifice of the Paschal lamb; and the prayer of *musaf* added on the Sabbath and festivals both explicitly mentioned and was named after the sacrifice of the same name and function. The synagogue itself was known as "a lesser temple" (מקדש מעט, *mikdash me'at*) and within it there lit "an eternal flame," as a remembrance of the eternal flame that was constantly alight in the Temple (Exodus 27:20). Each of these parallels was achieved through the application of midrashic hermeneutics to biblical texts, thus drawing the Temple into Jewish daily life.

The same hermeneutic methodology of midrash, which enabled the connection of ancient Temple practices to the day-to-day affairs of modern life, informed Portaleone's approach to music. It is very possible that he understood that the etymologies he proposed for the names of the kinnor and the 'ugav were historically inaccurate. He may also have understood that the notational systems used in contemporary polyphony were not literally part of ancient Temple practice and that the instruments of seventeenth-century Italy could not have existed in the time of the Temple. In fact, though, the question of Portaleone's historical awareness misses the point. By adopting the midrashic techniques, and by bringing them to bear on both questions of communal affiliation and those of halakhic practice, his treatise subsumed contemporary Italian musical tradition—a tradition in which the Jewish community of Mantua was deeply involved—within the framework of traditional Judaism. He thus recast modern music as a central component of Jewish life and learning. In his telling, neither music theory nor musical practice, in fact, constituted "Greek wisdom." Instead, as part of the system of knowledge that was once embedded within Jewish life and halakhah, music was inherently Jewish.

As such, *Shilṭei ha-giborim* and its midrashic approach activated a synchronic collectivity, giving its Jewish readers a sense of belonging within their time and place, as it affirmed that participation in Italian musical life was not only permitted to them, but also encouraged as a component of Jewish tradition. This synchronic collectivity was as paradoxical as the ghetto itself: the Jews of Mantua were, after all, being subjected to a process of physical separation from their non-Jewish neighbors, but that separation placed them in the very heart of the city. Simultaneously integrated into the topography of the city and cut off from it by means of the newly constructed ghetto walls, the Jewish community was also both integral to and separate from Mantua's soundscape. Portaleone's treatise served to approve their continued engagement with the musical life of the city's collective whole.

At the same time, the *Shilṭei ha-giborim* effected a process of time travel to a period when the Jews determined their own fate—musical and otherwise. In this sense, the treatise created a sense of diachronic collectivity, connecting Jews to their ancient forebears and bolstering their centuries-long traditions of learning, spirituality, and ritual. These traditions and the collectivity that they engendered were alive and well when the Jews made music among themselves, as Portaleone asserted that their music-making was part of their Jewish heritage. Yet even when the Jews of Mantua exited their communal space to teach or perform for their non-Jewish contemporaries, in Portaleone's understanding, they did so as Jews. The diachronic collectivity that he cultivated would thus enhance Jews' sense of identity and belonging because they would be aware, through reading Portaleone's treatise and internalizing his ideas, that they were rightful heirs to the contemporary Italian theories and practices of music.

NOTES

1. On the history of the ghetto's construction, see Shlomo Simonsohn, *History of the Jews in the Duchy of Mantua* (Jerusalem: Ktav Publishing House, 1977), 39–46.
2. Robert Bonfil, *Jewish Life in Renaissance Italy* (Berkeley: University of California Press, 1994), 90.

3. Ibid., 89.

4. David B. Ruderman, *Early Modern Jewry* (Princeton: Princeton University Press, 2010), 62.

5. להביא עבדי ה' ... אל האושר הטוב והנצחי הצפון בחסדו יתברך לצדיקים כלם.
Abraham Portaleone, Shilṭei ha-giborim (Mantua: Published by the author, 1612), title page.

6. The full contents of Portaleone's treatise are discussed in Gianfranco Miletto, *Glauben und Wissen im Zeitalter der Reformation: Der Salomonische Tempel bei Abraham Ben David Portaleone (1542–1612)* (Berlin: De Gruyter, 2004). Miletto interprets the volume as "encyclopedic" and analogous to an early modern *Kunstkammer* (cabinet of curiosities).

7. See Don Harrán, "In Search of the 'Song of Zion': Abraham Portaleone on Music in the Ancient Temple," *European Journal of Jewish Studies* 4, no. 2 (2010): 215–239. An English translation of the music-theoretical portions of Portaleone's volume and an essay about his approach can be found in Don Harrán, *Three Early Modern Hebrew Scholars on the Mysteries of Song* (Leiden: Brill, 2014), 208–253. Harrán's writings on Portaleone—along with his work on the musical thought and practice of figures such as Judah Moscato, Leon Modena, and Salamone Rossi—form a foundation of much of the current literature in this area; references to his work appear throughout these notes. However, our interpretation of Portaleone's project differs considerably from that of Harrán.

8. Portaleone owned, for example, a copy of Ercole Bottrigari's treatise *Il Patricio*, which offers an interpretation of the theories of Aristoxenus on the monochord. See Gianfranco Miletto, "The Library of Abraham Portaleone," *European Journal of Jewish Studies* 7 (2013): 97; and Gianfranco Miletto, *La biblioteca di Avraham Ben David Portaleone secondo l'inventario della sua eredità* (Florence: Olschki, 2013), 83.

9. See Miletto, *La biblioteca di Avraham Ben David Portaleone*, 95 and 97.

10. For a recent summary of the evidence for widespread Jewish participation in the musical culture of early modern Italy, see Daniel Jütte, "The Place of Music in Early Modern Italian Jewish Culture," in *Musical Exodus: Al-Andalus and Its Jewish Diasporas*, ed. Ruth F. Davis (Lanham, MD: Rowman and Littlefield, 2015), 45–61.

11. Ibid., 46.

12. Abraham Portaleone, *De Auro dialogi tres: In quibus non solum de Auri in re Medica facultate, verum etiam de specifica eius, & ceterarum rerum forma, ac duplici potestate, qua mixtis in omnibus illa operatur, copiose disputatur* (Venice: Apud Io. Baptistam à Porta, 1584). On Portaleone's Latin treatise in comparison to his Hebrew one, see Alessandro Guetta, "Avraham Portaleone, le scientifique repenti," in *Torah et science: Perspectives historiques et théoriques—Etudes offertes à Charles Touati*, ed. Gad Freudenthal, Jean-Pierre Rothschild, and Gilbert Dahan (Paris: Peeters, 2001), 213–227; and Alessandro Guetta, "Can Fundamentalism Be Modern? The Case of Abraham Portaleone (1542–1612)," in *Acculturation and Its Discontents: The Italian Experience Between Inclusion and Exclusion*, ed. David N. Myers, Massimo Ciavolella, Peter H. Reill, and Geoffrey Symcox (Toronto: University of Toronto Press, 2008), 99–115.

13. Guetta, "Can Fundamentalism Be Modern," 100.

14. Ibid., 102.

15. פשפשתי במעשי וראיתי אחרי ראי כי נוסף לעונותי אשר רבו משערות ראשי גדלה צעקת בטול תורה לפני ה' כי בילדי חכמי היונים ספקתי. הגבהתי עוף ללכת אחרי הפלוסופיא והרפואה אשר כחלקלקות אמריהן הציקוני ללחם לחם רשע בדרך אפלה ולא הגיתי במורשת קהלת יעקב כדין וכשורה.
Portaleone, *Shilṭei ha-giborim*, introduction; translation cited after Guetta, "Can Fundamentalism Be Modern," 103. The page numbers in Portaleone's volume begin again

with each chapter; as such, our references to the original Hebrew will include only chapter numbers.

16. In Jewish traditions of learning, transfer of traditional knowledge over the generations is often referred to in familial terms: "and you shall tell your son" (Exodus 13:8). Thus, in multiple places (endings of Tractates *Berakhot*, *Yevamot*, *Keritut*, and *Nazir*), the Talmud understands the word *bannayikh* (your sons) in terms of the phonetically similar word *bonayikh* (your builders) as referring to scholarship, the building of the Jewish edifice of knowledge. As we argue below, Portaleone was a creative participator in this technique of misreading based on phonetic similarity.

17. Ruderman, *Early Modern Jewry*, 121.

18. Simonsohn, *History of the Jews in the Duchy of Mantua*, 638.

19. See Abraham Melamed, "The Myth of the Jewish Origins of Philosophy in the Renaissance: From Aristotle to Plato," *Jewish History* 26, nos. 1– 2 (May 2012): 41– 59 and Abraham Melamed, *Myth of the Jewish Origins of Science and Philosophy /* המיתוס: רקחות וטבחות על מקור החכמות (Haifa: Haifa University Press; Jerusalem: Magnes Press, 2010); Melamed discusses Portaleone on p. 258.

20. Despite Portaleone's apparent intention to direct his book toward a Jewish readership, he was soon cited by Christians discussing the identity of the ancient Hebrew sources. Perhaps the earliest of these was Athanasius Kircher, *Musurgia universalis, sive ars magna consoni et dissoni* (Rome: Corbelletti, 1650), 1:48–53.

21. Babylonian Talmud, Gittin, 7a. A survey of this and later halakhic sources on music can be found in Boaz Cohen, *Law and Tradition in Judaism* (New York: Ktav, 1959), 167–181.

22. זמר יווני לא פסק מפומיה; Babylonian Talmud, Ḥagigah, 15b.

23. That Coimbram was objecting on the basis of the passage in Gittin 7a is clear from his citation of Hosea 9:1, which is also quoted there: "'Rejoice not, oh Israel, to exultation like the [other] nations." Harrán has attributed this listener's objection to the "proximity of the Sabbath to the doleful Ninth of Av" (the anniversary, according to tradition, of the destruction of both the First and Second Temples in Jerusalem in 587 BCE and 70 CE, respectively), but this interpretation seems incorrect. See Harrán, "'Dum recordaremur Sion,'" 23.

24. Modena's responsum as it appeared in Rossi's *Shirim* is reproduced and translated in Salamone Rossi, *Sacred Vocal Works in Hebrew: Hashirim 'asher lishlomo / "The Songs of Solomon"*, ed. with introduction and notes by Don Harrán as part of *Salamone Rossi: Complete Works* (Middleton, WI: American Institute of Musicology, 2003), 13a:193–194.

25. For information on the Dall'Arpa family, including an account of Abramino Dall'Arpa's forced conversion, see Gianfranco Miletto, "Rabbi Yehuda Moscato and a Case of Forced Conversion," *Frankfurter Judaistische Beiträge* 34 (2007–2008): 149–163.

26. Emily Wilbourne, "*Lo Schiavetto* (1612): Travestied Sound, Ethnic Performance, and the Eloquence of the Body," *Journal of the American Musicological Society* 63, no. 1 (Spring 2010): 1–43. Christian composers such as Orazio Vecchi and Adriano Banchieri incorporated stylized "Hebrew" in imitation of the Jewish music that they heard; see Don Harrán, "Between Exclusion and Inclusion: Jews as Portrayed in Italian Music from the Late Fifteenth to the Early Seventeenth Centuries," in David N. Myers, Massimo Ciavolella, Peter H. Reill, and Geoffrey Symcox, *Acculturation and Its Discontents*, 72–98. In addition, Shlomo Simonsohn's study of inventories of book collections owned by Jews in Mantua suggests that some owned books of music and music theory. See Shlomo Simonsohn,

"Sefarim ve-sifriyot shel yehudei Mantova, 1595" [Books and libraries of Mantuan Jews], *Kiryat Sefer* 37, no. 1 (1961–1962): 103–122.

27. Harrán, *Three Early Modern Hebrew Scholars*, 208.

28. ועל כי רבו המנגנים וכלי הנגון והמשוררים גם יחד, ראוי הוא להאמין, שיהיו ללוים ספרים רבים המלמדים כל מיני הנגונים בכלים, וגם כל מיני השיר על תהלות דוד בן ישי, ועם הספר ישירו ביום הזה.

Portaleone, *Shilṭei ha-giborim*, chapter 4; translation adapted from Sandler, "The Music Chapters," 76–77.

29. A discussion of music literacy and the significance of notation among early modern Italian Jews is in Lynette Bowring and Rebecca Cypess, "Orality and Literacy in the Worlds of Salamone Rossi," in *Music and Jewish Culture in Early Modern Italy: New Perspectives*, ed. Lynette Bowring, Rebecca Cypess, and Liza Malamut (Bloomington: Indiana University Press, 2022).

30. See Sandler, "The Music Chapters," 123–125.

31. Portaleone, *Shilṭei ha-giborim*, chapter 4; translation cited after Sandler, "The Music Chapters," 71.

32. שבביאת המשיח תשוב העטרה ליושנה ולימדו אותנו כהנינו לוינו ונביאנו במצות ה' הקולות הנאותים אל הזמרה המיוסדים על זרקא, שרי כו', אשר שכחנו בגלותנו, ה' יחוס ויחמול עלינו.

Portaleone, *Shilṭei ha-giborim*, chapter 179; translation cited after Sandler, "The Music Chapters," 158–159. The term *sharey*, little used or known today, is the equivalent of the *segol*; the term was used especially in the Italian rite. Our thanks to Aharon Gal and William Gewirtz for providing this explanation. Portaleone owned a medieval manuscript treatise on the te'amim; see Miletto, *La biblioteca di Avraham Ben David Portaleone*, 29.

33. See Sandler, "The Music Chapters," 91.

34. ". . . quell'armonia soavissima de i moti delle sfere, amata molto da essa natura." Ovid, *Le metamorfosi . . . ridotte da Giovanni Andrea Dell'Anguillara, in ottava rima . . . con l'annotationi di M. Gioseppe Horologgi . . . con postille, & con gli argomenti nel principio di ciascun libro di M. Francesco Turchi*, 6th ed. (Venice: Appresso Camillo Franceschini 1578), fol. 14r.

35. Giambattista Marino, *Dicerie sacre* (Turin: Luigi Pizzamigio 1614), 1:95r–95v.

36. While Miletto's interpretation of the inventory of Portaleone's library conflates multiple volumes by Ovid, his verbatim transcription of the inventory includes "Le me[t]tamorfosi di Ovidio tradotte da Gio. Andrea Anguillara; Le metamorfosi di Ovidio tradotti dal medemo"; as in the source cited in endnote 34, nearly all editions featuring Anguillara's translation in the second half of the sixteenth century also included Horologgi's commentary. See Miletto, *La biblioteca di Avraham Ben David Portaleone*, 70 and 118.

37. כי לא יתקע בשופר לנגן בשיר אלא לחובה בשביעי בא' לחדש והוא לחרדת הלב לא לנעימת הנגון.

Portaleone, *Shilṭei ha-giborim*, chapter 5; translation cited after Sandler, "The Music Chapters," 81.

38. שהמלך דוד, בכלים אשר בחר לנגן בשיר, לא הזכיר התוף בשום פנים.

Portaleone, *Shilṭei ha-giborim*, chapter 5; translation cited after Sandler, "The Music Chapters," 82. Portaleone does not refer to a specific passage in I Chronicles where the tof is omitted. He may have been thinking of Chapter 15, verses 16–22. The tof is mentioned elsewhere; see, for example, I Chronicles 13:8.

39. "... che i rustici agricultori nel cultivare i campi & i pastori per le selve." Translation quoted in Vincenzo Galilei, *Dialogue on Ancient and Modern Music*, trans. with intro. and notes by Claude V. Palisca (New Haven, CT, and London: Yale University Press, 2003), 93.

40. "... io non ardirei affermare questo essere il canto nelle Greche, e nelle Romane favole usato." Translated by Margaret Murata in *Strunk's Source Readings in Music History*, gen. ed. Leo Treitler (New York and London: W. W. Norton and Company, 1998), 660.

41. Simonsohn, "Sefarim ve-Sifriyot shel Yehudei Mantova 1595."

42. See Sandler, "The Music Chapters," 101–102.

43. For Portaleone's discussion of the clavichord, see Sandler, "The Music Chapters," 107–110.

44. כלי אחד נכון לנגון. מפני שעם רב חלקיו יחד, לא יעשה אלא כלי אחד בלבד עם המתרים עליו. כי מונוס ר"ל יחיד, או אחד, וקוורדה ר"ל מתר מתוקן לנגן.

   Portaleone, *Shiltei ha-giborim*, chapter 7; translation cited in Sandler, "The Music Chapters," 107.

45. Babylonian Talmud, Berakhot, 64a; Shemot Rabbah 33:7

46. הנבל הוא כלי מכלי הנגון ידוע אצלנו, נקרא בלעז ליאוטו, ובלשוננו הקדוש נקרא נבל: או מפני שמרב נעימותו הוא מנבל כל מיני כלי זמרה, כמו שאמרו במדרש תהלים, או מפני שבצורתו הוא כדמות נבל יין, חלול מתוכו, שיש לו צואר וכרס.

   Portaleone, *Shiltei ha-giborim*, chapter 7; translation cited after Sandler, "The Music Chapters," 111. Portaleone refers to Midrash Tehilim, Psalm 81:3.

47. וכזה, לפי דעתי, היה נבל דוד המלך באמרו בנבל עשור אזמרה לך. היינו, בנבל של עשרה סדרים.

   Portaleone, *Shiltei ha-giborim*, chapter 7; translation cited after Sandler, "The Music Chapters," 112.

48. Portaleone, *Shiltei ha-giborim*, chapter 7; translated in Sandler, "The Music Chapters," 117.

49. דְּאָמַר רַב אַחָא בַּר בִּיזָנָא, אָמַר רַבִּי שִׁמְעוֹן חֲסִידָא: כִּנּוֹר הָיָה תָּלוּי לְמַעְלָה מִמִּטָּתוֹ שֶׁל דָּוִד, וְכֵיוָן שֶׁהִגִּיעַ חֲצוֹת לַיְלָה, בָּא רוּחַ צְפוֹנִית וְנוֹשֶׁבֶת בּוֹ וּמְנַגֵּן מֵאֵלָיו, מִיָּד הָיָה עוֹמֵד וְעוֹסֵק בַּתּוֹרָה עַד שֶׁעָלָה עַמּוּד הַשָּׁחַר.... אָמַר רַב יִצְחָק בַּר אַדָּא, וְאָמְרִי לַהּ אָמַר רַב יִצְחָק בְּרֵיהּ דְּרַב אִידִי: מַאי קְרָא "עוּרָה כְבוֹדִי עוּרָה הַנֵּבֶל וְכִנּוֹר אָעִירָה שָּׁחַר".

   Babylonian Talmud, Tractate Berakhot 3b. *The William Davidson Talmud*, trans. Adin Steinsaltz; https://www.sefaria.org/texts/Talmud (accessed February 28, 2021).

50. Judah Moscato, *Sefer nefutsot Yehudah: Derushim le-khol ḥeftsehem* (Venice: Zuan de Gara, 1589), Translated in Harrán, *Three Early Modern Hebrew Scholars on the Mysteries of Song*, 87.

51. Gianfranco Miletto, "The Human Body as a Musical Instrument in the Sermons of Judah Moscato," in *The Jewish Body: Corporeality, Society, and Identity in the Renaissance and Early Modern Period*, ed. Maria Diemling and Giuseppe Veltri (Leiden and Boston: Brill, 2009), 390.

52. Translated in Harrán, "Sounds for Contemplation on a Lyre," 48.

53. Translated in ibid., 113.

54. Here, too, Portaleone relies upon the midrashic device of *noṭariḳon*, deriving the word *kinor* from *ken* (straight) and *'orekh* (across).

55. אם תיקח הארפה ותשים אותה לצד רוח הצפוני... אז, כשיקיש הרוח הזה מזה ומזה במתרים, ישמיע קול דממה דקה מהנגון, ולא זמר ונגון פרטי מתוקן ומיושר כמו שעושים המקישים בו בדעת ובמזמה, כי זה יהיה נס מוחלט, שאין צורך בו. וה' אלהינו יתברך שמו לא ישדד הטבע וירצה בנסים, אלא בעתים מיוחדים לסבה מה מהסבות לכבוד שמו, תהלתו ותפארתו.

   Portaleone, *Shiltei ha-giborim*, chapter 9; translation cited after Sandler, "The Music Chapters," 116.

56. In explaining the apparently miraculous story of King David's harp through natural causes, Portaleone seems to be addressing the debate over the nature of miracles in Jewish tradition. Most famously, some of the writings of Maimonides provide a purely natural, rational explanation for the apparent miracles described the Torah. On Maimonides' position and the evolution of his thought on this subject, see, for example, Y. Tzvi Langermann, "Maimonides and Miracles: The Growth of a (Dis)belief," *Jewish History* 18 (2004): 147–172. Most rationalist Jewish thinkers in subsequent centuries accepted the approach of Maimonides with few modifications.

57. That Portaleone owned this book is attested in the inventory of his library; see Miletto, "The Library of Abraham Portaleone," 99; and Miletto, *La biblioteca di Avraham Ben David Portaleone*, 84.

58. "À far sonare la citara, o la lira al vento. Fa in questo modo, quando gliè grandißimo vento mette l'istromento all'incontro, che gli percuota drento il vento, che quanto el soffia, suona leggiermente, e corre per tutte le canne ancho del instromento, se gliè di canna, talche ne sentirai un soavißimo concento." Giovanni Battista Della Porta, *De i miracoli et maravigliosi effeti dalla natura prodotti IIII* (Venice: Lodovico Avanzi, 1560), II:98. This volume was an Italian translation of Della Porta's original Latin edition: Giovanni Battista Della Porta, *Magia naturalis sive de miraculis rerum naturalium libri IIII* (Naples: Cancer, 1558). The many reprintings and translations of this volume throughout the sixteenth and seventeenth centuries attest to its widespread and lasting influence.

59. See Rebecca Cypess, "Giovanni Battista Della Porta's Experiments with Musical Instruments," *Journal of Musicological Research* 35, no. 3 (2016): 1–17.

60. Harrán, "In Search of the 'Song of Zion,'" 216. Harrán also comments elsewhere on Portaleone's cavalier approach to historical accuracy, yet he makes no attempt to contextualize this approach, still less to frame it within traditional Jewish methods of exegesis. See Harrán, *Three Early Modern Hebrew Scholars*, 201.

61. On the emergence of the *ars historica* in the last quarter of the sixteenth century, see Anthony Grafton, *What Was History?* (Cambridge: Cambridge University Press, 2007), and Grafton, "The Identities of History in Early Modern Europe: Prelude to a Study of the Artes historicae," in *Historia: Empiricism and Erudition in Early Modern Europe*, ed. Gianna Pomata and Nancy G. Siraisi (Cambridge, MA: MIT Press, 2005), 41–74.

62. For an edition of the *Me'or 'einayim*, including an extensive introductory essay, see Azariah dei Rossi, *The Light of the Eyes*, trans. with intro. and annotations by Joanna Weinberg (New Haven, CT, and London: Yale University Press, 2001). For a discussion of Azariah dei Rossi in the context of the ars historica, see Anthony Grafton, "Dating History: The Renaissance and the Reformation of Chronology," *Daedalus* 132, no. 2 (Spring 2003): 79.

63. That Portaleone owned a copy of this volume is attested in Miletto, *La biblioteca di Avraham Ben David Portaleone*, 26.

64. Guetta, "Can Fundamentalism Be Modern," 105.

65. Yosef Hayim Yerushalmi, *Zakhor: Jewish History and Jewish Memory* (Seattle & London: University of Washington Press, 1982), 72.

66. Ibid., 73.

67. Translation cited after Yerushalmi, *Zakhor*, 70–71.

68. Yerushalmi, *Zakhor*, 42, 44.

69. The midrashic reinterpretation of earlier texts to make them relevant for later writers is sometimes referred to as "actualizing midrash"—midrash that "actualizes" the original text. See, for example, Ekaterina Matusova, "Allegorical Interpretation of the Pentateuch

in Alexandria: Inscribing Aristobulus and Philo in a Wider Literary Context," *The Studia Philonica Annual* 22 (2010): 3, and Robert Bonfil, "Can Medieval Storytelling Help Us Understand Midrash? The Story of Paltiel: A Preliminary Study on History and Midrash," in *The Midrashic Imagination: Jewish Exegesis, Thought and History*, ed. Michael Fishbane (Albany, NY: State University of New York Press, 1993), 229–254.

SELECT BIBLIOGRAPHY

Bonfil, Robert. *Jewish Life in Renaissance Italy*. Translated by Anthony Oldcorn. Berkeley: University of California Press, 1994.

Bowring, Lynette, Rebecca Cypess, and Liza Malamut, eds. *Music and Jewish Culture in Early Modern Italy: New Perspectives*. Bloomington: Indiana University Press, 2022.

Cypess, Rebecca. "Giovanni Battista Della Porta's Experiments with Musical Instruments." *Journal of Musicological Research* 35, no. 3 (2016): 1–17.

Guetta, Alessandro. "Avraham Portaleone, le scientifique repenti." In *Torah et science: perspectives historiques et théoriques–Etudes offertes à Charles Touati*, edited by Gad Freudenthal, Jean-Pierre Rothschild, and Gilbert Dahan, 213–227. Paris: Peeters, 2001.

Guetta, Alessandro. "Can Fundamentalism Be Modern? The Case of Abraham Portaleone (1542–1612)." In *Acculturation and Its Discontents: The Italian Experience Between Inclusion and Exclusion*, edited by David N. Myers, Massimo Ciavolella, Peter H. Reill, and Geoffrey Symcox, 99–115. Toronto: University of Toronto Press, 2008.

HaCohen, Ruth. *The Music Libel Against the Jews*. New Haven, CT: Yale University Press, 2011.

Harrán, Don. "In Search of the 'Song of Zion': Abraham Portaleone on Music in the Ancient Temple." *European Journal of Jewish Studies* 4, no. 2 (2010): 215–239.

Harrán, Don. *Salamone Rossi: Jewish Musician in Late Renaissance Mantua*. Oxford: Oxford University Press, 1999.

Harrán, Don. *Three Early Modern Hebrew Scholars on the Mysteries of Song*. Leiden: Brill, 2014.

Jütte, Daniel. "The Place of Music in Early Modern Italian Jewish Culture." In *Musical Exodus: Al-Andalus and its Jewish Diasporas*, edited by Ruth F. Davis, 45–61. Lanham, MD: Rowman and Littlefield, 2015.

Melamed, Abraham. "The Myth of the Jewish Origins of Philosophy in the Renaissance: From Aristotle to Plato." *Jewish History* 26, nos. 1–2 (May 2012): 41–59.

Melamed, Abraham. Myth of the Jewish Origins of Science and Philosophy / החכמה מקור על המיתוס: וטבחות רקחות. Haifa: Haifa University Press; Jerusalem: Magnes Press, 2010.

Melamed, Abraham. "The Perception of Jewish History in Italian Jewish Thought of the Sixteenth and Seventeenth Centuries: A Re-Examination." *Italia Judaica* 2 (1986): 139–170.

Miletto, Gianfranco. *Die Heldenschilde des Abraham ben David Portaleone*. 2 volumes. Frankfurt: Peter Lang, 2003.

Miletto, Gianfranco. *Glauben und Wissen im Zeitalter der Reformation: Der salomonische Tempel bei Abraham ben David Portaleone (1542–1612)*. Berlin: De Gruyter, 2004.

Miletto, Gianfranco. "The Human Body as a Musical Instrument in the Sermons of Judah Moscato." In *The Jewish Body: Corporeality, Society, and Identity in the Renaissance and Early Modern Period*, edited by Maria Diemling and Giuseppe Veltri, 377–393. Leiden: Brill, 2009.

Miletto, Gianfranco. *La biblioteca di Avraham Ben David Portaleone secondo l'inventario della sua eredità*. Florence: Olschki, 2013.

Modena, Leon. *The Autobiography of a Seventeenth-Century Venetian Rabbi: Leon Modena's Life of Judah.* Translated and edited by Mark R. Cohen, with introduction and essays by Mark R. Cohen, Theodore K. Rabb, Howard E. Adelman, and Natalie Zemon Davis, with historical notes by Howard E. Adelman and Benjamin C. I. Ravid. Princeton, NJ: Princeton University Press, 1988.

Patuzzi, Stefano. "Music from a Confined Space: Salomone Rossi's *Ha-shirim asher lishlomoh* (1622/23) and the Mantuan Ghetto." Special issue "Sacred Space," *Journal of Synagogue Music* 37 (Fall 2012): 49–69.

Rossi, Salamone. *Sacred Vocal Works in Hebrew: Hashirim 'asher lishlomo / "The Songs of Solomon."* Edited, with introduction and notes by Don Harrán as part of *Salamone Rossi: Complete Works.* Middleton, WI: American Institute of Musicology, 2003.

Ruderman, David B. *Early Modern Jewry.* Princeton, NJ: Princeton University Press, 2010.

Ruderman, David B., and Giuseppe Veltri, eds. *Cultural Intermediaries: Jewish Intellectuals in Early Modern Italy.* Philadelphia: University of Pennsylvania Press, 2004.

Sandler, Daniel. "The Music Chapters of the *Shiltei Ha-Gibborim.*" PhD diss., Tel Aviv University, 1987.

Seroussi, Edwin. "Ghetto Soundscapes: Venice and Beyond." In *Shirat Dvora: Essays in Honor of Professor Dvora Bregman*, edited by Haviva Ishay, 157–171. Beer-Sheva: Ben Gurion University in the Negev Press, 2019.

Shear, Adam, and Joseph R. Hacker, ed. *The Hebrew Book in Early Modern Italy.* Philadelphia: University of Pennsylvania Press, 2011.

Simonsohn, Shlomo. *History of the Jews in the Duchy of Mantua.* Jerusalem: Kiryath Sefer, 1977.

Spagnolo, Francesco. "Scritto in italiano, ascoltato in ebraico: A proposito delle fonti scritte della musica ebraica in Italia." In *Ebraismo in musica: Da Mantova all'Europa e ritorno*, edited by Stefano Patuzzi, 87–101. Mantua: Di Pellegrini, 2011.

Wilbourne, Emily. "*Lo Schiavetto* (1612): Travestied Sound, Ethnic Performance, and the Eloquence of the Body." *Journal of the American Musicological Society* 63, no. 1 (Spring 2010): 1–43.

Yerushalmi, Yosef Hayim. *Zakhor: Jewish History and Jewish Memory.* Seattle & London: University of Washington Press, 1982.

10

SONIC TRANSFORMATIONS

Urban Musical Culture in the Warsaw Ghetto, 1940–1942

J. MACKENZIE PIERCE

IT has long been known that the Warsaw Ghetto was a noisy, musical place. Beggars sang for alms on its street corners, and starving professional musicians busked in courtyards. Audiences gathered for performances that lasted into the morning hours in the large ghetto buildings. Nearly one hundred cafés lined the central streets of the ghetto, many offering musical entertainments. The official governing body of the ghetto, the Judenrat, sponsored an orchestra, which performed canonic repertoire on a regular basis, and over a thousand artistic events were overseen by Jewish aid organizations. Nor are such instances of the ghetto's music-making evident only to the historian: in recent years, the music of the Warsaw Ghetto has achieved world-wide fame thanks to the release of the Academy-Award-winning film *The Pianist* (2002), based on the memoirs of Władysław Szpilman.

Despite these numerous sonic traces, there have been few scholarly discussions of the Warsaw Ghetto's music-making. Those that have been written, at least in English and Polish, have been broad surveys of musical activities, usually framed around questions of whether music enabled internees to resist Nazi persecution, or instead, inspired complacency among ghetto audiences.[1] While this line of inquiry is not inherently misguided, it does have limitations, as scholars such as Barbara Milewski, Amy Lynn Wlodarski, and James Loeffler have pointed out.[2] Approaching music of the Holocaust through the lens of resistance and complacency, they observe, shoehorns the diverse experiences of persecuted musicians into a standard mold. It is an approach that often reflects present-day anxieties about the power and limitations of music as an artform, and it can, in turn, foreclose an engagement with the beliefs and experiences of the victims themselves. This chapter proposes an alternative line of inquiry, one that situates music within the urban spaces of Nazi-created ghettos.[3] This approach asks how the ghetto's music was both an outgrowth and transformation of the prewar urban musical culture in which many ghetto musicians had once participated. In turn, it analyzes how victims invoked music to comment on the experience of ghettoization and on the radical remaking of their cities under German rule.

As for the case of Warsaw, within a matter of weeks in fall of 1940, a new collectivity had been created within the city out of the hundreds of thousands of prisoners confined to the ghetto walls. The ghetto's extreme population density (of over 200,000 people per square mile), rampant poverty, soaring disease, and widespread death stretch to the limit any comparison between it and prewar Warsaw. Yet, for all this undeniable upheaval, the ghetto's 1.2 square miles were still a part of the city, carved out of Warsaw's dense urban fabric, in an area just north of the city center. Unlike Nazi concentration and death camps, which were often isolated from population centers, the ghetto and its musicians had countless ties to both prewar Warsaw and to the so-called Aryan side beyond the ghetto walls.[4] If the ghetto had been created through a violent transformation of Warsaw, one that never fully erased the ghetto's urban qualities, how did the music that had helped define Warsaw as a metropolis before the war—its vibrant concert life, cabarets, and dance halls–continue within the ghetto? To answer this question, I suggest that we attend to the places in which music was made in the ghetto and ask how these often-familiar locales were both outgrowths and transformations of the prewar city.

Examining the continuities and ruptures in the music-making of Warsaw Jews across the period of ghettoization is a methodologically fraught task. As the historian Amos Goldberg has noted, the scholar is faced with a fundamental challenge when embarking on such a study: "how is it possible to write the history of *helplessness*" in the Nazi ghettos, he asks, "without sliding into heroization on the one hand, or obscuring the magnitude of the crisis on the other, but also without [helplessness] becoming a sanctified and melodramatic icon?"[5] A focus on the continuities in institutions, people, and projects between the prewar city and the ghetto can, he notes, downplay the trauma that the ghetto's prisoners faced, erasing their helplessness and its myriad impacts on their sense of self. But it is also possible to go too far in the other direction, by aestheticizing and romanticizing the victim's experiences, a recurring trope, he believes, in how the Holocaust has entered mass awareness in the West.[6] Musicologists have been especially attuned to this second tendency, because music of the Holocaust has sometimes been programmed and marketed in ways that suggest that it is uniquely posed to offer audiences access to Holocaust experience.[7]

In response to this challenge, Goldberg urges scholars to study the "transformations" that took place within what he describes as the "deep level of the fundamental concepts that constitute culture" in the ghetto.[8] Put differently, he asks scholars to consider how ghettoization changed not only the everyday lives of internees, but moreover the practices of meaning-making through which they organized their lives. I argue here that such transformations in ghetto culture were not only embedded in language and discourse, Goldberg's primary focus, but also evinced through the musical and listening practices of the ghetto. Sound became a way for prisoners to describe the newness of the ghetto and its various crises, as well as a way of commenting on the relationship between the present realities of the ghetto and its prisoners' prewar lives.

This chapter considers how three aspects of ghetto performance culture took shape out of prewar Warsaw: the courtyard and house-based performances, the cafés, and, finally, the performance traditions of the cabaret. The bulk of the chapter is devoted to two essays written for the Oyneg Shabes archive. The first, by the actor Jonas Turkow, explores the rapid growth in courtyard performances in the ghetto, while the second, by Stanisław Różycki, focuses on the café as a space of musical listening and sociability. The focus on these essays allows for a closer view on the Oyneg Shabes, an underground, secret archive situated in the ghetto named after the traditional Sabbath gathering, in light of its organizers holding their regular, clandestine meetings on the Sabbath.[9] Although one of the most significant sources concerning the Warsaw Ghetto, it has seen little attention from music scholars. Begun by the historian Emanuel Ringelblum in its earliest form in October 1939, it preserves thousands of contemporary documents, mostly in Polish and Yiddish, which in 1942 and 1943 were buried in metal boxes and milk canisters below the ghetto and partially recovered after the war.[10] Because the archive's dozens of associates believed that evidence drawn from everyday life in the ghetto would be crucial to creating a history of Jewish persecution, the reports it commissioned and collected preserve keen observations about the catastrophe engulfing Jewish Warsaw. The Oyneg Shabes sources are supplemented, in this chapter, with musical works and memoirs, although as explored in the conclusion, relying uncritically on memoirs can be problematic, since they inevitably reflect the postwar conditions in which they were written.

MUSIC IN THE JEWISH METROPOLIS

In the decades prior to the Holocaust, Warsaw had a Jewish population of over 300,000, making it one of the world's largest Jewish metropolises.[11] Jews also played an integral role in the city's musical life. Biographical surveys of Polish-Jewish musicians shed light on many dimensions of Jewish music-making in the city, from Yiddish-speaking klezmer musicians, to cantors, to big-band musicians, to classical virtuosos, composers, and orchestral players.[12] These latter two categories—the stars of the popular music and classical scenes—are especially salient to this chapter's focus on the links between music and urban experience in the ghetto. Indeed, Jewish patronage has been central to the establishment of some of the main institutions of classical music in Warsaw, most notably the Warsaw Philharmonic, and by the interwar years, the prominence of Jewish audiences and musicians in the Philharmonic was a topic of ongoing commentary.[13] If anything, Jews were even more important to the ebullient world of "light" or popular music in interwar Poland, where Jewish musicians and songwriters led the creation of Polish-language tangos, foxtrots, and rumbas, among other dance genres.[14] Such music was not only frequently performed in the city's dance halls and cabarets; it also often commented on urban experience—its dislocation, confusion, and anonymity.[15] Although popular and classical music were certainly not confined to Poland's metropolises, music was, for city denizens, a significant component of what it meant to participate in metropolitan modernity.[16]

The Jewish musicians active in Warsaw's classical and popular music worlds had a wide range of views on Jewishness. Many belonged to Warsaw's middle class and, as was common for this group, spoke Polish and were acculturated into Polish culture. This did not necessarily mean that they were assimilationists or rejected Jewish identity, however.[17] Other musicians had chosen to baptize, or their parents had done so. Although they did not necessarily see themselves as Jewish, they were still considered as such by the German occupiers. Still other figures such as the historian Emanuel Ringelblum and actor Jonas Turkow were multilingual, but chose to write and work in Yiddish, the language of the Jewish masses that they believed could form the basis for a secular Jewish culture.[18]

The beginning of World War II in September 1939, the rapid defeat of the Polish defense of Warsaw, and the city's subsequent occupation by Germany threw the city's musicians into crisis. Unlike in France, where the German occupation allowed performances to continue to a significant degree, the occupation of Warsaw involved a rapid closure of cultural institutions.[19] Major performance venues for classical music such as the Warsaw Philharmonic and the Polish Radio were shuttered, forcing musicians to find work elsewhere, often in cafés. In the early days of the war and occupation, some Jewish musicians were able to flee the city, most commonly to the east, where they soon found themselves under Soviet rule.[20] Some converts and acculturated Jews managed to hide their backgrounds and continue to live outside the ghetto. But many had no choice but to move into the ghetto.

The area of Warsaw in which the ghetto was established, slightly north of the city center, had been a center of Jewish inhabitance before the war. But it was not exclusively a Jewish neighborhood, and Jews had also lived elsewhere in Warsaw. In March 1940, the German authorities began to fence off Jewish-inhabited areas on the pretense of containing a typhus pandemic, the first phrase in the creation of the ghetto. The ghetto was officially decreed on October 2, 1940, at which point Jews were required to live within its arbitrary boundaries and Poles were required to leave said territory. The decreeing of the ghetto unleashed a panic as Jews attempted to find apartments within the ghetto boundaries; all told, around 138,000 Jews and 113,000 Poles had to change their residence (a process that would be repeated as the ghetto's boundaries were changed several times over the following years). By the time the ghetto was sealed in November 1940, nearly 400,000 Jews were confined to an area of just under 1.2 square miles. In addition, the ghetto also saw the influx of around 150,000 refugees who had been deported to the ghetto from elsewhere. These conditions persisted until the so-called *Großaktion Warschau*, when from July 22 to September 21, 1942, over 300,000 ghetto prisoners were deported and murdered in Treblinka.[21]

The ghetto's relation to both the prewar city and the so-called Aryan side were complex. Ghetto internees could not leave the ghetto, at least not easily and certainly not legally. The ghetto was cut off from the city by walls and barbed wire, and the entry points were guarded by Jewish and Polish police, as well as German gendarmes. Poverty, hunger, and infections were rampant, and thousands died per month of disease and starvation even before the deportations to death camps began. Yet there were also reminders that the ghetto prisoners were still living in Warsaw; there were postal deliveries, tram services, telephone connections, and continuous smuggling across the ghetto walls, on which the ghetto internees depended to survive. As Barbara Engelking has noted, the ghetto existed "behind a 'half-drawn curtain'"; its prisoners still lived in the city of Warsaw, but a city remade in countless horrifying ways.[22]

An Emerging Public for Ghetto Performances

The traumatic remaking of the city was audible to those writing in or about the ghetto. Witnesses observed how the collapse in musical employment meant more and more musicians were performing on ghetto streets. Stanisław Gombiński, who was a police officer in the ghetto, mentions in the first chapter of his memoirs from April 1944 that the "noise of the ghetto street was loud."[23] His ear was drawn not only to the sounds of people begging and selling wares, but also to the less expected sounds made by musicians. "Singing and music with every step, on the street, blocking traffic, in courtyards, on squares," he wrote. Some of what he heard were beggars singing for alms, but he also described the sounds of trained musicians. "Again, scales of the most varied types—singers, excellent opera arias and beautiful songs, voices, which had sung in concert halls and opera houses. Verdi, Puccini, Meyerbeer, Moniuszko, Niewiadomski and—oh Jewish impudence—Schubert, Schumann, and Wagner."[24] The repertoire that Gombiński heard (or chose to list) included Italian, Polish, and German composers that far exceeded the "Jewish" music the ghetto prisoners were exclusively supposed to perform. Beyond this, his description of such sounds early in memoirs conjures the aural newness of the ghetto, underscoring how ghettoization had dislocated music from the concert hall onto the street.

The *Gazeta Żydowska* (Jewish newspaper) gave this phenomenon a positive veneer. It described how "With the lyre in her hand, Polyhymnia, the muse of music, has left behind those venues that are today no longer needed. She has left the stifling and always crowded venues of the night-time dance halls as well as the serious temples of this art. She has gone onto the cobbled street in order to survive the difficult period of the war."[25] This statement should be interpreted within the context of its publication in the *Gazeta Żydowska*, the official paper of the Jewish community in occupied Poland, which was published in Polish. Although this periodical is an important source about musical life in the ghetto because of its extensive concert reviews, it was also widely despised by ghetto prisoners for promoting German propaganda and downplaying the severity of ghetto life.[26] The article quoted above, titled "Art on the Street," was written less than a week before the ghetto would be sealed from the city, at a time when thousands of Jews had just moved into the ghetto and others were desperately attempting to find apartments in it.

The writer euphemizes ghettoization by describing it as the "difficult period of the war" and paints the mass unemployment among musicians, which was the reason musicians went onto the street in the first place, as a democratization of art. The critic's attempt to project normalcy onto the transformation of the ghetto's aural spaces does, if nothing else, suggest that the changing sounds of the ghetto street were becoming ubiquitous, so difficult to ignore that they called for a euphemistic interpretation.

In addition to playing on the streets, unemployed musicians also began touring among the ghetto's courtyards, offering makeshift concerts in these large spaces that were enclosed by the ghetto buildings. These performances began in the first months of the occupation, before the ghetto was created, at a time when a "fever for entertainment" swept Jewish Warsaw, according to the actor and impresario Jonas Turkow, who wrote an essay on this topic in Yiddish in 1941.[27] The courtyards became important venues for performances in part because Jewish life turned inward, and the courtyard became a focus of socializing for those living within a building. The predominant housing stock in the ghetto were large buildings that could house hundreds of residents, if not more. These buildings had become a basic unit of social organization in the ghetto, and most of them had a house committee dedicated to various self-governance tasks.[28] As the dangers of the street grew during the occupation, Turkow described how "in almost every house [in Jewish Warsaw] there are either night-long parties, or at the very least, ones lasting until curfew."[29] These events were often organized by the house committees, and they could be rather formal, advertised through posters that listed performers and dates.[30] Unemployed musicians and actors could earn some money pooled from the inhabitants of the building.[31] "People who for years occupied renowned places on global stages, now travel from courtyard to courtyard in order to not die from hunger and often captivate us with their splendid sounds," Turkow observed.[32]

The creation of the ghetto briefly paused, but did not stop, this fervent artistic activity. Turkow described the newness of the sealed ghetto by recounting the sounds and sights of its streets, much like Gombiński and the critic writing for *Gazeta Żydowska* had done, albeit in more gruesome terms:

> A few steps further—there is a corpse covered with paper, from which a hand or leg sticks out; next to it—a violinist, who with a trembling hand and faded eyes bows the strings; a little farther, a woman with a small child in a pushcart, singing opera arias to the accompaniment of her child's cries; next to her, a cantor with a child in hand singing liturgical melodies . . . such scenes take place along all the streets and passages [of the ghetto].[33]

The courtyard performances and events organized by the house committees were, as Turkow described, set away from the misery of the street. That he saw the courtyards and houses as part of an emerging semi-public artistic space in the ghetto is further suggested by his overriding concern with shaping these performances. He not only worried that organizers were passing their parties off as charitable fundraisers, but also that the events were of low artistic quality and conducted in Polish, rather than Yiddish.[34] Turkow's concern with the language of performance in the ghetto reflected a broader interest, namely in treating Yiddish, the vernacular of the Jewish masses in eastern Europe, as a foundation for a national Jewish culture.[35] Indeed, before the war, Turkow, along with his brother Zygmunt, had been especially influential in the movement among Jewish intellectuals to reform the Yiddish theater and to turn it into a venue for high art.[36]

Turkow was able to act on these concerns because in September 1940 he had been put in charge of the newly created Centralna Komisja Imprezowa (Central Commission for Events, CKI). The CKI was intended to regulate the performances organized in the ghetto houses, a task it could carry out because it operated under the auspices of the Żydowskie Towarzystwo Opieki Społecznej (Jewish Society for Public Welfare), under whose aegis the house committees also operated.[37] The idea was that every performance to be organized in the houses first had to be vetted by the CKI, who would use this power, Turkow hoped, to "raise the cultural level of events" and "to fight with assimilation by supporting Yiddish during performances and events, to create in this manner a center of Jewish culture."[38]

In addition to approving events, the CKI also organized its own performances, some in coordination with house committees and others in the extensive network of soup kitchens and orphanages run by the self-help organization.[39] Turkow claimed that the CKI organized 1,814 performances (not all of them musical).[40] This volume of performances was crucial to enacting the regulation and betterment of artistic life that Turkow believed was sorely needed. Over 250 artists registered with the CKI, turning it into what he described as a "camouflaged professional union," and this in turn allowed the CKI to gain "control over all the events" and "in most cases decide on the program," while also "engag[ing] the most serious artists performing in Yiddish and performers of Jewish music."[41] Nor must we only take Turkow's word: the extant archives of the CKI confirm that it operated on a wide scale.[42] Suggestive of the volume of musical performances that it facilitated, in one representative month, May 1941, thirty-nine musical programs were to be performed on twelve different days. Most of these concerts involved singers, violinists, or pianists.[43] Virtually no lists of repertoires are preserved in the CKI's archive, but one exception is a June 1941 program of the singer Dina Turkow, the wife of Jonas, who went by the stage name Diana Blumenfeld. Her program was primarily in Yiddish, with songs by Mordechai Gebirtig, Dawid Bajgelman, and Iso Szajewicz, among others.[44]

More intriguing than the CKI's reach, however, is how Turkow frames his actions in terms of regulating, shaping, and bettering the ghetto's public. His is not only a description of the artistic "chaos" that he saw prevailing in Jewish Warsaw, but also an attempt to transform the new performances in the ghetto in line with his commitment to highbrow artistic production and Yiddish culture.[45] In asserting that the CKI was successful in this endeavor, he painted a picture of a new Jewish public coming into focus around the events:

> In contrast to other venues and private ventures, the broad crowds of the Jewish masses and intelligentsia attended the events organized by the Central Commission

for Events. These audiences had finally found a place where they could gather in a warm, cultured atmosphere and listen to artistic performances of recitations, songs, and music while not being exposed to the company of the so-called new "elites." These events enjoyed a good opinion in the better environments of Jewish society and were attended by them on a wide scale.[46]

The clear optimism in this passage is, in no small part, due to the time at which the essay was composed and the period it covers—late 1940 into early 1941 was the high point of the house committees' activities.[47] Even so, we see him here placing the CKI within the ghetto's social worlds, positioning its events as bridging masses and intelligentsia while implicitly excluding the smugglers, criminals, and others who had become wealthy in the ghetto and formed its "new elite." In positioning the CKI against the exclusivity of both "private ventures" and spaces frequented by the half-world of criminals, he alludes to the emergence within the ghetto of other publics, to which he was opposed but over which he could exercise little control. The most significant of these spaces was the ghetto café.

OVERHEARING THE GHETTO'S CAFÉS

Whereas the CKI and house-committee performances grew out of the ghetto's social-welfare organizations, the dozens of cafés in the ghetto operated on a commercial rather than charitable footing.[48] More problematically, in the minds of many, they were associated with the so-called new elites who had gained wealth in the ghetto from the dangerous, lucrative, yet essential work of smuggling food and goods into the ghetto. Some ghetto chroniclers, such as Ringelblum and Turkow, noted that the cafés depended on protection from the Jewish police and Gestapo, too.[49] For others, the cafés epitomized the disregard shown by the wealthy for the plight of their immiserated neighbors. Chaim Kaplan wrote in his diary, for instance, about the contrast between "the lavishly dressed crowds enjoying the music, pastries, and coffee [in a luxurious café]" and how "[s]ometimes at the very entrance of one of these elegant cafés [a visitor] might stumble on the corpse of a victim of starvation."[50] Guided by such remarks, prior scholarship has pointed to the cafés as an example of how access to musical performance had become restricted within the ghetto.[51]

A more ambivalent view of the ghetto cafés is presented by Stanisław Różycki in an essay titled "Kawiarnie" (Cafés), written for the Oyneg Shabes archive. Little is known about Różycki, although he was likely a high school teacher in Warsaw before the war and, in 1939, had fled to Soviet-occupied Lviv, before returning to the Warsaw Ghetto in October 1941.[52] His essays for the Oyneg Shabes archive are written in an elegant Polish. They focus on the Jewish street, documenting the sights, smells, and dangers of the ghetto's most public domain. In reading his essay of the cafés, we should keep in mind that for intellectuals of the 1920s and 1930s in Poland, cafés were far more than places to drink coffee or eat cake. Indeed, Warsaw's prewar cafés had been mythologized as a quasi-public sphere in which forward-looking artistic movements of the 1920s and 1930s had been born.[53]

A trace of the idea that the café held a social function exceeding its culinary one is evident in the very opening of Różycki's essay. In the second and third sentences, he observed:

> The ghetto cafés play a very significant role, not only in the ghetto's social life, but also in its public life due to the lack of clubs, unions, associations, markets, parks, cinemas, fields, dance halls, and so forth. The café thus substitutes for the theater, the cabaret, the variety show, the cinema—but not only— because alongside cabaret and music, the café is also a grocery store and restaurant, illicit trade occurs here, smugglers meet here to discuss their business, exchanges take place, goods are offered and searched for, there are rooms for lovers, and trade in living wares also finds protection here, not to mention that prostitution—as always—is rife in bars.[54]

In these two dizzying, list-filled sentences, Różycki underscores the simultaneous narrowing and widening of the café's role in the ghetto. He distinguishes only to collapse the difference between "social" (*towarzyski*) and "public" (*publiczny*) life in the ghetto, suggesting that the cafés had now been asked to fulfill the role formerly played by institutions of the public sphere, such as professional unions and voluntary associations. On the cafés writ large, he reserves judgement, underscoring the essential social function they serve while enumerating, in the same breath, their sordid aspects. In concluding his essay on the cafés, he returned to this point. He noted that "the existence of venues of this type is not in itself bad." Rather, he wished that the cafés would "not only be for snobs and layabouts, smugglers and speculators, but also for working people, office workers, the working intelligentsia, the proletariat."[55] While the promise of the café as public space was valid, he believed, the ghetto conditions prevented the cafés from fulfilling their potential.

Różycki's views on the ghetto café were further developed against his observation on the collapse of the Jewish street, much like Turkow had also done. To leave one's apartment was a treacherous undertaking, which required navigating children begging for food, strangers infected with typhus, and dead bodies.[56] In essays written for Oyneg Shabes with titles such as "Street Scenes from the Ghetto" and "Morality of the Street," he described streets littered with human waste and a collapse in public decency.[57] He saw the elitism of the cafés, which offered shelter from these conditions, as reflecting this broader collapse. "Because—if such a general and shameless public demoralization rules, such places [as the cafés] must exist and are only a natural emanation of the general conditions."[58]

Różycki describes the interiors, people, and sounds of the ghetto cafés in order to paint a picture of the differences among the ghetto's various well-to-do subgroups and their reactions to ghettoization. Despite the many reasons that led patrons to the cafés, he noted, "All have or wish to have the delusion that the atmosphere of the café separates them from the reality of the street, from the darkness of everyday life."[59] To make this point when he visits L'Ours, one of the ghetto's larger cafés, he calls attention to the difference between the trappings of the café and the conversations of its patrons. "There are no traces of the war, imprisonment, the ghetto. The faces are not at all haggard, rather the opposite—they look normal, well fed."[60] The patrons are, as he describes, a mix of those who still have savings and those who have become rich off of illicit activity in the ghetto. But as he listens more intently to the patrons, he notes that "the topic of conversation is the same, reduced to a common denominator. What's new, when's the offensive, how are you doing today with bread? . . . Neither the content nor the form is different from all our everyday, identical, stubbornly repeating questions, the answers to which are monotonously sad and hopelessly desperate."[61]

Różycki repeatedly evokes music in the essay to describe the patrons and atmosphere of each venue. When he visited the café Arizona, which he claimed was almost exclusively frequented by smugglers, his description of the café's music paints its patrons as isolated from the everyday concerns of the ghetto. They "dance, and dance with verve, with temperament, with humor, speeding up, stamping their feet to the beat, demanding encores."[62] When one of the musicians sang about a poor orphan begging for bread on the street, Różycki describes how one of the richest patrons, Jerzyk Kupfer, began to cry. "The asshole indeed shed a teardrop and quickly poured a drink of advocaat as consolation, though it made no difference."[63] Różycki's description of Kupfer's single teardrop points to the chasm separating him from the ghetto's realities: his reaction is trite compared with the immense and quotidian misery of the ghetto, Różycki implies, while his attempt to ameliorate the emotion through expensive alcohol is both futile and self-centered.

If Różycki described the song about the orphan to cast into relief the distance between street and café, elsewhere in the essay music serves to underscore the division between the present reality of the ghetto and memories of the pre-ghetto life. When visiting the café Splendid, where Artur Gold played with what Różycki considered to be the best jazz band in the ghetto, he wrote that the "wild rhythms, unbridled jazz orchestra, playing in a negro tempo is a dissonance, a clash with the slow, monotonous life, entirely ruled by everyday dullness. And this expresses, this creates a kind of un-natural, sick atmosphere; it appears as something unreal, not from this world. The contrast is too brutal."[64] He was more sympathetic to the music that he heard in the café Fontanna, which offered performances by Leon Boruński (a laureate of the 1932 Chopin Competition), Erwin Wohlfeiler, and songs from the soprano Marysia Ajzensztadt (the daughter of a well-known cantor). But here too, music seemed to express first and foremost a disjunction between sound and reality: "The mood that dominated here was as if in essence people had escaped to hell to listen to music, to raptly take in melodies, to remind themselves of the content of songs on which they had once been intoxicated."[65]

That Różycki discusses the music of each café that he visited not only confirms that the cafés were a major venue in which music was made. It also suggests that music played a central role in how he grasped the café's function in the ghetto. In some instances, he turns to music to sharpen the distinction that he draws between interior and exterior, bringing into focus the distance between the café audiences and the street. At other times, music serves as an emblem of the past, appearing to him to conjure the audiences' links to and desires for the world before the ghetto. Put differently, the contradictions that Różycki believed defined the ghetto cafés were as much heard as they were seen. Similar to Gombiński, who chose musical and sonic terms to evoke the newness of the ghetto street, Różycki heard in music a way of describing the café as social space, a sonic marking of the distance between audiences' hopes and their reality.

Café Sztuka and the Polish-Speaking Intelligentsia

On one level, the ghetto's courtyard and café performances were indebted to the architecture of the city and its prewar practices of urban socializing. Their social role in the ghetto was further defined by how they offered refuge from the street and its noisy, musical poverty. A third aspect of Warsaw's urban culture that both continued and changed through ghettoization pertains to the music and performances of the Polish-speaking intelligentsia interned in the ghetto. The bastion for such artists was the café Sztuka (Art), whose patrons would have been familiar with the cultural touchstones of the prewar intelligentsia, having frequented the famous literary café Ziemiańska, read the *Wiadomości Literackie* (Literary news), and attended the witty and urbane Qui pro Quo cabaret.

Turkow and Różycki both wrote with disdain about Sztuka, a stance that at least in part reflects larger concerns among those working with the Oyneg Shabes archive about language and assimilation within the ghetto.[66] Turkow, after insinuating that the café had connections to German officialdom, quipped about how "Yiddish grated unpleasantly on the ears" of Sztuka's patrons.[67] Różycki went even further, describing Sztuka's audience as "converts, educated bourgeoisie" who were "proud that before the war they had been rich . . . [and] can't stand the fact that they have been made equal with the 'scabs, Yids' with whom they share a common fate."[68] These observations do represent one point of view on Sztuka, but such dismissals should not be taken at face value: the fate of the acculturated, the baptized, and the Polish-speaking intelligentsia within the ghetto is also a part of the ghetto's history.

Many of the performers at Sztuka had cut their teeth in prewar Warsaw's cabaret scene, including Leon Boruński, Wiera Gran, Pola Braun, and Władysław Szlengel. The interwar cabaret had been distinguished by its topical commentary, satire, and quick-paced production schedules in performances that integrated Jewish and Polish performers, who played to a mixed audience. This Polish-language cabaret was also noteworthy for combining music—especially "light" music of internationally popular dance genres—with scenarios penned by some of the most eminent poets of the Polish language, such as Julian Tuwim.[69] The artists at Sztuka did not abandon these values when they were interned in the ghetto. One audience member, Mary Berg, a teenager imprisoned in the ghetto, described in her diary that at Sztuka, "one can hear songs and satires on the police, the ambulance service, the rickshaws, and even the Gestapo in a veiled fashion." Perhaps she had in mind Szlengel's *Żywy dziennik* (The living newspaper), a literary-artistic satire on events in the ghetto. In discerning such meanings,

Berg believed that the songs of Sztuka carried a significance that could not be reduced to escapism or nostalgia: "It is laughter through tears, but it is laughter. This is our only weapon in the ghetto—our people laugh at death and at the Nazi decrees."[70]

We gain a sense of what Berg might have had in mind by turning to one of the extant works premiered at Sztuka: a musical composition titled "Jej pierwszy bal" (Her first ball), which was originally premiered as part of one of *The Living Newspaper* performances.[71] The piece for voice and two pianos is around fifteen minutes long and includes narrative recitation as well as singing. The text was written by Szlengel, a prominent poet in the ghetto and the key figure behind *The Living Newspaper*. Its music was composed by Władysław Szpilman, a stalwart performer at Sztuka. Before the war, he had established himself as a respected interpreter of Chopin and a composer of classical music, having studied during the early 1930s with the renowned pedagogue Franz Schreker in Berlin.[72] *Her First Ball* was sung by Wiera Gran, who had risen to fame before the war by performing in the Warsaw cabarets while still a teenager, and whose popularity ballooned in the ghetto.[73] Szpilman, and his duo partner Andrzej Goldfeder, accompanied her.

Her First Ball is a series of variations on a waltz from Ludomir Różycki's opera *Casanova* (1922). The title alludes to the plot of a recent French film (*Un carnet de bal*, 1937) in which the widowed protagonist revisits the fates of her suitors twenty years after her debut ball. To reflect the varied life paths of the suitors, Szpilman composed each variation in a different musical style, including a slow-fox, rumba, tango, Tyrolian waltz (complete with yodeling), and a mazurka "à la Chopin."[74] The work's blending of genres—drawing from opera and the dance hall, Chopin and yodeling—evinces an interest in blurring high-low divides that was also characteristic of the prewar Polish-language cabaret.[75]

For many listening closely to *Her First Ball*, the piece was likely more than a light-hearted commentary on the foibles of past flirtations. Consider this following passage, sung about the final suitor, a "melancholy composer":

Bicie naszych serc
W nokturn się zmieniło
Będzie dłużej żył
Niż nasza miłość
Rytmy, rytmy łzy
Ścielą się pod stopy
Umrze może wielka miłość
Lecz zostanie Chopin

The beating of our hearts
Turned into a nocturne
It will live longer
Than our love
The rhythm, rhythm of tears
Flows under our feet
Perhaps great love will die
But Chopin will remain

The music here transforms from a waltz into a mazurka, both dances that share the same triple meter but have distinct rhythmic profiles. Audiences would have doubtless understood that the interpolation of the mazurka was no accident; indeed, it was the genre of Chopin's that had become most closely interwoven with Polish national identity.[76] Within the context of occupied Warsaw, the piece's allusion to Chopin in both text and music was daring. Outside the ghetto, his music was banned for the first years of the occupation, because of its strong associations with the Polish national cause.[77] Inside the ghetto, meanwhile, Jews were ostensibly banned from performing all "Aryan" music, although this ban was routinely ignored. Interpreted against this background, the line "But Chopin will remain" is not only a claim that musical works are more enduring than youthful love. It was also a suggestion that Chopin—and perhaps Polish nationhood along with it—will endure the latest cataclysm visited upon it.[78] Gran, who sang the piece, recalled that audiences understood the weight of Chopin allusion. She described how it felt risky to include the line and how it brought Sztuka's audiences to tears.[79] In this brief musical moment, the connections between the Szutka performers and the prewar milieu of the Warsaw cabaret, defined by double meanings and social commentary, comes to the fore. But we also gain a glimpse of how Sztuka's artists understood themselves in terms of the Polish musical and literary culture to which they had long belonged and which, for years prior, they had been integral to creating.

CODA: THE DEATH OF A CITY

Several traces of Warsaw's prewar musical world persisted in the ghetto: from the musicians interned within it, to the urban housing stock that became the stage for hundreds of performers, to the musical genres popular in the ghetto, to the salience of the café and cabaret as sites of public life and social commentary before and during ghettoization. Despite these continuities, there are notable shifts in what music meant to ghetto listeners and commentators. The texts of Turkow, Różycki, Szlengel, Szpilman, and others elucidate a hermeneutics of listening that developed within the ghetto. They suggest how the noisy, chaotic, and immiserated street was never far from performers' and commentators' ears, forming a sonic counterweight to artistic performances in houses and cafés. They also reveal how musical performance could index the world beyond and before the ghetto, providing these authors with tools for describing and perhaps critiquing the illusions and realities of the ghetto. In this sense, the music of the ghetto both was shaped by the place and spaces of the ghetto and also became a way of commenting on this space. Doubtless, there were other ways of listening to—and in—the ghetto. But these examples suffice to remind us that listening in the ghetto was constituted as much by the social relations created in the ghetto's spaces as by musical performance itself.

To conclude, I will shift from wartime documents to postwar memory, and consider how the most famous account of music in the urban space of the ghetto—that of

Władysław Szpilman—entered the public. Decades before Szpilman's story would reach worldwide audiences through the film *The Pianist*, a book appeared in Warsaw in 1946 with the title *Śmierć miasta: Pamiętniki Władysława Szpilmana, 1939–1945* (The death of a city: The memoirs of Władysław Szpilman, 1939–1945).[80] Szpilman's memoirs were published during a brief moment between the end of the war and the consolidation of Stalinist rule in Poland. During this time, organizations such as the Central Jewish Historical Commission collected thousands of survivor testimonies, and at least some Polish intellectuals showed considerable interest in the moral issues raised by the Holocaust.[81] The title of the 1946 memoirs is significant, because it frames Szpilman's experiences in terms of the destruction of Warsaw. Indeed, the memoirs document not only the German invasion and Szpilman's forced relocation into the ghetto, but also his harrowing survival of the ghetto's liquidation and his hiding in the ruined city following the systematic destruction of Warsaw in fall 1944. The city-based perspective would have resonated with a Polish-speaking readership in 1946, many of whom would have witnessed the destruction of the city first-hand. Portraying the fate of Polish Jews as part of the history of the city was also a trope embedded in prominent postwar Polish films, most notably *Zakazane piosenki* (Forbidden songs, 1946) and *Ulica graniczna* (Border street, 1948).[82]

It is significant, then, that the English-language reissue of the Szpilman memoirs has changed the title to *The Pianist: The Extraordinary True Story of One Man's Survival in Warsaw, 1939–1945*.[83] The focus of the title has shifted from Szpilman as a metonym for Warsaw's destruction to Szpilman as the exceptional individual.[84] While the new version has often been discussed as if it were more complete or uncensored than the 1946 publication, the text is almost entirely identical to it. Indeed, as the literary scholar Jacek Leociak has pointed out, there appear to be no passages in the memoirs that were restored in the new version.[85] Yet, the new version does make one crucial change: it rearranges the chapter order, such that the memoirs begin *in medias res* with Szpilman in the ghetto. Not only is the chronology of the memoirs disrupted, but readers also lose a sense for how the establishment of the ghetto was a rupture in Szpilman's relation to the city of Warsaw and his artistic milieu.[86]

The most significant change to the memoirs, however, concerns their authorship. Recent publications of the memoirs describe the book as if Szpilman had written it alone, but this is incorrect. In the original (1946) edition we see that the music critic Jerzy Waldorff "opracował" the memoirs, a word that can mean to "edit," "work through," or in music, "to arrange." Waldorff was a non-Jewish Pole and had not been interned in the ghetto. Before the war, he had expressed anti-Semitic views and shown sympathy for Italian fascism.[87] After the war, in the preface to *The Death of a City*, he explained how he saw in Szpilman's story a distillation of German brutality.[88] He also commented on how the memoirs had come into being: "in writing Szpilman's odyssey, I tried to give it a literary form that would," in addition to being factually accurate, "most faithfully convey the emotional content of the story of my friend."[89] He spelled out the relationship between Szpilman and himself in even more explicit terms in 1947, when he complained that the publisher, Wiedza, had removed his name from the cover of the book. After noting that Szpilman had approached him about writing the memoirs, he claimed,

As concerns our collaborative technique, we worked together in such a manner that [Szpilman] recounted his experiences to me and gave me chronological notes, and I composed this information into a literary whole, giving it the form of a book in which—I underscore—Szpilman wrote not a word.

Because of his name's removal from the cover, he quipped, "Szpilman was turned into the writer, the author of *Death of a City*, when he was not the author of the book, but rather its main character."[90]

We are not obliged to take Waldorff at his word, and the boundaries between author and protagonist are routinely blurred in collaborative memoir. Nonetheless, the widely available present-day editions of the memoirs have gone fully in the other direction, excising Waldorff's role altogether and ignoring his literary ambitions for the text. They do not mention Waldorff at all, they remove the preface he authored, and they have replaced it with a preface by Andrzej Szpilman, Władysław's son, which asserts Szpilman's authorship.[91] When the 1998 German translation appeared without Waldorff's name, he was furious: an act of literary collaboration has been passed off as one of individual testimony.[92]

Ultimately, Waldorff's removal from the new editions of the memoirs distances Szpilman from the literary and intellectual community through which his story first circulated and thanks to which it entered the public. Unlike Turkow, who left Poland soon after the war concluded, Szpilman had a flourishing career in postwar Poland, leading the popular music section at the Polish radio for nearly two decades, composing dozens of songs, and concertizing with his classical quintet.[93] The fact that he had met Waldorff before the war (in the spa town of Krynica in 1938) and that the two met again at the Polish radio studios shortly after liberation exemplifies that both belonged to the Polish-speaking intelligentsia. In the early postwar years, Waldorff not only saw the memoirs into print, but also promoted Szpilman's music, celebrating *Her First Ball* as an example of a popular yet artistic composition that should be emulated.[94] Other intellectuals, most notably Czesław Miłosz, also became fascinated by Szpilman's story and planned to turn it into a film.[95] But because Waldorff's role in giving Szpilman's experiences "a literary form" has been excised, today's readers—the vast majority of whom cannot find much less read the 1946 version—lose a sense of how this text was shaped by an early postwar intellectual community. Although the memoirs themselves remain (largely) in their original form, the erasure of authorship behind the present editions means that readers have lost insight into how the music of the Warsaw Ghetto was first transmitted into the postwar imagination: as part of the history of Warsaw's urban space.

Notes

1. See Marian Fuks, "Muzyka w gettach," *Muzyka* 16, no. 1 (1971): 64–76; Marian Fuks, "Życie muzyczne w gettach," *Biuletyn Żydowskiego Instytutu Historycznego* 82, no. 2 (1972): 41–56; and Shirli Gilbert, *Music in the Holocaust: Confronting Life in the Nazi Ghettos and Camps* (Oxford: Oxford University Press, 2005), chapter 1.

2. See Barbara Milewski, review of *Music in the Holocaust: Confronting Life in the Nazi Ghettos and Camps* by Shirli Gilbert, *Holocaust and Genocide Studies* 21, no. 1 (2007): 129–132; Amy Lynn Wlodarski, "Musical Memories of Terezín in Transnational Perspective," in *Dislocated Memories: Jews, Music, and Postwar German Culture*, ed. Tina Frühauf and Lily E. Hirsch (New York: Oxford University Press, 2014), 54–74; and James Loeffler, " 'In Memory of Our Murdered (Jewish) Children': Hearing the Holocaust in Soviet Jewish Culture," *Slavic Review* 73, no. 3 (2014): 585–611.

3. I build here on the work of historians who have applied the methods of urban studies to the ghettos of German-occupied Europe. See, for example, Gordon J. Horwitz, *Ghettostadt: Łódź and the Making of a Nazi City* (Cambridge, MA: Belknap Press of Harvard University Press, 2008) and Tim Cole, *Holocaust City: The Making of a Jewish Ghetto* (New York: Routledge, 2003).

4. Barbara Engelking, *Holocaust and Memory*, ed. Gunnar S. Paulsson and trans. Emma Harris (London: Leicester University Press, 2001), 81–214.

5. Amos Goldberg, "The History of the Jews in the Ghettos: A Cultural Perspective," in *The Holocaust and Historical Methodology*, ed. Dan Stone (New York: Berghahn Books, 2012), 95.

6. Amos Goldberg, "The Victim's Voice and Melodramatic Aesthetics in History," *History and Theory* 48, no. 3 (2009): 220–237.

7. See Lily E. Hirsch, "Righting and Remembering the Nazi Past: 'Suppressed Music' in American Concert Performance," *Music and Politics* 10, no. 1 (Winter 2016): https://doi.org/10.3998/mp.9460447.0010.102; and James Loeffler, "Why the New 'Holocaust Music' Is an Insult to Music—and to the Victims of the Shoah," *Tablet Magazine*, July 11, 2013.

8. Goldberg, "The History of the Jews in the Ghettos," 95. See also his study of the transformation of the ghetto's public sphere in "Rumor Culture among Warsaw Jews under Nazi Occupation: A World of Catastrophe Reenchanted," *Jewish Social Studies* 21, no. 3 (2016): 91–125.

9. The definitive account of the archive is Samuel D. Kassow, *Who Will Write Our History? Emanuel Ringelblum, the Warsaw Ghetto, and the Oyneg Shabes Archive* (Bloomington: Indiana University Press, 2007).

10. The content of the archive has been published by the Jewish Historical Institute in Warsaw as *Archiwum Ringelbluma: Konspiracyjne Archiwum Getta Warszawy*, 35 vols. (Warsaw: Żydowski Instytut Historyczny, 1997–2018).

11. Anthony Polonsky, "Warsaw," in *The YIVO Encyclopedia of Jews in Eastern Europe*, www.yivoencyclopedia.org.

12. See Leon Tadeusz Błaszczyk, *Żydzi w kulturze muzycznej ziem polskich w XIX i XX wieku: Słownik biograficzny* (Warsaw: Stowarzyszenie Żydowski Instytut Historyczny w Polsce, 2014); Isaschar Fater, *Muzyka żydowska w Polsce w okresie międzywojennym*, trans. Ewa Świderska (Warsaw: Oficyna Wydawnicza, 1997); and Marian Fuks, *Muzyka ocalona: Judaica polskie* (Warsaw: Wydawnictwa Radia i Telewizji, 1989).

13. See Halina Goldberg, " 'On the Wings of Aesthetic Beauty Toward the Radiant Spheres of the Infinite': Music and Jewish Reformers in Nineteenth-Century Warsaw," *Musical Quarterly* 101, no. 4 (2019): 407–454; Marian Fuks, *Żydzi w Warszawie: Życie codzienne, wydarzenia, ludzie* (Poznań: Sorus, 1992), 241–249, 342; and Magdalena Dziadek, "Zdzisław Birnbaum: Zapomniany kapelmistrz filharmonii," *Ruch Muzyczny* 45, no. 22 (2001): 13–17.

14. Tamara Sztyma, "On the Dance Floor, on the Screen, on the Stage: Popular Music in the Interwar Period— Polish, Jewish, Shared," in *Jews and Music-Making in the Polish Lands*,

ed. François Guesnet, Benjamin Matis, and Antony Polonsky, Polin: Studies in Polish Jewry 32 (Oxford: Littman Library of Jewish Civilization, 2020), 165–175; Robert A. Rothstein, "The Polish Tin Pan Alley, a Jewish Street," in Guesnet, Matis, and Polonsky *Jews and Music-Making in the Polish Lands*, 147–163; and Beth Holmgren, "Cabaret Nation: The Jewish Foundations of Kabaret Literacki, 1920–1939," in *Poland and Hungary*, ed. François Guesnet, Howard Lupovitch, and Antony Polonsky, Polin: Studies in Polish Jewry 31 (Oxford: Littman Library of Jewish Civilization, 2019), 273–288.

15. See Beth Holmgren, "The Polish-Language Cabaret Song: Its Multi-Ethnic Pedigree and Transnational Adventures, 1919–1968," in *Being Poland: A New History of Polish Literature and Culture since 1918*, ed. Przemysław Czapliński, Joanna Niżyńska, Agnieszka Polakowska, and Tamara Trojanowska (Toronto: University of Toronto Press, 2019), 258–272.

16. On the emergence of urban identities in Poland, see Nathaniel D. Wood, *Becoming Metropolitan: Urban Selfhood and the Making of Modern Cracow* (DeKalb: Northern Illinois University Press, 2010).

17. See Anna Landau-Czajka, *Syn będzie Lech: Asymilacja Żydów w Polsce międzywojennej* (Warsaw: Wydawnictwo "Neriton," 2006).

18. See David E. Fishman, *The Rise of Modern Yiddish Culture* (Pittsburgh, PA: University of Pittsburgh Press, 2010).

19. See Leslie A. Sprout, *Musical Legacy of Wartime France* (Berkeley: University of California Press, 2013).

20. See Beth Holmgren, "How the Cabaret Went to War," *Cosmopolitan Review* 6, no. 3 (2014): http://cosmopolitanreview.com/how-the-cabaret-went-to-war/.

21. See Barbara Engelking and Jacek Leociak, *The Warsaw Ghetto: A Guide to the Perished City*, trans. Emma Harris (New Haven, CT: Yale University Press, 2009), 36–72.

22. See Engelking, *Holocaust and Memory*, 82–83.

23. Stanisław Gombiński (Jan Mawult), *Wspomnienia policjanta z warszawskiego getta*, ed. Marta Janczewska (Warsaw: Stowarzyszenie Centrum Badań nad Zagładą Żydów, 2010), 47. "Odgłosy ulicy ghetta brzemią donośnie."

24. "Śpiew i muzyka na każdym kroku, na ulicach—tamując ruch, w podwórzach, na placach i skwerach. Znów gama najprzeróżniejszego rodzaju—śpiewacy i śpiewaczki, wspaniałe arie operowe i pieśni cudowne, głosy, które się na salach koncertowych i w gmachach operowych rozlegały, Verdi, Puccini, Meyerbeer, Moniuszko, Niewiadomski i o bezczelności żydowska! —Schubert, Schumann i Wagner." Ibid., 47.

25. "Wyszła Polihymia, muza muzyki z lirą w ręku z niepotrzebnych dziś dusznych i zawsze tłoczonych lokali nocnych dancingów oraz poważnych przybytków tej sztuki, wyszła na bruk uliczny, by ciężki okres wojny przetrwać." Sara W., "Sztuka na bruku," *Gazeta Żydowska*, November 8, 1940.

26. See Engelking and Leociak, *The Warsaw Ghetto*, 35–36; Goldberg, "Rumor Culture," 95.

27. Jonas Turkow, "Warszawa się bawi . . .," trans. Aleksandra Geller, *Archiwum Ringelbluma*, 26:16.

28. Kassow, *Who Will Write Our History?*, 119–124.

29. Turkow, "Warszawa się bawi . . .," 16.

30. Ibid., 9. See also, Marcel Reich-Ranicki, *The Author of Himself: The Life of Marcel Reich-Ranicki*, trans. Ewald Osers (Princeton: Princeton University Press, 2001), 153.

31. See the entry of April 26, 1941, in Emanuel Ringelblum, *Notes from the Warsaw Ghetto: The Journal of Emanuel Ringelblum*, trans. Jacob Sloan (New York: McGraw-Hill, 1958), 158;

and Jerzy Jurandot, *City of the Damned: Two Years in the Warsaw Ghetto*, trans. Jolanta Scicińska (Warsaw: Museum of the History of Polish Jews, 2015), 75.

32. Turkow, "Warszawa się bawi . . .," 9.

33. Ibid., 20.

34. Ibid., 12.

35. See Fishman, *The Rise of Modern Yiddish Culture*, chapters 6 and 7.

36. See Debra Caplan, *Yiddish Empire: The Vilna Troupe, Jewish Theater, and the Art of Itinerancy* (Ann Arbor: University of Michigan Press, 2018); and Mirosława M. Bułat, "Turkow Family," *YIVO Encyclopedia of Jews in Eastern Europe*, https://yivoencyclopedia.org/article.aspx/turkow_family.

37. See Kassow, *Who Will Write Our History?*, 123.

38. Turkow, "Warszawa się bawi . . .," 16.

39. See ibid., 17.

40. See Jonas Turkow, *C'était ainsi: 1939–1943, la vie dans le ghetto de Varsovie*, trans. Maurice Pfeffer (Paris: Austral, 1995), 169–171.

41. Turkow, "Warszawa się bawi . . .," 18.

42. See copies of performance schedules sent to the Abteilung für Volksaufklärung und Propaganda by the CKI. Archiwum Żydowskiego Instytutu Historycznego (AŻIH), 211 (Żydowska Samopomoc Społeczna), Aneks 252 (ŻTOS Centralna Komisja Imprezowa), pp. 4–60.

43. CKI to Abteilung für Volksaufklärung und Propaganda, April 30, 1941, AŻIH 211, Aneks 252, p. 13.

44. Dina Turkow to Abteilung für Volksaufklärung und Propaganda, AŻIH 211, Aneks 252, pp. 17–32.

45. Turkow, "Warszawa się bawi . . .," 16.

46. See ibid. 19.

47. See Kassow, *Who Will Write Our History?*, 128.

48. [Stanisław Różycki], "Kawiarnie," in *Archiwum Ringelbluma*, 5:67–76, here 68. Engelking and Leociak find evidence of ninety-five ghetto cafés or similar establishments. *The Warsaw Ghetto*, 634–640.

49. See Turkow, *C'était ainsi*, 168; and Ringelblum, *Notes from the Warsaw Ghetto*, 125.

50. Chaim Aron Kaplan, *Scroll of Agony: The Warsaw Diary of Chaim A. Kaplan*, trans. Abraham Isaac Katsh, rev. ed. (New York: Collier Books, 1981), 291.

51. See Gilbert, *Music in the Holocaust*, 28–30.

52. Kassow, *Who Will Write Our History?*, 253.

53. See Shachar Pinsker, *A Rich Brew: How Cafés Created Modern Jewish Culture* (New York: New York University Press, 2018), 55–97; and Andrzej Z. Makowiecki, *Warszawskie kawiarnie literackie* (Warsaw: Isrky, 2013).

54. "Kawiarnie gettowe spełniają bardzo doniosłą rolę w życiu nie tylko towarzyskim, ale i publicznym wobec braku klubów, związków, stowarzyszeń, giełd, parków, kin, boisk, dancingów, itd. Jest to miejsce zastępujące więc teatr, kabaret, rewię, kino, ale nie tylko to, bo obok kabaretów i muzyki jest tu i sklep spożywczy i restauracja, odbywa się handel pokątny, spotykają się szmuglerzy dla umawiania swych interesów, kwitnie tu pośrednictwo, oferuje się i poszukuje towaru, są gabinety dla zakochanych, a również handel żywym towarem znalazł tu schronienie nie mówiąc już o tym, że i prostytucja—jak zawsze—panoszy się w knajpach." [Różycki], "Kawiarnie," 67.

55. Ibid., 76.

56. See Kassow, *Who Will Write Our History?*, 251–255.

57. See Stanisław Różycki, "Obrazki uliczne z getta," and [Stanisław Różycki?], "Moralność ulicy," in *Archiwum Ringelbluma*, 5:19–36, 37–51.

58. "Bo — jeśli panuje taka ogólna i bezwstydna demoralizacja publiczna, takie lokale muszą istnieć i są tylko naturalną emanacją warunków ogólnych." [Różycki], "Kawiarnie," 76.

59. "Wszyscy mają lub chcą mieć złudzenie, że atmosfera kawiarni oddzieli ich od rzeczywistości ulicy, od czarnej codzienności." Ibid., 67.

60. "Nie ma żadnych śladów wojny, niewoli, getta. Twarze wcale nie wymizerowane, wprost przeciwnie, normalne, dobrze odżywione." Ibid., 69.

61. "Temat ten sam, zglajchszachtowany. Co nowego, kiedy ofensywa, jak tam dziś z chlebem . . . Ani treść, ani forma nie różnią się od wszystkich naszych codziennych, tych samych, uporczywie powtarzających się pytań, odpowiedzi, jednostajnie smutnych, beznadziejnie rozpaczliwych." Ibid., 70.

62. ". . . tańczą, tańczą z werwą, temperamentem, humorem, przyśpieszają, przytupują do taktu, żądają bisu." Ibid., 71.

63. "Drań uronił istotnie łezkę i prędko na pocieszenie wychlał ajerkoniak, choć był do niczego." Ibid., 71.

64. ". . . rytm dzikiej, nieokiełzanej orkiestry jazzowej, dającej murzyńskie tempo jest dysonansem, zgrzytem na tyle powolnego, jednostajnego życia, i zupełnie opanowanego przez szarzyzny dnia. A to razi, tworzy jakąś nienaturalną, chorobliwą atmosferę; wydaje się czymś nierzeczywistym, nie z tego świata. To zbyt brutalny kontrast." Ibid., 74.

65. "Nastrój panuje tu, jakby istotnie lud[dzie uciekli do] piekła, aby posłuchać muzyki, wsłuchać się w melodie, [przypomnie]ć sobie treść pieśni, które ich upajały kiedyś." Ibid., 74.

66. See Katarzyna Person, *Assimilated Jews in the Warsaw Ghetto, 1940–1943* (Syracuse: Syracuse University Press, 2014), 21–23; Justyna Majewska, " 'Czym wytłumaczy Pan . . .?': Inteligencja żydowska o polonizacji i asymilacji w getcie warszawskim," *Zagłada Żydów: Studia i Materiały* 11 (2015): 325–346; and Kassow, *Who Will Write Our History?*, chapters 1–4.

67. See Turkow, *C'était ainsi*, 168.

68. [Różycki], "Kawiarnie," 73. "mechesi, wykształcona burżuazja . . . dumni, że i przed wojną byli bogaci, z pogardą patrzą na nowobogackich paskarzy. . . . nie znoszą faktu, że są zglajchszachtowani z 'parchami, Żydłakami,' że dzielą wspólny los."

69. See Holmgren, "Cabaret Nation."

70. Mary Berg, *The Diary of Mary Berg: Growing up in the Warsaw Ghetto*, ed. Susan Lee Pentlin (London: Oneworld Publications, 2006), 104.

71. Engelking and Leociak, *The Warsaw Ghetto*, 588.

72. Filip Mazurczak, "Władysław Szpilman's Post-War Career in Poland," in Guesnet, Matis, and Polonsky *Jews and Music-Making in the Polish Lands*, 219–234.

73. See Agata Tuszyńska, *Vera Gran: The Accused*, trans. Charles Ruas (New York: Knopf, 2013), 69–71. On Tuszyńska's powerful and controversial probing of Holocaust memory in *Gran*, see Jolanta Wróbel Best, "The Other Heroine Is Memory (A Conversation with Agata Tuszyńska)," *The Polish Review* 60, no. 1 (2015): 85–95.

74. Katarzyna Naliwajek-Mazurek and Andrzej Spóz, eds., *Okupacyjne losy muzyków: Warszawa 1939–1945* (Warsaw: Towarzystwo im. Witolda Lutosławskiego, 2015), 2:143–146.

75. Holmgren, "Cabaret Nation," 288.

76. See Barbara Milewski, "Chopin's Mazurkas and the Myth of the Folk," *19th-Century Music* 23, no. 2 (1999): 113–135.

77. See Katarzyna Naliwajek-Mazurek, "The Use of Polish Musical Tradition in the Nazi Propaganda," *Musicology Today* 7 (2010): 243–259.

78. On a similar portrayal of Chopin in the film *Zakazane piosenki* (1946), see Barbara Milewski, "Hidden in Plain View: The Music of Holocaust Survival in Poland's First Post-War Feature Film," in *Music, Collective Memory, Trauma, and Nostalgia in European Cinema after the Second World War*, ed. Ewelina Boczkowska and Michael Baumgartner (New York: Routledge, 2020), 111–137.

79. See Tuszyńska, *Vera Gran*, 87–88.

80. See Jerzy Waldorff, ed., *Śmierć miasta: Pamiętniki Władysława Szpilmana, 1939–1945* (Warsaw: Wiedza, 1946).

81. See Laura Jockusch, *Collect and Record! Jewish Holocaust Documentation in Early Postwar Europe* (New York: Oxford University Press, 2012), chapter 3; Bret Werb, "'Vu ahin zol ikh geyn?': Music Culture of Jewish Displaced Persons," in Frühauf and Hirsch, *Dislocated Memories*, 75–96, especially 81–82; and Rachel Feldhay Brenner, *Polish Literature and the Holocaust: Eyewitness Testimonies, 1942–1947* (Evanston, IL: Northwestern University Press, 2019).

82. See Milewski, "Hidden in Plain View."

83. See Władysław Szpilman, *The Pianist: The Extraordinary Story of One Man's Survival in Warsaw, 1939–45*, trans. Anthea Bell (New York: Picador USA, 1999).

84. See Piotr Kuhiwczak, "Mediating Trauma: How Do We Read the Holocaust Memoirs," in *Tradition, Translation, Trauma: The Classic and the Modern*, ed. Jan Parker and Timothy Mathews (Oxford: Oxford University Press, 2011), 283–97. The English translation is not based on the original Polish, but most likely on the prior German translation.

85. See Jacek Leociak, "Pamiętniki Władysława Szpilmana: Zdumiewająca przemiana," *Rzeczpospolita*, March 1, 2001. The nationality of Wilm Hosenfeld, who helped Szpilman survive, was corrected from Austrian to German, however.

86. See Kuhiwczak, "Mediating Trauma."

87. See Jerzy Waldorf, "Totalisytczne finezje," *Muzyka Polska* 6, no. 2 (1939): 74–77; Jerzy Waldorff, *Sztuka pod dyktaturą* (Warsaw: Biblioteka Polska, 1939).

88. See Waldorff, *Śmierć miasta*, 7–8.

89. "Pisząc szpilmanowską odyseję, starałem się jedynie przekazać ją czytelnikowi w takiej formie literackiej, która by oddała jak najwierniej także i treść emocjonalną opowieści mego przyjaciela." Ibid., 8.

90. "Technicznie współpracowaliśmy w ten sposób, że on opowiadał mi swoje przeżycia i dostarczał chronologicznych notatek, a ja te wiadomości komponowałem w literacką całość, nadawałem im formę książki, w której—podkreślam—Szpilman nie napisał ani słowa. . . . Na literata, autora "śmierć miasta" został kreowany Szpilman, będący nie autorem, lecz bohaterem książki." Jerzy Waldorff, "Moja sprawa," *Przekrój*, July 16, 1947, 18.

91. Szpilman, *The Pianist*, 8.

92. Waldorff eventually ceded his authorial rights in exchange for 12,000 German marks, a substantial sum for Poland's literary market of the late 1990s, but likely a small amount considering the royalties the memoirs eventually generated. Mariusz Urbanek, *Waldorff: Ostatni baron Peerelu* (Warsaw: Iskra, 2008), 153–163.

93. See Mazurczak, "Władysław Szpilman's Post-War Career."

94. See Jerzy Waldorff, "Życie muzyczne w kraju: Warszawa," *Ruch Muzyczny* 1, no. 5 (1945): 12–13.
95. The film was released in 1950 as *Miasto nieujarzmione* (The unvanquished city) but Szpilman's story was changed beyond recognition and Miłosz had backed out of the project.

Select Bibliography

Archiwum Ringelbluma: Konspiracyjne Archiwum Getta Warszawy. 35 volumes. Warsaw: Żydowski Instytut Historyczny, 1997–2018.

Błaszczyk, Leon Tadeusz. *Żydzi w kulturze muzycznej ziem polskich w XIX i XX wieku: Słownik biograficzny.* Warsaw: Stowarzyszenie Żydowski Instytut Historyczny w Polsce, 2014.

Engelking, Barbara. *Holocaust and Memory.* Edited by Gunnar S. Paulsson and translated by Emma Harris. London: Leicester University Press, 2001.

Engelking, Barbara, and Jacek Leociak. *The Warsaw Ghetto: A Guide to the Perished City.* Translated by Emma Harris. New Haven, CT: Yale University Press, 2009.

Fater, Isaschar. *Muzyka żydowska w Polsce w okresie międzywojennym.* Translated by Ewa Świderska. Warsaw: Oficyna Wydawnicza, 1997.

Flam, Gila. *Singing for Survival: Songs of the Lodz Ghetto, 1940–45.* Urbana: University of Illinois Press, 1992.

Fuks, Marian. *Muzyka ocalona: Judaica polskie.* Warsaw: Wydawnictwa Radia i Telewizji, 1989.

Gilbert, Shirli. *Music in the Holocaust: Confronting Life in the Nazi Ghettos and Camps.* Oxford: Oxford University Press, 2005.

Goldberg, Amos. "The History of the Jews in the Ghettos: A Cultural Perspective." In *The Holocaust and Historical Methodology*, edited by Dan Stone, 79–100. New York: Berghahn Books, 2012.

Goldberg, Amos. "Rumor Culture among Warsaw Jews under Nazi Occupation: A World of Catastrophe Reenchanted." *Jewish Social Studies* 21, no. 3 (2016): 91–125.

Guesnet, François, Benjamin Matis, and Antony Polonsky, eds. *Jews and Music-Making in Polish Lands,* Polin: Studies in Polish Jewry 32. Oxford: Littman Library of Jewish Civilization, 2020.

Kassow, Samuel D. *Who Will Write Our History? Emanuel Ringelblum, the Warsaw Ghetto, and the Oyneg Shabes Archive.* Bloomington: Indiana University Press, 2007.

Loeffler, James. "'In Memory of Our Murdered (Jewish) Children': Hearing the Holocaust in Soviet Jewish Culture." *Slavic Review* 73, no. 3 (2014): 585–611.

Naliwajek, Katarzyna. "The Racialization and Ghettoization of Music in the General Government." In *Twentieth-Century Music and Politics*, edited by Pauline Fairclough, 191–210. Farnham, UK: Ashgate, 2013.

Pierce, J. Mackenzie. "Messianism Refigured: Tadeusz Zygfryd Kassern's Musical Monument to the Warsaw Ghetto Uprising." *Holocaust and Genocide Studies* 36, no. 2 (2022): 242–265.

Wlodarski, Amy Lynn. "Musical Memories of Terezín in Transnational Perspective." In *Dislocated Memories: Jews, Music, and Postwar German Culture*, edited by Tina Frühauf and Lily E. Hirsch, 54–74. New York: Oxford University Press, 2014.

....

11

SOUNDING OUT THE GHETTO

Spatial Aspects of Jewish Musical Life during the Nazi Era

....

TOBIAS REICHARD

IN the summer of 1933, a small circle of German Jews around the neurologist and musicologist Kurt Singer and the stage director Kurt Baumann founded the Kulturbund Deutscher Juden, later renamed to Jüdischer Kulturbund in Deutschland. The Jewish Culture League was conceived as a cultural self-help organization by and for Jews with the aim of providing financial and spiritual support for the thousands of artists who had lost their positions on "racial" grounds after 1933. It consisted at its peak of more than seventy regional and local branches in one hundred German cities and had approximately 70,000 members (artists, audiences, and administrative personnel). Since 1935, the single branches were centrally governed by the umbrella organization of the Reichsverband jüdischer Kulturbünde in Deutschland (Reich Association of Jewish Culture Leagues in Germany), under Singer's leadership. Nazi politicians supported this initiative, albeit with severe restrictions and strict control by the Propaganda Ministry and police agencies: artists and audiences had to obtain a membership and identify themselves as members at control points, neither public ticket sales nor advertising outside the Jewish press was permitted, artistic programs were subjected to strict censorship and had to be approved in advance by Nazi officials, performances had to be staged as closed events exclusively by and for Jews, and most of the events were attended by members of the Gestapo who surveilled the behavior of artists and audiences and controlled whether the repertoire corresponded with prior approvals. With these provisions, Nazi officials hoped to create a solution for the thousands of jobless artists who would otherwise have fallen to the state welfare system and to achieve a maximally segregated and fully controlled Jewish cultural life. Ultimately, these measures aimed at driving Jews into exile or permanent emigration.

In light of these circumstances, it is hardly surprising that contemporary Jewish accounts of music and theater life in the Nazi state are permeated by spatial metaphors to describe individual experiences. Former members of the Culture League have characterized it as an "island,"[1] "oasis,"[2] "refuge,"[3] or a space of "spiritual resistance,"[4] while others have called it a "prison"[5] or "ghetto theater."[6] Spatial semantics of isolation, confinement, and withdrawal as well as of subversiveness and resistance refer to a central aspect that impacted not only Jewish musical life, but also Jewish everyday experiences in the Nazi dictatorship in general. These experiences were the result of an increasingly strict regulation of public space, which succeeded in completely expelling Jews from society during the Nazi era.[7]

The term perhaps most reflective of these spatial dimensions of Jewish daily life and certainly one of the most disputed with regard to the Jewish musical life was "ghetto." In fact, before it even existed, the Culture League had been called a "ghetto enterprise" by one of its founders, Julius Bab, in June 1933.[8] Former members built on this concept: organist and composer Herbert Fromm, for example, who was active in the Frankfurt branch of the League, described it as a "spiritual ghetto for educated people."[9] The term *ghetto* was also used by fierce opponents of the League like the Austrian writer Joseph Roth, who in 1937 called it the regime's "officially sanctioned centerpiece of the new ghetto."[10] Similarly, the writer and satirist Kurt Tucholsky had expressed his opinion about the League in a letter to Arnold Zweig in December 1935, only six days before he would commit suicide in exile:

> There you see that the same people who in many domains played first violin accept the ghetto—the idea of the ghetto and its realization. . . . They are being locked up; they are crammed into a theater for Jews with four yellow badges on their front and back and they have . . . only one ambition: "Now for once we will show them that we have a better theater."[11]

Regardless of their respective opinion of the League or the various ways in which they suffered persecution at the hands of the Nazi regime, the term ghetto allowed Jews to place their experiences within a familiar framework of Jewish exclusion, separation, and persecution. In most uncertain times, some would find solace in situating their own experiences within a historical continuum of Jewish suffering (and survival). Others found themselves all the more desperate as they realized that the centuries-long exclusion of Jews had obviously not been overcome by emancipation. Yet, German Jews were well aware that they lived in a very different kind of ghetto in 1930s Nazi Germany than their ancestors did. The Berlin Rabbi Joachim Prinz provided perhaps the most famous description of what he would call "Ghetto 1935": "The ghetto is no longer a geographically defined district, at least not in the sense of the Middle Ages. It is the 'world' that is the ghetto. It is outside that the ghetto exists for us. In the markets, in the street, in hotels—everywhere is the ghetto."[12]

This brief overview already demonstrates that the term ghetto rarely means one and the same thing, even when the frame of reference is limited to the years of Nazi rule before the beginning of the "Final Solution." It can serve as a metaphor for the feeling of social isolation and estrangement or refer to a political strategy of "racial," cultural, and organizational segregation; it could be applied as a historically shaped concept in comparisons between the segregation of the 1930s and that of previous eras; it could be conceived as an imagined entity that does not exist in a material sense, but one that had quite tangible effects such as changes in public space and mobility options for Jews. From a postwar perspective, "cultural ghettoization" could be understood as a first step in the regime's effort toward the annihilation of European Jewry during the Second World War.

Before addressing all these aspects in greater detail, it is necessary to state that it can be problematic to operate on the basis of a single perspective and fixed notion of what the ghetto is and was. For the purpose of this chapter, the ghetto is thus conceived not only as a place in the sense of a "compulsory, segregated and enclosed area" where Jews or other minority group or groups lived.[13] It is also understood as a space, that is, as a "topographic reality and discursive metaphor," encompassing physical and imagined, material, and metaphorical qualities.[14] Following the approach of Daniel B. Schwartz and others, I will take into consideration the different uses of *ghetto* and the underlying concepts as they apply to different aspects of Jewish musical life under National Socialism, instead of essentializing or codifying the term.[15] This chapter predominantly focuses on the discussions and experiences of Jews in Germany in the years 1933 to 1938—who were by no means a homogeneous group, but were targeted collectively by the regime's racially motivated policies of persecution and segregation from the very first days of its rule. A later section offers a brief outlook on the developments during the Second World War.

In this context, "sounding out the ghetto" has a double meaning. On an analytical-descriptive level, it is intended as an exploration of various concepts of ghetto and the different applications of the term by a variety of actors—Jews and Nazi officials alike. Indeed, to what extent do places and spaces shape the character and perception of musical events?[16] Which agents and which practices were involved in the creation, transformation, or disappearance of places or spaces with significance for Jewish musical life in the Nazi state? On a more general level, it offers an opportunity to inquire what knowledge can be gained through a historiographic approach that is sensitive toward spatial contexts of musical life. How helpful are spatial concepts, like ghetto, as heuristics for understanding Jewish musical experiences under National Socialist dictatorship?

According to the historian Karl Schlögel, the complexity of histories of spaces and places always wields "a power of veto against the segmentation of the object, its subdivision into neat parcels, that academic historiography, and its division of labor favored."[17] Although Jewish musical life under National Socialism is hardly uncharted territory anymore, there are still major research gaps that more often than not seem to be the result of disciplinary (self-)restrictions.[18] This becomes obvious when looking at the Jewish Culture League. Its almost complete monopoly of Jewish artistical activities until the final dissolution in 1941 made the League an obvious starting point for research on cultural life under the Nazis in general and Jewish musical life in particular.[19] An extensive body literature on the League—particularly an anthology published by the Akademie der Künste Berlin and the work of Gabriele Fritsch-Vivié, Lily E. Hirsch,

Barbara Müller-Wesemann, and Rebecca Rovit—provides details on the organizational history and local chapters, its protagonists and relations to Nazi officials, the repertoire, and the debates regarding the orientation of the artistic programs.[20] Yet, despite the fact that Jews were often forced to move to other venues like synagogues, sports halls, or restaurants for musical events, and despite recent calls to take these spatial dimensions into account,[21] research on the League and on Jewish musical life in Nazi Germany in general rarely goes beyond the mere mention of addresses, including sometimes information on capacity and technical equipment of performance venues.[22] Although most Jewish musical activities took place right in the center of urban topographies (albeit under strict separation from the public), regional or local conditions that influenced Jewish musical life or the impact of performance venues on musical perception are rarely addressed.[23] Considering the significance of spatial contexts for musical events, while bearing in mind that the exclusion of Jews from German music culture was not only a matter of legal policy but a complex array of decrees, propagandistic efforts, and strategies of spatial dominance, the question of space and place in Jewish musical life in Nazi Germany is crucial. This complexity can only be grasped through an interdisciplinary approach that does not conceive of place as a "dash of local color or flavor to 'dry history,'" but whose guiding principle it is to "think history in conjunction with place."[24]

"Spiritual Ghetto"

In January 1934, an article in the periodical *Der Schild*, the journal of the Reichsbund jüdischer Frontsoldaten (Reich Association of Jewish Frontline Soldiers), looked back on the first months of activities of the Culture League. The author, Hans Samter, acknowledged the initiative as "unparalleled also outside the Jewish world." Not only did the League provide the necessary material and spiritual support for the hundreds of Jewish artists forced out of their jobs and for Jewish audiences in dire need of distraction from daily hardship, but according to him, it was also an opportunity to actively counteract one central goal of Nazi policy, namely to "put the German Jews into a spiritual ghetto." He was convinced that an active Jewish cultural life would be the only way to resist the Nazis' policy of forced "Judaization" and spiritual ghettoization and to express the German identity of Jews by "fighting for the active part [of Jews] in German culture over and over again."[25]

When Samter used the expression "spiritual ghetto," he could expect most of his readers to be familiar with what he was specifically referring to. Since the mid-nineteenth century, the term ghetto, or combinations such as "spiritual" or "cultural ghetto," had served as a metaphor for "a purportedly specifically 'Jewish' form of backwardness and Otherness" in Jewish and non-Jewish German discourse.[26] After the abolition of Western European ghettos in the course of the nineteenth century, the term became a symbol of a barbaric, medieval past. At the end of the Weimar era, the large majority of German Jews was still convinced that emancipation was instrumental in transcending the inheritance of the ghetto. According to historian Steven Aschheim, this required the "disappearance of the conspicuous ghetto Jew" by "a change of dress, a modulation of tone, a lowering of the decibel level."[27] Jewish modernization thus entailed more than just the acquisition of legal and social equality, but was conditional upon overcoming a state of mind that the term ghetto came to connote. Precisely this understanding of ghetto as a state of mind was what the term "spiritual ghetto" referred to in Samter's article. And this is why the author was confident, as were many other German Jews, that there *would* actually be a way for them to fight against such ghettoization under Nazi rule.

Against this background, leaders of Jewish organizations like the Culture League faced the well-known dilemma of creating an agenda reflective of the needs, identities, and self-perceptions of the various factions within German Jewry (naturally, these factions were themselves hardly homogenous in their members' opinions): Orthodoxy denied the Culture League the authority and the ability to represent Jewish culture altogether as it had, according to them, no foundation within Jewish law.[28] Liberal Jews, who represented the majority of German Jewry, tried to uphold the legacy of emancipation, Enlightenment, and acculturation by remaining "in active connection with the great cultural goods of Germany and the world," as Julius Bab explained in November 1933,[29] as would Hans Samter a few months later. Their national and cultural self-identification was emphatically German (which, however, did not automatically exclude the sense of belonging to the Jewish world at the same time). Especially the Culture League's leadership vehemently defended its agenda against repeated accusations of creating a "spiritual ghetto."[30]

Regional and genre-dependent variations in musical programs notwithstanding, the overall guiding principle for the League's events, at least initially, could be described as a commitment to the classical canon of bourgeois concert and opera life while gradually expanding into works of Jewish and foreign composers and playwrights.[31] Within the liberal faction, however, there were some, like the theater critic Ludwig Davidsohn of the *Jüdisch-liberale Zeitung*, who rejected this approach. Echoing Zionist views, Davidsohn demanded the inclusion of genuinely Jewish plays in the programs instead of the well-established classics.[32] Even his editors had to admit that many Jews felt degraded ("degradiert") by having to go to a special theater for listening to a Mozart opera, which was Jewish only insofar as the librettist, Lorenzo Da Ponte, and the translator, Hermann Levi, had been Jews.[33] Since the attendance of cultural events was not forbidden to Jews until 1938, many preferred to hear the classical repertoire in regular theaters.[34] Zionists saw in the Culture League and other initiatives the necessary groundwork for building their own nation with its own genuinely cultural life. Especially in the beginning, when Jews were still allowed to play German works, they critiqued the League's programming as not Jewish in character and as not reflective of the experiences of Jews in Germany, which in both cases would not help to foster a Jewish cultural or religious awareness.[35] In the absence of genuinely Jewish works, Zionists increasingly regarded the culture of eastern European Jews as religiously more authentic and spiritually more sincere and therefore more suited as a model for a future Jewish culture. However, works by Yiddish authors, for example *Di goldene keyt* (The golden chain) by Isaac Leib Peretz or the Leivick Halpern's *Golem*, repeatedly triggered polemical responses by liberal Jews who rejected such works as "ghetto culture" or claimed to understand them in the same vein as "Chinese theater."[36]

The Nazi regime tried to enforce the segregation between Jews and Germans in the music sector by influencing repertoire and personnel decisions. Authorities constantly urged the League's leadership to stage works by Jewish or foreign authors in order to prevent any signs of assimilatory tendencies. Police agencies especially, like the Gestapo and the Security Service of the SS, feared that without strict supervision, the League's events could become uncontrollable centers of resistance. They repeatedly (if largely un-successfully) demanded that the leadership had to consist of Zionists, whose drive to-ward emigration and the creation of a genuinely Jewish culture seemed to be most in keeping with the regime's goals.[37] To this end, they issued bans on the performance of "German" composers until virtually no "German" works were allowed anymore after 1938.[38] These bans were important steps in the regime's efforts to achieve cultural segre-gation and to abolish all symptoms of acculturation of German Jews in order to foster a feeling of collective estrangement from German society among them.

These measures fueled the inner-Jewish debates about the "Jewishness" of the Culture League's activities. To address these and other issues, the League's leadership organ-ized a conference in 1936 and invited musicians and musicologists to elaborate on their perspectives on Jewish music.[39] Also present were Hans Hinkel, who supervised the Culture League's operations for the Propaganda Ministry, and other Nazi representa-tives, who were to make sure that the regime's demands of a "Judaized" agenda were met. The aim of the conference was to bring about a broad consensus on the League's future directions that was more reflective of the various self-images and national identities of its members. For this purpose, the Jewish element in the Culture League's program was to be accentuated more than before in order to foster a stronger Jewish consciousness as demanded by Zionists. At the same time, however, participation in European cultural assets of the past—Jewish and non-Jewish—should continue. Although this general formula met with approval among the liberal and Zionist factions, the presentations by music experts made it clear that it was not possible to overcome some fundamental contradictions in the conception of a Jewish music. The scholars, among them Hans Nathan, Karl Adler, and Anneliese Landau, did not agree, for example, on whether Jewish music had fixed stylistic characteristics or whether the origin of the authors or the use of Jewish themes was already sufficient to designate a work as Jewish. Arno Nadel acknowledged, as would Kurt Singer later, that a "true Jewish music" was to be found only in "liturgical and folk music."[40] Nevertheless, they had to admit that, spirit-ually, there was no single, coherent, and representative lineage of synagogue music and, nationally, that a true Jewish folk music in the sense of being dependent on the land of its origin could not exist outside Palestine. More so, Nadel's assessment that "true Jewish themes and melodies have an eastern character"[41] brought the argument dangerously close to the polemical debate about "ghetto culture" that had sparked the controversy in the first place.

In his closing address, Kurt Singer boldly declared that "Jewish music is not orchestral music; it is vocal, ardent prayer, singing by individuals or the many, but not instrumental." Mirroring this view, he announced a competition for an orchestral prelude of solemn character for festive occasions, a choral work on a biblical or Jewish theme with orchestral accompaniment, a choral work for youth choirs, and a song and choral cycle, respectively, based on either German or Hebrew texts.[42] This was certainly a remarkable initiative to encourage Jewish composers at a time when the regime's anti-Semitic measures were intensifying. Even if about half of the more than 120 entries had to be rejected due to poor quality and no first prize was awarded in two of the five categories, the League's leadership considered the competition a success. First prizes were granted to Werner Seelig-Bass' Overture and Fugue for orchestra, to Richard Fuchs' choral work *Vom jüdischen Schicksal*, and to Hugo Adler's *Sechs hebräische Volkslieder* for choir a cappella (other compositions by Oskar Guttmann, Arno Nadel, Herbert Fromm, and Julius Chajes received honorable mentions). Yet, when Singer announced that the next edition of the competition would be extended to the category of chamber music, he was apparently softening his earlier conception of Jewish music as primarily festive and vocal in character.[43] This rather narrow perspective did not seem representative of the preferences of composers and their audiences, nor of the various positions taken at the conference, so that the question of Jewishness in music remained unanswered. Nevertheless, the promoters of the competition and the participants of the conference seemed to be satisfied with the general consensus to further engage in the pursuit of an emphatically Jewish cultural agenda.

According to the German press, the Nazi officials who had attended the conference in 1936 were equally pleased with its outcome—or so it seemed.[44] While the measures of influencing repertoire and personnel choices certainly managed to significantly increase the pressure on Jews, resulting in rising emigration, the strategy of cultural segregation proved to be less effective than politicians and police agencies had hoped for.[45] The overall increase of works by Jewish and foreign authors in the League's events throughout the 1930s and the inner-Jewish debates about artistic directions cannot deny the fact that Jews by and large held on to the familiar repertoire of European music culture to express their identity as long as it was permitted. And when Jews left Germany, they usually did so not because but in spite of the League's existence. Additionally, many of those who were supposed to be subjected to cultural segregation chose to avoid it in the first place. The leaders of the League were very much aware of the fact—as were Nazi officials—that around 90 percent of German Jews would refuse to join the League because they rejected artistic choices or would not let themselves be "ghettoized"—or simply decided against making long term commitments to the subscription conditions in times of financial duress.[46]

This, however, raises a crucial question about the nature of the Culture League as a "spiritual ghetto," which Daniel Schwartz has formulated as: "Can one chose to live in a ghetto?"[47] At least until 1938 Jewish audiences could indeed decide to a certain degree whether they should expose themselves to the increasingly "Judaizing" tendencies enforced by the Nazi leadership (artists who had to earn a living, however, had less of a choice). That a debate about the "spiritual ghetto" could exist after all is evidence for this fact. Thus, the concept of the spiritual ghetto, especially with regard to Jewish musical life under the Nazi dictatorship, comes closest to reality when it refers to the distinct experiences of individual (but not all) Jews. As a descriptive framework for the regime's anti-Semitic strategy, it misrepresents the goals and, as we shall see, their actual realization. Schwartz's assessment is therefore accurate, that "before 1938 both the concept and indeed specter of 'ghettoization'—as well as the word ghetto itself—were much more a part of an intra-Jewish discourse than of German policy or propaganda."[48] However, the concept of the ghetto did not remain a mere object of inner-Jewish debates. Nor was it exclusively a matter of legislation and cultural policy. Even if its walls were invisible, the Nazi ghetto of the 1930s had a very real and material side to it, one that influenced Jewish musical life significantly and one that almost no Jew in Germany was able to escape, regardless of his or her cultural identity or stance toward Jewish organizations like the Jewish Culture League.

THE GHETTO AS TOPOGRAPHICAL REALITY

In his aforementioned reflections on the world as the ghetto, Joachim Prinz captured the feeling of isolation Jews encountered all over Germany on a daily basis. About six months later, in November 1935, Prinz returned to the subject once more. Although his argument remained largely the same, one fundamental aspect had changed compared to his previous assessment. For him, it was no longer "the world" that was the ghetto. Instead, "the new ghetto is a life within the four walls."[49]

It is hardly coincidental that Prinz's localization of the ghetto shifted within 1935 from "the world" to "the four walls." That year saw not only the adoption of the Nuremberg Laws in September but witnessed some of the most violent acts against Jews since the Nazis came to power. In June, a number of Jewish-owned stores, such as the music store of Sigmund Koch in Munich, were boycotted and customers—Jews and non-Jews— violently attacked in broad daylight.[50] One month later, the Kurfürstendamm in Berlin, which was considered by anti-Semites to be particularly "Judaized" due to numerous Jewish inhabitants of the upper middle class and was regarded as a symbol for Weimar culture (Kurt Weill's *Aufstieg und Fall der Stadt Mahagonny*, for example, had its Berlin premiere in the Theater am Kurfürstendamm in 1932), became the site of brutal riots.[51] Prinz's change of perspective is therefore not only indicative of the fact that Jews lived in constantly changing conditions of public space, but that this space itself became increasingly precarious for them.

This has to do with public space being an area rigorously claimed by Nazi agitators, who saw dominance in the streets as a first step toward assuming power. Already in 1926, Joseph Goebbels, then executive manager of the NSDAP Gau of the Northern Rhineland, proclaimed that "whoever can conquer the street can also conquer the state."[52] Consequently, the symbolic occupation of villages and cities by SA troops with marches, anti-Semitic songs, the ubiquitous display of Nazi banners and boycotts of Jewish stores—often accompanied by physical violence—became a key feature in early Nazi propaganda and remained central after 1933.

This dramatically influenced mobility options for Jews. Under the impression there could be anti-Semitic attacks in the first weeks of Nazi rule, the newsletter of the Jewish community of Nuremberg-Fürth had called on its readers in May 1933, "in light of the circumstances of the time," to "abandon the old habit of gathering in groups and talking after leaving the synagogue."[53] Similarly, for fear of violent attacks, the Jewish community in Munich made the "urgent request" to its members in September that year "to leave the synagogue as little as possible during the service, and to avoid any gathering afterwards." Instead, meetings should be arranged "not in the immediate vicinity, but at more distant locations."[54] In August 1935, the community's newsletter cautioned again that "every responsible Jew . . . avoids large restaurants and places of entertainment, he refrains from superfluous promenades, and prefers to stay in his own house"[55]—or, as Joachim Prinz would call it a few months later, in the "ghetto of the four walls."

These precautions reveal two issues. Firstly, the possibility to recognize Jews in public was already considered such an acute danger that they were immediately forced to adapt everyday behavior. Violence thus played a central role in the "experiential space" of National Socialism from the very beginning, affecting everyone, but above all, Jews.[56] Secondly, this recognizability was apparently more dependent on spatial than personal conditions. The vast majority of German Jews were usually not identifiable as such, neither by behavior nor by outward appearance (for example, by not wearing the kippah)—a symptom not only of their embourgeoisement, but also a conscious protective measure against assaults.[57] In his memoirs, the long-time cantor of the Munich main synagogue, Emanuel Kirschner, describes a situation in the spa town of Bad Tölz south of Munich, where a SA guard in front of the local *Führerhaus* saluted him several times upon passing. "What high military animal the guard suspected in the ex-chasan from Munich" remained a mystery to Kirschner at the time, but can be explained by this reason.[58] Public places, on the other hand, had a particularly high threat level if they had a Jewish connotation. This is why warnings against public gatherings were usually issued with regard to synagogues, but not mainstream venues (as for example the so-called Museum in Munich, a concert hall that belonged to a private bank and was used for events regardless of whether organizers, performers, and audiences were Jewish). Conversely, the threat could be reduced by moving public gatherings to more distant locations. In this way, violence led to a restructuring of public space.

This transformation of public space through violence was central to National Socialist anti-Semitism, in which mental configurations of "Jewish topographies" played a key role.[59] On the one hand, the knowledge of when and which places could be visited or should better be avoided took on a completely new, at times lifesaving, importance for Jews.[60] It also led some members of the Culture League to perceive its events as their "own public space."[61] On the other hand, it was the imagination of "Jewish spaces" that guided the anti-Semitic violence of the persecutors. For centuries, Jews had been portrayed by others not only by their views, beliefs, daily rituals, and lifestyle, but also by their physical, gestural, performative, and sonic appearances, for example their customs of dressing or way of speaking.[62] Expressions like the German "Lärm wie in einer Judenschule" (noise like in the synagogue) or the Italian "fare un ghetto" (literally, "to make a ghetto," i.e., to create a tumult by talking at the same time), both still in use in the nineteenth and early twentieth centuries, hinged on the premise that Jews were recognizable not only by their physical but by their acoustic appearance as well, typically to be encountered in places of worship and dwelling.[63] While the political leadership rather tried to downplay or to conceal physical violence against Jews in the early years, a spatially oriented practice of violence allowed their public and media-effective stigmatization.[64] It was precisely the inherent theatricality of spatially oriented anti-Semitic violence—the devastation of stores, the display of "Jew" signs, or the placing of SA guards in front of shop entrances—that served to mark a place as Jewish in public. The Jewish publicist Robert Weltsch aptly characterized this strategy in his response to the boycotts of Jewish stores on April 1, 1933: "Not out of inner belief, not out of loyalty to their own community, not out of pride in a great past and human achievement, but because of the imprint of the red pamphlet and the yellow patch, they suddenly found themselves to be Jews."[65] Thus violence not only was a central component in the destruction of "Jewish spaces," but also often constituted them in the first place.

Yet, although Jews undoubtedly experienced severe segregation, they were by no means the only target. The Nazi boycotts of Jewish stores (and the accompanying violence) for example were not only intended to change the business behavior of the traders, who rarely sold goods produced exclusively by and for Jews, but rather the buying behavior of the customers.[66] In a similar vein, the numerous publications and encyclopedias regarding Jews and music that adhered to the NSDAP's racial doctrine obviously did not address a Jewish readership.[67] The party-sanctioned *Lexikon der Juden in der Musik* by Herbert Gerigk and Theophil Stengel, for instance, was written as "a safe guide . . . for cultural policy-makers, stage managers and conductors, for the radio, for leading personalities in the party organizations and affiliated associations and, last but not least, for the leaders of entertainment bands"[68]—which, of course, was not intended as a well-meaning recommendation, but a semi-official form of blacklisting with the goal of enforcing segregationist agendas.[69] Anti-Jewish policy was therefore bidirectional and affected people on either side of the imagined ghetto borders.

Existing tangible evidence for this bidirectionality of segregation and the spread of "Jewish topographies" are lists and in some cases even city maps with Jewish shops that were published in several German cities as well as registers of suppliers (Bezugsquellen-Anzeiger), in which only "Aryan" stores were mentioned.[70] The SA regularly concentrated their attacks either on places where Jewish shop owners were known (often based on these registers) or where Jews could be expected, for example during synagogue services or Jewish cultural activities. One of the most notorious attacks, which was to foreshadow many later assaults of this kind, had already taken place before 1933. In November 1930, Habimah, the famous Hebrew-speaking theater company of Russian origin, had performed in the city of Würzburg in Lower Franconia. A large group of people, mobilized by the local NSDAP group, had gathered in front of the Stadttheater, screaming anti-Semitic insults and violently attacking members of the audience upon leaving the theater.[71] Such attacks continued after 1933. Hanna Bernheim for example, who sang in the choir of a small branch of the Culture League in the Black Forest region, reports in her memoirs about an incident during a synagogue concert in the town of Hechingen in South-Western Germany in summer 1935, where a mob surrounded the synagogue while shouting anti-Semitic slogans and smashing windows with stones.[72] The actor Ernest Lenart remembered the fear of League members "that people would not show up" for performances, because "the SA was on the streets."[73] The dancer Hannah Kroner-Segal equally recalled her anxiety after events when she had to pass by SA members standing guard outside the venue. It is hardly surprising that to her, like to many others, the League felt like an "oasis," being separated from the frightening surroundings that reminded her of her actual status in German society.[74]

There is also evidence that these spatial conditions and experiences of violence directly influenced musical perceptions. In Munich for example, the Culture League increasingly used the main synagogue on Herzog-Max-Straße as a concert venue after Jewish artists had been banned from regular concert stages. A performance of the Kroyt-Quartett on December 10, 1933, playing string quartets by Mozart, Beethoven, and Haydn provided the first occasion to hear chamber music in this synagogue, which, unlike many other synagogues in Germany, had rarely been used for such non-liturgical purposes prior to 1933.[75] However, a subsequent review "could immediately state as a pleasant fact: The acoustics are quite excellent." In addition, the interior of the synagogue was atmospherically suitable for the perception of art, which, at least for the reviewer, took on religious traits: "The holiness of the room also helps one to 'devoutly' indulge in the artistic pleasures on offer. How closely religion and art are connected."[76] Thus, the experience of art in the sacred space of the synagogue could become an experience of faith even when the repertoire itself was neither Jewish nor sacred in nature.

On the very same day that the Kroyt-Quartett enchanted its Munich audience, the *New York Times* correspondent Herbert F. Peyser reported on what he deemed an unusual performance of *Le nozze di Figaro* in the Berliner Theater on Charlottenstraße (Nazi officials only occasionally allowed foreign journalists to attend the performances of the Culture League, hoping to elicit positive press coverage to counter accusations from abroad of the inhumane treatment of the Jews in Germany—an objective Peyser was obviously not willing to grant). For him, the secludedness of the "closed event" and the behavior of the audience had a direct impact on his own musical experience:

> Something in the manner and in the tranquil dignity with which that gathering listened to the unfoldment of Mozart's divine comedy presently became inexplicably but incredibly affecting—something of a spirit that somehow called to mind a congregation of early Christians at worship in the catacombs. And when the opera ended and one emerged on the street, the sight of the crooked cross and the thud of the Storm Troopers' boots seemed more than ever odious.[77]

Although Mozart's opera was neither thematically nor musically Jewish (or sacral in any way), for him, it took on a quite different, almost religious meaning (even if the comparison with early Christian worship may seem inappropriate within this context). Moreover, his experience was not limited to the duration of the performance, but also led to a changed perception of public space afterward: in contrast to the harmonious experience of the opera inside the theater, the symbols of National Socialist rule on the outside—the swastika on the walls and the sound of marching boots on the streets—were not simply omnipresent, but seemed "more than ever odious."[78]

The aforementioned spatial expressions as descriptions of Jewish cultural life under National Socialism—"oasis," "island," "refuge," and "ghetto," among others—were therefore not only signifiers of debates on artistic directions, religious believes, or national self-identification. They were also rooted in inherent characteristics of public space under National Socialist rule that affected Jewish everyday life in general and musical life in particular. This is not contradicted by the fact that some League members later claimed that they did not know what was happening on the "outside," since the League events became their whole life, while others seemed well aware of their predicament even during performances.[79] The key point is that in both opinions an "outside" (and consequently an "inside") existed in the first place. This divide and the resulting feelings of isolation and narrowness or of security and seclusion were, as it seems, the result of practices of spatial dominance and violence rather than of artistic debates and identities.

THE GHETTO AS PLACE

The violent pogroms in November 1938 not only represented a new escalation in anti-Semitic politics, but also had far-reaching consequences for the Jewish Cultural League. Across the Reich, synagogues had been set on fire, Jewish businesses vandalized, and hundreds of Jews attacked. In the days and weeks following the pogroms, thousands of Jews, including many members of the Culture League, were interned, expropriated, and resettled in the so-called Jewish houses (*Judenhäuser*), which marked the beginning of systematic physical concentration of Jews in the Reich.[80] Although the League continued operations in larger cities after 1938, Jewish musical activities were largely reduced due to emigration and persecution, and the deportation of former members to the ghettos and concentration camps that emerged in the months after the beginning of the Second World War. Had there actually been a strategy of cultural ghettoization of Jews in Nazi Germany, its leadership, at this point, had seemingly abandoned it.

This raises the question of whether there was an intrinsic connection that linked the anti-Semitism of the prewar years, the founding of the League, its gradual abolition beginning in 1938, and the establishments of ghettos in German-occupied territories since the outbreak of the war, beginning with Piotrków Trybunalski in October 1939. On first glance, there are indeed some striking parallels. Musical activities in the ghettos of Warsaw, Vilna, and Lodz, just to name the largest and most important of the nearly one thousand ghettos that existed in eastern Europe, resembled those of the Jewish Culture League in many ways, since they were regularly and exclusively staged by and for ghetto inmates (occasionally attended by SS guards). In some places, with Terezín being the most famous though certainly not the only example, inmates developed a broad range of activities, from chamber-music concerts, recitals, and cabarets to symphony concerts as well as theatrical and opera productions. The artistic programs were in most cases planned by a central Jewish committee and had to be approved in advance by the Nazi authorities.[81]

This is why historians as well as contemporaries have repeatedly suggested a continuity between the cultural ghettoization in the 1930s and the physical ghettoization during the Second World War. Saul Friedländer, for example, claimed that the Culture League "foreshadowed the Nazi ghetto, in which a pretense of internal autonomy camouflaged the total subordination of an appointed Jewish leadership to the dictates of the masters."[82] Herbert Freeden, a former Culture League official and the first to write its history after 1945, maintained that there was a "parallel between ghetto and Culture League," adding with regard to Terezín that the artistic activities there "were somewhat a continuation of the league, even if in a kind of distorting mirror."[83] The journalist Eike Geisel went one step further by suggesting that the Culture League developed the "early shapes" of what would emerge as "final form" in Terezín: a "fully controlled forced community."[84] As a matter of fact, Terezín was established only weeks after the League was officially abolished by the Gestapo on September 2, 1941, making it at least chronologically its successor.[85] Nazi leaders similarly exploited the imprisoned for propagandistic purposes. They allowed extensive cultural activities, which would then be used to deceive foreign observers about the true nature of the place. Equally deceived were the inmates themselves. Terezín served as an internment site for the so called "privileged Jews"—"celebrities," artists, scientists, members of the intelligentsia, and elders—many of whom, like the founding member and leader of the Reichsverband, Kurt Singer, were lured to apply for deportation under the pretense of being "resettled" to a "privileged camp" (*Vorzugslager*).[86]

This leads to the most obvious continuity between the Culture League and the ghettos: the people (although only a fraction of German Jews was deported to ghettos; the majority was sent to transfer and extermination camps[87]). Just like Singer, Elisabeth Baerlein, a former member of the orchestra of Munich's Culture League branch, was deported to Terezín in June 1942. Both continued their previous musical activities, Singer as an organizer and critic, Baerlein as a violinist and double bass player in the various music ensembles. Singer died in Terezín in February 1944 due to the catastrophic hygienic conditions, as did an estimated 33,500 other inmates. Baerlein was deported to Auschwitz in October that same year, where she was murdered upon arrival.[88]

Yet, while it seems tempting to compare the cultural activities between League and the ghettos, there are substantial differences, which put the assumption of a continuity between both in question. Firstly, neither the term "ghetto" and its offshoots of "spiritual" and "cultural ghetto," nor the concept of a forced confinement for Jews in one place, had been used by Nazi officials in the first years of Nazi rule. Perhaps most strikingly, the only time that the Jewish Culture League has been explicitly called a "spiritual ghetto" (and "ghetto" at all) in official documents was in a brief report by the SD from April 1937. These reports were usually intended to inform the political leadership about the moods and opinions of the population in Germany on different matters. Accordingly, the report seems to reflect the current status of inner-Jewish debates rather than Nazi policy.[89] This coincides with recent research on anti-Jewish policy during the Nazi era that has shown that the leadership did not seriously consider physical concentration of Jews before the establishment of the Jewish houses.[90] Ghettoization may have been a recurring topic in segregationist thinking and discourse, but was not acted upon until after the pogroms of November 1938.[91]

Secondly, historians have repeatedly emphasized that it would be misleading to assume a preconceived plan for the physical extermination of European Jewry before 1941. Despite the regime's prewar efforts to make life unbearable for Jews in Germany, the plans for mass extermination did not materialize until the war against Russia began in June 1941—a significant date given that the League's events seized precisely at that moment, with large deportations following in late summer/early autumn of 1941.[92] During its existence, the Jewish Culture League was essentially a compromise the Nazi regime made between expulsion and acceptance of Jews, with the latter being temporary until the former could be implemented. With the inception of the "Final Solution," the regime abandoned this approach almost immediately.

Thirdly, if the Culture League had indeed served as a precursor for the later cultural policies in the ghettos, as Friedländer, Freeden, and others suggested, then there is no obvious reason why the measures in the ghettos would often fall short of previous regulations. This is evident in the permissions for performing works by "Aryan" composers, which had been completely banned from league performances after 1938. Culture League affairs were mainly governed by the Propaganda Ministry and were centrally organized by the Reichsverband; in contrast, cultural policies in the ghettos were mostly left to local authorities, such as the Jewish-led ghetto administration or the SS. Since the surveillance structures inside the ghettos at times had loopholes, cultural life differed substantially from ghetto to ghetto. In Warsaw, local authorities allowed the creation of a symphony orchestra under the condition that no works of "Aryan" composers would be performed. Yet, when the first concert of the ensemble featured Beethoven's *Coriolan* overture, authorities raised no objections. This is similarly true for other works by German composers. In the Vilna Ghetto, repertoire restrictions were entirely absent, so that works by Beethoven, Bach, Schubert, and Mozart could be performed.[93] Reasons for this are not documented. It may be that the SS guards, who occasionally (if unofficially) attended recitals by ghetto inmates, may have appreciated hearing familiar music and were thus more inclined to allow such repertoires to be performed by Jews.[94] More likely, however, is the argument that different functionalities of musical life governed league and ghetto. The main goal of banning "German" works from the Culture League was that of forced Judaization to achieve cultural segregation and control. In the ghettos, music was equally a quite effective measure for exerting social control and creating an impression of normalcy, autonomy, and self-sufficiency (although it also played a significant role in various resistance movements). However, officially tolerated performances did not serve a policy of identity—after all, in the eyes of the occupiers, the ghettos in eastern Europe already constituted the "natural habitat" of their inmates.[95] Instead, they were intended to indirectly support the main goals of the ghettos—concentration, containment, exploitation for forced labor, and ultimately deportation and mass murder.

And lastly, a political strategy of "cultural" or "spiritual ghettoization" was, obviously, not a necessary step toward enabling concentration, mass deportations, and planful extermination in eastern Europe, where most of the ghettos were created during the Second World War (the Culture League, notably, never extended beyond the borders of the Reich[96]). Especially after the implementation of "Final Solution," the directionality of ghettoization was reverse, with cultural strategies of domination following the physical concentration and segregation of Jews in the occupied territories (and not the other way around as in the Reich). In order to establish control over the Jewish population in eastern Europe, the authorities transformed already existing areas of dense Jewish population on site into strictly sealed-off zones on site by use of extreme force. Cultural activities then certainly played an important role in maintaining control in the ghettos, but were not instrumental in their establishment. This further supports the notion that the Culture League was less a preliminary stage than it was a dead end on the road toward the "Final Solution."

The most decisive difference, however, was that the Jews active in the Culture League were usually still integrated in a familiar urban topography, which had a direct impact on the musical event. While still being embedded in their surroundings and trying "to remain in active connection with the great cultural goods of Germany and the world,"[97] Jews were constantly and painfully made aware of their own isolation by the proximity to their non-Jewish neighbors. The ghettos of eastern Europe on the other hand were mostly hermetically sealed-off districts, consisting of a polyglot Jewish community of various national backgrounds that had almost no possibility to interact with the non-Jewish population outside the now very visible ghetto walls.[98] There, according to Joachim Prinz's assessment—"the world is the ghetto"—had practically been reversed: for the inmates who were shut off completely from their surroundings, the ghetto became their world.

LIMITS AND BOUNDARIES OF THE "GHETTO"

Jewish musical life under National Socialism was eminently influenced by spatial conditions. These had transformative, at times disruptive and paradoxical, effects on performances as well as on the perception of cultural events. While performances of Yiddish plays or songs rarely succeeded in fostering a sense of Jewish identity, because they were regarded by many as "ghetto culture," works that were not Jewish by association could convey a feeling of "Jewishness" due to the particular circumstances in which they were presented (for example classical string quartets in a synagogue). Jews were therefore forced not only to develop an artistic agenda that reflected their self-image and national identity while coping with the growing pressure and many restrictions imposed by the regime. They also had to reconcile these efforts with a constantly changing public space that was becoming increasingly unsafe due to massive anti-Semitic violence. Jewish musical life therefore represented a much more complex space than descriptions expressing an "artistic oasis" or "cultural ghetto."

Using the concept of "ghetto" to describe the metaphorical and even actual space of Jewish musical life in Nazi Germany can therefore become problematic, as it is too far-reaching and yet not far-reaching enough. Unlike the newly established ghettos of the 1940s, the Culture League never became part of the "Final Solution." By using the term ghetto for both, a continuity between both could be implied (and is sometimes explicitly claimed as afore discussed by Friedländer, Freeden, and Geisel), ignoring the fact that they were guided by two very different or even opposite political agendas. The common notion that ghettos are, among other things, compulsory and not voluntary institutions further complicates the situation. Undoubtedly, the decrees of the Nazi regime did make it not only de jure, but also a de facto segregated undertaking. However, organizations like the Culture League were initially designed as self-help organizations and "emergency communities" for jobless Jewish artists and their audiences, which none of the later ghettos were.[99]

Concepts like *spiritual ghetto* and *cultural ghetto* are not far-reaching enough, if they are understood as a preliminary stage of actual ghettoization. This would simply distort the function of the League in relation to the numerous other segregationist efforts of the Nazi regime. In a call for a more nuanced understanding of the ghetto, Benjamin Ravid coined the phrase that "all ghettos were Jewish quarters but not all Jewish quarters were ghettos."[100] Although he had the premodern ghetto in mind, his assessment can easily be adapted to the situation of Jews in Nazi Germany: all ghettos were places of Jewish musical life, but not all places of Jewish musical life were ghettos. As shown above, Jews had a choice, albeit within a very restrictive environment, whether to become engaged in organizations like the Jewish Culture League and whether to be subjected to the "Judaization" efforts of the regime as a result. Of course, this does not mean that German Jews could avoid segregation in the 1930s (let alone the 1940s) by simply choosing not to "live in a ghetto." A case in point is the philologist Victor Klemperer, who, unlike his cousin acclaimed conductor Otto Klemperer, chose to remain rather than to go into exile. His sentiments of increasing isolation are well documented in his famous diary, as is his contempt for the Culture League.[101]

Whether or not the League should be regarded as a "ghetto" or an "oasis" needs to be approached from an interdisciplinary perspective and with nuance and should be distinguished from other anti-Semitic measures of the Nazi regime and the manifold ways they affected Jewish experiences. Future research needs to take into consideration the particularity of the Jewish musical life in Nazi Germany, in light of the fact that it *could* take on so many different meanings. This should not imply that "ghetto" or other spatial concepts—real or imagined, physical or metaphorical—are not useful theoretical frameworks for Jewish musical life in Nazi Germany. On the contrary, there is no doubt that spatial contexts such as urban environments, mental topographies, or architectural characteristics, and especially the restructuring of public space by violence had major effects in shaping the perception of musical events. Contemporaneous descriptions of the musical life, despite seeming to contradict each other at times, therefore deserve to be taken seriously, precisely *because* they so often coincide in their general relatedness to space.

NOTES

1. "Das Theater war unsere Rettung, wie eine Insel." Actor Martin Brandt in *Premiere und Pogrom: Der Jüdische Kulturbund 1933–1941–Texte und Bilder*, ed. Eike Geisel and Henryk Broder (Berlin: Siedler, 1992), 126.
2. "Der Kulturbund war plötzlich wie eine Oase, wo man anfangen konnte, den Beruf auszuüben." Dancer Hannah Kroner-Segal, ibid., 91.
3. "Das Theater . . . war für die Juden die einzige Zuflucht, wo sie mal ein paar Stunden auf andere Gedanken kommen konnten." Actress Steffi Ronau (Hinzelmann), ibid., 150.
4. Herbert Freeden, "Vom geistigen Widerstand der deutschen Juden: Ein Kapitel jüdischer Selbstbehauptung in den Jahren 1933 bis 1938," in *Widerstand und Exil 1933–1945*, ed. Otto R. Romberg (Bonn: Bundeszentrale für politische Bildung, 1985), 47–59. Paradoxically, Freeden has also interpreted the Culture League as a "prison," see the following note.
5. Herbert Freeden, *Jüdisches Theater in Nazideutschland* (Berlin: Ullstein, 1985), 5.
6. "Es war mehr oder weniger doch ein Ghetto-Theater." Dancer Steffi Ronau (Hinzelmann), in Geisel and Broder, *Premiere und Pogrom*, 150.
7. Jacob Boas, "The Shrinking World of German Jewry, 1933–1938," *Leo Baeck Institute Year Book* 31, no. 1 (1986): 241–266; Guy Miron, " 'Lately, Almost Constantly, Everything Seems Small to Me': The Lived Space of German Jews under the Nazi Regime," *Jewish Social Studies* 20, no. 1 (2013): 121–149.
8. "Ich freue mich über Ihren Enthusiasmus, obschon ich ihn ehrlich gesagt nur halb teile—denn es bleibt doch eine bittere Sache—ein Ghetto-Unternehmen—das wir freilich so gut machen wollen, daß sich die Deutschen schämen müssen." (I'm glad about your enthusiasm, although, to be honest, I only share it partly – because it remains a bitter thing—a ghetto enterprise—which, of course, we want to do so well that the Germans should be ashamed of themselves.) Julius Bab to Fritz Wisten, June 9, 1933, Akademie der Künste (Berlin), Fritz Wisten Archiv, 74/68/996; quoted after Barbara Müller-Wesemann, *Theater als geistiger Widerstand: Der Jüdische Kulturbund in Hamburg* (Stuttgart: M & P, 1996), 375.
9. Quoted after Tina Frühauf, *The Organ and Its Music in German-Jewish Culture* (New York: Oxford University Press, 2012), 148.
10. Preface to the 1937 edition of Joseph Roth, *The Wandering Jews: The Classic Portrait Of a Vanished People*, trans. Michael Hofmann (New York: W.W. Norton & Company, 2001), 130 (1st ed.: *Juden auf Wanderschaft*, Berlin: Die Schmiede, 1927).
11. "Da sehen Sie, daß dieselben Leute, die auf vielen Gebieten die erste Geige gespielt haben, das Getto *akzeptieren*—die Idee des Gettos und ihre Ausführung. . . . Man sperrt sie ein; man pfercht sie in Judentheater mit vier gelben Flecken vorn und hinten, und sie haben . . . nur einen Ehrgeiz: 'Nun warden wir ihnen mal zeigen, daß wir das bessere Theater haben!' " Kurt Tucholsky to Arnold Zweig, Zurich, December 15, 1935, in Kurt Tucholsky, *Politische*

Briefe, ed. Fritz J. Raddatz (Reinbek/Hamburg: Rohwolt, 1990), 118 (spelling and italicization according to the original); translation quoted after Saul Friedländer, *Nazi Germany and the Jews*, vol. 1: *The Years of Persecution, 1933–1939* (New York: HarperCollins, 2007), 172.

12. "Das Ghetto ist kein geographisch umgrenzter Bezirk mehr, wenigstens nicht in dem Sinne, wie es das Mittelalter kannte. Das Ghetto, das ist die 'Welt.'" Joachim Prinz, "Das Leben ohne Nachbarn: Versuch einer ersten Analyse—Ghetto 1935," *Jüdische Rundschau: Allgemeine jüdische Zeitung* 40, nos. 31–32 (April 17, 1935): 3.

13. Benjamin Ravid, "All Ghettos Were Jewish Quarters, but Not All Jewish Quarters Were Ghettos," *Jewish Culture and History* 10, nos. 2–3 (2008): 5.

14. Jürgen Heyde and Katrin Steffen, "The 'Ghetto' as Topographic Reality and Discursive Metaphor," *Jahrbuch Simon-Dubnow-Institut* 4 (2005): 423–430. The debate on the distinction between "place" and "space" is now quite differentiated. In what follows, "place" is understood as a static structure with a physical materiality; "space" can be imagined, symbolic or metaphorical, medial or narrative and can be created, changed or eliminated by discursive or performative actions (though this ideal-typical distinction is often met with overlap in reality). For an overview of the debate see Stephan Günzel, *Raum: Eine kulturwissenschaftliche Einführung* (Bielefeld: transcript, 2017), 45–60.

15. Daniel B. Schwartz, *Ghetto: The History of a Word* (Cambridge, MA, London: Harvard University Press, 2019), 5; Bryan Cheyette, *The Ghetto: A Very Short Introduction* (New York: Oxford University Press, 2020), 2.

16. See Susanne Rau, *History, Space, and Place* (London, New York: Routledge, 2019), 109–110. By perception I understand the cognitive processing of sensory impressions.

17. Karl Schlögel, *In Space We Read Time: On the History of Civilization and Geopolitics* (New York: Bard Graduate Center, 2016), xviii.

18. For a comprehensive and recent overview on the persecution of Jews in the culture sector, see Jörg Osterloh, *"Ausschaltung der Juden und des jüdischen Geistes": Nationalsozialistische Kulturpolitik 1920–1945* (Frankfurt am Main: Campus, 2020).

19. See Volker Dahm, "Kulturelles und geistiges Leben," in *Die Juden in Deutschland 1933–1945: Leben unter nationalsozialistischer Herrschaft*, ed. Wolfgang Benz and Volker Dahm (Munich: C.H. Beck, 1993), 75–267.

20. See also Judith Freise and Joachim Martini, *Jüdische Musikerinnen und Musiker in Frankfurt 1933–1942: Musik als Form geistigen Widerstands* (Frankfurt am Main: Otto Lembeck, 1990); Thomas Schinköth, *Jüdische Musiker in Leipzig 1855–1945* (Altenburg: Kamprad, 1994); Rainer Licht, "Hawa naschira—Auf laßt uns singen! Jüdisches Musikleben in Hamburg 1933–1945," in *Zündende Lieder—verbrannte Musik: Folgen des Nazifaschismus für Hamburger Musiker und Musikerinnen*, ed. Peter Petersen (Hamburg: VSA, 1995), 9–22.

21. Rebecca Rovit, "Assessing Theatre Under Duress in National Socialism: Tracking Theatre Repertoire in the Jewish Kulturbund and in the Camps," in *Theater unter NS-Herrschaft: Theatre under Pressure*, ed. Brigitte Dalinger and Veronika Zangl (Göttingen: Vandenhoeck & Ruprecht, 2018), 18; on the spatial influences of exile on musicians, see Anna Langenbruch, *Topographien musikalischen Handelns im Pariser Exil: Eine Histoire croisée des Exils deutschsprachiger Musikerinnen und Musiker in Paris 1933–1939* (Hildesheim: Olms, 2014).

22. Regarding the League's venues in Berlin, see Fritsch-Vivié, *Gegen alle Widerstände*, 84–87; regarding, for example, the technical equipment of the Conventgarden, a concert hall in Hamburg, see Müller-Wesemann, *Theater als geistiger Widerstand*, 209–212.

23. For recent inquiries into this subject, see Maria Kublitz-Kramer, "Die Aktivitäten des Jüdischen Kulturbunds in Ostwestfalen," in *Echolos: Klangwelten verfolgter Musikerinnen in der NS-Zeit*, ed. Christine Rhode-Jüchtern and Maria Kublitz-Kramer (Bielefeld: Aisthesis, 2004), 127–142; Dana Smith, "Female Musicians and 'Jewish Music' in the Jewish Kulturbund in Bavaria, 1934–38," in *Dreams of Germany: Musical Imaginaries from the Concert Hall to the Dance Floor*, ed. Neil Gregor and Thomas Irvine (New York: Berghahn, 2019), 123–144.

24. Schlögel, *In Space We Read Time*, xix.

25. "Das Bedenken aber, das so viele deutsch-jüdisch denkende Menschen immer wieder äußern, ist dies: daß es im Sinn der heute herrschenden Rassenlehre liegt, die deutschen Juden in ein geistiges Ghetto zu bringen. Und eins nur hilft dagegen: sich den tätigen Anteil an der deutschen Kultur immer aufs neue zu erkämpfen." Hans Samter, "Der Kulturbund—ein Träger unserer Zukunft?," *Der Schild* 13, no. 2 (January 26, 1934): n.p.

26. Katrin Steffen, "Connotations of Exclusion: 'Ostjuden,' 'Ghettos,' and Other Markings," *Jahrbuch Simon-Dubnow-Institut* 4 (2005): 459.

27. Steven Aschheim, *Brothers and Strangers: The East European Jew in German and German Jewish Consciousness, 1800–1923* (Madison, London: University of Wisconsin Press, 1999), 9.

28. Herbert Freeden, "Jüdischer Kulturbund ohne 'jüdische' Kultur," in *Geschlossene Vorstellung*, ed. Akademie der Künste (Berlin: Hentrich, 1992), 56.

29. "Wir wollen im lebendigen Zusammenhang bleiben mit den großen Kulturgütern Deutschlands und der Welt." Julius Bab, "Kulturarbeit der deutscher Juden," *Der Morgen* 9, no. 5 (November 1933): 326.

30. "Schon gelingt [das Werben für unser Theater] bei diesem, bei jenem, der gehört hat, daß es in diesem sogenannten geistigen Ghetto mehr Arbeit und fruchtbares Wirken geben kann als draußen im Betrieb provinzialer Theater." Kurt Singer, "Was tut uns not? Gedanken zum ersten Geburtstag des Kulturbunds," *C.V.-Zeitung* 13, no. 39 (September 28, 1934): n.p.

31. See Rebecca Rovit, *The Jewish Kulturbund Theatre Company*, 55–77; and Dana Smith, *The Jewish Kulturbund in Bavaria, 1934–1938: Art and Jewish Self-Representation under National Socialism* (PhD diss., Queen University of London, 2015), 186–191; https:// qmro.qmul.ac.uk/xmlui/bitstream/handle/123456789/27224/Smith_Dana_PhD_040815. pdf?sequence=1&isAllowed=y (accessed January 21, 2021).

32. Ludwig Davidsohn, "Kulturfragen: Antwort an Kurt Singer," *Jüdisch-liberale Zeitung* 14, no. 19 (March 6, 1934): n.p.

33. "Bund der Kultur," ibid.: n.p; the musicologist Ludwig Misch particularly emphasized the Jewish background of the libretto, see Mi. [Ludwig Misch], "'Figaros Hochzeit' im Berliner Theater," *Jüdische Rundschau* 38, no. 92 (November 17, 1933): 815.

34. See Yehoyakim Cochavi, "Kultur- und Bildungsarbeit der deutschen Juden 1933–1941: Antwort auf die Verfolgung durch das NS-Regime," *Neue Sammlung* 26 (1986): 396.

35. See Hirsch, *A Jewish Orchestra*, 42.

36. Freeden, "Jüdischer Kulturbund," 63.

37. See Yehoyakim Cochavi, "Georg Kareski's Nomination as Head of the Kulturbund: The Gestapo's First Attempt—and Last Failure—to Impose a Jewish Leadership," *Leo Baeck Institute Yearbook* 34 (1989): 227–246.

38. Hirsch, *A Jewish Orchestra*, 30.

39. Unless stated otherwise, the following remarks on the conference are based on ibid., 47–55.

40. "Die Kulturbünde sollen und müssen echte jüdische Musik, d.h. wertvolle Liturgie und Volkslied pflegen." Arno Nadel, "Jüdische liturgische Musik und jüdisches Volkslied," in Akademie der Künste, *Geschlossene Vorstellung*, 285.

41. "Selbst in . . . der ältesten deutschen-hebräischen Notenhandschrift . . . haben die echten jüdischen Motive und Melodien östlichen Charakter." Arno Nadel, "Jüdische liturgische Musik und jüdisches Volkslied," in Akademie der Künste, *Geschlossene Vorstellung*, 284.

42. Kurt Singer, "Abschlussrede," in Akademie der Künste, *Geschlossene Vorstellung*, 296–297.

43. "Das musikalische Preisausschreiben," *Jüdische Rundschau* 42, no. 35 (May 4, 1937): 5.

44. See Hirsch, *A Jewish Orchestra*, 54.

45. Michael Wildt, "Einleitung," in *Die Judenpolitik des SD 1935 bis 1938: Eine Dokumentation*, ed. Michael Wildt (Munich: Oldenbourg Wissenschaftsverlag, 1995), 16.

46. See Dahm, "Kulturelles und geistiges Leben," 120; and Rovit, *The Jewish Kulturbund Theatre Company*, 119.

47. Schwartz, *Ghetto*, 4.

48. Ibid., 137.

49. "Das neue Ghetto ist ein Leben in den vier Wänden." Joachim Prinz, "Zur Analyse der Zeit," *Jüdische Rundschau* 40, no. 89 (1935): 1.

50. See Tobias Reichard, "Eine 'abgeschlossene Sache'? Zu einer Topographie jüdischen Musiklebens im NS-Staat am Beispiel Münchens," in *Jüdische Musik im süddeutschen Raum / Mapping Jewish Music in Southern Germany*, ed. Claus Bockmaier and Tina Frühauf (Munich: Allitera, 2021), 54–57.

51. See Sonja Miltenberger, *Jüdisches Leben am Kurfürstendamm* (Berlin: Text-Verlag Edition, 2011).

52. "Der Machtstaat beginnt auf der Straße. Wer die Straße erobern kann, kann auch einmal den Staat erobern." Joseph Goebbels, *Wege ins Dritte Reich* (Munich: Eher, 1927), 28, quoted after Gerhard Paul, *Aufstand der Bilder: Die NS-Propaganda vor 1933* (Bonn: J.H.W. Dietz Nachf., 1990), 133.

53. "In alter Gewohnheit wird noch immer der Unsitte gehuldigt, nach dem Verlassen des Gotteshauses auf der Freitreppe, im Vorhof oder gar auf dem Gehsteig sich zu sammeln, um Begrüßung oder Unterhaltungen zu pflegen. Es wird wohl jeder Verständnis dafür aufbringen, wenn wir angesichts der Zeitumstände nachdrücklich um Abstellung dieser üblen Gepflogenheit bitten." "Mahnung," *Nürnberg-Fürther Israelitisches Gemeindeblatt* 13, no. 3 (May 1, 1933): 38; quoted after Jacob Borut, "Jüdisches Leben in Franken während des Nationalsozialismus," in *Die Juden in Franken*, ed. Michael Brenner and Andreas Heusler (Munich: Oldenbourg, 2012), 227.

54. "Wir richten . . . an die Gemeindmitglieder die dringende Bitte, das Gotteshaus während des Gottesdienstes so wenig wie möglich zu verlassen, bei Beendigung des Gottesdienstes ebenfalls jegliche Ansammlung zu vermeiden und in kürzester Zeit die Umgebung des Gotteshauses freizumachen. Ein Zusammentreffen wäre, wenn überhaupt nicht in unmittelbarer Nähe, sondern an etwas entfernteren Orten zu vereinbaren." Israelitische Kultusgemeinde München, "Bekanntmachung über die Gottesdienste an den hohen Feiertagen," *Bayerische Israelitische Gemeindezeitung* 9, no. 18 (September 15, 1933): 289.

55. "Heute wie jederzeit ist äußerste Zurückhaltung die selbstverständliche Pflicht eines jeden verantwortungsbewußten Juden. Er meidet die großen Gast- und Vergnügungsstätten, er unterläßt überflüssige Promenaden, er zieht den Aufenthalt im eigenen Hause vor." Israelitische Kultusgemeinde München, "Der Vorstand der Israelitischen Kultusgemeinde München," *Bayerische Israelitische Gemeindezeitung* 11, no. 16 (August 15, 1935): 347.

56. See Sven Reichardt, "Formen faschistischer Gewalt: Faschistische Kampfbünde in Italien und Deutschland nach dem Ersten Weltkrieg—Eine typologische Deutung ihrer Gewaltpropaganda während der Bewegungsphase des Faschismus," *Sociologus* 51, nos. 1–2 (2001): 57.

57. See Dirk Walter, *Antisemitische Kriminalität und Gewalt: Judenfeindschaft in der Weimarer Republik* (Bonn: J.H.W. Dietz Nachf., 1999), 104.

58. Emanuel Kirschner, *Erinnerungen aus meinem Leben, Streben und Wirken*, unpublished typoscript, Munich 1937, Leo Baeck Institute Archives, New York, LBINY, ME361, 216.

59. See Walter, *Antisemitische Kriminalität*, 102.

60. See Miron, " 'Lately, Almost Constantly, Everything Seems Small to Me,' " 124.

61. "Wir hatten unsere eigene Öffentlichkeit." Trumpet player Shabtai Petrushka (Siegmund Friedmann), in Geisel and Broder, *Premiere und Pogrom*, 189.

62. For overview see Julius H. Schoeps, Joachim Schlör, eds., *Bilder der Judenfeindschaft: Antisemitismus—Vorurteile und Mythen* (Augsburg: Bechtermünz, 1999).

63. See Schwartz, *Ghetto*, 136. The use of the phrase "Lärm wie in einer Judenschule" during the Nazi era is documented in Marcel Reich-Ranicki, *Mein Leben* (Munich: Pantheon, 2012), 76.

64. See Dietmar Süß, "Gewalt und Gewalterfahrung im 'Dritten Reich,' " in *München und der Nationalsozialismus*, ed. Winfried Nerdinger (Munich: C.H. Beck, 2015), 427–434.

65. "Nicht aus innerem Bekenntnis, nicht aus Treue zur eigenen Gemeinschaft, nicht aus Stolz auf eine großartige Vergangenheit und Menschheitsleistung, sondern durch den Aufdruck des roten Zettels und des gelben Flecks standen sie plötzlich als Juden da." Robert Weltsch, "Tragt ihn mit Stolz, den gelben Fleck!," *Jüdische Rundschau* 38, no. 27 (April 4, 1933): 131.

66. See Hannah Ahlheim, *"Deutsche, kauft nicht bei Juden!": Antisemitismus und politischer Boykott in Deutschland 1924 bis 1935* (Göttingen: Wallstein, 2011), 8.

67. See Pamela M. Potter, "Jewish Music and German Science," in *Jewish Musical Modernism, Old and New*, ed. Philip V. Bohlman (Chicago: University of Chicago Press, 2008), 81–101.

68. Theophil Stengel and Herbert Gerigk, eds., *Lexikon der Juden in der Musik: Mit einem Titelverzeichnis jüdischer Werke, zusammengestellt im Auftrag der Reichsleitung der NSDAP auf Grund behördlicher, parteiamtlich geprüfter Unterlagen* (Berlin: Bernhard Hahnefeld, 1940), 8–9.

69. See Tobias Reichard, "Verfolgungsinstrument Schwarze Liste: Antisemitische Musikpolitik im Zeichen der 'Achse Berlin-Rom,' " *Quellen und Forschungen aus italienischen Archiven und Bibliotheken* 100 (2020): 114–133.

70. See Ahlheim, *"Deutsche, kauft nicht bei Juden!"*, 184–204.

71. See Michael Wildt, *Volksgemeinschaft als Selbstermächtigung. Gewalt gegen Juden in der deutschen Provinz 1919 bis 1939* (Hamburg: Hamburger Edition: 2007), 93–94.

72. See Hanna Bernheim, *"History of my Life": Der Rückblick einer deutschen Jüdin auf ihr Leben vor der Emigration 1939*, ed. Benigna Schönhagen and Wilfried Setzler (Darmstadt: Theiss, 2014), 141–143.

73. "Die verantwortlichen Leute im Kulturbund hatten Angst, daß niemand kommen würde, auf den Straßen war die SA . . ." Ernest Lenart in Geisel and Broder, *Premiere und Pogrom*, 243.

74. See Geisel and Broder, *Premiere und Pogrom*, 91–93.

75. For further details and context on this concert, see Reichard, "Eine 'abgeschlossene Sache'?," 39–40.

76. "Es war das erste Mal, daß ein Streichquartett in unserer Synagoge erklang; und man muß gleich als erste erfreuliche Tatsache feststellen: Die Akustik ist ganz ausgezeichnet. Die Heiligkeit des Raumes verhilft aber auch dazu, sich 'andächtig' den gebotenen Kunstgenüssen hinzugeben. Wie eng sind doch Religion und Kunst miteinander verbunden." I. Z., "Synagogenkonzert des Hebräikon-Quartetts (Kroyt-Quartett) am 10. Dezember," *Bayerische Israelitische Gemeindezeitung* 9, no. 24 (December 15, 1933): 403.

77. Herbert F. Peyser, "Germany's Jewish Cultural League," *New York Times*, December 10, 1933.

78. Interestingly, the actor Kurt Katsch, who had played the main role in the League's very first performance of Lessing's *Nathan der Weise* a few weeks earlier, left an account quite similar to that of Peyser (although in his case, the play had a very clear religious meaning): "Das war kein Theater mehr, das war ein Erlebnis, das in seiner Inbrunst etwas Religiöses hatte. Man glaubte, in einem Tempel, nicht auf einer Bühne zu stehen." (This was no theater anymore; it was an experience that in his fervor had something religious. One had the feeling to be in a Temple rather than on a stage.) Kurt Katsch, *Memoirs: From Ghetto to Ghetto*, unpublished typoscript, undated, LBINY, ME419, 197–198.

79. "Andererseits hatte der Kulturbund auch eine negative Seite, denn weil er unser ganzes Leben war, haben wir gar nicht so genau mitbekommen, was draußen los war." Alice Levie, wife of the League's secretary Werner Levie, in Geisel and Broder, *Premiere und Pogrom*, 158.

80. Schwartz, *Ghetto*, 140.

81. See Gila Flam, *Singing for Survival: Songs of the Lodz Ghetto, 1940–45* (Urbana: University of Illinois Press; 1992); and Shirley Gilbert, *Music in the Holocaust: Confronting Life in the Nazi Ghettos and Camps* (Oxford: Oxford University Press, 2005).

82. See Friedländer, *Nazi Germany and the Jews*, 1:66; similarly, Bernd Sponheuer, "Musik auf einer 'kulturellen und physischen Insel': Musik als Überlebensmittel im Jüdischen Kulturbund 1933–1941," in *Musik in der Emigration 1933–1945: Verfolgung, Vertreibung, Vernichtung*, ed. Horst Weber (Stuttgart: J.B. Metzler: 1994), 110; Lionel Richard, "Die Jüdische Kultur unter nationalsozialistischer Kontrolle," in *Das "Dritte Reich" und die Musik*, ed. Stiftung Schloss Neuhardenberg, Cité de la musique, Paris (Berlin: Nicolaische Verlags-Buchhandlung, 2006), 195.

83. H. G. Adler, *Theresienstadt 1941–1945: Das Antlitz einer Zwangsgemeinschaft* (Tübingen: J.C.B. Mohr 1944), 579–585. ". . . in der Tat erscheint der Kunstbetrieb in Theresienstadt in gewisser Weise wie eine Fortsetzung des Kulturbundes – wenn auch in einem Zerrspiegel." Freeden, *Jüdisches Theater in Nazideutschland*, 7.

84. "Mit dieser . . . Gesamtorganisation waren die Konturen einer total erfaßten Zwangsgemeinschaft entstanden, deren Vollendung H[ans].G[ünther]. Adler am Beispiel von Theresienstadt beschreibt." Eike Geisel, "Ein Reich, ein Ghetto: Zwei Karrieren," in Geisel and Broder, *Premiere und Pogrom*, 319; Geisel even went so far as to compare the role of the League's leader, Kurt Singer, to that of a Jewish Elder (Judenältester), a term that described the leaders of the Jewish-led and Nazi-controlled self-administration in the ghettos, ibid., 320. For a more differentiated view, see Rebecca Rovit, "Cultural Ghettoization and Theater During the Holocaust," *Holocaust and Genocide Studies* 19, no. 3 (2005): 459–486.

85. It is disputed whether Terezín constituted a ghetto or a camp. It was originally conceived as a transit camp, but was never subordinate to the central administration of the camps

(SS-Wirtschafts-Verwaltungshauptamt) and, unlike other camps, had no specific mission of mass extinction. Also, everyday life was probably more similar to that of a ghetto. Yet, due to its unique function as a propaganda tool, the regime euphemistically referred to it as "Jewish settlement" to cover the true function as a transitional site of deportation; see Dan Michman, *The Emergence of Jewish Ghettos During the Holocaust* (New York: Cambridge University Press, 2011), 134–137; *United States Holocaust Memorial Museum Encyclopedia of Camps and Ghettos, 1933–1945*, vol. 2, part A: *Ghettos in German-Occupied Eastern Europe*, ed. Martin Dean, Mel Hecker (Bloomington: Indiana University Press, 2012), 180–184. On musical activities, see Amy Lynn Wlodarski, "Musical Memories of Terezín in Transnational Perspective," in Frühauf and Hirsch, *Dislocated Memories*, 57–72.

86. Fritsch-Vivié, *Gegen alle Widerstände*, 159.

87. Avraham Barkai, "Das letzte Kapitel," in *Deutsch-jüdische Geschichte in der Neuzeit. IV: Aufbruch und Zerstörung 1918–1945*, ed. Avraham Barkai and Paul Mendes-Flohr (Munich: C.H. Beck, 1997), 346.

88. About 84,000 other former Terezín inmates were deported and killed in Auschwitz and Treblinka; see Friedrich Geiger, "Deutsche Musik und deutsche Gewalt: Zweiter Weltkrieg und Holocaust," in *Geschichte der Musik im 20. Jahrhundert*, vol. 2: *1925–1945*, ed. Albrecht Riethmüller (Laaber: Laaber Verlag, 2006), 261.

89. The entire passage reads as follows: "Die Tätigkeit der jüdischen Kulturbünde, die sich besonders in den Großstädten bemerkbar macht, führt die Juden langsam in ein geistiges Ghetto, das ihm [sic!] als Lebensform seit Jahrtausenden durchaus vertraut ist." (The activities of the Jewish Culture Leagues, which are particularly noticeable in the big cities, are slowly leading the Jews into a spiritual ghetto, a way of life that has been familiar to them for thousands of years); Report of the SD-Hauptamt II 112, Berlin, April 8, 1937; quoted after *Die Juden in den geheimen NS-Stimmungsberichten 1933–1945*, ed. Otto Dov Kulka and Eberhard Jäckel (Düsseldorf: Droste, 2004), 227.

90. See Michman, *The Emergence of Jewish Ghettos*, 40–41.

91. Schwartz, *Ghetto*, 137–138.

92. See Rovit, *The Jewish Kulturbund Theatre Company*, 202.

93. See Gilbert, *Music in the Holocaust*, 42–43, and 61.

94. See ibid., 117.

95. Michman, *The Emergence of Jewish Ghettos*, 74–75.

96. The Jewish artistic activities at the Joodse Schouwburg in Amsterdam between August 1941 and July 1942 were a derivative copy of the League, but had no administrative connection with it; see Eike Geisel, "Da capo in Holland," in Akademie der Künste, *Geschlossene Vorstellung*, 189–214.

97. Bab, "Kulturarbeit der deutscher Juden," 326.

98. Flam, *Singing for Survival*, 13; and Wlodarski, "Musical Memories of Terezín," 69.

99. Rovit, *The Jewish Kulturbund Theatre Company*, 61.

100. Benjamin Ravid, "All Ghettos Were Jewish Quarters, but Not All Jewish Quarters Were Ghettos," *Jewish Culture and History* 10, nos. 2–3 (2008): 5–24.

101. On September 9, 1936, after Kulturbund officials had publicly distanced themselves from criticism of the regime from abroad—which was in the interest of their own self-preservation—Klemperer irreconcilably wrote in his diary: "The Jewish Cultural Leagues, they should be hanged." Victor Klemperer, *I Shall Bear Witness, 1933–1945* (New York: Random House, 1998), 1:189.

SELECT BIBLIOGRAPHY

Akademie der Künste, ed. *Geschlossene Vorstellung: Der Jüdische Kulturbund in Deutschland 1933–1941*. Berlin: Hentrich, 1992.

Borchard, Beatrix, and Heidy Zimmermann, eds. *Musikwelten—Lebenswelten: Jüdische Identitätssuche in der deutschen Musikkultur*. Cologne: Böhlau, 2009.

Brinkmann, Reinhold, and Christoph Wolff, eds. *Driven into Paradise: The Musical Migration from Nazi Germany to the United States*. Berkeley: University of California Press, 1999.

Dahm, Annkatrin. *Der Topos der Juden: Studien zur Geschichte des Antisemitismus im deutschsprachigen Musikschrifttum*. Göttingen: Vandenhoeck & Ruprecht, 2007.

Dahm, Volker. "Kulturelles und geistiges Leben." In *Die Juden in Deutschland 1933–1945: Leben unter nationalsozialistischer Herrschaft*, edited by Wolfgang Benz and Volker Dahm, 75–267. Munich: C.H. Beck, 1993.

Flam, Gila. *Singing for Survival: Songs of the Lodz Ghetto, 1940–45*. Urbana: University of Illinois Press, 1992.

Freeden, Herbert. *Jüdisches Theater in Nazideutschland*. Berlin: Ullstein, 1985 (1st ed. 1964).

Fritsch-Vivié, Gabriele. *Gegen alle Widerstände: Der Jüdische Kulturbund 1933–1941—Fakten, Daten, Analysen, biographische Notizen und Erinnerungen*. Berlin: Hentrich & Hentrich, 2013.

Frühauf, Tina. *The Organ and Its Music in German-Jewish Culture*. New York: Oxford University Press, 2012.

Geisel, Eike, and Henryk M. Broder, eds. *Premiere und Pogrom: Der Jüdische Kulturbund 1933–1941—Texte und Bilder*. Berlin: Siedler, 1992.

Gilbert, Shirley. *Music in the Holocaust: Confronting Life in the Nazi Ghettos and Camps*. Oxford: Oxford University Press, 2005.

Hirsch, Lily E. "Germany's Commemoration of the Jüdische Kulturbund." In *Dislocated Memories: Jews, Music, and Postwar German Culture*, edited by Tina Frühauf and Lily E. Hirsch: 243–264. New York: Oxford University Press, 2014.

Hirsch, Lily E. *A Jewish Orchestra in Nazi Germany. Musical Politics and the Berlin Jewish Culture League*. Ann Arbor: University of Michigan Press, 2010.

Levi, Erik, ed. *The Impact of Nazism on Twentieth-Century Music*. Vienna: Böhlau, 2014.

Michman, Dan. *The Emergence of Jewish Ghettos During the Holocaust*. New York: Cambridge University Press, 2011.

Müller-Wesemann, Barbara. *Theater als geistiger Widerstand: Der Jüdische Kulturbund in Hamburg*. Stuttgart: M & P, 1996.

Reichard, Tobias. "Eine 'abgeschlossene Sache'? Zu einer Topographie jüdischen Musiklebens im NS-Staat am Beispiel Münchens." In *Jüdische Musik im süddeutschen Raum / Mapping Jewish Music in Southern Germany*, edited by Claus Bockmaier and Tina Frühauf, 33–60. Munich: Allitera, 2021.

Rovit, Rebecca. *The Jewish Kulturbund Theatre Company in Nazi Berlin*. Iowa City: University of Iowa Press, 2012.

Rovit, Rebecca. "Assessing Theatre Under Duress in National Socialism: Tracking Theatre Repertoire in the Jewish Kulturbund and in the Camps." In *Theater unter NS-Herrschaft: Theatre under Pressure*, edited by Brigitte Dalinger and Veronika Zangl, 17–32. Göttingen: Vandenhoeck & Ruprecht, 2018.

Rovit, Rebecca, and Alvin Goldfarb, eds. *Theatrical Performance During the Holocaust: Texts, Documents, Memoirs*. Baltimore, MD: Johns Hopkins University Press, 1999.

Schwartz, Daniel B. *Ghetto: The History of a Word*. Cambridge, MA: Harvard University Press, 2019.

Stompor, Stephan. *Jüdisches Musik- und Theaterleben unter dem NS-Staat*. Hannover: Europäisches Zentrum für Jüdische Musik, 2001.

Weber, Horst, ed. *Musik in der Emigration 1933–1945: Verfolgung, Vertreibung, Vernichtung*. Stuttgart: J.B. Metzler: 1994.

PART IV

STAGE—בימה

12

HASIDIC CANTORS "OUT OF CONTEXT"

Venues of Contemporary Cantorial Performance

JEREMIAH LOCKWOOD

IF a cantor sings too much *khazones*, he is at risk of being kicked "outta there." This is what Yaakov "Yanky" Lemmer (1983–), who has served the Modern Orthodox Lincoln Square Synagogue in Manhattan since 2013, asserted in an interview in July of 2017. Lemmer was born into the Belz community of Brooklyn, New York. As a child he listened to records of early twentieth-century cantors with his father, an avid fan of cantorial music, and went with him to hear services led by internationally famed cantors such as the Hungarian-born Israeli cantor Moshe Stern (1935–). Lemmer describes himself as having been the only "oddball" among his cohort of friends who was interested in cantorial music when growing up. Indeed, he committed to a repertoire that was out of step with current tastes. Lemmer is one of the leading stars of the current generation of cantors and known for his interpretations of classic cantorial records. But in his prestigious pulpit position at the Lincoln Square Synagogue in Manhattan, he is limited by local tastes and customs, which prevent him from employing the historical performance practices he spent years developing. Instead, many of the musically marked moments in the services he leads focus on participatory music in a folk-pop vein.

A similar case is David Reich (1981–), a cantor with a more modest public career than Lemmer; as an amateur singer and keyboard accompanist, he performs at private parties within the Satmar community into which he was born. David expresses a chastising attitude toward what he perceived as a general lack of interest in old styles of cantorial music; this attitude is pervasive in his scene of cantors and cantorial music fans:

> Davening has become very routine. There's very little place for creativity. They might get someone to *daven* for an *omud* [lead prayer at the reader's lectern] . . . But being too creative is frowned upon. Most of the people don't necessarily appreciate khazones. People don't have the patience. It requires you to get in touch with certain

things in yourself that some people aren't comfortable with. They'd rather just sing melodies, easy stuff. This is deep.[1]

Lemmer and Reich are two examples of a cohort of young male singers born into Hasidic communities in Brooklyn in the 1980s who connect to what they call *khazones*, a Yiddish term for hazanuth that connotes not only cantorial performance but also a periodization that foregrounds what has come to be known as the cantorial golden age. The conception of the golden age is framed around the work of eastern European–born cantors active in the first three decades of the twentieth century who were stars of the emerging record industry and whose careers embraced synagogue prayer leading, recording for commercial record labels and performance in secular venues. After 1945, khazones experienced a diminished footprint as a popular-culture phenomenon in the United States. Prayer leading by "star" cantorial soloists as a model for the organization of synagogue ritual became increasingly rare as new worship music trends emerged. From the perspective of young Hasidic cantors who are enamored with the mythologized figure of the star cantor and invested in cultivating the musical skills and repertoires heard on early cantorial records, the contemporary synagogue is a limiting musical environment for the kind of liturgical music they love and have trained to sing.

This chapter focuses on three "out of context" sites of cantorial performance—the concert stage, streamed video, and *kumzits* (music making party)—that afford Hasidic cantors opportunities to pursue their aesthetic aspirations in venues that are not specific to Jewish liturgical music. For at least the past two centuries, cantors have performed outside of the synagogue for a variety of reasons, including seeking economic gain, representing the Jewish collective to non-Jews, or in pursuit of opportunity to fulfill musical desires and career ambitions that embrace the aesthetics of music worlds beyond the liturgical. While these motivations are still relevant, present-day Hasidic cantors have a more pressing concern about how to function as a cantor in the musical form they consider to be uniquely desirable.

In general, golden-age cantorial repertoires are not the stylistic norm in contemporary synagogue prayer leading. Performing outside of the synagogue allows Hasidic cantors to sing the repertoire that they have studied. Whereas cantors a century ago sang in concerts or on records in a style that was developed within the context of worship, Hasidic cantors today have learned and developed cantorial aesthetics largely by listening to old records as a mediating source. Unlike their early-twentieth century predecessors, for Hasidic cantors, "out of context" performances are the primary site for their work. Indeed, for some of the most talented singers, concerts, internet videos, and parties are the only forums available for performing their repertoire.

The phenomenon of Hasidic singers performing in the early twentieth-century recorded cantorial style does not reflect normative musical practices but rather emerged relatively recently, around the beginning of the twenty-first century.[2] As such, the cantors strike unusual and occasionally controversial figures in their birth communities. Self-presentation in the Hasidic community is governed by a conception of *tsniut*, or modesty, that is interpreted to require sartorial conformity and a self-effacing approach to personal comportment that stresses communal values.[3] The sensual press-photo images and assertive performance personas presented by cantorial record stars of the 1920s are strikingly different from contemporary Hasidic behavioral norms and even today, a century later, sometimes attract negative attention from conservative voices in ultra-Orthodox communities.[4] Hasidic cantors are buffeted on two sides by obstacles to finding sites of performance and connecting to audiences—on the one hand, their work is not tailored to the musical life or social norms of their birth community, and on the other, few synagogues hire cantors who sing in the golden-age style.

This chapter considers the work of a half dozen Hasidic cantors working out of New York City and is informed by an international scene of several dozen comparable ultra-Orthodox artists working primarily in Brooklyn and Montreal, as well as in Europe and Israel. Through ethnographic observation and historical analysis of concerts, internet videos of cantorial performances, and private home presentations, this chapter illuminates the ways in which Hasidic cantors are able to articulate their musical aesthetics. By developing performance careers in venues outside of the institutions of Jewish religious life, they are able to hone their musical careers around a form of expressive culture that poses a challenge to the role played by music in the Hasidic community and in other contemporary Orthodox communities. Rather than accentuating the collective through a broadly understood and popular music form, singing khazones affords Hasidic cantors an avenue for non-conforming self-expression. "Out of context" performances of cantorial music foreground a conception of cantorial music as an aesthetic experience with its own values distinct from the life of ritual in the synagogue.

SETTING THE STAGE: CANTORS AS ARTISTS IN THE TWENTIETH CENTURY

The frequently invoked concept "cantorial music of the golden age" refers to the repertoire of a cohort of star cantors active between the 1900s and 1930s who worked across the transnational Jewish world, in Europe and the United States. The key figures representing this style—among them Gershon Sirota (1874–1943), Zavel Kwartin (1874–1952), and Yossele Rosenblatt (1882–1933)—were born in eastern Europe and worked in elite urban synagogues throughout eastern and central Europe before emigrating to the United States. While they maintained positions as cantors, often well paid, they gave concerts, appeared on the radio, and recorded for major record companies. Their records sold in the hundreds of thousands. Through newspaper criticism in the Jewish press, and later through reissue LP liner notes, a "standard" cantorial biography emerged that highlights the aesthetic and commercial achievement of cantors who provided continuity, spiritual and otherwise, in the context of trans-Atlantic migration. However, while cantors in Europe and the United States sang in synagogue and on stage, only a small proportion of talented and ambitious singers appeared on records.

The primary sound of cantorial music found on the interwar-period records is commonly known, for lack of a better term, as a "non-metrical" setting of prayer texts, usually featuring a sizeable ambitus. Cantors repurposed the term *recitative*, borrowed from opera, to refer to their compositions in a heavily ornamented vocal style.[5] The style of cantorial prayer leading in the synagogue associated with star cantors was characterized by extended soloist compositions utilizing an idiomatic vocabulary of vocal techniques, including coloratura, ornamentation, and vocal gestures such as the *krekhts*, or sob, that thematize emotion through noises suggestive of the sound of shedding tears.[6] Oftentimes cantors were themselves composers or skilled improvisers. Cantorial vocal practices specific to the synagogue that were understood by Jewish audiences to represent a folkloric style were synthesized with elements of opera, which was undergoing its own popularization on record. Cantorial music was associated with a diaspora nationalist consciousness emerging in the same period. The well-known Russian-born socialist activist and author Chaim Zhitlowsky (1865–1943) included cantorial music in a list of Jewish communal matters that "reveals the ideals of the people's culture."[7] The conception of cantorial music as a distillation of Jewish historical experiences, especially related to persecution and displacement, is frequently cited in the writings of eastern European cantors working in the United States.[8] Numerous cantors moved over the course of their own lifetimes between semi-rural and urban environments; they drew on their own experiences hearing small-town prayer leaders as the basis for liturgical music that offered a memorialization of the Jewish past. As recording star cantors such as Kwartin and Samuel Vigoda (1895–1990) highlight in their memoirs, the work of eastern European cantors offered an oppositional response to the nineteenth-century urban Jewish choral music that was influenced by European classical music conventions.[9] At the same time, the new cantorial sound emerging around the turn of the twentieth century was highly influenced by the formal innovations of the choral synagogue repertoires that most professional cantors had studied.[10] As Mark Slobin has argued, the Jewish liturgical music of Europe must be understood as multiple, consisting of contrasting styles and ideologies that complemented and at times conflicted with one another.[11]

Cantorial performance outside of the synagogue has played an important part in the economy of Jewish sacred music since at least the nineteenth century. The Viennese cantor Salomon Sulzer (1804–1890), the figure most associated with the modernization of Jewish liturgical music and the professionalization of the cantorate, performed in official state concerts at which he represented the Jewish community, as well as collaborating with the elite of the Viennese classical music scene.[12] In his concert performances Sulzer presented a public face of the Jewish community that highlighted the ease of movement of Jews in non-Jewish spaces and their integration into the life of the modern nation-state (although the community did not always approve). Philip Bohlman suggests that cantors were responsible for inventing a modern conception of Jewish music, establishing the cantorate as a professional identity in relationship to a new domain of liturgical music expertise.[13] The cantor performed a paradoxical role, claiming to preserve tradition while simultaneously creating new repertoires that sought to elevate congregants through appeals to the sounds of elite European concert and church music. As cantorial concerts became a feature of Jewish life, they were popularly embraced but also inspired controversies about new cantorial repertoires, spaces of performance, and engagements with technology. The choices cantors made in their concert programming aimed to illustrate that Jewish liturgical music could be compatible with elite concert music while articulating a set of social and political ambitions for themselves and their community, and simultaneously appealing to the broad musical tastes of an increasingly urban and educated Jewish public.

Recorded cantorial music addressed both the cultural fluidity of modern Jewish life and the retrospective melancholy that attended communal memory of disappearing small-town Jewish life and religious practices. Star cantors performed their own compositions that were tailored to showcase their vocal powers and performance charisma. The music, detached from its ritual context, took on a variety of new meanings, including "nostalgia, ethnic solidarity, or the musical demonstration of Jewish identity for non-Jewish listeners," as Joshua Walden enumerates in an essay on Jewish music and electronic media.[14] The mediatization of cantorial music and its subsequent emergence as a form of popular culture did not occur without substantial pushback from cantorial ideologues, seeking to chastise and curtail new technologies that threatened to unmoor the sensual power of Jewish sacred vocal music from its safe containment in the synagogue. Foremost among the critics was Pinchas Minkowsky (1859–1924) of Odessa, one of the leading cantors of the day, who published a book-length diatribe against cantorial records in 1911.[15] Minkowsky claimed that cantorial records were being played in brothels and bars of ill-repute. In a pungent and surreal episode, he imagined a carnival in Texas where an animatronic model in a fun house sings with the voice of Gershon Sirota. Minkowsky cites these immoral contexts to suggest that cantorial ethics were compromised by the juxtaposition of sacred music with new media and popular culture. James Loeffler has written that Minkowsky reflects the zeitgeist of Odessa-based Jewish intellectuals and Zionists who sought to maintain an image of elevated purity in representations of Jewish folklore.[16] Minkowsky was not alone in his critique of cantors as corrupted by commerce; his anti-gramophone polemic suffused the public discourse around cantorial music, with critics in the Yiddish press on both sides of the Atlantic echoing his views.[17]

Cantorial performance outside of synagogues involved a breaking of ritual boundaries that invited skepticism of cantorial ethics. In order to establish the ethical profile of cantorial concerts, cantors carefully constructed narratives around their performance that established the dignity or seriousness of the sacred artist. These performances of identity were achieved through selection of venue and through concert programming. The writings and performance career of Elias Zaludkovsky (1888–1943) are illustrative of anxieties about concertizing. Zaludkovsky was a cantor and intellectual who published criticism influenced by Minkowsky and who seems to have coined the term *hefker khazones* (wanton cantorial music) to chastise his contemporaries who engaged in recording and other forms of suspect "popular" culture.[18] Despite his ethical concerns, Zaludkovsky concertized frequently both in synagogues and theaters, programming cantorial pieces between operatic arias and his own art song settings of Yiddish secular poetry. Zaludkovsky's concerts are illustrative of how cantors in the first decades of the twentieth century appealed to the tastes of a broad Jewish listening public that was conversant with the elite and popular musics of the day while maintaining a profile as a sacred artist in the rarified lineage of Sulzer.[19] To the consternation of conservative critics such as Zaludkovsky, star recording cantors in the United States performed in a broad variety of settings, ranging from elite concert halls like Carnegie Hall to vaudeville houses on bills that included acrobats and jazz singers.[20]

Opera, a popular form of entertainment in the nineteenth and early twentieth centuries, posed a particular conundrum for cantors whose vocal powers were ideal for stage roles. In the Jewish popular imagination, opera was represented as the paradigmatic path of corruption for a cantor. In the frequently retold and mythologized story of Yoel Strashunsky (1816–1850), a cantor in Vilna, an opera role posed a path toward apostacy and, ultimately, crippling madness for a cantor who failed to resist the temptation of a secular music career.[21] In a fascinating twist on the narrative of opera as path of corruption, Yossele Rosenblatt famously rejected an engagement with the Chicago Opera, but performed frequently on the vaudeville circuit.[22] According to his son, Rosenblatt justified his stage performances in part by suggesting that performing cantorial music for non-Jewish audiences created a positive image of Jews for the general population, echoing Sulzer's approach to the cantorate as constitutive of a public face of Jewish humanity, seeking social equality through appeals to aesthetics.[23] As Jeffrey Shandler asserts, Rosenblatt carefully constructed a public persona through multiple methods, including promotional images and a personal narrative that drew upon images of cantorial piety, to invoke a conception of the sanctified Jewish past.[24]

While cantors continued to have popular followings and release records in the 1940s and 1950s, albeit on smaller community-focused record labels, the growth of the Jewish community in this period was focused outside of the urban immigrant milieu that favored the offerings of star cantors. In the years following the Second World War, the Reform and Conservative seminaries established institutions of cantorial education intended to provide clergy for the efflorescence of new synagogues sprouting in the centers of Jewish life in the suburbs.[25] The cantorial training programs were helmed by cantors such as Abraham Binder and Israel Goldfarb, who sought to establish an approach to prayer music that would meet the needs of the changing Ashkenazic Jewish populace that was increasingly confident in its "American" identity and less attracted to or familiar with the music of their European-born parents' generation.[26] The founders of the Cantors Assembly, established in 1952 as a union for cantors in the Conservative movement, rejected the figure of the star cantor, opting for a model of "dignity and decorum" that they saw lacking in the dramatic virtuoso style of the immigrant era.[27] Beginning in the 1960s and 1970s, a new style of synagogue song arose epitomized by the work of acoustic guitar-playing songwriters such as Shlomo Carlebach (1925–1994) and Debbie Friedman (1951–2011), emerging from Orthodoxy and Reform, respectively. These composers and others who they inspired provided congregations with songs that facilitate group singing, often in a style influenced by commercial folk-pop genres.[28]

Stylistically and in terms of the structure of prayer experience, synagogues have moved away from the music of the golden age and its focus on cantors as arbiters of the synagogue sound space, although these changes have not occurred without dissatisfaction from the professional cantorate.[29] As Mark Slobin noted in his 1989 monograph on the "American cantorate," a cleft had emerged between presentational and participatory forms of worship music, with the cantors bowing to pressures from their communities to limit the quantity and moderate the stylistic content of their soloist repertoire.[30] This evolution away from presentational to participatory music, which emphasizes the collective,[31] impacted cantors, their performances, and their records. The perceived lower status of cantors in general and diminished popularity of khazones in particular is discernible in a decline narrative that permeates cantorial discourse, frequently articulated in the *Journal of Synagogue Music*, the professional publication of the Cantor's Assembly.[32]

Meanwhile in the Hasidic community, professional cantorial prayer leading in the golden-age style was never the norm. According to Mayer Boruch Kohn (1963–), an elder prayer leader in the Brooklyn Satmar community, prayer-leading duties are usually reserved for members of prestigious rabbinic families, regardless of their level of musical knowledge or talent.[33] Despite a dearth of communal support for professional cantorial performance, in the late twentieth century several prominent cantors emerged from the Hasidic world, including Benzion Miller (1945–) and Yitzchak Meir Helfgott (1969–). Notably, both Miller and Helfgott were born outside of the United States, Miller in a Displaced Persons camp in Germany in the aftermath of the Holocaust, and Helfgott in Israel. Miller and Helfgott are singers with exceptional vocal talents who became international stars working in prestigious orchestral concert contexts, even as the secure place of cantorial performance in the synagogue was in retreat. The prominence of these cantors drew attention to the existence of the golden-age style within the Brooklyn Hasidic community, inspiring artistically minded young men with its rarified formal complexity and dramatic emotional depth.

The work of young Hasidic cantors foregrounds repertoire and vocal stylistic markers they have learned from records of khazones. While some Hasidic cantors hold pulpit positions, their self-driven musical educations are aligned more closely with a musical style than with the imperatives of institutions and communal norms. Commenting on his own perception that his chosen musical style is held in disfavor among people in his congregation and the broader public, Yanky Lemmer said:

> I really don't care that much. Because I have to do what I feel is right . . . I just feel that's the right thing for me, it's what I do, and I need to cultivate that . . . there comes a point when you have to define what you do. I enjoy singing regular stuff [i.e., pop songs] as well. But the stuff that moves me, that really moves me, is khazones.[34]

Reliance on their own aesthetic concept places some Hasidic cantors in the perilous position of having no congregation to pray for, but also pushes cantors to seek other sites that can serve as venues for sacred performance. These "out of context" sites of performance lean into the cantorial traditions of stage performance and technological mediation. Bypassing the pulpit, Hasidic cantors direct their music toward scenes and stages where they can realize their conception of sacred music.

STAGING CANTORIAL MUSIC IN THE TWENTY-FIRST CENTURY

On January 31, 2018, Yanky and his brother Shulem Lemmer (1989–) came to Stanford University to perform a concert in the Campbell Recital Hall. For this special event, the Lemmers had hired clarinetist Michael Winograd, an important figure in klezmer music who has served as the director of KlezKanada, the annual klezmer music camp, and Yiddish New York, a new annual festival dedicated to Yiddish culture. Winograd contracted trumpet player Jonah Levy, an active participant in jazz and klezmer scenes, to fill out the horn section. The band displayed a cultural schism running down the middle of the stage. On stage left stood Winograd and Levy, neither of whom are observant. On stage right, the drummer and the keyboard player were Hasidic musicians from Brooklyn. The Lemmer brothers stood center stage (Figure 12.1). The Hasidic

FIGURE 12.1 Yanky Lemmer in concert at the Campbell Recital Hall, Stanford University, on January 31, 2018. Photographer: Linda Huynh. Reproduced by permission of the Taube Center for Jewish Studies, Stanford University.

musicians wore long jackets, white shirts, and yarmulkes, while the others wore "un-marked" suit jackets. In interviews, Yanky Lemmer has referred to his Hasidic iden-tity as a "look" or "gimmick" that is helpful in establishing his connection to audiences, especially in Europe, where, he seems to imply, stereotyped images of Jews are more prevalent. At this performance in Stanford, the audience consisted of mostly older Jews, seated together.

In his concert appearances, Lemmer typically performs for non-Hasidic Jews with mixed-gender audiences seated together. As a rule, gender segregation in public events is enforced in the Hasidic community. Performing for mixed-gender audiences is con-troversial for Hasidic singers and has emerged as source of conflict between rabbis and musicians. The Lemmer brothers have mostly managed to steer clear of explicit conflict around the issue, although Yanky has mentioned that vitriolic comments about his per-formance for mixed seated audiences in a concert he gave at a non-Orthodox synagogue was a source of discomfort and anxiety for himself and his family.[35] While for non-Hasidic audiences the association of Hasidic Jews with classics of cantorial music may appear natural, even inevitable, singing cantorial music fits uneasily with the Hasidic cultural landscape. Hasidic cantors bear a similarity to their peers in the "Orthodox pop" world in that singers also occasionally run afoul of rabbinic authorities enforcing local norms of piety and personal comportment. Orthodox pop, a somewhat nebulous term, is the descriptor used by Jews in the Hasidic and other Haredi communities to refer to the work of artists from Haredi backgrounds that is stylistically derived from contem-porary commercial music genres, but with pious lyrics often in Yiddish or prayer book Hebrew and sometimes employing melodic elements derived from Yiddish folk song or Hasidic nigunim. Orthodox pop is the dominant genre heard in public spaces in Hasidic neighborhoods in Brooklyn.[36] Unlike Orthodox pop, which has a broad popular fan base, golden-age cantorial music is comparatively fringe in the Hasidic community.

The pop-inflected rhythms and synthesizer presets favored by the Orthodox instrumentalists in Yanky and Shulem's backing band reflect the styles and timbres of contemporary Orthodox music, evoking the sound of "one-man band" wedding musicians who perform hit songs on Casio keyboards. The synthesizer pop style was in conflict with the aesthetic presented by Winograd, a folklorist and avant-garde improvising musician. Winograd's playing draws on the sound of early twentieth-century klezmer records and contrasts starkly with the sonic world of the Hasidic players, whose musical terrain mostly hews to drum-machine beats and synthesizer pop sounds.

For the opening numbers of the concert, the Lemmer brothers performed nostalgic Yiddish songs such as "Di naye hora" (The new hora) and "Mamele" (Mother), associ-ated with Moishe Oysher (1906–1958) and Molly Picon (1898–1992), respectively. While "Di naye hora" is a Zionist song that celebrates the founding of the state of Israel, in this concert setting and arrangement as a klezmer wedding dance number its political meaning was subsumed into an ethos of nostalgia. These pieces were presented in up-beat arrangements that skirted the line between klezmer and pop sounds and served as fitting showcases for the Lemmer brothers' charismatic and energetic stage personas.

For one of Yanky's solo numbers, about twenty minutes into the concert and after the audience had been wooed by a string of entertaining and familiar pieces, the instrumentation and musical style shifted. Winograd switched over to keyboard, replacing the Hasidic musician, and accompanied Yanky in a duo format. Winograd set the keyboard to an acoustic piano setting, removing the stylized synthesizer effects that the Hasidic player had been using. Yanky introduced "Ono Bohoach,"[37] a setting of the centuries-old sacred poem of unknown authorship, Ana bekoaḥ, which Joseph Shlisky recorded in 1924, by telling the dramatic story of the cantor's childhood abduction by a choir leader who brought the boy singer to America—a story that has become part of cantorial lore through repetition in liner notes on reissue albums.[38] Yanky then went on to discuss the mystical prayer the piece sets, a poetic and evocative text that calls upon God to untie the knots of the spirit. His spoken introduction prepared the audience to hear the cantor's voice as offering a forum for contemplating the experience of pain and an opportunity for mystical introspection. Yanky's speech invited the listeners to hear the music through the prism of the experiences of loss, vulnerability, and the political and economic vicissitudes of Jewish history.

Musically, "Ono Bohoach" was a radical departure from what had preceded it in the concert. Winograd's playing was minimalistic, eschewing flamboyant arpeggios and dance beats for a sparse sound that referenced the kinds of accompaniment heard on early records. On cantorial records the organ, or less frequently piano or orchestra, provides instrumental accompaniment, mostly played with great restraint, with sustained pedal points and only occasional figuration in imitation of the antiphonal responses that would have been sung by a choir. The austerity of Winograd's choices sounded intentional. His harmonization of the melody was a straightforward transcription from Shlisky's record, bringing to mind other early twentieth-century records that feature sparse and "raw" accompaniment, such as early country blues and Dixieland jazz records.

Yanky gradually built up the dynamics of the recitative, exploring its emotional potentials over the course of the five minutes or so during which he was singing. As the piece gradually moved into the upper register of his voice, the characteristic krekhts accentuating the beginning of phrases became more prominent, matching the idiomatic styling of Shlisky's recorded performance. Not only vocal quality but also pronunciation of the Hebrew prayer text was informed by the recorded source material. Hasidic Jews in Brooklyn today generally pronounce Hebrew prayer texts with a Polish or Hungarian accent, regional variants that correlate to the origins of different Hasidic communities in Europe. However, Hasidic cantors imitate the pronunciation of gramophone-era cantors in their cantorial performance, who employed a "standardized" Ashkenazi pronunciation that is described by Hasidic Jews as "Litvish" (Lithuanian). A more important influence on norms of golden-age cantorial pronunciation is likely the prestigious central European cantors who set standards for the modern cantorial style.[39]

Yanky's bodily gestures modeled the responses intended for the audience to experience; eyes closed, face slightly clenched, hands upturned in supplication. Yanky began to sweat. He looked as though he might be about to break into tears. The hall was silent as he sang, the sparse texture of the piano acting as a spotlight, drawing Yanky's voice into the center of a meditative attention. At the end of the piece, the audience, made up predominantly of older, non-Orthodox Bay Area Jews for whom golden-age cantorial music is almost certainly not part of a synagogue-based ritual practice, burst into rapturous applause.

Yanky's emotive concert persona orients the audience to a conception of the cantor as arbiter of aesthetic experience and conduit to pleasure through music. In the concert format, Yanky is able to invoke both the classic sound of the records he loves, and the presentational liturgical experience associated with the cantorial golden age. The concert hall is a forum in which participants are willing to engage in stylized listening practices that cede authority to presentational performers and allows artists to set the parameters for Jewish liturgical experience. Yanky's stage performance connects to a history of cantorial concerts, but unlike cantors of the golden age for whom the pulpit was also a concert-like setting for performance, for Yanky, concerts play a pivotal role as a site for the performance of his concept of cantorial artistry that he can only rarely access in the synagogue.

THE INTERNET AND CANTORIAL CULTURE

Leaders in the Hasidic community have taken a variety of approaches to the internet, with the Chabad embrace of the web as a means of religious outreach representing an extreme liberal stance. A mass event held at Citifield in 2012 represents a more conservative approach that is well represented among Hasidic leadership. At the 2012 gathering, rabbinic leaders implored their followers to abandon use of the internet, citing fears about its deteriorative effects on youth and general morality.[40] Despite these qualms, anecdotal evidence suggests that internet use and social media are widespread among Brooklyn Hasidic Jews, used for both commerce and entertainment. In the Hasidic cantorial community, the internet plays a significant role both as a source for learning golden-age cantorial repertoire and as a site for performance.

Yanky Lemmer's 2007 video of "Misratzeh B'rachamim," which is based on the 1924 record of Mordechai Hershman (1888–1940), is a live recording of a concert held at the Young Israel Beth El Synagogue in Borough Park Brooklyn, where Yanky was serving as a choir singer for Cantor Benzion Miller.[41] Founded in 1902 and boasting superb acoustics in its cavernous Moorish-style sanctuary, Beth El has an important history as a center for cantorial music and has employed numerous star cantors at its pulpit, including Hershman himself. In the present day, Beth El holds a unique position in the liturgical music world of Jewish New York as a holdout of prayer leading in a style that is reminiscent of the golden-age presentational approach. Once a month on the Sabbath preceding the new month in the Jewish calendar, Miller presides over a special service focused on cantorial performance, attended by a small but devoted self-selecting community of aficionados, many of them women seated separately in the balcony section.

In his Beth El concert video, Yanky, at the time twenty-four years old, sings the piece a whole tone lower than Hershman, rendering his vocal tone darker than Hershman's original. There is a hesitance in his performance, his eyes downcast and his body still throughout (he had not yet developed his showman's bravura). Yet his performance is marked by attention to coloratura and ornamentation that immediately marks his performance as informed by the golden-age style. Although the view count of this video has hovered around 50,000 for over a decade, a modest reach for a "viral" video, according to Yanky posting this video on YouTube directly led to a spate of work as a cantor and ultimately to his being hired at Lincoln Square, one of the most prestigious cantorial positions in New York. Yanky continues to regularly post videos on his Facebook and Instagram accounts that range in production values from cell-phone documentation of concerts to more professional music videos.

For Yoel Kohn (1985–), social media has provided his primary forum in which to perform as cantor after leaving the Hasidic community. Kohn has adopted a secular appearance and lifestyle and no longer considers himself to be a Hasidic Jew. His break with the Satmar world of his birth left him without recourse to employment in the Brooklyn and Kiryas Joel synagogues, where he had worked previously as a prayer leader on the High Holiday. He describes the role social media played in creating opportunity for him as a cantor as follows:

> I became non-religious, and I didn't actually pursue cantorial at all. For some reason I was recorded singing [Pierre Pinchik's 1928 record] "Rozo D'Shabbos" . . . a friend of mine was just pointing a camera at me. And we started recording . . . And suddenly, things started happening. People were contacting me. It became viral . . . so I thought, you know what, I'm gonna start producing, because as soon as I wanted to warm up, it became a big production, I became busy . . . Somebody posted it on Facebook, for friends only, and not just that, with a warning, please do not share, because I didn't want there to be a video of me singing without a yarmulke. I figured if my parents see this, it's gonna hurt them. But by the time it got back to my parents, my mother told me, Oh my God! You're famous! You're viral! I figured, alright. Fuck it. I'll produce some more. I'll put myself out there. Maybe get some work out of it. And that's it. That's the story of me.[42]

The 2015 video performance that altered Kohn's professional prospects was an impromptu, cell-phone recording that captured a display of virtuosity in the interpretation of old cantorial records.[43] The same is true for early videos of Yanky Lemmer. These raw documentarian videos allow cantors to inhabit the role of "viral" celebrities, using the internet as a venue for their style of sacred music. As cultural critics have noted, video-sharing sites like YouTube have a unique capacity to negotiate between commerce and community with content driven by the roughhewn aesthetics of amateur videos.[44] For Yanky, viral internet moments helped stage a major career development. However, in his pulpit position Yanky is extremely limited in performing the kinds of early recorded cantorial repertoire that he initially attained notoriety for and that make up the bulk of his internet videos. For Kohn, the videos helped him frame a space as a cantor who had left his community, paving the way for making a modest "comeback" as a cantor, mostly singing at private events in the Hasidic community, always outside of synagogues. That his visual appearance is mainstream while he interprets classic cantorial records has been perceived as a paradox and a source of his charisma.[45]

Yanky Lemmer and other Hasidic cantors have suggested that the internet helped draw Hasidic singers to cantorial performance by providing access to otherwise difficult-to-find old records. Aryeh Leib Hurwitz (1989–), a cantor who was born in the Brooklyn Chabad community, comments that he does not own any records of his own and listens and learns from cantorial records exclusively online, especially on a cantorial WhatsApp group where fans share mp3 files. Online archives, especially the Florida Atlantic University Recorded Sound Archive Judaic Collection, grant access to an enormous body of historical Jewish records that effectively make individual collections superfluous. The web-based archive contains an estimated 100,000 songs, featuring cantorial records from the earliest gramophone-era records through mid-century American cantorial albums, and on into the present. Private collectors have uploaded their cantorial records to streaming sites such as YouTube, making them widely accessible. On file-hosting sites and social-media platforms, Hasidic cantors interweave uploads of old records with new videos of interpretations of classics, signaling an orientation toward music making that blurs chronology and a pastiche approach to self-presentation that is well suited to the medium of the internet.

In their online videos, Hasidic singers inhabit the role of the cantor as presentational artist, directing the experience of liturgy through historically informed performance in ways that are rarely possible at the pulpit. With their video productions, cantors present themselves as artists with a relevant musical message, utilizing the most contemporary media platform to reach a broader public. The artistry demonstrated on these videos serves an overt role as a form of self-promotion, putatively toward the goal of getting jobs as a cantor in concert or in the pulpit. At the same time, making videos functions as an end in itself, affording Hasidic singers a virtual site in which to perform their public identities as cantorial artists in the golden-age style. The production of videos connects Hasidic singers to the musical world of the golden age, asserting the role of technological mediation as an expression of cantorial identity. Indeed, for Hasidic cantors, the mediated sound of cantorial voices on records are the key source of legitimate knowledge about their art form. Producing recordings of themselves connects Hasidic cantors to the kinds of musical practices typical of the artists they revere.

CANTORIAL *KUMZITS* IN HASIDIC BROOKLYN

The Hasidic kumzits is a music-making party that in its essence and aims can be traced back to the first generation of Hasidim in eastern Europe. In the early eighteenth century, Hasidic rabbinic leadership cultivated support from their followers through collective singing of paraliturgical music. Musical forms performed at kumzits parties include *deveykes* (spiritual cleaving) nigunim, which are intended to aid participants in achieving a meditative state, and nigunim in dance rhythms that foster states of shared enthusiasm.[46] The term *kumzits* itself derives from Yiddish and literally refers to sitting together. As such, it signifies a central space for collective engagement in music. The *khazones kumzits*, as these parties are sometimes referred to by participants, differ from typical music parties in the community in terms of both the music being sung and the format of presentation. Instead of Hasidic nigunim, performers sing covers of early twentieth-century cantorial records of liturgical pieces derived from synagogue ritual (not paraliturgical pieces), and instead of a group vocal texture, soloist voices are featured. As such, the khazones version of the kumzits is a relatively new phenomenon, seeming to have emerged in the twenty-first century. For the new generation of Hasidic cantors, such parties are an important outlet for the performance and development of their artistry.

On a hot summer night in 2018, Yoel Kohn sang at a kumzits in the home of a Satmar friend of his in Brooklyn, New York, just a few blocks from the Williamsburg Bridge. Like the other men in attendance at the kumzits, Kohn was born and raised in the Satmar community. Despite his break with Orthodoxy, Kohn has maintained his passionate interest in cantorial music and is considered to be a star performer among a small cohort of Hasidic cantorial fans. On that summer night, Kohn had been invited to lead a private prayer service and then to participate in a round-robin impromptu recital of cantorial classics sung by a small invited group of knowledgeable singers, all Hasidic men. Kohn began the party by leading the Maariv, a prayer service held in the evening; the focal point of his prayer leading was a rendition of Hashkivenu, the second blessing following the Shema during Maariv, using the setting recorded by Cantor David Roitman in April 1925.[47] Kohn's solo vocal performance was over eight minutes long, mirroring the length of Roitman's double-sided 78-rpm record. His voice captured nuances of Roitman's original with a timbral specificity and fidelity to the intonation and stylistic details captured on the old record. Yoel, like his peers in the small community of cantors who are committed to historical performance practices, has cultivated coloratura singing techniques that closely follow the models provided by old records, including attention to microtonal inflection and ornamentation. In his performance of Hashkivenu, Yoel executed a virtuosic falsetto coloratura passage typical of golden-age cantorial performance. As in a concert setting, the kumzits attendees sat with eyes focused on the singer, some with looks of intense emotional engagement, mirroring the dynamic arcs of the music, others relaxed, sitting back in their chairs as passive and satisfied audience members. The men present, mostly singers themselves, sang choral responses at appropriate moments in the piece.

Mirroring Roitman's recording, which featured a chamber ensemble made up of organ, flute, and string accompaniment, Kohn's rendition also relied on instrumental accompaniment, provided by David Reich, who used the string setting on his synthesizer keyboard, recalling the timbre of the historical performance. Departing from the original, Reich improvised a short passage to "fill in" the space when the 78-rpm record would be turned over to hear its completion. This Maariv service was distinct from norms of Orthodox practice, not only because of the focus on cantorial performance, but also in regard to the use of a musical instrument during prayer. Instrumental accompaniment is forbidden in Orthodox synagogues but is a typical element in the sound of early cantorial records. The use of the keyboard in Yoel's prayer leading in this kumzits setting was a notable instance of aesthetic concerns appearing to override norms of ritual practice.

When Kohn finished, after a confusing and cacophonous interlude of everyone seeming to talk at once, other singers began to perform. One after another, the attendees took turns performing virtuosic vocal pieces recorded by early twentieth-century cantors, at the forefront Yossele Rosenblatt, Samuel Malavsky, and Zavel Kwartin. Some of the singers were youthful and raw, and others were seasoned artists who had worked as professional cantors, such as Yossi Pomerantz (1978–), who until recently held a pulpit at the prestigious Modern Orthodox Congregation Beth Tikvah in Montreal, and Yoel Pollack (1981–), Kohn's cousin and a prominent singer in the Satmar community whose original compositions are sometimes performed at mass gatherings, such as the Satmar Rebbe's Hanukkah celebration.

For the final number of the evening, the group sang Israel Schorr's "Yehi Rotzon Sheyibone Beis-Hamikdosh," a ubiquitous favorite originally recorded in 1927 and covered by countless cantors in concert and on record. The end of the piece was approached as an improvisatory jam session, with each of the singers taking a phrase, treating it as a virtuoso improvised cadenza, and then passing on the solo to the next singer, and ending with the entire group singing the chorus together, resulting in a roaring, brassy swell of voices as each singer sought to assert his own presence.[48]

The kumzits thus offered a powerful space for the performance and experience of golden-age repertoire, an outlet for creativity and religious feeling. As such, the kumzits that night had much in common with "classic" Hasidic social music-making parties: it was a homosocial gathering for religious music-making, but with the difference that the musical focus was on the individual not the collective. Rather than reinforcing the social norms of the community, the party made room for the articulation of non-conformist approaches to prayer and aesthetics. The meaning of the party was transformed by the music itself, the presentational performance format, and the ambitions of the artists to reach across time to locate an aesthetic of Jewish prayer that they find to be uniquely compelling.

"KHAZONES IS DEAD": LONG LIVE KHAZONES

After the kumzits party in Williamsburg described above, a young man who had attended noted with disgust that none of the excellent singers present at the party could get a pulpit position as a cantor, including a few singers who are not so very young and already have substantial experience as professional artists. Switching into English from Yiddish, the young man proclaimed that "khazones is dead," echoing, perhaps intentionally, the old adage from the 1980s that "punk is dead," an articulation of the fear among members of a subculture that the anti-normative stance of their music-loving community is at risk of imploding under the social pressures of non-conformity. But unlike punk, which putatively died due to commercial overexposure and mindless imitation by non-cognoscenti, fans of cantorial music fear the death of the genre due to its artists being faced with indifference.

Performance in venues outside the synagogue grant Hasidic cantors opportunities to present their desired concept of liturgical expressive culture, pushing against commonly held cantorial narratives of communal indifference to golden-age cantorial styles in the synagogue by accentuating other sites of presentation as forums for sacred music. "Out of context" spaces of cantorial performance allow Hasidic cantors to connect with the musical past that is the focus of their aspirations, but with a changed approach to the sociality and function of the music. Whereas cantors of the golden age presented the sacred music style that they developed in synagogue prayer leading contexts using new mediated technologies and in secular concert spaces, for today's Hasidic cantors the opposite is the case. A form of cantorial music they have learned primarily from mediated sources provides the repertoire and stylistic norms of their performance, which is usually conducted outside of the synagogue ritual context. Instead of deriving their sacred-music practice from a communally constructed worship-music culture, Hasidic cantors are focused instead on the aesthetics of their own subculture, invoking a temporally displaced locus of authority that values the music of the past over that of the present while articulating a form of subjectivity that strains limits placed on expressive behavior in their birth community. By singing cantorial music outside of the synagogue, Hasidic cantors seek to reconcile their alienation from the musical life of the contemporary synagogue by framing cantorial performance as an art experience independent of ritual, but one that is suffused with the spiritual authority of the liturgical roots of their musical offering.

The music of golden-age cantors was described by practitioners as serving a variety of functions, including addressing communal desires for cultural preservation, seeking aesthetic elevation of the congregation through artistry, and as a means of generating deeply felt experiences of prayer. While contemporary Hasidic cantors share these goals as a foundational point of reference, their work points to another set of possibilities for the meaning of cantorial performance and its relationship to the Jewish collective. For Hasidic cantors, pursuing aesthetic excellence through khazones is a practice that engages critically with the norms of the Jewish community and surfaces a conception of cantorial music as a non-conforming practice. Khazones offers the cantors a means to articulate artistic impulses and feeling within a Hasidic social context that places limits on expressions of individualism. Their work challenges the norms of multiple Jewish communities, creating a musical experience through repertoires and vocal techniques that are instantly recognizable as markers of difference from the norms of any contemporary synagogue.

Hasidic cantors surface an alternative history of cantorial music as an art form that directly addresses and even accelerates points of tension in the Jewish collective response to modernity. The music of golden-age cantors attained the status of a recognized representation of the Jewish collective through a system of aesthetics, not through adherence to rabbinic values. The challenges that cantors have posed to religious authority resonate in the non-conforming stylistic choices of Hasidic cantors. Khazones offers the cantors an alternative to what they perceive as parochialism in synagogue music and challenges the status of normative definitions of Jewish law and custom as the deciding factor in personal comportment in their birth community. By highlighting non-synagogue sites of performance, whether by choice or necessity, Hasidic singers foreground one possible history of cantorial music that resonates with their own life stories in which Jewish sacred music is a practice that is dependent on performance outside of synagogues in order to achieve its fullest expression. In this version of cantorial history, new technologies and secular venues allow artists to represent Jewish collectivity in ways that push at the boundaries of rabbinic authority, framing aesthetics and performance as central organizational principles in the music of prayer.

Notes

1. David Reich, in discussion with the author, January 13, 2019.
2. See Akiva Zimmermann, "The Hasidic World's Attitude towards Hazzanut," *Journal of Synagogue Music* 34, no. 10 (2009): 148–150.
3. David Biale, David Assaf, Benjamin Brown, Uriel Gellman, Samuel C. Heilman, Murray Jay Rosman, Gad Sagiv, Marcin Wodziński, and Arthur Green, *Hasidism: A New History* (Princeton, NJ: Princeton University Press, 2018), 747–755.
4. See Yehoshua Kahana, "When Hasidic Singers Perform in a Litvish Accent," *Forverts*, September 10, 2019, https://forward.com/yiddish/431118/when-hasidic-performers-sing-in-a-litvish-dialect/; and David Olivestone, "Shul or Show? The Golden Age of Cantorial Music," *Segula: The Jewish History Magazine*, September 2020, 30–39.
5. See Noah Schall, *Yossele Rosenblatt: Classic Cantorial Recitatives* (New York: Tara Publications, 2015); Zavel Kwartin, *Smiroth Zebulon: Recitative für Kantoren* (self-published, 1928).
6. Descriptions of cantorial prayer leading services in the soloist presentational style abound in the Yiddish press. See Pinchos Jassinowsky, "In der velt fun khazones un idisher negina," *Der morgn zhurnal*, January 23, 1948. Bootleg recordings of "star" cantors, made in the 1960s or after and frequently documenting star cantors in their elder years, have survived through a network of circulation among fans, originally on homemade cassette tapes, and today accessible on YouTube and file-sharing sites. See "Chazzanut For All," http://www.mediafire.com/?u8j92uzbihc30 (accessed June 4, 2021).
7. Chaim Zhitlowsky, *Der sotsializm un di natsionale frage* (New York: A. M. Evalenko, 1908), 35.
8. See Leib Glantz, "Khazones—der 'shir ha shirim' fun di idishe masn," in *Khazonim zhurnal*, ed. Mordechai Yardeini (New York: Jewish Ministers Cantors' Association of America, 1950), 13–14; Gershon Ephros, "The Hazzanic Recitative: A Unique Contribution to our Music Heritage," *Journal of Synagogue Music* 6, no. 3 (1976): 23–28.
9. See Zevulun Kwartin, *Mayn leben* (Philadelphia: Aroysgegeben fun a gezelshaflikhen komitet, 1952), 148; and Samuel Vigoda, *Legendary Voices: The Fascinating Lives of the Great Cantors* (New York: S. Vigoda, 1981), 22–23.
10. See Vladimir Levin, "Reform or Consensus? Choral Synagogues in the Russian Empire," *Arts* 9, no. 72 (2020): https://doi.org/10.3390/arts9020072.

11. See Mark Slobin, *Chosen Voices: The Story of the American Cantorate* (Chicago: University of Illinois Press, 1989), chapter 1.

12. See Tina Frühauf, *Salomon Sulzer: Reformer, Cantor, Icon* (Berlin: Hentrich & Hentrich, 2012), 54–55.

13. See Philip V. Bohlman, *Jewish Music and Modernity* (New York: Oxford University Press, 2008), 73–104.

14. Joshua S. Walden, "Jewish Music and Media of Sound Reproduction," *The Cambridge Companion to Jewish Music*, ed. Joshua S. Walden (Cambridge: Cambridge University Press, 2015), 60.

15. See Pinchas Minkowsky, *Moderne liṭurgiye in unzere sinagogen in Russland* (1909/10), reproduced in Akiva Zimmermann, *Peraḳim be-shir: Sefer Pinḥas Minḳovski* (Tel Aviv: Sha'are Ron, 2011).

16. See James Loeffler, "The Lust Machine: Commerce, Sound, and Nationhood in Jewish Eastern Europe," in *Jews and Music-Making in the Polish Lands*, ed. François Guesnet, Benjamin Matis, and Antony Polonsky, Polin: Studies in Polish Jewry 32 (Oxford: Littman Library of Jewish Civilization, 2020), 257–278.

17. See Elias Zaludkovski, "Der khazonisher matsev," *Der morgn zhurnal*, November 17, 1926; B. Shelvin, "Di tsukunft fun khazones in amerike," *Di geshikhte fun khazones*, ed. Aaron Rosen (New York: 'Agudat ha-ḥazanim de-Ameriqa, 1924), 77–78.

18. Elias Zaludkovsky, "Der khazonisher matzev," *Der morgn zhurnal*, November 17, 1926.

19. Jeremiah Lockwood, "*Prière et crime dans la Pologne de l'entre-deux guerre: l'agenda musical 1924 du chantre Elias Zaludkovsky*," trans. Marie Schumacher-Brunhes, *Germanica*, no. 67 (December 2020): 49–68.

20. Henry Sapoznik, *Klezmer! Jewish Music from Old World to Our World* (New York: Schirmer Books, 1999), 83.

21. See Joachim Stutschewsky, *Der Ṿilner Balebesl, (1816–1850)* (1968; Amherst, MA: The National Yiddish Book Center, 2009); https://www.yiddishbookcenter.org/collections/yiddish-books/spb-nybc208890/stutschewsky-joachim-der-vilner-balebesl-1816-1850-legende-vegn-a-yidish-muzikalishn.

22. Samuel Rosenblatt, *Yossele Rosenblatt: The Story of His Life* (New York: Farrar, Straus and Young, 1954), 140–151.

23. Ibid., 261–262.

24. See Jeffrey Shandler, *Jews, God and Videotape: Religion and Media in America* (New York: New York University Press, 2009): 26–34.

25. See Neil Levin, "Music at JTS," *Tradition Renewed: A History of the Jewish Theological Seminary*, ed. Jack Wertheimer (New York: The Seminary, 1997); and Judah M. Cohen, *The Making of a Reform Jewish Cantor: Musical Authority, Cultural Investment* (Bloomington: Indiana University Press, 2009), 34–40.

26. See Geoffrey Goldberg, "The Development of Congregational Song in the American Conservative Synagogue: 1900–1955," *Journal of Synagogue Music* 44, no. 1 (2019): 35–88.

27. Israel Goldfarb, "An Analysis of the Hazanic Styles of Kwartin, Roitman and Rosenblatt," *Proceedings of the Seventh Annual Conference-Convention of The Cantors Assembly of America* (New York: Jewish Theological Seminary, 1954), 27.

28. See Ari Y. Kelman and Shaul Magid, "The Gate to the Village: Shlomo Carlebach and the Creation of American Jewish Folk," *American Jewish History* 100, no. 4 (2016): 511–540; and Judah M. Cohen, "Sing unto God: Debbie Friedman and the Changing Sound of Jewish Liturgical Music," *Contemporary Jewry* 35, no. 1 (2015): 13–34.

29. See Mark Slobin, *Chosen Voices: The Story of the American Cantorate* (Chicago: University of Illinois Press, 1989), chapter 9.

30. Ibid., 195–209.

31. See Thomas Turino, *Music as Social Life: The Politics of Participation* (Chicago: University of Chicago Press, 2008), 23–65.

32. Lachrymose views of the present and future of the cantorate are a recurrent feature of articles in the *Journal of Synagogue Music*, the publication of the Conservative movement Cantors Assembly. See Samuel Rosenbaum, "Epitaph for Jewish Music," *Journal of Synagogue Music* 1, no. 4 (1968): 30–41.

33. Mayer Boruch Kohn, in discussion with the author, April 20, 2021.

34. Yanky Lemmer, in discussion with the author, July 16, 2019.

35. Yanky Lemmer, in discussion with the author, July 16, 2019.

36. See Abigail Woods, "Pop, Piety and Modernity: the Changing Spaces of Orthodox Culture," in *Routledge Handbook to Contemporary Jewish Cultures*, ed. Lawrence Roth and Nadia Valman (New York: Routledge, 2014), 286–296.

37. The spelling employed on Shlisky's 1928 Victor records release is typical of early cantorial records, mixing German spelling conventions with idiosyncratic phonetic spelling of Ashkenazi liturgical Hebrew.

38. Benedict Stambler and Helen Stambler, *Cantor Joseph Shlisky: Faith Eternal*, Collectors Guild, CG619 (1962), LP, liner notes.

39. See Lewis Glinert, "Toward a Social Study of Ashkenazi Hebrew," *Jewish Social Studies* 2, no. 4 (1996): 85–114.

40. See Biale et al., *Hasidism*, 783–787.

41. "Chazzan Yaakov Lemmer-Beth E-l," March 25, 2007, YouTube video, https://youtu.be/tWrXQv19-kQ.

42. Yoel Kohn, in discussion with the author, January 15, 2019.

43. Yoel Kohn's video of Rozo D'Shabbos, originally posted in 2015, was deleted. Another account holder reposted the video, "Ruzu D'Shabbos Kohn," September 22, 2016, YouTube video, https://youtu.be/-6MbS2DybAE.

44. See Pelle Snickars and Patrick Vonderau, eds., *The YouTube Reader* (Stockholm: National Library of Sweden, 2009).

45. Sarah-Rachel Shechter, "Stirring Yiddish Singing by an Ex-Hasid," *The Yiddish Daily Forward*, November 27, 2015; http://yiddish.forward.com/articles/192080/stirring-yiddish-singing-by-an-ex-hasid/ (accessed April 28, 2021).

46. Biale et al., *Hasidism*, 209–211.

47. "Cantor Yoel Kohn: Hashkiveinu (Roitman)," August 19, 2019, YouTube video, https://youtu.be/S5yXzJjjLRU.

48. "Sheyibone – Yoely Kohn, Yossi Pomerantz," June 28, 2018, YouTube video, https://youtu.be/sa35i-Rfc00.

SELECT BIBLIOGRAPHY

Allen, Wayne R. *The Cantor: From the Mishnah to Modernity*. Eugene, OR: Wipf & Stock, 2019.

Cohen, Judah M. *Jewish Liturgical Music in Nineteenth-Century America: Restoring the Synagogue Soundtrack*. Bloomington: Indiana University Press, 2019.

Fader, Ayala. *Hidden Heretics: Jewish Doubt in the Digital Age*. Princeton, NJ: Princeton University Press, 2020.

Frigyesi, Judit. *Writing on Water: The Sounds of Jewish Prayer*. New York: Central European University Press, 2018.

Klein, Amit. "Changing Performance Styles of Twentieth Century Ashkenazi Cantorial Recitatives." *Analytical Approaches to World Music* 3, no. 2 (2014): 1–42.

Lockwood, Jeremiah, and Ari Kelman. "From Aesthetics to Experience: How Changing Conceptions of Prayer Changed the Sound of Jewish Worship." *Religion and American Culture: A Journal of Interpretation* 30, no. 1 (2020): 26–62.

Lockwood, Jeremiah. "Prière et crime dans la Pologne de l'entre-deux guerre: L'agenda musical 1924 du chantre Elias Zaludkovsky." Translated by Marie Schumacher-Brunhes. *Germanica*, no. 67 (December 2020): 49–68.

Loeffler, James. "The Lust Machine: Commerce, Sound, and Nationhood in Jewish Eastern Europe." In *Jews and Music-Making in the Polish Lands*, edited by François Guesnet, Benjamin Matis, and Antony Polonsky, 257–278. Polin: Studies in Polish Jewry 32. Oxford: Littman Library of Jewish Civilization, 2020.

Pasternak, Velvel. "The Golden Age of Cantors." *Journal of Synagogue Music* 31, no. 1 (September 2006): 160–164.

Schleifer, Eliyahu. "Current Trends of Liturgical Music in the Ashkenazi Synagogue." *The World of Music* 37, no. 1 (1995): 59–72.

Shandler, Jeffrey. *Jews, God and Videotape: Religion and Media in America*. New York: New York University Press, 2009.

Slobin, Mark. *Chosen Voices: The Story of the American Cantorate*. Urbana: University of Illinois Press, 1989.

Summit, Jeffrey. *The Lord's Song in a Strange Land: Music and Identity in Contemporary Jewish Worship*. New York: Oxford University Press, 2000.

Tarsi, Boaz. "Observations on Practices of Nusachot in America." *Asian Music* 33 no. 2 (2002): 175–219.

Walden, Joshua S. "Jewish Music and Media of Sound Reproduction." In *The Cambridge Companion to Jewish Music*, edited by Joshua S. Walden, 56–72. Cambridge: Cambridge University Press, 2015.

Wood, Abigail. "Pop, Piety and Modernity: The Changing Spaces of Orthodox Culture." In *Routledge Handbook to Contemporary Jewish Cultures*, edited by Lawrence Roth and Nadia Valman, 286–296. London: Routledge, 2014.

13

JEWISH MUSIC AND TOTALITARIANISM IN THE POST-STALINIST SOVIET UNION

JASCHA NEMTSOV
TRANSLATED BY TINA FRÜHAUF

THE death of Joseph Stalin on March 5, 1953, marked the end of an era for the Soviet Union and particularly for its Jewish inhabitants. Incidentally, the onset of this caesura coincided with the last day of Purim on March 1, the day Stalin suffered a stroke and was paralyzed. Political and Jewish collective memory would become intertwined in this "Miracle of Purim 1953." The mortal danger to Jewish existence in the Soviet Union—the apparently planned deportation of the entire Jewish population to Siberia at that time— came to a halt at the last moment. In the following decades, political anti-Semitism was no longer as aggressive as it had been during the final years of Stalinist rule. Soviet Jews no longer feared for their lives as they had in the years 1948 to 1953, they were no longer deported to the Gulag, and there were neither anti-Semitic purges in state institutions nor corresponding propaganda campaigns in the media. But anti-Semitism would remain virulent. State-directed hatred affected Jewish life in its various manifestations in the Soviet Union. Among other things, the expression of Jewish cultural identity in all its forms was largely taboo, and the suppression of everything Jewish would last until the end of communist rule. The restrictions, which were gradually lifted during the perestroika beginning in 1987, were the final phase in a long process of state-directed planned destruction of Jewish collective identity in the Soviet Union. It was to be achieved primarily through the annihilation of Jewish culture, which predated Stalinism, going back to the first years after the Bolshevik Revolution of 1917.[1]

While foreign anti-Soviet propaganda often portrayed the Bolshevik regime as a Jewish conspiracy, in actuality the Bolsheviks fought Jewish culture, which initially flourished with the bourgeois revolution of February 1917, and the subsequent abolition of centuries-long discrimination. The attitude of the Bolsheviks toward the Jews at that time was ambivalent. Their main theorists—Marx, Lenin, and Stalin—denied the existence of the Jews as a people and a nation in their writings, but demanded their complete acculturation and dissolution.[2] As such, the Bolsheviks could not simply ignore millions of Jews in their sphere of power. They therefore saw it as an urgent task to initially include the Jews in the socialist transformation of society, while suppressing Jewish religious practice and the Zionist movement.

In its fight against Jewish culture, the regime mainly used militant Jewish communists from the Commissariat for Jewish National Affairs, known under Russian acronym YEVKOM, and the Jewish section of the Bolshevik Party known as Yevsektsiya. The two organizations were used for the brutal and thorough eradication of the complete infrastructure of Russian Jewry.[3] The use of the Hebrew language was considered a crime and was subject to draconian punishments. As pianist and Zionist activist David Schor noted in his diary of 1924: "The Jewish people are in a most precarious situation. . . . The joy of long-awaited freedom and equality is poisoned by the complete suppression of national culture. The language is banned, the economic persecution mainly affects the Jews. . . . There is so much sorrow."[4] The last remaining cultural institution devoted to Hebrewism, the famous Moscow theater Habimah, disbanded in early 1926 with performers leaving the country.

Yiddish culture, especially Yiddish songs imbued with communist values, was tolerated as the expression of the Jewish "proletariat" at odds with Hebrew culture (Hebrewism), which was completely abolished. Indeed, through the 1920s the Soviet Union was the only country in the world with state-sponsored Yiddish-language schools, newspapers, theaters, writers' groups, town councils, and even courts.[5] During the early Soviet period, the state created such secular institutions to foster a specifically Jewish Soviet culture supposedly divorced from religious Jewish practice. Still, Yiddish, accepted as one language of the Soviet people, faced a stark decline as the mother tongue of large parts of the Jewish population.

Shortly after the rise of Stalin, the subsequent period beginning in 1928/1929, known as the Great Turn (or Great Break), saw the dissolution of all independent Jewish cultural institutions, many of which had been established in the course of the Revolution. Among them were also publishing houses, libraries, clubs, and organizations such as the Institute of Jewish Proletarian Culture in Kiev, closed in 1949, including its folklore department with its section for musical folklore founded and headed by Moisey Beregovsky (1892–1961). Jewish culture was thus completely nationalized and reduced to a level only necessary for propaganda purposes. At the same time, the Yevsektsiya was dissolved; the YEVKOM had already ceased to exist in 1924. And yet, there were exceptions. In May 1937, a dozen aged klezmers from smaller cities south of Kiev formed a klezmer band for the purpose of making a number of recordings and toured, giving concerts.[6] Their existence was cut short when, beginning in 1939, the Soviet Union experienced political anti-Semitic discrimination, which also led to the closure of most previously state-supported Jewish cultural, educational, and other institutions, and the removal of Jews from important positions in public life. In parallel to the anti-Semitic purges, which also affected institutions such as the Moscow Conservatory, Stalin initiated the creation of the Yevreyskiy antifashistskiy komitet (Jewish Anti-Fascist Committee) in 1941, whose primary task was to strengthen international Jewish solidarity with the Soviet Union in the struggle against Nazi Germany.

With the assassination of Solomon Mikhoels (1890–1948)—ordered by Stalin on January 12, 1948—chairman of the Jewish Anti-Fascist Committee and actor and director of the Moscow State Jewish Theater known by its Russian acronym GOSET, the last phase of the destruction of Jewish "national" life in the Soviet Union began: the few Jewish institutions that had remained until then were terminated, and Jews experienced massive anti-Semitic discrimination in all areas of society. Political show trials were explicitly directed against renowned Jewish personalities, and most of the accused, including almost all of the important Yiddish poets and writers, were executed. This anti-Semitic campaign, which apexed in late 1952, was supposed to culminate in the aforementioned deportation of all Soviet Jews to remote areas of the country; the relevant preparations were apparently cut short by Stalin's death.[7]

Even if the worst did not come to pass, Jews remained the only people who, until the definitive end of the Soviet Union, were not granted the national-cultural "blossoming" of all nationalities under socialism promised by the ruling party.[8] Any preoccupation with Jewish culture, including the commemoration of the Holocaust, was classified as "Zionist propaganda" and "nationalism," and suppressed by all means. While some support was provided for the music of all other peoples—no matter how few—within the Soviet federal system, Jewish music was, with rare exceptions, taboo in official cultural life. Moreover, the shock of the anti-Semitic persecutions during the preceding years was so deep-seated that many Soviet Jews did not dare articulate their Jewish identity publicly. Even singular Jewish cultural events during the Thaw period (the period of Nikita Khrushchev's government from 1953 to 1964, named after the eponymous title of a novel by the Russian Jewish writer Ilya Ehrenburg published in 1954)—such as the 1959 release of the collected works of Sholem Aleichem in Russian translation or concerts and recordings of Yiddish folk songs—did not ease the anxiety. For some, their Jewish identity became particularly important under these circumstances, mainly as a form of cultural demarcation from the totalitarian state. Some were even willing to risk their social existence for it; they became part of the Jewish national underground movement that emerged at the end of the 1950s. And yet others, from classical musicians like David Oistrakh and Emil Gilels to Yuri Levitan's ubiquitous voice on the radio during the war, were comfortably involved in mainstream Soviet culture.

Turning the focus to musicians and repertoires, this chapter focuses on the presence (and absence) of Jewish *music* in the public sphere, specifically in the concert hall and other stages in the post-Stalinist Soviet Union, encompassing the years 1953 to 1991. It asserts that through various types of musical activities, a certain part of the Jewish population was able to maintain a collective cultural identity. Captured as a *musical* community, this collectivity, however, was by no means homogenous and also extended to non-Jewish composers, musicians, and audiences. This chapter shows in which ways Jewishness was thematicized, performed, represented, and received in the face of Russian Jewish identity being generally understood as uniform and fixed.[9]

MOMENTS OF YIDDISH MUSIC ON STAGE

Much has been written about Soviet Yiddish music and theater in the 1920s and 1930s, and its violent destruction 1948 to 1952,[10] but less about the fact that state-sponsored Yiddish culture, however marginalized, continued to be produced and consumed in the post-Stalinist Soviet period. Indeed, the first years after Stalin's death were filled with hope for a revival of Jewish culture. As early as the summer of 1954, Yiddish songs were once again allowed to be heard sporadically in concerts in the USSR. One of the first to perform was the former GOSET actor Emil Gorovets (1923–2001) with a concert program titled *Freylekhs*, a nod to the lively circle or line dance. Several performers, including Nehama Lifshitz (1927–2017), Mikhail Aleksandrovich (1914–2002), Sidi Tal (Sorele Birkental, 1912–1983), or Bin'yamin Khaytovsky (Khayatauskas, 1917–1966), came from the territories in the west that had been annexed to the Soviet Union in 1939/40: Lithuania, Latvia, Moldova, or Western Ukraine. Jewish acculturation was not yet as advanced there as in central areas of the Soviet Union, and the Yiddish musical traditions had been preserved.[11]

Some of these musicians had fallen victim to the anti-Semitic campaign of 1948–1953 and survived the Gulag. Among them was Mikhail Epelbaum (1894–1957), once hailed internationally as the "Jewish Chaliapin" in tribute to his great voice. He spent the years 1949 to 1954 in labor camps. Upon his release and despite having been diagnosed with progressive cancer, he gave numerous concerts throughout the Soviet Union during the last two years of his life. While there is no information on the venues and contexts, a private letter from 1955 describes how his performances were received: "Among those who were alive after the great epidemic is Mikhail Epelbaum. He gives concerts all over Ukraine and Moldova. I heard that when he came on stage in a shtetl and said only one word: 'Jidn' (Jews), a general crying began, and it took a very long time before people calmed down and he could finally start the concert."[12] The Stalinist repressive measures are euphemistically described here as a "great epidemic." The unknown author of the letter was obviously afraid to call them by name. Epelbaum was taken to the hospital right after his last concert in Leningrad in the spring of 1957, where he died shortly thereafter.

Baritone Saul Lyubimov (Leybman, 1900–1968) had been among the best-known performers of Yiddish songs in the 1920s–1930s, recording several dozen records at the time. Lyubimov was arrested in 1949, sentenced to ten years in a labor camp, then freed in 1954. He returned to the concert stage in 1955 and released two recordings of Yiddish songs. Two years later he suffered a severe stroke that ended his concert activities forever. Zinovy Shulman (1904–1977), who had sung Yiddish songs for the first Israeli ambassador, Golda Meir, in 1948, had been also arrested in 1949 after a concert. He was tortured and sentenced to ten years in a labor camp, after he was forced to do hard labor in Kazakhstan, where he injured his hand. He was released in 1956 but was only able to perform again in the early 1960s. In the 1960s–1970s he released several recordings, and a compilation of sheet music with Yiddish folk songs from his repertoire, which Sovyetskiy Kompozitor published in 1973. Indeed, with Shulman and others, Yiddish song would have continuity on the stages of the post-Stalinist era.[13]

On November 16 and 17, 1959, two evenings of so-called Jewish song and humor (Russian does not distinguish between Jewish, Hebrew, or Yiddish culture, but captures all under the umbrella of еврейская, i.e., "Jewish") took place in the hall of the Komissarzhevskaya Theater (Figure 13.1). The star of this concert was announced as Khayatauskas, who, together with Ester Roytman and Yakov Klebanov, presented Yiddish folk, humorous, and everyday songs. The program also included vaudeville, feuilletons, songs and wedding tunes, and stories by Sholem Aleichem and Leyb Kvitko, among others. Such events necessarily cultivated a superficially entertaining and often clichéd image of Jewry. They presented a mix of various genres and forms of popular Jewish culture, typical of cabaret, in which music, literature, and theater were represented. Moreover, amateurs often performed alongside professional artists, which meant that the artistic level was uneven.

FIGURE 13.1 Poster of a concert on November 16 and 17, 1959, Leningrad. Private collection of the Jewish Community Center in St. Petersburg. Reproduced by permission of the Hochschule für Musik Franz Liszt Weimar.

Such events enjoyed extreme popularity and were usually sold out (ticket prices are unknown), the need so strong—especially of the older generations who still knew the Yiddish language and could remember the once-vibrant cultural context—for their culture and thus for the collective identity that the state had been trying to eradicate for decades with changing approaches. Except for such events, Jewish culture was hardly visible in Soviet *public* life. Historian Aleksandr Frenkel asserts that the concerts of Yiddish folk songs were "the most widespread and accessible form of existence of Jewish culture in the USSR. They were practically the only 'meeting places'—apart from the synagogue and the cemetery—where Soviet Jews could legally gather as part of a collective 'national action,' not only to jointly familiarize themselves with their heritage, but also simply to communicate, get to know each other, and maintain social contacts. The 'Jewish concerts' functioned, de facto, as a surrogate for a communal life under the conditions of prohibition of all other forms of ethnic consolidation."[14]

Each of these events represented the struggle against the arbitrariness and paternalism of the authorities and was, at the same time, a victory. The singers were often forced to perform "internationalist" programs in which Yiddish songs were allowed to form a small part alongside folk songs in other languages. Each program had to be approved by cultural supervisors, and all song texts in Russian translation had to be submitted for examination prior to the concert. Individual songs or even individual lines of the song texts often had to be deleted, even if the program as a whole had been approved. In many places, Jewish artists were met with open hostility. "In Minsk, they would not allow my concert, and when I went to the party's Central Committee, I was told that 'Jews and Gypsies have no place in Minsk,'" singer Nehama Lifshitz, who was admired as a "Jewish nightingale," later recalled of a concert tour in the late 1950s. Eventually the concert in the Belarusian capital was permitted after all, but the subsequent newspaper review stated that "the concert was imbued with the spirit of nationalism."[15] The poet Sara Pogreb later recalled a concert by Nehama Lifshitz in Dnepropetrovsk, Ukraine:

> There was a rumor that a singer was coming to sing in Yiddish. There were no posters. The run-down culture club of the tailors' union. A hall with about one hundred people in the audience. The singer amazed me: she didn't just sing, she showed her unwavering Jewish dignity, indomitability, self-confidence. She was filled with national feeling. How courageous! Nehama was the continuation of the Warsaw Ghetto Uprising.[16]

The year 1962 marked another noteworthy moment in the preservation of Jewish culture. Thirteen years after GOSET's closure, Bin'yamin Shvartser (1892–1979) founded the Moscow Jewish Drama Ensemble (MEDA) and with it revived Yiddish theater in Moscow. Among the troupe were several former students of Solomon Mikhoels from the GOSET troupe, disbanded in 1949, including Shvartser himself. He also acted as the artistic director of the new ensemble. The ensemble combined theatrical performances and concert programs with Yiddish songs. As such, the productions followed the custom of eastern European Yiddish theater, in which music played such a prominent role that it can be considered to be *musical* theater. Many actors served as interpreters of Yiddish songs on the concert stage. The theater worked closely with composer Yevgeny Rokhlin (1912–1995), who made a name for himself outside the Jewish music scene as a writer of jazz music, composer of popular songs, and music director of the Stanislavsky and Nemirovich-Danchenko Academic Music Theater in Moscow. The production of Sholem Aleichem's *Der farkishefter shnayder* (The bewitched tailor) with music by Rokhlin was a significant event in Moscow's Jewish cultural life:

> The premiere took place in the summer of 1974 in the crowded hall of the Sovietsky Hotel. . . . It had the effect of a powerful explosion. It is difficult to put into words the enthusiasm of the audience, which from that time on included more and more young people. To say that the audience just sang along would not be enough. The audience seemed to breathe every measure of the music, enjoyed the dialogues, and danced along with the actors. . . . *Der farkishefter shnayder* remained on stage until the end of 1987. . . . From the very beginning an almost mystical atmosphere arose around this play of Sholem Aleichem. It was almost impossible to get tickets for it. Everything was sold out in advance. And I remember well how an activist of the Jewish underground movement, Mikhail Nudler,[17] bought tickets at some suburban theater box offices (apparently, they were sent there on purpose to prevent a full house) and then distributed them among refuseniks [those who were denied the opportunity to emigrate during the Soviet period] and closest friends.[18]

The MEDA had come into being at a time when the liberal tendencies of the Thaw period were already mostly rescinded. A foreboding emerged in 1957, when the First World Festival of Youth and Students was held in Moscow, an event that caused euphoria among national-minded Soviet Jews. An Israeli delegation attended as well. Afterward, several dozen people were sentenced to camp imprisonment for unauthorized contacts with the Israelis. These were the first overt anti-Jewish repressions of the post-Stalinist period. In the following years, "the bureaucratic system developed a new model for Jewish culture in the USSR, which can be captured by the words 'restriction' and 'minimization.'"[19] After the end of the Thaw and especially after the Six-Day War in 1967, when the Soviet Union broke off relations with Israel, these modest manifestations of Jewish culture also disappeared from public view.

In parallel, Jews were used for propaganda purposes. In 1968 the cantor of the Leningrad synagogue, David Stiskin (1909–1982), was sent to the United States together with the Moscow rabbi Yehuda Leyb Levin (1894–1971). During several events Stiskin and Levin declared that there was no anti-Semitism in the Soviet Union and that there was complete religious freedom. The internal report of the Soviet mission to the United Nations confirmed that the visit contributed to the "spread of the truth" about the situation of Jews in the USSR and to the "exposure of hostile propaganda" in the United States on this matter.[20] In 1972 the KGB prepared a document containing information on the situation of people of "Jewish nationality" for possible use at press conferences with foreign journalists during the visit of the president of the United States, Richard Nixon, to the USSR. This document listed Jewish ensembles presumed to still be active at the time, including the Leningrad Jewish Comedy Ensemble and other ensembles that no longer existed.

In reality, Jewish culture together with Jewish music entered a time of "official non-existence."[21] The revitalization of Yiddish music had come to a halt, and the scene was largely extinguished.[22] The Leningrad Jewish Comedy Ensemble, founded in 1959, had already closed in 1970.[23] Initiatives in other major cities did not find approval or had again disbanded. From the early 1970s on, public performances of Yiddish folk songs were no longer possible. Most Yiddish-speaking singers who had remained in the country emigrated to Israel soon thereafter, among them Nehama Lifshitz, Mikhail Aleksandrovich, Anna Gusik, and Emil Gorovets. However, through their records published earlier, Yiddish song continued to be a significant cultural factor in the lives of many Soviet Jews. The author of this chapter (born in 1963) can well remember the joyful excitement of his father, who in 1970 was able to find an LP record in a department store, of Yiddish songs interpreted by Mikhail Aleksandrovich. This LP and singles featuring this repertoire were frequently played, always at a low volume such that neighbors could not hear the music. Aside from the private sphere, the MEDA would remain as the only Jewish cultural organization the Soviet Union in the public eye.[24]

While Yiddish song struggled to exist as an autonomous musical genre, it made subtle appearances in the Russian-Soviet soundscape without, however, being perceived as an expression of Jewishness. Soviet popular music was largely influenced by composers of Jewish descent who came from the former Pale of Settlement and had grown up in the sound sphere of Jewish musical culture. They incorporated some of its elements into their musical language, which, thus, became part of everyday Soviet life by way of hits and songs for the masses. By far the most important composer to synthesize Yiddish song into popular genres was Isaak Dunayevsky (1900–1955), grandson of a well-known cantor and synagogue composer; his film scores and songs were familiar to every Soviet citizen. The songs of Matvey Blanter (1903–1990), Yuli Khait (1897–1966), Zinovy Kompaneyets (1902–1987), and the brothers Dmitry Pokrass (1899–1978) and Daniil Pokrass (1905–1954) also became a central part of Soviet musical culture and socialist propaganda. Another brother, Samuil Pokrass (1894–1939), likewise a composer, had emigrated to the United States in the mid-1920s. The brothers used Mark Varshavsky's popular song "Oyfn pripetchik" as a model for their song "To ne tuchi—grozovïe oblaka" (These are not clouds—Thunderclouds), part of the score for the Soviet propaganda film Sïnï trudovogo naroda (The children of the working People, 1937). (During the Second World War the Pokrass brothers' melody was then outfitted with a new Yiddish text, "Zog nit keyn mol" [Never say] by Hirsh Glick. As such it became the anthem of Jewish partisans.)

The most famous composer of popular song and film music of the 1970s was Vladimir Shainsky (1925–2017). Hardly any other piece of Soviet music enjoyed the popularity of his songs from the animated film Tcheburashka (1971). During the Thaw, Shainsky had written songs to Yiddish texts by Moisey Geyf, Josef Kerler, and Aron Vergelis. He later claimed that all of his work was inspired by Jewish music:

"All my songs are Jewish"—Shainsky explained—"They're Kaddish [Jewish prayers] remodeled into what are supposed to be Russian songs. Look," he sat down at the piano and began playing first his songs and then the corresponding Jewish prayer melodies, explaining in detail how he adapted them to Russian taste. The evening ended with general laughter.[25]

Finally, the unofficial genres of Soviet urban folklore are imbued with Jewishness, especially the so-called Russian chanson or *blatnaya pesnya*, a type of song influenced by the demimonde and underworld milieu and not infrequently politically subversive. Blatnaya pesnya relies on Russian criminal slang, which follows the grammatical structure of Russian, but borrows vocabulary and idioms from Ukrainian and Yiddish, among other languages, not only absorbing the sonic inflections of Yiddish, but also relying on melodic fragments. Singers such as Leonid Utesov (Leyzer Vaysbeyn, 1895–1982), Villi Tokarev (1934–2019), and Mikhail Shufutinsky (1948–), among others, promulgated these genres, imbuing them with musical Yiddishism.[26]

MOMENTS OF JEWISHNESS IN ART MUSIC

In his article on Jewish art music in the era of its official nonexistence in Russia, Abram Yusfin mentioned covert forms of Jewish music in the post-Stalinist period, including elements of Jewish music in such genres as the quartet, sonata, instrumental concerto, or prelude without an overt reference to their Jewish derivation and content.[27] It is significant that among the composers, whose works at that time belonged to both overt and such "covert" forms of Jewishness in music, were musicians not exclusively of Jewish descent. After Stalin's death, Soviet audiences were able to experience for the first-time compositions by Dmitry Shostakovich, originally composed in the late 1940s but excluded from public performance due to the anti-Semitic campaigns. These included, above all, Shostakovich's song-cycle *Iz yevreyskoy narodnoy poėziy* (From Jewish folk poetry, 1948), whose premiere on January 15, 1955, was accompanied on the piano by the composer himself.[28] In 1963 he created an orchestral version of this cycle, which Kurt Sanderling premiered in East Berlin. For decades this piece remained the only work of Soviet music repertoire whose title contained the word "Jewish." But this is not where Jewishness ended.

Premiered on October 29, 1955, and deemed an extraordinary success, Shostakovich's Violin Concerto no. 1 (1947–1948) relied on motifs associated with klezmer in its second movement, a Scherzo.[29] The String Quartet no. 4 (1949), with its equally unmistakably Jewish themes in the finale, had already been included in concert hall repertoires since 1953.[30] In 1960 *Skripka Rotshil'da* (Rothschild's violin) received its world premiere. Shostakovich had completed and orchestrated it since its composer, his student Veniamyn Fleyshman, had died in the Second World War. The music does not simply quote traditional Jewish motifs; it is a significant attempt at the artistic development of Jewish musical thought.[31] Shostakovich's compositions with Jewish themes from that period also include the Violoncello Concerto no. 1 (1959) and the String Quartet no. 8 (1960), in which he quotes his own Jewishly melody from the Piano Trio no. 2 of 1944. This series of musical works with Jewish references in Shostakovich's oeuvre concluded in 1962 with the Symphony no. 13, discussed below. Most of them fall into a period when the composer was denounced as "formalist." They may be read as identification with an oppressed minority. And yet, it is noteworthy that all these works were premiered or performed by noteworthy ensembles and orchestras such as the Leningrad Philharmonic Orchestra and the Moscow Philharmonic Society, and on important stages from the Grand Hall of the Leningrad Philharmonic to the Composers' House in Ivanovo outside of Moscow.

Shostakovich's engagement correlated with his championing the performance and publication of Jewish music, which had inspired him in the first place. He supported the work of the most prominent Soviet researcher in the field of Jewish musical folklore, Moisey Beregovsky, with whom he had been closely associated since 1948, specifically the publication of his folklore collections.[32] Shostakovich also supported the anthology *Naye yidishe lider* compiled by Zinovy Kompaneyets; Shostakovich acted as general editor, and he also wrote a preface to this publication, in which he stated: "The appearance of new songs of national character always fills me with a feeling of joy. Jewish folk music is unique in its emotional emphasis, and one hears its echoes in the musical works of numerous great composers."[33]

Orally transmitted Jewish folk tunes also found their way into art music through Yury Shaporin (1887–1966). His "Vokalise" of 1948 for voice and piano draws on a melody that Solomon Michoels shared with him. Another non-Jewish composer in whose works Jewish culture reverberates was Aleksandr Vustin (1943–2020), beginning with *Slovo* (The word, 1975) for winds and percussion, and dedicated to his first composition teacher, Grigory Frid, whose text forms the basis of the work. In the years 1977 to 1982 Vustin then conceived *Capriccio* for mezzo-soprano, male voices, and ensemble, for which he draws from nigunim found in the aforementioned collection by Beregovsky. All these composers are part of a lineage established in the nineteenth century by Mikhail Glinka and the members of the so-called Five, also known as Mighty Handful—the group of Russian composers who aimed to develop a distinctly national style of classical music while relying on folklore. Almost all of them showed a certain interest in Jewish culture and wrote compositions containing Jewish elements starting with *Yevreyskaya pesnya* (Hebrew song, 1840) by Glinka. Particularly noteworthy was Modest Musorgsky's preoccupation with the Jewish traditional melos in several of his works including *Kartinki s vïstavki* (Pictures from an exhibition), the unfinished opera *Salammbô*, and the choral works *Porazheniye Sennakheriba* (The destruction of Sennacherib) and *Iisus Navin* (Jesus Navinus), or *Yevreyskaya pesnya* (Hebrew song).

Among the Jewish-born composers of this lineage is Aleksandr Veprik (1899–1958). In the 1920s he, along with Mikhail Gnesin (1883–1957) and the brothers Grigory Krein (1879–1955) and Aleksandr Krein (1883–1951), had been among the so-called Moscow Four, the protagonists of the Society for Jewish Music in Moscow, at that time the most important institution of the New Jewish School in music. In the early 1930s, Veprik, together with Krein, had attempted to secure the right of Jewish music to exist in accordance with Soviet ideology and to distance himself from developments in Palestine and the United States. After this project failed at the end of the 1930s, he turned to national folklore, devoting himself for many years to the folk melos of Kyrgyzstan. But as early as 1944, Veprik began to compose in parallel his *Pastoral* for small orchestra, which revived the material of the third movement of his own 1925 Suite op. 7, for violin and piano, with its unmistakable Jewish sound. In 1950 two colleagues denounced him and he was sent to the Gulag. After his return in 1954, he wrote further orchestral works imbued with Jewish elements.

In her diary—which chronicles cultural censorship, suppression, and anti-Semitism, and recalls the destinies of composer Samuil Senderey and conductor Leonid Pyatigorsky—Esfir Veprik affirmed ten years after her brother's passing: "And Sasha is a Jewish composer even in his last work 'Two Poems.'"[34] Several entries are devoted to the only memorial concert for the composer, which took place, not least through her own efforts, on November 16, 1964, at the Composers' House outside of Moscow (Figure 13.2). The concert presented music by Veprik and another important composer of the New Jewish School, Grigory Krein. However, it was self-evident that the Jewishness of their works would not be mentioned in public. From the 1960s onward, not even the word "Jew" could be uttered publicly, even in a "neutral" context—it was "somewhere between a dirty word and a state secret."[35] Esfir Veprik noted in her diary that the performers, the pianist Grigory Singer and the singer Dina Potapovskaya, both of Jewish descent, were startled when they saw the original title of the composition, *Kaddish*, in

Союз композиторов СССР
Союз композиторов РСФСР
Московский союз композиторов

ПРИГЛАШАЮТ ВАС

в понедельник, 16 ноября 1964 года

НА ВЕЧЕР,

посвященный
творчеству композиторов
ПРОФЕССОРА
Александра Моисеевича
В Е П Р И К А
и
Григория Абрамовича
К Р Е Й Н А

А. М. ВЕПРИК
(1899—1958 гг.)

Начало в 19 часов

Г. А. КРЕЙН
(1879—1955 гг.)

FIGURE 13.2 Title page of the program for the concert on November 16, 1964, with Aleksandr Veprik (left) and Grigory Krein (right) pictured. Reproduced by permission of the Hochschule für Musik Franz Liszt Weimar.

the sheet music during the preparation of the concert. Potapovskaya canceled on short notice, which Esfir Veprik ascribed to her perception of the Jewishness of the work and her anxiety that a performance would jeopardize her position at the Stanislavsky and Nemirovich-Danchenko Moscow Academic Music Theater.[36] Veprik's account stands in contrast to the fact that Potapovskaya recorded Jewish songs in 1965, even including a song in Hebrew by Mikhail Gnesin.

Surely, the concert is testimony that Jewish musical expression was by no means completely extinguished, despite anti-Semitic cultural policies, harassment by the authorities, and fears on the part of artists. While these factors had massively impaired Jewish collective identity, music—one of its few remaining living and effective forms of expression—was all the more significant for the self-assurance of many Jews in the Soviet Union. As such, production of art music imbued with Jewishness continued in the following decades.

Another noteworthy composer of Jewish descent who contributed to this production is Moisey Vaynberg (Mieczysław Weinberg) (1919–1996). Aside from a significant corpus of works dedicated to the remembrance of the Holocaust, discussed below, he conceived works imbued with different facets of Jewishness. The most notable one is the chamber opera *Pozdravlyayem!* (Congratulations! 1975/1982) after Sholem Aleichem's play *Mazl tov*, which had become popular in Russia especially through performances at the GOSET in Moscow. It had been first presented there in 1921 with sets by Marc Chagall, with Solomon Mikhoels as Reb Alter, and had remained in the repertory until the 1930s. By the time Vaynberg wrote his chamber opera, however, the Yiddish language had long ceased to be of cultural significance in the Soviet Union. Although the works of Sholem Aleichem—unlike those of many other Yiddish poets—were not banned, they were accessible only in Russian. Nevertheless, the Yiddish language remained immensely important for the opera as the speech melody shapes much of its musical material. Yiddish is a language with many diphthongs and is very vowel-focused. As such, the sliding intonation on vowels is related to the falling second, which can be found in the melodies of many Yiddish folk songs, often conveying a melancholy expression. Eastern European Jewish melos was influenced by Yiddish, whose trochaic basic rhythm, with its strongly stressed first syllable, differs substantially from the iambic structures of the Hebrew language. For Vaynberg, who had grown up in the Jewish milieu of Warsaw and surrounded by Yiddish, elements of its music became an organic part of his own musical language. The world of this chamber opera, however, does not have much in common with that of Sholem Aleichem's Tevje. Neither does one find oneself in a seemingly "authentic" Jewish shtetl, nor can the protagonists of the opera match Tevje's wisdom, humor, or wealth of spirit. The characters appear rather limited and whimsical. Thus, even the Jewish musical elements resound in a grotesque and parodic context. As such, the opera is one of the few examples of the humor in Vaynberg's "Jewish" compositions. It was premiered in 1983 at the Moscow Chamber Musical Theater under the direction of Boris Pokrovsky.

Composers were inspired by a variety of Jewish cultural markers. Aleksandr Manevich (1908–1976) conceived several works inspired by klezmer music, including the Clarinet Concerto (1955) and *Pyat' yevreyskikh narodnykh pesen* (Five Jewish tradi-tional songs, 1965); a year after his emigration to Israel, he conceived the cycle *Freylekhs* with six pieces for solo clarinet (1974). A contemporary, Boris Klyuzner (1909–1975), only occasionally drew from Jewish traditional music, such as in his Violin Concerto (1950), which premiered in 1955 and as of a few years ago has become standard rep-ertoire in Russia. The concerto opens with a recitative for solo violin based on motifs from biblical cantillation following Eastern Ashkenazic practice. It plays a key role, acting like a leitmotif for the whole composition. Other themes are reminiscent of klezmer music.[37]

Among the subsequent generations of composers, born Jewish, several con-tinued to create works that would bring Jewish sounds into the concert hall. Of note is Rafail Khozak (1928–1989) and works such as the orchestral suites *Bibleyskaya syuita* (Biblical suite) and *Heroy Sholom-Aleykhema* (Heroes of Sholem Aleichem), *Yevreyskiye liricheskiye tantsy* (Jewish lyrical dances) for string orchestra, the suite for vi-olin and piano *Stranitsy dalekoy yunosti* (Pages of a distant youth), and Jewish wedding pantomimes for viola and piano *Choreographer's soul* (The soul of a choreographer)—dates for all these compositions cannot be ascertained. Like many other composers born Jewish, Khozak worked in parallel in the fields of film and popular music to make a living.

One of the few composers who consistently explored Jewish themes was Sergey Berinsky (1946–1998). Aside from his works that memorialize the Holocaust, discussed below, are the *Sonata-partita a la barocco* (1985), which has been oddly called the "first Jewish organ piece,"[38] and the partita for violoncello *Menora* (1991)—both rely on Jewish spirituality in its broadest sense. According to Marina Boikova, it is precisely the Jewish spirit of Berinsky's music that led to the alienation felt in some musical circles.[39] And yet in spite of facing exclusion, unlike some of his Jewish colleagues Berinsky remained instead of emigrating. Noteworthy is the approach of Vladimir (Zeev) Bitkin (1947–), who was among the first Jewish musicians to resume fieldwork, after a fifty-year hiatus, in order to preserve the last remnants of Jewish musical culture in the Soviet Union. Between 1982 and 1987 he undertook several expeditions to Moldova and Ukraine, collecting over three hundred Jewish traditional songs, many of the melodies of which found their way into his own works. In 1993 he emigrated to Israel and has since lived in the Jewish quarter of Hebron. As folklorist-composer of the post-Stalinist period, he followed in the footsteps of Maksis Goldins (1917–2009) from Riga, who began to focus on Jewish musical tradition in the late 1940s and as a composer created works al-most exclusively in a Jewish style. In 1972 his twenty-one arrangements of Jewish folk songs for choir with piano accompaniment were published in Moscow. In all, Goldin created over forty choral arrangements and about eighty arrangements for voice with piano. Some of these arrangements were performed in two concerts in Riga in 1981 and 1982—extraordinary events at the time. Goldin also composed several works for various chamber ensembles and orchestras, all rooted in Jewish folk music. He also conceived the libretto (in Russian) for his purimshpil; and in 1987 he initiated the first recording of Yiddish songs since the 1960s with singer Ada Svetlova (1939–). His anthology

Yevreyskaya narodnaya pesnya (Jewish traditional song), with a total of 256 songs, was published in St. Petersburg in 1994 and is still widely in use.

However, the activities of these composers should not obscure the fact that, overall, there were only a few who risked turning to Jewish themes. Most avoided this inroad in order not to jeopardize their careers, or they were not interested. And unlike their colleagues or earlier generations, for both Jewish composers like Mikhail Gnesin or Aleksandr Veprik, and their non-Jewish colleagues such as Dmitry Shostakovich or Aleksandr Vustin, Jewish music was understood less as folk music. It had become a political and moral symbol.

Performing the Holocaust in Music

In contrast to anti-Semitic policies in Nazi Germany, the Soviet Union never *openly* expressed anti-Semitism. In its official pronouncements, the Communist Party and the Soviet state it controlled always professed friendship among nations, equal rights for all nationalities, and, even if not specifically, the fight against anti-Semitism, which was declared a vestige of the capitalist system. All anti-Semitic measures of the state were therefore either publicly disguised in euphemistic terms—as campaigns against "cosmopolitanism" and "Jewish bourgeois nationalism" during the Stalin period or as "anti-Zionism" from the late 1960s onward—or they were ordered through direct administrative channels and enforced with due secrecy through the structures of the party apparatus and the secret service, which were not subject to public control. There were no laws that would have justified bans on the performance of Jewish musical works, but various reasons were found to restrict if not inhibit it. The regime used subversive methods to further intimidate those involved in its practice. Many Soviet musicians, who still had fresh memories of the repressions of the Stalin era, interpreted even the slightest hint of Jewishness in music as a danger—if not to their lives, then to their careers.

However, the absence of anti-Semitic legislation and of a fundamental ban on Jewish culture allowed a certain amount of leeway and repeatedly generated new hopes when, for example, the one or other performance of Jewish-themed works was eventually permitted, in spite of harassment, and then actually took place—such moments seemed like miracles given the circumstances.[40] One such moment was the premiere of Dmitry Shostakovich's Symphony no. 13 "Babiy Yar" on December 18, 1962, in the Grand Hall of the Moscow Conservatory. The first movement is based on a poem by Yevgeny Yevtushenko, written in September 1961, on the occasion of the twentieth anniversary of the massacre in the Babyn Yar ravine on the outskirts of Kiev, which openly denounced the concealment of this mass murder of Kiev Jews as well as the hatred of Jews in general. In this context, a look back at previous works addressing the atrocity is significant.

In 1946 Symphony no. 1 "Pamyati muchenikov Bab'yego Yara" ("In memoriam of the martyrs of Babyn Yar" [1945] by the Ukrainian-Jewish composer Dmitry Klebanov (1907–1987) was to be premiered in his hometown of Kharkov (the venue remains unknown). After the dress rehearsal, however, at which several cultural functionaries were present, it was dropped from the program:

> What they [the functionaries] heard, however, left them speechless at its audacity: the entire thematic material of the symphony was permeated with distinctly Jewish motifs. For the mourning apotheosis of the finale, the soprano sang a vocalise in the style of synagogue song, highly reminiscent of the Jewish prayer for the dead (Kaddish). The scandal was perfect.[41]

Klebanov's symphony was finally heard in March 1949 at a private performance of the Union of Soviet Composers of Ukraine in Kiev, after which the composer faced repression. Klebanov escaped imminent arrest by fleeing to Moscow, where he was protected by the Union of Soviet Composers' chairman, Tikhon Khrennikov.[42] The work was not allowed to be premiered publicly until 1990, one year before the fall of the Soviet Union.

In contrast, the Yiddish lullaby "Babi Yar" (1953/1954) by Revekka (Rivka) Boyarskaya (1893–1967), based on a poem by Ovsey Driz, *was* performed, but with consequences. The aforementioned Nehama Lifshitz sang it in a concert at the Kiev National Theater of Operetta on November 13, 1959, which Vera Drizo documents as follows: "After the 'lullaby' the audience was numb until the silence was broken by someone's shouting: 'Why, people, stand up!' The audience rose, and immediately the curtain fell. The next day the singer was summoned to the Central Committee, where they demanded the lyrics of the song and banned her performance. It didn't help—Nehama sang it anyway and was punished by cutting her tour in Kiev from seven concerts to three. After that, by order of the Minister of Culture, she was not allowed to perform for almost a whole year."[43] The concert was her first and last performance in Kiev, where anti-Semitism was particularly strong at the time. This moment also attests not only to censorship in the aftermath of performance, but to the audience's reactions. Indeed, the genocide, which was consistently concealed in the Soviet Union, became an important, perhaps even the most important, theme of identification for Soviet Jews, no matter whether as audience, performer, or creator. Lifshitz's first encounter with the song supports this assertion:

> Rivka Boyarskaya was already bedridden then. Without tearing, but with an unbearable depth that terrified on the spot, she "howled" this lament. I sat petrified in her miserable little apartment. . . . I could not get up. Driz almost had to carry me out. I took this lament with me. The pianist Nadezhda Dukyatulskayte, who was with me in Moscow at that time, had herself lost her only child in the Kaunas ghetto, she found chords to the song and together we were searching for interpretation, as this cannot be called a song or cry, it is like a continuous pain, which is further intensified by touch. How was it possible to touch her, stretching in a monotonous melody with unexpectedly intermittent screams and then each time dying and fainting in this terrible "Lyulenki-lyu-lyu"? "Kinah"—this is what our people call it, "lament over the lost and destroyed."[44]

With the Hebrew word *kinah* (plural, kinot) for a dirge or lamentation, Lifshitz referred to Jewish songs performed especially at funerals but also on occasions of national mourning, such as commemorating the destruction of the Jerusalem Temple on the festival of Tisha B'Av, since biblical times. A clear alignment of the song with Jewish tradition.

In contrast to Klebanov and Boyarskaya, Shostakovich's Symphony no. 13, composed in the years 1961 and 1962, was performed just a few months after the composer completed it, though it was preceded by a struggle with the authorities and the composer faced all kinds of obstacles and setbacks.[45] The musicians involved were put under pressure in the hope that they would cancel. The conductor Yevgeny Mravinsky and the vocal soloists Boris Gmyrya and Askold Besedin bowed to this pressure—Gmyra even shortly before the dress rehearsal, so that the premiere was in jeopardy. Besedin then nevertheless became the soloist of the second performance in Minsk on March 19 and 20, 1963. Fortunately, another soloist, Vitaly Gromadsky, had also rehearsed the part as a precaution and was able to step in at the last moment. No publicity was permitted, yet the hall was full and the work received a rapturous ovation. After the premiere, the Central Committee summoned Yevgeny Yevtushenko, demanding changes to the poetic texts that underlie the five movements of the symphony, specifically to dilute the Jewish associations. After two performances in Minsk in March 1963, the symphony was hardly performed in the Soviet Union. The recording was also sabotaged, with the electricity in the studio being cut off several times during the session; most of the records were not playable, and the small remainder that survived were shipped abroad.[46] Such an unequal struggle with the powerful but no longer omnipotent Jew-hating Soviet state is characteristic of the situation of Jewish musical culture in the post-Stalinist era at large. (A written testimony to this can be found in the aforementioned diary of Esfir Veprik.)

The Holocaust was permitted to be mentioned only in reference to "Soviet citizens" but not specifically Jews. A case in point is Vasily Grossman and his epoch-making novel *Zhizn' i sud'ba* (Life and fate, 1959), which among other things addressed the genocide on Soviet territory. The novel not only was banned but, according to the orders of the party leadership, was supposed to disappear forever. All copies of the manuscript, as well as the drafts, were confiscated by the KGB in 1961. Fortunately, a friend of the writer was able to hide a copy, which was later smuggled to the West after Grossman's death.

The memory of the Holocaust, which was not supposed to be a subject of open discussion during the Soviet era, became nevertheless central to the work of several Soviet Jewish composers, albeit often in a covert manner. One of the few Holocaust documents published at the time was the diary of Anne Frank, printed in Russian translation in 1960, when her fate became a worldwide symbol of anti-Semitic persecution and Jewish suffering. Her name is mentioned in the first movement of Shostakovich's Symphony no. 13. Grigory Frid dedicated his monologue-opera *Dnevnik Anni Frank* (The diary of Anne Frank, 1969) to her; the work is based on excerpts from this publication. The opera premiered with piano accompaniment at the Composers' House outside of Moscow, in May 1972. As Frid recalled:

I suffered many agonies with this opera. That was because Gennady Rozhdestvensky wanted to perform it right away in the Grand Hall of the Moscow Conservatory. There were large concert posters, the performance was also mentioned in the Philharmonic's concert schedule with the exact date. But the concert was cancelled. I was summoned to the Cultural Department of the Central Committee, where I was told: "Grigory Samuilovich, we have to wait until the wave of Jewish emigrants subsides" (this was already in the early 1970s). "Besides, you must understand: the Party Congress."[47]

In 1977 a concert performance took place in a small and provincial town. The opera saw its staged premiere only in 1985, in the city of Voronezh.

Among the composers who addressed the Holocaust, the work of Moisey Vaynberg stands out due to the sheer volume of relevant compositions. Vaynberg was originally from Warsaw and the only member of his family to survive by fleeing to the USSR. The memory of the perished Polish-Jewish culture and his murdered family members form the common thread of his work. His Symphony no. 6 for boys' choir and orchestra in five movements (1962–1963) also addresses the Babyn Yar massacre and was inspired by Shostakovich's Symphony no 13. In the second movement he sets a text by the Leyb Kvitko and in the fourth movement by Samuil Halkin—both poets fell victim to the Stalinist anti-Semitic campaign of 1948–1953; each translated from the Yiddish into Russian—and in the last by Mikhail Lukonin. Unlike the first movement of Shostakovich's symphony, these texts do not explicitly reference Jewishness. The word "Jew" does not appear, not even in the fourth movement, in which mass shootings and children's screams are mentioned. But Vaynberg's music contains numerous Jewish elements (these were not necessary in Shostakovich's symphony because Jewishness was clearly articulated in the text), which, similarly to several of his other compositions, rarely rely on folklore. Rather, now in parallel to quite a few of Shostakovich's works from the 1940s to 1950s, he relies on musical symbolism: in Vaynberg's work, Jewishness generally extends, above all, to tragic associations. It relies on melodic and rhythmic phrases that directly link to Jewish traditional music. And there are structures that refer to Polish-Jewish musical culture in a broader sense, such as characteristic genres and forms of Polish popular music from the interwar period, a time during which Jews predominantly shaped and represented musical culture in a kind of Polish-Jewish musical symbiosis. And finally, certain musical images and associations—mainly somber and dramatic—relate to the Jewish experience of war as well as the catastrophe of the Holocaust. Such subtle incorporation of absolute music representing Jewishness obviously could not be grasped by Soviet cultural supervision. There were no censorship concerns regarding the symphony, especially in light of Lukonin's text in the last movement conveying the obligatory optimistic perspective. The Symphony no. 6 was premiered in Moscow in November 1963, under the baton of Kirill Kondrashin, who had conducted the premiere of Shostakovich's Symphony no. 13 a year earlier.

In the following years, Vaynberg wrote numerous other works in which the memory of the Holocaust had a formative influence. Among them are several symphonic and chamber-music works dedicated to the personal memory of Vaynberg's murdered family members: the String Quartet no. 16 (1971) is dedicated to his sister, the afore-mentioned Symphony no. 13 (1976) and the Sonata for Violin and Piano no. 6 (1982) to his mother, the Sonata for Solo Violin no. 3 (1979) to his father. He also wrote the cantata *Dnevnik lyubvi* (The notebook, 1965) for tenor, boys' choir, and chamber orchestra (1965). The Polish-Jewish poet Stanisław Wygodzki, whose entire family was murdered in Auschwitz, had written the texts in 1945 while hospitalized after his liberation from Dachau concentration camp. All of these works also have in common that they address Jewish suffering only indirectly on a textual level. Only Vaynberg's last completed Symphony no. 21 (1991) bears the unmistakable subtitle "Kaddish"; it is dedicated to the victims of the Warsaw Ghetto.

Vaynberg's most significant work with regard to processing the Holocaust is his opera *Passazhirka* (The lady passenger, 1967–1968), based on an autobiographical novella by the Polish writer Zofia Posmysz. Although the opera was commissioned by the Bolshoy Theater, it was not performed there. Neither the positive assessment of the Composers' Union, which recommended publication of the piano score, nor the advocacy of Shostakovich, who also wrote an enthusiastic preface for the print edition published in 1974, could bring it on stage. Although the opera focuses on Auschwitz, Jewishness is only marginally present when the Jewish girl Hannah from Salonika, an episodic character in the opera, recalls the extermination of the Jews. In accordance with the official "internationalist" Soviet view, the Jews are thus not mentioned as "exclusive" victims. Nevertheless, the subject of Auschwitz alone was reason for rejection. The opera was first performed in concert only in December 2006 at Moscow's International Performing Arts Center. The staged premiere followed in July 2010 at the Bregenz Festival. In the meantime, *Passazhirka* has become one of the most performed twentieth-century operas and has become a subject in musicological literature as well.[48]

Noteworthy is Vustin's *Tri stikhotvoreniya* (Three poems, 1966) for bass and piano, which set texts on the Holocaust by the renowned Yiddish poet Moisey Teif, albeit in Russian translation. Stylistically these songs are reminiscent of Shostakovich's *Iz yevreyskoy narodnoy poèziy*. Sergey Berinsky came to terms with the Holocaust with three works, composed in quick succession: the cantata *Kamni Treblinki* (The stones of Treblinka, 1977) for soloists, choir, and orchestra on Yiddish texts by Aron Vergelis; and the song cycle *Gvozdiki na snegu* (Carnations in the snow, 1978–1979) on poems in Yiddish by Khaim Beyder—both were part of a few Yiddish-language poets contributing to the Yiddish-language literary magazine *Sovetish heymland*, which was published from 1959 onward. Other noteworthy works are the *Rekviyem pamyati Yanusha Korchaka* (1979) in memory of the Polish Jewish educator and writer Henryk Goldszmit, who showed resistance against the Nazis and was murdered in Treblinka in 1942. All these works carefully navigate the Soviet and the Jewish, the individual and the collective experience through coded, yet clear messages or ambiguities hidden in music, text, and dedication.

FROM SOVIET STAGE TO JEWISH STAGE

Against all odds, in May 1957 a Jewish choir formed in Riga. This choir rehearsed at the trades club in the city center, at 17 Blauman Street. (Shortly thereafter a Yiddish drama group and orchestra formed as well, after receiving express permission from local officials.) Two hundred Jews applied to participate and rehearsals began in July that year. Eventually the government interfered, leading to rehearsals being held in secret and outside the club. The choir first performed on February 12, 1958, in the hall of the Riga Conservatory; music critics and a few officials from the party and state authorities attended. Thereafter the choir faced restrictions, being forced to reduce and eliminate Jewish identifiers, though it still included ghetto and other songs in Yiddish in their programming. From April 1958 until May 1962 the choir gave thirty-eight more concerts in Riga and beyond, some of them together with Nehama Lifshits.[49] As one of the few examples of Jewish collectivity in the absence of a Jewish community, the choir embodies the importance of a musical community.

A second similar collective formed twenty years later, in the midst of Brezhnev's suffocated era (1964–1982). In late 1977 the Jewish Autonomous Oblast in the Russian Far East unexpectedly got permission for its own music theater troupe, the Birobidzhan Chamber Jewish Musical Theater known under its Russian acronym KEMT; it formed the following year. The international criticism of the anti-Semitic cultural policy in the Soviet Union had given impetus for allowing the establishment of performing organizations focused on Jewish culture (a Yiddish theater group also formed in Kiev). Since the administrative center of Birobidzhan did not have the necessary infrastructure, in 1981 the theater moved its base to Moscow, from where the troupe toured all over the USSR, especially to the places that retained large Jewish populations, first under its director Yuri Sherling (1944–) and from 1984 under Mikhail Gluz (1951–2021). The young actors did not speak Yiddish and received language coaching from those of the former GOSET cast who were still professionally active at the time. Its first production *A shvarts tsayml far a vays ferdl* (A black bridle for a white mare) with music by Sherling was a huge success. The subsequent production *Lomir ale in eynem* (Let us all together) was conceived as a theatrical concert, with Gluz arranging many well-known Yiddish songs with classics by Mordechai Gebirtig, Mark Varshavsky, and Abraham Goldfaden. This production was also presented internationally in Eastern Bloc countries and in the United States. The history of the KEMT provides a more nuanced version of the common narrative that discusses the trajectory of Soviet Jews from authentic Jewish expression to acculturation, from Yiddish to Russian, from Judaism to atheism. It encapsulates the persistence of Yiddish culture, as both a vernacular and a post-vernacular means of identification.[50]

After Gluz parted with the troupe in 1991, the theater fell into crisis and was finally disbanded in 1995. At that time, however, the situation of Jewish musical culture on the territory of the former Soviet Union had already changed fundamentally.

With perestroika, a new era in the history of Jewish music began as well. Leningrad was the forerunner. Already in May 1988 an International Festival of Cantorial Music took place in the Leningrad's Grand Choral Synagogue. Within two days, six concerts were held, which were advertised throughout the city and were all sold out. A total of thirteen thousand people attended. These concerts, as well as the guest appearance of Shlomo Carlebach in the Leningrad's Grand Choral Synagogue in 1989 (and subsequent appearances in Kiev, Vilnius, and Moscow) and in the city's Yubileynïy Sports Palace in 1990, marked a breakthrough for Jewish musical life.[51] Indeed, since perestroika, a comprehensive reshaping of Jewish life has begun. Judaism in all its facets and forms is now no longer taboo and discriminated, but an important and respected part of the multinational culture not only in Russia, but also in the Ukraine, Belarus, and other former Soviet states.

In light of the recent developments, Jewish music in the post-Stalinist era is often misjudged in its significance, seen as a reflection of a period of stagnation, in which purely propagandistic musical activities were intended to conceal the actual absence of a "real" Jewish life in the Soviet Union. And yet, Soviet Jews developed their own forms of Jewish practices in private and public spheres, with music and theater perhaps being their only collective representation "on stage"—regardless whether as a musical community in distinct moments or in distinct collectives such as the choir or the theater troupe. As such, the musical community was highly temporary in nature, a fluid collectivity that anew formed each moment. Nonetheless, concerts and works conceived for the Soviet stages showed that Jewishness mattered, with music taking on new symbolism as a coded message and becoming imbued with new meaning. Most importantly, and perhaps unexpectedly, Soviet Jews and non-Jews were vigorously producing Jewish music from the 1950s through about 1970, a time Elie Wiesel had called the era of the "Jews of silence."[52] Aleksandr Galich, Vladimir Vysotsky, and Yuz Aleshkovsky used new recording technology in the 1960s and 1970s to spread their subversive songs. Following in their footsteps, in 1982 and 1983, in the era of the refuseniks, singer-songwriter Aleksandr Rosenbaum wrote a cycle of songs reimagining Isaac Babel's *Odessa Stories*. Composers, musicians, and audiences contributed to the awareness of a common Soviet-Jewish historical heritage, with music providing a paradoxical alternative to the silencing of all things Jewish.

Notes

1. For a comprehensive study on Jewish musical life in Russia half century before 1917, see James B. Loeffler, *The Most Musical Nation: Jews and Culture in the Late Russian Empire* (New Haven, CT: Yale University Press, 2010).

2. See Jascha Nemtsov, "Antisemitic Tendencies in Stalinist Music Policy," in *"Samuel" Goldenberg and "Schmuyle": Jüdisches und Antisemitisches in der russischen Musikkultur*, ed. Ernst Kuhn, Jascha Nemtsov, and Andreas Wehrmeyer (Berlin: Ernst Kuhn, 2003), 205–224. Among the authoritative writings that shaped Soviet state-directed anti-Semitism were Karl Marx's *Zur Judenfrage* (On the Jewish question, 1843), Lenin's

Положение Бунда в партии (The situation of the Bund in the party, 1903), and Stalin's Марксизм и национальный вопрос (Marxism and the national question, 1913).

3. See Arno Lustiger, *Rotbuch: Stalin und die Juden* (Berlin: Aufbau Taschenbuch, 2000), 72.

4. "Еврейский народ в очень необычной ситуации. Радость от долгожданной свободы и равенства отравлена полным подавлением национальной культуры. Язык запрещен, экономические преследования в основном затрагивают евреев. . . . Так много горя." David Schor, diary entry of June 18, 1924, Ives Schor Archive, folder 450, p. 137, Department of Manuscripts, ARC. 4* 1521, The National Library of Israel, Jerusalem.

5. See David Shneer, *Yiddish and the Creation of Soviet Jewish Culture, 1918–1930* (Cambridge: Cambridge University Press, 2004).

6. See Jeffrey L. Wollock, "Soviet Recordings of Jewish Instrumental Folk Music, 1937–1939," *ARSC Journal* 34, no. 1 (March 2003): 14–32; and Jeffrey L. Wollock, "The Soviet Klezmer Orchestra," *East European Jewish Affairs* 30, no. 2 (2000): 1–36.

7. Documents that evidence these plans were first summarized in Louis Rapaport, *Stalin's War Against the Jews: The Doctors' Plot and the Soviet Solution* (New York: Free Press, 1990). Subsequently, a number of historians have discussed the findings as controversial.

8. This postulate was first formulated by Stalin in his speech at the 16th Congress of the Bolshevik Party on June 27, 1930: "As a matter of fact, the period of the dictatorship of the proletariat and the building of socialism in the U.S.S.R. is a period in which national culture, socialist in content and national in form, blossoms." *Joseph Stalin: Marxism and The National Question, Selected Writings and Speeches* (New York: International Publishers, 1942), 208. It remained in effect until the end of communist rule.

9. See Larissa Remennick, *Russian Jews on Three Continents: Identity, Integration, and Conflict* (New Brunswick, NJ: Transaction Books, 2006), 31.

10. See, for example, Jeffrey Veidlinger, *The Moscow Soviet Jewish Theater: Jewish Culture on the Soviet Stage* (Bloomington: Indiana University Press, 2000); Anna Shternshis, "May Day, Tractors and Piglets: Yiddish Songs for Little Communists," in *The Art of Being Jewish in Modern Times*, ed. Barbara Kirshenblatt-Gimblett and Jonathan Karp (Philadelphia: University of Pennsylvania Press, 2008), 83–97; and Ber Kotlerman, "Positivist Romanticism on the Soviet Jewish Stage: Moyshe Goldblatt's New Yiddish Theatre (1937–1938)," *Aschkenas: Zeitschrift für Geschichte und Kultur der Juden* 24, no. 1 (2014): 101–127.

11. For further details, particular on Sidi Tal, see Asya Vaisman, "Sidi Tal and Yiddish Culture in Czernowitz in the 1940s–1980s"; http://czernowitz.ehpes.com/stories/vaisman/vaisman.html (accessed July 31, 2022).

12. "Среди тех, кто остался в живых после большой эпидемии, и Михаил Эпельбаум. Он разъезжает с концертами по Украине и Молдавии. Мне рассказали, что когда в одном местечке он вышел на сцену и произнёс одно только слово: 'Yidn' (евреи), поднялся всеобщий плач, длившийся очень долго, прежде чем публика наконец успокоилась и он смог приступить к программе." Quoted after Aleksandr Frenkel, "'Соним аф цулохес'—'Врагам назло': Еврейская эстрада в Ленинграде эпохи оттепели" ["Sonim af tsulokhes"—"Defying the enemies": Jewish Popular music in Leningrad during the Thaw], in Из истории еврейской музыки в России [On the history of Jewish music in Russia], ed. Galina Kopytova and Aleksandr Frenkel (St. Petersburg: Jewish Community Center Publishing House, 2015), 205.

13. For further details, see the extended text of the booklet by Joel Rubin and Rita Otens, accompanying the CD *Shalom Comrade! Yiddish Music in the Soviet Union, 1928–1961* (Mainz: Schott Wergo, 2010).

14. ". . . сделались в СССР основной, самой массовой и доступной формой существования еврейской культуры. Они стали практически единственными за пределами синагог и кладбищ 'местами встречи,' где советские евреи могли легально собираться для коллективного 'национального действия'—причём не только совместного приобщения к наследию своего народа, но и просто общения, знакомства, выстраивания социальных связей. Фактически 'еврейские концерты' играли роль специфического суррогата общинной жизни в условиях запрета на все прочие формы этнической консолидации." Ibid., 193.

15. "В Минске вообще не давали выступать, и когда я пришла в ЦК, мне сказали, что 'цыганам и евреям нет места в Минске'. . . . В конце концов мне позволили выступить в белорусской столице, после чего в газете появилась рецензия, в которой говорилось, что 'концерт был проникнут духом национализма.'" Lyudmila Kligman, "От молитвы до хохмы" [From prayer to humor], https://www.migdal.org.ua/times/66/5832/ (accessed January 31, 2021).

16. "Прошел слух, что приезжает певица, будет петь на идиш. Афиш не было. Захудалый клуб швейников. Зал человек на сто... Она меня поразила — она не только пела, она проявляла несгибаемое еврейское достоинство, несклоненность, уверенность в своей правоте. Она была насыщена национальным чувством. Какое мужество! Нехама была продолжением восстания в Варшавском гетто . . ." Shulamit Shalit, "Чтоб все видели, что я жива . . ." [Let everyone see that I am alive . . .], https://jennyferd.livejournal.com/6681813.html (accessed January 31, 2021).

17. Mikhail Nudler (1944–) organized a Purimshpiler troupe in Moscow in 1977. The performance took place in his apartment and included seventeen performers and twenty spectators. Dmitry Yakirevich wrote the music for it. Nudler has lived in Israel since 1980.

18. "Летом 1974 года в переполненном зале гостиницы 'Советская' прошла премьера спектакля. . . . Премьера произвела эффект мощного взрыва. . . . Трудно передать словами энтузиазм зрительного зала, в котором с этого раза стала присутствовать и молодёжь. Сказать, что публика только подпевала, было бы мало. Публика, казалось, дышала каждым тактом музыки, наслаждалась диалогами и пританцовывала вместе с актёрами. . . . В дальнейшем "Заколдованный портной" не сходил со сцены до конца 1987 года. . . . вокруг спектакля по Шолом-Алейхему возникла какая-то чуть ли не мистическая атомосфера. Билеты на него достать было почти невозможно. Всё раскупалось заранее. И я хорошо помню, как активист еврейского движения Михаил Нудлер скупал билеты в каких-то пригородных кассах (видимо, они направлялись туда специально, чтобы предотвратить аншлаги) и затем распространял их в кругу отказников и самых близких друзей." Dmitry Yakirevich, "Юбилейные ассоциации" [Biblical associations], https://belisrael.info/?p=115 (accessed January 31, 2021).

19. ". . . бюрократическая система выработала для еврейской культуры в СССР новую модель, характеризовавшуюся, прежде всего, словами 'ограничение' и 'минимизация.'" Aleksandr Frenkel, "Sonim af tsulokhes," 222.

20. See "The Central Committee of the Communist Party of Ukraine, 1968–1988," fond 1, inventory 25, folder 42, p. 4447, Central State Archives of Public Organizations of Ukraine, Kiev.

21. See Abram Yusfin, "Die jüdische Kunstmusik in der Epoche ihrer offiziellen Nichtexistenz in Russland," in *Verfemte Musik: Komponisten in den Diktaturen unseres Jahrhunderts—Dokumentation des Kolloquiums vom 9.–12. Januar 1993 in Dresden*, ed. Joachim Braun,

Vladimir Karbusický, and Heidi Tamar Hoffmann (Frankfurt am Main: Peter Lang, 1997), 183–194. The original Russian version of this article is published in Dmitry Elyashevich, Евреи в России: История и культура (Jews in Russia: history and culture) (St. Petersburg: St. Petersburg Jewish University Publishing House, 1995), 197–205.

22. See also Frenkel, "Sonim af tsulokhes,"/IBT> 238.

23. See ibid., 242. The musical director of the ensemble was the pianist and composer Semen (Zalman) Freydenberg (1901–1972), who had toured as a pianist together with Mikhail Epelbaum in the 1930s and was later imprisoned in the Gulag in 1947–1953.

24. The MEDA survived perestroika. In the late 1980s, it was restructured into the Jewish Theater "Shalom" under the direction of the well-known actor and director Aleksandr Levenbuk (1933–), with performances are in Russian.

25. "'Все мои песни—еврейские,' —заявил Шаинский. — 'Это кадиши, переделанные под якобы русские песни. Смотрите,'—сел он за рояль и начал играть сначала свои песни, а потом соответствующие им еврейские молитвы, подробно объясняя, как он их подгонял под русский колорит. Вечер закончился всеобщим повальным хохотом." Grigory Zhelnin, "Его песни распевает вся страна" (His songs are sung by the whole country), https://jewish.ru/ru/people/culture/3108/ (accessed July 26, 2021)

26. Robert A. Rothstein, "How It Was Sung in Odessa: At the Intersection of Russian and Yiddish Folk Culture," *Slavic Review* 60, no. 4 (2001): 781–801.

27. Yusfin, "Die jüdische Kunstmusik," 183.

28. Much has been written about the song cycle, especially by Russian scholars. Two noteworthy recent publications are Camilla Bork, "Aus jiddischer Volkspoesie: Schostakowitschs Liedzyklus Opus 79 und die musikalische Lyrik des 20. Jahrhunderts—Versuch einer historischen Standort-Bestimmung," in *Jüdische Musik und ihre Musiker im 20. Jahrhundert*, ed. Wolfgang Birtel, Joseph Dorfman, Christoph-Hellmut Mahling, Schriften zur Musikwissenschaft (Mainz: Are Edition, 2006), 183–202; and Evgenia Khazdan, "Cycle 'From Jewish Folk Poetry' by Dmitry Shostakovich: The Ethnomusicological Viewpoint," in *Jüdische Musik Als Dialog der Kulturen / Jewish Music as a Dialogue of Cultures*, ed. Jascha Nemtsov and Jüdische Musik (Wiesbaden: Harrassowitz, 2013), 243–258.

29. See Dethlef Arnemann, "Der jüdische Tanz in Schostakowitschs Erstem Violinkonzert op. 77: Ein Tanz gegen den Tod?," in *Dmitri Schostakowitsch und das jüdische musikalische Erbe / Dmitrij Šostakovič and the Jewish Heritage in Music*, ed. Ernst Kuhn, Andrea Wehrmeyer, and Günter Wolter, Schostakowitsch-Studien 3 (Berlin: Verlag Ernst Kuhn, 2001), 229–269.

30. For a detailed analysis of Shostakovich's reliance on Jewish folk idioms in the string quartet, see Jada Watson, "Aspects of the 'Jewish' Folk Idiom in Dmitri Shostakovich's String Quartet. No.4, Op. 83" (MA thesis, University of Ottawa, 2008).

31. See Izaly Iosifovich Zemtsovsky, "Schostakowitsch und der Jiddischismus in der Musik," in Kuhn, Wehrmeyer, and Wolter, *Dmitri Schostakowitsch und das jüdische musikalische Erbe*, 160. See also Sigrid Neef, "'Glory" oder "Gorje": Das jüdische Element in Schostakowitschs Opern (unter Einbeziehung von Flejschmans Oper Rothschilds Geige)," ibid., 200–228.

32. See Moisey Beregovsky, Еврейские народные песни (Moscow: Sovyetskiy Kompozitor, 1962).

33. Dmitry Shostakovich, preface to *Naye Yidishe lider* (Moscow: Sovyetskiy Kompozitor, 1970).

34. Esfir Veprik, Кто есть кто? [Who's who], diaries, April, 19, 1968, Russian State Archive of Literature and Art (RGALI), fond 2444, part 2, folder 136. The *Dve poemy* for orchestra (1956–1957) belong to Veprik's last compositions, but they are not his last works. This comprehensive diary is an important document attesting to the suppression of the music produced by the New Jewish School in the post-Stalinist period, as well as the anti-Semitic state policies of the time in general.

35. Mikhail Krutikov, "Constructing Jewish Identity in Contemporary Russian Fiction," in *Jewish Life after the USSR*, ed. Zvi Gitelman, Musya Glants, and Marshall I. Goldman (Bloomington: Indiana University Press, 2003), 252.

36. See Veprik, Кто есть кто?, September 13, 1965.

37. It is noteworthy that the well-known musicologist of Jewish descent Genrikh Orlov (1926–2007) devoted a chapter to Klyuzner's Violin Concerto in his monograph Русский советский симфонизм [Russian Soviet symphonic music] (1966), but without mentioning the Jewish influences.

38. Marina Boikova, "Unveröffentlichte Werke jüdischer Komponisten in Russland," in *Die Musik des osteuropäischen Judentums—totalitäre Systeme—Nachklänge: Kolloquium vom 02.–04.07.1994*, ed. Udo Zimmermann (Dresden: Dresdner Zentrum für zeitgenössische Musik, 1997), 96.

39. See ibid., 95.

40. See also James Loeffler, " 'In Memory of Our Murdered (Jewish) Children': Hearing the Holocaust in Soviet Jewish Culture," *Slavic Review* 73, no. 3 (2014): 585–611. Loeffler focuses on Mikhail Gnesin's Piano Trio, op. 63 (1943). Aleksandr Manevich's oratorio *Kaddish* (1946) for choir and wind orchestra is not mentioned, but Mendel Bash's memorial to the victims of Babyn Yar, the oratorio of 1961, is.

41. "Was sie [die Funktionäre] zu hören bekamen, verschlug ihnen allerdings die Sprache ob seiner Dreistigkeit: Das gesamte Themenmaterial der Symphonie war durchzogen von ausgesprochen jüdischen Motiven. Zur Trauer-Apotheose des Finales sang der Sopran eine Vokalise im Stile der synagogalen Gesänge, die sehr stark an das jüdische Totengebet (Kaddisch) erinnerte. Der Skandal war perfekt." Irma Zolotovitsky, "Zufälliges und Nicht-Zufälliges in Schostakowitschs 'Jüdischen' Kompositionen," in Kuhn, Wehrmeyer, and Wolter, *Dmitri Schostakowitsch*, 110.

42. Inna Dvuzhil'naya, Тема Холокоста в академической музыке [Holocaust as subject in art music] (Grodno: Grodno University Press, 2016), 72.

43. "На первом же концерте после 'Колыбельной' зрители оцепенели, пока тишину не разорвал чей-то крик: 'Что же вы, люди, встаньте!'. Зал встал, и тут же дали занавес. На следующий день певицу вызвали в ЦК, где потребовали текст песни и запретили ее исполнение. Не помогло—Нехама все равно ее спела и была наказана сокращением гастролей в Киеве с семи концертов до трех. После этого ей целый год распоряжением едва ли не министра культуры не давали выступать." Vera Drizo, "Как Нехаму Лифшицайте после 'Колыбельной Бабьему Яру' в Киеве гастролей лишили" [How Nehama Lifshitz was not allowed to perform after the "Lullaby to Babi Yar"], *Hadashot: Newspaper of the Association of Jewish Organizations and Communities on Ukraine*, no. 9 (September 2018), http://archive.hadashot.kiev.ua/content/kak-neh amu-lifshicayte-posle-kolybelnoy-babemu-yaru-v-kieve-gastroley-lishili   (accessed January 31, 2021).

44. "Ривка Боярская уже тогда была прикована к постели. Без надрыва, но с невыносимой глубиной, от которой окаменевают на месте, она "провыла" этот Плач. Я сидела, окаменев, в её убогой квартирке в запущенном доме, что напротив Московской консерватории, где она жила с мужем, театральным критиком Любомирским. Я не могла подняться с места. Дриз почти вынес меня на улицу. Я унесла с собой этот Плач. Пианистка Надежда Дукятульскайте, которая тогда была со мной в Москве, сама потерявшая единственного ребёнка в гетто Каунаса, нашла к песне строгие аккорды, и вместе с ней мы искали пути к исполнению, ведь это нельзя назвать ни песней, ни плачем, весь художественный и литературный опыт кажется фальшью. Это невозможно назвать ни звуком, ни словом, это как сплошная боль, которая ещё усиливается от прикосновения. Как же было прикоснуться к ней, тянущейся в монотонной мелодии с неожиданно прерывающимися вскрикиваниями и затем каждый раз мёртво замирающей и слабеющей в этом ужасном 'Люленьки-лю-лю'? "Кина'—вот как это называют в нашем народе—'Плач над Погибшим и Разрушенным.'" Nehama Lifshitz, excerpts from the memoirs quoted after https://jennyferd.livejournal.com/7906825.html (accessed January 21, 2021).

45. See also Francis Maes, *A History of Russian Music: From Kamarinskaya to Babi Yar* (Berkeley: University of California Press, 2002), 366–368.

46. See Yusfin, "Die jüdische Kunstmusik," 191.

47. "Я с этой оперой много мучений перенёс. Дело в том, что Геннадий Рождественский решил тогда сразу исполнить её в Москве в Большом зале консерватории. Были расклеены громадные афиши, выпущена программа филармонии с точным числом, когда это будет. Но концерт сняли. Меня вызывали представители ЦК, отдел культуры и сказали: 'Григорий Самуилович, нам надо подождать, во-первых, когда схлынет волна отъезжающих евреев' (это было уже начало 70-х гг.). 'Во-вторых, Вы понимаете—съезд.'" Quoted after Dvuzhil'naya, Тема Холокоста, 119. Frid most likely refers to the 24th Congress of the Communist Party of the Soviet Union held in 1971.

48. Among the most recent publications are Ludwig Steinbach, *Weinbergs Passagierin: Eine Analyse der Auschwitz-Oper* (Friedberg: Verlagshaus Schlosser, 2015) and Alexander Gurdon, "Sinfonisches Erinnern: Mieczysław Weinberg und Dmitrij Šostakovič als Musikalische Chronisten," in *Mein 20. Jahrhundert: Musikforschung zwischen Subjektivität und Fachlichkeit*, ed. Thomas Erlach and Klaus Oehl, Dortmunder Schriften zur Musikpädagogik und Musikwissenschaft 2 (Berlin: Lit Verlag, 2018), 67–91.

49. For further details on the choir's infrastructure and repertoire, see David Garber, "Choir and Drama in Riga," *Soviet Jewish Affairs* 4, no. 1 (1974): 39–44.

50. For a history of KEMT, see Yuri Sherling, Парадокс (Moscow: Feniks, 2007).

51. For a detailed account of the tour, see Natan Ophir, *Rabbi Shlomo Carlebach: Life, Mission, and Legacy* (Jerusalem: Urim Publications, 2014), 275–282.

52. Elie Wiesel, *The Jews of Silence: A Personal Report on Soviet Jewry* (New York: Holt, Rinehart, and Winston, 1966).

SELECT BIBLIOGRAPHY

Braun, Joachim. "The Double Meaning of Jewish Elements in Dimitri Shostakovich's Music." *Musical Quarterly* 71, no. 1 (1985): 68–80.

Geiger, Friedrich. "Alexander Weprik und die russisch-deutschsprachige Musikmoderne." In *Jüdische Musik in Sowjetrussland: Die "Jüdische Nationale Schule" der zwanziger Jahre*, edited by Ernst Kuhn and Jascha Nemtsov, 343–352. Studia Slavica musicologica: Texte und Abhandlungen zur slavischen Musik und Musikgeschichte sowie Erträge der Musikwissenschaft Osteuropas 15. Berlin: Ernst Kuhn, 2002.

Geiger, Friedrich, ed. *Komponisten unter Stalin: Aleksandr Veprik (1899–1958) und die Neue jüdische Schule*. Hannah-Arendt-Institut für Totalitarismusforschung: Bericht und Studien, 25. Dresden: Hannah-Arendt-Institut für Totalitarismusforschung, 2000.

Gitelman, Zvi. *A Century of Ambivalence: The Jews of Russia and the Soviet Union, 1881 to the Present*. Bloomington: Indiana University Press, 2001.

Klokova, Antonina. "'Meine moralische Pflicht': Mieczysław Weinberg und der Holocaust." *Osteuropa* 60, no. 7 (July 2010): 173–182.

Kuhn, Ernst, Andreas Wehrmeyer, and Günter Wolter. *Dmitri Schostakowitsch und das jüdische musikalische Erbe / Dmitrij Šostakovič and the Jewish Heritage in Music*. Schostakowitsch-Studien 3. Berlin: Ernst Kuhn, 2001.

Mogl, Verena. *"Juden, die ins Lied sich retten": Der Komponist Mieczyslaw Weinberg (1919–1996) in der Sowjetunion*. Musik und Diktatur. Münster: Waxmann, 2017.

Rothstein, Robert A. "How It Was Sung in Odessa: At the Intersection of Russian and Yiddish Folk Culture." *Slavic Review* 60, no. 4 (2001): 781–801.

Sheinberg, Esti. "Jewish Existential Irony as Ethos in the Music of Shostakovich." In *The Cambridge Companion to Shostakovich*, edited by Pauline Fairclough and David Fanning, 350–367. Cambridge: Cambridge University Press, 2008.

Sherling, Yuri. Парадокс. Moscow: Feniks, 2007.

Shneer, David. *Yiddish and the Creation of Soviet Jewish Culture, 1918–1930*. Cambridge: Cambridge University Press, 2004.

Shternshis, Anna. "Russian Militia Singing in Yiddish: Jewish Nostalgia in Soviet and Post-Soviet Popular Culture." In *Choosing Yiddish: New Frontiers of Language and Culture*, edited by Lara Rabinovitch, Goren Shiri, and Hannah Pressman, 179–194. Detroit: Wayne State University Press, 2012.

Yusfin, Abram. "Die jüdische Kunstmusik in der Epoche ihrer offiziellen Nichtexistenz in Rußland." In *Verfemte Musik: Komponisten in den Diktaturen unseres Jahrhunderts: Dokumentation des Kolloquiums vom 9.–12. Januar 1993 in Dresden*, edited by Joachim Braun, Vladimír Karbusický, and Heidi Tamar Hoffmann, 183–193. Frankfurt am Main: Peter Lang, 1995.

14

ART MUSIC IN THE YISHUV AND IN EARLY-STATEHOOD ISRAEL

JEHOASH HIRSHBERG

ISRAELI art music originated in the unique conditions of the Yishuv (literally, "settlement"), a term used to signify the Jewish community in Palestine under Otoman and British rule, prior to the establishment of the State of Israel in 1948. The beginnings of a musical life that would lead to the development of an art music unique to the region can be traced back to Tel Aviv, when it was still a small garden suburb of the city of Jaffa, one that evinced the inner urge of its residents to become a place for a collective.[1] In 1910 the Jewish population of Jaffa-Tel Aviv numbered about 10,000 within a general population of some 40,000. That year German-born singer Selma (Shulamit) Ruppin opened the first music school in Jaffa (after her untimely death in childbirth in 1912, it was named the Shulamit Music School in her memory). Ruppin invited violinist Moshe Hopenko (1880–1949), a recent immigrant from Russia, to serve as violin teacher and school director. On his first evening in what was still a small but fledgling town, Hopenko, who had rented a room from the local pharmacist, picked up his violin and, to the accompaniment of a piano, began to play. Moldovan-born painter and writer Nahum Gutman (1898–1980) poetically chronicled the magical experience of that very first concert:

נפתחו התריסים בבית הרוקח. מן החלונות המוארים נראה הכנר, ראשו מוטה אל הכינור ויד-ימינו מחליקה בקשת בקלות, כאותה רוח על פני החול... על הגדרות שסביב לבית התיישבו אנשי השכונה... מן הבתים הקרובים הוציאו כסאות למרפסות. אנשים שכבו בחולות שמסביב...וכי יודעים אנו מה בכוחה של מוסיקה לעשות באדם?

The shutters . . . were wide open. Through the lighted window one could see the violinist . . . the bow in his right hand gently caressing the instrument, like the breeze over the sand . . . the neighborhood residents sat on the surrounding fences . . . From nearby houses people took their chairs outside to listen. Others lay down on the sand all around. I said, "Do you know how music can affect us?"[2]

Gutman's accompanying drawing depicts the violinist and pianist as seen through the windows and surrounded by the impromptu audience sitting or reclining in the unpaved street, in the mild Mediterranean weather (Figure 14.1). Together, illustrating the collective power of live music, the musicians and the listeners represent a community of music lovers in the first days of Tel Aviv, likely to meet again on a similar occasion. As such, this concert marked the onset of a transition of art music in the Yishuv from (semi-)private to the public space, from informal to institutionalized.

Several years after what was presumably the first public performance of art music in the Yishuv, there was a hesitant beginning of professional concert activity when Yuly (Joel) Engel (1868–1927), a respected music critic, composer, and a researcher of Jewish music, immigrated from Russia to Palestine (via Berlin) in 1924. As such he followed three members of his Society for Jewish Folk Music (founded in 1908 in St. Petersburg with branches elsewhere). Engel's sudden death three years later cut the activity of that

FIGURE 14.1 Nahum Gutman, הקונצרט הראשון (The first concert), black and white drawing, 1910. Reproduced by permission of the Nahum Gutman Museum, Tel Aviv.

society, but it did not halt the movement it had created. Indeed, the early 1920s marked another shift.

Shortly after his much-acclaimed arrival in Tel Aviv, in the summer of 1923, Russian-born conductor Mark (Mordechai) Golinkin (1875–1963) founded the first opera ensemble with funds raised back in St. Petersburg with the help of a benefit concert, the Palestine Opera or האופרה הארץ ישראלית (Opera of the Land of Israel). Its repertoire was mainstream. The first season opened on July 28, 1923, with Verdi's *La traviata* and continued with Leoncavallo's *Pagliacci*, Gounod's *Faust* and his *Romeo et Juliette*, and Halévy's *La juive*. In the absence of an opera house, these were staged at the Eden Cinema in Tel Aviv and the Zion Theater in Jerusalem. Golinkin forced the singers to learn the librettos in Hebrew translation. But the singers mechanically memorized a text that they could hardly follow, and the audience did not understand what was being sung—as critic Aharon Zeev Ben-Yishai noted: "Was it in Hebrew? I doubt it."[3] Nevertheless, it was the symbolism of opera sung in Hebrew that counted.

As such, the emergence of Israeli art music was closely related to the renaissance of Hebrew as a living language. A shift in the status of Hebrew among the enlightened Jews in Europe and the Jewish immigrants to Palestine had become evident in the course of the 1880s. From a language of ancient religious texts, it became a central factor in the concept of a national literary and spoken revival. As Benedict Anderson asserts, "emerging nations imagined themselves antique."[4] The legitimacy of the Jewish community in Palestine, at first as an autonomous collective and, from 1948, as an independent state, was rooted in a mythological biblical past, with the long history of the language serving as a link, especially with the proliferation of newly emerging Hebrew poetry and literature during the Haskalah, the European Jewish movement toward secularization in the late eighteenth and early nineteenth centuries. Still, this is not to suggest the immediate adoption of Hebrew as the sole spoken language of the Jews in Palestine. Anderson emphasizes the significance of bilingualism in his discussion of the origins of nationalism.[5] Indeed, musicians in Palestine conversed mostly in German, and the languages heard on the street included Yiddish, Arabic, Ladino, and a profusion of European languages, all alongside modern Hebrew. But the primary language in the emerging art music, the concert hall, and on the stage was Hebrew.

Opera had been the most important medium in European national music schools. In the Yishuv, it relied on the utmost dedication of Golinkin, but it suffered from constant lack of funds. In 1927, after merely four seasons, the frail venture collapsed, leaving behind first attempts at a new repertoire for the local stages. The first opera written in the Yishuv was clearly Zionist: *The Pioneers*, a naïve and idealistic work composed in 1924 by Jacob Weinberg (1870–1958), a member of the St. Petersburg Society for Jewish Folk Music. Weinberg's libretto was translated into English by Arthur Mendel, into Hebrew by Joseph Markovsky, and into Yiddish by Meyer Chartiner. The first act takes place in a small Jewish town, a *shtetl* in Poland, where a motivated group of young pioneers—the halutzim of its title—organizes to immigrate to Palestine and establish a kibbutz there. Leah, the daughter of a wealthy family, stays behind, preferring the security of her pampered life, but soon afterward joins her boyfriend, Zeev, leader of the pioneers, and finally the parents of the young couple, the rich family and the poor one, follow suit; the opera concludes with the then Zionist anthem "Hatikvah" (The hope). The most noteworthy number of the opera is the coloratura aria "Ani havatselet ha-sharon" (I am the lily of the Sharon). Weinberg's heroine Leah sings her aria in Act I, while she still being in Poland, as an expression of her longing for the Jewish homeland, Zion. Stylistically it suggests the influence of Russian Orientalism and is reminiscent of the aria sung by the Queen of the Desert in Rimsky-Korsakov's *Zolotoj petušok* (The golden cockerel). As such it marks another transition.

This chapter concerns itself with transitions—from informal to institutionalized spaces and the evolving repertoires that filled them. It does so by focusing on the critical period of pre- and early-statehood Israel, specifically the 1930s to 1960s, and it discusses the stylistic aspects of the music in its historical and social context, including institutions and performing organizations. It also concerns itself with the question to what extent the construct of "Israeli art music" features or correlates with a collective identity within a community in transition.[6]

The Emergence of Institutions and Compositional Constraints

The ascent of Nazism in the 1930s witnessed an outburst of mobility. Irit Youngerman asserts that during this period seventy-five composers reached the shores of the Yishuv—sixty-one, if one eliminates those who came as children.[7] Nearly all the immigrant composers of the 1930s belonged to the category of "anticipatory refugees," defined as those who leave their hostile home country well before its final deterioration, with sufficient financial means and adequate preparation so that they can resume professional work soon after arrival.[8] Still, their migration was not without stress, as reflected in a letter from Paul Frankenburger to his father while the composer was on an exploratory tour of Palestine in the summer of 1933 (a typical action for an anticipatory refugee). The letter also suggests that his migration was motivated by expediency and temporary, and not a life-long commitment to a new place.[9]

Nearly all of the immigrant composers settled in the only urban centers of the time, Jaffa-Tel Aviv and Jerusalem. They arrived concurrently with several hundred professional performers and music teachers, and a seasoned audience eager for the resumption of a European-style concert life. And yet, the composers in the Yishuv comprised an immigrant community totally lacking a receiving community.

However, although much outnumbered by the immigrants from Poland, home to the largest concentration of Jews in Europe in the 1930s, the influence of the German newcomers was so overwhelming in all walks of life that the entire fifth wave of immigration at the time was referred to as "the German aliyah." (Rife with qualitative meaning, the term used to denote Jewish immigration to Palestine and to Israel to this

Table 14.1 A comparative survey of the pioneers of art music in and for the Yishuv.

Germany	German periphery	French influence
Erich Walter Sternberg (1891–1974)	Oedoen Partos (1907–1977). Born into a German-speaking family in Hungary, studied in Budapest under Zoltan Koday	Alexander U. Boskovich (1907–1964). Born in Cluj, Transylvania, trained almost entirely in Paris
Paul (Frankenburger) Ben-Haim (1897–1984)	Joachim Stutschewsky (1891–1976). Born in Russia, completely absorbed in Vienna's German culture	Mordecai Seter (Mark Starominsky) (1916–1994). Born in Russia, trained in Paris
Stefan Wolpe (1902–1972)	Marc Lavry (1903–1967). Born in Riga, Lithuania, almost entire professional career as conductor and composer spent in Berlin	Verdina Shlonsky (1905–1990). Only female composer among founders of Israeli music, born in Russia, trained in Berlin and, mainly, Paris
Josef (Grünthal) Tal (1910–2008)		Menahem (Mahler-Kalkstein) Avidom (1908–1995). Born in Poland, reached Palestine in 1925, later trained at Beirut's American University and then Paris
Hanoch (Heinrich) Jacoby (1909–1990)		
Haim (Heinz) Alexander (1915–2012)		
Abel Ehrlich (1905–2003)		

day is aliyah, literally, "ascent.") Philip Bohlman has pointed out that "the most pervasive ethnic music in the Central European Jewish community is Western art music."[10] Among the immigrant composers of those early years, the ones from Germany or the German periphery were all trained in Germany; the eastern Europeans among them had been attracted to Paris (Table 14.1). The preponderance of the German influence is noteworthy indeed.

Although most of the composers immigrated to Palestine in the 1930s, they did not form a national school nor did they recognize any mentor, as distinct, for example, from the Russian Five. Consequently, their responses to the challenge of creating new music for an emerging if imagined community were individual. In addition to the usual test facing all composers, that is, to compose good music, they faced an additional threefold constraint, either self-imposed or impelled by their surroundings.

Firstly, their attitude toward Jewishness. Assaf Shelleg asserts that most of the immigrant composers who chose to record their ideas of Jewishness in art music had hardly any exposure to Judaism, save for sporadic visits to the synagogue or domestic rituals and that "their impressions were often filtered through a musical language that charted their geocultural background and as such became pertinent to the non-Jewish majority."[11] At times the situation was even more complicated, for example, in the case of Paul Frankenburger (who later changed his name to Ben-Haim; literally, "the son of Haim," rendering his father's name Heinrich in Hebrew); his family visited the Munich synagogue only on the most important Jewish holidays, yet his father, the respected jurist Heinrich Frankenburger, was leader of the large Jewish community in Munich. The second constraint was the composers' attitude toward the East, which was dialectical to their heritage. And lastly, the composers faced ideological pressure to create a new and distinct "Israeli" style; as Shelleg notes, "No immigrant composer could have ignored the high voltage of Zionist rhetoric and its projection onto its burgeoning folk repertoire—authentic, borrowed, or newly invented—that transmitted the Yishuv's collectivist ethos."[12]

A representative example of this threefold constraint is the trajectory of Paul Ben-Haim. While using German in his daily life, immediately upon his immigration in 1933, he took daily Hebrew language lessons for the dual purpose of composing Hebrew art songs and for teaching music theory to children at the aforementioned Shulamit Music School. Lieder had been Ben-Haim's principal focus since the age of thirteen, and he came to Palestine already having created a corpus of eighty. It was only natural that in 1938, a mere five years after arriving, he established the genre of Hebrew art song, beginning with three biblical songs. In one, "Ani havatzelet ha-sharon" (I am the lily of the Sharon), drawn from the Song of Songs, the symmetrical fixed rhythm that he used for his German settings was replaced by a flexible rhythmical organization in 5/8 time, with frequent shifts of stress within the bars and changes of meter. Immediately after his biblical songs, Ben-Haim turned to modern Hebrew poetry, such as Rachel's "Akara" (The barren one).[13]

Aside from the creation of new genres, the most consequential event of the 1930s concerned Bronisław Huberman (1882–1947), one of the acclaimed violinists at the time. An equally great humanist, he embarked on uncompromising efforts to create an orchestra in Palestine, not only as a musical aim but also as a rescue operation for Jewish musicians who had been dismissed from their positions in leading European orchestras by anti-Semitic administrations. Assisted by colleagues, Huberman recruited the musicians through auditions all over Europe, never relaxing the strictures of professional excellence despite his humanitarian motivation.

The inaugural concert finally took place on December 26, 1936, in Tel Aviv and was a national holiday. After rigorous preparation under Swiss conductor Hans Wilhelm Steinberg (1899–1978), the orchestra was soon deemed ready to meet the stringent standards of the legendary Arturo Toscanini, who directed it. The festive concert with Mendelssohn on the program became a powerful anti-Nazi demonstration.[14] For the most part, the Palestine Symphony Orchestra played mainstream works, yet during its first decade, it also premiered a total of 116 new creations by immigrant composers.[15] It inaugurated a subscription series of ten annual programs; the number of subscribers immediately reached 16,000,[16] an impressive figure for a city with a population of

120,000 at the time. (The ongoing joke was that in order to become a subscriber, one needed to wait for another subscriber to pass away). Each program was repeated several times, with performances also held in Jerusalem and in Haifa. Offshoots of the Palestine Symphony Orchestra included several fine chamber-music ensembles, mostly string quartets, whose regular musical activity encompassed weekly Saturday-night concerts in the lobby of the original Tel Aviv Museum building, each program played twice, at 7 p.m. and at 9 p.m.[17] In 1950 it would become the Israel Philharmonic Orchestra.

A few years after the establishment of the Palestine Symphony Orchestra, the British Mandate administration inaugurated the Palestine Broadcasting Service (PBS). A third of its programs consisted of mostly live music broadcasts, from which the PBS Orchestra developed. As an official radio station, it aired music by Jewish and Yishuv composers in nearly each of its programs. Palestine can be said to have become a center of Jewish music with the inauguration of the World Centre for Jewish Music in Jerusalem on March 1, 1938, and the ensuing performance of Ernest Bloch's *Avodath Hakodesh* also known as *Sacred Service*, in 1940.[18] The outbreak of the Second World War cut the initiative short. But the groundwork was laid for the collective power of the orchestra as an institution that represented and catered to an imagined community.

In parallel, further attempts at establishing opera took place. After the initial failure of Mordechai Golinkin's early attempt to create a local opera company, performances resumed in 1931 by the renamed the New Palestine Opera Corporation (still under Golinkin's baton), now accompanied by a larger orchestra. These performances were sporadic, and the company disbanded five years later. Between 1935 to 1940 the Chamber Opera Group put on shows on the stages of the Heifetz and Ohel Shem halls in Tel Aviv, accompanied by two pianists in place of an orchestra. In 1941 a group of musicians inaugurated the short-lived Opera Amamit, also known as Palestine Folk Opera, which used the Moghrabi, a theater with two halls built on the instigation of Tel Aviv's first mayor, Meir Dizengoff, and completed in 1930. The company performed the first original Hebrew opera to be actually staged in Palestine. This was דן השומר (Dan the guard, 1944/45) by Marc Lavry, set to a libretto by Max Brod (1884–1968) and based on the play *Yeriot el ha-kibuts* (Shots fired at the kibbutz) by Shalom Shapira. A patriotic opera, it featured a love story played out against the background of life in a kibbutz during the 1936–1939 Arab uprising in Palestine. The great aria toward the end of the opera specifically identifies the settlement as Kibbutz Hanita, an isolated pioneer community at the northern tip of the country. The opera premiered on February 17, 1945, in Tel Aviv and was staged a total of thirty-two times. The plot revolves around two social groups, each with its own well-identified musical style: the young secular pioneers, and their traditional parents. By 1946 Opera Amamit had staged sixteen productions, but disbanded the following year.

In a sequence of transitions, opera companies emerged, performed, and disbanded, such as the Israel Opera, founded by American operatic soprano Edis De Philippe in 1948. During its decades of existence, it would suffer constant financial difficulties and political-personal straits. It closed after De Philippe's death in 1978. Despite the slim chances of a local opera actually being staged, composers were nevertheless not deterred from taking up the genre. An impressive number of eighty-three operas were written between 1917 and 2012, many of them never staged. The richest source for the plots of these operas was contemporary regional history, a trope that spans the whole century of compositions.

With the foundation of performing organizations, ensembles, and institutions as well as associations such as the Jerusalem Musical Society in 1932 and the Palestine Philharmonic Society in 1934, foundations were laid for Israeli art music and its ideologies by the "founding fathers," all anticipatory refugees. These, however, would face their own transitions.

Compositional Attitudes and Ideological Directions

Leonard Meyer has described the state of music in the mid-twentieth century as "the persistence over a considerable period of time of a fluctuating stasis—a steady-state in which an indefinite number of styles and idioms, techniques and movements, will co-exist."[19] Meyer's approach is a fitting point of departure for the analysis of the contribution of the first generation of composers in Palestine. Resuming composition in new surroundings under the looming threat of war implied that the composers functioned artistically under severe ideological pressures, both from the political and intellectual leadership of the Yishuv, as well as from their own reactions to their relocation. None of the first generation of immigrant composers had known one another prior to immigration, and as previously stated, there was no receiving community of composers in the country whatsoever. None of the new arrivals was recognized as an authority over the others. All of them, however, espoused three prevailing attitudes: collectivism, individualism, and the preservation of the European heritage, and folkloristic nationalism. These were by no means separate, but overlap and transition even within the domain of a single composer.

The most strongly codified (compositional) attitude was collectivism, which was initiated and practiced by Alexander Uriah Boskovich. In 1924 he embarked on piano studies in Vienna, and from 1932 to 1935 he studied in Paris under Paul Dukas and Nadia Boulanger. He then returned to Cluj and was active as an opera conductor and as musical director of a Jewish amateur orchestra. Having arrived in Tel Aviv in 1938 for the premiere of his suite *Chansons populaires juifs* (1936), later renamed *Sharsheret ha-zahav* (The golden chain) by the recently founded Palestine Orchestra, he decided to settle in Tel Aviv rather than return to Cluj, which by then had become dangerously fascist.

In a 1943 lecture for the Jewish-Hungarian community in Tel Aviv, Boskovich shared his ideology, which was already apparent in his Violin Concerto (1942) and Oboe Concerto (1943), deepened with the *Semitic Suite* (1945) for piano, orchestrated a year later, and further unfolded in his writings, a two-part article and an unfinished book.[20] Written five years after the establishment of the State of Israel, Boskovich's article contends that every artist carries within himself a deeply rooted national heritage. Accordingly, he asserted that "Israeli music" could be written only by composers who live in Israel. He formulated his concept of the "where" and the "when" as compulsory for the composer, claiming that under the blue skies and hot sun of the Mediterranean, things are sharply delineated and people are grounded in reality. Music should express the objective collective, and there should be no romantic, personal expression in Israeli music. He named as his representative work the *Semitic Suite*, stressing its origins in the Semitic people rather than in the Jewish spirit, and in his detailed performance instructions he sought to avoid emotional expression altogether, with the piano emitting a dry, percussive sound. He insisted that Israeli music find its symbolism in the melody of Arabic music. Making a detailed transcription of the melodic patterns of the maqām bayātī, he eschewed direct quotes of widely known Eastern tunes, and stressed in the "Introduction" that the *Semitic Suite* is "imagined folklore." Boskovich's doctrine received the support of Max Brod, an influential music critic (Boskovich himself was music critic of the daily *Ha'aretz* between 1956 and 1964). But Boskovich was not consistent in his so-called Mediterranean style; in the first version of the orchestration for the *Semitic Suite*, he instructed the two trumpets to play quarter tones, but he dispensed with them in the final version. He made much use of the piano, which he justified in a special article, in which he stated that the Jewish psyche ought to use the piano as a percussion instrument for rhythmic motoric expression and that the rhythmic potential of nation-building was best expressed by the rhythmic percussive qualities of the piano.[21]

After the *Semitic Suite* there was a long hiatus in his output, in part because Boskovich's artistic search proved difficult, and in part because of daily pressures, such as writing incidental music and creating new versions of the *Semitic Suite*. His orchestral *Shir ha-ma'alot* (Song of ascent, 1960) retains the Mediterranean style, but his subsequent composition, the cantata *Bat Yiśra'el* (Daughter of Israel, 1960), composed to Hayim Nahman Bialik's poem of the same name, was dedicated to the memory of his mother, who had been murdered in Auschwitz, and was composed in a tonal, Romantic manner. He then went through an extreme transformation and turned to serial technique, akin to that of Pierre Boulez, in which he composed his *Concerto da camera* for violin (1962) and *Ornaments* for a large orchestra (1964) before his sudden death at the age of fifty-seven. He had an admiring group of composition students, but they did not comprise an organized school.

The striving for collectivism reached its peak in the kibbutz movement during the Yishuv years, when the number of kibbutzim grew from eleven to one hundred thirty. Each kibbutz had its own musical life, from individual music-making to the kibbutz chorus and amateur orchestra. Almost every kibbutz had its own composer who was in charge of all aspects of musical life in the settlement. The function of music was paramount on the Jewish holidays, which were celebrated in the central dining hall or outdoors. The seder, the most important family ceremony of the Passover holiday, became the climactic collective kibbutz event. Several large kibbutzim created seder ceremonies of their own, which were then adopted by many others. For instance, the seder on

Kibbutz Yagur, the music for which was partly compiled, partly composed by Yehudah Shertok (Sharett, 1901–1979), was a project that originated in 1936 and was completed with its publication in 1951.[22] It earned him the Yoel Engel Prize, named for the father of modern music in Israel and awarded since 1945 by the municipality of Tel Aviv-Jaffa.

A contrasting attitude to collectivism was individualism, with two initial representatives: Erich Walter Sternberg and Stefan Wolpe. Sternberg was the first composer to settle in Palestine, in 1931, having made annual visits there since 1925. In 1938 he composed *The Twelve Tribes of Israel*—שנים-עשר שבטי ישראל. A set of orchestral variations on an original theme, it was the first large-scale orchestral work composed in the Yishuv, albeit following the rhetoric of late Romanticism. Anticipating a critical reaction, Sternberg published a precursory statement in German, along with translations in English and Hebrew, in which he emphasized that composers came to Palestine from the four corners of the earth and from different schools; he goes on to outline their objective: to find their own way and speak their language from within—regardless whether the audience, heterogenous as it were, expects to hear Palestinian folklore, synagogue chants, or Russianisms.[23] It would take a full four years before Sternberg's work would receive its world premiere by the Palestine Orchestra in Tel Aviv.

As it turned out, even the leading critics in the country had contradictory conceptions of what Jewish music was or, later, of what Israeli music ought to be. Sternberg's second orchestral composition, *The Story of Joseph*, composed in 1938 and premiered in November that year in Jerusalem, triggered conflicting responses by two leading critics. David Rosolio (1898–1963) pointed to the salient Jewish idiom of the piece,[24] while Menashe (Rabinowitz) Ravina (1899–1975) opined that Sternberg avoided the interpolation of Eastern motives.[25] Such clashing reviews left Sternberg confused and devoid of the needed support in his new surroundings. His settling-in did not progress well—he never mastered the Hebrew language, could not teach, and despite the appreciation he always received from his colleagues, he was not deemed prolific. His influence on the development of music in Israel remained limited.

New works were always a target for ideological criticism that demanded that they be "Jewish," and later on that they be "Israeli," a frustrating demand since there was no consensus whatsoever among music critics and commentators as to the musical essentials of the desired compositional identity. The blunt style of many of the reviews and public reactions had disastrous consequences, as in the unhappy case of the uncompromising, individualistic composer Stefan Wolpe.[26]

Wolpe differed from the other immigrant composers in that he had escaped from Berlin in 1933 not only as a Jew but also as a communist. He reached Palestine in 1934, after a short exploratory foray to Russia and a few months of studies with Anton Webern in Vienna. His compositional activity in Jerusalem was based on the dialectics of educational activity as choral composer, arranger, and director among kibbutz members, as contrasted with avant-garde compositions as teacher at the music conservatory that later became the Jerusalem Academy of Music and Dance. In 1935 and 1936, respectively, Wolpe composed *Four Studies on Basic Rows* for piano and *Drei kleinere Canons in der Umkehrung zweier 12tönig correspondierender Hexachorde* for viola and violoncello (note the German title);[27] the reaction of the musical establishment in Jerusalem was utterly negative. After hearing the performance of the *Four Studies* in 1936 by Irma Wolpe in Jerusalem, violinist Emil Hauser wrote Wolpe that topical up-to-date items should not be imported here.[28] The newly founded Palestine Orchestra rejected Wolpe's *Passacaglia* (1937), an orchestrated version of the *Four Studies*. An anonymous commentator perceived the music to be alien to the life in Palestine and uttered the hope that local composers will leave the path taken by Schoenberg, Webern, and their followers, and instead consider the music that surrounds them in their new locale.[29] Wolpe was inordinately sensitive and could not abide the vitriolic criticism hurled at him. Despite the deep regard and appreciation of his many students and friends in Jerusalem, he left for the United States in 1938. He was the only one of the immigrant composers who began a Schoenberg-like "school" of young admiring students.

Among the individualistic composers, Paul Ben-Haim became quite influential and internationally successful.[30] He had immigrated to Palestine at the age of thirty-six with 117 opus numbers composed in Germany already behind him. His attitude to his former life was paradoxical: he wanted to treat his past works as a closed chapter, but still felt attached at least to a few of them, which he performed in Palestine, such as his Concerto Grosso (1931). He continued to feel much admiration for Johann Sebastian Bach, whom he deemed the greatest composer who ever lived, evidenced in particular in his *Symphonic Metamorphosis on a Bach Chorale* (1968; note the English title), and for the French music of Debussy and Ravel, such as in his Serenade for flute and string trio composed in 1952. Ben-Haim's innovativeness derived from combining European art music forms together with Eastern elements. These elements included quotes from the traditional songs of Sephardic Jewry, as in the third movement of his large-scale 1949 Piano Concerto, which is based on the Persian-Jewish song "Lailah lo nim" (A sleepless night). He also composed his own imaginative "Eastern" music, such as the opening of his 1962 Violoncello Concerto and the *Sonata a Tre* (1968) for mandolin, guitar, and harpsichord.

Several composers clung to their European heritage and to the German avant-garde, while nurturing individualism. The leading proponent of this attitude was Josef Tal, who had immigrated to Palestine in 1934. After a short spell as a photographer in Haifa (the skill that had gained him an "entry certificate" into Palestine from the British authorities), and a brief and unsuccessful attempt at agriculture in Kibbutz Gesher, he settled in Jerusalem. Tal reacted to the pressures of the critics by rejecting the early direction of music in Israel as he felt it was not established through individual search.[31] As the leading avant-garde composer in the country, Tal maintained the intense, atonal style he had developed when he was still Josef Grünthal in Germany. In all his interviews, he declared that his music was Israeli by virtue of his living in Israel and speaking Hebrew. He occasionally made use of quotations as a means of national identification, such as in his Symphony no. 1 (1952), in which the second and third movements draw on a traditional Jewish-Persian lament derived from Abraham Zvi Idelsohn's *Hebräisch-orientalischer Melodienschatz—Thesaurus of Oriental Hebrew Melodies*. Indeed, Tal became the leading symphonist in Israel, ultimately creating six symphonies. Staying in touch with the European heritage, he pioneered a studio for electronic music at the Hebrew University of Jerusalem; but electronic sonorities always combine with solo instruments in Tal's work, such as his three concertos for piano and tape. He would be joined in this approach by Tzvi Avni.

In the Yishuv and during the first three decades of Israel's statehood, folkloristic nationalism enjoyed the strong political support of Mapai, the dominant political party in Israel until its merger into the modern-day Israeli Labor Party in 1968. The most powerful agent that spread the spoken Hebrew language was public education, and one of its most effective tools was the enormous repertoire of thousands of popular songs in Hebrew. These were performed by professional singers in public concerts, frequently outdoors, on radio and later on television broadcasts, spread by records and audiotapes, as well as regularly sung by school and amateur choirs. As an independent area of research, this subject is beyond the scope of the present chapter.[32]

The folkloristic approach in art music was firmly established by Marc Lavry, who immigrated to Palestine in 1935. In polar opposition to Boskovich, Lavry avoided verbal definitions of his music, asserting that he did not want to enter the debate on whether there was an "Israeli" musical style. He considered himself a composer of "the Land of Israel" because he was part of that land. Lavry established this life-long approach in the first work he composed in Palestine, *Emek*, op. 45 (1937), music set to the paean of praise to the Valley of Jezreel, a fertile area that epitomized Jewish agriculture in Palestine, written by Bulgarian-born poet Rafael Eliaz. Demonstrating his desire to blur any distinction between popular and art music, Lavry expanded *Emek* into an oft-performed symphonic poem based on the hora, the most popular folk dance in the Jewish community (Example 14.1). The *hora* that was danced in Palestine and later Israel has nothing to do with the Romanian *hora lunga*; originating in eastern European Hasidic dances, its regular characteristics were short, symmetrical rhythmic phrases in double meter and repeated syncopations.

Lavry's only seriously committed follower has been Shimon Cohen (1937–). But in the 1950s, during the first years of Israeli statehood, several of his colleagues temporarily adopted his approach as a mark of national identification: Haim Alexander, whose *Six Israeli Dances* for piano (1950) depict an idealistic rustic scene, adopted such a folkloristic attitude in only a few of his early works; Ben-Haim's orchestral suite *From Israel* (1951), with a quote from Bracha Zefira; Menahem Avidom's Symphony no. 3 *Mediterranean Sinfonietta* (1952); and Hanoch Jacoby's *Capriccio Israelien* for symphony orchestra (1951). But by then a shift had already begun to take place, with the foundation

EXAMPLE 14.1 The hora rhythm in Marc Lavry, *Emek* (The valley). Tel Aviv: Israel Music Institute, 1936.

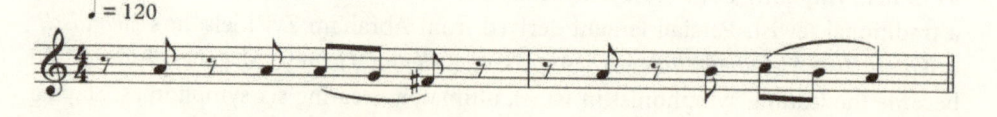

of the State of Israel and with a generation of composers that had been born in the 1920s and had been brought up in the Yishuv.

THE YEMENITE TURN AND PLURALISM

After the reclusiveness that dominated the Yishuv during the decade of World War II and the 1948 War of Independence, the most momentous cultural development of early statehood was the opening of Israeli culture to the West. Three composers born in the 1920s in Germany who immigrated to Palestine as children—Yehezkel Braun (1922–2004), Ben-Zion Orgad (1926–2006), and Tzvi Avni (1927–)—opened the art music of Israel to the pluralism that began to dominate the art-music scenes of Europe and the United States in the 1960s. It is noteworthy that they received their initial training under several of the founding fathers of music in the country, most notably Ben-Haim, Tal, Boskovich, and Seter, and continued their approach. But they also pursued advanced studies in the United States and visited Europe. Tzvi Avni, who had at first perpetuated an individualistic approach, has explicitly stated that his short study period in New York from 1962 to 1964 caused an upheaval in his entire way of thinking.[33] All his explorations at that time found expressions in *Meditations on a Drama*—הרהורים על דראמה (1966). Composed for chamber orchestra, the powerful work makes use of heavy clusters, a large battery of percussion, and some aleatoric sections, but the leading theme of the work is a blast from a solo horn that resembles the sound of the shofar, the ram's horn used in some solemn Jewish synagogue rituals (Example 14.2).

Braun, Orgad, and Avni paved the dialectical way for future generations of Israeli composers: while seeking contacts with the (Arab) East and seeking Jewish expression, they remained in close touch with directions taken in Europe and the United States. To this extent would Avni establish, in 1971, an electronic music studio at the Jerusalem Academy of Music and Dance, and with that Israel kept pace with the most recent developments in this field.

A unique development in Israeli art music was the transformation of the East from a foggy Orientalist ideology to a musical reality through mediators and by means of quotation of traditional melodies derived from publications, such as Idelsohn's *Hebräisch-orientalischer Melodienschatz—Thesaurus of Oriental Hebrew Melodies* and field-work

EXAMPLE 14.2 The horn call emulating the shofar. Tzvi Avni, *Hirhurim 'al drama*, mm. 48–50. Tel Aviv: Israel Music Institute, 1966.

transcriptions, as well as the inclusion of Eastern singers into performances of new compositions. The first mediator between Eastern traditions and Western composers was Bracha Zefira (1910–1990), a singer, song collector, composer, and painter. Born in Jerusalem into a poverty-stricken Yemenite family, she was orphaned when she was three years old and was raised by foster families from different Jewish communities, including Bukharan, Russian, and Sephardic; later she was sent to the Meir Shfeyah youth village and agricultural boarding school in northern Israel. Because she was brought up in several different cultural households, she was exposed to a variety of songs from different ethnic origins. Her teachers, who appreciated her talent, enrolled her at the Jerusalem School of Music, where she studied piano for a short time under British pianist Sidney Seal.[34] She later went to study theater in Berlin. There she met a fellow-member of the Yishuv, pianist Nahum Nardi (born Narodizky, 1901–1977), whom she married. They returned to Palestine and embarked on a career that culminated in several recordings and a series of successful concert tours. Zefira's Yemenite appearance and her unique and well-developed vocal quality were significant elements in her success.

The song "Bein nehar prat unehar ḥideḵel" (Between the Tigris and Euphrates) is a case in point for Zefira's art. It reveals a process of Westernization of an Arab song that reaches its transformation with the addition of piano accompaniment and operatic coloraturas, which enhanced reception of the song in the context of public concerts. Zefira's process takes off from a field recording of a Palestinian song performed by unknown Arab informant, which she designates in her book as "Adouk al-mawwāl," most likely referring to "Qadduk al-mayyās" (Your graceful shape, قدك الموال), a Syrian love song popular in the 1920s.[35] In her singing of the song in Arabic, Bracha Zefira presents her own interpretation, a slight adaptation. The song then goes on to become a textual and musical adaptation by underlaying the poetry of Hayim Nahman Bialik's Hebrew poem, "Bein nehar prat unehar ḥideḵel," set to the Arab tune, but now in regular meter. The same Hebrew song recorded by Zefira reveals another adaptation, by way of interpretation, with Nahum Nardi at the piano underlaying new harmonies and Zefira improvising operatic coloraturas at the end of each stanza.[36] In both the recording studio and life on stage, Nardi improvised his accompaniments to Zefira's singing.

With basically everything being improvised, Bracha Zefira was left with no notated music and no accompanist when she and Nahum Nardi separated in 1938. Under pressure to continue performing, she approached immigrant composers and commissioned them to transcribe and arrange "her" songs: She was the sole performer, refusing to allow any other performers access to them. Seeking prestige, she hired musicians from the Palestine Symphony Orchestra. Zefira performed also with the orchestra at large, such as on July 26 and August 10, 1939. Not unjustifiably, Zefira regarded her performances with the entire orchestra as her greatest achievements, and indeed she continued to be sporadically included in the programming. On the program of a concert taking place on February 4, 1942, was a movement from Paul Ben-Haim's Symphony no. 1 (1940); Israel Brandman's *Variationen über eine Thema von Engel* for piano and string orchestra (ca. 1934), with Ben-Haim as piano soloist; Marc Lavry's *Emek*; and six arrangements for

Zefira by Ben-Haim, Nardi, and Lavry—a clear turn of the singer to art music. But such concerts were rare; and her performances with ensembles were limited to Tel Aviv.

Ben-Haim became Zefira's foremost collaborator and piano accompanist, and he composed thirty-five arrangements for her, some of which of the same song.[37] An examination of these arrangements reveals a process of metrical regularization, as is evident in Ben-Haim's arrangement of "Lailah lo nim" (A sleepless night). The melody was originally part of the canon of traditional Persian Jewish circumcision ceremonies; Zefira asked poet Rafael Eliaz to write secular lyrics for the tune and thus was born a mellifluous love song. Ben-Haim made an equally dulcet arrangement in triple meter. He regularly incorporated his arrangements into large-scale instrumental works, and the present arrangement was interpolated, as previously mentioned, into the Piano Concerto of 1949, where it became part of the spirited Scherzo.

Zefira herself was critical of composers' ability to integrate Eastern song into art music, stating that they had no such experience, and despite their efforts they picked up the least characteristic and authentic elements of the songs.[38] The result, according to Zefira, was Oriental songs in cumbersome Western garb, and its interpretation she found lacking as well. In turn, as Ronit Seter has ascertained, Ben-Haim never credited Zefira for inspiring his work, silencing altogether the role she played in his conception of thirty-three of his works, that is, more than a third of his compositional oeuvre during the time of their collaboration, from 1939 to 1957.[39] Zefira stated several times that her sole interest was to sing in concert.[40] However, she also presented herself as protector of the traditional Eastern song, expanding her repertoire through interviews with informants from different Jewish communities as well as Bedouins and Arabs—a pluralism in its own right. As such she was not the only musician who drove such attempts at pluralism.

In the 1940s similar efforts were also made by the Yemenite singer and choreographer Sara Levi-Tanai (1911–2005). Like Zefira, she was orphaned at a young age and was raised in the same Meir Shfeyah youth village, where she was trained to be a kindergarten teacher. It was in that milieu that she composed her first songs. When she joined a social club of young Yemenites, she was exposed to the Yemenite traditions, which she avidly absorbed. In 1949 she founded the Inbal Dance Theater, which showcased Yemenite dance and folklore.[41] The theater company became very popular and was often used by Israel's Ministry of Tourism as a colorful cultural agent. Levi-Tanai made use of Yemenite dance movements in stylized theater style, arranged to suit her own music, such as in her choreography of the biblical Song of Songs, set to the music to Levi-Tanai's own highly popular setting of "El ginat egoz." Here a Yemenite melody is transformed into a popular song and, further, into an artistic scene in an ethnic dance theater.

In 1956 Levi-Tanai commissioned Mordecai Seter to write for the Inbal Dance Theater company. The result was his *Tikun hatsot* (Midnight vigil). A first version was performed by the company. Four versions followed between 1957 and 1961, the last of which is a monumental oratorio for tenor representing the worshipper, three choruses that sing out the apocalyptic visions, and orchestra (small revisions continued later on). *Tikun ḥatsot* is a monodrama, written to a libretto by Yemenite author Mordechai Tabib (1910–1979), whose action consists of visions experienced by a lone worshipper who prays all night in an empty synagogue.[42] As such it presents the Zionist narrative of destruction, exile, and redemption.

Seter interpolates into the work several traditional Yemenite songs that are sung by the chorus, representing the People, among them the paraliturgical melodies "Ahavat hadasah" (The love of Hadasah), which allegorically expresses a yearning for salvation, and "Elohim eshalah" (I pray to God) as well as "Elekha dodi nafshi eśa" (I will carry my soul to you), which is presented monophonically by the chorus in unison against the dissonant, tempestuous orchestra. A juxtaposition of Jewish-Yemenite materials and Western compositional technique rooted in pluralism, as it were.

As a Western composer, Seter with his aim of East-West synthesis came closest to the Yemenite tradition. *Tiḳun ḥatsot* won him the Israel State Prize in 1965. And although singers such as Bracha Zefira slowly fell out of fashion, subsequent generations of composers continued to be drawn to their Yemenite songs—Russian-born Mark Kopytman's (1929–2011) encounter of Yemenite singer Gila Beshari led him to revise his acclaimed orchestral work *Memory* (1981) to include her rendition of "Mi nishḳani mineshiḳot ahavah." Michael Wolpe (1960–), one of the leading contemporary composers in Israel, as well as professor of composition at the Jerusalem Academy of Music and Dance, dedicated his programmatic Symphonic Poem no. 5 *Song of Blessing—Shirat Bracha* (2005) to Bracha Zefira, interpolating several recordings of her voice into a continuous orchestral texture that responds to those songs. However, these encounters of East and West on the grounds of the Jewish Middle East are rather isolated attempts, as the insertion of an *invented* East was a much more frequent approach.

THE CONCERT HALL AS TRANSITIONAL SPACE

In his now classic article "Eastern Sources in Israeli Music," Amnon Shiloah famously labeled the compositions of the first generations as Orientalist, essentially a pejorative term.[43] Indeed, one of most controversial topics with regard to "Israeli music" was the pull of the East, whether through quotes of traditional prayer melodies or through fabricated Arabic-sounding material in the parameters of maqām-derived melody and harmony, as well as in orchestration. Shiloah's perspective, at odds with his claim of an "Israeli music" right in the title, reveals the belief that Israel is a Western state, founded on the predominantly European composition of the pre-statehood Jewish community. During the early years of statehood this relatively homogenous society evolved with the arrival of hundreds of thousands of Jewish immigrants from Middle Eastern countries who in spite of a state-driven massive acculturation project sowed traces of their own cultures, as audiences and composers.

As such, concert halls, and the compositions that filled them with sound, were rather spaces of transition for an emerging imagined community that as yet had not found itself as a nation. This transitional state that defined the community—in this case its composers and audiences—from the 1930s to the 1960s and to various degrees beyond, is evident in musical elements (be they Orientalist or not), compositional methods, and in the titles of the works that are not stringently Hebrew, but that also appear in German (reflecting origin) or English (reflecting international reach), and that are often published with parallel titles. And yet, a central marker in the music of Israel has been the employment of Hebrew lyrics, whether biblical citations or modern poetry. What ties these approaches together is the search for a music for a new collective, to establish or bolster a culture of belonging, even if it sometimes arbitrarily straddled the notions of the Jewish, Hebrew, and Israeli. In this straddling between East and West, between individualism and collectivism, composers revealed the search for musical solutions.

Initially geographically isolated, at least in the 1930 and 1940s, composers' contributions to the concert hall roughly continued or sought to continue a lineage in which such fellow composers as Arnold Schoenberg, Ernest Bloch, Darius Milhaud, and Mario Castelnuovo-Tedesco at the forefront had sought to find a modern voice for the (Jewish) concert hall.[44] If they modeled themselves on European trends first, by the 1960s their gaze shifted toward the United States, another transition, as it were. (And from the 1970s on an ever-increasing pluralism would leave their mark.) Another transition paralleled this shift that concerned the creation of an "Israeli music" as distinct from a "Jewish music" with all the contradictions that both concepts have entailed. For certain composers, critics, and commentators, any composition written in Israel implied "Israeli music," whereas for others it had to satisfy an entire range of requirements to qualify as "Israeli." Indeed, in the early years of Israeli statehood, as a rule, any performance of a work composed in Israel instigated arguments about whether it was "Israeli." The shift away from "Jewish music," which reflects the identity of a people, to music that represents a nation underlines the understanding of the new collective. The art music and concert life of the imagined community of British Mandate Palestine and early-statehood Israel overarchingly represents these transitions and shifts.

Notes

1. Yehoshua Ben-Arie, "Ha-nof ha-yishuvi shel Erets-Yisrael erev ha-hityashvut ha-zionit" [The residential landscape of the Land of Israel on the eve of Zionist settlement], in *History of the Jewish Community in Eretz-Israel since 1882* / תולדות היישוב היהודי בארץ־ישראל: מאז העלייה הראשונה, ed. Moshe Lissak and Gavriel Cohen (Jerusalem: The Israel Academy for Sciences and Humanities, 1989), 87.

2. Nahum Gutman, *A Little City and Few Men within It: Stories of the Beginnings of Tel Aviv* / עיר קטנה ואנשים בה מעט: סיפורים על ראשיתה של אחוזת בית היא תל אביב (Tel Aviv: Am Oved Dvir, 1959), 41.

3. Aharon Zeev Ben-Yishai, "Ha-livriṭit shel ha-operah ha-erets-yisralit" [The librettos of the opera of the Land of Israel], *Ha'aretz*, November 11, 1923. See also anon., "Mordechai Golinkin and the Palestine Opera (1927)," in *The Origins of Israel, 1882–1948: A Documentary History*, ed. David Sorkin, trans. Marganit Weinberger-Rotman (Madison: University of Wisconsin Press, 2011), 194–195. The original Hebrew article appeared in *Ha'aretz*, November 11, 1923.

4. Benedict Anderson, *Imagined Communities* (London: Verso, 1983), xiv.

5. See ibid., 38.

6. The term "Israeli art music" commonly refers to works composed by Jewish composers living in Palestine under the rule of the British Mandate and in the State of Israel. Taking into consideration time and place, it comprises an enormous repertoire. The first edition of Alice Tischler's bibliography of Israeli art music composers, published in 1988, included 3,200 works by 63 composers. All of them were retained in the expanded second edition of 2011, which includes nearly 6,000 works by 103 composers, and, naturally, the repertoire has further grown since then. Alice Tischler, *A Descriptive Bibliography of Art Music by Israeli Composers*, rev. ed. (Sterling Heights, MI: Harmonie Park Press, 2011). Tischler's criteria for adding composers to the original bibliography were "those born around and after 1947 whose works were performed and published, those who were settled in their profession as composers, and those who live and work in Israel." Tischler's purpose was to include each composer's entire output, with the exceptional case of Abel Ehrlich, who himself selected 135 of his enormous output of 3,500 works for inclusion in the volume. Tischler's bibliography does not include the works of Israeli-Arab composers who have recently been accepted into the performance canon of music in Israel, such as in the annual Israeli Music Fest.

7. Irit Youngerman, "In Search of a New Identity: European-born Composers in the Jewish Yishuv and Early Israeli Statehood, 1933–1958" / "בחיפוש אחר זהות חדשה מלחינים יוצאי אירופה ביישוב היהודי ובשנים הראשונות למדינת ישראל, 1933–1958 (PhD diss., Hebrew University of Jerusalem, 2013).

8. Egon Kunz, "The Refugee in Flight. Kinetic Models and Forms of Displacement," *International Migration Review* 7, no. 2 (1973): 132.

9. Paul Frankenburger to Heinrich Frankenburger, June 26, 1933, Paul Ben-Haim Collection, Mus 055, G 36, The National Library of Israel, Jerusalem. As of March 15, 2021, the letter is lost.

10. Philip V. Bohlman, *The Land Where Two Streams Flow: Music in the German-Jewish Community of Israel* (Urbana: University of Illinois Press, 1989), 11.

11. Assaf Shelleg, *Jewish Contiguities and the Soundtrack of Israeli History* (New York: Oxford University Press, 2014), 16.

12. Ibid., 74.

13. רחל is the *nom de plume* of Rachel Bluwstein (1890–1931). Born in Russia, she immigrated to Palestine in 1909 and, until her death at an early age, lived in the small settlement of Kinneret near the Sea of Galilee. She has been recognized as one of the greatest lyrical poets of Israel.

14. For the orchestra members' countries of origin, see Barbara von der Lühe, *Die Musik war unsere Rettung! Die deutschsprachigen Gründungsmitglieder des Palestine Orchestra* (Tübingen: Mohr Siebeck, 1998), 118. See also Josh Aronson and Denise George, *Orchestra of Exiles: The Story of Bronislaw Huberman, the Israel Philharmonic, and the One Thousand Jews He Saved from Nazi Horrors* (New York: Berkley Books, 2016).

15. For a recent historical survey of the orchestra, see Uri Toeplitz, *The History of the Israel Philharmonic Orchestra /* סיפורה של התזמורת הפילהרמונית הישראלית (Tel Aviv: Sifriyat poʻalim, 1992).

16. Lühe, *Die Musik war unsere Rettung*, 189.

17. The first Tel Aviv Museum on Rothschild Boulevard was originally the residence of Meir Dizengoff, who donated his home to the community.

18. See Philip V. Bohlman, *The World Centre for Jewish Music in Palestine 1936–1940* (Oxford: Oxford University Press, 1992).

19. Leonard B. Meyer, *Music, the Arts, and Ideas: Patterns and Predictions in Twentieth-century Culture* (Chicago: Chicago University Press, 1967), 172.

20. See Alexander U. Boscovich, "Baʻayot ha-musiḳah ha-mekoriṭ be-Yisrael" [The problem of original music in Israel], *Orlogin* 9 (November 1953): 280–294.

21. See Alexander U. Boscovich, "Musiḳah yisraelit lefsanṭer" [Israeli music for the piano], *Bat-ḳol: Ketav-ʻet le-musiḳah* (September 1957): 9–12.

22. See Muki Tsur, "Pesach in the Land of Israel: Kibbutz Haggadot," *Israel Studies* 12, no. 2 (2007): 74–103.

23. See Erich Walter Sternberg, "'The Twelve Tribes of Israel': Theme and Variations for Orchestra / 'Die zwölf Stämme Israels: Ein Thema mit Variationen für Orchestra (Selbstanzeige)," *Musica Hebraica* 1–2 (1938): 24; the Hebrew translation is printed on p. 71. This was to be the periodical of the World Centre of Jewish Music; the outbreak of the Second World War limited its publication to this sole double issue.

24. For the review, see David Rosolio, *Haʼaretz*, January 2, 1939.

25. For the review, see Menashe Ravina, *Davar*, February 23, 1939.

26. For an in-depth study of Wolpe's exile in Palestine, see Brigid Cohen, *Stefan Wolpe and the Avant-Garde Diaspora* (Cambridge: Cambridge University Press, 2012), 140–201; Jehoash Hirshberg, "A Modernist Composer in an Immigrant Community: The Quest for Status and National Ideology," in *On the Music of Stefan Wolpe: Essays and Recollections*, ed. Austin Clarkson (New York: Pendragon Press, 2003), 75–94.

27. For a discussion of the latter work, see Thomas Phleps, "Stefan Wolpe: Drei kleinere Canons in der Umkehrung zweier 12tönig correspondierender Hexachorde für Viola und Violoncello op. 24a," in *Klassizistische Moderne: Eine Begleitpublikation zur Konzertreihe im Rahmen der Veranstaltungen "10 Jahre Paul Sacher Stiftung"*, ed. Felix Meyer (Winterthur: Amadeus, 1996), 143–144.

28. See Stefan Wolpe's "Abschiedrede an die Kollegen (1938)," published in "'Die Lieder dieser Völker sind keine Museumsstücke': Vier Vorträge Zum Musikleben in Palästina 1938–39," ed. Heidy Zimmermann, *Musik-Konzepte*, no. 150 (July 2010): 40.

29. For the anonymous review, see *Haʼaretz*, August 7, 1936.

30. Audio recordings of Paul Ben-Haim's works can be accessed through the Israel Music Institute, www.imi.org.il.

31. For details, see Josef Tal, *Der Sohn des Rabbiners: Ein Weg von Berlin nach Jerusalem* (Berlin: Quadriga-Verlag Severin, 1985).

32. For an in-depth study with a detailed bibliography, see Natan Shahar, *Song of Songs Rise and Soar: The History of Hebrew Song /* שיר שיר עלה־נא: תולדות הזמר העברי (Moshav Ben Shemen: Modan, 2006); see also the repository of Hebrew songs composed up to the establishment of the State of Israel, which is regularly updated and expanded, www.zemeres het.co.il.

33. See Tzvi Avni, *Personal Notes: A Life in Music* / במפעם אישי: פרקי חיים במוסיקה (Kfar Saba: Maba', 2012), 58.

34. See Bracha Zefira, *Many Voices* / קולות רבים (Ramat Gan: Masada, 1978), 16. The book is both an autobiography and a transcription of all the songs she performed. The chronology of Zefira's school years as presented here is vague and cannot be reconstructed, but it has no bearing on the discussion of her professional activity.

35. See ibid., 218 and 220.

36. The music was compiled and collected by Gila Flam as part of her fieldwork in the 1970s; it explains the enormous difference in voice quality between Flam's tape-recorded version and the 78-rpm recording of the young Zefira in the 1930s. The recording of the four versions is held at The National Library of Israel, Jerusalem. The 1937 studio recording made by Columbia as well as later recordings have been uploaded to YouTube into several channels and are openly accessible. See also Gila Flam, "Bracha Zefira: A Case Study of Acculturation in Israeli Song," special issue "Music in the Ethnic Communities of Israel," *Asian Music* 17, no. 2 (1986): 108–125.

37. To date, five of Ben-Haim's arrangements for Zefira have been published as *Melodies from the East* (Tel Aviv: Israeli Music Publications, 1971). The rest are retained as manuscripts in The National Library of Israel, Jerusalem; arrangements by other composers are kept as manuscripts in individual archives.

38. See Zefira, *Many Voices*, 220.

39. See Ronit Seter, "Hirshberg's Ben-Haim: Three Decades Later," *Israel Studies in Musicology Online* 9 (2011): 108.

40. See Bracha Zefira, in discussion with the author, January 14, 1979.

41. See Shahar, *Song of Songs Rise and Soar*, 100. For further details, see Dina Roginsky, "Orientalism, the Body, and Cultural Politics in Israel: Sara Levi Tanai and the Inbal Dance Theater," *Nashim: A Journal of Jewish Women's Studies & Gender Issues*, no. 11 (2006): 164–197.

42. For a detailed history and discussion of the work, see Uri Golomb and Ronit Seter, "Mordecai Seter's *Midnight Vigil* (*Tikkun Ḥatzot*, 1961): Deconstructing Israelism, National and Biographical Myths," *Journal of Musicological Research* 38, no. 3–4 (2019): 329–347.

43. Amnon Shiloah, "Eastern Sources in Israeli Music," *IMI News* 93, nos. 2–3 (1993): 1–4.

44. See also Shelleg, *Jewish Contiguities*, 64.

Select Bibliography

Bohlman, Philip V. *The Land Where Two Streams Flow: Music in the German-Jewish Community of Israel*. Urbana: University of Illinois Press, 1989.

Bohlman, Philip V. *The World Centre for Jewish Music in Palestine 1936–1940*. Oxford: Oxford University Press, 1992.

Braun, Yehezkel, Rotem Luz, and Jehoash Hirshberg. Yehezkel Braun: His Life and Work / יחזקאל בראון: חייו ויצירתו. Tel Aviv: Israel Music Institute and Carmel, 2017.

Brod, Max. *Die Musik Israels*. Rev. ed. with 2nd section, "The Future and Development of Music in Israel," by Yehuda Cohen. Kassel: Bärenreiter Verlag, 1976.

Cohen, Brigid. *Stefan Wolpe and the Avant-Garde Diaspora*. Cambridge: Cambridge University Press, 2012.

Eisenstadt, Michael, ed. *From Dream to Reality: Twenty Years of the Israeli Opera*. Tel Aviv: The Israeli Opera, 2005.

Golomb, Uri, ed. *Alexander Uriyah Boskovich (1907–1964)*. Tel Aviv: Israel Music Institute, 2003.

Golomb, Uri, and Ronit Seter. "Mordecai Seter's *Midnight Vigil* (*Tikkun Ḥatzot*, 1961): Deconstructing Israelism, National and Biographical Myths." *Journal of Musicological Research* 38, nos. 3–4 (2019): 329–347.

Hirshberg, Jehoash. "Alexander U. Boskovich and the Quest for an Israeli National Musical Style." In *Modern Jews and their Musical Agendas*, edited by Ezra Mendelsohn. Studies in Contemporary Jewry 9 (New York: Oxford University Press, 1994), 92–109.

Hirshberg, Jehoash. "Kopytman's Heterophonic Trail: From Memory to Beyond All This." In *Mark Kopytman: Voices of Memories—Echoes and Dialogues*, edited by Yulia Kreinin, 67–80. Tel Aviv: Israel Music Institute, 2004.

Hirshberg, Jehoash. *Music in the Jewish Community of Palestine 1880–1948*. Oxford: Oxford University Press, 1995.

Hirshberg, Jehoash. "New Operas in the Yishuv and in Israel." In *Judaism in Opera / Judentum in der Oper*, edited by Isolde Schmid-Reiter and Aviel Cahn, 311–336. Schriften der Europäischen Musiktheater Akademie 11. Regensburg: Con Brio, 2017.

Hirshberg, Jehoash. *Paul Ben-Haim, His Life and Works*. 3rd rev. ed. Tel Aviv: Israel Music Institute, 2010.

Hirshberg, Jehoash. "The Vision of the East and the Heritage of the West: Ideological Pressures in the Yishuv Period and their Offshoots in Israeli Art Music during the Recent Two Decades." *Min-Ad: Israel Studies in Musicology Online* 4 (2005), https://www2.biu.ac.il/hu/mu/min-ad/min-ad05/en/JehoashH.pdf (accessed April 22, 2023).

Hirshberg, Jehoash, and Rakefet Bar-Sadeh. *Tsvi Avni: Ḥayav ve-yetsirato* [Tzvi Avni: His life and works]. Jerusalem: Carmel Publishing, 2020.

Kletinich, Yevgeny. "The 1960's: Kopytman in Moldova." In *Mark Kopytman, Voices of Memories*, edited by Yulia Kreinin, 81–128. Tel Aviv: Israel Music Institute, 2004.

Kreinin, Yulia. *The Music of Mark Kopytman: Echoes of Imaginary Lines*. Berlin: Verlag Ernst Kuhn, 2008.

Lühe, Barbara. *Die Emigration deutschsprachiger Musikschaffender in das britische Mandatsgebiet Palästina: Ihr Beitrag zur Entwicklung des israelischen Rundfunks, der Oper und der Musikpaedagogik seit 1933*. Frankfurt am Main: Peter Lang, 1999.

Lühe, Barbara, *Die Musik war unsere Rettung! Die deutschsprachigen Gründungsmitglieder des Palestine Orchestra*. Tübingen: Mohr Siebeck, 1998.

Nemtsov, Jascha. "Vermittler zwischen den Kulturen: Marc Lavry." In *Doppelt vertrieben: Deutsch-jüdische Komponisten aus dem östlichen Europa in Palästina/Israel*, edited by Jascha Nemtsov, 89–150, Jüdische Musik: Studien und Quellen zur jüdischen Musikkultur 11. Wiesbaden: Harrassowitz Verlag, 2013.

Seter, Ronit. "Hirshberg's Ben-Haim: Three Decades Later." *Min-Ad: Israel Studies in Musicology Online* 9 (2011): 97–113.

Seter, Ronit. "Israelism: Nationalism, Orientalism, and the Israeli Five." *Musical Quarterly* 97, no. 2 (2014): 238–308.

Seter, Ronit. "Verdina Shlonsky, 'The First Lady of Israeli Music.'" *Min-Ad: Israel Studies in Musicology Online* 6 (2007–2008), https://www2.biu.ac.il/hu/mu/min-ad/07-08/Seter-SHLONSKY.pdf (accessed 22, 2023).

Shelleg, Assaf. *Jewish Contiguities and the Soundtrack of Israeli History*. New York: Oxford University Press, 2014.

Shelleg, Assaf. *Theological Stains: Art Music and the Zionist Project*. New York: Oxford University Press, 2020.

Shmueli, Herzl, and Jehoash Hirshberg. *Aleksander Uriyah Boskovits': Ḥayav, yetsirato ve-haguto* [Alexander Uriah Boskovich: His life, work, and thought]. Jerusalem: Carmel Publishing, 1995.

Toeplitz, Uri. *Sipurah shel ha-tizmoret ha-filharmonit ha-yiśraʾelit* [The history of the Israel Philharmonic Orchestra]. Tel Aviv: Sifriyat poʾalim, 1992.

Youngerman, Irit. "Immigration, Identity, and Change: Émigré Composers of the Nazi Period and Their Perceptions of Stylistic Transformation in Their Creative Work." *Naharaim* 3 (2009): 117–134.

15

THE YIDDISH THEATER REPUBLIC OF SOUNDS AND THE PERFORMANCE OF LISTENING

RUTHIE ABELIOVICH

WHEN in 1903 Moyshe Hurwitz staged his four-act opera *Yetsies mitsraim* (The Exodus from Egypt) at the Windsor Theater (located on Bowery Street, in the Lower East Side) in New York City, a larger exodus was unfolding. Between 1875 and 1924, approximately two and a half million Jews crossed the Atlantic, immigrating to the United States from eastern Europe. Staging the biblical myth, Hurwitz—himself a migrant from eastern Europe—animated the physical itinerant act of the departure from Egypt, a mass-liberation movement that delivered the Israelites from slavery. By doing so, he transposed this myth into a theatricalized symbolic movement that resonated with the modern experience of the Jewish mass migration.[1] As in the biblical story, in Hurwitz's opera the Israelites departed from their home and, under the leadership of Moses, crossed the Red Sea in their long journey and passage to the Promised Land.

Hurwitz's opera conveys a typical example of the turn-of-the-century Jewish popular entertainment's predilection for biblical themes. Accompanied by music composed by Arnold Perlmutter and Herman Wohl, the opera was repeatedly performed during the first two decades of the twentieth century, on both sides of the Atlantic.[2] Recognizing the current Jewish sentiment, Hurwitz rendered the Jewish experience of displacement according to the storyline of the Israelites' founding myth, thus reshuffling emotional poignancy into box-office success. Staged across a central migratory trajectory—in eastern Europe and the United States—the biblical epos of the Exodus from Egypt thus transcended the mythical context, to become a national fiction whereby the newly uprooted reality in *di goldene medina* could be reconceptualized and imagined as a cultural metanarrative of modern Jewish emigration.

Moyshe Hurwitz (1844–1910) himself embodied this narrative. Born in Stanislav, eastern Galicia, to a Hasidic family, he had a short experience as an educator before he began producing theater in Romania. His big success came after he emigrated to New York in 1886, where his theater entrepreneurship grew massively. For the next thirty years, Hurwitz wrote a new work almost every week, composing more than one hundred and twenty melodramas and music-theater plays. During the first years of the Yiddish theater, Hurwitz was dominant in the New York theater scene as resident dramatist and prompter of the Romanian Opera House company, and later as the manager of the Windsor Theater. During the following decades, the repertoire of Yiddish stages across Europe (mainly in Galicia and the Pale of Settlement) and in the United States heavily resorted to the popular works of Hurwitz. Although they enjoyed enormous popularity, his works were considered *shund* (literally, "trash"), a pejorative reference to lowbrow entertainment that lacks artistic value.[3]

Like many other popular Yiddish performances, Hurwitz's opera *Yetsies mitsraim* stretched beyond the theater stage, to materialize in various commercial forms. Sheet music of the popular opera was available for purchase, and its songs were recorded by prominent performers and disseminated by commercial gramophone companies. Foraying from the fictional stage into the so-called reality, the songs and melodies of the biblical opera continued to accompany its listenership long after its performances had ended, and when the listeners were able to encode its sounds, it drew them into a "powerful collective experience," in Michael Steinlauf's words.[4] This affective experience was premised upon feedback and resonance between the songs and melodies performed in the Yiddish theater and the social, migratory conditions under which it was shaped.[5]

Like many other Yiddish theater performances at the outset of the twentieth century, Hurwitz's opera fostered sonority as its primary epistemology: the vocal execution of the language, songs, and melodies acted in the Yiddish theater as a performative conduit for affective expressions, through which society could be interpreted.[6] Categorized as operas, operettas, melodramas, vaudeville, and the like, Yiddish theater created and evoked, according to Mark Slobin, "a community of song," organized around its spoken Yiddish, songs, and melodies, enabling individuals to connect through a shared aural sensation.[7] Whatever preoccupied Jewish communities found its way onto Yiddish theater songs—assimilation and acculturation processes, anti-Semitic persecutions, migration, and uprooting.[8]

Modern Yiddish theater evolved in relation to Jewish sociopolitical changes. It gained momentum in 1876 Iași, Romania, with the wake of Abraham Goldfaden and his ragtag group of actors and musicians.[9] Thereafter, the genre rapidly expanded to the Russian Empire, and, alongside massive waves of migration to the United States, it was imported to New York, transforming from a regional phenomenon into a transnational entertainment network across the migratory enclaves of eastern European Jews.[10] As Nahma Sandrow has shown, it developed from pre- and early-modern Jewish expressive culture, originating in unwritten and improvised Jewish performance practices, familiar from the *purimshpil's* carnivalesque celebrations, and from wandering entertainers, such as the wedding *badkhan* and the Broder singers.[11] In tandem with the gradual modernization of eastern European Jews, folkloristic performance themes and practices were remolded vis-à-vis the popular culture that emerged around them. Among the most popular musical forms of the period were the opera and the operetta.[12] Yiddish theater scholars such as Edna Nahshon, Debra Caplan, Nina Warnke, and Tova C. Markenson have demonstrated how the mass-Jewish migration movement at the turn of the century transfigured the traditional wandering Jewish performers into theater transmigrants, traveling back and forth between continents, developing from exchanging prolific reciprocities between Jewish and non-Jewish actors and theater makers to performing a shared mobile dramatic repertoire.[13]

The transnational cultural network of theater songs that mobilized melodies and songs between Jewish cultural centers, mediating and disseminating musical theatrical forms could be well defined as the Yiddish theater republic of sounds, drawing from the appellation The Republic of Letters—an intercontinental intellectual community established through the dissemination and exchange of ideas, and objects in late seventeenth and eighteenth centuries in Europe and the Americas.[14] The musical performances of an international Yiddish theatrical repertoire encircled temporal communities. Stemming from embodied theatrical practices, the Yiddish theater republic of sounds resonated in the bodies of its listeners, binding together its audience under the same rhythmic beats and melodies. As theater performers and sound recordings spread out, mainly throughout the United States and eastern Europe, they became a cultural lifeline that knotted together remote communities.

The Yiddish theater republic of sounds thus renders spatial notions of detachment and dispersion into a creative condition of multiple performance locations. During times of accelerated social diffusion, the Jewish "community of song"—to reiterate Slobin's term—was not created through bodily co-presence of performers and spectators in the theater houses, but rather through the reproduction and circulation of an international repertoire of melodies and songs across continents. The Yiddish theater republic of sounds thus invites us to formulate the multimodalities of togetherness as based upon the faculty of listening, and to explore how listening to and in the theater generated new forms and experiences of the social.

Scholars of Jewish culture have researched the role played by music and songs in the Yiddish theater mainly by drawing on archival materials, such as music sheets, press reviews, and memoires. In "Music as Social History: American Yiddish Theater Music, 1882–1920," Irene Heskes provides an overview on the uses of music in the Yiddish theater, its musical roots, and on possible audience responses to the visual and aural spectacle. Based on the vast sheet music collections at YIVO, Slobin's *Tenement Songs* categorizes and contextualizes different kinds of songs and their appeal to Yiddish-speaking listenership. More recently, Nina Warnke has explored Yiddish theater composers and the reception history of Yiddish theater in the Yiddish press; Daniela Smolov Levy has focused on the contact points between canonical European opera in turn-of-the-century popular Yiddish theater in America, examining how Yiddish cultural elites sought points of contact between Yiddish popular theater and the highbrow operatic world. Joshua Walden emphasized the dramatic and musical traditions of Ashkenazi Jews in eastern Europe, significant musical performances and prominent figures behind the development of the Yiddish theater scene at the turn of the century.[15] Current perspectives in the study of Yiddish theater, as Joel Berkowitz explains in his introduction to *Yiddish Theater: New Approaches*, have mostly centered on textual sources for deciphering its artistic and social significance.[16] These, however, do not address the affective qualities and the sensuous impact of the performances; neither do they account for the perceptual qualities fashioned by the Yiddish theater, and on how these reflected, overtly or otherwise, prevailing social and political concerns.

Focusing on Moyshe Hurwitz's four-act opera *Yetsies mitsraim*, this chapter probes into performances of listening generated by the Yiddish theater as a fulcrum in shifting actual and imaginative configurations of the Jewish collective at the turn of the century. The collectiveness that lies at the heart of the following analysis encompasses theater makers and musicians, as well as the audiences that attended the theater houses; it pertains not only to the happenstances on or off stage, but also to the global circulation of its live or recorded performances. Highlighting the transnational route between the United States and eastern Europe during the first two decades of the twentieth century, this chapter traces the evolution of ways of listening in and to the Yiddish theater by considering two simultaneous and parallel processes: the invention of sound technology and the mass-Jewish migration movement that unfolded a salient phenomenon at the turn of the century. As subsequently discussed, listening played a central role in creating a transnational Yiddish theater scene, comprising various kinds of theatrical and social actors. Listening in and to theater became a basic practice for people to connect and grasp the new Jewish modern realm, both practically and imaginatively; listening would become, thus, a shared communal performance and a form of participation in the public sphere.

While listening is often thought of as a passive mode of consumption of knowledge, this chapter is premised upon the notion that listening entails more than the comprehension of words, the semiotic analysis of music and dramatic recitation; it signifies an entrance into a broader cluster of communication factors revolving around auditory attention. Listening, as Sophia Rosenfeld explains, depends not only on physiology, but also on incidental and contrived alterations in technology, environment, aesthetics, and social relations, and is also a product of those changes. Rosenfeld coins the term "historical ear" to historicize listening as a cultural phenomenon. Listening, according to Rosenfeld, is part of a politicized work of the senses and is structured and conceptualized by social power relations and technological developments. This is what she terms "regimes of listening," depicting this act of attention as a cultural effect that depends not only upon the sounds themselves, but also on the specific interpreters and their settings.[17]

Historians and musicologists who investigate the phenomena of modernity have begun, in the last two decades, to probe into histories of listening, attempting to reconstitute sounds of the past and their reception.[18] Shifting the focus from the musical score and its analysis to the musical event, its social dramaturgy and theatrical dynamics, these studies are premised on the idea that hearing and auditory perception are historically construed, and are subject to changes in the face of environmental and technological developments, as well as social relations.[19] Jonathan Sterne argues that changes in listening practices and in the scientific knowledge of hearing have shaped the emergence of sound-reproduction technologies. According to Sterne, human and sensory cultural practices preceded the invention of sound recordings and paved the way to the changes in timely perceptions of sound. Technologies, he argues, are repeatable social, cultural, and material processes crystallized into mechanisms. The recording of sound and its reproduction, thus, not only preserves voices, but also reflects historical and epistemological processes.[20]

The Yiddish theater emerged as a significant cultural phenomenon during times in which sound was rendered a commodity, via entertainment shows and commercial sound recordings. The concomitant processes of industrialization and urbanization, in tandem with the burgeoning mechanically reproduced sound, and the spiking Jewish mass migration during the late nineteenth century, yielded a transformative effect on modes of listening. Thus, the study of the ways whereby Yiddish theater fashioned the act of listening might foster an understanding of the modes in which people consumed and perceived culture, and deepen our grasp of the knowledge embedded in these forms.

Focusing on the central venues of listening yielded by the Yiddish theater, the following analysis firstly probes into the forms and meanings of listening in and to the Yiddish theater; secondly, it explores the changes that listening to theater underwent against the backdrop of the technological and economic development of the Yiddish commercial sound-recording industry. Finally, it examines the spatial ramifications of recorded theater sounds in public Jewish culture.

THEATRICAL LISTENING: *THE EXODUS FROM EGYPT*

Among the songs featuring in Hurwitz's opera, "Die nevuoh" (The prophecy)—sung by the dramatis persona of Moses—stood out in its popularity, mainly due to its incorporation into the concert repertoire of America's celebrity cantor Joseph (Yossele) Rosenblatt, which included both sacred and secular songs.[21] Written and composed by Arnold Perlmutter and Herman Wohl, this song become one of Rosenblatt's most favorite performed numbers, and in 1915 the song was recorded and produced by Columbia Gramophone Records as a commercial 78-rpm record.

The title of the song prefigures it as a prophetic speech act whereby the present moment encapsulates visions, claims, and rebukes regarding the future. The lyrics of this song unfold the prophecy of the rebirth of Jerusalem and Zion, in which "Israel's songs will be heard again."[22] Rosenblatt sang this prophetic chant, delivering his hopeful redemptive vision for the Israelites. In the recording, Rosenblatt, accompanied by piano music, enacted the blend between the synagogue and the theater stage, moving gradually from an operatic cantorial vocal execution onto a more rhythmic and lighter lyrical singing, familiar from both folk and theater songs.

Ghosted by the dramatic role of Moses, Rosenblatt's virtuoso vocal performance of the song, emerging from the recording, amalgamated the biblical-dramatic prophecy with his religious public authority and theatrical charm. Chanting a prophetic calling, Rosenblatt's performative speech act addressed his audience as a Jewish congregation. In tandem, through his vocal delivery as a prophet, he enacted timely social disputes and fissures between the old and the new world—between his charismatic cantorial presence and his mediated vocal performance. How did the towering biblical figure of Moses cast its aura on Rosenblatt? Did the theatrical context of the song enhance Rosenblatt's religious authority? Did the audience associate his voice with prophetic sincerity or with melodramatic duplicity?

Rosenblatt's religiosity, as Jeffrey Shandler explains, manifests the embrace, rather than the disparagement, of modern technology and cultural capitalism, in versatile ways compatible with traditional religious precepts and values.[23] Rosenblatt recorded all kinds of music, including popular liturgies from his cantorial repertoire, Jewish art music, Zionist anthems, Yiddish folk songs, and popular theater songs. Additionally, he performed regularly in concerts and recitals, and made occasional appearances in music halls and vaudeville stages during the 1920s. In all his performances, he emphasized his cantorial voice as well as the religious musical grain. The infusion of theatrical practices and religious singing patterns was thus built into Rosenblatt's public persona.

When Rosenblatt performed on grand theater stages, he infused the performative space with vocality familiar from the synagogue. However, in the theater, Rosenblatt's cantorial singing was emptied of its liturgical context and holy experience, becoming a performative scaffold for demonstrating his vocal virtuosity and charisma. During these moments, the listeners simultaneously became a theater audience and a pseudo-religious assembly. While listening to a vocal performance associated with prayer, they could nostalgically reimagine their congregation whose gradual drifting apart they had witnessed. The cantorial singing in the theater thus served as a displaced performance through which the audience could negotiate their changing identity, against the background of accelerated acculturation processes and their growing alienation from the traditional Jewish life.

Much of the music performed in the Yiddish popular theater comprised an alloy of heavily adapted music of the European canon, folk songs and melodies, chants, and spoken and sung liturgies performed at the synagogue. As such, the transaction between the synagogue and the theater was bidirectional. Many of the theater-music composers acquired their professional training as *meshorerim* and cantors, and some composed music for both the theater and the synagogue.[24] Abraham Goldfaden has left behind an eloquent description of the theatrical logic behind the eclectic musical logic he interlaced in his staged dramas. In his 1899 essay on music from his music productions, he explains the stylistic synthesis he invented for his theater performances as comprised of canonical operatic arias and melodies, marches, assembling Jewish and Ukrainian folk songs, gypsy, and French and Germanic influences with synagogue and choral music.[25] With no formal music education, Goldfaden defines his role as a compiler rather than a composer. His lack of formal musical knowledge gave him the freedom to interlace musical fragments borrowed or adapted from various sources, according to the dramatic impact he wished to create in his performances.[26] Theatergoers attending popular Yiddish performances listened to the unsystematic motely mixture of these very different musical legacies, discerning the contrafacts between them, the nuances embedded in their rendering and the connotations they provoked. Listening to a heterogeneous assortment of sounds became a basic way of knowing—an epistemic means for understanding and negotiating their new realm. Theatergoers would recognize the alterations and encode the modifications made to liturgies and folksongs played in the theater.

Synagogue music and songs played a significant role in eliciting and mobilizing the sought-for emotive dimension of the theater. Much like the theater, the synagogue afforded a common cultural venue, in which Jews could meet and be together, listen to the Jewish sonority, and actively participate in the event. During the same evening, as Goldfaden explains, the same musical repertoires could have and probably were intoned both in the synagogue and on the theater stage, albeit with variation.[27] Their inclusion in theater performances, much like the cantorial performance of a theater song, were functional for capturing and riveting the attention of the audience. Thus, the theater performed segments of Jewish liturgies not in order to construe theater as a sacred place or render it respectable, but in order to establish it as the center of Jewish communal life.[28]

The synagogue music performed in the theater also affected the audience's listening modes. Unlike the stringent rules of silence, and the focused listening convention binding concert-hall audiences, the synagogue shaped listening as an engaged social activity. Franz Rosenzweig points to the social role of liturgical music, arguing that the fundamental "togetherness" of the congregation is formed by the shared listening of the collective within a distinct religious space.[29] At the synagogue, Rosenzweig explains, the congregation sings together, synchronizing voices and bodies under the same rhythmic order, assuming an active role in the performance. The Yiddish theater reproduced this mode of listening. When performed in the theater, religious songs and melodies created a feeling of unity around a shared belief system; it consolidated the audience as an actual community. Against the backdrop of the radical disintegration that occurred outside the theater, during times of mass migration from eastern Europe, the theater afforded a place whereby individuals could imagine unity in a social reality fraught with defragmentation.

Jewish audiences did not abide by the stringent bourgeois codes of silent spectatorship. Going to the theater was an experience of togetherness revolving around shared engaged listening and loud participation in the staged drama. Theatergoers who filled the Yiddish theater often knew songs and skits by heart, and were thoroughly involved with the stage action.[30] The turmoil in the theater also emerged from the noisy audience. In his book on etiquette, describing the behavior of Jewish theater audiences at the turn of the century,[31] Yosef Tashrak argues that Yiddish theater has become synonymous with chaos, noise, and raucous behavior. When Jews enter the theater, Tashrak writes, they talk, stretch in their seats, eat peanuts, chew gum, and constantly interrupt other people in their surroundings.[32] Tashrak describes the engaged, lively, albeit boisterous behavior of the audience. The role played by theater, hence, transcended by far that of staged fiction. It was a social arena that enabled its audience to tune in to a charged manifold aurality—*qua* assembly, theater audience, and community; listening in and to the theatrical event entailed a simultaneous experiencing of this multilayered social event.

The interaction and exchange between sacred and secular songs, and melodies performed in the theater, structured an experience of polygonal listening, in which the theater and the synagogue penetrated each other, reflecting the multiplicity and divides entailed in displacement, assimilation, and acculturation processes characteristic of modern Jewish life. The diverse simultaneous aural performances that took place in the theater—encompassing the staged drama and the exchange among audiences—rendered a listening experience that demanded from the audience to split their attention, to simultaneously be in several realms at the same time. Thus, while listening to and in the theater afforded a gathering place for the community, its sounds enwrapped the audience as liminal subjects of divided in-between cultural worlds: eastern Europe and the United States; the theater and the synagogue.

ACOUSMATIC LISTENING: YIDDISH THEATER SOUND RECORDINGS

Rosenblatt's 1915 recording of "Die nevuoh" conveys the fundamental perceptual divides associated with modern cultural transformations. Mediated through the new sound technology, the theatrical prophetic performance paradoxically infused spiritual authority into Rosenblatt's celebrity public persona. As a performative speech act, the recorded prophetic calling manifests the power of the new technology to capture and simulate voices of non-embodied entities.[33] The novel sound technology enabled the crossover of presence and absence, at once enacting the disappearance of the physical presence, as well as an embodiment of the voice. This chiasmus opened up a space of intimacy between the individual listener and the voice, akin to a religious or mystical experience.[34]

Emanating from the gramophone, Rosenblatt's recorded voice performs the rupture between sound and its source, defined by Pierre Schaeffer as an "acousmatic" experience. The acousmatic, according to Schaeffer, "marks the perceptive reality of sound as such as distinguished from the modes of its production and transmission."[35] Film theorist and composer Michel Chion explains that the "acousmatic situation" is riddled with perceptual implications for modalities of listening. According to Chion, when sound is detached from its visible source, a concentrated listening experience is created—"sight and hearing are dissociated, encouraging listening to sound forms for themselves (and hence, to the sound object)."[36] Extrapolating from Chion's explanation, we could, then, regard sound recordings of theater songs as instantiations that offer a refuge from the vast aural jumble of the theater; inscribing sound into small, bite-size objects collected for single listening, they preserve a focused, in-depth mode of listening to a single event—one record at a time.

Yet, Chion's explanation of acousmatic listening overlooks the performative and social context of listening and the symbolic meanings invested in it as a recorded performance.[37] From this perspective, Rosenblatt's recorded song facilitated an acousmatic listening experience that simultaneously displaced the cantorial voice from the synagogue and from its ritualistic context, detaching his vocal rendering from the background noise prevalent in its original social performative event, and, in tandem, mentally and imaginatively reconnected its listeners to the sort of togetherness familiar from the theater and the synagogue. Under an accelerated migration movement, this togetherness also entailed negotiating with translocal cultural specificities and discrepancies along various Jewish centers. The gesture of migration, therefore, manifested itself not only in the dramatic theme, as in the example of the Exodus from Egypt, but also through the breakdown of its performances into live and recorded performance stages, in Europe and in the United States, and in the perceptual modes of listening they structured.

The sound-recording industry saw a surge over the course of the decade and a half preceding the First World War. As phonograph and gramophone companies developed their business across continents, music of all kinds was intensively recorded. In tandem with the flourishing of Yiddish popular theater, a massive commercial recording industry of Yiddish theater that developed in eastern Europe and the United States at the turn of the century produced hundreds of gramophone records of theater songs. Wherever a vibrant theater scene emerged, a prolific recording industry thrived. Among the prominent loci, Warsaw, Lemberg, and New York stand out as inexhaustible theater recording centers. The *Discography of Early European Recording of Jewish Music* lists at least six hundred recordings produced between 1904 and 1913 in Lemberg alone, featuring songs and skits from the popular theater repertoire, including extracts from plays written by Abraham Goldfaden, Josef Lateiner, Moyshe Hurwitz, and others.[38] Recordings of theater sketches, songs, and melodies performed by renowned actors are now stored at sound archives, mainly in the United States, Europe, and Israel. These sound recordings harbor a musical repertoire that was originally part of Yiddish theater performances. Some were composed by renowned music theater writers, while others feature folk songs, Yiddish translations of popular songs, adaptations to Jewish liturgy and religious songs. Commercial theater sound recordings enable us to experience a significant dimension of the theatrical aura attributed to iconic performers. Yet, these recordings have been detached from their original theatrical context. The profusion of commercial sound recordings of Yiddish theater songs attests to the fact that Yiddish theater actors did not only travel between continents in their tours; they also traversed performative modes of presence between the live theater event and its recorded manifestations.

The gramophone sound-recording industry was tightly connected with migration. Emil Berliner, a German Jew who had emigrated from Hannover to Brooklyn and settled in Washington, DC, developed the flat disc we know today (patented in 1887), which enabled the mass production of records. In 1901 he founded, together with engineer Eldridge Johnson, *The Victor Talking Machine Company*, which soon spread and developed from North America to London and thence to Europe. As the gramophone industry expanded globally, the beloved and familiar theater songs and the renowned voices of its performers became a natural arena.[39] During the first two decades of the twentieth century, Berliner's company produced hundreds of records in many eastern European cities such as Lemberg, St. Petersburg, and Warsaw and in the United States. Recordings produced in eastern Europe, as Henry Sapoznik explains, were hardly exported to the United States; the export of American Jewish recordings to Europe happened in far greater numbers.[40]

The Yiddish theater sound-recording industry emerged at a critical period of transition in social, cultural, and economic life, reconfiguring embodied practices and spatial configurations of both performers and audiences. This transnational theater enterprise operated by establishing an economic cultural network between touring theater performances and various paraphernalia—mainly commercial sound recordings, sheet music, booklets of dramatic scripts, and other ephemera. Following the successful performances of melodies or songs for an opera, operetta, or revue show, hit songs were produced as gramophone recordings that were played in private homes, cafes, gardens, or in backyards, streets, and working-class districts. In this way, the popular songs found their way from the theater stage onto other public spaces and were performed on various occasions. Thus, a feedback loop was generated between the stage and the street, as hit songs and numbers disseminated and were sung wherever possible. The result was physical distance and social proximity under the conditions of disembodied presence and immaterial space.

Theater sound recordings fostered communication across national borders, among Jewish cultural centers, enabling correspondence between Yiddish speakers. As Joshua Walden explains, the phonograph altered the careers of professional performers, as well as opened up new possibilities for musicians, who would previously had been known primarily among local listeners, to garner international attention. The phonograph also introduced a new way to experience elements from theater performances—the recordings. As Walden puts it, one need no longer attend the synagogue or concert hall to hear music once intended for these venues, but could rather choose to listen to this repertoire at home.[41]

The sound recording liberated the theater from its ephemeral, bodied incarceration, while imprisoning it in the new medium as a form of witness to the unseen. Once recorded, theatrical iterations are no longer confined to a specific place and time, nor are they bound to their corporeal anchor. Thus, the focus on reproduced sound and recorded theater voices gravitates around the productive tension between presence and resonance. Stemming from a specific social event, the sound recording defragments the visual, interactive elements from the aural experience. Correspondingly, Yiddish theater sound recordings provide an aural "close-up" into the atmosphere summoned in the theater, conjuring a fragment of a poignant, perhaps admired, musical moment. For those who watched the performances, the recording might have elicited memories from the actual shows. At the same time, these recordings were also perceived regardless of their theatrical context, as musical performances played on gramophones. Recordings of Yiddish theater songs made it possible to listen to familiar theatrical moments in an expanding number of spatial locations and situations.

Commercial sound recordings of Yiddish theater songs transmitted and propagated aural performative modes that connected eastern European Jewish cultural centers (such as Warsaw, Odessa, and Lemberg) with the new Jewish migratory realm in the United States, imbuing quotidian spaces with Yiddish theatricality, thus transgressing the boundaries of the stage to permeate the daily life of its audiences. Wherever theater melodies and songs were played, a new theater landmark was created. Yiddish theater sound, thus, connected different Jewish societies, forming a transnational Yiddish theater sounds republic.[42] Literary critic Bruce Smith identifies such collectives as "acoustic communities" organized around "soundmarks," through which their members made sense of their social space.[43] Within this scheme, theater songs engendered social gatherings that defined Jewish public and private spaces. As such, recorded theater songs gave way to new public performances that did not replicate or reproduce their theatrical origin. The presence of recorded voices in the private and public spheres brought Yiddish theater beyond the theater houses, creating new performances that involved Yiddish theater songs and melodies mediated through gramophones.[44]

THE PHONOGRAPH BY DAVID PINSKI

What did the gramophone mean for Jewish listeners as a material object, a cultural artifact, and a lavish status symbol? How were the sounds emanating from this machine perceived and deciphered? David Pinski's 1918 one-act drama *Der fonograf* (The phonograph) provides a witty description of the reception of sound technology in a traditional eastern European community, the *shtetl*. The play, defined by Pinski as a comedy, takes place in a "remote Russo-Yiddish town, where the Jews lived upon wind and miracles."[45] Pinski, himself a migrant from the Jewish Pale of Settlement to the United States, presents the phonograph as a marvelous object, smuggled from America across borders into the shtetl by Nahmen Riskin—a local young entrepreneur. A cutting-edge modern technology, the phonograph is intended to cater to the thirst of the Jewish public for entertainment and music, sounding the renowned voices of famous cantors and performers.

Riskin arrives from America equipped with old-new technology: a phonograph for his new business and a revolver for keeping dodgy locals away from him. Through the dialogues with typical characters of the shtetl—the informer, the thief, and the merchant—Pinski describes the widening rift between the new, migratory American cultural milieu and the European traditional habitus. Riskin contemplates the phonograph as a business opportunity, while his local surrounding is fascinated by the magical object; Riskin exhibits the composure of a merchant, while his family and friends are committed to the "old" hierarchies of the traditional Jewish community. The phonograph is, thus, presented in this play not only as a musical apparatus, but also as a social medium that exposes and embodies social tensions and communal complexities.

Upon the arrival of the phonograph in town, Riskin's domestic salon brims with locals—mostly family and curious neighbors—expecting to listen to the miraculous machine play. The fortunate ones huddle in the living room and nearby rooms. Others, left outside, crowd near the windows. Inside the house, everyone is waiting for those important guests who must arrive for the concert to begin: the rabbi, the cantor, the merchant, and their wives. As the audience awaits, various other guests arrive in the salon, introducing typecasts of the shtetl: Riskin's family circle—including his mother and mother-in-law, uncles, and brothers—as well as the town thief and the informer, who negotiates pecuniary issues with Riskin vis-à-vis the phonograph.

The peak of the drama transpires when the concert begins. All the attendees crowd silently around the phonograph, amazed by the wondrous invention. "This box here"—the cantor inquires skeptically—"sings like a cantor and his choir, and speaks Hebrew?" "I thought it was some sort of huge box, and the cantor and his choir got inside . . .," the rabbi's wife adds. These remarks portray the audience as old-fashioned characters mesmerized by the new technology, as if it were either a novel kind of supernatural or theatrical trickery. Riskin, in response, reassures them as he places a record upon the revolving disc and announces: "The cantor in the box will now sing 'Lay us down,' accompanied by his choir." Riskin refers to Hashkivenu, a blessing sung following the Shema, as part of the evening prayer (Maariv) before going to sleep, and on the Sabbath and holidays in a more elaborate version. It is a petitionary prayer in which a person asks to lie down in peace at night and return to life in the ensuing morning. In Pinski's drama the Hashkivenu played on the gramophone bears a symbolic meaning beyond its religious assignment. The gramophone in this scene is animated by the chant it sounds, thus replacing the cantor who is listening to a prayer that heralds his symbolic hibernation. As the first tunes begin to issue from the machine, the eyes of the attendees fill up with tears of astonishment. "Oh, dear me!" cries the cantor's wife, "just listen to that! A choir! And a real cantor!" topped by the merchant's wife's enthusiastic remark that "the thing is really praying!" clinched by the rabbi, who dubs the machine "a miracle of creation!"[46]

Riskin addresses the sounds of the prayer stemming from the curious apparatus: "I guess that when the Holy Days come around again, we'll rather put this phonograph before the altar, instead of the cantor." He, thus, deems the voice emanating from the phonograph to be at the same level as the (virtuoso) performance delivered by the cantor and the festive atmosphere of the congregation assembling in the synagogue during the High Holidays. The cantor in Pinski's comedy is intrigued by the sounds of the prayer emanating from the phonograph. His query, "Whose composition?," attests to the attempts of cantors to devise a traditional, if modern music; to render a liturgical music that would cater to the ascending Jewish bourgeoisie, and yet preserve the core of Jewish music.[47]

The phonograph reduced the majestic dimensions of the live cantorial singing, capturing the virtuoso cantorial vocal range within domestic surroundings. During these moments, the recorded voice of the cantor infiltrated into the mundane domestic space, and sounds associated with the pious atmosphere of the synagogue were performed as an aural theater. The group assembled in Riskin's house experienced a new mode of attention: listening to sounds wedged from their visible source. This perceptual shift, as Christoph Cox explains, was not only phenomenological but also ontological.[48] Rather than amount to mere reproductions of live events, recordings disclosed ontologically distinct, virtual aural worlds. The Hashkivenu played in *Der fonograf* with a machine brought from the "new" world, is, thus, detached from the daily reality of its listeners. This separation manifested the perceptual differences forged by mass migration and displacement, figuring the rift between the source—the shtetl—and the sounds emanating from the new modern Jewish culture in the form of the new aural technology.

The group gathered in the salon also performs its aural presence throughout the play. Pinski's drama presents the audience with various vocal organizations of the collective: the group huddled in the house speaks in concert to Riskin. Later, when the guests arrive and are transposed to the back room, their voices permeate the fictional space as disembodied sounds that echo the choral sounds issuing from the gramophone. The recording played in the fictional world includes the performance of a choir that accompanied the cantor; the cantor, in turn, expresses his strong impression (with a tinge of jealousy): "The cantor isn't so much, but the choir, the choir! If I only had such a choir, and those upper notes." Yet, when perpetuated through the gramophone, the synchronized voices of the chorus summon an image of a collective wedged by a deep fissure, as it is detached from its physical presence.

In this play, Pinski presents the phonograph as a transformative social vehicle: it magnetizes the people into the salon to experience the magic, while capitalizing on greed. It breaks down communal solidarity, and finally, it metamorphoses Riskin from an ambitious entrepreneur into a shrewd businessman who does not hesitate to adopt codes of behavior from the underworld. Pinski, thus, mocks not only the primitive, old-fashioned eastern European shtetl mentality, but also the ruthless and criminal intersection between the continents.

The phonograph connected various temporalities and places and, consequentially, altered the way people experienced their personal past and their collective being in the present. The experience of acousmatic listening conveys the distance between the voice and its source as a prism through which social reality could be refracted and better understood. In this manner, in Pinski's *Der fonograf*, the typical shtetl, with its established hierarchies, personal intrigue, and corruption, intersects with the new transmigratory reality, *di goldene medina* and its opportunities, as well as the latest technologies.

Peripatetic Listening: Theater Sound in the Streets

The nineteenth century saw intense transformations in urban sonic environments. Following the rise of sound-recording technologies, the soundscapes of cities and metropolises became more diversified. Daniel Morat examines the transformation in urban listening habits at the turn of the century. Listening to popular music, according to Morat, was part of the aestheticization of everyday life brought about by the rise of popular culture since the mid-nineteenth century.[49] As music became part of a growing capitalist entertainment industry, disseminated through commercial recordings, it became more available. The considerable bulk of sound recordings of popular theater and their broad distribution launched the Yiddish theater into new performance venues—the market, private homes, cafes, gardens, and the street—submerging urban centers with the renowned voices of prominent Yiddish performers emerging from new sound technologies.

Up until the beginning of the twentieth century, the organ grinder (also known as hand organ, or barrel organ) was the most common instrument heard on the streets.[50] However, along with the commercialization of the sound-recording industry, the streets became suffused with music emanating from phonographs and gramophones, the mechanical automobile and the movies. By the end of 1920, the streets of Europe were riddled with devices that superseded the manual organ grinder.

Samuel Jacob Harendorf (1900–1969), a Yiddish playwright and journalist, describes the particular relationship between sound recordings, Yiddish theater, and Jewish urban soundscapes in a short story titled "An aktiorisher fonograf vos vil nisht mkhll-zayn Shabes" (An actor phonograph, that does not want to violate the Sabbath).[51] Based on his memoires from his decade of traveling with theater troupes, between 1921 and 1931, Harendorf recounts the story of Moyshe Vaynberg and his old phonograph. According to the story, Vaynberg was an actor who performed with the renowned Gimpel theater troupe (originally from Lemberg). In order to secure a larger income, he decided to leave the theater group, buy an old gramophone, and travel around Galicia, playing records for money.[52] The audience admired the magical machine, and Vaynberg's wealth grew accordingly. Upon arriving in the small town of Monstrich on a Sabbath, Vaynberg wanted to produce a phonograph concert in the main square, playing a selection of recordings. Naturally, the Jewish community was outraged, lest the concert would violate the Sabbath sanctity. Opposing the community, Vaynberg played the phonograph, even when the rabbi exhorted him to stop. And then, suddenly, the phonograph stopped playing. Vaynberg inspected the phonograph, but could not find anything wrong with it. At the end of the Havdalah, the rabbi approached Vaynberg and asked him to play some nigunim at the meal customarily held by Jews after the Sabbath. Miraculously, the phonograph began to work again, as if nothing were wrong. Harendorf's story interlaces supernatural fascination with the new technology and Jewish religiosity. The gramophone, according to the story, is not a passive medium, but rather an object endowed with volition of its own that harbors understanding and sensitivity toward Jewish practices. It does not only play religious songs, but also abides by their preferred performative context.

A visual documentation of Jewish street-gramophone players features in Menachem Kipnis' ethnographic photographs that depict the daily life of the Jews of Warsaw and its vicinities prior to the Second World War.[53] One of Kipnis' photos shows a man tattered in old rags, standing next to a baby stroller carrying a gramophone (Figure 15.1). The placement of the sound machine bears a symbolic stance on the newly created Jewish soundscapes as originating in deeply ingrained traditional sonority. The baby-stroller sounding recorded Jewish folk songs, religious melodies, or theater songs created a "sonorous envelope," to borrow Didier Anzieu's fitting term, described as a "bath of sounds" and associated with the primary listening experience surrounding the infant, soothing, supporting, and stabilizing it during the initial phases of life. According to Anzieu, the "bath of sound" is comprised from the coupling of the infant's internal auditory sensation, and the external sounds produced by the caregiver. This imaginary sound envelope, according to Anzieu, provides the child a fiction of unity with the outer world. Anzieu's analysis presents this formative listening as a binding experience that provides the subject with an imaginary sonorous protection against the otherwise diffusive and disintegrating conditions of sound itself. The tunes and melodies arising from the gramophone, performing a musicality that lies at the core of Jewish culture, were familiar to Jewish bypassers. Theater songs and melodies were interlaced within the acoustic urban texture, coloring the streets with theatrical "social imaginaries."[54]

The Yiddish songs and melodies aired in the public domain yielded an ephemeral, non-material Jewish tinging of a shared space, engraved through sound that expanded throughout town squares and other public arenas—a form of public culture shared by the community at large. This aural street culture gave rise to a listening environment that was inseparable from the background music of daily noises.[55] Listening thus became a spatial practice of the various street users and reproduced a general ordering of the space. The crowd on the street that stopped by the gramophone surrounded the played sound, which transformed the passers-by into an audience. Once the audience constituted, a specific and temporal form of theatrical social relations was established in the street. People might have stood next to each other in proximity to listen to the music, or they might have listened from afar. The audio range of the gramophone, then, dictated the boundaries of its audience: anyone who can listen to the songs and melodies became part of the acoustic community mobilized by the gramophone. Thus, circles of belonging were formed by way of proximity to the performance and the source of sound. The temporary collectivity created by these performances lacked unity, and they varied in their attention and commitment to the performance. Yet the passers-by were all encircled within the same aural envelope. Street listening presents a way by which noise is captured, socially arranged, and then, as music, geared to order social life.

Listening to theater on the streets was a performative activity, connecting different geographical places, linking together the node through which the transnational theater

FIGURE 15.1 A street gramophone player in Warsaw during the interwar period, undated. Photographer: Menachem Kipnis. Menachem Kipnis Collection, RG 1343-f.086. Reproduced by permission of the YIVO Archives, New York.

network could be mediated across national borders. Sounding from old gramophones, the disembodied Yiddish theater songs that permeated the streets were captured by people "on the go" and attained symbolic meanings. Based upon a perceptual rift between the projected expression and its source, theatrical Jewish sonority fostered imaginations of coherence, unity, and connection, thus positioning its listeners in the very ontological tension under which they lived.

THE DECLINE OF THE REPUBLIC: BUILDING A MEMORY STAGE

Huwitz's opera *Yetsies mitsraim* manifests the circulation of the Yiddish theater among geographical locations, media, and modes of performances. Emerging as a significant cultural force, in tandem with Jewish migration from eastern Europe to the United States, modern Yiddish theater was, from its inception, entangled with transnational modes of mobility and communication. Travelling between eastern Europe and the United States, Yiddish theater constituted a sound republic—namely, the dispersion of Yiddish theater songs between continents—which partook in the consolidation of a transnational community by performing distinct Jewish sonorities.

At a time of profound social and geographical disintegration, the Yiddish theater catalyzed the communal ruptures through the performances of listening it inscribed. As such, it encompassed multiple simultaneous stages: the live theater event, recorded theater songs, and their performances in the public sphere. Listening to Yiddish theater, as shown in this analysis, depended upon a multilayered net of manifestations, gravitating between the ephemeral embodied theater performance and its reproduction through sound recordings that created virtual audio performances, triggering distinct sensuous experiences. Alongside the synagogue, the theater, and opera houses, the bourgeoise salon and street performances developed as parallel theatrical arenas. In each of these stages, audiences enacted different modes of listening. Furthermore, each of these stages relied on a different phenomenology of listening, through which the Jewish collective was conceived—as an actual embodied entity, a fictional construct, and a transnational collective. Through shifting modes of listening—entangled in mixed physical, embodied, and virtual technological realities—the audience could process, practice, and fictionalize new social relationships.

As a live social event, listening to Yiddish theater entailed an active engagement that was split between the staged drama and the havoc that took place in the theater. The audiences thus listened in and to theater songs that created a mental image of another place. The perceptual experience of displacement was further enhanced when listening to Yiddish theater sound recordings. Defined as acousmatic listening, listening to recorded theater entailed the separation between the sound and its corporeal source. Acousmatic listening implies the penetration of the sound into the body, as if it were a resonating instrument, vibrating through the ears and flesh. Acousmatic listening renders audiences as a medium. When played in the street, acousmatic listening assumed the gist of mobility, characterizing the modern migratory experience. As recorded sound, theater becomes nested in the mind of its listeners. Thus, by way of audio street performances, Yiddish theater songs took part in creating a network that propagated Jewish cultural identity. These performances of listening created and reflected a split consciousness, reformulating the ways theater was experienced into perceptual modes that resonated with the shifting social structures.

By the end of the Great War, the Yiddish theater republic of sounds declined, along with the downturn of the Yiddish theater.[56] Subsequently, the stages and social performances it produced also perished. However, the music and songs, iconic voices and rhythms of the Yiddish theater republic of sounds remained through reminiscent commercial sound recordings. When played today, these recorded sounds pierce our present, enabling us to experience, once again, fragments of idiosyncratic, specific expressions from the bygone theatrical world of the Yiddish theater during its foundational years. The reiteration of Yiddish theater sound recordings, displaced from their historical and performative context, produces a new stage in which the voices and sounds of the past are animated—a stage of cultural memory-building in the minds of its listeners. This stage permits the circulation of past aural formations, and conveys the modes whereby acting bodies talked, sung, and listened. Yet, the stage of memory does not draw its listeners into a different realm; rather, it stratifies their present and opens it, allowing a glimpse to past performances.

Hurwitz's opera *Yetsies mitsraim* resonates with the stage of memory. The opera dramatized the biblical myth at the core of the Passover Seder night—a ritual of collective remembrance in which Jews retell the story of the Exodus of the Israelites from slavery in Egypt. The Talmudic dictum iterated in the Seder—"In each and every generation let each person regard himself as though he had emerged from Egypt" (Mishnah, Pesaḥim 10:5)—prescribes the theatrical "as if" experience as a way to keep the memory alive.[57] Reenactment thus becomes a way to link the past with the present, in the ritual, theater, and beyond. Listening today to theater sound recordings from *Yetsies mitsraim* enables to embody the time-space ruptures entailed both in its varied performances, as well as in the flow of time. Infused and mediated by the corporality of its listeners, the fragmentary sounds and voices remnant from the Yiddish theater republic of sounds transform into a living memory—a corporal sensation created by the performance of listening.

ACKNOWLEDGMENTS

This article was written in the framework of the DYBBUK project (www.dybbuk.co) that received funding from the European Research Council (ERC) under the European Union's Horizon 2020 research and innovation program. Grant agreement No. 948150.

NOTES

1. The first modern Yiddish theater production in New York City related to the theme of Exodus took place as early as December 1887, when Reuben Weissman—the first and most famous prompter of the Yiddish theater—staged his five-act operetta *Moyshe rabeynu oder kries yam-suf* (Our teacher Moses, or, The parting of the Sea of Reeds) at the New York Oriental Theater, featuring the newly arrived immigrant Jacob A. Adler in one of the small roles, prior to his breakthrough. Neither the libretto nor the music of Weissman's operetta have been traced. Furthermore, the scene and dramatic gesture of the Exodus was also depicted in the curtain of the People's Theater (at 201 Bowery Street), featuring a rendition of Moses on top of mount Sinai presenting the Ten Commandments to the Israelites. See Edna Nahshon, ed., *New York's Yiddish Theater: From the Bowery to Broadway* (New York: Columbia University Press, 2016), 21; "The Jewish King Lear," *The New York Dramatic Mirror*, February 16, 1901, 15.

2. Dramatic manuscripts of the opera are kept in the Sholem Perlmutter Collection at YIVO Archives in New York, and in the Yiddish theater collection at the St. Petersburg State Theater Library. The manuscript was submitted to the drama censorship committee of the Russian Empire for approval in 1910.

3. See Shlomo Perlmutter and Jacob Mestel, eds., *Yidishe dramaturgn un kompositors* (New York: YKUF, 1952), 66–72; Zalman Zylbercweig, *Leksikon fun yidishn teater* (New York: Farlag "Elisheva", 1931), 1:591–605; Nahma Sandrow, *Vagabond Stars: A World History of Yiddish Theater* (Syracuse, NY: Syracuse University Press, 1996), 76, 104–108.

4. See Michael C. Steinlauf, "Fear of Purim: Y. L. Peretz and the Canonization of Yiddish Theater," *Jewish Social Studies*, New Series, 1, no. 3 (1995): 44–65.

5. See Gur Alroey, "From the Pale of Settlement to the Lower East Side: Early Hardship of Russian Immigrant Jews," in *The Jewish Metropolis*, ed. Daniel Soyer (Boston: Academic Studies Press, 2021), 62–90.

6. See Nina Warnke, "Yiddish Theater History, Its Composers and Operettas: A Narrative without Music," *Pismo Muzykalia 7 Judaica* 2 (2009): 1–11; and Mark Slobin, "The Music of the Yiddish Theater: Manuscript Sources at YIVO," *YIVO Annual of Jewish Social Sciences* 18 (1983): 372–390.

7. Mark Slobin, *Tenement Songs: The Popular Music of The Jewish Immigrants* (Urbana: University of Illinois Press, 1982), 199.

8. For studies on the rise of the Yiddish theater and its cultural significance against the background of the mass Jewish migration movement, see, for example, Joel Berkowitz, ed., *Yiddish Theater: New Approaches* (Oxford: The Littman Library of Jewish Civilization, 2003); Debra Caplan, *Yiddish Empire: The Vilna Troupe, Jewish Theater, and the Art of Itinerancy* (Ann Arbor: University of Michigan Press, 2018); Nina Warnke, "Immigrant Popular Culture as Contested Sphere: Yiddish Music Halls, the Yiddish Press, and the Processes of Americanization, 1900–1910," *Theater Journal* 48, no. 3 (1996): 32–335; and Vivi Lachs, *Whitechapel Noise: Jewish Immigrant Life in Yiddish Song and Verse, London 1884–1914* (Detroit, MI: Wayne State University Press, 2018).

9. For an extensive study on the development of modern Yiddish theater, through the life and work of Abraham Goldfaden, see Alyssa Quint, *The Rise of the Modern Yiddish Theater* (Bloomington: Indiana University Press, 2019).

10. See Mark Slobin, "Music in the Yiddish Theater and Cinema, 1880–1950," in *The Cambridge Companion to Jewish Music*, ed. Joshua S. Walden (Cambridge: Cambridge University Press, 2015), 215.

11. On the development of the Modern Yiddish theater, see Nahma Sandrow, *Vagabond Stars: A World History of Yiddish Theater* (Syracuse, NY: Syracuse University Press, 1996); on Jewish folkloristic forms in Yiddish theater and film, see Zehavit Stern, *From Jester to Gesture: Eastern European Jewish Culture and the Reimagining of Folk Performances* (PhD diss., University of California, Berkley, 2011).

12. For more on the development of the nineteenth-century operetta, in its European context, see Anastasia Belina and Derek B. Scott, eds., *The Cambridge Companion to Operetta* (Cambridge: Cambridge University Press, 2019).

13. On the transnational perspective for the study of modern Yiddish theater, see Debra Caplan, "Nomadic Chutzpah: The Vilna Troupe's Transnational Yiddish Theater Paradigm, 1915–1935," *Theater Survey* 55, no. 3 (2014): 296–317; Nina Warnke, "Theater as Educational Institution: Jewish Immigrant Intellectuals and Yiddish Theater Reform," *The Art of Being Jewish in Modern Times* (Philadelphia: University of Pennsylvania Press, 2013), 23–41; C. Tova Markenson, "Jewish Immigrant Theater and the Argentinean Avant-Gardes: The Case of Ibergus in 1926 Buenos Aires," *Modern Drama* 63, no. 4 (2020): 455–476; and Edna Nahshon, ed., *Jewish Theater: A Global View* (Leiden: Brill, 2009).

14. On the republic of letters, see Lorraine Daston, "The Ideal and Reality of the Republic of Letters in the Enlightenment," *Science in Context* 4, no. 2 (1991): 367–386; Peter Burke, "The Republic of Letters as a Communication System: An Essay in Periodization," *Media History* 18, nos. 3–4 (2012): 395–407; and Dena Goodman, *The Republic of Letters: A Cultural History of the French Enlightenment* (Ithaca, NY: Cornell University Press, 1994).

15. See Irene Heskes, "Music as Social History: American Yiddish Theater Music, 1882–1920," *American Music* 2, no. 4 (1984): 73–87; Nina Warnke, "Yiddish Theater History, Its Composers and Operettas: A Narrative without Music," *Pismo Muzykalia* 7 (*Judaica* 2, 2009): 1–11; Daniela Smolov Levy, "*Parsifal* in Yiddish? Why Not?," *The Musical Quarterly* 97, no. 2 (Summer 2014): 140–180; Joshua S. Walden, "The 'Yidishe Paganini': Sholem Aleichem's Stempenyu, the Music of Yiddish Theater and the Character of the Shtetl Fiddler," *Journal of the Royal Musical Association* 139, no. 1 (2014): 89–136; and Mark Slobin, "Music in the Yiddish Theater and Cinema, 1880–1950," in Walden, *The Cambridge Companion to Jewish Music*, 215–227.

16. See Berkowitz, *Yiddish Theater*, 6–9.

17. See Sophia Rosenfeld, "On being heard: A Case for Paying Attention to the Historical Ear," *The American Historical Review* 116, no. 2 (2011): 317–319.

18. On listening in the nineteenth century, see Christian Thorau and Hansjakob Ziemer, eds., *The Oxford Handbook of Music Listening in the 19th and 20th Centuries* (New York: Oxford University Press, 2019). On concert listening, see James H. Johnson, *Listening in Paris: A Cultural History* (Berkeley: University of California Press, 1995); and Peter Gay, *The Naked Heart: The Bourgeois Experience Victoria to Freud* (New York: W.W. Norton & Company, 1996), 4:11–35. On the development of musical listening, see Matthew Riley, *Musical Listening in the German Enlightenment: Attention, Wonder and Astonishment* (New York: Routledge, 2004).

19. For recent studies on performative knowledge encoded in our auditory culture, see Gina Bloom, *Voice in Motion* (Philadelphia: University of Pennsylvania Press, 2007); Bruce S. Smith, *The Acoustic World of Early Modern England* (Chicago: University of Chicago Press, 1999); Lynne Kendrick, *Theater Aurality* (London: Palgrave Macmillan, 2017); Susan Bennet, *Theory for Theater Studies: Sound* (London: Bloomsbury, 2019); Mladen Ovadija, *Dramaturgy of Sound in the Avant-garde and Postdramatic Theater* (Montreal: McGill

University Press, 2013); and Ruthie Abeliovich, *Possessed Voices: Aural Remains from Modernist Hebrew Theater* (Albany, NY: SUNY Press, 2019).

20. Jonathan Sterne, *The Audible Past* (Durham, NH: Duke University Press, 2003), 8–9.

21. For Yossele Rosenblatt's biography, see Samuel Rosenblatt, *Yossele Rosenblatt: The Story of His Life as Told by His Son* (New York: Farrar, Straus, and Young, 1954).

22. The lyrics of the song appear in the sheet music in the Florida Atlantic University Digital Library, http://fau.digital.flvc.org/islandora/object/fau%3A1782.

23. See Jeffrey Shandler, "Sanctification of the Brand Name: The Marketing of Cantor Yossele Rosenblatt," *Chosen Capital: The Jewish Encounter with American Capitalism*, ed. Rebecca Kobrin (New Brunswick, NJ: Rutgers University Press, 2012); Jeffry Shandler, "A Tale of Two Cantors: Pinhas Minkowski and Yossele Rosenblatt," *Academic Angles* (New York: Museum at Eldridge Street, 2008), 24–28; for a more extended discussion on the role of recordings and other media in the American cantorate, spanning through the twentieth century, see Jeffrey Shandler, *Jews, God, and Videotape: Religion and Media in America* (New York: New York University Press, 2009), chapter 1.

24. On the religious training of the pioneers of Modern Yiddish theater, see Slobin, *Tenement Songs*, 32–48; Nahma Sandrow, "Popular Yiddish Theater: Music Melodrama and Operetta," in *New York's Yiddish Theater: From the Bowery to Broadway*, ed. Edna Nahshon (New York: Columbia University Press, 2016), 64–83; and David Mazower, "Stories in Song: The *Melo-deklamtsyes* of Joseph Markovitsh," in Berkowitz, *Yiddish Theater*, 120–122n5.

25. Abraham Goldfaden, "Di muzik fun mayne gezangshpiln" (The music from my musical performances), in *Avrom Goldfaden: Oysgeklibene shriftn*, ed. Shmuel Rozshanski (Buenos Aires: YIVO Press, 1963), 255–261. This article was first published in German, in the Zionist newspaper *Die Welt*, no. 40 (Vienna, 1899). It was later translated into Yiddish and published in *Literarishe bleter*, no. 464 (Warsaw, 1933).

26. On the music of Abraham Goldfaden, see Irene Heskes, *The Music of Abraham Goldfaden, Father of the Yiddish Theater* (New York: Tara Publication, 1990).

27. Goldfaden, "Di muzik fun mayne gezangshpiln," 256.

28. As Andrea Most explains, in the late nineteenth and early twentieth century, the Yiddish theater played a crucial role in easing the transition for Jewish immigrants from religious to secular life. See Andrea Most, *Theatrical Liberalism: Jews and Popular Entertainment in America* (New York: New York University Press, 2013), 10 and 21.

29. See Franz Rosenzweig, *The Star of Redemption*, trans. Barbara E. Galli (Madison, WI: The University of Wisconsin Press, 2005), 381–382.

30. On the Yiddish theater audience, see Ilana Bialik, "Audience Response in the Yiddish 'Shund' Theater," *Theater Research International* 13, no. 2 (1987): 97–105; Nina Warnke, "The Child Who Wouldn't Grow Up: Yiddish Theater and Its Critics," in Berkowitz, *Yiddish Theater*, 201–216.

31. Yoysef Zevin Tashrak, *Etikete: A veg vayzer fun laytishe oyffihrung, heflikhkayt un shehne manieren far mener un froyen* (New York: Hebrew Publishing Co., 1912), 87. This quotation is also discussed by Nina Warnke, "Reforming the New York Yiddish Theater: The Cultural Politics of Immigrant Intellectuals and the Yiddish Press, 1887–1910" (PhD diss., Columbia University, 2001), 136–137.

32. Tashrak, *Etikete*, 87.

33. On nineteenth-century spiritual approaches to sound technologies, see Steven Connor, "The Machine in the Ghost: Spiritualism, Technology and the 'Direct Voice,'" in *Ghosts: Deconstruction, Psychoanalysis, History*, ed. Peter Buse (London: Macmillan, 1999),

203–225; and Jeffrey Sconce, *Haunted Media: Electronic Presence from Telegraphy to Television* (Durham, NC: Duke University Press, 2000).

34. Many thanks to Talia Trainin for this insight.

35. Pierre Schaeffer, "Acousmatics," in *Audio Culture: Readings in Modern Music*, ed. Christoph Cox and Daniel Warner (New York and London: Continuum, 2004), 77. For more on the sound object in Schaeffer's thought, see Brian Kane, *Unseen Sound: Acousmatic Sound in Theory and Practice* (Oxford: Oxford University Press, 2014), 15–44.

36. Michel Chion, "Acousmatique," in *Guide des objets sonores* (Paris: Buchet-Chastel, 1983), §2b, 19. For more on the sound object in Schaeffer's thought, see Brian Kane, *Unseen Sound: Acousmatic Sound in Theory and Practice* (Oxford: Oxford University Press, 2014), 15–44.

37. For an extensive discussion of the term *acousmatique* as interpreted by Michel Chion, see Kane, *Unseen Sound*, 4–7.

38. See Michael Aylward, "Early Recordings of Jewish Music in Poland," in *Focusing on Jewish Popular Culture and Its Afterlife*, ed. Michael C. Steinlauf and Antony Polonsky, Polin: Studies in Polish Jewry 16 (Oxford: Littman Library of Jewish Civilization, 2003), 59–69; and Michael Aylward, "Gimpel's Theater, Lwów: The Sounds of a Popular Yiddish Theater Preserved on Gramophone Records 1904–1913," in *Jews and Music-Making in the Polish Lands*, ed. François Guesnet, Benjamin Matis, and Antony Polonsky, Polin: Studies in Polish Jewry 32 (Oxford: Littman Library of Jewish Civilization, 2020), 125–145.

39. For further reading on the development of the early gramophone industry, see Geoffrey Jones, "The Gramophone Company: An Anglo-American Multinational, 1898–1931," *The Business History Review* 59, no. 1 (1985): 76–100; and Pekka Gronow, "The Record Industry: The Growth of a Mass Medium," *Popular Music* 3 (1983): 53–75. For more on the Jewish dimensions of the sound recording industry, see James Loeffler, "The 'Lust Machine': Recording and Selling the Jewish Nation in the Late Russian Empire," in Guesnet, Matis, and Polonsky, *Jews and Music-Making in the Polish Lands*, 257–277; Joshua S. Walden, "Jewish Music and Media of Sound Reproduction," in Walden, *The Cambridge Companion to Jewish Music*, 56–72.

40. See Henry Sapoznik, *Klezmer: Jewish Music from Old World to Our World* (New York: Schirmer Trade Books, 1999), 61.

41. See Walden, "Jewish Music and Media," 58.

42. The migration routes of Yiddish popular theater actors reveal dynamic transnational bidirectional tracks. Nina Glick Schiller, Linda Basch, and Cristina Blanc-Szanton's developed the concept of transmigration in order to describe immigrants whose daily lives depend on multiple and constant interconnections across international borders and whose public identities are configured in relationship to more than one nation-state. Transmigrants, according to this definition, position themselves both in their country of origin and in their country of settlement. See Nina Glick Schiller, Linda Basch, and Cristina Blanc-Szanton, "From Immigrant to Transmigrant: Theorizing Transnational Migration," *Anthropological Quarterly* (1995): 48–63.

43. Bruce S. Smith, *The Acoustic World of Early Modern England* (Chicago: University of Chicago Press, 1999), 56.

44. Georgina Born suggests to conceptualize sound recordings beyond the paradigm of reproduction or copy, to a conception of recording as representation. See "Recording: From Reproduction to Representation to Remediation," in *The Cambridge Companion to*

Recorded Music, ed. Nicholas Cook, Eric Clarke, Daniel Leech-Wilkinson, and John Rink (Cambridge: Cambridge University Press, 2011), 294–300.

45. David Pinski, "The Phonograph," in *Ten Plays*, trans. Isaac Goldberg (New York: B. W. Huebsch, 1920), 1–35.

46. Ibid., 20–23.

47. The cantor in Pinski's drama puts forward three names of prominent cantors: Joshua (Osias) Abrass, also known as "Pitshe" (1820–1884); the Lithuanian cantor and composer Nissi Belzer (originally Nissan Spivak, 1824–1906); and Salomon Sulzer (1804–1890).

48. Christoph Cox and Daniel Warner, "Modes of Listening: Introduction," in *Audio Culture: Readings in Modern Music*, ed. Christoph Cox and Daniel Warner (London: Bloomsbury Publishing, 2017), 87–89.

49. See Daniel Morat, "Music in the Air—Listening in the Streets: Popular Music and Urban Listening Habits in Berlin ca. 1900," in Thorau and Ziemer, *The Oxford Handbook of Music Listening*, 341.

50. On the performance of the barrel-organ, see Arthur W. J. G. Ord-Hume, *Barrel Organ: The Story of the Mechanical Organ and Its Repair* (South Brunswick, NJ: A.S. Barnes, 1978).

51. See Samuel Jacob Harendorf, *Teater karavanen: Maysehlekh un epizodn fun mayne vanderungen mit yidish teater* (London: Fraynt fun yidish loshn, 1955), 35–38. This anecdote is mentioned in Michael Aylward, "Gimpel's Theater," 145.

52. Another account of traveling gramophone is provided by Eddie Portnoy, who narrates a similar practice in the story of Puny Khane and Shimshon Gramophone, who made a living out of gramophone street performances. For twenty years, Portnoy writes, Khane would play the gramophone and Shimshon would dance. See Eddie Portnoy, *Bad Rabbi: And Other Strange but True Stories from the Yiddish Press* (Stanford, CA: Stanford University Press, 2017), 121–122.

53. Menachem Kipnis (1878–1942) was a singer, photographer, and ethnographer of Jewish music and folklore. He himself was a tenor at the Warsaw Opera, spending sixteen years on stage. See Zylbercweig, *Leksikon fun yidishn teater*, s.v. "Kipnis, Menakhem," 5:3799–37803; and Itzik Nakhmen Gottesman, *Defining the Yiddish Nation: The Jewish Folklorists of Poland* (Detroit, MI: Wayne State University Press, 2003), 56–66.

54. Charles Taylor defines social imaginaries as "the ways people imagine their social existence, how they fit together with others, how things go on between them and their fellows, the expectations that are normally met, and the deeper normative notions and images that underline these expectations." See Charles Taylor, *Modern Social Imaginaries* (Durham, NC: Duke University Press, 2004), 23.

55. Paul Simpson, "Sonic Affect and the Production of Space: 'Music by Handle' and the Politics of Street Music in Victorian London," *Cultural Geographies* 24, no. 1 (2017): 89–109; and Paul Simpson, "Street Performance and the City: Public Space, Sociality, and Intervening in the Everyday," *Space and Culture* 14, no. 4 (2011): 415–430.

56. See Judith Thissen, "Reconsidering the Decline of the New York Yiddish Theatre in the Early 1900s," *Theatre Survey* 44, no. 2 (November 2003): 173–197.

57. See Josef H. Yerushalmi, *Zakhor: Jewish History and Jewish Memory* (Seattle: University of Washington Press, 1982), 43–45.

SELECT BIBLIOGRAPHY

Aylward, Michael. "Gimpel's Theater, Lwów: The Sounds of a Popular Yiddish Theater Preserved on Gramophone Records 1904-1913." In *Jews and Music-Making in the Polish Lands*, edited by François Guesnet, Benjamin Matis, and Antony Polonsky, 125–145. Polin: Studies in Polish Jewry 32. Oxford: Littman Library of Jewish Civilization, 2020.

Berkowitz, Joel. *Shakespeare on the American Yiddish Stage*. Iowa City: University of Iowa Press, 2005.

Berkowitz, Joel, and Barbara Henry, eds., *Inventing the Modern Yiddish Stage: Essays in Drama, Performance, and Show Business*. Detroit, MI: Wayne State University Press, 2012.

Caplan, Debra. *Yiddish Empire: The Vilna Troupe, Jewish Theater, and the Art of Itinerancy*. Ann Arbor: University of Michigan Press, 2018.

Nahshon, Edna, ed. *New York's Yiddish Theater: From the Bowery to Broadway*. New York: Columbia University Press, 2016.

Quint, Alyssa. *The Rise of the Modern Yiddish Theater*. Bloomington: Indiana University Press, 2019.

Rotman, Diego. *The Yiddish Stage as a Temporary Home: Dzigan and Shumacher's Satirical Theater (1927–1980)*. Translated by Rebecca Wolpe. Berlin: De Gruyter, 2021.

Sandrow, Nahma. *Vagabond Stars: A World History of Yiddish Theater*. Syracuse, NY: Syracuse University Press, 1996.

Schaeffer, Pierre. "Acousmatics." In *Audio Culture: Readings in Modern Music*, edited by Christoph Cox and Daniel Warner, 76–81. New York and London: Continuum, 2004.

Slobin, Mark. "The Music of the Yiddish Theater: Manuscript Sources at YIVO." *YIVO Annual of Jewish Social Sciences* 18 (1983): 372–390.

Slobin, Mark. "Some Intersections of Jews, Music, and Theater." In *From Hester Street to Hollowood*, edited by Sarah Blacher Cohen, 29–43. Bloomington: Indiana University Press, 1983.

Slobin, Mark. *Tenement Songs: The Popular Music of The Jewish Immigrants*. Urbana: University of Illinois Press, 1982.

Steinlauf, Michael C., and Antony Polonsky, eds. *Focusing on Jewish Popular Culture and Its Afterlife*. Polin: Studies in Polish Jewry 16. Oxford: Littman Library of Jewish Civilization, 2003.

Thissen, Judith. "Reconsidering the Decline of the New York Yiddish Theatre in the Early 1900s." *Theatre Survey* 44, no. 2 (November 2003): 173–197.

Veidlinger, Jeffrey. "Theater: The Professionalization of Performance." In *Jewish Public Culture in The Late Russian Empire*, edited by Jeffrey Veidlinger, 165–195. Bloomington: Indiana University Press, 2009.

Warnke, Nina. "Yiddish Theater History, Its Composers and Operettas: A Narrative without Music." *Pismo Muzykalia* 7 Judaica 2 (2009): 1–11.

PART V

COLLECTION—
זאמלונג

16

THE YIVO SOUND ARCHIVE AS A LIVING SPACE

Archiving and Revitalizing Klezmer Music

ELÉONORE BIEZUNSKI

IN 1987 Michal Goldman directed the documentary film *A Jumpin' Night in the Garden of Eden*, which traced the efforts of two ensembles, Kapelye and the Klezmer Conservatory Band, to recover the lost history of klezmer music. In one central scene, two emerging figures, Henry Sapoznik and Hankus Netsky, walk into the YIVO Institute for Jewish Research, then located at Fifth Avenue and 86th Street in New York City, in the building facing Central Park that now houses the Neue Galerie. In a small room, Sapoznik shows the treasure trove contained in the newly founded Max and Frieda Weinstein Archive of YIVO Sound Recordings (henceforth, YIVO Sound Archive) to Netsky, and hands him a photograph of a young boy playing the balalaika, with his mother at his side. "Can you name that Jew?" Sapoznik asks with a smirk. They laugh. Netsky does not recognize the musician in the picture.

This anecdote is a humorous manifestation of what this chapter aims to show: how the archive functions as a living space, where the circulation of people and of materials is both generated by and generative of "cultural transfers," thus allowing one to connect with and revisit the past, to formulate new knowledge, and to inspire artistic creations. The archive offers a space where the living and the dead can interact, where the artifacts become closest to life, albeit in a fragmentary way.

Returning to the photograph, "this Jew" was Dave Tarras (189?–1989), one of the best-known klezmer clarinetists of the twentieth century. Born in Ternovka, Ukraine, he was the son of a klezmer trombonist and *badkhn* (wedding entertainer). He grew up surrounded by music and played various instruments. In 1915 he was drafted into the Imperial Russian Army; his musical abilities kept him away from the trenches. In 1921 he emigrated to the United States, settling in New York City. After initially working in a garment factory, he eventually made a living as a musician, working as a klezmer clarinetist with several ensembles. He also recorded Greek, Polish, and Russian melodies for

Columbia Records under different pseudonyms. He participated in approximately five hundred recordings during his career. During the revitalization of klezmer music in the 1970s and 1980s, Dave Tarras mentored many young musicians who would later become well known, including the clarinetist and mandolinist Andy Statman.

In November 1978 the Balkan Arts Center (now Center for Traditional Music and Dance) started a series of concerts in honor of Dave Tarras, at the Club Casa Galicia at 119 East 11th Street, with the master himself performing, accompanied by Sam Beckerman and Max Goldberg (Figure 16.1).[1] Walter Zev Feldman describes both this first concert and the subsequent "ecstatic dance party" as a "major cultural catharsis for New York Jews."[2] Many then-younger musicians and singers who would later involve themselves professionally in klezmer music or in Yiddish song (such as David Krakauer, Frank London, Hankus Netsky, Bob Cohen, Joshua Waletzky, Paula Teitelbaum, Alicia Svigals, and Janet Leuchter) avow that the series of concerts had a "galvanizing effect."[3] They were key events in the klezmer revitalization movement.

This was also the night the young Sapoznik, then a bluegrass and old-time banjo player who had recently become interested in Jewish music, met the discographer Richard Spottswood of the Library of Congress, a specialist in European and American jazz, blues, bluegrass, and country recordings. They would eventually collaborate on the documentation of pre-1942 Jewish music recordings produced in the United States, and later, joined by the multi-faceted artist and activist Jenny Romaine, issue a discography of 78-rpm discs.[4] Sapoznik was interested in both the recordings produced in the United States and those issued between circa 1906 and 1952 in Europe—access to all of them was key to the revitalization of klezmer music as they served as a "*major* source of repertoire and inspiration."[5] Around the same time musicians in California were turning to Martin Schwartz's private collection of klezmer music and that of the Judah L. Magnes Museum (now The Magnes Collection of Jewish Art and Life), where Lev Liberman had just discovered the 78-rpms.[6] In Philadelphia, Hankus Netsky was accessing primary sources from his family's collection and those at the Gratz College Archives.[7] Indeed, the revitalization unfolded in many places throughout the United States, where sound recording of klezmer music could be found.

In his now-classic sociological examination of art as collective action, Howard Becker underlines the major role of organizations in artistic change.[8] For revitalization to take place, musicians and scholars need to work together with organizations to create institutional structures that will support their research and creativity. This is what led the creation of the YIVO Sound Archive. As the current YIVO sound archivist, lead singer and multi-instrumentalist of the Grammy-winning band the Klezmatics, Lorin Sklamberg, affirmed in 2005, "it is not an overstatement to say that the 'klezmer revival' of the last 25 years would not have happened without the holdings in the YIVO Sound Archive."[9] The concept of revival used by Sklamberg has been both embraced and contested, and amply theorized.[10] For some it presents an all-too-linear sense of the phenomenon that unfolded as a dynamic process as encapsulated in the prefix "re-." Michael Alpert prefers the concept of revitalization, given its insinuation of "a rebirth of the vitality of something, rather than bringing back to life."[11]

FIGURE 16.1 Poster of the Dave Tarras Concert at Casa Galicia, on November 19, 1978. New York City. Reproduced by permission of the YIVO Institute for Jewish Research.

This chapter aims at uncovering the links between the establishment of the YIVO Sound Archive—now housing over 20,000 sound recordings dating from 1901 to the present—and the phenomenon of klezmer music's revitalization, by focusing on distinct moments in the 1970s and 1980s when the archive was created. As such, its formal establishment at YIVO in the early 1980s by a small group of musicians and scholars and the revitalization of klezmer were two facets of a single phenomenon. This had historical precedence, mirroring in essence the revitalization of Jewish music in Russia at the turn of the twentieth century by the Society for Jewish Folk Music, whose objective was to collect and arrange Jewish popular melodies, to present lectures and performances of this material, to establish and maintain an archive or a library of Jewish music, to publish a journal, and to encourage individual creativity in the domain of Jewish music.[12] If Jewish music was perceived as needing to be elevated at the turn of the century by way of art music, within a hierarchy that placed folk music at the bottom, such thinking was still extant at the time when the YIVO Sound Archive took shape.[13]

In order to (re)discover the sound of the past, to reconnect with practices once in full bloom, one had to turn to the few musicians who could act as agents of transmission, and to the remaining sound recordings that needed to be archived. In the absence of archivists, however, performers themselves became archivists, such as Henry Sapoznik, for whom "these scratchy records were a passport to a vanished land."[14] Simultaneously new and old, for him they "*were* the old country, a ticket back to that time and place."[15]

The very nature of sound recording raises questions of temporality and the vitality of the material, the movement that animates the object of study from within. Taking the temporality of the sound recording further by considering its function, Mark Slobin asserts that it provides a "cohesive feeling about place and time that tends to assimilate the immediate moment to larger patterns of local knowledge"—a "sonochronotope," as it were.[16] The recordings have the ability to blend the sense of time and of space between the here and now and the time-space represented by and on the recording itself. The microscale of the recordings as chronotope turn the archive into an "other space," a heterotopia in the Foucauldian sense: intense, incompatible, contradictory, or transforming.[17] The archive, as a heterotopic space of superposition of time, is the site of an accumulation of knowledge, pertaining not only to the artifacts it contains, but also to the history of how the artifact as well as the archive as a whole came to existence.

CREATING THE LIVING SPACE

The term *archive* designates both a container—the place where one goes to consult stored documents, a location—and its content, the documents themselves. Thus, the archive is both a real space and a metonymic space. As for the sound archives and their holdings, the recordings themselves exist in their materiality as well as in their content. Observing this level of the multiple and sedimented meanings of the archive implies the analysis of cultural artifacts as facts, as dynamic processes, and as representations.

The archive is also a living space and as such mappable—with its shelves, boxes, and folders, located in a building, in a street of a neighborhood, within a city. The collections in their materiality, composed of shellac 78-rpm records, and vinyl LPs, magnetic tapes, compact discs, and a variety of other media, need the care of the archivist to be preserved, and must be mapped to be accessible. The archivist thus becomes cartographer by creating inventories, catalogs, finding aids; by linking the information of what is where, and by making this information accessible. In the absence of this type of map—in what is technically called "hidden collection"—the archivist becomes a guide in an unmapped territory.

In the case of the YIVO Sound Archive, processes of displacement of intellectual and scholarly practices from one cultural context to another through migrations—a set of cultural transfers, as it were—add spatial complexity. The tumultuous history of the Yidisher Visnshaftlekher Institut (Yiddish Scientific Institute, known as YIVO), goes back to the early collecting enterprises of folklore in the Pale of Settlement as an element of national construction, and later evolves in parallel to the development of performance studies in a postmodern American intellectual context.[18] Founded in 1925, YIVO was, as historian David Fishman explains, "a modern research academy that employed the methods of the humanities and social sciences to study Jewish life."[19] In 1941 a group of intellectuals salvaged and shipped part of the holdings of the YIVO archives from Vilna to New York under tragic circumstances, including from inside the Vilna Ghetto by a group of poets and scholars known as the "Paper Brigade." Seventy years later, the institution's archive contains 23 million objects linked to a large library of 400,000 volumes, including large collections of sheet music, and other material related to music. The YIVO Sound Archive, officially established in 1981, holds recordings of music as well as spoken-word and other types of sound recordings, such as field recordings, lectures, and radio programs.

Both Samuel Norich, current president of the *Forward* and executive director of YIVO from 1980 and 1992, and Sapoznik assert that a sound archive already existed at YIVO prior to the formal creation of the Max and Frieda Weinstein Archives of YIVO Sound Recordings.[20] Recordings were scattered throughout different collections or were hidden away in the basement closet of the large Vanderbilt Mansion, where YIVO was then located. As Sapoznik states, "In the beginning, people would clean out their attics and donate records to YIVO. They were stored in the general YIVO Archives, where they went virtually unnoticed for years."[21] It was to this neglected treasure that Barbara Kirshenblatt-Gimblett would draw Sapoznik's attention when he began to study klezmer music. When, in 1976, he tried to find repertoire for his concerts, she "invited him to come and browse through the boxes of old records."[22] Adrienne Cooper (1946–2011), a renowned interpreter of Yiddish song and then the assistant to Norich at YIVO, describes the collaborative atmosphere at the time as follows:

> So there was creativity in the air. There was also a government program for folk artists called CETA, the Comprehensive Employment Training Act. There was a center [Martin Steinberg Center] just a few blocks from the YIVO, where other people,

> Carol Freeman and Zev Feldman, and others who were part of other music scenes, the American folk music scene, or the Balkan music scene, were rediscovering this music. It was a nice little community to start working with.[23]

As Cooper indicates, in the general context of the "roots movement" of the early 1970s, a number of young folk musicians sought to rediscover, learn, and revitalize the music of their grandparents, including klezmer music.

In 1977 the Martin Steinberg Center at the American Jewish Congress, located next door to YIVO, hired Sapoznik with federal funding from the Comprehensive Employment and Training Act, to direct a research project on Jewish music beginning in 1978. This position offered Sapoznik an opportunity to create a platform for various research projects and to create a body of accessible sources at a time when there was not yet a single reissue of old recordings of klezmer music (in contrast to the abounding reissues of cantorial and theater music). Freeman and Alpert, who had recently moved to New York (in 1981 and 1982 he would serve as program director of the Soviet Jewish Traditions Festival), were both employed in this program. Their task was to interview immigrants, including a few remarkable individuals such as the Yiddish singer Bronya Sakina (1910–1988) and klezmer drummer-badkhn Ben Bazyler (1922–1990), specifically asking them to recall songs, instrumental pieces, and dances from their hometowns.[24] During its short existence, this small research center provided musicians, directors, writers, poets, puppeteers, and playwrights with the means to express and develop artistic creativity rooted in Jewish continuity. It was through this program that Sapoznik began the project of archiving old records and radio recordings, and to interview Jewish musicians from Eastern Europe. The YIVO 78-rpm disc collection became the laboratory for this project.

Meanwhile, a few months after Dave Tarras' historic 1978 concert at Casa Galicia, Kirshenblatt-Gimblett conceived a two-part project on klezmer music: YIVO would sponsor a concert by the legendary klezmer clarinetist Dave Tarras, and Kirshenblatt-Gimblett would conduct a research project on klezmer music that would result in the creation of a sound archive, including a listening station, and the production of two records.[25] For this purpose, she submitted to YIVO's Research, Grants, and Special Projects Sub-Committee the grant application she had previously submitted to the National Endowment for the Arts. The proposed two-part project focused on a detailed documentation of the traditional instrumental music of Eastern European Jews (which Kirshenblatt-Gimblett called "klezmer-muzik") on the basis of interviews and recordings of the last surviving European-born klezmer musicians, including Dave Tarras; and on disseminating the music through the reissuing of records, thus providing access to the original sources of klezmer music. Though a pioneer, Kirshenblatt-Gimblett was not the first. In 1975 Janet Elias had already interviewed Dave Tarras (Kirshenblatt-Gimblett possessed a copy of the transcript, a twenty-eight-page typed and annotated text, which she subsequently deposited with YIVO). And in the early 1970s she had already conducted the "YIVO Folksong Project: East European Jewish Folksong in its Social Context" with a group of graduate students, aimed at documenting Yiddish songs together with their context, by interviewing extensively Yiddish singers.

The process of revitalization relied heavily on the active cooperation between institutional actors, such as Norich, Cooper, and Ethel Raim of the Balkan Arts Center; musician-researchers such as Feldman, Sapoznik, Alpert, Freeman, Joshua Waletzky, and accordionist-singer Lauren Brody who learned this style (and other folk styles, especially American and Balkan) through a combination of fieldwork, interviews, direct transmission from European-born musicians, and study of early recordings; as well as academics, such as Barbara Kirshenblatt-Gimblett and Mark Slobin, who began writing about the phenomenon of klezmer revitalization in the early 1980s. Slobin played an especially significant role in bringing the musicians to the archives and the sound archives to life; in two articles he addressed the "complex process" at the time of "bringing back the klezmer sound" and encouraged the researcher to go beyond the "traditional notions of loss and revival, of authenticity and acculturation," and to acknowledge "flexibility and ingenuity."[26] The boundary between researcher—whether officially affiliated with an academic structure or not—and musician was blurred, creating a collective that can be characterized as hybrid, porous, and intergenerational; even more so, with the creation and development of the YIVO Sound Archive, the figure of the sound archivist-performer emerged.

YIVO's main sound archivists, Henry Sapoznik, Jenny Romaine (who served as director after Sapoznik's departure in 1994 until 1999), and Lorin Sklamberg, have all been influential professional musicians and artists who had trained as archivists on the job, in direct contact with the material. Sapoznik started to research and study the music in order to imitate early twentieth-century recordings with his bands Kapelye (founded in 1979 with Michael Alpert) and the Youngers of Zion. As he began the work of gathering the neglected 78-rpms from the vast archives of YIVO, he gradually became more interested in the records themselves. All three figures saw in the recordings not only a source of knowledge and thus a space for transmission, but also a possible breeding ground for creation. They related to the recordings both within and beyond the space of the archives, "as a process," where collecting, accessing (selecting what belongs to the archive), describing and cataloguing, and disseminating and creating new materials based on archival materials all put both people and artifacts in motion.[27] Echoing Derrida's idea that the archive "opens out of the future,"[28] Niamh Moore reflects on the dynamics between the making of archives, their arrangement, their access, the production of knowledge, and in a broader sense, the cultural productions resulting from them: "The concept of an archival imaginary suggests that it is not merely that archives are sites where social science knowledge can be produced (or social science methods can be applied), but also that the archival imaginary is constitutive of the possibilities for knowledge-making."[29] The position of the archivist, emerging as the main actor and central figure of the archives, is liminal, looking simultaneously into the past and toward the future, while linking both in the present as they participate in a mode of cultural production that Barbara Kirshenblatt-Gimblett calls "heritage," which "produces something new in the present that has recourse to the past."[30]

As the main actor of the archive "whose role is to collect, organize, preserve and provide access to archival documents,"[31] the archivist is at times the guardian of sacred relics, the manufacturer, and cartographer of knowledge, the servant of the institution and its users, and in the case of the YIVO Sound Archive also an artist, sometimes an activist (if not a political, at least a cultural, one). As a space of collective interaction, the archive spans wide concentric circles: the innermost circle is composed of scholars and musicians who use the materials and incorporate it into their creations, whether artistic or academic. As such, they become ambassadors of the archives. The second circle is in contact with the archives only indirectly, or through the consumption of performances or documentary films, recordings or broadcasts, and teaching produced by the core group. As users from around the world seek to access materials and use them as sources of creation and teaching, the archive as a living space and as a process turns into a cutting-edge site of creativity, which finds ramification within an international community as materials are being circulated, taught, and performed on stages and through a network of Yiddish music workshops and festivals.

Henry Sapoznik describes the artifacts at YIVO's pre-establishment of the Sound Archive as "orphans on the cathedral steps."[32] According to him, the different technologies of sound recordings, paper-centric archival practices inherited from the nineteenth century, and a certain culture that prevailed at the time caused a general lack of interest in these materials. For Sapoznik, there was a dichotomy between the worldview held by the library and the archive, which saw "the klezmer thing along with the sound recordings . . . as a comedy relief of Yiddish culture," an amusing component of culture through an elitist prism, and the zeitgeist, which is "what young Jews wanted, . . . this tactile facile entry to an accessible culture."[33]

This tension, partly generational, can also be explained by the cultural changes that were taking place within YIVO during those years. YIVO had acted as a bridge between different worlds, with archivists and researchers still present and active at the time who had known the prewar institution in Vilna. The archives themselves are the result of cultural transfers, a process of territorialization, deterritorialization, and reterritorialization of everyday-life objects becoming artifacts as they are being transplanted into an archive, and the reception of new creations that draw their material from the archives.[34] But YIVO's staff increasingly saw young people born in the United States who came to replace older employees who had witnessed prewar Yiddish life (note that YIVO in Vilna was considered by some to be an elitist institution); English was supplanting Yiddish as the lingua franca, and the institution "abandoned its historic commitment to Yiddish as not only the subject but also the medium of its work."[35] This institutional resistance, however, was met with a real demand for more access to sound sources, with music attracting a growing number of enthusiasts. Kuznitz explains this phenomenon as a consequence of declining "Yiddish literacy, which made cultural forms such as literature inaccessible to growing numbers of Jews."[36] The enthusiasm for music was nonetheless real and profound, and access to this knowledge required special efforts.

At the beginning of the revitalization of klezmer music in the late 1970s, early recordings were difficult to obtain for study.[37] Sapoznik was given a corner table in the library on the second floor to consult the records he found dispersed in various places in the building, sometimes in a closet, sometimes on a shelf, which he gradually gathered. The records were listed only by a number corresponding to their order of acquisition on 3x5 index cards, in an acquisition inventory, not a reference catalog with cross-referencing.[38] At that time, YIVO was not equipped with a device to play 78 rpms, and Sapoznik brought his own, an old Garrard 40-B. He connected it to the sound system, and little by little uncovered the songs and arrangements beyond the hiss and clicks of the old record shellac.

Sapoznik played a major role in the watershed moment of klezmer's revitalization when musicians were seeking access to old recordings and suggesting the idea of reissuing archival recordings. This not only triggered interest in the sound collection, but also led to other forms of this buried knowledge such as a films and books. Released in 1981, the 33-rpm vinyl disc *Klezmer Music 1910–1942* became the first reissue of old recordings of klezmer music.[39] According to Sapoznik, "[a]ll the reissues that had come out previously on Folkways Records were made for an immigrant and nostalgia audience, so did not need context. If you're into nostalgia, you don't need context, because the person who is being nostalgic has their own context."[40] As Sapoznik explains, *Klezmer Music 1910–1942* reissue "was meant to be a showcase, not just for the record collection, but for the intellectual framework of the YIVO":

> So Barbara Kirshenblatt-Gimblett was the fairy-godmother, and we worked out the analysis of approaching it. The booklet, the Yiddish was type-set at the Forward, when they still had the Linotype machine, and they did all of that the old way. And it was a very homey, in-house kind. . . . And because we were making it up as we went along, it was this really exciting moment of discovery. . . . So I asked Andy Statman to do some writing, I asked Zev Feldman. I had a vision, because I knew— my advantage was: I knew reissue backwards and forwards, 'cause I had been doing old time music at that point for ten years. So I knew everything about how early country music had been documented. I knew Dick Spottswood, I had read his work.[41]

A favorable conjuncture, funding opportunities, engaged individuals, a cultural "necessity" caught up in a broader "roots" movement—all these factors combined allowed the YIVO Sound Archive to become institutionalized and, at the same time, to provide the bearers of klezmer's revitalization with both a source for the rediscovery of the repertoire and the style, a place of encounter and study, but also a certain legitimacy. Due to a donation from the Weinstein Family in 1981, redirected to this project in the wake of grant proposals written by Kirshenblatt-Gimblett to conduct research on klezmer music, and through the mediation of the then-director Norich and his assistant Adrienne Cooper, the Max and Frieda Weinstein Archive of YIVO Sound Recordings came into being at the end of December 1981.[42]

On December 29, 1981, Samuel Norich wrote to the Weinstein family, thanking them for their "most generous gift" to "further the cataloging, preservation and dissemination of our vast holdings of Jewish music."[43] In this letter, Norich details in five points the coming year's projects made possible by this gift:

1. To copy our entire connection of over 6000 musical items, represented on some 1200 discs and 600 hours of tape, onto high quality reel-to-reel and cassette tapes, and to make the entire collection, carrying your parents' names, accessible to scholars, students, performers and the public, at a listening facility at the YIVO Institute;
2. To foster the reissue of selected recordings and identify certain out-of-print scores and sheet music for reprinting;
3. To encourage and hopefully produce public programs and concerts based on material in the YIVO music collections;
4. To continue the cataloging of our 130 linear feet of archival holdings in Jewish music, consisting of manuscripts, printed scores, biographical materials, text of folk songs, as well as the sound recordings; and
5. To publicize the creation of the Max and Frieda Weinstein Archive of YIVO Sound Recordings and the availability of its numerous precious contents, and to thereby encourage further contributions both of financial support and Jewish music.[44]

Attached to this letter was the aforementioned *Klezmer Music 1910–1942* album as a "a small sampler of the sort of reissue records and tapes your donation will be used to support," as well as the review of the record by the historian, novelist, and music critic Nat Hentoff (1925–2017), which appeared in the September issue of *The Progressive* magazine (not found with the copy of the letter placed in the archive). Norich also shared that Sapoznik and Kirshenblatt-Gimblett, would be responsible for creating the archive of sound recordings.[45]

In April 1982, after he had just published his book *Tenement Songs*, Mark Slobin wrote a draft for a booklet in which he detailed the contents of YIVO's music archives, initiating an early mapping of the collection:

> Scattered among the treasures of YIVO are priceless collections of Jewish music. Acquired by chance and design over nearly six decades, the YIVO music holdings offer a broad panorama of media, genres, styles, composers, and resources. Little by little the archivists, librarians, and researchers are putting the music material in order so they will become accessible to scholars, musicians, and visitors.[46]

In this paper, Mark Slobin divides YIVO's musical materials into seven categories, noting that the list he offers is not exhaustive and cannot be considered a catalog, but rather is intended to provide entry points for the researcher. He concludes by inviting donations of new collections, as well as "gestures of support toward the endowment of a permanent YIVO Music Collections Fund."[47]

FIGURE 16.2 Members of the klezmer group Kapelye entertaining visitors outside the YIVO building at the tenth annual Museum Mile Festival, as depicted in the 1988 "YIVO Annual Report." Photographer: Layle Silbert. Reproduced by permission of the YIVO Institute for Jewish Research.

On the night of June 8, 1982, as Henry Sapoznik recalls, "a free concert was staged to celebrate the inauguration of the YIVO Sound Archives. . . . Nearly a thousand people jammed the corner of Fifth Avenue and East Eighty-Sixth Street to hear Kapelye play, the first of numerous concerts on this corner [Figure 16.2]. After the festivities, the difficult work of organizing the archives began"[48]—only a few months after the release of Kapelye's first vinyl album entitled *Future and Past* (Flying Fish Records, 1981).

MAPPING THE LIVING SPACE

As a social space, the archive escapes in a sense the possibility of its own cartography, for how many maps, in the descriptive (geographical) sense, would be needed to exhaust a social space, to encode and decode all of its meanings and contents?[49] Cataloging and inventory systems such as finding aids can serve as mental, if not spatial, maps of the intellectual space of an archive. The archive as a space of "possible knowledge" requires this particular kind of cartography to enable determining what knowledge is even possible, by showing the way to its access. In reverse, the existing unmapped collections in an archive remain terra incognita if and when not yet described, unknown zones remain silent—sometimes because they are simply absent, or because their descriptive information (metadata) connecting the artifact to a broader context is fragmentary or missing. The archive thus presents itself, according to Paul Ricoeur, as a physical place that shelters the fate of this kind of trace (the testimony) that we have carefully distinguished from the cerebral trace and the emotional trace, namely the documentary trace.[50]

As the archivists who created, collected, and organized the YIVO Sound Archive have copiously asserted, this archive functioned as a community within the institute and for the klezmer music revitalization at large. It consisted of YIVO's "old guard" from Eastern Europe and a cohort of young musicians.[51] As Mark Slobin has pointed out, Eleanor (Chana) Gordon Mlotek (1922–2013) took the role of mediator, embodying a bridge between continents and historical periods, spanning the divide of a catastrophe of cataclysmic proportions, "between generations of European-born and American-born Yiddishists; between a Yiddish-bred audience and mainstream American culture; between the practices of scholarship and archiving and those of everyday community life."[52] Through her training in folklore at UCLA (supported by a grant from YIVO), the bridge she formed also connected Eastern European and American scholarly practices. According to Slobin, "Seemingly detached from community work . . . Chana turned the shelves of hard-won materials into a hub of activity."[53] A major figure in the transmission of Yiddish music, Mlotek was YIVO's music archivist from 1984 to 2013, after having been the assistant of Max Weinreich, himself a "transitional figure between Europe and America."[54] She stood out as a major figure in the revival of Yiddish song, along with her husband Joseph (Yosl) Mlotek (1918–2000), a Yiddish educator and cultural impresario. Aside from her editions of song and poetry collections, and her role as a consultant until the very last months of her life, she was the driving force of the so-called autonomous fifth floor, a nickname given to a space that included the Sound Archive and derived from the circumstance that this space was difficult to access by elevator.

In the Vanderbilt Mansion, the Sound Archive was perched in the tiny former servants' quarters next to the photo and video archive. Sapoznik recalls that individuals in the rest of the building—the archives, the offices, and the beautiful reading room on the second floor—wondered: "what's going on up there? What is this parade of people going up and down all day?"[55] He also recalls the atmosphere in this "autonomous territory" in terms that reflect both the youth and Jewishness of those (or the majority of those) who hung out at the time: "It was a club house! All of the self-taught record collectors in the city would congregate there, and we would play records, and we would argue: "no, no, that's take 2!" and there was just this—it was like a beys medresh! It was like Rashi on records"[56] (Figure 16.3).

The topography of YIVO reflects the tensions between the generation that saw itself as the harbinger of the "paper archive" as window to scholarly erudition (sometimes perceived as culturally superior) and a younger generation for whom the archival movement meant elements of popular and mass culture beyond folklore; between those whose national agenda in Europe no longer corresponded to the identificatory needs of young American Jews integrated (or seeking to be integrated) into a multicultural society and that same cohort. But this topography also saw the merging of physical and mental spaces.

FIGURE 16.3 Staff of the YIVO Sound Archive: Henry Sapoznik, Jennifer Romaine, and Lorin Sklamberg (from left to right), as depicted in the 1987 "YIVO Annual Report." Photographer: Scott Areman. Reproduced by permission of the YIVO Institute for Jewish Research.

Considering the catalog, finding aid, or inventory as a "mental map," as a tool for navigating through the collections, implies considering the archive as a territory with landscapes, actors, dynamics, and circulation routes. This raises further questions, such as how the map modifies the territory, or at least the representation and the knowledge we have of it; in what way the map itself is a production of knowledge; and how the technology and the mode of description effect the ways in which archives are organized. For example, numbered and cataloged tapes do not necessarily need to be physically arranged by subject, or by provenance, as long as they are ordered by call number, whether that call number leads to the physical object or to a file containing a digital version of the object. It is then the description tool, a database, a spreadsheet, a catalog (formerly often a notebook or cardboard cards) that will allow the physical object to be found in its place and provide the documentation necessary to understand this object within a broader context.

The appraisal—the act of choosing whether to keep certain artifacts and documents— is one of the key functions of the archive as an agent of knowledge production, for it is this sorting that determines "what is remembered and what is forgotten, who in society is visible and who remains invisible, who has a voice, and who does not."[57] It determines "what the future will know about its past, which is often our present."[58] This is the same idea that Carolyn Steedman, echoing Derrida, captures as follows: "The grammatical tense of the archive is thus the future perfect, 'when it will have been.'"[59] For Derrida, the very structure of the archive determines what can be archived: "the technical structure of the archiving archive also determines the structure of the archivable content even in its very coming into existence and in its relationship to the future. The archivization produces as much as it records the event."[60]

The process of linking the artifact with its description (or metadata) is complex and requires both appropriate funding and staffing, for the skills involved can be manifold, from linguistic to technical abilities. The value of a collection depends on the quality of its documentation. As the folklorist and singer Ruth Rubin (1906–2000) repeatedly asserted, Yiddish folk songs "belong to the people"; but there was legitimate doubt concerning the possibility of ever finding documentation on the individuals she recorded in her pioneering collection, which is held at YIVO. In 2019, while coordinating the publication of her collection online, at the bottom of box 30, underneath the small binders that Rubin used to collect her reading notes and materials for her lecture-recitals, I found a blue notebook that looked like a copy of the index of the songs that had previously escaped my gaze. It was in fact an alphabetical index of the interlocutors, containing personal data; though sometimes very scarce (sometimes nothing more than a place and approximate date of birth), the index illuminates the lives of the people recorded by Rubin, especially when entries also contained a performer's profession or details on how they learned the songs they knew. The discovery of this binder completed a set of data that was already very well structured, but nonetheless had a lacuna. It brought a new level of liveliness and realness of voices from the past to this one-of-a-kind work of collecting Yiddish folk songs. This knowledge introduces spaces exterior to the physical presence of the voices as well as their historical dimension. Reconnecting the thread, stitch by stitch, between the artifacts and the lives that created them turns the archive into a place of knowledge.

The complex descriptive process of the artifacts, varying from one medium, collection, and object to another, requires skills that Sapoznik would acquire in part while working with Richard Spottswood on the discs found at YIVO; as he asserts, "tracking fifty years' worth of American-made 'foreign' records was a reasonably ambitious task, and even if you were the ever resourceful and methodical Dick Spottswood, you'd still need help—which is where I came in."[61] Indeed, as Lynn Dion recounts in her article on the Sound Archive, Spottswood "hired Sapoznik shortly after their meeting to be his New York researcher and to work specifically on the YIVO collection of 78's."[62] This experience helped Sapoznik establish a cataloging system for the Jewish records at YIVO, "based on more sophisticated methods of 'reading' every conceivable identifying mark both on the label and on the shellac body of the disc, Spottswood, in addition to developing procedures to transfer recordings using his special needle collection, created a discographic timeline and set each individual disc into its proper chronological context for the first time."[63] This cross-referencing of sources provided the basis for YIVO's Sound Archive catalog, while offering "the foundation for a future history of recorded Jewish music in the United States."[64]

Sapoznik remembers the painstaking cross-referencing work that led to the establishment of the discography of Jewish music on 78-rpms as follows:

[W]hile working on the catalog, we were going through the original Columbia and Victor recording ledgers and their paper. But [Columbia and Victor] didn't have any records [of Jewish music]. YIVO didn't have terribly many records, but at least what was there we could then cross-check. . . . The Victors were actually ledgers, they were actually books. They were the notes of the recording engineers, so that's where you found your sequential matrix numbering, that's where—if they chose to—they put in the personnel, they put in the date, they put in the take number. So, that was Victor. Columbia had what they called the blues, they were blue cards and they basically had the same information. So some of them had all the information, some of them had some of the information, some of them had none of the information. . . . Dick is a national treasure. He can just look at a disc and: "oh yeah, I know it says [so-and-so], but it's really Tarras because you could tell by the matrix number." And he could just decode them. He just memorized these series.[65]

According to the annual report of the YIVO Sound Archive of September 1987, Sapoznik and Romaine, who became Sapoznik's assistant that year, had been working as research assistants for the Ethnic Discography Project of the Library of Congress, under the direction of Spottswood in Washington, DC. Various tasks were detailed, pointing to the project being prelude to the computerization of the catalog of the YIVO Sound Archive: discographic records were extracted from the card-catalog source; the shelf collection was updated, that is, duplicates in better condition were moved to "active files," damaged covers were replaced with new ones; the discography established by Spottswood, of recordings published before 1942, was completed.[66] These pioneer discographers opened the possibility to access the world of early klezmer recordings. Creating discographies and catalogs, they drew the maps that musicians could use to find the recordings, learn the music, and use it as a springboard to express themselves.

A LIVING SPACE IN MOTION

The revitalization of klezmer music has been historicized in two main phases, followed by a "post-revival." The first phase, corresponding to the "roots movement" of the 1970s (spearheaded in part by the advent of Alex Haley's book *Roots: The Saga of an American Family* and its subsequent network television mini-series adaptation), saw young Jewish musicians playing bluegrass and American folk music, interpreting the music of their roots, that is, the music sung, played, and listened to by their ancestors. This continued into the 1980s and then also saw the rise of institutional structures that offered access to sources of a musical style that had been just rediscovered by a small group of activists, among them Michael Alpert, Lauren Brody, Zev Feldman, Hankus Netsky, Andy Statman, Alicia Svigals, and Joshua Waletzky. These pioneers and others learned from recordings and firsthand from the klezmorim and singers of previous generations, both born in Eastern Europe or the United States, who were still alive at the time. Among them were Leon Schwartz (1901–1989), Sid Beckerman (1919–2007),

Max Epstein (1912–2000), Pete Sokolow (1940–), Ray Musiker (1926–), Elaine Hoffman Watts (1932–2017), and, as far as singers are concerned, Bronya Sakina (1910–1988), Mariam Nirenberg (1906–1991), and Ben Bazyler (1922–1990). Oral transmission was the starting point of this learning process, with a focus on imitating what was heard as closely as possible, in order to be able to innovate from this solid foundation, to create new arrangements and to write new compositions.

These musicians also reestablished the repertoire, standardized the genre of klezmer music as well as its teaching, and integrated singing and dancing practices. Their initiatives, at the intersection of historical continuity and authenticity, arose from their need "to root their contemporary approach in a meaningful past, which is not the same thing as searching for roots, although for many the two go hand in hand."[67] The first generation of "revivalists" benefited from the groundwork laid by these musicians, as transmitters of culture. Together, they created the conditions for this transmission to take place on the scale of an entire community, notably through the creation of KlezKamp, an annual klezmer music and Yiddish culture festival in the Catskill Mountains of Upstate New York, produced by Henry Sapoznik between 1985 and 2015. It played a major role in the dissemination and teaching of klezmer music and in the formation of musical and aesthetic approaches.[68]

Sapoznik formally proposed the idea of a Yiddish music retreat to YIVO officials in 1982. Through a rich cultural program "based on values of cultural continuity" focusing on various aspects of Eastern European Jewish expressive culture, including language and literature, theater, and cuisine, the event aimed to place Yiddish music and dance in a broader context.[69] The program was initially named the Yiddish Folk Arts Program, also sometimes called Yiddish Folk Art Institute (Institute of Yiddish Folk Art), but soon, "with [his] weakness for nicknames" (he referred to YIVO as the "'VO"), Sapoznik coined KlezKamp, which would become its brand name.[70] Adrienne Cooper, then assistant director at YIVO, immediately understood the importance of the program and acted on its behalf, as Sapoznik recalls:

> By February 1984, Cooper and I were meeting with Becky Miller, hired to coordinate KlezKamp. I had already lined up veterans Ruth Rubin, Max Epstein, Leon Schwartz, Bronya Sakina, and younger players like Michael Alpert, Lauren Brody, Hankus Netsky, and dance ethnographer LeeEllen Friedland to serve as its staff.[71]

The idea behind the festival was to bring the sources to the people rather than the people to the sources, or, as Sapoznik himself states, "to make the sound archives—and YIVO itself—more active."[72] His notion of "dynamic transmission" was indeed central to the design of the program, a week-long retreat aimed at creating an intergenerational environment where novices, from the youngest to the oldest, could mix and train young and old practitioners in the various Yiddish folk arts.

The first Yiddish Folk Arts Program, or KlezKamp, was held during Christmas week 1985 at the somewhat "run-down" Paramount Hotel in Parksville, New York, and was attended by about one hundred twenty people, almost all of them musicians, thirty of whom were hired to teach.[73] While at the time there were no Jewish educational programs offered during Christmas week, Sapoznik's innovation challenged Jews "to de-camp from their assimilationist holiday making to immerse themselves in the Yiddish tradition."[74] This initiative created not only a suitable context for learning music, but also a community around klezmer; in Sapoznik's words: "It created a curriculum, a standardized repertoire, a teaching standard."[75] According to klezmer violinist Alicia Svigals, the interlocking scenes of klezmer music beyond Klezkamp, including those that emerged from it, were associated with youth subcultures and truly intergenerational.[76] However, KlezKamp did not remain under the auspices of YIVO. Sapoznik and Lorin Sklamberg created the non-profit organization Living Traditions to continue to run the annual event independently, after both were laid off by YIVO's Board of Directors, which did not seem to appreciate the vitality, youthfulness, creativity, and queerness of the KlezKamp constituency. This was also a result of an inner conflict within the Board of Directors over whether to emphasize the survival of Yiddish, or whether to give the institution a more American orientation.[77]

By 1996 klezmer had taken its course. KlezKamp, according to Mark Slobin, "had expanded to 450 people of all ages and persuasions (ranging from Orthodox to members of the New York's 'queer' scene). Meanwhile klezmer had spread across Europe, to the avantgarde 'downtown' music world of New York City, and up to the highest spheres of classical music, violin superstar Itzhak Perlman."[78] This second phase of revitalization, which began in the late 1980s and continued into the 1990s, saw a proliferation of musical groups, such as the Klezmatics, whose members continued to draw materials to different extents from the YIVO Sound Archive. While deepening their knowledge of the old styles, they pursued a fusion that is inherent in klezmer music, a merger of styles. Just as Yiddish is a fusion language, klezmer is a fusion music. This analogy became ever-more tangible in that the definition of klezmer music has come to include Yiddish song. This analogy also permits to consider klezmer as post-vernacular.[79] The network of significations that arise from its existence, and its "resemantization" in a present that is partly cut off from its vernacular linguistic, cultural, and anthropological context, are at the heart of what is at stake in the use of archives.[80] If these actors in the revitalization of Yiddish music at YIVO and those around them were, as in the case of Sapoznik, Alpert, and Feldman, indirectly exposed to Yiddish culture and the Yiddish language as a vernacular—if only within their family—then they were effectively cut off in the United States from the actual social and cultural context in which this music had not only an aesthetic and artistic function, but also a religious and ritual one. In this way sound archives have participated in a dialectical dynamic of musical revitalization from the very beginning of their creation.

The successive phases of revitalization have subsequently led to a "post-revival" phase, characterized "first and foremost by the recognition that a revived tradition has become firmly established in a new context where it can no longer be described as either moribund or threatened and is therefore no longer in need of rescue."[81] This phase is also marked by explorations of repertoires, and styles, as well as timbres and textures, giving way to a burgeoning of new works, both sung and instrumental. The concept of post-revival also opens the possibility to "acknowledge the significance of the original revival impulse and to identify a new musical or social culture as part of its legacy."[82] The pendular movements of the interaction between the United States and Europe are remarkable, and the many workshops created in the wake of and to some extent modeled on KlezKamp, reinforce the transnational dimension of the community around Yiddish music. This moment, when "no one remembers that at one time there was nothing," characterizes the current phase and testifies to the success of the popularization of klezmer music through the creation and publication of archives and spaces organized for its transmission, promoting in particular encounters between the generations.[83]

If archives (especially national archives) are considered a *lieu de mémoire* (place of memory), and among the most concrete of them (along with war memorials, as opposed to the "more abstract and intellectually constructed, such as the notion of lineage, generation, or even region and 'man-memory'"), archivists are the essential vector of that memory.[84] For, as Jonathan Boyarin asserts, "the 'place' of memory on the most material level remains the individual brain."[85] An archive is also a space where individual and collective memories meet, where group and communal identities are negotiated. As Francis Xavier Jr. Blouin and William G. Rosenberg capture it:

> An archive is a place where complex processes of "remembering" occur, creating and recreating certain kinds of social knowledge. We use quotation marks for remembering to emphasize that the processes that bring the past to life in an archive involve much more than simply accessing documents. Through acquisition, classification, and preservation, archives provide those who come to learn about the past with a mixture of materials, sometimes carefully selected and ordered, sometimes quite disorganized and arbitrary, through which particular forms of individual and social visions are structured and produced.[86]

In this vein, the YIVO Sound Archive can be understood as a space in motion. It serves as a repository of documents (in this case sound recordings) and possible sources, and is thus a historical phenomenon in its own right. As a spatialized territory, it forms "a complex tangle of dynamic, multidimensional and multiscale socio-spatial relations."[87] This space, always reconfiguring itself, is the product of dynamics generated by actors—individuals with their own creativity, caught in a web of social and cultural, intellectual and scientific, institutional and artistic contexts. In short, the archive is considered as a living process.

2020, A VIRTUAL SPACE ODYSSEY: PERFORMING AND ARCHIVING THE LIVING SPACE

In recent times, technology and the pandemic of 2020 have paradoxically enabled the transnational community of klezmer aficionados to approach the archives under new circumstances.[88] As musicians from around the world interested in Jewish music suddenly found themselves stranded at home, the demand for digitized material became stronger. Deprived of touring, they saw an opportunity to bring to the forefront some activities that they had not been able to prioritize until then. One such project is the study of the older sources of klezmer music, and in particular the work of Moisey Beregovsky (1892–1961).

Beregovsky was a pioneer. Zev Feldman credits him for introducing the term *klezmer* to refer to the style of music rather than to the musicians. Between 1929 and 1947, he was the only person making wax cylinder recordings of Jewish music in Ukraine (aside from Sofia Magid, who was working independently in St. Petersburg). By the mid-1940s, he had amassed 7,000 musical documents, including the cylinder recordings from the earlier An-Sky and Zusman Kiselgof folklore expeditions, which he cataloged. Only a small portion of the five volumes of musical transcriptions, texts, and essays he prepared during his lifetime were published. A compilation, under the English title *Old Jewish Folk Music*, edited and translated by Mark Slobin, appeared in the United States in 1982, making it possible for some of the melodies he collected to be learned and performed by contemporary klezmer musicians. His archive was thought to have been destroyed during the Second World War, but in the mid-1990s it surfaced in the Vernadsky National Library of Ukraine in Kiev.

The collaborative projects of 2020 were a late ripple effect of the renewed interest researchers in Russia took in Jewish music from the early twentieth century onward. A few initiatives took place over Zoom, beginning in April 2020. The Berlin-based American violinist Craig Judelman created the Facebook group "Beregovski Online Forum," offering a series of discussions with musicians and scholars about the life and work of klezmer's preeminent ethnomusicologist. London-based violinist Ilana Cravitz launched an international project involving thirty-five violinists to explore, revisit, record, and share pieces from an unpublished volume of Beregovky's nigunim; each participant was scheduled in a series of daily Zoom concerts entitled "A Nign a Day," broadcast live on Facebook and archived on YouTube. Inspired by these initiatives, I started a *leyenkrayz* (reading group) to collectively read one of Beregovsky's Yiddish articles, titled "Yidishe klezmer, zeyer shafn un shteyger" (Yiddish klezmer music, their creations and practices, 1941). The nearly thirty Sunday sessions during which we completed the reading of this article and started reading a second one, "Tsu di ufgabes fun der yidisher muzikalisher folkloristik" (Concerning the goals of Jewish music folkloristics, 1932), never saw fewer than a dozen participants, and by early 2021 the group was growing to about two dozen. Renowned klezmer and Jewish music specialists as well as passionate amateurs, whose presence may have been motivated solely by curiosity, attended the sessions. Everyone contributed their knowledge to the group's discussions, which shed light on the texts that brought us together.

Another major collaboration that took off during the pandemic is the 2018 Kisselgof-Makonovetsky Digital Manuscript Project of the Klezmer Institute, a crowdsourced initiative born out of the online publication of the manuscripts of the Kiselgof-Makonovetsky collection, including original notebooks of the An-Sky expedition archived in the Vernadsky National Library of Ukraine. The Klezmer Institute is also leading a Klezmer Archive Project, which aims at creating new tools to not only connect different archival collections, but also to analyze their musical content, both written and recorded.[89] Collaborative projects that explore newly accessible digitized archives have blossomed, deepening the complex dialectic between history and memory that opens up issues of community and identity formation in the present. As Jonathan Boyarin suggests, "memory is neither something preexistent and dormant in the past nor a projection from the present, but a potential for creative collaboration between present consciousness and the experience or expression of the past."[90] The interactivity of the archives, which started before the pandemic, in part due to new technologies and the internet, has become even stronger in the realm of Jewish music.

These initiatives not only base themselves in the study of archives, but create their own archives, documenting their work as it is happening. Archivists and activists, especially with repositories that are halfway between community and institutional archives, play a major role as agents of cultural transfer and revitalization of the music. By selecting objects worthy of remaining in the archive, mapping them physically and intellectually, re-editing them, transforming them, archivists become the window, the doorway, the mirror of the archival space.

The crucial roles of all actors involved in the archive—whether they are archivists, users, or receivers of works created from the archive—reveal the essential aspect of the collective, if not communal investment. But the archive's potential to reinvent the present and imagine the future also points to its temporality. Barbara Kirshenblatt-Gimblett uses the concept of anachronism to express the complex relationship to time that arises from the archives and their use, and elaborates on as it follows:

> Anachronism is a productive principle, a musical aesthetic, which operates by unsettling temporal direction. There is no smooth continuity from yesterday's *klezmorim* to today's *klezmers*. There is no dramatic rupture, no simple sequence of life, death, and rebirth, as the term revival would imply. Instead, old and new are in a perpetually equivocal relationship. The future precedes the past, the new precedes the old, the revival precedes its historical models.[91]

This transformative dimension of the archive into a new object over time can lead to creative displacements, as Adrienne Cooper asserts: "I can listen to the field recordings, I can absorb them, and then they are completely translated through me. What I'm going to emit is absolutely different."[92] Indeed, the question of what is new and what is old generates a friction, a tension that can be found in Dan Ben-Amos' definition of folklore (building on Benjamin Botkin): "Folklore may be 'old wine in new bottles' and also 'new wine in old bottles' but rarely has it been conceived of as new wine in new bottles."[93] Applied to the Yiddish sound archive, this view sheds a brighter light on the vitality that springs from this space, departing from the notion of it being inert, even dead, and putting in the abyss the representations of Yiddish culture that oscillate between the moribund and the subversive, as it is appropriated, absorbed, and transformed. Indeed, what is more alive than subversion?

NOTES

1. Dave Tarras Trio, "Klezmer Music: Dave Tarras Tribute Concert 1978," March 16, 2016, YouTube video, https://youtu.be/V6zKleJSYi4.
2. Walter Zev Feldman, *Klezmer: Music, History, and Memory* (New York: Oxford University Press, 2016), xii.
3. See ibid.
4. See Richard K. Spottswood, *Ethnic Music on Records: A Discography of Ethnic Recordings Produced in the United States, 1893–1942*, vol. 3: *Eastern Europe*, 7 vols. (Chicago: University of Illinois Press, 1990).
5. Joel E. Rubin, *New York Klezmer in the Early Twentieth Century: The Music of Naftule Brandwein and Dave Tarras* (Rochester, NY: University of Rochester Press, 2020), 3. Michael Aylward has documented over 15,000 recordings produced in Europe between 1899 and 1956. For an interview with him and other collectors, under the auspices of the Klezmer Institute's series "Gramophone in Focus," see https://klezmerinstitute.org/gramophone-in-focus/, consulted on October 31, 2020.
6. Sincere thanks to Mark Slobin for making me aware of this fact.
7. Hankus Netsky, in discussion with the author, November 14, 2021.
8. See Howard S. Becker, *Art Worlds*, updated and expanded ed. (Berkeley: University of California Press, 2008).
9. "Jewish Music Begins at Home: The YIVO Sound Archive and the Rebirth of Klezmer," *YIVO News—Yedies fun YIVO*, no. 199 (Winter 2005): 21.
10. See Caroline Bithell and Juniper Hill, eds., *The Oxford Handbook of Music Revival* (New York: Oxford University Press, 2016); Tamara E. Livingston, "Music Revivals: Towards a General Theory," *Ethnomusicology* 43 (1999): 66–85; Barbara Kirshenblatt-Gimblett, "Sounds of Sensibility," in *American Klezmer: Its Roots and Offshoots*, ed. Mark Slobin (Berkeley: University of California Press, 2002), 129–173.
11. Michael Alpert, in discussion with the author, January 6, 2020.
12. See Irene Heskes, *The St. Petersburg Society for Jewish Folk Music* (Owings Mills, MD: Tara Publications, 1998), 28.
13. Sincere thanks to Hankus Netsky for making me aware of the parallelisms and differences.
14. Henry Sapoznik, *Klezmer! Jewish Music from Old World to Our World* (New York: Schirmer Trade Books, 2005), 185.
15. Ibid., 186.
16. Mark Slobin, *Fiddler on the Move: Exploring the Klezmer World* (Oxford: Oxford University Press, 2000), 73.
17. See Michel Foucault, "Des Espaces Autres," *Empan* 54, no. 2 (2004): 12–19; Michel Foucault, *Les Hétérotopies: Le corps utopique* (Paris: Éditions Lignes, 2009).
18. For a history of YIVO, see Cecile E. Kuznitz, *YIVO and the Making of Modern Jewish Culture: Scholarship for the Yiddish Nation* (New York: Cambridge University Press, 2014).
19. David E. Fishman, *The Book Smugglers: Partisans, Poets, and the Race to Save Jewish Treasures from the Nazis* (Lebanon, NH: ForeEdge, 2017), 20.
20. Samuel Norich, in discussion with the author, October 30, 2019; and Henry Sapoznik, in discussion with the author, May 6, 2020.
21. Lynn Dion, "Old Record Keep on Turnin'," *The Book Peddler* (Winter 1988): 42.
22. Ibid.
23. Adrienne Cooper, in discussion with the author, May 9, 2006.

24. See Pete Rushefsky, "Michael Alpert and Zev Feldman: Saving Yiddish Dance," *Center for Traditional Music and Dance* (blog), January 1, 2007, https://ctmd.org/magazine/master-artists-profiles/michael-alpert-and-zev-feldman-saving-yiddish-dance/.

25. Barbara Kirshenblatt-Gimblett analyzes the obstacles to knowledge of the music as it was played in Eastern Europe as a combination of factors: immigration and acculturation; commercialization of music, leading to changes in repertoires, instrumentation and re-cording techniques; changes of musical trends. See Barbara Kirshenblatt-Gimblett, "Grant Application for Project to Document Traditional East European Jewish Instrumental Music (Klezmer-Muzik) and to Issue Two Records," February 16, 1979, RG 100, box 1, YIVO Archives, New York.

26. Mark Slobin, "The Neo-Klezmer Movement and Euro-American Musical Revivalism," *The Journal of American Folklore* 97, no. 383 (January 1984): 99. See also Mark Slobin, "Klezmer Music: An American Ethnic Genre," *Yearbook for Traditional Music* 16 (1984): 34–41; and "A Fresh Look at Beregovski's Folk Music Research," *Ethnomusicology* 30, no. 2 (1986): 253–260.

27. Niamh Moore, "Weaving Archival Imaginaries: Researching Community Archives," in *The Archive Project: Archival Research in the Social Sciences*, ed. Niamh Moore, Andrea Salter, Liz Stanley, and Maria Tamboukou (New York: Routledge, 2016), 129.

28. Jacques Derrida and Eric Prenowitz, "Archive Fever: A Freudian Impression," *Diacritics* 25, no. 2 (1995): 45.

29. Moore, "Weaving Archival Imaginaries," 150.

30. Barbara Kirshenblatt-Gimblett, "Theorizing Heritage," *Ethnomusicology* 39, no. 3 (1995): 369–370.

31. Moore, "Weaving Archival Imaginaries," 159.

32. Henry Sapoznik, in discussion with the author, May 6, 2020.

33. Henry Sapoznik, in discussion with the author, May 6, 2020.

34. Pirkko Moisala, Taru Leppänen, and Milla Tiainen, eds., *Musical Encounters with Deleuze and Guattari*, Bloomsbury Sound Studies (New York: Bloomsbury Academic, 2017), 17.

35. Kuznitz, *YIVO*, 187.

36. Ibid.

37. Henry Sapoznik, comp., *Cantors Klezmorim & Crooners 1905–1953: Classic Yiddish 78s from the Mayrent Collection*, 3 vols. (London: JSP Records, 2009), liner notes.

38. Henry Sapoznik, in discussion with the author, May 6, 2020.

39. See Henry Sapoznik, comp., *Klezmer Music 1910–1942: Recordings from the YIVO Archives* (New York: Folkways Records, 1981), liner notes.

40. Henry Sapoznik, in discussion with the author, May 6, 2020.

41. Henry Sapoznik, in discussion with the author, May 6, 2020.

42. Samuel Norich, "Establishment of the 'Max and Frieda Weinstein Archive of YIVO Sound Recordings,'" December 29, 1981, RG 100, box 1, YIVO Archives, New York.

43. Ibid.

44. Ibid.

45. Ibid.

46. Mark Slobin, "First Draft of Copy of Brochure on the Music Holdings," April 15, 1982, YIVO Archives, New York.

47. Ibid.

48. Sapoznik, *Klezmer!*, 213.

49. See Henri Lefebvre, *La production de l'espace* (Paris: Anthropos, 2000), 103.

50. See Paul Ricoeur, *La mémoire, l'histoire, l'oubli* (Paris: Seuil, 2000), 210.

51. Jenny Romaine, in discussion with the author, October 3, 2019; Lorin Sklamberg, in discussion with the author, May 1, 2019; Henry Sapoznik, in discussion with the author, May 6, 2020.

52. Mark Slobin, "Eleanor & Chana: The Musical Mediators," *Musica Judaica* 20 (2013–2014): 249.

53. Ibid., 254.

54. Ibid., 249.

55. Henry Sapoznik, in discussion with the author, May 6, 2020.

56. Henry Sapoznik, in discussion with the author, May 6, 2020.

57. Terry Cook, "Remembering the Future: Appraisal of Records and the Role of Archives in Constructing Social Memory," in *Archives, Documentation and Institutions of Social Memory: Essays from the Sawyer Seminar*, ed. Francis Xavier Jr. Blouin and William G. Rosenberg (Ann Arbor: University of Michigan Press, 2007), 169.

58. Ibid.

59. Carolyn Steedman, "'Something She Called a Fever': Michelet, Derrida and Dust (Or, in the Archives with Michelet and Derrida)," in Blouin and Rosenberg, *Archives, Documentation, and Institutions of Social Memory*, 6.'

60. Derrida and Prenowitz, "Archive Fever," 17; Jacques Derrida, *Mal d'archive: Une impression freudienne* (Paris: Editions Galilée, 2008), 34.

61. Sapoznik, *Klezmer!*, 215.

62. Lynn Dion, "Old Record Keep on Turnin'," 42.

63. Ibid.

64. Ibid.

65. Interview with Henry Sapoznik, May 6, 2020.

66. "YIVO Annual Report," 1987, RG 100, YIVO Archives, New York.

67. Barbara Kirshenblatt-Gimblett, "La renaissance du klezmer: Réflexions sur un chronotope musical," *Cahiers de littérature orale*, no. 44 (1998): 237–238.

68. Sapoznik, *Klezmer!*; Mark Slobin, "Searching for the Klezmer City," in *People of the City: Jews and the Urban Challenge*, ed. Ezra Mendelsohn, Studies in Contemporary Jewry 15 (New York: Oxford University Press, 2000), 35–48.

69. Interview with Henry Sapoznik, May 6, 2020.

70. Henry Sapoznik, "Klezkamp and the Rise of Yiddish Cultural Literacy," in *American Klezmer: Its Roots and Offshoots*, ed. Mark Slobin (Berkeley: University of California Press, 2002), 178.

71. Ibid.

72. Henry Sapoznik, in discussion with the author, May 6, 2020.

73. Slobin, *Fiddler on the Move*, 4.

74. Ibid.

75. Henry Sapoznik, in discussion with the author, May 6, 2020.

76. See Barbara Kirshenblatt-Gimblett, "Sounds of Sensibility," *Judaism* 47 (1998): 58.

77. Jenny Romaine, in discussion with the author, October 3, 2018.

78. Slobin, *Fiddler on the Move*, 4–5.

79. See Jeffrey Shandler, *Adventures in Yiddishland: Postvernacular Language & Culture* (Berkeley: University of California Press, 2006), 22.

80. Michel Espagne, "La notion de transfert culturel," *Revue sciences/Lettres*, no. 1 (April 18, 2013): 1.

81. Bithell and Hill, *The Oxford Handbook of Music Revival*, 29.

82. Ibid.

83. Henry Sapoznik, in discussion with the author, May 6, 2020.

84. "Plus abstrait et intellectuellement construit, comme la notion de lignage, de génération, ou même de région et d''homme-mémoire," *Les lieux de mémoire*, ed. Pierre Nora, Quatro (Paris: Gallimard, 1997), 1:15.

85. Jonathan Boyarin, *Remapping Memory: The Politics of Timespace* (Minneapolis: University of Minnesota Press, 1994), 23.

86. Blouin and Rosenberg, vii.

87. "Le territoire forme donc un écheveau complexe de relations socio-spatiales dynamiques, multidimensionnelles et multiscalaires." Guy Di Méo, *Géographie sociale et territoires* (Paris: Nathan Université, 2001), 12.

88. See also Mark Slobin, "COVID-Era Online Collective Research Initiatives in Yiddish Traditional Music," *Ethnomusicology* 65, no. 3 (Fall 2021): 630–633.

89. The Klezmer Archive project, which I am a team member of, has been awarded a NEH grant to research new tools "to create a universally accessible, useful resource for interaction, discovery, and research on all available information about klezmer music"; https://klezmerinstitute.org/klezmerarchive/ (accessed on November 3, 2020).

90. Boyarin, *Remapping Memory*, 22.

91. Kirshenblatt-Gimblett, "Sounds of Sensibility," in Slobin, *American Klezmer*, 138.

92. Adrienne Cooper, in discussion with the author, May 9, 2006.

93. Dan Ben-Amos, "Toward a Definition of Folklore in Context," *Journal of American Folklore* (1971): 5.

Select Bibliography

Biezunski, Eléonore. "East Side Story: Mémoires sédimentées de l'expérience migratoire juive à New York à travers une chanson yiddish." In *Mémoires des migrations, temps de l'histoire*, edited by Marianne Amar, Hélène Bertheleu, and Laure Teulières, 19–34. Tours: Presses Universitaires François Rabelais, 2015.

Feldman, Walter Zev. *Klezmer: Music, History, and Memory*. New York: Oxford University Press, 2016.

Fishman, David E. *The Book Smugglers: Partisans, Poets, and the Race to Save Jewish Treasures from the Nazis*. Lebanon, NH: ForeEdge, 2017.

Fox, Sandra. " 'The Passionate Few': Youth and Yiddishism in American Jewish Culture, 1964 to Present." *Jewish Social Studies*, 26, no. 3 (October 2021): 1–34.

Goldberg, Sylvie-Anne. "Olam, histoire d'un monde." In *Olam*, edited by Mark Zborowski and Elizabeth Herzog, 444–451. Terre Humaine. Paris: Plon, 1992.

Gottesman, Itzik Nakhmen. *Defining the Yiddish Nation: The Jewish Folklorists of Poland*. Detroit, MI: Wayne State University Press, 2003.

Joyeux-Prunel, Béatrice. "Les transferts culturels: Un discours de da méthode." *Hypothèses* 1, no. 6 (2003): 149–162.

Kelman, Ari Y. *Station Identification: A Cultural History of Yiddish Radio in the United States*. Berkeley: University of California Press, 2009.

Kuznitz, Cecile E. *YIVO and the Making of Modern Jewish Culture: Scholarship for the Yiddish Nation*. New York: Cambridge University Press, 2014.

Moore, Niamh, Andrea Salter, Liz Stanley, and Maria Tamboukou. *The Archive Project: Archival Research in the Social Sciences*. New York: Routledge, 2016.

Rubin, Joel E. *New York Klezmer in the Early Twentieth Century: The Music of Naftule Brandwein and Dave Tarras*. Rochester, NY: University of Rochester Press, 2020.

Slobin, Mark. *American Klezmer: Its Roots and Offshoots*. Berkeley: University of California Press, 2002.

Veidlinger, Jeffrey, ed. *Going to the People: Jews and the Ethnographic Impulse*. Bloomington: Indiana University Press, 2016.

Wollock, Jeffrey. "Historic Records as Historical Records: Hersh Gross and His Boiberiker Kapelye (1927–1932)." *ARSC Journal* 38, no. 1 (Spring 2007): 44–106.

Wood, Abigail. *And We're All Brothers: Singing in Yiddish in Contemporary North America*. Burlington, VT: Routledge, 2016.

17

JEWISH MUSIC SOUND-RECORDING COLLECTIONS IN THE UNITED STATES

JUDITH S. PINNOLIS

Recorded sound is more than music and entertainment;
it encompasses the sounds of the streets, of nature,
and of the vanished folk heritage of indigenous and transplanted cultures,
as well as of important national events and precious moments in our own
personal lives.[1]

IN a recent interview, Charles Bernhaut recalled a visit to a large downtown Philadelphia law firm where he happened to meet Robert Freedman, who worked there as a lawyer.[2] The two began to talk about Jewish music, a topic of interest to both of them. Freedman invited Bernhaut to walk down the hall to his office. There, Bernhaut saw hundreds of LPs in packing boxes and scattered on every surface where Freedman was temporarily housing them for safety during a move. Those LPs represented only part of Freedman's massive collection of Jewish music, the other part being in an apartment he rented for storage. Both collectors would later contribute their rare and vast collections to major institutions: Freedman's initial donation in 1996 of three thousand LPs would become the foundation of the Robert and Molly Freedman Jewish Sound Archive at the University of Pennsylvania, and Bernhaut's more than seven thousand LPs and four thousand five hundred cassettes would ultimately be sent to the National Library of Israel in 2020, although he still maintains an archive of over five hundred two-hour recorded programs online.

These men's stories are paradigmatic for collecting Jewish music sound recordings in the United States (and perhaps elsewhere, too). Becoming enthralled with music and with sound recordings in particular gives impetus for creating a collection. In a process that often leads to the amassing of expansive collections over years, the collector becomes more than merely a consumer. The collector's obsession with finding more and more recordings often results in an expansion of musical tastes and interests with deep focus often concentrated in certain domains, as Bob Freedman's was in Yiddish music, and Charlie Bernhaut's in *khazones* (cantorial singing). Some collectors manage to keep track of what they own. Others lose track. Eventually, either they or their families decide to donate their huge number of recordings and seek out an institution to take over the collection. The collector becomes a donor, turning to an archive or library with an interest in building collections in a certain domain. From there, the sound-recording collections take on new lives, often being digitized, and becoming part of the institution, where they continue to grow. This seemingly common narrative does not account for the many deep complexities for the institutions or the resulting scholarship they support in result. While the origin stories vary in slightly different iterations, essential patterns of collecting, with exceptions, are repeated over and over throughout the United States.

The sound recordings of Jewish music in libraries, archives, and museums have contributed to shaping the idea of an American Jewish culture. They echo a trifold story of transplanted culture, the early emergence of twentieth-century American Jewish culture, and a later matured one. These sound recordings reflect not only the collectors' communities, but also their individual musical desires, tastes, and adventures. For the collectors, their Jewish identity is tied up with their collections, as Freedman asserts:

> First of all, I've considered the collection in relation to Jewish identity, history, or American music. I can only say that my Jewish identity has been the defining feature of my life, of which the interest in Yiddish song has played a part. The dominant influences were my father and the curriculum (especially history) of the Yiddish school which I attended. My father and the school taught me to take pride in, proclaim and affirm my *Yiddishkayt* and be comfortable in my skin.[3]

As this attestation makes clear, Freedman's recorded sound collection has a deeper meaning for him than merely being music and entertainment.

While each collector's focus is different, most have rather broad definitions of Jewish music. This eclecticism and fluidity of the concept through time and space allow the inclusion of myriad repertoires and genres. Yet specifying these collections as "Jewish" creates—at the same time—an "in-group" or exclusivity that seems to define them. As such, they represent a self-reflective value, designating any music declared by the creator of a recording collection to be Jewish. Such description mirrors the very act of collecting, which appears to be motivated by a desire to "save" or "preserve" a Jewish musical culture, and to serve as an identity marker of the collector as well. While academic debates and discussions to define "what is Jewish music" have continued unabated, they were not key for the collectors. Their own internal sense of Jewishness determined inclusion in their collections, and each individual set the parameters and limits of inclusion.

Judah Cohen observes that Jewish music is "a product of those who study it and assert their authority on the topic."[4] This idea, in which Cohen describes the outsized influences of musicologists and their agendas in the early twentieth century on the study of Jewish music, can easily be expanded to apply to sound-recording collections. These collections are the products of their collectors and have already proven influential in steering the direction of research. Their influence over future intellectual histories will undoubtedly continue, and with similar outcomes as described by Cohen of the musicologists and their agendas in the early twentieth century.

Development of a library's sound-recording collection from a personal collection is not at all unusual, as noted in a comprehensive study by the Library of Congress, which concludes, "Privately held recording collections are often more comprehensive than publicly available collections held by institutions. Record and sound collectors often have sharply focused interests, defined by genre of music, specific performer, or both."[5] Jewish sound-recording collections, constructed from privately held collections, follow this pattern.

Certain sound-recording collections of Jewish music focus on a specific genre or subgroup, such as Joel Bresler's collection of Sephardic music, which is held outside of Boston, Massachusetts. Emily Sene, who captured field recordings on reel-to-reel tape of Jews from Turkey between 1940 and 1970 in California, created a collection now held in La Archivera at the University of California, Los Angeles. Benedict Stambler's collection, which he donated to the New York Public Library, consisted of over four thousand cantorial, Hebrew, and Hasidic recordings. At the time of Stambler's death in 1967, his collection was believed to be one of the largest in the world focused on Jewish liturgical music.[6] The pattern of an individual trying to collect as comprehensively as possible in an area of Jewish music continues to this day. As recently as 2017, yet another collection became accessible: the North African Jewish music collection, by Christopher Silver, professor of Jewish history and culture at McGill University, who started collecting around 2009, now comprises around five hundred recordings of old shellac 78 rpms. Selections are available online through *Gharamophone*. Silver's process of building a collection of the music of the Jews of the Mahgreb echoes the approaches of Joel Bresler and Sherry Mayrent discussed further below.

Other collections are highly focused by topic, such as that in the United States Holocaust Memorial Museum in Washington, DC, which exclusively holds music created within a specific geographical and time span. The Memorial Museum focuses on specific song types, such as concentration camp songs, partisan songs, and Displaced Persons songs. Their collections also encompass oral histories from Gratz College, which they digitized and made available online.[7] A smaller but significant collection with a similar focus, the Ben Stonehill Archive Collection, is now available online through the Center of Traditional Music and Dance, with the original archival tapes held by the Library of Congress. Stonehill recorded more than one thousand songs from Holocaust survivors in 1948 who were then temporarily housed at the Hotel Marseilles in New York City.[8]

Some larger academic collections, of course, are the work of professional librarians. The Harvard University Library Judaic collection of sound recordings is described by Violet Gilboa and Charles Berlin in a three-volume catalog published in 1996, when the sound-recording collection comprised seven thousand recordings, with special focus on Israeli music.[9] Since then, that collection has continued to grow as part of the greater collection of musical sound recordings and has expanded in scope.

Jewish music sound-recording collections discussed in this chapter are primarily identified, labeled, or set aside as "Jewish music collections" in academic libraries in universities. This is unlike general sound-recording collections, which grow organically based on the development of curricula over time. For this reason, I define these collections as "constructed." As this chapter asserts, these collections are atypical, but not exclusively so, by comparison with other "ethnic music" holdings in American institutions.[10] (In library science, Jewish music is often thought of as a segment of American "ethnic music" or part of "world music."[11]) Even those libraries with reasonably sized collections of Jewish sound recordings do not normally maintain separate designations, nor do they separate these materials from their general holdings.

This chapter focuses on the origins of large Jewish music sound-recording collections residing in academic institutions, as well as their cultural impact and factors determining present and future uses of these materials. Observations are mostly based on four of the largest collections in the United States: the Dartmouth College Jewish Sound Archive, the Judaic Collection of the Recorded Sound at Florida Atlantic University (formerly the Judaic Sound Archive), the Robert and Molly Freedman Jewish Sound Archive at the University of Pennsylvania, and the Mayrent Collection of Yiddish Recordings at the University of Wisconsin. Also addressed, especially because of its highly specialized and rare content, is the privately held collection of Sephardic music by Joel Bresler. The chapter delves into how these collections correlate with different understandings of Jewish music and mirror the many complexities of this concept, with contextualized focus on issues of conservation and preservation, unique problems, access, and authenticity. The discussions ultimately reveal the fine line of individuality and collectivity that the Jewish music sound-recording collections navigate.

CONSTRUCTING COLLECTIONS: MOTIVATIONS AND SCOPE

Sound recording in the early twentieth century, especially for the Jewish communities still establishing themselves in America, had the impact of standing in for the collective and presenting a unique culture that had value.[12] Additionally, recording makes it possible for that culture to be preserved outside of a concert hall or a live event. Recording serves as a type of musical memory, albeit a commercialized and westernized one, as "ethnic phonograph records intensified a more self-conscious, modern, and commercialized experience of aural culture."[13] While Jewish musicians and performers could be viewed or see themselves as representing the "folk" or as the living symbols of their traditions (whether those were cantorial, Yiddish, klezmer, or Sephardi),[14] from the very beginning, the "exotic" sounds of America's diverse communities were mixed with what William Kenney refers to as "reassuring" American musical elements.[15] One of the earliest recordings of Hebrew music, a 1905 Edison Company cylinder recording, was performed by the Edison Military Band, with the US company convinced it could appropriately perform in any style.[16]

Much like "ethnic" recordings of other European immigrant groups, Jewish immigrant involvement in recorded music opened up economic opportunity. Jews, along with Italian, Poles, and Hungarians, produced and purchased more recordings, and seemed "to have more interest in recorded music than others."[17] Further, the commercial nature of these recordings lent credence to and emphasized the notion that the very ability to market their music to a large audience, and to reach the intellectual elite as well as the Jewish masses, meant that this music was both distinctive and "American." These were products of mass marketing and culture, but they were also social products that enabled Jews to see themselves as culturally unique and worthy amid the great swath of immigrant cultures. Recordings play an important part in what Kenney calls "ethnogenesis," that is, "the development and public presentation of a more self-conscious ethnic group identity."[18] In short, if you listened to recorded Jewish music, it meant you "identified." Owning and listening to recordings helped build and maintain your identity as a Jew in the United States.

These sentiments of self-worth and identity are reflected in the motivations of the creators and owners of sound recordings, and they continue to be echoed in present mission statements in the websites of today's collections. Sound recordings aided the cultural continuity and preservation of the Jews. Bob Freedman stated succinctly that his mission was to "collect, preserve, and promote the cultural legacy contained in Judaic sound recordings."[19] Roger Bennett and Josh Kun's exploration of about five hundred LP recordings in *And You Shall Know Us By the Trail of Our Vinyl* describes their LP collecting as "an exercise in identity archaeology."[20] They view their sound-recording collecting of the Jewish sonic past as "shedding light on our own futures, on who we would become." Sherry Mayrent wanted to collect "every" 78 rpm of Yiddish or Hebrew music to ensure the music's survival. As a klezmer musician, she had noted the lack of resources, and especially the distinctions in continuity between klezmer and other folk cultures. Mayrent was concerned about the loss of two generations of musical legacy, both from the Holocaust and through acculturation in the United States. She felt that listening to and enjoying the music increases Jewish identity and you "don't have to understand the words."[21] As such, Mayrent focused on tracing changes to aesthetic tastes and interests from 1908 to around 1942, and the bulk of her collection falls within that period.

Henry Sapoznik spoke of "salvaging," even from dumpsters, attics, and rummage sales, radio transcriptions on single-cut, acetate-coated aluminum discs for his collections. Some of those recordings became part of his NPR *Yiddish Radio Project* program and ultimately went to the American Folk Life Center at the Library of Congress.[22] Nate Tinanoff, a founding member of the Florida Atlantic University's Judaic Sound Archive, described collecting the sound recordings as a "rescue" operation.[23] For him, the preservation of Jewish sound culture was a primary motivator in assembling the collection in the first place. Alexander Hartov, of the Dartmouth College Jewish Sound Archive, termed the origin of his project a personal interest, based on the discovery of a family history. His collection of Jewish recordings came from the *Joseph Tall Hour*, a daily Yiddish radio show produced by a member of his wife's family that had started as early as the 1920s.[24] Christopher Silver in Montreal remarked that he "wanted to collect in order to bring the music back into conversation with people."[25] Interviews with many individuals involved in collecting or curating Jewish sound-recording collections reveal fundamental and common motivations: among them are personal fulfillment, the wish to share this culture with a greater community, and a desire to ensure the continuity of Jewish culture for future generations. There is also the overarching desire to preserve Jewish musical culture and the aim to be comprehensive in scope in a genre or in a format. While there are certainly highly specialized field recordings in some of these collections, for the greater part, they represent the aggregation of commercialized interests in Jewish music. Still, these sound recordings provide historical perspective— definitions of Jewish culture reflected back to the community.

The scope of some collections is so massive that the materials themselves pose multiple challenges. One such collection is the Judaica Sound Archive at Florida Atlantic University (FAU), which started in 2002 with just one thousand 78-rpm recordings, selected by volunteers. Once the initial collection was announced to the public, the archive started receiving boxes of records nearly every day from Jewish collectors, and from other Jewish institutions all over the country, soon holding LPs and tapes as well. A gift of four thousand recordings from the National Yiddish Book Center in 2003, along with other gifts from several Jewish institutions, spurted their growth. However, it was Cleveland furniture dealer Jack Saul's initial gift of more than thirty-six thousand recordings that made FAU's one of the world's most expansive Jewish music sound recordings collections in breadth as well as depth. After Jack Saul's death in 2009, another gift packed up in Cleveland and bound for FAU yielded an additional twenty-four thousand recordings. Within the first three years of operation, the Judaica Sound Archive had set out to "welcome all recorded voice and music of the Jewish experience such as Yiddish theater, sacred songs, folk songs and klezmer."[26] With Saul's gifts, this ambitious scope was made possible. Despite its huge size, this collection's major unifying principle with other Jewish recording collections is being constructed largely based on a private collection. At FAU, one of the archive's strengths has been their concerted effort to find "best copies," to do digital cleanup of music for better listening, and to gain the copyright permission needed to make the materials freely available to the public online. As of this writing, FAU had gleaned more than sixty thousand recordings from which to choose its online offerings, making it one of the most significant Jewish music sound-collections in the United States.[27]

In some cases, such as collections defined by format, the scope may exceed individual taste, but reflects what commercial interests felt would sell to a Jewish public at the time they were published. One such comprehensive collection based on format is the Mayrent Collection of Yiddish Recordings at Mills Music Library at the University of Wisconsin. This collection began with Sherry Mayrent's gift of recordings of 78 rpms and is part of a major endowment of the Institute for Yiddish Culture. Mayrent started out with a modest collection of klezmer music, but then purchased the Yiddish music collection of Dick Spottswood, famous for cataloging and reissuing discographies of vernacular music. Ultimately, the collection covers a wide swath of interests, from Sabbath and High Holiday musics including rare cantorial recordings to Yiddish theater and spoken humor. It includes surprising items, such as South American Yiddish music, and spoken-word commercial recordings by Sholem Aleichem.[28] To date, there are probably about nineteen thousand individual sides with over five thousand individual performances in the collection, of which approximately four thousand pieces of music have been transferred to a digital format. The online site includes gallery images of the recordings. Wisconsin's collection is a leader not only in its comprehensive nature, but by the special quality of cataloging, care given to the digital copies, and easy and open access through their portal. In addition to comprehensiveness, the great strengths of this collection are that it has been pristinely transferred, has deep and accurate metadata, and represents a near entirety of Jewish music items in that format.

Likewise navigating individuality and collectivity at the other end of the spectrum is Joel Bresler's private collection, the most comprehensive one of Sephardic music recordings. Bresler has made selections of the collection available to the Jewish Music Research Centre of the Hebrew University of Jerusalem, which in turn has been able to produce several scholarly guided CD anthologies, with comprehensive booklets. The majority of the materials in Bresler's collection are not yet available in American libraries. Neither are they accessible via social-media platforms such as YouTube, nor on commercial platforms such as Spotify, save for a few songs. Sounds clips are available through his *Sephardic Music* website. This collection is specific and yet comprehensive in content. As the collection is still held privately, and there is no standard orthography of Ladino for many of the song titles, names, and so on, creating solid metadata is challenging. Bresler himself has pointed out that he had, for one song, seventeen variant spellings. Multiply that by thousands of recorded songs, and the enormity of the need for title authority files becomes apparent.[29]

BIBLIOGRAPHIC CONTROL AND PRESERVATION

The bibliographic control of sound recordings, that is, the cataloging and access of sound recordings through library and archive portals, has been an issue since libraries began to acquire them beginning in 1911, about twenty years after the appearance of commercial recordings.[30] Although libraries acquired sound recordings, they were only added to library catalogs in the 1920s.[31] Music requires more sophisticated cataloging than many general library holdings, and questions still plague music librarians about the depth of cataloging. Issues include whether to catalog at the "band" or "track" level, or the level of the individual musical work (which may take multiple tracks), or at the level of the "physical item." For example, a single CD can hold many pieces of music, each possibly by a different composer or of a different genre, or associated with different subgroup (such as Ashkenazic or Sephardic), or from different time periods. In addition, the composer and the performers can be equally important and are often co-creators. Folk-music adaptations by certain performing groups or by a specific singer may be as, or even more, important an identifying element as the origin of the piece. Often, its creators or origins may be unidentifiable. Creative credit can extend today to the production teams including sound engineers or production designers who are essential parts of the creative group that produces the final sound and product of a piece of music.

In terms of cataloging Jewish sound-recording collections, the skill levels of those involved vary as greatly as the level and depth of the collections. It is standard that archival sound-recording collections are cataloged differently than items held in a library general collection. However, some curators describe their cataloging as "sort of ad hoc," with no library or archival standards applied.[32] In other collections, such as the Mills Music Library at the University of Wisconsin, strict adherence to high professional standards have been applied under the direction of the head librarian, Jeanette Casey.[33] In the case of the Freedman Jewish Sound Archive collection at the University of Pennsylvania, most of the indexing and cataloging was done by the original owner, Bob Freedman.[34] It was so detailed and meticulous that other institutions have considered trying to create collaborative connections to his cataloging—individual agency turned into collective effort. Unfortunately, some of those early efforts for joint project development in bibliographic control have been unsuccessful. Nevertheless, future projects will be able to take advantage of the high-level indexing of this important collection.

One study of sound recordings in the United States indicates that academic collections range from just a few hundred to one hundred seventy-five thousand and more items, with an average (in that study) of just over eighteen thousand five hundred. Fewer than two-thirds of the US collections in that study indicated that their LP collections were fully cataloged.[35] Key Jewish music sound-recording collections, such as those at Dartmouth, FAU, Pennsylvania, and Wisconsin, do not fit this mold and have succeeded in sustaining ongoing cataloging efforts. In recent years, the Library of Congress Working Group on the Future of Bibliographic Control has highlighted "hidden collections," referring to the vast numbers of sound recordings hidden from public use due to lack of cataloging. Frequently, limited resources prevent retrospective cataloging projects necessary to make these collections findable and accessible.[36] This may be the condition of Jewish music holdings in many libraries. The proportion of backlog in cataloging the collections in departments at other major institutions is currently unknown. Thus, the existence and scope of Jewish music intermingled in academic settings may be "hidden" by being uncatalogued. In addition, those academic library collections with Jewish music holdings that are not as a result of the efforts of passionate individuals are often haphazard and sporadic, and frequently show a lack of understanding of the culture. They often have the nature of an afterthought. In terms of decontextualization, many of these collections lack any real evaluation.

Format reissues, transfers, and updates constitute another issue for Jewish music as with other sound recordings. In a study by Tim Brooks in 2009, data indicates, for example, that 57 percent of the recordings of any genre published between 1950 and 1964 never saw CD reissue, making cultural-heritage preservation in multiple formats a necessity.[37] Roger Bennett and Josh Kun's examination of their five hundred LP recordings include only those not rereleased on CD, thus highlighting this issue. They assert that "the bulk of LP releases didn't make the cut and were left to live out their years in their original forms, risking extinction with each move. . . . LPs that stayed LPs, and, as a result, drifted swiftly to the invisible margins of history."[38] Digital recordings distributed over the internet, including radio, are not systematically collected for preservation, and this is certainly the case for most recordings of Jewish music.[39]

Anecdotal evidence suggests that thousands of easily made cassette recordings have never been rereleased in another format. That is certainly the conclusion of some major collectors, such as Charlie Bernhaut, whose cassette collection of cantorial music has proved rare, and some items even unique.[40] That cassette collections are often fragile and rare is echoed by Alexander Hartov at Dartmouth, who received a major collection of Hasidic music that originated as cassettes made during community events over a period of decades.[41] The phenomenon of a distinct community recording their events or community elders' song repertoires is repeated in many collections known to exist. Others are most certainly held in private collections or under the auspices of Jewish communities. Other "homemade" recordings by amateurs were made in settings such as at Reform Jewish camps. Followers of Shlomo Carlebach "donated tons of homemade recordings made when he appeared in people's homes."[42] These rare items wound up in Dartmouth. Other amateur recordings are held in many aggregated institutional collections. So much of that sort of material is in dire need of basic cataloging, as well as digitization for preservation purposes, and for dissemination and access.

Other issues pertain to categorization, which cannot fully rely on Library of Congress subject headings for detailed help, given the structures and complexities of some genres for which subject names, to date, have not yet been adapted. What Edwin Seroussi describes as "binaries" have, to some extent, been carried problematically into the Jewish music "cataloging" used by many of the collectors themselves.[43] Binaries such as "religious versus secular," "folk or popular versus art," or "vocal versus instrumental" are far from applicable to many Jewish musical pieces, which often fall into an in-between spectrum. These binaries came out of the commercial music world and may have been useful ways to market, but they are less useful in collections used by scholars. As Keller points out with regard to traditional music, the problematic nature of classification is, in general, a long-known phenomenon.[44] In Jewish music in particular, there is still no extant and certainly no standardized vocabulary to define or even identify the various pieces for in-depth library cataloging, although tagging and some note field annotations may help remedy this in some cases and to some extent. In addition, generic terms such as "klezmer" are descriptors that no longer contain their original meanings and require qualification—terms which have yet to be added to taxonomies.

Another issue is that of preservation. US copyright law, as currently written, prohibits many activities necessary for audio preservation, although the law does provide exceptions for libraries and archives, allowing for some audio preservation. For years the laws dealing with sound recordings were so restrictive and anachronistic in light of available technologies that they created only the narrowest of paths on which making copies is fully permissible. Thus libraries, archives, museums, and other institutions found it "virtually impossible" to reconcile their "responsibility for preserving and making accessible culturally important sound recordings with their obligation to adhere to copyright laws."[45] More than two decades have passed since the US Congress passed the National Recording Preservation Act of 2000 (Public Law 106-474). That legislation "affirmed the nation's collective interest in preserving sound recordings for posterity; and, to promote greater public awareness of the issues involved, established the Library of Congress National Recording Preservation Board and the National Recording Registry."[46] The Music Modernization Act of 2018 has now modified some of the restrictions on pre-1972 sound recordings passing into the public domain. December 2021 marked the end of a "transition" period allowing all 1923 recordings to pass into public domain. Items published between 1923 and 1946 will have a ninety-five-plus-five- (effective hundred-year) term before transitioning into the public domain. Items published in 1947–1956 will have a one-hundred-and-ten-year rolling term. Items published between 1957 and 1972 will be in the public domain in 2067 as previously scheduled. These changes will allow free access to preserve most 78 rpm collections and, within a few years, to fully disseminate many of the early Jewish music sound recording collections. This will affect the majority of items held at Wisconsin, without fear of violating US copyright. Beginning January 2022, Dartmouth, FAU, Pennsylvania, and others now may release many recordings to the public. With these clear guidelines, parameters for releasing music online can be further planned and scheduled.

And yet, digital formats are not inherently safe harbors of preservation. Protecting and maintaining digital audio recordings poses problems that go beyond those associated with the preservation of analog recordings, and they require a totally new set of preservation techniques. Thus, there is no specific correlation between the risk to sound recordings and their age. Recordings originally created in digital formats are actually at particular risk.[47] Another barrier is that institutions may not receive funding if its collection is in need of preservation but will not be available for off-site listening. Thus, for sound recordings today, preservation and access have become inextricably linked.[48]

The issue of how libraries ensure an audio heritage still challenges librarians, archivists, and museum curators. According to a report by *Heritage Health Index* that measured conditions of US collections, there are approximately 46.4 million sound recordings held by US institutions, from archives to scientific research organizations.[49]

These holdings do not necessarily reflect the cataloging, the condition of the recordings, or their state of preservation. In addition, specialized equipment may be necessary to play these many sound recordings (such as those for 78 rpms, LPs, reel-to-reel, and cassette tapes), and some of this equipment is increasingly rare.

By way of comparison, of those items held in specifically designated collections of Jewish music sound recordings, there are very broadly estimated to be possibly between five hundred thousand to one million items, or approximately 1.07 to 2.15 percent of the country's estimated holdings. Estimates are difficult because each Jewish music collection enumerates its collection differently: some keep track by number of individual tracks, others by "song or work" (this may represent several tracks or even sides), others by "side" of a disc, others by "item" level, or "album" so a recording with fifteen or even thirty songs could count as one item in their inventory or catalog. Some curators can give statistics based only on already cataloged or digitized items, but not the entire collections. Thus, there is no uniformity in the methods of enumeration among the various institutions. Furthermore, such estimates would necessarily include all duplications, because there is currently no way to assess exact duplicates between institutions over the vast arrays of their collections through a single catalog or database. The inability to exclude duplicates means that, logically, the actual number of individual items would inevitably be far fewer. Until there is a better and comprehensive way to assess Jewish sound collections in a more specific manner, the actual numbers are unknowable.

The rough estimate based on averages includes physical sound recordings held in formats such as cylinders, 78 rpms, LPs, audiocassettes, videocassettes, videodiscs, and CDs, and all types of tape recordings such as reel-to-reel, cassette, or metal tapes. (Aluminum and glass acetate are much rarer media but do exist in some collections, as do some transcriptions of radio programs.) This estimated aggregated size of Jewish music sound recordings in large collections specifically excludes sound recordings held on institutional servers such as sound and video files such as mp3, mov, or mp4a, or those recordings in streaming formats held in aggregated subscription databases, as cultural preservation for Jewish sound recordings implies the preservation and maintenance of sound recordings primarily created or released between 1890 and 2020 and held in physical formats by institutions.

A new project by UCLA's Lowell Milken Center for Music of American Jewish Experience employing a SQL database and the Tableu software is attempting to provide a qualitative analytical tool for Jewish music sound recordings that could be utilized to solve the dilemmas of enumeration and duplication. This experiment is in its early phases. The project's first target consisted of analyzing the constructed Milken Archive collection—a few hundred recordings from the modern period from a single label with regularized data. To analyze the vastly larger sets of widely diverse sound recordings of Jewish music has taken a coordinated effort between musicologists, data scientists, and librarians. Regularization was needed to align data from the various catalogs to allow importing to a data-aggregator system for analysis. After that, a massive intake was possible, with regularization of data (itself a herculean task). This will ultimately allow the

type of analysis that can give a better picture of the actual diversity as well as the duplication in the various collections. From there, further analysis will eventually be possible,
and quantification of the variety of Jewish musics held in physical formats will be fea-
sible. This sequence of highly desirable tasks has been enormously complex in its scope.
In the future, musicologists will be able to use the tool to learn all sorts of information,
such as various recordings of particular songs in all its versions, and to create statis-
tical and other broad analyses. With some additional work, the data can also provide
the additional benefits of being able to find out *where* needed items are kept and housed
within a single searchable database or portal, and whether they are available in digitized
formats for study and access.

The ever-present question remains about the continued relevance of such relatively
static collections as music continues to develop, being created over time. In addition to
preserving, storing, digitizing, and providing access through solid metadata and digital portals to these materials, academic libraries now face the dilemma about providing
continued access to digitized sound recordings. Digitally licensed music has required
adaptations as recording companies (facing their own challenges) have little incentive to share or lend files to libraries. Various solutions—from the negotiation of rights
agreements and preservation of websites of artists to collaborations with archives to
save digital files—have had various levels of success.[50] Until legislative reform further
loosens the copyright restrictions strangling libraries' ability to deal with digital music
free of confining legal constraints, there will continue to be overwhelming challenges.
One solution that has been suggested is to require online-only copyrighted music to
be deposited at the Library of Congress, as had been done with physical formats, but
this solution is not in place yet, and is not currently enforceable, given that music is
constantly appearing on new and ever-expanding varieties of social-media venues.[51]
This same issue certainly exists for Jewish music being created today. In the past, there
seemed at least to be a possibility of capturing the knowledge of Jewish music sound
recordings. No doubt, new technologies will arise, but the political and legal solutions
may continue to lag behind, making true answers years down the road. Some of those
advocating for the distribution of Jewish music through apps see new technologies as a
way of further preserving and distributing on-demand and just-in-time music in danger
of dying out.[52] While these are certainly helpful tools of dissemination and distribution for education and entertainment, the task of capturing all—or even most that is
created—is not yet commonly available. In today's digital age, longevity of even award-
winning music is at risk.

The tasks of both preservation and bibliographic control are even more daunting, and
those who attempt to understand this music will find that many interest groups must be
consulted. Jewish music, as it continues to express the culture and aspirations of Jews,
will continually be morphing, adapting, and growing with the people it serves. Having
long ago moved beyond functional music and entertainment, Jewish music sound
recordings today capture "the *folks-neshome* of the Jewish communities,"[53] as Joshua
Walden has termed it, and will likely continue to do so for the future. Walden, in a 2015
essay, concludes that "changes in the medium of transmission ineluctably contribute

to changes in the message."[54] With all the technological changes, we can expect today's rapid pace of change in genres and styles of Jewish music, as well as hybridizations of the same, will continue.

AUTHENTICITY OF HISTORICAL ACCURACY

Issues of authenticity abound when dealing with commercial recordings. Nevertheless, the recordings themselves as well as their record jackets, liner notes, and advertisements may serve as historical documentation. Commercial recordings were created for immediacy and were intended for the tastes and likes of the perceived audiences and market of their day. They were dressed in the garb of entertainment and were often idealized versions of the culture. Peter Goldsmith, in *Making People's Music: Moe Asch and Folkways Records*, points out that a recording "stamps that performance with an aesthetic value. . . . Never mind that the idea of aesthetic value may have no currency within that cultural context."[55] Dealing with authenticity in sound has been an issue for researchers and musicians of this music from the start. Both must decide what can be gleaned from recordings that is "authentic" for their purposes. Indeed, the revitalization of klezmer music of the 1970s relied heavily on imitating recorded performance stylistics from 78 rpm recordings. Old sound recordings, along with the elderly musicians who were surviving veteran performers, played a major role in providing role models for the artists in very disparate locations who began to study and imitate this musical style. In doing so, their "discoveries" actually created a new cultural phenomenon in instrumental and vocal performance practice.

Authenticity is a question in commercial recordings of every genre. Sound recordings created cultural "memories" and "preserved" sounds that had never really existed in community practice. Cantors who had never sung in a synagogue with instrumental accompaniment were recorded with organ or orchestra. Children's holiday songs and ditties were given lush harmonic renditions. Aesthetic needs outweighed normative authenticity, transforming original practices. As Owe Ronström captures it, "the importance of representations lies not so much in the relation to what really happened there and then, but in the meanings and functions here and now."[56] In the case of sound recordings of Jewish music, for many performing musicians, they became the "historical record" that encapsulated an "authentic" Jewish sound, rather than a misrepresentation, or contrived or faux documentation.

Using the commercially produced sound-recording collections now held in academic libraries and archives to understand Jewish music or to do research holds many pitfalls. As noted above, the presentation and interpretation of the music can give a false impression of style and performance practice. Most often the use of contrafacta is not indicated in any commercial recording, and the origins of songs in general is often not indicated, frequently omitting even the name of the composer and assuming that a song is "traditional." Attribution to a composer is a major issue, as many of the people performing the music had no idea where or when the songs had been written. Synagogue music is especially prone to this omission, in what Rachel Adelstein refers to as "engineered forgetting."[57] Klezmer music on 78 rpms, often held by the so-called klezmer revivalists as authentic objects worthy of imitation, allowed only short three- or four-minute limited pieces in what would traditionally have been extended sets of music. Thus, not only was the music taken out of context—it was massively truncated. (Never mind that wedding music was never intended to be listened to "in concert" by people sitting in halls.)

Legends and tales abound about the importance that 78 rpm recording collections had in the revitalization of klezmer music, whether finding 78 rpms in long-neglected collections or being brought "down from the attic" from families.[58] The basic narrative is that recordings formed the basis for what came to be known as "the revival," which generally meant overcoming, as Barbara Kirschenblatt-Gimblett has termed it, a "rupture" in cultural transmission from the European immigrant generation to postwar America.[59] There is little doubt that the reissues Sapoznik and Kirshenblatt-Gimblett facilitated through Folkways label's first re-release of old klezmer music, *Klezmer Music 1910–1942*, invigorated the process of revitalization and aided the rapid growth of the culture that later led to music camps and new recordings by new artists and groups.[60] This is an early example of how archival Jewish music sound-recording collections morphed from being merely scholarly repositories to serving as transmitters of culture that allowed for an evolution of that culture. Fifty years later, the process has been accelerated by the growth of online digital repositories of sound recordings, as can be gleaned from Jeremiah Lockwood's chapter in this handbook.

Authenticity issues linger concerning the Jewish languages used in commercial recordings. Linguistic issues abound, from YIVO-trained modern singers performing in accents and pronunciations that never existed in Europe or real life to a Sephardic "modern" Hebrew pronunciation being assigned to choral music from nineteenth-century Germany, which was originally written with an Ashkenazic pronunciation in mind. Poetic license is taken with liturgical or sacred texts. Summaries and even mistranslation often appear in liner notes, if English translations are added at all. Linguistic issues and non-standard orthography also appear in the transliterations used in commercial recordings. For obvious reasons, variations over time and location affected both Yiddish and Hebrew transliteration. Even today, although a standard Library of Congress orthography exists, it is not always used for a variety of reasons. One curator stated, "I know what the Library of Congress system does with Hebrew and it's crazy. So we've got a much simpler system and it works."[61] Individual decisions not to use this system lead to additional variations and complication for future possible aggregation efforts. Titles listed that are not in compliance will not correspond with title authority fields at institutions using Library of Congress's standards.

These linguistic concerns are significant. Matching pieces between recordings is already difficult, but without standardization even matching the same exact piece from another copy of the same recording between institutions becomes problematic. There is also the linguistic issue of hybrid language usage within songs, such as so-called Yinglish, which relies on Yiddish or English words to varying degrees, depending on the era during which the song was recorded. Some such hybridizations were used for comic effect, others were standard usage in the mixing of languages during periods of acculturation. The transliteration and translation of these hybrid texts creates particular issues for metadata and digital presentations.

Commercialized or homogenized musical elements, such as the rendering of Jewish modal music in major or minor for organ or guitar accompaniment, is frequently a problem in Jewish sound recordings. As entertainment, these are perfectly acceptable adaptations and uses of music. Performers and creators are free to express, edit, use, and interpret music as they see fit. The problem lies in attempting to use these materials for an understanding of a history of this music. American recordings are often songs "dressed up in Sabbath best" clothing, or an Americanized "made-for-TV" version with lush full orchestrations behind a woman *khanzante*, for example. Many of these stylizations reflect not the actual experience of that music, but an idealized, entertainment version.

De-contextualization occurs, for instance, when geographically diverse Ladino songs from many lands seemingly are presented together as a repertoire. Ladino songs may have lost their geographical origins over time, been learned through various recorded performances, or even gained popularity through a myriad of recordings.[62] Ladino recordings are frequently made by "outsiders" to the traditions, including non-Jewish Spanish-speaking musicians, who may not be familiar with the meanings of the words in context, among other interpretive issues.[63] In special cases, such as the collection of Sephardic folk songs by ethnomusicologists, field-recording efforts (such as those by Susana Weich-Shahak in Israel) effected new interpretations culminating in a wide range of performances in commercially recorded sound, which used "musical markers to tell its own story (or stories) about where Sephardic music comes from—and, in some cases, where it should belong today."[64] Sephardic song, which had been orally transmitted in the past, became industrialized and divorced from geographical affiliation. Instead, commercial recordings became the source for a new "revival" of the music. In the case of Sephardic music recordings, as noted earlier concerning klezmer music, the word "revival" is used, examined, and defined within wide parameters.[65] "Historical" recordings, such as those produced by the Jewish Music Research Centre in Jerusalem, encapsulate and reduce large numbers of the original 78 rpms into a few anthologies. Joel Bresler's private collection was able to provide a massive variety of versions, offering the scholars in Israel, in one instance, more than two hundred performances of a single song.[66]

AUDIENCES

While Jewish music sound-recording collections sometimes coincide with departments of Jewish studies in universities, many such departments in the United States do not offer courses in Jewish music. Musicology departments fare no better, possibly because of a lack of a way to easily define or pigeonhole Jewish music within the greater context of current music scholarship, or the absence of the knowledge and skills necessary required to do serious research. Studying the Jewish soundscape intersects with many other fields and subject areas, while elucidating much about Jews and Judaism in a lived environment and giving context to a co-territorial environment in history.

Jewish sound-recording collections provide access to students, faculty, and researchers of all disciplines who seek access to them. They are especially important to Jewish studies in universities because so many students in classes that incorporate music rely on sound recordings rather than on scores or manuscripts, due to the peculiar nature of baseline knowledge and the prerequisites for entry to these classes. Students with significant knowledge of Jewish studies may not necessarily be expected to know how to read music or to have a significant background in music history. If students are not able to read and learn from a score, faculty must often rely on listening, the common denominator of sound recordings, for primary documentation of the material. Sound-recording collections are one of the most intuitive ways to include Jewish music in university courses of history, culture, or area studies. They allow a more democratic and a broader approach and wider appeal and are useful for primary materials, class resources, and assignments. Jewish music sound-recording collections can serve not only as a way of providing access for learning, but also as an impetus for students to increase creativity and to use as musical resource materials when repurposing.

In turn, the academy can shape Jewish sound-recording collections by being interactive with them in various ways. For instance, Dartmouth's Jewish Sound Archive does have a significant and large collection of sound recordings produced by individual synagogues. These recordings reflect music as it was actually experienced by members of the congregations in the context of their spiritual lives. However, there has been as yet no concerted effort to inventory or list those recordings, and no analysis of what those represent in terms of the history of music that Jews actually "identify with" in their communities. Fieldwork needs to be done for the smaller and more isolated communities, which may have local composers and songwriters whose music is being lost.

While the primary sources of musical manuscripts and scores exist in libraries and archives, major field-recording projects of contemporary Jewish Americans await collection under the direction of a musicologist, anthropologist, or other scholar. American Jewish music still needs to be gathered, as thousands of amateur tapes of venues such as Jewish summer camps, adult retreats, and synagogues, as well as celebrations and festivals across denominations, have yet to be collected in any comprehensive way. Some archival collections, such as those of American Hasidic women's songs or Jewish dances, will require continued collecting efforts to create a comprehensive repository. Finding, preserving, and providing access to thousands of recordings of America's cantors is at present crucial work as members of the older generation trained in Europe retire. Some cantors' recordings languish without proper attention or the funds to achieve the desired access at the institutions where they reside. Most of the music of American cantors and prominent in-group musicians, composers, and performers has yet to be systematically collected. Wesleyan University's oral-history project, *American Cantors*, available online and curated by Mark Slobin, is a significant start in this.

The fact that the current abundance of cantor-composers and singer-songwriters may have works available on YouTube or other streaming services is a worthwhile effort, but to date there is no systematic bibliographic control, lists, or metadata capturing this important moment. Commercial services are not reliable long term, as anyone who has stored their music on many of the shared sound spaces understands. Without a systematic effort to capture and preserve it, this community-building through sound across denominational spectrums is in danger of passing into oblivion. Many libraries and governmental groups understand and support the preservation of cultural heritage. Through their networks and organizations, resources might be tapped for help in accomplishing these goals.[67]

The Jewish music sound-recording collections at Dartmouth, FAU, Pennsylvania, and Wisconsin have served a wider community than students and faculty at their respective institutions. Most reported heavy usage by music students and scholars at other institutions. People involved in non-music disciplines and professions, including anthropologists, historians, and sociologists as well as film makers and journalists, were also reported users. Most significantly perhaps, practicing musicians interested in Jewish music performance are heavy users of these collections. Being located in the United States or other countries, they have found the web portals of these large Jewish sound-recording collections and use them for study and inspiration. Cantors are especially significant users of the online collections. During interviews, questions of usage of the online collections also revealed a keen interest by the general public around the country and the world.

The growth of end-user active audiences—a collective of individual listeners, as it were—shows the manifold importance of Jewish music sound-recording collections. Created by individuals and being handed over to libraries for broader consumption, in the twenty-first century, they do not merely present a process and a product (as collectibles), but facilitate the process of gathering those together who wish to listen. Just as the new technology of sound recordings in the early twentieth century had provided access removed from the concert hall, the aggregation of these recordings through online portals today reaches audiences across time and space and of various backgrounds. As Josh Kun has succinctly opined, the recordings as products demonstrate "what music can tell us about the past, how it helps us survive the present, and how it can help people imagine new futures."[68] For some of those who listen, these sound-recording collections provide the "sound track" to Jewish history—sought after, but elusive. Ultimately these collections facilitate plural listening experiences rather than invoking a single listening collectivity. By bringing widely dispersed audiences together through shared resources, the collections create, in effect, a collectivity of listeners.

ACKNOWLEDGMENTS

The author would like to thank the many collectors and informants for their time and professional expertise, including Charles Bernhaut, Eléonore Biezunski, Joel Bresler, Jeanette Casey,

Paula Eisenstein-Baker, Robert Freedman, Lewis Glinert, Alexander Hartov, Jeff Janeczko, Sherry Mayrent, Henry Sapoznik, Nate Tinanoff, and Bret Werb.

NOTES

1. Robert Bamberger and Sam Brylawski, *The State of Recorded Sound Preservation in the United States: A National Legacy at Risk in the Digital Age*, CLIR Publication 148 (Washington, DC: Council on Library and Information Resources and The Library of Congress, 2010), 2.
2. Charles Bernhaut, in discussion with the author, March 19, 2021.
3. Robert Freedman, in discussion with the author, April 15, 2020, and April 26, 2020.
4. Judah M. Cohen, "Whither Jewish Music? Jewish Studies, Music Scholarship, and the Tilt between Seminary and University," *AJS Review* 32, no. 1 (April 2008): 31.
5. Bamberger and Brylawski, *State of Recorded Sound Preservation*, 4.
6. See "Benedict Stambler, Musicologist, Dead," *The New York Times*, July 5, 1967.
7. Bret Werb in discussion with the author, April 16, 2020.
8. See Miriam Isaacs, *Collecting Jewish Cultural Treasures in a Post-WWII New York Lobby: Jewish Folksong, Ben Stonehill and the Hotel Marseilles*, The American Folklife Center at the Library of Congress, Washington, DC, November 13, 2013, video, https://www.loc.gov/item/webcast-6252/.
9. See Violet Gilboa and Charles Berlin, *Judaica Sound Recordings in the Harvard College Library: A Catalog* (Cambridge, MA: Harvard College Library, 1996).
10. See William H. Kenney, *Recorded Music in American Life: The Phonograph and Popular Memory, 1890–1945* (New York: Oxford University Press, 1999), 215. "Ethnic" is used here as Kenney has, to refer "to a group of people sharing cultural characteristics that may include language, religion, folklife, customs, and/or history"; ibid.
11. See also Judith S. Pinnolis, "Jewish Diasporas," in *A Basic Music Library: Essential Scores and Sound Recordings*, vol. 2: *World Music*, ed. Liza Vick, 4th ed. (Chicago: American Library Association, 2018), 175–178.
12. See Peter D. Goldsmith, *Making People's Music: Moe Asch and Folkways Records* (Washington, DC: Smithsonian Institution Press, 1998), 5.
13. Kenney, *Recorded Music*, 54.
14. Goldsmith, *Making People's Music*, 5.
15. Kenney, *Recorded Music*, 54.
16. Ibid., 55.
17. Ibid., 59.
18. Ibid., 87.
19. Robert Freedman, in discussion with the author, April 15, 2020, and April 26, 2020.
20. Roger Bennett and Josh Kun, *And You Shall Know Us by the Trail of Our Vinyl: The Jewish Past as Told by the Records We Have Loved and Lost* (New York: Crown Publishers, 2008), 16.
21. Sherry Mayrent, in discussion with the author, April 27, 2020.
22. Henry Sapoznik, "Yiddish Radio," *Henry Sapoznik*; https://www.henrysapoznik.com/yiddish-radio (accessed August 11, 2021).
23. Nate Tinanoff, in discussion with the author, May 5, 2020.
24. Alex Hartov and Lewis Glinert, in discussion with the author, April 14, 2020.

25. Asaf Shalev, "This Historian is Preserving North African Jewish Music from a Bygone Era," *Jewish Telegraphic Agency*, March 12, 2021.

26. "JSA: Our History," Judaic Sound Archive, December 7, 2006, https://web.archive.org/web/20060620222456/http://faujsa.fau.edu/06A/history.html

27. Nate Tinanoff, in discussion with the author, May 5, 2020.

28. Jeanette Casey, in discussion with the author, May 6, 2020.

29. Joel Bresler, in discussion with the author, April 7, 2020, and April 21, 2020.

30. See Kenney, *Recorded Music*, xiii.

31. See Stradler, "Cataloging Music Sound Recordings," 278.

32. Alex Hartov and Lewis Glinert, in discussion with the author, April 14, 2020.

33. Jeanette Casey, in discussion with the author, May 6, 2020.

34. Robert Freedman, in discussion with the author, April 15, 2020, and April 26, 2020.

35. See Andrea Imre and Elizabeth J. Cox, "Are We on the Right Track? Issues with LP Record Collections in U.S. Academic Libraries," *Notes* 65, no. 3 (March 2009): 477.

36. Ibid., 485.

37. See Tim Brooks, *Survey of Reissues of U. S. Recordings*, CLIR Publications 133 (Washington, DC: Council on Library and Information Resources and Library of Congress, 2005).

38. Bennett and Kun, *And You Shall Know*, 226.

39. See Bamberger and Brylawski, *State of Recorded Sound Preservation*, 4.

40. Charles Bernhaut, in discussion with the author, March 19, 2021.

41. Alex Hartov and Lewis Glinert, in discussion with the author, April 14, 2020.

42. Ibid.

43. Edwin Seroussi, "Music: The 'Jew' of Jewish Studies," *Jewish Studies* / מדעי היהדות, no. 46 (2009): 48.

44. Marcello S. Keller, "The Problem of Classification in Folksong Research: A Short History," *Folklore* 95, no. 1 (1984): 100.

45. Bamberger and Brylawski, *State of Recorded Sound Preservation*, 7.

46. Ibid., vi.

47. See ibid., 2–3.

48. See ibid., 7.

49. See Institute of Museum and Library Services, "Condition of Collections," in *A Public Trust at Risk: The Heritage Health Index Report on the State of America's Collections* (Washington, DC: Heritage Preservation, 2005), 28.

50. See Judy Tsou and John Vallier, "Ether Today, Gone Tomorrow: 21st Century Sound Recording Collection in Crisis," *Notes* 72, no. 3 (March 2016): 475–479.

51. See ibid., 480–481.

52. See Joshua S. Walden, "Jewish Music and Media of Sound Reproduction," in *The Cambridge Companion to Jewish Music*, ed. Joshua S. Walden (Cambridge: Cambridge University Press, 2015), 69.

53. Joshua S. Walden, "Music of the 'Folks-Neshome': 'Hebrew Melody' and Changing Musical Representations of Jewish Culture in the Early Twentieth Century Ashkenazi Diaspora," *Journal of Modern Jewish Studies* 8, no. 2 (July 2009): 151.

54. Walden, "Jewish Music and Media," 69.

55. Goldsmith, *Making People's Music*, 6.

56. Owe Ronström, "Traditional Music, Heritage Music," in *The Oxford Handbook of Music Revival*, ed. Caroline Bithell and Juniper Hill (New York: Oxford University Press, 2014), 43.

57. Rachel Adelstein, "Engineered Forgetting: Migration, Cultural Trauma, and Anonymization in Synagogue Repertoire" (paper, Society for Ethnomusicology, Ottawa, ON, October 24, 2020).

58. See Henry Sapoznik, *Klezmer! Jewish Music from Old World to Our World* (New York: Schirmer Books, 1999), 185; and Seth Rogovoy, *The Essential Klezmer: A Music Lover's Guide to Jewish Roots and Soul Music, from Old World to the Jazz Age to the Downtown Avant-garde* (Chapel Hill, NC: Algonguin Books, 2000), 77; as well as Hankus Netsky, "American Klezmer: A Brief History," in *American Klezmer: Its Roots and Offshoots*, ed. Mark Slobin (Berkeley: University of California Press, 2002), 20.

59. Barbara Kirshenblatt-Gimblett, "Sounds of Sensibility," in Slobin, *American Klezmer: Its Roots and Offshoots*, 129.

60. See Saposnik, *Klezmer!*, 186.

61. Alex Hartov and Lewis Glinert, in discussion with the author, April 14, 2020.

62. See Edwin Seroussi, "From Spain to the Eastern Mediterranean and Back: A Song as a Metaphor of Modern Sephardic Culture," in *Garment and Core: Jews and Their Musical Experiences*, ed. Eitan Avitsur, Marina Ritzarev, and Edwin Seroussi (Ramat Gan: Bar Ilan University Press, 2012), 71.

63. See Judith R. Cohen, "Judeo-Spanish ("Ladino") Recordings," *The Journal of American Folklore* 112, no. 446 (Autumn 1999): 533.

64. Julia Randel, "Musical Constructions of History: Performance Practices in Recent Recordings of Judeo-Spanish Song," in *Studies in Jewish Musical Traditions: Insights from the Harvard Collection of Judaica Sound Recordings*, ed. Kay Kaufman Shelemay, Harvard Judaica Collection Student Research Papers Series 7 (Cambridge, MA: Harvard College Library, 2001), 114.

65. See ibid., 115; and Ronström, "Traditional Music, Heritage Music," 43.

66. In the case of Joel Bresler, because a 78 rpm recording tracks are so short, he estimated it took fewer than a dozen of the Jewish Music Research Centre's released anthologies to use about half of the main repertoire of his massive collection of Sephardic music.

67. See John DiConsiglio, *Connecting to Collections: A Report to the Nation* (Washington, DC: Institute of Museum and Library Sciences, 2010), 44.

68. Josh Kun, "Jewish Listening: A Reckoning," in *Josh Kun: 2019–2020 Etta and Milton Leve Scholar-in-Residence* (Los Angeles: University of California, Center for Jewish Studies, 2019), video, https://levecenter.ucla.edu/2019-2020levescholar/ (accessed August 16, 2021).

Select Bibliography

Bamberger, Robert, and Sam Brylawski. *The State of Recorded Sound Preservation in the United States: A National Legacy at Risk in the Digital Age.* CLIR Publication 148. Washington, DC: Council on Library and Information Resources and The Library of Congress, 2010.

Goldsmith, Peter D. *Making People's Music: Moe Asch and Folkways Records.* Washington, DC: Smithsonian Institution Press, 1998.

Heskes, Irene. "A Duty of Preservation and Continuity: Collectors and Collections of Jewish Music in America." *Journal of Synagogue Music* 13, no. 2 (January 1984): 45–52.

Isaacs, Miriam. "Stonehill Jewish Song Archive: About the Archive." *Center for Traditional Music and Dance.* https://stonehilljewishsongs.wordpress.com/.

Jacobson, Bernard. "The Milken Archive of American Jewish Music: Recordings in the Naxos American Classics Series." *Journal of Synagogue Music* 31, no. 1 (Fall 2006): 221–230.

Kenney, William H. "The Phonograph and the Evolution of 'Foreign' and 'Ethnic' Records." In *Recorded Music in American Life: The Phonograph and Popular Memory, 1890–1945*. New York: Oxford University Press, 1999.

Kirshenblatt-Gimblett, Barbara. "Sounds of Sensibility." In *American Klezmer: Its Roots and Offshoots*, edited by Mark Slobin, 129–173. Berkeley: University of California Press, 2002.

Pinnolis, Judith S. "Jewish Diasporas." In *A Basic Music Library: Essential Scores and Sound Recordings*. II: *World Music*, edited by Liza Vick, 175–178. 4th ed. Chicago: American Library Association, 2018.

Pinnolis, Judith S. "Jewish Music on the Internet: Digital Media Reviews." *Notes* 61, no. 1 (September 2004): 194–197.

Shelemay, Kay Kaufman, ed. *Studies in Jewish Musical Traditions: Insights from the Harvard Collection of Judaica Sound Recordings*. Harvard Judaica Collection Student Research Papers Series 7. Cambridge, MA: Harvard College Library, 2001.

Walden, Joshua S. "Jewish Music and Media of Sound Reproduction. In *The Cambridge Companion to Jewish Music*, edited by Joshua S. Walden, 56–71. Cambridge: Cambridge University Press, 2015.

18

POSTCUSTODIALISM IN THE
JEWISH MUSIC ARCHIVE

JOSEPH TOLTZ

Music (in its myriad forms) functions in archives and library collections in a very different way to other material and is marked by unique rules of engagement. It is often governed by legal constraints (jurisdictional copyright law) regarding replication and transcription. It presents its own technical challenges when considering preservation and the move to digitization. Music in archives is a material treasure trove for those who carefully venture within: a fertile ground for those wishing to reconnect to traditions imagined to have been lost or forgotten; a place to find objects that tell radically different stories of cultural experience to accepted narratives; a space to challenge long-held beliefs about approaches to interpretation in performance; a repository to reunite individuals and collectives with works of their ancestors captured by anthropologists and ethnomusicologists and preserved by archivists; and, occasionally, a moment to dissolve history itself by resonating the past in present bodies through performance. Music always lies dormant in archives, waiting to resound and reverberate at an undefined point in future time.

The notion of archive as a repository of neutral, dispassionate historical content has been well and truly dismantled in the past fifty years,[1] and important decolonization principles are now actively effecting change in the way communities, scholars, archivists, librarians, and artists view, review, reclaim, reconstruct, perform, and (occasionally) dissolve archival hierarchies. One of the ways that decolonization addresses and interrogates meaning in archives is via a thorough examination of the aesthetics, politics, and power relations that construct archival and museum collections.[2] In the context of archival holdings for Indigenous and minority populations, decolonization harnesses postcustodialism to reconnect and revitalize cultural property, reclaim ownership, and re-center the dynamic between cultural knowledge holders, archives, and museums. From its initial coinage in 1981 by Gerald Ham, postcustodialism recognized that the encounter of the archive with digitization would force archivists to transform traditional understandings of physical custodialism.[3] This added to the ongoing debate around control and decentralization of records as expressed by traditional owners of the material held in archives, reinforced by support from postcolonial theorists and activists.[4]

This chapter asks if such an approach can be taken with regard to Jewish music holdings in archives and if, in doing so, would such a degree of focus in post-Holocaust and other Jewish communities displaced from their traditional lands enhance and re-frame our understanding of this material.[5] It engages two case studies of such collectives on opposite sides of the globe, one situated in Australia, the other in the United States,[6] places of migration where issues of decolonization remain unresolved. These are a set of archives of which I am intimately familiar through my research career: they hold narratives of migration, displacement, suffering, relocation, and reinvention of musicians born Jewish.

Australia, which is ranked number nine among the countries of the largest Jewish populations, holds music collections of fragmentary material from Jewish migrants, refugees, internees, and survivors of the Holocaust. Their holdings speak to the value assigned to migrant musical cultures in a society struggling with an unresolved colonial past. Substantive material is held in archives at the National Library of Australia, the Sydney Jewish Museum, the Jewish Museum of Australia, and the Jewish Holocaust Centre in Melbourne, with smaller holdings in other state and private libraries around the country. But the only dedicated space for archival Jewish music holdings is the Australian Archive of Jewish Music, held at Monash University in Melbourne, a public institution founded in 1958 (part of the Group of Eight most distinguished universities in Australia), and this will be the focus of the first case study.

The archival landscape of Jewish music in the United States is too long to allow for a list, with many of the lists that currently exist incomplete.[7] In light of its sheer breadth, and in diametrical opposition to Australia, it is defined by a diversity of sources, some of which are addressed in the chapters by Judith Pinnolis and Eléonore Biezunski for this handbook. The case study at hand focuses on the United States Holocaust Memorial Museum, a partly federally funded institution founded in 1980 dedicated to telling narratives of the Holocaust, reconstructing the history leading up to the conflagration, and revealing the history of the immediate aftermath. The fragmentary, heterogenous nature of both case studies allows for a rich, problematic complexity to emerge, a neces-sity when considering a postcustodial reading of such archives when they are accessed for use in present and future reconstructions for performances.

Historical amnesia is a powerful state that is utilized politically to silence discussion around the traumatic impact of the colonial mindset on First Nations people. This am-nesia also extends to silences about the ways in which migrant communities were and still are treated under conditions established by colonialism. At the height of the age of assimilation, that is, after World War II, a great wave of migrants arrived to alleviate Australian labor shortages. Despite Australian Jewish communal protests, hundreds of Nazis and their willing collaborators gained entry, qualifying as "healthy Balts," the right types for assimilation into Anglo-Australia. Despite Australia's best efforts to re-strict Jewish migration after the war as much as possible,[8] the Jewish population of the continent was transformed and reinvigorated by thousands of Holocaust survivors and Jewish refugees. At the same time, systematic violence continued (and continues to this day) against First Nations people and their cultures. In the scholarly space, non-Indigenous scholars have had to transform their work to a model of intercultural knowledge production,[9] working with and in community and recognizing the act of research as "a symbolic, interpretive, transactional, contextual process."[10]

The application of a postcustodial lens to the Jewish archive takes inspiration from this methodology, which works to decolonize archives cooperatively with First Nations partners. The archives I have examined and worked with come from and are generated by community priorities and individual desires to preserve. They already follow postcustodial principles of custody, care, control, and collaboration.[11]

JEWISH MUSIC MIGRATION: FRAGMENTARY DIREMPTION OR REPAIR?

At the opening address of an international conference in Potsdam on preserving Jewish archives in 1999,[12] the then-director of the Jewish Historical Institute in Poland, Felix Tych, observed that the course of events in Europe from 1933 to 1945 transformed scholars of Jewish history into archaeologists, sifting through fragments of tombstones and rubble of synagogues, in the hope of unearthing well-preserved documents of Jewish history, only to find destruction or displacement of crucial collections.[13] In the area of ethnomusicology, such "sifting" began as early as 1941, where Moisey Beregovsky, in the relatively safe area of Ufa, Bashkiria (Soviet Central Asia), collected songs of Jewish refugees from Poland, Ukraine, and Russia. In doing so, the folklorist was emulating the work of the first Jewish ethnographers into Yiddish societies under threat earlier in the century: Joel Engel and S. An-ski.[14] From 1945, Israel Kaplan, Shmerke Kaczerginski, Aleksander Kulisiewicz, Yehuda Eismann, David Boder, and others would collect songs from survivors and refugees in Europe,[15] while Ruth Rubin would start her collecting in 1947 in Montreal,[16] and Ben Stonehill in 1948 in the United States.[17]

This collecting activity refutes Foucaultian and Derridean notions of the use of the archive to assert collective power,[18] as it was primarily intended to serve a temporary juridical purpose, that is, to act as mnemonics of wartime atrocities and displacement, and not as permanent artistic expressions—and was rarely embraced and reintegrated into the reconstructed Yiddish sound world, but portrayed rather as examples of the diremption of Yiddish culture before and after the war. Scholars, such as Shirli Gilbert, have utilized this diverse material to present musical expression as a force of agency that challenges more hegemonic readings of musical activities particularly in camps and ghettos (e.g., narratives of resistance, complicity, capitulation).[19] In the field of concert music, works written in camps and ghettos rarely survived, the exception being the relatively large body of material preserved from Terezín, which has now entered regular concert repertoire and has had much written about its structure, quality, and meaning.[20]

Surveying the nature of these activities, what unites the creators and the *zamlers* is the need to collect. Identity is of secondary concern, the immediate imperative being the preservation of the history of the material, over and above aesthetic concerns of musical quality. The case studies presented further below will demonstrate that this need continues to be imperative, guiding the collection of "Jewish music" in archives across the globe, with privilege of historical function over concerns of aesthetic value and power relations. And yet these case studies also reveal distinct differences, with the United States Holocaust Memorial Museum's prime collection focus on global consolidation of its subject matter, while the Australian Archive of Jewish Music seems comfortable in its national focus and fragmentation, an issue that other archives on this continent face as well.

Fragmentary Snippets: A Brief Survey of Jewish Music Holdings in Australian Archives

Jewish music holdings in Australian archives are often not identified in collections as "Jewish," the exception being the Australian Archive of Jewish Music. Trove, the online catalog of the National Library of Australia and gateway for searching holdings of all significant public libraries in Australia, does not allow for Boolean search. When using the term *Jewish music* together with the geographic restrictor "Australia," 879 records appear, including general news items pertaining to the Jewish community next to recordings of Jewish music, music scores, and miscellanea. Graeme Skinner, who has written on synagogue music in the early colonies, such as consecration music from the York Street Synagogue in Sydney (1840), the Hobart Hebrew Congregation (1845), and the order of service of the consecration of the Launceston Synagogue (1846),[21] tagged the source material referenced in Trove as "synagogue music," thus enabling more accurate searches for scholars.[22] But Skinner comments that it is only possible to search specifically by theme when other users of Trove tag subject matter in this way (in essence, creating metadata for future searches).[23]

Despite these search issues, the National Library of Australia holds in its own collection significant content by Jewish Australian composers (especially material from the period of migratory flux, i.e., 1933–1960), but this content is not identified as "Jewish music" and difficult to identify as such until one examines scores and origin stories. The modernist composer Felix Werder (1922–2012) donated his entire collection of scores to the National Library of Australia. He had a lifelong involvement in Jewish music from an early age with his father Boaz Bischofswerder a well-known cantor in Berlin (later in London).[24] The pair were unjustly identified as "hostile enemy aliens" and transported with over two thousand other men of Jewish origin to Australia on the HMT *Dunera* in 1940,[25] imprisoned first in Hay and then Tatura, remote rural towns in Australia. By 1942 the Australian government had recognized this British error and released the men, many of whom then enlisted in Army Employment companies, to assist the war effort against the Nazis. Werder's avant-garde aesthetic gained wide interest from artistic directors in Australia in the 1960s and 1970s (his one-act opera *The Affair* was the first Australian-written opera performed at the new Sydney Opera House in 1974), but following retirement from his music criticism work, he received more attention in the land of his birth, with his last opera being performed at the Berlin Festival in 1987. He remains a neglected figure on the concert platform, both in Australia and overseas. In the scholarly field he is mentioned in important surveys of Australian concert music, and only two theses are devoted to close analysis of his works, one of which examines his work as a music critic rather than analysis of his compositional output.[26]

The composer Werner Baer (1914–1992), steeped in the Berlin tradition of Jewish organ music, leader in the Jüdischer Kulturbund's *Kleinkunst* division until his imprisonment in 1938 during Kristallnacht and subsequent departure to Singapore in early 1939, was a prominent repetiteur, composer, conductor, and organist in Australia (primarily Sydney) from the late 1940s until his death.[27] He and his first wife and child were also unjustly transported to Australia from Singapore in 1940 on the *Queen Mary* and imprisoned in Tatura before release in 1942.[28] Baer wrote and arranged music for the Australian Broadcasting Corporation (ABC) during his time as New South Wales State supervisor of music. All his original scores and symphonic arrangements were preserved in the ABC archives until funding cuts forced the Australian Music Centre to lobby for the works (as part of the Symphonies Australia-ABC archive) to be conserved at the National Library of Australia.

Another section of the National Library of Australia houses papers and materials (including musical scores) from Gertrud Bodenwieser (1890–1959), one of the most important dance pedagogues in Vienna. Bodenwieser escaped the Nazi's annexation of Austria in May 1938 to Colombia, whence she arrived in Australia in August 1939. Her influence on dance in Australia cannot be overstated, for she used local composers like Baer and others, as well as her Jewish repetiteur Marcel Lorber, to write original scores to her highly innovative modern dance works. In 2017, with permission from the Australian Music Centre, I brought a selection of this material back to the listening public at the opening night Out of the Shadows: Rediscovering Jewish Music and Theatre, a festival curated for the UK Arts and Humanities Research Council project, Performing the Jewish Archive.[29]

Other fragmentary records of Jewish musical life can be found at the Jewish Museum of Australia, including the most significant collection of material from German-speaking internees of Jewish origin transported on the HMT *Dunera* and the *Queen Mary*, and imprisoned in the rural towns of Hay and Tatura from 1940 to 1943. The Sydney Jewish Museum, and its equivalent in Melbourne, the Jewish Holocaust Centre, also hold fragmentary collections of music, donated exclusively by survivors and descendants in the case of the latter, and additionally by families of active Jewish musicians in the former (the Sydney Jewish Museum covers Jewish life in Australia as well as Holocaust education). As these were donated in haphazard fashion, they are challenging to navigate for researchers. Consolidated into one collection (be it online or physical), all this material would weave an interesting narrative about the story of migrating Jewish musicians to Australia, and the impact their work had on the local scene.

FRAGMENTATION IN THE AUSTRALIAN ARCHIVE OF JEWISH MUSIC

The idea for a Jewish music archive in Australia sprung from an encounter at the Australian Centre for Jewish Civilisation at Monash University in Melbourne. Margaret Kartomi, a distinguished Australian ethnomusicologist with expertise in the music of South Asia, met Dov Noy, legendary pioneer of folklore studies in Israel, who described to her his archival research in Jewish music and folklore.[30] Incorporated into Noy's lecture was a performance of Yiddish songs by local artist Freydi Mrocki. During talks with the folklorist, Kartomi had the idea of starting an Australian archive of Jewish music. Later she traveled to New York to visit the YIVO Institute for Jewish Research, where she was impressed by the research and archival holdings. Later still, while giving a keynote on the music of Surabaya at SOAS in London, Kartomi encountered London's burgeoning klezmer scene and observed the dynamic interaction between research, archive, and performance.

All these encounters with the Jewish music archive inspired the launch of the Australian Archive of Jewish Music in 1995 at Monash University, with a small seed grant from the vice chancellor. Kartomi's first act was to enlist Bronia Kornhauser to be its archivist. By 1999 an advisory board was in place, with representation from distinguished professors across the university and prominent musicians of the Jewish community in Melbourne. The funding that established the sustainability of the archive came through two successful Australian Research Council grants awarded to Kartomi, to study the music of the Baghdadi Jewish diaspora in Singapore, Bombay, Yangon, Penang, Surabaya, and Sydney. The first grant (1997–1999) was entitled "Musical Outcomes of Jewish Diasporas in Southeast Asia and Australia, 1930–45"; the second grant (1999–2001) was entitled "Music and Musicians in Locations along the Southern Asian-Jewish and Northern Asian-Jewish Diaspora Routes in the 20th Century." Kartomi published several articles on the topic of the Baghdadi Jewish diaspora and deposited her ethnographic recordings in the Australian Archive of Jewish Music for access by future scholars, descendants of interviewees, and members of the general public.[31] A follow-up Australian Research Council Linkage Infrastructure, Equipment, and Facilities Grant, *Preserving Australia's Sound Heritage* (2004–2008) enabled the archive's administrators to create a web-based catalog and digitize rare and/or fragile recordings.

While Kartomi was busy researching overseas, Kornhauser continued her own field-work in Melbourne, attending Jewish music performances and events, gathering ethnographic interviews with prominent Jewish musicians of all varieties. Kornhauser then moved from collecting interviews to approaching Jewish community members, to encouraging people to donate material that they were listening to, and especially material their parents had been listening to when they came to Australia, as a cultural record of migration. This part of the archival collection was particularly aimed at the large Holocaust survivor population in Melbourne. Per capita, Australia is second only to Israel in proportion of survivors, with the majority of Yiddish-speaking Eastern Europeans (mostly of Polish, Russian, or Lithuanian origin) settling in Melbourne, and mostly non-Yiddish speaking Czech, Slovak, Hungarian, German, and Austrian Jews settling in Sydney.[32]

Kornhauser's first acquisition was a large collection from the Jewish Museum of Australia, containing some early 78 rpm records that were produced under license in Australia from overseas commercial labels. At the start, Kornhauser accepted any and every donation in order to build a foundation to the archive; however, her practice soon changed so that only items that were not held by the archive were accepted. From 1996 to 1999, at an annual community festival called Concert in the Park, Kornhauser set up a stall to promote the collecting activities of the Australian Archive of Jewish Music; this produced a snowball effect in Melbourne's Jewish community, and soon she began assessing numerous private collections for potential ingestion. As well as recordings, the archive also accepted important ephemera relating to musical events and activities.

Concurrent with the collecting activities, Kornhauser began to record important Jewish music events for the archive. In these early collective endeavors, there were only basic permissions to record, garnered from donors (and no permissions given for public accessibility), and collections were often anonymized at the request of the donors. Similarly, in early ethnographic interviews, respondents were anonymized rather than permission being garnered for identification and disseminated. This has shaped not only the way that the collection can be referenced, but also the way in which it can be accessed, with only seven items available on the open-source digital platform of the Music Archive of Monash University. An example of access problems can be seen in the collection donated by the protégé of Miriam Rochlin, an important pianist and accompanist in the Melbourne Jewish scene for many decades. The donor was unsure about permissions, and with only distant relatives unable to be contacted, the collection remains digitally closed but physically accessible to researchers.

The peak intensity of collecting for archival purposes occurred between 1995 and 2008, with a subsequent large gap until collecting recommenced in 2018. Kartomi explained that there were two major reasons for this: leading forces on the advisory board became inactive; and fundraising attention was directed to the development of five fully funded professorships at the Australian Centre for Jewish Civilisation, the Jewish studies department at Monash. Only through Kartomi's continued success in ARC grants did the archive continue to function, and for a ten-year hiatus, Kornhauser's Jewish communal research efforts had to be focused elsewhere.

As well as traditional research outputs, the Australian Archive of Jewish Music released two recording efforts to the general public to reflect collection holdings and broaden access to its material. The first contained just over sixty-three minutes of 78 rpm recordings taken from the archive, cleared with copyright permissions from composers, arrangers, and performers or rights holders.[33] The second comprised field-recordings undertaken by Kartomi in the various communities of the Baghdadi-Jewish diaspora in Southeast Asia and Australia.[34] Both Kartomi and Kornhauser expressed disappointment at the lack of engagement with this particular collecting endeavor, giving as an example the attendance at the launch of the *Out of Babylon* CD at the Jewish Museum of Australia. Many people who had registered their interest canceled at the last minute when they realized that the recording was not of music from the Sephardi diaspora, but rather from the Mizrachi Baghdadi diaspora.[35]

Similar to the National Library of Australia and others, the collection of the Australian Archive of Jewish Music is thus disparate and fragmented—a combination of professionally produced (copyright) material, ethnographic interviews from Australia and Southeast Asia, amateur recordings, and communal concerts. The collection has been shaped by the two ethnographers involved in its establishment, with occasional participation from other Monash University musicologists at the time: Aline Scott-Maxwell, Kay Dreyfus, Greg Hurworth, and Joel Crotty. Access to the archive by other scholars has been lackluster. For my doctoral dissertation, I accessed some of Kornhauser's ethnographic interviews for background purposes before conducting my own interviews with Holocaust survivors residing in Melbourne in 2008. The Australian Archive of Jewish Music holds music recordings from Melbourne's Jewish Holocaust Centre, in a format more easily accessible than that at the Centre itself. This is an example of how the emphasis on music as the center of the collection provides more accessible resources for music researchers.

Other internal Monash researchers have accessed other aspects of the collection for research purposes, and the occasional researcher interested in the material on the aforementioned Felix Werder, who eventually settled in Melbourne after the war. Kerryn Hancock utilized the recordings donated by Cantor Abraham Adler for a master's thesis. Adler, born in Vienna, was the cantor at Elwood Synagogue from 1957 to 1975 and was active in promoting Jewish liturgical music to the wider listening community through broadcasts on local radio 3GB, before returning to the city of his birth to take up the position of Obercantor at the Stadttempel at Seitenstettengasse. A prominent scholar who utilized the holdings of the Australian Archive of Jewish Music was Albrecht Dümling, during the period he was researching his study of Jewish refugee artists fleeing to Australia.[36]

In the context of artistic research, the archive has been used extensively by klezmer musicians in the Melbourne community. David Krycer and Freydi Mrocki, two members of one of the earliest Australian klezmer ensembles, Klezmania, are frequent visitors to the archive for inspiration for their own original compositions. Many members of the general public also access the archive for their own musical pleasure and interest, but during the COVID-19 pandemic, this had to be curtailed.

At present, with the retirement of Kartomi, most of the original material from the archive has moved to a secured basement facility. Monash University has invested time and energy into protecting the holdings, and digitizing and preservation works has seen a full-time project manager appointed. With such resources being invested, it is clear that the current collection in the Australian Archive of Jewish Music is in secure hands for the immediate future. The expiration of copyright on some historically important recordings will hopefully lead to more material added to the digital open-access resource. There is great potential in this archive to expand with enthusiasm, link to other significant collections in Australia, and garner financial support, and it has much material that would be of interest to scholars interested in patterns of migration and cultural production. Time will tell if the latter is forthcoming.

FRAGMENTARY MUSIC COLLECTING: THE UNITED STATES HOLOCAUST MEMORIAL MUSEUM

The founding director of the United States Holocaust Memorial Museum (USHMM) was Jeshajahu (Shaike) Weinberg. The USHMM was always conceived to be both a museum and research center, with objects on permanent and rotating display, and an archival collection that was far deeper than the immediate needs of the permanent exhibition space.[37] Within its research mission was an imperative to gather, catalog, and make available primary documentation pertaining to Holocaust history, and as much as possible, to make available this material as open source to all researchers. The only material in the museum that is restricted usually comes with conditions from other institutions, for example, the large amount of primary material scanned in the early days from the Bundesarchiv, the Federal Archives of Germany that hold much of the unprocessed original paper documents related to specific subjects—roundups, deportations, camp architecture, ghetto administration, and slave labor consignments.

In the course of the USHMM's institutional evolution, its mission broadened to include the documentation of Jewish life before the Holocaust, in order to contextualize the war and the genocide. At this point, photographs and the moving image became intrinsic to the USHMM's collective efforts.[38] Weinberg, who prior to his curatorial work was a successful theater director, saw music as co-equal to the gathering of these other cultural material, as its own form of documentation. In this way, he corresponded to the mindset of the first collectors who began transcribing songs from survivors in the Displaced Persons camps, who recognized that such songs memorialized persons, places, and events that might otherwise remain unknown. At a time when there was no possibility for physical documentation, the songs remained in the minds of survivors, and this is what gave weight to such material. In the initial project a learning center was established,[39] so museum visitors would be able to research in more depth subject matters that they had encountered during their visit—for example, if wanting to know more about the concentration camp Buchenwald, they could access an encyclopedia entry and also hear the camp songs that were collected and digitized.

The focus on music received new emphasis with ethnomusicologist Bret Werb joining the staff of the USHMM in 1993. Werb's main mission in the early years was to link music to such subject matter featured in the Wexler Learning Center. Although there was a good deal of material that had been recorded, his own archival searches were uncovering references to particular works of music (mostly songs) but no recordings. In order to address this, a recording studio was set up at the USHMM, and five CDs were produced over a period of seventeen years, along with extensive booklets. The first was drawn from published collections made by Eleanor (Chana) Mlotek, the esteemed musicologist and folklorist from YIVO.[40] The second recording utilized an acquisition for the collection, a facsimile of a very rare copy of the wartime notebook of Mordechai Gebirtig, troubadour of Krakow.[41] The third was linked to the Resistance segment of the museum's permanent exhibition;[42] the fourth, similarly, linked to a temporary exhibition on the Kovno (Kaunas) Ghetto.[43] The very last recording comprised material written and transcribed by Aleksander Kulisiewicz (1918–1982), one of the most important collectors of concentration-camp songs, whose vast archive was acquired by the museum in the early 1990s.[44] In this recording, the USHMM focused only on Kulisiewicz's collection of originally composed Polish songs that told, in diary fashion, his experiences in the concentration camp Sachsenhausen.

As well as the recording project, Werb was co-curator for chamber concerts at the USHMM across a period of eight seasons, from 1994 to 2002, with a cellist from the National Symphony Orchestra, Steven Honigberg. These concerts showcased some of the discoveries from the archives, at the same time that the distinguished recording label DECCA was publishing its *Entartete Musik* series of recordings. The first interest came from music composed in Terezín, but the programming also presented the works of émigré composers like Ernst Toch, Erich Zeisl, Karl Weigl, and Leon Levitch, and premieres of the works of Mieczesław Weinberg. With Washington Musica Viva (a local ensemble), Werb and Honigberg presented Hans Gál's music revue *What a Life* in a performance that for the first time interspersed the musical numbers with readings from the composer's camp diaries (later published as *Music Behind Barbed Wire*).[45]

In March 2000, the players staged a tour of this repertoire to Phoenix, Los Angeles, and Portland, Oregon. In the context of popular genres, the revival of the musical *Cabaret* on Broadway in 1998 gave impetus to some cabaret performances, but given the solemn nature of the permanent exhibition in the building, such presentations had to be accompanied by fairly serious, academic narratives. In 2002 one particularly important program, *Lavender Songs*, presented Weimar cabaret, focusing on the persecution of gay artists, narrated by Alan Lareau from the University of Wisconsin, Oshkosh.[46] Similar aesthetic concerns about presentation in the USHMM were considered by the Roma ensemble *Khanci Dos*, which decided that the museum constituted a graveyard, and as such, inappropriate as a venue for dancing and singing. As with the cabaret evening, the presentation of this 2003 performance was in concert form, informed by scholarship.

When I asked Werb why the performance program ceased, the answer was that financial constraints limited its continuation.[47]

I first met Bret Werb online in 2008, having been recommended his advice during the course of my ethnographic doctoral research. During my Barbara and Richard Rosenberg fellowship at the USHMM from late 2010 to June 2011, I worked closely with him on musical contents in the archive. As with all who work at the USHMM, Werb is not only a fountain of knowledge about Jewish life before, during, and in the immediate aftermath of the Holocaust, but also incredibly generous in sharing his specialized musical knowledge with all researchers who approach him. He is consummately equipped to speak not only about collection practices, priorities, and content, but also about the development and priorities of the museum in relation to the collecting of musical material.

Collecting material at the USHMM continues apace, despite a considerable backlog of collections waiting to be cataloged because of the COVID-19 pandemic. There is a significant, growing amount of material emerging from individuals who worked as entertainers in Displaced Persons camps in the immediate aftermath of the war. In the course of our conversation, Werb mentioned that he had just received another orchestral composition from The Happy Boys Ensemble, a touring troupe of musicians who were survivors of the Lodz Ghetto.[48] Collecting this material still adheres to the mission of the USHMM: the musical culture of the Displaced Persons camps dealt directly with life before the war, acts of commemoration, and at that time, current events such as the Exodus Affair, difficulties with attempted immigration, the Zionist push for Displaced Persons to go to British Mandate Palestine or later Israel, and the basic problems of reestablishing life after camps and ghettos.

The collections currently most used by performer-researchers are the aforementioned Kulisiewicz collection and the David Bloch collection. Bloch was a pioneer musicologist in this field, and I was lucky enough to have him as a mentor and friend during the last ten years of his life. When his widow Emilie Berendsen Bloch was considering institutions to deposit his vast collection, I advocated for the collection to be deposited at the USHMM, precisely because of the open-source policy that the institution maintains, and Emilie Bloch agreed with this advice. Currently there are performers interested in works by the German composer James Simon (1880–1944), held only in the David Bloch collection. There have also been a number of Terezín-related performances of lesser-known composers in the Netherlands, Canada, and the United States. The USHMM also holds concert music from the German Jewish composer Edwin Geist (1902–1942), who fled to Kovno, Lithuania, but was entrapped by the Nazis an eventually perished. His works are currently under examination.

One of the most noteworthy recent acquisitions is the Moisey Beregovsky collection, originally preserved in the Vernadsky National Library of Ukraine in Kiev. Prior to this important acquisition, the USHMM only had the fragmentary songbook of *Jewish Folk Creations during the Great Patriotic War*,[49] which Beregovsky had failed to publish. For the first time since the 1940s, the entire archive that the musicologist and folklorist created in the years 1941–1943 in Ufa is now accessible.[50] During this time in

Central Asia, Beregovsky interviewed many other Jewish refugees who had fled there and was able to capture rare accounts of life in nineteenth-century Jewish shtetls, as well as music, artworks, jokes, and anecdotes. Beregovsky was also the custodian of material from the early expeditions of Jewish ethnographers and ethnomusicologists, Joel Engel and S. An-ski.

Werb provides other examples of how the archival music resources at the United States Holocaust Memorial Museum are accessed for different purposes. Polish music researchers have reengaged with the phenomenon of interwar tangos, a beloved popular dance form at the time. Much of the musical material collected by Kulisiewicz was based on these popular songs, which were invariably written by Polish-Jewish composers and lyricists who ended up in camps and ghettos. The interest in reviving this material in Poland has seen a curious circularity occur, where researchers consult the contrafactum material that Kulisewicz faithfully recorded, and then track down or reconstruct the melodies (and presumably source original words). Another interesting development has seen the works of the teenage composer-pianist Josima Feldshuh (1929–1943). Although she died under tragic circumstances at the age of thirteen, her notebook of original compositions was preserved, along with records of her performances with the ghetto orchestra. Since the rediscovery of her works, the Polin Museum in Warsaw has held events that honor her memory, where young Polish artists feature her music and learn more about the history of this particular individual.[51]

VALUING FRAGMENTATION

The post-Holocaust world transformed the *zamler* from a salvage folklorist to a crisis ethnographer, or to paraphrase Shmerke Kaczerginski, from a crank to a maniac.[52] This informs the concentration and disparity of material at the USHMM as well as some other institutions. The advantage and vulnerability of such fragmentary collections is that, viewed holistically, their diversity naturally resists grand themes that serve hegemonic arguments about the function of music in times of oppression and displacement.[53] The power of collective activity at USHMM through its continuing mission to gather and preserve is buoyed by an open-source online philosophy that allows all to access as much of this material for whatever purposes. This vulnerability is reinforced by its fragmentary nature; standing out of context, it can also be used opportunistically to tell a certain narrative to the detriment of others.

The Australian Archive of Jewish Music, far smaller in scale, provides a no-less-disparate perspective to view Jewish music through an Australian and East Asian lens. Driven by the enthusiasm and research agendas of two individuals, it stands at a crossroad, with future developments uncertain but present material assured of preservation. Without support for a continued collecting mission, it is in real danger of atrophy. Yet in the digital age and with willingness across institutions, other Australian archives could link their holdings to this archive, providing a locus for a larger body of material of Jewish musical development at the far end of the globe for scholars to study and absorb.

Unlike the real, present digital inequalities that Australian First Nations communities face in access to material,[54] researchers working with material at the USHMM have unfettered access to an enormous amount of recorded and scanned material online. Physical presence is sometimes warranted, and the USHMM relies on scholars to improve collection accessibility during research fellowships.[55]

One of the least compatible relations between postcustodialism and music archives is the current copyright situation. Originally formulated to benefit composers and performers through the provision of rights, the unintended consequence of copyright is to restrict broader audience access to works that, in a pre-copyright context, would have been disseminated through community and/or oral tradition. This narrowing of musical options contributed to the further promotion of "canonical" composers in the European-derived Jewish music repertories, in the absence of free access to the diversity of music in archives.

Postcustodialism is incompatible with notions of canonicity and is, in fact, a refutation of this system. The two institutions examined in this chapter operate under a deliberately postcustodial rubric, through open-access policies where possible, encouragement of scholar-performers, and ongoing relationships with donors. Many institutions across the world that hold prominent Jewish music collections still lag in considering the implications of postcustodial practices in archives. They refuse access to material to the general public (including descendants of those communities who have moved out of the locale) and question scholars who have not received imprimatur to study this material via other scholarly introductions. They restrict the provision of open access to holdings, often ostensibly under the rubric of custodianship, but more often with an unspoken curatorial gatekeeper ethos, desiring to control access to the material. They do not provide clear and accessible collection guides, do not follow critical metadata principles and, as a consequence of both of these, do not collate holdings in a systematic fashion. Such institutions often argue that their archives have a characteristically fixed geographic location, and for those interested in their contents, travel and permission must be sought to obtain access. To be fair, many of these institutions also struggle with funding for maintenance of their collections, let alone developing protocols for enhanced access, and these problems are not restricted to Jewish music holdings. However, in a digital age, it is hard to see such policies as doing more than privileging those with means (to travel, to develop contacts, to overcome access issues through scholarly reputation) over those without. The consequence of gatekeeper ethos combined with under-resourcing is to restrict greater understanding of the diversity of the Jewish music archive in the wider public, as well as in the academy.

Postcustodial challenges remain for the Jewish archive. With the absence of living collaborators and the phenomenon of "Holocaust fatigue," there is a reluctance to explore archival material by Jewish communities who are often focused solely on future potential, not the traumatic past. But postcustodial studies of material in these archives are imperative, in order to continue to nuance the way in which Jewish culture survives, changes, and adapts. The use of musical material in archives to represent Holocaust experience treads the same boundaries of Holocaust memory[56] and is vulnerable to the same sort of synecdochic vulnerabilities that could catapult the performer and listener into their own personal experience,[57] moving them from the historical context in which the work arose. It is in this way that appropriation of this material for heated, contested political spaces operates, adding a further layer of complication and distortion to the mix. A postcustodial approach that allows open access to all members of the public, removal of scholarly gatekeepers, participation of the collector and acknowledgement of their role as curator, reintroduction of cultural material to descendants, and above all, precise scholarly attention to a rich, wide spectrum of creations will not only ensure preservation of the Jewish (music) archive, but also maintain its fragmentary integrity as a history and resource of culturally embodied mobility.

NOTES

1. See Marlene Manoff, "Theories of the Archive from across the Disciplines," *Portal* (Baltimore, MD) 4, no. 1 (2004): 9–25.

2. See Taylor R. Genovese, "Decolonizing Archival Methodology: Combating Hegemony and Moving Towards a Collaborative Archival Environment," *AlterNative: An International Journal of Indigenous Peoples* 12, no. 1 (2016): 32–42.

3. See Jeannette A. Bastian, "Taking Custody, Giving Access: A Postcustodial Role for a New Century," *Archivaria* 53 (2002): 77–93.

4. See Frank Gunderson, Robert C. Lancefield, and Bret Woods, eds., *The Oxford Handbook of Musical Repatriation* (New York: Oxford University Press, 2019).

5. See also Edwin Seroussi, "Music: The 'Jew' of Jewish Studies," *Jewish Studies / מדעי היהדות*, no. 46 (2009): 51.

6. See Philip Joseph Deloria, *Playing Indian*, Yale Historical Publications (New Haven, CT: Yale University Press, 1998); and "The New World of the Indigenous Museum," *Daedalus: Journal of the American Academy of Arts and Sciences* 147, no. 2 (2018): 106–115.

7. See, for example, the selective overview "Libraries and Archives with Jewish Music Collections," Jewish Music WebCenter, http://jmwc.org/jewish-libraries-and-archives/.

8. See Ruth Balint, *Destination Elsewhere: Displaced Persons and Their Quest to Leave Postwar Europe* (Ithaca, NY: Cornell University Press, 2021), 115–134.

9. See Sally Treloyn, "Music in Culture, Music as Culture, Music Interculturally: Reflections on the Development and Challenges of Ethnomusicological Research in Australia," *Voices: A World Forum for Music Therapy* 16, no. 2 (2016), https://doi.org/10.15845/voices.v16i2.877.

10. Myron W. Lustig and Jolene Koester, *Intercultural Competence: Interpersonal Communication across Cultures*, 2nd ed. (New York: HarperCollins College Publishers, 1996), 25.

11. See Bastian, "Taking Custody, Giving Access," 37–38.

12. For the proceedings, see Jean-Claude Kuperminc and Rafaële Arditti, eds., *Preserving Jewish Archives as Part of the Cultural Heritage: Proceedings of the Conference on Judaica Archives in Europe, for Archivists and Librarians, Potsdam, 1999, 11–13 July* (Paris: Nadir de l'alliance israélite universelle, 2001).

13. See James Jordan, Lisa Leff, and Joachim Schlör, "Jewish Migration and the Archive: Introduction," *Jewish Culture and History* 15, no. 1–2 (2014): 1–5.

14. See James Loeffler, *The Most Musical Nation: Jews and Culture in the Late Russian Empire* (New Haven, CT: Yale University Press, 2010).

15. See Bret Werb, "'Vu ahin zol ikh geyn?': Music Culture of Jewish Displaced Persons," in *Dislocated Memories: Jews, Music, and Postwar German Culture*, ed. Tina Frühauf and Lily E. Hirsch (New York: Oxford University Press, 2014), 75–96.

16. See "Ruth Rubin," The Ruth Rubin Legacy: Archive of Yiddish Folks Songs; https://ruthru bin.yivo.org/exhibits/show/ruth-rubin-sound-archive/who-was-ruth-rubin   (accessed July 24, 2022).

17. See Janina Wurbs, "A Treasure Trove in a Hotel Lobby-Songs of the Ben Stonehill Collection at the YIVO Sound Archives," *European Journal of Jewish Studies* 8, no. 1 (2014): 127–136.

18. See Michael O'Driscoll, "Derrida, Foucault, and the Archiviolithics of History," in *After Poststructuralism: Writing the Intellectual History of Theory*, ed. Michael O'Driscoll and Tilottama Rajan (Toronto: University of Toronto Press, 2002), 284–309.

19. See Shirli Gilbert, "Buried Monuments: Yiddish Songs and Holocaust Memory," *History Workshop Journal* 66, no. 1 (2008): 107–128.

20. See, for example, Michael Beckerman, "Postcard from New York—Trio from Terezín," *Music & Politics* 1, no. 1 (2007), https://doi.org/10.3998/mp.9460447.0001.101; and Joža Karas, *Music in Terezín, 1941–1945*, 2nd ed. (Hillsdale, NY: Pendragon Press, 2008).

21. See Graeme Skinner, "Australian Composers and Arrangers of Early Colonial Synagogue Music: New Light on Isaac Nathan, James Reichenberg, and Herman Hoelzel," *The Australian Jewish Historical Society Journal* 20, no. 2 (2011): 193–294.

22. For nineteenth-century holdings, "Hebrew" was the preferred nomenclature over "Jewish." Graeme Skinner, email to author, January 24, 2022.

23. See Graeme Skinner, "Mapping Australian Colonial Music with Trove: New Paradigms for Music Research, Teaching, and Librarianship," *Music Reference Services Quarterly* 14, no. 1–2 (2011): 1–13.

24. Bischofwerder's small archive and some of his compositions are held at the Archive of Australian Judaica at the University of Sydney; https://judaica.library.sydney.edu.au/cata log/collect3.html#bischopswerder (accessed February 5, 2022).

25. See Ken Inglis, Bill Gammage, Seumas Spark, and Jay Winter with Carol Bunyan, *Dunera Lives*, Australian History (Clayton, Victoria: Monash University Publishing, 2018).

26. See Adrian Thomas, "The Composer as Critic: Three Australian Case Studies, 1950–1975" (PhD diss., University of Queensland, 1996); and Melanie Walters, "Avant-garde or Rearguard? The Flute Music of Felix Werder: A Portfolio of Recordings and Exegesis" (PhD diss., University of Adelaide, 2016).

27. For a detailed biography, see Albrecht Dümling, "Baer, Werner," in *Lexikon verfolgter Musiker und Musikerinnen der NS-Zeit*, https://www.lexm.uni-hamburg.de/object/ lexm_lexmperson_00001347.

28. See Albrecht Dümling, *The Vanished Musicians: Jewish Refugees in Australia* (New York: Peter Lang, 2016).

29. Out of the Shadows Gala Opening Night, Verbrugghen Hall, Sydney Conservatorium of Music, August 5, 2017. Sydney Symphony Orchestra Fellows, Sydney Conservatorium of Music Symphony Orchestra conducted by Roger Benedict, https://vimeo.com/238401306.

30. Margaret Kartomi and Bronia Kornhauser, in discussion with the author, October 4, 2021.

31. See Margaret J. Kartomi, "Tracing Jewish-Babylonian Trade Routes and Identity through Music, with Reference to Seven Versions of a Song of Praise Melody," in "Silk, Spice and Shirah: Musical Outcomes of Jewish Migration into Asia c. 1780–c.1950," special issue, *Ethnomusicology Forum* 13, no. 1 (2004): 75–100; "Continuity and Change in the Music-Culture of the Baghdadi-Jews throughout Two Diasporas in the Colonial and Post-Colonial Periods: An Introduction," *Australian Journal of Jewish Studies* 16 (2002): 90–110; "Singapore, a South-East Haven: The Sephardi-Singaporean Liturgical Music of Its Jewish Community, 1841 to the Present," *Musicology Australia* 22 (1999): 3–17.

32. See Sharon Kangisser-Cohen, "Why We Chose Australia," in *Holocaust Survivors: Resettlement, Memories, Identities*, ed. Dalia Ofer, Françoise Ouzan, and Judith Tydor Baumel-Schwartz (New York: Berghahn Books, 2012), 274–292.

33. *Taʿam: The Flavours of Jewish Music in Australia*, comp. and prod. Bronia Kornhauser (Melbourne, Australia: Monash University, 2002).

34. *Out of Babylon: The Music of Baghdadi-Jewish Migrations and Beyond*, prod. Bronia Kornhauser and Margaret Kartomi (Tuscon, AZ: Celestial Harmonies, 2007)

35. At that time, the term *Sephardi* was used by the Jewish population of Australia to describe any Jews who were not part of the majority Ashkenazic ethnic grouping, which included Mizrachi Jews with no discernible links to the Spanish diaspora.

36. See Dümling, *The Vanished Musicians*. Dümling provides important accounts of Baer's and Werder's lives, based on extensive interviews with family members (and Werder himself).

37. See Adrian Dannatt and Timothy Hursley, *United States Holocaust Memorial Museum: James Ingo Freed*, Architecture in Detail (London: Phaidon, 2002).

38. See Jeshajahu Weinberg and Rina Elieli, *The Holocaust Museum in Washington* (New York: Rizzoli International Publications, 1995), 62.

39. Ibid., 182–183.

40. *Remember the Children: Songs for and by Children of the Holocaust*, with program notes by Gila Flam (Washington, DC: United States Holocaust Memorial Museum, 1991).

41. *Krakow Ghetto Notebook of Mordecai Gebirtig* (Port Washington, NY: Koch International, 1994). The original Gebirtig manuscript is held in the archives of the YIVO Institute for Jewish Research, Mordecai Gebirtig Papers, 1920–1967, RG 740 (bulk 1920–1942).

42. *Rise Up and Fight! Songs of Jewish Partisans* (Washington, DC: United States Holocaust Memorial Museum, 1996).

43. *Hidden History: Songs of the Kovno Ghetto* (Washington, DC: United States Holocaust Memorial Museum, 1997).

44. *Ballads and Broadsides: Songs from Sachsenhausen Concentration Camp, 1940–1945* (Washington, DC: United States Holocaust Memorial Museum, 2008).

45. Hans Gál, *Music Behind Barbed Wire: A Diary of Summer 1940*, trans. Anthony Fox and Eva Fox-Gál (London: Toccata Press, 2014). In a post-interview email, Bret Werb remarked that the practice of integrating the music with Gál's diary is now common when presenting the work. Bret Werb in discussion with the author, July 15, 2022.

46. Alan Lareau, "Lavender Songs: Undermining Gender in Weimar Cabaret and Beyond," *Popular Music and Society* 28, no. 1 (2005): 15–33.

47. Bret Werb, in discussion with the author, November 3, 2021.

48. Bret Werb, in discussion with the author, November 3, 2021.

49. See Bret Werb, "Fourteen Shoah Songbooks," *Musica Judaica* 20 (2013): 39–116.

50. The collection is digitally available for research on-site only. For a finding aid, see https://collections.ushmm.org/findingaids/RG-31.137_01_fnd_en.pdf.

51. See "Josima Feldschuh—a Wunderkind," Polin: Museum of the History of Polish Jews, March 15, 2021, https://polin.pl/en/josima-feldschuh-a-wunderkind (accessed February 3, 2022).

52. See Abigail Wood, "Commemoration and Creativity: Remembering the Holocaust in Today's Yiddish Song," European Judaism 35, no. 2 (2002): 44.

53. See Shirli Gilbert, Music in the Holocaust: Confronting Life in the Nazi Ghettos and Camps (Oxford: Oxford University Press, 2005).

54. See Petronella Vaarzon-Morel, Linda Barwick, and Jennifer Green, "Sharing and Storing Digital Cultural Records in Central Australian Indigenous Communities," New Media & Society 23, no. 4 (2021): 692–714.

55. See the work of Miriam Isaacs, Stonehill Jewish Song Archive, https://stonehilljewishsongs.wordpress.com/ (accessed February 3, 2022).

56. Edward T. Linenthal, "The Boundaries of Memory: The United States Holocaust Memorial Museum," American Quarterly 46, no. 3 (1994): 429.

57. Michael Bernard-Donals, "Synecdochic Memory at the United States Holocaust Memorial Museum," College English 74, no. 5 (2012): 417–436.

Select Bibliography

Dümling, Albrecht. The Vanished Musicians: Jewish Refugees in Australia. New York: Peter Lang, 2016.

Harris, Amanda. Representing Australian Aboriginal Music and Dance 1930–1970. New York: Bloomsbury Academic, 2020.

Kartomi, Margaret. "Tracing Jewish-Babylonian Identity through Music, with Reference to Seven Versions of a Song-of-Praise Melody." Ethnomusicology Forum 13, no. 1 (2004): 75–100.

Kornhauser, Bronia. "Australian Archive of Jewish Music". Australasian Music Research 4 (1999): 131–138.

Kornhauser, Bronia. "Jewish Music: Beyond Nation and Identity?" Australasian Music Research 7 (2003): 113–120.

Kornhauser, Bronia. "Songs to Heal Times Past: Miriam Rochlin's Collaborations with Immigrant Jewish Performers in Melbourne after World War II." Musicology Australia 33, no. 2 (December 2011): 223–239.

Sandmeier, Rebekka. "'. . . In die vier Winde unter dem Himmel zerstreut.' (Sacharja 2,10): Die Schallplattensammlung liturgischer Musik der Jüdischen Reformgemeinde Berlin und die Bestände im Archiv des Leo Baeck Instituts." In Traveling Sounds: Dokumentation zum 6. Berliner Salon des Leo-Baeck-Instituts am 29. April 2009, 37–45. Schriften aus dem Archiv der Universität der Künste. Berlin: Universität der Künste, 2009.

Toltz, Joseph. "Ethnography and the Empathic Imperative: Negotiating Histories in the Sydney Brundibar Project." Studies in Musical Theatre 14, no. 1 (2020): 23–36.

Toltz, Joseph. "'My Song, You Are My Strength': Personal Repertoires of Polish and Yiddish Songs of Young Survivors of the Łódź Ghetto." In Jews and Music-Making in the Polish Lands, edited by François Guesnet, Benjamin Matis, and Antony Polonsky, 393–410. Polin: Studies in Polish Jewry 32. Oxford: Littman Library of Jewish Civilization, 2020.

Toltz, Joseph. "Transcendent Innocence: Red-Riding-Hood Redeemed?" In *Creative Research in Music: Informed Practice, Innovation and Transcendence*, edited by Anna Reid, Neal Peres Da Costa, and Jeanell Carrigan, 169–177 New York: Routledge, 2021.

Toltz, Joseph, and Anna Boucher. *The First Holocaust Songbook*. Manchester: Manchester University Press, 2024.

Werb, Bret. "'Vu ahin zol ikh geyn?': Music Culture of Jewish Displaced Persons." In *Dislocated Memories: Jews, Music, and Postwar German Culture*, edited by Tina Frühauf and Lily E. Hirsch, 75–96. New York: Oxford University Press, 2014.

PART VI

SACRED AND RITUAL SPACES—עירוב / חופה/ כותל

19

REIMAGINING SPIRITUAL EXPERIENCE AND MUSIC

Perspectives from Jewish Worship in the United States

JEFFREY A. SUMMIT

RABBI Abraham Isaac Kook (1865–1935) was the first chief rabbi in Palestine under the British Mandate. Beloved for his inclusiveness of all people, respected for his rabbinic scholarship, known as both a philosopher and a mystic, Kook was a founder of the school of religious Zionism.[1] In a poem, from his collection of writing from different periods, *Orot ha-Kodesh* (Holy lights), he used the metaphor of "the fourfold song" for how Jews performed their complex identities in pre-State Israel in the tumultuous days of the First World War and the Russian Revolution: "There is one who sings the Song of Self. And within one's self, finds everything; the full of one's spiritual satisfaction within one's own fullness." Kook continues, "And there is one who sings the Song of Nation. He steps out from the circle of his private concern . . . attaches himself with gentle love to the ensemble of *kneset Yisrael*—the Jewish people, and with her sings her songs, shares in her distresses, delights in her hopes." Kook then expands the circle and writes, "And there is one who broadens further her sense of self, until it extends and expands beyond the boundary of Israel, to sing the Song of Humanity. . . . She is drawn to common destiny and yearns for humanity's sublime self-actualization." Kook then writes of the fourth song, "the Song of World-Creation," where "one unifies one's self with all existence, with all creatures, and with all worlds." Finally, Kook speaks about an integration of the four songs, "And then there is one who arises with all these songs together in concert, all parts contributing their voices, all together harmonizing their melodies. . . . The Song of Self, the Song of Nation, the Song of Humanity, the Song of World-Creation—they all symphonize together within this person at every moment and at all times."[2]

With a historical distance of nearly a century, Rabbi Benjamin J. Samuels looks back at the concept of "the fourfold song," stating that it "resounds with the competing, and often conflicting, secular socio-political movements and ideologies of the first quarter of the twentieth century—Zionism, nationalism, socialism, universalism—and yet harmonizes them within a redemptive Jewish religious framework of soulful lyricism, rabbinic reference, kabbalistic allusion, and messianic longing."[3]

While Rav Kook did not intend his metaphors in this poem to be a way to understand music and spiritual expression in Jewish worship, these four categories can be helpful in exploring an increased focus on spirituality in the early twenty-first century in Jewish congregational prayer. This chapter relies on the concept of Rav Kook's "fourfold song" to suggest a typology of categories that can be employed to consider how Jews in the twenty-first century experience music in worship—the song of self, the song of nation, the song of humanity, and the song of all existence.[4]

These four areas can be understood as expanding concentric circles—concentric eruvin—domains that move from the individual, to the Jewish people, out to all humanity, and finally, an expanding boundary encompassing all creation. The parameters of each circle or eruv contain and define their own relationship to worship and how one experiences the sacred. But in that the term *eruv* also connotes a mixture, these concentric domains are permeable, at times blending into one another and drawing meaning and power from that movement over boundaries, a movement facilitated and experienced through music.[5]

In the late nineteenth and early twentieth centuries, the study of religion focused on the concept of experience. According to Anne Taves, it was commonly held that "a certain kind of experience, whether characterized as religious, mystical, or spiritual, constituted the essence of 'religion' and the common core of the world's 'religions.'"[6] She references scholars such as Mircea Eliade, Rudolf Otto, and Gerard van der Leeuw, all of whose works have shaped the study of religion in the twentieth century.[7] When in 1902 William James published his now-classic work, *The Varieties of Religious Experience*, he understood these experiences to entail a powerful encounter with the divine. James wrote that personal religious experience "has its root and center in mystical states of consciousness" of which he described four features: ineffability, an experience that "defies expression . . . in words"; a noetic quality providing "insight into depths of truth unplumbed by the discursive intellect"; "transiency, cannot be sustained for long"; and "passivity, [as if one's] own will were in abeyance . . . as if grasped and held by a superior power."[8]

In my work—analyzing the meaning and experience of chanting Torah, and melody choice in Jewish worship, in hundreds of interviews—this is not the way Jews speak about their deep connection to Jewish worship and musical traditions, or why and how they find meaning in prayer. They do not talk about the sacred or encounters with the numinous. In these conversations, I found that cross-denominationally, many Jews were not that comfortable speaking about God. Mark Slobin observed that these Jews "do not talk about God because contemporary religious expression is primarily about themselves."[9] And yet, even at a time when religious affiliation is declining in the United States, spirituality is on the rise. A 2017 Pew Research Center Study found that 27 percent of adults think of themselves as spiritual but not religious—an increase of 8 percentage points in five years.[10] The sociologist of religion Wade Clark Roof describes spirituality as "the quest for wholeness," and references the philosopher Peter H. van Ness who speaks about spirituality as having "an outer and inter-complexion." As such, an outward spiritual orientation faces the world as an inclusive whole while an inward orientation focuses on the most vital aspects of the self.[11] Roof writes that contemporary spirituality encompasses four themes, "a source of values and meaning beyond oneself, a way of understanding, inner awareness, and personal integration."[12]

Longtime scholar of liturgy and religion at the Hebrew Union College in New York, Professor and Rabbi Lawrence A. Hoffman examined contemporary spirituality among American Jews in focus groups that he assembled while lecturing at synagogues across North America.[13] If he asked congregants for "moments when God is in your life," he discovered that "Jews don't know from God." But if he asked for "moments of profundity in your life," people replied affirmatively and gave illustrations that matched those given by parallel Christian focus groups where people identified them as God. The experience of Jews and of Christians is the same, Hoffman concluded, but Jews lack comfort with traditional spiritual language, like "God." He referenced philosopher Richard Rorty, who said that we make progress not by arguing better but by speaking differently,[14] and said, "The question is, therefore, not just how people find spirituality in prayer, but how they find a language adequate to describe their experience."[15]

In my previous research, as many Jews reflected upon the participatory music of the synagogue and their experiences chanting from the scroll of the Torah, they described meaningful encounters with forces larger than the self, connections that stood out as especially important in their lives. In describing these experiences, the language employed by Ann Taves is helpful; she focuses on "experiences deemed religious (and by extension, other things considered special) rather than 'religious experience.'"[16] Some of the worshippers I interviewed saw these experiences as positioning themselves in the flow of Jewish history, a vertical connection back through time that—even if imagined—linked them to something authentic, ancient, and true. Others spoke about the power of performing a ritual while knowing that Jews around the world were chanting the same text at the same time. In this way, the performance of sacred text enabled them to experience peoplehood, a horizontal connection to Jews around the world, bridging the isolation that many experienced in their lives. When chanting the Torah, or singing traditional prayers in Hebrew, others experienced a feeling of ownership and connection to a ritual that had been performed for thousands of years, a visceral affirmation of their membership in the Jewish people. For others, the feeling of being part of a long line of transmission—practices passed from generation to generation—created a sense of larger purpose as they taught and passed these rituals to their children. Some spoke of grasping a deeper intellectual understanding of their Judaism after embodying biblical and liturgical text in performance. When chanting sacred text, some felt a profound connection to relatives who perished in the Holocaust and saw their participation in synagogue as an affirmation that Judaism would continue to survive as a tradition. When describing these profound connections—"experiences deemed religious"—many Jews said they sensed something larger and transcendent, something that some were willing to call God.

In the changing landscape of congregational worship, if spiritual language is made accessible and understandable, more Jews are willing to use "God language" to describe their experiences. Rabbi Noa Kushner, the founding rabbi of The Kitchen in San Francisco described this work—constructing impactful worship and teaching people how to pray—as "translation not innovation."[17] Music is one of the most important vehicles for this translation. In their study of the congregation B'nai Jeshurun on Manhattan's Upper West Side, Ayala Fader and Mark Kligman focus "on the experience of God that so many congregants reported feeling during prayer."[18] They conducted their research in 2000 and 2001, and since that time, the approach of B'nai Jeshurun to music and Jewish spirituality in worship has had a deep impact both on the formation of new intentional congregations and the approach to worship in established synagogues that are exploring new ways to facilitate meaningful experiences in prayer. According to Fader and Kligman, B'nai Jeshurun's rabbis and cantor/music director Ari Priven work to create a worship experience that feels authentically Jewish while focusing on personal relevance to individuals and accomplish this "through a musically driven, emotionally engaged, and embodied form of prayer."[19] One of the congregation's rabbis, Marcelo R. Bronstein, explains: "We have to change the paradigm from the idea of God to the experience of God."[20]

This chapter grew out of conversations with Jewish prayer leaders, rabbis, cantors, and music leaders, who are focused on "the experience of God" and are building this new language of spirituality, as well as creating deeply spiritual services where music is a core component of Jewish worship. By providing opportunities to articulate spirituality, they are creating the possibility for congregants to access that experience. A number of these leaders are part of the Jewish Emergent Network, described on their website as "path-breaking Jewish communities" that, while not affiliated with mainstream denominations, share "a devotion to revitalizing the field of Jewish engagement, a commitment to approaches both traditionally rooted and creative, and a demonstrated success in attracting unaffiliated and disengaged Jews to a rich and meaningful Jewish practice."[21] These are congregations that all see, and refer to themselves, as communities, bound together not only by worship but also by educational programming, social-justice initiatives, and structures of interpersonal support. As creative and innovative as these congregations are, they represent only a sample of synagogues that are actively addressing what it means to create Jewish worship experiences that are spiritually meaningful for their congregants. There is essential research to be done with talented cantors, rabbis, and musical leaders cross-denominationally throughout North America in order to present a fuller picture of the dynamic changes that are currently impacting synagogue practice. In addition, Jews in Generation Z are using music in powerful ways in Jewish movements for environmental, political, and social justice, forms of activism that many see as an important component in their spiritual lives, an area that requires further study.

The interviews for this chapter were conducted during 2020 at the height of the COVID-19 pandemic. As such, many of these leaders were struggling with how best to conduct worship services on virtual platforms. While there is important research to be done on Jewish congregational music during the pandemic, this is not the focus of this chapter. Yet, in all of the interviews conducted for this study, these leaders spoke passionately about the loss of the ability to sing together in worship. Noa Kushner said, "not being able to actually sing and pray with my community has been like having my limbs cut off." This sense of acute loss as actual communities became virtual during the pandemic viscerally underscored the centrality of music in worship in all of my interviews.

New paradigms can be helpful as we approach and analyze this increased focus on spirituality in Jewish worship and the role of music and prayer in the religious lives of Jews today. The expanding circles of Rav Kook's fourfold song—moving from the self, to the Jewish people, to humanity as a whole, and then to all creation—encompass a broad range of the experiences described by the leaders interviewed for this chapter. While these experiences move toward a larger inclusion, harmony, and integration, they begin with the individual worshipper, the song of the self.

THE SONG OF THE SELF

In the course of the twentieth century, self-agency played an increasingly larger role in individuals' approach to religion.[22] By the late 1980s, a vast majority of Americans felt that individuals should arrive at their own religious beliefs, independent of churches or synagogues.[23] These broader trends in our culture have impacted and shaped Judaism in the United States over the past fifty years. This stress on the individual led to the primacy of the home and family in Jewish practice, places where it was easier to assert personal agency and control. The synagogue worship service, on the other hand, was under the control of religious authority, where the individual was secondary to the congregation. This is in concert with Philip Bohlman's broader perspective on the impact of congregational worship in America, where congregational song and experiences subsume the individual. But music, Bohlman writes, can be "a means of re-dressing the frequent historiographic tendency to consider religion as a primarily collective experience."[24] So too, the leaders I interviewed described how they are working to create musical experiences where the communal space of the synagogue can be a stage for personal experience, and where that experience feels real, authentic, and emotionally true.

When many Jews discuss authenticity in Jewish worship, they reference aspects of tradition—real or imagined—that have historical and cultural lineage: Hebrew liturgy, traditional *nusaḥ* (prayer chant), or tunes that are attributed back to the revelation at Mount Sinai. But the leaders spoke about another kind of authenticity, one that focused on creating and "holding" a space where participants could be emotionally authentic and personally real. Rabbi Arthur Green, scholar of Jewish mysticism, founder of the Hebrew College Rabbinical School, and one of the founders of the Havurah movement, spoke about what it meant to make the "business of prayer," in his words, real: "For me, it's about opening the heart."[25] He illustrated this with a story from his early experiences in synagogue: "I went to my grandparents' shul, a corner of Eastern Europe in Northern

New Jersey." He related that his main memory of that synagogue was Yizkor (the memorial prayers for the dead) and said that his grandmother had lost both her daughter and her only brother within two years: "She cried the whole day when she came to say Yizkor and everybody came over to comfort her. And then there was Mrs. Marcovich, who sat as quietly as a stone throughout the service, but when the rabbi read Mrs. Marcovich's husband's name from the memorial tablet, everyone knew that she was going to scream. It was emotionally real. There was room for people to feel something."

Many other leaders spoke about the importance of creating prayer communities where something "real" could occur in the course of worship. Noa Kushner reflected on real, authentic experience and used the analogy of tourists and pilgrims, a metaphor she credited to her teacher, Lawrence Hoffman. She continued, "Tourists mediate their experience with cameras and phones. But pilgrims have to get close enough to what's going on unmediated because they want a transformational experience." She explained that she was more interested in creating an experience for "pilgrims" who could bring their honest, authentic self to worship: "If that means you need to sit and cry your eyes out, that's what I want you to do. If that means you need to dress up, do that. And if you're a joker, I hope you would sit in the back and make some jokes. People should be who they really are." This approach is very different from that of large, formal synagogues where, as one joke goes, the rabbi stops the college student entering the synagogue in jeans and a tee shirt and says, "Of course, you can pray in jeans. You just can't pray *here* in jeans." Kushner explained that her reason for structuring this authentic informality was so worshippers could "catch air" and, as a congregation, "rise above the ground just a bit." She continued, "As we sing, sometimes I imagine a ladder unfolding. If we're able to do something real, the ladder will reach higher." The idea that a person can build ladders to ascend to the heavens, and that a nigun, a melody sung to vocables, can be such a ladder, has its roots in Hasidic teachings that stress the connection between music and spiritual ascent.[26]

Rabbi David Ingber, the senior and founding rabbi of Romenu, a Jewish community in Manhattan whose tag line is "Jewish life, elevated," reflected on the role of music in facilitating this kind of experience where one rises to a higher plane. He spoke about how music invites a state of change for people: "Almost every piece of music is a *madeleine de Proust*: It allows us to access memories, our lived experience, the soundtrack of our life."[27] Continuing the metaphor of food, he said, "Then, like salt to meat, it teases out the feeling and deepens the experience. Music in worship tenderizes a person's experience and makes their affective qualities rise." In this way, music becomes a catalyst for intensified feelings, drawing singular meaning from the personal experiences and life journey of the worshipper.

While these leaders stressed the importance of the emotional transformation in worship, Jewish prayer is a structured experience with a set liturgy. In Hebrew, the name of the Jewish prayerbook, the siddur, literally means "order." Those praying engage with the liturgy, whose language has been developed and structured over the past two millennium. This dynamic between the liturgy and the experiential affect that the worshippers bring to the act of prayer has been discussed throughout the development of the synagogue service.[28] As Abraham Joshua Heschel asserts, "Jewish prayer is guided by two opposite principles: order and outburst, regularity and spontaneity, uniformity and individuality, law and freedom. These principles are the two poles about which Jewish prayer revolves."[29] These "two poles" are *keva* and *kavanah*; the former meaning "set" or "fixed" generally refers to the traditional text of the liturgy, the latter referring to focused intention in prayer, the work of the heart. Much of the current discussion on spirituality in Jewish prayer focuses on the role of music to intensify kavanah in worship.

Rabbi Ebn Leader, scholar of Jewish prayer and faculty member at the Hebrew College Rabbinical School, reflected on the ability of music to heighten kavanah. By personalizing and intensifying the experience of prayer, music can serve as a commentary on the meaning of the liturgy. In this way, music functions as an "oral Torah" bringing new vibrancy to the written text of the prayerbook. Leader explained that just as Jews have both a written Torah and an oral Torah—the commentaries that make the written text alive and relevant—the same is true for prayer. He continued this analogy, equating the written Torah to the prayerbook, while the oral Torah is the music: "The role of the written Torah is to anchor you to generations past, and the purpose of the music is to anchor you to your own reality—what does this history look like when it actually exists in your life?"[30] The music of the service becomes a commentary, shaping the affective meaning of individual prayers and structuring an emotional arch over the course of the worship service.

When the "oral Torah" of music works this way, it can open the worshipper to deeper levels of understanding and devotion. Worshippers might reject or dismiss certain prayers, but music can facilitate new ways to approach and embrace the liturgy. This musical commentary can introduce new interpretations of the prayers' meanings. David Ingber commented, "You hear a new melody for a particular prayer and think, maybe sin and asking for forgiveness doesn't always have to be in this mode? Maybe I can approach this differently?" In this way, for example, the emotional affect of the music might help the worshipper reconceptualize the process of *teshuvah*, that is change, turning, or repentance, not as guilt-laden but as reflective, joyous, and positive.

While the use of music to intensify kavanah can bring new relevance to worship, the spiritual journey that the worshipper experiences between these poles of "order and outburst," to use Heschel's words, has an inherent tension that entails negotiating risk. While worship requires kavanah, this intensity can subsume a worshipper's focus and even be a distraction from saying the prayers that are obligatory in the service. In a discussion of the dynamics of prayer in the Babylonian Talmud, Berakhot 29b, Rabbi Zera commented that he could insert something new into his prayers but was afraid to do so lest he became confused.

Joey Weisenberg is a musician and the founding director of Hadar's Rising Song Institute, an organization that brings together musicians and prayer leaders with the goal of reinventing music as a communal Jewish spiritual practice. He is known for composing and popularizing the singing of nigunim in contemporary Jewish worship. Weisenberg reflected on this tension between these two poles in the experience of prayer, characterizing this process as a dialogue between "the form and the fire." He went deeper by interpreting the Hebrew word for the Jewish people, *'Ivrim*, playing on the word's root meaning, "to cross over," and connecting it to the Hebrew word "sinners," *ha'avaryanim*, those who transgress or cross over. He continued, "On Yom Kippur, when we say, [before the recitation of the Kol nidrei prayer], 'we are allowed to pray in a congregation together with the transgressors,' it's not only that we are *allowed* to pray with those transgressors, but we actually *need* the transgressors. We need the transgressive side of ourselves—the side that's willing to take the risk of crossing over some of the boundaries."[31] It is this sense of possibility on the edges, feeling the power just at the edge of the eruv, that brings the vibrancy and the "fire" to spiritual expression.

Music can be a place to negotiate a sense of creative transgression. Through song, the worshipper is able to engage in this tension—the obligation to recite the same fixed liturgy every day coupled with the obligation to bring something new and personal into prayer. Weisenberg reflected, "The norms of Jewish life tend to keep you in a box. But music is the agent, for me, that allows the boxes to disappear." This ability for music to enable the worshipper to transcend boundaries and make worship authentically real deepens the potential for impactful prayer. This concept of sacred journey is a recurring theme in American worship,[32] but here the worshipper's journey is neither exile, exodus, nor pilgrimage: this journey is focused inward, pushing against the boundaries of set liturgical structure seeking deeper personal meaning and spiritual intensity.

While the worship dynamics of kevah and kavanah have intellectual and emotional dimensions, Jewish prayer is an embodied experience. The service has a defined choreography to which the worshipper quickly becomes accustomed: standing, sitting, stepping forward and backward, bowing, and in both traditional and neo-traditional settings, shucking.[33] Even the Yiddish word for praying, *davenen*, has the connotation of swaying, rhythmic movement. When a worshipper is davening, prayer is expressed physically and, in turn, becomes known through the body.[34] Many Jewish prayer leaders come to know this intrinsically.

Joey Weisenberg spoke about how the highest level of *emunah* (faith) is an embodied experience, something we feel deep within our bones. Quoting from *Netivot Shalom* (thoughts on the Torah portion *Beshalaḥ*) by Rabbi Shalom Noah Barzofsky, the Slonimer Rebbe (1911–2000), Weisenberg described three levels of faith: "The first one is the lowest, that of the mind. The next level is the heart. But the highest level of faith is that of the body, the limbs and bones. That's when you're not even thinking or feeling, but it's vibrating through you." This Hasidic teaching asserts that when the Jewish people sang their first song together crossing the Red Sea—Who is like you, God!—they were on this highest level of faith, trembling in their bodies. In this way, the faith expressed through song is more than an emotional affect or an intellectual belief. It is an embodied expression emanating from the core of the individual connecting the worshipper back to the moment when Jewish slaves moved from bondage to freedom and coalesced into the Jewish people.

Here, the body—and as David Ingber explained, the breath—together become the locus for deeper spiritual experience. Ingber, who has taught Pilates and practices yoga, stressed that it is specifically by connecting with one's breath and locating it in the body that singing becomes a powerful, transformative experience. The singing breath enables the worshipper to access a range of emotions with more intensity: "We want the music to be stretching people in there in their affective zone—joy, sadness, it's also pathos," Ingber said that singing is the Jewish version of breath work, a kind of pranayama, the practice of breath control in yoga.

In Hebrew, the concept of breath and soul are both found in the same word, *neshamah*. The physical act of singing brings worshippers deep within their bodies, shaped by the rhythm of their breathing. During the COVID-19 pandemic, many leaders expressed how tragically ironic it was that the very thing that brought life to their communities— engaged participatory song—had become a potential source of deadly transmission. In fact, this was a time when the embodied, healing experience of song was needed more than ever.[35] Rabbi Mónica Gomery, one of the co-founders of the initiative Let My People Sing, and rabbi and music director at Kol Tzedek Synagogue, amplified this idea in a sermon on Yom Kippur 2020. She wrote, "Our resilience lies in our ability to slow down, breathe deep, and open up more space within our bodies. For millennia, Jewish rituals and practices have been designed for just that, and at their core is song."[36] Gomery stressed that living during the pandemic, a period of profound trauma, people needed to sing. She imagined a section of the Talmud the rabbis might have written if they had been living through the pandemic and been asked how do we know that when one sings alone over Zoom, the *shekhinah* (God's sheltering feminine presence) is with them? She envisioned this answer: "Because ours is a tradition that has known, intimately, the hole in the heart, the bottomless well of loss." She deepened her reflection by quoting the thirteenth-century Spanish kabbalist Abraham Abulafia, who taught that the shekhinah dwells in the cavities of the human body, the hollow places that amplify and generate sound. She concludes, "We are never alone because we are echoed."[37] In this sermon, Gomery does more than provide comfort to her congregation as they suffer loneliness and loss during a time of isolation and trauma. She teaches that each person intrinsically embodies God's presence. Congregants might feel empty or hollow, but in fact, it is in those spaces within that one experiences the resonance of holiness. Music works transformation in one's corporal being and, in doing so, open possibilities for more impactful spiritual experience.[38]

There are studies of Americans' search for spirituality that evidence a move away from institutional religion and traditional liturgy.[39] However, the spiritual experiences described by these leaders take place in the realm of structured Jewish worship and congregational affiliation. Here, leaders engage their congregants through traditional prayer but explore and find new meaning in the worship service. Creating opportunities for experiences that feel "real," where the worshipper can be their authentic selves, using music to intensify affective experience, taking risks to reach higher levels of expression while powerfully grounding their experiences in the body, these leaders open new ways to engage with and articulate spiritual experience. While for many of their congregants the sovereign self remains the arbiter of religious experience, they engage with their Judaism in the context of their congregations. This communal expression provides a broader and deeper platform for the individual, amplified by the merging of one voice with many. While they sing the song of the self, by desire and necessity, this song moves beyond that personal realm and merges with the congregation, into the song of the Jewish people.

The Song of the Jewish People

The spiritual leaders I interviewed all discussed whether Jewish worship is primarily about the experience of the individual or the larger collective. Arthur Green reflected, "What do people long for in worship? I would say that 80 percent of it is community, and 20 percent is prayer and some kind of spiritual inner work. There is some of that, but the majority of it is community." The requirement of a *minyan*, a quorum of ten adult Jews in order to say core parts of the liturgy, has long privileged the importance of the group. Yet the individual and the congregation are not always in lock step during worship. Using the metaphor of a train conductor for the *shaliah/shalihat tsibur*, the leader in prayer, might offer further insight. Everyone on a train is headed down the track in the same direction. Yet while they are on the train, the passengers do not all do the same thing at the same moment. Some stand, some sit, some walk around, some talk in the club car. The leader is there to announce where the service is, but not necessarily where the individual worshipper is in the service.[40]

To underscore this tension, Ebn Leader reflected on the dynamic between individual and communal worship. He noted that this is one of the oldest arguments in the Talmud (Babylonian Talmud, Berakhot 26b), and to illustrate how worshippers today still deal with this issue, he asked: "What does a person do when they walk in late to synagogue?" He observed that there are two standard options: "If you sit down, look at the person next to you and say, 'Oh, what page are we on?' and you open to that page and begin praying, you are a communal prayer person, that is, the main thing that's happening in the service is the action of the community." He continued, "If on the other hand, you come in, you sit down, look at the person next to you and say, 'Oh, you guys are two minutes before the Amidah. I'll do these key prayers to catch up.' Then, you're a person focused on individual prayer."[41] The question is whether the individual serves communal prayer or public prayer exists to serve the needs of the individual. While the "song of the self" is very much about the individual's prayer experience, it is the collective that both amplifies individual expression and creates the necessary structure, locus, and set times that support Jewish worship.

Joey Weisenberg reflected on this tension and noted that this is not only about how one views the religious obligations connected to prayer. It is also about whether one finds meaning in individual experience or group experience, and how the worshipper negotiates between the two poles: "There is this constant interplay between the plurality and the individual, and that is what makes prayer rich. Some of us are naturally hermits, and it's helpful to move toward the collective from time to time. Others can't even think about being alone and might need to learn how to be alone in the middle of the congregation." While discussions about religious experience have privileged and focused on the individual, these congregational leaders stressed that a core aspect of Jewish prayer is only found in the experience of the collective.

The power of song to forge a group of individuals into a collective has long been recognized. From the use of music in movements for racial and social justice, to labor organizing and political initiatives, organizers have learned that the act of blending voice and breath creates a singular, visceral bond among people. It is now common practice in liberal Jewish institutions to begin a study session by singing a nigun together, a practice that I have used in my undergraduate ethnomusicology classes. Students are more willing to speak openly, take risks, and listen once they have joined together in song. Yet, the leaders I interviewed took this power of music to a higher level. Mónica Gomery observed that it was specifically through song that the Jews coalesced into a people, after the exodus from Egypt. She references a midrash (Shemot Rabbah 23:4), which teaches that "Shirat hayam" (The song of the sea) was the first song ever sung to God and until that moment of liberation there was no possibility to sing as a community: "That song only emerged from this tremendous formative experience when the group of Israelite slaves were forged into a people."[42] Gomery said that the act of singing together allows for the dissolution of the individual self: "Song is our language for being the children of Israel, for being a people, for being a family." She stressed that through song, Jews express themselves—and experience themselves—as an interconnected, collective body.

In fact, the only opportunity that many congregants have to sing in a group is in synagogue worship. This experience of the collective is especially impactful in a culture that puts so much stress on the empowered individual. In liberal Jewish congregations, where the individual often functions as the arbiter of Jewish observance and practice, collective singing opens congregants to a different experience where primary value is placed on their synagogue community. Gomery said that one of the most profound lessons congregants learned by singing together in worship is that the collective is more important than the individual. She explained that after services, she would often receive conflicting feedback from congregants: "Somebody needs the prayers to be faster, or slower. Somebody wants new tunes and somebody wants old tunes. Somebody loves this and hates that." It was impossible to construct a service that met each congregant's personal needs. Gomery observed that the core issue was how to build communities where individual preferences were not at the center of the worship experience. She said that the experience of singing together can condition participants to compromise. Congregants learned how to yield and make space for others. Prayer, Gomery said, is a "dance" where the worshipper both needed to find a comfortable space for themselves while surrendering their individuality and accepting that one's desires and preferences are not always met. Noa Kushner also stressed that part of the emphasis on group participation through song was teaching the importance—and the power—of compromise: "The process is a way of saying that this worship space is not about your personal idiosyncrasies. There is plenty of room for that in your daily lives." Kushner said that in the synagogue, worshippers had the luxury of entering a communal chamber and leaving the intensity of self-focus behind.

In the late twentieth and early twenty-first centuries, there are many ways that American culture supports empowered individuals as they fulfill their personal needs and values. Technology has facilitated the increase in personal agency in our society, and people have learned that social media can amplify their personal opinions and expressions in any discourse. It is common to look to the internet when one has religious questions, asking "Rav Google" for an answer rather than meeting with one's congregational rabbi. While technology has created new avenues for education and personal expression, it has also challenged traditional structures of authority and the primacy of local Jewish communities. Conversely, participatory song provides a balance, an active way to experience, and model, the value of the collective. Many of these leaders felt that the give-and-take learned in the course of communal singing taught lessons that were a prerequisite for cooperative, functioning communities.

One of the steps in establishing that kind of participation was creating an atmosphere where worshippers could overcome their self-conscious preconception that singing belonged to trained, professional musicians. "We're not here to sound good. We're here to reach for something much deeper that happens when we're all in song together. It's about learning that each of us is needed," stressed Gomery. She continued, stating that congregants needed to let go of the idea that a person either was, or was not, a singer. In this participatory experience people came to see themselves as "co-creators," as part of the larger whole. In this way, creating music together in worship can be liberating and healing, transforming how participants understand the role and function of music in the synagogue.

In my cross-denominational research on music and melody choice in Jewish worship in the late 1990s, performance had given way to participation as a value embraced simultaneously by congregants and leaders in all of the worship communities I studied. This move toward participation took many forms, including the creation of "break-away" communities that stressed congregational singing, a restructuring of congregational leadership, and the adoption of new musical repertoires. But the leaders interviewed for this chapter conceptualized and discussed the impact of participatory singing in new ways. Such congregational singing moved the focus from "front of the room" performance to, in Gomery's words, "democratized singing." And like in any working democracy, each individual's voice is powerful in the way it affirms one's individual expression while amplifying the larger power of the collective. Noa Kushner saw this approach to congregational music as one of the differences between going to a concert and being engaged with music in worship: "Art provides ultimate freedom but religion, at the end of the day, is tethering." She explained how the personal relationships among congregants are grounding, an experience of belonging underscored by the responsibilities worshippers felt, both to one another and to the tradition. Kushner stressed that worship was able to "rise" specifically because the community was bound together through commitment and obligation. Music in a concert could be a soaring experience, but it could not provide a solid place for participants to land, held by the webs of connection that a worship community was able to provide.

Similarly, in the course of his research with synagogues throughout the United States, Lawrence Hoffman explored the deeper factors that made synagogue worship meaningful. Participatory congregational music, Hoffman said, builds interpersonal connections among congregants:

> In shared music, particularly, worshipers appreciate the extent to which relationships matter. The music underscores the way they, and those assembled with them, have committed their lives to something important, not just to their synagogue, but to the causes for which the worship service—prayers, music, sermon and all—stands.

Such connection challenges current analysis on the decline of civic engagement in American society. While some scholars have argued that religious beliefs and sentiments in the United States were defined more by the empowered individual than by institutional affiliation,[43] the perspectives of these prayer leaders show that even as congregants are concerned with their own personal journeys, such experiences happen especially powerfully in the context of a worshipping community.

It was specifically the experience of recognizing the power of the collective that opened worshippers to think beyond their own narrow vision and personal concerns. The impact of these webs of connection was greater than simply valuing community: it provided a lens through which congregations could see beyond themselves, and even consider the existence of a higher power. Sharon Brous, founding rabbi of the congregation IKAR in Los Angeles, spoke about the role of music in prayer to create horizontal connections among members of their community. It was only after experiencing these powerful personal associations that they were able to conceptualize something larger than the self. She said, "It's hard for a lot of people to imagine a vertical connection. They bring cynicism and obstacles to really connecting with something bigger than themselves, with God." But she stressed that when congregants experienced powerful horizonal connections in worship, they were able to move beyond their protective cynicism.[44]

Brous told the story of a man in their community who was experiencing a painful divorce and was present one Friday night when the congregation broke into joyous dance and song celebrating a couple who had just become engaged. She worried that the couple's joy might deepen this man's sadness and pain. Instead, he joined enthusiastically in the dance. When she approached him after services, he replied that the couple had what everybody wants and asked, "Why wouldn't I dance with them?" Brous reflected, "This man overcame his own heavy-heartedness. The couple's love didn't undermine his own truth—Instead, it affirmed his own humanity as we sang and danced together." Brous called this "the horizontal connection in worship" that afforded people the opportunity to move beyond themselves, to sense others' joy, pain, loss, and love, an experience that was truly the antidote to loneliness. She said that by being in conversation with each other through song, these congregants are sustained and enriched by the life experience of the collective.

These horizontal bonds do more than create bonds among members of a congregation. They extend to connect worshippers to diverse Jewish communities around the world. Many of these emerging Jewish communities draw their musical repertories from diverse Jewish sources, extending beyond what is often referred to as "Ashkenormative tradition," that is, music that privileges the dominant Ashkenazi traditions in the United States and assumes its primacy in Jewish worship. B'nai Jeshurun describes its music as a "rich kaleidoscope of Jewish diversity," and all of these emerging congregations draw heavily from Sephardic and Mizrachi traditions as well as contemporary Jewish composers in Israel and the United States. David Ingber spoke about how music expanded these connections to Jews throughout the world, amplifying worshippers' ownership of their Jewish identity and creating a connection with their ancestors. He said, "People have a tribal need, a need to be part of a people. When music has Jewish context and content, they sense their personal story is part of a larger story." He continued and said that if a congregant had only grown up with Ashkenazi traditions, and then heard a Sephardic version of a familiar prayer, or Iraqi Torah chant, it opened them to the diversity of Jewish culture. The music underscored that their personal connection with the Jewish people extended far beyond the boundaries of their particular congregation. Joey Weisenberg also reflected on the subtle ways that musical choice conveyed association with different Jewish communities and, with that, brought worshippers to the experiences core to those particular groups: "How you sing, and how you speak, has encoded meaning." He continued, "When I close my eyes while davening, I default to Ashkenazi Hebrew. That pronunciation brings up a set of feelings that were transmitted to me, and then I can become a vessel and transmit it onwards."[45] He continued, speaking about the linguistic coding that subtly conveyed association with particular Hasidic groups:

> When you sing a nigun, a wordless melody, you have a choice of which syllables [vocables] to use. If you're singing with Chabadniks, you might be more likely to sing, "yum a moi moi." Whereas, the Modzitzers are going to be singing "bim bam," and then some of us are singing "lai, lai lai." These mean nothing, and yet, they are loaded with meaning. Sing the wrong nonsense syllable, and we quickly demonstrate our outsider status.

The ability to know and recognize these coded distinctions in the performance of Jewish prayer deepened these horizontal connections as worshippers came to a fuller understanding of the rich complexity of Jewish culture.

Once experienced, there was tremendous power in affirming these shared connections. Weisenberg observed that worshippers wanted to put their whole being into the act of prayer and come together in a recognition of the power of their shared experience. This could be felt viscerally in how the congregation responded together at a prayer's conclusion: "People just want to say a hardy amen." He said that this is the essence of what people want to experience in community: "We're trying to feel this depth—not just from our heads and our hearts, but out of our guts, in our *kelayos* (kidneys, Ashkenazi pronunciation of Hebrew, *kelayot*).[46] People want to dig into their inner being and let their deepest feelings out where they can merge with the feelings of others." In this way, the journey inward is only the first step in a more expansive experience, amplified by horizontal connections—interpersonal, intergenerational, and to the Jewish people as a whole.

Just as a "hearty amen" conveyed the essence of shared congregational experience, David Ingber stressed that the real power of communal worship was experienced in the silence after the singing stopped. He called this process "prayformance" and explained, "Prayformance is the art of stirring and then inviting people to store what has been stirred. Stir and then store." Like Ingber, many leaders discussed how an essential part of a song's power was created in the control of the silence held together at the conclusion of the singing rather than, in Inger's words, "spilling it out," and wasting that moment by clapping, talking, or playing instrumental flourishes. Mónica Gomery also expressed that after singing in harmony, the power of community was felt most intensely by "being alone together," silently turning inward while being part of a larger community. Lawrence Hoffman reflected similarly on the power of holding the space after the music stopped: "It's the feeling of everybody converging on a melody, a song, the harmony where a group has coalesced and you don't want it to end. But then, it's about savoring the silence. Because how often in life do we get to be silent together?"

This power of silence is experienced in other religious traditions as well. In her ethnography of the Sufi ritual of Sama' as practiced by the Nematollahi order in Toronto, Katayoun Ghanai speaks about the role of "focused silence" in the ritual.[47] She describes how the music begins slowly and then accelerates during the ritual. When it reaches its peak, the music stops and the assembled hold a silence that is understood to be a specific part of the ritual. Ghanai explains that this practice of music and silence in a group has a profound impact on the participants: they experience an altered state, a trance that helps them "feel lighter, to have a clearer mind and less ego," as well as "to overcome the emotional burdens of daily life."[48] So too, Jewish tradition has long recognized the power of silence. In the Midrash (Shemot Rabah 29:9) Rabbi Abbahu quotes Rabbi Yochanan, who taught that in the moment that the Torah was given, the world fell perfectly silent: no bird twittered, the sea did not roar, even the angels stopped their continuous praise. Only when the whole world was in silence were the Jewish people able to hear and experience God's revealed presence.

The silence that these prayer leaders discuss is not the absence of sound: it is the defining moment when the swelling sound of the collective has ceased. That shared experience of quiet underscores and contains the music. The silence has been created by the song and, as such, is an integral and transformative aspect of the music experience. It is this creative, generative silence that follows and holds the collective musical expression of the congregation, the song of the Jewish people.

THE SONG OF ALL HUMANITY

When I was a song leader in Jewish youth group in the mid-1960s, some of the most important music in my formative years, music that framed and defined my experience as a Jew, was not Jewish music. Judah Cohen writes that when campers at the Reform Movement's Oconomowoc summer camp first heard "The Hammer Song" ("If I Had a Hammer") in a secular setting in the mid-1960s, they said "this is our song!—'The Hammer Song' is Jewish!"[49] So too, a repertoire of songs from the civil rights movement defined my experience as much as any liturgical selection or Israeli song we sang in the National Federation of Temple Youth. Songs such as "Follow the Drinking Gourd," "Oh, Freedom," and "We Shall Overcome" were part of my Jewish soundscape. This music signified the core values that were taught in liberal Jewish youth movements at that time: a passion for racial justice, courage to take a moral stand, and a belief that the Jewish tradition was actively committed to positive social change for all. Partly, the inclusion of this repertoire into Jewish contexts rests on the fact that that the American Jewish experience is essentially an American experience.[50] But it also grows out of a larger focus in liberal Judaism stressing that all humanity was created in the image of the divine, a teaching that is reinforced by rabbis' sermons, congregational study groups, and in the music of communal worship.

The leaders I interviewed believed that while their congregational worship was grounded in being distinctively Jewish, the experience should open participants to a much larger vision of human connection. David Ingber spoke about why people were drawn to worship at Romemu: "People come to be human and the Jewish worship service, in its particular way, reminds them of that." As the community prays for people who are sick and remembers people who have died, congregants experience a sense of "collaborative vulnerability," a feeling that is reinforced by the music in worship. Ingber explained that congregants knew that they needed the person next to them to create a greater sense of beauty. But this experience had an impact beyond the immediacy of worshipping and singing together, extending to their actions and interactions outside of the congregation. Through deep musical participation, worshippers came to understand that they had a responsibility to be actively present in the larger world. In this way, part of the power of worship was that it enabled congregants to situate their place in "the tapestry of humanity" and realize they had a role to play in "a more expansive collective." Ingber concluded, "They want to come to synagogue and feel *Jewishly* human." While this experience of worship is enriched by its particularism, it aspires to the universal.

Worshippers' feelings of connection and empathy deepened as they realized they were singing and praying with others who held a diverse range of life experiences. Sharon Brous also spoke about how music can help worshipers access their vulnerability in a way that provides a deeper connection to the holiness of all humanity. She said, "At IKAR, at any moment in the room, there's grief and there's love fulfilled. There's new life and there's loss. There's someone in the room who is at the edge between life and death and there's someone who feels totally centered and profoundly grateful." Brous stressed that their worshipping community was able to encompass and contain those powerful emotions and experiences, an expression best manifested in their participatory music, a time when "all of our voices are part of a holy chorus."

At IKAR, and at many of these congregations, the worship space itself is arranged to facilitate that connection. Congregants sit so that everyone in the room can see one another and everyone can be seen. When worshippers see one another's faces and sing together, they begin to understand the range of life experiences, emotions, and transitions that are held in the room. They then feel that they are taking part in something greater than a particular worship service. Brous said that singing together as a community enabled worshippers to move beyond their separate selves and that experience of connection engendered a sense of mutual responsibility and the potential for positive personal transformation: "I often think about what it means to have all of that openheartedness and vulnerability in one space and time—each person begins to realize that their presence could be a source of healing for someone else, even someone who they don't know." Brous explained that when individuals become acutely aware of their place in the worshipping congregation, that experience opens "a sense of possibility, that collectively, I think is God." While Judaism stresses the credal belief that God is One, which is to say that God is ultimately about a sense of unity and oneness, communal singing is one of the few accessible ways to understand that truth experientially. The fluid engagement of a worshipper creating music in a group offers a singular possibility for the individual to simultaneously perceive one's own voice and hear it merge, join, and disappear into the collective, underscoring the connection to a greater harmony.

Scholars describe Judaism at the beginning of the twenty-first century as being individually centered, focused on the self rather than on the collective.[51] Yet, in the interviews conducted for this chapter, leaders stressed the power that they, and their congregants, experienced in prayer when they came to see themselves as a valuable, and valued, part of a greater whole. Rabbi Sharon Cohen Anisfeld, former dean of Hebrew College's Rabbinical School and current president of Hebrew College, spoke about how prayer, and the music of worship, enabled her to feel the sanctity of being a part of something larger. She told this story: "I was teaching [the fourth blessing of the Sabbath morning Amidah] *Yiśmaḥ Moshe bematnat ḥelḳo* (Moses rejoiced in the gift of his portion/his part) and had just been sharing a Hasidic teaching that stresses we are all just a part, a *ḥelek*—we're not complete without each other."[52] Anisfeld continued, explaining that it is one thing to teach a text: it can be a very different experience when one sings that text in prayer. She said that when they came to the portion of the service where the congregation sang that verse as part of the liturgy, she was overpowered with emotion as she heard those words in an entirely new way:

> I've thought a lot about the importance of experiencing one's "partialness"—but it has usually been connected to accepting one's limitations, vulnerabilities, insecurities, jealousies—all the ways that a person can feel diminished. But to connect that to joy was a revelation for me! I understood that if you can't truly embrace your partialness, your helek-ness, then how can you feel a part of anything?

Anisfeld explained that accepting one's partialness is the only way to open the gates of the heart to the joy of belonging to a more expansive collective.

It is through the specific act of making music together that being a part can be seen as valuable. The individual need not feel lessened but rather supported and amplified by the group. Anisfeld continued, "In the swell and the power, the joy of harmony, the whole experience is lifted up and made more beautiful by every voice that is contributing. Through the music, we experience this lesson of our worth and the fact that each of us is really a contributing part of a much larger whole. It's a lesson that in so many ways we spend our whole lives trying to learn." While that experience was centered on congregational music, the act of singing together taught profound spiritual lessons about how to construct a meaningful life of generative interpersonal connection. Similarly, Mónica Gomery observed that while congregants focus on music, the issues at stake are much larger: "How do we learn to be with ourselves and with others?" In their own ways, the leaders all referenced these worship dynamics—the embodied contribution of one's voice and breath, the negotiation entailed in joining with others to create harmony, a complex tapestry, creations of palpable but ethereal power, to feel oneself to be a valuable and necessary part of the whole. Many worshippers entered these communities as individuals following the particular path of Jewish worship, but then found themselves singing the song of all humanity.

THE SONG OF ALL EXISTENCE

In the age of the Anthropocene, spirituality increasingly encompasses humanity's relationship with the natural world. Jeff Todd Titon writes that this idea is characteristic of many religious traditions and states, "If all beings are connected, then all are related; that is, all beings are our kin." He continues, saying that knowing the world through sound "opens a space for empathy, sociability, and a participatory public ecology."[53] Humanity's connection to "the earth and its fullness," *ha'arets umelo'ah*, as one congregational leader quoted from Psalm 24:1, is an increasingly important component in Jewish spirituality. In the past forty years, the movement of eco-Judaism has grown significantly, with conferences, retreat centers, summer camps, powerful activism, interfaith work, and a developing musical repertoire.[54]

Eco-spirituality extends beyond the connection with other human beings, expanding worshippers' understanding of their place in relation to all creation. This entails a reformulation of our relationship to the natural world, focusing on obligation, kinship, and responsibility as opposed to personal liberty and economic prosperity.[55] Sharon Cohen Anisfeld described how worship can open congregants to confront this responsibility: "When a prayer experience is deeply moving it starts to build a bridge to something beyond ourselves and then we ask a question: What is that thing and what does it ask of me?" Anisfeld referenced one of the most moving experiences she ever had in worship, as the congregation sang the prayer, Ahavah rabah (Great love): "I was filled with an overwhelming sense of being on the receiving end of so much love in my life. There was an awareness of all life and living beings—the blessings of existence. It made me overflow with tears, and I thought: 'How can I possibly live my life in response to that? How do I love the world back enough to do justice to all that I have received?" The leaders discussed a range of worship experiences in which they, and their congregants, felt a connection to the larger physical world. In these experiences, they moved from a narrow sense of privileging their own well-being toward a greater obligation to value and protect all creation. Many of these leaders used natural imagery—water, waves, wind, the rhythms of change—to convey these experiences with holiness.

In a world where our lives—and the health of our planet—depend on water, leaders referenced examples of how Jewish liturgy and teaching use images of water to convey divine power and life-giving sustenance. From the teaching in the Psalms that God's power can be found in the mighty breaking waves of the ocean (Psalm 93) to the image of the Torah as life-giving waters (Babylonian Talmud, Bava Kamma 82a.), Jewish tradition connects water to a conception of the divine. So too, water is seen as an agent of personal and spiritual transformation, both in the experience of ritual immersion in the "living waters" of the mikveh, and on a larger scale, in the Exodus story of redemption as Jewish slaves are transformed into a people when passing through the birth canal of the parting waters of the Red Sea. Anisfeld continued, "The living waters are everywhere and the question is: are our wells blocked up or not?"[56] She continued, "There are times when we feel connected, or not connected, to this source of life, depleted or not depleted." Anisfeld stressed that those living waters are always present and that every person, in their own way, is trying to find how to access them. She said that for her, it was the music that opened up the channels as she was carried by the waves of the music. Anisfeld explained that she came to experience God in this way through participatory singing in prayer: "Music is like water in the sense that it is flowing over you and through you. You can enter in, as opposed to standing apart. Both music and water allow for the experience of immersion—you can lose yourself." Rabbi Lizzi Heydemann, founding rabbi of Mishkan Chicago, spoke similarly about the flow of worship and how one can feel swept up by forces larger than the self:

> I studied religion and was introduced to the language of collective effervescence, and the sense of the numinous and I think that's what is happening. It's feeling that you are part of a swell and something is happening in the room. And then afterwards, you say, "Did that just really happen? It almost feels like God was in this place, and I did not know."[57]

These connections between music and water—a surge of power, depth, movement, liquid waves of sound—offer rich imagery as worshippers articulate spiritual experience. Ecological consciousness has long been associated with spirituality. Roger S. Gottlieb describes how early conservationism developed from a religious sense that the earth was God's creation and should not be despoiled.[58] So too, the wilderness is often seen as a locus for religious experience, awe, wonder, and revelation.[59] At a time when our fragile planet is increasingly imperiled, these experiences of eco-spirituality are accessible, relevant, and impactful for worshippers. These images of music as a natural force—like water or wind—create language for the individual to understand and articulate the feelings of being immersed in, and connected to, the larger world. This state of flow, to use Mihaly Csikszentmihalyi's concept, a feeling of intense focus, deep immersion, and transcendent harmony, moves the worshipper to experience the world and themselves from a more integrated and engaged vantage point.[60]

Music also has the ability to connect worshippers to processes of change, an essential component of the natural world. In my previous research, I spoke to many congregants who would come to services religiously every week to make sure that nothing in the service was ever changed. But in fact, dynamic communities would regularly change and introduce new music. Coming to terms with that process provided opportunities for spiritual growth on deeper levels. Mónica Gomery observed that nothing is static or constant in life: "Part of the spiritual learning of our relationship to God is to have an enduring relationship to change, to process and transformation." She explained how the experience of congregational singing could open worshippers to that truth: "If we're not attached to the 'right way' to do it, or 'my way' to do it, or the things that I like and don't like, then we become available to our actual experience" as it changes over time. Gomery believed that music could be the ultimate tool in a congregation's spiritual toolbox, a way to teach congregants about other things that cannot be seen but have the ability to impact and move the worshipper. In this way, music is like the wind. These things that move us but cannot be seen have the power to cultivate our relationship to mystery—which, she said, "Is also about God." The dynamics of musical change—inherent both in the music itself, and in the rhythms of a worshipping congregation—mirror life transformations. Through the interactive process of singing together, worshippers come to appreciate and understand deeper elemental transformations, the wonder and ineffable nature of the universe.

It made little difference if participants and leaders named these experiences as religious experiences, experiences deemed religious, or profound realizations in the course of Jewish prayer. The power of congregational song brought them into a larger harmony—with themselves, with the congregation, with the world writ large. Sharon Brous believed that the goal of music in prayer went far beyond the act of bringing people into sacred conversation with each other. Ultimately, the goal was to break through the bonds of the self, "creating access to something beyond any of us or all of us." It was specifically the experience of transcending personal, communal, and anthropocentric boundaries that the worshipper came to know God's omniscient presence. So too, Joey Weisenberg reflected that the act of singing together aspired to allow worshippers to feel in tune with the deepest parts of themselves and connect to the fullness of creation. In this way, he said, one's deepest spiritual expression became: "Here I am. I am a part of the world, with the world, at the world's mercy. I am part of the interdependence of all life." The song of all existence brings the worshipper into encounter with the complex, interlocking polyphony of creation. The larger forces of music—swell, flow, waves, harmonic connections—transport the worshipper to a higher vantage point, where the self is perceived as an integrated, valued, and sacred part of the fullness of existence.

ALL SONGS IN ONE ENSEMBLE

At the conclusion of their study on spirituality at B'nai Jeshurun, Ayala Fader and Mark Kligman asked the congregation's rabbis to reflect and comment on the findings of their report. Together, Rabbis J. Rolando Matalon, Marcelo R. Bronstein, and Felicia L. Sol stressed that it was not possible to understand Jewish spirituality at BJ if one just focused narrowly on Sabbath services. They observed that when visitors came to their services, they were moved by the number of people in attendance as well as the beauty and intensity of worship: "But what they don't know, what they don't see, is that this experience is created by the myriad of deeds that take place daily, building and strengthening the fabric of the community and feeding back into the vitality of the service."[61] These rabbis go on to stress that hundreds of people in their congregation are engaged together every day in social-justice projects—visiting the sick, comforting the bereaved, housing the homeless, feeding the hungry, and participating in literacy programs, as well as in Jewish study and the communal work of running the congregation. These rabbis emphasized that they are constantly involved in teaching "a Judaism in which we live our lives as a response to the question "what does God ask of us?"[62] Worship on the Sabbath became a culmination and celebration of this committed participation, as well as a gathering place to seek energy and inspiration for the week to come.

This truth was reiterated by all of the religious leaders I interviewed. They stressed that there are additional aspects of congregational life that undergird and create the opportunity for such integrated spiritual experience through music. While their successful emerging congregations are known for their impactful approaches to music, spirituality, and prayer, all of these leaders stressed that social justice, committed community engagement, active Torah study, and the cultivation and support of real relationships, as well as a broad-based ownership of the congregational experience, were key to building authentic connection among members. The music in these congregations then relied on leaders and worship teams who were highly skilled at creating and holding space for community participation. The experience of singing together was both deeply grounded in the interactions of the congregation and broadly supported by members' communal engagement.

It is noteworthy that while Rav Kook's fourfold song speaks about people who have different approaches to expressing and performing their identities—the song of the self, the song of the Jewish people, the song of humanity, and the song of all existence—Kook never privileges one song over another. All of those voices are valued and necessary in a congregation. It is only in their coming together, with "all parts contributing their voices, all together harmonizing their melodies. One with another creating polyphonic vitality and life," that they create "a song of holiness." Indeed, Rav Kook ends his poem "The Fourfold Song" emphasizing integration.

Referencing the Jewish legal code, the *Shulhan Arukh*, Joey Weisenberg said, "when leading prayer, if one only sings to hear their own voice, that is a travesty."[63] He quoted

Rav Naḥman of Bretslav, who taught that the job of the leader in prayer is to consider each person in the room because every person has a point of goodness: "The leader's job is to link those points together and turn them into a nigun. They each hold one note, but if you put them together, then they turn into a melody."[64] While William James saw religious experience as individuals approaching the divine "in their solitude,"[65] all of the experiences examined in this chapter take place in the context of worshipping congregations, first centered in individual experience but moving outward to encompass ever-larger concentric circles of connection, created, brought together, and facilitated by the music of the service.

Eruv is the strangest of boundaries. While in Jewish law an eruv delineates a space where one can carry on the Sabbath, its root meaning is "mixture." It is a boundary that allows one to extend and blend private and public space, creating expanding, permeable concentric domains. An eruv positively impacts the individual, for example, allowing a worshiper to carry house keys or parents to push children in strollers on the Sabbath. But in empowering individuals, it facilitates community, enabling people to congregate together and families to transport food to join with friends for Sabbath meals. It is a fence that does not separate, a border that impacts the individual by allowing for greater contact and deeper communal connection. So too, the expanding circles delineated in Rav Kook's poem are not meant to be hard boundaries. Each song can permeate the next and Kook teaches that it is specifically in their integration that one finds holiness. When viewed as categories of contemporary religious experience, these musical expressions move and flow into one another—each song adding depth and richness to the next, pulling together many separate notes to create melody and harmony.

NOTES

1. For a biography of Abraham Isaac Kook during the British Mandate, see Yehuda Mirsky, *Rav Kook: Mystic in a Time of Revolution* (New Haven, CT: Yale University Press, 2019).
2. Abraham Isaac Kook, *Orot ha-Kodesh*, trans. Benjamin J. Samuels, "'Shir Meruba':* Rav Kook's "The Fourfold Song," *Tradition: A Journal of Orthodox Jewish Thought* June 25, (2020), https://traditiononline.org/the-best-rav-kooks-fourfold-song/ (accessed November 10, 2020).
3. Samuels, *"Shir Meruba"*. While each of these movements has aspects in common with Kook's four songs, I do not equate these movements and ideologies with Kook's four songs in this chapter.
4. While Samuels translates the fourth song as "Song of World-Creation," in this chapter, I use the translation "the song of all existence," in that he describes this song as encompassing "all existence, all creatures and all worlds."
5. For a comprehensive examination of Western ideas about the nature of experience, see Martin Jay, *Songs of Experience: Modern American and European Variations on a Universal Theme* (Berkeley: University of California Press, 2005).
6. Ann Taves, *Religious Experience Reconsidered: A Building-Block Approach to the Study of Religion and Other Special Things* (Princeton, NJ: Princeton University Press, 2009), 3.

7. See Mircea Eliade, *The Sacred and the Profane: The Nature of Religion*, trans. W. R. Trask (New York: Harcourt, 1987 [1957]); Rudolf Otto, *The Idea of the Holy* (London: Oxford University Press, 1958 [1923]); G. van der Leeuw, *Religion in Essence and Manifestation* (1933, repr. Princeton, NJ: Princeton University Press, 1986).

8. See William James, *The Varieties of Religious Experience* (1902, repr. New York: The New American Library, 1958), 292–294.

9. Mark Slobin, in discussion with the author, December 1999. Also see Summit, *The Lord's Song*, 152.

10. See Michael Lipka and Claire Gecewicz, "More Americans now say they're spiritual but not religious," Pew Research Center, September 6, 2017, https://www.pewresearch.org/fact-tank/2017/09/06/more-americans-now-say-theyre-spiritual-but-not-religious/ (accessed March 21, 2021).

11. Wade Clark Roof, "Modernity, the Religious and the Spiritual," *The Annals of the American Academy of Political and Social Science* 558, no. 1 (1998): 215, 216.

12. Wade Clark Roof, *Contemporary American Religion* (New York: MacMillan Reference Books, 1999), 34, 35.

13. Hoffman co-founded Synagogue 2000, an interdenominational initiative to transform synagogues into spiritual and moral centers for the twenty-first century.

14. Richard Rorty, *Contingency, Irony, and Solidarity* (Cambridge: Cambridge University Press, 1989), 7.

15. Lawrence Hoffman, in discussion with the author, November 18, 2020. All quotes without citations are from ethnographic interviews conducted on the virtual platform Zoom in the fall of 2020. The first time a person is quoted, their title and position are listed. Subsequent quotes only reference the person's name.

16. Taves, *Religious Experience Reconsidered*, xiii.

17. Noa Kushner, in discussion with the author, December 7, 2020. The Kitchen and other communities mentioned in this chapter—Let My People Sing, IKAR, and Mishkan Chicago—provide in-depth descriptions of their aims on their websites.

18. Ayala Fader and Mark Kligman, "The New Jewish Spirituality and Prayer: Take BJ, For Instance." *S3K Report*, no. 7 (November 2009): 2.

19. Ibid.

20. Ibid., 3.

21. See *The Jewish Emergent Network*; http://www.jewishemergentnetwork.org (accessed March 21, 2021). Also see Steven M. Cohen, J. Shawn Landres, Elie Kaunfer, and Michelle Shain, "Emergent Jewish Communities and their Participants: Preliminary Findings from the 2007 National Spiritual Communities Study" sponsored by The S3K Synagogue Studies Institute & Mechon Hadar (November 2007), https://www.synagoguestudies.org/wp-content/uploads/2008/10/NatSpirComStudyReport_S3K_Hadar.pdf (accessed March 21, 2021).

22. See Steven M. Cohen and Arnold M. Eisen, *The Jew Within: Self, Family and Community in America* (Bloomington: Indiana University Press, 2000), 13–42.

23. The Gallup Organization, *The Unchurched American* (Princeton, NJ: Princeton Religious Research Center, 1989), 31.

24. Philip V. Bohlman, "Prayer on the Panorama: Music and Individualism in American Religious Experience," in *Music in American Religious Experience*, ed. Philip V. Bohlman, Edith L. Blumhofer, and Maria M. Chow (New York: Oxford University Press, 2006), 237.

25. Arthur Green, in discussion with the author, October 28, 2020.

26. Kalonymus Kalman Shapira, *To Heal the Soul: The Spiritual Journal of a Chasidic Rebbe*, trans. and ed. Yehoshua Starrett (New York: Rowman and Littlefield, 1995), section 36, 119, 120.

27. David Ingber, in discussion with the author, November 13, 2020.

28. The rabbis in the Talmud felt so strongly about the importance of kavanah that when they discussed the recitation of the central prayer in the morning and evening service, the Shema, they said that if one lacks focused intention when reciting the prayer, one does not fulfill the obligation to pray (Babylonian Talmud, Berakhot 13a). Maimonides, who was well known for distrusting the place of music in prayer, said that prayer without kavanah is not prayer at all and stated that if one prayed without kavanah, one had to go back and repeat the prayer with focused attention (Mishneh Torah, Tefillah 4:15, 16). Even though Maimonides' view was disputed by later commentators, Joseph Caro's sixteenth-century legal code the *Shulḥan Arukh* stressed that it was better to do a little supplication with kavanah, than a lot without it (*Shulḥan Arukh: Oraḥ Ḥayyim* 1:4).

29. Abraham Joshua Heschel, "The Spirit of Jewish Prayer," in *Moral Grandeur and Spiritual Audacity: Essays*, ed. Susannah Heschel (New York: Farrar, Straus and Giroux, 1997), 111.

30. Ebn Leader, in discussion with the author, November 3, 2020.

31. Joey Weisenberg, in discussion with the author, November 17, 2020.

32. Philip V. Bohlman, "Introduction: Music in American Religious Experience," in *Music in American Religious Experience* ed. Philip V. Bohlman, Edith L. Blumhofer, and Maria M. Chow (New York: Oxford University Press, 2006), 8.

33. For a chart of movement in Jewish worship, see Shulamit Saltzman, "Movement of Prayer," in *The Second Jewish Catalog: Sources and Resources*, ed. Sharon and Michael Strassfeld (Philadelphia: Jewish Publication Society, 1976), 292–295.

34. Tomie Hahn, *Sensational Knowledge: Embodying Culture through Japanese Dance* (Middletown, CT: Wesleyan University Press, 2007), 1.

35. Much has been written on the power of music in physical healing; see Gregory Barz and Judah M. Cohen, eds., *The Culture of AIDS in Africa: Hope and Healing Through Music and the Arts* (New York: Oxford University Press, 2011); and Benjamin D. Koen, ed., *The Oxford Handbook of Medical Ethnomusicology* (New York: Oxford University Press, 2011).

36. Mónica Gomery, "Eych Nashir: How Can We Sing in Exile?," *Hebrew College* (blog), October 13, 2020, https://hebrewcollege.edu/blog/eych-nashir-how-can-we-sing-in-exile/.

37. Ibid.

38. See also Bohlman, "Prayer on the Panorama," 244, 245.

39. Linda A. Mercadante, *Belief without Borders: Inside the Minds of the Spiritual but not Religious* (New York: Oxford University Press, 2014), 1–19. Wade Clark Roof, *A Generation of Seekers: The Spiritual Journeys of the Baby Boom Generation* (San Francisco: Harper, 1993), 63–88.

40. Jeffrey A. Summit, "Searching for a Metaphor: What is the Role of the *Shaliach/Shalichat Tzibur* (Leader of Prayer)?," in *Studying Congregational Music: Key Issues, Methods, and Theoretical Perspectives* ed. Andrew Mall, Jeffers Engelhardt, and Monique Ingalls (New York: Routledge, 2021), 230–245.

41. Ebn Leader explains that the rationale for this argument is found in the Babylonian Talmud, Berakhot 26b, and connected to the dispute about source of the three daily prayer services. In this discussion, Yossi b. Hanina argued that the daily prayers were established by the Patriarchs. R. Yehoshua b. Levi objected, asserting that the prayer services were established in correspondence to the daily *temidim* (regular burnt offerings at the Temple).

In that the sacrifices were brought by the community, not by individuals, prayer would be primarily a communal enterprise.

42. Mónica Gomery, in discussion with the author, December 15, 2020.

43. See Robert D. Putnam, "Bowling Alone: America's Declining Social Capital," *Journal of Democracy* 6, no. 1 (1995): 69.

44. Sharon Brous, in discussion with the author, December 8, 2020.

45. For a discussion of code switching and melodic choice in Jewish worship, see Summit, *The Lord's Song*, 129–146.

46. In the Hebrew Bible, the kidneys are often understood to be the site of emotion. See Job 19:27, Psalm 73:21, and Proverbs 23:16.

47. Katayoun Ghanai, "The Sound of Silence: An Ethnography on the Sama' Ritual in the Nematollahi Kaneqah in Toronto" (MA Thesis, York University, Toronto, ON, 2018), 33.

48. Ibid., 39, 40.

49. Judah M. Cohen, "Singing Out for Judaism: A History of Songleaders and Songleading at Olin-Sang-Ruby Union Institute," in *A Place of Our Own: The Rise of Reform Jewish Camping* ed. Michael M. Lorge and Gary P. Zola (Tuscaloosa: University of Alabama Press, 2006), 185.

50. See Summit, *The Lord's Song*, 147–155. See also Jonathan D. Sarna, *American Judaism: A History* (New Haven, CT: Yale University Press, 2004).

51. See Cohen and Eisen, "The Sovereign Self," 20.

52. Sharon Cohen Anisfeld, in discussion with the author, October 1, 2020.

53. Jeff Todd Titon, "Ecojustice, Religious Folklife and a Sound Ecology," *Yale Journal of Music & Religion* 5, no. 2 (2019): 113.

54. See Hava Tirosh-Samuelson, "Judaism," in *The Oxford Handbook of Religion and Ecology*, ed. Roger S. Gottlieb (New York: Oxford University Press, 2006), 25–64; Martin D. Yaffe, ed., *Judaism and Environmental Ethics: A Reader* (Lanham, MD: Lexington Books, 2001); Arthur O. Waskow, ed., *Torah of the Earth*, vol. 1: *Exploring 4,000 Years of Ecology in Jewish Thought: Zionism & Eco-Judaism* (Woodstock, VT: Jewish Lights, 2000).

55. Titon, "Ecojustice," 113.

56. For a discussion of the imagery of wells and water in Hasidic writings, see the commentary of the Sefat Emet on the Torah portion *Toledot* in Arthur Green, *The Language of Truth: The Torah Commentary of the Sefat Emet, Rabbi Yehudah Leib Alter of Ger* (Philadelphia, PA: Jewish Publication Society, 1998), 37–42.

57. Lizzi Heydemann, in discussion with the author, November 19, 2020. Here, she is referencing the verse Genesis 28:16.

58. See Roger S. Gottlieb, "Introduction: Religion and Ecology—What Is the Connection and Why Does it Matter?," in *The Oxford Handbook of Religion and Ecology*, ed. Roger S. Gottlieb (New York: Oxford University Press, 2006), 15.

59. Roger R. Gottlieb draws from Michael P. Nelson, "An Amalgamation of Wilderness Preservation Arguments," in *The Great New Wilderness Debate*, ed. J. Baird Callicott and Michael P. Nelson (Athens: University of Georgia Press, 1998), 168.

60. See Mihaly Csikzentminalyi, *Flow: The Psychology of Optimal Experience* (New York: Harper and Row, 1990).

61. Fader and Kligman, "The New Jewish Spirituality and Prayer," 12.

62. Ibid.

63. Joseph Caro, *Shulḥan Arukh: Oraḥ Ḥayyim* 53:11. Quoted in Weisenberg, *The Torah of Music*, 209.

64. Naḥman of Bretslav *Likkutei Moharan* (1808), 282. Quoted ibid., 226.
65. William James, *The Varieties of Religious Experience*, 42.

SELECT BIBLIOGRAPHY

Bellah, Robert. "The New Religious Consciousness and the Crisis of Modernity." In *The Robert Bellah Reader*, edited by Robert N. Bellah and Steven M. Tipton, 265–284. Reprint. Durham: Duke University Press, 2006 [1976].

Bohlman, Philip V. "Prayer on the Panorama: Music and Individualism in American Religious Experience." In *Music in American Religious Experience*, edited by Philip V. Bohlman, Edith L. Blumhofer, and Maria M. Chow, 233–253. New York: Oxford University Press, 2006.

Cohen, Steven M., J. Shawn Landres, Elie Kaunfer, and Michelle Shain. "Emergent Jewish Communities and their Participants: Preliminary Findings from the 2007 National Spiritual Communities Study." Sponsored by The S3K Synagogue Studies Institute & Mechon Hadar (November 2007). https://www.synagoguestudies.org/wp-content/uploads/2008/10/NatS pirComStudyReport_S3K_Hadar.pdf.

Eliade, Mircea. *The Sacred and the Profane: The Nature of Religion*. Translated by W. R. Trask. New York: Harcourt, 1987 [1957].

Fader, Ayala, and Mark Kligman. "The New Jewish Spirituality and Prayer: Take BJ, For Instance." *S3K Report*, no. 7 (November 2009): 2–11.

Gottlieb, Roger S. "Introduction: Religion and Ecology – What is the Connection and Why Does it Matter?" In *The Oxford Handbook of Religion and Ecology*, edited by Roger S. Gottlieb, 3–21. New York: Oxford University Press, 2006.

Green, Arthur. *The Language of Truth: The Torah Commentary of the Sefat Emet, Rabbi Yehudah Leib Alter of Ger*. Philadelphia, PA: Jewish Publication Society, 1998.

Heschel, Abraham Joshua. "The Spirit of Jewish Prayer." In *Moral Grandeur and Spiritual Audacity: Essays*, edited by Susannah Heschel, 100–126. New York: Farrar, Straus and Giroux, 1997.

Illman, Ruth. *Music and Religious Change Among Progressive Jews in London: Being Liberal and Doing Traditional*. Lanham, MD: Lexington Books, 2018.

James, William. *The Varieties of Religious Experience*. Reprint. New York: The New American Library, 1958 [1902].

Jay, Martin. *Songs of Experience: Modern American and European Variations on a Universal Theme*. Berkeley: University of California Press, 2005.

Leeuw, Gerard van der. *Religion in Essence and Manifestation*. Reprint. Princeton, NJ: Princeton University Press, 1986 [1933].

Mall, Andrew, Jeffers Engelhardt, and Monique Ingalls, eds. *Studying Congregational Music: Key Issues, Methods, and Theoretical Perspectives*. New York: Routledge, 2021.

Mercadante, Linda A. *Belief without Borders: Inside the Minds of the Spiritual but not Religious*. New York: Oxford University Press, 2014.

Mirsky, Yehuda. *Rav Kook: Mystic in a Time of Revolution*. New Haven, CT: Yale University Press, 2019.

Nelson, Michael P. "An Amalgamation of Wilderness Preservation Arguments." In *The Great New Wilderness Debate*, edited by J. Baird Callicott and Michael P. Nelson, 154–200. Athens: University of Georgia Press, 1998.

Otto, Rudolf. *The Idea of the Holy*. Reprint. London: Oxford University Press, 1958 [1923].

Roof, Wade Clark. *Contemporary American Religion*. New York: MacMillan Reference Books, 1999.

Roof, Wade Clark. *A Generation of Seekers: The Spiritual Journeys of the Baby Boom Generation*. San Francisco: Harper, 1993.

Roof, Wade Clark. "Modernity, the Religious and the Spiritual." *The Annals of the American Academy of Political and Social Science* 558, no. 1 (1998): 211–224.

Rorty, Richard. *Contingency, Irony, and Solidarity*. Cambridge: Cambridge University Press, 1989.

Saltzman, Shulamit. "Movement of Prayer." In *The Second Jewish Catalog: Sources and Resources*, compiled and edited by Sharon and Michael Strassfeld, 292–295. Philadelphia, PA: Jewish Publication Society, 1976.

Summit, Jeffrey A. *The Lord's Song in a Strange Land: Music and Identity in Contemporary Jewish Worship*. New York: Oxford University Press, 2000.

Summit, Jeffrey A. "Searching for a Metaphor: What is the Role of the Shaliach/Shalichat Tzibur (Leader of Prayer)?" In *Studying Congregational Music: Key Issues, Methods, and Theoretical Perspectives*, edited by Andrew Mall, Jeffers Engelhardt, and Monique Ingalls, 230–245. New York: Routledge, 2021.

Summit, Jeffrey A. *Singing God's Words: The Performance of Biblical Chant in Contemporary Judaism*. New York: Oxford University Press, 2016.

Taves, Ann. *Religious Experience Reconsidered: A Building-Block Approach to the Study of Religion and Other Special Things*. Princeton and Oxford: Princeton University Press, 2009.

Tirosh-Samuelson, Hava. "Judaism." In *The Oxford Handbook of Religion and Ecology*, edited by Roger S. Gottlieb, 25–64. New York: Oxford University Press, 2006.

Weisenberg, Joey. *The Torah of Music: Reflections on a Tradition of Singing and Song*. Translations by Joshua Schwartz. New York: Hadar Press, 2017.

20

SONIC COLLECTIVITY AT THE KOTEL HA-MAʿARAVI (WESTERN WALL)

ABIGAIL WOOD

IT is 1:00 am the night before Yom Kippur 5780, October 8, 2019, and the Western Wall Plaza is packed to capacity for the final *Seliḥot* before Yom Kippur, recited according to the Sephardi rite. These penitential prayers are recited nightly during the month before the High Holidays, traditionally after midnight; the following evening, the same texts will form a central part of the Yom Kippur liturgy. It is half an hour after the service began, but standing at the back of the plaza, my friend and I struggle to stay on our feet and open our prayer books as still more people crowd into the packed space, jostling us from all sides. The prayer area in front of the Western Wall itself is divided into men's and women's sections, but here at the back of the plaza the crowd is mixed: men of all ages, teenage boys and girls, older couples, families, a policeman in uniform. A stream of teenaged boys in jeans and trainers push past us, reciting the Hebrew texts from memory as they read WhatsApp messages on their phone screens. Meanwhile, the voice of Moshe Habusha, son of Iraqi immigrants and today the most esteemed cantor of the Jerusalem-Sephardic musical tradition, rings out via loudspeakers across the Western Wall Plaza, his face projected onto giant screens. Reciting the liturgical poem ʿAnenu (Answer us), Habusha opens each line of text with a long, improvised vocal melisma on the first word of each line, breaking the regular rhythm of this piyyut as he explores different Arab maqāmāt in free tempo, increasing each time the emotional energy of his supplications, then snaps back into rhythm as he continues each line in the familiar, simple refrain of the piyyut. The crowd answers each phrase loudly, repeating his words to the same rhythmic melody:

עננו בזכותיה דבר יוחאי עננו
עננו רחום וחנון עננו
רחום וחנון חטאנו לפניך רחם עלינו

Answer us, by the merit of Bar Yochai, answer us.
Answer us, merciful and gracious One, answer us.
Merciful and gracious One, we have sinned before you.

Habusha and a group of prominent rabbis are located on a balcony above the crowds; high above their heads glow the green lights of one of the minarets of the Al-Aqsa Mosque. As Habusha transitions to the next piyyut, there is a wave of anticipation in the crowd: we have reached Adon haselihot (Master of forgiveness), the most well-known piyyut of the Selihot service. Structured around an alphabetic acrostic, the short verses of the piyyut are easy to memorize; the melody is catchy and rises to a satisfying high pitch for the supplicatory refrain "Ḥaṭanu lefanekha, raḥem ʿaleinu" (We have sinned before you, have mercy on us). While liturgically this is not the most significant point of the service, it is clearly the peak experience the crowd has been waiting for. The floodlights illuminating the plaza are reflected in a sea of phone screens, as thousands of those present hold their phones high to try to record the moment, seeking to store the experience to recall it later or to send to friends and family. Habusha sings the first two words, then leaves the crowd to continue; any tiredness due to the late hour does not show as the voices of tens of thousands soar through the plaza:

אדון הסליחות בוחן לבבות
גולה עמוקות דובר צדקות
חטאנו לפניך רחם עלינו

Master of forgiveness, examiner of hearts,
Revealer of our inner depths, speaker of truths,
We have sinned before you, have mercy on us

The musical moment described above (see also Video Example 20.1 for recording) illustrates a peak moment of sonic collectivity at the Western Wall—the *Kotel ha-Maʿaravi*, known in Hebrew simply as the Kotel (Wall). On the eve of Yom Kippur, the tens of thousands present made their way from across the country to the place from which, according to a frequently cited Midrashic text, the divine presence (*shekhinah*) has never departed since the destruction of the Temple in 70 CE (Exodus Rabbah 2:2).[1] The liturgy at the event follows the Sephardi rite (*nusaḥ ʿedot hamizraḥ*), but the format of the massed prayer gathering is relatively new, an outgrowth of the Sephardi *teshuvah* movement that since the 1990s has promoted a "return" to religious practice among Israeli Jews who may not otherwise be strictly observant. The large proportions of the plaza allow tens of thousands of Jews to join together as a physical collective,

VIDEO EXAMPLE 20.1 Erev Yom Kippur selihot prayers at the Western Wall, October 8, 2019. Filmed by the author.

symbolically joining the tens or hundreds of voices heard reciting the same seliḥot in individual synagogues across the country into tens of thousands present together in one space. The structure of the plaza itself enables them to form a sonic collective, as the sound produced by their voices rebounds off the three stone walls that enclose the paved space. This sonic collective then echoes into more distant spaces, as a live broadcast and phone videos transport its sounds to those physically distant from this service. Meanwhile, the political and cultural context of the event continues to develop: while during his lifetime the event was strongly associated with Rabbi Ovadia Yosef (1920–2013), former Sephardic Chief Rabbi of Israel, spiritual leader of the Shas political party and a key figure in the teshuvah movement, by the mid-2010s prayer pamphlets that circulated at the event with a picture of Ovadia Yosef and the Shas logo had been replaced by a new edition printed by the Western Wall Heritage Foundation, the administrative body responsible since 1988 for matters concerning the Western Wall, indicating that the event had been absorbed into the "official" calendar and rhetoric of the site.

More than any other contemporary Jewish place, the Western Wall Plaza is an iconic space of Jewish prayer. It is also a unique sonic space, whose soundscape refracts and amplifies diverse historical, religious, national, and political narratives of Jewish collectivity, which are continually retold and re-created as people and voices jostle in this often-crowded space. Despite the momentary unity created at times like that described in the vignette above, the Kotel plaza is frequently a place of symbolic—and sonic— tension. It is a place of prayer, yet unlike Jerusalem's grand churches and mosques, and the historical Jewish Temples of which it is a remnant, its spatial and acoustic nature is defined not by architecture but by the lack thereof: an open space whose bare walls recall the destruction both of the Jewish Temple and of the Mughrabi neighborhood that was razed immediately following the 1967 Six-Day War in order to create the current open prayer space. Orthodox Jewish norms dominate everyday practices at the site, yet it functions daily as a meeting point of different types of collectivity: diaspora Jews pray alongside Israelis; religious observances take place alongside military swearing-in ceremonies and state ceremonies; civil and religious authorities lock horns about religious restrictions at the site; and the melodies of different Jewish communities intertwine and occasionally compete for dominance. At the same time, those praying at the Kotel are constantly aware of religious Others, whether through the sound of the muezzin from the Al-Aqsa Mosque high above, or through the presence of Christian pilgrims, who, enamored by the historical authenticity of the site, whisper prayers to Jesus alongside women reciting psalms.

In this chapter, the soundscapes of prayer and ritual serve as a prism to refract and reflect on these contested narratives of Jewish collectivity. I will read the sonic landscape of the Kotel plaza through two lenses: the first considers the resonances of the Jewish sonic past that echo through the current plaza and continue to shape its soundscape today; the second turns to contemporary soundscapes, considering how the co-presence of divergent Jewish collectives is negotiated every day through sound.

HISTORICAL RESONANCES

The huge, chiseled limestone blocks of the Kotel, their surfaces beaten by nearly two millennia of weather and polished smooth by the touch of the faithful, are among Jerusalem's most visually recognizable sites. This fifty-seven-meter stretch of a retaining wall built by Herod to reinforce the Temple Mount is one of the few remaining physical traces of the Second Temple, which stood above it. During its existence, the Second Temple and its predecessor, the First Temple, which stood in the same location until its destruction in 586 BCE, were not only the physical and conceptual centers of the religious Jewish world; they were also the center of the Jewish musical world. The Book of Chronicles recounts in great detail the appointment of musicians from among the Levites under King David (1 Chronicles 15:16–16:43; 23:1–5; 25:1–7), later describing of the Levites singing and playing in the Temple under King Hezekiah (2 Chronicles 29:25–30; 30:21–22). While compiled after the destruction of the Second Temple, during the third to sixth centuries CE, the Babylonian Talmud discusses the construction and use of instruments in the Temple in detail (Arakhin 10a–11a). The destruction of both the First and Second Temples not only silenced these musical practices themselves, but also marked a turning point in Jewish religious attitudes to music, which was often silenced as a sign of mourning for the Temple. If Psalm 137, referring to the Babylonian exile after the destruction of the First Temple, describes the Levites hanging up their harps and asking "How can we sing the Lord's song in a strange land?," after the destruction of the Second Temple, the Mishnah says that "song ceased in drinking-houses" (Sotah 9:11). By the sixteenth century, Rabbi Joseph Caro stated in the *Shulḥan Arukh*, the primary code of Jewish law, that in order to remember the destruction of Jerusalem, the rabbis "decreed that one should not play instruments of song and all kinds of music, and all things that make the sound of song, in order to derive pleasure from them. And it is forbidden to hear them because of the destruction [of the Temple in Jerusalem]. And even vocal song sung over wine is forbidden, as it is written (Isaiah 24:9) 'They will not drink wine with a song'" (*Shulḥan Arukh: Oraḥ Ḥayyim* 560:2–3). Only the Yemenite Jewish community continued strictly to observe this ban on instrumental music following the destruction of the Temple; nevertheless, it influenced a nineteenth-century Ashkenazi ban on instrumental music at weddings held in Jerusalem following a cholera epidemic; this later ban is still followed in some strictly Orthodox communities.[2]

Following the destruction of the Second Temple in 70 CE, religious and historical sources document that Jews returned to the wall or the nearby Mount of Olives to lament the destruction of the holy places. Jewish vocal lamentation at the site—from which the English term *Wailing Wall*, and the Arabic *al-Mabka* (the place of weeping), were derived—has been described by Christian visitors since the fourth century, including by Jerome.[3] This practice was described frequently by nineteenth-century Christian visitors, for whom it served as a tourist attraction, even if it is often unclear whether they are indeed describing lamentation, or are simply projecting meaning upon the everyday soundscape of Jewish prayer: in 1888, a reporter in New Zealand's *Waikato Times* reported, "It is one of the most affecting sights in that city of strange memories to see the 'ancient people' standing there, psalter in hand, wailing out words which have a singular significance in that place. The place is sacred with the tears of many generations."[4] Recalling a visit to the wall in 1932, Harvard's George Sarton identified the weeping practice with older, religious men, whom he explicitly contrasts with the younger Jewish colonists creating the modern State of Israel.[5]

From the mid-nineteenth century onward, European Jews attempted to acquire the land in front of the Western Wall from the Ottoman Empire in order to enlarge the prayer area available to Jewish visitors, and in 1915 military governor Cemal Pasha allegedly made an offer to sell the land to Jewish communal leader Albert Antébi. Historian Robert Mazza attributes the failure of this deal both to growing political tensions and to the marginal place that the Kotel held at that time in Zionist ideology.[6] Meanwhile as increasing numbers of Jews immigrated to Palestine from the late nineteenth century onward and began to visit and pray at the wall, tensions rose between local Arab and Jewish populations. During the British Mandate period, the prayer space next to the Wall—part of a passageway less than four meters wide, belonging to a North African endowment and leading to houses in the Mughrabi Quarter built in the thirteenth century to house Muslim Moroccan pilgrims—was an increasingly focal point of national, political, and religious disputes between Zionist Jews and Muslims, the latter countering Jewish claims to the wall by identifying the wall with the place where the prophet Muhammad tethered his miraculous beast—*al-burāq*—during *al-mirāj*, his nocturnal journey from Mecca. In 1929 disputes between Muslims and Jews about rights at the wall became more heated, eventually leading to major violent riots in August 1929 throughout Palestine in which 133 Jews and 116 Arabs lost their lives. Sari Nusseibeh locates the beginning of the "al-Buraq revolt" in a sonic moment, when young supporters of Revisionist Zionist leader Ze'ev Jabotinsky, marching to the wall, shouted, "The Wall is ours!," and sang the then Zionist anthem "Hatikvah" (The hope).[7]

In the wake of the riots, the British authorities, supported by the League of Nations, appointed a commission "to determine the rights and claims of Moslems and Jews in connection with the Western or Wailing Wall at Jerusalem."[8] In the commission's 1930 report, both sides cite sound in their claims for rights at the space: the Muslim representatives refer to an 1840 decree from Ibrahim Pasha cautioning the Jews against "raising their voices" at the Wall,[9] whereas the Jews entreat that "the Arabs should be prohibited from disturbing the Jewish services by leading donkeys through the passage or by installing a muezzin in the neighborhood of the Wall or by conducting the Zikhr [*sic*] ritual in the courtyard at the southern end of the Pavement, to which the Jews object because of the concomitant disagreeable noise."[10] In 1931 the commission concluded with recommendations that spoke directly to the sound disputes:

> (5) The Jews shall not be permitted to blow the ram's horn (Shofar) near the Wall nor cause any other disturbance to the Moslems that is avoidable; the Moslems on

the other hand shall not be permitted to carry out the Zikr ceremony close to the Pavement during the progress of the Jewish devotions or to cause annoyance to the Jews in any other way. . . . (7) It shall be prohibited for any person or persons to make use of the place in front of the Wall or its surroundings for all political speeches or utterances or demonstrations of any kind whatever.[11]

This history of sound disputation and perceived domination forms an important backdrop to the recent history of the Western Wall and its environs. From 1948 to 1867, the Western Wall, along with the rest of the Old City, was under Jordanian control. Its capture by Israeli forces, iconized in David Rubinger's photograph of three paratroopers standing at the foot of the wall, was a defining moment of the 1967 Six-Day War.[12] The Israeli victory was marked by sounds, broadcast on Israeli radio: paratroop commander Motta Gur's live-broadcast announcement "Har habayit beyadenu!" (The Temple Mount is in our hands!); soldiers singing "Hatikvah," and Major-General Shlomo Goren, the chief rabbi of the Israel Defense Forces, sounding blasts on the shofar on the Temple Mount and at the foot of the Western Wall.[13]

In this context, Goren's shofar blasts were doubly resonant. First, due to the symbolism of the instrument, he juxtaposed this particular historic moment with significant biblical moments linked to the shofar, from the binding of Isaac, to the Sinaitic revelation, to the capture of Jericho by Joshua. In the latter three cases, the sound of the shofar is mentioned in the biblical narrative itself; later Rabbinic literature additionally links the shofar with the ram Abraham sacrificed instead of his son Isaac (Mishnah Berurah on *Shulḥan Arukh: Oraḥ Ḥayyim* 596:1), traditionally understood to have taken place on the Temple Mount itself. These meanings resounded with the moment of Israeli euphoria, and also with fervor of religious-nationalist groups who read the 1967 victory in messianic terms; a concrete indication of God's intervention in the future of the Jewish people. Second, the shofar blasts were an emphatic statement of Israeli presence and sovereignty, simultaneously overturning the explicit ban of the 1931 British commission on sounding the shofar in the Western Wall space and the years of Jordanian rule under which access to the wall was impossible for Israeli Jews. Daniel Monk identifies Goren's shofar blasts—which index the transformation of the soundscape of the Western Wall from one of mourning for the lost Temple to one of celebration—not only as instant icons of the Israeli victory, but also as intervening in the convergence of religious and national collective ideologies at the newly captured Western Wall.[14]

The immediate wake of the Six-Day War marked a further transformation of the sound space at the wall as these religious and national ideologies immediately intersected. On the night of June 10, 1967, the Mughrabi Quarter bordering on the Western Wall, then home to 135 Muslim families, and Muslim holy places including two mosques, was knocked down to clear a large plaza in front of the wall. Gershom Gorenberg notes that the decision to raze the neighborhood, "in a twilight time between war and the first formal government discussions of postwar policy," created facts on the ground that emphasized Israeli control over the Old City.[15] Meanwhile, control of the Western Wall was handed to the chief rabbinate in line with the control of religious authorities over other religious sites in Jerusalem. The end of the war neatly dovetailed with the Jewish pilgrimage festival Shavuot, celebrated that year on June 13–14, during which 200,000 Jewish Israelis streamed to the newly cleared plaza.[16] Overnight, then, the voices of Muslims of the Mughrabi Quarter were silenced by expulsion; while today the sonic juxtaposition of Jewish and Muslim sacred spaces continues to resound in the Western Wall plaza, Jewish and Muslim prayer spaces are firmly delineated and distanced both conceptually and by hard security infrastructure.

CONTEMPORARY COLLECTIVITY

While the creation of the Western Wall Plaza in 1967 distanced everyday spatial contestation between Muslims and Jews from the immediate environs of the wall, the formation of this resonant physical space created a new kind of sonic proximity between those now using the space. Approaching the wall, this proximity is first articulated by the physical nature of traveling toward the wall through the crowded Old City streets. The plaza is situated in a valley, the approach is therefore downward: by steps or a steep road from the Jewish Quarter; down stepped market streets from the Jaffa Gate, or along the valley itself, via El Wad (HaGai) Street in the Muslim Quarter. Descending via the steps from the Jewish Quarter, beggars and charity collectors rattle cups of coins toward passersby, calling "tsedakah!" (charity!); others hold up red strings, a popular talisman, for visitors to tie on their wrist. As a paved balcony affords a first view of the full plaza, the steps turn downward toward a security gate, a familiar secular ritual (bag in x-ray machine, step through gates, banter with bored guards, or jostle with fellow visitors) that marks a formal entry point into the Western Wall area. In combination with the heavy symbolic meaning attached to the Western Wall, this process of isolation from the everyday world, and clearly bounded yet penetrable space, resonate with Michel Foucault's designation of certain cultural spaces as "heterotopias."[17] For Foucault, heterotopias—literally, "other spaces"—act as a mirror to society; both physically within yet symbolically removed from everyday space, they are places where cultural meanings are simultaneously created, enacted, and superimposed.

Empty of fixed furniture apart from a wall marking off the lower prayer section, which is divided by a metal *mehitsah*, a partition that is particularly used to separate men and women, the Western Wall Plaza provides a flexible space for Jewish religious activity.

Recent book-length critical studies explore the debates that have shaped the development of the site over the last half-century from the perspectives of architecture (Alona Nitzan-Shiftan), archaeology (Raz Kletter), social history (Kobi Cohen-Hattab and Doron Bar), and gender roles in Jewish prayer (Yuval Jobani and Nahshon Perez). The current bare plaza reflects a lack of consensus between religious authorities, secular authorities, and archaeologists, which stalled architectural development. Following the 1967 war, there was much public debate about plans for the site; finally plans by architect Moshe Safdie, which proposed a stepped, amphitheater-like approach to the wall, were approved in 1977.[18] However, these plans were never implemented owing to rabbinic objections to planned commercial and tourist facilities at the site.[19]

Today, the stone plaza, sunk into a valley with high stone walls on two of the three open sides, creates a resonant box within which sounds are reflected, joining all present into a shared acoustic space. This resonance is noted by signs at the entrance from the Jewish Quarter, requesting people not to bring drums and musical instruments into the plaza, in order to avoid disturbing fellow worshippers. Shared religious and national meanings at the Western Wall Plaza emerge from the polyphony of voices that resound in this open space. While the soundscape of the plaza constantly changes, it articulates Jewish and Israeli calendars of prayers, life-cycle events, and ceremonies, both on a daily basis and following the yearly prayer cycle, inflected by the constant flow of different individuals and prayer groups who gather there. On a few occasions during the year—such as the midnight Selihot described above, or the Priestly Blessing on the intermediate days of Passover and Sukkot—the entire plaza functions as a single prayer space. At these times, tens of thousands of worshippers listening to the voice of the hazan (prayer leader) relayed over speakers function as a single congregation, enacting a shared sense of religious intention and practice. Most of the time, however, individuals and small groups circulate in the plaza and jostle for space at the wall, a constant polyphony of practices. Individual prayer is prominent: many visitors whisper prayers directly to the wall—or hold up mobile phones to the stones to enable an interlocutor to do so—reflecting the belief that the divine presence is directly manifested in this place. Men pray in *minyanim* (small prayer groups), several often operating simultaneously a short distance apart. Meanwhile, outside the prayer area nearest the wall, the plaza frequently hosts secular national ceremonies including swearing-in ceremonies for Israeli Defense Force soldiers whose shouting of "Ani nishbaʿ! Ani nishbaʿ! Ani nishbaʿ!" (I swear! I swear! I swear!) resounds throughout the plaza. On Yom HaZikaron, Israel's memorial day, sacred use of the space temporarily gives way to the secular collective, as the prayer area is briefly cleared for the national memorial ceremony.

Within this temporal cycle, moments in which the sonic practices of multiple groups converge articulate shared intention. Suzy, an Orthodox immigrant, originally from the United States, and her husband related to me how they walked down to the Western Wall from their home in the Jewish Quarter to pray at *nets* (sunrise) every morning, noting that although several minyanim regularly met at this time, a silence was palpable exactly at sunrise, as everyone consensually began the silent Amidah prayer at the same time—only disturbed sometimes by groups of visitors "straight off the plane" who failed to fall silent at the relevant time.[20] By contrast, sometimes moments of convergence are expressed through heightened activity: Monday and Thursday mornings are busy with bar mitzvah celebrations, and on Friday evenings the plaza is packed with visitors welcoming the Sabbath: on a Friday in February 2014, secular Israeli teenage girls in tight trousers participating in a weekend of religious activities rubbed shoulders with large groups of diaspora Jewish teenagers visiting Israel part of organized tour programs. The teenagers sang and danced in circles—Sabbath services, religious songs, or Israeli popular songs, depending on the group, while a substantial Breslov Hasidic minyan prayed at the front of the plaza near the wall, all observed by many curious non-Jewish tourists who come to watch the Sabbath celebrations.

The recurring rhythms produced by the layering of multiple events such as these serve to articulate a collective sense of co-presence at the Western Wall, linking very different events and protagonists into a shared articulation of a Jewish-Israeli calendar. Nevertheless, the open, resonant plaza and polyphonic nature of the soundscape simultaneously allows dissenting voices to emerge. Sonic collectives in and around the Western Wall Plaza re-articulate the plaza as a space of ideological contestation, contributing to wider debates about freedom of religious expression in public spaces in the state of Israel. As Kobi Cohen-Hattab and Doron Bar observe, this contestation in turn invokes the wider physical and symbolic context of the Western Wall:

> Though ostensibly the conflicts surrounding the Western Wall related to the right to pray there and control its status and appearance, they in fact touched on more basic questions: the acceptance or rejection of religious authority; the upholding of tradition or the revolt against it; the place of scientific research; the question of archaeology at religious sites – religion versus science; the place of the state and its institutions at holy sites; collaboration with, or rejection of, other Jewish traditions in the State of Israel and its institutions, including the traditions of Diaspora Jewry belonging to the non-Orthodox movements.[21]

Scholars examining the ways in which these debates play out at the Western Wall have largely focused on textual sources through which competing positions are articulated in government discussions, legal opinions, architectural plans, and the news media; sound rarely factors into these discussions. Nevertheless, in *The Political Life of Sensation*, Davide Panagia compellingly argues that the politics of voice in the public sphere transcend conventional questions of meaning, or "making sense" of utterances.[22] A word, he notes, is both sound and sense; "though a political utterance may be retroactively tuned to sound like a reasonable expression of interests, its first pitch is an interruptive noise."[23] The following two examples—two alternate forms of Jewish collectivity that have sought in recent years to assert their presence in the Kotel—illustrate how "interruptive noises" at the Western Wall Plaza bring sonic presence to the heart of the ongoing debate about the religious and ideological meanings of the site.

WOMEN OF THE WALL

The most prominent ideological contestation at the Western Wall in recent years has concerned religious authority, amid ongoing campaigns for the recognition of non-Orthodox religious rights in Israel, particularly focusing on women's roles in prayer. While debates about non-Orthodox prayer at the Western Wall date back to 1967, they have been more prominent since the late 1980s, when groups espousing egalitarian prayer or women's Torah readings have met at the wall, resulting in regular scuffles with groups of Haredi Jews shouting offensive insults.[24] This contestation, based upon fundamentally different understandings of the common good and collective rights, has direct resonances for the relationship of Israeli and diaspora Jews: while most religious Israeli Jews identify with Orthodox norms, in which women do not serve as prayer leaders or count in a minyan, non-Orthodox denominations with an egalitarian approach to gender roles are far more common in diaspora communities and among English-speaking immigrants to Israel.

Meanwhile, despite many legal attempts to change the status quo, under the auspices of the Ministry of Religion and the state-appointed Orthodox Rabbi of the Western Wall, the prayer plaza reflects the norms of an Orthodox synagogue: Torah scrolls are exclusively used on the men's side, bookshelves hold traditional prayer books, and a cadre of religious personnel uphold rules of conduct, including enforcing women's modest dress.[25] Signs ask visitors to respect the holiness of the site, to dress modestly, and not to take photographs on the Sabbath; the enforcement of Orthodox prayer norms at the Western Wall has been the matter of ongoing debate in Israeli society as well as various court cases, as will be discussed in the case of the Women of the Wall below. Following traditional Jewish practice, men's prayer in the plaza tends to be formal and communal, gathering in minyanim; women almost exclusively pray individually, their communal practices largely restricted to activities such as dividing the Book of Psalms among a group of women in order to complete reading the whole book in one session.

In recent years, the most prominent challenge to Orthodox religious hegemony in shaping religious practices at the Western Wall has been mounted by Women of the Wall, a women's prayer group seeking since 1988 to pray as a group, read from a Torah scroll, and permit those members who desire to pray with tallit and tefillin at the Western Wall. The religious and legal struggles of this group have received sustained attention from the Israeli and Jewish press, in Jewish feminist circles, and scholars.[26] Throughout the group's history, and spanning a series of decisions by regional courts and the Supreme Court, its members have continued to meet every month at the Western Wall. In accordance with police directives, they normally pray within the women's section and then read Torah at the Robinson's Arch egalitarian prayer area. Located in a neighboring archaeological park next to an adjacent stretch of the same wall, this prayer area was established by an Israeli government commission in 1998 to serve as a location for egalitarian Conservative and Reform services; it was expanded in 2013.

Sound has repeatedly been referenced during this contestation. Both supporters and detractors of the group have linked the Women of the Wall's practice of singing certain portions of the prayers to models in wider Jewish thought. For some of the women, song is a direct way to connect to the redemptive model of Miriam, who sang with the women during the biblical account of the exodus from Egypt (Exodus 15:20–21).[27] Conversely, strictly Orthodox opponents of the group have raised the halakhic issue *kol b'ishah ervah*, referring to a rabbinic prohibition for men to hear the singing voices of women during prayer. During the prayers themselves, sound has frequently served as a direct arena of contestation, the singing voices of the women juxtaposed with male (and female) opponents shouting insults, and by pointedly loud male prayer services on the other side of the meḥitsah; typically, harmonies sung with Western vocal production by the Women of the Wall are counterposed with the unharmonized heterophony of simultaneous male prayer services and hoarse, shouting voices of male and female protestors.

During a brief period in 2013, however, sound assumed a more instrumental role in the contestation between Women of the Wall and their detractors. Following a ruling in May 2013 by the Jerusalem District Court that it was indeed permissible for women to pray with prayer shawls and tefillin at the Western Wall, a harsh war of words erupted between Women of the Wall and religiously conservative factions, including a newly created opposing group, Women for the Wall. On July 8, 2013, Rosh Ḥodesh of the month of Av, the opposition came to a head. Ahead of the Women of the Wall's scheduled service, the opposing group, together with political allies, brought thousands of women and teenaged seminary girls to the Western Wall, completely filling the women's prayer area; in response the police moved the Women of the Wall to a cordoned-off area at the back of the upper plaza. Here, the opposition to the women's prayer moved from verbal contestation—whether via legal work or via shouted insults—to sheer noise. A large number of strictly Orthodox men and women used shrill plastic whistles to try to drown out the sound of the Women of the Wall's prayer; meanwhile, loudspeakers were installed in the men's prayer section for a prayer service led by the official rabbi of the Western Wall, marking a significant change from the usual unamplified prayer in independent minyanim, and effectively drowning out the women's prayer. The women's prayer continued as usual, ending with an emotional rendition of "Hatikvah," Israel's national anthem.

These protests were widely covered by Israeli and international media, which was largely sympathetic to Women of the Wall, framing these events within larger debates, both local and global, about religious fundamentalism and modernity. Mirroring the acoustic dimensions of the conflict, sound—implied in photographs—assumed a prominent role in the visual language of the media coverage. Whereas in previous years, press photographs had focused particularly on religious practices (women reading Torah or praying with tallit and tefillin) and on police arrests of various members of the group, several widely circulated press photographs in 2013 transposed the sounds of the conflict into visual form. In one memorable image, a member of Women of the Wall in dungarees and short sleeves, her mouth closed and her face relaxed, reaches out to embrace a strictly Orthodox woman whose face is contorted and mouth wide open in a shouting gesture, a copy of the Book of Psalms in her hand. In a second image, a blonde girl in a blue T-shirt, smiles at a young yeshiva student who appears to be shouting and gesticulating at her. A photograph of the strictly Orthodox women who flooded the plaza shows a woman wearing a turban facing the camera, metal whistles in her mouth and that of a teenaged girl standing beside her, and a camera in the hand of the third pointing at the viewer.

While the ebb in the conflict between Women of the Wall and their detractors subsided during the following months, these images—and the sounds that accompanied them—stand as a powerful intervention into the struggle between the Women of the

Wall and their detractors, at least temporarily reframing it from a conflict about specific religious practices with norms enforced by the Israeli police and challenged in the court system, to a more global contestation of communal norms played out in the brute, interruptive rhetoric of acoustic volume and popular protest.

SIVUV SHEARIM AND RIKUDGALIM

A different contestation of the Western Wall as ideological space is embodied by participants of the monthly Sivuv Shearim (Circling the Gates) ritual, which has taken place on the eve of Rosh Ḥodesh most months since 2000, pausing during the COVID-19 restrictions. Identified by its organizers as the renewal of a ceremony documented in the Cairo Genizah, and building upon a modern ritual circling of the gates of the Old City on the fast of Tisha B'Av, organizers present the march as an outlet for Jewish hopes for the building of the Third Temple. Beginning from the Western Wall Plaza, the group circles the Temple Mount via streets inside and outside the Old City, stopping at each of the historical gates to recite psalms connected with the Levites of the biblical Temple. Like the Women of the Wall, the organizers of Sivuv Shearim see their relatively small community as representative of a broader public: "Sivuv Shearim is not an event that belongs to a small group, but is undertaken as emissary of the whole of the Jewish people."[28]

While the organizers of Sivuv Shearim place emphasis on the antiquity of the ritual, its form and the musical elements employed are new ones. Unusually for a Jewish religious ceremony, Sivuv Shearim uses recorded music and amplification. Participants, most of them teenage members of religious youth movements, push pram bases with loudspeakers precariously attached. When the group stops near each gate, the speakers convey the leader reciting psalms to a Sephardic nusaḥ. The rest of the time, they play loud religious popular music connected to Jerusalem or relevant religious holidays. (In accordance with religious prohibitions, no recorded music is used on Rosh Ḥodesh of the month of Av.) The group is gender segregated—men first, followed by women, the front row of whom hold up a curtain, which serves as a portable meḥitsah. The group moves through seemingly empty streets: all businesses are closed by this time in the evening, and a mobile framework of police roadblocks prevents Palestinians from passing along the streets while the Sivuv passes.

Intertwined with the widely articulated religious goal of connecting to the Temple is a religious-nationalist narrative that seeks to expand current Jewish spaces in predominantly Palestinian parts of the Old City, which resonates with broader Jewish nationalist and settlement movements active in the Old City. A 2011 article in "Ha-ḳol ha-yehudi" (The Jewish voice), a news site set up in 2005 to protest Israel's disengagement from Gaza, protested the police's decision to cancel that month's Sivuv Shearim because of Ramadan, quoting anonymously one of the organizers: "The police tries to prevent Jewish presence in the Old City, but we will not give up, and will continue to circulate here freely. The police canceled one 'Sivuv Shearim' and got two [impromptu rituals]."[29] Within this framework, music forms a means, at least temporarily, for the group to achieve its political goals.

Within the carnivalesque atmosphere created by recorded music, singing, and tambourines, various sounds serve as a vehicle for the fusion of religious and political ideology. Songs from the popular religious repertory—including Shlomo Carlebach's "Am Yisrael chai" (The people of Israel live) and "Yibaneh hamikdash" (Rebuild the sanctuary)—segue into "Am hanetzach lo mefached" (The eternal people are not afraid, a text set to a Breslov Hasidic melody and associated with protests against the 2005 Israeli disengagement from Gaza) and "Zochreini Na" (Remember me), a song recorded by Dov Shurin on his album *Biblical Revenge*, released during the Second Intifada in 2002. Shurin sets Judges 16:28, a verse in which Samson calls for God's revenge on the Philistines, to a fast melody and heavy rock beat. His setting clearly replaces the biblical "plishtim" (Philistines) with "falastin" (Palestine), a replacement followed by participants in the Sivuv.[30]

This fusion of nationalist ideology and religious repertories sung while moving through the Old City streets recalls the Rikudgalim, the annual flag dance through Jerusalem on Yom Yerushalayim, the anniversary of the reunification of Jerusalem under Israeli control in 1967. Much larger than Sivuv Shearim, the Rikudgalim is attended by thousands, primarily secular-nationalist and religious-nationalist teenagers, who stream through the main streets of the Old City, cordoned off by the police, toward an ecstatic evening of live music, speeches, and dancing at the Western Wall. In footage of the 2011 Rikudgalim passing through the Old City, neo-Hasidic songs with nationalist overtones are interleaved with explicitly racist football songs and chants associated with supporters of Beitar Jerusalem: "Mohammed is dead"—"Death to Arabs."[31]

Beyond serving as a vehicle for ideology, however, in the Sivuv Shearim sound itself plays an instrumental role in reframing unfamiliar geographies, using sound temporarily to extend the consensual Jewish communal space of the Western Wall Plaza to streets in the Muslim Quarter of the Old City. During the Sivuv, singing, recorded music, and the loud jingling of specially produced tambourines reverberate in the resonant, empty stone streets, literally amplifying the presence of the relatively small group of participants (tens or hundreds) taking part in the event.

Both Sivuv Shearim and Rikudgalim rely on the Israeli civil control of East Jerusalem in order to take place free of physical threats, physically articulating a narrative of united Jerusalem with security cooperation from the police. Nevertheless, they simultaneously undermine the reality of the united city by performing a heroics of conquest in contested space and by provoking the status quo: in 2021 the Yom Yerushalayim Rikudgalim was eventually canceled and rerouted in the context of the inflamed tensions that led to eleven days of violent conflict between Israel and Gaza militants. Referring to Yom Yerushalayim celebrations, ethnomusicologist Tanya Sermer suggests that "[b]lasting music through loudspeakers at multiple stages and on moving vehicles, and marching and dancing with Israeli flags does not just celebrate Israel's military victory in 1967 and the annexation of East Jerusalem and the Old City, it in fact re-conquers that territory anew each year and unifies the city for the duration of the performance."[32] If the participants in these marches thus place themselves in the role of the Israeli soldiers who liberated the Western Wall in 1967, at the same time they call the solidity of that liberation into question. The secure auditory space of the Western Wall Plaza is frayed, and the wall is repositioned within a narrative that renders the 1967 victory as incomplete, waiting for a political resolution that would turn the whole Old City into Jewish space, and religious resolution in the building of the Third Temple.

Sound and the Politics of Presence

As an iconic space for Jewish collectivity, the Kotel stands alone among contemporary Jewish spaces, with no close parallel in terms of size, topography, or religious significance. These qualities, coupled with the physical separation of the Kotel plaza other Jewish spaces in Jerusalem, leads it to function as the type of space that Foucault labeled "heterotopia": sociocultural spaces set aside from everyday life where cultural meanings are simultaneously created, enacted, and superimposed. The weighty historical roots of the Kotel have drawn Jews to pray in this location for centuries, yet since 1967 lack of agreement among Israel's political and religious echelons regarding the development of the space has left an almost blank architectural canvas, affording different groups including those discussed above scope to imagine new ritual contexts for the performance of Jewish prayer and Jewish-Israeli nationhood. Notably, since massed prayers at the Kotel on the Sabbath and holidays are not practical—loudspeakers are not permitted by *halakhah*, and the Kotel is relatively far from most Jewish neighborhoods in Jerusalem— and during the middle of the day the prayer plaza is busy with tourists, these new (or renewed) prayer rituals give shape to a parallel calendar of early-morning and late-night prayer gatherings marking new months and approaching holidays, practiced alongside Israeli national and military ceremonies in the adjoining plaza. From these prayers and ceremonies emerge a counterpoint of different voices as each group temporarily stakes a claim to the site then disperses; meanwhile, the proximity of the muezzin sounding from the Al-Aqsa Mosque just above the wall is a constant reminder that these ceremonies take place on a contested political and religious seam line.

If, as I suggested at the beginning of this chapter, the stones of the Wall are a visual icon of a remarkably consensual Jewish space, sound complicates this space. As political scientist Davide Panagia suggests, listening to public spaces offers a shift in analytical paradigm that goes beyond conventional historical and sociological approaches to the site: one focused less clean, coherent narratives grounded in clearly articulated texts, than on parsing dynamic spaces in which competing utterances and ideologies sometimes speak to each other, sometimes interrupt each other, and sometimes simply exist in the same space.[33] In the discussion above, echoing Daniel Monk's sonic analysis of the Western Wall Plaza immediately following the 1967 war, I have illustrated how the changing soundscape of the Western Wall plaza emphasizes the dynamic process of contesting discourses and identities that continue to shape this site, highlighting the embodied interaction between physical space and the politics of individual and collective presence.

NOTES

1. This text probably refers to the original western wall of the Temple itself.
2. See Edwin Seroussi, "Music in the Religious Experience of Israeli Jews," in *The Garland Encyclopedia of World Music. VI: The Middle East*, ed. Virginia Danielson, Dwight Reynolds, and Scott Marcus (New York: Routledge, 2017), 199–206.
3. Four fourth-century Christian accounts of this practice are cited by William M. Christie, "The Wailing Wall at Jerusalem," *The Expository Times* 42, no. 4 (1931): 176–180.
4. "The Jews' Wailing Place," *Waikato Times*, October 27, 1888.
5. See George Sarton, "The Jerusalem Congress," *Isis* 45, no. 1 (1954): 63–77.
6. See Robert Mazza, "The Deal of the Century? The Attempted Sale of the Western Wall by Cemal Pasha in 1916," *Middle Eastern Studies* 57, no. 5 (2021): 696–711.
7. See Sari Nusseibeh and Anthony David, *Once Upon a Country: A Palestinian Life* (New York: Farrar, Straus and Giroux, 2007), 30–32. For wider background to these events, see also Kobi Cohen-Hattab and Doron Bar, *The Western Wall: The Dispute over Israel's Holiest Jewish Site, 1967–2000* (Leiden: Brill, 2020), 35–36.
8. "Report of the Commission appointed by His Majesty's Government in the United Kingdom of Great Britain and Northern Ireland, with the approval of the Council of the League of Nations," December 1930, https://www.un.org/unispal/document/auto-insert-183716/.
9. Ibid., section V: The Evidence; and appendix 6: Moslem Exhibit.
10. Ibid., section IV: The Respective Claims of the Two Parties. The Jewish Claims.
11. "Report by His Majesty's Government in the United Kingdom of Great Britain and Northern Ireland to the Council of the League of Nations on the Administration of Palestine and Trans-Jordan for the Year 1931," December 31, 1931, appendix 1: Palestine (Western or Wailing Wall) Order in Council, 1931, http://unispal.un.org/UNISPAL.NSF/0/C2567D9C6F6CE5D8052565D9006EFC72.
12. For discussion of the symbolic nature of this photograph, see Daniel Monk, "Diskotel 1967: Israel and the Western Wall in the Aftermath of the Six Day War," *RES: Anthropology and Aesthetics* 48 (2005): 166–178.
13. See ibid., 170–171.
14. See ibid.
15. Gershom Gorenberg, *The Accidental Empire: Israel and the Birth of the Settlements, 1967–1977* (New York: Henry Holt, 2006), 44–45.
16. See also Yitzhak Reiter and Jon Seligman, "1917 to the Present: Al-Haram Al-Sharif/Temple Mount (Har Ha-Bayit) and the Western Wall," in *Where Heaven and Earth Meet: Jerusalem's Sacred Esplanade*, ed. Oleg Grabar and Benjamin Z. Kedar (Jerusalem: Yad Ben Zvi Press, 2009).
17. Michel Foucault and Jay Miskowiec, "Of Other Spaces," *Diacritics* 16, no. 1 (1986): 22–27.
18. Safdie's plans can be found at https://www.safdiearchitects.com/projects/western-wall-precinct (accessed February 2, 2021).

19. See Alona Nitzan-Shiftan, *Seizing Jerusalem: The Architectures of Unilateral Unification* (Minneapolis: University of Minnesota Press, 2017), 234, and Cohen-Hattab and Bar, *The Western Wall*, chapter 3.

20. Suzy [real name redacted], in discussion with the author, November 28, 2009.

21. Cohen-Hattab and Bar, *The Western Wall*, 14.

22. Davide Panagia *The Political Life of Sensation* (Durham, NC: Duke University Press, 2009), 61.

23. Ibid, 48–49.

24. See Tanya Sermer, "Women of, for, and at the Wall: A Performative Analysis of Gender Politics at the Western Wall in Jerusalem," *Women and Music: A Journal of Gender and Culture* 23, no. 1 (2019): 48–74; and Yuval Jobani and Nahshon Perez, *Women of the Wall: Navigating Religion in Sacred Sites* (Oxford: Oxford University Press, 2017).

25. See Cohen-Hattab and Bar, *The Western Wall*, 131.

26. See Phyllis Chesler and Rivka Haut, eds., *Women of the Wall: Claiming Sacred Ground at Judaism's Holiest Site* (Woodstock, VT: Jewish Lights, 2002); Stuart Charmé, "The Political Transformation of Gender Traditions at the Western Wall in Jerusalem," *Journal of Feminist Studies in Religion* 21, no. 1 (2005): 5–34; and Sermer, "Women."

27. See Bonna Devora Haberman, "Women of the Wall: From Text to Praxis," *Journal of Feminist Studies in Religion* 13, no. 1 (1997): 5–34.

28. Ofer Kapach, May 2008, http://binyamin.org.il/?CategoryID=553&ArticleID=1138 (accessed June 20, 2021).

29. See "Hamishṭarah biṭlah Sivuv Shearim eḥad" [The police canceled one Sivuv Shearim], August 1, 2011; https://www.hakolhayehudi.co.il/item/Jewish_identity/-המשטרה-ביטלה-סיבוב-שערים-אחד-וקיבלה-שניים (accessed June 21, 2021).

30. For a recording, see Dov Shurin's "Zochreini Na," November 29, 2009, YouTube video, https://youtu.be/DbZbygwuqfI.

31. For "Death to Arabs," see Just Jerusalem, "Solidarity: Yom Yerushalayim," June 1, 2011, YouTube video, https://youtu.be/JrWFg6S-Xas. For further discussion of singing as nationalist activity during Yom Yerushalayim in the Old City, see Tanya Sermer, "The Politicization of Neo-Hasidic Popular Music: The Musical Discourse of Religious Zionism and Its Role in the Struggle to Claim the Public Sphere of Jerusalem," *Moods and Modes of Jewish Music*, ed. Yuval Shaked (Haifa: Department of Music, University of Haifa, 2014).

32. Ibid., 3–4.

33. See Panagia, *The Political Life of Sensation*, 52.

SELECT BIBLIOGRAPHY

Charmé, Stuart. "The Political Transformation of Gender Traditions at the Western Wall in Jerusalem." *Journal of Feminist Studies in Religion* 21, no. 1 (2005): 5–34.

Cohen-Hattab, Kobi, and Doron Bar. *The Western Wall: The Dispute over Israel's Holiest Jewish Site, 1967–2000*. Leiden: Brill, 2020.

Jobani, Yuval, and Nahshon Perez. *Women of the Wall: Navigating Religion in Sacred Sites*. Oxford: Oxford University Press, 2017.

Kletter, Raz. *Archaeology, Heritage and Ethics in the Western Wall Plaza, Jerusalem: Darkness at the End of the Tunnel*. New York: Routledge, 2019.

Mazza, Roberto. "The Deal of the Century? The Attempted Sale of the Western Wall by Cemal Pasha in 1916." *Middle Eastern Studies* 57, no. 5 (2021): 696–711.

Monk, Daniel B. "Diskotel 1967: Israel and the Western Wall in the Aftermath of the Six Day War." *RES: Anthropology and Aesthetics* 48, no. 1 (2005): 166–178.

Nitzan-Shiftan, Alona. *Seizing Jerusalem: The Architectures of Unilateral Unification.* Minneapolis: University of Minnesota Press, 2017.

Sermer, Tanya. "Women of, for, and at the Wall: A Performative Analysis of Gender Politics at the Western Wall in Jerusalem." *Women and Music: A Journal of Gender and Culture* 23, no. 1 (2019): 48–74.

Sharabi, Asaf. "Religion and Modernity: Religious Revival Movement in Israel." *Journal of Contemporary Ethnography* 44, no. 2 (2015): 223–248.

Wood, Abigail. "The Cantor and the Muezzin's Duet: Contested Soundscapes at Jerusalem's Western Wall." *Contemporary Jewry* 35, no. 1 (2015): 55–72.

Wood, Abigail. "Performative Languages I: Sound, Music and Migration in Jerusalem's Old City." In *Rescripting Religion in the City: Migration and Religious Identity in the Modern Metropolis*, edited by Jane Garnett and Alana Harris, 51–61. New York: Routledge, 2016.

21

SINGING AT THE SABBATH TABLE

Zemiroth as a Family History

NAOMI COHN ZENTNER

THE singing of zemiroth accompanying Sabbath meals is the most widespread domestic musical custom performed by observant Ashkenazic Jews from the Middle Ages until the current day.[1] The term *zemiroth*, which is derived from *zemer* (song), has also been used in Italian and Sephardic Jewish congregations, but there it refers to the psalms intoned before the main section of the Sabbath morning prayers.[2] Within the Ashkenazi world *zemiroth shabbat* (henceforth simply called zemiroth) specifically refers to the paraliturgical songs sung around the Sabbath table during mealtimes.[3] The poetic texts of zemiroth address the commandments of keeping the Sabbath and the spiritual rewards to those who uphold it. Most of them originated in medieval Spain implementing the Arabic poetic meter, while a handful of poems were added to the textual canon later, among them "Ya ribon alam" by Rabbi Israel ben Moses Najara (1555–ca. 1625), "Ya ekhsof" by Rabbi Aharon ben Jacob Perlov "the Great" of Karlin (1736–1772), and "Yom shabbat ḳodesh hu" by Yonathan (dates unknown). Sephardic Jews began singing zemiroth in the modern era, inspired by the Ashkenazi custom and after having access to printed collections of zemiroth; and yet their repertoire and performance is distinct.[4]

Since at least the tenth century, zemiroth were sung to elevate the family mealtime to a festive occasion with religious meaning beyond the mere consumption of food. Indeed, zemiroth, recounting the sacredness of the Sabbath, turn mealtimes into rituals of religious significance. Singing zemiroth also creates intimacy among those sitting at the table and constructs the family as a musical collective bound by time and place. At the same time, it connects the family with others performing the same custom, not only in the present but in the past and future. Singing the same melodies as others expands this rite further by signifying which social group the family feels part of and by formulating a (multilayered) cultural sense of self. As Frederick Bird asserts, "By means of ritual, people represent themselves to themselves."[5] In other words, the act of singing zemiroth is part of the construction of the family's religious, local, ethnic, and even Zionist allegiance. The choice to sing one melody and not another is part of a dialogue with other collectives such as those of Hasidic courts, yeshivas, and kibbutzim, and within this choice lies identification. Statements, such as "we sing the *regular* zemiroth tune" or "we sing the same tunes as everyone else," underline the importance of belonging to a common religious culture, one that is shared beyond the private and domestic sphere.[6] In Edmund Leach's words people "engage in ritual in order to transmit collective messages."[7]

This chapter traces the different modalities of collective musical experience in the home, a performance space rarely considered in Jewish music scholarship (even though major ceremonies of Judaism that include music take place within the nuclear or extended family). It asserts that while the practice of singing zemiroth has largely remained a family custom taking place during the Sabbath meals within the confines of the home, in the early twentieth century it began to extend beyond the boundaries of the home (and by extension, the metaphoric eruv) into public spaces; with that a specifically religious Zionist repertoire was formularized and popularized.

Since most secular families discontinued the practice of singing zemiroth, this chapter relies on observant Ashkenazic families in Israel during the twentieth and twenty-first centuries as an example, especially those connected to various religious Zionist spaces such as yeshivas, kibbutzim, and youth movements. This focus is natural as collectivity is a definitive quality of religious Zionism as a result of two opposing forces: one being the gravitation of religious Jews toward each other and toward houses of prayer as a way of life, particularly in the diaspora; the other being an expression of the socialist ideals absorbed from secular Zionism and its attempt to create a closely knit society, in which all members contribute to the social structure. This common religious culture is shared even when it is private and domestic. Broadening this point beyond religious Zionism, Michael Kramer elaborates on the importance of collective connection as follows:

> the question we should be asking about contemporary [American and Israeli] Jews is not how heavily or lightly they wear their Jewishness, whether they lean towards the traditional or the innovative, whether they prefer *yeshivot* or Jewish film festivals, whether they wear their Jewishness on their sleeves, or tattooed on their bodies. The first question we should be asking about contemporary Jews is whether their expressions of Jewishness make them feel connected to other Jews, however and wherever they may be.[8]

Certain melodies in a family's zemiroth repertoire connect them to other Jewish ethnic and regional collectives, while others link them to communities related to innovative religious, social, or national movements. This diversity is explored by looking at the layers of the zemiroth repertoire of one family from the perspective of its head, Baruch Vessely. His life story and social affiliations connect him to collectives of different kinds as can be discerned from the zemiroth repertoire sung in his home, which is a weekly link to the various social webs of geographic, familial, religious, and even national, that is, Zionist, affiliations in the course of a single meal. And yet in order to understand the meaning of zemiroth today, one must also have an understanding of their early history.

ORIGINS AND SOURCES

One of the earliest sources for zemiroth is the famous *Maḥzor Vitry* (ca. twelfth century), named after its compiler Simḥah ben Samuel of Vitry, a student of Rashi.[9] In contrast to other piyyutim appearing in this maḥzor that often have textual references, indicating which melodies they should be sung to, no such musical indication is mentioned for the zemiroth. The maḥzor specifies the purpose of the zemiroth to be sung during the Sabbath day meal, along with the legal reasoning that this was a means of dividing the whole second meal into two smaller meals (resulting in the three Sabbath meals) thus accommodating the scarcity of food at the time. Until the fifteenth century the number of zemiroth sung during the afternoon mealtime was much larger than those designated for the evening meal, but eventually the canon of poems intended for the evening mealtime grew as later collections of zemiroth attest.

Zemiroth appearing in manuscripts from the thirteenth to sixteenth centuries, such as central European Ashkenazi prayerbooks and the *Birkat hamazon* (the Hebrew blessings that the Jewish law prescribes following a meal), attest to a varying selection of zemiroth poems, depending on location. It was only after the Birkat hamazon appeared in print (Prague, 1514) that selected zemiroth poems became staples throughout central Europe and a canon formed.[10] Indeed, all subsequent publications of zemiroth poems followed the order of the Prague publication and do so until the present day, thus rooting the order of the ritual in the conventions of a specific time (the sixteenth century) and place (central and eastern Europe). A poignant example is "Kol meḵadesh shevi'i" (He who sanctifies the Sabbath as befits it), the first poem of the Friday night zemiroth in the Prague print and subsequent editions. This placement endures until the present day, as it continues to be the first zemer sung on Friday nights by many families.

That the second book ever to be printed in Hebrew in Prague (the first, printed two years earlier, was a siddur) was the Birkat hamazon is further testament to the widespread custom of singing Sabbath table songs.[11] In comparison, Italian printers who started producing Hebrew books as early as 1475 printed zemiroth much later, suggesting that the custom was less prevalent in their communities. The 1618 testimony of the rabbi and poet Menachem ben Judah de Lonzano confirms that singing zemiroth was essentially an Ashkenazi custom, one that was practiced by Italians, too.[12]

The Prague manuscript of 1514 became the prototype for the *bentsherl*, that is, printed booklets of the Grace after Meals, which were the next generation of zemiroth prints. These publications, of which over seventy editions appeared between 1600 and the 1870s throughout central Europe, featured Yiddish translations of the zemiroth side by side with the original Hebrew and Aramaic texts.[13] Since the Yiddish translations were rhymed, it is safe to assume that they were sung in lieu of the Hebrew texts. The Yiddish translation transfigured the Hebrew poetic material according to contemporaneous norms by retaining accepted rites of religious piety and domestic entertainment, and at the same time making it accessible and coherent for those singing it.[14] The use of Yiddish, alongside Hebrew, and the prevalence of zemiroth in many different publications appearing in the Ashkenazic realm suggest that the singing of table songs had become a widespread custom during the early modern period through the late nineteenth century.

While the canon of zemiroth texts, with their variances from one place to another, is relatively easy to trace through manuscripts and printed collections, locating the musical settings of these poems is much more challenging. First and foremost, the singing of zemiroth began as, and still is, an oral tradition. The melodies of zemiroth first appeared in print only in 1856.[15] Therefore, it can be assumed that families would choose their own selection of melodies, according to their tastes and ancestral customs—and that the repertoire could change frequently. Edwin Seroussi asserts that in the domestic sphere musical repertoires remain flexible: "Family singing around the Sabbath table is one such fluid activity in which established traditions interplay with novelties."[16] The selection of zemiroth and the time involved in singing them could change at every meal. Some melodies are considered staples, while others undergo change more frequently. Thus, even upon finding the notation of a zemiroth melody, there is no guarantee that this was part of a long-lasting or widespread musical custom.

While the literary content of zemiroth was sacred, the characteristics of the melodies show an unusual degree of openness to vernacular songs and dance repertoires of local and regional music. The few extant musical notations of zemiroth in manuscripts before the mid-nineteenth century attest to local non-Jewish melodies and musical styles finding their way into the domestic soundscape of Ashkenazi Jews centuries before such an acculturation occurred to their synagogue music. The privacy of the domestic sphere, in the absence of strict rabbinic supervision, allowed families to adopt melodies and styles in dialogue with the surrounding non-Jewish environment. One of the Hungarian repertoires of zemiroth melodies is a case in point for this co-territoriality, since, as Judit Frigyesi has shown, it was similar in form to Hungarian songs and instrumental music, especially with regard to modal shifts.[17]

One of the earliest notations of a zemiroth melody can be found in a manuscript of South German provenance dating from 1510/11. As a number of scholars have outlined, the melody for "Tsur mishelo akhalnu" (The Rock from whose bounty we have eaten) shows influences of the contemporaneous surrounding culture.[18] Similar influences can be observed in a later zemiroth manuscript from mid-eighteenth-century Bohemia leaning on late Baroque instrumental music from the same locale.[19] Among the known melodies German-speaking Jews borrowed, several of which are still in use today, are the folk songs "Fuchs, du hast die Gans gestohlen," Bernard Anselm Weber's melody for "Mit dem Pfeil dem Bogen" to a text from Friedrich Schiller's *Wilhelm Tell*, and the aria "Quell'uom dal fiero aspetto" from Daniel Auber's opera *Fra Diavolo* (1830). These melodies were all sung to the text of "Tsur mishelo," the most popular Sabbath table song text among German Jews.

The adoption of surrounding melodies to zemiroth was due to the latter's fluidity and variability. After being adopted into the home to be sung to a sacred poem, these melodies could then be more easily introduced into the liturgy. This intersection of synagogue with home can be evidenced in Maier Kohn's 1870 manuscript "Der Vorbeter in der Synagoge von München", which includes a melody for the piyyut Sisu ve Gilu besimhat torah, still used today for the zemer "Yom ze mehubad" (This day is honored from among all days).[20]

Local or regional influences can be observed with regard to the paraliturgical songs, particularly songs of the Haggadah, piyyutim for Hanukkah and Purim, and piyyutim and songs for life-cycle events such as weddings and circumcisions. However, since some of these occasions occurred only sporadically, turnover of the family repertory of these festive songs was less frequent than that of the Sabbath zemiroth, which invited a sometimes-weekly transformation following changing trends and tastes.

As for regional differences, it is important to note that whereas the zemiroth sung in German-speaking lands adopted non-Jewish secular melodies of a broad variety, eastern European Jewry did not generally rely on local or regional vernacular song. Here, zemiroth melodies were closely related to the musical language of the synagogue and later to Hasidic nigunim as well as to instrumental music such as klezmer dance tunes.[21] "Yom ze mekhubad," for instance, was sung to the melody of "A holem," a Yiddish song that served as a klezmer tune, and "D'ror yikra" (Freedom he shall proclaim), which will be discussed further below, was sung to the melody of a Hasidic nigun.[22]

Secondary literature on the music of the zemiroth is scarce. Scholarly articles tend to focus on individual songs such as "Ki eshmera shabbat" or "Ma yafit."[23] Zemiroth anthologies often offer extensive introductions. In one such introduction from 1937, Arno Nadel provided references to the origin of zemiroth melodies, focusing on eastern European and Hasidic melodies, in line with the authenticity discourses at the time.[24] About twenty years later Chemjo Vinaver published the *Anthology of Jewish Music*, which includes zemiroth he assembled during his long journey from Poland to Berlin to New York City and many Sabbath table songs from the Cohen-Danciger family.[25] Neil Levin's 1981 publication, which he edited together with Velvel Pasternak, is noteworthy for its detailed and meticulous introduction to the anthology of Ashkenazic and Sephardic zemiroth melodies.[26]

Written and recorded documentation of the melodies to which zemiroth have been sung by Ashkenazic families from the last a hundred and forty years, show that musical styles vary immensely, ranging from simple tunes made of one or more short motifs repeated in strophic form, to longer pieces that could contain a medley of melodies, each sung to a different strophe of the poem, from melodies with a regular beat to those in free-flowing rhythm. Of the latter, some were performed as complex solos, resembling hazanuth, while others were more speech-like, echoing the *nusah*-style to which much of the liturgy in Ashkenazi synagogues at the time was intoned. The most widespread style was derived from dances with upbeat tempo and a regular beat, such as Hasidic dance nigunim, well suited for communal singing. But zemiroth melodies could also be slow and contemplative such as the *hitvaadut* nigunim of the Hasidim. The music of the zemiroth was at once sacred and folk, and it could be connected to liturgical soundscapes as well as to secular and non-Jewish contexts. All this underlines the impossibility to categorize zemiroth melodies according to distinct musical traits. These melodies were highly diverse in form, tempo, length, ornamentation, performance style, and character. Furthermore, many of them overlapped with klezmer music, Hasidic nigunim, liturgical songs, and vernacular songs. Judit Frigyesi aptly describes the diversity and heterogeneity of synagogue songs, which were often interchangeable with zemiroth, as follows:

> The songs bravely face whatever happens to come along: czardas, mazurka, tango or march—sentimental or insipid, nostalgic or vulgar. They are the garbage and the waste, the forbidden and the appalling—a heterogeneous mass, a collage of haphazardly gathered, eclectic fragments. Heterogeneity is courage. It is the daring acceptance of *anything that comes*.[27]

Finding musical cohesiveness within this diversity is an ever-more-elusive effort, as every family relies on its own idiomatic and idiosyncratic collection of melodies derived from different sources. And yet, certain similarities in the zemiroth repertoire can be found among families from the same geographic area and social surrounding. In light of this, a suitable inroad into exploring zemiroth melodies is collectivity.

ZEMIROTH AND COLLECTIVITY

Kay Kaufman Shelemay has argued that music has a central role in the process of creating community by strengthening collectivity.[28] With regard to zemiroth repertoires several collectives are at stake, the first being the family: the intimate family and the extended family that share similar repertoires. As such, the family, with its zemiroth repertoire rooted in distinct locales, represents what Shelemay has called a "musical community of descent."[29] Indeed, the zemiroth melodies sung in a family have delineated the home and have characterized the family's sonority, since melodies were often part of a unique or well-known family heritage linking the family to a branch of their ancestry.

After the eighteenth century, Ashkenazi families encountered and embraced new zemiroth melodies, challenging the families' role as musical communities of descent. Reactionary movements such as Hasidism or Zionism and even certain yeshivas produced repertoires of zemiroth melodies that inadvertently expressed a new collective identity, uniting those who sought to align with the new religious or national movements. In light of their revolutionary ideology and instigation of social change, as well as being disseminators of new collections of zemiroth melodies, Hasidism and Zionism can be considered, following Shelemay, "musical communities of dissent," especially around the time of their inception.

The distinct body of melodies sung at the Hasidic *tishen* (Sabbath or holidays gatherings for Hasidic Jews around their rebbe) was eventually also sung around the family table, often replacing older family or regional customs through new patterns of transmissions that diverged from the transmission of descent, that is, from father to son.[30] A similar process, in which a new zemiroth repertoire succeeded the older one of descent, occurred in eastern European yeshivot, such as those of Volozhin and Slabodka.[31] After the establishment of the State of Israel, Zionist families sang what they called "Israeli" zemiroth melodies as a way of fitting into a new society and of aligning themselves with it as well as its ideals. The families who adopted these melodies chose to do so not only for aesthetic reasons, but mainly because they were part of a shared culture. The association of certain melodies with a certain collective that produced or embraced them led to designations such as "Hasidic zemiroth," "Israeli zemiroth," or "Slabodka yeshiva zemiroth," even if this was not their original source.

While in sociological terms the familial collective is not a community, with regard to curation processes of their zemiroth melodies the musical behavior of families is in line with communal practices and categories. Thus, in certain cases, when a family adopted melodies that belonged to another collective, the family became, following Shelemay's categorization, a "musical community of dissent." Once these new melodies were established within a family and new generations were born, their reactionary nature faded and they became part of the family's standard repertoire and were transmitted as melodies of descent. Other melodies in the family repertoire inevitably connected it to other social groups and collectives, to the non-Jewish musical worlds (especially through vernacular song), or later on to the transnational eastern European musical culture at large.

The case study provided below shows a certain tension between the melodies Baruch Vessely learned by descent and those he learned in communities of dissent. This is typical since musical communities of dissent are mainly created on the basis of their resistance to communities of descent and can be minority groups that go against majority or hegemonic collectives. Often members of musical communities of dissent originate in the descent communities that they are challenging, leading to strained relationships between them.

ZEMIROTH OF IMMIGRANTS IN ISRAEL

Scholarly discourses have portrayed the musical aspects of new immigrants' religious life in Israel as a dynamic process of acculturation and accommodation.[32] Indeed, while immigrants had a strong desire to hold on to, and partake in, familiar religious soundscapes, encounters with new norms and aesthetic sonorities brought changes to the synagogue service and of course to the home. When families immigrated to Israel, their zemiroth repertoires, performance practices, and patterns of transmission often show a negotiation between preservation and modification due to encounters with other musical traditions and with secular Israeli music.

A case in point is Baruch Vessely (1924–) whose zemiroth traverse repertoires of at least three different kinds of musical collectives, linking him to others singing the same tunes. Vessely was born and raised in Dunajská Streda (Slovakia). Almost all of his family perished in the Holocaust. He survived and in 1947 immigrated with his father to British Mandate Palestine, where he later met and married his wife Rivka, and where his two children and many grandchildren and great grandchildren were born.[33] In an interview about his zemiroth repertoire, he asserts that he has forgotten most of the tunes he used to sing with his family in Slovakia, save for one, "Kol meḳadesh shevi'i," which he sings until today.

The poem "Kol meḳadesh" is a four-lined stanza with varying numbers of syllables in each line, challenging any attempt to set it neatly to melodies with a fixed number of beats to a consistent meter. The melody Baruch Vessely sings is one of the most widespread melodies for zemiroth sung among eastern European Jews before the Holocaust. It consists of four differing, musical phrases corresponding to the mono-rhymed quatrain of the poetic strophe and is sung in the flexible recitation known as nusaḥ. Within this style, an unrestricted number of recitation tones can adapt to the irregular number of syllables in the text, while remaining within the melodic framework. "Kol meḳadesh" stands out among Baruch's body of zemiroth melodies—which are all metered and mostly upbeat—due to its free-flowing rhythm and modality (in the *yishtabaḥ* mode), typical of the Ashkenazi performance practice of sections of the morning service.

Variations of this melody are documented in scores and recordings of the Ashkenazi diaspora, showing how the dispersion of one melody can serve as a cultural map of Jewish mobility and migration (Example 21.1).[34]

Despite its widespread popularity among eastern European Jews before the Holocaust, several musical characteristics in Baruch's rendition affirm it to be part of a

EXAMPLE 21.1 Comparison of versions of "Kol meḳadesh shevi'i" from Hungarian-speaking regions. Baruch Vessely's version is given in the third line. Transcriptions by the author.

local variant. His pronunciation and intonation point to a local variant that originated from Hungarian-speaking lands. His ornamentation (F – G – A – B-flat – A on the word "lo," at the end of the first segment) appears in many other Hungarian renditions and is a typical regional variant. Indeed, Baruch's rendition is not as much a local melody as a local rendition, a sort of accent or dialect, of a pan-eastern-European melody.

The "Kol meḳadesh" melody in nusaḥ style was known by many families. Baruch mentions that both his father and his maternal grandfather knew it. Commenting on his singing, I mention that it is similar to how a common acquaintance renders it, and Baruch says: "Of course! We are from the same place!" While at first "Kol meḳadesh" is the only melody that Baruch recalls from his childhood, when I play recordings of other zemiroth that originated near his hometown, he can identify them. Thus, for example, upon hearing a recording of "Shalom aleikhem," or as the Hungarians pronounce it, "Shuloym aleykhem" (Example 21.2)—sung by the Erloy Hasidim, who originated from the Hungarian city of Eger—he begins to sing along and affirms that his family used to sing this melody when he was growing up. Likewise, he recognized a "Eshet ḥayil" sung by other Jews from the region who had later migrated to Israel. These tunes connect Baruch to his ancestral home and local musical customs.

The earliest layer of Baruch's zemiroth repertoire consists of melodies he learned during childhood and are rooted in his family's tradition. These tunes are tied to his birth place, in a region in southern Slovakia that he refers to as "Oberland" (known in Slovakian as Horná zem and in Hungarian as Felvidék). During the time of his up-bringing, Baruch's hometown, which he refers to in Hungarian as Dunaszerdahely, was part of Slovakia, Hungary, Nazi Germany, and after 1945 Czechoslovakia; Hungarian was but one of the spoken languages at the time, attesting to the multiethnic and multi-lingual fabric of the town and region.

EXAMPLE 21.2 "Shuloym aleykhem," as sung by the Erloy Hasidim. Transcription by the author.

The customs of the Oberland Jews showed similarities to the Jewish traditions of the so-called sheva kehilot, that is, the seven towns within easy traveling range of Vienna where Jews could reside after the 1675 expulsion from the capital. In the course of the nineteenth century, they absorbed western European Jewish influences, particularly of Moravia and southern Germany (in contrast to the Jews of the "Unterland," who closely aligned with the customs of eastern European Jewry). Their zemiroth repertoire included both eastern and western European melodies, and performance practice, thus reflecting this intersection. The Oberland Jews sang both the upbeat, dancelike melodies in major modes that are typical of the zemiroth repertoires of Western European Jews, as well as the Hasidic nigunim, klezmer tunes, and liturgical formulas characteristic of the eastern European zemiroth.

While "Kol mekadesh" is the only zemiroth melody from his family home that Baruch still sings today, it is not the only melody from his youth he has preserved. Indeed, another type of zemiroth prevalent among Oberland Jews is still part of Baruch's current repertoire as well, connecting him even more tightly to the eastern European Jewish culture of the region. In his hometown, Baruch had attended the local Hasidic yeshiva. He recalls that for *shaleshudes*, the third Sabbath meal at the yeshiva, they would sing two Hasidic zemiroth that he had not heard at home: "Atkinu seudata" (Let us prepare for meal) and "Azamer beshvahin" (I will sing on the praises, Example 21.3). The text of "Azamer beshvahin" is attributed to Ha'ari, Rabbi Isaac ben Solomon Luria (1534–1572), the founder of the Lurianic school of Kabbalah. Although he did not distinguish himself as a writer, Ha'ari wrote three widely known hymns used to accompany the Sabbath meals of the Sephardim and Hasidim that were included in many prayer books.[35] A number of Hasidic yeshivas, such as those in the cities of Pápa and Galanta, adopted such kabbalistic texts.

Baruch asserts that the yeshiva's liturgy followed Ashkenazic customs practiced by eastern European Jews, and not the nusah Sepharad practiced by Hasidic communities

EXAMPLE 21.3 "Azamer bishvahin." Transcription by the author.

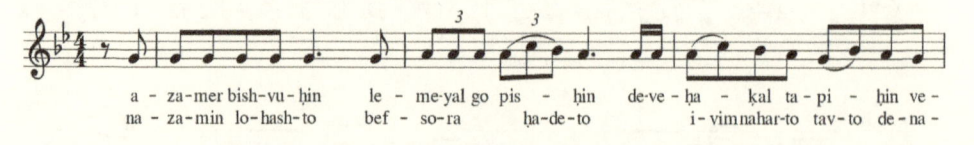

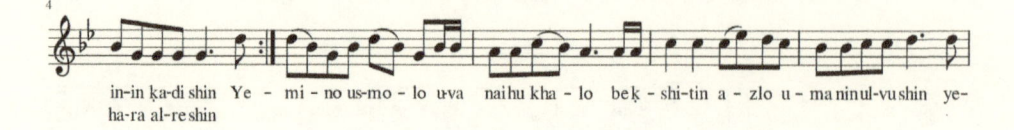

elsewhere. Still, those attending the yeshiva learned zemiroth poems rooted in kabbalistic texts, which they shared with other Hasidic courts. Baruch also recalls how after the Friday night meal held at home, all the students would go to the house of Rabbi Asher Ansel Katz, who led the yeshiva, to join his family's meal, receive *sheyrayim* (holy leftovers) from the rabbi, and sing zemiroth together. He perceives these melodies as distinct from the zemiroth tunes of his father, indicative of the larger disparities between the Hasidic melodies and the western European religious practice he grew up in. Indeed, the Hasidic movement was revolutionary also in the sense that it offered a reservoir of nigunim, which from the early nineteenth century would serve some families with an alternative to older regional and domestic musical customs. Since these melodies and kabbalistic texts had not been part of the family as a musical community of descent, when adopting them into the space of the home the family often supplemented and, in some cases, even substituted previously used ones. Thus, melodies that represented a social and spiritual Hasidic collective were sung by those who lived in proximity but did not share the Hasidic ideology and way of life. The Sabbath table's flexibility and variability facilitated the integration of Hasidic zemiroth melodies and kabbalistic texts into the Oberland zemiroth repertoire.

After his immigration to British Mandate Palestine, Baruch's zemiroth repertoire gradually diverged from that of his youth and grew more similar to that of his contemporaries and peers, a process that can be observed in many other religious Zionist families. Shortly after his arrival, in 1947 he joined kibbutz Masuot Yitzḥak, which belonged to the religious kibbutz movement. He asserts that he learned the rest of his zemiroth repertoire at the kibbutz from members who had founded it two years earlier. After fighting in the War of Independence defending his kibbutz, he was taken prisoner and spent over a year in Jordan in a camp of prisoners of war, before finally moving to Jerusalem after the foundation of the State of Israel. By then, due to his kibbutz experiences, he was already familiar with the zemiroth tunes that were sung by members of his religious Zionist circle at the time. One of them is "D'ror yiḵra," which he had learned in the kibbutz. Baruch recalls this melody easily, and not only because he acquired it most recently, that is, in his early days as a new immigrant, but because he is surrounded by people who sing it as well, including his family, close and extended. His current zemiroth repertoire consists mainly of melodies learned in a religious Zionist context.

After singing "D'ror yiḵra" during an interview about his zemiroth repertoire, he looks at me and says, "This! You know this." Baruch and I live in the same neighborhood and are members at the same synagogue. I know his children and grandchildren. We are from the same social and religious "tribe," and he thus assumes that our zemiroth melodies must be common. And of course, he is right. I do know this tune. Not because I am a musicologist who researches and collects zemiroth melodies, but because I heard it growing up. This and others were tunes that everyone around me knew and sang during the Sabbath meals. I learned them from my father who, like Baruch, learned them in a religious Zionist context, disconnected from his family's zemiroth repertoire. In my father's case the context was the religious Zionist youth movement of Bnei Akiva. My previous research on zemiroth in the religious Zionist community has revealed that a pool of about thirty melodies were familiar to anyone belonging to this collective and its various spaces.[36] These melodies were sung in youth movements, schools, and dining halls of religious kibbutzim, and singing them was indicative of belonging to the Zionist social collective with its ideology and beliefs. The melodies themselves were neither composed by Zionists nor created for Zionist contexts; most of them were well-known eastern European zemiroth tunes, some Hasidic in origin.

One such melody is a Hasidic nigun attributed to the spiritual leader of the Hasidic court of Ruzhin, Rabbi Israel Friedman (1796–1850). It is sung till today in the tishen of the Boyan dynasty as the "Nigun of Rabbi Israel of Ruzhin." At some point, this melody was set to the words of the piyyut "D'ror yikra," written by medieval poet Rabbi Dunash ben Labrat (920–990). Traces of the melody's origin as a nigun without a clear regular beat are apparent in the unusual 6/4 time signature and in its performance practice in which the number of beats in each measure changed frequently. It has become one of the most well-known zemiroth sung in religious Zionist circles (Example 21.4).

All of the religious Zionist participants interviewed for this research sang or at least knew this melody for "D'ror yikra." Those born between the 1920s and the 1950s learned it from their time in religious Zionist spaces, usually in Israel; some learned it during Sabbath meals in religious kibbutzim in the 1940s and 1950s, others in religious Zionist high schools and Zionist yeshivas, and yet others in Bnei Akiva, a religious Zionist youth movement. Those who were born in Europe during 1930s and 1940s recalled learning "D'ror yikra" along with Zionist songs in Jewish orphanages for child Holocaust survivors in Budapest and Switzerland. Although this was clearly not a new melody, in the 1940s it was perceived as such in religious Zionist social circles and therefore had a certain youthful revolutionary air of dissent when sung by youngsters in Israeli youth movements and religious kibbutzim. This melody was sung during the

EXAMPLE 21.4   "D'ror yikra" as sung by Baruch Vessely. Transcription by the author.

Sabbath mealtime in many young religious Zionist families in the 1960s and 1970s. For the generation born after 1970, both in Israel and abroad, "D'ror yiḳra" became known as a family tune, shared with other religious Zionist families and the community at large. This melody is a prime example of the versatility of its collective meaning, being at different points in time an integral part of Hasidism, of the new religious "Israeli," and of families—of musical communities of dissent and descent.

With "D'ror yiḳra" becoming known abroad as an "Israeli" tune, it is important to ask, at what stage do zemiroth begin to be associated with a new locale, and specifically with Israel. Learning and singing zemiroth was part of the socialization process of new immigrants in Israel and of a younger Israeli-born generation of religious Zionists during the 1940s to the 1970s. This socialization process, an "Israelization," as it were, differed significantly from that of local communities in Europe—such as Oberland—and consequently patterns of zemiroth transmission in Israel diverged from those in Europe. The strong social ties connecting individuals in Israel with their peer strata (in state schools, youth movements, the army) meant that the musical repertory of thirty widespread zemiroth melodies that circulated in religious Zionist institutions were an important part of social belonging and identity.

In the case of Baruch, singing these tunes at his Sabbath table after learning them in large communal settings was a way to show alignment with the ideology, social norms, and cultural practice of a new society coming into being. This repertory was often detached from the family or local tradition of zemiroth and incorporated the youthful spirit present in these (mostly educational) institutions for youth. Certain musical characteristics of zemiroth melodies, such as melodies with a slower or changing tempo, nusaḥ-style melodies like "Kol meḳadesh," and long complex melodic structures, were deemed unsuitable for the emerging body of "Israeli" zemiroth melodies, and their practice in family homes fell out of fashion. The preferred melodies, especially by the youth, tended to be upbeat, with short repetitive phrases, sung in a fast tempo—the beat often emphasized by banging the rhythm on the dining table at which the meal took place. Thomas Turino sees such short repetitious melodies as conducive to communal participation:

> Rather than leading to boredom, as it might for a seated audience, highly repetitive forms and rhythms actually add to the intensity of participatory performance because more people can join in and interact. . . . and it is this stylized social interaction that is the basis of artistic and spiritual pleasure and experience. Repetition of the rhythmic groove and predictable musical forms are essential to getting and staying in sync with others. Social synchrony is a crucial underpinning of feelings of social comfort, belonging and identity. In participatory performance, these aspects of being human come to the fore.[37]

Between 1940 and 1970, the performance of these "Israeli" zemiroth often took place during large meals in communal dining rooms, sung in a similar manner to the Zionist practice of singing Hebrew folksongs in public singalongs known as *shira betsibur*.

Utilizing the power of simultaneous communal singing of a shared melodic and textual repertoire—creating what Ruth HaCohen has called a "vocal community"—can be observed particularly in Israel's youth movements.[38] Religious Zionist youth sang zemiroth tunes during Sabbath mealtimes in the communal dining rooms of religious kibbutzim, Zionist yeshivot, and youth movements' *shabatonim* (retreats), that is, in public settings. In this way, zemiroth melodies became part of a mainstream repertoire and were transmitted as such to religious Zionists abroad. The younger generation of these communities used zemiroth alongside Israeli folksongs to prepare for their future life in Israel as a cultural socialization, as it were. After immigration, singing zemiroth together became critical in forging a sense of camaraderie among individuals arriving from different countries, many of whom had at first little to no common language.

Since the nineteenth century, waves of migration and displacement led family customs to be displaced and replaced. For Baruch, singing "Israeli" zemiroth melodies with his new family in Israel led to him gradually forgetting his childhood zemiroth repertoire, to a degree that even recalling it was a challenge. His trajectory represents a recurring theme that accelerated throughout the twentieth century: the demise of established regional zemiroth repertoires in favor of new transregional ones. For the younger generation, singing zemiroth melodies learned in Zionist settings in Israel served to perpetuate religious and Zionist ideals in a public space. This younger generation, in turn, would influence their families' repertoires, moving the newly learned pieces back into a domestic setting, albeit to varying degrees. Indeed, different religious Zionist families living in Israel had different approaches to the question of preservation versus change of zemiroth melodies. Some zealously sought to hold on to their family traditions, others added new melodies to their repertoire, or replaced it in its entirety.

While mobility affected the zemiroth repertoire of families as musical communities of descent throughout history, what had changed in the twentieth century pertained to the types of melodies sung, their modes of transmission, and the new social ties they facilitated when singing with others in various Zionist spaces. This musical soundscape, disconnected from its ancestral and geographic roots brought families closer to those who lived in the same social and religious environments.

ZEMIROTH BETWEEN INDIVIDUALITY AND COLLECTIVITY, PRIVATE AND PUBLIC SPACES

In her book about Jewish prayer and its sounds, Judit Frigyesi relates the memories of various Hungarian prayer leaders, one of which, Márton Fóti, describes his father's modest leadership in singing zemiroth:

> My father sang the *zmires*. He knew all the verses by heart. We joined in for some of the songs, but at other times we just listened. He had a special style. He sang as if he

were telling a story. He withdrew into himself, afraid almost of being at the center of attention. It was so modest, so . . . unpretentious, that you had to listen.[39]

In some homes it was customary that the head of the family sings zemiroth on his own, and the quiet listening of the family members was acknowledged as silent participation, while in others he could assert his authority in deciding what will be sung in the course of the Sabbath by everyone present. Whether the head of the family accepted new melodies brought in by the younger generation depended on the interfamily dynamics and on the extent of his accommodation of unfamiliar zemiroth melodies during the family meals.

This negotiation of individuality and collectivity in the domestic sphere can also be observed in the case of Baruch Vessely, and yet the foundation on which it occurs is unique given his trajectory: Baruch's zemiroth repertoire consists of a tapestry of different melodies, each connecting him with a different part of his personal history and the related collective. There is the local tune from his childhood home that is tied to his family as well as his hometown if not region. There are the melodies learned in the local Hasidic yeshiva. And there are the many melodies he learned during his time in the kibbutz that link him to the religious Zionist community that he eventually joined. The latter had the strongest presence in his family's Sabbath mealtime, most likely because these melodies were the most recent ones he acquired; they were experienced by his children and their peers, and they were known among other families in his environs. These melodies embodied the shifts and dynamics of belonging to different collectives and to new social and religious milieus. In this way, the zemiroth transcend the distinction between home and public, family and community at large.

In many ways the use of zemiroth melodies is comparable to what sociolinguistics studies call "code switching," the alternation between two or more languages, pronunciations, vocabularies, or accents depending on social identifications. Jeffrey Summit has applied this strategic linguistic alignment to melody choice in Jewish communal settings; he asserts, "The use of the term *code* . . . as opposed to repertoire or style is meant to imply that melodies [for public worship] are infused with particular associations, coded meaning, and symbolic significance."[40] Even after leaving the environment of a social group—be it the native family, a youth movement, or a yeshiva—zemiroth melodies would remain in the repertoire of the individual, not solely to enable code switching, but rather as an act of adherence, fidelity, nostalgia, and sometimes mere habit. Continuing to sing the zemiroth melodies even after the active participation and physical proximity to that social sphere or place of learning has ended is an act of tenacity and alliance, transcending boundaries of time and place.

Due to the blurring borderlines between public and private spheres, individuals can perform their belonging to numerous (musical) collectives while seated at their own dining room table. For those singing zemiroth, certain melodies have meaning beyond being an assortment of pleasant sounds; a tune can be a tangible connection to a lost world and those inhabiting it, thus resounding the Jewish family and region that one had belonged to. A melody can connect to a revolutionary Jewish movement, and finally, newly learned melodies, even if they are old in origin, can serve in new contexts.

But the zemiroth melodies can be also understood in a different context or space, created by eruvim, to which they can be even compared. The outcome of erecting an eruv—the artificial blurring of the domestic sphere into the public, usually by winding a wire around posts to demarcate an extended private domain—is analogous to the absorption of new melodies into the home, in effect making the intimate family table part of the public sphere. While the introduction of additional melodies into the home effectively make the domestic an offshoot of the public, the melodies also act as a sort of reverse eruv by establishing a private ritual enclosure. More so, approaching the zemiroth-eruv metaphorically, each melody constitutes an invisible thread encircling the singers and concurrently connecting them with individuals and collectives who once shared or still share them, in and through time and space. In this way examining how a melody, as delicate as the string of the eruv, can serve as a musical connection between individual and community leads to an understanding of how significant belonging to a community was and continues to be for Ashkenazi Jews, especially in the course of the long twentieth century, impacting the choice of song in the most intimate of all places, the home.

Notes

1. Albert Evan Kohn, "Domestic Piety in a Jewish Key: Sabbath Table Singing in Medieval Europe, 1200–1600" (BA thesis, Jewish Theological Seminary, 2018), 6.
2. See, for example, Mark Kligman, "Chanting Psalms Today: The Zemirot in Syrian Sabbath Prayers," in *Psalms in Community: Jewish and Christian Textual, Liturgical, and Artistic Traditions*, ed. Harold W. Attridge and Margot E. Fassler (Leiden: Brill, 2004), 325–340.
3. See Ernst Daniel Goldschmidt, "Zemirot," in *Encyclopaedia Judaica*, ed. Michael Berenbaum and Fred Skolnik, 2nd ed. (Detroit, MI: Macmillan, 2007), 21:507.
4. See Edwin Seroussi, "Jüdische Musik," s.v., *MGG Online*, https://www.mgg-online.com/mgg/stable/372426.
5. Frederick Bird, "Ritual as Communicative Action," in *Ritual and Ethnic Identity: A Comparative Study of the Social Meaning of Liturgical Ritual in Synagogues*, ed. Jack N. Lightstone and Frederick B. Bird (Waterloo, ON: Wilfred Laurier University Press, 1995), 35.
6. Despite the firm-held claims of these practitioners, since religious Jews are forbidden from recording or documenting in any way on the Sabbath, any actual evidence supporting this idea could not be substantiated since it was gleaned from encounters with friends and family in near proximity.
7. Edmund Leach, *Culture and Communication: The Logic by which Symbols are Connected: An Introduction to the Use of Structuralist Analysis in Social Anthropology* (Cambridge: Cambridge University Press, 1976), 45.
8. Michael Kramer, "There's No Place Like Home," in *Jews at Home: The Domestication of Identity: Jewish Cultural Studies*, ed. Simon Bronner, 2 vols. (Portland, OR: Littman Library of Jewish Civilization, 2010), 322.

9. The original *Maḥzor Vitry* is lost; later non-identical copies, dating from the late twelfth to mid-fourteenth century, are the only extant sources. This chapter relies on the copy MS Opp. 59 (cat. Neubauer 1100), Bodleian Library, Oxford.

10. *Grace after Meals, Birhat ha'mazon* / ברכת המזון, facsimile ed. (Prague, 1514; London: Valmadonna Trust Library, 1984).

11. See Marvin J. Heller, *Printing the Talmud* (Leiden: Brill, 2019), 125.

12. See Menachem de Lonzano, *Shtei yadot* [Two hands] (Venice 1618), 100b.

13. See Chava Turniansky "The 'Bentsherel' and the Sabbath-hymns in Yiddish" / ה"בענטשערל" והזמירות ביידיש, *Alei Sefer: Studies in Bibliography and in the History of the Printed and the Digital Hebrew*, no. 10 (1982): 51–92.

14. See Andrea Schatz, "Introduction: 'Yiddish: A Diasporic Path to Modernity," *Jewish Studies Quarterly* 15, no. 1 (2008): 1–4.

15. Melodies to "Ya ribon" and "Tsur mishelo" were first printed in Israel Mayer Japhet, *Schire Yeschurun: Gottesdienstliche Gesänge—Eingeführt in die Synagoge der Israelitischen Religionsgesellschaft zu Frankfurt am Main* (Frankfurt am Main: J. Kauffmann, 1856), 142–143. The first printed collection of numerous zemiroth appeared in Abraham Baer, *Baal Tfillah: Oder, Der practische Vorbeter* (Göthenburg: author, ca. 1877), 105–107.

16. "Das Singen in der Familie am Schabbattisch ist eine solche sich verändernde Aktivität, bei der gewachsene Traditionen mit Neuem interagieren. Der Vortrag dieser Lieder, in der aschkenasischen Tradition zemirot genannt, markiert auch Zeit in dem Sinne, dass er das Schabbatmahl von anderen Mahlzeiten trennt." Edwin Seroussi, "Jüdische Musik," s.v., *MGG Online*, https://www.mgg-online.com/mgg/stable/372426.

17. Judit Frigyesi, "Is There Such a Thing as Hungarian-Jewish Music?," in *Between Minority and Majority: Hungarian and Jewish/Israeli Ethnical and Cultural Experiences in Recent Centuries*, ed. Pál Hatos and Attila Novák (Budapest: Balassi Institute, 2013), 141–143.

18. For a description of the manuscript and references to pertinent literature, see Tina Frühauf, "Resonating Places, Mapping Jewish Spaces: Jews, Music and Southern Germany," in *Jüdische Musik im süddeutschen Raum / Mapping Jewish Music of Southern Germany*, ed. Claus Bockmaier and Tina Frühauf (Munich: Allitera Verlag, 2021), 19–21.

19. See also Israel Adler and Edwin Seroussi, "Musical Notations of Zemîrôt (Sabbath Table Songs) in an Eighteenth Century Manuscript at the Prague National Library," *Studies in Bibliography and Booklore*, no. 20 (1988): 5–24.

20. Maier Kohn, "Der Vorbeter in der Synagoge von München," *Eduard Birnbaum Music Collection*, Mus. Add. 4a (Cincinnati: Hebrew Union College, 1870), 98.

21. See Walter Zev Feldman, *Klezmer: Music, History and Melody* (New York: Oxford University Press, 2016) 214, 235–247.

22. See Abraham Zvi Idelsohn, *Thesaurus of Oriental Hebrew Melodies*, vol. 9: *The Folk Songs of the East European Jews* (Leipzig: Friedrich Hofmeister, 1932), 21 ("A cholem hot sich mir gecholemt," no. 72).

23. See, for example, Rachel Kolander, "Hapiyut ki eshmera shabat," *Meḥkarey ḥag*, no. 8 (1997): 80–99; Macy Nulman, "Mah Yafit: The Intriguing Fate of the Sabbath Table Hymn," *Journal of Jewish Music and Liturgy*, no. 1 (June 1976): 23–38; Avigdor Herzog (with Andre Hajdu), "A la recherché du 'tonus peregrinus' dans la tradition musicale Juive," *Yuval Studies of the Jewish Music Research Center* 1 (1968): 194–203.

24. See Arno Nadel, *Die häuslichen Schabbatgesänge* (Berlin: Schoken Verlag, 1937).

25. See Chemjo Vinaver, *Anthology of Jewish Music* (New York: Edward B. Marks Music Corp., 1955).

26. See Neil Levin, "Zemiroth: An Overview—The Growth of a Musical Tradition," in *Z'mirot Anthology*, ed. Neil Levin and Velvel Pasternak (Cedarhurst: Tara Publications, 1981).

27. Judit Frigyesi, *Writing on Water: The Sounds of Jewish Prayer* (Budapest: CEU Press, 2018), 141.

28. See Kay Kaufman Shelemay, "Musical Communities: Rethinking the Collective in Music," *Journal of the American Musicological Society* 64, no. 2 (2011): 349–390.

29. Ibid., 367–368.

30. For the Hasidic contribution to the body of zemiroth melodies as well as their dissemination beyond Hasidic social circles, see Levin, "Zemiroth: An Overview," vii–viii.

31. The adoption of a new repertoire of zemiroth melodies in Israel through the transmission of the Slabodka yeshiva in Lithuania (also known as Yeshivat Knesset Yisrael) is apparent in the ethnographic recording of Yisrael Schneider, singing the zemiroth that his father learned from Rabbi Eliezer Zeev Loft, who was the communal mentor. Yisrael Schneider, undated recording, National Sound Archives, NSA Y-10099-CAS_B, Jerusalem.

32. See, for example, Amnon Shiloah and Eric Cohen, "The Dynamics of Change in Jewish Oriental Ethnic Music in Israel," *Ethnomusicology* 27, no. 2 (1982): 227–252.

33. Baruch Vessely, in discussion with the author, January 23, 2011.

34. Among the notated sources for "Kol meḳadesh" are Israel Goldfarb and Herbert Levinthal, eds., *Song and Praise for Sabbath Eve: For Use at Synagogue Gatherings in Connection with the Late Friday Evening Sermon or Discourse* (New York: n.p., 1920), 89; Herbert Loewe, ed., *Mediaeval Hebrew Minstrelsy: Songs for the Bride Queen's Feast—16 Zemiroth Arranged according to the Traditional Harmonies* (London: Clarke and Co., 1926), 32–33; Abraham Moses Bernstein, ed., *Musikalisher Pinkes* (Vilna: B. Szulman, 1927), 5; Idelsohn, *Thesaurus of Oriental Hebrew Melodies*, 9:10–11; Herman Meyerovitsch, ed., *Oneg Shabbos: Anthology of Ancient Hebrew Table Songs* (London: Edward Goldstein and Sons, 1951), 6.

35. See Yehuda Liebes, "Zemirot les'eudat shabat sheyasad ha-Ari haḳadosh" *Molad* 4, no. 23 (1972): 540–555. For further insights on the text of "Azamer beshvaḥin" and its kabbalistic connotations, see Israel Gutwirth, *The Kabbalah and Jewish Mysticism* (London: Philosophical Library/Open Road, 2021).

36. See Naomi Cohn Zentner, "Ancient Melodies for a New Society: *Zemirot Shabbat* in 'Bnei Akiva' and among Religious Zionist Youth in Israel" / ניגונים עתיקים לחברה חדשה: זמירות שבת בקרב בני עקיבא וצעירי הציונות הדתית, in *Music in Israel*, ed. Tuvia Friling, Gideon Katz, and Michael Wolpe (Iyunim Bitkumat Israel 6; Beer-Sheva: Ben-Gurion Research Institute for the Study of Israel and Zionism, 2014), 713–740.

37. Thomas Turino, *Music as Social Life: The Politics of Participation* (Chicago: University of Chicago Press, 2008), 41–44.

38. Ruth HaCohen, " 'The Sound of Music': The Birth and Demise of Vocal Communities," thematic issue "The Sound Issue," in *AJS Perspectives: The Magazine for the Association for Jewish Studies*, ed. Jonathan M. Hess and Laura S. Lieber (Spring/Summer 2016): 12–13.

39. Frigyesi, *Writing on Water*, 178.

40. Jeffrey A. Summit, *The Lord's Song in a Strange Land: Music and Identity in Contemporary Jewish Worship* (New York: Oxford University Press: 2000), 131.

SELECT BIBLIOGRAPHY

Adler, Israel, and Edwin Seroussi. "Musical Notations of Zemîrôt (Sabbath Table Songs) in an Eighteenth Century Manuscript at the Prague National Library." *Studies in Bibliography and Booklore* 20 (1988): 5–24.

Bird, Frederick. "Ritual as Communicative Action." In *Ritual and Ethnic Identity: A Comparative Study of the Social Meaning of Liturgical Ritual in Synagogues*, edited by Jack N. Lightstone and Frederick B. Bird, 23–52. Waterloo, ON: Wilfred Laurier University Press, 1995.

Bronner, Simon, ed. *Jews at Home: The Domestication of Identity*. Jewish Cultural Studies 2. Portland, OR: Littman Library of Jewish Civilization, 2010.

Cohn Zentner, Naomi. "Ancient Melodies for a New Society: *Zemirot Shabbat* in 'Bnei Akiva' and among Religious Zionist Youth in Israel" / ניגונים עתיקים לחברה חדשה: זמירות שבת בקרב בני עקיבא וצעירי הציונות הדתית. In *Music in Israel*, edited by Tuvia Friling, Gideon Katz, and Michael Wolpe, 713–740. Iyunim Bitkumat Israel 6. Beer-Sheva: Ben-Gurion Research Institute for the Study of Israel and Zionism, 2014.

Cohn Zentner, Naomi. "Kol mekadesh shevi'i: Resounding Synagogue and Home in Early Modern Ashkenaz." *Report of the Oxford Centre for Hebrew and Jewish Studies* 2019–2020 (Oxford: Oxford Centre for Hebrew and Jewish Studies, 2020): 30–32.

Frigyesi, Judit. *Writing on Water: The Sounds of Jewish Prayer*. Budapest: Central European University Press, 2018.

Gosfield, Avery. "Gratias Post Mensam in Diebus Festiuis Cum Cantico העבריים: A New Look at an Early Sixteenth Century Tzur Mishelo." In *Revealing the Secrets of the Jews: Johannes Pfefferkorn and Christian Writings about Jewish Life and Literature in Early Modern Europe*, ed. Jonathan Adams and Cordelia Heß, 275–296. Berlin: De Gruyter, 2017.

Herzog, Avigdor. "Familial Music Repertory: Shabbat Table Songs" / רפרטואר מוסיקלי משפחתי. *Proceedings of the World Congress of Jewish Studies* 11, Division D, II: Art, Folklore, Music (1993): 43–48.

Levin, Neil, and Velvel Pasternak. *Z'mirot Anthology*. Cedarhurst: Tara Publications, 1981

Turniansky, Chava. "The 'Bentsherel' and the Sabbath- hymns in Yiddish" / ה"בענטשערל" והזמירות ביידיש. *Alei Sefer: Studies in Bibliography and in the History of the Printed and the Digital Hebrew*, no. 10 (1982): 51–92.

22

EARLY MODERN YIDDISH WEDDING SONGS

Synchronic and Diachronic Functions

DIANA MATUT

אונ' וואו מן טוט טנצן אונ' שפרינגן. בייא דיא ברוילפֿט לייט וואו מאן
טוט זינגן

And where one dances and jumps / Is with the bride and groom, where one sings.[1]

THE early modern period was one of the most decisive times in the formation of Ashkenazic customs on the grounds of central and eastern Europe. Many aspects of what is today considered as normative Orthodox solidified during these centuries. Moreover, the very concept of "Orthodoxy" was in itself a result of Jewish practices of that time.[2] But this was also a period during which Ashkenazic society changed fundamentally, especially due to factors that David B. Ruderman defined as "accelerated mobility," "a heightened sense of communal cohesiveness," "knowledge explosion," a "crisis of rabbinic authority," and the "blurring of religious identities."[3] The texts of wedding songs are insightful sources for the adjustments Ashkenazic society underwent as a result of these changes, since songs served as didactic tools for the implementation of new religious ideals, social norms, morals, and customs.

While singing can be considered to have been the customary default version for changing wedding customs and never stood to debate, questions such as gender and behavioral norms for singers, performance practices, and repertoire came under increased scrutiny.[4] As will be shown below, early modern sources mention women as the main performers; they sang for other women, and occasionally for the couple. By the end of the early modern period, however, they and their unpaid singing services were replaced by a male cast of singers and entertainers called *badkhonim* who permanently took over at least some of the core women's singing functions as paid professional wedding entertainers.

One of the most important inner-Jewish arguments that continuously supported song was the religious obligation of making bride and groom joyful on their wedding day and to honor them. In the early modern Yiddish כלה 'איין היפשר זמר פֿר חתּן אונ (A lovely song for groom and bride, ca. 1676), this is mentioned explicitly: "We will jump while dancing, we will raise our voices, and we will multiply our praise in order to honor bride and groom."[5] In order to make the newlyweds happy, many kinds of entertainment were permissible and employed during the early modern period, including the telling of stories and jokes, learned and pious Bible interpretations, instrumental music, dancing, and other activities for which the songs themselves bear witness.

More than twenty Yiddish or bilingual Hebrew-Yiddish wedding songs are known from the early modern period, but only few of their melodies have been transmitted. They were explicitly intended for the bride and/or the groom, variously known as *kale-lid* (bride song), *khosn-lid* (groom song), or *khosn-kale-lid* (groom-and-bride song). In spite of this slim body of transmitted songs, the fact that singing featured so prominently during the preparation and celebration of a wedding in central and eastern Europe during the entire period in question, it is safe to assume that a comprehensive and varied song repertoire once existed. The various *genizot*, that is, storage areas in a Jewish synagogue or cemetery containing writings or printed matter no longer used but for religious reasons not destroyed—especially those found in recent years in Germany—bear witness to the wealth of literature and songs lost.[6]

In the Yiddish-speaking world, songs were usually collected and copied by hand or printed with a maximum of up to five texts. Such booklets could be produced at relatively low costs and were easy-to-carry objects. And while Yiddish songs where frequently printed and distributed, Yiddish or bilingual Hebrew-Yiddish song collections were a rare exception at a time when vernacular song books in many European languages became an artifact of everyday life. Among such rare collections are Elijah ben Moses Loanz's זְמִירוֹת וְתוּשְׁבָּחוֹת (Songs and praises), which appeared in Basel in 1599; the so-called Wallich-manuscript (ca. 1600), and Elhanan Henle Kirchhan's שמחת הנפש (Joy of the soul), published in Fürth in 1726/27.

It was also common to insert one or two songs into larger works such as manuscripts and books on ethics and morals, stories, prayers, or miscellaneous house books for a bride or newlywed. One bride song, for example, was printed with the book מצות הנשים (Women's commandments) (Venice, 1588)—which as a guide for women's religious obligations was of special importance for every bride and wife-to-be. At the same time, oral transmission of songs was still commonplace. Indeed, the printing of a song text did not necessarily mean the end of the latter's presence in oral tradition and songs transferred from the written medium to the oral sphere and vice versa. The vast majority of material, however, is presumed to be lost due to prevalent orality, material decay and reuse, wars, fires, and other means of destruction, but also because of inner-Jewish (self-) censorship and changing tastes.

The twenty-odd songs at the heart of this chapter may seem like a rather thin textual base, but they are important sources for early modern social, religious, and ethical norms, the development of personal piety, and the broad attempt at moral "normativization" of Ashkenazic Jewry by religious authorities. Conveying (wedding) customs as well as general societal and religious rules and admonitions, they served as important tools and were widely embraced in light of being sung to popular, much-loved melodies.

Little is known about the spectrum of songs not explicitly labeled as bride- or groom-song, but befitting the occasion. However, contemporary moralistic sources mention the singing of "imprudent songs" and the equally bewildering behavior of the (female) guests during wedding feasts.[7] It can therefore be assumed that drinking, love, evening, or humorous songs were performed as well. While certain wedding song topics remained extant during the entire course of the early modern period (as, for instance, mentioning of the three essential religious obligations for women), others disappeared (such as those that referenced the physical appearance of bride and groom or the impending wedding night) and new ones emerged (as for instance new rules pertaining to the behavior of the future housewife).

This chapter relies on a diverse body of sources and uses first and foremost songs to provide insight into the wedding customs of the so-called early modern Ashkenazic Jewry, a somewhat disputed term for a heterogenous collectivity, which in the early modern context can be understood as being "coterminous with those who spoke Yiddish in its various dialects and followed Mosheh Isserles' glosses to the Halakhic code, *Shulḥan 'arukh*."[8] And yet the focus on what follows is on a distinct collective, that of those involved in wedding customs in various capacities, as facilitators and listeners of song, and specifically on women as important agents of the same. Only those songs are used as sources that were explicitly intended for the wedding festivities. I will not include others here—such as Yiddish drinking, love, farewell, riddle or evening songs—that might have been performed at a wedding but were not exclusively bound to the occasion and performed in different contexts throughout the year. Other common and prominent forms of musical entertainment will be considered as well.

The Wedding as Social Event: Singing as Communal Experience and Performance

Yiddish wedding songs were neither sung during *erusin*, the legally binding engagement that is performed under the *khupe*, nor during *niśuin*, the actual marriage ceremony with its seven blessings (since the Middle Ages the two parts together form the traditional wedding). Instead, they are integral parts of various rituals leading up to the wedding proper as well as the celebrations thereafter. In her study on central European wedding songs, Alice Elscheková captured them as social songs:

[T]he wedding song repertoire as a whole is well known, for each member of the community takes part in innumerable weddings during the decades during which he or she lives in the community. These weddings correspond to a more or less unified, repeated scenario and progressive model. The music and song repertoires are a particularly characteristic part of the wedding's structure.[9]

These observations also apply to the Yiddish songs, although with subtle differences between the different Ashkenazic communities scattered through Europe.

Although there is no universal standard given that wedding customs depended on region and each respective community as well as the financial means of the families and status of the bride (a virgin, a widow, or a divorcee), distinct social occasions explicitly mentioned in early modern sources as moments of performance and/or communal singing can be identified.[10]

The first important event in which wedding songs were heard is the so-called *shpinholts*, which in itself consisted of several stages. During the day of the shpinholts, bride and groom received friends and relatives who entertained them with songs and dances. They also visited the Jewish community's dance house, where more dancing, singing, and music making with larger groups took place, including musical processions from their respective houses to the dance hall and back.

Yuspa Shammes (1604–1678), beadle, *soyfer* (religious scribe), and chronicler originally from Fulda, described in his book about the customs of the Jewish community in Worms—the singing, and even more explicitly, the performance of khosn-kale-lider for the shpinholts:

> After the festive morning meal on Shabbat, the helper of the *shamash* [the sexton or beadle of a Jewish congregation] calls *Tsu der shpinholts*, as (he did) the day before. Then, the women and ahead (of them) the *rabbanit*, wife of the *av bet din* [rabbi who presides over a rabbinical court], come to the house of the bride and put the bride on a chair and dress her in women's clothing called *reklé* [gown] and sing a tune and a groom-and-bride-song.[11]

The days of separation before the wedding were (and are) a custom that prevented groom and bride from seeing each other up to eight days before the wedding proper. During this time, they were visited by their friends and peers, mostly other unmarried young men or women of the community. Singing was a common pastime during these visits, and while neither Jewish nor Christian literature on the shpinholts reference wedding songs specifically, it can be safely assumed that songs were performed that at least befitted the situation. One account that corroborates this stems from the converted Jew Ernst Ferdinand Hess, who in 1598 wrote about the engagement and wedding of the Jews:

> When the time has drawn near until the eighth day (before the wedding) / bridegroom / and bride do not leave the house / thereupon the bachelors come to the bridegroom / and the maidens to the bride / sing and play with them / so that time does not hang heavy on their hands.[12]

FIGURE 22.1 The colored copper engraving shows a "Jewish braiding of the bride." Detail from *Jüdische Ceremonien* (Nuremberg: Johann Peter Wolff Seel. Erben, 1830); Bilderbogen 61, Graphische Sammlung, Inv. Nr. HB 22997, Kapsel 1279, Germanisches Nationalmuseum, Nuremberg.

The braiding and veiling of the bride, however, appears to have been the most important moment for singing in preparation of the wedding (Figure 22.1). It was, with the exception of the veiling, an all-women event and happened before the bride was being led to her wedding in a procession. Before the braiding, the bride was already dressed in her wedding gown and given a place of honor. She would hold a bowl in her lap into which presents such as rings, money, and other gifts were thrown. In the meantime, the guest did enjoy light refreshments that had been prepared.[13] Her hair was loosened, combed, and braided, which seems to have been a joyous affair that sometimes lasted a significant amount of time, according to the Yiddish work *Many Pious Women* (the title page and beginning of this manuscript is lost, and it was thus aptly named by the editors Fox and Lewis): "Some of them put a bridal bonnet on her head. Others comb and braid her locks. If the bride's hair just happened to be long, there would never be an end to this!"[14] The Christian Hebraist Johannes Buxtorf (1599–1664) described such a scene in 1603:

> During this braiding and combing, the women take exceptional joy / in singing beautiful songs / in dancing and all kinds of pastimes / in order to make the bride happy. And in order for the very wise rabbis to convince the pious women more easily / they wrote in the Talmud / God himself made Eve braids in Paradise / and he sang to her / and danced with her in Paradise.[15]

It is important to note that the custom of shaving a women's hair before or after the wed-ding was not the standard during the early modern times, but it began to gain currency during this period as a sign of piety.[16] Instead, married women covered their hair with scarfs, hats, or bonnets.

A great variety of songs accompanied this elaborate preparation of the bride. Depending on the community, as well as the time and place, the repertoire could encompass humorous and joyful songs, meant to fulfil the religious obligation of making the bride happy on her wedding day. As the Christian Hebraist Paul Christoph Höpfner described it: "Adorning [the bride] was a special pleasure for the women which they showed in all sorts of manners through singing, dancing and playing in order to please the bride; and they thought that in doing so they'd render a pleasant service unto God."[17]

Some texts sung for this occasion described the future spouse and his qualities while others were quite explicit in the depiction of the forthcoming wedding night, already with erotic undertones. Didactic songs with religious and moral-ethic content, how-ever, featured prominently, reminding the bride of her future obligations, her new pri-vate roles and social functions, strongly emphasizing behavioral norms expected by the community.

This particular moment of singing, when the bride was adorned, veiled, and prepared for the khupe, is significant for the development of religious practice since it reveals a custom-in-the-making as reflected in the choice of songs: an excepted Orthodox norm today is to make the bride weep before her wedding, a custom with many-layered retro-spective interpretations. During the early modern period, however, not all authorities and influential writers agreed on the issue of weeping. Some, like the ספר ברנט שפיגל (Magnifying glass), a morality anthology first published Cracow in 1596, deemed this ritualistic shedding of tears superfluous, stressing that only a solemn mind was re-quired.[18] Indeed, there are differing descriptions of the mood for the braiding and veiling and songs were chosen accordingly. Paul Christian Kirchner, a Jewish convert to Christianity who published a book on the customs and religious beliefs of his former coreligionists, offers one such description:

> So far as I was able to see / once when I was observing this ceremony of braiding from beginning to the end / I noticed / that exactly those women / who braid her / also sing songs to her in the German-Jewish language / while the bride is sitting with her face veiled / and weeps about her virginity / but with such seriousness / as the Armenian wailers in Constantinople weep for their dead for money / and even a little less / because they look out from beside the veil at the smallest opportunity / and laugh heartily.[19]

Processions were yet another occasion for singing; either private ones, for example when the bride was being led to the chamber where she was to be braided or public ones when she was led through the streets to the wedding canopy. Johannes Buxtorf described one such procession, which given its nature most likely took place indoors, in 1603:

> On the day when she is to be blessed / she dons her wedding clothes / and adorns herself most beautifully in Jewish manner: afterwards, she is led by the women into a special chamber / they sing lovely wedding songs going before her/ seat her on a fine armchair/ comb her hair/ make nice tresses of braids for her/ put bonnets on her / and put the veil before her eyes.[20]

While the wedding songs themselves are not specified in this source, their exact context and practice are detailed. They are sung by the group that leads the bride as processionals.

After the wedding ceremony and various different processions, the festive meal took place, providing yet another and perhaps the most elaborate occasion for singing. R. Selig, son of R. Hezekiah of Prague, captured this in song from 1676:

I will sing a song	איין גיזנג וויל איך טאן זינגין
I will gobble good wine	גוטין וויין וויל איך שלינגין
With joy and merriment	מיט פרייד אונ' פריילייכקייטי
To honor the bridegroom.	צו ערין דען ברייטי:
. . .	. . .
With dancing will we jump	מיט טנצין וועלן מיר שפרינגין
We will raise our voices	אויף היבין וועלן מיר אונזר שטימן
And we will increase praise	אונ' לוב וועלן מיר מערין
To honor bride and groom.[21]	ברויט אונ' ברייטי צו ערין:

In the wedding songs themselves, this aforementioned joyous (evening) celebration is addressed. Some didactic literature, however, expressed the view that the attending guests were in dire need of higher moral standards. One such complaint was made by Elhanan Kirchhan (1666–1757), who in 1727 wrote that "there are women who drink a lot of wine at a wedding or circumcision. . . . When the *droshe* [short Bible interpretation] is over, the *khutspe lider* [insolent songs] emerge again. They cheer and romp and sing, clap with their hands and feet and jump on the table."[22]

Singing was as much part of the communal experience as it was a performative moment. Thus, after having identified the various occasions for singing during the Ashkenazic wedding, the important question of who sang for whom arises. While the singing and vocal performance of men in the form of professional wedding entertainers, known as badkhonim, became an established and still practiced norm, the focus here is on those whom primary (the songs themselves) as well as secondary sources (by Christian Hebraists or Jewish contemporaneous authors) present as early modern wedding singers—women of the community.[23]

In various Jewish cultures worldwide, women singing was (and is) an ordinary part of wedding festivities.[24] In general, women's songs were not performed during the

wedding proper while the couple stood under the khupe, but on various occasions before and after the ceremony, as discussed above. Performance practices and spaces, languages, content of the songs, use of instruments, voice techniques, times for singing,
performers, and audiences naturally differed greatly between the various Jewish cultural
spheres. But the most significant difference lies in the fact that up to the modern period, women's singing for various wedding festivities was (and partly still is) the norm
in most Jewish communities worldwide. Among the Ashkenazim, however, this custom
was eventually lost.

One source that attests to women singing is the aforementioned publication by Paul
Christian Kirchner, who wrote that "Around noon, before the marriage, the bride is
braided delicately by invited married women (a), there are also two maidens (b) appointed who sing for her about how she has to behave towards her husband and in her
married status."[25] He details not only the braiding and those who carry it out in this specific collective (married women), but also the singers (in this case, two "maidens") and
the content of the songs. The bride is being taught through song in order to adhere to
religious obligations and social norms. These are, indeed, major themes in Yiddish and
bilingual wedding songs as elaborated further below.

Similarly, an inner-Jewish, Yiddish source, the sixteenth-century *Many Pious Women*,
provides important information about women's singing practice, namely that unmarried and married women were standing around the bride while only "some" sang to her,
but those who did performed "loudly."[26] This indicates a modus of self-assured and un-
inhibited performance that might not conform to expected norms of modesty. The late
twentieth-century ethnographic observations by Zelda Kahan Newman, on wedding
songs of contemporary Jewish women from the Satmar Hasidic community, reveals
that this custom has not been forgotten: "We see . . . the beginnings of a folk-tradition.
Satmar women have initiated a custom, even as they claim that this custom is rooted
in tradition."[27] This raises the question of why women's singing has disappeared as a
custom among Ashkenazim, and probably latest among this rather strict Hasidic group.

The present absence of the feminine voice at the Ashkenazi wedding is partly the result of larger developments that took hold in the early modern period and became normative in eastern Europe. There, some of the most important moments for singing, the
seating (*kale bazetsn*), veiling (*kale badekn*), and weeping for (and with) the bride (*kale
baveynen*) were transformed into a solely male domain. Instead of women performing
with and for women, a professional class of vocal wedding entertainers (*badkhonim*)
and instrumental musicians (*klezmorim*) were hired who received renumeration for
their services and sang and played for the bride and her guests at these important wedding functions. In fact, entire instrumental klezmer repertoires now bear the names of
these wedding-preparation stages.

As men, badkhonim were allowed to sing before both sexes. In Yiddish-speaking
western Europe, issues surrounding *kol ishah* at weddings and other singing occasions
were frequently mentioned, and authorities struggled to implement the strict prohibition of women singing in public—a male professional singer thus was one way of avoiding
possible dilemmas. Other factors certainly contributed to this development, such as the

general professionalization and organization of music making by klezmer guilts during the early modern period and thus, a monetary interest, or the supersession of women by men in religious functions and so on—this question certainly merits further investigation.

While at the end of the early modern period, Yiddish in western Europe was nearing the time of its decline and passing, it would continue to thrive in eastern Europe until the Second World War. Women continued to sing in Yiddish for a bride while preparing her for her public wedding appearance—but obviously in increasingly less prominent (and un-paid) functions. It seems, however, that this tradition has experienced a tremendous rupture since it is not practiced in Orthodox circles anymore and only recently has received renewed attention.

The Wedding as Musical Event

An early modern Ashkenazic wedding could be a lush musical affair, depending, of course, on the community's size, importance, and location (which determined whether musicians could reach it easily), as well as the financial means of the family. It included first and foremost instrumental music, but also singing in Hebrew, general communal singing of Jewish and non-Jewish song repertoires, as well as the art of professional wedding-entertainers. Music making and singing, as well as performers such as badkhonim and klezmorim, are frequently mentioned in early modern wedding songs, such as in the twenty-first verse of the אײן שיהן כלה ליד (A nice bride song, ca. 1750), which describes the archetypical moment of the klezmorim's performance, when the bride is being led to the khupe:

Strike up, letsonim and klezmorim!	שפיהלט אויף איהרי לצנים אונ' כלי זמרים
It is almost time to go to the khupe!	צו דער חופה גיהן איזט נוהן בלד צייט
Dear bride, your hair is covered now	ליבה כלה נוהן זיין בדעקט דייני האַרן
Thus, you have to leave your childhood behind.	זוא מוזטו פֿר לאזן דייני קינדישקייט

It is followed by a verse that amplifies the precarious financial situation of musicians when the bride is being asked to give "to poor people, and don't forget fools, servants, and klezmorim."[28] Almost the same phrase appears in the אײן שיהן חתן ליד (A nice groom song, ca. 1750) bound together with the aforementioned bride song, as the twenty-second verse goes: "Give presents today, too, to fools (jesters), servants and klezmorim. If not, they won't be merry and will shout like dead animals."[29]

Klezmorim played during various stages of the wedding (predominantly for the various processions) and were considered essential for the fulfilment of the religious obligation to make the bride (and groom) happy—this according to the ruling of Rabbi Jacob ben Moses Moellin (known as the Maharil, 1365–1427).[30] Thus, instrumental music at weddings was religiously accepted and flourished in the centuries after.[31] And yet, the reconstruction of the instrumental wedding repertoire for the time before 1750 is a difficult endeavor, given the limited sources (Figure 22.2). In turn, the transmitted melodies of Yiddish wedding songs provide clearer evidence for the music history of this genre.

FIGURE 22.2 "Wedding ceremony of German Jews." Three musicians are depicted with their instruments: hammered dulcimer, violin, and viola da gamba. Bernard Picart, *Histoire générale des ceremonies, mœrs, et coutumes religieuses de tous les peoples du monde*, vol. 1 : *Qui contient les ceremonies des Juifs & des Chrétiens Catholiques* (Amsterdam: J. F. Bernard, 1723), 176a, lower part. Courtesy of the Library of the Jewish Theological Seminary of America.

As was common during the early modern period, well-known songs or texts written to a preexisting melody, commonly known as contrafacta, were generally printed without their melodies. Most people were unable to read music, and since publishing musical notation always required particular printing skills and technical equipment, it was costlier and thus avoided when unnecessary. Most of the early modern Yiddish wedding song texts therefore have no melodies accompanying them. But in some instances, authors (or printers) referenced the melody intended for the rendering of a particular song. This was done by way of naming the first line or title of a contemporary song that the audience was sure to know, often introducing it with a term like *benign* (in/ with the melody [of]). This method of writing a new text to an existing melody not only provided immediate performability and enhanced memorability, but could also serve other means, such as creating humor or sarcasm—depending on the melody chosen and the text that originally belonged to it.

Yiddish song writers often gave the singers great freedom in either providing more than one possible melody or suggesting that, should the melody they had in mind be unknown or not to the performer's liking, they could simply choose or even compose another one. A good example for this is a Purim song, written by Moses Melamed from Prague in the seventeenth century, where the author states that "The melody of Rav Rabeynu Shimen

FIGURE 22.3 Elhanan Henle Kirchhan, שמחת הנפש (Joy of the soul), vol. 2 (Fürth: Bonfat Shneur, 1726/27); fol. 13v.

zetsal fits this very well. Whoever knows a better one may (continue) to use it."[32] Melodies used for wedding songs were either taken from non- Jewish sources (e.g., the German songs *Es ist auf Erden kein schwerer Leiden*[33] and *Halb schwarz, halb weiß*[34]) or the Jewish paraliturgical corpus (e.g., גוט שבת גוט שבת, Good Sabbath, good Sabbath).

Only two genuinely Yiddish wedding songs have been published with their melodies, both of them in the moral work by the aforementioned Elhanan Kirchhan, which is one of the most exceptional sources for the history of Yiddish song, being the first such publication and, for a long time, the last to include musical notation intended for the Yiddish songs (Figure 22.3). While its first part, published in 1707, was a prose volume on morals, ethics, and behavior, the second part of 1727 reinforces the earlier writings through song. Kirchhan had a clear aim, that is, to further the moral edification of his coreligionists. Thus, he made it abundantly clear that his bride songs were intended as a substitute for all the "imprudent" or "insolent" songs, as he states in the heading of one of them, "So that one lets the insolent songs be I have written this song for weddings and circumcisions" (Figure 22.3).

Kirchhan did not compose any of the melodies for his poems. Instead, existing Baroque tunes were used that either he or the person who wrote the notation chose. However, words and music do not match, and it is doubtful whether Kirchhan truly intended his poems for the particular tunes or even had them in mind while writing.

SONG TEXTS: BETWEEN EROTICISM
AND MORALITY

Early modern Yiddish wedding song texts reveal social and religious practices as well as the development of Ashkenazic ethics, morals, and piety. Verbalizing social expectations and religious obligations in light of the transition that the couple undergoes and their new functions within their community, the texts aid the attempted "normativiziation" of Jewish society and are didactic in nature.[35] They are multilayered and equally serve various other functions, such as entertaining the couple and making them merry (thus fulfilling a religious obligation), describing the virtues of the respective partner and bringing them closer to each other, preparing them for a joyful wedding night, and describing patterns of behavior that will ensure a successful marriage in mutual respect.

Except for the songs themselves, only few early modern secondary sources provide references as to the content of wedding songs. An important example is the manuscript called *Many Pious Women*, a work on *muser un hanhoge* (ethics and behavior) as well as *minhogim* (customs), published in Yiddish. As the unknown author writes:

> On top of that, look—at a wedding, when the call goes out "to the braiding!," see how eagerly, poor things [referring to women], they would like to make themselves busy. So there they stand, around the bride. Some of them sing to her, very loudly, the very loveliest bridal songs, which are based upon verses from the Torah reading of the week. [The songs say] that she should keep the menstrual laws and light her candles, take the dough-offerings and make three thin loaves for blessings. She should not be a stranger to her husband, but take off her chemise quickly; she should not resist strongly, but very quickly grant him his first request.[36]

The subjects mentioned here cover a wide spectrum, ranging from Torah-related topics to the common three commandments for women (lighting the Sabbath candles, making the dough offering, and keeping the laws of purity) as well as preparation for the wedding night in being specific about the behavior expected of her before sexual intercourse takes place.

In diachronic analysis certain topics are a constant through the centuries while others appear or disappear in clusters over time. Among those specific ones that vanish in the course of the early modern period are, for example, the explicit mentioning of love, the appearance/beauty of the bride, or the couple being brought together or led to bed as in this twelfth verse of a Yiddish song from around 1600:

נון פוירט זיא הין אין ערין:
וואל היים אין איר גימאך:
איר זאמין זול זיך מערין:
אלש גאט צו אברהם שפר[ך]:
אלדי צו גוטיר נכט:

Now lead them honorably
Home to their chamber.
Their seed shall multiply,
Just as God said to Abraham.
Farewell, good night.[37]

This moment of the wedding festivity, when the couple is about to be escorted to their home, is captured in yet another song from the same manuscript:

מיר האבן גיזונגין מיט פרויליכקייט:
חתן אונ׳ כלה צו ער אך אנדרי גוטי לייט:
קומט נון הער עש איזט קומן דיא צייט:
דש דער חתן מיט דער כלה צו בעטי איילט:

> We sung with joy
> To honor bridegroom and bride and other good people, too.
> Come now, the time has come
> That bridegroom and bride hurry to bed with each other.[38]

Sexuality, the virginity of the bride, and that a woman should not be forced are topics that disappeared at the end of the seventeenth century. In a wedding song from Prague 1676, the author still emphasizes that intercourse should take place "lovingly":

[6] טוט אייך ניט לנג במיאן
טוטש דיא ברויט אויז ציהן
אירי קליידר אויז צו טאן
אונ׳ זיא ליגן צון אירן מאן:

. . .

[9] מיט ליב שפֿט זאלן זיא גייגין
אז וויא דיא הינר אין דיא שטייגן ...
איין צוגישלאסניר ברון
צו איין בשניטנין זון ...

[10] איין ווירדגי מייד
איר ברישט זיין בירייט
זאל איבר רעט ווערין
פֿון אירן ברייטי גאר גערין:

> [6] Don't trouble yourselves for too long
> And undress the bride
> Take off her clothes
> And lay her beside her husband.
> . . .
>
> [9] They shall have intercourse[39] lovingly
> Like the chickens on the perch . . .
> A closed well [a virgin]
> With a circumcised son . . .
>
> [10] A worthy maiden
> Her breasts are ready
> She shall enjoy being persuaded
> By her bridegroom.[40]

Equally rare and diminishing over time was the admonishment or cautioning of men. Seldom do sources present such sensible and intimate insight into the ideal husband's behavior as in a song from around 1600. In this source, the groom is being advised as how to behave toward his pregnant wife:

ביפעל דיינם וייב ווען דוא ציכסט וייט:

ניט גיא פֿון איר אין און איניקייט:

ווען זיא שון איזט נוהט אן דער צייט:

מיט גוטן ווארטן דיך צו איר נייג:

Order your wife when you travel far,
Do not part from her in discord.
When she is already close to the time [close to giving birth]
Bend towards her with good words.[41]

Some of these songs were intended for either bridegroom or bride because of their highly specific content. They would probably not have been performed for the opposite sex. For most of the material, however, this is not the case. Even if the title states otherwise, often either bride and groom are addressed in the text proper or the content is such that no clear boundaries can be drawn. What is more, even themes such as the three particular religious obligations for women are no indication either, since they are also mentioned in songs that clearly address both partners.

Newly introduced in the course of the seventeenth century are in the main "recommendations" for women such as: they should stay home rather than go out, attend synagogue services, pray, buy and read Yiddish books in order to learn proper religious and social conduct, cook well, be obedient to the husband and not dance with or sing before other men, cover their hair and treat the servants well. This is expressed in the אײן שין נייא כלה ליד (A nice new bride song), probably from Frankfurt on the Main, around 1700, which reads like a litany of prohibitions for the future house wife:

[16]　זיוה ווייד וויוא גנוטבֿא בֿעג וֿילטשטנרע

אוני׳ לויפֿן זאלשטו אויך ניט פֿיל אויז

[21]　שטאלץ קייט אוני׳ דייני הַאר זאלשטו ניט לאזן זעהן

דיין היבש זינגן פֿר פֿרעמדי מאנן זאל אך ניט גישעהן

[24]　טרינק דיך קיין מאל פֿאל עש זייא פֿון וויין אודר ביר

רעבֿט איבל שטיט עש אן איינם פֿר שווייגן פֿון דיר

יוא פֿר מיידן זאלשטו אויך צו שפֿילן מיט קארטן

ריבֿטיג האשטו זונשט דעז (דלוֹת) צו ער ווארטן

[25]　... פֿלייסיג טוא אין טייטשן ספֿרים לייאן

אלזו ווערשטו דיך אופֿֿט דרינן ערפֿרייאן

[16] Diligently care for your house
And, moreover, do not go out often

[21] You shall neither show pride nor let your hair be seen
Also, your lovely singing shall not take place before other men

[24] Never fill yourself up with wine or beer
It does not befit a man, never mind you
Avoid playing in cards, too,
Otherwise you have to expect poverty.

[25] . . . read diligently in Yiddish books
So you will enjoy them often[42]

Another example stems from the equally rich source איין שין כלה ליד (A nice bride song, ca. 1700):

[18] טוא אין דיא תפֿלה ניט שמואתֿן נאך שוועצין
אך זיך לויף ניט פֿיל אויש דיין הויז
פֿון אויס לויפֿן קומט רבֿילתֿ אוני׳ לשון הרע וויא עש גרעט ווערט אויף אלין פלעצין

[18] Do not talk or chatter during prayers
And do not leave your house very often.
From going out comes gossip and defamation the way it is spoken everywhere[43]

What can be said with certainty is that the range of topics covered in these songs is vast and despite certain repeating key themes never static—in neither diachronic nor synchronic perspective. Conceptionally, the songs encompass subject areas extending to biblical stories and characters, women's commandments, lawful ethical and moral behavior and possible repercussions, expected social and religious norms and implementations of normativity, the wedding day (its customs and religious dimensions), the wedding night and sexual behavior, attributes of bridegroom and bride, singing and music making, author's strophe, and Messianic hope.

Ashkenazic wedding songs served synchronic as well as diachronic functions.[44] On the particularly consuetudinary synchronic level, they are bound to the stages of the festivity. They are descriptive and "explain the action taking place," which also facilitates "appropriate emotional responses."[45] In diachronic perspective, they are at the same time mirror of and motivator for changes in social, religious, and legal history. Moreover, in contemporary feminist theory on the writing of women's histories, wedding songs are explicitly mentioned as sources that need to be reevaluated as material that has been performed (and in part written) by women and present "excellent documentations of the everyday."[46] These topical changes point, all in all, to the progressing religious, ethical, and moral "normativization" or reshaping of Ashkenazic society in general and Jewish women in particular. It is clear just how didactically charged wedding songs became in the course of the early modern period. They certainly were one of the most practical and popular means of getting the message across that Jewish communities entered a new era, shaped by new standards that were enforced through social control.

NOTES

1. Moshe N. Rosenfeld, *The Book of Cows: A Facsimile Edition of the Famed Kuhbuch, Verona 1595—From a Unique Copy in a Private Collection* (London: Hebraica Books, 1984), 6.

2. David B. Ruderman, *Early Modern Jewry: A New Cultural History* (Princeton: Princeton University Press, 2010), 146–158.

3. Ibid., 14–16.

4. For further details on this subject, see Harry Fox and Justin Jaron Lewis, *Many Pious Women: Edition and Translation*, Studia Judaica 62 (Berlin: De Gruyter, 2011), 294–295; Don Harrán, "'Keḥi kinnor' by Samuel Archivolti (d. 1611): A Wedding Ode with Hidden Messages," *AJS Review* 35, no. 2 (2011): 253–291; Debra Kaplan, "Rituals of Marriage and Communal Prestige: The *Breileft* in Medieval and Early Modern Germany," *Jewish History* 29 (2015): 273–300; Samuel N. Rosenberg, "The Medieval Hebrew-French Wedding Song," *Shofar* 11 (1992): 22–37; Roni Weinstein, *Marriage Rituals Italian Style: A Historical Anthropological Perspective on Early Modern Italian Jews*, Brill's Series in Jewish Studies 35 (Leiden: Brill, 2004).

5. Noah Abraham Asher Selig b. Hiskija, אויין היפשר זמר פֿר חתן אונ' כלה (A lovely song for groom and bride), Prague, ca. 1676, Opp. 8° 460 (17), Bodleian Library Oxford.

6. For ongoing projects that focus on genizot, see "Genisa Bayreuth," http://genisa.ikgbayre uth.net; "Genizat Germania," http://www.hebrewmanuscript.com/partner/country/germ any-11.htm; and "Genizat Germania," https://www.genizatgermania.uni-mainz.de.

7. See Elhanan Henle Kirchhan, שמחת הנפש (Joy of the soul), 2 vols. (Fürth: Bonfat Shneur, 1726/ 27), http:// nbn- resolv ing.de/ urn:nbn:de:hebis:30:2- 2949; or Jacob Shatzsky, ed., *Simḥath Hanefesh (Delight of the Soul): A Book of Yiddish Poems by Elḥanan Kirchhan* (New York: Max N. Maisel, 1926), 84.

8. Ivan G. Marcus, "Ashkenaz," *YIVO Encyclopedia of Jews in Eastern Europe*, https://yivoe ncyclopedia.org/article.aspx/Ashkenaz (accessed July 15, 2021).

9. Alica Elscheková, "Functions and Transformational Processes of Central European Wedding Songs," trans. Linda Fujie, *The World of Music* 39 (1997): 43.

10. For early modern Jewish wedding customs see Kaplan, "Rituals of Marriage and Communal Prestige," and Daniel Sperber, *The Jewish Life Cycle: Custom, Lore and Iconography: Jewish Customs from the Cradle to the Grave* (Ramat Gan: Bar-Ilan University Press, 2008), Weinstein, *Marriage Rituals Italian Style*.

11. אחר סעודת שחרית בשבת, הנער של שמש קורא: צו דער שפּינהולין, כדאתמול. אז הנשים באין והרבניי אשת האב ב"ד בראשם, לבית הכלה, ויושבין הכלה על כסא, ולובשין לה מלבושים וכלה. נשים שקורין רעקלי, ומשוררת זמר ושיר חתן וכלה. Benjamin Salomon Hamburger, Erich Zimmer and Israel Mordechai Peles, eds., *Wormser Minhagbuch des R. Jousep (Juspa) Schammes: Nach Handschriften des Verfassers zum ersten Male vollständig herausgegeben . . . von Jair Chajim Bacharach*, 2 vols. (Jerusalem: Mifal Torat Chachme Aschkenas, 1992), רכ"ז (# ז-ו).

12. "So die zeit nun biß auff acht Tage verlauffen / gehet der Breutigam / wie auch die Braut nicht auß dem Hause/ alsdann kommen die Jungen Gesellen bey dem Breutigam/ und die Megde bey die Braut / singen und spielen mit ihnen / daß ihnen die zeit nicht lang wehret." Ernst Ferdinand Hess, *Flagellvm Iudeorvm: Juden Geissel / Das ist: Eine Neuwe sehr nútze vnd gründliche Erweisung*... (s.l.: n.p., 1598), 82. Flagellum Iudeorum, Juden Geissel.

13. See Christian Gottlieb Seeligman, *Jüdischer Ceremonien: Von der Jüden Hochzeiten, Fest- und Feyer-Tagen durchs gantze Jahr* . . ., 2nd ed. (Lund: Königliche Academische Buchdruckerey, 1737), 6–7.

14. Fox and Lewis, *Many Pious Women*, 230–232.

15. "Bey diesem flechten oder straelen haben die Weiber ein sonderbare frewde / mit schoenen Liedern zu singẽ/ mit tantzen vnd allerley kurtzweil / daß sie die Braut froelich machen. Vn daß solches die Hochweisen Rabbinen/ die fromen Weiber desto ehe vberzeugẽ / schreiben sie im Talmud / Gott selbst habe der Eua im Paradeiß Zoepffe ge-macht/ vñ ihr vorgesungen/ vñ mit ihr im Paradeiß getantzet." Johannes Buxtorf, *Synagoga iudaica: Das ist Jüden Schul darinnen der gantz jüdische Glaub und Glaubensubung mit allen Ceremonien, Satzungen, Sitten und Gebräuchen, wie sie bey ihnen offentlich und heimlich im Brauche . . . gründlich erkläret wird* (Basel: Sebastian Henricpetri, 1603), 575–576.

16. See Ruth Berger, *Sexualität, Ehe und Familienleben in der jüdischen Moralliteratur (900–1900)* (Wiesbaden: Harrassowitz, 2003), 116.

17. "Dieser Putz war den Weibern eine sonderbare Freude, welche sie mit singen, tantzen und spielen auf alle Weise bezeigeten, damit sie die Braut erfreueten, und meyneten, sie thaeten Gott einen angenehmen Dienst damit." Paul Christoph Höpfner, *Hierosolyma antiqua Oder Kurtze Fragen Von denen Profan-Gebräuchen der Juden; Welche In Bürgerlichen, Gelehrten, Krieges- und Haus-Sachen bestehen* . . ., ed. Christoph Semler (Halle: Renger, 1732), 158.

18. See Sigrid Riedel, ed., *Moses Henochs Altschul-Jeruschalmi "Brantspigel": Transkribiert und ediert nach der Erstausgabe Krakau 1596* (Frankfurt am Main: Peter Lang, 1993). An edition published in Hanau in 1626 can be accessed at http://sammlungen.ub.uni-frankfurt.de/jd/content/titleinfo/1709573; see fol. 109r for the passage in question.

19. "So gut ich es gesehen / wie ich dann diese Ceremonie des Flech=tens einesmals vom Anfang bis zum Ende beobachtet / habe ich befunden / daß eben diejenige Weiber / welche sie flechtē / auch die Lieder in teutsch-juedischer Sprach singen / da unterdessen die Kalah mit verhueltem Angesicht sitzet / und ihre Jungfrauschafft beweinet / aber mit solcher Ernsthaftigkeit / als die Armenischen Klag-Weiber in Constantinopel ihre Todten ums Geld zu beweinen pflegen / und noch ein klein bisgen weniger / weil sie bey der gering=sten Gelegenheit neben dem Schleyher weg gucken / und so herzlich lachen." Paul Christian Kirchner, *Juedisches Ceremoniel, oder Beschreibung dererjenigen Gebraeuche, welche Die Juden so wol inn- als ausser dem Tempel, bey allen und jeden Fest-Taegen, im Gebet, bey der Beschneidung, bey Hochzeiten, Ausloesung der Erst-Geburt, im Sterben, bey der Begraebnueß und dergleichen, in acht zu nehmen pflegen* (Nuremberg: Peter Conrad Monath, 1726), 178–179.

20. "Am tag / wenn sie soll eyngesegnet werden/ legt sie ihre Hochzeitliche Kleider an / vnnd mutzet sich auffs schoenest nach juedischer weise: wird darnach auch von den Weibern in ein besonder Gemach gefuehrt / die singen liebliche Hochzeitlieder vor jr her/ setzen sie auff einen schoenen Saessel/ straelen ihr das Haar/ machen ihr schoene Flaechten der Zoepffe/ setzen ihr schoene Hauben auff/ vnd mache˜ ihr den Schlaeyer fuer die Augen." Buxtorf, *Synagoga iudaica*, 575–576.

21. R. Selig (Son of) R. Hezekiah, אײן גיזאנג וויל טאן איך זינגין (A song I will sing), Prague, 1676, Opp. 8° 460 (17), fol. 1r, Bodleian Library, Oxford.

22. Kirchhan, שמחת הנפש, fol. 17r.

23. See Walter Zev Feldman, *Klezmer: Music, History & Memory* (New York: Oxford University Press, 2016), 61–63.

24. See Judith R. Cohen, "'Ya salió de la mar': Traditional Judeo-Spanish Wedding Songs," in *Women and Music in Cross-Cultural Perspective*, ed. Ellen Koskoff (Westport, CT: Greenwood Press, 1987): 55–67; Susana Weich-Shahak, "'Dice la nuestra novia' (Says our Bride): Music and Poetry in the Wedding Songs of the Moroccan Sephardim," *European Judaism* 52, no. 2 (2019): 95–110, including further references; Kay Kaufmann Shelemay, *Let Jasmine Rain Down: Song and Remembrance among Syrian Jews* (Chicago: University of Chicago Press, 1998); Marilyn Herman, "The Secular Music of the Yemenite Jews as an Expression of Cultural Demarcation Between the Sexes," *JASO* 27, no. 2 (1996): 113–135; Martine Chemana, "Women Sing, Men Listen. Malayalam Folksongs of the Cochini, the Jewish Community of Kerala, in India and Israel," *Bulletin du Centre de Recherche Français à Jérusalem* 11 (2002): 83–92.

25. "Um den Mittag, ehe die Copulation geschieht, wird die Braut durch gebettene Ehe-Weiber zierlich geflochten (a), daben sind zwey Jungfrauen (b) bestellet, welche ihr vorsingen, wie sie sich gegen ihrem Mann und ihrem Ehestande zu verhalten hat." Kirchner, *Juedisches Ceremoniel*, 178–179.

26. See Fox and Lewis, *Many Pious Women*, 230–232.

27. Zelda Kahan-Newman, "Women's Badkhones: The Satmar Poem Sung to a Bride," *International Journal of the Sociology of Language* 138 (1999): 94.

28. Anon., אײן שיהן כלה ליד (A nice bride song), ca. 1750, Oriental Collections / 1979.c.16, fol. 2v, British Library, London.

29. Anon., אײן שיהן חתן ליד (A nice groom song), ca. 1750, Oriental Collections / 1979.c.16, fol. 4v, British Library, London.

30. See Abraham Z. Idelsohn, *Jewish Music: Its Historical Development* (1929; New York: Dover Publications, 1992), 206.

31. For further details on klezmorim during the early modern period, see Feldman, *Klezmer*, 59–98.

32. Moses Melamed, זמר נאה לפורים (A fine song for Purim), Prague?, c. 1650, Opp. 8° 605 [olim 546], title page, Bodleian Library, Oxford.

33. For an edition of text and melody, see Diana Matut, *Dichtung und Musik im frühneuzeitlichen Aschkenas*, Studies in Jewish History and Culture 29 (Leiden: Brill, 2011), 1:260–266; 2:71 and 251–260.

34. R. Selig (Son of) R. Hezekiah, אײן גיזאנג וויל איך טאן זינגין (A song I will sing), Prague, 1676, Opp. 8° 460 (17), fol. 1v, Bodleian Library, Oxford.

35. Fox and Lewis call this "didactic poetry," see *Many Pious Women*, 31.

36. Ibid., 230.

37. For the edition see Matut, *Dichtung und Musik*, 1:270–271.

38. See ibid., I:350–355; and II:304–306.

39. The word used in the original is "geigen" (to fiddle). On its euphemism for intercourse, see Lutz Röhrich, *Lexikon der sprichwörtlichen Redensarten* (Freiburg: Herder, 1994), s.v. "geigen."

40. R. Selig (Son of) R. Hezekiah, אײן גיזאנג וויל איך טאן זינגין (A song I will sing), Prague, 1676, Opp. 8° 460 (17), fol. 1v–2r, Bodleian Library, Oxford.

41. For the edition and commentary, see Matut, *Dichtung und Musik*, 1:350–355 and 2:304–306.

42. Josef of Treves,אײן שין נײא כלה ליד (A nice new bride song), Frankfurt[?], ca. 1690–1715, Opp. 8° 556 (9) [olim 494 (9)], Bodleian Library, Oxford.

43. Anon.,אײן שין כלה ליד (A nice bride song), ca. 1700, Opp. 8° 1103 (32B), Bodleian Library, Oxford.

44. Ingeborg Weber-Kellermann, "Hochzeits- und Ehestandslieder," in *Handbuch des Volksliedes*. I: *Die Gattungen des Volksliedes*, ed. Rolf Wilhelm Brednich, Lutz Röhrich, and Wolfgang Suppan (Munich: Wilhelm Fink Verlag, 1973), 551–574.

45. Smita Tewarsi Jassal, *Unearthing Gender: Folksongs of North India* (Durham, NC: Duke University Press, 2012), 127.

46. K. M. Sheeba, "Interrogating Disciplinary Boundaries: Feminist Alternatives and Writing Women's Histories," *Proceedings of the Indian History Congress* 74 (2013): 487.

Select Bibliography

Baumgarten, Jean. *Introduction to Old Yiddish Literature*. Edited and translated by Jerold C. Frakes. New York: Oxford University Press, 2005.

Feldman, Walter Zev. *Klezmer: Music, History and Memory*. New York: Oxford University Press, 2016.

Fox, Harry, and Justin Jaron Lewis. *Many Pious Women: Edition and Translation*. Studia Judaica 62. Berlin: De Gruyter, 2011.

Gosfield, Avery. "'I Sing it to an Italian Tune . . .': Thoughts on Performing Sixteenth-Century Italian-Jewish Sung Poetry Today." *European Journal of Jewish Studies* 8 (2014): 9–52.

Grossman, Avraham: *Pious and Rebellious: Jewish Women in Medieval Europe*. Waltham, MA: Brandeis University Press, 2004.

Matut, Diana. *Dichtung und Musik im frühneuzeitlichen Aschkenas*. Studies in Jewish History and Culture 29. Leiden: Brill, 2011.

Matut, Diana. "'Lid, ton, vayz—shir, nign, zemer': Der einstimmige jiddische Gesang im 15. und 16. Jahrhundert." In *Creatio ex unisono: Einstimmige Musik im 15. und 16. Jahrhundert*, edited by Nicole Schwind, 149–174. Troja: Jahrbuch für Renaissancemusik 13. Münster: Universität Münster / Institut für Musikwissenschaft und Musikpädagogik, 2017.

Matut, Diana. "'With Kind Words Lean Towards Her . . .': Singing for a Bride and Groom in Early Modern Ashkenaz." In *Worlds of Old Yiddish Literature*, edited by Simon Neuberg and Diana Matut, 199–258. Studies in Yiddish 13. Cambridge: Legenda, 2023.

Rosman, Moshe. "The History of Jewish Women in Early Modern Poland: An Assessment." In *Jewish Women in Eastern Europe*, edited by ChaeRan Y. Freeze, Pauly Hyman, and Antony Polonsky, 25–56. Polin: Studies in Polish Jewry 18. Oxford: Littman Library of Jewish Civilization, 2005.

Ruderman, David B. *Early Modern Jewry: A New Cultural History*. Princeton, NJ: Princeton University Press, 2010.

Weinstein, Roni. *Marriage Rituals Italian Style: A Historical Anthropological Perspective on Early Modern Italian Jews*. Brill's Series in Jewish Studies 35. Leiden: Brill, 2004.

Weissler, Chava. "The Religion of Traditional Ashkenazic Women: Some Methodological Issues." *AJS Review* 12, no. 1 (1987): 73–94.

23

BUKHARIAN JEWISH WEDDINGS AND CREATIVE USES OF THE CENTRAL ASIAN PAST

EVAN RAPPORT

BUKHARIAN Jews, the collective name of Jews who historically lived in and around Central Asian cities, have had an essential role in performing and maintaining the urban classical repertoire known as shashmaqom, or more generally, maqom. Bukharian Jews typically perform this repertoire in concerts for people outside of the community, especially in the United States, where many Bukharian Jews have resettled, and Bukharian performances of the shashmaqom can be heard on such recordings as the Ilyas Malayev Ensemble's stirring and nuanced *At the Bazaar of Love*.[1] Bukharian Jews themselves link their history and identity quite strongly to this music. However, at internal celebrations Bukharian Jews rarely request shashmaqom. At weddings, musicians perform mainly pop songs at an extreme volume, singing in many different languages, including Russian, Hebrew, Spanish, and Persian. Central Asian music is typically represented with exuberant solos on the doira (frame drum), heralding blasts on the karnai (long trumpet), and pop songs with lyrics that create romantic images of Central Asian cities or the past.[2]

The striking differences between the ways that Bukharian Jews internally represent themselves at community events, the myriad stories that they tell about themselves, and the ways that others represent their community raise a number of questions. For example, are these many different styles and approaches all considered to be "Bukharian music" among Bukharian Jews themselves, and do Bukharian Jews understand these various aspects of musical life to be in conflict? At first, these differences might appear as a contradiction between an idealized representation of Bukharian Jews as exotic keepers of an ancient tradition and the reality of a diverse society with little connection to classical Central Asian music among the general populace.

Other scholars of Jewish music have faced similar complexities while researching various Jewish communities. In her classic text of 1995, "Mythologies and Realities in the Study of Jewish Music," Kay Kaufman Shelemay explores the persistent tensions between distinct mythologies and realities, such as the belief in an underlying continuity of Jewish music reaching back to antiquity versus the reality of extremely different musical styles practiced by Jewish communities the world over.[3] In the past several decades, the gulf has widened between scholars and those outside of Jewish music research, as scholars have continued to dismantle mythologies but popular conceptions remain rooted in them. And a concern with this widening division seems to now be a fundamental feature of Jewish music scholarship. Why then does this gap remain?

Experiences with Bukharian Jewish music and musicians offer insights into the issue of mythologies and realities more generally. Indeed, both are intertwined: scholars and musicians both use mythologies strategically, reality is interpreted with and through mythology, and mythologies have their own histories and genealogies rooted in real-life experiences. In this chapter, using the Bukharian Jewish wedding as a case study, the differences between mythologies and realities are recognized but understood to be related products of various creative uses of the past, with the term *creative* signaling both the act of creating (for instance, ideas and experiences of the past are used to create one's present reality) and an imaginative process (that is, people use ideas and experiences of the past in resourceful and original ways). As such, the discussion of Bukharian Jewish weddings will focus on two facets: remembrances of old Central Asian weddings and performative representations of old Central Asia in contemporary celebrations.

Jewish weddings are ideal sites for rethinking the ways that the past—in terms of lived experiences, memories, narratives, and mythologies—can be used by many different actors in creative ways. Weddings are the central events in the life of a community, uniting people from different backgrounds and also, though ritual, music, and dance, linking the celebrating families to the shared histories and customs of all Jewish people, underscoring the widespread belief that Jews are "irrevocably linked" and "mutually responsible" for one another.[4] As such, weddings are events where Jewish people perform ideas of their communities, identities, and histories to themselves and one another, making weddings moments in which mythologies are affirmed and give meaning to the participants. Furthermore, since weddings are the lifeblood of a community, they are also frequently invoked when individuals remember the past and create historical narratives. Yet at the same time, from the standpoint of professional musicians, the wedding celebration cannot be only a space for mythology and idealization, since these events are their primary source of income.[5] To have a successful career as a wedding musician, one must address the realities of the celebrants as thoroughly and in as many ways as possible, and since young people are usually the primary focus of the wedding event, changing realities for members of different generations are also brought to the fore. At a wedding, mythologies and realities come together in dramatic fashion in the present, while being rooted in multiple historical narratives.

BUKHARIAN HISTORIES

The term *Bukharian Jew* today broadly refers to all of the Jews who lived in Central Asian cities, primarily in Uzbekistan and Tajikistan, including not only Bukhara but also Samarqand, Dushanbe, Tashkent, Khiva, Mary, and Shahrisabz.[6] Bukharian families have lived for many years in Afghanistan, Israel, Iran, Russia, and the Caucasus.[7] Central Asian Jews are like other Jews, "among the most migratory peoples in the history of world."[8] Although linked together as "Bukharian Jews," the histories of Jews in these various cities can be quite different; for example, at the end of the nineteenth century, Samarqand was under Russian rule while Bukhara remained nominally under the rule of the Manghit emirs, and Jewish life in these two cities was subject to distinct restrictions. But Bukharian Jews themselves connect their history to shared roots in Central Asia dating as far back as the Babylonian exile of the Jews in the sixth century BCE. Bukharian Jews are also a branch of Persian Jewry, like Iranian Jews, and the Persian Empire once spread far into contemporary Central Asia.[9] The Bukharian Jewish mother tongue is Persian as it is generally spoken in Central Asia, where it is also a dominant language among other city-dwellers; however, Bukharian Jews all over the world have been typically multilingual, also speaking Russian and Turkic languages, as well as often Hebrew and English.

The concept of a specifically Bukharian Jewry, consisting of those communities in Central Asian cities that eventually became part of the Soviet Union, emerged in the late nineteenth century through Bukharian immigration to Palestine and encounters with Jewish travelers.[10] Nineteenth-century writings by outsiders generally refer to Jewish populations in terms of specific cities, not in terms of one distinct ethnicity, and Jews simply called themselves *Yahudion* ("Jews"). The term *Bukharskie evrei* (Russian, "Bukharian Jews"), in use both within and outside the community, became commonplace only in the twentieth century.[11]

Bukharian Jews established the Bukharian Quarter in Jerusalem at the end of the nineteenth century, and regular emigration to Palestine and later Israel continued through the twentieth century. This history is distinct from that of Bukharian Jews in the United States. Since the 1940s, a small number of Bukharian Jews began settling in New York, eventually establishing enough of a foothold to start a Bukharian Jewish center and synagogue in 1963.[12] But it was not until the dissolution of the Soviet Union that Bukharian Jews left Central Asia en masse and began immigrating to New York in greater numbers. In 1990 Jews leaving the Soviet Union were granted presumptive refugee status through the Lautenberg Amendment to the Foreign Operations Appropriations Act, which allowed the Bukharian Jewish community in the United States to grow considerably. In 2006 the population in the United States was roughly 30,000.[13]

The Bukharian Jewish community in New York has continued to grow and change. Many Bukharians have moved to and from New York and Israel, as well as other cities with significant Bukharian populations in the United States, such as Atlanta and Denver, and in Europe, such as Vienna. Bukharian Jews who moved to New York as young children, or who were born in New York, are now adults or having children of their own. Queens College, a public school and part of the City University of New York, located near Forest Hills, Rego Park, Kew Gardens Hills, and other neighborhoods with the largest Bukharian populations, has become a vital center for Bukharian youth.[14]

There are major differences between mythologies and realities in the telling of Bukharian history generally, not just in the sphere of musical life. Since the nineteenth century, scholars, journalists, and travelers have portrayed Bukharian Jews as an isolated, homogeneous group—and at times, Bukharian Jews present themselves in a similar manner. Isolation is typically characterized as a result of geography, due to Central Asia's deserts and mountains, or as a result of a political schism between Iran and Central Asia at the beginning of the Safavid era. In reality, Bukharian Jews were not historically isolated from the rest of world Jewry, at least not to a degree beyond that of any other Jewish community. And the narrative of isolation directly conflicts with another notion about Bukharian Jews as living in the "crossroads of Asia" and thriving as merchants along the famous silk routes.

For understanding the dynamics at play in the Bukharian Jewish wedding, it is necessary to avoid an uncritical acceptance of the narrative of isolation, which mainly serves to support the idea of an unbroken chain to antiquity. The myth of an isolated Bukharian Jewish community, established after the Babylonian exile and then cut off from the rest of the Jewish world until modern times, is an enticing fantasy of a link to the ancient Jewish past but not supported by historical research. Instead, it is best to consider how Bukharian Jews, a variously constituted and ever-changing population, creatively define themselves by combining ideas of uniqueness and links to antiquity (narrated in historical terms through the trope of isolation) with ideas of cosmopolitanism (narrated through the trope of the crossroads). Stories about weddings of the past, and performances at contemporary weddings that aim to represent the past, help bring together contrasting notions of Bukharian Jewish history at a time when people with disparate backgrounds have newly come together in New York, Israel, and Europe.

BUKHARIAN WEDDINGS AND CREATIVE REMEMBRANCES OF THE CENTRAL ASIAN PAST

The wedding, referred to by the specific term *arusi* or the more generic terms for banquets *tūi* or *bazm* (all Persian), has been one of the most consistent aspects of Bukharian Jewish life from pre-Soviet times to today. The wedding is so central to Bukharian Jewish life that the celebration dedicated to ending and beginning the yearly cycle of reading the Torah, Simchat Torah, is modeled on a wedding ritual; Bukharian Jews call this holiday the *Sefer Tūi*, or "[Torah] scroll wedding." In the Sefer Tūi, the

Torah scroll is adorned in the style of a traditional bridal costume from Central Asia, and an honored male who has donated to the synagogue for the privilege is treated as the groom (see Figure 23.1).[15] At the Sefer Tüï, professional musicians perform a wide range of celebratory music in the manner of a traditional wedding, although all of the songs are on religious themes. Simchat Torah repertoire might include standard up-tempo songs for the holiday, such as "Simkhu No," and newer songs by Bukharian poets and composers, such as Avrom Tolmasov's "Ajab Ajab," or original text-settings such as Nison Niyazov's poem "Chi Ajab Umri Javoni" set to "Ufori Iroqi Bukhoro," a melody from the classical shashmaqom repertoire.[16] The Sefer Tüï effectively combines multiple histories and experiences by merging the Jewish holiday, which connects Bukharian Jews with the larger Jewish community, with the specifically Bukharian Jewish traditions exemplified by wedding celebrations.

In the early 2000s, musicians and Bukharian Jews in general in New York regularly referred to weddings when discussing the changes and challenges faced by their im-migrant community. In these exchanges, the old Central Asian wedding was typically depicted as a bastion of tradition and remembered with nostalgic overtones. The Soviet era in particular often took on romantic qualities when described by older immigrants and when imagined by younger Bukharian Jews. These memories can be striking be-cause those who lived in Soviet Central Asia also remember difficult living conditions

FIGURE 23.1 Adorned Torah at a Sefer Tüï in Queens, October 2009. Photo by the author.

and restrictions on Jewish religious practice. However, life in Soviet Central Asia was generally recalled with fondness, and the wedding celebration was a natural event with which to associate those sentiments.

For musicians of the older immigrant generation who lived most of their lives in Central Asia (i.e., they moved to New York at fifty years of age or older and probably came as refugees), their former homes are remembered as part of a timeless premigration period during which Bukharian Jews celebrated weddings with "Bukharian music," "ethnic music," or other formulations describing music and traditions that are distinctly or uniquely their own. In these particular remembrances, "Bukharian music" centers on maqom as played on quintessentially Central Asian instruments, especially the ṭanbūr (long-necked lute), although such weddings seem to have been rare during Soviet times. For example, Roshel Amin (1951–), a master classical musician, often recalled a specific wedding in Panjrud, Tajikistan, that he dated to the 1960s:

> We went to this wedding, me, my father, and my brother, with this ṭanbūr. There were a thousand people sitting there, no microphone, nothing, just the ṭanbūr. And we sang with these shashmaqom books in front of us. The people listened, all the people only listened to this maqom art (san'at) music, shashmaqom art music.[17]

Several musicians explained that only older guests or those from cities with strong Bukharian traditions would prefer classical maqom at a wedding, which speaks to the disparities between those from various Central Asian cities, now all living together in New York. I once asked Ilyas Malayev (1936–2008) what he thought the difference was between a wedding in Uzbekistan and in the United States. Malayev came to New York City in 1995, after leading an illustrious career in Uzbekistan as a poet and performer of light classical music and popular stage (estrada) entertainment. In New York, Malayev continued to write poetry for popular wedding musicians, although he remade his image on world music stages, where he mostly played classical Central Asian music to non-Bukharian audiences. He answered:

> The difference? It's a very significant difference. There, it was much more national (milli) music. In Tashkent, in Uzbekistan, in Tajikistan—except in the last years of the Soviet Union—Bukharians only sang maqom. After a little, bit by bit, technology appeared and with it our music disappeared. Now here—to me, weddings here [in America] are unacceptable. If they were from years and years ago from Samarqand, from Tashkent, from Bukhara, only these immigrants want, for example, [classical singers such as] Ezro Malakov, Avrom Tolmasov, Roshel Rubinov, or Muhabbatkhon [Muhabbat Shamayeva].[18]

In this assessment, Malayev was also speaking as someone who was a prominent artist in Central Asia, and whose personal repertoire and musical style were much more versatile and generally appreciated before immigration (although he remained the most prominent poet in the community). Malayev and other musicians from Central Asia frequently contrasted the idea of an old, maqom-filled Central Asian wedding to the contemporary Bukharian Jewish wedding in New York, where the bride and groom, their families, and their friends want current international pop- and dance-music hits. Roshel Rubinov (1966–), although a poet and musician of a younger generation, echoed Malayev's thoughts. Rubinov had immigrated to New York in 1995 and became one of the most active Bukharian wedding musicians as well as a prominent maqom performer. He asserted:

> [In New York people] want pop music. They want to dance. Today everything is completely changed. Old people come to the party and ask me, please, sing one song, our songs, an Uzbek song, a Tajik song, a Bukharian song. They understand, they want it, they listen to it, not only old people but people that grew up there. Those that were born in Uzbekistan, Tajikistan, they like this music, maybe they're about forty years old, fifty years old, forty-five and up, people from Samarqand, Bukhara, Shahrisabz, Navoi, or Kattakurgan.[19]

But although musicians in New York typically recall Central Asian weddings with a heavy emphasis on the shashmaqom, an objective interpretation of the data and ethnographic reports indicates that those particular kinds of weddings would seem to be rather unusual in the broader context of Soviet-era Central Asian musical life. In reality, most weddings in Central Asia seem to have featured a mix of international styles and an emphasis on estrada and popular music, just the same as contemporary Bukharian weddings in New York and throughout the diaspora. In post-Soviet Uzbekistan, the shashmaqom has taken on even more powerful associations of the past and Uzbek tradition as a crucial part of a nation-building project, as Tanya Merchant has pointed out. In contemporary Uzbekistan maqom is played at the morning *osh* men's celebration, simultaneously invoking the Uzbek past and rejecting associations of the Soviet era.[20] For contemporary Bukharian Jews, the wistful linking of the shashmaqom to the Central Asian past through stories about weddings seems to be less about their actual experiences in Central Asia than it is about life after immigration and the challenges that people face when their lives have been completely uprooted and they must navigate unfamiliar territory.

In addition to the classical shashmaqom repertoire, a key part of remembering the old Bukharian Jewish wedding in Central Asia is the female wedding entertainer called *sozanda*.[21] Historically, sozandas presided over several parts of a wedding and other life-cycle events for both Jews and Muslims, such as the women's parties held for the bride before the wedding. According to Yafa Pinkhasova (Tühfakhon, 1928–2010), the most famous Soviet-era sozanda, these events would include birth celebrations and circumcisions, as well as eyebrow-threading (*qoshchinon*) ceremonies for women before a wedding; tefillin-tying (*tfillin bandon*) events when Jewish boys become bar mitzvah at age thirteen and begin observing the commandment of praying with phylacteries; and turban-binding (*salla bandon*) rituals for honoring Muslim women elders.[22] Sozandas also entertained the emir's mother during the pre-Soviet era. Sozandas play percussive music in small ensembles of one leader with several accompanists, and most songs are performed in a call-and-response style.

The role of sozanda is now frequently associated with Jewish women, in a parallel to the world of the classical shashmaqom repertoire, which in the United States and Israel has also become linked to Jewish performers. Female Jewish sozandas were among the best known, such as those who entertained the Emir's mother, including Mikhali Karkigi (1888?–1978) and her mother, Tovoi Karkigi (Tovoi Namatiyeva, 1857–1959), and Buluri Oshma (Shishakhon).[23] But in another example of mythologies conflicting with realities, although Jews were very strongly represented as musicians and entertainers since the nineteenth century and the period of the last Manghit emirs, the association of the term *sozanda* with Jewish women in the city of Bukhara is a twentieth-century development. Many, but not all, of the major sozandas were Jewish, and very few Jews had access to the court—and Jews, being such a small minority in Central Asia (less than 1 percent), could not have been responsible for providing the necessary music and entertainment for all weddings in Bukhara, and definitely not throughout the region. Similarly, despite the many important Jewish figures in the history of the shashmaqom, most classical Central Asian musicians have been Muslims.[24]

Scholars, more than musicians or typical members of the Bukharian community, have been instrumental in remembering the sozanda's role in weddings. For example, Theodore Levin and Otanazar Matyakubov documented some of the repertoire on the Smithsonian Folkways collection *Bukhara: Musical Crossroads of Asia*, as performed by Tühfakhon's ensemble.[25] In the notes, obligatory live music at a celebration is described as "provided by an ensemble usually consisting of between three and seven *sozanda*-s." The 92nd Street Y, a major cultural institution on the Upper East Side of New York City, staged a sozanda performance in a re-creation of a Bukharian wedding as part of the "Music and Dance of the Jewish Wedding" series, organized by Walter Zev Feldman, in 2004. In cases such as this staged wedding re-creation, it is mainly scholars who are encouraging Bukharian Jews to explore creative uses of the past in order to affirm particular perspectives of old Central Asia. And these creative expressions have also brought together scholars and musicians who have sympathetic views of the past, generating more creative products.

In my many interviews, musicians did not discuss the sozanda role without prompting. Besides Tühfakhon, who had relocated to Denver, and Nina Bakayeva in Israel, hardly any women are known to specifically call themselves "sozanda."[26] Noted sozandas of the Soviet era such as Hevsi Bakayeva (Noshputi, 1908–1961) and Hevsi Aronova (Gubur, 1907–1971) were known as concert and stage performers, and although they may have sung at weddings, these women are not generally described as wedding entertainers. Part of the conflict seemed to be the general association of the sozanda role with a kind of folk musician, essential to celebrations but not on a level with the refined professional classical singer role that many Jewish women occupied in Soviet

Central Asia. Tühfakhon was famous as someone who brought the sozanda repertoire to the concert stage, a performer in the same category as Ilyas Malayev and Muhabbat Shamayeva, and different from an average sozanda.

Tamara Katayeva (1947–), a prominent singer and dancer specializing in classical lyric songs, comments on sozandas at weddings today, describing sozanda-style singing as a continuing role for women, but limited to female-only parties after the Sabbath following the wedding. She also makes a point to make a distinction between herself and the role of a sozanda:

> Now, there are sozandas but they don't sing at our weddings here. They only sing for Shabbat, only for ladies, Jewish ladies, after *seudah* [*seudah shlishit*, the "third meal" eaten on Saturday evenings]. After eating, they'll call a lovely artist, Muhabbat can go, they might call me, but only for women. It's called *shabbat poïtakht* [Sabbath throne]. And for men they'll call Ezro Malakov, or Roshel Aminov. It was a tradition in Central Asia, and I'm very glad this tradition is continuing here, because we sing for people how they have to get along, keep Shabbat, and respect family and older people, his mother and her mother. But here there isn't a "sozanda." I only go if I want to; this is not my job.[27]

In the United States specifically, musicians and scholars have wrestled with the status of the maqom and the sozanda repertoires with respect to weddings, in many ways the essential life-cycle event for Bukharian Jews. Although wedding bands play some songs from the sozanda repertoire, and although maqom is performed at weddings and at community celebrations, their performance is typically limited and serves a symbolic purpose. Young brides and grooms are often blamed for the dwindling state of Bukharian Jewish traditions at weddings as a generation uninterested in tradition because of their experiences growing up in America. However, these characterizations seem to describe generational conflicts and the fears of those who fled Central Asia more than they describe the actual concerns of younger Bukharian Americans or the complexities of Central Asian musical life.

Characterizations of past Bukharian weddings as bastions of tradition, either by musicians discussing classical maqom or by scholars describing sozanda performance, differ in many respects from many accounts of weddings that took place in pre-Soviet and Soviet Central Asia. In pre-Soviet times, only wealthy families would be able to hire ensembles of musicians and dancers, including professional sozanda ensembles.[28] The role of the sozanda in the average wedding during the Soviet era seems to be overemphasized by scholars, given the extremely small numbers of sozandas at the end of the twentieth century and the lack of spontaneous remembrances by my interviewees, both male and female; intermittent sozanda singing by semi-professionals seemed to be more typical in Soviet Central Asia, and the sozanda and her repertoire have long had a mostly symbolic role at weddings.[29] Similarly, older male musicians focus on the small parties surrounding the groom and held for men, where classical tunes would be played, and exceptional circumstances such as the one particular wedding, cited by Roshel

Amin, in which everyone listened to him and his father perform only classical music.[30] These same musicians avoid describing aspects of Central Asian weddings that they deem untraditional, such as the Soviet civil ceremonies known as ZAGS and promoted by Soviet authorities seeking to replace religious practices, which grew in prominence at least since the 1960s.[31]

Musicians often downplay direct connections between today's Bukharian Jewish weddings and many non-classical aspects that are clearly consistent with the Soviet era, such as the use of heavy amplification, popular songs with the characteristic West and Central Asian 6/8 dance rhythm, and songs in Russian and other languages.[32] The contemporary Bukharian Jewish wedding style is unmistakably an extension of the weddings held in Central Asia, perhaps an obvious notion, but confirmed by footage of the 1990s. A 1994 wedding in Samarqand mentioned by anthropologist Alanna Cooper in her monograph featured karnais heralding the bride and group, keyboard and percussion primarily playing loud 6/8 dance music, a male wedding singer performing upbeat Persian-language and Russian-language songs, and at one point during the celebration, an older sozanda singing blandishments for donations.[33] In *The Hundred Thousand Fools of God*, Theodore Levin describes two similar weddings—a Muslim celebration in Tashkent and a Jewish wedding in Queens, both presumably held in the early 1990s (dates are not given)—with the same "earsplittingly" loud music and "grossly amplified *tar*, synthesizer, and pop vocalists."[34] These showy weddings, so similar in both Central Asia and New York, are contrasted with the "older style of *toy*" (tŭĭ), described as more spiritual and less secular.[35] However, these contemporary weddings seem to be mostly different from the ways that older musicians such as Ma'ruf Khoja *describe* weddings in the past, and not necessarily unlike the majority of earlier weddings, and it is unclear what time period is exactly meant by "older." As noted, musicians' remembrances of "old" weddings only partially resemble the wide variety of practices of actual weddings in different cities and time periods, and documented weddings in both New York and Uzbekistan for at least thirty years point to many shared characteristics.

During the Soviet era in which older Bukharian musicians lived, maqom and the sozanda repertoires were already presentational and concertized forms. However, in New York, the Bukharian wedding of the Central Asian past, marked especially by performances and reception of classical maqom, has become a symbol of difference and loss, contrasted with today's loud and extravagant weddings—even though such weddings were (and still are) also actually an important part of Central Asian life. Because young people are typically the ones getting married, and because professional musicians must address the desires of the bride and groom, their families, and their guests, the older musicians' narrative of decline from Central Asia to New York is a larger statement on their opinions regarding the state of young first- and second-generation Bukharians in New York. Through their idealization of the Central Asian past, older immigrants are expressing concerns and fears about losing meaningful aspects of their lives, which also brought definition to their community, as younger Bukharian Jews come of age in New York.

Bukharian Weddings and Performances of the Central Asian Past

The tŭĭ, the large party for the bride and groom held for both families and their guests, with men and women celebrating together, is the central event of the contemporary Bukharian wedding. Among Bukharian Jews in New York, as is typical among other communities in the United States, the mostly secular party often overshadows other aspects of the traditional rituals leading up to the wedding. At all of these Bukharian parties, musical symbols and representations of the Central Asian past can be found. Reflecting diasporic circumstances, Bukharian Jews have retained some elements of a shrinking traditional wedding repertoire, and also replaced older material with newly invented symbols of the Central Asian past.

The classical maqom style continues to be played at wedding parties but transformed, not as dance music or even entertainment, but as background music during times such as the "sweet table" of desserts. During these moments, maqom is played on the typical contemporary wedding band instrumentation consisting of electric guitars, keyboard, doira, clarinet, percussion, and electronic drums. Musicians do not switch to acoustic instruments or those instruments marked as symbolic of the maqom repertoire, such as the ṭanbūr. Furthermore, wedding musicians usually prefer to play newer songs written in a classical style, such as compositions by the prominent middle-aged musicians Roshel Rubinov and Avrom Tolmasov (such as "Hofiz Shuda Bin," or "Ṭanbūr Manam"), instead of canonical melodies. This classical music segment of the wedding party, while typical, is not deemed mandatory. Even so, these occasions are considered important emblems of Bukharian tradition, and especially geared toward the older people in attendance, who wish to be reminded of their lives before immigration. And not only older people enjoy classical music; as Menashe Khaimov, a younger Bukharian community activist told me, "these songs bring me back to Uzbekistan. I came to this country at the age of fourteen and it's great sometimes to go back, at least mentally."[36] Khaimov's evocative turn of phrase of traveling through music, "to go back mentally," reminds us that "attachment to the culture of the birthplace is more than nostalgia; it is for many a function of the construction of identity."[37]

The Central Asian past is mostly symbolized at weddings by the *jomma* dance, which is considered essential, and the percussive doira music accompanied by the long karnai. The jomma is the beautiful heavy embroidered coat with designs and patterns, reserved for honors and special occasions; Jewish jommas are often adorned with symbols such as Stars of David and menorahs, and in New York, some have American iconography such as the Great Seal of the United States (see Figure 23.2). After the honorees don the jomma, they dance in Central Asian style, with arms outstretched and hands and feet rhythmically marking a two-beat feel of a constant 6/8 pulse. In today's wedding

FIGURE 23.2 Musicians playing doira and karnai at a Sefer Tūĭ in Queens, and jomma (embroidered celebratory coat) worn by celebrant in center, October 2009. Photo by the author.

bands, a drum machine (or drum sounds played on the keyboard) often keeps the 6/8 pulse going without breaks or variations, while doira players play virtuosic solos and embellishments of the underlying rhythm; the doira is typically played throughout the wedding party, but these dances offer opportunities for flashy improvisations. The main songs accompanying these dances would be previously associated with the folkloric and sozanda repertoire, generally called "Bokharcha" (Bukhara-style music), such as "Shastu shastu chor" or "Boy boy boy, abrukash dumi mora."[38] These are consistent features of the Bukharian Jewish wedding, much more characteristic of the Central Asian wedding than maqom.[39] And as noted, much of this music had already taken on a symbolic quality in Central Asia itself.

In addition to these signals of the Central Asian past, certain Russian-language pop songs played at weddings also hark back to Central Asia, such as "Samarkand" by the Uzbek singer Nasiba Abdullayeva (1961–), which features nostalgic lines such as "I remember my beloved Samarqand / Enchanted fairy tale" and "Magical nights, dear ancient streets / The distant roads won't separate us / You are always with me, my beloved Samarqand."[40] Many of these songs about Central Asia are of more recent vintage than some of the English, Spanish, Russian, or Hebrew pop songs heard at weddings. Another example is the popular song "Moya Mama Samarkand, Moya Papa Bukhara" by the Bukharian wedding singer Yuhan Benjamin. This Russian-language song features prominent instrumental symbols of the past: the doira and tār, a lute often associated with classical music.[41] Ruben Shimonov, who came to the United States at the age of six and who worked at the Queens College Hillel during his twenties, referred to these newer songs and "dancified versions of probably traditional songs" as what most young Bukharian Americans associate with Central Asia and the past, rather than maqom.[42]

The performance of the Central Asian past mainly in songs such as "Samarkand" and "Moya Mama Samarkand," as well as the jomma dances, have had a significant impact on younger generations. In New York, the music played at contemporary Bukharian weddings clearly has different resonances for those who emigrated as adult refugees in the early 1990s than it does for those such as Shimonov, who were born in the United States or immigrated as children.[43] Most significantly, for many younger Bukharian Jews today, weddings may be the only times that they encounter "Bukharian music." One young interviewee recalls a conversation with a prominent wedding musician:

> He is very upset at the community today in the sense that all these youngsters that come to him, they don't want Bukharian music. And he can play all these beautiful songs, and the parents are asking for beautiful songs, but the kids are saying if you play those, we're not going to invite you anymore. So now, he's competing between his "bread" [making a living] and the culture. If he's going to try to preserve the culture and play the music to preserve it, they're not going to invite him and he won't be able to feed himself and his family. Or he goes with the flow, but yet, then what makes a Bukharian wedding a Bukharian wedding? So he told me he still tries, he puts two or three Bukharian songs, and says, "it's just for the grandparents."[44]

Most members of this generation, who from the standpoint of the early 2020s may now be parents themselves, connect most strongly to American pop, hip hop, electronic music, reggaetón, and Russian and Israeli songs. For instance, David Aminov was mostly a fan of hip hop as a young man in his twenties, a music he related to the "blue collar, hard nose, scrappy" upbringing and lifestyle that he experienced as a first-generation American.[45] These younger Bukharians may only know a little bit of "Bukharian" (Tajik Persian) from living and communicating with their parents and grandparents, so anything in Persian, including recent songs in a popular style, are heard as representations of Central Asia and mapped onto the past. The instances during the wedding in which songs about Central Asia are sung and when the doira and karnai are featured certify the wedding as a specifically Bukharian wedding, since most of the repertoire at Bukharian wedding celebrations today resembles other wedding celebrations in New York, including those of other diasporic communities and other Jewish American communities. At a Bukharian wedding with music played by a band such as the in-demand ensembles led by Yuhan Benjamin or Albert Narkolayev, one hears dance music accompanied by a steady 6/8 or 4/4 beat; American pop and rock; Spanish-language songs; and Russian, Israeli, and Eurodisco songs. DJs often play a similar eclectic mix as well as electronic dance music and hip hop. Bukharian weddings also of course feature the song that is now common to all Jewish weddings, "Hava nagila."

The dizzying combination of languages and styles at Bukharian Jewish weddings constitutes an eclectic party repertoire that has deep historical roots for the community.

Some Bukharian Jews have embraced this eclecticism as an anchor to the past, revealing the mutability of the concept of tradition. This is especially true for those Bukharian Jews with urban backgrounds. As Ruben Shimonov put it, the performance of different kinds of music is "just what we do," a reflection of urban life in Central Asia and the "same thing" in New York.[46] Shimonov also understood Bukharian Jewish interest in international popular styles historically, remembering his grandfather proudly telling him about his childhood: "he used to tell me, 'I used to go on my roof, in the 1930s Soviet Union, when Western music was prohibited, to listen to foxtrots and catch radio signals from Germany'... and he loves classical Russian music."[47]

Nevertheless, the very different experiences that older and younger Bukharians have had with Central Asia itself necessitate different creative uses of the past. Most young Bukharian Jews relate to Central Asia primarily through *representations* of the past, in music and other cultural forms, created by their parents' or grandparents' generation as a product of mass migration. Older immigrants perform these ideas of the Central Asian past as they seek to remember their personal Central Asian experiences, and in turn, the younger generation remembers these performances by their elders. Younger Bukharian Jews' childhoods are filled with these symbolic performances and mediated stories, heard at weddings, Sefer Tŭĭs, and other celebrations, reinforcing the meaning and power of the symbols. At weddings, where young people and their future lives are the focus, these generational concerns and multiple representations come together in dramatic ways—and continue the cycle—as remembrances and performances of the Central Asian past are combined with an eclectic repertoire that speaks directly to the needs of the younger generation.

Reconsidering Mythologies and Realities

At a time when Bukharian life is so rapidly changing, the stakes are high for remembering and performing ideas of the past at weddings. It is in this light that mythologies and realities in the study of Jewish music invite reconsideration, especially with regard to the meaning of creation and creativity. While there are clear inconsistencies between the stories of past weddings as steeped in ancient Bukharian traditions and the reality that older weddings were often the same eclectic pop music affairs that they are today, linking old Bukharian Jewish weddings to music associated with the past serves an important purpose of anchoring Bukharian people to the Central Asian cities where they lived for centuries and then left en masse in an extremely short span of time. Telling stories about the old Bukharian Jewish wedding in this way also reminds the community of the celebrated stature in Central Asia of many older immigrants, and it positions older people as essential carriers of tradition and history at a time when younger people have little direct experience of Central Asia and its current and past realities. Similarly, contemporary songs with idealized depictions of Central Asia and symbolic remnants of distinctly Central Asian music may be critically assessed as simplistic and romantic, but such creative uses of the past also imbue Bukharian Jews with distinctiveness and a sense of pride, especially as a little-known and often marginalized group among other Jewish communities internationally. Most of all, these performances give wedding celebrants joy, unity, and opportunities to dance.

Furthermore, Bukharian Jews themselves may understand these specific representations of the past to be constructions and acts of creativity, and thus easily reconcilable even when they may seem contradictory. For some Bukharian Jews, the ability to harmonize ostensibly conflicting narratives and perspectives can be a point of pride. People in general often understand mythologies as stories that give meaning to their individual lives, group identities, and histories, and they also accept that such stories and representations are the products of human creativity and not reflections of verifiable facts. Shimonov's sophisticated interpretation of Bukharian Jewish wedding music and musicians' "balancing act" expresses some of the multiple ways that the past, and creative uses of the past, can be understood:

> We live in a time right now, especially in New York, there are so many different musical traditions and so many different generations, and we want to bring everyone under one roof. Musicians have their finger on the pulse of the community and they will know, ok, people right now are into reggaetón so I'm going to play some reggaetón. The simple answer is that the crowd wants it, so they give the crowd what they want. We don't want to be pigeonholed, and the musicians understand that more than anybody. . . .
>
> We [Bukharian Jews] can say: we have what we have constructed, what we have envisioned as our traditional music, it's not going anywhere, we have it, but we're also good at all this other stuff. The same ones who are spinning hip hop records will then take a break and do this [doira playing] for you. It's this balancing act that we take a lot of pride in and *that's* what makes it distinctly Bukharian.[48]

While describing the eclectic musical potpourri of a typical Bukharian Jewish wedding, Shimonov also explained that "traditional" Bukharian Jewish music as performed at a wedding is something constructed as well as something that belongs to them: "we have it." Ultimately, it is all of these various products of creativity, such as the sounds Bukharian Jews "have envisioned as our traditional music," that are the distinct property of the community.

Creative uses of the past persist and thrive because they generate vital experiences and because they give meaning to the stories and memories of individuals and their families. More generally, creative engagements of culture and history can be said to be the essence of Jewish musical life, sustaining people not only at weddings, but bar and bat mitzvah parties, b'rit milah celebrations, and other life-cycle events. For what is left if musicians cannot creatively engage with the pasts they imagine, and the myths that they and their audiences find meaningful? And as academics interrogate myths in the pursuit of realities, scholarship that interprets the past should be understood as its own paradoxical combination of mythology and reality, and contingent upon research that is shaped by subjective experiences. Creative uses of the past are not myths opposed to reality, but rather interpretations of experience and history that, when set to music and dance, are undeniably powerful and self-affirming forms of celebration.

NOTES

1. Ilyas Malayev Ensemble, *At the Bazaar of Love: Timeless Central Asian Maqam Music*, Shanachie 64081, 2003.
2. Ethnographic information in this chapter stems from the author's field research, which was mainly conducted in New York between 2002 and 2014.
3. Kay Kaufman Shelemay, "Mythologies and Realities in the Study of Jewish Music," *The World of Music* 37, no. 1 (1995): 24–38.
4. Yossi Shain, *Kinship and Diaspora in International Affairs* (Ann Arbor: University of Michigan Press, 2007), 2.
5. See Theodore Levin, *Hundred Thousand Fools of God: Musical Travels in Central Asia (and Queens, New York)* (Bloomington: Indiana University Press, 1996), 281–282.
6. In English, the spellings *Bukharan* and *Bukharian* are both commonly used to refer to the Jewish community of Central Asia. Although scholars have tended toward *Bukharan*, Bukharian Jews themselves overwhelmingly use the spelling *Bukharian,* and I follow their preference. The spelling *Bukharian* applies to the Jewish community and not the city of Bukhara in general (e.g., Bukharan court).
7. Afghanistan was a particularly important place for Bukharian Jews in the twentieth century. For example, the last emir of Bukhara, Olim Khon, lived in exile in Afghanistan after being deposed by the Russians; in Afghanistan, Olim Khon was entertained by the Eliezerofs, Jewish musicians who stayed in Afghanistan from 1935 to 1937 on their way to Palestine. Jacob Nasirov, the rabbi of Bet El, the Afghan Jewish synagogue in Queens, is a Bukharian Jew whose family emigrated to Afghanistan in 1932 before emigrating to Israel in 1949. See Sara Koplik, "The Experiences of Bukharan Jews outside the Soviet Union in the 1930s and 1940s," in *Bukharan Jews in the 20th Century: History, Experience, and Narration*, ed. Ingeborg Baldauf, Moshe Gammer, and Thomas Loy (Wiesbaden: Reichert, 2008), 91–109; Sara Y. Aharon, *From Kabul to Queens: The Jews of Afghanistan and their Move to the United States* (New York: Decalogue Books, 2011); and for an Uzbek Muslim perspective, Yousof Mamoor's memoir, *In Quest of a Homeland: Recollections of an Emigrant* (Eden, SD: Nettleberry, 2005).
8. Margaret Kartomi and Andrew D. McCredie, "Introduction: Musical Outcomes of Jewish Migration into Asia via the Northern and Southern Routes c. 1780–c. 1950," *Ethnomusicology Forum* 13, no. 1 (May 2004): 13.
9. See Houman Sarshar, ed., *Esther's Children: A Portrait of Iranian Jews* (Beverly Hills, CA: Center for Iranian Jewish Oral History, 2002), 5.
10. See Alanna E. Cooper, *Bukharan Jews and the Dynamics of Global Judaism* (Bloomington: Indiana University Press, 2012), 128–134.
11. See Robert Valiyevich Al'meyev, "K etnologii bukharskikh evreyev" [On the ethnology of Bukharian Jews], in *Evrei v srednei azii: Voprosy istorii i kul'tury*, ed. Edvard Vasil'evich Rtveladze (Tashkent: Izdatel'stvo "Fan" Akademii nauk Respubliki Uzbekistan, 2004).

12. See David Ochildiev, *A History of the Bukharan Jews* (New York: Mir Collection, 2005), 177. There is very little information on the early Bukharian Jewish population in the United States. This monograph by a local historian in the Bukharian community is an exception.

13. Numbers of the US or New York Bukharian Jewish population are often much higher in articles, magazines, and websites, e.g., 50,000 or 60,000, although given without evidence or citations. In his 2008 study, Kaganovitch estimates 28,000 in the entire United States for the year 2006, which seems realistic when compared with other population estimates; Albert Kaganovitch, "The Bukharan Jewish Diaspora at the Beginning of the 21st Century," in *Bukharan Jews in the 20th Century: History, Experience, and Narration*, ed. Ingeborg Baldauf, Moshe Gammer, and Thomas Loy (Wiesbaden: Reichert, 2008), 111–116. For one history of Soviet Jewish immigration to the United States, see Stuart Altshuler, *From Exodus to Freedom: A History of the Soviet Jewry Movement* (Lanham, MD: Rowman & Littlefield, 2005).

14. For a map of Bukharian Jewish neighborhoods in Queens, see Evan Rapport, *Greeted with Smiles: Bukharian Jewish Music and Musicians in New York* (New York: Oxford University Press, 2014), 11.

15. Photographs of traditional Bukharian Jewish wedding dress can be seen in Hetty Berg, ed., *Facing West: Oriental Jews of Central Asia and the Caucasus* (Zwolle: Waanders, 1997).

16. For more on the Simchat Torah celebration, see Rapport, *Greeted with Smiles*, 106–107; a medley of Simchat Torah tunes can be heard through the book's companion website (http://www.oup.com/us/greetedwithsmiles). Bukharian Simchat Torah songs can also be heard on Ezro Malakov, prod., *Musical Treasures of the Bukharian Jewish Community / Muzykal'naya sokrovishchnitsa bukharskikh evreev/Otser ha-muzykah shel kehillat yehudei bukharah* (Tel Aviv: World Bukharian Jewish Congress, 2007); and Yosi Niyazov, *Yosi Niyazov* (B'nei Baraq: Bukharian Organization Ateret Menaḥem, n.d.).

17. Roshel Amin in discussion with the author, December 2, 2003. Translated from Persian by the author. Interview transcriptions in this chapter are sightly edited to improve intelligibility and readability.

18. Ilyas Malayev in discussion with the author, January 16, 2006. Translated from Persian by the author.

19. Roshel Rubinov in discussion with the author, December 2, 2005. Translated from Persian by the author. See also Rapport, *Greeted with Smiles*, 91.

20. See Tanya Merchant, "Imagined Homogeneity: *Maqom* in Soviet and Uzbek National Projects," in *Routledge Handbook of Asian Music: Cultural Intersections*, ed. Lee Tong Soon (London: Routledge, 2021).

21. Prior to the twentieth century, the term *sozanda* was used more generically to refer to male and female musicians of both light and serious repertoires, just as the term is used in Afghanistan and parts of Iran, and this is still the case and among the general populace in Central Asia. Sāsān Fātemi, "La musique légère urbaine dans la culture iranienne: Réflexions sur les notions de classique et populaire" (PhD diss., Universite Paris X–Nanterre, 2005), 228.

22. See Alexander Djumaev, "Musical Traditions and Ceremonies of Bukhara," *Anthropology of the Middle East* 3, no. 1 (Spring 2008): 52–66. For photographs of a *qoshchinon*, see Joan Roth, *Jewish Women: A World of Tradition and Change* (New York: Jolen Press, 1995), 130–133.

23. Tovoi Karkigi was also known as Tovoi Urus, *rus* meaning "Russian," because she could speak Russian at a time when very few Central Asians did.

24. See Ol'ga Aleksandrovna Sukhareva, *Bukhara: XIX–nachalo XX v. (Pozdnefeodal'nyĭ gorod i ego naseleniye)* (Moscow: Nauka, 1966); Fātemi, "La musique légère urbaine," 227–229. For more on the sozanda, see also Djumaev, "Musical Traditions"; Nizam Nurjanov, "Traditsii sozanda v muzykal'no-tantseval'noĭ kul'ture tadzhikov na rubezhe XIX–XX vekov," in *Muzyka narodov Azii i Afriki*, ed. Viktor Sergeyevich Vinogradova (Moscow: Sovyetskiĭ Kompozitor, 1980), 3:111–157; Elena Reikher, "The Female Sozanda Art from the Viewpoint of Professionalism in the Musical Tradition: A Preliminary Survey," *Musica Judaica* 18 (2005–2006): 70–86; Manṣūrah Sābet'zādeh, "Musiqi-ye shādi va sorur dar Tājikestān," *Mahoor* 2, no. 6 (Winter 2000): 69–82; and Zoya Tajikova, "O muzikal'nom iskusstve bukharskikh zhenshchin-sozanda," in *Traditsii muzykal'nykh kul'tur narodov Blizhnego, Srednego Vostoka i sovremennost'*, ed. Dilbar A. Rashidova and Tukhtasin B. Gafurbekov (Moscow: Sovetskii Kompozitor, 1987).

25. Theodore Levin and Otanazar Matyakubov, recorders, *Bukhara: Musical Crossroads of Asia* (Smithsonian Folkways, 1991). Jean During also recorded some of the sozanda repertoire in Bukhara in 1990, available on *Musique d'Asie centrale: l'esprit de la tradition* (Arles: Cité de la Musique/Actes Sud, 1998) and *Transoxania: Folk Music of Persian-Speaking People* (Tehran: Mahoor Institute of Culture and Art, 2003).

26. See Reikher, "The Female Sozanda Art."

27. Tamara Katayeva in discussion with the author, May 11, 2006. Translated from the Persian by the author.

28. See Sukhareva, *Bukhara*, 315; Reikher, "The Female Sozanda Art," 81–82.

29. See Fātemi, "La musique légère urbaine," 214–216.

30. See also Edith Gerson-Kiwi, "Wedding Dances and Songs of the Jews of Bokhara," *Journal of the International Folk Music Council* 2 (1950): 18; this information was based on observations made in Israel.

31. See Levin, *The Hundred Thousand Fools*, 45; Cooper, *Bukharan Jews*, 159. ZAGS (Zapis Aktov Grazhdanskogo Sostoyaniya) is the registry office where marriages and other changes in civil status were recorded in the Soviet Union, and still in Russia.

32. See Levin, *The Hundred Thousand Fools*, 45; Cooper, *Bukharan Jews*, 156; Rapport, *Greeted with Smiles*, 136–139.

33. See Cooper, *Bukharan Jews*, 156. Thanks to Alanna E. Cooper for generously sharing this unreleased video footage with me.

34. Levin, *The Hundred Thousand Fools*, 44–45, 280–284.

35. Ibid., 284, 41–42.

36. Menashe Khaimov in discussion with the author, July 24, 2015.

37. Kartomi and McCredie, "Introduction: Musical Outcomes," 14.

38. Fātemi concludes that the term *bokharcha* has only recently become used to describe the sozanda repertoire; "La musique légère urbaine," 242–247. Recordings of these songs can be heard on Bukharan Jewish Ensemble Shashmaqam, *Central Asia in Forest Hills N.Y.* (Smithsonian Folkways, 1991).

39. See Rapport, *Greeted with Smiles*, 136–139.

40. Translated from the Russian by Michael and Wendy Grinberg.

41. Yuhan Benjamin (Юхан), Моя Мама Самарканд, February 27, 2015, YouTube video, https://youtu.be/jeXl_YDa3_A.

42. Ruben Shimonov in discussion with the author, July 29, 2015.

43. Bukharian Jewish American generations are heavily tied to the refugee experience, more than to broad age cohorts of first- and second-generation immigrants, underscoring

the need for understanding migrant generations in their particular historical context, including "the impact of historically grounded features of the host society context that migrants confront *after* migration." Nancy Foner, "Mobility Trajectories and Family Dynamics: History and Generation in the New York Immigrant Experience," *Diaspora: A Journal of Transnational Studies* 18, nos. 1–2 (Spring/Summer 2009): 25. See also Mette Louise Berg and Susan Eckstein, "Introduction: Reimagining Migrant Generations," *Diaspora: A Journal for Transnational Studies* 18, nos. 1–2 (Spring/Summer 2009): 1–23.

44. [name withheld] in discussion with the author, August 10, 2015.
45. David Aminov in discussion with the author, July 29, 2015.
46. Ruben Shimonov in discussion with the author, July 29, 2015.
47. Ruben Shimonov in discussion with the author, July 29, 2015.
48. Ruben Shimonov in discussion with the author, July 29, 2015.

SELECT BIBLIOGRAPHY

Al'meyev, Robert Valiyevich. "K etnologii bukharskikh evreyev" [On the ethnology of Bukharian Jews]. In *Evrei v srednei azii: Voprosy istorii i kul'tury*, edited by Edvard Vasil'evich Rtveladze, 26–38. Tashkent: Izdatel'stvo "Fan" Akademii nauk Respubliki Uzbekistan, 2004.

Baldauf, Ingeborg, Moshe Gammer, and Thomas Loy, eds. *Bukharan Jews in the 20th Century: History, Experience, and Narration*. Wiesbaden: Reichert, 2008.

Berg, Hetty, ed. *Facing West: Oriental Jews of Central Asia and the Caucasus*. Zwolle: Waanders, 1997.

Cooper, Alanna E. *Bukharan Jews and the Dynamics of Global Judaism*. Bloomington: Indiana University Press, 2012.

Djumaev, Alexander. "Musical Traditions and Ceremonies of Bukhara." *Anthropology of the Middle East* 3, no. 1 (Spring 2008): 52–66.

During, Jean. *Musique d'Asie centrale: l'esprit d'une tradition*. Arles: Cité de la Musique/Actes Sud, 1998.

Gerson-Kiwi, Edith. "Wedding Dances and Songs of the Jews of Bokhara." *Journal of the International Folk Music Council* 2 (1950): 17–18.

Levin, Theodore. *The Hundred Thousand Fools of God: Musical Travels in Central Asia (and Queens, New York)*. Bloomington: Indiana University Press, 1996.

Nurjanov, Nizam. "Traditsii sozanda v muzykal'no-tantseval'noi kul'ture tadzhikov na rubezhe XIX–XX vekov" [Sozanda tradition in Tajik music and dance culture at the turn of the 19th–20th centuries]. In *Muzyka narodov Azii i Afriki*, edited by Viktor Sergeyevich Vinogradova, 3:111–57. Moscow: Sovyetskii Kompozitor, 1980.

Ochildiev, David. *A History of the Bukharan Jews*. New York: Mir Collection, 2005.

Rapport, Evan. *Greeted with Smiles: Bukharian Jewish Music and Musicians in New York*. New York: Oxford University Press, 2014.

Reikher, Elena. "The Female Sozanda Art from the Viewpoint of Professionalism in the Musical Tradition: A Preliminary Survey." *Musica Judaica* 18 (2005–2006): 70–86.

Roth, Joan. *Jewish Women: A World of Tradition and Change*. New York: Jolen Press, 1995.

Sukhareva, Ol'ga Aleksandrovna. *Bukhara: XIX–nachalo XX v. (Pozdnefeodal'nyi gorod i ego naseleniye)* [Bukhara: 19th–early 20th century. The late feudal city and its people]. Moscow: Nauka, 1966.

PART VII

DESTRUCTION / REMEMBRANCE—
זכר / חורבן

REMEMBERING THE DESTRUCTION, RE-ANIMATING THE COLLECTIVE

Romaniote Liturgical Music after the Holocaust

MIRANDA L. CROWDUS

It is a blistering day near Athens, Greece, in the summer of 2017. I am at the Restion Jewish Senior Home with Cantor Haim Ischakis. Restion is some distance from Athens in a peaceful spot, surrounded by green hills and scrub characteristic of the region. The senior home is replete with a mikvah and a synagogue on its lower floor as well as living quarters. In the synagogue, I take recordings with my hand-held Zoom device while Haim Ischakis reads a section from the Torah: "Vayosef hurad mitsraimah va'yiḵnehu Poṭifar . . . " (And Joseph was brought down to Egypt. And Potifar bought him . . . , Genesis 39:1). Listening to the cantillation that highlights the drama of the Joseph story, I am struck how this excerpt is at once familiar and unfamiliar. The story is familiar, as is the declamatory style and the consistency of the musical patterns; however, the melodies themselves did not correspond to any trope that I had ever heard. The melodic and spoken patterns are neither of Ashkenazic, nor are they of Sephardic provenance; the cantillation lacks the quarter tones heard in the cantillation of Jews of Middle Eastern origins, as well as the nasal inflection and blend of Arabic and Aramaic in some of the Yemenite cantillation styles. Some features, such as the "spoken" almost cut-off sound on the word "mitsraima" (to Egypt), as well as the leap of a fifth followed by a florid melisma on the name "Potifar," are unlike any other documented cantillation. Despite these differences, the consistency of the melodic pattern, and the overall structure and its application to the biblical text, clearly identify it as Torah trope. In fact, Torah cantillation arguably represents the cornerstone of community and the collective survival through liturgical traditions.[1] In this case, the liturgical tradition is a present-day version of the long-enduring, distinctive Romaniote Jewish practice.

Over the past two thousand years, the Romaniote Jews have survived in Greece and surrounding areas under different rulers and regimes. They are identified by distinctive, unique religious and cultural practices, including their language (Yevanic or Judeo-Greek), clothing, cuisine, and particular musical repertoires. Historically, these repertoires included hymns in Judeo-Greek, a particular mode of Torah cantillation, as well as Judeo-Greek folk songs.[2] Romaniote liturgical musical practices emerged from a Jewish tradition that has experienced many changes throughout the centuries in light of oral transmission. In turn, the transmission of Romaniote repertoires was cut off by the Holocaust. As community leader, Allegra Matsa, one of the few Romaniote Jews still resident in Ioannina, remarked: "My parents never imagined that devastation like that could happen, so we never wrote down the melodies. We never thought that they might get lost."[3] Arguably, the Romaniote musical repertoire that remains has undergone drastic transformation reflecting its adaptation to new environments, and also owing to gaps in memory resulting from the near destruction of the community during the Holocaust.[4] Thus, study of contemporary Romaniote music, both current and historical, is imperative, in particular a focus on its interconnectedness with historical rupture, liturgy, and self- and historical identification.[5]

The concepts *ḥurban* (literally, "destruction") and *zekher* (literally, "memory," "remembrance," or "memorial") and their relationship to musical practices form a particularly apt triangulation through which to examine Romaniote musical practices today, give their long-enduring history characterized by rupture and persecution. Traditionally, ḥurban or *ḥurban habayit* refers to the destruction of the Second Temple by the Romans in 70 CE. Since the Holocaust it has also been used as a designation for the genocide of the European Jews. Indeed, the term *ḥurban* has been applied to the destruction, not only of a building or physical structure, but also of a populated zone and a population. This chapter focuses on how ḥurban—understood as the destruction inflicted during the Holocaust, specifically of the Jewish population of Ioannina—is remembered through zekher, remembrance, as a fundamental part of the contemporary Romaniote religious experience. As such, zekher is understood as a process, in the sense of remembering and commemorating, but also as the "making present" of no-longer-present Jewish objects, events, and people through religious ritual and the musical transmission of the liturgy.

Focusing on performances by Haim Ischakis in Greece in 2017, this chapter looks at two instances of how ḥurban and zekher are evoked simultaneously. The first is the Romaniote Yom Kippur service in Ioannina, where the two concepts surface through direct references in the liturgy and in the music in a process called "re-animation," that is, the transformation of ḥurban into an active Jewish space through the sounds of Jewish—here, specifically Romaniote—prayer. The second pertains to the reactions to the service of the congregants, both local and from abroad, who actively remember the destruction of former Jewish presence through homage made to people and places connected with their personal pasts. They use these tropes to reclaim and strengthen the present individual participants and their families as a collective.

Very little critical scholarship focuses exclusively on Romaniote history, religious and musical practice, and identity. The sources that do so hail from disciplines such as Jewish studies, Byzantine studies, history, and archaeology. The seminal publication on contemporary Romaniotes is *The Jews of Ioannina* by Rachel (Rae) Dalven, a New York–based scholar, who fostered the self-identification of Romaniote in the 1980s.[6] Dalven's book presents a historical overview of the Jewish community of Ioannina from the tenth century until the early 1990s and includes important details about unique Romaniote practices. As such, the book also includes descriptions and transcriptions of three Romaniote hymns. Marcia Haddad Ikonomopolous, the director of the Kehila Kedosha Janina Museum and Synagogue in New York, is another important figure who has documented the history of the Romaniotes. She has done so both through creating and facilitating numerous resources accessible through Kehila Kedosha Janina's website. Other critical histories exist that do not deal specifically with Romaniotes, but investigate Judeo-Greek history at large.[7]

Several musicologists have written about Jewish music in Greece. Among them is Amnon Shiloah, who has contributed several short articles on Judeo-Greek music in the early 1970s accompanied by his important recordings, *Greek Jewish Musical Traditions*.[8] But scholarship on specifically Romaniote music is sparse. Yosef Matsa's anthology of sixteen hymns written by Jews of Ioannina and transcribed from two unpublished nineteenth-century manuscripts is the first and so far only edition of the song repertoire of the Romaniote.[9] Leo Levi's entry for the first edition of the *Encyclopedia Judaica* attempts an overview of the different Jewish musical traditions in Greece, categorized as "Romaniote, Sephardic and Italian."[10] Rachel Dalven and Israel Katz have contributed a short article on Romaniote melodies.[11] Yitzchak Kerem's article on the music of the Greek Jews in the Holocaust, while focusing on Sephardic musical practices in Greece, contains some reflections on Romaniote practices.[12]

As with any music rooted in oral tradition that existed before notated scores, there is very little documented evidence of Romaniote musical and musical-liturgical practices, particularly before the twentieth century. To discuss Romaniote liturgical music, musicologists are not only confronted with a lack of sources but also with a challenge of categorization, specifically at what point in time one chooses to designate the beginning of the category Romaniote and whom to identify as Romaniote. The approach taken in this chapter is holistic in that Romaniote refers to the practitioners and their audiences who self-identify as Romaniote—many of whom trace their ancestry to at least the eighteenth century. However, such definition does not exclude historical definitions of Romaniote referring to the Greek-speaking Jews of Roman Palestine, categorized as Romaniote by Jewish studies scholars and historians, or to the Jews of Byzantium or the Greek-speaking Jews of the Ottoman Empire. Indeed, the contemporary Romaniote described here view their historical "timeline" as originating in antiquity, and this idea shapes their individual and communal self-understanding. Thus, current Romaniote musical practitioners and their audiences are not so much bearers of a "timeless tradition," but rather contemporaries who negotiate a broad range of present-day (Jewish) contexts and surroundings, while being informed by their long-enduring Romaniote heritage. It is for this reason—the importance of self-identification that is built in part through a changing and ruptured oral tradition—that the subsequent analyses rely mainly on linguistic descriptions of musical traditions and associated practices. It is beyond the scope of this chapter to provide the array of transcriptions necessary to begin a large-scale process of musical note-based comparisons.

EARLY HISTORY, DISRUPTION, AND DESTRUCTION

The history of the Jews in Greece goes back to biblical times, but the earliest evidence of their presence on the Greek mainland dates only to the third century BCE. According to Rachel Dalven, oral accounts maintain that a Roman slave ship was destroyed on the Albanian coast, resulting in the Jewish survivors settling in the area. Although there are no precise historical records of this event, it should be noted that there have been remains of Roman slave ships discovered off the coast of the Epirus region and that Romaniotes from Ioannina still describe their origins in this way. Rabbi Benjamin of Tudela (1130–1173), a rabbi who traveled through the Byzantine Empire and left one of the earliest and most important accounts of Byzantine Jewry, notes that there were Jews in Corfu, Ioannina, Arta, Patras, Chalkis, Salonika, Thebes, and Aphilon.[13] The Jewish community in Ioannina is one of the oldest in Greece, and its presence is largely responsible for conserving the distinctive culture of the Romaniotes until the Second World War.

Although concrete evidence is sparse, it is highly probable that the Romaniote Jews have been living in Greece for more than two thousand years, residing on the Greek mainland and the islands, as well as in Constantinople and Asia Minor. They are especially associated with the Epirus region of northwest Greece in which Ioannina is their social, cultural, and historical capital. The term *Romaniote* generally denotes the Greek-speaking Jews of the Byzantine Empire, even if they primarily used Hebrew in their writings.[14] The term derives from the Latin designation for the Eastern Roman Empire, *Romania*, which became Byzantium after 330 CE.

Over the past two thousand years, many different regimes—Byzantine, Venetian, Ottoman, Greek Nationalist—have ruled over Greece and have left their trace on the life and culture of the Romaniotes. Romaniote history has been influenced not only by external non-Jewish populations but also by intra-Jewish tension and cultural exchange. As the Byzantine Empire began to deteriorate in the thirteenth century, an influx of Jews of Italian origin influenced the culture—including the liturgical-musical practices—of the Romaniote Jews, particularly on the island of Corfu.[15] Following the Alhambra Decree of 1492 in Spain, the Sultan of the Ottoman Empire, Bayzeid II (1481–1512), extended an invitation to the Jews who had been exiled from the Iberian Peninsula, including Jews who had found a temporary home in Sicily, to settle in the empire.[16] The newly formed Sephardic communities were rife with social and religious tensions, both internally and externally, with the Romaniotes. The two groups gradually reconciled their differences, but they remained relatively distinct, especially with regard to their liturgy. For instance, the Romaniotes continued to practice the triennial Torah reading cycle (rather than the annual cycle practiced by the Sephardim),[17] which suggests that for a time the Romaniote rite followed the Palestinian rather than the Babylonian Talmud.

Until the sixteenth century, the Romaniote Jews used the *Maḥzor Romania* (Venice, 1527), which originated during the Byzantine Empire and is one of the oldest extant compilations of prayers and paraliturgical hymns in Europe. Archeological and iconographic evidence such as synagogue architecture, depictions of instruments and song in areas where Romaniote resided, and surviving literature and responsa all suggest that musical-liturgical processes were experienced cyclically, as part of the phenomenological experience of traditional Judaism. Vocal declamation, in particular, played an important role in religious and social identity of the Romaniote. Bowman observes that "throughout their history, the Romaniotes expended great effort on religious poetry, which reached its peak during the period 1350–1550."[18] A change came in 1577, when the Romaniotes adopted the Sephardic prayers "so that they could be united as Jews."[19] Elisabeth Hollender and Johannes Niehoff-Panagiotis assert that "[t]he result of these very complex acculturation exchanges is the subsequent disappearing of most of the communities with a distinctive Romaniote identity and the retreat of Romaniote Judaism into the former provincial towns of western Greece."[20]

Throughout the centuries, the Romaniotes continued to be caught between the power struggles of their environment that often caused major disruption to their ways of life and stability, such as during the Greek War of Independence of 1821. At this time, all the Jews of Greece found themselves not only in a position of instability but also often pitted between Ottoman and Christian Orthodox factions.[21] The Ottoman domination over Greece was overthrown in 1913, at which point the Romaniotes found themselves to be part of a united Greece. During the Greeks' struggle for independence from Ottoman rule, the city of Ioannina was laid under siege by Ottoman forces and was only liberated after a lengthy struggle.[22]

Before the Holocaust, the Jewish community in Ioannina was the largest Romaniote community in Greece and was the heart of the Romaniotes—both literally and symbolically.[23] The long and distinctive history of the Romaniote Jews almost ended during the Nazi occupation of Greece which began on April 4, 1941, when the Allied forces on the Albanian side were defeated. By the end of May, Greece had fallen under the control of Nazi Germany. After May 1941, Greece was divided into three zones of occupation overseen by the Germans, Bulgarians, and Italians. Both Athens and Ioannina were at first under Italian control, which improved life for the Romaniotes, as the Italians did not deport the Jews living in areas that they controlled. A German division arrived in Ioannina in 1943 and, on March 25, 1944, deported nearly all of the Jewish population to Auschwitz. Of approximately two thousand men, women, and children, only approximately 163 adults survived.[24] Other Greek cities with Romaniote Jews, such as Chalkis, Patras, and Athens, suffered similar losses, as did Sephardic communities in Greece, particularly in Salonica, a hub for Sephardic rabbinical leadership. As in the case of the Jews of Ioannina, many survivors chose not to return to Greece.

The decimation of the Jewish population of Greece caused many distinctive Romaniote practices to dwindle and some to disappear. However, owing to late nineteenth-century immigration of Romaniote Jews to the United States, the practices live on in New York at the Kehila Kedosha Janina established by Romaniotes from the city of Ioannina in 1906. Synagogue membership in New York grew and peaked in the 1930s. In Israel, too, some Romaniote traditions continued for a time in Jerusalem at the Beth Avraham and Ohel Sarah Synagogue in the Montefiore district and in Kfar Shalem at Shalom Synagogue. The Shalom Synagogue was established by the former Romaniote Jewish community of the island of Zakynthos, which, unlike other Jewish communities in Greece, survived the Holocaust.[25] In Greece itself, Romaniote practices have lived on in specific locales, such as Ioannina, Chalkis, and Athens. In all locations in which Romaniote traditions survive today, perseverance despite major historical disruptions (the arrival of the Sephardic Jews to Greece in the fifteenth century and, later, the near annihilation of the Romaniotes during the Holocaust) form a major component of the Romaniotes' narrative. This narrative continues to shape constructions of group identity and the sense of Romaniote distinctiveness.

CONTINUANCE: PILGRIMAGE TO IOANNINA

When I returned to Greece in the fall of 2018 to observe Yom Kippur in Ioannina, I witnessed a new kind of religious pilgrimage unique to Romaniotes—their physical and spiritual return. While some Jewish groups travel for High Holidays, in my experience, it is rare for observant Jews (myself included) to travel away from their homes and extended family at these pivotal points in religious ritual observance. Indeed, many Romaniote participants experience the travel as a return; they leave (whether from Athens, New York, or elsewhere) to come "home." In contemporary forms of Judaism emerging in later modernity—communities, youth initiatives, organizations, and so on—this feeling is commonly associated with "returning" to Israel, but very rarely associated with pilgrimages to Europe. Even for Romaniotes whose descendants did not originate in Ioannina, the place has taken on a pivotal significance in this Romaniote revival. Annette Fromm describes this pilgrimage-return in her vivid ethnographic tableaux of Romaniote life. She explores how, through the periodic return of individuals associated with the Jews of Ioannina as pilgrims, a new avenue of the expression of Romaniote identity has been created. While Jewish pilgrims often hail from New York and neighboring states, such as Connecticut and New Hampshire, most of whom are affiliated with the Kehila Kedosha Janina Museum and Synagogue in New York, others come from farther afield, from Texas, California, and Toronto in Canada. Many of them have actual Romaniote ancestry (a grandfather or a grandmother or, in some cases, both parents), but some are practicing and non-practicing Jews without any claim to

Romaniote heritage. Yet, they come together in this remote village in Greece, once the center of the Romaniotes, to observe the holiest day in the Jewish calendar, assembling in a new collective for the Yom Kippur Service.

While the city of Ioannina today has only about fifty year-round Jewish inhabitants, one of whom is its current mayor, Moses Elisaf, Ioannina's Jewish population grows significantly over Yom Kippur. I myself experienced a sense of ingathering, having traveled from Hannover in Germany, first by plane and then by chartered bus from Athens, together with members of the Jewish community there. The trip to Ioannina from Athens by bus takes about five hours. The scenery is particularly striking, especially the waterways by the town of Patras, once home to a thriving Romaniote community. The road into Ioannina ascends a large hill, allowing passengers an almost full view of the beautiful city. One can see small cobbled streets, the walls surrounding the old town, and a sparkling lake on the eastern side. The bus makes its way to the Grand Serai Congress & Spa, a luxury hotel where most of the Jewish visitors stay over the holiday, gathering as a collective.

While exploring the town both before and after the Yom Kippur service, I notice remnants of Jewish culture here and there, especially in the medieval town center—a Star of David on the metalwork of a fence or carved into the stones of a dwelling, and similar indicators of a once thriving Jewish presence. These markers evoke Eva Hoffman's description of the former Jewish communities of Eastern Europe in that, both there and in Ioannina, the absence of Jews is experienced as a presence. In other words, their absence is somehow "inescapable" owing to signs and knowledge of their former presence.[26]

The synagogue Kahal Kadosh Yashan (Holy Old Congregation) stands inside the walled city at the edge of what was once the old Jewish quarter. The name of the synagogue itself denotes remembering the "old" (or former) community, as the Hebrew word "kahal" refers not to the building, but to its congregants. White-walled and spacious, it was erected in 1829 on the site of an older synagogue, which dated back to the Byzantine period. The bimah is elevated on a high platform facing the Ark on the opposite wall, according to the distinctive layout of Romaniote synagogues. The men's section is on the left side of the bimah while the women's section lies to the right of it. During the German occupation, the synagogue escaped destruction because it had been requisitioned as a municipal library. In addition, many wooden and silver *tikim* (Torah cases), prayer books, and religious garments were hidden in a crypt and thereby escaped destruction. Right after the Second World War, the then-mayor of Ioannina, Demetrios Vlachides, returned these items, many of which he had taken precautions to preserve, along with the building itself, to the surviving Romaniote Jews. Artemis Batis Miron, who survived Auschwitz, recalls the events of 1943–1945 as follows:

> When the Germans entered Ioannina, he [the mayor] went into the synagogue, took out all of the contents, hid them, and promised when the Germans left he would replace everything. He purposely turned the synagogue into a temporary library, so that the Germans wouldn't destroy it. And true to his word, when the Nazis left, he returned everything, all of the religious objects, to the synagogue exactly as they were, renovated the synagogue, and today there are twenty four pure white panels

and on them, carved in black letters, are the names of the victims. So it's exactly like it was plus these memorial plaques.[27]

This testimony is corroborated by Dalven's account.[28] As Batis Miron describes, a marked feature of today's synagogue today is the large plaques on either side of the Ark, upon which the names of the Romaniote Jews of Ioannina who perished in the Holocaust are engraved. Indeed, these plaques are frequently the focus of visitors, not only during informal visits, but also during key points at prayer services in the synagogue as surviving Romaniotes and others explicitly remember those who perished. This synagogue, full of religious and social significance for the Romaniote Jews and a survivor of destruction in its own right, is where the annual Yom Kippur service is held.

The Yom Kippur service in Ioannina is led by Cantor Haim Ischakis, a resident of Athens. Ischakis leads services for many life-cycle and commemoration events in Greece as well as other parts of Europe, using the musical-liturgical tradition that he learned from his father who was an Auschwitz survivor and a cantor. He was born in 1959 in Athens to Romaniote parents. He graduated from the Greek-French high school Lycée Léonin in 1976 and then left Greece briefly as a young man to pursue university studies at the Hebrew University of Jerusalem. Upon his return to Greece in 1981, he became involved in his family's wholesale commercial business and began to become interested in Romaniote traditions. In the 1990s he began to take an active interest in practicing the repertoire that he had learned from his father. Upon the death of his father in 1996, Ischakis dedicated himself full-time to teaching others about Judeo-Greek traditions, including the musical-liturgical practices. He continues to lead services and serve as a rabbi for local Judeo-Greek communities as well as a tour guide for visitors to cultural heritage sites. Unlike other Romaniote leaders, Ischakis does not serve a single congregation, but rather prays with different groups, both local and international, at different locations revolving around festivals and commemorative events, which are attended by Jews and non-Jews.[29] On Rosh Hashanah, for example, he leads the Jewish community of Chalkis for services.

The Yom Kippur service in Ioannina is one of many commitments that Ischakis takes on in order to revitalize Jewish-Romaniote life in Greece and for Romaniote visitors from "out of town." The liturgy of the Yom Kippur service interpreted and transmitted musically by Haim Ischakis can be understood to be a contemporary Romaniote variant of an older Romaniote service. The different components of the liturgy—traditional prayers and piyyutim—are chanted during the five main prayer services of Yom Kippur: Maariv (beginning with Kal nidrei, in Romaniote pronunciation), Shacharit, Musaf, Minchah, and Neilah. The Torah is chanted during Shacharit and Mincha. Prayer tunes are skillfully chanted by Ischakis using a combination of old and new elements. Whether or not the tunes are familiar to them, attendees find the melodies engaging and meaningful for their holiday observance. Some parts of the service are more virtuosic, such as the Ioannina version of Unetaneh tokef. It is sung by Ischakis in Greek and is a fascinating blend of presumed Romaniote and contemporary Israeli tunes such as one composed by Yair Rosenblum in 1990. Other parts of the service tie the congregants together through call and response, as well as melodic repetition to incite a trance-like state of religious unification, particularly at the conclusion of the Yom Kippur service.

The *selihot*, penitential poems and prayers recited during the period leading up to the High Holidays to prepare the congregation for *teshuvah* (penitence), are distinct. They receive special emphasis through melodic embellishment, but they also have declamatory passages to facilitate congregational singing. Destruction and an incitement to remember it are central tropes of the selihot and in the way in which they are interpreted and performed by Ischakis. Two such examples are El melekh yoshev (The king sits [on his throne of mercy]) and El nora alilah (God of awe). For the congregation of Ioannina, the former is connected to remembering the destruction experienced during the Holocaust. The words describe God as a compassionate, merciful king who has the ability to mitigate the "stern decrees" of former years if successfully petitioned to do so. El nora alilah emphasizes similar themes, but with more forward-looking, positive feelings.

At the heart of the selihot are the Thirteen Attributes of Mercy that depict God sitting on a throne of mercy, emphasizing a divinity who pardons people for their transgressions. The text is rooted in Exodus 34:5–7. In most services, El melekh yoshev directly precedes the Thirteen Attributes and functions as a quasi-introduction to their recitation. In many Ashkenazi congregations, the attributes are given special musical emphasis through florid cantorial solos and/or communal singing, with several commonly used melodies in minor keys; conversely, in Sephardic practices, the Thirteen Attributes tend to be recited quickly, with little melodic variation (while the recitation of El melekh varies).[30] In his service, Ischakis combines the two approaches creating a new musical interpretation all his own. El melekh yoshev is sung to a virtuosic E-minor, highly embellished recitation, while the subsequent Thirteen Attributes are declaimed in Sephardic fashion—almost read like a list, especially when compared to the sonorous, highly improvised part that precedes them. Ischakis employs this contrast quite deliberately with two results: he differentiates the service from both Sephardic and Ashkenazi versions while simultaneously referencing them, and he prompts introspection, owing to the abrupt contrast between the "factual" declamation of God's merciful attributes and the musical introduction. This contrast suggests that God's attributes remain unchanging and transcend musical embellishment.

Ischakis' singing of the El nora alilah, a piyyut that begins the Neilah service in most Romaniote and Sephardic services at the conclusion of Yom Kippur, sparked a change in the melancholic, contemplative atmosphere of the previous Minchah service. This shift might well occur in many Sephardic communities that chant this piyyut; however, the intensity of the shift between the "present" deceased ancestors of Ioannina, the destroyed community, and the possibility of salvation charged the space and participants with particular renewed energy and optimism. In his recitation, Ischakis reinforces this shift by stimulating congregational participation, through creating an unusual rendering of the piyyut that incites the congregation to call-and-response (described in more detail below). The poem is attributed to Moses Ibn Ezra, a twelfth-century poet from Spain. Each stanza consists of four lines with five syllables to the line; the fourth line of each verse repeats the words "besha'at ha-neilah" (at the time of the closing of the gates), as verses 4–6:

אֵל נוֹרָא עֲלִילָה
אֵל נוֹרָא עֲלִילָה
הַמְצִיא לָנוּ מְחִילָה
בִּשְׁעַת הַנְּעִילָה

זְכֹר צִדְקַת אֲבִיהֶם
וְחַדֵּשׁ אֶת יְמֵיהֶם
כְּקֶדֶם וּתְחִלָּה
בִּשְׁעַת הַנְּעִילָה

קְרָא נָא שְׁנַת רָצוֹן
וְהָשֵׁב שְׁאָר הַצֹּאן
לְאָהֳלִיבָה וְאָהֳלָה
בִּשְׁעַת הַנְּעִילָה

תִּזְכּוּ לְשָׁנִים רַבּוֹת
הַבָּנִים וְהָאָבוֹת
בְּדִיצָה וּבְצָהֳלָה
בִּשְׁעַת הַנְּעִילָה

God of great deeds
God of great deeds
Grant us forgiveness
At the time of the closing of the gates

Renew their days by remembering,
The righteousness of their ancestors,
As in the days of origin.
At the time of the closing of the gates.

And return the scattered flocks, please,
Declare a year of blessing
To Aholiva and Ahola.[31]
At the time of the closing of the gates.

May old and young
Look forward to long lives,
In gladness and delight,
At the time of the closing of the gates.[32]

The text entreats God to inscribe the congregation in the Book of Life before the "closing of the gates," namely, the conclusion of Yom Kippur at sundown. The poem evokes final thoughts of repentance as the service draws to a close. The text expresses several points relating to the Romaniote pilgrims' Yom Kippur experience. The continued existence, for which God is entreated, is a collective, prosperous, "delightful" one, full of "light," an

EXAMPLE 24.1 Haim Ischakis, El nora alilah (opening), transcription by the author.

existence that transcends generational boundaries and that anticipates rebirth and renewal. The gathering of the "scattered flocks" is a messianic reference to the ingathering of the exiles, but for many participants, it is the righteous ancestors, namely, the Holocaust victims whose names appear on the plaques who they remember. This experience was recounted by some of the participants—although, the "return" that they describe does not involve "Zion" or modern Israel, but rather, a return to Ioannina. Cantor Ischakis renders the piyyut using a unique melody, which is repetitive and energetic, as is often the custom in many traditions in which it is sung (Example 24.1).

The phrase "el nora alilah" and the verses are sung to the same melody, with varying improvised ornamentations. The verses "core" motive spans B-flat to E-flat below middle C. The first two lines of the verses are rendered slightly slower by Ischakis in tempo rubato. This dramatic section contrasts with the last line of the verse and the refrain, both of which are sung using a simple melody without ornamentation or variation in tempo. The lower range and consistent tempo encourage the congregation to join in on the refrain "grant forgiveness to us, at this hour of closing prayer," reinforcing the supplications introduced in the verses. Although not identical, there are striking similarities between the tune used by Ischakis in this service and Sephardic used in other locations in Greece, as well as Iraqi and even Spanish and Portuguese variants practiced in the Netherlands.[33] However, in contrast with other Greek variants, in Ischakis' version, the tones tend to be less nasal and the melody is devoid of quarter-tones. While the melody used by Ischakis is similar to local Sephardic (and more distant Mizrahi), Ischakis imbues the tune with distinctiveness. Essentially, Ischakis relies on a melody associated with Sephardic practice and interprets it uniquely for the Romaniote congregations, a Romaniotization, as it were. Thus, his interpretation reclaims Romaniote identity through musical transmission and interpretation.

Ischakis' diverse collage of melodies, textures, and declamations creates a contemporary Romaniote service that is a newly composed and improvised corpus, a blend of the old and the new. In some instances, different musical layers blend and are indiscernible from one another; in other instances, the differences are not only heard, but deliberately emphasized. This process shapes music that expresses, in itself, rupture and gaps in both musical and communal history and memory. Rather than abandoning or replacing previous musical traditions, the music has been restructured in a rich reworking constituting what Frigyesi terms "liturgical folk music," which is differentiated from formal cantorial practice.[34] While Ischakis' musical-liturgy may or may not resemble a Romaniote ritual that was performed several hundred years ago, it constitutes meaningful heritage since it has been created in a manner typical of the shaping and transmission of historical Jewish oral musical forms.

Many congregants described how the text and melodies of the piyyutim trigger thoughts of their ancestral families who perished in the Holocaust.[35] The recitations of the piyyutim prompted them to recollect members of their families and others who perished and whose names are on the wall of the synagogue.[36] Although this might be more evident to the observer, a melancholic irony emerges. While the participants urge God to inscribe them in the Book of Life, the Jews who perished are inscribed on a list of the dead, on memorial plaques. Indeed, at the Kahal Kadosh Yashan, the memorial plaques have been placed not in the entrance hall, as is the custom in many synagogues, but directly next to the Ark. Thus, the Romaniote community that was destroyed during the Holocaust becomes a focal point during many of the Yom Kippur prayers; those who remember former community members can recall their absence more potently. But hymns like El nora alilah also move the participants from moments of melancholic recollection or spiritual supplication to a more forward-looking, optimistic mood with the relatively energetic melody and hopeful language of the poem. Many of the verses of this piyyut are positive and look forward toward forgiveness and prosperity, rather than mere survival and collective continuance.

Looking Ahead: Destruction and Its Remembrance

The Yom Kippur experience in Ioannina emphasizes how pilgrimage functions to sustain Romaniote identity—as one of the participants from New York City remarked: "When I come to this place, I remember who I am."[37] The annual pilgrimage is one of several religious and non-religious events through which Romaniote identity is remembered and reaffirmed in the present. This reaffirmation of community occurs through shared oral-history narratives of remembering the recent destruction of the Holocaust as well as the long-enduring Romaniote existence in Greece defined by survival, notwithstanding instability and disruption. In this, music is of significance as it triggers and perpetuates a process of remembering. As Ischakis' selection presents a continuation of a synthesis of musical traditions, it is not the specific style or character of the repertoire that initiates this process, but rather, the presence of the music within the context of the liturgy itself.

While ḥurban as the destruction experienced during the Holocaust is a core experience of the Romaniote Jews, it also applies in another sense and temporal context. In his lexicon, or treatise, *Sefer ḥeshek Shelomoh* (The desire of Solomon, 1802), the Hebrew linguist and poet Rabbi Solomon Pappenheim (1740–1814) explains that the biblical usage of the word *ḥurban* denotes that which is not inherently damaged but can be considered destroyed owing to its disconnection from what it requires to "live." Thus, a ghost town can be termed a ḥurban because it is abandoned by human inhabitants, despite the buildings being intact.[38] Empty synagogues, town quarters, and city districts where Jews once resided: the places themselves are not visibly damaged, yet their lack of a living, practicing Jewish population precludes them from being considered a thriving settlement. In the case of a synagogue, the absence of regular prayer and other religious activities is what generates the state of ḥurban. The Kahal Kadosh Yashan synagogue, and even Ioannina as a whole, can thus be designated ḥurban. Indeed, the absence of Jewish life in the city has been marked by its current mayor of the city, Moses Elisaf, who comments on the difficulty of keeping Judaism alive in Ioannina with such a small community.

It is the process of zekher that fills the emptiness that constitutes ḥurban. Once a year, the town of Ioannina, now relatively devoid of a Jewish presence, is suddenly replete with Jewish visitors. Through the annual Yom Kippur pilgrimage, a ritual in its own right, the ḥurban of both city and synagogue is negated, as the city is restored and "re-animated" through the service. While the pilgrimage and the service are temporary, they are cyclical, thus Jewish presence in all its splendor is both short- and long-lived. The impact, however, on both the few Jewish residents of Ioannina and the pilgrims is long lasting. As such the Romaniote experience can serve as paradigm that ḥurban is not a permanent state, but one that can be altered through human agency and occupation. This removal of ḥurban in places marked by Jewish inhabitation is central to the Jewish experience at large and is repeatedly evoked in Jewish liturgy, with many prayers articulating the desire for the restoration of the Temple, such as at the end of the Amidah.

A well-known passage in the Babylonian Talmud (Makkot 24b) recounts different responses to the ḥurban habayit. Upon observing the destroyed Temple, a group of rabbis begins to weep; but Rabbi Akiva laughs. The rabbis respond to Rabbi Akiva's laughter by telling him that he has "consoled" them. While laughter as a reaction might seem unexpected, an ongoing trajectory of Jewish interpretation, beginning with this Talmudic passage, understands Rabbi Akiva's response to be both optimistic and practical. The destruction of the Temple, as with everything, was decreed by God and is part of an ultimate religious redemption. The concept of consolation after destruction—common in both the Hebrew Bible and the liturgy—prompts the obligation to remember what was lost. Therefore, not only is zekher imperative, but laughter as consolation signifies that life cannot be lived looking backward, mourning destruction, but must be anchored in the present with a gaze toward the future.

Such interpretation is fitting for capturing the performance and experience of Romaniote liturgical music in Ioannina today. Different parts of the service encourage the remembrance of and the dead in different ways. The El nora alilah is a forward-looking conclusion to the Yom Kippur service and the Romaniote practice of remembering destruction; as such it echoes Rabbi Akiva's laughter as once deserted spaces are filled with musical Jewish sounds of the past and the present through Ischakis' synthetic musical performance. The fact that the repertoire is newly formed, a blend of the old and the new, prompts participants to remember the past, but also to look forward to the future. The destruction of the community is remembered, not only symbolically through commemoration, but through an active embodied affirmation of Jewish collectivity, in a religious service that honors the continuity of Jewish life and Romaniote distinctiveness in the present.

NOTES

1. For a discussion of the importance of the practice of Torah cantillation as the cornerstone of Jewish identity, historically and in present times, see Jeffrey Summitt, *Singing God's Words: The Performance of Biblical Chant in Contemporary Judaism* (New York: Oxford University Press, 2008).
2. See Rachel Dalven, *The Jews of Ioannina* (New York: Cadmus Press, 1990); Rachel Dalven and Israel Katz, "Four Traditional Judeo-Greek Hymns and their Tunes," *Musica Judaica* 18 (2005): 106–124.
3. Allegra Matsa, in discussion with the author, September 30, 2018.
4. The degree to which these musical transformations or lacunae represent either normative changes in orally transmitted repertoires or lost traditions owing to trauma and rupture or both of these will not be debated here.
5. For a discussion of Romaniote musical practices in relation to cultural sustainability, see Miranda L. Crowdus, "Kulturelle Nachhaltigkeit als relationales Konzept in der Aufführung jüdischer Musik," in *Jüdisches Kulturerbe MUSIK: Divergenzen und Zeitlichkeit— Überlegungen zu einer Kulturellen Nachhaltigkeit aus Sicht der Jüdischen Musikstudien*, ed. Sarah M. Ross, Jüdische Musikstudien / Jewish Music Studies 2 (Bern: Peter Lang, 2021), 89–129.
6. See Dalven, *The Jews of Ioannina*.
7. See K. E. Fleming, *Greece: A Jewish History* (Princeton, NJ: Princeton University Press, 2008); Steve Bowman, *The Jews of Byzantium* (Tuscaloosa: University of Alabama Press, 1985); Giorgis Antoniu and A. Dirk Moses, eds., *The Holocaust in Greece* (Cambridge: Cambridge University Press, 2018).
8. See Amnon Shiloah, "Greek-Jewish Musical Traditions" (Washington, DC: Smithsonian Folkways, 2001).
9. See Yosef Matsa, *G+anniōtika Evraïka tragoudia* (Ioannina: Ekdosis, 1953).
10. Leo Levi, "Greece: Musical Traditions of Greece and the Balkans," *Encyclopedia Judaica*, ed. Cecil Roth (Jerusalem: Keter Publishing House, 1971), 7:882–883. The entry contains no transcriptions or specific descriptions of the music.
11. See Dalven and Katz, "Four Traditional Judeo-Greek."
12. See Yitzchak Kerem, "The Music of the Greek Jews in the Holocaust," *Proceedings of the First International Conference on Jewish Music*, ed. Steve Stanton and Alexander Knapp (London: City University, Department of Music, 1994), 46–53.
13. See Benjamin of Tuleda, *The Itinerary of Rabbi Benjamin of Tudela*, vol. 1: *Text, Bibliography and Translation*, trans. and ed. Adolf Asher (London: A. Asher & Co., 1840), 46–57.
14. See Elisabeth Hollender and Jannis Niehoff-Panagiotis, "*Mahzor Romania* and the Judeo-Greek Hymn ἕνας ὁ κύριος—Introduction, Critical Edition and Commentary," *Revue des études Juives* 170 (2011): 118.
15. Sources of musical-liturgical practices in Corfu provide insights into practice may be relevant to the practices of the mainland Romaniote Jews; see, for instance, the Hebrew collection of responsa relating to a dispute regarding the singing of the Shema in Corfu (פסק על נגון קריאשמע בצבור בעיר קורפו), Greece, 1753, MS X893 Sh354. See also: Samuel Krauss, *Talmudische Archäologie* (Leipzig: G. Fock, 1910–1912), 3:283–274.

16. See Hollender and Niehoff-Panagiotis, "*Mahzor Romania*," 118.

17. The chanting of the Torah in a triennial, rather than an annual, cycle derives from the ancient Palestinian practice. References to the triennial cycle, including Talmudic (Megillah 29b), see *Encyclopedia Judaica*, s.v. "Triennial Cycle," accessed April 30, 2021.

18. Steve Bowman, *The Jews of Byzantium* (Tuscaloosa: University of Alabama Press, 1985), 129.

19. Dalven, *The Jews of Ioannina*, 19.

20. Hollender and Niehoff-Panagiotis, "*Mahzor Romania*," 118.

21. See Fleming, *Greece*.

22. See Guy Chantepleure, *La ville assiégée: Janina octobre 1912–mars 1913* (Paris: Calmann-Lévy, 1913), for a complete account of day-to-day activities in Ioannina both before and after the siege. It should be noted that "Guy Chantepleure" is the pen-name of Jeanne-Caroline Violet, the wife of a French diplomat who lived in Ioannina during the fighting between the Greek and the Ottoman forces, and therefore this volume is her eyewitness account.

23. Dalven discusses the social and religious significance of Ioannina for the Romaniotes throughout *The Jews of Ioannina*.

24. See Steve Bowman, *The Agony of Greek Jews 1940–1945* (Stanford, CA: Stanford University Press), 71–72.

25. For a history of the Jewish population of Zakynthos and a recounting of how the entire Jewish community was saved during the Holocaust through the heroic actions of the island's Christian leaders, see Dino Seder, *Miracle at Zakynthos: The Only Greek Jewish Community Saved from Annihilation* (Washington, DC: Philos Press, 2014).

26. Eva Hoffman, *Exit into History: A Journey Through Eastern Europe* (New York: Penguin, 1993), 276.

27. Kathryn Berman and Liz Elsby, "An Interview with Artemis Batis Miron, A Survivor from Ioannina Greece," https://www.yadvashem.org/articles/interviews/batis.html (accessed April 30, 2021).

28. See Dalven, *The Jews of Ioannina*, 77.

29. The Jewish religious events, as opposed to cultural events, have a much higher percentage of Jewish participants and are sometimes only attended by Jews.

30. For more information on the Thirteen Attributes of Mercy, their placement in the service, and how they are recited, see Arnold Rosenberg, *Jewish Liturgy as a Spiritual System: A Prayer-by-Prayer Explanation of the Nature and Meaning of Jewish Worship* (New York: Rowman and Littlefield, 2000). For specific discussions on the musical setting this part of the service, see Maxine R. Kanter, "Leitmotifs in Sephardic High Holiday Liturgy," *The Journal of Synagogue Music* 21 (1991): 33–52; Joseph A. Levine, "The Hidden Subdivisions of S'lihot," *The Journal of Synagogue Music* 33 (2008): 108–139; and for a detailed musical analysis of Ashkenazi tradition highlighting modulation as a central device, see Judith Niran Frigyesi, "Modulation as an Integral Part of the Modal System in Jewish Music," *Musica Judaica* 5, no. 1 (1982–83): 52–71.

31. Aholiva and Ahola refer to the Ancient Kingdom of Israel and the Kingdom of Judah. They are pejorative terms used by the Prophet Ezekiel to refer to these places.

32. Translation by Natalie C. Polzer. Other translations try to emulate the rhyme scheme, foregoing this literal approach, which takes into account not just the poetics but the religious context and placement in the liturgy of the piyyut.

33. See, for example, Abraham Zvi Idelsohn's *Hebräisch-orientalischer Melodienschatz*, vol. 4: *Gesänge der orientalischen Sefardim* (Vienna: Benjamin Harz, 1923), 156. For a detailed

comparison of the melody in different Sephardic traditions using musical transcriptions, see Avner Bahat, "El Nora Alila (God of Awe, God of Might): From Spain to the Four Corners of the Earth," *Inter-American Music Review* 17, nos. 1–2 (2007): 77–90. For recordings of different traditions, see Edith Gerson-Kiwi's 1958 recording of El nora alilah (Baghdad), sung by Yaakov Huri, and Amnon Shiloah's 1970 recording (Larissa, Greece), sung by Itzhak Meizan, both held at the National Library of Israel; and the author's recording of Haim Ischakis on the CD *Synagogue Music of the Romaniote Jews of Greece* EZJM Ethnographic Fieldwork Recordings Series, 2018.

34. Judit Frigyesi, "Orality as a Religious Ideal in East-European Jewish Prayer," *Yuval 7* (2002): 115.

35. Asking people to reflect on experiences of their family during the Holocaust is not easy and requires extreme sensitivity. Moreover, responses are not always straightforward. Any errors of interpretation are my own.

36. Observations collected through conversations with participants in September and October 2018, during and after the post-Yom Kippur breaking of the fast.

37. "Batya" and "Koula," in discussion with the author, September 30, 2018.

38. See Rabbi Shlomo Pappenheim, *Yeri'ot Shemoh: An Investigation of Synonyms in the Hebrew Bible*, ed. Moshe Tzuriel (Jerusalem: Rabbi Kook Institute, 2018), 826–827.

SELECT BIBLIOGRAPHY

Benjamin of Tuleda. *The Itinerary of Rabbi Benjamin of Tudela*. Volume 2, *Text, Bibliography and Translation*, translated and edited by Adolf Asher. London: A. Asher & Co., 1840.

Bowman, Steve. *The Jews of Byzantium*. Tuscaloosa: University of Alabama Press, 1985.

Bowman, Steve. "Survival in Decline: Romaniote Jewry Post-1204." In *Jews in Byzantium*, edited by Robert Bonfil, Oded Irshai, Guy G. Stroumsa, and Rina Talgam, 101–132, Leiden: Brill, 2012.

Chantepleure, Guy [Jeanne-Caroline Violet]. *La ville assiégée: Janina octobre 1912 mars 1913*. Paris: Calmann-Lévy, 1913.

Crowdus, Miranda L. "Cantor Haim Ischakis – Musical Highlights Synagogue Music of the Romaniote Jews of Greece." CD Liner notes: EZJM Ethnographic Fieldwork Recordings Series, 2018.

Crowdus, Miranda L. "Rescuing a Nearly-Lost Liturgical Tradition: Synagogue Music of the Romaniote Jews of Greece." *Journal of Synagogue Music* 44, no. 1 (2019): 132–148.

Dalven, Rachel. *The Jews of Ioannina*. New York: Cadmus Press, 1990.

Doxiadis, Evdoxios. *State, Nationalism and the Jewish Communities of Modern Greece*. London: Bloomsbury, 2018.

Fleming, K. E. *Greece: A Jewish History*. Princeton, NJ: Princeton University Press, 2008.

Matsa, Yosef M. *Gianniōtika Evraïka tragoudia*. Ioannina: Ekdosis, 1953.

Plaut, Joshua Eli. *Greek Jewry in the Twentieth Century, 1913–1983: Patterns of Jewish Survival in the Greek Provinces before and after the Holocaust*. Madison, NJ: Farleigh Dickinson University Press, 1996.

Seder, Dino. *Miracle at Zakynthos: The Only Greek Jewish Community Saved from Annihilation*. Washington, DC: Philos Press, 2014.

Stavroulakis, Nicholas. *The Jews of Greece*. Athens: Talos Press, 1990.

Weinberger, Leon J. *Romaniote Penitential Poetry*. Tuscaloosa: University of Alabama Press, 1980.

"WE LIVE FOREVER"

Music of the Surviving Remnant in Sweden

SIMO MUIR

In 1948, after having spent more than a year among Holocaust survivors in Sweden, Polish Jewish actor Josef Glikson (1899–1992) wrote about his and his actress wife Cypora Fajnzylber's (1913–?) experience performing for them. In his emotional account, Glikson describes their visits to sanatoria and convalescent homes with survivors, who had gone through all the "seven circles of hell" and were now rebuilding their lives in a strange new environment.[1] Glikson testifies how important and meaningful a familiar Yiddish song or a scene from a prewar Yiddish play could be for the survivors, who had lost nearly all their loved ones, their country, and their homes.

After the Second World War had ended, several hundred thousand Jews gathered in Displaced Persons (DP) camps in Central Europe, especially in Germany. Sweden became a Nordic center of Holocaust survivors after 11,500–12,000 Jews were brought there from concentration camps or DP camps as a result of two relief efforts in 1945: the Red Cross White Buses expedition and the United Nations Relief and Rehabilitation Administration action.[2] The majority of the survivors brought to Sweden were young women, many of whom were from Poland, with others from Hungary, Czechoslovakia, and Romania. Between 1946 and 1948 there was another wave of several thousand Jews, the so-called transmigrants and skilled workers who came mostly from Poland and German refugee camps.[3] In 1947, owing to remigration, the number of Jewish survivors and refuges in Sweden totaled about 7,000, the same amount as the local Jewish community that had survived the war unharmed.

In the case of Sweden, frontline Polish Jewish performing artists like Josef Glikson, Cypora Fajnzylber, Khayele Grober (1898–1978), Shloyme Prizament (1889–1973), and Niusia Gold (1909–?) attained a prominent role in the cultural life of the *sheyres-hapleyte* (following 1 Chronicles 4:43, *she'erit hapletah*), the surviving remnant, as the survivor community called itself in Yiddish. Many of these actors and singers, who either settled temporarily in Sweden or came there on tour, had evaded the *ḥurban*—the destruction of European Jewry (in Yiddish, the *khurbn*)—as refugees in the Soviet Union.

Along with the performing artists, some notable Yiddish authors from Poland settled in Sweden and contributed to the cultural revival of the survivor community, among them Rokhl Korn (1898–1982), one of the major poets of modern Yiddish literature. Fürth-born cantor and composer Leo Rosenblüth (1904–2000), who was appointed cantor at the Great Synagogue in Stockholm in 1931, collected Yiddish songs from among the survivors soon after the war ended. The Mosaiska Församlingen i Stockholm (Mosaic Congregation of Stockholm) played a key role in organizing the cultural out-reach among the survivors and in 1946 employed Bessarabian-born Yiddish poet and Hebrew teacher Mordechai Husid (1909–1988), who had come to Sweden in 1944 as a refugee from Axis-allied Finland to coordinate these activities.[4] In addition, the Svenska Sektion (Swedish Section) of the World Jewish Congress, Di yidishe dramatishe amater gezelshaft (The Yiddish Dramatic Amateur Society) founded in Stockholm in 1906, and emerging survivor organizations, especially Der fareyn fun geratevete yidn in 1945 yor (The Association of Rescued Jews of 1945) founded in Malmö in July 1946, organized multiple concerts and performances.[5]

While there is a growing literature on the musical life in DP camps and survivor communities on German soil—from Sophie Fetthauer's *Musik und Theater im DP-Camp Bergen-Belsen: Zum Kulturleben der Jüdischen Displaced Persons 1945–1950* and Tina Frühauf and Lily H. Hirsch's collection of essays *Dislocated Memories: Jews, Music, and Postwar German Culture*, to Frühauf's monograph *Transcending Dystopia: Music, Mobility, and the Jewish Community in Postwar Germany, 1945–1989*—there has been very little research about other countries.[6] This chapter will fill one such gap by focusing on Yiddish songs and musical performance among the survivors in Sweden. Glikson's recollections titled "Bay der sheyres hapleyte in Shvedn" (Among the surviving remnant in Sweden), in 1948 serialized in the journal of the Swedish Section of the World Jewish Congress, *Yedies* (News), serves as a key source.[7]

According to Atina Grossman, "in many ways this Jewish collective of the She'erit Hapletah was only invented, not in the crucible of the Holocaust but later in the transi-tional protected and highly ideologized life of the DP camps."[8] Compared to the DPs in postwar Germany, a proportionally large number of the survivors in Sweden remained in the country, while others emigrated to Israel and the West. Having had different experiences of survival—some under the Nazi occupation in the ghettos, camps, and in hiding, others in the gulags and under the terror of the Soviet Union—the sheyres-hapleyte were not a uniform group. Among them there were Zionists of various political shades, leftist Bundists, and those who wanted to restore their Orthodox way of life. And yet, one can observe the music of the sheyres-hapleyte through Kay Kaufman Shelemay's concept of musical community, which she distinguishes further as communities of de-scent, dissent, and affinity. The survivors in Sweden represent all three types, and their Yiddish culture is an embodiment of these different communal structures. First and foremost the sheyres-hapleyte can be considered a descent community, "united through what are understood from within to be shared identities, whether they are grounded in historical fact, are newly invented, or emerge from some combination of historical circumstance and creative transformation."[9] In a descent community "music moves beyond a role as symbol literally to perform the identity in question and serves early on in the process of community formation to establish, maintain, and reinforce that collective identity."[10] According to Shelemay, rather than separate types, the three categories of collectivity can exist along a "continuum that can move in different directions or become part of a multidimensional framework."[11] A musical community "might span the entire length of the continuum at a given point in time,"[12] which can be seen in the case of the sheyres-hapleyte in Sweden, where Yiddish song promulgated feelings of affinity between the survivors and the local Jewish community, but also fomented dissent between these communities.

The meaning of Yiddish song among survivors during the years of 1945 and 1948 is at the core of this chapter and as such is discussed from different angles: firstly, as part of *kleynkunst* (literally, "little art"), cabaret shows and ghetto and concentration-camp songs collected among the descent community of survivors in sanatoria and convalescent homes; secondly, as part of melo-declamations of poetry, Jewish art music and dance, and choral repertoire performed in cities and larger towns where a wider affinity community formed; and finally, as part of early Holocaust commemoration among survivors in newly established communities detached from the Swedish Jewish community. As such, *zekher* as the remembrance of the *ḥurban* is a central theme in the music of the survivors. This remembrance is twofold as they commemorate the victims of the Holocaust and recall their own experiences of persecution and survival.[13] The case of Sweden exemplifies the meaning of singing and performing as an act of remembering and reconnecting with the pre-Holocaust Yiddish culture.

Kleynkunst Performances and Singing in Sanatoria and Convalescent Homes

Soon after their arrival in Sweden at the end of 1946, Josef Glikson and Cypora Fajnzylber started to tour sanatoria and convalescent homes, financed by the Swedish state in southern Sweden. They were hired by the Mosaic Congregation of Stockholm, which along with the Jewish communities of Malmö, Gothenburg, and Norrköping took responsibility for the survivors.[14] While the physical care of the survivors was covered by the state, the Jewish communities took it upon themselves to give them "cultural and religious care," as they called it. Indeed, the survivors in these facilities suffered physical and psychological after-effects from their time in concentration camps, and many spent long periods, even years, recuperating.

Before the war, Glikson and Fajnzylber were members of the experimental and politically radical Yiddish theater group called Yung-teater (Young theater) in Warsaw. Founded by Michał Weichert, this avant-garde theater company had been among the leading Yiddish art theaters in Poland in the interwar period. For the troupe, according to Glikson, theater was not just "empty entertainment, but a means of struggle for human and social liberation."[15] With the outbreak of the Second World War, Glikson and Fajnzylber fled to the Soviet Union, as did a few hundred thousand Polish Jews, only to endure harsh conditions under Stalinist terror.[16] They ended up in Tashkent, where they became members of a local theater troupe and, after repatriation to Poland, in 1946, took part in Yiddish performances in Warsaw (Figure 25.1).[17] Like many other Polish Jews, after the Kielce pogrom in August 1946, they sought to leave the country and were able to acquire visas to enter Sweden.

Glikson and Fajnzylber performed Yiddish songs as part of their kleynkunst performances. Kleynkunst or *minyatur teater* (miniature theater) became a fashionable genre among Yiddish-speaking audiences between the world wars and has been described by Nahma Sandrow as "a sort of cabaret revue, witty, gay, and irreverent, rapidly winging from music to dance to monologue to sketch."[18] Glikson and Fajnzylber's performance arranged by the Yiddish Dramatic Amateur Society in Stockholm on December

FIGURE 25.1 Yiddish actors Josef Glikson (on the left) and Cypora Fajnzylber with David Minster in Tashkent, Uzbekistan, USSR, ca. 1945, id. no. 1550.90, Collection of the Museum of Jewish Heritage, New York. Reproduced by permission of the Museum of Jewish Heritage, New York. Courtesy of Cypora and Josef Glikson.

21, 1946, and a concert from their visit to Helsinki on January 24, 1948, included solos and duets of Yiddish songs, monologues and scenes from classic and modern Yiddish prose and drama, and recitations of contemporary poetry.[19] The programs were carefully balanced, with the first part being serious and the second, lighter.

Songs by the popular Krakow-born songwriter and singer Mordechai Gebirtig had a prominent place in Glikson and Fajnzylber's repertoire. Gebirtig's songs, which spread from kleynkunst stages to all of Poland and beyond, appeared in most Yiddish singers' programs.[20] Some became especially meaningful in the ghettos and concentration camps, such as his 1938 song "S'brent" (It burns) about a pogrom in the Polish town of Przytyk. Gebirtig continued to create songs under the German occupation until he was shot during deportation in 1942. His wartime songs were published by the Centralna Żydowska Komisja Historyczna (Jewish Historical Commission) in Krakow in 1946. The same year, one of the editors of the anthology, journalist and activist Nella Rost, emigrated to Sweden, where she worked for several years for the Swedish Section of the World Jewish Congress.[21]

Gebirtig's "Es tut vey" (It hurts) served as the opener for Glikson's and Fajnzylber's programs, always sung by Glikson. The song described the pain caused by the indifference and *Schadenfreude* of the non-Jewish Polish neighbors toward the persecution of Jews during the German occupation, as the first verse subtly captures:

S'tut vey!
S'tut shreklekh vey!
Nisht azoy der has,
vos in soyne brent.
Afile nisht di klep
fun vildn soynes hent,
nisht der mogn-Dovid
oyf der hant.
A shand!
Oyf doyres lang,
a shand!
Vet dos zayn far zey.

It hurts!
It hurts terribly!
Not so much the hatred,
that burns in the enemy.
Not even the blows
from the wild enemy's hands,
not the Star of David
on the arm.
A disgrace!
For generations,
a disgrace!
It will be for them.[22]

The poem allowed survivor audiences to commemorate, actively processing their painful experiences and trauma through performances and art.

Another Holocaust-era song by Gebirtig, sung by Glikson, was titled "Kol nidrey" (All vows) after the Aramaic prayer recited at the beginning of Yom Kippur. Gebirtig's Yiddish song describes how Jews, after being forbidden to assemble for Yom Kippur service, were singing the Kol nidrei in secret. Recitations of poetry that commemorated the destruction of Eastern European Jewish communities followed, among them Simha-Bunim Shayevits' emotive poem " . . . Lekh lekho . . . " (Go forth), written during a mass deportation from the Lodz Ghetto, and American poet Dora Teitelboim's poem "Geven amol a hoyz" (There once was a house) about Jewish life in *shtetls*, the small towns in prewar eastern Europe, which no longer existed.

The second part of Glikson and Fajnzylber' programs was altogether lighter, even containing humorous pieces from the prewar repertoire of the Yiddish stage. It featured Gebirtig's duet "Motele" (Little Mordechai), which is a dialogue between a *heder* boy who runs into trouble, and his concerned father. The programs ended with Yisroel Ashendorf's contemporary version of the popular folk song "Yidl mitn fidl un Berl mitn bas" (Yidl with the fiddle and Berl with the bass), in an arrangement by a L. Tajtelbaum. Like Glikson and Fajnzylber, Ashendorf had survived the war in exile in the USSR and soon after repatriation left Poland.

The conditions for Glikson and Fajnzylber's performances in the sanatoria and convalescent homes were by no means welcoming. In most instances, they had to perform in spaces with neither a stage nor the professional facilities they were accustomed to in Warsaw, and they even had to sing without a piano or other musical accompaniment. Apparently, many survivors were not familiar with the Yiddish stage, or Jewish—only non-Jewish theater in general. Nonetheless, the survivors' displacement created a yearning for Yiddish culture, as Glikson recalls:

> If we are successful in reviving their hearts and to lift up their spirits, we do not consider it as our achievement. It is above all a merit of the listeners themselves. . . . The overwhelming thirst for a Yiddish word that dominates these people contributes to the success [of the performances]. The strangeness of the environment where they find themselves, strengthens the longing for everything Yiddish.[23]

According to Glikson, through these performances, survivors who had witnessed the destruction of eastern European Jewry and lost everything were now reconnecting with their past, their culture, and even with their loved ones:

> Their eyes have absorbed the most dreadful images and the awful torture that the Jewish people have experienced in the German camps, in the Auschwitzes and Majdaneks, and so on. Their hearts are filled with the yearning to connect with the roots of the Jewish people, with its essence, with the spirit of hope that streams in Yiddish literature. They feel that through it they come closer to their nearest ones, to those who died tragically.[24]

Glikson, in an emotional tone, recounts their encounters with audiences, especially in a sanatorium in Västerås near Stockholm, with women suffering from tuberculosis who, despite their serious condition, had "an interest in Yiddish literature and a longing for a Yiddish melody."[25] Upon hearing that Glikson and Fajnzylber were coming for a visit, some of the women were able to persuade their doctor to grant them special permission to go and greet the actors at the train station, several kilometers from the sanatorium. According to Glikson, it was apparent that the day was a special *yontev* (Yiddish, celebration) for the women: "Today they will unite themselves with the Yiddish word, they will feel close to the Jewish people, they will start to believe in their own future as well as in the future of the entire Jewish collective."[26]

Glikson's account reflects his belief in the transformative power of performance and art in general, which transcends mere entertainment. He saw that through performance in Yiddish, they were reuniting the survivors with the *yidishn klal* (Jewish collective). As Shelemay has stated, performance of music can become "an important force in reconstituting a fractured community as an integrated whole in distant homelands."[27] In this way, by traveling from one place to another, often revisiting the sites, Gligson and Fajnzylber's performances served as a link between the sheyres-hapleyte, who were scattered in small groups over southern Sweden, sometimes grouped according to lifestyle. The convalescent center in Hälsingmo, north of Stockholm, for example, housed observant Jews (hence Glikson called the center the *kosher-lager*, kosher camp, referring to the observancy of the center's inhabitants). Initially Glikson and Fajnzylber were apprehensive about how they would be received with their secular Yiddish repertoire by this religious collective. To their pleasant surprise, they were "thanked with the old Jewish *yasher-koyekh* [thank you], exactly like one thanks the Cohens after the Priestly Blessing."[28]

In his recollection of visits to a convalescent home in Korsnäs, in Falun north-west of Stockholm, Glikson makes references to songs sung by the survivors. In Korsnäs the survivors, most of whom were young working men, lived in a big villa that had a dining room with a long table, around which they would eat their meals and spend time together, and sing; as Glikson asserts:

> At the table one could hear a Jewish melody from time to time, a Yiddish folk song. Depending on the time, the songs were: at *shalesh-sudes* [the last of the Sabbath meals] someone starts to hum a Hasidic melody, a *nigun* of the Modzitzer rebbe; during a workmen's holiday, like the First of May—workmen's songs.[29]

According to Bret Werb, "repertoire remembered from before the war that was connected to sentimental constructions of the DPs past," was the largest category of songs among survivors in postwar Germany, and these songs "acted as an anchor, giving DPs a needed sense of place and comfort located in memories of home."[30] Besides the prewar songs, survivors sang songs from ghettos and concentration camps, in remembrance, zekher, of their loved ones but also reliving their own experiences. Shirli Gilbert maintains that, through the songs sung by the survivors, we can explore "how surviving victims shaped their understanding of what had happened to them and their relationship to the individual and collective future."[31]

While Glikson does not mention the singing of ghetto or camp songs, cantor and composer Leo Rosenblüth, a central figure in the Swedish Jewish music scene, did collect songs among the survivors in Sweden. German-born Rosenblüth had become part of the Swedish Jewish collective that for the most part represented Reform Judaism and was highly acculturated and Swedish-speaking. In addition to singing and composing liturgical music for the Great Synagogue of Stockholm, Rosenblüth took great interest in Yiddish music and was clearly fascinated by the songs of the sheyres-hapleyte. Soon after the survivors were brought to Sweden in 1945, he visited a refugee center in Kalhyttan, west of Stockholm, and it is possible that he even came in contact with the men in Korsnäs, since he resided at the time in Falun.[32] His anthology *Mir lebn ejbig: 13 jidische lider wos men hot gesungen in di konzentrazionsläger* (We live forever: 13 Yiddish songs that were sung in the concentration camps) was published in Stockholm in 1946 (Figure 25.2). The collection is among the first publications of such songs worldwide.[33] In the Romanized Yiddish-language introduction Rosenblüth states that he had collected "a lot" of these songs. According to him, many of the lyrics in his anthology were set to existing melodies (a very common practice in the ghettos and camps), but there were also original compositions. The selection of the songs was arranged for piano, guitar, and accordion by Walter Cohn (1911–1978), who also originated from Germany and had arrived in Sweden prior to the Second World War. The booklet with the scores was published through the initiative of Swedish linguist and Yiddishist Bertil Maler (1910–1980), the Mosaic Congregation of Stockholm, and the Judiska Musiksällskapet i Stockholm (Jewish Musical Society in Stockholm).[34]

Several of the songs in Rosenblüth's collection are well known, and most of them can be found in poet and partisan Shmerke Kaczerginski's large anthology published in New York in 1948.[35] These songs include: Hirsh Glik's "Zog nit keynmol!" (Never say), Gerbirtig's above-mentioned "S'brent," and Kaczerginski's "Shtiler, shtiler" (Quieter, quieter) about the Ponar killing site near Vilna.[36] There are also three pieces by Leyb Rosenthal, who wrote songs for the Vilna ghetto cabaret that became very popular: "Ikh benk aheym" (I long for home), "Tsu eyns, tsvey, dray" (One, two, three), and "Mir lebn eybik," which also provided the name for Rosenblüth's collection. The other songs in Rosenblüth's collection are less known. They deal with the bitter fate of the Jews during the Holocaust, with their suffering and loss.[37] For instance, "Der shvartser tsug" (The black train) tells about deportation to the deathcamp of Auschwitz-Birkenau and from there to slave labor in Germany, and about longing for home and a loved one. Only one of the songs in Rosenblüth's anthology, "Shpalt zikh, himl!" (Split open, sky!), deals with hope and the ending of the war and suffering.

Survivors also created new songs.[38] Among the DPs in postwar Germany, according to Shirli Gilbert, these songs "frequently functioned as a medium for expressing desperation and continued suffering, they were also a forum for raising morale, confirming affirmative responses, and imagining possible futures."[39] While there are no examples currently available from survivors in Sweden, it is likely that similar songs were

FIGURE 25.2 Cover of Leo Rosenblüth's collection of Yiddish ghetto and concentration-camp songs published in Stockholm in 1946. Reproduced by permission of the Judiska Biblioteket, Stockholm.

conceived; an indication are a few postwar Yiddish poems that were published in the papers of the sheyres-hapleyte. For instance, two poems by the Vilna-born Moyshe Gurin (1921–1990) from 1947 appeared in *Unser Blatt—Undzer blat* (Our paper): "Shtil-lebn in katset" (A still-life in a concentration camp) and "Vemen s'iz bashert" (Whoever is destined). The latter deals with the trauma and mental aftereffects of the genocide that cast a shadow on the daily lives of the survivors (first stanza):

> Vemen s'iz bashert tsu shlofn baydernakht—
> kumt der ovnt, shteln shotns zikh oyf vakh,
> ringlen mikh arum un tsipn shtiker kop.
> Nisht far dir iz bashafn ot der shlof.

> Whoever is destined to sleep at night—
> the evening comes, shadows stand guard,
> surround me and pluck bits of my head.
> Sleep has not been created for you.[40]

Aside from the singing Glikson encountered in Korsnäs, he asserts that "there is no Yiddish cultural life in the convalescent homes scattered around Sweden, and unfortunately no one is interested in creating such a thing."[41] Glikson's experiences and thoughts are highly subjective and might not reflect the actual situation accurately.[42] And yet Glikson's observations underline that among the sheyres-hapleyte there were many who did not know Yiddish, or speak and read the language fluently. Moreover, gradually the number of survivors in the convalescent centers declined. As they recovered physically, they either emigrated or settled in towns, engaging with the Jewish cultures they encountered.

Guest Performances and Concerts in Cities and Towns

In addition to the sanatoria and convalescent homes, Glikson and Fajnzylber performed their kleynkunst shows in cities and towns where many survivors had settled. Among them was Stockholm, which already had an existing Yiddish cultural scene. The Jewish community in Sweden originated when German Jews arrived during the second half of the eighteenth century. Yiddish-speaking immigrants from eastern Europe followed at the turn of the nineteenth and twentieth centuries. At the heart of their cultural life was the Yiddish Dramatic Amateur Society, which would eventually play an important part in rebuilding the cultural life of the Holocaust survivor community by arranging performances. Already in October 1945, the society, in collaboration with the theater section of Judiska klubben (The Jewish Club), organized special performances for survivors of their production of author and ethnographer S. An-ski's play *Der dibuk* (The possessed).[43] The play, embedded in Jewish folklore, had been an interwar success on stage and screen. The Stockholm production was directed by Jura Tamkin, and the music for it was composed by Leo Rosenblüth.[44]

In addition to the Yiddish Dramatic Amateur Society's events, the Culture and Press Office of the Swedish Section of the World Jewish Congress arranged Yiddish-language concerts and gala evenings, which often took place in the halls of the Medborgarhuset (Citizen's house), in the Södermalm district of Stockholm. They invited prominent Yiddish performers to visit Sweden, with the revenue often going to the rehabilitation of the "Rescued of 1945." Their tours were part of a wider phenomenon of performing artists visiting DP camps and survivor communities in Europe, many coming from the United States and Britain. Such performances helped to heighten morale among the survivors and were steps toward normalization of their cultural life.[45] Moreover, the Yiddish-language concerts and performances in the bigger Swedish towns formed a wider affinity community, bringing together members of the indigenous Swedish Jewish community with the newly arrived survivors. They also performed together and even created new music together, proving what Shelemay has called "a particularly powerful mechanism for catalyzing affinity communities."[46]

In September 1947 the talented Białystok-born comic actress and singer Khayele Grober gave three performances in Stockholm, accompanied by Vienna-born composer and pianist Hans Holewa (1905–1991), who had fled the Nazis to Sweden in 1937.[47] Grober was a former member of the famed Habimah theater troupe from Moscow who toured prewar Poland with a kleynkunst troupe called Di yidishe bande (The Yiddish gang). She had become familiar to the Swedish Jewish community through her tour to the Scandinavian countries in 1935, before emigrating to Canada in 1939.[48] The program for her Yiddish Dramatic Amateur Society concert in Stockholm on October 11, 1947, began with the song "Likht bentshn" (Candle lighting). The lyrics by Montreal-based poet Yakov Yitzhak Segal were dedicated "to the memory of our 6 million victims."[49] This was followed by a sentimental prewar song "Benkshaft" (Longing), with lyrics by Zishe Weinper and melody by Solomon Golub. The song tells how "in the night of black sorrow two white doves" bring comfort in the longing for a loved one. Grober generally dedicated the first part of her concerts to the victims of the Holocaust and the vanished prewar Jewish life, an overt expression of zekher or remembrance. She then sang three songs by Gebirtig, including "Dray tekhter" (Three daughters), a standard in the program of prewar Yiddish cabaret.[50] The second part of the concert offered the audience new perspectives: Grober sang traditional and modern songs in Hebrew, such as Mordechai Zeira's (1905–1968) "Khay Israel" (Israel is alive).[51] With this and in contrast to Glikson and Fajnzylber, Grober revealed Zionist leanings. The concert ended with "Der klezmer in dzshez-land" (The klezmer musician in jazz land), about a "rootless" eastern European musician in the United States longing for his shtetl, recalling that in their new destinations her audiences would long for their homes. After her third performance to a packed hall in the Medborgarhuset, the audience was ready to "carry their hearts on a silver platter to her."[52] The Swedish press wrote enthusiastically about Grober's concerts. *Dagens Nyheter* (Daily news) commented that with the "Likht bentshn" that started her show "the singer struck a serious tone, and in the deeply moving solemn song there was an almost all-consuming intensity of pain."[53] During her visit to Sweden, Grober most likely met with Leo Rosenblüth, as some years later she would record two of his arrangements of Yiddish songs.[54]

Warsaw-born actress Niusia Gold was actually the first touring performer to come to Sweden after the war. She had already visited Sweden in August 1946 and returned in the spring of 1948.[55] Before the war, Gold had toured widely in eastern Europe. She and her two daughters survived the Holocaust hidden by a French family, and after the war she worked in Paris for the Yiddish art theater Yikut.[56] In 1947 she performed the role of a director of a children's home for surviving orphans in the Polish semi-documentary film *Undzere kinder* (Our children), also featuring Shimen Dzigan and Isroel Schumacher with their kleynkunst performances.[57] Gold's programs in Malmö on February 15, 1948, and Stockholm on March 7, 1948, featured dramatic excerpts of familiar prewar repertoire as well as melo-declamations (rhythmic and melodic recitations) of Holocaust poetry accompanied by Malmö-born pianist Gudrun Goldman (1927–).[58] Melo-declamations were fashionable, performed with much facial expression and gesture, and accompanied by appropriate music.[59] According to the review in *Di shtime*, published by the Association of Rescued Jews in 1945, Gold's rendering of poet Itzhak Katzenelson's "Tsu di himlen" (To the heavens), the ninth poem from his epic poem "Dos lid fun oysgehargetn yidishn folk" (The song of the murdered Jewish people), was "spine-chilling."[60] In the poem, written in an internment camp in Vittel, France, before deportation to Auschwitz, Katzenelson expressed anger and utter disappointment toward humankind.[61] The reviewer of *Di shtime* considered the absolute high point of the evening Gold's performance of Sholem Asch's (the most prolific and popular Yiddish novelist before the war) "Der marsh fun kedoyshim" (The march of the martyrs):[62]

> To the tune of Chopin's Funeral March, the lyrics describe the encounter between the victorious [Red] army, that is greeted with enthusiasm in the liberated Warsaw, and the endless procession of Jewish martyrs, whose suffering the poet has described with stirring images.[63]

As historian Margarete Myers Feinstein asserts, through watching performances that retell the horrors, survivors could imagine the fate of their loved ones, and could attain emotional release.[64] For Swedish Jews, especially those with more recent connections to Eastern Europe, who had lost loved ones in the Holocaust, these performances were also deeply meaningful. Despite the harrowing images Gold brought to her audiences, the reviewer in *Di shtime* likened her performance to a folk song where a rabbi's teaching made children feel warm in a cold room: "Niusia Gold's art made us feel warm in a similar way."[65]

Dutch Jewish dancer-singer Lin Jaldati (1912–1988), a survivor of Auschwitz and Bergen-Belsen, and her German husband, Eberhard Rebling (1911–2008), performed in Stockholm, Malmö, and Norrköping during their first European tour to Scandinavia at the end of 1946 (Figure 25.3).[66] Already in the late 1930s they created a Yiddish variety show featuring dance, music, and song.[67] David Shneer asserts that before the war their "performances were heavily didactic, teaching Dutch audiences, both Jewish and

TANZ UN GESANG-OWENT

fun der barimter jidisher kinstlerin

LIN JALDATI

fun Holand

Ejngeordnt durch der Jidisher Dramatisher Amatergeselshaft.

Montik dem 25 Nowember 1946 acht asejger punktlich
in Medborgarhuset klejner sal Medborgarplatsen.

Numrirte biljetn zu 3:50, 2:50 un 1:50 kenen nor bashtelt wern
durch telefon 53 91 23.

Di zol plezer sajnen bagrenizt.

FIGURE 25.3 Advertising for the performance of dancer-singer Lin Jaldati and pianist Eberhard Rebling on November 25, 1946, JUD01174. Reproduced by permission of the Judiska Museet, Stockholm.

otherwise, about eastern European Jewish culture."[68] After the war their performances acquired a new meaning as they started performing for survivors who "were attempting to rebuild their lives . . . and to restore some semblance of normalcy, which included such mundane and joyous activities as attending concerts." For Jaldati's audiences in Sweden, with many survivors from Bergen-Belsen, her performance must have been especially meaningful, as she sang as one camp survivor to another. Jaldati, though, was not a native Yiddish speaker, but had learned the language before the war.

Jaldati's and Rebling's performance in Stockholm on November 25, 1946, was arranged by the Yiddish Dramatic Amateur Society.[69] The program, titled *Tants un gezang ovnt* (Dance and song soiree), consisted of two dance sets, two piano recitals, and two sets of songs. The dance sets featured a scene from the Bible and several scenes from eastern European Jewish life, including a dancing Hasid (performed in crossed-dressing) and a mother during the Havdalah. These were accompanied by piano arrangements of music by notable Jewish composers and introduced with a brief storyline. The dances included a number called "Der mes un dos meydl" (The deceased and the girl), based on the *dance macabre* from above-mentioned *Der dibuk* and performed to the original music for the play by the Russian Jewish composer and ethnographer Yoel Engel. Engel was the chief musicologist in S. An-ski's ethnographic expeditions. He also played a prominent role in the Society for Jewish Folk Music, which was founded in St. Petersburg in 1908 and strove for modern national style of Jewish concert music. The storyline in Jaldati's program introduced the dance as follows:

> According to an eastern-Jewish legend, the soul of a human, who has not fulfilled its life's purpose, is doomed to hover between heaven and earth. This soul (dybbuk) descends to earth and takes its refuge in a body of a person it has loved the most. . . . In this dance a girl is possessed by a dybbuk and longs to be united with him, which can only happen through death.[70]

For an audience of survivors, whose family members and loved ones had perished in the Holocaust and had not thus "fulfilled their lives purpose," the dance scene from An-ski's play must have been emotionally charged and meaningful. Jaldati's program also featured two dance scenes that addressed khurbn, "Yid 1943" (Jew 1943) and "Di mame oyf Keynems-land" (The mother in No Man's Land), performed to the music by Joseph Achron, a member of the Society for Jewish Folk Music and a prominent representative of Jewish art music in Russia. The storyline of "Di mame oyf Keynems-land" describes the helpless situation of Polish Jews, who were cast out from Germany after the pogroms of 1938. The piano interludes by Rebling, between the dance scenes and songs, featured Jewish dances by Aleksandr Krein (also a member of the Society for Jewish Folk Music and one of the leading modernist composers in the Soviet Union), and interpretations of *nigunim* by Rebling himself.

In addition to folk songs, Jaldati included a number of the theater songs of Mordechai Gebirtig in her repertoire. She sang three of his prewar songs, including the popular "Reyzele" (Little rose), a sentimental song about a girl named Rose and her sweetheart.[71]

During her tour in Sweden, Jaldati traveled to Falun to meet Leo Rosenblüth, who gave her his song anthology *Mir lebn ejbig*.[72] Some of the song arrangements from this anthology later appeared in her repertoire, among them Gebirtig's "S'brent." The only Holocaust-related song in Jaldati's and Rebling's Scandinavia performances was Hirsh Glik's "Zog nit keynmol!," which closed their program.

Along with guest performances by visiting artists, the Yiddish Dramatic Amateur Society and the Swedish Section of World Jewish Congress arranged concerts in collaboration with the Swedish Jewish community and the sheyres hapleyte. On April 10, 1948, together with several survivor organizations, they arranged a gala concert in Medborgarhuset in honor of Rokhl Korn, who was about to emigrate to Canada.[73] Korn had survived the war in the Soviet Union and had spent nearly two years in Sweden, often reading her poetry at literary soirees with Mordechai Husid, and alongside Glikson's and Fajnzylber's performances. Later in 1948, Korn's book *Heym un heymlozikeyt* (Home and homelessness) was published in Buenos Aires featuring poems commemorating life before the Holocaust and experiences of exile and displacement.[74] The gala concert opened with a performance of Yiddish folk songs by a newly founded group of three Swedish Jewish women: Rakel Lazaroff, T. Magnus, and Hanna Meilach. One of the high points of the evening was Rosenblüth's performance of Yiddish songs featuring one with Korn's lyrics. Rosenblüth's archives contain two songs he composed to Korn's poetry, "Mit vos . . ." (With what . . .) and "Oyf mayne shikh" (Upon my shoes).[75] "Mit vos" was also published in *Yedies* in 1946, and expresses the poet's difficulty in finding words with which to comfort the sheyres-hapleyte as the first stanza reveals:

Mit vos zol ikh kumen tsu dir itst, mayn folk,
ikh, dos blut fun dayn blut un di rip fun dayn rip—
Vu ken ikh gefinen dos vort far dayn tsar,
ven s'shtarbt yeder ershtling oyfn rand fun mayn lip.

With what shall I come to you now, my people,
I, the blood of your blood, the rib of your rib
Where can I find the word for your pain,
When every firstborn dies on the edge of my lip.[76]

The song ends with a plea: "vil ikh betn, az s'zol undz bashert zayn di gnod, / far mir un dir, di gnod fun a trer" ("I want to pray, that we would be blessed with the mercy, / for me and you, the mercy of a tear").[77] The gala evening closed with another set of Yiddish folk songs sung by Polish Jewish actress-singer Gizi Hajdn and accompanied on piano by her husband, the composer, director, and actor Shloyme Prizament. Like Glikson and Fajnzylber, Hajdn and Prizament had evaded the Holocaust in Soviet exile. After repatriation they settled in Sweden, where they worked for a while before leaving to Argentina.[78]

In addition to concerts by singers, the sheyres-hapleyte and the wider Yiddish-speaking community could enjoy Yiddish music performed by choirs visiting from neighboring Finland and Denmark. For the New Year's celebration of 1948, the amateur

FIGURE 25.4 The choir of the Jewish Song Association in Helsinki, in 1947, prior to their Scandinavian tour. The Finnish Jewish Photograph Collection, file 21, National Archives of Finland, Helsinki. Reproduced by permission of the Helsingin juutalainen seurakunta, Helsinki.

choir of the Judiska Sångföreningen i Helsingfors (The Jewish Song Association in Helsinki), under the baton of Isaac Skurnik (1898–1975), performed in Malmö and Stockholm (Figure 25.4). The sheer size of this mixed choir, with ninety singers, and their appearance with women in long white dresses and men wearing white ties, made a huge impression on the audiences.

Their performances were different from those described above in that they did not sing any songs related to the Holocaust or evoking remembrance. Their repertoire consisted mostly of Yiddish folk songs, contemporary Yiddish songs composed by Finnish Jews, liturgical pieces in Hebrew (sung in Ashkenazic pronunciation), and some choral pieces by classical composers such as Beethoven and Grieg.[79] Most of the modern choral arrangements of the Yiddish folk songs, such as the love song "Tif in veldele" (Deep in the forest) and the children's song "Hob ikh a por oksn" (I have a couple of oxen), were by Helsinki-born conductor and composer Simon (Pergament) Parmet (1897–1969). Parmet had studied piano under Aleksandr Glazunov at the St. Petersburg Conservatory and was influenced by the ideals of the Society for Jewish Folk Music. Parmet's elder brother Moses Pergament (1893–1977) had also studied in St. Petersburg and became a well-known composer and music critique in Sweden. In 1944 he composed a choral symphony, titled *Den judiska sången* (The Jewish song), based on the poems of Swedish poet Ragnar Josephson. When it premiered in 1947 and was broadcast on the radio, it included the epigraph "a lament for the six million Jews who fell victim to the cruelty of the Third Reich."[80] The lack of Holocaust-related songs in the repertoire of the Jewish choir from Helsinki somewhat accentuates the history of the community during the war. Even though Finland had been allied with Nazi Germany, the community had evaded the Holocaust (Nazi Germany officially never demanded ghettoization and deportation of the small Finnish Jewish community) and under the watchful eye of the Soviet Union tried to distance itself from it in public. Nevertheless, according to *Di shtime* the sheer existence of the choir, which had been founded in 1917, reminded the sheyres-hapleyte, in a moving way, of the choirs in their own communities that had been eradicated by the Holocaust.[81]

Only three weeks later, the Hazomir (Hebrew, nightingale) choir from Copenhagen performed in Malmö and Landskrona.[82] The choir's background differed from the Helsinki choir. As most of its members were Danish Jews who had fled across the gulf to Sweden in 1943 in order to evade deportation to concentration camps, it epitomized survival and the rebuilding of Jewish culture.

CULTURAL LIFE AND HOLOCAUST COMMEMORATION IN NEW COMMUNITIES

While most Jewish survivors settled in Stockholm, Malmö, and Gothenburg, many set up home in smaller towns that, up until then, had no Jewish communities. These emerging new communities across southern Sweden rebuilt their cultural lives independent of the preexisting Swedish Jewish community. For many of their members, the Yiddish-language played a vital role. Especially those who supported the Labor Bund or Labor Zionism, without sharing their political views, envisioned a Yiddish-speaking future in Jewish Sweden. Given their bonding through the Yiddish language and culture and their disagreement with the Swedish Jewish community—an act of "resistance against an existing collectivity," they represented a community of dissent.[83]

An editor of *Di shtime* considered the situation of the survivors in Sweden as favorable compared to Germany and Austria, but nevertheless emphasized that they belonged to the wider shreyres-hapleyte that "shared an aspiration to build a new life on Jewish-national grounds." The editor deemed the goals of the survivors different from the Swedish Jews, speaking for the community as a whole:

> Our mentality is different. We feel bound by unbreakable threads to the Jewish tradition and to Jewish lifestyle. None of us can agree with the current Jewish-cultural situation in Sweden. . . . In several larger and smaller towns throughout the country, the refugees themselves have established associations, clubs, and in smaller places committees that do their best to look after their needs, creating at least a sparkle of Yiddish-cultural life wherever they are.[84]

In his column "A heymisher vinkl" (A cozy corner), Mordechai Husid writes about his visit to Uppsala, near Stockholm, in 1947, observing that the growing community of survivors, many working in a tile factory, were among the first to organize a cultural club in Sweden.[85] After a while, the club that had started as Bundist became nonaligned so that everyone could feel welcomed. At the time it was common for Jews with a working-class background and no formal education to be culturally inquisitive.[86] The cultural activities of the club included an amateur theater section that organized literary and kleynkunst soirees with visiting actors, singers, musicians, and authors. Aside from members of the Yiddish Dramatic Amateur Society, Glikson and Fajnzylber were among their frequent guests, along with Korn and Husid.[87] The club even had a dance group that rehearsed and performed Hungarian dances, as many of the survivors originated from Hungary and Rumania.

The emerging survivor communities also began to arrange Holocaust commemorations.[88] In 1945 the Association of Rescued Jews in Malmö rented a hall for the days between Rosh Hashana and Yom Kippur and arranged for *hazkores*, memorial services "for the holy martyrs of our last destruction," led by their prayer leaders.[89] The post-Holocaust version of the traditional El male raḥamin (God full of mercy), with additional references to the death camps, became a central prayer-song during these services. April 19, the date of the Warsaw Ghetto Uprising, became a memorial day, observed annually (both the Zionist-oriented World Jewish Congress and the leftist Bund promoted this date).[90] Gradually these commemorations began to take the form of secular rituals, with speeches in Yiddish and witness testimonies, Yiddish song and poetry. As Simon Perego has argued, the use of Yiddish in these contexts "contributed to its promotion to the status of a 'modern sacred language.'"[91] Yiddish became known as the *loshn hakeydoyshim*, language of the martyrs and language of the murdered culture.[92] For instance, in the 1948 program of the local group of Bundists in Eskilstuna near Stockholm as well as the usual speeches and the lighting of six candles, there was a recitation of author Hayim Nahman Bialik's Yiddish poetry, Yiddish songs, Chopin's Funeral March, and the memorial event ended with the "Zog nit keynmol!" sung in unison.[93]

On February 21, 1948, the sheyres-hapleyte and members of the wider Yiddish-speaking community in Stockholm gathered for Glikson's and Fajnzylber's farewell concert in the Medborgarhuset.[94] A representative of the Mosaic Congregation of Stockholm wrote that "a great number of letters from the refugees bear witness of the enormous popularity of the Glikson-couple."[95] One by one, all of the Polish Jewish authors and professional performing artists, like Rokhl Korn, Shloyme Prizament, and Gizi Hajdn, emigrated to the West. Mordechai Husid, as one of the important coordinators of cultural programs for the survivors, moved to Canada in 1949. Visiting artists would, however, continue to tour Sweden, such as in January 1949, when the well-known Polish Jewish actor, director, and playwright Zygmund Turkow and his actress wife Rozi Turkow performed in Stockholm.[96]

As such the Polish Jewish actors and singers, who either temporarily settled in Sweden or came there on a tour, played an important role in rebuilding and revitalizing

Yiddish culture among the survivors. Through their performances of Yiddish song, they helped to contribute to formations of community. Yiddish song bolstered the survivors' origin, uniting them through a common experience of destruction, loss, and displacement, where music maintained and reinforced their collective sense of self. In cities and towns concerts and other performances of Yiddish song gathered a wider community of affinity, bringing together the sheyres-hapleyte with Yiddish-speaking members of the Swedish Jewish community and those interested in this repertoire. In parallel, the emerging communities of Jewish survivors in southern Sweden created their own Yiddish cultural institutions—voices of dissent toward acculturated and linguistically assimilated Swedish Jewish community, as it were. These different functions and representations of Yiddish song ultimately suggest a temporal understanding of zekher, as remembrance for the future.

ACKNOWLEDGMENTS

The author would like to thank Helen Beer, Vivi Lachs, and Pontus Rudberg for their comments on earlier drafts of this chapter as well as Carl Henrik Carlsson, Oren Cohen Roman, Izabela Dahl, Yael Fried, Malin Norrby, Andreas Schein, and Bret Werb for assisting in locating archival material and information.

NOTES

1. "Shive medure genem." Yosef Glikson, "Bay der sheyres hapleyte in Shvedn," *Yedies*, February 6, 1948.
2. See Johannes Heuman and Pontus Rudberg, eds., *Early Holocaust Memory in Sweden: Archives, Testimonies and Reflections* (Basingstoke: Palgrave Macmillan, 1921), 17.
3. See ibid., 18.
4. See D. Köpnisvsky, "Her Mordco Husid . . .," May 16, 1950, Mordco Husid collection, Archives of the Jewish Community of Stockholm, National Archives of Sweden, Stockholm.
5. See "A nayer yidisher fareyn in Malme," *Yedies*, July 26, 1946.
6. For references to Yiddish cultural activities among Bundist survivors in Sweden, see Håkan Blomqvist, *Socialism på jiddisch: Judiska Arbeter Bund i Sverige* (Stockholm: Carlssons, 2021), 61–62, 70–77, 132–135, 148–149.
7. See Yosef Glikson, "Bay der sheyres hapleyte in Shvedn," *Yedies*, January 9, 1948; January 16, 1948; January 23, 1948; February 6, 1948; February 20, 1948.
8. Atina Grossman, "Entangled Histories and Lost Memories: Jewish Survivors in Occupied Germany, 1945–49," in *"We Are Here": New Approaches to Jewish Displaced Persons in Postwar Germany*, ed. Avinoam Patt, and Michael Berkowitz (Detroit, MI: Patt Wayne State University Press, 2010), 24–25.
9. Kay Kaufman Shelemay, "Musical Communities: Rethinking the Collective in Music," *Journal of the American Musicological Society* 64, no. 2 (2011): 367.
10. Ibid., 368.
11. Ibid., 376.
12. Ibid., 376.

13. According to Margarete Myers Feinstein, who has studied theater in DP camps in postwar Germany, through performance "survivors re-live their trauma, not to wallow in it, but to gain some control for it and to imagine new endings, new coping mechanisms." "Re-imagining the Un-imaginable: Theater, Memory and Rehabilitation in Displaced Persons Camps," in *After the Holocaust: Challenging the Myths of Silence*, ed. David Cesarani and Erich J. Sundqvist (London: Routledge, 2012), 64.

14. See Michael Wächter, "The Jewish Community of Stockholm hereby certifies," August 27, 1947, id. no. 1569.90, Collection of the Museum of Jewish Heritage, New York.

15. Michael C. Steinlauf, "Yung-teater," in *YIVO Encyclopedia of Jews in Eastern Europe*, https://yivoencyclopedia.org/article.aspx/Yung-teater (accessed June 4, 2021).

16. On music among Polish Jewish refugees in the USSR, see Eliyana R. Adler, "Singing Their Way Home," in *Jews and Music-Making in the Polish Lands*, ed. François Guesnet, Benjamin Matis, and Antony Polonsky, Polin: Studies in Polish Jewry 32 (Oxford: Littman Library of Jewish Civilization, 2020), 411–428.

17. See the certificate issued to Josef Glikson by the Związek Patriotów Polskich w Z.S.R.R., Tashkent, May 1, 1946, id. no. 1575.90, Collection of the Museum of Jewish Heritage, New York; advertisement for a literary cabaret of the Teatr "Praska Rewia," Warsaw, October 20, 1946, id. no. 1562.90, Collection of the Museum of Jewish Heritage, New York.

18. Nahma, Sandrow, *Vagabond Stars: A World History of Yiddish Theater* (Syracuse, NY: Syracuse University Press, 1996), 323.

19. See "Artistisher owent," Stockholm, December 21, 1946, JUD01174, Judiska Museet, Stockholm; "Detta är vad ni hungrat efter … Program," Helsinki, January 24, 1948, Finland, RG 116, file 74, YIVO Archives, New York. The Stockholm performance was accompanied by G. Katzenstein.

20. See Natan Gross, "Mordechai Gebirtig: The Folk Song and the Cabaret Song," in *Focusing on Jewish Popular Culture and Its Afterlife*, ed. Michael C. Steinlauf and Antony Polonsky, Polin: Studies in Polish Jewry 16 (Oxford: Littman Library of Jewish Civilization, 2003), 107.

21. See Mordechai Gebirtig, *S'brent (1939–1942)*, ed. Mikhal Borvits, Nela Rost, and Yosef Volf (Krakow: Tsentrale yidishe historishe komisye, 1946).

22. Gebirtig, *S'brent*, 16–17.

23. "Oyb es gelingt undz dokh tsu derfrishn di hertser un tsu dermuntern di gemiter, nemen mir dos nisht oyf undzer kheshbn. Dos iz koydem kol dos fardinst fun di tsuherer aleyn. … Tsu hilf dem derfolg kumt di umgeheyere durshtikeyt tsum yidishn vort, fun velkher di mentshn zenen bahersht. Di fremdkeyt fun der svive, in velkher zey gefinen zikh, farshtarkt di benkshaft tsu alts, vos iz yidish." Yosef Glikson, "Bay der sheyres hapleyte in Shvedn," *Yedies*, January 9, 1948.

24. "Zeyere oygn hobn ayngezapt di shreklekhste bilder un inuyim, vos dos yidishe folk iz durkhgegangen in di daytshe lagern, in di Oshvientshims, Maydaneks, u. a. v. Zeyere hertser zenen durkhgenumen mit der benkshaft, zikh tsu baheftn mitn shoyresh fun yidishn folk, mit zayn mehus, mit dem hofnungs-gayst, vos shtromt in der yidisher literatur. Zey filn, az durkh dem dernentern zey zikh tsu zeyere noentste, tsu di tragish umgekumene." Yosef Glikson, "Bay der sheyres hapleyte in Shvedn," *Yedies*, January 9, 1948. Diego Rotman writes about the return of the famed comedians Shimen Dzigan and Isroel Shumacher to Poland from their exile in USSR (they also ended up in Tashkent) during the Second World War and about the important role the re-telling and remembering their

prewar repertoire had for the audiences in reconnecting with their pre-Holocaust life in Poland. Diego Rotman, "Performing Homeland in Post-vernacular Times: Dzigan and Shumacher's Yiddish Theater after the Holocaust," in *The Cultural Experience of Exile, Place and Displacement among Jews and Others*, ed. Asher D. Biemann, Richard I. Cohen, and Sarah E. Wobick-Segev (Berlin: De Gruyter, 2019), 87–89.

25. Yosef Glikson, "Bay der sheyres hapleyte in Shvedn," *Yedies*, February 6, 1948.

26. "Zey veln zikh haynt baheftn mitn yidishn vort, zey veln zikh derfiln noent tsum yidishn folk, onhoybn gloybn in zeyer eygener tsukunft vi in der tsukunft fun gantsn yidishn klal." Yosef Glikson, "Bay der sheyres hapleyte in Shvedn," *Yedies*, February 6, 1948.

27. Shelemay, "Musical Communities," 371.

28. "Men hot undz gedankt mitn altn yidishlekhn yasher-koyekh, punkt vi men dankt koyanim nokhn dukhnen." Yosef Glikson, "Bay der sheyres hapleyte in Shvedn," *Yedies*, January 23, 1948.

29. "Baym tish hert zikh fun tsayt tsu tsayt a yidish zeymerl, a yidish folks-lid. Ophengig fun der tsayt zaynen di gezangen: baym shales sudes khapt emetser unter a heymishn nign, a nign fun Modzshitser rebn; in an arbeter yom tev vi der ershter may—arbeterlider." Yosef Glikson, "Bay der sheyres hapleyte in Shvedn," *Yedies*, January 16, 1948.

30. Bret, Werb, "'Vu ahin zol ikh geyn?': Music Culture of Jewish Displaced Persons," in *Dislocated Memories: Jews, Music, and Postwar German Culture*, ed. Tina Frühauf and Lily H. Hirsch (New York: Oxford University Press, 2014), 75.

31. Gilbert, "We Long for a Home," 290.

32. Survivors in a refugee center in Kalhyttan to Leo Rosenblüth, ca. 1945, Leo Rosenblüth Collection 4.5.1., Musik- och teaterbibliotek, Stockholm.

33. Leo Rosenblüth, *Mir lebn ejbig: 13 jidische lider wos men hot gesungen in di konzentrazionsläger* (Stockholm: Lundén, 1946). On early songbooks of ghetto and concentration camp songs, see Bret Werb, "Fourteen Shoah Songbooks," *Musica Judaica* 20 (2013–2014): 39–116; and Joseph Toltz and Anna Boucher. "Out of the Depths: Complexity, Subjectivity, and Materiality in the Earliest Accounts of Holocaust Song-Making," *East European Jewish Affairs* 48, no. 3 (2019): 309–330.

34. Rosenblüth was one of the founders of the Jewish Musical Society, besides Hans Holewa and Moses Pergament. During the war they arranged concerts and produced records in Yiddish in order to raise funds for relief to Jews in ghettos and camps. Pontus Rudberg, *The Swedish Jews and the Holocaust* (London: Routledge, 2017), 165–221.

35. Shmerke Katsherginski, *Lider fun di getos un lagern* (New York: CYCO bicher farlag, 1948).

36. In Rosenblüth's original titles: "Der lezter weg" (The final way), "Der weg kejn Panar" (The way to Ponar), "'S brent."

37. The songs are "Diselbn gassn" (The same streets), "Ich schtej bam tajchele" (I stand by a stream), "Kirchengloken" (Church bells); "Bremen" (Bremen; lyrics and melody by Dr. Eva Ledig), "Ich such ejn ejze" (I am looking for advice; lyrics and melody by Jakob Weingarten); "Der schwarzer zug" (The black train) and "Schpalt sich, himl!" (Split open, sky!). The songs "In such ejn ejze," "Kirchengloken," and "Bremen" could not be located in other anthologies of ghetto and concentration camp songs.

38. See also Werb, "Vu ahin zol ikh geyn," 77; Gilbert, "We Long for a Home," 295–300.

39. Gilbert, "We Long for a Home," 295.

40. Moyshe Gurin, "Shtil-lebn in katset" and "Vemen s'iz bashert," *Unser Blatt / Undzer blat*, no. 3 (1949): n.p..

41. "Keyn yidish kulturel lebn iz dokh in di rekonvolestsentn hayzer, vos zenen tsevorfn iber Shvedn, nisht faran un layder iz keyner nisht farinteresirt es tsu shafn." Yosef Glikson, "Bay der sheyres hapleyte in Shvedn," *Yedies*, January 23, 1948.

42. Blomqvist makes some references to singing and performing taking place in convalescent homes, see *Socialism på jiddisch*, 74, 77, 79.

43. See "Judiska flyktingar ser judisk teater," *Dagens Nyheter*, October 15, 1945. The Yiddish Dramatic Amateur Society also organized a program of Yiddish music and poetry for the survivors broadcast on the Swedish radio on February 13, 1946, featuring Leo Rosenblüth and Hungarian-born actress-singer Kay Whitt, née Katharina Weitz (1886–1965) from Denmark. "I samband med . . .," *Judiska hem*, nos. 2–3 (1946): 43.

44. See "Sch. An-skis Der Dibuk," ca. 1945, JUD01174, Judiska Museet, Stockholm.

45. See Gilbert, "We Long for a Home," 291.

46. Shelemay, "Musical Communities," 373.

47. The Bund also arranged some performances in the countryside; see Blomqvist, *Socialism på jiddisch*, 119–120. On Holewa, see Henrik Rosengren, "'Vi har redan tillräckligt med judar här:' Tonsättaren Hans Holewa och exilens dubbelhet," *Scandinavian Jewish Studies* 27, no. 1 (2016): 4–23.

48. See "Chayele Grober, Sång och drama," November 3, 1935, JUD01174, Judiska Museet, Stockholm.

49. "Chajele Grobers konsert," October 11, 1947, JUD01174, Judiska Museet, Stockholm.

50. Ibid., 111. The other songs by Gebirtig were "Viglid" (Lullaby) and "Avreymele un Yosele" (Abraham and Joseph).

51. In May 1948 singer Bracha Tsipora from Palestine gave concerts of Hebrew songs in Stockholm. "Groyser derfolg fun der erets yisroeldiker zingerin Brokhe Tsipore," *Yedies*, May 28, 1948.

52. "Der oylem—der tsolraykher fun ale dray ovntn—hot ir 'antkegn getrogn di hertser oyf a zilbernem tats' . . . " "Khayele Grobers aroystrit in Shtokholm," *Yedies*, October 17, 1947.

53. "Här slog sångerskan an en allvarligen ton, och i den djupt gripande halvt mässartade sången tonade en smärta av nästan förtärande intensitet." "Chajele Grober väckte jubel," *Dagens Nyheter*, December 10, 1947.

54. Khayele Grober, "Jewish Folk Songs," [no label], https://www.discogs.com/Chayele-Grober-Jewish-Folk-Songs/release/5762422 (accessed June 4, 2021).

55. See "Niussia Gold, Wort-Konzert," August 25, 1946, JUD01174, Judiska Museet, Stockholm; "Nusia Gold vider in Malme," *Di shtime (fun sheyres-hakhurbn in Shvedn)*, February 6, 1948.

56. Veronica Belling, "'S'iz nisht dos vos amol iz geven': Max Perlman (1909–1985)," *Digital Yiddish Theatre Project*, April 21, 2020, https://web.uwm.edu/yiddish-stage/siz-night-dos-vos-amok-is-geven-max-perlman-1909–1985 (accessed August 29, 2022).

57. See J. Hoberman, *Bridge of Light: Yiddish Film between the Two World Wars* (New York: The Museum of Modern Art, 1991), 331.

58. See "An aroystrit fun der parizer aktrise Nusia Gold," *Yedies*, March 12, 1948.

59. See, for instance, David Mazower, "Stories in Song: The Melo-deklamatsyes of Joseph Markovitsh," in *Yiddish Theatre: New Approaches*, ed. Joel Berkowitz (Oxford: Littman Library of Jewish Civilization, 2003), 119–137.

60. Ele, "Vos shraybt di shvedishe prese vegn Nusia Gold," *Di shtime*, February 27, 1948.

61. See David Roskies and Naomi Diamant, *Holocaust Literature: A History and Guide* (Waltham, MA: Brandeis University Press, 2012), 204.

62. The piece was a dramatization of Asch's "Triumf-marsh" (Triumphal march) published in his anthology *Der brenediker dorn* [The burning bush] (Nyu-york: Farlag funem idishn fraternaln folks-ordn, 1946).

63. "Tsu di tonen fun Shopens troyer marsh vert bashildert a tsuzamentref tsvishn di zigraykhe armey, velkhe vert bagrist mit bagaysterung un [unclear] in der bafrayter Varshe, un an umendlekhn tsug fun yidishe martirer, velkhes leydn der dikhter hot geshildert in farbshtarke bilder." Ele, "Vos shraybt di shvedishe prese vegn Nusia Gold," *Di shtime*, February 27, 1948.

64. Meyers Feinstein, "Re-imagining the Un-imaginable," 43.

65. Ele, "Vos shraybt di shvedishe prese vegn Nusia Gold," *Di shtime*, February 27, 1948.

66. See David Shneer, "Eberhard Rebling, Lin Jaldati, and Yiddish Music," in *Dislocated Memories: Jews, Music, and Postwar German Culture*, ed. Tina Frühauf and Lily E. Hirsch (New York: Oxford University Press, 2014), 162–166.

67. See ibid., 162–165.

68. Ibid. 164.

69. See "Tanz un gesang-owent," November, 25, 1946, JUD01174, Judiska Museet, Stockholm.

70. "Enligt en östjudisk legend är själen av en man, som icke fullgjort sin livsuppgift, dömd att evigt sväva mellan himmel och jord. Denna själ (Dybuk) söker sig ner till jorden och tar sin tillflykt i den människas kropp, som den älskat mest av allt.... I denna dans är flickan besatt av en Dybuk och längtar att bli förenad med honom, vilket endast kan ske genom döden." The program for Jaldati's and Rebling's Helsinki performance has the storylines of the dances in Swedish. "Judisk konst," November 28, 1946, file 459, Finnish Jewish Archives, The National Archives of Finland, Helsinki.

71. The other songs by Gebirtig were "Hey tsigelekh" (Hey little goats) and "Ver vet der ershter lakhn" (Who will laugh the first). The folk songs in the program were "Fun shtot tsu shtot" (From town to town), "Raboysay" (Gentlemen), "A katarinke lid" (Barrel organ song), and the Yemenite folk song "Gamal gamali."

72. See Shneer, "Eberhard Rebling, Lin Jaldati," 166.

73. "A fayerlekher gezegenungsovnt lekoved der dikhterin Rokhl Korn," *Yedies*, May 16, 1948. Besides Korn, authors Nokhum Bomze (1906–1954), Moyshe Grosman (1904–1961), Leo Finkelshteyn (1895–1950), Yoysef Rubinshteyn (1905–1978), Yisroel Tabaksblat (1891–1950), and Rachmil Bryks (1912–1974) settled in Sweden for a short time. The Swedish Section of the World Jewish Congress had in 1946 a special rescue project to bring Jewish authors and their families to Sweden. "Retungs-aktsye far yidishe shrayber in Poyln," *Yedies*, August 30, 1946.

74. See Rokhl Korn, *Heym un heymlozikeyt: Lider*, Dos poylishe yidntum 39 (Buenos Aires: Tsentral-farband fun poylishe yidn in Argentine, 1948).

75. "Mit wos sol ich kumen," sheet music. Leo Rosenblüth Collection 2.1.17., Musik- och teaterbibliotek, Stockholm; "Ojf majne schich," sheet music. Ibid. Both poems were also published in Korn's book *Heym un heymlozikeyt*.

76. Rokhl Korn, "Mit vos," *Yedies*, September 6, 1946.

77. Rosenblüth also performed a song he had composed to Husid's poem. Rosenblüth's archive contains one song with Husid's lyrics: "Majn libe is gebojren ojf a schtejn" (My love was born on a stone), sheet music. Leo Rosenblüth Collection 2.1.17., Musik- och teaterbibliotek, Stockholm.

78. Hajdn, for instance, gave concerts together with tenor Marcel Kaufler, who had become familiar to Polish Jews through performances for Warsaw and Krakow radio, and who

settled in Sweden for a while. Prizament composed the music for Abraham Goldfaden's classic operetta *Tsvey Kuni-Lemls* (Two Kuni-Lemls), which was performed by the Yiddish Dramatic Amateur Society in 1948 under his direction. "A kontsert fun yidishn lid un vort in Shtokholm," *Yedies*, October 1, 1948; M., "Wegen jidischen Theater: Di zwej Kuni-Lemelss," *Unser Blatt / Undzer blat*, no. 2 (1948): 11–12.

79. See "Program vid sångarfesten i Medborgarhusets stora sal," Stockholm, January 4, 1948. file 456, Finnish Jewish Archives, The National Archives of Finland, Helsinki.

80. "Ett sorgekväde över de sex miljoner judar som föll offer för Tredje rikets grymhet." See also Henrik Rosengren, *"Judarnas Wagner": Moses Pergament och den kulturella indetifikationenes dilemma omkring 1920–1950* (Stockholm: Sekel, 2007), 206–208.

81. See L. T., "Der yidisher gezangfareyn fun Helsingfors in Malme," *Di shtime*, January [day unclear], 1948.

82. See "Tsvey gelungene kontsert-ovntn fun 'Hazomir,' Kopenhagen, in Landskrona un Malme," *Di shtime*, February 6, 1948.

83. Shelemay, "Musical Communities," 370.

84. "Andersh iz undzer mentalitet, mir filn zikh gebundn mit umtseraysbare fedim tsu der yidisher traditsye un yidishn lebns shteyger. Keyner fun undz ken nisht maskim zayn mit dem itstikn yidish-gaystikn matsev in Shvedn. . . . In a gantser rey shtet un shtelekh ibern land zenen geshafn gevorn durkh di pleytim aleyn fareynen, klubn, in kleyne erter komitetn, velkhe bamien zikh tsu gebn an entfer oyf zeyere noytn, shafndik khotsh a shayn fun yidishe-kultur lebn oyfn ort." "Di noytikeyt tsu shafn a tsentrale kerpershaft fun der sheyres-hakhurbn in Shvedn," *Di shtime*, February 6, 1947.

85. M., "A hejmisch winkl: Uppsala," *Unser Blatt / Undzer blat*, no. 4 (1947): 9–10.

86. See Gross, "Mordechai Gebirtig," 109; on disputes between Bundists and (left-wing) Zionists in Sweden, see Blomqvist, *Socialism på jiddisch*, 119–121.

87. Husid also mentions in his article actor Isak Inwentash, who apparently was among the actors who arrived in 1946 and resided in Sweden for a short time.

88. See Gilbert, "We Long for a Home," 301–303.

89. "A nayer yidisher fareyn in Malme," July 26, 1946. For similarities in memorial practices in Paris, see Perego, "Yiddish or not?," 224–225; For Holocaust commemoration among Swedish Jews, see Malin Thor Tureby, "The Holocaust and the Jewish Survivors in the Swedish-Jewish Press, 1945–1955," in *Early Holocaust Memory in Sweden: Archives, Testimonies and Reflections*, ed. Johannes Heuman and Pontus Rudberg (Basingstoke: Palgrave Macmillan, 1921), 264–269. M. [Mordechai Husid], "A hejmisch winkl," *Unser Blatt / Undzer blat*, no. 7 (1947): 9–10.

90. See also Blomqvist, *Socialism på jiddisch*, 123–124.

91. Simon Perego, "Yiddish or Not? Holocaust Remembrance, Commemorative Ceremonies, and Questions of Language Among Parisian Jews, 1944–1967," *Journal of Modern Jewish Studies*, 20, no. 2 (2021): 223, 230.

92. See Jan Schwarz, *Survivors and Exiles: Yiddish Culture after the Holocaust* (Detroit, MI: Wayne State University Press, 2015), 185.

93. Blomqvist, Socialism på jiddisch, 138–139.

94. "A gezegenungsovnt fun di aktyorn Tsipore Faynzilber un Yosef Glikson," *Yedies*, February 13, 1948; "A fayerlekher gezegenungskontsert lekoved di gevezene 'Yung teater' mitglider Tsipore Faynzilber un Yosef Glikson," *Yedies*, February 27, 1947.

95. Michael Wächter, "The Jewish community hereby certifies."

96. "Teaterafton, Zygmunt Turkow och Rozi Turkow," January 15, 1949, JUD01174, Judiska Museet, Stockholm.

SELECT BIBLIOGRAPHY

Adler, Eliyana R. "Singing Their Way Home." In *Jews and Music-Making in the Polish Lands*, edited by François Guesnet, Benjamin Matis, and Antony Polonsky, 411–428. Polin: Studies in Polish Jewry 32. Oxford: Littman Library of Jewish Civilization, 2020.

Blomqvist, Håkan. *Socialism på jiddisch: Judiska Arbeter Bund i Sverige*. Stockholm: Carlssons, 2021.

Feinstein, Margarete Myers. "Re-imagining the Un-imaginable: Theater, Memory and Rehabilitation in Displaced Persons Camps." In *After the Holocaust: Challenging the Myths of Silence*, edited by David Cesarani and Erich J. Sundqvist, 39–54. London: Routledge, 2012.

Frühauf, Tina, and Lily H. Hirsch, eds. *Dislocated Memories: Jews, Music, and Postwar German Culture*. New York: Oxford University Press, 2014.

Gilbert, Shirli. "'We Long for a Home': Songs and Survival among Jewish Displaced Persons." In *"We Are Here": New Approaches to Jewish Displaced Persons in Postwar Germany*, edited by Avinoam Patt and Michael Berkowitz, 289–307. Detroit, MI: Patt Wayne State University Press, 2010.

Muir, Simo. "'Mother Rachel and Her Children': Artistic Expressions in Yiddish and Early Commemoration of the Holocaust in Finland." *East European Jewish Affairs* 48, no. 3 (2018): 284–308.

Perego, Simon. "Yiddish or not? Holocaust Remembrance, Commemorative Ceremonies, and Questions of Language among Parisian Jews, 1944–1967." *Journal of Modern Jewish Studies* 20, no. 2 (2021): 222–247.

Rotman, Diego. "Performing Homeland in Post-Vernacular Times: Dzigan and Shumacher's Yiddish Theater after the Holocaust." In *The Cultural Experience of Exile, Place and Displacement Among Jews and Others*, edited by Asher D. Biemann, Richard I. Cohen, and Sarah E. Wobick-Segev, 81–97. Berlin: De Gruyter, 2019.

Rudberg, Pontus. *The Swedish Jews and the Holocaust*. London: Routledge, 2017.

Shneer, David. "Eberhard Rebling, Lin Jaldati, and Yiddish Music in East Germany, 1949–1962." In *Dislocated Memories: Jews, Music, and Postwar German Culture*, edited by Tina Frühauf and Lily E. Hirsch, 161–186. New York: Oxford University Press, 2014.

Schwarz, Jan. *Survivors and Exiles: Yiddish Culture after the Holocaust*. Detroit, MI: Wayne State University Press, 2015.

Toltz, Joseph, and Anna Boucher. "Out of the Depths: Complexity, Subjectivity, and Materiality in the Earliest Accounts of Holocaust Song-Making." *East European Jewish Affairs* 48, no. 3 (2019): 309–330.

Thor Tureby, Malin. "The Holocaust and the Jewish Survivors in the Swedish-Jewish Press, 1945–1955." In *Early Holocaust Memory in Sweden: Archives, Testimonies and Reflections*, edited by Johannes Heuman and Pontus Rudberg, 249–286. Basingstoke: Palgrave Macmillan, 2021.

Werb, Bret. "Fourteen Shoah Songbooks." *Musica Judaica* 20 (2013–2014): 39–116.

"FERRAMONTI WE DO NOT FORGET"

Jews, Music, and Internment in Italy

SILVIA DEL ZOPPO

Nelle ore grigie ed oscure di Auschwitz, abbiamo sempre visto davanti noi, come un miraggio, il luminoso giardino d'Urbisaglia in Italia, paese di sole e di brava gente.[1]

"IN the gray and dark hours of Auschwitz, we have always seen before us, like a mirage, the bright garden of Urbisaglia in Italy, a sunny country of good people." With these words, Paul Pollak, former chief doctor of the Vienna Police Department, reminisced about his captivity in the small internment camp near Macerata, where he had been deported just weeks after it was established inside the Villa Giustiniani Bandini on June 16, 1940. The site had already been used to detain Austrian and German prisoners during the First World War.[2] It housed about one hundred inmates at a time, among them Italian Jews who were deemed dangerous for political reasons, foreign Jews from countries where racial policies were enforced, antifascists, and Slovenians. Prisoners came and went until the camp's closure in August 1943. During Pollak's time, they were reportedly in good health. They had access to a small library; they could stroll through the lush park that surrounded the grounds of the villa. They engaged in playing bocce and held chess tournaments. At one time a small ensemble existed, consisting of accordion and violin, "which masterfully managed to get through many sad hours."[3] In light of this and despite the "sad hours," it might be unsurprising that Pollak captured the internment site with the metaphors of "mirage" and "bright garden," the latter evoking a biblical allusion to the Garden of Eden—a stark contrast to the experiences of most other prisoners who describe the darkness and desolation in camps. Terezín, for instance, often named a "model camp-ghetto," had been captured by František Petr Kien, librettist of Viktor Ullmann's *Der Kaiser von Atlantis*, as "a hostile desert."[4] Such varying perceptions ultimately underline that the term *concentration camp* refers to a variety of systems that greatly differ in their severity, mortality rate, and architecture, while having in common that inmates are held outside the rule of law. And yet describing sites like Urbisaglia as *internment camps* would be a euphemism.

Urbisaglia was one of the forty-eight sites in Central and Southern Italy established under War Ministry Circular no. 3/227 of January 31, 1936 (with subsequent amendments of June 10, 1940, Circular no. 22897), that between May 1940 until the end of 1943 served as camps for enemies, political opponents, generally "undesired people," and especially foreign Jews.[5] Jews in Italy had been already affected by the *leggi razziali*, a set of laws beginning to be issued in September 1938 that enforced racial discrimination. After ninety years of equality, freedom, and property rights, granted in March 1848 with the Statuto Albertino, Jews were no longer allowed to hold professional positions and public appointments, and render services such as in the military. They could no longer enter schools and universities or take part in cultural life; they were affected by the ban of Jewish books and by the prohibition of so-called mixed marriages.[6] Around 60,000 native and foreign Jews living in Italy faced such persecutions.[7] To make matters worse, foreign Jews—including those who had been naturalized after January 1, 1919, but had their citizenship revoked on September 7, 1938, days after the Council of Ministers Mussolini approved the Royal Decree-Law no. 1381—faced expulsion.[8] For most of them a return to their homeland or emigration to nearby countries was not a possibility, given the anti-Jewish persecutions pervading much of Europe. With no place to go, foreign Jews were first imprisoned and then deported to concentration camps. Italy thus turned out to be a *rifugio precario* (a precarious refuge), as such defined by Klaus Voigt in his seminal book with the same title.[9]

The vast majority of camps in Italy were located in the central and southern parts of the country, spreading along the peninsula, which Michael Ebner has designated as a "fascist archipelago," as Mussolini's regime ruled there through violence.[10] Most of these camps were situated in remote or isolated areas, far away from the centers that drove the economic and political life of the country. Most were quite small; only fourteen had more than a hundred inmates, and few reached an overall number of a few thousand.

As such, the concept of camp was not new to Italy. Italian camps had been previously erected in Albania, Somalia, Libya, and Slovenia, where between 1930 and 1933 an estimated 40,000 people died of starvation, illness, or hard labor. The earliest known attempt to create an extermination camp for Italian political prisoners can be traced to 1932, in Gasr Bu Hadi (Libyan Sahara); financial constraints stalled the project.[11] The plan alone, however, questions the notion of Italians as *brava gente* (good people), although reports of former inmates, such as Pollak, have supported this myth.[12]

What is more, after the fall of the fascist regime and Italy's surrender on September 8, 1943, the newly founded Repubblica Sociale Italiana (Italian Social Republic), Mussolini's last venture though under asphyxiating German control, did not change course.[13] Just the opposite, the Campo di Fossoli in the north, for example, which had been erected in 1942 for prisoners of war, was enlarged by sixty wooden and twenty stone barracks. Renamed Fossoli di Carpi, it became the "national concentration camp" for Jews. Before it came under German control in March 1944 and served as a transit camp, two trains had already left for Auschwitz. (From November 1945 to May 1947 the camp was in use for foreign refugees, some of them Jewish Holocaust survivors.)[14] The same is true for another camp further north, in Bolzano. A transit camp, it was however solely operated by Nazi Germany. Risiere di San Sabba near Trieste, a former rice-processing factory, erected in October 1943, constituted the main camp of the Adriatic Coast. During its time of existence, first under Italian and then under German control, it facilitated the deportation of circa 20,000 inmates to Auschwitz and other extermination camps. About 5,000 inmates were murdered on site.[15]

As far as camps in Central and Southern Italy are concerned, Ferramonti di Tarsia stands out. Not only did it occupy a vast territory of 16 hectares and counted around 2,000 inmates at a time (a total of 3,823 Jews, out of which only 141 with Italian citizenship, were detained between June 20, 1940, and September 1943),[16] it was one of the few camps in Italy built for the purpose of internment, other than the majority of the sites, which repurposed abandoned or confiscated buildings for imprisonment and surveillance through agents of public security. The erection of its ninety-two barracks came with remarkably high costs as well as particular difficulties: Ferramonti, originally named Media Valle Crati for its setting, is situated in the inaccessible Calabrian hinterland, 23 miles from Cosenza, in the Crati River Valley. Malaria afflicted the area due to swampy grounds and water shortages in summer, a place deemed unsuitable by any medical standards.[17] But it was a place deemed suitable for internment due to its low strategic relevance and the distance from localities. It was a *non-lieu* located in the middle of nowhere and unknown to most of the deportees and others.[18]

Ferramonti also stands out, for on September 14, 1943, it became the first camp in Europe to be liberated by the Allies. Inmates, who until then had lived under significant restrictions, regained their freedom, but were de facto unable to leave the camp, as the war was still raging in most of Europe. Emigration to Palestine or the United States from ports like Bari and Naples would only be possible from June 1944 onward. Given these constraints, many of the former inmates remained in the camp, which the British administration maintained as a Displaced Persons camp until December 1945. Thus, Ferramonti's purposes correlated with distinct historical events: Italy's entry into the Second World War on June 10, 1940, and the Allies' invasion and subsequent liberation.[19]

During the time when it served as a concentration camp, Ferramonti housed about a third of the foreign Jews in Italy, with 30 percent of the prisoners stemming from Yugoslavia, 25 percent from German-speaking lands, 8 percent from Czechoslovakia, and 6 percent from Poland, as well as 15 percent from Albania, Benghazi, and elsewhere. But there was also a small number, about two hundred, non-Jews. Among them were Italian political opponents and communists, Chinese immigrants who with Japan's entry into the war had become enemies, and Greeks, Yugoslavs, and French from Italian-occupied Corsica. As such, the prisoners of Ferramonti were a heterogenous group of people, having different origins and different religions, or none. In contrast to other camps, men, women, and even entire families who were held there were able to preserve their ties. Several couples got married at the camp, and over twenty children were born there.

The prisoners of Ferramonti at large certainly did not form a community in the conventional sense, in that they had little in common and had no incentive to distinguish themselves from other individuals or groups outside the camp. This is also true for the Jewish prisoners within the camp, perhaps with the exception of the five hundred survivors of the Pentcho shipwreck, a particularly distinct group. The Pentcho was a refugee ship that sailed from Bratislava down the Danube, on May 18, 1940. The voyage was the last one to be organized by the Betar, the right-wing Revisionist Zionists who tried to help Slovak and Austrian Jews escape to Palestine. After being rescued by the Italian Navy, the refugees were transferred first to Rhodes and from there, in January 1942, to Ferramonti.

Diversity was defined not only by place of origin and reason for internment, but also by denomination. And while the different Jewish groups were in close contact and even housed together in the barracks, they would eventually maintain religious autonomy through different spaces for worship—liberal, Orthodox, and another for the Zionist Betar organization. (Similarly, Catholic and Greek Orthodox maintained different houses of worship.) And while the culture of the prisoners—their language, worship, and music—enhanced distinctiveness and/or difference, *symbolically* they were a community as they shared the condition of internment in all that it entailed. Nowhere is this more obvious than in a Hanukkah concert on December 6, 1942, discussed below, to which all the prisoners regardless of their faith were invited (apparently camp guards attended events as well).

What all prisoners had in common were the life conditions they faced in Ferramonti. These were unhealthy and inhospitable. Inmates suffered from malaria because of the surrounding marshes. At first, the prisoners were subjected to heavy restrictions in all aspects of their lives: they had to answer to roll-calls, and patrol towers were located all along the external fence. Initially, any form of assembly including teaching and praying was forbidden or limited, and prisoners required special permission to read certain books or foreign publications. Repeated requests and petitions to improve welfare, written between July 1940 and July 1943, reflect the harsh conditions and ultimately led to the loosening of restrictions and support, with the Italian Jewish relief agency, the Delegazione per l'assistenza degli emigranti ebrei (DELASEM), supplying books, food, and liturgical objects and setting up an infrastructure for the children. (The Vatican, which had looked favorably on the establishment of Jewish internment, also deployed small charity funds.) Some restrictions—especially those limiting public assembly, praying, and teaching—were eventually being lifted.

And yet, inmates were called by name rather than by number. They were neither forced to work nor abused, physically mistreated, or threatened with death, and nearly all survived their imprisonment unharmed. Most of the detainees were allowed to roam freely on the grounds during daytime. And inmates had limited and supervised contact and exchanges with civilians living nearby or coming from afar. Aid organizations and clerics were allowed to visit: notably, Izrael Markovič Kal'k (Israel Kalk) of the Mensa dei Bambini, a private aid organization focused on helping the youngest victims of the persecution by providing them with both material and educational support, visited the camp several times. The chief rabbi of Genoa, Riccardo Pacifici, paid one visit in 1942, and Francesco Borgongini Duca, who served as Apostolic Nuncio to Italy, came once as well. Despite censorship, it was possible to send and receive letters, thereby maintaining contact to relatives and friends.

The improving conditions also allowed for a variety of cultural expressions and experiences, which in turn reflected the prisoners' heterogeneity while being a symbolic community. Similar is true for other camps. In much of the musicological literature, the various repertoires and practices have been captured with the term *concentration camp music* or *Lagermusik*, a controversial umbrella-term that was used by the inmates as well, as evidenced in Buchenwald song "Wenn so beim Ausmarsch die Lagermusik spielt" and other sources. Such a concept refers to almost boundless musical practices, styles, and repertoires connected with concentration camps throughout Europe and beyond. And yet, as James Loeffler has contended with a view on a related concept, "by labeling certain works of art as 'Holocaust music,' we risk creating a genre that turns the details of history and the complex meanings of music into one saccharine lesson in universalist tolerance." Loeffler's concern is directed toward turning "Jewish composers into shadow images defined only by their status as Hitler's victims." He concludes that "No art, even that which is produced in the most extreme conditions, can be reduced to a one-dimensional message, however important. Doing so risks suffocating music by over-inoculating it against the very freedom of interpretation that is the lifeblood of all art."[20] As such, this chapter forgoes the discussion of repertoires, genres, styles, and performance in Ferramonti as "concentration camp music," focusing instead on the presence and absence of musical expressions of Jewishness within the confines of the camp in light as well as their meaning.

During its short existence, Ferramonti saw a variety of cultural and especially musical activities on the initiative of the prisoners.[21] These are thoroughly documented due to the initiative of Israel Kalk, who, as the founder and leader of the Mensa dei Bambini, not only supported persecuted Jews but also, until 1943, while forced to take refuge in Switzerland, documented tracks of their existence. After his death, his collection became part of the Centro di Documentazione Ebraica Contemporanea in Milan and represents one of the most abundant and complete documentations of an Italian concentration camp. Within this collection the memoirs of the Austrian pianist and composer Kurt Sonnenfeld (1921–1997) stand out and serve as the one source for this chapter.[22] Similarly noteworthy is the diary of the Capuchin Franciscan monk Calliste Lopinot (1876–1966), who was in close contact with all detainees during his stay from 1941 to 1944 (he came ostensibly to assist Catholic prisoners but also—as revealed by his diary—to encourage and support new converts).[23] Both individuals played a key role in reporting on the collective, as witnesses of musical activities.[24]

But still, while the music history of fascist Italy has been well covered with Fiamma Nicolodi's *Musica e musicisti nel ventennio fascista* and Harvey Sachs' *Music in Fascist*

Italy, and more recently with the edited volume by Alessandro Carrieri and Annalisa Capristo, *Italian Jewish Musicians and Composers under Fascism*, music researchers have largely overlooked Ferramonti and other camps in Italy. There are several hundred publications on music in concentration camps, with the vast majority focusing on Nazi Germany, Poland, and specifically Terezín, but Italy has hardly been considered.[25]

Only very recently studies emerged on music and musicians in the concentration camps of fascist Italy—most notably Raffaele Deluca's *Tradotti agli estremi confini*. Similarly, musical practices in Displaced Persons camps have only recently and sporadically received attention, with Sophie Fetthauer's study on Bergen-Belsen and several essays in Tina Frühauf and Lily Hirsch's volume *Dislocated Memories* being the most in-depth studies.[26] Bret Werb has discussed the various ways the Displaced Persons anchored their sense of place and comfort in musical memories of home, infusing them with new memories of the recent past and visions of the future.[27] In his analysis of the film *Long is the Road*, Joshua Walden has shown how the trauma of dislocation gave way to creativity, and how music functions as a bearer of memory—a significant connection between music and displacement.[28] From a methodological viewpoint, these may be regarded as paradigmatic, but they focus on camps where life conditions significantly differ from the situation in Ferramonti. More so, most of these studies hardly take into account the different phases of a camp as a site of oppression and liberation as well as commemoration. The transitory existence of the camp unfolding within two different phases that defined the site and how these presented themselves in the musical events organized by the Jewish inmates and, in a third phase, expressed *zekher*: these are the subjects of this chapter. Distinguishing among these distinct phases is all the more important as scholars lump distinct chapters in the history of ghettos and camps together, assessing them as one historical record, testimony, and memory.

THE CONCENTRATION CAMP
(JUNE 1940 TO SEPTEMBER 1943)

After the initial restrictive period, the fascist militia in charge of Ferramonti never interfered with cultural and leisure activities as long as they observed camp regulations and did not undermine order.[29] It thus can be safely assumed that informal music making was part of Ferramonti's culture as early as January 1941, with inmates relying on sheet music sent by relatives.[30] Later on Kurt Sonnenfeld himself contributed some repertoire, composing the *Ferramonti-Walzer*, based on lyrics by Ferdinand Kaska, who arrived in Ferramonti in January 1942. (A "Ghettoliedchen" by Isco [Isak] Thaler and a "Ferramonti-Lied" are documented, but neither lyrics nor music has been found.) Given the conditions in the camp, it is unclear, however, whether the lyrics should be understood as irony or naiveté, as he describes life as follows:

Das schönste Land, war so bekannt
Das kann man sag'n ganz ohne Schand:
Das ist ja nur Ferramonti.
Und wer es hat so oft gesehn
Der kann es sagen wie wunderschön
Es ist in Ferramonti.
Zeitig am Morg'n wo man erwacht
Und die Sonn' durchs Fensterlacht
Da kann ja nur sein Ferramonti.
Und jede Frau die es hier gibt
Ist gleich in jed'n stark verliebt.
Ferramonti vergessen wir nicht.

The most beautiful land, was so well known
That can be said without shame:
That's just Ferramonti.
And he who has seen it so often
Can say how beautiful
It is in Ferramonti.
Early in the morning when you wake up
And the sun is shining through the window
There can only be Ferramonti.
And every woman there is
Is instantly in love with everyone.
Ferramonti we do not forget.

Staged performances by and for the community of inmates are documented beginning on March 23, 1941, when Siegbert Steinfeld (1909–?), a baritone previously active in the Jewish Culture League of Berlin and now waiting for his visa to emigrate, gave a so-called *Opernabend*, accompanied on the accordion by pianist Bogdan Zins (1905–1994), a former student of Rudolf Serkin, whose extreme mastery and virtuosity ("mit unglaublicher Fingerfertigkeit") was recognized by fellow pianist Kurt Sonnenfeld.[31] The duo was joined by amateur violinist Walter Behrens (1901–?), a medical doctor who had moved from his native Karlsruhe to Rome due to restrictions Jewish students faced in Germany, and he had graduated there prior to his internment. As such, the concert attests to a common practice in Ferramonti, namely that within the narrow perimeters of the camp, amateur and professional musicians often shared the stage. With a program consisting of lieder by Ludwig van Beethoven, Franz Schubert, and Robert Schumann—as well as composers forbidden or persecuted by the Nazis, including Max Kowalski, Edvard Moritz, and the Schreker student Isco Thaler from Bohorodchany in Galicia who was interned in Ferramonti—it embraced European art music in a holistic and integrative way. An encore performance, with slightly different repertoire, was given on April 14. In absentia of a keyboard instrument, Zins again accompanied on the accordion.

A decisive impulse for further musical activities came with the arrival of Yugoslav prisoners, among them the conductor Lav Mirski (1893–1968) on October 26, 1941, and several singers during the winter of 1941/1942. As duly documented by Sonnenfeld in his memoirs, shortly after his arrival Mirski assembled a choir, which sang regularly during Jewish services, Friday evenings, and Saturday mornings, with tenor Rudi Marton, baritone Bruno Weiss, and bass Michael Adler taking over the solo. As Sonnenfeld put it with a rhetoric of spiritual resistance: "one almost did not have the impression of being interned at all. . . . Especially the psalm, Adonaj malakh remained unforgettable for us."[32] But such perspective also warrants caution. As Shirli Gilbert writes in *Music in the Holocaust*, a descent into sentimentality and mythicization could lead to unrealistic assumptions and ahistorical narratives.[33]

According to Sonnenfeld, there had already been music in worship before Mirski's arrival—documented for a bar mitzvah—but not with an organized choir and conductor. Over time the choir grew and began to concertize, a development deemed by Sonnenfeld as "quite incredible" (Figure 26.1). The choir, then consisting of about forty male voices, also appeared in concert, such as on March 8, 1942, deemed one of the most significant events taking place in the camp due to its scale. It featured repertoire by canonical composers such as Beethoven's "Die Ehre Gottes aus der Natur" (from the six

FIGURE 26.1 The choir of Ferramonti, with its founder Lav Mirski (back row, on the right), Israel Kalk Collection, "II. Ferramonti di Tarsia: Il campo di Ferramonti di Tarsia, 1940–1943: Fotografie con didascalie in italiano," album 6, p. 38. Reproduced by permission of the Historical Archive, Fondazione Centro di Documentazione Ebraica Contemporanea, Milan.

songs op. 48, after Christian Fürchtegott Gellert) as well as Schubert's hymn *Hymnus an den heiligen Geist*, D.748, and an unspecified *Sanctus* (presumably from the *Deutsche Messe*, D.872 in light of its German text and arrangement by Fritz Spies, who did not arrange any other Mass parts). Right after these works, which would be well suited for a Catholic service, two arrangements of liturgical texts were programmed as well: a setting of Adonai malakh (Psalm 93) by Samuel Naumbourg (possibly the same that Sonnenfeld had mentioned in conjunction with synagogue service), and a setting of the Yigdal by Mirski himself, which concluded the first part of the concert. Sprinkled in were the "Winzerchor" from Mendelssohn's unfinished opera *Die Lorelei* and the "Pilgerchor" from Wagner's *Tannhäuser*—one by a composer forbidden by Nazis, the other fully embraced.

Apparently, the choir also formed subdivisions, with mainly Slovenian singers appearing in Catholic services and Bruno Weiss, Paul Gorin, and Elly Laqueur Silberstein singing solo, accompanied by a harmonium. A female choir had been planned as well, but the escalation of war events apparently prevented its formation.[34] A pivotal point for the male choir came on April 5, 1942, Easter Sunday, when it sang a Stabat Mater under the baton of Mirski to great acclaim. According to Calliste Lopinot, several of the Jewish singers participated as well.[35] As Kalk reported, part of the Jewish community was disturbed by this and Mirski justified his action with the assertion that although he himself is a practicing Jew, he is also an artist, and thus the direction of a choir in a church would not invalidate his Jewishness. The choristers advanced the same argument; and while rooted in their self-understanding as musicians, it is also a testament of religious tolerance (as is the Catholics' acceptance of Jews singing in a choir on Easter and other holidays). Indeed, religious celebrations were open to the whole community of prisoners regardless of their beliefs. But not everybody embraced this. With regard to the Easter Sunday service, Cantor Isaac Weiss argued that his conscience would not allow him to continue the Jewish services if the choir did not expel the singers who appear in the church.[36] The debates led to the split of the community and the foundation of a third synagogue by and for the Orthodox Jews (the Betar group had created their own space for services before). It is unclear how matters settled in the long run, but on Monday, September 7, 1942, the choir gave a so-called Yom Kippur concert under the direction of Mirski (it took place just a few days before the High Holidays).[37] Still, the musical experiences of that year attest to the fact that inmates placed value in Jewish-liturgical music, regardless of their level of observance.

A musical turning point came on May 19, 1942, with the arrival of a harmonium, which the Vatican sent from Lecco on request of the Catholic authority at the camp.[38] In absentia of a Catholic pianist or organist, Sonnenfeld accompanied the small choir that sang during worship; as mentioned in his memoirs, he also played works by Girolamo Frescobaldi and preludes and fugues by Johann Sebastian Bach. Whether the harmonium was used during Jewish worship is unknown. But keyboard instruments were surely in high demand given the presence of a number of pianists, among them Isco Thaler, Anita Falk Hoffmann, Ladislav Sternberg, and the young Leon Levitch.[39] By July 1942 the prisoners had access to a grand piano, brought into the camp by the Mensa dei Bambini. With this arrival the pianists had an instrument to practice and to teach, and musical activities could now diversify. Photographs attest to other instruments being used in the camp, especially string instruments such as the violin, guitar, and mandolin.[40] And Isco Thaler founded a small ensemble of five instrumentalists, which he conducted. Some musicians received the necessary upkeep and repairs for their instruments from the local luthiers Nicola and Vincenzo De Bonis of Bisignano, an attestation to the aforementioned contacts with the outside world, but also a sign that the prisoners had funds available. Indeed, prisoners received financial support from families and also were paid a small stipend from the regime.

Of the documented performances that took place between March 1941 and the discontinuance of Ferramonti as a concentration camp in the fall of 1943, one was a decidedly Jewish expression. It took place in the so-called Allgemeiner Tempel, on the third day of Hanukkah, on December 6, 1942, at two-thirty in the afternoon, and was followed by a religious service with choral music. The concert featured an appropriate program for the occasion. It began with a children's choir singing the "Al ha-nisim" (About the miracles), a prayer of gratitude added to the Amidah and Birkat hamazon that thanked God for saving the Jewish people. Here it was sung in a German translation by the twelve-year-old Paul Hirsch, thus catering to the German-speaking Jewish prisoners. The subsequent part, called "Hanukkah in der Kwuzah"—referring to an intimate communal meeting or group and as such designating the earliest form of small, voluntary, agricultural, collective community before the rise of the kibbutz—featured the children singing other well-known Hanukkah songs, in Hebrew: "Mi yimalel gevurot Yisrael?" (Who will speak of the valorous acts of Israel?), a secular rewording of Psalm 106:2, and "Hayo haya melekh rasha" (Once there was an evil king), which retell the holiday's story—as well as a Hebrew song of the pioneers or halutsim, "Anu nihyeh harishonim" (We shall be the first). The children then sang in different groupings "Yeled ḳat," a song about a little boy celebrating Hanukkah. The most central prayer of the holiday, Maoz tsur, ensued—all under the direction of Lav Mirski and accompanied by Brčko-born Ladislav Sternberg on piano. Thereafter came a dramatization of the biblical episode of David and Goliath, a "small ballet" (Reigenspiel) by the smallest children, followed by three songs that related life in Palestine: the workers' song "Shir ha-emeḳ" (Song of the valley music by Daniel Sambursky, lyrics by Nathan Alterman), a nigun, and "Nihyeh kulanu halutsim" (When all of us pioneers). Speeches followed and the concert closed with the "Hatikvah," at the time still the Zionist anthem and an expression of Jewish unity. The event displayed two pillars of Jewish identity through song: traditional practices associated with the holiday and Zionism—both interlinked through the notion of victory.[41] As such, it also attests to the education of children and youth by older prisoners, instilling in them a sense of their Jewish heritage through song. Singing lessons and choral music were part of their education in the camp, alongside foreign languages, science, and other subjects, bearing testimony of the forward-looking efforts spent to cultivate the youth, both as individuals and as a growing community.

But these and other activities would face a rupture. Half a year later, in early summer of 1943, the fascist Ministry of the Interior planned the relocation of the prisoners from

Ferramonti farther north to Fossoli. They were an added burden on a country already deep in financial crisis. This move would have ultimately condemned them to *ḥurban*, a destiny that many other prisoners faced after the dismantlement of the camps in Central and Southern Italy, among them those who had been interned in Urbisaglia, which after September 1943 fell into the hands of the Nazis (of the prisoners who were deported via Fossoli to Auschwitz, only Pollak survived).[42] This plan, however, did not materialize.

THE DISPLACED PERSONS CAMP (SEPTEMBER 1943 TO DECEMBER 1945)

On July 25, 1943, the king of Italy and the Grand Council of Fascism deposed Mussolini, and secret negotiations for an armistice with the Allies ensued. But war operations threatened Ferramonti on several occasions, such as on August 27, when a Canadian plane flew over the area and bombed the site, causing the death of four prisoners, wounding eleven, and setting two of the barracks on fire.[43] Events accelerated with the surrender of Italy to the Allies on September 8, 1943. By that time, Anglo-Canadian forces had already disembarked in Sicily from their North African bases, crossed the Strait of Messina, and began landing in the southernmost tip of Calabria. Ferramonti was officially liberated by the Eighth Battalion of the British Army on September 14. More than half of the survivors fled the site to surrounding areas, but the other half remained. Indeed, the withdrawing German troops in September and October still posed great danger to the Jews, as did the civil war consuming Italy. With the Allies' dismantling of the bureaucratic structures of the "first Ferramonti," it became a Displaced Persons camp under the auspices of the Welfare Commission of the Allied Military government in the Occupied Territories. The "second Ferramonti," under Anglo-American control, was born. As such Ferramonti was the first camp to have a purpose as a Displaced Persons camp. Lengthy investigations and trials did not take place there, in part because Lav Mirski, who in light of the self-governance of the survivors now served as its director (Sonnenfeld took over the musical directorship), did not see any cause as no atrocities had been committed.

Although between September 1943 and the end of 1944 Ferramonti's population shrunk by half, it was home to one of the largest and most active Jewish communities in Italy at the time. The survivors established a more structured system by quickly setting up small businesses and enhancing social and cultural services. The changes led to improvements in several aspects of everyday life; it also affected the musical practices, with an increased number of performances taking place. But more so, music making was no longer confined to being behind barbed wire. This new gained freedom is obvious in a charity concert the inmates organized on November 9, 1943. Called *Concerto per i sinistrati*, it stood under the patronage of the Allied Command and was intended to raise funds for people injured in the Royal Air Force's bombings of Cosenza on April

12, that year.[44] Unlike previous events organized by the musicians, this concert took place at the Cinema Italia in Cosenza, under the direction of Mirski and with Sternberg on piano. It featured a program of Italian favorites with popular arias from the operas of Umberto Giordano, Puccini, and Verdi. But sprinkled in were also composers born Jewish such Mendelssohn and Meyerbeer. The Polish bass Jeremias Metzger (1903–?) sang an unspecified aria from Halévy's *La juive* (possibly "Rachel, quand du Seigneur"), the only piece with a more overt Jewish association. Clearly the concert was geared toward a different audience: the inhabitants of Cosenza.

In a bitter twist of fate, just days after this concert the Italian Social Republic drafted a manifesto, the Carta di Verona of November 14–16, 1943, declaring all Jews foreign enemies regardless of their previous citizenship and thereby facilitating the confiscation of property and deportation. Even though the Italian Social Republic constituted itself in the northern part of Italy, racial persecutions were exacerbated throughout Italy. In Ferramonti the survivors, under the protection of the British, remained relatively safe. Being in a transitory state, they continued with their activities, including musical events. A concert on March 22, 1944, is noteworthy as it highlighted Austrian music performed by Jewish musicians mostly from Vienna, a clear turn to their place of origin, a reimagining of home in reaction to displacement, a bearing of zekher as a significant connection between music and displacement.

Perhaps during this phase, the undated parodies of Viennese songs by Hermann Leopoldi, Hans Lang, and Fritz Spielmann with lyrics in German originated. Through slang terms, substitution of toponyms, use of nicknames to point to fellow inmates, hyperboles, and the abundant use of figurative language, they present scenes of ordinary life in Ferramonti, specifically with reference to the black market and the illegal trade of goods ("In einem Cafe in Hernals") and gambling ("Schön ist so ein Kartenspiel"), but also the desire to leave Ferramonti and seek fortune elsewhere. These songs could have been conceived during either phase of the camp, and yet given that gambling had been prohibited then and leaving the site was not possible, it is likely that these songs originated after September 1943. With regard to their themes and function, they compare to similar songs conceived in Terezín and the transit camp of Westerbork.[45] To be sure, the songs were not merely intended for amusement. The refrain of "Schinkenfleckerl" (Hams and noodle casserole), for instance, addresses the recurring problem of starvation. And yet the consciousness of a shared condition, simultaneously as survivors and Displaced Persons, found expression in other self-representational performances and song lyrics of cabaret and varieté, magic numbers, revues, theatrical sketches, and similar forms of entertainment (also common practices in the Bergen-Belsen Displaced Persons camp),[46] which increased in their frequency and relevance in the second historical phase of Ferramonti.

In this regard, a Hanukkah event on December 10 and a Purim event on February 26, 1945, are noteworthy as two seemingly pronounced expressions of Jewishness, although the programs nuance this assumption. The Hanukkah celebration of 1944 resembled all but the event taking place two years prior. It featured piano solos by Anita Falk Hoffmann, who performed an Andante by Beethoven and a waltz by Chopin.

Sonnenfeld accompanied the ball following the formal program (in the Purim celebration organized by the Zionists, he was replaced by Manfred Eisenhardt) as Sternberg had already left the camp, playing concerts in the South of Italy before leaving for Palestine. Annie Lazar sang one unnamed song and one Yiddish song. There were hardly any traditional Hanukkah songs, save for the Maoz tsur sung by the children's choir. The "Hatikvah" was programmed as the closing piece of the first part of the program, which formed the official Hanukkah celebration. The same is true for the Purim event, which featured a very similar program.

Thereafter activities began to disintegrate. Lav Mirski had already left for Palestine in May 1944, together with over two hundred other survivors (the first emigration transport authorized by the British mandatory government), and Sonnenfeld took over the direction of the choir during Catholic and Jewish worship. In the summer, 982 Jews were transferred to the Fort Ontario Emergency Refugee Shelter in Oswego, New York: among them the young Leon Levitch (he founded a youth choir with "some leftover from Ferramonti," i.e., members of the Zionist youth organization, and harmonized folk—including Zionist—tunes he had learned in Italy, but considering himself "politically kind of apolitical").[47] With many musicians gone, Kurt Sonnenfeld had the piano to himself. In a letter to him, written in March 1945 from Salerno by the Romanian clinician and amateur violinist Joseph Lax (1905–1990), the former internee called Ferramonti a "cursed place."[48] He encouraged Sonnenfeld to move as well. In September 1945 Sonnenfeld left Ferramonti for Milan, hopeful that he could resume his career as conductor and composer there. Three months later the camp was abandoned.

TOWARD A SITE OF REMEMBRANCE

As differentiated from concentration camps such as Auschwitz, Buchenwald, or Sachsenhausen, music in Ferramonti was never used as a means of torture, to humiliate or persecute inmates; it did not accompany punishments or executions. The authorities never superimposed music making. It was not tied to propaganda and did not lead to social inequality as elsewhere.[49] As such music provided agency. Musical performances in Ferramonti served relaxation and recreation, the spiritual overcoming of the war experience. They were a form of expressing the will to live under extreme conditions—with their repertoires representing individual and collective identities, Jewish or other, in concert, worship, and school. As the first Hanukkah event reveals, Jewish identity could be performed freely through traditional holiday songs, Zionist songs, in Hebrew or in German. There were no restrictions to the (musical) expression of Jewishness during much of the first phase of the site. The same is true for events that did not take place to celebrate a Jewish holiday per se. And yet Ferramonti, with its specific characteristics of location and purpose, followed—with substantial difference in the degree of oppression and, above all, its outcome—the model of other historical cases of segregation of the Jews, such as the ghettos in Papal Rome or occupied Warsaw.

With regard to Jewish music, Ferramonti was a place of in-betweenness, which becomes obvious during its second phase as a Displaced Persons camp. Surprisingly, after officially gaining "freedom," the second Hanukkah event points to a reversal of displaying Jewish identity through music, save for the "Hatikvah," as the only common denominator. If liberation led to a greater variety of performances representing the tastes of the acculturated Jews of Central Europe, this expression extended into the Jewish realm as evident in the mainstream classical music repertoire during the Hanukkah event, where Jewish musical expressions were nearly absent.

As such, the two Hanukkah celebrations are diametrical opposites in seemingly oblique contexts. They reveal different approaches to Judaism and the progressive shift from the sacred Jewish tradition to the secular Hebrew culture. As Yael Zerubavel asserts in her analysis of the transformation of the holiday cycle, the Zionist Jews sought to underrate the religious character of traditional Jewish feasts in order to emphasize their national-political meaning.[50] The reinterpretation of Hanukkah as the celebration of human rather than divine success in liberating the Maccabees from oppressors unfolds in Ferramonti, and more specifically in the choice of Zionist Hanukkah songs in the 1942 program. Additionally, the programs reveal that during the oppressive phase Jewish music was emphasized and after liberation deemphasized. Reasons for this might be found in the changing demographics of the internees after liberation, or in the fact that their trajectory more clearly began to point toward the future, as artists came predominantly from mainstream musical venues and hoped to return to them.

Thereafter a third Ferramonti surfaces, one of the survivors who remember it and of zekher, prefigured as such in the last line of the aforementioned *Ferramonti-Walzer*, which reads "Ferramonti vergessen wir nicht"—a verse in anapestic rhythm, which seems to both urge the duty of collective memorialization and ascertain the impossibility of forgetting. Zekher in its common meaning as "remembrance" finds itself more concretely in the memories of the Ferramonti, and already before 1945. Aside from the above-mentioned comment by Lax, a title page of a printed score of Tomaso Vitali's Chaconne, found among the scores of Ferramonti and played in the camp, bears the dedication "for the happy hours spent together." And there is also a photo on whose backside the Greek archimandrite Damaskinos Hatzopoulos wrote a note in French to thank Lav Mirski for the music, calling the concerts in Ferramonti "bright spots of a very dark age."[51] Looking back, Leon Levitch asserts in a rhetoric of spiritual resistance similar to Sonnenfeld's: "Making music . . . helped us to keep up some kind of a morale . . . otherwise we would all have lost our minds."[52]

Clearly, the efforts of the musicians, regardless of repertoire and level of music making, helped to distract and to preserve dignity at both an individual and a collective level, contributing to a relatively peaceful coexistence of all the groups present at Ferramonti, including the guards. This is not to discount other experiences. In a 2012 interview, Peter Silberstein, son of the soprano Elly Laqueur Silberstein, reported the loss of his sister Ruth, who had suffered mental illness and attempted suicide during internment. She tragically died in an explosion, killed by a grenade, while walking outside the camp just after it was liberated. In light of her traumatic experiences, their mother never returned to the stage again after the war.[53] Aside from personal tragedies, the survivors collectively experienced freezing winters, scorching summers, hunger, and uncertainty. Ferramonti might indeed have been a "cursed place."

Reminiscing from a more distant, twenty-year perspective, Kalk asserts that "the Jews, . . . tempered by adversity, enlivened by a fraternal solidarity, united by the commonality of sufferings, immediately found a self-defense, a secret weapon that allowed them to resist all opposition."[54] He ascribed this to their "genio organizzativo" (organizational genius), which he saw unfold in several areas, among them "la sezione musicale" (the music section) and "il concistoro religioso" (the religious consistory), with the former having helped to maintain the high spirit.[55]

Kalk's retrospective and how he remembered Ferramonti temporally coincided with plans to build a highway that would connect Calabria to the rest of Italy. Prioritizing infrastructure over history and memory, the new motorway bisects Ferramonti. Since its completion in 1974, uncountable numbers of Italians and tourists have rushed through this site, perhaps hearing the sounds of their engine, the noise of the highway, a conversation of fellow travelers, or perhaps music on the radio. And according to author and journalist Paul Paolicelli, who came across Ferramonti in 2002, the local residents did not want to remember what happened there.[56] Around that time, however, Oscar Klein (1930–2006)—a boy at the time of internment who became a world-renowned jazz musician, often collaborating with Mussolini's third son, the jazz pianist Romano Mussolini—planned a commemorative concert on site, which did not come to fruition.[57]

And yet, on April 25, 2004, on Festa della Liberazione (Liberation Day), the national holiday in Italy commemorating the end of the fascist regime and of the Nazi occupation, the Museo della Memoria Ferramonti di Tarsia opened in one of the former barracks, displaying documents and photos. It expanded over the course of the following years. The renovation of the barracks, now painted in warm yellow tones and in some cases rebuilt, underlines Calabria as a "safe haven," and "southern paradise" for Jewish refugees. But such late efforts also cast a shadow. Nonetheless, High Holiday services have taken place there since at least 2019. And as recently as March 11, 2021, the eightieth anniversary of Kurt Sonnenfeld's arrival at the site, the Museo della Memoria celebrated that moment, for being interned at Ferramonti did not lead to death but to "a hope of salvation." Students of the local school presented a musical program. As the museum asserts, "The prisoners' commitment to promoting a dignified life in the camp through democratic relations, attitudes based on solidarity and tolerance, cultural, artistic and sporting institutions and activities has always been alive and well, leaving an indelible mark on the history of the camp and of Europe."[58] The problematic rhetoric of spiritual resistance evident in earlier accounts apparently continued to persist. While civic awareness and commemoration were finally under way, such late efforts often combined with triumphalist and uncritical narratives also cast a shadow.

Be it as it may, in the twenty-first century another symbolic community has emerged at the site of Ferramonti, underlining Anthony Cohen's definition of it being created by outsiders as well as insiders who repeatedly and deeply engage with it, at an analytical and imaginative level.[59] In essence, those who engage with or gather at Ferramonti today form a collective in the imaginary sense, constructed symbolically, with the aim of commemorative or other belonging, relating through the shared meanings of and knowledge about the site, and through the collective ritual of zekher.

Notes

1. Paul Pollak, "Il campo di concentramento d'Urbisaglia (Macerata)," Israel Kalk Collection, "VII. Testimonianze e documentazione," box 6, folder 76, p. 8, Historical Archive, Fondazione Centro di Documentazione Ebraica Contemporanea, Milan. The collection is fully digitalized and can be accessed at http://digital-library.cdec.it/cdec-web/storico/det ail/IT-CDEC-ST0006-000000/israel-kalk.html.

2. See Carlo Spartaco Capogreco, "Urbisaglia," in *The United States Holocaust Memorial Museum Encyclopedia of Camps and Ghettos, 1933–1945*, vol. 3: *Camps and Ghettos under European Regimes Aligned with Nazi Germany*, ed. Geoffrey P. Megargee and Joseph R. White (Bloomington: Indiana University Press, 2018), 469–470.

3. ". . . che riuscì magistralmente a far sorvolare su molte ore tristi." Pollak, "Il campo di concentramento d'Urbisaglia (Macerata)," p. 5.

4. ". . . aber wie Sand vor dem Herbststurm / werden wir nach den vier Winden wirbeln / jeder einsam in feindliche Wüsten." Peter Kien, "Ein Psalm aus Babylon" (1941–1945). For a bilingual German-English edition of his poetry, see Ira Rabin and Elena Makarova, eds., *Franz Peter Kien* (Terezín: Pro Památník Terezín vydalo nakl. Oswald, 2009). On the varying perceptions of Terezín, see Amy Lynn Wlodarski, "Musical Memories of Terezín in Transnational Perspective," in *Dislocated Memories: Jews, Music, and Postwar German Culture*, ed. Tina Frühauf and Lily E. Hirsch (New York: Oxford University Press, 2014), 57–72.

5. For a complete account of these camps, see Gina Antoniani Persichilli, "Disposizioni, normative e fonti archivistiche per lo studio dell'internamento in Italia (giugno 1940–luglio 1943)," *Rassegna degli Archivi di Stato* 38, nos. 1–3 (1978): 77–96. For a list of all foreign Jews interned in Italy, see Anna Pizzuti, comp., *Ebrei stranieri internati in Italia durante il periodo bellico*; http://www.annapizzuti.it/database/rubrica.php (accessed June 4, 2021).

6. For further details on Italian legislation against Jews, see Mario Toscano, *Ebraismo e antisemitismo in Italia: Dal 1848 alla guerra dei sei giorni* (Milan: Franco Angeli, 2003); Enzo Collotti, *Il fascismo e gli ebrei: Le leggi razziali in Italia* (Bari: Laterza, 2003); and Marie-Anne Matard-Bonucci, *L'Italia fascista e la persecuzione degli ebrei* (Bologna: Il Mulino, 2016).

7. See Michele Sarfatti, *Mussolini contro gli ebrei: Cronaca dell'elaborazione delle leggi del 1938* (Turin: Zamorani, 1994), 158.

8. See Michele Sarfatti, *The Jews in Mussolini's Italy: From Equality to Persecution*, trans. Anne C. Tedeschi and John Tedeschi (Madison: University of Wisconsin Press, 2006), 129–131.

9. See Klaus Voigt, *Il rifugio precario: Gli esuli in Italia dal 1933 al 1945*, trans. Loredana Melissari (Florence: La Nuova Italia, 1996). See also the German original, *Zuflucht auf Widerruf: Exil in Italien, 1933–1945*, 2 vols. (Stuttgart: Klett-Cotta, 1989).

10. Michael R. Ebner, *Ordinary Violence in Mussolini's Italy* (New York: Cambridge University Press, 2010), 3.

11. See Dan Stone, *Fascism, Nazism and the Holocaust: Challenging Histories* (Abingdon: Routledge, 2021), 187.

12. On the revision of this stereotype, see Filippo Focardi, *Il cattivo tedesco e il bravo italiano: La rimozione delle colpe della seconda guerra mondiale* (Bari: Laterza, 2013).

13. For further details on the Italian Social Republic, see Amedeo Osti Guerrazzi, *Storia della Repubblica Sociale Italiana* (Rome: Carocci, 2012).

14. For a full account on Fossoli, see Danilo Sacchi, *Fossoli: Transito per Auschwitz—Quella casa davanti al campo di concentramento* (Florence: Giuntina, 2002).

15. For recent literature on the subject, see Carlo Spartaco Capogreco, *Mussolini's Camps: Civilian Internment in Fascist Italy (1940–1943)*, trans. Norma Bouchard and Valerio Ferme (Abingdon: Routledge, 2019); and Simon Levis Sullam, *The Italian Executioners: The Genocide of the Jews of Italy* (Princeton, NJ: Princeton University Press, 2018).

16. See Carlo Spartaco Capogreco, "Ferramonti di Tarsia," in *The United States Holocaust Memorial Museum Encyclopedia of Camps and Ghettos, 1933–1945*, vol. 3: *Camps and Ghettos under European Regimes Aligned with Nazi Germany*, ed. Geoffrey P. Megargee and Joseph R. White (Bloomington: Indiana University Press, 2018), 424–426.

17. See the report of Mario Collina, March 3, 1942, Ministero dell'interno, Direzione generale Pubblica Sicurezza, series AA.GG.RR., cat. M4–16, box 26, Archivio Centrale dello Stato, Rome. See also Carlo Spartaco Capogreco, *Ferramonti: La vita e gli uomini del più grande campo d'internamento fascista* (Florence: La Giuntina, 1987), 40–41.

18. See Persichilli, "Disposizioni," 80–81.

19. Michele Sarfatti has proposed a distinction between two phases of terror against the Jews in Italy: one before July 1943, when the rights of the Jews were threatened ("the period of attack on Jewish rights"), and the second after September 8, 1943, when the lives of many Jews were in danger ("the period of attack on Jewish life"); see *La Shoah in Italia: La persecuzione degli ebrei sotto il fascismo* (Turin: Einaudi, 2005), 75.

20. James Loeffler, "Why the New 'Holocaust Music' Is an Insult to Music—and the Victims of the Shoah," *Tablet*, July 11, 2013.

21. Similar activities in Italian camps are also documented in Campagna, Alberobello, and Urbisaglia, among others. See Raffaele Deluca's *Tradotti agli estremi confini: Musicisti ebrei internati nell'Italia fascista* (Milan: Mimesis, 2019).

22. See Kurt Sonnenfeld, "La vita musicale a Ferramonti di Tarsia," Israel Kalk Collection, "II. Ferramonti di Tarsia: Istituzioni culturali e artistiche," box 2, folder 25, pp. 37–47, Historical Archive, Fondazione Centro di Documentazione Ebraica Contemporanea, Milan. All programs of the concerts performed in Ferramonti and sheet music discussed in this chapter can be found in the same folder.

23. The diary is published as "Diario 1941–1944, Ferramonti-Tarsia," in *Ferramonti: Un lager nel sud—Atti del convegno internazionale di studi: 15/16 maggio 1987*, ed. Francesco Volpe (Cosenza: Orizzonti meridionali, 1990), 156–207.

24. There are several shorter accounts of musical activities, such as by Siegfried Kuttner, Israel Kalk Collection, "II. Ferramonti di Tarsia: Istituzioni culturali e artistiche," box 2, folder 25, pp. 5–17; Walter Berent, 1656/3/9/66, pp. 13–18, The Wiener Holocaust Library, London; and David Henry Ropschitz, *Ferramonti: Salvation Behind the Barbed Wire*, ed. Yolanda Ropschitz-Bentham (La Vergne: Grosvenor House, 2002).

25. On music making in concentration camps, including a literature review, see Guido Fackler, "Cultural Behaviour and the Invention of Traditions: Music and Musical Practices in the Early Concentration Camps, 1933–6/7," *Journal of Contemporary History* 45, no. 3 (July 2010): 601–627. For a more recent literature review, see also Juliane Brauer, "How Can

Music Be Torturous? Music in Nazi Concentration and Extermination Camps," *Music and Politics* 10, no. 1 (Summer 2016): 1–34.

26. See Sophie Fetthauer, *Musik und Theater im DP-Camp Bergen-Belsen: Zum Kulturleben der jüdischen Displaced Persons 1945–1950* (Neumünster: von Bockel, 2012); and Tina Frühauf and Lily E. Hirsch, eds. *Dislocated Memories: Jews, Music, and Postwar German Culture* (New York: Oxford University Press, 2014).

27. See Bret Werb, "'Vu ahin zol ikh geyn?': Music Culture of Jewish Displaced Persons," in Frühauf and Hirsch, *Dislocated Memories*, 75–96.

28. See Joshua S. Walden, "'Driven from Their Home': Jewish Displacement and Musical Memory in the 1948 *Movie Long Is the Road*," in Frühauf and Hirsch, *Dislocated Memories*, 121–140.

29. See Mario Rende, *Ferramonti di Tarsia: Voci di un campo di concentramento fascista 1940–1945* (Milan: Mursia, 2009), 71–74.

30. See Ernst Bernhard to Dora Bernhard, January 20, 1941, in *Lettere a Dora dal campo di internamento di Ferramonti (1940–41)*, ed. Luciana Marinangeli (Turin: Aragno, 2011).

31. See Sonnenfeld, "La vita musicale a Ferramonti di Tarsia".

32. "Man hatte fast gar nicht [den] Eindruck interniert zu sein. . . . Besonders der Psalm, 'Adonaj Maloch' blieb uns unvergesslich." Ibid., 39.

33. See Shirli Gilbert, *Music in the Holocaust: Confronting Life in the Nazi Ghettos and Camps* (Oxford: Oxford University Press, 2005), 14–16.

34. See Sonnenfeld, "La vita musicale a Ferramonti di Tarsia," 39.

35. See Rende, *Ferramonti di Tarsia*, 112.

36. See untitled and undated typescript, Israel Kalk Collection, "II. Ferramonti di Tarsia: Vita religiosa ebraica," box 2, folder 26, p. 46, Historical Archive, Fondazione Centro di Documentazione Ebraica Contemporanea, Milan.

37. See also Rende, *Ferramonti di Tarsia*, 124.

38. The harmonium was manufactured in Borgo Valsugana (Trento) by Egidio Galvan. See Lopinot, "Diario," May 19, 1942. The harmonium is still extant and housed at the Capuchin Monastery in Cosenza. On the instrument and its features, see Antonio Carlini and Mirko Saltori, *Cent'anni di musica a Borgo: Le armoniche di Egidio Galvan, 1901–1944* (Borgo Valsugana: Amici della musica, 2001). See also Rende, *Ferramonti di Tarsia*, 115, 120, 169.

39. At the time a teenager, Leon Levitch (1927–2014) received piano lessons from Otto Strauss and instruction in four-part harmony by Isco Thaler; according to his own accord, he "was not considered as a member of the 'professional' musical community." Thomas Bertonneau, "Interview of Leon Levitch: A Twentieth Century Romantic Temperament— L'artiste doit aimer," Center for Oral History Research, University of California–Los Angeles, 1984, p. 38, https://oralhistory.library.ucla.edu/catalog/21198-zz0015vgm2 (accessed on June 12, 2021).

40. See Israel Kalk Collection, "II. Ferramonti di Tarsia: Il campo di Ferramonti di Tarsia: Fotografie con didascalie di Israel Kalk in italiano, yiddish e inglese," album 5, Historical Archive, Fondazione Centro di Documentazione Ebraica Contemporanea, Milan.

41. On the relationship between Zionism and Hanukkah as well as other Jewish holidays, see Yael Zerubavel, *Recovered Roots: Collective Memory and the Making of Israeli National Tradition* (Chicago: University of Chicago Press, 1995), 18 and 126.

42. About Urbisaglia, see Giovanna Salvucci, "Il campo di internamento di Urbisaglia (1940–1943)," in *Carissimi Primo, Anne ed Elie: Studi e interventi per la Memoria della Shoah*

nelle università, nelle scuole e nei musei d'Italia, ed. Clara Ferranti (Macerata: Edizioni Università di Macerata 2004), 235–248; and Roberto Cruciani, *E vennero 50 anni di libertà, 1943–1993: Campi di concentramento, prigionieri di guerra, internamento libero nelle Marche, 1940–1945* (Macerata: Cooperativa Artivisive,1993).

43. See Capogreco, *Ferramonti,* 146.

44. See Lopinot, "Diario," April 12, 1943. See also Rende, *Ferramonti di Tarsia,* 133.

45. See Ulrike Migdal, ed., *Und die Musik spielt dazu: Chansons und Satiren aus dem KZ Theresienstadt* (Munich: Piper, 1986); and Edward Hafer, "Cabaret and the Art of Survival at the Concentration Camp Westerbork," in *Colloque "Musique et camps de concentration": Conseil de l'Europe 7–8 novembre 2013,* ed. Amaury du Closel (Strasbourg: Council of Europe, 2015), 145–163.

46. See Fetthauer, *Musik und Theater im DP-Camp Bergen-Belsen;* and "The Kazet-Teater and the Development of Yiddish Theater in the DP Camp Bergen-Belsen," in Frühauf and Hirsch, *Dislocated Memories,* 97–120.

47. Thomas Bertonneau, "Interview of Leon Levitch," 59.

48. "Vedo molta gente qui che era con noi a Ferramonti. Hanno tutti un buon aspetto e si 'arrangiano' bene. Spero ormai di rivederti presto. Abbi coraggio. Prendi le tue poche cose e parti da quel luogo maledetto. Vedrai che qui è più bello e rimpiangerai ogni giorno in più del necessario che hai trascorso là." Deluca, *Tradotti agli estremi confini,* 157.

49. See also Gilbert, *Music in the Holocaust,* 23.

50. See Yael Zerubavel, *Recovered Roots: Collective Memory and the Making of Israeli National Tradition* (Chicago: University of Chicago Press, 1995), 218.

51. ". . . [les] points lumineux d'une époque très obscure," Israel Kalk Collection, ""II. Ferramonti di Tarsia: Il campo di Ferramonti di Tarsia, 1940–1943: Fotografie con didascalie in italiano," album 6, p. 26, Historical Archive, Fondazione Centro di Documentazione Ebraica Contemporanea, Milan.

52. Thomas Bertonneau, "Interview of Leon Levitch," 41.

53. See Peter Silberstein (Silton), interviewed by Lauren Taylor, July 13, 2012, https://www.parc hiletterari.com/eventi-scheda.php?ID=05941 (accessed April 19, 2023).

54. "Gli ebrei invece, temprati dalla avversità, vivificati da una fraterna solidarietà, uniti dalla comunanza delle sofferenze, hanno subito trovato un'autodifesa, un'arma segreta che ha permesso loro di reistere a tutte contrarietà." Israel Kalk, "I campi di concentramento italiani per ebrei profughi: Ferramonti di Tarsia (Calabria)," in *Gli ebrei in Italia durante il fascismo,* ed. Paolo Foa, Quaderni della Federazione Giovanile Ebraica d'Italia 1 (Sala Bolognese: Forni Editore, 1961), 67.

55. See ibid., 67–68.

56. See Paul Paolicelli, *Under the Southern Sun: Stories of the Real Italy and the Americans it Created* (New York: St. Martin's Press, 2003), 101.

57. See Riccardo Schwamenthal, "Oscar Klein. Storia e cronaca," *Il sismografo: Bollettino della SISMA,* no. 29 (1999): 23–26.

58. "Sempre vivo è stato il loro [dei prigionieri] impegno a favorire nel Campo una vita dignitosa con relazioni democratiche, con atteggiamenti improntati a solidarietà e tolleranza, con istituzioni ed attività culturali, artistiche e sportive, lasciando nella storia del Campo e della Europa una traccia indelebile." Museo della Memoria Ferramonti di Tarsia, https://www.campodiferramonti.it/2021/03/09/ferramonti-day-11-marzo-1941-11-marzo-2021/ (accessed June 4, 2021)

59. See Anthony Cohen, *Symbolic Construction of Community* (London: Routledge 1985), 13.

SELECT BIBLIOGRAPHY

Capogreco, Carlo Spartaco. *I campi del Duce: L'internamento civile nell'Italia fascista (1940–1943)*. Turin: Einaudi, 2004.

Carapella, Eleonora. "Musicisti ebrei nell'Italia delle persecuzioni: Il caso Aldo Finzi." In *Italian Music during the Fascist Period*, edited by Roberto Illano, 301–329. Speculum Musicae. Turnhout: Brepols, 2004.

Carrieri, Alessandro, and Annalisa Capristo, eds. *Italian Jewish Musicians and Composers under Fascism: Let Our Music Be Played*. Basingstoke: Palgrave MacMillan, 2021.

De Felice, Renzo. *The Jews in Fascist Italy: A History*. Translated by Robert L. Miller. New York: Enigma Books, 2001.

Deluca, Raffaele. "Musik und Musiker im italienischen Lager Ferramonti." *mr-Mitteilungen*, no. 91 (2016): 7–17.

Deluca, Raffaele. *Tradotti agli estremi confini: Musicisti ebrei internati in Italia*. Milan: Mimesis, 2019.

Del Zoppo, Silvia. "Beiträge süddeutscher und österreichischer jüdischer Gefangener: Zum Musikalischen Leben in einem faschistischen Internierungslager: Die Fallstudie von Ferramonti Di Tarsia." In *Jüdische Musik im süddeutschen Raum / Mapping Jewish Music in Southern Germany*, edited by Claus Bockmaier and Tina Frühauf, 173–188. Musikwissenschaftliche Schriften Der Hochschule für Musik und Theater München 16. Munich: Allitera-Verlag, 2021.

Del Zoppo, Silvia. *Ferramonti: Interpreting Cultural Behaviors and Musical Practices in a Southern-Italian Internment Camp*. Frankfurt am Main: Peter Lang, 2021.

Del Zoppo, Silvia. "Suoni da Ferramonti: Lagermusik come esperienza corale in un campo di internamento fascista." In *Music, Individuals and Contexts: Dialectical Interactions*, edited by Alessandro Cosentino, Giacomo Sciommeri, and Nadia Amendola, 535–544. Rome: Universitalia, 2019.

Klein, Shira. *Italy's Jews from Emancipation to Fascism*. Cambridge: Cambridge University Press, 2018.

Nicolodi, Fiamma. *Musica e musicisti nel ventennio fascista*. Scandicci: Discanto, 1984.

Picciotto Fargion, Liliana. *Il libro della memoria: gli ebrei deportati dall'Italia (1943–1945)*. Milan: Mursia, 2002.

Rende, Mario. *Ferramonti di Tarsia: Voci da un campo di concentramento fascista 1940–1945*. Milan: Mursia, 2009.

Rosenberg, Jesse. "Race, Religion, and Jewish Identity in the Operas of Fascist Italy." *Journal of Jewish Identities* 10, no. 1 (2017): 105–129.

Sachs, Harvey. *Music in Fascist Italy*. London: Weidenfeld and Nicolson 1987.

Zuccotti, Susan. *The Italians and the Holocaust: Persecution, Rescue, and Survival*. New York: Basic Books, 1987.

27

"I SAY SHE IS A *MUṬRIBA*"

Faded Memories of Aleppo's Jewish Women Musicians

CLARA WENZ

IN 2012, *Darkhey "Eretz"*, the journal of the Tel Aviv–based World Center for Aleppo Jews Traditional Culture, published a Hebrew article entitled "Sipura shel asirat Zion Naziha Assis" (The story of the prisoner of Zion Naziha Assis). The article opens with a scene said to have occurred in 1962 during a cold night in the Syrian city of Aleppo. Two impoverished Jewish women—a mother and her daughter—are walking side by side through the dark alleys of their neighborhood. The father has already died and the two sons have moved to Israel, leaving them behind in a city that, as the author, the Syrian-born Israeli painter Avraham Shemi-Shoham describes, feels increasingly alien to them.[1]

Most of Syria's Jews have left the country. Many of their former houses stand abandoned or are inhabited by newly arrived, non-Jewish residents, and the movement of Syria's remaining Jewish population is severely restricted. State authorities are frequently imposing travel bans on them, and, with emigration to Israel being strictly illegal, many of those who want to leave the country are forced to pay smugglers to take them over the Turkish border. This is the plan of the two aforementioned women. Determined to leave their hometown of Aleppo, they are on their way to one of their Jewish neighbors, Naziha Assis. She, or so they have heard, would be able to assist them in their journey to Israel—a mission that she eventually accomplishes by convincing a smuggler to help, despite their being unable to pay the required fee, which, according to the author, amounted to three hundred US dollars per person (with Syria's GDP per capita estimated at two hundred twenty-eight dollars at that time,[2] even a middle-class Syrian would have had difficulties to afford this sum).

Born in Aleppo in 1920, Naziha Assis is described by Shemi-Shahom as a "tall and beautiful woman . . . endowed with unbelievable courage."[3] His article provides a detailed account of her life: her apprenticeship with a Jewish seamstress; her marriage to Leon; her role assisting to smuggle Syrian Jews over the Turkish border; her arrest by the Syrian Intelligence Service; the hardship she, her husband, and their eight children endured during the two years she spent in an Aleppian prison; their final escape to Israel in 1978; her subsequent recognition as *Asirat Zion* (Prisoner of Zion) by Israeli State authorities; and her tragic death in 2004 after being kicked by a horse while walking through her new hometown of Jaffa.

In portraying the life of Naziha Assis, the author not only celebrates her contributions and sacrifices to the Zionist project (thereby marking her place within Israel's society and collective national memory), but also depicts a Jewish world in Aleppo that existed separately from its non-Jewish and predominantly Muslim surroundings, with the relations that *did* exist characterized by hostility.[4] Indeed, the article refers to a time in which, following the 1948 war between the newly established state of Israel and many of its surrounding Arab countries, the number of Jews living in Syria had already drastically declined. While a census from 1943 estimated their number at 29,770 (with approximately 17,000 of them living in Aleppo), in the year 1959 this number had declined to only 6,500 (2,000 in Aleppo), with those having stayed facing an environment of increased marginalization.[5]

Yet in the article's depiction of hardship, oppression, and societal discord, there is one paragraph that stands out. Shemi-Shalom describes how, one day back in Aleppo, a Jewish woman named Sarah heard Naziha singing. Immediately fascinated by her voice and beauty, she persuaded Naziha to become a member of her band. As it turned out, Sarah was the leader of an all-women music ensemble that would regularly perform at Muslim women's weddings. And Naziha, who agreed to join her that same night, is said to have given a stunning first performance. As the author describes:

> She wore a red dress, her hair gathered in the back, with two ends of curly hair on her cheeks and earrings in her ear giving her the look of a flamenco dancer. That night, she sang a number of songs in Arabic and with great success.[6]

A (Syrian) Jewish singer performing Arabic songs is, as such, not unusual. Before the mass exodus of Jews from countries such as Syria, Egypt, Lebanon, or Iraq throughout the past century, local music traditions constituted a cultural sphere in which the region's Jewish and (predominantly) Muslim population interacted in an intimate manner. Not only were Jewish singers, instrumentalists, and composers actively involved in the performance and preservation of urban art-music repertoires such as the *qaṣīda*, the *muwashshaḥ*, or the *dawr*—in many cases, these repertoires were actually an integral element of their own religious musical traditions.[7] In Syria, and especially in Aleppo, one of the region's historical centers for the development of urban art music, Hebrew (para)liturgical hymns (the so-called *piyyutim* and *pizmonim*) were frequently structured according to Arab musical forms, modes (maqāmāt, sing. maqām), and/or borrowed melodies from local songs. As illustrated in the writings of ethnomusicologists Kay Kaufman Shelemay and Mark Kligman, this tradition is still being kept alive by Syrian Jews in North and South America, and in Israel today, where it plays a pivotal role in preserving and enacting their communal and cultural memories.[8]

Yet while Shelemay has stated that, within the Syrian-Jewish diasporic context of the United States she explored, "[e]vidently no Ḥalabi [= Aleppian] woman in memory played musical instruments; and only one, Sarah Tawil, has been praised as a singer of extraordinary talent,"[9] the above paragraph reveals a hitherto unacknowledged aspect in the history of Syrian Jewish music-making. Back in Aleppo, it was not only men but also women from the city's Jewish community who were active as musical performers—and not, as one may expect, within the context of Jewish life-cycle events or liturgical traditions, but in a Muslim context and in the sphere of Arab music-making.

Taking the life story of Naziha Assis as its point of departure, this chapter explores the world of Aleppo's Jewish women musicians and the manner in which their eclipsed memory lives on today. It draws on literary and historical sources as well as personal interviews with descendants of Aleppo's former Jewish community in Tel Aviv-Jaffa. Attending to the theme of *zekher*, preliminary understood as remembrance, it considers the reasons that have led to the history of Aleppo's Jewish women singers being largely forgotten, or at least having taken refuge in rather subtle registers. These include a history of conflict between Israel and Syria, religious concerns and condemnations about women performing in public, the association of women's music making with sexual transgression, and the gender dichotomies that characterize approaches within existing scholarship on (Syrian) Jewish music.

All these factors have contributed to a general reluctance to recognize Aleppo's Jewish women musicians (and their Muslim counterparts) as a *musical* community, defined by Shelemay as "a collectivity constructed through and sustained by musical processes and/ or performances."[10] Yet, through the stories and histories that *did* survive in the personal accounts of their descendants and constituencies, their memory not only challenges some of the collective values of a community regarding Jewish women's music making; it also exposes forms of musical belongings that contest the often drawn distinctions (and hierarchies) between "Muslim/Arab" and "Jewish," "male" and "female," "classical" and "vernacular," as well as "public" and "domestic" musical practice.

THE KHŪJAHS OF ALEPPO: A BRIEF INTRODUCTION

In his article, Shemi-Shalom makes no further mention of Naziha's musical activities except to state that she eventually gave up her singing career due to pressure received from a work colleague, despite her insistence on performing for women only, and that after her imprisonment, she refused to ever sing again.[11] Focusing on her contributions to the Israeli national cause, he treats her musical career as a side story. For example, what the article fails to mention is that back in Aleppo, the type of all-women band that Naziha joined was once a common phenomenon and that their members had a special name: they were called *Khūjahs*.

According to the *Comparative Encyclopaedia of Aleppo*, the term *Khūjah* has roots in both the Ottoman and Persian language, where it denotes "sheikh/sheikha" and "master," respectively.[12] In Aleppo, the term has a double meaning. First, it is an honorary title given to a woman who teaches the Quran, and second, it is the name given to the leader of an ensemble of women musicians. According to the encyclopedia, the majority of the latter, *musical* Khūjahs, were Jewish, and their main performance context was that of Muslim women's wedding celebrations, where they are said to have "married off" the bride and taken charge of the wedding procession known as *zaffah*.[13] In a similar vein, an article published by the Syrian media platform *Souriat* on Aleppian wedding rites of the past notes that the Khūjah would sing during the henna celebrations and on the wedding day itself when the bridegroom, returning to his house, passed under an umbrella of swords to be received by his female relatives.[14]

The assertion that, within the past century, many of Aleppo's Khūjahs were Jewish is supported by the Syrian historian Iyād Maḥfūẓ, who reports that most of them lived in Qilleh (pronounced in Aleppian dialect as "'Illeh"). Located in the northwest of the old town, this neighborhood, together with the adjacent quarter Baḥsīta in the south, developed into a predominately Jewish area when, during the sixteenth and seventeenth centuries and under the influx of Sephardic Jews, the city's growing Jewish population expanded westward from the area immediately surrounding the ancient synagogue.[15] Women from all social classes, writes Maḥfūẓ, would go there to employ Khūjahs for their wedding parties:

> those who wanted to enliven their daughters' weddings with a musical ensemble specialized in female entertainment would have to visit the Khūjahs in their houses, especially those living in Qilleh, to negotiate and arrange a price, the number of singers and instrumentalists and whether or not there was going to be a dancer.[16]

Ensembles of Jewish and/or Muslim women performers were not a phenomenon limited to Aleppo but once existed across the Mediterranean, the Middle East, and beyond. Within the Ottoman Empire, especially across the Balkans and Turkey, Sephardic percussionists, singers, and dancers—the so-called *tañaderas*—are said to have participated in life-cycle events and rituals of both Muslim and Jews;[17] in Iraq, Jewish women ensembles of drummers and singers were known as the *daqqaqāt*;[18] and in Central Asia, many of the women wedding and court entertainers—the so-called *sozandas*—belonged to the Bukharan Jewish community.[19]

The society of women musicians whose function and performance context perhaps most closely resembled that of the Khūjahs (despite the vast majority of them being Muslim) were the *'awālim* (sing. *'ālimah*). Literally "learned woman" in Arabic (notice the similar meanings of the Khūjah's and the *'ālimah's* professional title), the *'awālim* were singers and entertainers active in nineteenth- and twentieth-century Egypt. Their musical activities ranged from entertaining women audiences in Harems to performing at Cairo's cabarets and coffeehouses to recording songs for the region's record labels, especially a genre of popular strophic songs known as *ṭaqāṭīq* (sing. *taqṭūqa*), as well as taking part in women's life-cycle or (pre)wedding celebrations. According to Frédéric Lagrange, a well-known expert on Egypt's musical history, the 'awālim often served as "spokesperson" for the brides to be, presenting songs with lyrics that contained advice for the bride's future married life.[20] Moreover, they frequently traveled to Syria for training purposes, especially to Aleppo, where, as he has noted, "they met local Jewish female singers."[21] While he provides no further information on these singers—one can assume that it was Aleppo's Khūjahs whom they met—these encounters, according to Lagrange, facilitated an exchange of repertoires between the Egyptian ṭaqāṭīq and an Aleppian genre of songs known as qudūd, which will be discussed below.

Contrary to the history of the 'awālim, which has received significant scholarly attention, only fragmented information has been transmitted about the musical worlds and history of Aleppo's Jewish Khūjahs and their Muslim and Christian co-performers. The Syrian historians, Muḥammad 'Intābī and Najwa 'Uthmān, acknowledge al-Hajjah 'Āishah al-Muslimānīyah, presumed to be the only recorded name of an Aleppian Muslim Khūjah from the late nineteenth century.[22] And in the memoirs of the Aleppian writer Jamīl Wilāya, one reads that some Khūjahs were notorious for their beautiful voices and "held a special place in the hearts of their [female] admirers."[23]

Jewish Women Musicians: A Blind Spot in the History of Eastern Arab Music

Besides the predominantly Arabic sources already mentioned, the memory of Jewish women performers from Aleppo is largely absent from historical records. There are multiple reasons for this. Not only were their contributions to Aleppo's (male-dominated) musical life largely non-textual and non-recorded, but one can assume that their history was, at times, actively filtered out from the public imagination, for example, by actors from within the Aleppian Jewish community and motivated by (predominantly male) concerns and anxieties over their community's moral reputation. Such concerns will be explored below.

Another plausible reason for the scarcity of sources on the history of Aleppo's Jewish women musicians are the processes of disintegration that resulted from past wars between Israel and many of its surrounding states, including Syria. After their emigration from these states, not only did Jews face a lack of contact with the culture and people left behind, but at times their disintegration also implied the vanishing of their history from their former home countries' public discourse and memory. In other words, it meant that certain members of the region's former Jewish population, especially those who, after 1948, emigrated to Israel, were deliberately "forgotten" by official state authorities.

In the realm of music, the most infamous case took place in 1972, when Saddam Hussein ordered the erasure of the names of the famous al-Kuwaiti brothers—two Jewish composers and musicians who emigrated from Iraq to Israel in 1951—from official radio playlists, music publications, and academic curricula, despite the fact that their music is still being played across the Arab world today.[24] In Syria, as the anthropologist Jonathan Shannon has documented, state authorities, too, enacted a strategy of "willful forgetting" against the country's Jewish population, including its musicians.[25] And while Shannon has pointed out how the legacy of Jewish instrumentalists (such as the Aleppian qanūn-player Ya'qūb and his son Salīm Ghazālah) continues to live on in the private and embodied memories of some of the Syrian musicians he interviewed, none of them seem to have acknowledged the presence of either Jewish vocalists (men or women) or Jewish women performers.

Yet one of Aleppo's Jewish women singers continues to be remembered by at least some Syrians as a great musician of her time: Fairūz al-Ḥalabīyah (1895–1955), also known as Fairūz Mamīsh or Rachel Smocha, who is said to have recorded with local and regional record companies and publicly performed at the al-Shahbander, which, built at the beginning of the twentieth century and located west of Aleppo's Jewish quarter, was once one of the city's most famous musical theaters.[26] Moreover, she is often remembered for having sang before King Faisal I upon his visit to Aleppo in 1920—a story that highlights the role the memory of Jews in the Middle East played and continues to play in the formation of Arab national identities. While it remains unknown whether Fairūz al-Ḥalabīyah was locally referred to as Khūjah, her continued presence in Syrian public memory and scholarly discourse seems to be an exception.

Finally, other factors that have contributed to concealing the history of Aleppo's Khūjahs are existing approaches within academia itself. If, as Edwin Seroussi has stated, women are "the great absent of Jewish music research,"[27] then perhaps the greatest absentee within existing scholarship on the subject is the history of Jewish women's engagement with Arab music or Arabic songs. The trend to disregard women within scholarship on the history of Jewish music, on one hand, and a general lack of engagement with the musical life of Jewish minorities within scholarly material on (Eastern) Arab music, on the other, has resulted in the fact that studies on Jewish women musicians within the Arab world are almost non-existent.[28] This is despite the fact that singers such as Layla Mūrād (Egypt), Fairūz al-Ḥalabīyah (Syria), and Salīma Mūrād (Iraq) are still remembered across the region today.

Studies that *do* focus on the musical cultures of Syrian and especially Aleppian Jews have largely concentrated on text-based liturgy and ritual performances, that is, on a musical heritage that has been codified in Jewish song and prayer books, and which is almost exclusively performed by men. Within this context, scholars have tended to draw a distinction between melody and/or musical form ("Arab/secular") and sacred Hebrew text ("Jewish/religious"). As Shelemay writes with regard to the pizmonim, "the song texts provide insight into a world of explicitly Jewish experience, while the melodies relate primarily to extra-Jewish sources and frames of reference."[29] While serving as a frame for identifying surviving traces of a "Judeo-Arab" musical community,[30] this distinction has filtered out other, non-textual histories of musical interaction, including the participation of Jewish women in Arab music. An exception is Shelemay's article

"The Power of Silent Voices: Women in the Syrian Jewish Musical Tradition," thus far the only existing study on the musical lives of Syrian Jewish women.[31]

Focusing on the absence of active women performers from the pizmonim performance in the Syrian community in Brooklyn, Shelemay works toward uncovering their presence and contributions to the public domain of music making from which they are traditionally excluded. Besides women's representation in song texts, their involvement in ritual and communal contexts, and their preservation of oral histories, she identifies her interlocutors' knowledge of and interest in Arab musical traditions as "one of the most active ways in which they participate in the *pizmon* tradition."[32] Yet she frames this engagement exclusively in terms of women's contribution to transmitting their own community's liturgical traditions and ritual contexts. The case of Aleppo's Khūjahs, by contrast, suggests that Jewish women's knowledge (and practice) of Arabic music tied them not only to their own religious community, but also to places and people *outside* of it.

Café Orange and the Cabarets of Baḥsīta

According to Ivet, one of Naziha's daughters who now lives in Holon on the outskirts of Tel Aviv-Jaffa, women, both Muslim and Christian, including local politicians' wives, would come from near and far to listen to her mother's voice or invite her to their homes to sing at their private parties and life-cycle celebrations. The center of Naziha's musical life, however, was Café Orange, locally known as "'ahwet al-burt'ān." Regarded as one of the oldest cafés in the city and located southwest of Qilleh near a market area referred to as al-Swayqa, the café until recently served as one of Aleppo's most popular locations for women's wedding celebrations. Now in her fifties, Ivet recalls how, as a young child and together with her sisters, she used to accompany her mother to work. She remembers their visits to the café and how they used to watch the celebrations and listen to her mother's *jawqah* (musical troupe), which usually consisted of two Muslims singers as well as an 'ūd-player and a singer/dancer, both of whom were Jewish.

> Outside you had a sign that had "Café Orange" written on it. We would go up the stairs . . . there were a lot of chairs, it was a big salon . . . the chairs were made of wood. Oh, how our backs were aching from those chairs, because we sat there for hours! We would go at seven and stay until three at night! We wouldn't go to school the next day because we were up so late . . . There was more than one singer, so that if one got tired, the other one could sing. . . . it was a big salon and at the end of it was a stage, with the singers and the band, and the groom and the bride would be sitting on it as well. The women would sit and begin to sing their songs for the bride . . . and the party started.[33]

While Naziha performed at weddings and for women only, reports suggest that at least some of Aleppo's Khūjahs were also musically active in places where men and women would mix. According to Iyād Maḥfūẓ, they also performed in the cabarets and musical theaters of Baḥsīta.[34] Located just south of Qilleh, this neighborhood, too, was once predominantly inhabited by Jews. Moreover, it holds a distinct place in the collective memory of Aleppo's inhabitants, including the city's former Jewish population. "Whenever Baḥsīta is mentioned before an Aleppian, they smile," is how the Syrian lawyer 'Ala' Sayyid Sayyid opened his 2008 article on the neighborhood's history.[35] This observation also proved true among Aleppian Jews in Tel Aviv. Indeed, the first time I asked my interlocutors about Baḥsīta, it stirred laughter, especially among women. One giggled, blew out the smoke of her cigarette, and turned to her husband, "She is asking for Baḥsīta!" "Baḥsīta!"; another woman laughed out loud, asking if I knew what was at the center of this neighborhood?

Reminiscent of the French historian Pierre Nora's remarks on "immediate" and "true" memory, which, contrary to forms of commemoration that have been transfigured by their "passage through history," has taken refuge in spontaneous and embodied gestures, habits, and reflexes,[36] my interlocutors' laughter about Baḥsīta sounded out a local history of sexual transgression: besides a busy market area as well as several cabarets and nightclubs, Baḥsīta was also home to Aleppo's infamous red-light district, known locally as Manzūl.[37] 'Ala' Sayyid remembers the Manzūl as one of the places in which Aleppo's Khūjahs were musically active. At the beginning of the twentieth century, he writes in his article, its entrance street featured a cabaret extending over three floors where women dancers and singers—the Khūjahs—would perform. Notwithstanding his assertion that "it was not required of the Khūjahs to engage in prostitution,"[38] their association with "indecency" and Baḥsīta's dubious reputation still haunt the way they are being remembered by members of Aleppo's Jewish community today.

Aliza K., who grew up in Aleppo's old Jewish quarter and today, just like Ivet, lives in Holon, recounts her community's condemning attitudes toward women performers. More than six decades after having left Aleppo as a teenager, she still remembers Khūjah Fairūz (not to be confused with the aforementioned Fairūz al-Ḥalabīyah), the mother of one of her friends, who, back in Aleppo, used to sing and dance in Baḥsīta's cafés and cabarets and at local wedding parties before emigrating to Israel.

> The Jewish communities did not like them [the Khūjahs]. They thought of them badly. The father of my friend was not Jewish, he was Muslim. Her mother [Kūjah Fairūz] fled Aleppo and took all three children with her. She left and took a lot of gold with her. But the Jews in Aleppo did not like her. . . . I say, "This is art, she is a *muṭribah*," but the others said, "It's not good, she goes out with Arabs. . . ." But she was really nice. I loved her very much. Here, when they got to know her, they said dancing and singing is an art. In Aleppo, they did not say that; they did not like it. That's why she worked with Christians and Muslims, not with Jews. And she brought a lot of gold with her. She had an entire bag full . . . ![39]

Indeed, monetary income is a recurring theme in the memory of the Khūjahs, and one may assume that, similar to musicians in Egypt and Jewish singers in Tunisia,[40] it was mostly women born to underprivileged families who took up the profession of performers. For Naziha, her musical expertise, too, provided a way of escaping economic hardship. As she herself recounted in an interview with the social scientist Daniel Monterescu prior to her death in 2004:

> My life didn't start well. At a young age, around six or seven, my parents divorced, and my grandmother raised me. I had no father and my mother was ill. In short, when I was eight years old, I wanted to study, but we had no money. So my grandmother said to me, "Come, I'll teach you a trade." She took me to a dressmaker; I learned very well. I grew up and was sixteen. Then they married me off to someone forty-four years old because I had no parents. My husband took me to Beirut. But after a few months, I got divorced and came back. But I have a talent, I have a musical ear. I hear a melody - I go nuts. I hear Umm Kalthum, 'Abd al-Wahab, Farid al-Atrash. Until then I was a dressmaker at home. I left the sewing, said to my grandmother, "I want to buy a violin." The weddings in Syria were separate [between men and women]. I learned to be with the women. There, the Muslims have music bands that are all women.[41]

According to her daughter, Naziha loved performing so much that she refused to give it up even after she remarried and gave birth to seven daughters and one son:

> It was really hard because she was working at night and had a family. My sisters always had to cook so that she could get a bit of sleep. She was happy but she had eight children. She would work at night and come back in the morning, sleep a bit and then work as a seamstress. She had three jobs. She got so tired. When she worked, they would give her two gold liras.[42]

The cases of Naziha Assis and Khūjah Fairūz suggest that back in Aleppo, there were Jewish women whose engagement with Arab music was less motivated by intra-communal and religious concerns, than anchored in their social and economic relations to the communities that surrounded them. Yet, as expressed by Aliza K., these relations and their work as musicians were often negatively perceived, at least by some members of their own community.

MUSIC AT THE MARGINS: THE KHŪJAHS' PLACE IN ALEPPIAN JEWISH MEMORY

Condemning attitudes toward women singers, especially those performing before a male audience, is a theme that prevails throughout much of musical history (not only) in the Middle East. While in Aleppo, as elsewhere in the region, prohibitions on women's public music-making often varied according to a family's socio-economic status and religious practices, they can, at least in the Orthodox Jewish context, be traced back to the Talmudic dictum "kol b'ishah erva" (Berakhot 24a), which prohibits men from reciting a blessing or praying while being exposed to a woman's voice.[43] In Aleppo's synagogues, the effects of this dictum were discernible in the gendered segregation of seating and the women refraining from participating actively in rituals that would make their voices heard—a custom that continues in Syrian synagogues across the world.[44] As Claudette Sutton, daughter of an Aleppian-born Jew, remembered: "By orthodox practice, women and men sat separately in the synagogue. Women did not say the prayers or learn to read Hebrew. At the services, they would listen, talk with one another, and perhaps observe in a private quiet manner."[45]

Within Aleppo's Jewish community, anxieties over a woman's public voice also extended into the realm of profane music-making and the world of the Khūjahs. As the anthropologist Walter Zenner has noted in his historical study on Aleppian Jewry, women's work as entertainers was a profession generally considered "akin to prostitution and lacked honor."[46] And, already in 1913/14, Aleppo's Chief Rabbi Jacob Saul Dweck (1828–1919) had published a treatise in which he lamented about a new immorality in the city:

> There has increased in our times a new prohibited activity which never happened before. Many girls have desecrated God's Holy Name, singing and dancing in public. Men and women say to them, "Show me your face. Let me hear your voice, for your voice is pleasing." There they sit—men, their wives, and their children. Men—why do they go to graze in such places in the shade of the tree that Naaman has planted? Women – why do they go to display their beauty before commonfolk and notables alike? Children—why do they go to get an education in sinning? Woe to the eyes that see such things and to the ears that hear them. The city that was praised as the perfection of beauty, how has the faithful city become a harlot![47]

Throughout the past century, the association of publicly performing Jewish women with moral impurity continued to be disseminated in a variety of ways. It appeared in rumors as in the story of the Jewish singer and 'ūd-player Nathla, who, it is claimed, had "relations" with the red-light district before performing at women's weddings.[48] And it took the form of insinuations such as, for instance, those against the popular Jewish singer "F" and her sister "M," who are mentioned in the *Aleppo Chronicles* as examples of the city's "disreputable" Jewish women, considered "wild, probably prostitutes too."[49]

It is likely that in Aleppo, as elsewhere across the region, Jewish women such as Naziha Assis chose to sing in non-Jewish, women-only contexts to avoid these insinuations and condemnations. There, as "outsiders," they may have been less restricted by moral norms than their Muslim counterparts, who, in their own communities, often faced similar constraints in performing in public.[50]

Yet while the confinement of women to private, segregated spaces may have meant that their music making was regarded as less sinful, it did not necessarily lead to a decrease in its association with sexual transgression. Instead, this privacy at times seems to have aroused men's fantasies, such as, for example, that of the Aleppian writer Nihād Sīrīs. In his historical-fictional novel *Ḥālat Shaghf* (States of passion), he associates the Khūjahs, some of whom he remembers as being Jewish, with the *banāt al-ʿishrah* (Arabic for "girls of intimacy"). These women are said to have secretly cultivated intimate, romantic, and at times sexual relationships with one another, and would regularly meet to sing, dance, and make music—a phenomenon that, according to Sīrīs, was particularly widespread in Aleppo during the first half of the twentieth century.[51]

The Khūjahs' Association with "Women Songs"

The preoccupation with the Khūjahs' moral conduct and (sexual) bodies may be the reason that little is known about the actual *music* they performed. A few Arabic sources have associated their musical practice with music "special to women" or, more specifically, "folkloric" repertoires such as the *hanhūnāt*, a set of joyful popular songs indigenous to Aleppo and its countryside, with no particular mention being made of musical pieces specific to Aleppo's Jewish Khūjahs.[52] Given that they performed in contexts that relied on musical and vocal interaction with their Muslim or Christian co-performers, one can assume that Aleppo's Jewish Khūjahs, at least in their public capacity as wedding singers or entertainers at coffeehouses and cabarets, shared a common musical repertoire with their non-Jewish band members.

Of this repertoire, the most important would have been the local *qudūd ḥalabīyah* (sing. *qadd*), a genre of popular and strophic songs that are usually sung in colloquial Arabic and belong to the music most strongly associated with Aleppo. Most importantly, the qudūd are musical contrafacta, consisting either of religious lyrics set to the melody of a popular folk song, or the contrary, of profane lyrics set to the melody of a preexisting religious song.[53] As such, the qudūd's melodies travel through diverse performance contexts, ranging from Islamic *dhikr* ceremonies (set to religious, sacred texts) to secular musical gatherings and concerts where they form part of a musical suite known as the *waṣla* (featuring more "profane" and romantic lyrics). More recently, during the Syrian uprising, melodies were set to newly composed lyrics that articulated protesters' resistance to the Assad regime and denounced the brutality of its aerial bombardments (residents of besieged East Aleppo, for example, changed a line from the famous Aleppian qadd "al-bulbul nāgha" [The nightingale sang] from "we were six at the spring/the beloved one came, then we were seven" to "we were one hundred at the mosque, a barrel bomb came down and we were seven").[54] Finally, some qudūd, in this case set to Hebrew text, still form part of paraliturgical rituals by Syrian Jews around the world, such as, for example, the qadd "al-qarāṣīyah," named after a plum that grows in the countryside outside of Aleppo.[55] Most importantly, they form the core repertoire during local wedding celebrations.

Further insight into the performance of an Aleppian qadd during a woman's wedding celebration, albeit staged, is offered in a scene from an episode of the Syrian TV series 'Urs Ḥalabī (The Aleppian wedding) (1999).[56] The scene shows a large group of women gathered in the courtyard of a traditional Arab house. The bride sits on stage, surrounded by a traditional *takht* (musical ensemble) including a qanūn-, 'ūd-, and nāy-player, as well as two percussionists and several singers. The qadd they sing is called "Ta'ī 'al-Fay" (Come into the shade). Sung in responsorial style by several singers, its lyrics consist of a poetic duel between two women—a blonde and a brunette. Both praise their own beauty and merits while challenging and ridiculing their "opponent" with verses that mock their various flaws (for example, comparing the other's skin tone to the color of a zucchini). The audience, which sits on chairs in front of them, claps, sings, and dances along to the refrain: "Ta'ī 'al-fay, ta'ī 'al-fay, wa ana badī shūfak marrah wa yifarfaḥ 'albī shway" (Come into the shade, I want to see you for a moment and delight my heart). At the end of the women's verbal exchange, everyone sings in unison: "Color does not matter to us, what matters is the mind."

A comical way to deal with possible rivalry endured within a woman's marriage, this song, in its numerous melodic and lyrical variations, continues to be performed by women across the Middle East. Ivet, while acknowledging that the qudūd formed part of her repertoire, did not remember whether her mother had ever performed Ta'ī 'al-Fay. If she had, she would have shared this song—or at least its melody—not only with her Muslim or Christian co-performers but also with men from within and outside Aleppo's Jewish community, such as, for example, Yosef Antebi and Muḥammad Qadrī Dalāl.

Born in Aleppo in 1938, Yosef Antebi emigrated to Israel in his mid-twenties and lived nearby the old town hall of Tel Aviv until he passed away in 2021. "This song is a hundred years old!," he exclaimed when asked about Ta'ī 'al-Fay and recounted having been taught this song by his father in their family home in Qilleh. And Muḥammad Qadrī Dalāl, one of Aleppo's most distinguished contemporary musicologists and composers, has documented the song in his study on the religious Aleppian qudūd; according to him, its religious version is still traditionally performed during the mawlid al-nabī, the Islamic festivities that observe the birthday of the Prophet Muhammad.[57]

The presence of the melody of "Ta'ī 'al-Fay" in different performance contexts and memories exemplifies that in Aleppo, the lines between "secular" and "sacred," "Arab" and "Jewish," and ultimately "male" and "female" musical practices were much softer and more permeable than one may expect. However, the scene from the Syrian TV series paints a different picture, at least on first impression. In its display of Aleppian women's customs and performance traditions, and with the song's lyrics seemingly marking a typically "female" context, it appears to correspond to those few sources associating the Khūjah's repertoires with music "special to women" and/or folklore. Representations such as these not only risk obscuring the fact that Aleppo's Khūjahs may also have performed songs that did not correspond to this classification; they are also likely among the reasons for why their musical practice has received less scholarly attention.

The tendency to portray women's musical practice as "typically female" and "folk-loric," often in comparison to more "serious," "classical," or "male" musical repertoires, is a problematic theme that also appears throughout scholarship on Jewish music. Commenting on how this approach effectively mirrors women's exclusion from Jewish liturgical contexts and their social confinement to private, segregated spaces, Edwin Seroussi has stated in his article on *De-gendering Jewish Music*:

> Musicology perpetuated [the sexual] segregation [of women's voices] by treating sep-arately women and men's repertoires on the basis of a series of dichotomies based on the language of the texts of the songs (Hebrew for men/vernacular Jewish languages for women); contexts of performance (year cycle for men/life cycle for women) and style (recitative, cantillation, "great" music traditions for men / folk songs, "small" music traditions for women).[58]

The few memories that survive Aleppo's Jewish Khūjahs today challenge this distinc-tion. They expose that in Aleppo, musical performance and repertoires were impacted by the physical and social proximity, not only between Jewish men and women but also between the city's different faiths. To point this out, it is worthwhile to revisit Aliza K.'s remarks about her neighbor's mother.

THE KHŪJAH AS MUṬRIBA

"I say 'This is art, she is a *muṭribah*,'" is how Aliza commented on Khūjah Fairūz, bestowing upon her an Arabic title that signifies musical refinement and is tradition-ally reserved for professional singers of *ṭarab* music—the "classical" urban art music repertoires of the Eastern Arab world.[59] Reminiscent of the anthropologist Anthony Paul Cohen's observation that community boundaries tend to be largely symbolic in char-acter, so that "boundaries perceived by some may be utterly imperceptible to others,"[60] Aliza did not identify her neighbor's mother with the society of marginalized "loose women" that many members of her community condemned her for. Rather, she asso-ciated her with a *musical* community known in Arabic as the *ahl al-ṭarab* (the people of ṭarab) and as such laid claim to reinserting Fairūz's memory into a "great" musical tradition—not into the Syrian Jewish liturgical context but into the realm of "classical" Arab music. By doing so, she safeguarded the artistic legacy of her neighbor's mother against charges of inappropriate conduct and also, from within the private settings of her living room in Holon, challenged what the ethnomusicologist 'Ali Jihad Racy has identified as the "historical centrality of the male perspective" on ṭarab culture.[61]

Despite numerous (Jewish) women performers having excelled in the various urban art music traditions of the Eastern Arab world, "classical" musical canons and concepts of musical refinement, such as ṭarab, tend to be established through musical forms and repertoires considered to be "male." An example of this perspective is offered in a podcast series by the Foundation for Arab Music Archiving and Research (AMAR), in which Frédéric Lagrange and Muṣṭafa Saʿīd—another distinguished expert in the music history of the Arab world—provide a typology of the aforementioned ʿawālim, women singers and entertainers active in nineteenth- and twentieth-century Egypt whose performance context was, in many ways, similar to that of the Khūjahs. Contrary to those ʿawalim who mainly performed at weddings and whose musical repertoires consisted of "light" urban genres such as the ṭaqāṭīq or folk songs popular in the coun- tryside, the term *muṭribah*, so they state, traditionally remained reserved for the "first rank" ʿalimah who performed "male" repertoires and genres, such as the dawr or the qaṣīda, and showcased expertise in traditional Arab music's system of modes.[62]

Given that no details of Khūjah Fairūz's actual musical practice have been transmitted, it is unclear into which "category" she would have fallen. Naziha, however, would cer- tainly have qualified for the title of a muṭriba. According to her daughter, her repertoires included not only local repertoires such as the aforementioned Aleppian qudūd or the mass-mediated hits of the Egyptian superstar Umm Kulthum, but also compositions by the Egyptian Sayyid Darwīsh (1893–1923), widely regarded as one of the fathers of modern Egyptian music. Moreover, according to her daughter, she spent hours at their home listening to records of ʿAbdu al-Ḥāmūlī (1841–1901), another of Egypt's great modernizers of Arab music at the turn of the twentieth century. During these listening sessions, Naziha would express to her children her knowledge of the maqām system. As her daughter Ivet remembered:

> She would say things like, "This music is in maqām *nahawand*"; "This music is in this [maqām]". She knew all of them [maqāmat], and she would teach them to us as well! Whenever she would hear a song, she would say this is this [maqām] and this is that [maqām]. . . . When she listened, you could see how she changed, you could see how much she loved and interacted [with the music]. Also when she heard a bad voice. She was very sensitive to music.[63]

With her ability to recognize various maqāmat, as well as her engagement with two of the main representatives of Egypt's nineteenth- and early–twentieth-century ṭarab traditions (a repertoire that, according to the previously cited classification, would likely be referred to as "male"), Naziha transgressed the strict boundaries traditionally assigned not only to women's music-making but also to the musical practice of Aleppian Jews. This brief insight into Naziha's musical practice then opens the possibility to move beyond the text-based and "religious" paradigm with which studies on the musical practices of Aleppian Jews have approached histories of musical interaction.

Despite the fact that information about Aleppo's Jewish Khūjahs is scarce and arguments about their musical repertoires must therefore remain largely speculative, the participation of Jewish women singers at Muslim weddings and their activity in local music theaters and cafés highlights that, back in Aleppo, encounters between "Arab" and

"Jewish" musical practices were neither restricted to the synagogue nor limited to an exclusively male domain. Nor were they merely the result of the interaction of melody (Arab) and sacred text (Hebrew). Rather, they also occurred across networks of musical collaborations that relied on physical contact and proximity between women of different faiths. Yet many questions remain unanswered. What was the nature of the relations that existed between Aleppo's Jewish Khūjahs and their Muslim and Christian co-performers? Did they share a similar socioeconomic background? Were their musical interactions influenced by the environment of alienation and marginalization that the article that opened this chapter described? What exactly did their musical encounters look and sound like? Were their musical performances characterized by the kind of "sensorialized sociality" that scholars have argued is central for experiencing a sense of (musical) community?[64] In light of the departure of almost the entire Jewish community from Syria and with the last generation of Jews who were born in Aleppo and have an immediate memory of the city's musical life gradually disappearing, questions such as these are becoming ever more difficult to attend to.

FADED MEMORY

Naziha was one of the last Jewish Khūjahs in Aleppo. According to her daughter Ivet, there was only one remaining Jewish family living in Qilleh when they left the city in 1978. The rest had moved to the more affluent Jewish neighborhood of al-Jamīlīyah, or left the country altogether. Once in Israel, Ivet recalled, her mother stopped singing in public and never touched an instrument again. Moreover, she refused to allow any of her children to take music lessons for fear that they, too, would decide to pursue a singing career and relive the hardship she had experienced in Aleppo.

The memory of Aleppo's Jewish Khūjahs operates in a context of public and private redactions. Whether a local society of disreputable or secretly desired women, representatives of an authentic albeit less serious (because "female," "domestic," and folkloric) heritage, or, as in the case of Shemi-Shoham's article about Naziha Assis, a collective of national heroes honored by the Israeli state—the narratives that surround Aleppo's Jewish women singers affiliate them with different (real and imagined) "communities," while tending to overshadow memories of the actual *music* they performed. Today, the musical history of Aleppo's Jewish Khūjahs has become largely imperceptible, also on the ground. Most of the city's ancient Jewish neighborhood of Qilleh was destroyed in the context of urban redevelopment programs that occurred in the late 1970s.[65] Café Orange, the former workplace of Naziha, which until recently served as a space for wedding celebrations, was severely damaged in the course of the Syrian war. And as Aleppo's reconstruction has only just begun, archives on the ground that could provide more material on the Khūjahs' history remain inaccessible.

In the case of Aleppo's Khūjahs, the concept of zekher, then, implies a fragmented, eclipsed, faded, and at times "suppressed" memory and a form of remembrance that is largely absent from public and persistently male-dominated modes of commemoration. Zekher, here, refers to a history that lacks official memorials and archivization efforts, but that lingers instead in the personal stories of the musicians' dispersed descendants and constituencies. At times, their stories memorialize Aleppo's Khūjahs as members of a great musical community, the ahl al-tarab (as in the case of Aliza K.'s remarks about her neighbor's mother). Diversely, they reenact the loss of their memory. When recently urged by one of her daughters to allow her to attend singing classes, Ivet remembered her mother's fear. She, too, refused.

ACKNOWLEDGMENTS

This chapter was written with the support of the Martin Buber Society of Fellows at the Hebrew University of Jerusalem. It draws from fieldwork undertaken in Tel Aviv-Jaffa in the years 2016/17, which was supported by a doctoral studentship of the German National Academic Foundation and the Mildred Loss Studentship of the Jewish Music Institute (JMI) in London. The author would like to thank Ilana Webster-Kogen for her comments on earlier drafts of this chapter, Aliza K., Ivet Assis, and Yosef Antebi (1938–2021) for generously sharing their memories, and the anonymous reviewer for their thoughtful feedback and helpful suggestions.

NOTES

1. Born in Aleppo in 1935, Avraham Shemi-Shoham emigrated to Israel in the 1960s. He has exhibited his paintings in Israel and abroad and is the author of several articles and books, including *Sipurim mi-Ḥalab Suryah* [Stories from Aleppo, Syria] (self-published, 2017).
2. World Bank National Accounts Data, https://data.worldbank.org/indicator/NY.GDP. PCAP.CD?end=1962&locations=SY&start=1961 (accessed December 10, 2020).
3. Avraham Shemi-Shoham, "Sipura shel asirat Zion Naziha Assis," *Darekhey "Eretz"* 17 (2012): 36.
4. As such, the article corresponds to other Israeli media publications on the history of Syrian Jews, which, one could argue, tend to put forward a view that Mark Cohen has termed "the neo-lachrymose conception of Arab-Jewish history." According to Cohen, this perspective often transposes the history of Jewish suffering and persecution in medieval Christian Europe onto Jewish life under Muslim rule in order to associate the history of Middle Eastern Jewry with the cultural memory of Ashkenazi Jews as well as counter the narratives of an idealized inter-faith coexistence mobilized by Arab state regimes and their constituencies. Mark Cohen, "The Neo-lachrymose Conception of Jewish-Arab History," *Tikkun* 6, no. 3 (1991): 55–60. See also Joel Beinin, *The Dispersion of Egyptian Jewry: Culture, Politics, and the Formation of a Modern Diaspora* (Berkeley: University of California Press, 1998), 14–17.
5. Michael M. Laskier, "Syria and Lebanon," in *The Jews of the Middle East and North Africa in Modern Times*, ed. Reeva S. Simon, Sara Reguer, and Michael M. Laskier (New York: Columbia University Press, 2003), 325. See also Walter P. Zenner, *A Global Community: The Jews from Aleppo, Syria* (Detroit, MI: Wayne State University Press, 2000), 51–62.
6. Shemi-Shoham, "Sipura shel asirat Zion Naziha Assis," 36.

7. See Edwin Seroussi, "Music," in *Encyclopedia of Jews in the Islamic World*, ed. Norman A. Stillman (Leiden: Brill, 2010), 3:498–519. For more information on the mentioned repertoires and musical forms, see the glossaries of Ali Jihad Racy, *Making Music in the Arab World: The Culture and Artistry of Ṭarab* (Cambridge: Cambridge University Press, 2003), 226–230; and Jonathan H. Shannon *Among the Jasmine Trees: Music and Modernity in Contemporary Syria* (Middletown, CT: Wesleyan University Press, 2006), 227–230.

8. See Kay Kaufman Shelemay, *Let Jasmine Rain Down: Song and Remembrance Among Syrian Jews* (Chicago: University of Chicago Press, 1998); and Mark L. Kligman, *Maqam and Liturgy: Ritual, Music, and Aesthetics of Syrian Jews in Brooklyn* (Detroit, MI: Wayne State University Press, 2009).

9. Shelemay, *Let Jasmine Rain Down*, 129.

10. Kay Kaufman Shelemay, "Musical Communities: Rethinking the Collective in Music," *Journal of the American Musicological Society* 64, no. 2 (2011): 364.

11. Also of significance, states the author, was an incident at a wedding in which gunshots fired by celebrating guests accidently hit and fatally wounded the groom. Shemi-Shoham, "Sipura shel Asirat Zion Naziha Assis," 36 and 40.

12. Variations of the word continue to be used across the Balkans, Turkey, and the Middle East as well as Central and Southeast Asia, most often within a religious context and as an honorary title given to scholars of Islam.

13. Khayr al-Dīn Asadī, ed., *Mawsūʿat Ḥalab al-Muqāranah* (Aleppo: Jāmiʿat Ḥalab, Maʿhad al-Turāth al-ʿIlmī al-ʿArabī, 1981), 244, 367.

14. "al-ʿUrs al-Ḥalabī Qadīman Bikāfat Tafāṣīlihi," *Souriat* (August 16, 2015), http://souriat.com/2015/08/7548.html.

15. Abraham Marcus and Yaron Ayalon, "Aleppo," in *Encyclopedia of Jews in the Islamic World*, ed. Norman A. Stillman (Leiden: Brill, 2010), 1:119ff.

16. Iyād J. Maḥfūẓ, *Buyūt al-Khafāʾ fī Ḥalab al-Shahbāʾ - Khilāl al-Qarn al-ʿAshrīn: Khazāʾin Lam Tuftaḥ* (Latakia: Dār al-Ḥiwār lil-Nashr wa al-Tawzīʿa, 2017), 270–271.

17. Edwin Seroussi, "De-gendering Jewish Music: The Survival of the Judeo-Spanish Folk Song Revisited," *Music and Anthropology* 3 (1998), https://www.umbc.edu/MA/index/number3/seroussi/ser_0.htm; and Amnon Shiloah, *Jewish Musical Traditions* (Detroit, MI: Wayne State Univ. Press, 1992), 40–41.

18. Ibid. See also Yeheskel Kojaman, *The Maqam Music Tradition of Iraq* (London: Y. Kojaman, 2001); Sara Manasseh, "Daqqaqat: Jewish Women Musicians from Iraq," *Yearbook of the International Council for Traditional Music* 25 (1990): 7–15; and Sheherazade Hassan, "Female Traditional Singers in Iraq: A Survey," *International Journal of Contemporary Iraqi Studies* 4, no. 1–2 (2010): 25–39.

19. See Evan Rapport, *Greeted with Smiles: Bukharian Jewish Music and Musicians in New York* (New York: Oxford University Press, 2014).

20. Frédéric Lagrange, "Women in the Singing Business, Women in Songs," *History Compass* 7, no. 1 (2009): 30. See also Muṣṭafa Saʿīd and Frédéric Lagrange, "Durūb al-Nagham, Awalem 1," The Foundation for Arab Music Archiving and Research (AMAR) Audio Podcast 43, https://www.amar-foundation.org/043-awalem-1/ (accessed November 1, 2020).

21. Frédéric Lagrange, " ʿAlma," in *Encyclopaedia of Islam*, ed. Kate Fleet, Gudrun Krämer, Denis Matringe, John Nawas, and Everett Rowson, 3rd ed. (Leiden: Brill, 2014). For more on the history of Egypt's ʿawālim, see Frédéric Lagrange, *Musiques d'Égypte* (Arles: Cité

de la Musique, 1996); Virginia Danielson, "Artists and Entrepreneurs: Female Singers in Cairo during the 1920s," in *Women in Middle Eastern History: Shifting Boundaries in Sex and Gender*, ed. Nikki R. Keddie and Beth Baron (New Haven, CT: Yale University Press, 1991), 292–309; and Karin v. Nieuwkerk, *"A Trade Like Any Other": Female Singers and Dancers in Egypt* (Austin: University of Texas Press, 1995).

22. Muḥammad 'Intābī and Najwa 'Uthmān, *Ḥalab fī Mi'at 'Ām, 1850–1950* (Aleppo: Jāmi'at Ḥalab, Ma'had al-Turāth al-'Ilmī al-'Arabī, 1993), 69.

23. Jamīl Wilāya, *Ḥalab, Bayt al-Nagham* (Damascus: Dār Ṭlās lil-Dirāsāt wa al-Tarjamah wa al-Nashr, 2008), 162.

24. Seroussi, "Music."

25. Jonathan H. Shannon, "Jewish Fingers and Phantom Musical Presences: Remembrance of Jewish Musicians in Twentieth-Century Aleppo," in *Musical Exodus: Al-Andalus and Its Jewish Diasporas*, ed. Ruth F. Davis (Lanham: Rowman & Littlefield, 2015), 126.

26. See, for example, Qaḥṭān M. Muhannā, *Widād min Ḥalab* (Damascus: Dār Mamdūḥ 'Adwān lil-Nashr wa al-Tawzī'a, 2010), 118 and Sa'ad Z. Kawākibī, *Dhikrayāt min Māḍī Ḥalab* (Aleppo: Manshūrāt Nādī al-Sayyārāt wa al-Siyāḥah al-Sūrī, 2010), 154. Two of her songs have been re-issued on a French compilation of Judeo-Arabic music *Mélodies judéo-arabes d'autrefois, Maghreb er Moyen-Orient* (Paris: Blue Silver, 1997). See also Amnon Shiloah, "Identities and Multifaceted Music," in *Music in Israel*, ed. Michael Wolpe, Gideon Katz, and Tuvia Friling, *Iyunim Bitkumat Israel Thematic Series*, Vol. 8 (Beer Sheva: Ben-Gurion University of the Negev, 2014), 485.

27. Seroussi, "De-gendering Jewish Music."

28. This is less the case with regard to North Africa. See, for example, Ruth Davis, "Jews, Women and the Power to be Heard: Charting the Early Tunisian Ughniyya to the Present Day," in *Music and the Play of Power in the Middle East, North Africa and Central Asia*, ed. Laudan Nooshin (Farnham, UK: Ashgate Press, 2009), 187–206; and Vanessa P. Elbaz, "Judeo-Spanish Melodies in the Liturgy of Tangier: Morocco Feminine Imprints in a Masculine Space," in *Musical Exodus: Al-Andalus and Its Jewish Diasporas*, ed. Ruth F. Davis (Lanham: Rowman & Littlefield, 2015), 25–43.

29. Shelemay, *Let Jasmine Rain Down*, 11.

30. Ibid. and Kligman, *Maqam and Liturgy*, 8. See also Ruth Katz, "The Singing of Baqqashot by Aleppo Jews. A Study in Musical Acculturation," *Acta Musicologica* 40, no. 1 (1968): 65–85; and Kumiko Yayama, "The Singing of Baqqahot of the Aleppo Jewish Tradition in Jerusalem: The Modal System and the Vocal Style" (PhD diss., Hebrew University of Jerusalem, 2003).

31. See Kay Kaufman Shelemay, "The Power of Silent Voices: Women in the Syrian Jewish Musical Tradition," in *Music and the Play of Power in the Middle East, North Africa and Central Asia*, ed. Laudan Nooshin (Farnham, UK: Ashgate Press, 2009), 269–288.

32. Ibid., 283. For a more general exploration of women's roles in conserving Syrian Jewish cultural identity and rituals within diasporic contexts, see Faye Ginsburg, "When the Subject Is Women: Encounters with Syrian Jewish Women," *The Journal of American Folklore* 100, no. 398 (1987): 540–547; Paulette. K Schuster, "Stepping Out of Bounds: Communal Participation of Syrian Jewish Women in Mexico City," *Iggud: Selected Essays in Jewish Studies* 2 (2005): 235–246; and Yael Zerubavel and Dianne Esses, "Reconstructions of the Past: Syrian Jewish Women and the Maintenance of Tradition," *The Journal of American Folklore* 100, no. 398 (1987): 528–539.

33. Ivet Assis, in discussion with the author, February 2, 2017.

34. Maḥfūẓ, *Buyūt al-Khafā' fī Ḥalab al-Shahbā'*, 80–81; 86–87.

35. "Mā dhukurat baḥsītā amām ḥalabī ila wa ibtasam." 'Ala' Sayyed, "Baḥsīta . . . Ḥikāyah Buyūt al-Mut'ah' fī Ḥalab," *Watan*, June 23, 2008, https://www.watan.com/2008/06/23/1-2-2/ (accessed June 13, 2023).

36. Pierre Nora, "Between Memory and History: Les Lieux de Mémoire," *Representations*, no. 26 (1989): 13.

37. While oral accounts tell of Jewish prostitutes or Jewish women being compelled to reside there for being "morally loose," most of my research partners denied the presence of Jewish prostitutes, perhaps to safeguard their neighborhood's and community's reputation. See Shannon, "Jewish Fingers and Phantom Musical Presences," 131 and Joseph A. D Sutton, *Aleppo Chronicles: The Story of the Unique Sephardeem of the Ancient Near East, in Their Own Words* (New York: Thayer-Jacoby, 1988), 200; 236.

38. 'Ala' Sayyed, "Baḥsīta."

39. Aliza K., in discussion with the author, May 22, 2017.

40. See Danielson, "Artists and Entrepreneurs," 301; and Davis, "Jews, Women and the Power to be Heard," 204.

41. Daniel Monterescu, *Jaffa Shared and Shattered: Contrived Coexistence in Israel/Palestine* (Bloomington: Indiana University Press, 2015), 232. Naziha is one of four residents from Jaffa whose personal life stories Monterescu explores against the background of three themes: Nation and community, old age and liminality, as well as gender and family. With regard to Naziha, he argues, it was predominately the latter theme that characterized her memory of immigration to Israel which, according to him, she told mainly as a story of success and personal autonomy. See ibid., 232–239.

42. Ivet Assis, in discussion with the author, February 2, 2017.

43. See also the chapter by Jessica Roda in this handbook. For more on the genesis of this dictum, see Ellen Koskoff, *Music in Lubavitcher Life* (Chicago: University of Illinois Press, 2001), 126–134 as well as Shelemay, "The Power of Silent Voices," 273–274 and Seroussi, "De-gendering Jewish Music."

44. Shelemay, "The Power of Silent Voices," 274.

45. Claudette E. Sutton, *Farewell, Aleppo: My Father, My People, and Their Long Journey Home* (Santa Fe, NM: Terra Nova Books, 2014), 52.

46. Zenner, *A Global Community*, 45.

47. Jacob Saul Dweck, *Derekh Emūna* (Aleppo, 1913/14), 17b, quoted in Norman A. Stillman, *The Jews of Arab Lands in Modern Times* (Philadelphia, PA: Jewish Publications Society, 2003), 222. The treatise is full of references. As noted by Stillman, in the last cited sentence, Dweck paraphrases Lamentations 2:15 and Isaiah 1:21. Moreover, as Stillman explains in a further footnote to the treatise, here, Naaman—the name of the Aramaean commander who suffered from leprosy and approached the prophet Elisha to be cured—acts as "eponym for Gentile Syrians"; ibid., 222. Rabbi Dweck is still remembered today by the Orthodox Aleppian Jewish community as "a man of principle who . . . fought bitterly against immodest behaviour such as attending non-Jewish parties, listening to Arab love songs in coffeehouses, mixed dancing, and ladies going without hair coverings." See David Sutton and David T. Lanyado, *Aleppo: City of Scholars* (Brooklyn, NY: Mesorah, 2006), 182–183. For more on the writings of Aleppian rabbis, see Yaron Harel, *The Books of Aleppo: The Rabbinic Literature of the Scholars of Aleppo / ספרי אר"ץ: הספרות התורנית של חכמי ארם צובה* (Jerusalem: Ben-Zvi Institute, 1997).

48. Maḥfūẓ, *Buyūt al-Khafā' fi Ḥalab al-Shahbā'*, 271.

49. Sutton, *Aleppo Chronicles*, 236.

50. See Veronica Doubleday, "The Frame Drum in the Middle East: Women, Musical Instruments and Power," *Ethnomusicology* 43, no. 1 (1999): 111–113.

51. Nihād Sīrīs, *Ḥālat Shaghaf* (Beirut: Dar 'Atiyah lil-Nashr, 1998). For the recently published English translation, see Nihād Sīrīs, *States of Passion*, trans. Max Weiss (London: Pushkin Press, 2018).

52. "Al-'Urs al-Ḥalabī Qadīman" and Wilāya, *Ḥalab, Bayt al-Nagham*, 162, 297.

53. Jonathan H. Shannon, "al-Muwashshaḥât and al-Qudûd al-Halabiyya: Two Genres in the Aleppine Wasla," *Middle East Studies Association Bulletin* 37, no.1 (2003): 91.

54. On this example, see also Clara Wenz, *Music during the Syrian War: Displacement and Memory in Hello Psychaleppo's Electro-Tarab*, Elements in Music and the City Series (Cambridge: Cambridge University, 2023), 12.

55. A recording of a pizmon based on this qadd is available on the website of the Sephardic Pizmonim Project, a digital archive for the liturgical heritage of Aleppian Jews, https://www.pizmonim.org/book.php?manuscript=19 (accessed November 1, 2020).

56. "Musallsal al-'Urs al-Ḥalabī Ughnīyah Ta'ī 'al-Fay," February 11, 2016, YouTube video, 2'56" "Hassan Basha," https://youtu.be/JkShTnb3SII.

57. Muḥammad Qadrī Dalāl, *al-Qudūd al-Dinīyah: Baḥth Tārīkhī wa Mūsīqī fi al-Qudūd al-Ḥalabīyah* (Damascus: Wizārat al-Thaqāfah fi al-Jumhūrīyah al-'Arabīyah al-Sūrīyah, 2006), 288. A variation of the song Ta'ī 'al-Fay is already documented in Gustaf Dalman, *Palästinischer Diwan: Als Beitrag zur Volkskunde Palästinas* (Leipzig: J.C. Hinrichs'sche Buchlandlung, 1991 [1901]), 250–251; 360.

58. Seroussi, "De-gendering Jewish Music."

59. The different manifestations of ṭarab music have been studied in detail. In the English language, the standard work on the subject is Racy, *Making Music in the Arab World*. See also Shannon, *Among the Jasmine Trees*; Virginia Danielson, *The Voice of Egypt: Umm Kulthum, Arabic Song, and Egyptian Society in the Twentieth Century* (Chicago: University of Chicago Press, 1997); and Michael Frishkopf, "Tarab in the Mystic Sufi Chant of Egypt," in *Colors of Enchantment: Theater, Dance, Music, and the Visual Arts of the Middle East*, ed. Sherifa Zuhur (Cairo: American University in Cairo Press, 2001), 239–276.

60. Anthony Paul Cohen, *The Symbolic Construction of Community* (London: Routledge, 1993), 13.

61. Racy, *Making Music in the Arab World*, 18.

62. See Sa'īd and Lagrange, "Durūb al-Nagham, Awalem 1."

63. Ivet Assis, in discussion with the author, February 2, 2017.

64. Rachel Harris, "'A Weekly Mäshräp to Tackle Extremism': Music-Making in Uyghur Communities and Intangible Cultural Heritage in China," *Ethnomusicology* 64, no. 1 (2020): 27.

65. Heinz Gaube and Eugen Wirth, *Aleppo, historische und geographische Beiträge zur baulichen Gestaltung, zur sozialen Organisation und zur wirtschaftlichen Dynamik einer vorderasiatischen Fernhandelsmetropole* (Wiesbaden: Ludwig Reichert Verlag, 1984), 52–53.

Select Bibliography

Dalāl, Muḥammad Q. *Al-Qudūd al-Dīnīyah: Baḥth Tārīkhī wa Mūsīqī fi al-Qudūd al-Ḥalabīyah*. Damascus: Wizārat al-Thaqāfah fi al-Jumhūrīyah al-ʿArabīyah al-Sūrīyah, 2006.

Danielson, Virginia. "Artists and Entrepreneurs: Female Singers in Cairo during the 1920s." In *Women in Middle Eastern History: Shifting Boundaries in Sex and Gender*, edited by Nikki R. Keddie and Beth Baron, 292–309. New Haven, CT: Yale University Press, 1991.

Kligman, Mark L. *Maqam and Liturgy: Ritual, Music, and Aesthetics of Syrian Jews in Brooklyn*. Detroit, MI: Wayne State University Press, 2009.

Koskoff, Ellen. *Music in Lubavitcher Life*. Chicago: University of Illinois Press, 2001.

Lagrange, Frédéric. "Women in the Singing Business, Women in Songs." *History Compass* 7, no. 1 (2009): 226–250.

Laskier, Michael M. "Syria and Lebanon." In *The Jews of the Middle East and North Africa in Modern Times*, edited by Reeva S. Simon, Sara Reguer, and Michael M. Laskier, 316–334. New York: Columbia University Press, 2003.

Manasseh, Sara. "Daqqaqat: Jewish Women Musicians from Iraq." *Yearbook of the International Council for Traditional Music* 25 (1990): 7–15.

Nieuwkerk, Karin V. *"A Trade Like Any Other": Female Singers and Dancers in Egypt*. Austin: University of Texas Press, 1995.

Racy, Ali J. *Making Music in the Arab World*. Cambridge: Cambridge University Press, 2003.

Schuster, Paulette. K. "Stepping Out of Bounds: Communal Participation of Syrian Jewish Women in Mexico City." *Iggud: Selected Essays in Jewish Studies* 2 (2005): 235–246.

Seroussi, Edwin. "De-gendering Jewish Music: The Survival of the Judeo-Spanish Folk Song Revisited." *Music and Anthropology* 3 (1998): 1–15.

Shannon, Jonathan H. "al-Muwashshahât and al-Qudûd al-Halabiyya: Two Genres in the Aleppine Wasla." *Middle East Studies Association Bulletin* 37, no.1 (2003): 82–101.

Shannon, Jonathan H. *Among the Jasmine Trees: Music and Modernity in Contemporary Syria*. Middletown, CT: Wesleyan University Press, 2006.

Shannon, Jonathan H. "Jewish Fingers and Phantom Musical Presences: Remembrance of Jewish Musicians in Twentieth-Century Aleppo." In *Musical Exodus: Al-Andalus and its Jewish Diasporas*, edited by Ruth F. Davis, 125–140. Lanham, MD: Rowman & Littlefield, 2015.

Shelemay, Kay K. *Let Jasmine Rain Down: Song and Remembrance Among Syrian Jews*. Chicago: University of Chicago Press, 1998.

Shelemay, Kay K. "Musical Communities: Rethinking the Collective in Music." *Journal of the American Musicological Society* 64, no. 2 (2011): 349–390.

Shelemay, Kay K. "The Power of Silent Voices: Women in the Syrian Jewish Musical Tradition." In *Music and the Play of Power in the Middle East, North Africa and Central Asia*, edited by Laudan Nooshin, 269–288. Farnham, UK: Ashgate Press, 2009.

Sutton, Joseph A. D. *Aleppo Chronicles: The Story of the Unique Sephardeem of the Ancient Near East, in Their Own Words*. New York: Thayer-Jacoby, 1988.

Zenner, Walter P. *A Global Community: The Jews from Aleppo, Syria*. Detroit, MI: Wayne State University Press, 2000.

Zerubavel, Yael, and Dianne Esses. "Reconstructions of the Past: Syrian Jewish Women and the Maintenance of Tradition." *The Journal of American Folklore* 100, no. 398 (1987): 528–539.

PART VIII

SPIRIT—שכינה

28

ULTRA-ORTHODOX WOMEN AND THE MUSICAL SHEKHINAH

Performance, Technology, and the Artist in North America

JESSICA RODA

For those familiar with Hasidic music, it might come as a surprise to learn that among the most recent additions to its soundscape are performances by women and girls available on social media. Indeed, the strict gender segregation observed in Hasidism and more broadly in ultra-Orthodox Judaism—which includes Hasidic and Litvish-Yeshivish branches[1]—as well as codes of *tsniut* (modesty) require that women's and girls' voices be inaudible at religious events attended by men.[2] As a result, the public faces and voices of ultra-Orthodox communities are represented almost entirely by men, particularly in the arts. Therefore, there is a common assumption that the concept of the artist does not apply to ultra-Orthodox women and girls as they do not *publicly* perform, sing, or dance. Nevertheless, musical performances are central to the lives of Orthodox girls and women at schools, summer camps, or for *tsedakah* (charity) events. It is there that they can unfold and develop their creativity. Girls sing and perform at the third meal on the Sabbath, at lifecycle events such as bat mitzvahs, at engagements, or at weddings, where they are separated from men and have their privacy. They perform at family events during the holidays and, on rare occasions, at exclusive musical gatherings such as *kumzits* (a musical gathering that often takes place after the Sabbath) or other informal occasions. Women generally have fewer opportunities to perform than girls because their social positions as mothers and wives are traditionally at odds with the public figure of the performer on stage. However, married women still engage with the arts, for example by becoming involved in the production of plays and performances on a voluntary basis, or by writing lyrics and scripts to sell to schools and summer camps. Because of the norms of tsniut in ultra-Orthodox circles, these performances and related activities constitute a specifically feminine collective scene in parallel to masculine performances, as they define themselves as private and exclude men.

A recent example of the misapprehension that ultra-Orthodox women are silent in the arts is the popular miniseries *Unorthodox*, released in March 2020 and based on Deborah Feldman's 2012 memoir about her painful departure from her Hasidic community. The main character, Esty, struggles to play the piano and sing in her community. When she escapes and travels to Berlin, she meets a group of students from the Conservatory of Music and is confronted with a different conception of musical performance. The depiction of her character suggests that creativity, singing, and exploring the arts within her community are impossible because of her gender.

This portrayal of ultra-Orthodox women as silent and invisible echoes a conception of women's autonomy and agency that integrates Western ideas as universally accepted ideals, or missionary feminism (to follow the philosopher Serene Khader), and understands a woman's status and agency exclusively on the basis of her public position and presence.[3] Ultra-Orthodoxy has a distinct way of thinking about women's positionality in society, governed by a strict interpretation of the concept of tsniut—which in ultra-Orthodoxy requires women to often disengage from the public sphere to prevent the opposite gender and external audience from accessing the performance of the self. Tsniut relates to both men and women, but in recent times has come to be applied more specifically to women. It encompasses a spectrum of practices, often translated as modesty and humility, that women and girls should adopt for their self-representation in public and private spaces. With an intensification of supervision over tsniut observed among ultra-Orthodox groups, from rabbinical authorities to educators, tsniut is today at the core of various halakhic discussions as well as feminist debates and criticisms. The literature is driven by three main interpretations, aligned with specific feminist ideologies.[4] A first generation of scholars envisioned modesty, through the lens of Western universal feminism, as a mode of patriarchal regulation, discipline, and oppression of women's bodies and sexuality.[5] Others, echoing postcolonial feminist scholars in Islamic studies,[6] conceive modesty as a tool for agency and empowerment.[7] A third trend captures tsniut as a dynamic concept that reveals the way religious authorities and texts are challenged and reinterpreted in order to construct new feminine ideals of modesty and beauty.[8]

This chapter approaches tsniut as a spectrum of practices that provides information on the conflicts, negotiations, and agreements that dictate individual and collective interpretations of how and where women and girls should sing and perform. The spectrum of these practices is reinterpreted over time and between places, constantly influenced by its environment. It includes dress codes and hair coverings; appropriate thoughts, language, and body expressions; and choices of literature, images, and sounds. Regarding sounds, woman's voice (*kol ishah*) has been at the center of halakhic debates, and to a lesser degree a focus of feminist scholars, because of its perceived sexual implications. The basis of this debate on the "sexual implications" of woman's voice centers on the Talmudic interpretation of a passage in the *Tanakh* (Hebrew Bible), Song of Songs 2:14:

יוֹנָתִי בְּחַגְוֵי הַסֶּלַע בְּסֵתֶר הַמַּדְרֵגָה הַרְאִינִי אֶת־מַרְאַיִךְ הַשְׁמִיעִינִי אֶת־קוֹלֵךְ כִּי־קוֹלֵךְ עָרֵב וּמַרְאֵיךְ נָאוֶה

O my dove, in the cranny of the rocks, Hidden by the cliff, Let me see your face, Let me hear your voice; For your voice is sweet And your face is comely.[9]

In the sixth century, based on this passage, the Talmudic scholar Amora Samuel wrote "kol b'ishah ervah" (Talmud, Berakhot 24a), generally translated as "the voice of a woman is a sexual incitement."[10] Samuel's interpretation led other rabbinical scholars to debate whether the statement referred to a woman's voice in any context, or applied specifically to women when singing, engaging in religious study, being in the presence of a male reciting the Shema, or being nude.[11] While the comments on this sentence in the Talmud, and the passage in the Tanakh on which it is based, led to multiple interpretations, Maimonides' commentary on the word *ervah* has been adopted by ultra-Orthodox Jews as the basis for various halakhic prohibitions. As Ellen Koskoff states, "the word *ervah* in Maimonides' interpretation referred only to a woman of the 'forbidden unions'—that is, one who was not likely to become a marriage partner, one with whom a man might establish an illicit relationship."[12] According to Maimonides, sexual stimulation in itself was not prohibited; rather, it was the potential to create a context of sexual stimulation that was restricted. The concept of illicit relationships led to the restriction on men hearing the voices of women who are foreign to them (not a wife or family member) in the context of performance and, more specifically, of singing and entertainment. While the halakhic prohibitions are centered on preventing men from hearing women's voices, women and girls are not prohibited from singing or performing.

Practices regarding this prohibition have taken different forms. Some women will sing and perform only in a closed space with curtains (if there are windows), where they can be certain that no man will overhear them as long as they do not project their voices. This is the norm among Hasidim except for Lubavitch. Others will sing outdoors for a women-only audience, labeling their performance as "for women and girls only" and assuming that it is the responsibility of men to not listen. It is important to note that these pragmatic applications of halakhic restrictions correlate with the changing time and space of Jewish communities. For instance, in North Africa and among Sephardic or Mizrahi communities, women who live according to Jewish laws and customs have historically been active in singing for communal celebrations, performing publicly during Jewish holidays, weddings, and circumcisions.[13] Following the migration of North African Jews to France, Canada, Israel, and the United States in the 1960s and 1970s, as well as the Lubavitcher Rebbe's visit to Morocco in the early 1960s, interactions with Orthodox and ultra-Orthodox European Jews certainly inspired a stricter application of *halakhah* within many Sephardic and Mizrahi communities.

Because of the halakhic restrictions connected to tsniut, and more specifically kol ishah, ultra-Orthodox women and girls are often invisible in, or altogether absent from, so-called public representations and stages available to both genders. Nevertheless, they have created distinctive musical scenes exclusive to women and girls where they mobilize music to respond to spiritual and religious needs. Following the kabbalistic conception of feminine principles of the divine, the *shekhinah*, and Jewish feminist reinterpretations of this mystical concept, one can postulate a feminine musical scene or musical shekhinah.[14] If ultra-Orthodox women claim their productions to be sacred, and that their manifestation of God's message is exclusively available to women, then the shekhinah embraces this feminine attribute of the presence of God in musical production. Here, shekhinah is not understood as passive and receptive to patriarchal values.[15] Rather, it symbolizes the power and status of the ultra-Orthodox woman, seen in her presence as a "beckoning princess or a comforting mother, but also as a stern and punitive disciplinarian."[16] At the same time, shekhinah can also be an ambivalent concept in the mobilization of women, capable not only of challenging the divide between the masculine and the feminine, but also of reinforcing it. While ultra-Orthodox women and girls are listening to and embracing male musical productions, their musical shekhinah has a role, format, sound, and aesthetic that differs from masculine ones.

This chapter discusses the embodiment and the transformations of this musical shekhinah in ultra-Orthodox communities (except Lubavitch), specifically the multiple ways in which it can be expressed as communal and individual experiences in performances.[17] The analysis of the transformation of the musical shekhinah highlights a redefinition of the concept of creativity as multilayered and varied according to the performance scene.

DEFINING THE MUSICAL SHEKHINAH

Kyrias Joel, one of the most secluded Hasidic communities in North America, located in Monroe (Upstate New York), is a fitting locale in which to explore the feminine musical space. It is home to the Satmar, a Hasidic dynasty that originates from the city of Szatmárnémeti in Hungary (now Satu Mare, Romania), where it was founded in 1905 by Rabbi Joel Teitelbaum. In 2014 Kyrias Joel saw the advent of an all-woman band, driven by three married women who sing and play saxophone, harp, keyboard, guitar, violin, and accordion. They perform for women and girls only at various events in their Satmar and other ultra-Orthodox communities. In recovery homes for new mothers, at summer camps, and for tsedakah events, the band is invited to entertain. Their performances are reserved for intimate celebrations where the performers know the members of the audience, a key aspect that allows them to be on stage and to certify the event is private. In contrast to other events for women and girls, where anyone could buy a ticket and walk in, these events are restricted to insiders. The band usually performs cover songs, originally in Yiddish or *lashon ha-ḳodesh* (a mix of Hebrew and Aramaic, essentially comprising religious texts and prayers), which are known to their audience who have sung them as well. They singularize themselves by their live performance and never pre-record in the studio. If the band has many videos of their performance, this is essentially for personal use. They expand their audience through word of mouth. When people outside their local community heard about the band, they began inviting the group to their own events for women and girls. The band constitutes a group, rather than a community of women performers, and the members agree that Toby is their leader, "the artist," even though she does not consider herself that way: "Toby learns one instrument after another, proposes musical arrangements for each song, and always has innovative ideas."[18]

The story told by these three women from Kyrias Joel allows for several observations about the changes and the status of music therein. While scholars such as Ellen Koskoff assert that married women who have been Orthodox from birth have almost no opportunities to perform, focusing her observations on collective performances among young girls,[19] the increased presence of this musical band and other similar performances by married women, its participation at women-only gatherings across many ultra-Orthodox communities, and its focus on individual talent and voices highlight noteworthy transformations regarding the status of women's creativity and artistic consumption. The concept of the artist, and of having a professional career or generating *parnaśah* (income) from music or the performing arts, was once alien to ultra-Orthodox women and girls. The twenty-first century has seen an important change, with individual talent becoming increasingly celebrated. If one premise regarding ultra-Orthodox women's performances excludes the concepts of fame and of creativity for its own sake, as scholars such as Miriam Isaac stated,[20] another premise can interpret the recent increase in the professionalism of the arts among ultra-Orthodox women and girls as an alternative perspective on creativity for religious, social, and educational purposes.

While this feminine space is an integral part of ultra-Orthodox life, the sources regarding its development in North America are extremely limited due to the lack of women scholars in the field. Previously, research on ultra-Orthodoxy was highly dominated by men, who focused on sources and practices where women were invisible or silent. They often considered the movement and its music as an exclusively masculine domain, viewing women as peripheral.[21]

The first scholars who wrote about Hasidic women and performances in North America were Shifra Epstein and Ellen Koskoff, respectively, in the 1970s and 1980s. Epstein focused on the Bobov theater,[22] and Koskoff exposed the causal relationship between the socio-religious status of women and their musical practices. Koskoff also observed that women who were religiously observant from birth (named *frum* from birth or FFB) and married remained mostly absent from the musical scene, while young observant girls embraced performing arts in schools and camps; *baal teshuvot* (Jews from a secular background who become religiously observant) integrated secular sounds and conceptions of the arts into their new religious community, resulting in a greater presence of women in music and the arts.[23] Koskoff's observations remain valid, with the exception of married women observant from birth (as discussed further below). While pioneering in scope, Koskoff's focus was limited to the Lubavitch communities, and Epstein concentrated on one specific performance, the Purim play. Only later, in the 1990s and early 2000s, some of the first publications on non-Lubavitch women's performances emerged, with the works of Zelda Kahan-Newman on Satmar songs;[24] Asya Vaisman Schulman on various Hasidic dynasties across North America, Europe, and Israel;[25] and more recently, Rose Waldman on Hasidic women's voices in North America and Jill Gellerman on the history of Hasidic dance.[26] All of these scholars pointed out the communal experience of these performances, underlining that tsniut requires discretion in the public display of individual talent; however, they did not discuss the valorization and celebration of individual voices that now characterize ultra-Orthodox feminine productions. Indeed, if this musical shekhinah is defined by the common experience shared by women and girls when participating in a musical life that is exclusive to their gender because of tsniut and kol ishah, then the celebration of the individual and the making of "frum female artist" within the communal space has only recently emerged.

It is important to define how the women and girls discussed in this chapter interact with each other and recognize themselves as a community. First, the women and girls performing and singing collectively in summer camps or schools define their community on the basis of common affiliation to Jewish Orthodoxy. The community is further defined according to specific adherence to Hasidic and Litvish branches and localities. Nevertheless, within a large majority of performances outside these educational circles, for instance, at charity events, women and girls are defining themselves through their belonging to Orthodoxy in general, rather than by specific denominations and localities. Indeed, there are Hasidic women making music with women from the Litvish world or with Modern Orthodox performers. The women and girls at tsedakah events, on YouTube, or in the recording studio label themselves as professional artists, and more specifically as "frum female artists," a novel concept that serves as a self-identifier and reshapes the traditional interpretation of the feminine musical practice as a collective space, highlighting its ambivalence (discussed further below). The frum female artists use performances to connect with other women and girls across the world, creating a new community of belonging based on their common affinity with the arts as Orthodox women. This transformation in the creation of communities in the context of the musical shekhinah echoes the shift that has occurred within community studies, which now considers the communal experience beyond the local, looking at transnational interactions facilitated by technology.[27]

In his analysis of the relationship between music and community, Will Straw refers to two distinct ways in which a community may be constructed:

> One towards the stabilization of local historical continuities, and another which works to disrupt such continuities, to cosmopolitanize and relativize them. . . . The point is not that of designating particular cultural spaces as one or the other, but of

examining the ways in which particular musical practices "work" to produce a sense of community within the conditions of metropolitan music scenes.[28]

These two modes are reconciled in the concept of the scene, which forms a basis for the discussion that follows. By considering four musical scenes—the school/summer camp, the Broadway replica, the home studio, and the YouTube music video—this chapter demonstrates how this musical shekhinah functions to produce a sense of community beyond the logic of geographic space and local community belonging.[29] Inspired by Kay Kaufman Shelemay's tripartite framework for analyzing music and the collectivities it generates, it suggests that the production of a sense of community within these four scenes is based on common affiliation, common necessity, or common affinity.[30]

SCENE 1: SCHOOLS AND SUMMER CAMPS— THE ORIGIN OF WOMEN- AND GIRLS-ONLY PERFORMANCES

In the early twentieth century the formalized education of ultra-Orthodox girls began in Eastern Europe with the foundation of schools. In 1917 Sarah Schenirer opened a school in Krakow that became one of the models for the education of ultra-Orthodox girls in Europe during the interwar period:[31] the network of Bais Yaakov schools and summer camps. Schenirer was not the first to provide a formal Jewish education to girls in the region, but she was the first to do it in Krakow's Hasidic circles and focusing on performances. These educational programs valued youth, women, and innovation, and they integrated musical performances and songs into education, which deepened the shared identity (Jewish Orthodoxy), ethnicity (Ashkenazic Jew), and religious ties of students and faculty. Through performances as collective experiences, a sense of belonging to a community of shared affiliation was established.

Schenirer's goal was to address the lack of spiritual guidance available to girls and women, many of whom were leaving Judaism.[32] Her guidance, certainly influenced by her love of Polish theater,[33] ascribed a central role to performance, music, and dance, leading her to write scripts to be performed during Jewish holidays.[34] Schenirer also imbued girls' education with a Hasidic spirit, often ending her speeches with circle dances with her at the center.[35] Her theatrical work, complete with script, songs, dance, and acting, embedded into the transmission of a religious message a spirit of entertainment that constitutes the origin of women-only performances in the ultra-Orthodox world. The role of a song is particularly noteworthy, as it is treated as part of a broader performance used to achieve the religious, moral, and ethical goals that the community seeks to foster. Music is seen as a form of communication with God.[36] Schenirer's educational approach echoes the shekhinah as a collective place for girls' presence and power.

Schenirer's approach inspired many Hasidic and Litvish communities during its development in the interwar period in Europe and, after the Holocaust, in North America and Israel. Other ultra-Orthodox schools and summer camps for girls adopted the model to their needs, integrating performances and plays into their curriculum. Today, many schools and summer camps serving ultra-Orthodox girls around the globe offer performing arts in their curriculum, though they do not all follow the same pattern. Indeed, there is a spectrum of opportunities for listening, performing, dancing, singing, or playing an instrument, with learning the piano or guitar being the most popular. The extent to which girls participate in music-making in these spaces depends on the norms of tsniut and kol ishah followed by the Hasidic or Litvish group associated with the school or camp, and on the age of the students (pre– or post–bat mitzvah). Performances are considered beneficial for educational and religious purposes in that they define gender roles, reinforcing girls' sense of belonging and faith in these programs. The prevailing themes of the songs and scripts are historical events, faith, motherhood, holidays, redemption, self-sacrifice, tsniut, or the dangers of the outside world. As Asya Vaisman Schulman notes, wedding, love, and work songs are not part of the corpus.[37] (Nor are these themes present in the scripts.)

The repertoire of melodies used in schools and camps is taken from a variety of sources, sometimes from *nigunim* and *zmires* (Jewish hymns), but mostly from the recent popular music released by famous ultra-Orthodox male singers or composers or from non-Jewish sources. Today, depending on the audience and the community (Hasidic or Litvish), the language of the songs is either Yiddish (essentially Hasidim apart from Lubavitch), Loshen Kodesh (Hasidim and Litvish), modern Hebrew (Litvish), or English (mostly Litvish and Lubavitch).[38] Teachers and principals officially censure the use of non-Jewish music, though the generation of women born before the Second World War and in the 1950s–1960s used to listen to secular music and were well familiar with Jewish secular music. Despite this censorship, non-Jewish melodies are still entering the musical space as authorship in music is rarely attributed and non-Jewish music is seldom identified if non-exposed to it.[39] Though girls often write lyrics, few compose melodies, so the common practice is to do a cover or a contrafactum. The repertoire of songs used in schools and summer camps constantly changes, with new popular songs from the Jewish male and, more recently, music industry by and for women. Scripts for theatrical performances are often Yiddish or Hebrew adaptations or translations (depending on the community) from Jewish novels in another vernacular language. Original compositions by screenwriters, principals of schools, directors of camps, or directors of plays in schools are also used.

As scripts and songs travel via physical and digital support with girls and women when they visit family abroad, and travel from school to school or from camp to camp, they create a global corpus in which authors and composers are often forgotten. Thus, when a girl sings or acts at school or summer camp, she rarely knows who composed the melody or wrote the script. As lyrics are often written by girls and women directly involved in the performance, authorship, if it is known at all, is usually associated with the lyricist. The lack of attribution of authorship appears to be due to three main factors:

oral tradition, the codes of tsniut and the focus on the collective, and amateurism. The songs are transmitted from a group or an individual to another as an oral tradition. The materializations of melodies as transcriptions or scores that include names of lyricists, composers, or arrangers are rare.[40] With the increasing accessibility of the recording process (the cassette in the 1980s and the mini-cassette or the digital Dictaphone in the 2000s–2010s), many commercial and home recordings also circulated without authorship. As many girls have told me: "the music belongs to the community. This is our Jewish music." Authorship is traditionally subsumed into the category of the collective, something that is also true of the repertoire sung in ultra-Orthodox male circles but not to the same degree because of their public presence. If a name is mentioned, it is often the lyricist or the singer. In the case that she is a woman, sometimes only her initials appear, adhering to the codes of tsniut in most conservative settings. According to these codes, creativity aims to enrich the community and not personal artistic growth and fame. Thus, women and girls are rarely claiming their names in the most conservative circles. Being "tsniut" is also reflected in the rejection of the desire for individual attention. Lastly, because their performances are traditionally guided by educational, social, and religious motivations, they are associated with amateurism, where the sources of origin and the valorization of artistic personal development are rarely valued.

SCENE 2: BROADWAY MUSICALS IN BROOKLYN—THE RACHEL'S PLACE PRODUCTION

In the last two decades, the growth of an ultra-Orthodox middle class with a taste for consumerism and entertainment,[41] combined with secular Jewish women artists joining ultra-Orthodoxy (notably baal teshuvot among Chabad), has given rise to a scene of professional women performers. Though live performances for girls and women outside schools and summer camps do have a social dimension, motivated by tsedaḳah, they have become very similar to performances traditionally found only in the secular artistic scene, now involving dancers, singers, actresses, and professionally trained musicians. These professional scenes, supported by social organizations and purposes, entertain their audience while raising funds for charity. In the 2010s, one of the most famous and professional of these entertainment spaces for ultra-Orthodox women in North America was the Rachel's Place production, which staged its first performance in 2011 though the development of this professional scene for the purpose of fundraising can be traced back the early to mid-2000s.

With the growing interest in performing arts and entertainment within the ultra-Orthodox middle class at the time, these tsedaḳah events attracted sizable audiences, encouraging women to develop larger professional productions. Among the pioneers in this area were Malky Giniger, originally from Flatbush and belonging to a Modzitz

Hasidic family (a Hasidic dynasty well known for its musical compositions and its recordings by the Cantor Ben Zion Shenker). She founded the Ratzon program in 2003, which started out in 1992 as Voices of Youth. Ratzon now has branches around the world, and Giniger's first musical productions were released on DVD in 2010 (*Lost and Found*). The Girls' Night On, an open-mic night and concert hosted by women for women, was launched in New York in 2004 by Leslie Ginsparg, a Bais Yakov scholar and writer currently serving as academic dean of the Women's Institute of Torah Seminary and College, an Orthodox Jewish college for women. Miriam Leah Gamliel, a baal teshuvah trained as a professional singer and actress at Barnard College and Pennsylvania State University, created Atara in 2007, a transnational network that supports Orthodox women in the arts. Finally, Leah Forster, a comedian who produces comedy shows including music, released several DVDs and CDs in the late 2000s. These pioneers also performed with Rachel's Place at different points in their careers, but mainly developed other performances independently, as the Rachel's Place productions were a form of voluntary work and did not generate income.

Every year since 2011, Imeinu's Rachel's Place,[42] a transitional independent living program for runaway and homeless girls in New York, transplants a Broadway musical into the neighborhood of Little Odessa (South Brooklyn) at the Master Theatre for ultra-Orthodox women and girls: the Rachel's Place production.[43] When the organization's founding members were looking to renew their events to contribute to their annual fundraising in the early 2010s, they hired Miriam Handler as the production director and Chani Schick, Handler's sister, as the musical director. They considered hosting a charity event where a professional production could entertain women and girls. Both Handler and Schick were well known in the women-only artistic scene and were able to invite the most "talented" women and girls from their circles to participate. As the founder of the N'shei Tzedaka Players, an organization founded in the 1990s that produced musicals for girls and raised money for social needs in the community, Handler was well-connected and knowledgeable about musicals. While directing these musicals, she often adapted secular scripts or produced original ones based on Jewish stories; with Rachel's Place, she fully explored Broadway musicals while making small changes in the script, and the words of songs to fit Orthodox religious narratives. However, the choreography, the melodies, and the arrangements she uses from the original Broadway show for Rachel's Place productions are identical, information that is never advertised.

The Rachel's Place production reveals one of the most telling examples of the transformation of live performances since the 2010s: the integration of secular musicals into the musical shekhinah. If Broadway plays for women and girls only in North America have been documented as occurring in certain ultra-Orthodox circles such as Bais Yakov Schools in 1970s, it was then banned and documented as forbidden.[44] The normalization of Rachel's Place productions highlights an important shift in the integration of secular plays within Orthodoxy, the need for "highly professional entertainment" for female audiences without the need to exit Orthodox circles and the pragmatism in using professional artistic material (script, scores, lyrics) already existing. It also reveals the transformation of live performance from serving primarily educational and religious purposes into an experience anchored in entertainment and the arts for their own sake. In 2019 the production was entitled *Katalina*, a replica of *Anastasia* (written by Terrence McNally; music and lyrics by Lynn Ahrens and Stephen Flaherty). The production is immensely popular each year, with tickets ranging from 25 to 90 US dollars and generally selling out within a few days. Girls and women from different Orthodox backgrounds travel by bus organized for the occasion, by taxi, subway, and private car from various neighborhoods in order to attend. At the 2019 and 2020 editions of the production, booklets of almost 100 pages each were distributed to the audience containing the program and information about the production: the synopsis, the name of each participant (including production staff, cast, musical ensemble, and dancers) alongside a short biography and photo, a list of sponsors, photos from behind the scenes, advertisements for DVDs from previous years, and publicity from sponsors. One important element was missing: the names of the composers and lyricists, as including these would have revealed the connection between the production and the Broadway musical *Anastasia*.

Though many women involved were aware that *Katalina* was a replica of *Anastasia*, some did not seem to notice it, and others did not talk about it. The production encompasses paradoxes and contradictions about performance according to ultra-Orthodox norms. Some baal-teshuvot women artists who participated expressed their discomfort. Among them, Rivka, a famous artist in ultra-Orthodoxy, explained:

> I do not really understand how Rachel's Place exists. I know that Miriam Handler tried to produce some Broadway in the past, but I think the organization was shut down because of it. It is kind of a taboo. Nobody talks about it, but many know. In the early 2010s, when Rachel's Place was created, it rapidly became popular. Maybe the rabbinical authority could not stop it or only ignored it as it was too popular and could bring better to the community with its fundraising dimension. I do not know, but it might be several parameters. In any case, having a Broadway and telling our girls they can't watch secular movies or listen to secular music does not make sense. Rachel's Place is a fully non-Orthodox production. For sure you essentially have Orthodox women on stage and in the audience, but is it what makes a production kosher?[45]

As one of the most popular performances for women and girls in ultra-Orthodox circles at the time, Rachel's Place interrogates the transformation of the musical shekhinah over the last decade. A closer look at the 2019 production of *Katalina* indicates the various strategies implemented to assist the integration and celebration of Broadway scripts, choreography, and music in ultra-Orthodox feminine circles. The booklet presents *Katalina* as a story about "one girl's search for her identity." *Anastasia*, however, is a love story, a theme traditionally non-existent in ultra-Orthodox performances. The 2019 production utilizes the love story in its script. Musicals used in Rachel's Place productions are always renamed, allowing all connections with the original Broadway production to be erased to advertise the musical's themes in ways that could resonate with religious values. A production of *Mary Poppins* in 2014 became *That's My Nanny*, *Fiddler on the Roof* in 2016 *Shtetl*, and *Oliver!* in 2020 became *Ragamuffin*.

Though the themes addressed in these musicals may be different from those usually presented in live performances for summer camps and schools, the musicals are still accepted because of the effort taken by producers and directors to respect the norms of tsniut for dress codes on stage as well as kol ishah, and certainly because of their long-standing good reputation. Only women and girls are present on stage and in the audience, costumes cover elbows and knees, married women have their hair covered, and DVDs sold a few months after the live performance are labeled "for women and girls only," with no traces of the performance available online for download or streaming. The fact that Rachel's Place productions are replicas of Broadway musicals is unspoken by the audience and the participants. Some women also explain that the status of Rachel's Place as a home for girls at risk could be another reason for this acceptance, alongside the independence of Rachel's Place from religious schools and institutions.

Rachel's Place productions offer a different interpretation of the "kosher" entertainment scene for women only and of what count as "acceptable scripts and stories." They have opened avenues for professionalization in the domain of performing arts for women, and for the recognition of the arts for their own sake, while tying women's performance to tsedakah. Directors at Rachel's Place need people able to dance, sing, act, and even play instruments for the productions. As the large majority of these need to be female and Orthodox, the productions have fostered a growing community of women artists consisting of not only girls performing in high schools and summer camps, but also married women who had years of experience performing for private occasions and learning in private settings with professionals in the arts.

With Rachel's Place productions, secular popular culture is adapted and normalized as a product of Orthodoxy. Women and girls from various backgrounds are able to watch the performance live in the theater or on DVD a few months later. The most conservative Hasidic schools do not offer screenings of these DVDs on their premises, but some girls and women from these schools still watch them in their spare time and/or attend the performances. Most women and girls acting, dancing, and singing in Rachel's Place come from the Litvish/Bais Yakov circles, but some women from more conservative groups—such as Belz, Bobov, Satmar, and other Hasidic dynasties—participate anonymously, changing or omitting their names.

By preserving the content of secular popular culture and changing only its frame, Rachel's Place reshapes the musical shekhinah in light of new norms of tsniut. The gender division created through kol ishah allows women and girls to integrate concepts of fame, celebrity, and professionalism, previously associated only with men's performances and once considered detrimental to tsniut, into their artistry. This way of negotiating tsniut implicitly impacts women's agency through the arts. Although summer camps and schools were and still are the home of the musical shekhinah, some married women have found new ways of acquiring agency and positions of authority in the arts. The integration of Broadway musicals into this ultra-Orthodox entertainment scene, where singers, actresses, and dancers perform every year to serve their community locally and transnationally (with the release of DVDs across the globe), and are recognized as professionals, highlights a transformation in the format and potentiality of performances. The musical shekhinah expands the sound and performative experience of women and girls into an artistic experience valued for its own sake with the aim of women's empowerment. This creative space has led women aspiring to professional careers in the arts to invest in other resources to promote their artistic activity, such as by producing albums and building home studios.

SCENE 3: THE HOME STUDIO

While the scene of live performances is still extremely vibrant, music for and by women only is now recorded, promoted, and marketed. As the circulation of DVDs of Rachel's Place underlines, the musical shekhinah exists as live performances and as part of a commercial and non-commercial recordings market. The commercial recordings began with female singers around the 1980s, while the non-commercial ones are the result of the digital turn and the emergence of home studios owned by ultra-Orthodox women in the 2000s.

The first commercial recordings were essentially made by baalot teshuva, as increasing numbers of women artists joined Orthodoxy in the 1980s and 1990s. Trained in secular professional musical schools, baalot-teshuva women brought their knowledge to ultra-Orthodox circles and shifted their careers as artists from secular stages to Orthodox ones. Among them, Ruthi Navon Zmora, an Israeli singer who performed on Broadway, recorded her first album in 1988 (Independent) labeled "for women only" on the cover; Julia Blum recorded *Stand Tall* (Independent) in 1990 and *Songs of the Heart* (Firefly) in 1998, though her albums did not mention "for women only" on the cover; and Kineret Sarah Cohen recorded her first album in 1998. The first women born into ultra-Orthodoxy who composed, recorded, and commercialized their music in North America were Rochel Miller, a Litvish woman who grew up in the Bronx; Malky Giniger mentioned earlier; and Chanale Fellig-Harrell, a Chabad woman from Florida who now lives in Israel. This first generation was a small group of women working mostly with male sound engineers and producers. They were rarely considered professionals at this point, as their performances were envisaged as an amateur hobby serving social and educational purposes.

Following the technological and digital revolution of the early 2000s, from the mid-2010s women started to invest in building home studios to record and provide instrumental accompaniment to their music for women and girls in summer camps, schools, and charity events. Principals of schools and directors of summer camps saw studio-recorded backing tracks as a way of including instrumental accompaniment without the need for instrumentalists to be on stage during live performances or rehearsals, and to be independent of male studio owners. Through this process, music for women and girls only transformed into a tool to generate income.

Today, ultra-Orthodox women with home studios are exploring two market avenues. One is part of the official music industry, producing recordings of women singers that anyone can access on streaming and downloading platforms, or by walking into a Jewish-run store selling music. The other is an underground and informal avenue accessible only from within, by participating in the women and girls' collective life, with women artists producing music in studios for summer camp and school projects within the community. The digital turn makes both avenues possible, particularly the increasing miniaturization and distribution of recording and listening equipment since the 2000s.[46] This move to digital production offered new possibilities for ultra-Orthodox circles at large, but particularly for women struggling to produce music while respecting kol ishah and not interacting with the outside world or with men while doing so. The digital turn facilitated easy access to equipment and the acquisition of technical knowledge, which in turn enabled women to create and distribute their music in the comfort of their homes.[47] Though the emerging albums were initially considered marginal and difficult to market, by the late 2010s both forms of distribution (formal and informal) began to be celebrated and promoted, as evidenced by an article featuring women in the recording studio in the ultra-Orthodox magazine *Ami Living* in January 2021.[48]

The home studio is thus envisaged as providing professional, economic, and artistic opportunities for women, their families, and their communities. Women and girls have started learning the basics of recording, editing, arranging, and mixing with online classes or other music production experts, often outsiders such as secular Jews and non-Jews.[49] A few have even specialized in composing melodies and arrangements, among them Chanale Fellig-Harrell and Shaindel Antelis from Chabad-Lubavitch; and Chayala Neuhaus, Nechama Cohen, and Franciska from other Hasidic and Litvish-Yeshivish communities. Women with home studios opened and are still opening new possibilities for providing others with soundtracks, arrangements, and recordings to facilitate their creative experience.

The home studio also impacted the musical aesthetic of women's performances. It has supported modernization (e.g., the use of electronic instruments) as well as the individualization of women and girls' musical performances. Every woman or girl who enters a home studio wants to exit with a song that sounds "professional." This means having a pre-recorded instrumental accompaniment made using a high-quality MIDI (Musical Instrument Digital Interface), and being able to equalize her voice if she gets out-of-tune, or voice-changer (deepfake voice) in case they do not want their voice to be recognizable. These women and girls want to record their own versions of recent popular hits of the Jewish music world or new compositions. They are not seeking to perform traditional melodies, instead being attracted to the most "modern" and recent recordings. This style of music production echoes the making of music in the popular music industry, where a song's popularity is sudden and declines rapidly as the audience soon forgets the latest hit and moves on to the next one. It also mirrors secular music consumption as well as the establishment of a work community based on economic and professional necessity.

Concerning the individualization of musical performance, while performances in summer camps and schools focus on the collective experience, the home studio also celebrates the soloist. The studio is linked to the emergence of ultra-Orthodox women as professional singers and celebrities, who self-identify as frum female artists or singers. Utilizing the studio to make recordings available in the musical market at large allows girls and women to create a professional space to develop their artistic personalities. Frum female artists such as Dobby Baum, Devorah Schwartz, Bracha Jaffe, or Franciska enter and participate in the music industry alongside ultra-Orthodox men as singers, while serving only women and girls.

The home studio has also contributed to the traceability and circulation of music, creating a corpus of songs shared transnationally among women and girls. The cover of the song "Charasho" (recorded by the famous Lubavitch singer Benny Friedman in 2019) by Hasidic girls from Brooklyn illustrates the phenomenon particularly clearly. A few months after the release of Friedman's hit, composed by Yitzy Waldner with lyrics by Aliza Spiro, the principal of a girls' high school in Borough Park took the melody and added her own lyrics to it, narrating her struggles with the closure of her school while explaining the need to be resilient and accept the closure as God's will. The song was recorded, arranged, and mixed in a studio in Borough Park, sung by girls from the same school. The refrain goes as follows: "Yes, I can accept this plan. I accept, I accept it's how Hashem wanted to be. And I trust that it must be designed with love for me. Yes, it's hard, and it hurts It's so tough but so am I. I say yes to Hashem plans I won't ask why." The song was entitled "I Accept." It circulated via email, WhatsApp, and file exchange and rapidly became a "hit" heard in schools, summer camps, and dance and gym classes across the United States and Canada. It was then reinterpreted among various circles even in the United Kingdom and Israel. In early 2020, Elisha, a woman from Borough Park in her seventies, was inspired to write a Yiddish version of the song. She kept the message of resilience and acceptance, and added the idea of "understanding." The song, entitled "Ich farshtei" (I understand), was recorded in a home studio in Borough Park and distributed via email to schools and via a hotline. The MP3 files of "I Accept" and "Ich farshtei" circulated without naming either the singer or the lyricist. The name mentioned as the artist was the name of the home studio owner, listed alongside her email and phone number. If the song has now been appropriated collectively, a new artist has emerged too: the home-studio owner.

The home studio owned by women and girls has transformed the musical shekhinah traditionally known through live performances in schools and camps. Home studios allow girls to diversify their music, providing a "sophisticated" musical background to their performances while respecting kol ishah as the music production remains in the hands of women. The home studio has also created new ways to consume and produce music at the individual level. Many girls and women record music as individual singers hoping to build an artistic career. These individual and collective opportunities for the production and the consumption of music have led to a rising need for professional training in music and its related disciplines (sound engineering, mixing, studio production, etc.). This is developing an array of careers and businesses in the arts that transcend the performing stage. Music is no longer just a collective experience anchored in religiosity, education, and entertainment. Music can provide parnaśah, become a career and profession, and lead to the growth of an individual's talent and fame. This transformation from a collective to an individual celebration, from live to digital expression, indicates the professionalization of some ultra-Orthodox women and girls' musical productions. The musical shekhinah expands the live experience of sharing sound and performance for religious and educational purposes to the digital skill of producing music for financial and professional reasons. This in turn implies new models of womanhood and girlhood, in which tsniut and fame may coexist.

SCENE 4: MUSIC VIDEOS ON YOUTUBE

The emergence of the music video in ultra-Orthodox women's circles follows the path of the development of the home recording studio. Since the late 2000s, and increasingly since the late 2010s, ultra-Orthodox singers who pursue careers as professional artists in the music industry are emulating non-Orthodox women and male ultra-Orthodox singers by producing professional music videos that they distribute on YouTube. Depending on the artist, these videos may be unlisted, meaning only a person who has the link can access them, or be available publicly, with a large majority of women releasing public videos.

These videos feature original compositions by women singers or other women composers, contrafacta of non-Jewish compositions and Orthodox male singers, and many covers of Orthodox male artists. The lyrics are mostly in English, sometimes in Loshen Kodesh when borrowed from a religious text (often Tehilim) or modern Hebrew, and only rarely in Yiddish. As the videos on YouTube tend to reach a broader audience than through other forums, crossing geographical and denominational borders, singers privilege English as it is understood by most, even those coming from a Yiddish home.

Releasing their videos on YouTube with the label "Kol isha—for women and girls only," these artists advocate an understanding of tsniut, and more specifically kol ishah, that makes the listener, rather than the producer, responsible for ensuring that only women and girls engage with their productions. They aspire to offer an artistic experience with sound and images that is similar to what male singers have been doing since the creation of YouTube. Today, many women singers want to emphasize women's potential to perform and provide professional music videos that equal those of male pop stars.

The three pioneers in North America of producing music videos for their original compositions are Shaindel Antelis, Franciska, and Nechama Cohen. Shaindel Antelis released her first two music videos in 2011 (*Change, The Light*) directed by Leah Gottfried, a director, writer, producer, and actor who also directed one of Franciska's music videos, *Shiru L'Hashem*, in 2017. None of Shaindel Antelis' videos are publicly available, though links to the unlisted YouTube videos are available on her website. Franciska produced *Lekha Dodi* in 2012,[50] and Nechama Cohen *Inside Out* in October 2014, both opening the path for women artists to post public music videos on YouTube in North America. The three women have different approaches to the composition of music and music videos. Shaindel and Nechama wrote their lyrics in English, giving the listener a taste of pop-rock music with spiritual and personal lyrics in their vernacular language. Franciska, however, drew inspiration from prayers and religious texts in Hebrew to compose her music, while at the same time being inspired by folk music, North American music, Israeli pop, blues, and even hip-hop.

Franciska is one of the only frum female singers to have produced music videos on a regular basis for several years. Moreover, she does so by providing and exploring different musical genres, visual aesthetics, and narratives in each video. In 2017 she released several music videos with professional dancers in different performance styles, such as hip hop (*Ata Takum*, directed by Raquella Raiz),[51] ballet (*Ruth*, directed by Rivka Cohen),[52] and contemporary dance (*Shiru L'Hashem*, directed by Leah Gottfried).[53] In 2019, inspired by the Japanese philosophy of *kintsugi*, she adapted the symbol of Japanese gold-repaired pottery into her music video *Vezakeni* (directed by Chris Cole) to express the scars of life passing. As Franciska is the composer of the songs she produces and releases, she also creates the narratives of her music videos:

> Everything comes from a very artistic place. Very often a vision or an idea comes to me, we (the videographer and other collaborators such as the dancers) develop it in a way that can be executed on a budget.... One idea comes and we figure out how to connect it.... Every music video is unique, different, new ideas inspire it and we need to figure out how to transmit it into images.[54]

While Franciska has mostly composed songs with Hebrew lyrics referring to prayers and religious texts, in 2021, she explored a new musical aesthetic with the song *If You Wanna Be*,[55] where she introduced lyrics written in English by the Lubavitcher rapper Rachel Samuels. This eccentric music video draws on North American hip-hop paradigms, with symbols such as a golden throne, gold coins falling, a crown, white and blue wigs, and high-speed rap (Figures 28.1–2). The song and music video offer a provocative version of feminine *frumkeit*, in terms of both sound and imagery, while transmitting an uplifting religious message about the need to trust God.

For Franciska, the music video is a way to explore and expand her creativity and fandom without the constraints of religious authority. Unlike other frum female artists, Franciska does not have her music on common "kosher" streaming platforms. For her, the percentage fee taken from her revenue in order to sell her music on those platforms is not financially compelling. The music video is a new way to promote her music through a free medium that could contribute to an increase in downloads and streaming. Since deciding to think about her art as a personal endeavor, expanding her sources of parnaśah outside her artistic practices, she has felt much more liberated and empowered artistically and economically.[56] In that vein, in 2018 she created a podcast,

FIGURE 28.1 Screenshot of the music video If You Wanna Be (Franciska featuring Rachel Sam). Reproduced by permission of Franciska.

FIGURE 28.2 Screenshot of the music video If You Wanna Be (Franciska). Reproduced by permission of Franciska.

FIGURE 28.3 Cover of the Franciska Show (photo by Enoch Purnell, March 2021, Philadelphia). Reproduced by permission of Franciska.

The Franciska Show, which initially focused on Jewish Orthodox women in the arts, in 2021 she expanded to discuss women, passion, and success (Figure 28.3), and then on "conversations worth having," discussing controversial topics within Jewish Orthodox circles. The launch of individual singles as music videos on YouTube facilitates Franciska's collaboration with other frum female singers, promoting artistic individuality as well as building a new community of frum female artists online. Franciska's recent collaborations with Rachel Samuels, Devorah Schwartz (*Modim* in May 2020), and Maayan Davis (*Tov Lehodot* in December 2020) are examples of her collaborative projects with dancers and other singers.

With live performances canceled during the COVID-19 pandemic, YouTube became a very popular platform for frum female artists to promote their music and expand their fandom, posting videos on the platform and promoting them on Instagram and other social media. Artists and their fans have also used YouTube to support each other during the pandemic. In this light, Dobby Baum released the single *It Is Meant To Be*, Bracha Jaffe and Shaindy Plotzker *AH-YAY!*, and Devorah Schwartz and Chayala Neuhaus *Ein Od Mildavo: Covid Cover.*[57]

Once videos are posted on the artists' individual YouTube channels, links to them are then shared by other frum female singers on other social media platforms. Frum female singers have between 5,000 and 35,000 Instagram followers. Promoting one another's videos drastically increases the number of views they each receive on YouTube. Since March 2020 the number of music videos produced by these artists has exploded, as has their followers on Instagram. As online performances and concerts became the sole performance space available to artists during the pandemic, many invested in their virtual presence by posting more on Instagram, hosting live Zoom performances and promoting them on their mailing lists, and performing in live online concerts advertised in Jewish magazines. Some artists have reached over 500,000 views on YouTube, an impressive achievement for singers who perform exclusively for a niche audience. Frum female artists do not yet reach the same number of followers, honorariums, and views as their male counterparts, but their willingness to challenge this gender inequality in the kosher music industry while performing for women and girls only is clear. If, for a long time, the gold standard of promotion for Orthodox women artists was the release of albums, in 2020 their focus definitively and by necessity shifted toward the release of music videos, a mode of representation that would market them as professional singers.

Regarding the financing of these music videos, some artists have been funding production independently, using them as a form of investment to generate future gigs, while others have received funding through collaboration with Orthodox organizations for charity campaigns or from individual donors and organizations. One of the most telling examples of this phenomenon is the video *Stronger All As One*, produced by the organization Chesed 24/7, which provides extensive and innovative services to the sick, the elderly, the disabled, and any individual or family facing a life challenge, and featuring Bracha Jaffe. It was released on the artist's YouTube channel on February 3, 2021, and gained over 100,000 views in its first two months. Almost all public music videos have very high production values; many collaborate with charity organizations, using a religious message to encourage donation, following the model of the tsedaḳah event using the digital. Another example is the network Thank You Hashem producing high-quality music videos of various frum artists including Bracha Jaffe, Judith Gerzi, Shaindy Plotzker, and Menucha Abraham.[58]

With the emergence of the kol-ishah market online, with music videos being made available on YouTube essentially as public video, the musical shekhinah takes on a new aspect, defying the gender divide that allows men to be the public face of the arts while rendering women invisible. If the scenes of the home studio and the Broadway replicas, made only for and by women, allow ultra-Orthodox women to exercise their artistic agency, the music-video scene offers an interpretation of tsniut and kol ishah where women are not limited in their actions and distribution of music as well as their process of gaining publicity. These music videos are available to anyone via a simple click. The initial lines that defined the musical shekhinah as secretive, unrecorded, and private are now being redrawn, leaving religious authority powerless in the face of this new and growing phenomenon.

CREATIVITY, COMMUNITY, AND THE FUTURE OF THE KOL-ISHAH MARKET

The ultra-Orthodox feminine musical space constitutes a multilayered social, cultural, and economic reality in which there is significant variation in how the musical shekhinah is understood, expressed, and performed. If the musical shekhinah is generally characterized as private, live, unrecorded, unmarketable, and outside the industry, the journey through the four scenes explored in this chapter underlines a different reality. The transformation of the musical shekhinah, from the centrality of the collective to the celebration of the individual, from the private scene of the summer camps and schools to the publicly accessible YouTube music video, highlights a redefinition of the concept of creativity and publicity among Orthodox women and girls that varies between different scenes. Contrasting with the traditional definition of creativity as collective experience with social, educational, and religious purposes, mostly confined to summer camps and schools, the digital turn has created a growing demand for kosher entertainment within which individualism, the concept of the "artist," and new careers for women and girls in music have emerged. These diverse understandings of creativity, varying between the collective and the individual, now coexist and should be interpreted in constant dialogue. Young girls in Hasidic schools continue to develop their creativity through school performances. They also witness new forms of creativity by attending fundraising events where frum female artists such as Bracha Jaffe, Dobby Baum, or Devorah Schwartz perform. Girls in schools and summer camps learn about these singers from their live performances, music videos, or DVDs of Rachel's Place productions, as the singers themselves increasingly become famous celebrities. The concept of art for its own sake, as well as art for the glory of the artist, is no longer peripheral to cultural norms. Rather, it has been integrated into new cultural norms of the musical shekhinah that coexist with more traditional ones.

Aside from the novelty of fame that is found among popular ultra-Orthodox women artists, where the culture of celebrity from global pop culture has been adapted to Orthodoxy, the musical shekhinah has allowed for new processes of community building among girls and women. In summer camps and schools, girls and women mobilize music to reinforce sisterhood based on common affiliation. In the home studio, Broadway productions in Brooklyn, or in music videos, girls and women form a community based on the common professional necessity to find artists embodying an "artistic professionalism." The community built by the collective experience of participating in these productions is based not on sharing a common affiliation to Orthodoxy, but on sharing a common desire to succeed in the arts. Contrary to experiences in schools or summer camps, alliances among frum female artists are based on professional expertise and stimulated by common necessity and artistic affinity. Music is no longer in service of a community created solely on the basis of common descent; instead, the musical community today is shaped by professional, economic, and artistic interests and development as well.

With their newly marketable and economically sustainable professions within the arts, frum female artists and home studio owners are transforming the social status of women and girls, and their ways of gaining publicity. This new artistic scene—where women and girls from various ultra-Orthodox backgrounds collaborate and interact, based on artistic and personal affinity, in search of the expression of shekhinah—suggests a reconsideration of ultra-Orthodoxy's definitions beyond religious groups, denominations, and dynasties. Lastly, the varying understandings of the musical shekhinah explored in this chapter reflect current debates in the wider society in which ultra-Orthodox women and girls build their identities. As a specifically feminine concept, the musical shekhinah is just one instance of a broader gender divide that can be interpreted as a tool for feminine empowerment or as a normative division that must be respected and maintained. At the same time, the musical shekhinah also acts upon the society in which it exists, transforming it, while simultaneously challenging, reinforcing, and complexifying the divide between masculine and feminine practices in contemporary ultra-Orthodox communities.

Acknowledgments

This chapter draws on fieldwork undertaken in Montreal, New York City, and online from 2018 to 2021, which was supported by a Georgetown Summer Grant and the 2021 Eakin Fellowship from the McGill Institute for the Study of Canada. I would like to thank Aashia Bose, my research assistant during my fellowship at McGill, for her precious data collection and analysis on the music video. I owe a tremendous debt of gratitude to all the women and girls, and frum female artists, who agreed to participate in my research and welcomed me into their homes and studios, rehearsals, and shabbat tables. A special thanks to Franciska for allowing me to publish the photos in the chapter.

Notes

1. This chapter uses the term *ultra-Orthodoxy* rather than the Israeli term *Haredi* to characterize the communities and individuals in question, in light of their location in North America and their self-definition in opposition to modern Orthodoxy and, more specifically, secular society and modernity. One of the elements that differentiates Orthodoxy and ultra-Orthodoxy is that ultra-Orthodox communities strongly disapprove of the internet for personal use. These attitudes are found among the Hasidic and Litvish-Yeshivish communities but not the Hasidic communities of Chabad-Lubavitch.
2. The distinction between women and girls is made according to their marital status and their age. Girls are unmarried and attend schools or seminaries, while women are married, divorced, or widowed.
3. See Serene J. Khader, *Decolonizing Universalism: A Transnational Feminist Ethic* (Oxford: Oxford University Press, 2019).

4. See Lea Taragin Zeller, "Modesty for Heaven's Sake: Authority and Creativity among Female Ultra-Orthodox Teenagers in Israel," *Nashim* 26 (2014): 75–96; and Lea Taragin Zeller, "Between Modesty and Beauty: Reinterpreting Female Piety in the Israeli Haredi Community," in *Love Marriage, and Jewish Families,* ed. Sylvia Barack Fishman (Cambridge: Cambridge University Press, 2015), 308–326.

5. See Tamar El Or, *Educated and Ignorant: Ultra-Orthodox Jewish Women and Their World* (Boulder, CO: Lynne Rienner, 1994), and Rhonda Berger-Sofer, "Pious Women: A Study of the Women's Roles in a Hasidic and Pious Community" (PhD diss., Brown University, 1978).

6. See Saba Mahmood, *Politics of Piety: The Islamic Revival and the Feminist Subject* (Princeton, NJ: Princeton University Press, 2005); and Leila Abu-Lughod, *Remaking Women: Feminism and Modernity in the Middle East* (Princeton, NJ: Princeton University Press, 1998).

7. See, for example, Yafeh Orit, "The Time in the Body: Cultural Construction of Femininity in Ultraorthodox Kindergartens for Girls," *Ethos* 35, no. 4, (2007): 516–553; and Rachel S. Harris and Karen E. H. Skinazi, eds., "Special Issue: The Feminism and Art of Jewish Orthodox and Haredi Women," *Shofar: An Interdisciplinary Journal of Jewish Studies* 28, no. 2 (2020); Heather Munro, "Navigating Change: Agency, Identity, and Embodiment in Haredi Women's Dance and Theater," *Shofar: An Interdisciplinary Journal of Jewish Studies* 28, no. 2 (2020): 93–124; Sima Zalcberg Block, "Shouldering the Burden of Redemption: How the 'Fashion' of Wearing Capes Developed in Ultra-Orthodox Society," *Nashim* 22 (2011): 32–55; and Barbara Goldman Carrel, "Hasidic Women's Head-Coverings: A Feminized System of Hasidic Distinction," in *Religion, Dress and the Body,* ed. Linda Arthur (New York: Berg, 1999), 163–180.

8. See Taragin-Zeller, "Modesty for Heaven's Sake: Authority and Creativity Among Female Ultra-Orthodox Teenagers in Israel," and Taragin-Zeller, "Between Modesty and Beauty: Reinterpreting Female Piety in the Israeli Haredi Community."

9. Songs of Songs 2, *Sefaria,* https://www.sefaria.org/Song_of_Songs.2.13?lang=bi (accessed September 23, 2022).

10. Ben Cherney, "Kol Isha," *The Journal of Halacha and Contemporary Society* 10 (1985): 57–75.

11. See Ellen Koskoff, "Miriam Sings Her Song: The Self and Other in Anthropological Discourse," in *Musicology and Difference,* ed. Ruth Solie (Berkeley: University of California Press, 1993), 149–163.

12. Ibid.

13. See Vanessa Elbaz, "Kol B'Isha Erva: The Silencing of Jewish Women's Oral Traditions in Morocco," in *Women and Social Change in North Africa: What Counts as Revolutionary?,* ed. Doris Gray and Nadia Sonneveld (Cambridge: Cambridge University Press), 263–288.

14. See Susanna Heschel, "Judaism," in *Her Voice, Her Faith: Women Speak on World Religions,* ed. Katherine Young and Arvind Sharma (Boulder, CO: Westview Press, 2004); Gershom Sholem, "Shekhinah: The Feminine Element in Divinity," in *On the Mystical Shape of the Godhead* (1976; New York: Schhoken Books, 1991), Chava Weissler, "Meanings of Shekhinah in the 'Jewish Renewal' Movement," in *Women Remaking American Judaism,* ed. Riv-Ellen Prell (Detroit, MI: Wayne State University Press, 2007), 51–58.

15. Katherine Young, "Judaism," in *Her Voice, Her Faith: Women Speak on World Religions,* ed. Arvind Sharma and Katherine Young (Boulder, CO: Westview Press, 2002), 156.

16. Chava Weissler, "Meanings of Shekhinah in the "Jewish Renewal" Movement," in *Women Remaking American Judaism,* ed. Riv-Ellen Prell (Detroit, MI: Wayne University Press, 2007), 60.

17. The Lubavitcher differentiate themselves from other ultra-Orthodox dynasties through their outreach approaches and their use of the internet, so are not central to this study. However, some Haredi women include Lubavitcher singers in a cross-communal approach, which will be addressed toward the end of this chapter.

18. Leah, member of the band in Kyrias Joel, in discussion with the author, July 27, 2020. To protect the identity of the artist, only their first name is used.

19. See Ellen Koskoff, *Music in Lubavitcher Life* (Urbana: University of Illinois Press, 2000).

20. See Miriam Isaacs, "Creativity in Contemporary Hasidic Yiddish," in *Yiddish Language and Culture: Then and Now—Proceedings of the Ninth Annual Symposium*, ed. Leonard J. Greenspoon (Omaha, NE: Creighton University Press, 1998), 165–188.

21. See David Biale et al., *Hasidism: A New History* (Princeton, NJ: Princeton University Press, 2017).

22. See Shifra Epstein, "The Celebration of a Contemporary Purim in the Bobover Hasidic Community" (PhD diss., University of Texas at Austin, 1979); "Josef Is Still Alive in Brooklyn: Tradition and Modernity in the Performance of a Musical in Yiddish by Hasidic Women," in *Di Froyen: Women and Yiddish, Tribute to the Past, Directions for the Future* (New York: National Council of Jewish Women, 1997); "Going Far Away in Order to Better Understand the Familiar: Odyssey of a Jewish Folklorist into the Bobover Hasidic Community," *The Journal of American Folklore* 112, no. 444 (1999): 200–212.

23. Ellen Koskoff, "The Sound of A Woman's Voice: Gender and Music in an American Hasidic Community," in *Women and Music in Cross Cultural Perspective*, ed. Ellen Koskoff (Westport, CT: Greenwood Press, 1987); and Koskoff, *Music in Lubavitcher Life*.

24. Zelda Kahan-Newman, "Women's Badkhones: the Satmar Poem Sung to a Bride," *International Journal of the Sociology of Language* 138 (1999): 81–99.

25. Asya Vaisman Schulman, "She Who Seeks Shall Find": The Role of Song in a Hasidic Woman's Life Cycle," *Journal of Synagogue music* 35 (2010): 155–183; and Asya Vaisman Schulman, "Seamed Stockings and Ponytails: Conducting Ethnographic Fieldwork in a Contemporary Hasidic Community," in *Going to the People: Jews and the Ethnographic Impulse*, ed. Jeffrey Veidlinger (Bloomington: Indiana University Press, 2016), 282–299.

26. See Rose Waldman, "Women's Voices in Contemporary Hasidic Communities," *Shofar: An Interdisciplinary Journal of Jewish Studies* 28, no. 2 (2020): 35–60; Jill Gellerman, "(Not Just) *Az der rebbe tantst*: Toward an Inclusive History of Hasidic Dance," in *The Oxford Handbook of Jewishness and Dance*, ed. Naomi M. Jackson, Rebecca Pappas, and Toni Shapiro-Phim (Oxford: Oxford University Press, 2022), 53–85.

27. The shift in community studies happened in the course of the 1980s and 1990s with the transformation of relationships with spaces and locality. The work of Benedict Anderson, Arjun Appadurai, and Anthony Cohen had a direct impact on this transformation. See Kay Kaufman Shelemay, "Musical Community: Rethinking the Collective in Music," *Journal of the American Musicological Society* 64, no. 2 (2011): 349–390; Benedict Anderson, *Imagined Communities: Reflections on the Origin and Spread of Nationalism*, rev. ed. (London: Verso, 1991); Arjun Appadurai, *Modernity at Large: Cultural Dimensions of Globalization* (Minneapolis: University of Minnesota Press, 1996); and Anthony P. Cohen, *The Symbolic Construction of Community* (Chichester, UK: Ellis Horwood, 1985).

28. Will Straw, "Systems of Articulation, Logics of Change: Communities and Scenes in Popular Music," *Cultural Studies* 5 (1991): 373.

29. See ibid. See also Will Straw, "Scenes and Sensibilities," *Public* 22–23 (2001): 245–257.

30. In her article "Musical Community" Kay Kaufman Shelemay suggested a tripartite model based on processes of descent, dissent, and affinity. I suggest that the increased role of technology in the creation of the ultra-Orthodox musical scene has given rise to a new community based on processes of necessity (economic and technical).

31. See Naomi Seidman, *A Revolution in the Name of Tradition: Sarah Schenirer and Bais Yaakov* (Oxford: Oxford University Press 2019).

32. See Seidman, *A Revolution in the Name of Tradition*; and Rachel Manekin, *The Rebellion of the Daughters: Jewish Women Runaways in Habsburg Galicia* (Princeton, NJ: Princeton University Press, 2020).

33. On Sarah Schenirer's enthusiasm for Polish theater, something she shared with many other Orthodox and Hasidic girls from Galicia, see Joanna Lisek, "'I Feel So Crazy, Like Flying the Coop': The Lesser-Known Sarah Schenirer. Side Reflections on Naomi Seidman's Book," *Shofar: An Interdisciplinary Journal of Jewish Studies* 38, no. 1 (2020): 272–290.

34. See Naomi Seidman, "Legitimizing the Revolution: Sarah Schenirer and the Rhetoric of Torah Study for Girls," *New Directions in the History of the Jews in the Polish Lands*, ed. Antony Polonsky, Hanna Węgrzynek, and Andrzej Żbikowskip (Boston: Academic Studies Press, 2018), 356–365.

35. See ibid.

36. See Abigail Wood, "Stepping Across the Divide: Hasidic Music in Today's Yiddish Canon," *Ethnomusicology* 51, no. 2 (2007): 205–237; and Koskoff, *Music in Lubavitcher Life*.

37. On the theme of these songs see Asya Vaisman Schulman, "Hold on Tightly to Tradition: Generational Differences in Song Repertoire among Contemporary Hasidic Women," in *Choosing Yiddish: Studies on Yiddish Literature, Culture, and History*, ed. Lara Rabinovitch, Shiri Goren, and Hannah Pressman (Detroit, MI: Wayne State University Press), 339–356.

38. Yiddish and Loshen Kodesh are the most frequent languages used among Hasidim, while English and modern Hebrew are the most frequent among Litvish-Yeshivish circles.

39. For more on the prohibition against non-Jewish sources and the generational discrepancies, see Asya Vaisman Schulman, "She Who Seeks Shall Find": The Role of Song in a Hasidic Woman's Life Cycle," *Journal of Synagogue Music* 35 (2010): 155–183.

40. Velvet Pasternak is one of the few who transcribed Hasidic songs from the supposedly old tradition from eastern Europe. Indeed, very few composers of melodies are able to read music. Ben Zion Shenker, a composer and hazzan associated with the Modzitz Hasidic dynasty, is one of the few who materialized the pre-war Modzitz songs along with his compositions in musical score. Among the materializations of music via recording, Ben Zion Shenker was a pioneer, with his first recording of Hasidic music in 1950 (Modzitzer Melaveh Malka Melodies), followed by David Wedyger in the 1970s.

41. See Yael Friedman and Yohai Hakak. "Jewish Revenge: Haredi Action in the Zionist Sphere." *Jewish Film & New Media: An International Journal* 3, no. 1 (2015): 48–76.

42. Imeinu's Rachel's Place was founded in 2006 by a group of women concerned about young girls on the street with no place to call home.

43. The Master Theatre is located in the neighborhood of Brighton Beach, also known as the Little Odessa because of its tight-knit Russian and Eastern European communities, Jewish and non-Jewish, but not ultra-Orthodox.

44. See Leslie M. Ginspard, "Defining Bais Yaakov: A Historical Study of Yeshivish Orthodox Girls High School education in America, 1963–1984" (PhD diss., New York University, 2009), 159.

45. Rivka, in discussion with the author, May 16, 2019. The name of the artist has been changed to preserve her anonymity.
46. Ons Barnat, "Vers une ethnomusicologie du studio d'enregistrement: Stonetree Records et la *paranda* garifuna en Amérique centrale," *Cahiers d'ethnomusicologie* 30 (2017): 121–135.
47. This practice was possible as neither male nor female authority figures saw any danger in it, and instead sought new opportunities to consolidate religiosity and sisterhood.
48. See Musia Kaplan, "Rochel Leah Reifer Creates Music and Helps Other To Do It Too," *Ami Living* 501 (2021): 36–39.
49. Artistic knowledge is often transmitted from professionals outside the community or via online training; this fact is usually kept secret as it implies external interaction on-site or online that is forbidden by religious authorities.
50. Franciska Kay, "Lekha Dodi," March 7, 2012, YouTube video, https://youtu.be/2UV2 5196M30.
51. Franciska, "Ata Takum," December 11, 2017, YouTube video, https://youtu.be/EZN-dQuN43s.
52. Franciska, "Ruth," May 25, 2017, YouTube video, https://youtu.be/d4GvMFhkBUo.
53. Franciska, "Shiru L'Hashem," November 7, 2017, YouTube video, https://youtu.be/YSYY gpBzz4M.
54. Franciska, in discussion with the author, January 24, 2021.
55. Franciska, "If You Wanna Be," February 21, 2021, YouTube video, https://youtu.be/l6J8 rJB3f6U.
56. Franciska, in discussion with the author, December 20, 2020.
57. Dobby Baum, "It Is Meant to Be," March 25, 2020, YouTube video, https://youtu.be/jQOf cUroJJo; Bracha Jaffe and Shaindy Plotzker, "AH-YAY!," May 17, 2021, YouTube video, https://youtu.be/ZSdK8EI_yz8; Devorah Schwartz and Chayala Neuhaus, "Ein Od Mildavo: Covid Cover," January 17, 2021, YouTube video, https://youtu.be/cVgX7CKOFas.
58. For the YouTube channel of Thank You Hashem, see https://www.youtube.com/@Tha nkYouHashem/videos.

SELECT BIBLIOGRAPHY

Elbaz, Vanessa Paloma. "Kol B'Isha Erva: The Silencing of Jewish Women's Oral Traditions in Morocco." In *Women and Social Change in North Africa: What Counts as Revolutionary?*, edited by Doris Gray and Nadia Sonneveld, 263–288. Cambridge: Cambridge University Press, 2018.

Epstein, Shifra. "Going Far Away in Order to Better Understand the Familiar: Odyssey of a Jewish Folklorist into the Bobover Hasidic Community." *The Journal of American Folklore* 112, no. 444 (1999): 200–212.

Fader, Ayala. *Mitzvah Girls: Bringing Up the Next Generation of Hasidic Jews in Brooklyn.* Princeton, NJ: Princeton University Press, 2009.

Harris, Rachel S., and Karen E. H. Skinazi, eds. "The Feminism and Art of Jewish Orthodox and Haredi Women." Special issue, *Shofar: An Interdisciplinary Journal of Jewish Studies* 28, no. 2 (2020).

Isaacs, Miriam. "Creativity in Contemporary Hasidic Yiddish." In *Yiddish Language and Culture: Then and Now—Proceedings of the Ninth Annual Symposium*, edited by Leonard J. Greenspoon, 165–188. Omaha, NE: Creighton University Press, 1998.

Koskoff, Ellen. *Music in Lubavitcher Life*. Urbana: University of Illinois Press, 2000.

Roda, Jessica. *For Women and Girls Only: Reshaping Jewish Orthodoxy Through the Arts in the Digital Age*. New York: New York University Press, 2024.

Seroussi, Edwin. "Music." In *Studying Hasidism: Sources, Methods, Perspectives*, edited by Marcin Wodzinski, 197–230. New Brunswick, NJ: Rutgers University Press, 2019.

Skinazi, Karen E. H. *Women of Valor: Orthodox Jewish Troll Fighters, Crime Writers, and Rock Stars in Contemporary Literature and Culture*. New Brunswick, NJ: Rutgers University Press, 2018.

Vaisman Schulman, Asya. "Contemporary Yiddish-language Productions at Hasidic Girls' Schools and Camps." In *Yiddish: A Jewish National Language at 100. Proceedings of Czernowitz Yiddish Language 2008 International Centenary Conference*, edited by Wolf Moskovich, 197–204. Jerusalem: Hebrew University of Jerusalem, 2010.

Vaisman Schulman, Asya. "Hold on Tightly to Tradition: Generational Differences in Song Repertoire among Contemporary Hasidic Women." In *Choosing Yiddish: Studies on Yiddish Literature, Culture, and History*, edited by Lara Rabinovitch, Shiri Goren, and Hannah Pressman, 339–356. Detroit, MI: Wayne State University Press, 2012.

Vaisman Schulman, Asya. "She Who Seeks Shall Find": The Role of Song in a Hasidic Woman's Life Cycle." *Journal of Synagogue Music* 35 (2010): 155–183.

Waldman, Rose. "Women's Voices in Contemporary Hasidic Communities." *Shofar: An Interdisciplinary Journal of Jewish Studies* 28, no. 2 (2020): 35–60.

Wood, Abigail. "Pop, Piety, and Modernity: The Changing Spaces of Orthodox Culture." In *The Routledge Handbook of Contemporary Jewish Cultures*, edited by Laurence Roth and Nadia Valman, 286–296. New York: Routledge, 2015.

Wood, Abigail. "Stepping Across the Divide: Hasidic Music in Today's Yiddish Canon." *Ethnomusicology* 51, no. 2 (2007): 205–237.

Yafeh Orit. "The Time in the Body: Cultural Construction of Femininity in Ultraorthodox Kindergartens for Girls." *Ethos* 35, no. 4 (2007): 516–553.

29

"ON A HARP OF TEN STRINGS I WILL SING PRAISES TO YOU"

Envisioning Women and Music in the Oppenheimer Siddur

SUZANNE WIJSMAN

In the Middle Ages, most Hebrew manuscripts were made for the transmission of texts used in Jewish ritual, education, study, and community life. Each manuscript is a unique entity, created in a process where texts were not only copied, but sometimes embellished with decorative or figural artwork, often in highly individualistic ways. The visual programming of Hebrew illuminated manuscripts reflects the mentality of the religious, social, and cultural collectivities that produced them, as well as the individual choices, imaginings, and viewpoints of their scribes, artists, patrons, and owners. As Katrin Kogman-Appel has observed, decorated and illuminated medieval Hebrew manuscripts represent a shared, complex, and interconnected "web of associations" between patrons, artists, and audiences.[1]

Among the paratextual elements present in medieval Hebrew manuscripts are images of instruments and musicians. Apart from the shofar—the ram's horn used for Jewish ritual purposes—it is unclear if, or to what extent, illustrations depicting musicians in Hebrew manuscripts relate to the use of contemporary medieval instruments in medieval and early modern Jewish communities. However, there are traces of activity by Jewish musicians during the late Middle Ages and early modern era, both men and women. In his pioneering research on itinerant Jewish musicians, Albert Wolf notes an account by Israel Isserlein (1390–1460), the prominent rabbi and Talmudic authority in Germany in the first half of the fifteenth century, that mentions Jewish women musicians performing at Christian weddings.[2] Wolf also cites an account from Prague, dated 1533, in which Jewish musicians were employed in aristocratic houses, performing before or after a meal for a small fee, and Jewish musicians are reported to have performed in a royal procession in 1512.[3] Abraham Idelsohn, Hayyim Schauss, and Naomi Feuchtwanger-Sarig all cite the fifteenth-century *Sefer Maharil: Minhagim* by the Ashkenazic rabbinic authority Rabbi Jacob ben Moses Moellin (known as the Maharil, 1365–1427), mentioning his ruling that weddings, as joyous occasions, require music, as well as details of a wedding celebration with instrumentalists accompanying the bride and groom to the synagogue in Mainz.[4]

Walter Salmen and András Borgó have examined the role of medieval Jewish instrumental musicians in Ashkenaz, also noting their role in providing music for weddings in the Jewish *Tanzhaus* or for other celebratory occasions.[5] A more recent study by Walter Zev Feldman gives an overview and analysis of early terminology for early Ashkenazic Jewish musicians and entertainers and its relationship to actual instrumental practice, including discussion of the foundation and activity of the Prague Jewish musicians' guild around 1540.[6] He concludes that, in the German-speaking lands of Ashkenaz, secular instrumental performance "was in the hands of a group of men (and perhaps occasionally women) who combined aspects of musician, singer, clown, and dancer" and that these musician-entertainers may have been itinerant, but they enjoyed a lower social status when compared with their Italian, Sephardic, or Bohemian counterparts.[7] Research by Richard Prior and Peter Holman into the early history of the violin has recognized that, beginning in the sixteenth century, some of the most prominent early string players in Italy, the Netherlands, and England were Sephardic Jews, including important musicians at the court of Henry VIII in England.[8]

Such fragments of documentary evidence concerning Jewish instrumental music-making in late medieval and early modern Europe are supported by iconographical evidence. For example, a harpist is pictured alongside a dancing trio in the important fifteenth-century dance treatise, *De pratica seu arte tripudii* (On the practice or art of dancing, 1463) by Guglielmo Ebreo da Pesaro (ca. 1420–ca. 1481), the Jewish dancing master who served Italian nobles such as Isabella d'Este at the court of Ferrara and the Sforza family in Milan.[9] Given the emphasis on the importance of music in this treatise and his role as dancing master to members of the Italian nobility, Guglielmo is likely to have been a highly trained musician himself. Even though he converted later to Christianity, Guglielmo's treatise pre-dates his conversion. *De pratica* begins with a declaration of Guglielmo's Jewish identity: "Here begins the little work in the vernacular on the practice or art of dancing by Guglielmo the Jew of Pesaro."[10]

Couples are also pictured dancing to instrumental accompaniment in two wedding images in an Italian Yiddish Miscellany from Italy dated circa 1503, now in the collection of the Paris Bibliothèque Nationale, containing an illustrated *Sefer minhagim* (Book of customs).[11] In the first image, two couples dance face-to-face while touching hands, accompanied by a lute player in an illustration for *Shabbat naḥamu*, the first Sabbath following Tisha B'Av. In the second, couples dance accompanied by instrumentalists who probably play the pipe and drum, though the image of the musicians is partially cut off. As Diane Wolfthal has observed, the illustrations in this manuscript were done by an amateur artist whose work represents an "insider's view" of Jewish customs, including wedding customs.[12] Instrumental musicians also appear in other books of customs, such as the illustration for Purim customs in the Venice *Sefer minhagim* (1593).[13] Although some of this evidence post-dates medieval times, it is reasonable to assume that, collectively, it points to the existence of lively musical cultures and instrumental performance within Jewish communities in the late Middle Ages as well as Jewish iconographic traditions depicting music-making.

The vast majority of medieval Hebrew manuscripts containing illustrations that include musical motifs were made for liturgical use or to illustrate biblical texts or commentaries.[14] Due to the rabbinic prohibition against instrumental music in the synagogue following destruction of the Second Temple, the depiction of instrumental performance in medieval Hebrew manuscripts is unlikely to have been intended to be read in a literal way as representing instrumental music performed in connection with Jewish worship or ritual.[15] Rather, the presence of musical imagery in such contexts may serve a decorative purpose or represent, symbolically, the idea of musical sound, including vocal sound such as musically delivered prayer. As Tilman Seebass has observed, "an instrument is almost an indispensable tool for the visualisation of the idea of music."[16] However, images of music-making and musical instruments in medieval art often have a deeper, semiotic function. As Richard Leppert states: "Reference to music occurs in visual art not because musical sound exists but because musical sound has meaning. . . . The visual representation of people making and listening to music, governed by conventions, encapsulates music's ideological use value, conscious or unconscious."[17]

Elisheva Baumgarten and Ivan G. Marcus have both convincingly argued the case for a process of appropriation that existed in medieval Ashkenaz, whereby aspects of local medieval Christian cultures were transformed when adapted in Jewish contexts.[18] As Baumgarten observes, theories of cultural appropriation imply not only multidirectionality in the process of appropriation, but that appropriation can be defined as "an act of possession" or "to make one's own," which she argues are fitting descriptors for the way such phenomena occurred in medieval Ashkenaz.[19] Art historians such as Kogman-Appel, Evelyn Cohen, Sarit Shalev-Eyni, Sara Offenberg, and Marc Epstein have examined this process at work in Hebrew illuminated manuscripts, in which the meanings of motifs seen in medieval Christian art have been changed when appearing in works made for Jewish audiences, and are even sometimes reversed in a polemical way.[20] As I will demonstrate in this chapter, we see this process of appropriation and transformation at work, too, in musical iconography from medieval Ashkenaz.

The musicians appearing in Hebrew illuminated manuscripts typically are figures of men, half-human half-beast hybrids, or sometimes animals. Women playing musical instruments also appear, but most often in archetypical scenes, such as in Passover Haggadot where depictions of Miriam playing the timbrel in celebration over Pharaoh's demise in the Red Sea illustrate the biblical account described in the Book of Exodus 15:20.[21] The numerous examples of Miriam performing on her timbrel in medieval Haggadot suggests that this recurring topos in Jewish medieval manuscript art is one that crosses geographical and temporal boundaries, perhaps highlighting Miriam's status in Judaism as *'eshet ḥayil* (אֵשֶׁת חַיִל)—the woman of valor (Proverbs 31:10–21).[22] However, images of women musicians in medieval Hebrew illuminated manuscripts outside such typological contexts are much rarer.

Among Hebrew manuscripts containing musical imagery, the Oppenheimer Siddur (Oxford, Bodleian Library MS Opp. 776) is exceptional for the thematic character of its musical iconography and the sheer number of illustrations of musicians it contains— forty-four across its thirty-three illuminated pages. The Oppenheimer Siddur is a small-format book of daily prayers according to the Ashkenazic Rhineland rite (*minhag Rinus*) that was finished in 1471 by a scribe, Asher ben Yitzḥaq, who says in its colophon that he made it for use in prayer by "my sons and the sons of my sons":

> סימתי זאת התפילה באחד לחודש הרביעי רל"א לפרט באלף הששי שבח לא'. אני אשר
> ב"ר יצחק השוא'. יהי רצון שיתפללו בה בניי ובני בניי לאל. ונפשי תאיבה ומצפה לביאת
> גואל. חזקינו ואמצינו בבינין אריאל. סלול השלו' פרו על עבדיך הואל. והראיני בשלום
> שאר אחי את עמך ישראל. סליק סליק.

> I finished this prayer on the first day of the fourth month in the 231st year in the sixth millennium, according to the Creation era [1 Tammuz, 5231/June 28, 1471]. I am Asher ben Rabbi Yitzḥaq who requests this. It is my wish that my sons and the sons of my sons will pray to God with it. And my soul desires and watches for the coming of the Redeemer. Make us powerful and strong in the building of the Temple. Grant peace, make fruitful and be pleased with all your servants. And show the rest of my brothers, your people Israel, peace.[23]

Codicological features suggest a German provenance because both sides of the parchment have been scraped to achieve an equalized texture, a practice known only in Hebrew manuscripts produced in Germany after 1300.[24] I have argued elsewhere that a German provenance is also supported by elements in its artwork.[25] Previous research on the Oppenheimer Siddur has revealed motifs appearing in both scribal copying and artwork, and the results of scientific analysis of pigments show that identical pigments were used in both text copying and painting, strongly supporting the hypothesis that the scribe Asher ben Yitzḥaq was also the artist of this manuscript.[26] That this manuscript was likely made by a single individual for his private family audience thus removes speculation about the respective roles and relationships of patron, scribe, and artist, since all were one and the same. It allows us to consider the iconographic programming of the Oppenheimer Siddur, and what Asher ben Yitzḥaq was trying to communicate to his family members through the images he created in his prayer book, as the vision of a fifteenth-century Ashkenazi Jew.

Three unusual scenes in the Oppenheimer Siddur feature a woman and music. In all three, the woman is paired with a man. In two, the women are shown alongside their male partners actively performing on an instrument, while in the third, the woman embraces a male musician. These three images have no antecedents in the aforementioned Haggadot, nor direct parallels in the illustration program of any other extant Hebrew illuminated manuscript. This chapter will explore how Asher ben Yitzḥaq appropriated motifs seen in the love iconography of the wider fifteenth-century collectivity within which he lived, and transformed them in these three images. It will also discuss possible interpretations for such images of women and music in the context of a medieval Ashkenazic prayer book by examining their resonances with Jewish art, literature, and theology. A focus on the feminine elements in the illustrations in this prayer book connects this chapter broadly with the theme of this section, *shekhinah*.

ENVISIONING HARMONY

אַשְׁרֵי יוֹשְׁבֵי בֵיתֶךָ עוֹד יְהַלְלוּךָ סֶלָה.
אַשְׁרֵי הָעָם שֶׁכָּכָה לּוֹ אַשְׁרֵי הָעָם שֶׁיְהוָה אֱלֹהָיו.

Happy are they that dwell in Thy house,
They are ever praising Thee. Selah.
Happy is the people that is in such a case.
Yea, happy is the people whose God is the Lord.

Psalms 84:5, 144:15

On fol. 12v (Figure 29.1), a facing couple plays long horns while supporting a rectangular panel containing the initial word in for the opening two lines of the Ashrei, which is recited at least three times daily in Jewish prayers: "Happy are those who dwell in Thy house; they are continually praising Thee" (Psalm 84:5), "Happy are the people that is in such a case; happy are the people whose God is the Lord" (Psalm 144:15).[27] Although the man and woman here are clearly playing animal horns and not metal trumpets, the thin, elongated shape of these suggests they are playing the horned trumpet, an instrument

FIGURE 29.1 The Oppenheimer Siddur, Bodleian Library MS Opp. 776, fol. 12v, detail. Courtesy of the Bodleian Libraries, University of Oxford.

that is distinct from the shofar used in Jewish ritual, which often has a more pronounced curve in the bell or a flattened shape when seen in Ashkenazic manuscripts of this era.[28]

Both the woman and man in this illustration wear head coverings: the man dons a pointed red cap, and the woman wears a wimple, the white cloth wrapped around the head and neck that was worn by married women during the medieval era to hide their hair and ensure their modesty. In Ashkenazic illuminated manuscripts of the late Middle Ages, women frequently are depicted wearing white wimples—indeed for the reader, the presence of a white wimple or other head covering often differentiates men from women.[29] Younger, presumably unmarried women are often depicted in Ashkenazic manuscripts without such head coverings, as seen in the fifteenth-century First Darmstadt Haggadah.[30] From this, we may infer that the woman and man in the illustration on fol. 12v are a married couple.

The symmetry and complementary elements in the composition on fol. 12v create a harmonious image. The roles of man and woman are equal and balanced: each figure supports one side of the panel containing the initial word of the Ashrei with one hand, while simultaneously holding a horned trumpet with the other. The bells of their horns are held in mirrored gestures, pointing gracefully upward, with the puffed red cheeks of both figures as they blow the instruments enlivening a musical scene by their actions, visualizing the sound of joyful praise of God expressed in the opening of the Ashrei.

The colors used here, too, serve to emphasize harmony: pigments have been mixed to achieve complementary shades of orange-red and crimson, resulting in chiaroscuro, the play of light and shade that creates the impression of soft folds in the garments worn by the couple, with the colors of each figure's robe complementing that of the facing figure. The bright red color of the man's cap is also mirrored by, and draws attention to, red outlining that surrounds the gilded letters of the initial word, אַשְׁרֵי (Ashrei), in the panel that the couple hold. The background of the panel is pale blue, often considered the color of the heavens in the Middle Ages,[31] providing a complementary support for the larger, red-outlined black letters of the initial word, as well as contrasting the red tones of the couple's clothing.

This balanced portrait suggests that this couple perhaps represents the "people," or עַם ('am), referred to in the opening lines of the Ashrei. In the Book of Psalms, loud sounds and instruments, such as trumpets and shofarim, are media used for praise of God, such as in Psalm 98:6:

$$\text{בַּחֲצֹצְרוֹת, וְקוֹל שׁוֹפָר הָרִיעוּ, לִפְנֵי הַמֶּלֶךְ יְהוָה}$$

With trumpets and sound of the horn shout before the King, the Lord.

and Psalm 150:3:

$$\text{הַלְלוּהוּ, בְּתֵקַע שׁוֹפָר}$$

Praise Him with the blast of the horn.

In the thirteenth-century Parma Psalter, Psalm 95 is illustrated with a horn and trumpet, referring to such loud, joyful sound in the opening verse: "O come, let us sing unto the Lord; let us shout for joy to the Rock of our salvation" (Psalm 95:1).[32] The image of two horned trumpets being blown by the facing couple on fol. 12v recalls such textual and pictorial references to trumpets and horns as sonic media of praise. Thus, the complementary elements of this composition are melded and united: they combine chromatically, spatially, and sonically to create a vision of harmony that reminds the reader of the content of the Ashrei that follows.

Additionally, the image of this facing horn-playing couple on fol. 12v recalls pairs of angel trumpeters that often appear in medieval Christian art, sometimes in eschatological scenes in which angel trumpeters are positioned alongside, below, or around a Christ figure at the top or middle of a composition, their trumpets announcing the end of days.[33] The positioning of the musical instruments and their sonic import in such images provide directional focus for the reader's attention and signal the hierarchy of importance of the elements in the frame of a scene. Artists of earlier medieval Ashkenazic illuminated manuscripts appropriated this convention from Christian art. For example, in the depiction of the Revelation of the Torah in the thirteenth-century Dresden Maḥzor, the two figures of Moses receiving the Torah and giving it to the people of Israel are framed by two facing, winged, trumpeting angels (Figure 29.2). This scene is highly reminiscent of representations of the Last Judgement in Christian religious art of the late Middle Ages.[34]

The appearance of this motif in the Dresden Maḥzor indicates that it was already known in thirteenth-century medieval Ashkenaz, and it is possible that Asher ben Yitzḥaq may have been aware of its use in earlier Ashkenazic illuminated manuscripts when planning the decoration program for his siddur. However, in the Oppenheimer Siddur, it is an earthly man and woman who are paired on fol. 12v, not otherworldly angels. And, rather than depicting an event such as the Revelation of the Torah, as seen in the Dresden Maḥzor, the sight of this couple's trumpeting sound draws the reader's attention to the texts that follow, evoking the opening of the Ashrei and praise of God both in sight and implied sound of the horned trumpets. This accords with the function of illuminated word panels in general in medieval Hebrew manuscripts and, later, in printed Hebrew books, since their primary purpose is that of a reading device to highlight texts and mark their divisions. Yet, as with historiated initials in Latin manuscripts, the space around such initial words provided the artists of medieval Hebrew manuscripts with the opportunity to include visual commentary relating to the texts in the form of figural decoration. In the case of the Oppenheimer Siddur, the inclusion of motifs with sonic import, as we see here on fol. 12v, is a defining characteristic.

In addition to the vision of trumpeting sound on fol. 12v, the musical couple here recalls images of wedding couples found in earlier Ashkenazic manuscripts; in particular, facing couples appear in several illuminations for the opening of the piyyut, Iti mi-levanon (Come with me from Lebanon), based on the Song of Songs and recited on *Shabbat ha-gadol*, the Sabbath preceding the start of the festival of Passover. Sarit Shalev-Eyni explains that the occurrence of this motif refers to a metaphorical wedding

FIGURE 29.2 The Dresden Maḥzor, Sächsische Landesbibliothek–Staats- und Universitäts-bibliothek Dresden, MS Dresd.A.46.a, fol. 202v. Courtesy of the Sächsische Landesbibliothek–Staats- und Universitätsbibliothek Dresden.

banquet and the Jewish allegorical reading of the Song of Songs as an expression of the bond of love between God and the Jewish people, *kneset Yisrael* (a Talmudic expression referring to the Jewish people as a whole).[35] Shalev-Eyni convincingly argues that the bride represents kneset Yisrael in such portrayals of wedding couples in Ashkenazic liturgical manuscripts.[36] It is perhaps no coincidence that, as in the Oppenheimer Siddur, one such image of a "loving couple" occurring in the Darmstadt Maḥzor frames the initial word of the Ashrei, though in the Darmstadt Maḥzor it appears in a different liturgical context: the *yozer piyyut* for Simchat Torah (Figure 29.3).[37]

The broader significance of what Shalev-Eyni terms "the loving couple" in medieval Hebrew manuscript art is open to interpretation.[38] For example, both Shalev-Eyni and Kogman-Appel discuss the image of a crowned bride and bridegroom in the Leipzig Maḥzor but arrive at different conclusions about the identity of the woman and meaning of the couple's presence. Shalev-Eyni contends that this image expresses the marriage allegory in the Song of Songs, as discussed above, but also suggests that it may be influenced by medieval love iconography and lyric poetry in Christendom, including the Marian cult, in which Mary—and by extension, the Christian faith— is portrayed as the bride of God. Kogman-Appel, on the other hand, offers a complex argument that, in the Leipzig Maḥzor, the crowned female figure in represents the feminine aspect of God, the *Shekhina*, and the male figure reminds the viewer of the "ultimate goal of the ritual of prayer" according to the medieval Ashkenazic Pietists: the mystical union of the male worshipper with the Glory, or *Kavod*, a process that is sometimes expressed metaphorically using erotic imagery in kabbalistic writings.[39]

Shalev-Eyni and Sara Offenberg discuss another, enigmatic version of this motif in the Levy Maḥzor.[40] There, a male figure kneels before a crowned and blindfolded bride, the blindfold a clear reference to medieval polemical representations of the Jews as blind *Synagoga* and Christian Church as the seeing *Ecclesia*. However, Shalev-Eyni and Offenberg both argue that, in the Levy Maḥzor, identification of the blindfolded woman with the Jewish people acquires a different connotation: here, *Synagoga* is crowned, signifying her status in the bridal couple as the true "bride of God," a pictorial visualization of the marriage allegory evoking the verse from Song of Songs that opens the piyyut Iti mi-levanon: "Come with me from Lebanon, my bride . . ." (Song of Songs 4:8). In appropriating the Christian convention of the "bride of God" that was associated with the Song of Songs, the "loving couple" in the Levy Maḥzor therefore expresses a Jewish theological viewpoint, asserting the primacy of the Jewish people as the true "bride."[41]

Irrespective of differences in interpretation of the "loving couple" motif by Shalev-Eyni, Kogman-Appel, and Offenberg, its prevalence suggests that this motif was an iconographic convention well-known by the artists of medieval Ashkenazic illuminated manuscripts. Perhaps we see it also here in the Oppenheimer Siddur. If associating such love iconography with particular liturgical texts, such as the piyyut Iti mi-levanon and the Ashrei, was part of this tradition, it helps to explain the inclusion of the facing couple

FIGURE 29.3 The Darmstadt Maḥzor, Universitäts- und Landesbibliothek, Darmstadt, Cod. Or 13, fol. 349v. Courtesy of the Universitäts- und Landesbibliothek, Darmstadt.

on fol. 12v: this illustration recalls such images and, by implication, the pictorial allegory of the loving bond between kneset Yisrael and her God.

However, in no other Ashkenazic manuscript illumination where the "loving couple" appears is there any allusion to music as seen on fol. 12v of the Oppenheimer Siddur. In this regard, the illumination for the opening of the Ashrei on fol. 12v diverges from this earlier group of "loving couple" images. It not only refers to the "loving couple," but additionally appropriates the convention of trumpeting angels seen in Christian medieval religious art, transforming it into a Jewish vision where the trumpets being blown, and imagined loud sound draw the reader's attention to the focal point of the illustration: the initial word "Ashrei" in the panel and its exhortation to joyful praise of God. These elements, along with the carefully planned color scheme and compositional symmetry, all contribute to the vision of harmony conveyed by this image.

SIN, MUSIC, AND FOLLY

וְהוּא רַחוּם יְכַפֵּר עָוֹן וְלֹא יַשְׁחִית.
וְהִרְבָּה לְהָשִׁיב אַפּוֹ וְלֹא יָעִיר כָּל חֲמָתוֹ.

But He, being full of compassion, forgiveth iniquity, and destroyeth not;
Yes, many a time doth He turn His anger away,
And doth not stir up all His wrath.

Psalm 78:38

Another scene with a woman in proximity of music-making appears on fol. 24v in the Oppenheimer Siddur (Figure 29.4) but makes a strikingly different impression. A vignette within a gothic tracery window in the right-hand margin contains a smiling young woman with blond, plaited hair wearing a purple-colored dress who is seated, embracing a man who is identified as a fool by his yellow, hooded tunic and the bagpipe he is playing. Yellow was often worn by fools or jesters, a mark of low social status in medieval times, and fools are often shown playing the bagpipe in medieval art.[42] The central word panel depicts nine dark-colored, fierce-looking wild men in battle with one another, and in the bottom margin below them, a brightly colored fiddler and shawm player are playing their instruments. The prayers of the long Taḥanun, said on Mondays and Thursdays in the Ashkenazic rite, begin here with the Hebrew phrase, *ve-hu' raḥum* (וְהוּא רַחוּם) in the main illuminated panel:

וְהוּא רַחוּם יְכַפֵּר עָוֹן וְלֹא־יַשְׁחִית וְהִרְבָּה לְהָשִׁיב אַפּוֹ וְלֹא־יָעִיר כָּל־חֲמָתוֹ. אַתָּה יְהֹוָה לֹא
תִכְלָא רַחֲמֶיךָ מִמֶּנּוּ חַסְדְּךָ וַאֲמִתְּךָ תָּמִיד יִצְּרוּנוּ. הוֹשִׁיעֵנוּ יְהֹוָה אֱלֹהֵינוּ וְקַבְּצֵנוּ מִן־הַגּוֹיִם
לְהוֹדוֹת לְשֵׁם קָדְשֶׁךָ לְהִשְׁתַּבֵּחַ בִּתְהִלָּתֶךָ׃... אֲדֹנָי בְּכָל־צִדְקֹתֶיךָ יָשָׁב־נָא אַפְּךָ וַחֲמָתְךָ מֵעִירְךָ
יְרוּשָׁלַם הַר־קָדְשֶׁךָ כִּי בַחֲטָאֵינוּ וּבַעֲוֹנוֹת אֲבֹתֵינוּ יְרוּשָׁלַם וְעַמְּךָ לְחֶרְפָּה לְכָל־סְבִיבֹתֵינוּ.
וְעַתָּה שְׁמַע אֱלֹהֵינוּ אֶל־תְּפִלַּת עַבְדְּךָ וְאֶל־תַּחֲנוּנָיו וְהָאֵר פָּנֶיךָ עַל־מִקְדָּשְׁךָ הַשָּׁמֵם לְמַעַן
אֲדֹנָי׃... הַטֵּה אֱלֹהַי אָזְנְךָ וּשְׁמָע פְּקַח עֵינֶיךָ וּרְאֵה שֹׁמְמֹתֵינוּ וְהָעִיר אֲשֶׁר־נִקְרָא שִׁמְךָ עָלֶיהָ
כִּי לֹא עַל־צִדְקֹתֵינוּ אֲנַחְנוּ מַפִּילִים תַּחֲנוּנֵינוּ לְפָנֶיךָ כִּי עַל־רַחֲמֶיךָ הָרַבִּים.

FIGURE 29.4 The Oppenheimer Siddur, Bodleian Library MS Opp. 776, fol. 24v. Courtesy of the Bodleian Libraries, University of Oxford.

And He, being merciful, forgives iniquity and destroys not: many times he turns his anger away, and does not stir up all His wrath. Withhold not thou thy tender mercies from us, O Lord: let thy loving-kindness and thy truth continually preserve us. Save us, O Lord our God, and gather us from amongst the nations, to give thanks unto thy holy name, and to triumph in thy praise. . . . O Lord, according to all thy righteous acts, let thy anger and thy fury, I pray thee, be turned away from thy city Jerusalem, thy holy mountain; because for our sins and for the iniquities of our fathers, Jerusalem thy people are become a reproach to all that are round about us. Now therefore hear O our God to the prayer of thy servant and his supplications and cause your countenance to shine on thy sanctuary that is desolate for the sake of the Lord. . . . Incline thine ear, O my God and hear. Open thine eyes and behold our desolations and the city which is called by thy name, for we do not lay our supplications before thee because of our righteous acts but because of thy abundant mercies.[43]

FIGURE 29.4A The Oppenheimer Siddur, Bodleian Library MS Opp. 776, fol. 24v, detail. Courtesy of the Bodleian Libraries, University of Oxford.

Zvi Ron suggests that the early sources relating to the long Taḥanun said on Mondays and Thursdays contain evidence that it only became standardized in Ashkenazic prayer books in the eleventh century, since it appears in approximately its current form for the first time in the *Maḥzor Vitry*, compiled by Simḥah ben Samuel of Vitry (d. 1105). Ron notes several repeating themes in the long Taḥanun: supplications for salvation from Israel's distress, an end to persecution by her enemies and God's punishments, including the Jewish Exile, and pleas for redemption.[44] The tripartite composition on fol. 24v echoes these themes.

In prayer texts for the long Taḥanun drawn from the Book of Daniel, Jerusalem is portrayed as suffering desolation and the exile of the Jewish people is likened to an outcast who has "become a reproach to all that are round about us." This personification of Jerusalem is reflected elsewhere in biblical literature, where Jerusalem is sometimes personified as a sinful woman and equated with the people of Israel. For example, in Lamentations chapter 1, Jerusalem is portrayed as a solitary widow who was formerly great among the nations and a princess but now none of all her lovers is there to comfort her (Lamentations 1:1–2), and is described as sinful, an unclean woman who is despised (לְנִידָה הָיָתָה) (Lamentations 1:8).

Though the image of the woman embracing the bagpiping fool occupies only a small portion of this elaborate, full-page illumination, this vignette is striking due to the amorous gesture of the woman toward the male bagpiper: she has her left arm around his shoulder, and her right hand rests provocatively on his knee. This scene has no apparent antecedent or parallel among surviving Hebrew illuminated manuscripts of the Middle Ages. However, it is strongly reminiscent of pictorial representations of the allegory of the folly of love, which was a popular subject in works by fifteenth- and sixteenth-century German printmakers. For example, an engraving by Israhel van Meckenem (ca. 1445–1503) shows a young woman adorned with a crown of flowers who is embracing a fool, pulling open the lower half of his garment in an unmistakably revealing and suggestive way (Figure 29.5). The woman's advances toward the fool on fol. 24v make her intentions similarly clear.

In fifteenth-century pictorial allegories of the folly of love, women are frequently shown assuming an active role in relation to men. For example, in an engraving by Master E. S. (ca. 1420–ca. 1468), a fool dressed in a hooded garment with donkey ears is shown losing his trousers while embracing a nude woman who is playing the lute and holding a mirror that reflects his grinning face (Figure 29.6). Keith Moxey asserts that the nude woman here is an allegorical personification of lust, and that in this composition the artist equates the sin of lust with folly.[45] Christa Grössinger likewise argues that the role of women in such pictorial allegories is that of a negative agent of temptation. She maintains that, in this particular image, it is the woman who is shown as having the upper hand in the power hierarchy: she is manipulating the fool by unbuttoning his tunic and showing the viewer his leering grin in the mirror she holds, asserting her power.[46] Similarly, on fol. 24v in the Oppenheimer Siddur it is the woman whose embrace and wanton behavior signals that she is the active partner in relation to the bagpipe-playing fool.

The instrument being played by the fool on fol. 24v, the bagpipe, also has symbolic meaning in fifteenth-century German prints. In another allegorical depiction of the folly of love, *The Small Garden of Love* by Master E. S., a bagpipe-playing fool is placed between a pair of lovers sitting on either side of a well, while in another scene to the left of this, an amorous couple appears in which the man's caresses are well received by the woman, who looks out of the picture at the viewer with a knowing smile (Figure 29.7).[47]

Though fools in art of this period are often depicted with the instruments they most often used in courtly entertainments, the pipe and drum, the bagpipe when played by a fool usually had a negative connotation. For example, a barefoot, bagpipe-playing fool with tonsured hair appears on the 1 of Bohemia, the card with the lowest value in the *Hofämterspiel*, a deck of courtly playing cards dated circa 1450, reflecting the fool's low status in the social hierarchy.[48] As Moxey has pointed out, the image of a bagpipe being played by a fool, with its erect pipes emerging from the air sack, also has obvious sexual connotations when pictured alongside such consorting couples.[49]

FIGURE 29.5 Israhel van Meckenem, *Bekräntztes Mädchen hält einen knieenden Narren am Gewand fest* (Woman wearing a wreath holding a kneeling fool by his robe), Berlin, Kupferstichkabinett. Reproduced as figure no. 6 in Eugen Diederichs, *Deutsches Leben der Vergangenheit in Bildern* (Jena: Diederichs, 1908), 1:2. Courtesy of the Heinrich Heine Universität, Düsseldorf, urn:nbn:de:hbz:061:1-18542. Public Domain.

A number of prints of this era show men and women together in musical scenes, and with other instruments, too, such as the lute and harp. Israhel van Meckenem's *Circular Ornament with Musicians Playing near a Well* (Figure 29.8), a copy of a similar engraving by Master E. S., shows a facing couple playing the harp and lute with a well in between

FIGURE 29.6 Master E. S., *Luxuria and the Fool*, Kupferstichkabinett, Staatliche Kunstsammlungen Dresden. Courtesy of the Staatliche Kunstsammlungen Dresden.

them—further evidence that musical activity in such scenes involving men and women represents their love interactions, and that the sexual connotations of the instruments used were not restricted to the bagpipes.[50] The lute and harp are also played by a man and woman in Israhel van Meckenem's *The Lute Player and Harpist* (Figure 29.9), where numerous pictorial details highlight the sexual implications of this scene: the position of the neck of the lute and its open case, the upright position of the man's accoutrements,

FIGURE 29.7 Master E. S., *The Small Garden of Love*, Munich, Staatliche Graphische Sammlung. Reproduced as plate no. 34 in Max Geisberg, *Der Meister E.S.* (Leipzig, Klinkhardt & Biermann, 1924).

FIGURE 29.8 Israhel van Meckenem, *Circular Ornament with Musicians Playing near a Well*. National Gallery of Art, Washington, DC. Courtesy of the National Gallery of Art, Washington, DC.

FIGURE 29.9 Israhel van Meckenem, *The Lute Player and Harpist*. The Metropolitan Museum of Art, New York. Courtesy of The Metropolitan Museum of Art, New York.

and presence of lighted candles in the background which, in the art of the period, some-times symbolized male sexual desire, as well as the woman's closed coffer, which Nadine Orenstein argues symbolizes her virginity.[51]

Grössinger argues that the woman's role as depicted in this print repertoire is a nega-tive one, expressing her sexuality and capacity to tempt men into sin.[52] Supporting this is the fact that three out of twelve engravings by Israhel van Meckenem in the series of engravings that was later innocuously entitled *Scenes from Daily Life* depict couples en-gaged in musical activity in scenes with sexually suggestive elements. This indicates that music-making and the instruments being played were part of the symbolic pictorial vo-cabulary used to represent the sexual dynamics between men and women in fifteenth-century Germany.[53] Such scenes, therefore, were not merely portrayals of contemporary "daily life" but rather intended to convey a moral message, warning against the tempta-tion of lust and sin.

The vignette on fol. 24v appropriates the fifteenth-century allegory of the folly of love and reinterprets it from a Jewish perspective to express the content of the Taḥanun texts that follow. The initial texts of the Taḥanun that begin on this page emphasize supplications for God's mercy and forgiveness of the sin.[54] In this context, the object of the woman's lustful behavior is the fool playing a bagpipe, implying that this vignette is intended to be read metaphorically, like the visual allegories of the folly of love, discussed above.

Tova Forti notes that both Wisdom and Lady Folly are often personified as sexually sinful women in the Bible, and Lady Folly is often equated with sexual promiscuity as the "other woman."[55] In Proverbs 9:13–18, Lady Folly, or *'eshet kesilut* (אֵשֶׁת כְּסִילוּת), is described in sexually suggestive terms as a woman who entices naïve and thoughtless men into her house, where they face mortal danger:

> The woman Folly is riotous; she is thoughtless, and knows nothing.
> And she sits at the door of her house, on a seat in the high places of the city,
> To call to them that pass by, who go right on their way:
> Whoso is thoughtless, let him turn in here;
> And as for him that lacks understanding, she says to him:
> "Stolen waters are sweet, and bread eaten in secret is pleasant."
> But he knows not that the shades are there; that her guests are in the depths of Sheol.

Midrash Mishlei 9:4 compares the behavior of Lady Folly with that of a prostitute, *'ishah zonah* (אישה זונה), and to Eve and her primal sin against God, *'eshet kesilut-this is Eve* (אשת כסילות ז חוה).[56]

Such teachings may also be reflected in Asher ben Yitzḥaq's Jewish appropriation of the folly of love allegory in the vignette on fol. 24v. The woman's active role suggests that its focus is her behavior, and that this image serves as a visual metaphor for the sins of the people of Israel that are frequently mentioned in the prayers of the long Taḥanun. The placement of this scene, immediately adjacent to the main panel containing the opening word of the main texts, also indicates its importance since it could hardly be missed in the right-to-left reading process of the Hebrew text. A group of nine violent wild men in battle appear in the main panel, a highly unusual scene in medieval Hebrew manuscript art. The mythical figure of the wild man can be seen in Christian religious and secular art of the late Middle Ages in a variety of guises: he appears as a humorous sprite clambering on leafy foliage in engravings and illuminations; a menacing super-human figure in battle with knights; a debased figure who is portrayed as less than human; a symbol of extreme Christian piety and asceticism; or a strongman and protector on the coats of arms of European noble families.[57] The wild man also appears in association with love imagery on tapestries, love caskets, and wedding boxes as a symbol of "untamed" male desire, implying that lust reduces a man's behavior to a bestial, subhuman level.[58]

Because of their brutality and violence, I argue that it is the negative, aggressive aspect of wild men that is portrayed on fol. 24v in relation to the prayers of the Taḥanun. Here, they are likely to serve as a pictorial metaphor for the non-Jews who are identified as Israel's persecutors in the long Taḥanun, from whom the supplicant asks to be saved. Moreover, on fol. 24v, the positioning of the scene of wild men in battle following the vignette, with its reference to the allegory of the folly of love, suggests that a direct relationship exists between these two scenes: the chaos and aggression depicted in the main panel, symbolizing the behavior of the persecutors of Israel, is a consequence of the sin and folly of kneset Yisrael represented in the vignette that precedes it.

The third element in this composition, two sweet-faced, colorful male musicians playing the shawm and fiddle in the bottom margin, recall the many other images of performing musicians who accompany texts throughout this prayer book, some of whom appear in association with high holiday prayers, such as those for Yom Kippur and the opening of the weekday Hoshanot said on Sukkot (fols. 72v–73r, 79v).[59] The musicians in the bottom margin of fol. 24v are seated on ornate corbels at the bottom of a thick architectural frame that was originally painted in gold with filigree scrolling ornaments, but on the outside of the frame, details that suggest that this part of the composition may represent the Jewish Exile—another important theme in the Taḥanun.

The spatial organization of the entire page on fol. 24v, with its implied opposition between the instruments being played in the upper and lower margins, serves to highlight the message the Taḥanun texts convey. While sin and folly are unmistakably represented by the yellow-clad bagpiper and woman embracing him, the instruments played by the musicians in the bottom margin—the fiddle and shawm—were commonly used by musicians in fifteenth-century Germany.[60] The music-making of the fiddler and shawm player in the bottom margin of this composition resonates with that of the many other pairs of performing musicians who appear in the illuminated initial word panels of the Oppenheimer Siddur, contributing a musical and sonic dimension to the reading of the prayer texts they accompany.

The way that Asher ben Yitzḥaq has employed and interconnected these three scenes creates an ironic visual play, referencing not only allegories of love in contemporary fifteenth-century Christian secular art, their moral warnings against sin, and the topos of the mythical wild man,[61] but also the theme of music as a visual metaphor associated with prayer that occurs throughout this siddur. This full-page, elaborate illumination thus forms a complex visual commentary on the Taḥanun texts that begin here.

It is safe to assume that, as an artist, Asher ben Yitzḥaq may have had access to engravings by artists such as Master E. S. and Israhel van Meckenem that were produced, copied and circulated in Germany during his lifetime. Indeed, the striking similarity between figures of animals and birds in the Oppenheimer Siddur and those in prints by the earliest fifteenth-century German engraver, the Master of the Playing Cards, supports this hypothesis, especially since we know that such prints were used as models by artisans who decorated other fifteenth-century Hebrew manuscripts.[62]

Most importantly, it is clear that Asher ben Yitzḥaq knew that the key elements in the three scenes of this full-page illumination on fol. 24v, as well as the implications of the sequential arrangement for their interpretation, would be understood by his prayer book's intended readers—his children. This composition thus exemplifies Baumgarten's "multidirectional" process of appropriation in medieval Ashkenaz. The way Asher ben Yitzḥaq has employed motifs such as music-making, the allegory of the folly of love, and images of wild men suggests they are imbued with deliberate multivalency, reflecting on the one hand meanings that were current in the wider fifteenth-century Christian society within which he lived, but transforming them for his Ashkenazic Jewish audience on the other. In this process, he made them his own.

The Harmony of Love

כהושעתה אב המון השליך עליך יהב.
בעדו רדתו ומלטתו מלהב. כן הושענא.

As You saved the father of the multitudes [Avraham], cast on You [our] burden.
For his sake You descended and rescued him from the blade, so please save now![63]

Hoshanot for the Sabbath, minhag Rinus

Our third and final illustration in the Oppenheimer Siddur, on fol. 83v, occurs in the middle of Hoshanot prayers recited on the Sabbath on the last day of Sukkot (Figure 29.10).[64] Here, we see a seated, smiling young woman with plaited blond hair who is strikingly similar to the woman pictured on fol. 24v, wearing again a purple-colored gown. This time, it is she who is playing an instrument: the medieval harp, which is resting between her knees with only her right hand visible plucking the strings. She faces a seated man wearing a crimson tunic and brimmed hat who is playing the shawm with his left hand. His right arm appears to be extended toward the woman. Whether this is a gesture of embrace is not discernible, as the man's right arm is obscured by the harp; however, if so, the image on fol. 83v may invert an important detail of the scene on fol. 24v, where it is the woman who is shown in active embrace of the male bagpipe-playing fool.

What stands out in the illumination on fol. 83v is the music-making of this "loving couple" and, in particular, the woman playing a harp, especially since earlier in the

FIGURE 29.10 The Oppenheimer Siddur, Bodleian Library MS Opp. 776, fol. 83v, detail. Courtesy of the Bodleian Libraries, University of Oxford.

siddur there are two illustrations with male harp-players (fols. 8v and 79v). Formally, and in terms of the way this scene features music-making together by a man and woman with a shawm and harp, there are no direct parallels for this image in extant medieval illuminated Hebrew manuscripts, and for comparable images we must again turn to medieval Christian sources.

Women are often shown playing the harp in fifteenth- and sixteenth-century artworks, sometimes in conjunction with another instrument being played by a man. Yet the significance of the instruments and musical performance on them is not always clear. The meaning of the harp as a feminine symbol in Christian art of this era is somewhat ambiguous. Is it the act of the woman's performance on the harp that is significant, as in the engraving by Meckenem in Figure 29.8, identifying the woman as an object of male desire? Or is the harp a symbol of female power or virtue? For example, a French tapestry from Arras made circa 1420 shows a female harp player on the left with a man facing her on the right, holding a banderole containing musical notation and the opening text for the fourteenth-century French chanson, *De ce que fol pensé remaint* (A fool's plans often come to nothing) (Figure 29.11). The musical incipit and text are centrally placed in this tapestry, implying a connection between folly and love; here, the object of the man's amorous desire is represented by the woman and the instrument she plays.[65]

FIGURE 29.11 Arras Tapestry, Pe 602, Musée des Arts Décoratifs, Paris.

In two other examples, a male lute player and female harpist appear in woodcuts in the fifteenth-century Strasbourg and Augsburg Calendars, representing "Flegmaticus," the phlegmatic temperament in the Four Temperaments that is characterized by the negative trait of lethargy,[66] while the 6 of the suit of France card in the *Hofämterspiel* (ca. 1450) depicts a young lady-in-waiting playing the medieval harp.[67]

Yet religious symbolism is also attached to the harp in both Jewish and Christian medieval art. It is the instrument most frequently pictured with King David, often at the beginning of the Psalms but also in other contexts. In Jewish art, the harp as a symbol of David is ancient: it is seen on coins of the second century and Bar Kokhba period as well as in a sixth-century synagogue floor mosaic.[68] In medieval Hebrew manuscripts and later Jewish books, the mere presence of the harp can signify an association with King David and the Book of Psalms.[69] In the Talmud (Berakhot 3b:29), special powers are ascribed to David's harp and linked to his piety, as in the following passage:

דָּוִד, סִימָנָא הֲוָה לֵיהּ, דְּאָמַר רַב אַחָא בַּר בִּיזְנָא, אָמַר רַבִּי שִׁמְעוֹן חֲסִידָא: כִּנּוֹר הָיָה תָּלוּי לְמַעְלָה מִמִּטָּתוֹ שֶׁל דָּוִד, וְכֵיוָן שֶׁהִגִּיעַ חֲצוֹת לַיְלָה, בָּא רוּחַ צְפוֹנִית וְנוֹשֶׁבֶת בּוֹ וּמְנַגֵּן מֵאֵלָיו, מִיָּד הָיָה עוֹמֵד וְעוֹסֵק בַּתּוֹרָה עַד שֶׁעָלָה עַמּוּד הַשַּׁחַר.

David had a sign indicating when it was midnight. As Rav Aḥa bar Bizna said that Rabbi Shimon Ḥasida said: A lyre hung over David's bed, and once midnight arrived, the northern midnight wind would come and cause the lyre to play on its own. David would immediately rise from his bed and study Torah until the first rays of dawn.[70]

Apart from the female harpist on fol. 83v, all other harpists depicted in the Oppenheimer Siddur are male. This is consonant with the instrument's appearance in other Hebrew illuminated manuscripts where the harp is predominantly played by a man and very rarely seen being played by a woman.[71] In no other surviving medieval Hebrew illuminated manuscript are the harp and shawm paired together. However, these two instruments do appear together played by women and men, respectively, in carved bone panels on fifteenth-century game boxes. For example, on the lid of a game box in the collection of the Metropolitan Museum of Art, a woman stands on the left playing a harp facing a man playing a shawm on the right, and a peacock with its tail fully open is between them (Figure 29.12). Not only is a musical couple pictured with harp and shawm on this box, but on the sides a boar hunt is pictured as well as two kneeling wild men flanking the keyhole that is placed in the center of a bushy treetop. Paula Nuttall has convincingly argued that these and other motifs had connotations of erotic love in late medieval art, and she notes that such scenes appear frequently on game boxes and marriage caskets during this period. She contends that these boxes are objects that were probably made as marriage gifts rather than intended to store games, as was once thought.[72] Among the motifs appearing on such game boxes are *moresca* dancers, fools, music-making by men and women, wild men, fruit-bearing trees, jousting, and hunt scenes. As Nuttall observes, the symbolism of sexual union within the contained context marriage is inherent in the function, form, and decorative themes of the game box.[73]

A scene on a side panel of one of the game boxes Nuttall discusses shows a woman playing a harp accompanying the beating of a pear tree—a symbol of a fruitful marriage union—making it clear that the harp in the hands of a woman in this context was associated with marriage, feminine sexuality, love, and fertility.[74] On another box mentioned by Nuttall, dated to the last quarter of the fifteenth century, a man plays the shawm behind two couples who are holding hands and engaged in a courtly dance.[75] Taken together, this evidence strongly suggests that the harp and shawm were gendered instruments in the love iconography of the era. Such gendered musical imagery and its marriage symbolism may help to explain the significance of the musical couple on fol. 83v in the Oppenheimer Siddur.

Yet the location of this illustration on fol. 83v in the siddur texts is also noteworthy. It occurs in the middle of Hoshanot prayers recited on the last day of Sukkot when this occurs on the Sabbath. It is preceded by another illumination overleaf on fol. 83r marking the end of the weekday Hoshanot, depicting a group of men at prayer, and

FIGURE 29.12 Game Box (15th–16th cents.), Metropolitan Museum of Art, New York. Courtesy of The Metropolitan Museum of Art, New York.

occurs after the texts of the Sabbath prayer, *'om netsurah* (אֹם נְצוּרָה), which is immediately above the illustration of the musical couple on fol. 83v:

אֹם נְצוּרָה כְּבָבַת בּוֹנֶנֶת בְּדַת נֶפֶשׁ מְשִׁיבַת. גּוֹמֶרֶת הִלְכוֹת שַׁבָּת. דּוֹרֶשֶׁת מַשְׂאַת שַׁבָּת. הַקּוֹבַעַת אַלְפַּיִם תְּחוּם שַׁבָּת...

The nation, guarded like the pupil of the eye,
[She] contemplates the doctrine that restores the soul,

[She] studies the laws of Shabbat,
[She] interprets the carrying of Shabbat,
Which establishes two thousand as the perimeter of Shabbat. . . .[76]

In this prayer, all verbs describing the carrying out of the Sabbath *mitzvot* in Hebrew are feminine, suggesting that the implied subject—the nation guarded like the pupil of an eye by God—*kneset Yisrael*, here is personified as a woman. The fact that the Sabbath is also often represented symbolically as a woman in Judaism further emphasizes the feminine aspect of the image on fol. 83v. In the well-known piyyut, *Lekhah dodi*, sung during the Kabbalat Shabbat service, the Sabbath is described as a bride:

לְכָה דוֹדִי לִקְרַאת כַּלָּה פְּנֵי שַׁבָּת נְקַבְּלָה

Come, beloved, to meet the bride. Let us welcome Shabbat.

Even though this piyyut was composed later, in the sixteenth century, earlier Jewish literature uses the metaphor of a bride when referring to the Sabbath, such as the following passage from the Midrash (Bereishit Rabbah 10:9):

גְּנִיבָא וְרַבָּנָן, גְּנִיבָא אָמַר מָשָׁל לְמֶלֶךְ שֶׁעָשָׂה לוֹ חֻפָּה, וְצִיְּירָהּ וְכִיְּירָהּ, וּמַה הָיְתָה חֲסֵרָה,
כַּלָּה שֶׁתִּכָּנֵס לְתוֹכָהּ. כָּךְ מֶה הָיָה הָעוֹלָם חָסֵר, שַׁבָּת.

Geniva said: This is comparable to a king who prepared a wedding chamber, but was missing a bride. Similarly, the world was missing Shabbat.

A similar passage in the Babylonian Talmud (Shabbat 119a:2) describes the Sabbath as a bride and queen:

רַבִּי חֲנִינָא מִיעֲטֵף וְקָאֵי אַפַּנְיָא דְמַעֲלֵי שַׁבַּתָּא, אָמַר: "בּוֹאוּ וְנֵצֵא לִקְרַאת שַׁבָּת הַמַּלְכָּה".
רַבִּי יַנַּאי לָבֵישׁ מָאנֵי מְעַלּוּ (שַׁבָּת) [וּמִיכַּסֵּי], וְאָמַר: "בּוֹאִי כַלָּה, בּוֹאִי כַלָּה".

Rabbi Ḥanina would wrap himself in his garment and stand at nightfall on Shabbat eve, and say: Come and we will go out to greet Shabbat the queen. Rabbi Yannai put on his garment on Shabbat eve and said: Enter, O bride. Enter, O bride.[77]

Furthermore, the harp or lyre also is mentioned in prayers said on the Sabbath. Psalm 92, also known as *Mizmor le-yom Shabbat* and recited on the Sabbath in the *minhag Ashkenaz*, mentions instruments used in praise of God: in particular, the *nevel 'asor*, the ten-stringed lyre, as in the following verses (Psalm 92:1–4):

מִזְמוֹר שִׁיר לְיוֹם הַשַּׁבָּת:
טוֹב לְהֹדוֹת לַיהוָה וּלְזַמֵּר לְשִׁמְךָ עֶלְיוֹן:
לְהַגִּיד בַּבֹּקֶר חַסְדֶּךָ וֶאֱמוּנָתְךָ בַּלֵּילוֹת:
עֲלֵי־עָשׂוֹר וַעֲלֵי־נָבֶל עֲלֵי הִגָּיוֹן בְּכִנּוֹר:

> A Psalm, a Song. For the Sabbath day.
> It is a good thing to give thanks unto the Lord, and to sing praises unto Thy name, O Most High;
> To declare Thy lovingkindness in the morning, and Thy faithfulness in the night seasons,
> With an instrument of ten strings, and with the psaltery; with a solemn sound upon the harp.

In the Talmud, the nevel 'asor or ten-stringed lyre is associated with the world to come, such as in this Talmudic commentary by R. Yehuda on Psalm 92:4 (Arakhin 13b:12): "The harp of the world to come has ten cords, as it is said: With an instrument of ten strings, and with the psaltery; with a solemn sound upon the harp."[78] Midrash Bamidbar Rabbah 15:11 also mentions the ten-stringed harp as the instrument of the world to come, as distinct from the instrument in the time of the Messiah, which will have eight: "In the days of the Messiah it will be made of eight cords; for so in fact says David in the melody, For the Leader; with string-music; on the Sheminith—eight-stringed. . . . In the time to come it will be made of ten; for it says, O God, I will sing a new song unto Thee, upon a psaltery of ten strings."[79]

It is therefore worth noting that, when this tiny image is digitally magnified, ten strings are visible on the harp being played by the woman on fol. 83v. In this regard, the woman's instrument is similar to the ten-string harp appearing in another illumination in the Oppenheimer Siddur for a different Sabbath Psalm (Psalm 19) on fol. 8v, where a bearded figure plays the harp, possibly representing King David as Psalmist (Figure 29.13). This suggests the possibility that the harp in the hands of the woman on fol. 83v may signify not only the Jewish marriage allegory, but may also evoke the metaphor of the Sabbath bride, the nevel 'asor and the world to come.

Interpreted as a reference to the world to come, the ten-string harp played by the woman on fol. 83v may also be a sign of Jewish redemption, especially because it occurs in the last illuminated word panel for the prayer texts in this siddur. Such a reading is consonant with the ending colophon of the Oppenheimer Siddur that follows a few pages later, where Asher ben Yitzhaq expresses his hope for the salvation of his people:

> And my soul desires and watches for the coming of the Redeemer.
> Make us powerful and strong in the building of the Temple.
> Grant peace, make fruitful and be pleased with all your servants.
> And show my brothers, your people Israel, peace.

Conclusion

The appearance of well-known, fifteenth-century love iconography conventions in the Oppenheimer Siddur shows that, as a Jewish artist, Asher ben Yitzhaq not only had

FIGURE 29.13 The Oppenheimer Siddur, Oxford, Bodleian Library MS Opp. 776, fol. 8v, detail.
Courtesy of the Bodleian Libraries, University of Oxford.

access to engraved prints and models in Jewish sources when illustrating his prayer
book, but also that he was intimately conversant with the multivalency of such imagery in the wider collectivities within which he and his family lived—both Jewish and
Christian. While the vignette with the woman and bagpipe-playing fool in conjunction
with the image of fighting wild men on fol. 24 is discordant, the illustrations on fols. 12v
and 83v express the harmony of love through the visual metaphor of coupled male and
female musicians with their reference to the convention of the "loving couple" in medieval Jewish art, and the Jewish marriage allegory. The semiotic function of the musical
instruments, appearing in all three illustrations, and image of music being played are
central to communicating this message.

These three images of women and music in the Oppenheimer Siddur, therefore,
create a "web of associations" through reflexive references across the siddur, and by the
appropriation and transformation of iconographic conventions that were known and
circulated in fifteenth-century Germany, in the Jewish community, as well as outside

it. By reimagining them in the context of in his family siddur, Asher ben Yitzḥaq has created a musical vision affirming the bond of love between kneset Yisrael and God, and expressing his hope for redemption of the Jewish people.

NOTES

1. See Katrin Kogman-Appel, *A Mahzor from Worms: Art and Religion in a Medieval Jewish Community* (Cambridge, MA: Harvard University Press, 2012), 187.

2. See Albert Wolf, "Fahrende Leute bei den Juden," *Mitteilungen zur jüdischen Volkskunde: Organ der Gesellschaft für jüdische Volkskunde in Hamburg und der Gesellschaft für Sammlung und Konservierung von Kunst- und historischen Denkmälern des Judentums in Wien* 27, no. 3 (1908): 92.

3. See Wolf, "Fahrende Leute," 92. For more extensive discussion of the Prague Jewish musicians' guild, see Gerben Zaagsma, "The Klezmorim of Prague: About a Jewish Musicians' Guild," originally published as "De klezmorim van Praag: Over een joods muzikantengilde," *Groniek. Historisch Tijdschrift* 143, no. 32 (1998): 223–230. English translation provided courtesy of the author.

4. See Abraham Z. Idelsohn, *Jewish Music Its Historical Development* (New York: Dover Publication, 1992), 206; Hayyim Schauss, *The Lifetime of a Jew* (New York: Union of American Hebrew Congregations, 1950), 170–174; and Naomi Feuchtwanger-Sarig, *Thy Fathers Instruction: Reading the Nuremberg Miscellany as Jewish Cultural History* (Berlin: De Gruyter, 2022), 340n199.

5. See Walter Salmen, ". . . *denn die Fiedel macht das Fest": Jüdische Musikanten und Tänzer vom 13. bis 20. Jahrhundert* (Innsbruck: Edition Helbling, 1991); "Klezmer in Schlesien," *Musik des Ostens* 12 (1991): 283–286; "Jüdische Hochzeits- und Tanzhäuser im Mittelalter," *Aschkenas* 5, no. 1 (1995): 107–120; and András Borgo, "'Pharao Barna ivadékai' és a klezmorim: A cigány és jiddis zenekultúra magyarországi kapcsolatai," *Muzsika* 36, no. 9 (1993): 32–40.

6. See Walter Zev Feldman, *Klezmer: Music, History, Memory* (New York: Oxford University Press, 2016), 59–98.

7. Ibid., 96.

8. See Richard Prior, "Jewish Musicians at the Tudor Court," *Musical Quarterly* 69, no. 2 (Spring 1983): 253–265; and Peter Holman, *Four and Twenty Fiddlers: The Violins at the English Court 1540–1690* (Oxford: Clarendon Press, 1995), 82–86.

9. See Barbara Sparti, ed. and trans., *Guglielmo Ebreo of Pesaro: 'De Pratica seu arte tripudii': On the Practice or Art of Dancing* (Oxford: Clarendon Press, 1993).

10. Ibid., 85.

11. See Diane Wolfthal, *Picturing Yiddish: Gender, Identity, and Memory in the Illustrated Yiddish Books of Renaissance Italy* (Leiden: Brill, 2004), 225, and 247.

12. Ibid., 117.

13. *Sefer minhagim*, Venice, 1593, postink-heb-90, fol. 73b, Royal Library, Copenhagen.

14. For a general overview of musical iconography in medieval Hebrew manuscript art, see András Borgó, "Die Musikdarstellungen in den mittelalterlichen illuminierten hebräischen Handschriften" (PhD diss., University of Innsbruck, 2000).

15. See Amnon Shiloah, *Jewish Musical Traditions* (Detroit, MI: Wayne State University Press, 1992), 84–86.

16. Tilman Seebass, "The Visualisation of Music through Pictorial Imagery and Notation in Late Medieval France," in *Studies in the Performance of Late Medieval Music*, ed. Stanley Boorman (Cambridge: Cambridge University Press, 2008), 26.

17. Richard Leppert, "Seeing Music," in *The Routledge Companion to Music and Visual Culture*, ed. Tim Shepherd and Anne Leonard (New York: Routledge, 2013), 9–11.

18. See Ivan G. Marcus, *Rituals of Childhood: Jewish Acculturation in Medieval Europe* (New Haven, CT: Yale University Press, 1996) and Elisheva Baumgarten, "Appropriation and Differentiation: Jewish Identity in Medieval Ashkenaz," *AJS Review* 42, no. 1 (2018): 40–42.

19. Baumgarten, "Appropriation and Differentiation," 41–42.

20. See Katrin Kogman-Appel, "Pictorial Messages in Mediaeval Illuminated Hebrew Books: Some Methodological Considerations," in *Jewish Manuscript Cultures: New Perspectives*, ed. Irina Wandrey (Boston: De Gruyter, 2017), 443–468; Evelyn Cohen, "The Teacher, the Father, and the Virgin Mary in the Leipzig Maḥzor," in *Proceedings of the Congress of Jewish Studies* 10, Division D, II: Art, Folklore, Music (Jerusalem, 1990), 71–76; Sarit Shalev-Eyni, *Jews Among Christians* (Turnhout: Brepols, 2011); Sara Offenberg, "Staging the Blindfolded Bride: Between Medieval Drama and Piyyut Illumination in the Levy Maḥzor," in *Resounding Images: Medieval Intersections of Art, Music, and Sound*, ed. Susan Boynton and Diane J. Reilly (Turnhout: Brepols, 2015), 281–294; and Marc M. Epstein, *Dreams of Subversion in Medieval Jewish Art and Literature* (University Park: Pennsylvania State University Press, 1997) and *Medieval Haggadah: Art, Narrative and Religious Imagination* (New Haven, CT: Yale University Press, 2011).

21. For a detailed discussion of this motif, see András Borgó, "Die Musikinstrumente Mirjams in spätmittelalterlichen hebräischen Darstellungen," *Music in Art*, 31 (2006): 175–193.

22. Miriam is named, along with eighteen other prominent Jewish women, as an example of the 'eshet ḥayil, in Midrash Mishlei 31:29, *Sefaria*, https://www.sefaria.org/Midrash_Mish lei.31.5?lang=bi (accessed September 3, 2022).

23. I gratefully acknowledge the assistance of Malachi Beit-Arié in obtaining the transcription and translating the colophon. The entire digitized manuscript may be viewed at Digital Bodleian, https://digital.bodleian.ox.ac.uk/objects/e0e188d1-75b0-4309-a085-8cde913c9 f3c/ (accessed September 3, 2022).

24. Both sides of the parchment leaves have been scraped to achieve an equalized texture, a practice seen only in Germany, mainly after 1300. See Malachi Beit-Arié, *Hebrew Codicology: Tentative Typology of Technical Practices Employed in Hebrew Dated Medieval Manuscripts*, 2nd ed. (Jerusalem: Israel Academy of Sciences and Humanities, 1981), 22–26.

25. Suzanne Wijsman, "The Oppenheimer Siddur: Artist and Scribe in a 15th-Century Hebrew Prayer Book," in *Crossing Borders: Hebrew Manuscripts as the Meeting-Place of Cultures*, ed. Piet van Boxel and Sabina Arndt (Oxford: The Bodleian Library, 2009), 69–84.

26. See ibid.; and Suzanne Wijsman, Sarah Neate, Sotiria Kogou, and Haida Liang, "Uncovering the Oppenheimer Siddur: Using Scientific Analysis to Reveal the Production Process of a Medieval Illuminated Hebrew Manuscript," *Heritage Science* 6, no. 15 (2018).

27. All translations of biblical texts are from *The Holy Scriptures According to the Masoretic Text* (Philadelphia, PA: Jewish Publication Society of America, 1955).

28. This is in accord with other illustrations of shofarim in medieval Hebrew manuscripts; see for example the prayer book MS Add. 662, fol. 65r, Cambridge University Library, Cambridge. On the flattening of horns for shofarim, see Jeremy Montagu, *The Shofar: Its History and Use* (Lanham, MD: Rowman & Littlefield, 2015), figure 1.1. The instrument

played on fol. 12v more closely matches images of the horned trumpet seen in other images of this instrument and the way it is played from the medieval period as illustrated in Jeremy Montagu, *The World of Medieval and Renaissance Musical Instruments* (Sydney: Ure Smith, 1976), 42.

29. Examples include the Tripartite Maḥzor, Add. MS 14762, fol. 15r, British Library, London, and the Hamburg Miscellany, Cod. Hebr. 37, fol. 29v, Staats- und Universitätsbibliothek Hamburg Carl von Ossietzky, Hamburg.

30. For a discussion of the Darmstadt Haggadah, Cod. Or. 8, fol. 37v, Universitäts- und Landesbibliothek, Darmstadt, see Katrin Kogman-Appel, "Portrayals of Women with Books: Female (Il)literacy in Medieval Jewish Culture," in *Reassessing the Roles of Women and "Makers" of Medieval Art and Architecture*, ed. Therese Martin, Visualising the Middle Ages 7 (Leiden: Brill, 2012), 2:525–559.

31. See Herman Pleij, *Colors Demonic and Divine: Shades of Meaning in the Middle Ages*, trans. Diane Webb (New York: Columbia University Press, 2004), 16.

32. Parma, Cod. Parma 1870, fol. 136r.

33. Examples can be found in the MS 969, fol. 9r, Bibliothèque Mazarine, Paris; the stained glass window of Chartres Cathedral, 15th c., http://musiconis.huma-num.fr/en/fiche/122/anges-sonnant-de-la-trompette.html (accessed April 11, 2021); and Jan van Eyck's *The Last Judgement*, ca. 1440–41, Metropolitan Museum of Art, New York, https://www.metmuseum.org/art/collection/search/436282 (accessed September 4, 2022).

34. For an example of pairs of trumpet-blowing angels in Christian art, see Book of Hours, France, ca. 1420, MS M. 1000, fol. 235v, The Pierpont Morgan Library, New York; and the MS 870, fol. 44v, Bibliothèque Mazarine, Paris.

35. See Sarit Shalev-Eyni in *Jews Among Christians: Hebrew Book Illumination from Lake Constance* (Turnhout: Brepols, 2010), 100–103, and "Iconography of Love: Illustrations of Bride and Bridegroom in Ashkenazi Prayerbooks of the Thirteenth and Fourteenth Century," *Studies in Iconography* 26 (2005): 27–57.

36. Shalev-Eyni, "Iconography of Love," 28.

37. See Shalev-Eyni, *Jews Among Christians*, 100–101.

38. Shalev-Eyni, "Iconography of Love," 27.

39. See Kogman-Appel, *A Mahzor from Worms*, 184–186. On the metaphor of mystical union in medieval Kabbalah, see Moshe Idel, *Kabbalah and Eros* (New Haven, CT: Yale University Press, 2005).

40. See Shalev-Eyni, "Iconography of Love," 36–39; and Sara Offenberg, "Staging the Blindfolded Bride: Between Medieval Drama and Piyyut Illumination in the Levy Maḥzor," in Boynton and Reilly, *Resounding Images*, 281–294.

41. Shalev-Eyni, "Iconography of Love," 27–57.

42. On the negative connotations of the color yellow, see Pleij, *Colors Demonic and Divine*, 77–80.

43. Simeon Singer, trans., *The Authorised Daily Prayer Book of the United Hebrew Congregations of the British Empire* (London: Eyre and Spottiswoode, 1935). It commences with Psalm 78:38, followed by Psalm 40:12, Psalm 106:47, and Daniel 9:16–18.

44. See Zvi Ron, "The Development of the Expanded Tachanun for Monday and Thursday," *European Journal of Jewish Studies* 12 (2018): 88–106.

45. Keith Moxey, "Master E. S. and the Folly of Love," *Simiolus: Netherlands Quarterly for the History of Art*, 11, nos. 3–4 (1980): 125–148.

46. See Christa Grössinger, *Humour and Folly in Secular and Profane Prints of Norther Europe 1430–1540* (London: Harvey Miller Publishers, 2002), 121.

47. See Moxey, "Master E. S. and the Folly of Love," 129–130.

48. See "1 (Fool) of Bohemia," from The Courtly Household Cards, Kunsthistorisches Museum Wien, Kunstkammer (KK 5077–5124), woodcut on paper, paint, pen, and ink (ca. 1450), in Timothy Husband, *The World in Play: Luxury Cards, 1430–1540* (New York: Metropolitan Museum of Art Exhibition Catalogue, 2016), https://www.metmuseum.org/art/collection/search/697329 (accessed September 8, 2022).

49. See Moxey, "Master E. S. and the Folly of Love," 125–148.

50. See no. 19, in Diederichs, *Deutsches Leben*, 1:6.

51. See Suzanne Boorsch and Nadine M. Orenstein, "The Print in the North: The Age of Albrecht Dürer and Lucas van Leyden The Age of Albrecht Dürer and Lucas van Leyden," *The Metropolitan Museum of Art Bulletin* 54, no. 4 (1997): 22. On candles as a symbol of male arousal, see the depiction of David and Bathsheba in the Morgan Picture Bible, MS M.638, fol. 41v, Pierpont Morgan Library, New York, and its discussion by Sarit Shalev-Eyni, "Purity and Impurity: The Naked Woman Bathing in Jewish and Christian Art," in *Between Judaism and Christianity: Art Historical Essays in Honor of Elisheva (Elisabeth) Revel-Neher*, ed. Katrin Kogman-Appel and Mati Meyer (Leiden: Brill, 2008), 200–203.

52. See Grössinger, *Humour and Folly*, 107–129.

53. See ibid., 74.

54. See Ron, "The Development of the Expanded Tachanun," 102.

55. Tova Forti, "Female Imagery in Wisdom Literature," in *The Wiley Blackwell Companion to Wisdom Literature*, ed. Samuel L. Adams and Matthew Goff (Hoboken, NJ: John Wiley & Sons, 2020), 179–180.

56. See Midrash Mishlei 9:4, *Sefaria*, https://www.sefaria.org/Midrash_Mishlei.9.4?lang=bi&with=all&lang2=en (accessed September 10, 2022).

57. See Roger Bartra, *Wild Men in the Looking-Glass: The Mythic Origins of European Otherness*, trans. Carl T. Berrisford (Ann Arbor: University of Michigan Press, 1994); and Timothy Husband, *The Wild Man: Medieval Myth and Symbolism* (New York: The Metropolitan Museum of Art, 1980).

58. See, for example, Minnekästchen with courtly scenes, ca. 1400–1500, wooden casket, Historisches Museum, Basel, as depicted in Husband, *The Wild Man*, 91, fig. 53.

59. See Suzanne Wijsman, "Silent Sounds: Musical Iconography in a Fifteenth-Century Jewish Prayer Book," in Boynton and Reilly, *Resounding Images*, 313–333.

60. See Keith Polk, "Vedel and Geige—Fiddle and Viol: German String Traditions in the Fifteenth Century," *Journal of the American Musicological Society* 42 (1989): 504–545; and "Instrumental Music in the Urban Centres of Renaissance Germany," *Early Music History* 7 (1987): 159–186.

61. A music-making couple appears with wild men in Israhel van Meckenem's engraving *Ornament with Flower and Eight Wild Folk*, The National Gallery of Art, Rosenwald Collection, Washington, DC, https://www.nga.gov/collection/art-object-page.3385.html#inscription (accessed September 2, 2022).

62. See Suzanne Wijsman, "The Oppenheimer Siddur," 76–77.

63. An uncorrected copying error occurs in the second verse of this piyyut in the Oppenheimer Siddur: ‏בעדו רדתו ומלטו מלהב‎.

64. I am grateful to Dr. Nahum Weissenstern of the National Library of Israel for his observations in private correspondence concerning the sequence of Hoshanot in this siddur.

65. For detailed discussion on the ambiguity in the meaning of this image, see Seebass, "The Visualisation of Music," 20–27.

66. Grössinger, *Humour and Folly*, 59.

67. "6 (Lady-in-Waiting) of France," from The Courtly Household Cards, Kunsthistorisches Museum Wien, Kunstkammer (KK 5077–5124), woodcut on paper, paint, pen, and ink (ca. 1450) in Husband, *The World in Play*; https://www.metmuseum.org/art/collection/search/697332 (accessed September 2, 2022).

68. See for example the Jewish coin of the Bar Kokhba Revolt, 134–135CE, The Israel Museum, Jerusalem; https://www.imj.org.il/en/collections/539339 (accessed September 10, 2022); and Asher Ovadiah, "Excavations in the Area of the Ancient Synagogue at Gaza (Preliminary Report)," *Israel Exploration Journal* 19, no. 4 (1969): 199, pl. 15.

69. For example, Masoretic Bible, Spain (1266), fol. 336r, Haverford College Library, Haverford.

70. The Babylonian Talmud, The William Davidson Edition, *Sefaria*, https://www.sefaria.org/Berakhot.3b.29?ven=William_Davidson_Edition_-_English&lang=bi&with=all&lang2=en (accessed September 10, 2022).

71. A woman playing the harp appears in the Floersheim Haggadah (Zurich: The Floersheim Collection, 1502), 18, https://cja.huji.ac.il/sch/browser.php?mode=alone&id=252214 (accessed September 10, 2022).

72. Paula Nuttall, "Dancing, Love and the 'Beautiful Game': A New Interpretation of a Group of Fifteenth-century 'Gaming' Boxes," *Renaissance Studies* 24, no. 1 (2010): 119–141.

73. Ibid., 140.

74. Ibid., 137.

75. Ibid., 134.

76. For *Shabbat Chol Hamoed, Sefaria,* https://www.sefaria.org/Siddur_Ashkenaz%2C_Festivals%2C_Sukkot%2C_Hosha'anot%2C_For_Shabbat_Chol_Hamoed?lang = bi (accessed September 10, 2022).

77. The Babylonian Talmud, The William Davidson Edition, *Sefaria*, https://www.sefaria.org/Shabbat.119a.2?lang=bi&with=all&lang2=en (accessed September 10, 2022).

78. Ibid; https://www.sefaria.org/Arakhin.13b.12?lang=bi (accessed September 10, 2022).

79. Midrash Bamidbar Rabbah, trans. Judah J. Slotki, ed. H. Freedman and Maurice Simon (London: Soncino Press, 1961), 2:651.

Select Bibliography

Baumgarten, Elisheva. "Appropriation and Differentiation: Jewish Identity in Medieval Ashkenaz." *AJS Review* 42, no. 1 (2018): 39–63.

Borgó, András. "Die Musikinstrumente Mirjams in spätmittelalterlichen hebräischen Darstellungen." *Music in Art* 31 (2006): 175–193.

Boynton, Susan, and Diane J. Reilly, eds. *Resounding Images: Medieval Intersections of Art, Music, and Sound.* Turnhout: Brepols, 2015.

Epstein, Marc M. *Dreams of Subversion in Medieval Jewish Art and Literature.* University Park: University of Pennsylvania Press, 1997.

Epstein, Marc M. *The Medieval Haggadah Art, Narrative and Religious Imagination*. New Haven, CT: Yale University Press, 2011.

Feldman, Walter Zev. *Klezmer: Music, History, Memory*. New York: Oxford University Press, 2016.

Grössinger, Christa. *Humour and Folly in Secular and Profane Prints of Northern Europe 1430–1540*. Turnhout and London: Harvey Miller Publishers, 2002.

Kogman-Appel, Katrin. *A Mahzor from Worms: Art and Religion in a Medieval Jewish Community*. Cambridge, MA: Harvard University Press, 2012.

Leppert, Richard. "Seeing Music." In *The Routledge Companion to Music and Visual Culture*, edited by Tim Shepherd and Anne Leonard, 7–12. New York: Routledge, 2013.

Marcus, Ivan G. *Rituals of Childhood: Jewish Acculturation in Medieval Europe*. New Haven, CT: Yale University Press, 1996.

Moxey, Keith. "Master E. S. and the Folly of Love." *Simiolus: Netherlands Quarterly for the History of Art* 11, nos. 3–4 (1980): 125–148.

Shalev-Eyni, Sarit. "Iconography of Love: Illustrations of Bride and Bridegroom in Ashkenazi Prayerbooks of the Thirteenth and Fourteenth Century." *Studies in Iconography* 26 (2005): 27–57.

Shalev-Eyni, Sarit. *Jews Among Christians*. Turnhout: Brepols, 2011.

Van Boxel, Piet, and Sabina Arndt, eds. *Crossing Borders: Hebrew Manuscripts as a Meeting-Place of Cultures*. Oxford: The Bodleian Library, 2009.

Wijsman, Suzanne. "Musicians and Wild Men: Signs of Identity in a Fifteenth-Century Jewish Prayer Book." In *Belonging and Detachment: Representing Musical Identity in Visual Culture*, edited by Antonio Baldassare and Arabella Teniswood-Harvey, 569–592. Vienna: Hollitzer Wissenschaftsverlag, 2023.

Wijsman, Suzanne. "Silent Sounds: Musical Iconography in a Fifteenth-Century Jewish Prayer Book." In *Resounding Images: Medieval Intersections of Art, Music and Sound*, edited by Diane Reilly and Susan Boynton, 313–333. Turnhout: Brepols, 2015.

Wolfthal, Diane. *Picturing Yiddish: Gender, Identity, and Memory in the Illustrated Yiddish Books of Renaissance Italy*. Leiden: Brill, 2004.

30

THE CONCEPT OF HARMONY IN PRE- AND EARLY MODERN JEWISH LITERATURE

ALEXANDRE CERVEUX

THE twelfth chapter of *Akedat Yitshak* (Binding of Isaac), a collection of philosophical commentaries on the Torah by Rabbi Isaac Arama (ca. 1420–1494), offers an interpretation of the sinful conduct of Noah's generation that resulted in the deluge. A short appendix, titled "Nigun 'olam," suggests a reading of this episode in seemingly musical terms. Arama compares the "human construction" (הבנין האנושי) to the "construction of the universe" (כעין בנין העולם הכולל); they constitute a "microcosm" (עולם קטן) and a "macrocosm" (עולם גדול), respectively, and are interrelated. Arama states that their relationship is of the kind that "those knowledgeable of melody" (חכמי הנגון) have found in two perfectly tuned instruments. Together, they form a cosmos shaped as a "unified body" (כאיש אחד). Arama further asserts that proper observance of the Torah guarantees the stability of their concordance; disobedience may however produce discordance, the ultimate consequence of which would be God's creation turning against the terrestrial creatures as in the episode of the deluge. If, on the other hand, a tuneful concord of both instruments is preserved, harmony will flow from the top to the bottom through their various strings, thereby providing a positive outpouring over humanity.[1] In a sense, "Nigun 'olam" may thus be understood as a Jewish transposition of the Pythagorean Harmony of the Spheres.

This short excerpt presents two ideas that will recur in this chapter. First, it introduces the notion of collectivity, as the "human construction" refers to humankind (האנשים) in general, and more specifically to the people of Israel. Second, it reveals the importance of the concept of harmony in a Jewish context, which corresponds here to its connection with and a manifestation of the *shekhinah*, understood as the divine, indwelling presence of God in the world. Indeed, the nature of this connection was the subject of debate among medieval thinkers and subsequent readers of their texts. Is harmony a specific substance, a force? Or is it a more abstract principle? As for the latter, Dov Schwartz asserts that toward the end of the Middle Ages and the beginning of the Renaissance thinkers came forward who particularly highlighted "music as a reflection of cosmic harmony."[2] He goes on to state that their reflection reveals the influence of Neoplatonic mysticism and a "softening of the radical rationalism" that was characteristic of this period.[3] In other words, Arama's elaborations on the music of the universe would be characteristic of an alternative worldview that is not strictly rationalist and mystically oriented. In the same vein, Chani Haran Smith discusses Arama's wide knowledge of both Jewish literature and Greco-Arabic philosophy, and suggests, in spite of a lack of sufficient evidence, that the Neoplatonic element in Arama's thought is owed to the influence of Marsilio Ficino (1433–1499), one of the most influential philosophers of the early Renaissance in Italy.[4] Schwartz and Smith base their elaborations upon previous writings by Moshe Idel, who had interpreted this text through the lenses of mysticism and magic, stating that it would depict the human capacity to influence supernatural forces and produce a change in the divine structure of the universe.[5] However thought-provoking these considerations may be, most significantly they are connected through a more general idea, that of analogy, which is raised only *en passant* by Idel and Smith. This chapter deepens the concern with analogy, showing that it is a crucial element to understanding the place of music in various premodern texts, whether they are theological, mystical, or philosophical in perspective or content. Analogies raise the question of what music, or harmony specifically, has to do with matters that are ontologically opposed, such as the microcosm and the macrocosm, terrestrial and celestial beings, or Israel and God.

As such, the aim of this chapter is twofold. It will first show the recurring themes of early mystic texts that relate to music, such as the perpetual praise in heaven, celestial liturgy, and praise in the lower part of the cosmos, to then expose the conceptualizations of harmony in major texts written by renowned thinkers, such as Philo, Abraham Ibn Ezra, Maimonides, and Yohanan Alemanno, between late antiquity and the early Renaissance. Their corpus will uncover the role music played in the general economy of Jewish knowledge, not simply as a discipline or an art, but more concretely as an activator of metaphorical thinking, as well as the roles the people of Israel as a collective body, the human collectivity, and the shekhinah play therein.

The Song-Filled Universe of Early Jewish Mystics

The destruction of the Second Temple in 70 CE caused irreparable damage to Jewish life and rite: the thread that linked the people of Israel to God was broken. In order to lessen the trauma caused by the Temple's destruction, Jewish sages provided an answer, namely that the Temple, including its rites and music, had been transposed into heavenly realms.[6] Following this, there is virtually no interruption in the permanent singing of praises to God, to which creatures on earth as in heaven lend themselves. This idea resonates in the so-called Merkavah and Hekhalot literature, a motley collection of early Jewish mystical texts in Hebrew and Aramaic, as well as in many midrashim of the same time, dating from late antiquity to the early Middle Ages. These texts contain accounts of visions, whose basic motif is the spiritual journey toward the divine chariot (מרכבה), following Ezekiel's prophetic vision in the first book. They also describe the grandiose architecture of heaven and earth. These texts are full of songs and litanies, written in a colorful language hitherto unknown in rabbinic literature. As Gershom Scholem has shown, they illustrate the importance of song in early mystic circles, in particular rhythmic recitation that may induce ecstasy and generate visions.[7]

Many of these texts do not refer to a concrete and circumscribed song, but rather to a constant and uninterrupted resounding, a song-filled universe that Karl Erich Grözinger called a "himmlisches Sangespleroma" (heavenly pleroma of song).[8] Like fire or water, song is an element in its own right, central in the portrayal of heaven; it materializes as a component used in the celestial architecture. This idea can be found, for example, in the fifth chapter of *Masekhet Hekhalot*, in the mystics' description of the seventh heaven and the seventh hall, where the throne of glory is surrounded by armies of angels and powerful heroes, hit by storms of snow, fire, and thunder, and where blessings, hymns, and songs are constantly resounding.[9] The authors of these lines tried to describe the indescribable, to give contours to the image of the divinity by mixing symbols of glory and power, music and song. But ultimately, the abundance of detail saturates the image and makes it indecipherable. According to this conception, the celestial singers and musicians emanate from song that, together with fire, water (or snow), and wind, is part and parcel of the material of the celestial realm. In this sense, some passages describing the supernal architecture, such as *Masekhet Hekhalot* 6, state that song alternates with other elements to form ramparts, in the form of concentric circles, around the throne of glory.[10] In a text known as *Merkavah rabah*, song is also the fabric and the ornament of this throne.[11] Other texts, such as *Hekhalot rabati* 24:1, also describe how the creatures, men and angels, weave crowns of song and prayer for God (an idea that still appears in Jewish liturgy, in the Keter) or that God is clothed with songs.[12]

If song solidifies as a component of the universe, it is also sometimes described as fluid and overflowing. A passage in *Hekhalot rabati* 8:4 speaks of torrents of joy, delight, and love, pouring out from the throne and flowing with the sound of the *ḥayot*'s lutes, of the ophanim's timpani, of the *keruvim*'s cymbals, and this sound swells and gushes out when Israel cries out before him: "ḳadosh, ḳadosh, ḳadosh" (Isaiah 6:3).[13] Here, Israel's voices add to the sonic saturation of the heavenly realm. They symbolize the earthly world and evoke the dimension of time, especially liturgical time, since this overflow occurs at the time of the Kedushah, the prayer that describes God's holiness. In other words, this passage describes the link that is created between the eternal realm of heaven and the temporal realm of earth in order to form, during the liturgy, a united collective in praise of the divine.

Some early mystical texts suggest that God not only formed creatures to sing his praise, but also gave them song, which can be considered a creature in its own right as it has been created and exists. In this sense, an excerpt from the early medieval cos-mographic midrash, *Seder rabah de-bereshit* (The great order of Creation), says: "He created man to rule over all things, and praise and song He planted in their mouths; and song and praise in their throats."[14] In other words, singing is the object of a specific act of creation and is not merely functional. By extrapolation, the same midrash refers to the singing of all beings, earthly and heavenly, at the moment of the completion of the Creation, when they celebrate what the text calls "the inauguration of heaven and earth" (חנוכת שמים וארץ). On this occasion, animals, plants, mountains, and all the angels parade before God, exulting him, glorifying him, and singing his praises. The ministering angels proclaim his glory, to which others respond that the Lord rejoices in his works. This passage describes a ritual performed before him, but above all a joint celebration of the Creator and the creatures he made. Given the context of the descrip-tion, the inauguration of heaven and earth is meant to be celebrated every week on the Sabbath. This celebration of joy resembles a wedding in which God and the Sabbath are the bride and groom, in whose honor creation, as a unified collectivity, dances and sings.

Other passages of early mystical texts speak of the celestial institution of music for the Sabbath. For instance, the *Alfa beta de-rabi Akiva* states that when the first man "saw the Sabbath" (שכיון שראי אדם הראשון את השבת), that is, personified as God's bride, he opened his mouth to praise God; at that moment, multitudes of ministering angels descended from heaven with all kinds of musical instruments, to play with him in song.[15] In other words, this text suggests that music for the Sabbath is of heavenly origin, promoted by angels, and an emanation of the music played and sung before the godly throne. Sabbath music thus appears as a primordial gift from God preserved in this world, and as the expression of an original celebration of the divine and the creation.

The excerpts from Merkavah and Hekhalot texts, and midrashim, illustrate how important song, indeed a very elaborate conception of song, is in the minds of early Jewish mystics. They introduce into Jewish literature the theme of the origin of song and music on earth, a godly gift to humankind, to give him thanks. Important themes also appear that delineate two collectives, those of humankind and those of angels, whose existence is motivated solely by the glorification of the Creator. Together they form a greater collectivity unified through song, which Karl Erich Grözinger conceptualized as a "panhymnische Einheit" (panhymnic unity).[16] By extension, such song, which permeates all parts of creation and bounds all creatures together and with God, is also what facilitates the *unio mystica*, the mystical union between the believer and the divine, a theme that runs through all subsequent mystical literature.

Compared to other rabbinic literature of the time, early mystical texts reveal a signifi-cant shift in the conception of music. In the former, song is part of the divine command to glorify God that all creatures must fulfil, which otherwise has no ontological reality. In the latter, music and song appear as a kind of constructive element of the heavenly realm that provide an ontological foundation for terrestrial song. This conception is comparable to, although independent from, the Pythagorean Harmony of the Spheres that influenced subsequent generations of Jewish thinkers.

Medieval Jewish Conceptions of Celestial Harmony

The Greco-Arabic translation movement that developed in ninth- and tenth-century Baghdad unleashed intense intellectual activity in Islamic and Jewish circles alike. Consequently, various elements of Greek philosophical doctrines influenced or penetrated Islamic and Jewish thinking, such as those attributed to the Pythagoreans. Harmony is central to their doctrine, primarily in an abstract and metaphysical sense. Pythagoreans considered harmony as the unification (or "bounding," etymologically speaking) of opposites, and they looked for evidence of this principle throughout the universe (*kosmos*), on the premise that harmony is found in all things and beings that involve proportion, symmetry, and commensurability. Pythagoreans then identified the concept of harmony with musical phenomena via numerical ratios. It is only through this analogy that the musical aspect of harmony was first revealed. Two attitudes in the medieval Jewish reception of this doctrine prevailed throughout the period, that of Abraham Ibn Ezra (1089–1164) and that of Maimonides (1138–1204).

In Ibn Ezra's *Sefer ha-'olam* (Book of the world, 1147–1148), on the fates of countries and wars, and other larger-scale issues, one passage focuses on what Shlomo Sela called "the musical tones of the planet."[17] Ibn Ezra attributes to Ptolemy the idea that "the ratio (ערך) of Jupiter to Saturn is not as noble (נכבד) as [the ratio of Jupiter] to Venus."[18] Ibn Ezra substantiates this idea in his *Sefer ha-ṭe'amim* (Book of reasons, 1148) in which he assigns a number to each of the seven planets and explains that a planet can have a positive influence if its number is in a noble and harmonious ratio to the number of another planet.[19] In this context, the idea of a "noble ratio" suggests a connection to the Pythagorean theory that each of the seven planets (as well as the fixed stars) have numbers that correspond to the musical tones produced by the rotation of the spheres in which they are enclosed. Ibn Ezra probably derived this idea from the fifth epistle of the Ikhwān al-Ṣafā', on music, which provides a thorough explanation of it.[20] As to whether such harmonies are audible, Ibn Ezra specifies that "those unable to hear these sounds are deaf, in the same manner as those who are unable to see the deeds of God are blind."[21] In his commentary on Isaiah 42:18, he further explains that "[h]earing and seeing originate in the heart: those that are deaf and blind in their hearts are, therefore, called here 'deaf and blind.'"[22] In other words, hearing and seeing are interpreted as characteristics of intelligent human beings. He suggests a mode of knowledge that is based on sensation and on the interpretation of meanings hidden in phenomena. This approach is the result of his desire to reconcile revealed knowledge and philosophy, or, faith and reason. In this spirit, in his commentary on the Psalms, Ibn Ezra attempts to explain the verse: "Above the voices of many waters the Lord is mightier on high" (Psalms 93:4).[23] He considers these "voices of many waters" to corroborate the idea that the heavenly spheres produce mighty sounds in their circular movement (וזה לאות כי לגלגלים קולות). He also relates this verse to another from the book of Ezekiel (1:24), which refers to these sounds. Given the context in Ezekiel, this juxtaposition suggests that these "voices of many waters" allegorically refer to the sounds that resonate in the spheres, more precisely to those of the wings of the creatures in the divine chariot. Ezekiel was thus an educated human being, able to read hidden signs.

Ibn Ezra shared Avicenna's basic Neoplatonic cosmology, including elements of Pythagoreanism. According to this conception, the physical world provides access to the metaphysical realm. He implemented this view in a philosophical tale entitled *Igeret Ḥay ben Meḳits*, in which he tells the story of Ḥay ben Meḳits' spiritual journey to the heavenly realm.[24] In this tale, Ibn Ezra questions the nature of the relationship between this earthly, material world, where sensible phenomena occur, and the heavenly, immaterial world. The former is linked with the latter, since the most beautiful elements of the visible world allow us to grasp the concept of beauty, whose absolute form belongs to the invisible world. For this reason, imagination plays a central role in philosophical activity: by taking over from the senses, it intersects *sensibilia* and bridges the gap between the world of phenomena and the intelligible realm. In the space of the text, this awareness of world's beauty is achieved through language. Thus, Ibn Ezra uses a rich language that derives from his experience of the sensual world, as for example in his elaborate description of the world of plants, the variety of fruits, or the birds singing in the foliage.[25] Although Ibn Ezra probably had in mind the beautiful Andalusian gardens, his descriptions implement biblical vocabulary and imagery, particularly from the Song of Songs and the Psalms. In this way, Hebrew, above all the language of revelation, makes it possible to describe the world, endows it with a sacred aura, and opens the way to the suprasensible dimension. Another passage exemplifies the potency of Hebrew, when Ḥay ben Meḳits, in his ascent through the spheres, has to pass through a devouring fire located on the border between the material and the intelligible world. The striking imagery used by Ibn Ezra overwhelms the senses and the imagination to better introduce the idea of order and harmony that reigns in the higher sphere. He then describes the great spheres that come into view, immense, polished like mirrors, completely intertwined, and their inhabitants:

> Their hosts are neither numbered nor countable.
> All of them sing praise
> In unison they lavish acclaim.
> They always stand still
> Constantly worshipping their Maker.
> They preserve their regular course
> Holding fast to their covenant . . .
> Their motion is that of those who strive
> Their worship that of those who yearn.
> Their forms crave
> Their souls desire.[26]

In this spiritual journey, Ḥay ben Meḳits thus realizes that he is approaching the shekhinah and becomes aware of the existence of a celestial community entirely devoted to the permanent praise of the divine. This concept of a harmonious celestial realm is also found in the passage corresponding to the last sphere, where angels stand guard, while other cherubim and seraphim praise and announce his unity, and the ophanim sing.[27] Thus, the anchoring in the terrestrial world is achieved through the language that allows the description of phenomena and, by abstraction, the invisible world. Such description stimulates the mystics' imagination and makes it possible for them to visualize its grandeur, to imagine the sound of praises beautifully sung by divinely created beings, more perfect than the mystics, who in an ever deeper ecstatic state, feel closer to the divine presence. In this perspective, the unified collectivity formed by the entire creation is fully driven by desire and love for God. This desire is based primarily on earthly beauty, which encapsulates the concept of heavenly beauty and harmony.

The example of *Sefer ha-ʿolam* mentioned above recalls that Neoplatonism agrees with astrology in conceiving a theory of influence. According to this theory, the stars exert a particular influence that determines the fate of peoples and individuals. The celestial image of the universe, conceived as a harmonious system, is reflected on everything in the sublunary world. Thus, the life of each being is influenced by an astral configuration, which upon observation would allow astrologists to predict and know.

Faithful to Aristotelianism, Maimonides refuted the idea that the celestial world imprints its image on the sublunary world. He rejected astrology in general, particularly because it is not based on experience or reasoning. He raised this idea in a passage devoted to astronomy in *The Guide for the Perplexed* (ca. 1190), written in Arabic using the Hebrew alphabet. According to him, the real purpose of this science is to show that the movement of the stars is uniform and circular, in accordance with what is observable.[28] Elsewhere in the guide, Maimonides expounds the ideas of the Pythagoreans and Aristotle on the music of the spheres.[29] He recalls the widespread opinion that the celestial spheres, in their movement, produce "fearful and mighty sounds" (קולות נוראים ועצומים מאוד). Indeed, as in the case of the bodies of the sublunary world, which, when moved rapidly, produce sound, so the large and rapid celestial spheres would also produce sound in their revolution. Maimonides mentions the idea of the Pythagoreans, according to whom such sounds are harmonious, "similar to the ratios of musical harmonies" (כערך נגוני המוסיקה), despite their considerable force. The Pythagoreans argued that one can no longer hear these sounds, as we have been accustomed to them since birth and are unable to distinguish them from silence. Maimonides claims that such a view is also held by the sages, who in the Babylonian Talmud describe the noise made by the sun's rotation (Yoma 20b). However, he agrees with Aristotle, who in his chief cosmological treatise *De caelo* (On the heavens, 350 BCE) demonstrated that the stars do not produce sounds: they are fixed in their own spheres, which move them in silent motion.[30] This interpretation allowed Maimonides and other philosophers after him to prove that Ezekiel's belief in celestial sound was wrong.[31]

This statement should be put into perspective with another passage in the *Guide*, where Maimonides discusses the heavens and celestial beings' ability to praise God on the basis of biblical verses.[32] He states that the spheres are animate and intellectual (חיים משכילים), or, as the philosophers say, "living beings" (בעלי חיים). Thus, when the psalmist writes that the heavens "*tell* the glory of God" (Psalms 19:2), the Hebrew turn of phrase necessarily implies that he refers to beings endowed with intelligence. However, heavens and spheres speak a language that is not that of humans. This passage echoes the many references in ancient Jewish texts to the praising of celestial beings. Furthermore, Maimonides also deals with the belief in angels, widespread during his time, whose function and manifestation are frequently discussed by Jewish scholars. Maimonides considers that angels are not corporal beings and conforms to Aristotle's opinion: "he would say separated intellects (שכלים נפרדים), and we would say angels (מלאכים)."[33] He then recalls the Aristotelian theory that intelligent beings are intermediate beings between the divine and other beings, and that they effect the motion of the spheres, on which the existence of all things depends. Maimonides claims that this idea appears in all parts of scripture, in which God's actions are described as being performed by angels. He says that the term *angel* (מלאך) also refers to the "messenger among men" (השליח מן האנשים). Hence everyone who is entrusted with a certain mission, who performs a movement that serves the purpose of the Creator, is a *malakh* (angel).

Although the Pythagorean Harmony of the Spheres did not suit Maimonides, his discussion of the heavens' language, inaudible to humans, and of the intellects' silent movements gave it an interesting resonance. Thus, the Maimonidean conception of cosmic harmony is only spiritual, beyond any harmony that is audibly perceptible in the sublunar world: it refers to the perfect order of the created world, in which superior intelligent beings mediate between God and the people of Israel, which may then mediate with the human collectivity at large.

MUSICAL KNOWLEDGE AS A FEATURE OF ANALOGICAL REASONING

Since Jewish culture does not have a formal music theory, tentative conceptualizations of music tried to fill the lacunae by borrowing material from surrounding cultures. An early manifestation of this can be found in the work of Philo of Alexandria (20 BCE–45 CE), a Jewish philosopher whose commentary on Moses' life, entitled *De vita Mosis*, reflects a strong Hellenistic influence. In the passage that relates to the Song of the Sea, Philo states that Moses, after the crossing, divided the nation into separate male and female choirs, which were respectively led by himself and Myriam; these two choirs sang in tuneful concord with the voices blended in due proportion, producing a melody "of the fullest and sweetest harmony" (*ēdiston kai panarmonion apoteleitai melos*).[34] Although the original biblical passage contains only vague references to music such as *shirah* (שירה) and *tof* (תוף), Philo's interpretation incorporates seemingly Pythagorean ideas that are used to clarify his understanding and explanation of this event. His Hellenized readership might thus understand that this joyful outpouring is spontaneously harmonious. This interpretation represents one of the earliest examples in a Jewish context where the concept of harmony is illustrated through the evocation of musical notions.

From the tenth century, Jewish thinkers employed new philosophical and scientific methods, acquired through the study of Greco-Arabic texts, such as the rationalist inquiry. Through Maimonides' efforts, Aristotelian rationalism soon formed the basis of medieval Jewish philosophy, which contemporary and later scholars largely relied on— or tried to undermine. From the twelfth century, this philosophy was introduced into Catalonia and Provence by Andalusian Jews. They translated philosophical texts from Arabic into Hebrew for their coreligionists. Hebrew then became an idiom of science and philosophy. Intellectual activity in Provence and northern Spain reached a peak in the thirteenth and fourteenth centuries, and then gradually declined until the early years of the sixteenth century.

The development of the philosophical mind involved the learning of sciences, considered foreign from the traditionalist Jewish point of view.[35] The science of music (חכמת המוסיקה) was one of them, as shown by the numerous lists and classifications of sciences.[36] These elementary inventories were also developed into full-fledged encyclopedic works and later, as far as music is concerned, into independent texts on the subject of music alone. From a strictly rationalist perspective, the purpose of musical knowledge does not necessarily include instrumental practice or composition. Considering music primarily as a quadrivial science (in fact, an elementary science), the Jewish rationalists were mainly concerned with its mathematical principles. From this perspective, they focused on specific technical aspects of music, such as the measurement of intervals and note values. The rationalist attitude toward music is characterized by the fact that thinkers scrupulously choose musical notions that conformed to their philosophical aim. For example, the anonymous treatise attributed to Abū al-Ṣalt, transmitted in Hebrew translation, but no longer extant in the original Arabic, and mostly based on Abū Naṣr al-Fārābī's *Kitāb al-mūsīqī al-kabīr* (The great book of music, ca. 940), excludes all notions deemed subjective.[37] Unlike the original, it only presents the most rational elements. By extension, music may feature in philosophical thinking as a discipline that teaches and demonstrates invariant harmonic ratios. Hence, the place of music in the rational curriculum is both consistent with and defined by the aim of philosophy.

Conversely, the strictly rational approach to musical knowledge is tempered (if not even counterbalanced) by a more intuitive knowledge of music. Jewish thinkers often used common, empirical conceptions of music in order to convey or imply the concept of harmony. As such, references to music adopt the analogical, metaphorical language—which Michel Foucault calls "resemblance"—that is associated with knowledge construction: indeed, this can be seen in Isaac Arama, in whose writings music figures in a "play of symbols" and enables "possible knowledge of things visible and invisible."[38] This explains why music is deeply embedded in the field of knowledge, to the point of being a common theme in disciplines as different as theology, medicine, poetics, ethics, and others. Here, elements of music theory are invariably referred to as a means of explaining, expressing, or evoking the concept of harmony or affiliated ideas, like proportion, symmetry, and structure. For example, Jewish commentators have tried to explain Avicenna's notion of a "musical blood pulse," that is, that aspects of music could be useful to physicians in taking the pulse and in making a diagnosis.[39] From this perspective, music can be conceived on a theoretical and epistemological level that is higher than the strict rationalist curriculum: the subject of music fosters thinking, because of its evocative power.

This approach to the understanding of music changes with Isaac Arama's conception of cosmic harmony in the above-mentioned *Akedat Yitshak*, which is based entirely on the comparison of microcosm and macrocosm to two perfectly tuned instruments. It highlights the theory of sympathetic resonance, which can be observed especially in string instruments, wherein if one string is played, other strings may also be excited via the body of the instrument. This phenomenon was known to theorists and natural philosophers of the premodern period but retained an occult reception until around 1600.[40] As such, Arama revitalized the ancient micro-macrocosmic theory by engaging in a developed analogy through which he compares the sublunar world, humankind and more precisely the people of Israel, to a small instrument, and the superior world, heavenly hosts and spheres, to a larger one. The concept of harmony is the key to understanding this passage, as it connects the two parts of the cosmos. From a Jewish perspective, it correlates the concept of harmony to the Torah, the apex of the macrocosm to the shekhinah, and the microcosm to the people of Israel as a collective body. According to this interpretation of the Torah and the commandments, the concept of harmony regains its etymological meaning (*armonia*), that of a binding and constraining principle, like the "fastenings" used by Odysseus to hold together the heterogeneous parts of his raft (Homer, *Odyssey* 5, lines 248 and 361).[41] Thus, if Idel's theurgical and magical interpretation of this passage is relevant, it seems that a philosophical reading of it is equally valid to understand that music is the link between emotion and reason. Arama aimed to foster moral education (i.e., by conforming to the teachings of the Torah) by eliciting the idea of harmony that should prevail within the people of Israel and, by extrapolation, within the human collectivity.

Arama's approach to place music at the crossroad of multiple analogies, surfaces in early modern Jewish literature, in which the subject of music is no longer approached from a quadrivial perspective. Discussing music may convey ideas that are a priori alien to music, but always related to the concept of harmony. A case in point is the work of Yohanan Alemanno (1435–1504), a rabbi, philosopher, and exegete active in Italy. His approach reflects the philosophical research cultivated in the circle of Cosimo da Medici (the sponsor of the Platonic Academy in Florence), which combined resurgent Neoplatonism, theology, and influence from the recently rediscovered Hermetic corpus. By combining these different doctrines, the Florentine humanists aimed to achieve intellectual completeness through embracing the hidden truths. For Marsilio Ficino, one of the main representatives of this movement, philosophy and theology have the same purpose, which is the knowledge of God; scripture sets forth the perfect revelation of God's love for his creatures, and philosophy makes him known as the origin of wisdom and truth. Alemanno transposed this Neoplatonic conception into a Jewish context.

In *Ḥeshek Shlomoh* (Solomon's desire), a commentary of the Song of Songs, Alemanno advances the idea that Solomon provides instructions on how to achieve mystical union with God. He further suggests that those who do not possess Solomon's qualities— wealth, noble lineage, intellectual abilities, among others— that is, those who have little wisdom, will have to struggle to achieve *devekut*, unity with the divine. Several passages in this commentary reveal how music illustrates and participates in this ultimate goal.[42] Firstly, music represents the real and sensitive world from which more abstract knowledge is constructed. Evidence for this is found in Alemanno's para-phrase of the song, in which the sensual dimension is exacerbated (i.e., even more than in the original).[43] In essence, the beautiful woman sitting within her walls talks with her companions about love and lovers. Together they sing praise to a handsome shep-herd, feeling desire for him. Then this shepherd, who, like David, plays all instruments, comes down from the hill. The sound "increases as he approaches" (ושירו עמו הולך וחזק). Then the sound of his voice "beats on the walls of [the beautiful woman's] heart" (השיר דופק על קירות לבה), while he sings songs about the passionate lover's heart, he who has achieved perfect wisdom, understanding, and knowledge. Alemanno goes on to discuss how she burns with desire in her entrails and bones.[44] The application of a traditional allegorical reading of this song would reveal a description of the intimate union with the divine, in which the beautiful woman stands for the people of Israel, whereas the shepherd descending from the mountain stands for Moses. The song he plays is the Torah, which is a song of love. From a literary viewpoint, Alemanno's par-aphrase is a skillful *mise en abyme*, featuring a shepherd in the guise of King Solomon singing his own song. In this passage, Alemanno intends to demonstrate that physical desire is analogous to spiritual desire. Both may intensify, leave their mark, but remain unsatisfied. As for music, it represents the link between the two main individuals that resurfaces in all possible interpretations aimed at defining their relationship. In this respect, music symbolizes the sensory dimension. Like the feeling of desire, it is intan-gible but nevertheless present and increases to the point of dizziness. Proceeding by way of analogy, Alemanno thus describes the physical sensation that the mystic may experience when trying to attain devekut.

In another passage of *Ḥeshek Shlomoh*, Alemanno explains that music, conceived in an abstract way, guarantees access to a higher and hidden knowledge.[45] He first points out that Solomon, among the sciences he mastered, was particularly knowledgeable of the "science of harmony" (מלאכת השיר הכולל), otherwise known as the "science of music" (חכמת המוסיקה), which made it possible for him to grasp the harmonious relations that exist between things, is comparable to those found between musical sounds. This passage suggests that Alemanno was convinced that musical knowledge has the ability to shape and train the mind, and thus help to recognize connections be-tween things. In other words, music renders the soul in a receptive disposition that cultivates the capacity to reflect on the structure of the world, which consists of multiple interrelations between all elements. Hence, it enables people to gradually acquire a rep-resentation of the world. The aim of this noetic process, that is, reasoning, is to approach higher and more abstract forms of intelligence, and ultimately to get closer to the divine presence.

Elsewhere in *Heshek Shlomoh*, Alemanno goes into more detail about the nature of these interrelations and the way in which the noetic process, which occurs through a movement of the soul, is achieved.[46] To this end, Alemanno makes an implicit reference to Arama's theory of resonance. He explains that spiritual desire oriented toward knowledge functions like the string of a lyre, which, when plucked, would set in motion a straw placed on a similar string on another lyre. He asserts that on the basis of what happens between both instruments, "this is what happens to the intellective soul who knows how to play according to the property by which melodies subdue (literally, "sadden" or "conform") the forces of nature."[47] Alemanno also refers to the all-encompassing power of song (שירה), that is, music, which is based on the understanding of the relationships (יחסים) between things, and thus endowed with a hidden secret force. Indeed, Alemanno explains that the world is built according to a combination of relationships that are analogous to the relationships hidden in song. One whose spirit is illuminated and understands these *yehasim* can command them. Moshe Idel has suggested that this conceptualization clearly implies a "magical interpretation" of music that, like other sciences (such as astrology and alchemy), possesses a hidden force that may be used to affect the course of events.[48] Yet Alemanno's conceptualization of music has profound implications that cannot be reduced to magical interpretation. In Alemanno's science of music, Neoplatonism, hermeticism, and Kabbalah fuse, thus facilitating an understanding of various concepts such as harmony, desire, knowledge, and reasoning, as well as the connections between things. As such, the science of music also supports speculative and spiritual activities. Furthermore, Alemanno emphasizes the seductive effect of music, such as through the paraphrase of the song, which illustrates and arouses desire, not only for higher forms of beauty, but even for its very essence and source, namely God.

In the esoteric tradition, the confidentiality of teaching and the transmission from master to disciple mean that the number of initiates is purposely reduced. The question that remains is whether others, that is, the vast majority of non-initiate worshippers, can benefit collectively from this individual experience, and to what extent. Initiates would only testify to their experience and share their visions without further detail. As for Alemanno, he offers a demanding intellectual and spiritual endeavor that is imbued with Kabbalism, and that would therefore be reserved for the elite. Another text by Alemanno, *Hei ha-'olamim* (The immortal life, 1470–1503), adds nuance to this idea.[49] There, he describes the ideal education for young men, which combines the Platonic model (i.e., as in Plato's *Republic*) and Florentine education. *Hei ha-'olamim* does not refer to music, but to the ideas it contains about the formation of the mind and sensibility of young men, paralleling those presented in *Heshek Shlomoh*. Most importantly, *Hei ha-'olamim* highlights the social dimension of education: Alemanno speaks of the Florentines collectively as models of virtue that, according to his theory, can only be of divine inspiration.[50] As to whether music is part of this education, as *Heshek Shlomoh* suggests, it would be thus featured in a solid intellectual education. In this perspective,

Alemanno considers Solomon as the true paragon, master of all knowledge and music, witness to a special relationship with the shekhinah and an incomparable model for the Jews as a collective body.

Conceiving the Covenant and the Unity of the People of Israel through Harmony

Whether it appears in the representation of parallel realities or in rationalist systems, this chapter stresses that music rarely stands only for itself. It can presume to represent something else, to convey new meanings, to inspire certain sentiments or the idea of a connection with the shekhinah, and ultimately to represent the people of Israel as a collective body. This conceptualization did not disappear after the Middle Ages. Indeed, during the Renaissance, and later among the Hasidim and the Maskilim, this theme reemerged, becoming the subject of different interpretations. Music, both ineffable and irresistible, continued to be a subject of inspiration to describe the particular relationship of the Jews and the divine.

In the context of Judaism, the term *harmony* can be applied in its etymological sense, that of a binding principle, in two ways: first, because it symbolizes the link between creation and God through the expression of praise, and also the covenant between God and the people of Israel, conceived as a harmonious relationship (the example of Arama could be read in this sense); second, because it symbolizes the unity of the people of Israel. These ideas are reflected in various aspects of contemporary Jewish life and culture. Some of the themes discussed here still feature in the liturgy, especially in the formulation of texts such as the piyyut El adon (God, Master), which illustrates the heavenly pleroma of song, or Keter, which exemplifies panhymnic unity. The sung interpretation of these texts reveals the fundamental role of music in the praise of God. Depending on local customs, *minhagim*, or individual sensibilities, singing may be considered as an activity that solidifies the relationship with God, with others, or with the Jewish tradition. The unity of Israel in prayer may also be considered from the perspective of ritual studies. Various references in rabbinic literature reveal that the children of Israel should pray in a tight group, forming a "bundle" (באגודה אחת), in reference to the various species, bound together in the *lulav*.

In later modernity, this proximity, which represents group cohesiveness, is brought about by various practices. The case of modern Israel provides many examples that reveal the importance of music in national culture.[51] A particularly interesting example is a type of music consumption that takes form in *shirah be-tsibur* (communal singing). It has emerged during the time of the first settlements in *Erets Yisrael*, as shown in Judah Leman's *A Land of Promise* (1935), one of Palestine's earliest sound films. This practice has continued over the course of successive *aliyot*. It has largely contributed to the development of Israeli folk-song repertoire, disseminated through specially designed *shironim* (songbooks). In this context, communal singing has a social function but also an educational one: it promotes the Hebrew language and Israeli culture. For this reason, the practice has been adopted into Israel's intensive Hebrew study program, known as *ulpan*.[52] It has also sprawled out to the diaspora, where it became relevant in youth movements and non-religious gatherings. A recent manifestation of this practice is the Koolulam, a social-musical initiative aimed at strengthening the fabric of society.[53] Founded in 2017 in Tel Aviv, it has become a transnational effort—reaching to the four corners of the earth, and with the new realities caused by the COVID-19 pandemic virtually *Across the Globe* (thus the title of a virtual event on April 19 and 20, 2021). As a "global engine" it focuses on mass-singing events, drawing thousands of people together for communal singing. It operates under the slogan "Singing is believing," sub-headed with the sentence: "Musical harmony can inspire harmony in humanity." As such, the ancient theme of harmony, transmitted through song and music, is still manifest and relevant today. Since biblical times, harmony has constituted a characteristic feature of the people of Israel and the greater collectivity that it is part of, and specifically served as a link between Jews and the shekhinah.

NOTES

1. For an edition of the Hebrew text, based on the 1522 print, see Israel Adler, ed., *Hebrew Writings Concerning Music in Manuscripts and Printed Books from Geonic Times up to 1800*, RISM, B/IX/2 (Munich: Henle, 1975), 92–96.

2. המוסיקה כמשקפת את ההרמוניה הקוסמית. Dov Schwartz, *Kinor nishmati: Ha-musikah ba-hagut ha-Yehudit* [Kinnor of the soul: Music in Jewish thought] (Ramat-Gan: Bar-Ilan University, 2014), 174.

3. Ibid.

4. See Chani Haran Smith, *Tuning the Soul: Music as a Spiritual Process in the Teachings of Rabbi Nahman of Bratzlav* (Leiden: Brill, 2010), 84–85.

5. See Moshe Idel, "The Magical and Theurgical Interpretation of Music in Jewish Sources from the Renaissance to Hasidism" / הפירוש המאגי והתיאורגי של המוסיקה בטקסטים יהודיים מתקופת הרנסנס ועד החסידות, *Yuval: Studies of the Jewish Music Research Centre* 4 (1982): 35–37.

6. See Rachel Elior, *The Three Temples: On the Emergence of Jewish Mysticism*, trans. David Louvish (Oxford: The Littman Library of Jewish Civilization, 2004).

7. See Gershom Scholem, *Die jüdische Mystik in ihren Hauptströmungen* (Frankfurt am Main: Suhrkamp Verlag, 1967), 61–67.

8. See Karl Erich Grözinger, *Musik und Gesang in der Theologie der frühen jüdischen Literatur* (Tübingen: J.C.B. Mohr, 1982), 299–300.

9. See Adolph Jellinek, *Bet ha-Midrasch: Sammlung Kleiner Midraschim und vermischter Abhandlungen aus der ältern jüdischen Literatur*, 6 vols., 2nd ed. (Jerusalem: Bamberg & Wahrmann, 1938), 2:43.

10. See ibid., 2:44.

11. See Shlomo Musayov, *Sefer Merkavah shelemah* (Jerusalem: Defus Solomon, 1920/21), 5r.

12. See Jellinek, *Bet ha-Midrasch*, 3:101. See also Arthur Green, *Keter: The Crown of God in Early Jewish Mysticism* (Princeton, NJ: Princeton University Press, 2014).

13. Jellinek, *Bet ha-Midrasch*, 3:90.

14. ולבסוף ברא אדם למשול בכל, והלל וזמרה נטע בפיהם ושיר ותשבחות בגרונם. Solomon A. Wertheimer, *Batei Midrashot*, with addenda and corrigenda by Abraham J. Wertheimer (Jerusalem: Ketav va-sefer, 1967/68), 1:26.

15. See Jellinek, *Bet ha-Midrasch*, 3:14–15.

16. Grözinger, *Musik und Gesang*, 300.

17. Abraham Ibn Ezra, *The Book of the World: A Parallel Hebrew-English Edition of the Two Versions of the Text*, ed. and trans. Shlomo Sela, 2 vols. (Leiden: Brill, 2010), 1:18.

18. Ibid., 70–71; for a note about this passage see 1:120.

19. See ibid., 1:230–231.

20. *Epistle on Music of the Ikhwan al-Safa*, ed. and trans. Amnon Shiloah (Tel Aviv: Tel Aviv University, 1978), 34–46.

21. See Shlomo Sela, *Abraham Ibn Ezra and the Rise of Hebrew Science* (Leiden: Brill, 2003), 309n196.

22. *The Commentary of Ibn Ezra on Isaiah* (London: Society for the Promotion of Hebrew Literature, 1873), ed. and trans. Michael Friedländer, 191.

23. *Rabbi Abraham Ibn Ezra's Commentary on Books 3–5 of Psalms: Chapters 73–150*, trans. Norman Strickman (Boston, MA: Academic Studies Press, 2016), 190–191.

24. For an analysis and an English translation of *Igeret Ḥay ben Meḳits*, see Aaron W. Hughes, *The Texture of the Divine: Imagination in Medieval Islamic and Jewish Thought* (Bloomington: Indiana University Press, 2004).

25. Ibid., 197–198.

26. Ibid., 200.

27. See ibid., 205.

28. Maimonides, *The Guide of the Perplexed*, trans. Shlomo Pines (Chicago: University of Chicago Press, 1963), 2:273–276.

29. Ibid., 2:267.

30. See Aristotle, *On the Heavens*, trans. William K. C. Guthrie (Cambridge, MA: Harvard University Press, 1939), 190–197.

31. They include Samuel Ibn Tibbon, Gersonides, Joseph Ibn Kaspi, Moses Narboni, and Profiat Duran. See Ofer Elior, "Ezekiel Is Preferable to Aristotle: Torah and Science in Four Interpretations of Ezekiel's 'I Heard'" / יחזקאל עדיף מאריסטו: דת ומדע בארבעה פירושים ל'ואשמע' ליחזקאל, *Pe'amim: Studies in Oriental Jewry*, 139–140 (2014): 55–80; and Charles Touati, "Le problème de l'inerrance prophétique dans la théologie juive du Moyen Âge," *Revue de l'histoire des religions* 174 (1968): 169–187 (in particular 180–182).

32. See Maimonides, *The Guide of the Perplexed*, 2:259–261.

33. Ibid., 2:261–265.

34. Philo, "Moses 1 and 2," in *Philo*, vol. 6 [On Abraham—On Joseph—On Moses], trans. Francis H. Colson (Cambridge, MA: Harvard University Press, 1935), 578–579.

35. See Gad Freudenthal, ed., *Science in Medieval Jewish Cultures* (Cambridge: Cambridge University Press, 2011).

36. See Nehemia Allony, "The Term *musiqah* in Medieval Jewish Literature / המונח מוסיקה בספרותנו בימי הביניים," *Yuval: Studies of the Jewish Music Research Centre* 1 (1968): 11–35 (Hebrew section), and 2 (1971): 29–39 (Hebrew section).

37. See Hanoch Avenary, "The Hebrew Version of Abu l-Ṣalt's Treatise on Music," *Yuval: Studies of the Jewish Music Research Centre* 3 (1974): 7–82.

38. Michel Foucault, *The Order of Things: An Archaeology of the Human Sciences* (London: Routledge, 2002), 19.

39. See for instance Amnon Shiloah, "*Ên-Kol*—Commentaire hébraïque de Šem Tov ibn Šaprût sur le canon d'Avicenne," *Yuval: Studies of the Jewish Music Research Centre* 3 (1974): 267–286.

40. See Penelope Gouk, "The Role of Harmonics in the Scientific Revolution," in *The Cambridge History of Western Music Theory*, ed. Thomas Christensen (Cambridge: Cambridge University Press, 2002), 224.

41. See Homer, *Odyssey*, trans. Augustus T. Murray (Cambridge, MA: Harvard University Press, 1919), 200–201 (line 248) and 208–209 (line 361).

42. For an edition of some of the passages related to music, mainly based on the manuscript housed at the Staatsbibliothek Berlin (Ms. Or. Qu. 832), see Adler, *Hebrew Writings*, 39–44.

43. MS Or. Qu. 832, f. 125r, Staatsbibliothek zu Berlin. See Adler, *Hebrew Writings*, 42.

44. MS Or. Qu. 832, f. 125r, Staatsbibliothek zu Berlin.

45. MS Or. Qu. 832, f. 128r, Staatsbibliothek zu Berlin. For an edition of this passage, see Moshe Idel, "The Magical and Theurgical Interpretation," 37–38.

46. MS Or. Qu. 832, f. 126v–127v, Staatsbibliothek Berlin. See Adler, *Hebrew Writings*, 42–44.

47. כן יקרה לנפש המשכלת היודעת נגן בסגולה שבה נגינות מעציבות כחות הטבע. MS Or. Qu. 832, f. 127v, Staatsbibliothek zu Berlin.

48. Idel, "The Magical and Theurgical Interpretation," 38.

49. Yoḥanan Alemanno, *Ḥay ha-ʿolamim / L'immortale*, vol. 1: *La retorica*, ed. and trans. Fabrizio Lelli (Florence: Olschki, 1995).

50. Ibid., 150.

51. See Motti Regev and Edwin Seroussi, *Popular Music and National Culture in Israel* (Berkeley: University of California Press, 2004).

52. See, for example, Deborah Golden, "'Now, like Real Israelis, Let's Stand Up and Sing': Teaching the National Language to Russian Newcomers in Israel," *Anthropology & Education Quarterly* 32, no. 1 (2001): 52–79.

53. See Chava Wiess and Rotem Maor, "Harmonizing Hearts with Many Voices—Analysis of Koolulam, a Mass-Singing Phenomenon, and Its Contribution to Resiliency," *Voices: A World Forum for Music Therapy* 22, no. 2 (2022). https://voices.no/index.php/voices/article/view/3295 and https://doi.org/10.15845/voices.v22i2.3295

SELECT BIBLIOGRAPHY

Elior, Rachel. *The Three Temples: On the Emergence of Jewish Mysticism*. Translated by David Louvish. Portland: The Littman Library of Jewish Civilization, 2004.

Grözinger, Karl Erich. *Musik und Gesang in der Theologie der frühen jüdischen Literatur*. Tübingen: J. C. B. Mohr, 1982.

Hicks, Andrew. *Composing the World: Harmony in the Medieval Platonic Cosmos*. Oxford: Oxford University Press, 2017.

Idel, Moshe. "Conceptualization of Music in Jewish Mysticism." In *Enchanting Powers: Music in the World's Religions*, edited by Lawrence E. Sullivan, 159–188. Cambridge, MA: Harvard University Press, 1997.

Idel, Moshe. "The Magical and Theurgic Interpretation of Music in Jewish Sources from the Renaissance to Hasidism" / הפירוש המאגי והתיאורגי של המוסיקה בטקסטים יהודיים מתקופת הרנסנס ועד החסידות. *Yuval: Studies of the Jewish Music Research Centre* 4 (1982): 35–63.

Ofer, Elior. "'The Conclusion whose Demonstration is Correct is Believed': Maimonides on the Possibility of Celestial Sounds according to Three Medieval Interpreters." *Revue des études juives* 172, nos. 3–4 (2013): 283–303.

Prins, Jacomien, and Maude Vanhaelen, eds. *Sing Aloud Harmonious Spheres: Renaissance Conceptions of Cosmic Harmony.* New York: Routledge, 2018.

Schwartz, Dov. *Kinor nishmati: Ha-musiḵah ba-hagut ha-Yehudit.* Ramat-Gan: Bar-Ilan University, 2013.

Smith, Chani Haran. "Music as a Spiritual Process in the Teachings of Rav Nahman of Bratslav." *Journal of Synagogue Music* 34 (2009): 8–47.

Smith, Chani Haran. *Tuning the Soul: Music as a Spiritual Process in the Teachings of Rabbi Naḥman of Bratzlav.* Leiden: Brill, 2010.

Werner, Eric, and Isaiah Sonne. "Philosophy and Theory of Music in Judaeo-Arabic Literature." *Hebrew Union College Annual* 16 (1941): 251–320, and 17 (1943): 511–572.

INDEX

....

For the benefit of digital users, indexed terms that span two pages (e.g., 52–53) may, on occasion, appear on only one of those pages.
Note: Tables and figures are indicated by *t* and *f* following the page number

Abitan, Michel, C3P41
absolute time, 14–15
accordion, 196–97, 199, 389, 594–95, 600, 640–41
acculturation, 47–51
acousmatic listening, 364–67
adamah/adamot (earth/lands). *See also* land
  Al-Andalus, 70, 73, 75–79
  biblocentrism and, 40–41, 42–47, 48–49, 51–53, 55–56
  deflations, 51–56
  introduction to, 17–18, 39–41
  returns to other lands, 56–59
Adler, Abraham, 436
Adler, Ferdinand, 125–26
Adler, Israel, 3–4, 9
Agambe, Giorgio, 16
Agrupación Nueva Música, 154
Akedat Yitsḥak (Binding of Isaac), 698, 707
Al-Andalus
  adamah in, 70, 73, 75–79
  ancestral relationship, 83–85
  founding of, 72–73
  introduction to, 70–72
  Jewish indigeneity and, 75–79
  Judeo-Andalusian music, 70, 71, 75, 76–77, 81–82, 84
  Judeo-Spanish music, 71, 73–75, 166–67, 168, 170–72, 175–76, 180n.10, 180–81n.12
  repertoire and place, 72–75
  Sepharadic music, 70–71, 72–75, 79–83
al-Ḥalabīyah, Fairūz, 619
al-Ḥāmūlī, 'Abdu, 627

al-Yahūdī, Mansūr, 72–73
Alcaide, Ana, 79–81
Aleichem, Sholem, 185–86, 320
Alemanno, Yohanan, 707, 709–10
Aleppo's Jewish Khūjahs (Jewish women musicians)
  association with women's songs, 624–26
  Baḥsīta cabarets, 620–22
  Café Orange and, 620–22
  as historically absent, 618–20
  introduction to, 614–16
  memory-making of, 622–24
  muṭribah, 24–25, 621, 626–28
  Naziha Assis, 614–16, 620–22, 627, 628–29
Aleshkovsky, Yuz, 328
Alexander, Haim, 346–47
Alexanian, Diran, 146
Alpert, Michael, 384
Alter, Robert, 49–51
American Jewish Studies Association, 9
American Society for Jewish Music, 9–10
American Women's Club, 126–28
Amichai, Yehudah, 51–52
Amin, Ash, 203
Amin, Roshel, 539–40
Aminov, David, 543
Anderson, Benedict, 337
Andreani, George, 145, 146, 156–57
Anisfeld, Sharon Cohen, 465–67
Antebi, Yosef, 625
Antelis, Shaindel, 652–53
anti-Jewish Campbell Riots (1931), 170

anti-Semitism. *See also* Nazism
  by European orchestras, 340
  Franco regime, 79
  Jewish émigrés in Buenos Aires, 144–45
  sounding out the ghetto, 267–73, 275–77
  in Soviet Union, 315–16, 317, 319–20, 322–28
  state- sponsored, 74, 309, 310–12
  of Wagner, Richard, 125–26
  of Waldorff, Jerzy, 253
  Yiddish theater and, 358
anti-Zionism, 16, 322
anticipatory refugees, 338, 342
Anzieu, Didier, 371
Arab Jews, 56–57
Arab Revolt (1936), 170
Arabic music, 71, 93–94, 342–43, 620
Arabic songs, 615, 619
Arabo-Andalusian music, 73, 81–82, 83–84
Arabo-Islamic culture, 91–92, 109–10
Aragoneses, Alfons, 81
Arama, Isaac, 698–99, 706–7
Arditi, Mister, 173
Argentina. *See* Jewish émigrés in Buenos Aires
Aris San, 175–77
Aristotelian rationalism, 706
Aristotle, 704–5
Arkette, Sophie, 190
Aronova, Hevsi, 538–39
ars historica, 230
art music
  compositional attitudes and ideological
    directions, 342–47
  deflations, 51–56
  Hebrewism of, 39–43, 41*f*, 56–63
  institutionalization of, 40–41
  institutions and compositional
    constraints, 338–42
  introduction to, 39–41, 335–38, 336*f*
  Israeli art music, 18–19, 53, 335, 337, 338, 342,
    347–48, 352n.6
  Jewishness in, 317–22
  pluralism and, 347–50
  role of concert hall in, 350–51
  Western art music, 57, 338–39
  Westernness as duty, 47–51
  the Yishuv and, 335, 337–50, 339*t*
Art Worlds (Becker), 146–47

Artist Club, 123–24, 125, 131–32
Aschheim, Steven, 264–65
Ashkenazic Jews/Ashkenazim, 16, 56–57, 148,
  166–67, 171, 176–77, 185, 188–91, 359–60,
  496, 508, 518–19, 667. *See also* feminine
  elements in Oppenheimer Siddur
Asociacion Cultural Israelita de Buenos
  Aires, 149
Association for Jewish Studies, 9–10
Association of Jewish Precentors, 129–30,
  131, 132
Association of Rescued Jews, 586
Australian Archive of Jewish Music, 23–24,
  430–32, 434–37, 440–41
Australian Broadcasting Corporation
  (ABC), 433
Australian Centre for Jewish Civilisation, 434
Australian Research Council, 434
avant-garde music, 153–55, 158–59
Avidom, Menahem, 346–47
Avni, Tzvi, 347*f*, 347
Avraham Mi-Sha'ar Aryeh. *See* Mantua ghetto
  music and Portaleone
Ayen erekh: Ahavah (Grossman), 61–62
"Az yeranen 'ets ha-ye'arim" (On that day
  the tree of the forest shall shout for
  joy), 104–8
"Azamer beshvaḥin," 502*f*, 502–3
Azoulay, André, 84–85

Babylonian Jewish music, 2–3, 48, 91–92, 93–
  94, 99, 103, 107–10
Babylonian Talmud, 58, 102, 106, 455, 458, 467,
  472n.28, 472–73n.41, 479, 556–57, 565,
  689, 704
badkhn (Jewish wedding entertainer), 23, 383–
  84, 388, 512–13
Baer, Hans, 119–20, 121, 124–25, 126–28
Baer, Werner, 433
Baerlein, Elisabeth, 273
Baghdadi Jewish community, 17–18
Baḥsīta cabarets, 620–22
Bakayeva, Hevsi, 538–39
Balkan Arts Center (Center for Traditional
  Music and Dance), 384
Bar, Doron, 484
Barzofsky, Shalom Noah, 456

Bashrav (Ehrlich), 53–56, 54*f*
Bashrav (Olivero), 60–61
bath of sounds, 371
Baum, Dobby, 655
Baumgarten, Elisheva, 666
Becker, Howard, 146–47, 384
Beethoven, Ludwig van, 125–26
Behrens, Walter, 600
Béla, Dajos, 155, 156–57
Ben Dor, Orna, 174
Ben-Haim, Paul, 42–43, 44*f*, 340, 345, 346–47, 348–49
Ben Stonehill Archive Collection, 410
Ben-Yishai, Aharon Zeev, 337
Beregovsky, Moisey, 310–11, 318, 400–1, 439–40
Berg, Mary, 250–51
Berinsky, Sergey, 321–22, 326
Berl, Heinrich, 133
Berlin, Shtetl, 205
Berliner, Emil, 366
Bern, Alan, 193–94
Bernhaut, Charles, 408–9
Bernheim, Hanna, 270–71
Bernstein, Leonard, 62–63
Besedin, Askold, 324
Bible, 17–19, 24–25, 216–18, 230
    Book of Psalms, 106, 220–21, 485, 486, 669–70, 686–87
    Ezekiel, 39–40, 42–43, 44*f*, 48–49, 700, 702–3, 704
    Genesis, 1, 75
    Psalms of David, 224
    Song of Songs, 93, 340, 349, 638–39, 670–72, 703, 708
biblical sovereignty, 39–40, 42
biblocentrism, 40–41, 42–47, 48–49, 51–53, 55–56
Binder, Abraham, 294–95
Bird, Frederick, 493–94
Birkat hamazon, 495, 603
Bischofswerder, Boaz, 432–33
Bitkin, Vladimir (Zeev), 321–22
Blanchot, Maurice, 16
blatnaya pesnya (Russian chanson), 317
Bloch, David, 439
Bloch, Emilie Berendsen, 439
Blouin, Francis Xavier, Jr., 400
Blum, Julia, 649

Bodenwieser, Gertrude, 433
Bohlman, Philip V., 4, 5–6, 292–93
Boikova, Marina, 321–22
Bolshevik Revolution (1917), 309–10
Borgó, András, 665
Boskovich, Alexander Uriah, 342–43
Boulanger, Nadia, 342
Boyarskaya, Revekka (Rivka), 323–24
Boym, Svetlana, 169
Braun, Yehezkel, 347
Bresler, Joel, 410, 411, 414
Brinner, Benjamin, 146–47
Broadway musicals, 645–49
Brod, Max, 342–43
Bronstein, Marcelo R., 469
Brous, Sharon, 461, 464–65
Brubaker, Roger, 165–66
Buenos Aires. *See* Jewish émigrés in Buenos Aires
Bukharian Jewish weddings of Central Asia
    in Afghanistan, 546n.7
    Bukharian histories, 533–34
    creative remembering, 534–40
    introduction to, 531–32
    jomma dance, 541–43, 542*f*
    mythologies and reality of, 544–46
    performances of Central Asian past, 541–44
    shashmaqom, 531, 534–35, 536, 537–38
    sozandas, 534–40, 541–42, 547n.21, 617
burial in Jewish music, 17–18, 42–43, 75–76, 79, 81–82
Busch, Fritz, 151
Buxtorf, Johannes, 516, 517–18
Buzeng Xu, 120–21

Café Orange, 620–22
cantillation markings, 224–25
cantorial music. *See* Hasidic cantors
Carlebach, Shlomo, 416
Caro, Joseph, 479
Casa del Teatro, 151–52
Castro, Juan José, 153–54, 155, 160*f*
Cazés, Moshé, 169–70
celestial harmony, 702–5
Central Asia Bukharian Jewish weddings. *See* Bukharian Jewish weddings of Central Asia

Centralna Komisja Imprezowa (Central Commission for Entertainments, CKI), 246–47
chalgidjís, 169–70
Chamber Jewish Musical Theater (KEMT), 327
Chamber Opera Group, 341
Chartiner, Meyer, 337–38
Chion, Michel, 364–65
choral music, 43, 267, 292, 302, 321–22, 327–28, 344–45, 369, 421, 571, 584–85, 603
Chronakis, Paris, 178
clavicordo, 226–27
code switching, 507
Cohen, Judah, 410, 463–64
Cohen, Kineret Sarah, 649
Cohen, Nechama, 652–53
Cohen, Shimon, 346–47
Cohen-Hattab, Kobi, 484
collections. *See also* klezmer music in YIVO Sound Archive; postcustodialism in Jewish music archive
    Ben Stonehill Archive Collection, 410
    Harvard University Library Judaic collection, 411
    Holocaust music collections, 430
    introduction to, 23–24
    Jewish culture in, 23–24
    Mayrent Collection of Yiddish Recordings at Mills Music Library, 414, 415
collective agency, 15–16
collective memory, 15–16, 24–25, 73, 309, 621
collectivism, 342, 343–44, 351
collectivity
    diachronic collectivity, 19–20, 218–19, 232
    Jewish émigrés in Buenos Aires, 145, 146–47, 159–60
    Jewish music studies and, 15–16
    singing zemiroth at Sabbath meals, 498–99
    synchronic collectivity, 19–20, 218–19, 232
Collegium Musicum de Buenos Aires, 159
Commissariat for Jewish National Affairs (YEVKOM), 310–11
commonsense groupism, 165–66
communities of affinity, 165–66
concentration camps. *See* Jewish music and internment in Ferramonti di Tarsia
concert stage, 126–28

concert streamed videos, 652–56
consolidation of Jewish music studies, 8–11
continuity of Jewish music, 135–36
convivencia, 71, 72–73, 78, 79–80, 81–82
Cooper, Adrienne, 387–88, 398, 402
cosmic harmony, 698–99, 705, 707
COVID-19 pandemic, 400–1, 439, 452–53, 457, 655, 710–11
creative signaling, 532
Csikszentmihalyi, Mihaly, 467–68
cultural appropriation, 666
cultural ghettoization, 262–63, 272, 273, 276
cultural mapping, 32n.41
Czernowin, Chaya, 59–63

Dalāl, Muḥammad Qadrī, 625
"Daled bavos" (Melody of four stanzas or gates), 2
Dalven, Rachel (Rae), 555
Darmstadt Maḥzor, 670–72, 673f
Darwīsh, Sayyid, 627
davenen, 456
Davis, Maayan, 653–55
De Auro dialogi tres (Portaleone), 219–20, 221
De Philippe, Edis, 341–42
decolonization, 429–30
Dei Rossi, Azariah ben Moses, 230
Della Porta, Giovanni Battista, 229
Deluca, Raffaele, 599
Der fonograf (The phonograph) (Pinski), 367–69
derashot (sermons), 106–7
Derrida, Jacques, 389, 395–96
destruction and remembrance
    ḥurban ha-bayit (destruction), 24–25
    introduction to, 24–26
    zakhor (to remember), 23–24
    zekher (remembrance), 24–25, 554, 565, 571, 575–76, 579–80, 587, 599, 605, 607, 608–9, 616, 628–29
deterritorialization, 17–18, 390
Deutscher, Isaac, 3–4
deveykes (spiritual cleaving) nigunim, 301–2
diachronic collectivity, 19–20, 218–19, 232
Die Tribüne, 125, 131–32
digital age/turn, 190, 440–41, 649–52, 657, 690
digital transnationalism, 190

digitization, 395–96, 413–14, 416, 417, 419

Dion, Lynn, 396

Displaced Persons, 2–3, 121–22, 389, 439, 605

Displaced Persons (DP) camps, 172–73, 569–71, 599, 604–6

Dizengoff, Meir, 341

Dori, Dafna, 93–94

Dreifuß, Alfred, 123–24, 125, 131–32

Dresden Maḥzor, 670, 671f

"D'ror yikra," 504–5, 504f

Drucker, Yosele, 185–86

Dukas, Paul, 342

Dümling, Albrecht, 436

Dunayevsky, Isaak, 316

Durkheim, Emile, 15–16

early modern period. See Yiddish wedding songs in early modern period

eco-spirituality, 466–68

Ehrlich, Abel, 53–56, 54f

Einheitsgottesdienste (unified services), 128–29

Eisler, Martín, 152

Elbaum, Moshe, 133

Elscheková, Alice, 514–15

Emek (Lavry), 346

emic philosophy, 72, 74

Enesco, George, 146

Engel, Yuly (Yoel), 336–37, 431, 439–40, 582

Engelbrecht, Richard, 146

Enlightenment era, 14, 23, 265

Entartete Musik (degenerate music), 155–56

Epelbaum, Mikhail, 312

Epstein, Shifra, 641–42

Erets Yisrael. See Greater Israel (Erets Yisrael)

Erlich, Ruwin, 153–54, 160f

eruv, 17, 21, 450, 455–56, 470, 494, 508

ethnomusicologists, 57–58, 71–72, 401, 422, 429, 434, 438, 439–40, 488–89, 615, 626

European Association for Jewish Studies, 9–10

European Jewish Artist Society, 123–24, 125–26

Ezekiel, 39–40, 42–43, 44f, 48–49, 700, 702–3, 704

Fader, Ayala, 452, 469

Fajnzylber, Cypora, 569, 571–78, 572f

Fefer, Itzik, 196–97, 197f

Feidman, Giora, 193–95

Felber, Erwin, 130–31, 133

Feldman, Walter Zev, 187

feminine elements in Oppenheimer Siddur
   envisioning harmony, 668–74, 668f, 671f
   harmony of love, 667f, 684–90, 685f, 688f
   introduction to, 7–8, 664–68
   sin, music, and folly, 674–84, 675f, 678f
   Yitzḥaq, Asher ben and, 667–68, 682–84, 690–92, 691f

feminine musical scenes, 2–3

Ferramonti di Tarsia. See Jewish music and internment in Ferramonti di Tarsia

fertility in Jewish music, 17–18, 75, 84, 687

film industry
   Buenos Aires, 156–57
   Greece, 175–77, 183n.46
   internment camps and, 599
   Jewish film festivals, 494
   klezmer music in YIVO Sound Archive, 383, 390
   in Sweden, 580
   totalitarianism and, 316, 321
   Warsaw Ghetto and, 240, 251, 252–53, 254
   Yiddish theater and, 364–65

First Nations people, 430–31

Fishman, David, 387

Five (Mighty Handful), 318

Flemming, K. E., 166–67, 172–73

folksongs, 58–59, 362–63, 505–6

Forshpil, 196–97, 197f, 198f

Forster, Leah, 645–46

Foucault, Michel, 482, 706–7

fourfold song, 21, 449–50, 453, 469

Fraenkel, Wolfgang, 128

Franciska, 652–55, 654f, 655f

Frank, Anne, 324

Frankenburger, Paul, 338, 339–40

Freeden, Herbert, 273

Freedman, Bob, 412, 415

Freedman Jewish Sound Archive, 415

Freie Deutsche Bühne (Free German Stage), 151–52

Frenkel, Aleksandr, 314

Frid, Grigory, 318, 324–25

Friedländer, Saul, 273

Friedman, Israel, 504

Friedmann, Hersch, 132, 134

Frigyesi, Judit, 497–98, 506–7

Fromm, Herbert, 262
Fruchter, Josef, 133–34
Fundacion Tres Culturas, 78–79, 84–85

Galich, Aleksandr, 328
Galilei, Vincenzo, 226
galut (exile), 12–13, 127–28
Gamliel, Miriam Leah, 645–46
Gazeta Żydowska (Jewish newspaper), 244–45
Gebirtig, Mordechai, 438, 573–74
Geisel, Eike, 273
Geist, Edwin, 439
Gellerman, Jill, 641–42
Gemeinschaft Jüdischer Kantoren, 129–30
Genesis, 1, 17–18, 42, 75, 119–20, 553–54
genocide, 24–25, 323–24, 437–38, 554–78
German Jews, 149, 195, 205–6, 261–62, 264–68, 269, 273, 276, 366, 439, 496–97, 517, 521f, 578
Gestapo, 247, 250–51, 261, 266, 273
Ghanai, Katayoun, 463
Ghetto Nuovo, 19–20
ghettos, 12–13, 19–20, 431–32. *See also* Mantua ghetto music and Portaleone; sounding out the ghetto; urban musical culture in Warsaw Ghetto
Giniger, Malky, 645–46, 649
Ginio, Eyal, 168
Ginsparg, Leslie, 645–46
Glazunov, Aleksandr, 584–85
Glikson, Josef, 569, 571–78, 572f
Glinka, Mikhail, 318
Gluz, Mikhail, 327–28
Gmyrya, Boria, 324
Gnesin, Mikhail, 318–19
Goebbels, Joseph, 268–69
Gofenberg, Jossif, 204
Gold, Niusia, 580
Goldberg, Amos, 241
goldene medina, 188–89
Goldfaden, Abraham, 358–59, 362–63
Goldfarb, Israel, 294–95
Goldins, Maksis, 321–22
Goldman, Michal, 383
Goldschmidt, Emil, 200
Goldsmith, Peter, 420
Goldszmit, Henryk, 326

Golinkin, Mark (Mordechai), 337–38, 341
Gombiński, Stanisław, 244
Gomery, Mónica, 457, 459–60, 463, 465–66, 468
Goren, Shlomo, 481
Gorovets, Emil, 312
Gottfried, Leah, 652–53
Gottlieb, Roger S., 467–68
Graetzer, Wilhelm (Guillermo), 146, 149–50, 159
gramophone sound-recording industry, 366
gramophone street players, 367–69, 372f
Great Turn (1928/1929), 310–11
Greater Israel (*Erets Yisrael*), 17–18, 40f, 62–63, 70–71, 73, 710–11
Grecian Jews. *See* Romaniote liturgical music
Greek Salonikan Jews. *See* Salonika
Greek wisdom, 219–23, 231–32
Greekness in music, 171, 175–77, 178–79
Green, Arthur, 453–54, 458
Grober, Khayele, 579–80
Groh, Matthias, 199
Gromadsky, Vitaly, 324
Grossman, Atina, 570–71
Grossman, David, 61–62
Grossman, Vasily, 324
Grözinger, Karl Erich, 700, 701
Grupo Renovación, 153–54
Guetta, Alessandro, 219–20, 227, 230
guitar, 79–80, 175, 193, 196–97, 294–95, 345, 422, 541, 576, 602–3, 640–41, 644
Gurs Relief Committee, 150
Gutman, Nahum, 335–36

ha-makom, 12
Habimah theater company, 22–23, 270–71, 310, 579–80
Habusha, Moshe, 476–77
Hajdu, Andre, 57–59
Ḥakham Yosef Ḥayyim ben 'Eliah al-Ḥakham
    "Az yeranen 'ets ha-ye'arim" (On that day the tree of the forest shall shout for joy), 104–8
    introduction to, 2–3, 91–93
    life, work, and leadership, 95–97, 108–10
    melodies used by, 102–3

music originating in Arab-Muslim
    countries, 93–94
paraliturgical music/songs, 97–100, 100t
virtue of singing praises to God, 97–99
ḥakhamim (rabbis), 91
ḥakhmey ha-sefaradim (the Sephardic/Middle
    Eastern rabbis/sages), 96
Halkin, Samuil, 325
"Hamelekh Shaul ve'ani" (King Saul and I)
    (Amichai), 51–52
Handler, Richard, 15
Hanukkah, 107, 125, 149–50, 205, 303, 497, 597,
    603, 605–7
Haredi/Haredim, 16, 186, 297, 484–85
Harendorf, Samuel Jacob, 370–71
harmonium, 129–30, 602–3, 611n.38
harmony
    celestial harmony, 702–5
    early Jewish mystics and, 699–701
    etymological sense of, 710
    introduction to, 698–99
    musical knowledge in analogical
        reasoning, 705–10
    in Oppenheimer Siddur, 667f, 668–74, 668f,
        671f, 684–90, 685f, 688f
    unity of the Israeli people through, 710–11
harp, 26–27, 222–23, 227–29, 237n.56, 479,
    640–41, 665, 678–82, 681f, 684–
    87, 689–90
Harrán, Don, 216–18, 228, 229–30
Hartov, Alexander, 412–13
Harvard University Library Judaic
    collection, 411
Hasidic cantors
    as artists, 291–96
    internet and, 299–301
    introduction to, 289–91
    kumzits (music making party), 290, 301–
        3, 637–38
    liturgical music, 290, 292–93, 299, 301–2
    non-metrical sound of, 292
    pressures of non-conformity, 303–5
    staging music of, 296–99
Hasidim, 1–2, 16, 301–2, 497–99, 502, 637–38,
    639, 650, 710
Hausdorff, Martin, 130–31, 133–34
Havassy, Rivka, 166

Hebräsch-orientalischer Melodienschatz/
    Thesaurus of Oriental Hebrew Melodies
    (Idelsohn), 5
Hebrew Bible. See Bible
Hebrew language, 39–41, 42–47, 135–36, 216,
    221, 310, 320, 340, 344, 346, 710–11
Hebrew songs, 126–27, 132, 183n.51, 318, 348,
    590n.51, 603
Hebrewism, 17–18, 39–43, 41f, 56–63, 310
hefker khazones (wanton cantorial music), 293–94
Helfgott, Meier, 295
Hellenization program, 168–69, 174–75
Her First Ball (Szpilman), 251–52
Hermerschmidt, Jan, 192, 193
Heschel, Abraham Joshua, 454–55
Ḥeshek Shlomoh (Solomon's desire), 708–10
Heskes, Irene, 359–60
Hess, Ernst Ferdinand, 515
heterotopia, 27, 386, 482, 489
Heydemann, Lizzi, 467
himmlisches Sangespleroma (heavenly pleroma
    of song), 700
Hindemith, Paul, 146
hip hop, 543, 545, 652–53
historiography, 23–24, 31n.32, 40–41, 178,
    230, 263–64
Hoffman, Lawrence A., 451, 460–61, 463
Hollender, Elisabeth, 557
Holman, Peter, 665
Holocaust. See also Jewish music and
        internment in Ferramonti di Tarsia;
        Romaniote liturgical music
    Australian Archive of Jewish Music, 434–
        37, 440–42
    Final Solution, 262–63, 274, 275, 276
    ḥurban (genocide of Jews), 24–25, 554, 564–
        65, 569–70, 571, 603–4
    Jewish music studies and, 13
    memory of, 24–25
    music collections and, 430
    survivors from Salonika, 172–73
    totalitarianism in post-Stalinist Soviet
        Union, 322–26
    United States Holocaust Memorial
        Museum, 23–24, 410, 432, 437–40
    urban musical culture in Warsaw Ghetto, 241
    Yiddish songs and, 133–34

Holocaust fatigue, 441–42
Holocaust Memorial Museum in Washington, DC. *See* United States Holocaust Memorial Museum
Holocaust survivors in Sweden
  commemoration in new communities, 585–87
  guest performances and concerts, 578–85
  introduction to, 569–71
  kleynkunst (little art), 571–80, 586
Hongkou Ghetto, 122
Honigberg, Steven, 438
Hopenko, Moshe, 335
Höpfner, Paul Christoph, 517
Horváth, Sándor, 155
Huberman, Bronisław, 340
hurban (genocide of Jews), 24–25, 554, 564–65, 569–70, 571, 603–4
Hurwitz, Aryeh Leib, 301
Hurwitz, Moyshe, 357–58, 360, 361, 373–74
Husid, Mordechai, 569–70, 586
Hussein, Saddam, 618–19

Ibn Ezra, Abraham, 1, 702–4
Ibn Ezra, Moses, 561–63
Idel, Moshe, 709
Idelsohn, Abraham Zvi, 5–6, 9, 49f
identity theory, 15
Īdishe Dramatishe Stude, 153
Ikonomopolous, Marcia Haddad, 555
immigrants. *See also* migrants/migration
  composers, 338–41, 342, 344–45, 348–49
  singing zemiroth at Sabbath meals, 499–506
individualism, 304, 342, 344, 345–46, 348–49, 351, 657
Ingber, David, 454, 456–57, 461–62, 463, 464
Institute for Yiddish Culture, 414
institutionalization, 8–11, 40–41
instruments. *See also* piano; individual instruments
  accordion, 196–97, 199, 389, 594–95, 600, 640–41
  clavicordo, 226–27
  guitar, 79–80, 175, 193, 196–97, 294–95, 345, 422, 541, 576, 602–3, 640–41, 644
  harmonium, 129–30, 602–3, 611n.38
  harp, 26–27, 222–23, 227–29, 237n.56, 479, 640–41, 665, 678–82, 681f, 684–87, 689–90
  keren, 226–27
  keyboard, 186, 196–97, 289, 296–98, 302–3, 540, 541–42, 600, 602–3, 640–41
  kinnor, 216–18, 226–29, 231–32
  lute, 216–18, 224, 227, 536, 542–43, 665–66, 677, 678–82, 681f, 686, 700
  lyre, 227–28, 244–45, 687, 689–90, 709
  nevel, 224, 226–27, 689, 690
  organ, 148–49, 225, 298, 302–3, 321–22, 370, 420, 422, 433
  sampogna, 225–27
  saxophone, 155, 169–70, 640–41
  shofar, 76, 225–27, 347, 347f, 480–81, 664–65, 668–69, 693–94n.28
  tof, 225–27, 235n.38, 705–6
  tsiltsal, 226–27
  tsiltsal shema, 226–27
  ʿugav, 216–18, 226–27, 231–32
  violin, 53–54, 54f, 146, 150, 155, 158–59, 245, 320–21, 335–36, 398–99, 401, 602–3, 640–41, 665
International Forum for Jewish Music Studies, 9–10
International Hebrew Wedding Music (Kostakowsky), 190
International Society for Contemporary Music (ISCM), 154
internet
  archives on, 401–2
  digital recordings, 416
  Hasidic cantors, 290, 291, 299–301
  search questions, 460
internment camps. *See* Jewish music and internment in Ferramonti di Tarsia
Ischakis, Haim, 560–64, 563f
Israeli art music, 18–19, 53, 335, 337, 338, 342, 347–48, 352n.6
Israeli music, 54–55, 342–43, 344, 346, 350–51, 411, 499

Israeli National Sound Archive, 9
Isserlein, Israel, 664–65

Jabotinsky, Ze'ev, 480
Jacob, Paul Walter, 149–50, 151–52, 154–55
Jacoby, Hanoch, 346–47
Jaffe, Bracha, 656
Jaldati, Lin, 191–92, 580–83, 581f
James, William, 450, 469–70
jazz, 150, 155, 158, 172, 189–90, 201, 249, 296–97, 298, 314–15, 384, 608
Jerusalem, 18–19, 20–21
Jerusalem Academy of Music and Dance, 344–45
Jerusalem Musical Society, 342
Jerusalem School of Music, 347–48
Jerusalem Temple, 24–25, 130, 131, 324
Jewish Autonomous Oblast, 327
Jewish collectivities, 16, 178
Jewish Community of Central European Jews, 128–29
Jewish culture. See also urban musical culture in Warsaw Ghetto
    in collections, 23–24
    ghettoization, 262–63, 272, 273, 276
    Jewish émigrés in Buenos Aires, 147–50
    in Jewish music studies, 13
    mapping of, 32n.41
    popular-music taste cultures, 178–79
Jewish Emergent Network, 452
Jewish émigrés in Buenos Aires
    anti-Semitism and, 144–45
    cultural infrastructure of, 147–50
    introduction to, 144–47
    music network of, 151–60
    Zionism and, 149–50
Jewish Enlightenment, 23
Jewish folk tunes, 318
Jewish Historical Ethnographic Society, 23–24
Jewish Holocaust Centre, 430, 433–34, 436
Jewish identity, 114n.77, 119–20, 124–25, 243, 275–76, 293, 311, 409, 412–13, 461–62, 603, 606–7, 665
Jewish liturgy, 9, 62–63, 365, 467, 565, 700
Jewish memory, 13, 622–24
Jewish Museum of Australia, 430, 435

Jewish music. See also Al-Andalus; postcustodialism in Jewish music archive; Salonika; sound recordings in US; Yiddish music
    Babylonian Jewish music, 2–3, 48, 91–92, 93–94, 99, 103, 107–10
    burial in, 17–18, 42–43, 75–76, 79, 81–82
    city and, 18–19
    collections, 23–24
    collectivity and, 15–16
    congregations of refugees in Shanghai, 130
    consolidation of, 8–11
    continuity of, 135–36
    destruction and remembrance, 24–26
    fertility in, 17–18, 75, 84, 687
    folksongs, 58–59, 362–63, 505–6
    ghetto and, 12–13, 19–20
    Hebrew songs, 126–27, 132, 183n.51, 318, 348, 590n.51, 603
    institutionalization of, 8–11
    introduction to mapping, 1–3
    Israeli music and, 54–55, 342–43, 344, 346, 350–51, 411, 499
    Jewish community and, 13
    Jewish culture in, 13
    land and, 17–18
    modeling of, 11–16
    organization of, 17–28
    overview of, 3–4
    sacred and ritual spaces, 20–22
    spatial approach to, 12–15
    stage space, 22–23
    temporal approach to, 14–15
    theory and methodology, 5–8
    topicality of, 135–36
    Western Jewish musical traditions, 48, 56
Jewish music and internment in Ferramonti di Tarsia
    concentration camp overview, 599–604
    Displaced Persons (DP) camps, 599, 604–6
    introduction to, 594–99
    as site of remembrance, 606–9
Jewish Music in Its Historical Development (Idelsohn), 5
Jewish Music Research Centre, 9, 422

Jewish musical community
    of affinity, 165–66
    Baghdadi Jewish community, 17–18
    klezmer music, 197–205
    Moroccan Jewish community, 73–74, 76–78, 83
    studies on, 13
Jewish musical indigeneity, 75–79
Jewish mysticism/mystics, 113n.55, 453–54, 698–701
Jewish National Fund, 134
Jewish Nazi refugees in Shanghai
    community of, 121–23
    concert music, 126–28
    continuity and topicality of Jewish music, 135–36
    introduction to, 119–21
    musical life of, 123–26
    synagogue music, 128–31, 129f
    Yiddish music, 131–35
Jewish songs. See also paraliturgical music/songs; spiritual expression in Jewish worship; Yiddish wedding songs in early modern period
    Aleppo's Jewish Khūjahs, 624–26
    folksongs, 58–59, 362–63, 505–6
    Hebrew songs, 126–27, 132, 183n.51, 318, 348, 590n.51, 603
    shirot ve-tishbaḥot (songs and praises to God), 97
    song of self, 21, 449–50, 453–58
    spiritual expression in, 21, 449–50, 453–63, 469–70
    theater songs, 23, 358–59, 362, 364–67, 371–74, 582–83
Jewish space/spaces, 13–14, 17, 19–21, 76, 150, 189, 269–70, 487–90, 554. See also sacred and ritual spaces
Jewish spirit/spirituality, 5–6, 321–22, 342–43, 452, 455–56, 466, 469
Jewish topographies, 268–72
Jewish voice, 17–18, 78, 79, 81–82, 84, 487–88
Jewishness
    Jewish music as marker of, 5–6
    by Nazi refugees in Shanghai, 127–28
    sounding out the ghetto, 266–67, 275–76

totalitarianism in post-Stalinist Soviet Union, 317–22
    urban musical culture in Warsaw Ghetto, 243
The Jews of Ioannina (Dalven), 555
Johnson, Eldgridge, 366
jomma dance, 541–43, 542f
Journal of Synagogue Music, 294
Judah de Lonzano Menachem ben, 495
Judaica Sound Archive at Florida Atlantic University (FAU), 413
Judelman, Craig, 202, 204–5, 401
Judeo-Andalusian music, 70, 71, 75, 76–77, 81–82, 84
Judeo-Spanish music, 71, 73–75, 166–67, 168, 170–72, 175–76, 180n.10, 180–81n.12
Jüdisch-liberale Zeitung, 265–66
Jüdische Gemeinde zu Berlin, 204
Jüdische Kulturgemeinschaft.
    See Asociacion Cultural Israelita de Buenos Aires
Jüdische Kultusgemeinde/Jüdische Gemeinde, 128–29
Jüdischer Kulturbund (Jewish Culture League), 125, 261, 263–77.
    See also Reichsverband Jüdischer Kulturbund
Judiska Sångföreningen i Helsingfors (The Jewish Song Association in Helsinki), 583–84, 584f

kabbalistic sources of music, 26–27, 93, 95, 96–97, 113n.55, 220–21, 223, 227–28, 502–3, 640, 709–10
Kaczerginski, Shmerke, 576
Kahal Kadosh Yashan (Holy Old Congregation), 559–60
Kahan-Newman, Zelda, 641–42
Kahn, Alfred, 132–33
Kahn, Daniel, 189, 196
Kalk, Israel (Izrael Markovič Kal'k), 597–98, 602, 608
Kapla, Chaim, 247
Karduan, Moshon, 173
Karoutchi, Maxime, 78
Karpen, Andreas, 193–94

Kartomi, Margaret, 434

Katayeva, Tamara, 539

Katz, Israel, 555

kavanah (conviction), 98–99, 454–55, 456, 472n.28

KEMT. *See* Chamber Jewish Musical Theater

Kenney, William, 411–12

ķeren, 226–27

keyboard, 186, 196–97, 289, 296–98, 302–3, 540, 541–42, 600, 602–3, 640–41

Khaimov, Menashe, 541

Khozak, Rafail, 321

Khrushchev, Nikita, 311

Khūjahs. *See* Aleppo's Jewish Khūjahs (Jewish women musicians)

kibbutz movement, 343–44, 503

kinnor, 216–18, 226–29, 231–32

Kinor David Maroc, 81–83, 84

Kinsky, Robert (Roberto), 146

Kipnis, Menachem, 371

Kirchhan, Elhanan, 518, 522, 522f

Kirchner, Paul Christian, 517, 519

Kirschner, Emanuel, 269

Kirshenblatt-Gimblett, Barbara, 387, 388–89, 391, 402, 421

Kisselgof-Makonovetsky Digital Manuscript Project, 401–2

Klebanov, Dmitry, 322–23

Kleiber, Erich, 151

Kleiner, Grete, 132

Klemperer, Victor, 276

kleynkunst (little art), 571–80, 586

KlezKamp (Yiddish Folk Arts Program), 398–99

Klezmer Institute, 401–2

klezmer music
  Berlin's changing scene, 191–97
  changing klezmer scenes, 205–7
  introduction to, 185–88
  Jewish community, 197–205
  shifting paradigms of, 188–91

klezmer music in YIVO Sound Archive
  cartography of, 393–97
  introduction to, 383–86, 385f
  as living space, 386–402
  in motion, 397–400

revitalization, 384–86, 389, 394, 397–98, 399–400, 402
  virtual performance and, 400–2

Klezmerstammtisch, 199–201

Kligman, Mark, 452, 469

Klyuzner, Boris, 320–21

Knoll, Andreani, 145

Kodaly, Zoltan, 146

Kogman-Appel, Katrin, 664

Kohn, Maier, 497

Kohn, Meier Boruch, 295

Kohn, Yoel, 300, 302–3

"Kol meķadesh shevi'i," 500–1, 500f, 502

Kondrashin, Kirill, 325

Kook, Abraham Isaac, 449–50, 453, 469, 470

Korn, Rokhl, 569–70

Kornhauser, Bronia, 434–35, 436

Koskoff, Ellen, 641–42

Kostakowsky, Wolff N., 190

Kotel ha-Ma'aravi. See sonic collectivity at Western Wall

Krein, Aleksandr, 318–19, 319f, 582

Krein, Grigory, 318–20, 319f

Kroyt-Quartett, 271

Krycer, David, 436

Kulisiewicz, Aleksander, 438

Kulthum, Umm, 627

Kumok, Joseph (George Andreani), 145

kumzits (music making party), 290, 301–3, 637–38

Kushner, Noa, 452–53, 454, 460

Kvitko, Leyb, 325

Kwartin, Zavel, 291

Lampe, Franka, 195

land, 17–18, 70, 73, 75–79, 80, 81–82. *See also adamah/adamot*

landsmanshaftn societies, 188–89

Lautenberg Amendment to the Foreign Operations Appropriations Act (1990), 533

Lavry, Marc, 346–47, 346f

Lax, Joseph, 606, 607

Leach, Edmund, 493–94

Leader, Ebn, 455, 458

leadership, 95–97, 108–10

Lemmer, Shulem, 296–98

Lemmer, Yaakov "Yanky," 289, 290, 295–301, 296f

Lenart, Ernest, 270–71

Lenhardt, Gunther, 125

Leningrad Jewish Comedy Ensemble, 316

Leningrad's Grand Choral Synagogue, 327–28

Leon, Judah Messer, 220–21

Leppert, Richard, 666

Levi-Tanai, Sara, 349–50

Levin, Neil, 497

Levin, Yehuda Leyb, 315–16

Levitch, Leon, 607

Levy, Daniela Smolov, 359–60

Levy, Jonah, 296–97

Lewin, Ossi, 127–28

Library of Congress, 421

Library of Congress National Recording Preservation Board, 417

libretto, 51, 61–62, 321–22, 337–38, 341, 349–50

Lifshitz, Nehama, 323–24

Lindberg, Friederike "Fritzi" Schlichter, 155

listening
    acousmatic listening, 364–67
    peripatetic listening, 370–73
    theatrical listening, 361–64

liturgical music. *See also* Romaniote liturgical music
    Hasidic cantors, 290, 292–93, 299, 301–2
    Torah tropes, 553–54, 556–57

Loeffler, James, 293, 598

Los Bohemios Vieneses, 155, 156f

Lowell Milken Center for Music of American Jewish Experience, 418–19

Ludus Paschalis (Hajdu), 57–59

Ludwig, Hermann, 153

Lurje, Sasha, 202–3

lute, 216–18, 224, 227, 536, 542–43, 665–66, 677, 678–82, 681f, 686, 700

lyre, 227–28, 244–45, 687, 689–90, 709

Lyubimov, Baritone Saul, 312–13

Maestro, Yaakov "Jako," 173–74

Maḥfūẓ, Iyād, 617

maḥshevet yisrael (Jewish thought), 94

Mahzor Romania, 557

Mahzor Vitry, 495, 676

Maimonides, 702, 704–5

Malayev, Ilyas, 536–37

Manevich, Aleksandr, 320–21

Mann, Barbara, 12

Mantua ghetto music and Portaleone
    complexity of, 223–29
    De Auro dialogi tres, 219–20, 221
    diachronic collectivity, 19–20, 218–19, 232
    Greek wisdom of, 219–23, 231–32
    introduction to, 215–19, 216f
    midrashic approach to, 229–32
    radical empiricism of, 219–20, 227, 230
    Shilṭei ha-giborim, 216–18, 217f, 219–32
    synchronic collectivity, 19–20, 218–19, 232

Marcus, Ivan G., 666

Margolinski, Henry, 125–26

marocanité music, 79–83

Martin Steinberg Center at the American Jewish Congress, 388

Marx, Karl, 16

Masekhet Hekhalot, 700

Master E. S., 677, 679f, 680f

Matalon, J. Rolando, 469

Matsa, Yosef, 555

Mayrent, Sherry, 412, 414

Mayrent Collection of Yiddish Recordings at Mills Music Library, 414, 415

Mazower, Mark, 170

Meckenem, Israhel van, 678–82, 678f, 680f, 681f

media and sacred spaces, 22

megorashim, 73–74

Meir, Golda, 312–13

Meisels, Ernst, 146

Meisels, Otto, 146

memory stage, 373–74

Mendelssohn, Felix, 125–26

Me'or 'einayim (Dei Rossi), 230

Metamorphoses (Ovid), 225

Meyer, Leonard, 342

Midrash Zelkhah academy, 95

midrashic approach to music history, 229–32

migrants/migration. *See also* immigrants
    anticipatory refugees, 338, 342
    dynamic transnational bidirectional tracks, 378n.42
    gramophone sound-recording industry, 366

immigrant composers, 338–41, 342, 344–45, 348–49

postcustodialism in Jewish music archive and, 431–32

Mikhoels, Solomon, 311

Miller, Benzion, 295

Miller, Rochel, 649

Mills Music Library, 414, 415

Minkowsky, Pinchas, 293

Miron, Dan, 11

Mirski, Lav, 601, 601f, 606

Miṣḥaf al-shbaḥot (The holy book of praises), 99–100, 100t

Mishnaic Hebrew, 58–59

Mizrahi music, 171, 174–79, 183n.51, 639

Mlotek, Eleanor (Chana) Gordon, 394, 438

Modena, Leon, 222

"Moladeti" (My homeland), 39–40, 40f

Monk, Daniel, 481, 489–90

Morgenstern, Lia, 132

Moroccan Jewish community, 73–74, 76–78, 83

Moscato, Judah, 227–29

Moscow Jewish Drama Ensemble (MEDA), 314–15

Motets (Seter), 48, 50f, 55–56

Moxey, Keith, 677

Mravinsky, Yevgeny, 324

Mrocki, Freydi, 436

Museo della Memoria Ferramonti di Tarsia, 608

music education in Buenos Aires, 159

Music Modernization Act (2018), 417

music theory, 6, 30–31n.27, 216–18, 221, 231–32, 340, 705–7

musical community, 16, 24–25, 191, 201, 311, 327, 328, 498, 499, 502–3, 570–71, 611n.39, 616, 619–20, 626, 627–28, 629

musical knowledge in analogical reasoning, 705–10

muṭribah, 24–25, 621, 626–28

muzikant, 186

Nadel, Arno, 266, 497

Naḥman, Rav, 469–70

Najara, Israel ben Moses, 493, 497

Nancy, Jean-Luc, 16

Nardi, Nahum, 347–49

Nation (the people of Israel), 17–18, 101–2, 670, 676–77, 699–700, 705–8, 710–11

National Library of Australia, 430, 432–33

National Recording Preservation Act (2000), 417

National Recording Registry, 417

National Socialism, 263–64, 269–70, 272, 275–76

National Yiddish Book Center, 413

Naziha Assis, 614–16, 620–22, 627, 628–29

Nazism. *See also ḥurban*; Jewish music and internment in Ferramonti di Tarsia; Jewish Nazi refugees in Shanghai; urban musical culture in Warsaw Ghetto

ascent of, 338

Jewish Argentines and, 144–45, 148, 151–52, 153–56, 158

policy of exterminating European Jews, 262–63, 274, 275, 276

postcustodialism in Jewish music archive and, 433–34

Neoplatonism, 704, 707, 709

Netsky, Hankus, 189–90, 383

Neuhaus, Chayala, 655

nevel, 224, 226–27, 689, 690

New Age mysticism, 79–83

New Palestine Opera Corporation, 341

Newman, Zelda Kahan, 519

Niehoff-Panagiotis, Johannes, 557

nigun/nigunim, 2, 97, 205, 297, 301–2, 318, 370–71, 401, 454, 455–56, 459, 462, 469–70, 497–98, 502–4, 575, 582, 603, 644, 698

noetic process, 450, 708–9

non-Jewish Jews, 3–4

non-metrical sound of cantorial music, 292

Nora, Pierre, 621

Norich, Samuel, 387, 392

nostalgia, 73, 167–70, 177, 178–79, 187, 189, 193, 250–51, 293, 297–98, 391, 507, 541

nusaḥ (prayer chant), 453–54

"O ergatis" (The worker) (Toundas), 170, 171f

Olivero, Betty, 59–63

"Ono Bohoach," 297–98

open-source digital, 435, 437

opera
    ancient temple and, 223, 226
    art music and, 51, 52, 61
    in early statehood Israel, 337–38, 341–
        42, 348
    by émigré musicians in Buenos Aires, 147,
        148–49, 150–52
    in ghettos, 244, 245, 251, 265–66, 271–73
    Hasidic cantors and, 292, 293–94
    in internment camps, 601–2, 604–5
    in Jewish music archives, 432–33
    by Nazi refugees, 123–24, 125, 132
    Sabbath table and, 494
    totalitarianism and, 318, 320, 324–25, 326
    Yiddish theater and, 23, 358, 359–60, 361–
        63, 373
Opera Amamit, 341
opera houses, 23
operettas
    by émigré musicians in Buenos Aires, 147,
        151–53, 155–56, 158–59
    klezmer music and, 190
    by Nazi refugees, 120–21, 123–26
    totalitarianism and, 323
    Yiddish theater and, 357–59, 360, 366, 373,
        374, 375n.1, 375n.2
Oppenheimer Siddur. See feminine elements
        in Oppenheimer Siddur
oral Torah, 455
oral tradition, 5, 57, 74, 75, 224, 226, 441, 496,
        513, 555–56, 644–45
oral transmission, 397–98, 513, 554
Orgad, Ben-Zion, 347
organ, 148–49, 225, 298, 302–3, 321–22, 370,
        420, 422, 433
Orientalism, 133, 337–38, 347–48, 350
Orot ha-Kodesh (Holy lights) (Kook), 449, 450
Otono Sefardi en Cordoba (Sephardi Autumn
        in Cordoba), 80
Ottoman Empire, 165, 167, 171, 480, 555–57, 617
Oyneg Shabes archive, 242, 247–48, 250

Pahlen, Kurt, 157
Palestine Broadcasting Service (PBS), 341
Palestine Folk Opera, 341
Palestine Orchestra, 342, 344–45
Palestine Royal (Peel) Commission, 42

Palestine Symphony Orchestra, 340–
        41, 348–49
Palestinian Talmud, 58–59
Panagia, Davide, 484, 489–90
panhymnische Einheit (panhymnic
        unity), 701
Pappenheim, Solomon, 564–65
paraliturgical music/songs. See also Ḥakham
        Yosef Ḥayyim ben 'Eliah al-Ḥakham;
        singing zemiroth at Sabbath meals
    melodies, 102–3
    Miṣḥaf al-shbaḥot (The holy book of
        praises), 99–100, 100t
    religious ethos in, 100–2
    virtue of singing praises to God, 97–99
Pasternak, Velvel, 497
Paul IV, Pope, 19–20
Paz, Juan Carlos, 153–54
Perego, Simon, 586
Pergament, Moses, 584–85
peripatetic listening, 370–73
Perlmutter, Arnold, 357
Pesaro, Guglielmo Ebreo da, 665
peṣrev form, 53–54
Pew Research Center Study, 450–51
Peyser, Herbert F., 271
Philipp, Michael, 120–21
Philippsborn, Fritz, 134
Philo of Alexandria, 705–6
piano
    art music and, 335, 342–43, 344–49
    émigré musicians in Buenos Aires, 150, 152,
        155, 159, 160f
    in ghettos, 251
    Hasidic cantors and, 297–99
    Holocaust survivors in Sweden, 574, 576,
        582, 583, 584–85
    in internment camps, 602–3, 604, 605–6
    Nazi refugees and, 126–27, 132–33, 135
    totalitarianism and, 317–19, 321–22,
        324, 326
    ultra-orthodox women and, 638, 644
    Yiddish theater and, 361–62
Pinkhasova, Yafa (Tühfakhon), 537–39
Pinski, David, 367–69
Pisk, Paul, 146, 154
Pitchon, David "Daviko," 175

pluralism and art music, 347–50
Pnina Nahmias, 172
Pogreb, Sara, 314
Pokrass, Daniil, 316
Pokrass, Dmitrij, 133–34, 316
Pokrass, Samuil, 316
Poliker, Yehuda, 174
Pollack, Yoel, 303
Pollak, Paul, 594–95
polyphonic music, 222
popular music, 178–79
Portaleone, Abraham. *See* Mantua ghetto
    music and Portaleone
postcustodialism in Jewish music archive
    Australian Archive of Jewish Music, 434–
       37, 440–42
    Australian archives, 432–34
    fragmentation in, 434–37, 440–42
    introduction to, 429–31
    migration and, 431–32
    United States Holocaust Memorial
       Museum, 432, 437–40
Potapovskaya, Dina, 319–20
prayer. *See also* singing zemiroth at
       Sabbath meals
    davenen, 456
    Mahzor Romania, 557
    seliḥot, 476, 477–78, 477*f*, 483, 561–63
    spiritual expression in song, 21, 449–50,
       453–63, 469–70
    at Western Wall Plaza, 476, 477–80, 481–
       87, 489
    women's roles in, 484–87
Prinz, Joachim, 262, 268–69
Prior, Richard, 665
Psalms, Book of, 106, 220–21, 485, 486, 669–
    70, 686–87
Psalms of David, 224
Purim, 108, 128, 309, 497, 521–22, 605–6, 641–
    42, 665–66
purimshpil, 321–22, 358–59
Pythagorean Harmony of the Spheres, 701
Pythagoreans, 698, 701–3, 704–5

Rachel's Place productions, 645–49, 657
radical empiricism, 219–20, 227, 230
radio stations in Buenos Aires, 155–56

Ratzon program, 645–46
Ravina, Menashe (Rabinowitz), 344
reterritorialization, 17–18, 390
rebetiko (Greek-language song style), 166
Rebling, Eberhard, 191–92, 580–83, 581*f*
recording/recording studios, 366, 412–13, 417.
       See also sound recordings in US
Reform Jewish camps, 416
Reform movement, 14, 16, 463–64
Reich, David, 289–90, 302–3
Reichsverband Jüdischer Frontsoldaten
       (Reich Association of Jewish Frontline
       Soldiers), 264
Reichsverband Jüdischer Kulturbund
       (Reich Association of Jewish Culture
       Leagues), 261–62. *See also* Jüdischer
       Kulturbund
religious music, 5–6, 120, 124, 130–31, 303,
    362, 615
remembrance. *See* destruction and
    remembrance
repertoire and place, 72–75
resonance, 358, 366–67, 457, 478, 479–82, 483,
    484–85, 543, 667–68, 705, 707, 709
Retzler, Max, 134
revitalization, 23–24, 84, 188, 189, 194–95, 203,
    206, 316, 383–86, 389, 391, 394, 397–98,
    399–400, 402, 420, 421
Rikudgalim dance, 488–89
Ringelblum, Emanuel, 242, 243
Riskin, Nahmen, 367–69
ritual spaces. *See* sacred and ritual spaces
Rohland, Peter, 191–92
Rokhlin, Yevgeny, 314–15
Romaine, Jenny, 384, 389, 395*f*
Romaniote liturgical music
    early history, 556–58
    introduction to, 7–8, 553–56
    process of remembering, 564–66
    religious pilgrimage, 558–64
    seliḥot, 561–63
Romanticism era, 344
Romero, Manuel, 147
Ron, Zvi, 676
Ronström, Owe, 420
Roof, Wade Clark, 450–51
roots movement, 388, 391

Rosenbaum, Aleksandr, 328

Rosenberg, William G., 400

Rosenblatt, Joseph (Yossele), 291, 294, 303, 361–62, 364

Rosenblüth, Leo, 569–70, 576, 577f, 583

Rosenfeld, Sophia, 360

Rosenzweig, Franz, 43–46, 363

Rosh Hashanah, 560

Rossi, Salamone, 14

Rozen, Mina, 168

Różycki, Stanisław, 247–50

Rubin, Joel, 196–97

Rubin, Ruth, 395–96

Rubinov, Roshel, 536–37

Ruderman, David B., 215, 512

Ruppin, Selma (Shulamit), 335

Russian Jews, 132, 135–36, 310, 311, 582

Sabbath meals. See singing zemiroth at Sabbath meals

Sachs, Curt, 3–4, 8

sacred and ritual spaces, 20–22

Sadik y Gazóz, 166, 169, 170

Salmen, Walter, 665

Salonika
    Greekness in music, 171, 175–77, 178–79
    introduction to, 165–67
    longing and belonging, 167–70
    popular-music taste cultures, 178–79
    Tel Aviv-Jaffa and, 18–19, 165–66, 171–77, 178

sampogna, 225–27

Samter, Hans, 264–65

Samuel, Simḥah ben, 495

Samuels, Benjamin J., 449–50

Samuels, Rachel, 653–55

Sapiro, Boris, 131–32

Sapoznik, Henry, 383–84, 386, 387, 388, 389, 390–91, 393, 395f, 396–97, 398–99, 412–13

Sattler, Henry, 134

Saul, Jack, 413

Saul at Ein-Dor (Tal), 51–53

saxophone, 155, 169–70, 640–41

Schaeffer, Arnold, 357, 361

Schaeffer, Pierre, 364–65

Scharwenka, Xaver, 146

Schenirer, Sarah, 643–44

Schlichter, Dora (Dolly), 146

Schlichter, Victor, 145, 146

Schlögel, Karl, 263–64

Schloß, Julius, 128

Schneerson, Menachem Mendel, 1

Schoenberg, Arnold, 146

Scholem, Gershom, 43–46

Schor, David, 310

Schuler, Ernst August, 58

Schulman, Asya Vaisman, 641–42, 644

Schwartz, Daniel, 267–68

Schwartz, Devorah, 653–55

Schwartz, Dov, 698–99

Schwartz, Leon, 397–98

Schwarz, Nikolai, 132

science of music, 708–9

secular Jews, 16, 148, 243, 645, 650

secular music, 5–6, 20–21, 294, 624–25, 644, 646–47, 650

Seder rabah de-bereshit (The great order of Creation), 700–1

Sefer ḥeshek Shelomoh (The desire of Solomon) (Pappenheim), 564–65

Seisanas, Aristides. See Aris San

Selig, R., 518

selihot, 476, 477–78, 477f, 483, 561–63

Semitic Suite (Boskovich), 342–43

Sephardic Jews/Sephardim, 16, 70–71, 73, 74–75, 79–81, 84, 176–77, 502, 556–57

Sephardic music, 13, 15, 70–71, 72–75, 79–83, 410, 411, 414, 422, 476, 555

Seroussi, Edwin, 5–6, 14, 416–17, 496

Serre, Michael, 75–76

Seter, Mordecai, 48–51, 50f, 55–56

Shainsky, Vladimir, 316–17

Shalev-Eyni, Sarit, 670–74

Shammes, Yuspa, 515

Shanghai Jewish Chronicle, 119–20, 127, 130–31

Shanghai Municipal Council, 126

Shanghai refugees. See Jewish Nazi refugees in Shanghai

Shank, Barry, 206

Shannon, Jonathan, 618–19

Shaporin, Yury, 318

Sharlin, William, 5–6

shashmaqom, 531, 534–35, 536, 537–38

shbaḥoth music, 91

shekhinah, 13, 20–21, 26–28, 98–99, 457. *See also* ultra-Orthodox feminine musical *shekhinah*

Shelemay, Kay Kaufman, 78, 165–66, 498, 532, 570–71, 575, 616, 620

Sherling, Yuri, 327

Shiloah, Amnon, 93–94, 350, 555

Shilṭei ha-giborim (Portaleone), 216–18, 217*f*, 219–32

shirah be-tsibur (communal singing), 710–11

shirot ve-tishbaḥot (songs and praises to God), 97

Shneer, David, 580–82

shofar, 76, 225–27, 347, 347*f*, 480–81, 664–65, 668–69, 693–94n.28

Shoshano, Rose, 133

Shostakovich, Dmitry, 317–18, 322, 324, 325

shpinholts, 515

shtetl, link to Jewish music, 12–13

Shulman, Zinovy, 312–13

"Shuloym aleykhem," 501–2, 501*f*

Shvartser, Bin'yamin, 314–15

Silberstein, Peter, 607–8

Silver, Christopher, 410, 412–13

Simon, James, 439

Singer, Grigory, 319–20

Singer, Kurt, 266–67, 273

singing zemiroth at Sabbath meals
  collectivity and, 498–99
  immigrants and, 499–506
  individual and collective nature of, 506–8
  introduction to, 493–95
  origin and sources, 495–98

Sirota, Gershon, 291

Sivuv Shearim (Circling the Gates) ritual, 487–89

Six-Day War (1967), 39–40, 481–82

Skinner, Graeme, 432

Sklamberg, Lorin, 384, 389, 395*f*

Slobin, Mark, 189, 294–95, 359–60, 392, 394, 401, 450–51

Smetana, Bedřich, 125–26

Sociedad de Proteccion a los Immigrantes Israelitas (Society for the Protection of Israelite Immigrants, or Soprotimis), 144–45

Society for Jewish Folk Music, 336–37

Society for the Promotion of Culture Among the Jews of Russia, 23–24

Sol, Felicia L., 469

song of self, 21, 449–50, 453–58

Song of Songs, 93, 340, 349, 638–39, 670–72, 703, 708

sonic collectivity at Western Wall
  historical resonances, 479–82
  introduction to, 20–21, 476–78
  politics of, 489–90
  Rikudgalim dance, 488–89
  seliḥot, 476, 477*f*, 477–78, 483
  Sivuv Shearim (Circling the Gates) ritual, 487–89
  as sonic proximity, 482–84
  women's roles in prayer, 484–87

Sonnenfeld, Kurt, 599, 600–3, 606

Sonnenschein, Siegrfied, 132–33, 134

sound recordings in US
  audiences of, 422–24
  authenticity and historical accuracy, 420–22
  bibliographic control and preservation, 414–20
  introduction to, 408–11
  motivation and scope of, 411–14

sounding out the ghetto
  cultural ghettoization, 262–63, 272, 273
  ghetto as place, 272–75
  introduction to, 261–64
  limits and boundaries of, 275–77
  spiritual ghetto, 262, 264–68, 273–74, 276
  as topographical reality, 268–72

sozandas, 534–40, 541–42, 547n.21, 617

spatiality, 11, 12–15, 17, 191, 205–6

Spencer, Herbert, 15–16

Spiller, Ljerko, 146, 155

spiritual expression in Jewish worship
  all songs in ensemble, 469–70
  eruv in, 17, 21, 450, 455–56, 470, 494, 508
  fourfold song, 21, 449–50, 453, 469
  introduction to, 449–53
  song of all existence, 466–68
  song of all humanity, 463–66
  song of Jewish people, 458–63
  song of self, 21, 449–50, 453–58

spiritual ghetto, 262, 264–68, 273–74, 276

Spottswood, Richard, 384, 396, 414
Srougo, Shai, 170
St. Petersburg Society for Jewish Folk
    Music, 337–38
stage space, 22–23
Stalin, Joseph, 309, 310–11
Stallings, W. Joseph, 17–18
Stambler, Benedict, 410
Steedman, Carolyn, 395–96
Steinberg, Hans Wilhelm, 340–41
Stern, Moshe, 289
Sternberg, Erich Walter, 42–43, 344
Steuermann, Eduard, 146
Stiskin, David, 315–16
Strashunsky, Yoel, 294
Straw, Will, 642–43
street sounds, 370–73
Sulzer, Salomon, 292
summer camps, 643–45
Sweck, Jacob Saul, 623
Swedish Holocaust survivors. *See* Holocaust
    survivors in Sweden
Sydney Jewish Museum, 430, 433–34
synagogue music, 128–31, 129*f*
synchronic collectivity, 19–20, 218–19, 232
Syrian Jewish women musicians. *See* Aleppo's
    Jewish Khūjahs
Szpilman, Władysław, 251–54

Tal, Josef, 51–53, 345–46
Talmud
    Babylonian Talmud, 58, 102, 106, 455, 458,
        467, 472n.28, 472–73n.41, 479, 556–57,
        565, 689, 704
    eruv hatserot in, 21
    kol b'ishah erva dictum, 622–23
    Mantua ghetto music, 218, 221–22, 227–
        28, 231
    musical studies, 57–58
    Oppenheimer Siddur and, 690
    Palestinian Talmud, 58–59
    woman's voice (*kol ishah*), 80, 622–23, 626,
        638–39, 641–42
Tarras, Dave, 383–84
Tashrak, Yosef, 363–64
Teatro Astral, 150
Teatro Colón, 147, 148, 150–51

Teatro de la Opera, 147
Teatro IFT, 153, 158–59
Teatro Odeon, 147
Teitelbaum, Joel, 640–41
Tel Aviv-Jaffa, 18–19, 165–66, 171–77, 178, 343–
    44, 616, 620
temporality, xv, 4, 14–15, 23–24, 47–48, 58–59,
    74, 386, 402
territorialism, 40–41, 56, 58–59
territorialization, 17–18, 390
teshuvah, 57, 455, 477–78, 561, 645–46
Thaler, Isco, 602–3
theater, Yiddish. *See* Yiddish theater
theater songs, 23, 358–59, 362, 364–67, 371–
    74, 582–83
theatrical listening, 361–64
Thibaud, Jacques, 146
Thirteen Attributes of Mercy, 561
Thrift, Nigel, 203
Tiḳun ḥatsot (Midnight vigil) (Levi-
    Tanai), 349–50
Tinanoff, Nate, 412–13
Titon, Jeff Todd, 466
tof, 225–27, 235n.38, 705–6
Tonkiss, Fran, 16
Tonnies, Ferdinand, 16
topicality of Jewish music, 135–36
Torah
    Bukharian Jewish weddings, 534–35, 535*f*
    concept of harmony in, 707
    Mantua ghetto music, 220, 221
    meaning and experience of
        chanting, 450–51
    oral Torah, 455
    paraliturgical music/songs and, 101–2
    tropes, 553–54, 556–57
Toscanini, Arturo, 340–41
toshavim, 73–74
totalitarianism in post-Stalinist Soviet Union
    Holocaust and, 322–26
    introduction to, 309–11
    Jewishness in, 317–22
    new era of Jewish music, 327–28
    Yiddish music and, 310, 311, 312–17
Toundas, Panayiotis, 170, 171*f*
Tragaki, Dafni, 167–68
Trailin, Sergey Aleksandrovich, 146

transnationalism, 190
Treaty of Lausanne, 168
Tri stikhotvoreniya (Three poems)
	(Vustin), 326
Troyke, Karsten, 192, 195–96
Trum, Albert, 127, 128
tsedaḳah (charity), 482, 637–38, 640–41, 642,
	645–46, 648, 656
tsiltsal, 226–27
tsiltsal shema, 226–27
tsniut (modesty), 290–91, 637–39, 640, 641–42,
	644–45, 648–49, 651–52, 656
Tucholsky, Kurt, 262
Turino, Thomas, 505
Turkow, Dina (Diana Blumenfeld), 246
Turkow, Jonas, 243, 245, 246
Tych, Felix, 431

ufaratsta, 1–2
ʿugav, 216–18, 226–27, 231–32
ultra-Orthodox feminine musical *shekhinah*
	Broadway musicals, 645–49
	defined, 640–43
	future of, 657–58
	home studio, 649–52
	introduction to, 26–28, 637–40
	schools and summer camps, 643–45
	tsniut and, 290–91, 637–39, 640, 641–42,
		644–45, 648–49, 651–52, 656
	YouTube music videos, 652–56
ultra-Orthodox Judaism
	Hasidim, 1, 16, 301–2, 497–99, 502, 639, 710
	Litvish-Yeshivish branches, 637–38, 650
	tsniut and, 290–91, 637–39, 640, 641–42,
		644–45, 648–49, 651–52, 656
Umayyad Caliphate of Cordoba, 72–73
UN Security Council, 17–18, 41
United States Holocaust Memorial Museum
	(USHMM), 23–24, 410, 432, 437–40
urban musical culture in Warsaw Ghetto
	ghetto cafés, 247–52
	impact of German occupation, 242–44
	introduction to, 240–42
	Oyneg Shabes archive, 242, 247–48, 250
	Polish-speaking intelligentsia, 250–52
	public performances of, 244–47
	traces of prewar musical world, 252–54

US copyright law, 417

Van Ness, Peter H., 450–51
Vaynberg, Moisey (Mieczysław Weinberg),
	320, 325–26
Veprik, Aleksandr, 318–19
Veprik, Esfir, 319–20
Vernadsky National Library of Ukraine, 401–2
Vessely, Baruch, 500–1, 500*f*, 502–4, 505, 507
Vinaver, Chemjo, 497
violin, 53–54, 54*f*, 146, 150, 155, 158–59, 245,
	320–21, 335–36, 398–99, 401, 602–3,
	640–41, 665
Vision of a Prophet (Ben-Haim), 42–43, 44*f*
voice. *See* choral music; opera; singing
	zemiroth at Sabbath meals; sonic
	collectivity at Western Wall; women's
	voice (*kol ishah*)
Volkshochschule, 159
Vustin, Aleksandr, 318, 322, 326
Vysotsky, Vladimir, 328

Wagner, Richard, 125–26
Walden, Joshua, 293, 359–60, 366,
	419–20, 599
Waldman, Rose, 641–42
Warkov, Esther, 93–94
Warnke, Nina, 359–60
Warsaw Ghetto. *See* urban musical culture in
	Warsaw Ghetto
Warsaw Ghetto Uprising, 133–34, 314, 586
Warsaw Philharmonic, 242–43
Warschauer, Max, 128
waṣla, 624–25
Weber, Bernard Anselm, 496–97
Weber, Carl Maria von, 125–26
Weber, Max, 95–96
Webern, Anton, 344–45
wedding music/musicians, 2–3, 186, 190, 297,
	420–21, 532, 536–38, 541, 543, 545. *See
	also* Bukharian Jewish weddings of
	Central Asia; Yiddish wedding songs
	in early modern period
wedding songs. *See* Bukharian Jewish
	weddings of Central Asia;
	Yiddish wedding songs in early
	modern period

Weinberg, Jacob, 337–38

Weinberg, Jeshajahu (Shaike), 432, 437–40

Weisenberg, Joey, 455–56, 458–59, 461–62, 468, 469–70

Weissman, Reuben, 375n.1

Weißtein, Curt B. M., 157

Werb, Bret, 438–39, 440, 575–76

Werder, Felix, 432–33, 436

Werner, Eric, 5–6

Western art music, 57, 338–39

Western Jewish musical traditions, 48, 56

Western Wall Heritage Foundation, 477–78

Westernness as duty, 47–51

Wiesel, Elie, 328

willful forgetting, 618–19

Winograd, Michael, 296–98

Wohl, Herman, , 357, 361

Wolf, Albert, 664–65

Wolpe, Michael, 350

Wolpe, Stefan, 4, 344–45

women and music. *See* Aleppo's Jewish Khūjahs; feminine elements in Oppenheimer Siddur; ultra-Orthodox feminine musical *shekhinah*

Women of the Wall, 485–87

women's voice (*kol ishah*), 80, 622–23, 626, 638–39, 641–42

World Centre for Jewish Music in Jerusalem, 341

World Congress of Jewish Studies, 9

World Jewish Congress, 569–70, 583, 586

World War II, 3

Wygodzki, Stanisław, 326

Yaakov Nahmias, 172

Yemenite music, 5, 107–8, 126–27, 347–50, 479, 553–54

Yetsies mitsraim (The Exodus from Egypt) (Hurwitz), 357, 358, 360, 374

Yevreyskiy antifashistskiy komitet (Jewish Anti-Fascist Committee), 310–11

Yevtushenko, Yevgeny, 324

Yiddish Dramatic Amateur Society, 578–80, 583, 586

Yiddish music. *See also* Jewish music
klezmer music, 189–95, 196, 197–99, 201–2, 204
in post-Stalinist Soviet Union, 310, 311, 312–17

postcustodialism in Jewish music archive and, 431–32

Yiddish theater
acousmatic listening, 364–67
Der fonograf (The phonograph) (Pinski), 367–69
emergence of, 23
introduction to, 357–61
Jewish émigrés in Buenos Aires, 152–53, 158–59
memory stage, 373–74
music in post-Stalinist Soviet Union, 310, 311, 312–17
peripatetic listening, 370–73
refugees from, 120–21
songs by Shanghai refugees, 131–35
theater songs, 23, 358–59, 362, 364–67, 371–74, 582–83
theatrical listening, 361–64
urban musical culture in Warsaw Ghetto, 245–46

Yiddish wedding songs in early modern period
braiding of bride, 516–17, 516f
as communal experience and performance, 514–20
introduction to, 512–14
as musical event, 520–22
shpinholts, 515
song texts, 522–27

Yidisher Visnshaftlekher Institut (YIVO), 23–24

Yitzḥaq, Asher ben, 667–68, 682–84, 690–92, 691f

YIVO Sound Archive (Yidisher Visnshaftlekher Institut/Yiddish Scientific Institute). *See* klezmer music in YIVO Sound Archive

Yom Kippur, 476, 477–78, 477f, 564–66, 683

Yosef, Ovadia, 477–78

Young Israel Beth El Synagogue, 299–300

YouTube music videos, 652–56

Yusfin, Abram, 317

zakhor (to remember), 23–24. *See also* destruction and remembrance

Zaludkovsky, Elias, 293–94

zamler movement, 23–24, 187, 195–96

Zefira, Bracha, 347–49, 350

zekher (remembrance), 24–25, 554, 565, 571, 575–76, 579–80, 587, 599, 605, 607, 608–9, 616, 628–29. *See also* destruction and remembrance

zemiroth at Sabbath meals. *See* singing zemiroth at Sabbath meals

Zernik, Herbert, 132–33

Zerubavel, Yael, 607

Zhitlowsky, Chaim, 292

Zimmermann, Heidy, 133

Zins, Bogdan, 600

Zionism
   adamah/adamot and, 42–47, 56–63
   anti-Zionism *vs.*, 16, 322
   art music and, 337–38
   biblical sovereignty, 39–40

   Holocaust survivors in Sweden, 570–71
   Jewish émigrés in Buenos Aires, 149–50
   Jewish music research, 5
   Kook, Abraham Isaac, 449
   in post-Stalinist Soviet Union, 311
   Salonika, 165, 175–76, 183n.47
   singing zemiroth at Sabbath meals, 494–95, 498, 504–6
   sounding out the ghetto, 265–66

Ziryāb, ʿAlī ibn Nāfiʿ, 72–73

Zmora, Ruthi Navon, 649

Zohar, Zvi, 94

Zomina, Raya, 132–34

Żydowskie Towarzystwo Opieki Społecznej (Jewish Society for Public Welfare), 246

Żywy dziennik (The living newspaper), 250–51